Media Business and Innovation

Series Editor:

M. Friedrichsen, Berlin, Germany

For further volumes:
http://www.springer.com/series/11520

Mike Friedrichsen • Wolfgang Mühl-Benninghaus
Editors

Handbook of Social Media Management

Value Chain and Business Models in Changing Media Markets

Editors
Mike Friedrichsen
Institute for Media Business
Media Business Transfer Center
Berlin, Germany

Wolfgang Mühl-Benninghaus
Institute for Media and Music Science
Humboldt University
Berlin, Germany

ISBN 978-3-642-28896-8   ISBN 978-3-642-28897-5 (eBook)
DOI 10.1007/978-3-642-28897-5
Springer Heidelberg New York Dordrecht London

Library of Congress Control Number: 2013933243

© Springer-Verlag Berlin Heidelberg 2013
This work is subject to copyright. All rights are reserved by the Publisher, whether the whole or part of the material is concerned, specifically the rights of translation, reprinting, reuse of illustrations, recitation, broadcasting, reproduction on microfilms or in any other physical way, and transmission or information storage and retrieval, electronic adaptation, computer software, or by similar or dissimilar methodology now known or hereafter developed. Exempted from this legal reservation are brief excerpts in connection with reviews or scholarly analysis or material supplied specifically for the purpose of being entered and executed on a computer system, for exclusive use by the purchaser of the work. Duplication of this publication or parts thereof is permitted only under the provisions of the Copyright Law of the Publisher's location, in its current version, and permission for use must always be obtained from Springer. Permissions for use may be obtained through RightsLink at the Copyright Clearance Center. Violations are liable to prosecution under the respective Copyright Law.
The use of general descriptive names, registered names, trademarks, service marks, etc. in this publication does not imply, even in the absence of a specific statement, that such names are exempt from the relevant protective laws and regulations and therefore free for general use.
While the advice and information in this book are believed to be true and accurate at the date of publication, neither the authors nor the editors nor the publisher can accept any legal responsibility for any errors or omissions that may be made. The publisher makes no warranty, express or implied, with respect to the material contained herein.

Printed on acid-free paper

Springer is part of Springer Science+Business Media (www.springer.com)

Contents

Part I Introduction

The Social Media Management Chain, How Social Media Influences Traditional Media 3
Mike Friedrichsen and Wolfgang Mühl-Benninghaus

Part II Management with Social Media

Traditional Media Companies in the U.S. and Social Media: What's the Strategy? 9
Alan B. Albarran and Terry Moellinger

Social Media in Companies. Integrated Approach for a Social Media Strategy 25
Mike Friedrichsen

Some Economics of New Media Content Production and Consumption, and Strategic Implication for Media Companies 49
Marco Gambaro

How (Social) Media Can Change "Change" in Organizations 59
Holger Sievert and Astrid Nelke

Employees' Conceptions of How Management Can Operationalize Employee Involvement 73
Stavros Georgiades

Book Industry Business, Concentration, Internet and Social Media of Management and Marketing 87
Paulo Faustino

New Venture Creation in Social Media Platform; Towards a Framework
for Media Entrepreneurship 125
Datis Khajeheian

New Marketing Communication in Social Media Business 143
Wolfgang Mühl-Benninghaus

Social Networks as Marketing Tools for Media Companies 161
Alfonso Sánchez-Tabernero, Julián Villanueva, and José Luis Orihuela

Managing New(s) Conversations: The Role of Social Media in News
Provision and Participation 179
François Nel and Oscar Westlund

Social Media: Managerial and Economic Opportunities
and Challenges 201
Francisco J. Pérez-Latrel and George Tsourvakas

Part III New Value Chain with Social Media

Social Media, Aggregation and the Refashioning of Media Business
Models 219
Charles Brown

How Media Companies Should Create Value: Innovation Centered
Business Models and Dynamic Capabilities 239
Hans van Kranenburg and Gerrit Willem Ziggers

Media Management and Social Media Business: New Forms of Value
Creation in the Context of Increasingly Interconnected Media
Applications 253
Reinhard Kunz and Stefan Werning

Managing Social Media Value Networks: From Publisher (Broadcast)
to User-Centric (Broadband-Narrowcast) Business Models 269
Zvezdan Vukanovic

Two Faces of Growth: Linking Customer Engagement to Revenue
Streams 289
Biser Zlatanov

Keys to Monetize Social Media in the Audiovisual Business 311
Mónica Herrero and Mercedes Medina

Digital Hollywood: How Internet and Social Media Are Changing
the Movie Business 327
Alejandro Pardo

Distributing Audiovisual Contents in the New Digital Scenario:
Multiplatform Strategies of the Main Spanish TV Networks   349
Enrique Guerrero, Patricia Diego, and Alejandro Pardo

Facebook: A Business Perspective on the Power of Intelligent Networking
and Social Media   375
Richard A. Gershon

Multimedia Strategies for FM Radio Stations in Moscow   391
Elena Vartanova, Mikhail Makeenko, and Andrei Vyrkovsky

Social Media in Russia: Its Features and Business Models   405
Marianna Blinova

China's Media Industry: Landscape and Development   417
Min Hang

Part IV Forms and Content of Social Media

Social Media Strategies and Practices of Integrated
Media Companies   431
Piet Bakker, Sanne Hille, and Marco van Kerkhoven

"Telekom hilft": Customer Service in the Social Web   443
Andreas H. Bock

Online Radio: A Social Media Business?   455
Paul Dwyer

Platform Leadership in Online Broadcasting Markets   477
Tom Evens

Ad Addressability and Personalized Content in IPTV Markets   493
Christoph Fritsch

The Social Media War: Is Google+ the David to Facebook's
Goliath?   513
Richard Ganahl

Applications for the Media Sector to Leverage Content in Social
Networks   533
Jochen Spangenberg and Birgit Gray

Star Management of Talent Agencies and Social Media in Korea   549
Moonhaeng Lee

Predicting the Future of Investor Sentiment with Social Media in Stock
Exchange Investments: A Basic Framework for the DAX Performance
Index   565
Artur Lugmayr

Branding with Social Media at RTS 591
Stéphane Matteo, Giulia Spolaor, and Cinzia Dal Zotto

Social Television, Creative Collaboration and Television Production: The Case of the BBC's 'The Virtual Revolution' 603
Nicholas Nicoli

Evolution of Strategy and Commercial Relationships for Social Media Platforms: The Case of YouTube 619
Sonya Yan Song and Steven S. Wildman

Part V   Social Media: Impact and Users

Social Media and New Audiences as a New Challenge for Traditional and New Media Industries 635
Germán Arango-Forero and Sergio Roncallo-Dow

Towards a Typology of Strategies for User Involvement 657
Arne H. Krumsvik

Social Media Monitoring Tools as Instruments of Strategic Issues Management 671
Johanna Grüblbauer and Peter Haric

Social Networks: The Question on Efficiency Remains 689
Harald Rau

How to Engage the Audience? A Study on Using Twitter to Engage Newspaper Readers 703
Aldo van Weezel and Cristóbal Benavides

Blogs and Social Media: The New Word of Mouth and its Impact on the Reputation of Banks and on their Profitability 715
Eleftheria (Roila) Christakou and George-Michael Klimis

Social Networks and Media Brands: Exploring the Effect of Media Brands' Perceived Social Network Usage on Audience Relationship ... 737
Sylvia Chan-Olmsted, Moonhee Cho, and Mark Yi-Cheon Yim

Social Media Involvement Among College Students and General Population: Implications to Media Management 751
Louisa Ha and Xiao Hu

Customer Integration and Web Interactivity. A Literature Review and Analysis of the Role of Transaction Costs in Building Value Webs ... 775
Paul Murschetz

All Businesses are Media Business: The Impact of Social Media on the Healthcare Market 795
Alexander Schachinger

The Impact of Facebook on News Consumption 805
Agnes Urban and Tamas Bodoky

The Usage and Advertising Effects of Social Media in China 819
Li-Chuan Evelyn Mai

Part VI Conclusion

What Social Media Are Doing and Where They Are Taking Us 835
Robert G. Picard

About the Authors 843

Part I
Introduction

The Social Media Management Chain, How Social Media Influences Traditional Media

Mike Friedrichsen and Wolfgang Mühl-Benninghaus

In the past, the opportunity to be a publisher or a broadcaster was open to a select few. Now anyone can become a global media brand. The job of finding, producing and distributing content has extended from the newsroom to the street. In some countries, traditional, mainstream media has got lazy; they stopped trying many years ago. They failed to take account of changing audience behavior.

The technology advanced and the tools were developed to enable anyone to research, create and disseminate content. And some traditional mainstream media companies—not all, but some—failed to see the significance.

And there is social media. At first there was a cacophony of noise that was hard to follow. But then those designing social media tools got smarter, and social media became more focused and personalized through tagging, lists, and other filters. The noise was reduced and meaningful communication and instant participation enabled. It empowered the individual who had a story to tell with the tools to proclaim their news to the world. But still, some traditional, mainstream media organizations failed to respond. And the audience moved away and found a new home in their preferred social networking space, where they met like-minded individuals and formed communities. Those bonds grew. Individuals who were once loan voices—sometimes heard, often ignored—became recognized. Based on the quality of the content they produced they began to gain followers through peer group recommendation. Those followers responded, added value to what was being said, and shared the information with their contacts. And with smart tagging, it all went viral. They lost touch with their audience.

And as this happened, a new middle media, made up of informed bloggers and social networkers, began to develop. These were individuals who wrote and broadcast with authority, not because they were paid to do so, but because they had knowledge and a passion that they wanted to share with the world. Gradually,

M. Friedrichsen (✉) · W. Mühl-Benninghaus
Humboldt Media Business School, Humboldt University Berlin, Berlin, Germany
e-mail: friedrichsen@hmbs.eu

networks began to be built; experts linking their skills and sharing information. At the same time—in some newsrooms—tired, lifeless professional journalists were rewriting news releases and handouts, or copy/pasting the news wires, publishing and broadcasting the resulting content and pretending it was journalism.

The traditional, mainstream media organizations that get it right are those that have formulated a social media strategy based on taking note of changing audience behavior. For many, social media is now a central part of the newsgathering, news production and news distribution strategy. They have joined the global social media conversation and contribute to that conversation. They ask questions and answer questions, and the content they produce contains audience input which the audience trusts and, because it is about the issues that concern them, they comment, add value and share. Because of that, the media landscape will never be the same again. Traditional media that fails to recognize and respond to this ongoing change is probably doomed. However, the continued growth of social media could awaken those traditional media houses that have failed in their duty to inform the public debate. It could signal the end of copy/paste journalism and result in a flourishing of vibrant people-focused journalism. Social media could go down in history as having been the resuscitator that jolted mainstream media back to life.

A few years back, one would get into the office and talk about a TV program from last night. You'd chat about a talk show host and the latest song, or having spotted the Audi or Heineken billboard on a specific highway. Traditional media ruled by relevance, content, circulation and ultimately, audience share.

Today, you are more likely to get an update on trending topics on Twitter/Facebook or ground breaking news via one of these platforms prior to watching the late night news or reading the afternoon print edition of a newspaper or listening to radio news on the hour.

It has become easy to recognize these social tools as part of the media marketing mix, from a marketer's perspective. But more scary is that new/social media has managed to get free air, as most shows now incorporate, or rather extend, their audience to these mediums for additional information and in the process, build stronger affiliations with their fans beyond the first media contact point, in this case TV, radio, outdoor or print.

So, taking this into consideration, traditional media houses need to start asking some questions.

- To what extent does new/social media have an impact on the long term strategic focus for traditional media houses?
- Are traditional media houses playing a role in diminishing their value and creating an audience shift phenomenon?
- Are traditional media houses seeking to find relevance to the extent that they have directly or indirectly become an ally in the process producing content that drives traffic to their future competitors?
- Are those that form part of the strategic team in traditional media houses aware that social media status as a secondary platform has the ability to convert into a primary media platform of preference?

- With diminishing newsroom expertise, and reliance on new media for content, what will be traditional media future currency be, considering readily available independently produced content?
- How best to monetize content produced by traditional media houses in these new platforms?

The battle to take pole position is evolving at the speed of light. Whilst traditional media is experiencing challenges in attracting future audiences, social media started with the same audience that traditional media disregarded and despite this, they failed to create relevance even with their current audience.

It's unfortunate that traditional media has failed to find content that their future audience could easily identify with beyond the music shows, matric results and the career sections. While circulation and audience ratings are diminishing for traditional media houses, the opposite is an hourly occurrence for new and social media. Traditional media houses are cutting costs of content production and staff, and social media has now become a source for traditional media looking for content.

Apps developers and content producers are all creating their communities in these new platforms. Even though this might differ with each type of traditional media, for print the following sections are no longer relevant to attracting new audiences: the food section, the car section, the property section, the classified section and it won't be long until the business section and the front page have their turn too.

1 Focus of the Book

More and more we can see a continuous change from the old Media Management to new strategic, operative and normative management options. Social Media Management has become an issue for every media company with a renewed "skill set"- specialized knowledge for the digital products and production and for marketing and target groups. This emerging development of media shift nowadays requires increasingly for active communication in the fundamental segments of these scholarly disciplines. The interface of media economy/media management provides the relevant arena in this matter.

2 Main Parts of the Book

- Management with Social Media.
- New Value Chain with Social Media.
- Forms and Content of Social Media.
- Social Media: Impact and Users.

Most of the chapters are interdisciplinary approaches. Main questions (among other) are:
- What are the specific effects of Social Media on Media Management Research?
- How is the value chain changing?

- What are the main changes of business models?
- Are there new theoretical approaches? Is it possible to combine "old" and "new" theories?
- Do we have some new empirical results?
- What are the proposals for the development in this research field?

Seventy-five Media Management researchers from the whole world are involved in this book. With very different content and methodical attempts the contributions also permit an interesting comparison of the developments in each country.

Part II
Management with Social Media

Traditional Media Companies in the U.S. and Social Media: What's the Strategy?

Alan B. Albarran and Terry Moellinger

Social media has existed in various forms for several decades, but came in to mainstream notoriety in the first decade of the twenty-first century with the debut of a number of sites (e.g. MySpace, Facebook, LinkedIn, YouTube, etc.) that soared in popularity and access. While still in its infancy, social media is impacting the way individuals communicate with one another and creating disruption across the media industries.

Social media has taken on greater importance by capturing the attention and interest of consumers, marketers, advertisers, and businesses. While the number of social media users changes literally by the hour, it is clear millions of people are using social media around the world. The wide adoption of social media has created more confusion and challenges for the media industries, as social media has become yet another platform to engage and interact with consumers. Media companies do not have a choice; they must now include social media as part of their overall digital strategy. But what exactly is the *strategy* in adopting and utilizing social media? That is the central question driving this particular study.

Our analysis draws as its theoretical basis Chan-Olmsted's (2006) meta-review of issues in strategic management as applied to media firms. The author notes that strategic management research as a field is relatively young, with its origins dating to the 1960s. Key authors who influenced the development of strategic management as an area of research include Chandler (1962), Porter (1980, 1985), Chafee (1985), and Mintzberg et al. (1998). A more limited body of research volumes regarding strategy among media firms exists, notably an edited volume on media firms (Picard 2002), and Chan-Olmsted (2008).

This chapter examines several "traditional" based media companies housed in the United States to discern how the company is utilizing social media from a strategic

---

A.B. Albarran (✉)
University of North Texas, Denton, TX, USA
e-mail: albarran@unt.edu

T. Moellinger
North Central Texas College, Gainesville, TX, USA

perspective. The companies examined include broadcast and film conglomerates The Walt Disney Company, Viacom, News Corporation, Time Warner, and CBS; newspaper publishers The New York Times, and Gannet; and the largest public radio company in America, Cumulus. Here are the research questions guiding this study:

RQ1: How are the traditional media companies addressing the strategic challenge of developing a social media presence?
RQ2: How is social media integrated into a comprehensive digital strategy?
RQ3: How is social media being monetized by these companies?
RQ4: Are new business models emerging?

Addressing these research questions required an examination of several sources including academic and business literature as well as corporate documents available in the public domain such as annual reports, SEC filings, and information on the companies' Web sites.

1 The Challenge of Integrating Social Media

How are the traditionally media based companies in the United States addressing the strategic challenge of developing a social media presence and how they integrating social media into a comprehensive digital strategy? The first research question can be easily answered by examining Table 1 below, drawing the data from Web sites and platforms used by the various companies. A content analysis of each company reveals similar involvement in areas like Web sites, social media sites, video sites, Twitter, blogs, and different forms of online gaming. As seen in the table, the companies are actively engaged in several forms of social media and once can conclude that most have developed a strong social media presence.

We now take a closer individual look at the companies to address the second research question regarding how social media is part of a larger digital strategy.

1.1 Walt Disney Company

The Walt Disney Company was one of the first large American media corporations to engage in social media. As *Go.com* was conceived, its mission was to promote Disney entertainment projects, theme parks, and merchandise, principally through their brick-and-mortar outlets, conforming to then Chief Executive Officer Michael Eisner's vision of "synergy." However it also invited comment and group discussion from fans in a fledgling social network (Eisner and Schwartz 1998). Although Eisner left in 2005 [a year after a surprising stockholder's meeting where Roy Disney and Stanley Gold engineered the withholding of 43 % of the proxies supporting Eisner's re-election of the board (Stewart 2005)]; his concept of synergy still dominates the company's utilization of social media. Whether it's the use of Blogs, Twitter, Facebook, YouTube or other platforms by their youthful stars, production and sports teams, or theme park, resort, cruse-line marketing managers, the goal is to promote the sale of Disney products, except now they are expanding their merchandise sales to include on-line offerings. The sole exception is gaming.

Table 1 U.S. media corporations and social media presence

Corporation	Internet Web sites	Facebook, MySpace, LinkedIn	YouTube and other video sites	Twitter	Blogs	Gaming
Belo	√	√	√	√	√	
CBS	√	√	√	√	√	
Cumulus	√	√		√	√	
Disney	√	√	√	√	√	√
Gannett	√	√	√	√	√	
NY Times	√	√	√	√	√	
News Corp	√	√	√	√	√	
TimeWarner	√	√	√	√	√	√
Viacom	√	√	√	√	√	√

Source: Compiled by the authors from company Web sites and digital platforms

Gaming falls under the direction of Disney Interactive Media Group (DIMG). Their mission "is to deliver Disney content to fans wherever and whenever they want it, through numerous interactive platforms." While on the surface that appears an extension of the synergy concept, the unit is also engaged in revenue generation as well, producing "console and handheld video games for the Nintendo Wii™, Nintendo DS™, Playstation® Portable, X-box 360® video game and entertainment system, [and] PLAYSTATION®3 computer game system" (Interactive Media 2011, p. 1). Again, this appears to be an extension of an older Disney goal of promoting synergy within product lines and the production of a new type of brick-and-mortar product. However, the interactive division is also concerned with engaging their potential consumers in direct feedback and "user generated content" through numerous Web sites and placing both content and games on Facebook and MySpace. They have also developed interactive on-line virtual worlds such as *World of Cars Online*, *Disney Club Penguin*, *Disney Fairies Pixie Hollow*, *Disney's Toontown Online*, and *Pirate of the Caribbean Online*. The division also purchased Playdom.com in 2010 which offers games on a subscription basis, to "more than 47 million monthly users" (Annual Report, DIMG 2011, p. 25). Playdom has also brought Disney's ESPN franchise into the gaming area.

In terms of Disney's gaming revenue generation, Bob Iger, current President and CEO, stressed that the company "approached games in kind of a blended way." While they will continue in their traditional role of providing products for console units that are linked to their entertainment programming, Iger also acknowledged the emerging use of games on all Internet-based platforms and the growing social media aspects of this use and the problems that creating a revenue stream caused. The CEO noted "there are a lot of business models out there now from free-to-play, micro transactions, subscriptions, sponsorship, box product now at multiple tiered pricing with downloadable content on the back end. And we in this group need to take advantage of every one of those revenue streams in a dynamic way to maximize our potential" (Iger 2011, p. 2).

1.2 News Corporation

Despite their problems with the acquisition and divesting of MySpace, News Corporation has remained interested in social media and the potential of social media outlets. The company established "Slingshot Labs," which hope to develop new Internet-based destinations and social media applications to promote new ventures and revenue streams (News Corporation Launches). News Corps' Dow Jones operation is now using consumer reaction as noted through social media portals as an indicator of consumer confidence in the economy (Thibault 2009).

The use of digital media, including social media formats, falls into line with the company's internal vision. In the 2010 Annual Report to shareholders, Rupert Murdoch stated that "core principle" of News Corporation is that they are "a creative media company that attracts and retains customers by giving them the news and entertainment that they value" (Murdoch 2010, p. 10). This vision is also directly applied to digital media, noting "as one of the leading suppliers of content worldwide, we've made strides in giving consumers an array of choice when it come to consuming digital content." Peter Levinsohn, President, New Media and Digital Distribution for the Fox Filmed Entertainment division, also mentions that the goal of News Corp was to build "distribution models that are both sustainable and durable over the long term" (Henderson and Horner 2009, pp. 1–2). However finding both a sustainable and durable model is proving difficult for all media companies. Murdoch has stated the company will depend on advertising revenue less in the future (Murdoch 2010); they are pursuing a two-tiered approach to revenue generation. While attempting to sell content, they are still dependent on advertising, with social media both supporting and promoting this effort.

News America Marketing, a division of News Corporation, began offering its advertising clients a coupon service that takes advantage of both an Internet location and Twitter notification for potential consumers (News America Marketing Upgrades 2009). News Corp as also attempted to link the viewers of their popular Fox Network properties, like *The X Factor*, with advertisers like Chevrolet on several social media sites (Fox Broadcasting Company 2011) and Pepsi on YouTube (Hudson 2011).

As an example to the second revenue stream, News Corporation is also attempting to sell their content, especially in the financial sector. Both *MarketWatch* and the *Wall Street Journal* itself are now offering social media applications to be used on *Facebook* and with other Internet-delivery platforms to be modeled on a subscription revenue stream (Huston 2011; MarketWatch App 2009).

1.3 Viacom

Viacom uses social media to attract consumers to their Web sites especially its youth oriented asset MTV, and MTV's popular cable program *Jersey Shore*. Once the viewer reaches these platforms, they are greeted with top-up advertising copy and links to other related sites (which also feature advertisements) and Viacom's promotional content. This program began in 2008 when the MTV networks acquired the *Flux Social Media* platform (MTV's Networks Acquires 2008), and has accelerated to include all of the popular social media sites favored by young consumers. In a further attempt to brand themselves to the youth audience, all of Viacom's cable networks are engaged in what they term the "Take Action, Right Now" program. Each network supports group discussion and other social media techniques about issues geared toward their audience, e.g., Comedy Central's "Address the Mess," MTV's "Lean to Green," and CMT's "One Country" and "Music for Kids" (Take Action 2001). Viacom also sponsors MTV U's network for college students (The Number 1 Media Network 2011), and President Clinton's social media "tool" for financial aid (President Clinton Announces 2011).

Viacom's use of social media is not limited to the youth market. During the most recent Super Bowl contest, they used Facebook and Twitter to attract people to their *"OnionSports"* and *"OSNGirlfriends"* sites ("Onion SportsDome" Delivers 2011). Viacom has attempted to link films produced from Paramount Pictures and Nickelodeon Movies with theme related games as an additional revenue stream (Freeplay social media game 2010).

1.4 Time Warner

Joining Disney and Comcast, Time Warner believes that in a few years all television content will be available on the Internet (Levine 2011). While the company claims to be "aggressively pursuing initiatives that give audiences more choice and quality at no addition cost to them" (Bewkes 2011, pp. 1–2), their CEO, Jeff Bewkes also claimed that "consumers are willing to pay for high quality content," and along with Comcast they have offered to provide visual content to their cable subscribers (LaVallee 2009). Their first attempt to use the Internet as a content delivery mechanism was their creation of Pathfinder.com in 1994, However in recent years they, along with Disney and CBS, have found that mobile applications provide more revenue. *The Hollywood Reporter* noted an increase in mobile video revenues grew in 2010 to $46.6 million, up from $43 million in 2008 (Szalai 2011). Although they were off the mark with regard to seeing the value of the Internet, Time Warner's use of social media outlets have been limited to encouraging the display of free content, primarily news and promotions, in order to establish a presence. In addition, they have retooled their traditional Web sites to provide the look of the newer social media portals, and have invited viewer response.

The one exception is Mousebreaker, a gaming provider owned by Time Warner's IPC Media division, which provided a football (soccer) game for Facebook users. This launch corresponded with the popular World Cup games and was aimed at the British and European markets (Gawn 2010). Mousebreaker follows the precepts outlined by CEO Jeff Bewkes, that the company should pursue dual revenue streams, offering content through subscription/licenses and incorporating advertising into the presentation (Mousebreaker Ltd 2011).

An example of how Time Warner is dressing up its Web offering to mimic social media sites can be seen in their CNN Tech portal. The site is designed to showcase "the latest news, products, perspectives and buzz in the world of technology," as well as cultural demands for mobile use, gaming, and new "gadgets." This site is "a user-friendly [with a] blog-inspired design," and ask their users for comments and "Facebook 'recommends' are integrated at every level" (Andrews 2010, p. 1).

Like most of the other media companies, Time Warner is attempting to make their content accessible for other Internet-delivery methods, making applications available for iPhone and iPod Touch, and feature their comments on Twitter (Andrews 2010).

1.5 Columbia Broadcasting System (CBS)

CBS has maintained an Internet presence for a number of years. CBS promotes their entertainment, sports, and news programming. In addition they also feature advertising for other programs and their corporate sponsoring partners as well as advising viewers to follow the development of their favorite programs on Facebook and Twitter. CBS also actively encouraged their on-the-air personalities to use those two social networks as well as video streaming sources such as YouTube. Their use of social media sources is an attempt to draw people to their Web sites. The NCAA® "March Madness®" (basketball tournament) on-demand site demonstrates the effectiveness of this strategy. Using promotions on Facebook and Twitter (along with normal fan interest) for the first day of the tournament, the site drew the largest single day traffic for a sporting event in the Internet's history (NCAA® March Madness® 2010). In addition to providing program content and promotions, as well as advertising on the Internet, CBS's publishing branch—Simon & Schuster—uses the Bookvideos.tv platform and social media site YouTube to feature their authors and promote the sales of their books (Simon and Schuster 2007).

In addition to the use of social media to draw consumers to their advertising based Web sites, CBS has coupled local blogs, and their social media reach, with their local station, national and local advertisers, and CBS news content together in a "locally focused venture" (CBS Television Stations Launch 2008). The focus on providing localized service to their advertising base as lead CBS to partner with CityGrid® Media to "provide businesses of all sizes the opportunity to be featured CBS's two dozen co-branded television and radio Web sites across the country" (CBS teams with CityGrid® Media 2011, p. 1).

1.6 The New York Times Company

The one sector in America's media that has embraced social networking as a potential revenue stream is newspaper publishing. The New York Times has entered into a relationship with LinkedIn to provide the users of the social network with personalized content drawn from the *Times* for business and technology reporting, where users can share and discuss these stories. This relationship is directed toward increasing advertising revenue. The Times press release announcing this new linkage, stated: "This relationship expands NYTimes.com's targeting capability and creates a powerful incentive for advertisers to leverage LinkedIn's and NYTimes.com's combined reach to the business community" (The New York Times and LinkedIn 2008, p. 1). The realization that a strategy was needed with social media sites were demonstrated when The New York Times joined the Facebook Ads system in 2007. Although this was mostly an attempt to allow "users to learn about New York Times, Boston Globe and the Times Company's Regional Media Group content" (McNulty 2007, p. 1), and not to generate additional revenues, it did provide the entry step into social media. In addition to LinkedIn and Facebook, the Times supplies news and financial updates on Twitter, and videos on both MySpace and YouTube (Social Media Channels 2011). The Times has created delivery applications for mobile platforms, like the BlackBerry, Sony Reader, the Palm Pre, Nook, Kindle, and iPhone. In addition, they have established *beta628*, a Web site that explores new interactive projects and invites comments and suggestions (Mason 2011).

While the Times generates advertising revenue through their Internet and social media presence, they have also created a second revenue source through the selling of their content online, including their popular travel section, book reviews, and crosswords. Their new "metered model will offer users free access to a set number of articles per month and then charge users when they exceed that number" (McNulty 2010, p. 1).

1.7 Gannet, Inc

Like The New York Times, Gannett, the publisher of USA Today and 81 other daily newspapers (Our Company 2011), has adopted "a pay for content" approach for their Internet portals. Although Craig A. Dubow, the former CEO of Gannett admitted that they are looking at "different prices for different content models," and sustainability of any model is an important determination, the company is convinced that "consumers value our content and are absolutely willing to pay for it" (Dubow 2010, pp. 2–3). In addition to charging readers for content, Gannett is actively engaged in providing businesses with advertising linked to these sites, creating additional revenue streams. Gannett's on-line solicitations mention their ability to present advertising messages "across a wide-range of platforms" (Our Marketing Solutions 2011, p. 1), including print, television stations, and Web sites "that reach 52 million unique users monthly" (Our Company 2011, p. 1). Dubow stated: "Central to these efforts is the idea that consumers will always seek relevant content and advertisers need to connect to those consumers" (Dubow 2008, p. 2).

Recognizing the potential of digital media, Gannett acquired social media outlet Ripple6 in 2008, (Gannett acquires 2008), and a year latter established a digital media network by incorporating such offerings as MomsLikeMe.com, HighSchoolSports. net, Metromix.com featuring local entertainment needs, and *BNQT* focusing on action and extreme sports, to their digital mix. Along with their Web portals, PointRoll, Ripple6 and *ShopLocal*, these sites were designed to support the company's local news offering and promote local advertising, thus adding "localism" as a third pillar to Gannett's revenue growth (Gannett Announces Formation 2009). In addition, they have HistoryBeat.com to serve people interested in local history into a potential consumer base (Gannett Digital Media Network partners 2009).

Taking the growth of digital media, including social media, and both revenue objectives into consideration, Gannett has launched their "It's All Within Reach" campaign. In announcing the campaign, Dubow stated "In today's changing media landscape, Gannett is in a unique position to help businesses reach, tailor and direct their messages to specific audiences on many different platforms" (Dubow 2011, p. 1).

Social media plays a substantial part in Gannett's strategic vision, claiming that 2009 was "a breakout year for digital content—from apps to tablets to social media." CEO Dubow said "We are putting a significant amount of time and energy into social media to further engage with our viewers and our readers" (Dubow 2010, pp. 1–2). In addition to supporting their Internet and local media offerings, Gannett also uses social media, especially Facebook and Twitter, to deliver local content and keep their audiences informed of emergency situations (Social media: Essential tools 2011).

1.8 Cumulus

With the 2011 acquisition of Citadel Broadcasting Corporation, Cumulus Media is the largest public radio company in the United States, with 570 stations in 120 markets (Hannan 2011). The financial operation of the company would be classified as a traditional advertising based model with each station responsible for, and judged on, the generation of sales revenue. Cumulus views their other media forms—primarily local television and newspapers—as their primary competition, and each station approaches their potential clients with the sentiment that "no media reaches more people more often for less" (Radio is the most cost-effective 2011, p. 1). Focusing on local advertisers, their sales force also discounts the Internet, and social media, as an expensive, too technologically complex, and unnecessary means of attracting customers. They argue that advertisers should "focus on building community, not on winning the search game" (Local Business...Untangle the Web 2011, p. 1). However, their local radio stations, reflecting a need to attract listeners, have embraced the Internet and many of their over-the-air personalities maintain Facebook pages and contribute information through Twitter and Blogs. Like the other media concerns, the individual stations, while constructed to appeal to their listeners tastes—sports information, talk radio issues, popular music personalities and upcoming events—also feature advertising copy and links. Although Cumulus has not constructed a potential revenue stream for social media, on an indirect level it does use a form of social media to enhance their revenue. They offer advertising clients an in-house newsletter designed to focus on both national and local economic trends. This newsletter is available on a subscription basis and distributed as both an email and a blog (Subscribe 2011).

1.9 Belo Corporation

Belo Corp. owns and operates 20 television stations, two regional cable news channels, two local cable news channels and manages two others, and operates 30 Web sites. The company had 2009 annual revenue of $590 million, and employs 2,300 (Belo Fact Sheet 2011). In attracting advertising clients, they contend "the majority of Belo television stations are the most-watched stations in their markets" (Belo Advertising 2011, p. 1).

Belo's primary revenue stream is advertising based, both on its television stations and Web sites. A good example is WFAA.com, the site associated with their flagship station in the Dallas, Texas market. This site features "in-depth features and interactive multi-media" drawn from their news operation, and also "covers late breaking news, streaming video, sports, entertainment, local classified listing and current weather updates highlighted by 57 up-to-the minute weather radars." Their on-the-air personalities, both anchors and reporters, are also encouraged to maintain an Internet presence. Of their 32 reporters/anchors, sports reporters, and weather forecasters, 19 have individual Facebook pages, 20 use Twitter, and all have an Internet page linked to the station's Web site. The station also provides mobile applications which receive "6 million page views per month" (WFAA Advertising 2011, p. 1). In addition to their local classified section, clients can place copy directly within the site, and link their own Web site to their advertising. Belo reached an agreement with Yahoo that "expands the audience reach that Belo stations can deliver to advertisers" (Television Company Belo Corp. Expands 2011, p. 1). Belo's use of social media is directed to support this traditional advertising model. In addition to posting videos on YouTube, all of their on-air personalities—news, sports, weather, traffic and special features/assignments—have a Facebook page and most are active in presenting a blog, and using Twitter.

In analyzing the integration of a social media strategy by these U. S. based companies we observe some similarities but many more differences. Some companies have a clearly defined strategy, while others are in various stages of development. Large conglomerates, as would be expected, are more engaged in a variety of social media activities and recognize the importance of monetizing their efforts. Print-dominated companies are perhaps a bit more limited in their use of social media, constantly using it to drive back to their main product lines. Smaller companies like Belo have a discernable strategy built around localism and news personalities. Table 2 offers some key quotes related to a strategy for social media activities from selected companies.

As Rupert Murdoch indicates all the media companies are attempting to place themselves in a position to "drive history," at least in terms of establishing a successful business model for the digital marketplace. They recognize social media is an important tool. However, finding the appropriate revenue generating combinations using social media has proven difficult. As Jeff Bewkes of Time Warner indicates this approach needs to be exactly that, a combination. Further, at least for the near future, advertising exposure needs to be an element in constructing a model. As Craig A. Dubow of Gannett and the press release from The New York Times indicate, social media is important not only to engage their readers and establish a corporate presence, but also drives these same readers to corporate Web sites where content can be purchased and advertisements viewed. The Times press release also mentions the power of the Internet as a tool to distribute content, and most of these companies have developed applications that are used on mobile platforms.

Marc Frons of The New York Times indicates the challenge is to "create a better online experience" (McNulty 2010, p. 1) to insure reader/viewer continued engagement, as well as promoting the company's financial success. In terms of engagement, the companies have not only established a social media presence but have also redesigned the Web sites to incorporate elements drawn from social media platforms. In terms of financial success, CBS indicates new partnerships are being formed to provide a localized consumer experience. Amy Powel of Viacom mentions another area of possible revenue that several media companies are pursuing is via gaming. Companies recognize that many game sites constitute a virtual gaming community. Given the popularity of video games, this area represents a growing revenue stream.

Table 2 Observations on social media as part of a digital strategy

Corporation	Key quote/reference
News Corporation	From the wheel to the Web, from the printing press to fiber optic cable, it has always been technology that has driven history. Those in the driving seat have always been those who fully understood and used that technology—Rupert Murdoch, CEO (2006, p. 5).
Time Warner	Today, there is widespread acknowledgement among content providers that free-ad-supported Web sites cannot replace powerful dual revenue stream business models—Jeff Bewkes, CEO (2011, pp. 1–2).
Gannett	We are putting a significant amount of time and energy into social media to further engage with our viewers and our readers—Craig A. Dubow, CEO (2010, pp. 2–3).
New York Times	The linkage of content and social media "give us the opportunity to distribute NYTimes.com content to a very engaged readership and a viral distribution platform"—*New York Times* Press Release (McNulty 2007, p. 1).
New York Times	We are challenging out talented staff and our community of users to publish ideas and concepts that can create a better online experience—Marc Frons, Chief Technology Officer, *The New York Times* (McNulty 2010, p. 1).
CBS	The CBS Local Ad Network, [is] a first-of-its-kind partnership between a major media company's television stations and local bloggers and social media Web sites—CBS Press Release (CBS Television Stations Launch 2008, p. 1).
Viacom	It is only natural to extend our interactive marketing to a social media game—Amy Powell, Viacom Spokesperson (Freeplay social media game 2010, p. 1).
Disney	There are a lot of business models out there now from free-to-play, micro transactions, subscriptions, sponsorship, box product now at multiple tiered pricing with downloadable content on the back end. And we in this group need to take advantage of every one of those revenue streams in a dynamic way to maximize our potential—Bob Iger, CEO (2011, pp. 1–2).

2 Monetizing Social Media

Regarding the third research question, no company has completely formed a successful model for producing revenue using social media. Most companies are looking at traditional methods to measure activity, namely the number of hits and their growth over time. Dubow of Gannett explains that "USA Today and our local sites served more than 1.6 billion mobile page views, that's up 267 %," in their 2010 Annual Report, (Dubow 2010). Some companies are attempting to measure success in terms of bottom-line revenue, but social media is not yet broken out but embedded within other revenue segments. A good example is CBS. The company generated advertising revenue of $2.21 billion for the first quarter of 2011, but does not reveal what percentage is contributed by digital platforms like social media. Likewise they report "content licensing and distribution" category of $889 million, yet it is unclear if this includes their locally focused advertisement venture along with station fees (Consolidated and Segment Statement 2011).

Both Gannett and Disney have created a "digital" or "interactive media" segment. In 2010 Gannett reported net operating revenue of $618,259,000 for their digital segment (Consolidated Statement 2011). This led former CEO Dubow to observe: "We are seeing tremendous growth with digital, which make up 20 % of our revenue in the first quarter of this year" (Dubow 2010). On the other hand, while Disney reported $761,000, when adjusted for operating expenses this total became ($234,000) for 2010. However, it is uncertain if their gaming operations fall into this category or their consumer products one which showed adjusted revenue of $677,000 (Summary Financial Highlights 2011).

What can be discerned is that media companies are beginning to monetize their social media efforts. All but one company (Cumulus) is using their social media platforms to direct their listeners to Web sites designed to promote revenue. The most direct revenue stream related to monetization remains advertising; primarily used to drive consumers to Web sites promoting various products and/or services.

The second revenue stream observed is with media content. One avenue is the promotion of an entertainment or informational product with the hope that the reader/viewer will later access the content through one of its platforms. Closely linked with this effort is an attempt to get the consumer to make a purchase entertainment, such as a movie, television program, music, book or other print product—by downloading the product online or making a traditional purchase via a retailer or other vendor. Some Web sites, especially those associated with print and newspaper providers, also attempt to encourage readers/viewers to purchase content either through subscription or as a metered model.

The only media company in this analysis that does not yet use social media to direct people to their Web site is radio giant Cumulus. They see locally based advertising as their primary revenue stream. Cumulus does use a form of social media to support a secondary stream, by offing advertising clients informational blogs in support of an in-house newsletter that is offered on a subscription basis. Along with the dual revenue approach adopted by most media companies, Disney, Time Warner, and Viacom use social media gaming to both promote entertainment programs and as a revenue source, providing games through downloads, subscriptions, or brick-and-mortar retailers.

Figure 1 illustrates how the American media companies in this study are using social media in their revenue generating strategies. Social media sites, blogs, and gaming platforms (where utilized) are used to drive audience traffic to company digital platforms and Web sites. At these locations, consumers are exposed to various forms of advertising messages, subscription offers, and the opportunity to purchase a product or service.

3 Are New Business Model Emerging?

Based on this initial analysis of nine traditionally-oriented media companies based in the United States, there is no evidence of any new business model emerging regarding social media. At this early stage, monetization of social media is happening primarily through traditional advertising, and that is limited. Further, the revenues are apparently so small that no company breaks out the exact contribution of social media income to their total revenues.

But this does not mean that we won't see new business models emerging. There are several areas which are ripe for growing revenues related to social media. We identify the following as distinct possibilities:

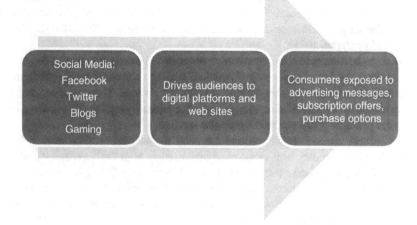

Fig. 1 Approaches to social media monetization. *Source*: Author's rendition

- Location Based Services (LBS). These services utilize a consumer's location (usually through GPS capabilities) to track customers as they enter restaurants, retail establishments, and other places of business. Foursquare is an early leader in this nascent industry. As customers "check-in" their location, customers can receive coupons and other discounts on their mobile phone. While Foursquare and similar services raise privacy concerns for some, many consumers will likely ignore the problem in order to receive promotional discounts. LBS services will help grow digital advertising, and also encourage and promote more point-of-sale shopping.
- Mobile Broadcast Video. In the United States, several mainstream television operators crated the Open Mobile Video Coalition in 2007 to promote the development of mobile television for portable devices. Testing has already begun in Washington, D. C., with other markets to follow. The debut of full-motion, live broadcast television on mobile devices is a short time away, opening the opportunities to engage social media efforts with live video and generate new revenue streams.
- Social Media Marketing. We know that social media offers new ways to promote and market products to both audiences and advertisers. Many retailers from different industries are just now experimenting with social media marketing. Small businesses at the local level have for the most part not at all engaged a social media marketing effort as yet. The potential of more business owners—whether large or small—adopting a social media marketing effort over the next 3 years is quite large. In fact, BIA/Kelsey predicts that social media advertising will reach $8.3 billion in the U. S. by 2015 (Wasserman 2011).
- Networks of Networks. One other area of expected growth and potential new business model is the ability of companies to harness data from individuals engaging social media via their network with those networks established by friends. An extension of database marketing, it will one day be possible for companies to leverage their network of networks to promote, market, and engage audiences. This is happening now as

research companies are "mining" data generated by social media sites; it will only become more sophisticated and more targeted moving forward.

These four areas appear to show promise as to where new business models may emerge, although we won't speculate as to what these new models may look like. Ultimately, the marketplace will determine what new models prove the most effective.

Conclusion

This study sought to explain how social media is being used strategically by nine different traditional-based media companies in the United States. The sample of companies selected for analysis ranged from large multidivisional conglomerates (e.g., News Corporation, Time Warner, Disney, Viacom, CBS) to print-based companies (New York Times and Gannett) to television (Belo Corp.) and radio (Cumulus).

All of the companies are engaged in a social media strategy with varying levels of development with the exception of Cumulus, which is minimally involved in a social media strategy. The companies do recognize the importance of social media, and are actively integrating social media across their digital platforms. Each company was individually analyzed to offer a complete picture of their efforts.

Many companies are attempting to monetize their social media activities, but at this early stage of development it is not possible to determine exactly what percentage social media revenues contribute to total revenues. By all estimates, it appears to be small yet all companies believe that social media revenues will grow over time, as does industry analysts like BIA/Kelsey (Wasserman 2011).

No evidence of new business models is yet present in the young marketplace for social media. However, several new applications and options in development (e.g., location based services, mobile video, expanded marketing, and network analysis) hold promise for growth.

This is an area where more research over time will be needed to understand the evolving marketplace in which social media operates, and how these traditional companies continue to adapt and grow. This analysis was limited in scope by the focus on a handful of companies representing one continent, and was also examined at a time when recessionary pressures were still being felt along with a muted business climate. The findings nevertheless will hopefully spur more research in to the discussion of understanding how traditional-based media companies adopt and integrate social media, leading to increased knowledge of the best practices and models to use to maximize revenues and a competitive strategic advantage.

References

Andrews, A. (2010, June 8). CNN.com's new tech section buzzes with breadth of experts, surfaces news based on social signals. Retrieved from http://www.timewarner.com/newsroom/press-releases/2010/06/CNNcoms_New-Tech-Section_Buzz.html

Annual report: Disney interactive media group. (2011, August 21). Retrieved from http://corporate.disney.go.com/investors/annual_reports/2010/kb_dirng_story.html

Belo Advertising. (2011, October 7). Retrieved from http://www.belo.com/advertising.html

Belo Fact Sheet. (2011, October 7). Retrieved from http://www.belo.com/about/facts.html

Bewkes, J. (2011, September 19). Content everywhere. Retrieved from http://www.timewarner.com/our-innovations/vontent-everywhere.html

CBS teams with CityGrid® Media to connect local advertisers with consumers across the web. (2011, March 29). Retrieved from http://www.cbscorporation.com/news-article.php?id=767

CBS television stations launch first-of-its-kind revenue sharing partnership with local blogs and social media websites. (2008, March 1). Retrieved from http://www.cbscorporation.com/news-article.php?id=604

Chafee, E. (1985). Three models of strategy. *Academy of Management Review, 10*, 89–98.

Chandler, A. (1962). *Strategy and structure*. Cambridge, MA: MIT Press.

Chan-Olmsted, S. M. (2006). *Competitive strategy for media firms. Strategic and brand management in changing media markets*. Mahwah, NJ: Lawrence Erlbaum Associates.

Chan-Olmsted, S. M. (2008). Issues in strategic management. In A. B. Albarran, S. M. Chan-Olmsted, & M. O. Wirth (Eds.), *Handbook of media management and economics* (pp. 161–180). Mahwah, NJ: Lawrence Erlbaum Associates.

Consolidated and segment results. (2011, October 11). *2011 first quarter report for CBS Corporation*. Retrieved from http://investors.cbscorporation.com/phoenix.zhtml?c=99462&p=irol-sec

Consolidated statements of income (loss). (2011, October 10). *Gannett Co, Inc. 2010 annual report*. Retrieved from http://www.gannett.com/section/INVESTORREL02.html

Dubow, C. A. (2008, December 10). Gannett executives speak at the UBS Media and Communications Conference. Retrieved from http://www.gannett.com/apps/pbcs.dill/artikkel?AID=9999100319010.html

Dubow, C. A. (2010). *Gannett's 2010 annual report*. Retrieved from http://www.gannett.com/section/INVSTORREL02.html

Dubow, C. A. (2011, March 7). Gannett launches "it's all within reach" national brand campaign. Retrieved from http://www.gannett.com/apps/pbcs.dill/artikkel?Dato=99999999&Kategori=PRESSRELEASE18&Lop.html

Eisner, M. D., & Schwartz, T. (1998). *Work in progress*. New York: Random House.

Fox Broadcasting Company, Sysco Television and FremantieMedia announce Chevrolet as official automotive sponsor of The X Factor. (2011, June 9). Retrieved from http://www.newscorp.com/news/bunews_444.html

Freeplay social media game and experience based on M. Night Shamalan's July 2, 2010 release. (2010, June 6). Retrieved from http://www.viacom.com/news/Pages/newstext.aspx?RID=1437433.html

Gannett acquires social media provider Ripple6. (2008, November 13). Retrieved from http://www.gannett.com/apps/pbcs.dill/article?AID=9999100419003.html

Gannett announces formation of the Gannett Digital Media Network. (2009, April 23). Retrieved from http://www.gannett.com/apps/pbcs.dill/article?AID=999100203042.html

Gannett Digital Media Network partners with Footnote.com to launch HistoryBeat.com websites. (2009, August 1). Retrieved from http://www.gannett.com/apps/pbcs.dill/artic;e?AID=9999100712011.html

Gawn, A. (2010, June 10). Mousebreaker launches first Facebook game. Retrieved from http://www.timewarner.com/newsroom/press-releases/2010/06/Mousebreaker_Launches-First-Facebook.html

Hannan, J. P. (2011, September 16). Cumulus Media Inc. announces completion of the acquisition of Citadel Broadcasting Corporation and related global refinancing. Retrieved from http://phx.corporate-ir.net/pheoenix.zhtml?c=105645&p=irol-newArticle_print&ID.html

Henderson, J., & Horner, J. (2009, April 1). News Corporation establishes digital leadership roles. Retrieved from http://www.newscorp.com/news/news_431.html

Hudson, J. (2011, June 2). The X Factor and Pepsi announce YouTube partnership. Retrieved from http://www.newscorp.com/news/bunews_442.html

Huston, A. (2011, September 20). *Wall Street Journal* launches "WSJ Social" app in Beta for Facebook. Retrieved from http://www.newscorp.com/news/bunews_476.html

How local businesses can untangle the web. (2011, September 21). Retrieved from http://dallas.cumulusradio.com/ideasForBuildingYourBusiness/UntanglingTheWeb/tabid/102.html

Iger, B. (2011, February 17). *The Walt Disney Company's 2011 investor conference.* Retrieved from http://corporate.disney.go.com/investors/archive.html

Interactive Media Group. (2011, August 21). Retrieved from http://disney.go.com/disneycareers/dimg.html

LaVallee, A. (2009, December 6). Time Warner CEO: There is a willingness to pay for quality content. *The Wall Street Journal.* Retrieved from http://blogs.wsj.com/digits/2009/12/08/TimeWarner-ceo-there-is-a-willingness-to-pay-for-quality-content.html

Levine, D. M. (2011, June 7). In 2 years nearly all TV content will be online, on mobile too, predict network execs. *Adweek.* Retrieved from http://www.adweek.com/internet-week-blog/2-years-nearly-all-tv-content-will-be-online-132322.html

MarketWatch app now available on App Store. (2009, November 2). Retrieved from http://www.newscorp.com/news/bunews_92.html

Mason, K. (2011, August 8). NYTimes.com launches site for innovative experimental projects. Retrieved from http://phx.corporate-ir.net/phoenix-zhtml?10517&p=irol-newsArticle_print&ID=1594171&highlight.html

McNulty, D. (2007, November 7). The New York Times Company joins Facebook Ad launch. Retrieved from http://phx.corporate-ir.net/phoenix-zhtml?10517&p=irol-newsArticle_print&ID=1074153&highlight.html

McNulty, D. (2010, January 20). The New York Times announces plans for a metered model for NYTimes.com in 2011. Retrieved from http://phx.corporate-ir.net/phoenix-zhtml?10517&p=irol-newsArticle_print&ID=1377114&highlight.html

Mintzberg, H., Ahlstrand, B. W., & Lampel, J. (1998). *Strategy safari: A guided tour through the wilds of strategic management.* New York: Free Press.

Mousebreaker Ltd. (2011, October 5). Retrieved from http://www.mousebreaker.co.uk.html

MTV Networks acquires social project. (2008, September 22). Retrieved from http://www.viacom.com/news/Pages/newstext.aspx?RID=1199485.html

Murdoch, R. (2006, March 13). Speech by Rupert Murdoch at the annual livery lecture at the worshipful company of stationers and newspaper makers. Retrieved from http://www.newscorp.com/news/news_285.html

Murdoch, R. (2010). *2010 Annual report.* Retrieved from http://www.newscorp.com/investor/annual_reports.html

NCAA® March Madness® on demand achieves record-breaking first day of traffic. (2010, March 1). Retrieved from http://www.cbscorporation.com/news-article.php?id=624

News America Marketing upgrade coupon website www.SmartSource.com. (2009, May 12). Retrieved from http://www.newscorp.com/news/bunews_31.html

Number 1 media network by and for college students. (2011, September 21). Retrieved from http://www.viacom.com/ourbrands/medianetworks/mtvnetworks/Pages/mtcu.aspx.html

"Onion SportsDome" delivers special social media Super Bowl coverage. (2011, February 4). Retrieved from http://www.viacom.com/news/Pages/newstext.aspx?RID=1525017.html

Our company. (2011, September 6). Retrieved from http://www.gannett.com/apps/pbcs.dill/artikkel?Dato=99999999&Kategori+WHOWEARE&Lopenr=10.html

Our marketing solutions. (2011, September 6). Retrieved from http://www.gannett.com/section/MARKETING&template=cover.html

Picard, R. G. (2002). *Media firms: Structure, operations, and performance.* Mahwah, NJ: Lawrence Erlbaum Associates.

Porter, M. (1980). *Competitive strategy.* New York: Free Press.

Porter, M. (1985). *Competitive advantage: Creating and sustaining superior performance*. New York: Free Press.

President Clinton announces MTV and College Board collaboration on first-ever social media tool for financial aid. (2011, April 4). Retrieved from http://www.viacom.com/news/Pages/newstext.aspx.html

Radio is the most cost-effective branding media available. Period. (2011, September 21). Retrieved from http://dallas.cumulusradio.com/TheSKinnyonRadioAdvertising/WhyUseRadio/ tabid/107.html

Simon & Schuster and Turn here premiere author videos on YouTube and Bookvideos.tv. (2007, June 14). Retrieved from http://www.cbscorporation.com/news-article.php?id=322

Social media: Essential tools for delivering content. (2011, September 6). Retrieved from http://www.gannett.com/apps/pbcs.dill/article?AID=9999100803002.html

Social media channels. (2011, October 7). Retrieved from http://www.nytco.com/company/innovation_and=Technology/index.html

Specific Media acquires MySpace from News Corporation. (2011, August 8). Retrieved from http://www.newscorp.com/news/news_489.html

Stewart, J. B. (2005). *Disney war*. New York: Simon & Schuster.

Subscribe to our newsletter. (2011, September 21). Retrieved from http://dallas.cumulusradio.com/ideasForBuildingYourBusiness/TheGrowthwireNewsletterBlog.html

Summary financial highlights. (2011, August 21). *Walt Disney 2010 annual report*. Retrieved from http://corporate.disney.go.com/investors/annual_report/2010/financials_highlights.html

Szalai, G. (2011, March 3). ESPN, CBS, CNN, others grew mobile video revenue in 2010. *The Hollywood Reporter*. Retrieved from http://www.hollywoodreporter.com/news/espn-cbs-cnn-others-grew-163992.html

Take action, right now. (2001, September 21). Retrieved from http://www.viacom.com/corpresponsibility/Pages/ourinitiative.aspx.html

Television company Belo Corp. expands advertising reach with Yahoo!. (2011, October 7). Retrieved from http://www.belo.com/newsroom/releases/Television-Company-Belo-Expands-Advertising-Reach.html

The New York Times and LinkedIn from strategic relationship. (2008, July 22). Retrieved from http://phx.corporate-ir.net/phoenix-zhtml?10517&p=irol-newsArticle_print&ID=1177390&highlight.html

Thibault, R. (2009, April 30). New economic sentiment indicator introduced by Dow Jones hints at first tentative signs of recovery. Retrieved from http://www.newscorp.com/news/bunes_05.html

Wasserman, T. (2011). Social media ad spending to hit $8.3B in 2015. Retrieved from http://mashable.com/2011/05/03/social-media-ad-spending-8b/

WFAA.com advertising overview. (2011, October 9). Retrieved from http://www.wfaa.com.html

Social Media in Companies. Integrated Approach for a Social Media Strategy

Mike Friedrichsen

1 Introduction

For commercial enterprises, the emerging set of new technologies and forms of communication in social media are leading to a whole new channel of interaction with customers, partners and employees. Given that 39 % of the fastest growing companies in the US have implemented e.g. blogging compared to only 11.6 % of Fortune 500 companies (Barnes and Mattson 2008), it cannot be ignored that social media can offer businesses a competitive edge. Today the potential of customer contributions and recommendations for products and services is more highly valued than ever before. In fact, Gartner estimates the amount of money spent annually on enterprise social software—also referred to as "Enterprise 2.0" by McAfee (2006)—will reach 1.06 billion US dollars by 2012 (Gibson 2009, eWeek, 26, p. 16). By definition, concepts like microblogging and social networks require unique communications and knowledge in addition to traditional advertisement strategies.

The aim of this chapter is to give in introduction on social networks and to contain a non-industry specific framework for social media that assists in identifying touch points and business objectives.

The first part of this chapter characterizes social networks. Since online social networks are a key highlight of the social media landscape, theories, models and analytic methods of social network research have to be considered. In particular, this includes an analysis of social networks and the exchange of information within them. The transition of the existing concepts of relationship marketing combined with social media in an enterprise environment is investigated the main part of this paper. In conjunction with feasible measurements, a definition of contact points for

M. Friedrichsen (✉)
Humboldt Media Business School, Berlin, Germany

Stuttgart Media University, Stuttgart, Germany
e-mail: friedrichsen@hmbs.eu

the implementation of social software derived from relationship marketing paradigms is also provided here. Within this conjunction a model termed as social media management chain is developed.

2 Social Networks

In existing relationships, social networks are vital for the exchange of resources such as information, an essential concept of social media.

> "When a computer network connects people or organizations, it is a social network. Just as a computer network is a set of machines connected by a set of cables, a social network is a set of people (or organizations or other social entities) connected by a set of social relations, such as friendship, co-working, or information exchange." (Garton et al. 1997)

The term *social network* was coined by Barnes (1954; cited by Wasserman and Faust 1994), who described it as nodes representing social entities (e.g. individuals or departments of an organization), which in turn are denoted as actors. Social relationships are linked by ties including interactive, political and economical relationships between pairs of actors.

The real-world networks present in a wide range of application fields are described by Barabási (2003). These networks are established by nodes and directed or undirected links between pairs of nodes. In the case of undirected links, the degree of a node indicates the number of links connected to that node, whereas the concepts of in-degree and out-degree describe the same characteristic for a node in a network composed of directed links. A path in the network determines a sequence of nodes connected by links. The distance between two nodes is defined as the number of nodes on the shortest path connecting these nodes (Harary 1967).

Barabási and Albert (1999) used the term "scale-free networks" to describe large real-world networks. Scale-free networks, like the World Wide Web, consist of a few nodes with a comparatively high degree of termed hubs and a large number of nodes with a small degree resulting from the preferential attachment of links to nodes that already show a large number of incoming links. Social networks can be characterized as scale-free networks based on links between individuals within a community who know each other. Large interpersonal networks are scale-free since there are particular individuals in the network who are more favored by others and thus more frequently connected to due to specific social relationships (Lehel 2007, p. 36).

From the individual user's standpoint, online interpersonal networks are established on social software platforms and focus on one individual, the focal person and his or her relationships with other individuals. These relationships with others are referred to as egocentric networks or personal networks, respectively (Haythornthwaite 1996; Wasserman and Faust 1994; Wellman 1999). Personal networks also represent role-based relationships in a particular social context, including close relationships such as friendships, affiliations and formal relationships (e.g. co-workers).

2.1 Social Network Analysis

Social network analysis (SNA) is an interdisciplinary research field that is based on the assumption of the importance of relationships among interacting units. The social network perspective encompasses theories, models, and applications which are expressed in terms of relational concepts or processes. Along with a growing interest and the increased use of network analysis, a consensus has arisen on the central principles underlying the network perspective. In addition to the use of relational concepts, the following aspects can be noted as relevant:
- Actors and their actions are viewed as interdependent rather than independent, autonomous units.
- Relational ties (linkages) between actors are channels for the transfer or "flow" of resources (either material or immaterial).
- Network models focusing on individuals view the structural network environment as a provider of opportunities for or constraints on individual action.
- Network models conceptualize structure (social, economic, political, etc.) as lasting patterns of relations among actors.

The unit of analysis in network analysis is not the individual person, but an entity consisting of a "collection" of individuals and the links between them. Network methods focus on dyads (two actors and their ties), triads (three actors and their ties) or larger systems (subgroups of individuals or entire networks) (Gretzel 2001; Wasserman and Faust 1994).

Wasserman and Faust (1994, p. 21) state that social network analysis can be characterized as a "generalization of standard data analytics techniques and applied statistics" since mathematical models are used to formalize metaphorical terms like popularity, social position and isolation. Mitchell (1969) defines three the levels, frequency, intensity and durability, to define the quality of interpersonal relationships, which are also subject to social network analysis. The social relationships of an interpersonal network can be visualized by a sociogram, a chart that plots the structure of interpersonal relations (Moreno 1937).

The vertices here represent actors and edges denote the ties between them. The two-dimensional sociogram shown in Fig. 1 presents a group of six individuals in an interpersonal network. Arrows indicate ties between these individuals. The size of each node depends on the quantity of degrees and in-degrees. There are a number of alternatives available when creating such illustrations with sociograms (e.g. computer-generated types with a three-dimensional perspective) thanks to further developments (Freeman 2000).

2.2 Information Exchange in Social Networks

Active ties between actors can be characterized by social interaction including the exchange of resources (e.g. information). Interpersonal relationships based on the exchange of information are defined by content, direction and strength attributes (Haythornthwaite 1996).

Fig. 1 Example of a sociogram (created with NetVis)

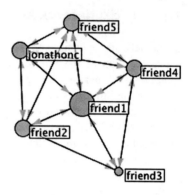

Information and knowledge are considered as content within the scope of their exchange in a social media environment. Haythornthwaite (1996, p. 326), for example, noted that "relationships can cover the sharing, delivery, or exchange of a wide variety of resources, including information."

The direction of information exchange relationships describes the way information is transferred between pairs of individuals. If the information being considered flows in both directions, the underlying relation is referred to as undirected or symmetric. Otherwise it is referred to as directed or asymmetric.

The intensity of a relationship is indicated by its strength. In such, a relationship with frequent transfers of information is considered stronger than one in which information is rarely exchanged. Furthermore, the strength of ties refers to the cumulative strength of all of the different social relationships between two individuals which is also affected by the continuity of the relationships (Haythornthwaite 1996). A close relationship with frequent exchange of information denotes a strong tie that implies, e.g., a sense of trust between the respective individuals. By contrast, a loose form of contact generally equates with a weaker tie. Individuals who are linked to another person by strong ties are also likely to share a large number of strong ties to other people (Granovetter 1973). On one hand, those linked by strong ties to the focal person tend to have access to the same information and therefore do not represent sources of new information. On the other hand, Granovetter (1973) observed that weak ties are essential in order to establish connections between different interpersonal networks and thus obtain new information.

For the appropriate measurement and analysis of information exchange in social networks, primary characteristics such as cohesion, structural equivalence, prominence range need to be examined and is not subject of this paper.

One primary aspect of the measurement and analysis of information exchange in social networks is that of brokerage. Brokerage can be measured by the actor's betweenness, which describes if an actor owns the role of an intermediary connecting clusters and cliques in the network. According to Burt (1992), these actors maintain an essential role in filling in the structural holes between clusters in the social network if these areas of the network have not yet been connected.

The outcome of this for the exchange of information in social networks is that an actor who has taken on the role of a broker is able to deliver information from one cluster to another, and thus maintain the control over the information flow, although he or she does need to be able to authorize the information disseminated to others, which is referred to as information legitimation, as in the case of e.g., digital rights management (Haythornthwaite 1996).

Range indicates the number of sources an actor has access to. It depends on factors like the size of an actor's personal network and access to other interpersonal networks. The range of an actor is determined by his or her direct and indirect ties with other actors in the available networks.

Analyzing information exchange relationships by measuring the aforementioned characteristics of social networks also reveals the information routes along which information flows between actors (Haythornthwaite 1996).

3   Relationship Marketing

Existing relationships with customers or other stakeholders have the potential of being expanded in online social networks or community platforms. Social media present a new situation and communication challenge for organizations, which subsequently call for a structured approach and integration. Relationship marketing recognizes the long-term value of relationships for organizations by continuously nurturing existing correlations throughout the entire life cycle, rather than focusing on the acquisition of new customers. Over time, the relationship-marketing initiative has developed procedures, strategies and key elements that can be adapted to multiple industries and situations (Payne and Rapp 2003). As Hougaard and Bjerre (2002, p. 40) note:

> "Relationship marketing is company behavior with the purpose of establishing, maintaining and developing competitive and profitable customer relationship to the benefit of both parties."

3.1   Customer Loyalty

Hougaard and Bjerre (2002) state that as a key success factor, customer loyalty has always been conventional wisdom in the development of superior market performance.

> "Customer loyalty is the seller's perception of a consumer's positive attitude to the product manifested by rebuying." Kunøe (1994; cited by Hougaard and Bjerre 2002, p. 109)

It follows that customer loyalty is a substantial intangible asset because it's the ultimate indicator of future sales and profits. Reaching this level in a customer-relationship implies attitude and behavioral dimensions. The economic value for an organization can be classified by three types. The ability to retain a customer for an extended period of time can be described as a *lifetime economy*. An *efficiency economy* refers to the ability to create dyadic cost advantages for both parties during the customer life cycle, which leads to a vertical integration. Customer participation in and contribution to a supplier's value generation is characterized as a *value adding economy*.

3.2 Six-Market Model

One approach that addresses all of the stakeholders of an organization is the "six-market model" developed by Payne (Ballantyne et al. 2001). This holistic model accommodates a fast changing and complex business world with the idea of taking vital customer and vendor relations into consideration. Taking these vital relations into account is a requirement for fulfilling customer needs within a complex value creation process. This includes a strong focus on internal marketing and activities in core markets and results in the six-market model (Fig. 2).

Customer markets lie at the center of the six-market model and customers remain the primary target of marketing activities here. This modified approach shifts from transaction-oriented marketing to customer relationships, concentrating on long-term success. The main characteristics of transaction-oriented marketing are its focus on quick sales to new customers, a spotlight on product features and irregular communications with customers, as well as a limited scope of dedication to customer needs and product service. In contrast, the relationship marketing approach recognizes customer value, longevity, quality as a mutual goal, and frequent and persistent communications combined with strong attention to the preservation of existing customer relations. The relationship marketing ladder (Fig. 3) shows the difference in the emphasis of marketing activities to develop advocates of a company, product or service. Within a partnership, the organization stays extremely close to customers and actively encourages an ongoing dialogue about all aspects of its business, as it seeks to achieve a competitive advantage and superior business relationships (Charlesworth et al. 2007). Payne and Rapp (2003) argue that a high proportion of customers at the upper level provide long-term competitive advantages in successful customer relations. Generating such a high level of customer loyalty is difficult and demands excellent knowledge about individual customer needs and previously purchased products.

In addition, supplier and alliance markets have been identified as a field of activity for relationship development that makes it possible to keep up the pace with the changing trend of new correlations between organizations and suppliers. To reach a partnership level with suppliers, companies tend to integrate vendors in early stages of product development, and establish mutual values and bonus systems oriented on customer expectations along with a closed-loop communication process. The task within a relationship marketing initiative is to sell and support this perception of a vendor relationship both internally and externally.

The scope of the six-market model also comprises the recruitment market. This market has to be included since human resources and a skilled workforce have

Fig. 2 Six-market model (Ballantyne et al. 1991, p. 21)

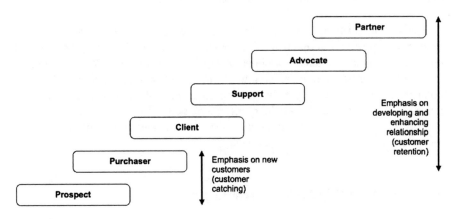

Fig. 3 Relationship marketing ladder (Payne 1994)

become essential for organizations, especially when it comes to customer service. Another cause for increased attention to this market is the demographic development and the continuous decline in the labor force of most industrialized countries.

Influence markets combine several relations of a company with its different stakeholders, which could affect the customer relationship. For example, companies on the stock exchange are facing a number of different stakeholders like analysts in addition to their customers or investors. Payne and Rapp (2003) claim that all market participants must be identified, integrated and resources allocated within a marketing plan, apart from public affairs and investor relation activities.

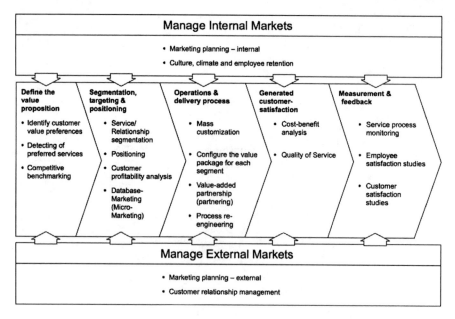

Fig. 4 Relationship management chain (Payne and Rapp 2003)

The six-market model also implements an internal view related to an internal marketing approach. Internal markets embrace that every individual and division of an organization is simultaneously internal supplier and customer. Referral markets have become more and more significant in recent years due to the fact that companies are using multiple distribution channels and participating in affiliate networks. The impact and potential of referral markets and internal markets need to be reviewed in a social media context. The six-market model allows an as-is analysis which considers every market.

3.3 Relationship Management Chain

The concept behind the relationship management chain (Fig. 4) by Payne and Rapp (2003) is based on the idea from Porter (1985) of linking all of the steps involved in a value chain. The focus of the relationship management chain is on how improved relations in business generate value creation. Like Porter's model and its "support activities", the relationship management chain also includes activities that influence every step. These "support activities" are the management of internal and external markets.

3.3.1 Management of External Markets

The management of external markets also includes non-customer markets and is a "support activity" that has an impact on every step within the relationship management chain and includes the marketing planning process for external markets along with the customer relationship management and customer loyalty as described in Sect. 3.1. Key features of the marketing planning process for external markets are an as-is analysis of the current situation of an organization, and the definition of objectives and how they can be accomplished.

3.3.2 Management of Internal Markets

The management of internal markets implies the administration and coordination of an organization's own profit centers along with the management of all internal customer–supplier relations. In addition, this includes a marketing planning process to identify and quantify all of the needs of internal customers, and develop methods and systems that will support their objectives at a cost-efficient level.

3.3.3 Definition of Value Proposition

The concept behind the relationship management chain is to emphasize tangible and intangible customer values aside from the core product or service performed by a structured procedure of establishing relations. The definition of value proposition comprises three main topics as follows:
- Identification of customer value preferences encompasses an analysis of how the value of service and each service component is appraised by consumers in comparison to other marketing activities. This approach allows us to classify and evaluate the effect of each service component for different customers and the feasibility of the potential substitution of services.
- Detection of preferred services identifies the importance of subliminal service components and allows to measure a predisposition. This method also offers the possibility of grouping customers according to their common service preferences.
- Competitive benchmarking discloses the value of each service, product and brand component as perceived by customers compared with an immediate competitor.

3.3.4 Segmentation, Targeting and Positioning

After exposing key service features and their impact and value from a consumer viewpoint, patterns are retrieved from the customer groups. This includes the ability of customer segmentation if there is a wide range of preferences within the extracted groups. Following this segmentation process, target groups have to be defined, as well as how services can be positioned against those from competitors.
- Service/relationship segmentation is used to extract segments. A cluster can be described as a group of relatively homogeneous customers.
- Positioning refers to differentiating an organization, product or service in such that it can be successful within a specific market segment (Payne and Rapp 2003). The quality of relationships is an additional asset when positioning a product or service.
- Customer profitability analysis refers to an application of segmented reporting and breaks down the costs of customer groups. Beside the fact that customers

purchase different quantities of products, Payne and Rapp (2003) note a strong divergence between service investments among multiple customers and state that key accounts are not necessarily cost-effective.
- Database marketing and micro-marketing is used to generate personalized communications in order to promote value preferences and preferred services. The services and values defined in the first step of the relationship management chain can be tailored through micro-marketing to meet the needs and desires of micro-segments on a market.

3.3.5 Operations and Delivery Process

Skills and competencies are an advantage in a competitive environment (Evans et al. 1994). This means that flexible business processes have to be modeled and managed within the value added chain due to the need for more flexibility in product configuration and a better quality of service.
- Mass customization describes the process of delivering wide-market goods and services customized to satisfy a specific customer wish so that customers receive optimal goods and services.
- Configuration of the value package for each segment includes the configuration of a value package for each segment and takes different customer needs into consideration by defining specific features for the whole product environment (e.g. concrete reaction rates).
- Value-added partnerships (partnering) refers to the value of partnerships with suppliers and other external partners. The close collaboration with reliable partners is a key factor for benefiting from a broad spectrum of instruments like secure deliveries to plants (Palmen 2007).
- Process reengineering is the ability of an organization to verify and audit existing business processes including comparative studies with industrial best practices and referential processes.

3.3.6 Generated Customer Satisfaction

Another differentiating factor in a competitive business environment is customer satisfaction, which is tied in to the entire product environment. Maintaining customer relationships depends on meeting a customer's original expectations of a product and service.
- Cost–benefit analysis takes all intangible and tangible values for a customer into consideration along with all direct and indirect investments related with the purchase or use of the product. The analysis is part of consumers' selection procedure for products or services. Relationships or potential relationships also represent a value in a cost–benefit analysis.
- Quality of service considers services as often experienced at a subjective level, yet generated multi-dimensionally. Grönroos (1983) describes three dimensions—technical, functional and the overall corporate image—which influence customers' perception of service quality.

3.3.7 Measurement and Feedback

The relationship management chain is a closed-loop concept and includes measurement and feedback as its last steps in order to ensure ongoing improvement of all processes. Efforts in this step are geared towards enhanced customer satisfaction.

- Service process monitoring includes the whole production processes alongside the relationship management chain. Key elements which could have a negative impact on customers' perception of service quality must be identified.
- Employee satisfaction studies consider employee satisfaction at the levels of activity, salary, opportunity for advancement and contentment with the department head, as well as general satisfaction amongst coworkers and must be monitored (Smith et al. 1969). In addition to these levels, new elements like satisfaction with the overall work environment, a corporation's internal communication culture, satisfaction with management's performance and the corporate image have all emerged as relevant factors.
- Customer satisfaction studies reflect the external impression of an organization. Measuring customer satisfaction provides an indication of how successful an organization is at providing products and/or services to the market. Findings should ideally be matched with competitors to identify any voids.

3.4 Relationship Economics in e-Businesses

A comprehensive study conducted by McKinsey & Company in 1999–2000 (Kemmler et al. 2001) helped to achieve a new level of understanding in the area of relationship economics in e-Business. Internet companies have suffered from a fatal attraction of sorts. These companies were very successful at luring visitors to their sites, but not at getting them to buy products or turning occasional buyers into frequent consumers. Indeed, the more visitors these sites drew, the more money they lost. Only a small, but solid, group of leaders succeeded in becoming profitable by turning visitors into returning customers. At the time, traffic was usually tracked according to page-views, advertising impressions and unique users. However, the foundation of long-term profitability is a life-long customer value, i.e., the revenue customers generate throughout their entire lives minus the costs of acquiring, converting and retaining them (Hougaard and Bjerre 2002, p. 331). Figure 5 offers an overview of performance indicators developed alongside Click-Through-Rate (CTR) and the number of unique page visitors.

Measuring the repeat customer base experience can also be applied to the performance of web applications and is useful in terms of reporting (Wong 2008). According to Forrester analyst Jean Pierre Garbani, web application performance has to be monitored and managed at the granularity of each individual transaction, not from a silo such as a cloud, logical server, piece of code, database or infrastructural component.

Evans et al. (2004) have outlined the key components of a successful relationship that can be relevant to the online marketplace as follows:

Attraction	Conversion	Retention
• Visitor base	• Customer base	• Repeat-customer base
• Visitor acquisition cost	• Customer acquisition cost	• Repeat customer acquisition cost
• Visitor advertising revenue	• Customer conversion rate	• Repeat customer conversion rate
	• Number of transactions per customer	• Number of transactions per repeat customer
	• Revenue per transaction	• Number of transactions per repeat customer
	• Revenue per customer	
	• Customer gross income	• Revenue per transaction of repeat customer
	• Customer maintenance cost	• Revenue per repeat-customer
	• Customer operating income	• Revenue-customer churn rate
	• Customer churn rate	
	• Customer operating income before marketing spending	

Fig. 5 Indicators in the e-performance scorecard (Kemmler et al. 2001)

- Trust—arises from an organization's ability to keep its promises on its deliverables so expectations are met. Evans et al. (2004) describes trust as a process with different elements varying in its importance in the acquisition and retention phases, e.g., brand experience, satisfaction of customer expectations, verified payment systems, etc.
- Commitment—relationships rely on mutual commitment from both parties even though the required investment may pose problems (Charlesworth et al. 2007, p. 237).
- Loyalty—as described in Sect. 3.1, this has been a strategic focus for many marketers during the past few years. Performance indicators include measures such as RFM analysis and the lifetime value (LTV), which represents the present value of future cash flows attributed to a customer relationship.
- Mutual goals—as described in the relationship marketing paradigm, mutual goals should be identified to achieve satisfactions for both parties in the exchange process. As Evans et al. (2004) points out, these goals do not need to be the same.
- Social bonds with customers are built by marketers by viewing them as clients instead of just nameless faces. Ways are found to keep in touch with consumers and interact with them in order to pinpoint their changing needs and offer solutions.
- Structural bonds are predominantly related to buyer–supplier relationships and may also generate strong competitive advantages because customers increase their business with the seller to take full advantage of these value-enhancing linkages.
- Adaption takes the flexibility and configuration of organizational systems into consideration such as orders and distribution. These systems need to support mutual benefits and must be convenient for customers.

- Satisfaction, as described in the fifth step of the relationship marketing chain, must be gained initially during exchange processes and over the long term throughout the consumer life cycle.
- Cooperation in an e-business environment includes many forms such as survey participation, writing online reviews or customer involvement in new product development.
- Non-retrievable investments have no value unless there is a possibility of a long-term relationship.
- Attraction in business relationships can vary. From a consumer's perspective, attraction may stem from the status and prestige attached to a brand, its reliability or street credibility.

The description of the social media landscape demonstrates that new communities emerge, multiple conversations are conducted, knowledge is shared and information is exchanged. The categorization of social software by Lehel (2007) facilitates a better understanding of the different social software applications.

Requirements of enterprises that could be mapped to the application of social media are at hand such as the enforcement of relationship or establish knowledge. Social media fosters interaction, communication and information exchange by several services. Each type of social software provides particular features to achieve the different requirements. It is incidental that social media could be come an asset of value creation. The application of social media in adding value is subject for further consideration.

4 Social Media

Social interaction on the World Wide Web, including the behavioral and cultural patterns of the people using social software, can be described as social media. Social software represents a significant class of "Web 2.0" applications that can act as mediators for interpersonal communication and the exchange of information (Evans 2008, pp. 33–34). Online tools that people use to share content, profiles, opinions, insights, experiences, perspectives and other forms of media itself, thus facilitating conversations and interaction online between groups of people, can be described as social software. These tools include weblogs, message boards, groups, podcasts, microblogs, lifestreams, bookmarks, networks, communities, wikis and video blogs (Solis 2007). Tepper (2003) asserts that the development of social software has been enhanced by a great increase in the number of individuals using social software. The implementation of these tools within a corporate environment is referred to as Enterprise 2.0.

A prominent characteristic of social software is the foundation of online social networks between users. Existing real-life personal networks of users form a basis for establishing networks on social software platforms. In such, online personal networks can represent a real-world context including social interaction by using social software and overlapping with interaction in the physical world. On the other hand, social software enables users to build entirely new relationships online.

Characteristics of these relationships depend on the kind of social software and available services. The services provided are for interpersonal or group communication use, the support of metadata management, information and user search functionalities, publications, sharing, subscriptions, commenting and collaborative classification. They ultimately allow individual users to link, exchange and organize information as pieces of content with selected contacts in a social network based on social software (Lehel 2007).

Since functional features and information models of social software reveal limitations from the individual user's perspective, the user-centered social software model proposes an integrated view on all available information by encompassing services for the acquisition of relevant information, controlled information dissemination to selected contacts and flexible metadata and semantic information relation management concerning the organization of distributed personal information.

5   Development of a Paradigm for Social Media in Business

This part presents a strategy blueprint for social media in business. Requirement of the described strategy is to outline a non-industry specific approach that utilizes latest social software for gaining competitive advantages. To encompass an advantage in competition, objectives of the relationship marketing initiative are implemented in this approach in addition to other features aiming on knowledge management and the support of interaction and communication of individuals.

The three-tiered strategy is structured as followed:
I.   Identification of Conversations
II. Operationalization of the Social Management Chain
III. Integration in Information Systems

5.1   Identification of Conversations

The six-market model is the starting point for identification of conversations and related activities in the social media space, assuming that all markets of the six-market model represent vital relations that can impact the business of an enterprise.

Identification of conversations concentrates on conversations in each market and an analysis of its author and readership termed as audiences. This also comprises the type of social media used in the existing conversations. All identified conversations need to be qualified as to its relevance (Evans 2008, p. 300). Identification of conversations is the first step that leads to an ongoing monitoring of the markets and its conversations. In addition disclose this first tier of the strategy objectives for future application needs of social media.

Enterprise information systems need to be considered for research of conversations and audiences, too. Information systems in the enterprise comprise multiple services and systems for content creation and management (e.g. ECM), communication and collaboration (e.g. Groupware) and business operations (e.g. CRM, ERP). All these system are using own or consolidated data repositories.

Operationalization of business objectives with social media assumes detection and qualification of conversations in social media. The domain of social media implies multiple types of social software. Conversations are conducted in different types of social software and demand adapted research and monitoring systems. Nevertheless universal metrics can be applied to all types of social software. However metrics in social media are evolving as social media does. Evans (2008, p. 299) states that developing a solid metrics base for activities involves a combination of well-understood data along with over a period of time developed trends based on a wider range of available data.

1. Content Metrics

    Content measures are aimed to reveal audiences and content in the social web. Contributors and detractors can be isolated. Collected metrics indicate how an individual, topic, organization, product or service is perceived. This leads to potential business objects such as prioritizing product improvements or scheduling a response to competitive moves (Evans 2008, p. 300).

    Search engines are a first step to detect conversations, content and audiences on specific topics. Monitoring services offer search reports in regular basis on specific keywords. Search functions within community platforms enable also a search inside social networking services. Several blog search engines can perform comprehensive research and monitor conversations and dependencies (e.g. blogroll, trackback) in the blogosphere. Thereby these search services accommodate specific features of weblog-related technologies.

    Conversations and audiences should also be identified in existing enterprise information systems. Enterprise search applications such as SharePoint Enterprise Search are able to integrate multiple data repositories of information systems (Hester 2007). Hence, enterprise search applications comprehend similar search functionalities like public search engines (e.g. Google) in addition to enterprise specific requirements such as people search.

2. Relevance Metrics

    Influence and engagement are parameters of a conversation that determine its relevance.Dimensions of influence in relationships can also be described as driving forces of customer relationships (Hougaard and Bjerre 2002).

    Dimensions of influence in the blogosphere are *function of topic* and readership. The *function of topic* describes the impact of a post within an associated domain and its higher degree of effectiveness (Finin et al. 2008). The influence of conversations can also be measured by on-site web analytics. Metrics are *time-on-site* and the *bounce rate* of referred visitors. *Time-on-site* is the difference between the time a visitor viewed the first and last page in a visit. This measure shows how long a referred visitor remained on a site and indicates the value of the conversation and source (Evans 2008). The *bounce rate* measures the percentage of landing page terminations compared with all landing page arrivals.

Engagement as a parameter of relevance metrics describes the interest level in a message, resource or product and the willing to pass it along. Ratings in e-commerce platforms, referrals in social networking service, "comment to post ratio" in the blogosphere, views, bookmarks and subscriptions indicate engagement.

Relevance metrics try to identify conversations that are being used as a part of the decision-making process from a sales perspective.

5.1.1 Recruitment Markets

Recruitment markets consider potential employees as a key resource for the enhancement of an organization (Michaels et al. 2001). The positive image of a company is significant for attracting potential workforce. With the evolving Web 2.0 employees and alumni started exchanging their views, comments and opinions of organizations (Twist 2004). These mostly uncontrollable conversations take place in the social media landscape, for instance in community platforms, social networks, blogs, etc. (Jäger 2008) and are also available for prospects, customers, suppliers, and competitors. On the other side enables Web 2.0 recruiters to perform a background check of applicants. Social networks for professionals (e.g. Xing) show insights of individuals, such as relations with employees of competitors, customers and partners. Key activities for recruitment markets is to identify Platforms, conversations or specific individuals in order to monitor the image and conversation about an organization. Social networking platforms can be located for background checks on applicants. Possible objectives for a social media initiative can be weblogs and feeds, or participation in relevant community platforms to create own conversations and awareness about the organization, its individuals and attractiveness.

5.1.2 Internal Markets

From a relationship marketing perspective are all individuals and divisions of an organization simultaneously internal supplier and customer, who are attached to the value chain. It follows that individuals and divisions are audiences that need to be identified. Social media in internal markets is aimed to improve communication, social networks, knowledge management and company-wide awareness on goals, strategy, values and mission. This includes the activities of Identification of relevant audiences (e.g. individuals, divisions, communities of practice and project teams), assessment of social software applications as facilitator for specific business objectives and social network analysis of already implemented social networks and information management systems, such as ECM.

5.1.3 Supplier and Alliance Markets

Supplier and alliance relationships are important. Organizations tend to integrate vendors from early stages of product development, establish mutual values and a closed loop communication process, considering customer expectations. The objective is to sell and support this perception of a vendor-relationship internal and external. Key activities for supplier and alliance markets is to identify and drive

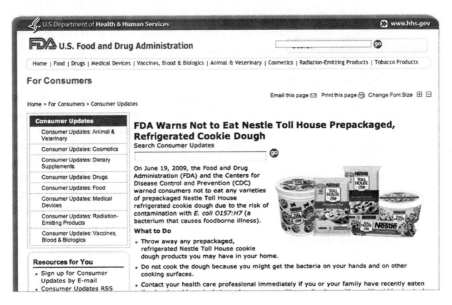

Fig. 6 FDA product notice for consumers (2009, FDA Warns Not to Eat Nestle Toll House Prepackaged, Refrigerated...)

conversations on mutual goals and values along with projects and products, affecting both entities. Social software can merge those conversations on joint platforms. Along with the evaluation of a joint social software platform that comprehends social networking services to connect counterparts along with unified collaboration, weblogs and wikis to transfer knowledge and support the relationship.

5.1.4 Influence Markets

Influence markets consider several relations respectively stakeholders that effect customer relationships. These stakeholders could be highly industry-specific in case of regulators or government agencies (e.g. FDA, BaFin).

Figure 6 shows a warning notice posted by the FDA relating to the contamination of a specific food product, in the section of consumer updates. In the mentioned case are consumers the assigned audience, and able to subscribe via a RSS feed to this website and receive updates on regular bases. This example shows how a government agency has utilized the weblog-related technology of feeds to communicate with its audience. Key activities for influence markets is to identify relevant conversation, sources and audiences in influence markets. Crises management should include social media for communication (e.g. corporate blog) (Eck 2007, p. 67).

5.1.5 Referral Markets

Referral markets consider multiple distribution-channels (e.g. wholesaler, distributor), existing customers and networks of experts as audiences that can leverage market coverage and brand awareness. Key activities for referral markets is to identify relevant audiences and conversations that are engaged with the product, service or related subjects. Another objective is to integrate relevant audiences in communication strategy or existing affiliate marketing programs.

5.1.6 Customer Markets

Customer markets are the center of the six-market model and primary target of social media activities. As described in Sect. 3.2 is the emphasis of the relationship marketing ladder to convert prospects into loyal customers and advocates of a company, product or service. From this it follows that audiences in customer markets comprise all levels of the relationship marketing ladder including prospects, purchasers and clients. With the increasing number of weblogs become individuals (e.g. blogger) market participants since they are able to recommend a product or a service. Key activity for customer markets is the Identification of relevant audiences and conversations and use social media as an instrument to understand customer needs and drive conversations.

5.2 Operationalization of the Social Management Chain

The second tier of this strategy describes operationalization, in terms of implementation, execution and measurement of a social media initiatives in an enterprise environment. The approach is modeled in a "social media management chain" shown in Fig. 7. The social media management chain provides a framework that has been assumed by the relationship management chain (Payne and Rapp 2003) and adapted to the scope of social media. The described model posses supporting activities along with four steps of activities. Preconditions are the identification of conversations and objectives for each market.

The focus of the social media management chain is on how social media in business generate value creation. This presented model is an integrated approach and implies that all steps of the social media management chain are vital for a successful implementation of a social media strategy. Support activities of social media that affect value creation are the management of internal and external markets.

5.2.1 Management of Internal Markets

The management of internal markets is an evolving field for social media adoption. This stage implements the determined findings and objectives of the first tier in a social media plan for internal markets. All activities are focused on developing methods and systems that will support internal customers at a cost-efficient level. Management of internal markets is a "support activity" and affects every step of the social media management chain. The first step is the providing of suitable social software for all relevant audiences and their needs, for example weblogs for knowledge workers to generate information (McAfee 2006, p. 22). The generated information could support every step of the chain. Appropriate social software applications act as facilitator for defined business objectives. Social network

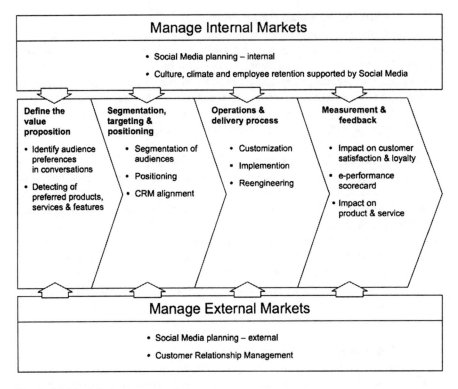

Fig. 7 Social media management chain

analysis can be utilized to detect "structural holes", and improve information exchange and knowledge transfer.

5.2.2 Management of External Markets

Management of external markets includes also non-customer markets. As part of the first step of the social media strategy audiences and objectives in all external markets, such as influence markets, supplier and alliance markets, etc. have been determined. Nevertheless does each segment of the external markets demand specific objectives to address relevant audience and achieve defined business objectives. This leads to the development of individuals social media plans for external markets. Weblogs dedicated for crises management (e.g. product recall) enable organizations to endorse an open and transparent communication with market participants of external markets (Eck 2007, p. 67). Customer relationship management provides basic functionalities (e.g. campaign management, after-sales services, etc.) that can support social media initiatives. It is incidental that CRM is a supportive activity that affects all steps of the social media management chain depending on the level of integration.

5.2.3 Definition of Value Proposition

Definition of the value proposition within the social media marketing chain is the next iteration after determining relevant audiences and conversations in customer markets. Identifying of audience preferences in relevant conversations discloses how the detected audience appraises a product or service. Detecting of preferred services and features exposes conversations and its content on a more detailed level in terms of product feature or service. Findings can be used for mapping of features and services to specific audiences compared to the grouping of customers.

5.2.4 Segmentation, Targeting and Positioning

After evaluating key products, features and services the second step of the social media chain is dedicated for segmenting, targeting and positioning in terms of social media. Segmentation of an audience maps a specific product or service configuration to a corresponding audience based on the findings of the first step of the chain. Positioning describes the selection of the appropriate social media facilitator such as community platforms or blogs for engaging conversations. The alignment with a customer relationship management system considers the integrated approach of the presented social media strategy. This activity connects findings of the research phase in social media with existing data and knowledge on customer behavior and characteristics.

5.2.5 Operations and Delivery Process

The aim of the operations and delivery process is to actively encourage an ongoing dialogue with relevant audiences and preserve existing customer relationships as a competitive advantage. Customization describes the development of a tailored social media solution. The parameters of the solution have been defined in the prior steps of the social media management chain. Common goal of all customer-focused social media solutions is the enhancing of relationships as described with the relationship marketing ladder. Loyalty has also been identified as a competitive advantage. The design of a social media application hence should foster the lifetime economy, efficiency economy and value adding economy of customer relationships.

Implementation of a social media application comprises the technical deployment, integration in an existing information management infrastructure and the organizational integration. Organizational integration encompasses individuals and divisions that will contribute. Integration of social media in an existing technical infrastructure is subject of the third tier of the outlined social media strategy.

Reengineering is aimed to improve established social media implementations. With the evolving characteristics of social media are established applications, metrics and environments in motion. A defined reengineering step ensures an ongoing evaluation of implementations, platforms and processes.

5.2.6 Measurement and Feedback

The measurement and feedback step defines several parameters to make social media activities measurable. A closed-loop concept with a reengineering phase in the previous step ensures ongoing improvement.

Key performance indicators are the impact on customer loyalty and satisfaction. Rebuying a product or referring it is expressed as loyalty. Respective data can be captured through social media and analytical CRM. The e-performance scorecard reveals additional data points and cost–benefit analysis for measuring social media initiatives. The impact (e.g. quality, design) on a product or service by social media activities should be measured and reflects the engagement of social media activities with a product or service. This metrics describes the influence of generated feedback and interaction in the social media landscape on a specific product or service and is an indicator for a value adding economy.

5.2.7 Integration in Information Systems

The integration tier of the social media strategy considers the integration of social media in an existing information systems infrastructure. The management and analysis of thousands of users of social media applications excludes an efficient manual management. To integrate functionalities of external social media platforms and services in existing enterprise information systems the implementation interfaces is required. Most public social networks are already offering application programming interfaces (API) for a machine-readable access and are using standardized web services (e.g. del.icio.us) (Richardson and Ruby 2007, p. 28). Enterprise middleware is the touch point for the technical integration of social software on the enterprise side. This application server allows the connection with existing applications and systems such as Business Process Management and CRM. The common data exchange format used by web services of social software is XML (Dostal et al. 2007, p. 199). All major ERP, ECM and CRM systems support this data format that enables a data integration of social software in business operations.

Integration of social media in information systems is an extensive field of application. Efforts and costs for integration need to be included in an evaluation process for implementation of social software.

Conclusion and Prospects

"Markets are conversations" is the first assumption of the cluetrain manifest (Locke et al. 2001). Social Media is a vehicle for conversation within a market. Millions of customers, employees and individuals are using social media for conversations. As a result companies that want to participate, understand and drive their key markets need to participate in this area of conversation. Avoidance of conversations operated by social media in key markets will result in a competitive disadvantage cause customers and competitors won't avoid it. Hence multiple organizations have started to use social media in their business.

Technology infrastructure like EAI and web services in addition to communication strategies of related areas such as the relationship marketing initiative and online marketing are at hand. Gainer of the evolving social media landscape will be organizations with the ability to adopt and integrate relevant areas of social media for their business quickly with a strong focus on business objectives within their strategy.

In addition are the company structures of public or commercial social media platforms to be considered. Many companies are financed by venture capitalist and are still searching for their business model such as twitter. The selection of partners within a social media strategy and the involved efforts for implementation must consider the fact that those companies and services can be fast substituted by other social media providers. However are other initiatives like OpenID and OpenSocial a perspective for universal interaction with multiple social media platforms.

References

Ballantyne, D., Christopher, M., & Payne, A. (1991). *Relationship marketing: Bringing quality, customer service, and marketing together*. London: Butterworth-Heinemann.
Ballantyne, D., Christopher, M., & Payne, A. (2001). *Relationship marketing: Creating stakeholder value (Chartered Institute of Marketing)*. London: Butterworth-Heinemann.
Barabási, A.-L. (2003). *Linked: How everything is connected to everything else and what it means for business, science, and everyday life*. New York: Plume.
Barabási, A.-L., & Albert, R. (1999). Emergence of scaling in random networks. *Science, 286*, 509–512.
Barnes, N. G., & Mattson, E. (2008). Social Media in the Inc. 500: The first longitudinal study. Retrieved April 1, 2009 from http://www.umassd.edu/cmr/studiesresearch/blogstudy5.cfm
Burt, R. S. (1992). *Structural holes*. Cambridge, MA: Harvard University Press.
Charlesworth, A., Gay, R., & Esen, R. (2007). *Online marketing: A customer-led approach*. Oxford: Oxford University Press.
Dostal, W., Jeckle, M., Melzer, I., & Zengler, B. (2007). *Service-orientierte Architekturen mit Web Services*. Munich: Elsevier, Spektrum.
Eck, K. (2007). *Corporate Blogs – Unternehmen im Online-Dialog zum Kunden*. Orell Fuessli
Evans, D. (2008). *Social media marketing – An hour a day*. Indianapolis, IN: Wiley.
Evans, M., O'Malley, L., & Patterson, M. (2004). *Exploring direct and relationship marketing*. London: Thomson Learning.
Evans, P., Stalk, G. J., & Shulman, L. E. (1994). Competing on capabilities: The new rules of corporate strategy. *Harvard Business Review*, 57–68.
FDA Warns Not to EAT Nestle Toll House Prepackaged, Refrigerated Cookie Dough. (2009). Retrieved June 11, 2009, from http://www.fda.gov/ForConsumerUpdates/ucm168012.htm
Finin, T., Joshi, A., Kolari, P., Java, A., Kale, A., & Karandikar, A. (2008). The information ecology of social media and online communities. *AI Magazine, 29*(3), 77–92.
Freeman, L. C. (2000). Visualizing social networks. *Journal of Social Structure, 1*(1).
Garton, L., Haythornthwaite, C., & Wellman, B. (1997). Studying online networks. *Journal of Computer Mediated Communication*. Retrieved June 1, 2009 from http://jcmc.indiana.edu/vol3/issue1/garton.html
Gibson, S. (2009). Web 2.0 tools gain enterprise acceptance. *eWeek, 26*(7), 16–18.
Granovetter, M. (1973). The strength of weak ties. *American Journal of Sociology, 78*(6).
Gretzel, U. (2001). Social network analysis: Introduction and resources. Retrieved May 12, 2009 from http://lrs.ed.uiuc.edu/tse-portal/analysis/social-network-analysis/
Grönroos, C. (1983). Innovative marketing strategies and organizational structures for service firms. *Emerging Perspectives on Services Marketing*, 9–21.
Harary, F. (1967). *Graph theory*. Reading, MA: Addison-Wesley.
Haythornthwaite, C. (1996). Social network analysis: An approach and technique for the study of information exchange. *Library & Information Science Research, 18*(4), 323–342.

Hester, M. (2007). Find It All with SharePoint Enterprise Search. Retrieved June 10, 2009 from http://technet.microsoft.com/en-us/magazine/2007.01.search.aspx

Hougaard, S., & Bjerre, M. (2002). *Strategic relationship marketing*. Berlin: Springer.

Jäger, W. (2008). Übersicht: Interaktive Internet-Tools für das Personalmanagement. *der arbeitsmarkt*. Retrieved June 4, 2009 from http://www.derarbeitsmarkt.ch/arbeitsmarkt/de/themen/archiv/103180/Übersicht_Interaktive_Internet_Tools_für_das_Personalmanagement

Kemmler, T., Kubicová, M., Musslewhite, R., & Prezeau, R. (2001). E-performance II: The good, the bad, and the merely average. Retrieved May 7, 2009 from http://www.mckinseyquarterly.com/E-performance_II_The_good_the_bad_and_the_merely_average_1079

Kunøe, G. (1994). *Metalojalitet*. Working Paper

Lehel, V. (2007). *User-centered social software – Model and characteristics of a software family for social information management*. München: Technische Universität München.

Locke, C., Levine, R., Searls, D., & Weinberger, D. (2001). *The Cluetrain manifesto: The end of business as usual*. New York: Basic Books.

McAfee, A. P. (2006). Enterprise 2.0: The dawn of emergent collaboration. *MIT Sloan Management Review, 47*(3), 21–28.

Michaels, E., Handfield-Jones, H., & Axelrod, B. (2001). *The war for talent*. Boston, MA: Harvard Business School Press.

Mitchell, J. C. (1969). The concept and use of social networks. In J. C. Mitchell (Ed.), *Social networks in urban situations* (pp. 1–50). Manchester: Manchester University Press.

Moreno, J. L. (1937). Sociometry in relation to other social sciences. *Sociometry, 1*(2), 206–219.

Palmen, N. (2007). Mercedes Benz – classy partnership with suppliers. Retrieved May 1, 2009 from http://www.allbusiness.com/company-activities-management/company-strategy/11711991-1.html

Payne, A. (1994). Relationship marketing - Making the customer count. *Managing Service Quality, 4*(6), 29–31.

Payne, A., & Rapp, R. (2003). *Handbuch Relationship Marketing: Konzeption und erfolgreiche Umsetzung*. Munich: Vahlen.

Porter, M. E. (1985). *Competitive advantage: Creating and sustaining superior performance*. New York: Free Press.

Richardson, L., & Ruby, S. (2007). *Web services mit REST*. Sebastopol, CA: O'Reilly.

Smith, P. C., Kendall, L. M., & Hulin, C. L. (1969). *The measurement of satisfaction in work and retirement – A strategy for the study of attitudes*. Chicago: Rand McNally.

Solis, B. (2007). The definition of social media. Retrieved May 6, 2009 from http://www.webpronews.com/blogtalk/2007/06/29/the-definition-of-social-media

Tepper, M. (2003). The rise of social software. *netWorker, 7*(3), 18–23.

Twist, J. (2004). US blogger fired by her airline. Retrieved May 5, 2009 from http://news.bbc.co.uk/2/hi/technology/3974081.stm

Wasserman, S., & Faust, K. (1994). *Social network analysis: Methods and applications (Structural analysis in the social sciences)*. Cambridge: Cambridge University Press.

Wellman, B. (1999). *Networks in the global village: life in contemporary communities*. Boulder, CO: Westview Press.

Wong, H. (2008). Real users really matter - Applying real user performance information to the application lifecycle. Retrieved May 3, 2009 from http://www.ddj.com/architect/210300296

Some Economics of New Media Content Production and Consumption, and Strategic Implication for Media Companies

Marco Gambaro

Internet has become part of our daily life and has reshaped roles and boundaries of traditional media through complex processes of complementarity and substitutability. Some functions, previously performed by specific media, go on the net like the explosion of keyword search seems to show, while on the other side traditional sources can gen new and wider audience. The cost reduction of information dissemination enabled new form of consumption and information acquisition, but despite the importance of internet in news and media consumption the experiences of content production specifically dedicated to the net are relatively rare and since the erosion of traditional media is advancing, some problem may emerge considering this line of development.

The problem is particularly compelling in the news. In the past together with traditional media emerged large professional organizations that collected and interpreted the news to the benefit of the whole society reducing information asymmetries and creating a countervailing power able to monitor the behaviour of business and politics.

Other kind of content experienced similar trajectories. In movie and audiovisual area, new distribution platforms, like Youtube, make available many interesting non professional contents and allow new diffusion opportunities and new ancillary streams of revenues for content originally produced for other media, but original production is not the main feature of these system. The aggregation capabilities allows new form of visibility to long tail products and transforms content otherwise dead in some archive in consumption opportunities (Anderson 2006).

This chapter discuss the economic condition of the content production for new digital platforms. I consider both entertainment and informative contents and the possible relationship with traditional media. News are an obvious centre of interest

---

M. Gambaro (✉)
Dipartimento di Economia Management e Metodi Quantitativi (DEMM), Università degli Studi di Milano, Milan, Italy
e-mail: marco.gambaro@unimi.it

since the whole society benefit from the dissemination activity of the media. On the economic side, in the market the benefit of the competition requires that every agent has access costless to relevant information, to prevent information rent for more informed part. On the same wave in democratic system only informed voter can monitor and eventually sanction politicians at the election. The process to select appropriate public policies require discussion that are possible only if relevant information are freely available.

Half of US citizens get most of national and international news from internet, a level not far from newspaper and television, and in the net they experience more variety and a multiplicity of sources (PEW 2011).

In Europe news consumption exhibit growing importance: 50 % of internet users reads news on internet but devote little time to them. The average reader devotes 25–30 min per day to its newspaper and can browse dozens of new and read 10–15 of them. In television average viewer watches more than half of a single newscast that means about ten different news. On the net emerge a greater selection: the average surfer of a news site watches only an handful of pages and therefore she concentrates on bigger events, a sort of star economy in news selection (European Commission 2011).

At the same time there is a multiplication of information sources that can be easily accessed and monitored and the interested consumer can easily check a news, visiting the same source that inspired the journalist. Moreover many specialised sites monitor and select news on specific topics adding enormous amount of variety.

In theory switching costs are low since in only a couple of clicks it is possible to pass from one site to another, but both in news site and blogs, brand plays an important role and leader gets a disproportionate number of visits and page views

Internet is becoming a platform for the delivery of very different media and pieces of news, and while traditional media evolved with specific position in vertical chain of information and offer a stable bundle of news in term of format and depth of range, on internet, professionals and final users can find themselves side by side very different type of information and news. Breaking news spreads on Twitter or Facebook same hours before the news agencies release and confirm them, so they are becoming a main source for journalists (Stanyer, Rohrmeier, Hess, 2007).

The degree of vertical integration or the share of value added is articulated. You find raw news, aggregation in a specific scheduling, general purpose news aggregation, comment and contribution, press releases and tread of comments opinion reaction or simple links that are substantially unbundled and that require a specific consumption capability.

For the news the main source of revenues remain advertising and the dominant business model is to attract visitors and sell their attention to advertising agencies and company both through traditional display advertising or keyword search. But many sites that display pieces of information or comment have only a virtual business model since they do not collect any revenues at all. The advertising is also more concentrated than unique visitors or page views and in each category only the more respected and visited sites get some advertising revenues.

The wide range in product variety and economic conditions reflect the same variety in juridical status and regulation. In traditional media information enjoy a special status that includes rules of separation with advertising, some specific rights for journalist, the right of reply and correction when wrong information are diffused. Many of these features become thinner on the net and it is not yet clear the impact of these differences on quality of information available.

We observe complex dynamics between traditional media and new content distribution on the net both on production than in consumption side.

Media operate in an ecological environment where they compete for resources as money, user attention and scarce factors of production. When a new media appears in the niche there is a general realignment with a role redefinition but hardly someone will disappear as happened to theatre with cinema or radio with television.

Also if web is changing everything and several niche audience are moving to new platforms, there are considerable inertia in media consumption. Watching video on line becomes a regular habit. In Europe one third of the population dedicate half an hour per day to this activity totalling 130 video a month in France, 186 in Germany, 114 in Italy and 165 in UK. Key factors for watching online video include convenience and flexibility (European Commission 2011). In US college students with internet connection are increasingly consuming video on devices different from traditional tv set. Different categories of video are consumed in different moments of the day: news mostly in the morning, short clip in the afternoon and longer form in the evening.

Although time spent surfing on the net is growing fast, television and radio continue to get the biggest share of population time spent for information and entertainment.

The average American watches television 6.5 h per day while in Europe the average consumption is around 4 h and this huge consumption does not appear to have declined in the last few years.

In the offer side the combination of technological innovation and accessibility of distribution channels allows a multiplication of content sources. Many content are simply side effect or spillover of other activities like administrative data or many webcams. Moreover users put on the net many contents that they create with simplified production means, but on the whole the larger of audiovisual and information contents consumed on internet are in one way or another produced by traditional offline media.

Usually at the beginning offline publishers look with fear to online environment. The main perceived threats are the possible substitution with traditional content delivery, the possible new content availability like ucg or aggregators that can substitute their main activity, the time and attention cannibalization and finally on the revenue side the rising of a cheaper advertising alternative.

Since internet attracts so much consumer attention it is interesting to reflect over the condition for new content production.

Let me point out some features of information goods that contribute to explain internet dynamics.

First they are a good example of public good with no rivalry in consumption. In general the fact that a specific piece of information is consumed by a particular client do not reduce the possibility that other user will eventually use that same information. Strictly speaking the use of information does not "consume" the good itself as happens in more traditional physical merchandises and also in many services. This feature leads to a substantial inappropriability and makes hard, without institutional arrangements, to exclude non paying consumers from use and to set up a proper market. Eventually technological development made easier to exclude non paying users like in pay tv and in these cases we have a shift to private good.

In information goods fixed costs play a crucial role since the first copy require a lot of effort while the variable costs to replicate and to distribute additional copy are relatively small and, in the digital environment, virtually converging to zero. Therefore they exhibit always strong scale economies and average costs is declining the larger is the diffusion of a specific product. Moreover scarce factors, able to capture important rents, are concentrated in production of original copy while production and distribution phases show more traditional industrial features. Since average cost are decreasing with diffusion, revenue considerations matter when we analyze cost, since the more practical way to reduce average costs is to increase diffusion with reduction in price or promotional activity.

Third, information goods are characterized by the absence of a well defined production function. There is not a fixed set of rules to produce a good movie or a good entertainment show. Sometime contingent factors play a crucial role in defining quality: in newsgathering if you are in the right place at the right time you get a valuable piece of information with very low production costs maybe just with a mobile phone.

But in general it is possible to add quality to an information product (for instance a video content), putting into production additional resources, but obviously with a declining marginal productivity. In a tv show a bigger studio or more cameras or more guests or more screenwriters, better lights, everything will make the show more attractive, but the problem is when to stop the additional resources. It is the traditional 27th dancers problem. If you add dancers the show will become more enjoyable and the effect is strong if you shift from four to eight dancers, but will decline when the step is from 24 to 28. But how to choice in advance the appropriate number of dancers. It is possible to guess the effect only on a probabilistic basis, based on experience, but no recipe is available nor is possible to write a production function able to drive both production decisions and cost controlling activities. The absence of definite production function make particularly hard to control cost increase since there is no clear ceiling to orient choices.

Finally information goods are usually sold in bundle in order to capture demand complementarities and to exploit different willingness to pay in consumer segments and for different product. The pay television is a bundle of channels offered together for a monthly subscription. A basic package includes usually something like 40–50 different television channels. Every consumer likes only a small subset of channels and the demand for single channels exhibit a large variance and unpredictability. If the channels are offered together in bundles the average price will rise and the variance of willingness to pay will shrink, making the demand more predictable and stable.

Also the newspaper can be considered a bundle of several pieces of news and advertising. The average reader consumes only a fraction of the total articles but continues to buy the newspaper if she values those articles enough for the cover price. Eventually different readers prefer different set of articles and the newspaper producer select the news in order to maximize the overlapping sets of readers.

The bundle allows the producer to charge a price that can rise above the monopoly price and sometime antitrust authorities were worried about that possible market power, but at the same time the alternative to sell each products individually often involves coordination and transaction costs that is far higher than the possible gain.

With a bundle approach if there is interdependency of preferences a publisher can serve also small markets that cannot sustain themselves independently.

But bundle equilibrium can be fragile. If in the market competing products emerge for specific components, bundle may not be able to recover total costs and eventually can collapse. American newspapers experienced a similar dynamics when specialized internet serviced like Monster or Craiglist deeply eroded their classified advertising revenues and forced (combined with declining diffusion) many papers to exit the market.

Also in new media content production one size does not fit all. There are different categories of content with different cost structures, product conditions and vertical chains. I will limit the analysis to some categories where professional subjects play a role: movie and TV programs; news and video news; UGC; applications on data bases.

As far as movies are concerned, for the moment internet is mainly a distribution platform with no additional costs. Also with this new distribution platform movies has remained substantially the same and no specific offer for the new medium has so far appeared. Since the new distribution channel generate only marginal revenues production costs remained the same as before.

But a new channel is not always a good deal. Movie are distributed through a temporal price discrimination device called windowing where the first release are placed in movie theatres, then after some month there is video rental and immediately later video sell-through; 12 month after theatrical release movie appears on pay tv and passed other twelve months in free tv. The key economic problem is to price discriminate among distribution channels in order to maximize total profit.

A new channel is attractive if its revenues are not subtracted to existing channels unless the unit price is higher than the other. Moreover a new channel can be dangerous for incumbents if it can alter vertical equilibrium or the channel leadership.

Terms and condition of new window are chosen taking into consideration cross elasticity, channel margin, channel leadership and risk bearing.

For existing products new windows operate like a gold pot that generate an unexpected revenue stream. But once the new platform is consolidated, the competition with endogenous fixed costs will dissipate additional profit in increase of production costs. Production budget is decided considering expected revenues over a portfolio of products. Movie industry already experienced this pattern with the emergence of cable television and with home video. So eventually production cost of movie can raise in a few year following the growth of internet consumption.

For television the landscape is more fragmented. Many viewers are spending more and more time on the net watching new content or short snack taken from traditional tv programs, as happens often on Youtube (Fointaine et al. 2010). While for the moment tv consumption does not decrease, tv stations fear the future trends and want to participate to the internet bonanza. Since they realized that anyway it was possible to find their programs on the net, they began to offer them directly in order to maintain viewer loyalty and to monetize potential demand.

After several experiments on a pay per view basis, advertising emerged as the dominant business model. Probably the turning point in the American landscape was the launch of Hulu founded in march 2007 by the major network to offer a catch-up tv service.

Hulu is owned by NBC, Universal, The Walt Disney Company and News Corporation and offer video of its parent networks and from other 250 content companies. The large and original content base fuelled the success and the growth. In 2011 Hulu attracted in the average month 2 millions of unique visitors and distributed 813 million streaming. The average user watches at its video content for more than 5 h per month, not a large consumption if compared with traditional television viewing, but a large number in internet landscape. With 650 advertises, Hulu realized 420 millions of revenues, not enough to realize a profit, but a huge success story in digital video distribution.

To increase the Arpu it offers also Hulu-plus a premium service with a monthly fee of 7.99 $, that allows to watch content in other devices beyond pc, and make available a wider range of contents. But advertising in the basic service remains the main source revenues. Compared to traditional television, Hulu get an higher unit price, but fill less commercials in every program hour.

In USA television networks sell advertising at 20 $ CPM (price per thousand viewer of a single commercial) while Hulu could charge a price of 25–30 $ slightly declining since the 35 $ of 2009. The differences in target (more young and affluent) and the novelty of the medium contribute to explain the difference. At the same time one hour of network tv is filled in US with 20 commercial while the limit on catch-up tv seems to be in the range of 6–8, probably because on the net there is less loyalty to a specific site or program. Therefore revenue per viewer are around 40 cent in television and around 20 cents in catchup tv. So in these conditions the same program cannot be produced only with Internet revenues, but the advertising saturation can grow. When revenue per viewer will approach television I expect the specific add on programs dedicated to internet window will be produced. One possibility is cheap sequel (as we witness on home video ten years ago) or program with specialized digital features like multiple ending or interactive content or more generally gamification of content production.

If we restrict the attention to information news the story is different. In video news production the typical issue is not the cost of the single story, but the cost of the full coverage for a specific unit of time, the management of the newsroom and the whole production flow. They are mainly fixed irrecoverable costs substantially independent from the single output.

The typical national television newscast of a major European country employ 100–150 journalists and 100–120 technicians with a total annual costs in the range of 30–35 million euros. If it deploys 3–5 editions every day, each one with 16–20 stories, a total of 50–70 stories is produced every day. A television newscast is a huge machine, able to deal with unexpected stories, designed not to miss any relevant story and to give every evening a relatively complete view of the events of the day. Compared with other program a newscast is a cheaper way to produce audience at least for television based on advertising model. The cost per hour per viewer is three four time less compared with entertainment or drama.

An all news channel exhibit substantially the same dimension. The cost per year can be around 40–50 million euros. Once the production feed is deeply reused the same resources needed to produce a traditional newscast can produce a full news channel.

Several news sites, notably those ones belonging to a newspaper have begun to offer news video, to complete their product range. Sometimes the clips came from the news agencies, or form some cheap source, but often they produce or commission these news coverage. A daily flow of 6–7 original stories can cost 1–1.5 million euros per year, only a fraction of the cost of a television newscast. Naturally the product is different: 6–7 stories, compared with 50–60 and the delivery model is a kind of best effort, but anyway the difference is huge and rely heavily on production methods. Moreover usually these news services offered on the net hardly recover their costs with the advertising clips they insert in. Technological innovation is the main factor that drives down video production costs. Digitalisation as usual reduce components, size and costs of the devices while at the same time enhance technical quality. The price of a professional video camera until 10 years ago was at least 100 thousand euro but now a small digital camera with similar or superior features can cost 3,000 euro. A similar decline in price occurred to editing stations that passed from 120 thousands euro to cheap software application for standard personal computers. The digital environment facilitates the creation and the growing use of video archive that if the video clips are completed with appropriate metadata, can reduce the cost of reuse the original footage both in different programs and along with time.

Finally a flexible and lighter production organization take advantage of specific technological innovations and of transformations that digital environment allows in labour capabilities In the past high technical costs supported heavy production organization. To make a simple interview was employed a four o five persons team. Some focal points of new organization are: smaller video team, less skill in the frontline and more centralised support through mobile equipments.

Newspapers and magazines have been suffering the internet competition both in reader than in advertising market and experienced an acceleration in their already established decline. Internet is acting as a disruptive technological innovation that transforms the entire economic environment in which publishers operate.

Three typical strategic answers are emerging: multiplatform distribution, to activate relationship in a specific value chain and to develop user generated contents.

The economic result depends on several factors. With multiplatform distribution there are new editorial costs to adapt the news flow to new platform, new technical costs to convert contents in specific format and language, but are possible also scope economies between different platforms. The possible additional revenues are linked to market dimension and substitution patterns. But in general internet revenues do not compensate losses in copies also if we consider only advertising. The average printed copy is read for thirty minutes every day and generate 0.7–0.9 euro of advertising revenues. A unique visitor spend typically 2–3 min on a newspaper site with 5–7 page view and 1–2 cent of revenues. On the cost side scope economies are not easy to exploit in a very traditional work environment, as happens in newspapers. A journalist could work at the same time writing for different platforms the same story, performing the basic research and treatment just once, but she has to adapt format, language and timing to communication and technical features of different platforms.

As a second strategy publishers can try to saturate the information space of a particular sector combining print and online media. The basis is often to reach the ability to enable the actors of a specific economic sector to communicate each other. With a similar strategy some publishers get 35–40 % of their revenues from the web. Aside with traditional printed offer they add interactivity background information, specific application. Sport Illustrated and Reed Business Information are good example of this kind of strategy.

A third strategy is related to user generated contents. A publisher can use technical devices like spiders or scraper to find them on the net. But the real problem is to organize them successfully in order to attract users and to monetize the attention.

UCG involve a production input provided by people without direct compensation and can be described with "private provision of public goods". The main economic issues when dealing with UCS are similar to the ones that emerge with open source and for what we have a growing stream of scientific literature (Lerner, Tirole, 2002).

A first important question is: why do user contribute with their knowledge and give work, mainly for nothing. A first explanation is to signal the their value for a possible future labour market, especially when in the labour market it is not easy to entry. A second possibility I related to externalities or spillover promotional effects linked to UCG. If contributing to a blog or posting a video I can have some beneficial subsequent effect, it is rational to perform this activity.

Also the production side can be important. If I have some exclusive information but I cannot exploit it in anyway, maybe because I lack the needed organization, then it easier to give it for free as user generated content, hoping eventually in some possible future positive result. Or if my marginal cost produce a valuable information are low, compared with other agent's cost, then other things being equal I would contribute with more and better UCG (Stoeckl, Rohrmeier, Hess 2007).

The second main economic question, similar again to open source software. is how the quality can remain high in a non professional environment. Peer review and self selection of real expert are probably the best explanations. Tweeter is already an important source for newsgathering but until now the news signalled by a tweet need to pass through the costly process of verification and confirm in the newsroom. But it is not impossible that a similar process could be performed in a collaborative way in a wiki environment and at that point the newsroom organization could be challenged.

If a publisher wants to organize and monetize UCG the basic problem is to obtain contribution and to maintain quality and at the same time to select contribution in order to exclude the low quality contents. Many blog or forum once opened to free contribution receive a lot of spam or unsolicited false advertising. If a publisher can observe quality costlessly the problem is largely one of production planning. And if reputation matter there can be sufficient social incentive to participate in the offer of content (Resnick et al. 2006). But the typical issue can be under provision of quality. On the other side if producer does not spend in content selection, consumer can contribute content that has negative value for the producer (MacKie-Mason 2009).

In the last few year several sites have developed intermediate business models, where publisher try to attract content from consumers but in a structured setting.

Demand Media, probably the best example of this approach, identifies topics with high online advertising potential and automatically generates the more attractive title for articles outsourced to freelance journalists. The business model is based on the long tail search: the content-driven websites attract visitors by showing up in multiword search engine queries, then Demand Media tries to keep them by offering related content. Demand Media is the largest contributor to You Tube uploading 20,000 video per months and gets about 1.5 page views per day on this site.

The production model relies on crowd sourcing where contributions are realized by freelance journalists, blogger or video makers that bid for each title. The resulting procurement price is very low for professional standard. In 2010 all the tiles between 25 and 30 $ were assigned and realized while titles for which Demand Media offered less than 20 $ remained unassigned.

Other sites are looking for production and business model to organize and value user contributions.

Squidoo is a community user generated content site that allows user to create pages for subject of interest. Contributions are grouped by topics in order to reduce search costs. 50 % of the advertising revenues goes to creators of the more than two million pages.

Hub Pages allows users to submit magazine-style articles which are posted as individual web pages that earns revenues through search engines and aggregators.

Examiner operates a network of local news websites, allowing "pro–am contributors" to share their city-based knowledge on a blog-like platform, in 238 markets throughout the United States and parts of Canada with two national editions, one for each country. During 2009 many of the writers were receiving $0.01 per page view

In conclusion technological innovations and redefinition of media landscape enable new entrants to unbundle traditional media contents and to offer specific information component to selected targets or general public. Therefore traditional cross-subsidization patterns collapse and media organization need to evolve quickly in order to remain in the market.

Declining production costs that characterize many information market reduce scale economies especially in new production organization making possible more flexible way to create and aggregate information contents.

If internet operations of traditional media will remain unprofitable is foreseeable a wave of consolidation that can involve not only digital branches. Different information sites will merge in order to reach sufficient scale economies.

In the new digital landscape some topics will require special attention. Companies tend to become content producers and to communicate directly with consumers disintermentiating the media role (Dellarocas 2006). The trend is stronger when specialised information is costly to produce for the media while can be an easy spillover for an incumbent company or when consumer group are specialized and well defined.

These companies will reduce advertising expenses with their own communication investments eventually in digital communication and magazines will suffer more than newspaper or television.

We can see first clues of the blurred boundaries between professional and amateur production. In many topics expert consumer can gather and organize information with a quality comparable with professional.

While in the end a specific space will remain for professional intermediaries many information stream originate from non professional sources and the same role of content producers need to find new definition and new boundaries.

References

Anderson, C. (2006). *The long tail: how endless choice is creating unlimited demand*. London: Random House.

Dellarocas, C. (2006). Strategic manipulation of internet opinion forums: Implications for consumers and firms. *Management Science, 52*(10), 1577–1593.

European Commission. (2011). *Internet usage and online content*. Digiital Agenda Scoreboard 2011

Fointaine, G., Le Borgne-Bachschmidt, F., & Leiba, M. (2010). Scenarios for the internet migration of the television industry. *Communication and Strategies, 77*, 21.

Lerner, J., & Tirole, J. (2002). Some simple economics of open source. *Journal of Industrial Economics, 50*(2), 197–234. http://ideasrepec.org/a/bla/jindec/v50y2002i2p197-234.html.

MacKie-Mason, J. (2009) Tom Sawyer Production on the INTERNET: getting the good stuff. In: *Keeping the bad stuff out*. WP Department of Economics and School of Information, University of Michigan

Project for Excellence in Journalism, (2011) *The State of the News Media: An Annual Report on American Journalism 2010*. http://www.stateofthenewsmedia.com

Resnick, P., Zeckhauser, R., Swanson, J., & Lockwood, K. (2006). The value of reputation on ebay: a controlled experiment. *Experimental Economics, 9*(2), 79–101.

Stanyer, J. (2008). Web 2.0 and the transformation of news and journalism: new possibilities and challenges in the Internet age. In A. Chandwick & P. N. Howard (Eds.), *The handbook of Internet politics*. New York: Routledge.

Stoeckl, R., Rohrmeier, P., Hess, T. (2007). Motivation to produce user generated content: differences between webloggers and videobloggers. In: *20th Bled eConferences Merging and Emerging Technologies, Processes and Institutions*.

How (Social) Media Can Change "Change" in Organizations

Holger Sievert and Astrid Nelke

1 Introduction

Global, fast-moving markets also require companies to provide increasingly flexible structures and thinking patterns. Transformation has become an omnipresent accompaniment of internationally operating companies. To survive successfully, companies must realign themselves to the market conditions at shorter and shorter intervals. The changes must be made rapidly and in a targeted manner without worrying the employees or bypassing the interests of stakeholders. The resulting demand placed on the company management is not only to constantly recheck and formulate the strategic milestones, but also to communicate these accordingly. Internal communication thereby plays a crucial role. It has served to pass on information to employees, e.g. through internal newsletters and company newspapers, in the past and has now, due to further features of computer-based systems, become even more important for the motivation of employees, their commitment to the company, and process optimization.

The functions of social media platforms in a company also widen the scope of internal communication and offer potential for corporate management, particularly in relation to change management processes. This paper first addresses the classic change communication in organisations. It will tackle the theoretical issue of cooperation between communication professionals and general management and determine how it can be realized in a more efficient way. Using the example of Deutsche Lufthansa AG, it will present the challenges that arise for "classic" internal online communication in an internationally operating company and how these problems can be successfully mastered, particularly with regard to involving all the employees.

H. Sievert (✉) • A. Nelke
MHMK University Media and Communication, Cologne, Germany
e-mail: h.sievert@mhmk.org

Subsequently, the article will turn to the current first steps of social media-based online-activities in the range of internal communication within organisations. After a look through existing academic and practitioners' literature on this subject, the examples of Lufthansa and the German Ministry of Foreign Affairs make clear that there are still big differences between the organisations pertaining to the use of social media as a communication tool—internally as well as externally.

Finally, the potential that social media and online communication bear for organisations will be laid out. Especially the opportunities offered by the use of social media in the change process will be emphasized with regard to data from a worldwide full survey that we conducted in the German Ministry of Foreign Affairs.

2 "The Past": Internal Change Communication and Its Classic Online Tools

2.1 General Problems of Change Communication Between the Conflicting Priorities of Overall Management and Communication Professionals

Change management can be defined as "a structured approach to transitioning individuals, teams, and organisations from a current state to a desired future state" (Gadd and Einbinder 2010, p. 63). According to this source, the current definition of change management includes both organisational change management processes and individual change management models, which together are used to manage the people side of change. However, it is quite disappointing that in this case, like in so many others, communication is not mentioned explicitly—although it really has become very crucial.

Thus leadership and communication advance to the decisive indicators in the change process. Thereby internal communication as an integrative part of holistic communication management will take on greater significance (Grunig et al. 2002, p. 480). Based on an interview survey involving 265 German PR professionals and 235 German general managers, Sievert and Westermann (2009) established that communication professionals and executives in general management have very different views on their respective roles in the change process. While just under a quarter (23 %) of the communication professionals was of the opinion that the company communication should control the change processes, only every tenth respondent (11 %) from general management agreed to this position. Likewise, the question pertaining to the function of communication revealed a clear discrepancy: Only 16 % of the managers attributed the leading role in the change process to communication. In contrast, this was demanded by a quarter (25 %) of the communication professionals (Sievert and Westermann 2009, p. 1122 et seq.).

In this context it is striking to note the differing expectations both groups have in terms of the qualification of communication managers: While the PR professionals distinctly stress working techniques (64 % rate them as "very important"), only

37 % of the general managers consider the working techniques of communication professionals "very important".

Their views vary on the evaluation of business knowledge and communication science, respectively, too: Only 29 % and 21 %, respectively, of the PR professionals rate these two qualifications as "very important". The general managers attach more importance to these skills, giving business knowledge (26 %) and proficiency in communication science (28 %) the highest ratings.

Sievert and Westermann infer from these results that PR professionals are quite application oriented while general management rather requires the communication professionals to focus more on management (Sievert and Westermann, 2005, p. 1124 et seq.).

Change processes can only be communicated to an optimal degree, if general management and communication professionals collaborate in a company efficiently, which in the past often has not been the case. To this end, the intranet is increasingly employed as a communication structure. In the following chapter the potential of the intranet for internal communication will be clarified using the example of the Deutsche Lufthansa AG.

2.2 Analysis of "Classic" Internal Online Communication in 2005: The Example of Deutsche Lufthansa AG

Internal communication creates transparency in enterprises and should motivate employees—not only, but especially in situations of change. Imparting the change process to the employees requires an internal communication that is both professional and tailored to the communication assignment. For this purpose, the tools of formal internal communication and the existent but hardly controllable informal internal communication in organisations should ideally interact and form a unified interactive whole. However, in the future the role of internal communication will shift its focus from a top-down communication to more modern approaches—we will come back to that later. Apart from classic internal media like the company newspaper, the equipment comprises "classic" computer-based instruments like the intranet, which has been introduced into more and more companies since the mid-1990s. These computer-based instruments can be employed as a link between formal and informal internal communication; opportunities that should be made use of especially in change processes.

The computer-based information exchange involving the active participation of employees plays an important role in this context. Döring (2003, p. 128) points out that the use of computer-mediated communication is preceded by the decision against another medium. Each individual's choice is limited by the media available at the work place. In addition, Döring assumes that in both their professional and private lives people are confronted with problems regarding communication and cooperation on the factual content level and the socioemotional level which differ in terms of demand and importance. To tackle these issues, individuals have divers media at their disposal which require different degrees of user knowledge and support varying reciprocity, i.e. the possibility of a mutual exchange. According to the theory of rational media choice, individuals in a concrete situation select exactly the medium that is best suited to meet the factual and social requirements to solve the communication problem at hand (media appropriateness).

Short et al. (1976, p. 64 et seq.) determined that with technically mediated interaction, the more the partners perceive the contact through a certain medium as personal, sensitive, and sociable, the more distinctive the social presence becomes. The opportunity to respond allows the participants to develop a common basis of information as a basis of understanding (Döring 2003, p. 132). Computer-based internal communication means like social media tools and the intranet offer the characteristics mentioned. Especially the latter seems to be very important in organisations: 87 % of the respondents in "Trendmonitor Interne Kommunikation 2010" of a German PR association rated the intranet as important or very important.

This is where a study on the "information pages" of the intranet platform eBase of the Deutsche Lufthansa AG by Astrid Nelke-Mayenknecht (2008) sets off. The Lufthansa group, Germany's largest airline, had 90,673 employees worldwide in 2004 (Nelke-Mayenknecht 2008, p. 170). In September 2005 they were interviewed about their use of the "information pages" by means of an online-questionnaire. On the "information pages" the employees were able to collect information in four different areas: topics, organisation (the Lufthansa group consists of a number of sub-organisations), regions and processes. It should be mentioned that the "information pages" chiefly provided facts that were available in reference books across the group and in the Yellow Pages. In the discussion forums connected to this section employees had the chance to interact. It is important to note, that it was only in these discussion forums that you could speak of real knowledge being inparted, namely when the staff members reported on their experiences. All the other components of the "information pages" were limited to furnishing information of a mostly one-sided type, from the company to the employee (Nelke-Mayenknecht 2008, p. 174 et seq.).

In this research the intranet was perceived according to Giddens (1984, p. 25) as a structure that is constantly reproduced and changed through the interaction of its users, the active protagonists (Nelke-Mayenknecht 2008, p. 63). The worldwide empirical survey within the Lufthansa group covering data from 5,464 returned questionnaires revealed that almost 80 % of the respondents used the "information pages"-part of eBase at least several times a month. That result argues for the established role of this intranet offer in the corporate group of Lufthansa as early as in 2005.

Interestingly, the outcome clearly showed that particularly the newcomers to the company and the apprentices used the "information-pages", whereas the managers mostly fell into the category of "rare users" (Nelke-Mayenknecht 2008, p. 181). This result can be accounted for by the well-developed networking contacts of the managers and corresponds to the statements maintained by the scientists (Rommert 2005, p. 132). As Nelke-Mayenknecht clearly indicates in her research, it is indispensable for the development of the "information pages" to also motivate the employee groups of managers and consultants to use them. Nelke-Mayenknecht follows Giddens in assuming that the "information pages" as a structuring element will only be ideally reproduced and developed with all protagonists, i.e. the users, working on them together. For this reason, the involvement of all employee groups is essential for the advancement of this part of the intranet eBase. The proposition "knowledge is power" did not seem to prevail in the Lufthansa group. Only a small number of employees refused to publish their project results on the "information pages" for fear of their personal replaceability (Nelke-Mayenknecht 2008, p. 205).

In the future, this aspect should be taken into consideration when thinking about the application of computer-based media in internal communication, especially in change processes. It will be necessary to ensure that all employees really use the internal intranet and the social media content by installing certain motivational systems. This might be accomplished by the insertion of headlines on the startscreens of the employees' computers.

3   "The Present": First Steps Within Social Media As a New Tool of Change Communication

3.1   General Acceptance of Social Media for Internal Communication in Academic and Practitioners' Literature[1]

So far, all the particulars in this paper were aimed at "classic" internal online communication (not only) in change processes, particularly the intranet. With the Web 2.0 becoming progressively established, however, the manner of electronic communication is increasingly changing. More and more passive recipients grow into actively producing participants. Nowadays, in the intra-organisational public both wikis (collectively compiled knowledge bases in the style of Wikipedia) and blogs (weblogs, online journals with forums for discussion), are found as documentational tools or newsportals. Social software is also applied in project- and knowledge management (Ebersbach et al. 2008, p. 211), e.g. while restructuring an organisation. This offers companies a whole new channel to communicate with their employees—but it also holds new risks, especially during transitory situations. Blogs, podcasts, and wikis allow interaction between people within a company and do not depend on the hierarchy of the firm, which can be both a blessing and a curse. Despite extensive research, specific literature on change and social media in the corresponding topical communication was not found; the authors of this paper appreciate complementary reference material. Reference books on internal communication in general may increasingly reflect the issue, but they by no means do so consistently. Particularly in topical papers concentrating on a single medium and in interdisciplinary writings social media are often not even mentioned, despite relatively recent dates of publication (cf. for example Ludwig 2008; Cauers 2009; Crijns and Janichs 2008).

Smith and Mounter (2008) explain the benefit of Web 2.0 for internal communication very comprehensively. In a separate chapter "They go it alone—online"

---

[1] The authors of this paper wish to thank Pia Körber, Leonie Schöne and Adriana Tkacz for helping with the research for his subchapter.

(p. 202) the subject of social media is examined. Both Britons advise against overrating the use of social media. Instead, they should be viewed as an addition to the former internal communication. "As ever it is essential to remember that social media is really just another tool in the communicator's box and should be considered as part of a wider media mix rather than as the single magic solution to all communication problems" (Smith and Mounter 2008, p. 209).

Nevertheless, they regard the use of social media for internal communication as extremely important. Companies therefore should train their employees so that they can utilize these communication channels and publish their opinions. Their motto "listen and learn" (Smith and Mounter 2008, p. 211) hints at how to handle criticism that might appear in the blogs. Smith sees the advantage of social media in company communication from several angles: On the one hand, there is the perspective of the employees who would be more actively involved in her view. Apart from that, the young employees could be reached this way and it simply would be fun. On the other hand, there is the perspective of the company which has created a simple system to exchange information, but also a platform on which one can get widespread and permanent feedback from the employees, so that improvements can be tackled on a much more systematic level (cf. Smith and Mounter 2008, p. 202 et seq.).

This principally positive attitude towards social media in Great Britain is opposed by an often sceptical one in the Romance language area. One example is Bustínduy (2010) who mainly suspects a close relation to time loss at the workplace: "De hecho, se puede afirmar que las nuevas tecnologias son los potenciales ladrones del tiempo del siglo XXI" (p. 55).[2]

Bustínduy (2010) compares the use of Web 2.0 in internal communication with the introduction of the telephone. Telephones were excessively and wrongly used for private conversations at first and are a very helpful means of communication nowadays. He believes that after a few years the "join in-web" would be seen as a necessary tool in internal communication in much the same way (cf. Bustínduy 2010, p. 55 et seq.). Rather descriptive-realistic than sceptical is the approach of German specialist authors. For example, Mast reasons that it is important for companies to integrate Web 2.0 into the intranet because people are getting more and more interactive and interlinked (cf. 2010, p. 237 et seq.). She especially puts emphasis on blogs, primarily CEO blogs. The author recommends continuous and current work and "real" personal content. Decisions that are explained, problems that are imparted—according to her, this all creates closer bonds between the different hierarchic levels that can be vey helpful, particularly in change processes. As one great advantage of social media, Mast lists the fast and inexpensive nature of the communication network that companies can benefit from (Mast 2010, p. 236 et seq.).

The previous concrete application of social media has been examined by Schick (cf. 2010, p. 195 et seq.). As reported by him, only a few companies, primarily

---

[2] In the context of a global publication this quotation was left in the original (Spanish) language. An English translation would be: "In fact, it is possible to affirm that the new technologies are the potential time thieves of the twenty-first century."

related to IT and telecommunications, utilized Web 2.0 tools on a large-scale basis in internal communication. Most companies, however, felt uncomfortable and overwhelmed with this subject. Due to lack of experience with Web 2.0 and the corresponding tools, Schick states, the firms confined themselves to meanwhile familiar strategies. Furthermore, in many enterprises it is difficult to determine an area of responsibility for social media. The companies fear new costs that may be incurred by the establishment of a specific department devoted to this purpose. Renowned authors in Great Britain and Germany view the further development of internal communication to Web 2.0 as a sensible extention to existing tools and a chance to make companies more transparent, attractive and ultimately more efficient for all reference groups. The latter is highly significant, notably in transition situations. The focus thereby stays on the intranet as "Plattform für verschiedene Anwendungen" (Thielke 2009, p. 12).[3] Employees as well as stakeholders and management benefit from tools like weblogs, wikis and network platforms in the fashion of Facebook or MySpace.

To what extent closed communities can or cannot be employed in external platforms beyond that, is not discussed by any of the examined authors. All in all, that development is still in its early stages and seems to be perceived rather sceptically, particularly in Romance countries. Nevertheless, it will be crucial for the successful management of change in the future.

3.2 Analysis of Internal Social Media Use in 2011: The Examples of Deutsche Lufthansa AG and the German Ministry of Foreign Affairs[4]

For this paper a small case study was carried out on the previous use of social media in the Deutsche Lufthansa and the German Ministry of Foreign Affairs. The Deutsche Lufthansa was selected because the data regarding the use of classic online communication in internal change processes was collected in this company (cf. Sect. 2.2); the Ministry of Foreign Affairs was chosen as a reference since, in the framework of a kind of cultural change project in June 2011, we will have the opportunity to question all employees there about social media context amongst others (cf. Sect. 4.2).

Thus, this sample here constitutes a link between the two companies that are the subject of each of the empirical papers presented.

This trial evaluated the online presence of the two institutions mentioned and their employees in the social networks and services Facebook, XING, LinkedIn,

---

[3] In the context of a global publication this quotation was left in the original (German) language. An English translation would be: "platform for different applications".

[4] The authors of this paper wish to thank Corinna Schwarz, Corinna Hübl, Heike Poley and Patricia Kurowski for helping with the research for this subchapter.

Twitter and MySpace[5] in mid-May 2011. At the centre of the analysis was the question, to what extent precisely social media are used for internal communication here, e.g. concerning change issues. The search was conducted with the search function that each service provided and a series of different short and long versions of the name of each company with the main focus on the German language.

In the first instance the results were deflating: On the whole and considering their respective size, the presence of both companies in social media, apart from two defined exceptions, is quite limited. Relatively speaking, there are only a few associated special pages and groups and the generally discernible involvement of employees in social media mostly ranges between one and 3 % of the employees in each company. The exceptions are the Lufthansa-fanpage on Facebook with over 200.000 "likes", which is official, but geared to the outside and a relatively high but privately initiated presence of Lufthansa employees on individual pages on LinkedIn plus employees of both organisations on XING. All this is to be observed before the general similarities and disparities of the two companies: Both are internationally, yes virtually globally positioned and active. However, in comparison to the Ministry of Foreign Affairs, which is deemed rather conservative, the Lufthansa AG is meanwhile clearly set up differently regarding its total number of employees and the disposition to take on technical and structural changes. Nevertheless, both organisations show interesting niches and trends that should at least be shortly examined within the framework of the permitted extent of this paper. The service with the widest reach for both organisations is Facebook. Five groups can be found there for the Ministry of Foreign Affairs (MOFA), 22 for Lufthansa. In turn, only two of the five MOFA-groups, merely 408 members altogether, match our focus of internal communication: one unofficial network of 127 current employees and one of 281 current or former interns. With Lufthansa the absolute figures are also higher internally: 14 of the 22 groups mentioned above are internal in the broadest sense and have 3,467 members; "Lufthansa Crew" (1,760 members) and "Lufthansa Cargo" (728 members) being the major ones. Relatively speaking, the corresponding groupings of both organisations are still rather small since they comprise only 3 % of the total number of employees each. Things look even bleaker in terms of clearly internal references on the special Facebook-site: Only 11 "likes" on a single, additionally specific page for the Ministry of Foreign Affairs ("Rainbow AA")[6] and also only two pages ("Assessment Center" and "Flight Attendants") with 292 "likes" at Lufthansa. Evaluating the external or not definitely recognizable sites, however, we can establish that Lufthansa certainly takes the lead due to the mentioned fansite etc. (in this area there are 111 "likes" on 13 pages for the MOFA and 266,694 "likes" on 28 pages for Lufthansa, while the official fansite obviously dominates). The second important social network with regard to the two organisations is LinkedIn. It contains neither official pages nor groups of the

---

[5] The two latter services were also completely examined, but led to hardly measurable, since very low figures—especially internally. For this reason, due to the lack of space and relevance, the results will not be depicted in this paper.

[6] AA here short for "Auswärtiges Amt" = Ministry of Foreign Affairs.

Ministry of Foreign Affairs, although 155 employees are individually listed with the service. At least you encounter 15,118 individual Lufthanseatics on the networking platform, which equals just under 13 % of the personnel. There are four groups with an internal focus that comprise 660 members altogether. Externally or not clearly recognizable there are decidedly more through marketing activities, yet still only a handful given the size of the corporation: 429 members in three groups or 5,977 followers on three LinkedIn sites.

That leaves XING as the third major network that is particularly important in Germany. With 1,628 members approximately 12 % of the MOFA-employees and more than 10,000 Lufthansa employees (that would correspond to just under 9 %, the real value is presumably higher but is not recorded by XING) are identifiably listed here. The MOFA is not featured on XING with any groups but with three inofficial sites. Lufthansa has ten groups with internal focus and 3,809 members as well as three further external groups with 488 members; there are notably more sites, namely two official and about 48 non-official ones. The examination of five of the most important social media services distinctly reveals: Externally, the services are increasingly utilized for advertising and communication purposes—measured against the significance of the organisation, however, these values are not phenomenal, either. Internally, the use is extremely rudimentary and mostly due to the initiative of a group or an individual. The relatively high number of members in the geographically most relevant networks (LinkedIn and XING) clearly indicates that the employees of both companies are relatively willing and, as a general rule, at least have the technical ability to communicate through social media. Thus, both the internal use of actually external services and the creation of equivalent, specifically internal offers[7] have great potential, especially for accompanying fundamental changes as a permanent process.

4 "The Future": What the Real Impact of Social Media Could Be on Change Communication

4.1 General Reflections on the Context of Social Media and Leadership in Change Situations

A past that displayed a basic but very particular acceptance and always rather trailed behind the technological developments and a present, in which the more recent services are used intensely on a private basis while they hardly ever structurally expand into internal communication, expressly in change processes. Disregarding many details, that could be this paper's highly abridged summary so far. Above all,

---

[7] For the MOFA at least the authors of this paper can officially report that this internal "imitation model" is not used, either. No reliable statement was available from Lufthansa. However, general experience at colleges, for example, has shown that "imitation models" of this kind seldom enjoyed a popularity that was even comparable to the original's.

this lays out two things: enormous heaps of potential for internal (change) communication going to waste and the lack of systematically knowledge to exploit just this potential, since the decision to join and use the Web 2.0 lies with the company's management and culture of communication. The above-mentioned Schick writes: "Der erfolgreiche, d. h. der nutzbringende Einsatz solcher neuen Kanäle hängt entscheidend von der Führungs- und Kommunikationskultur der einzelnen Unternehmen ab" (2010, p. 195).[8] His assumption: A targeted, professional and genuine application of Web 2.0 can lead to economic success. Schick (2010, p. 196 et seq.) illustrates this point by using the example of the already well-established "blogs": Managers who use this instrument in their companies should see to it that they do it genuinely. If the chairman of the board employs this tool, he or she should make sure to provide the texts themselves. To quote Schick (2010, p. 197): "Für den Erfolg (der Blog wird von vielen gelesen und möglichst auch kommentiert) ist entscheidend, dass hier in einer sehr persönlichen Art publiziert wird und bei den Mitarbeitern nicht der Eindruck entsteht, das alles sei die, Schreibe' des Vorstandsassistenten—ausgewogen, abgestimmt und glattgebügelt."[9]

There are at least three fundamental correlations between company management and communication culture on the one hand and social media as a tool for internal communication especially for, but not limited to, change processes on the other:

1. *Social media require leadership—particularly in change situations*
   Social media are still a tool that neither the company nor the employees really handle professionally, but in which we virtually all are beginners in some way. Which rules of decent behaviour, of sensible conduct will apply in the time to come? What am I allowed to say how about my boss or a definite change project in an internal social medium? What is appropriate on the external level if I am critical about maybe even the whole institution or oppose it in a particular aspect but still am its employee? How much am I allowed to communicate to the inside and outside about what is happening in the company, for example in change situations, which are not exactly confidential but may in total not paint a positive picture or possibly a too valuable one for the competition? These and many further questions have not been decided yet. Organisations therefore need a leadership that takes a clear stance on such issues and suggests—ideally dialogic-oriented—solutions. The "social media guidelines" that exist in companies to date do not incorporate this aspect comprehensively enough and are notably written with far too little relation to reorganisation and restructuring situations.

---

[8] In the context of a European conference this quotation was left in the original (German) language. An English translation would be: "The successful, i.e. beneficial application of such channels critically depends on the management- and communication culture of each company."

[9] In the context of a global publication this quotation was left in the original (German) language. An English translation would be: "To ensure the success of the blog (it is read by many and may even be commented on), it is important that it is published in a very personal way so that the employees do not get the impression that it is all the "writings" of the executive assistant—balanced, aligned, and smooth."

2. *Leadership needs social media—particularly in the starting phase*
   For a long time management at best has not meant bossing and pushing around employees but a "leadership" that provides and sets the example of objectives (and where this style does not yet exist, social media will obviously increase pressure to introduce it). In a time when the necessity to change and decide emerges at a faster and faster pace, it is vital for a modern "leader" to notice problems in the organisation as early as possible in order to react to them and make use of the much-invoked "collective intelligence" of every single employee. Given their dialogic, very symmetric communication approach, social media can offer essential support—which unfortunately is hardly taken advantage of up to now. How much leverage can be developed here, particularly concerning necessary changes, is best assessed by those who have worked successfully with "change agents" and other selective models in the past.
3. *Social media and leadership will mutually define one another anew—basically and longterm*
   What is more, through social media the boundaries between "top" and "bottom" as well as between "inside" and "outside" of organisations will be newly defined in the long run. The "grenzenlose Unternehmung",[10] a demand that Picot, Reichwald and Wigang (cf. 2008) already voiced at the turn of the millennium and repeated 3 years ago, could then actually become true.
   Especially big corporations with distinctive hierarchies could develop a new dialogical culture of openness, medium-sized companies might form an advanced, efficient type of network that will enable them to better play to their strengths, particularly in change situations. Every artificial hierarchy that is not also constructed by department or qualification, however, will face problems in this new world. And reversely, the way management applies social media will also continue to crucially influence the perception and development of the networks and services themselves. But this is not the attempt to paint the pure picture of a "beautiful new world" of social media communication. The subject is also linked to various problems. The authors of this paper will revisit them in the conclusion (cf. Chap. 5).

4.2 Analysis of the Possible Acceptance of Social Media as a Tool of Internal Change Communication in 2015/16: The Example of the German Ministry of Foreign Affairs

In a study conducted by the authors of this paper in and with the Ministry of Foreign Affairs (MOFA) in June 2011, the employees of the office around the world were questioned about their general use of media, including social media, in an online survey that involved the entire staff. Simultaneously, for the second part of this

---

[10] In the context of a global publication this quotation was left in the original (German) language. An English translation would be: "boundless enterprise".

project a content analysis of the internal media of the Ministry of Foreign Affairs was carried out and evaluated from January 1, 2010 to May 30, 2011, counting in possible references to the use of social media (cf. Nelke and Sievert 2013).

For the online survey a total of 5,826 staff members from the MOFA accessed a questionnaire that was provided on the website of an external survey tool. The return rate amounted to 1,562 individually filled in questionnaires, which corresponds to nearly 27 % of the people surveyed. The comparison of singular features between population and samples spoke for the fact that the survey feedback was relatively highly representative. Selective results may be outlined as follows: All in all, nearly 67 % of the employees use classic internet websites for work purposes. Social networks such as Facebook, XING and LinkedIn are employed significantly less for professional use by the staff of the MOFA. Only 16 % of the employees state that they draw on these social media tools for work purposes. The results for forums and blogs (9 %), RSS-Feeds (4 %) and social networks like Twitter (2 %) are even worse. This outcome shows that the range of social media currently does not play a very important role in the professional communication of the Ministry's staff. However, earlier in Sect. 3.2 we mentioned that 1,628 employees of the Ministry of Foreign Affairs were registered on XING, which points in another direction. It reveals that nearly 28 % of the Ministry's staff use this social network. In contrast, Facebook groups with focus on internal communication are only applied by 7 % of the employees. These results lead to the assumption that the employees of the MOFA use social networking sites to a much greater degree in the (half-) private realm than in a purely professional context.[11] In order to ensure a more future-oriented internal communication in the Ministry of Foreign Affairs social media-activities must be expanded and transferred from the half-private to a primarily also professional context.[12] The survey also disclosed that the employees wish for considerable changes with regard to communication: 62 % advocated more transparency in communication, 53 % of which wanted staff members on every level of the hierarchy to be able to influence communication equally. 32 % of the employees of the MOFA supported an expanded intranet. Thus it is clear that the internal communication of the MOFA needs to take advantage of the potential that social media offer for more transparency and participation. The department of communication should refocus its strategic planning for the next years on this

---

[11] For a second complementally substudy a sample of 516 sampling units from the internal media of the Ministry of Foreign Affairs was drawn out in the time period from July 2010 to June 2011. Analysis indicated that the internal media of the MOFA sparsely mention and respectively refer to external media. It is also striking that in all the studied content of the internal media there were only 58 references to the internet in "intern AA" (internal MOFA), "FFD-Rundbrief" (FFD-Newsletter) and the intranet. Only 1.4 % of the external references lead to the Web 2.0-area and here to social networking sites. Furthermore, there are virtually no links at all connecting the individual internal media of the MOFA.

[12] The separation of private and professional context is a general problem in connection with social media (Facebook is increasingly also employed professionally while LinkedIn and XING are progressively used for private purposes.) This issue cannot be further addressed.

area and execute it stringently. On the other hand, the data show that particularly in the realm of internal communication there is a great need for development when it comes to the application of social media. It needs to be determined whether the familiar social media-platforms and prospective official groups are to be used for internal communication or whether it is preferable to build up an internal network under the umbrella of the existing intranet. Since in some branches of the MOFA the internet is not readily accessible the internal version via the intranet platform may be the more promising one here. Apart from that, blogs and wikis can be integrated into the existing intranet and provide for a faster and more transparent communication. The employees of the MOFA make use of social media privately rather than in connection with their job. At the same time nearly two thirds of the staff wish for greater transparency in the communication of the MOFA. Hence, one can conclude that communication via social media will gain more relevance in the Ministry of Foreign Affairs in the future. One instance that demonstrates how much the employees desire social media is the fact that this time the regular internal list of job openings was not first accessible through official channels or at least over the intranet of the MOFA but was privately exchanged among the employees on Facebook. Therefore, the management of the Ministry of Foreign Affairs must establish whether the social media-activities of its staff should continue mainly privately or whether the organisation will participate in this dialogue itself.

Conclusion

Based on experiences in similar organisations from three time frames, the present paper endeavoured to outline how organisational change through (social) media could be more people-friendly and effective, in short: better in every respect, in the future. The three theoretical observations and the three concrete analyses for the past, the present and the future should have shown that there are a considerable need and substantial possibilities that have remained unexploited to date. Yet, in connection with change, the authors do not want social media merely to be viewed as a further tool, but as the general expression of a modern understanding of leadership—that exists in quite a number of, albeit by far not in all cases. The new tools described, however, can surely help advance its expansion and acceptance. Nevertheless, let us finally not conceal the risks linked to such a development: For example, there is a chance that participants too devoted to hierarchies may use the new technologies to control rather than for the dialogue. Or the risk of the progressive disappearance of the boundaries between private and public and between personal and professional matters. Or the risk that lies in the permanent traceability of information and statements that one might prefer a little less publicly accessible after a few years—just to name a handful. But given the global competitive pressure, the organisations will not be in the position to choose *if* they want to open up further to social media. It is merely the *how* that they can help design for the benefit of the company and its employees. Making a contribution in order to make this happen preferably on a scientific-reflected, yet practice-oriented basis was the object of this paper.

References

Bustínduy, I. (2010). *La comunicación interna en las organizaciones 2.0*. Barcelona: Editorial UOC.
Cauers, C. (2009). *Mitarbeiterzeitschriften heute. Flaschenpost oder strategisches Medium* (2nd ed.). Wiesbaden: VS Verlag für Sozialwissenschaften.
Crijns, R., & Janichs, N. (2008). *Interne Kommunikation von Unternehmen. Psychologische, kommunikationswissenschaftliche und kulturvergleichende Studien* (2nd ed.). Wiesbaden: VS Verlag.
Döring, N. (2003). *Sozialpsychologie des Internet. Die Bedeutung des Internet für Kommunikationsprozesse, Identitäten, soziale Beziehungen und Gruppen* (2nd ed.). Göttingen, Bern, Toronto, Seattle: Hogrefe-Verlag.
Ebersbach, A., Glaser, M., & Heigl, R. (2008). *Social Web*. Konstanz: UVK Verlagsgesellschaft.
Gadd, C. S., & Einbinder, J. (2010). *Transforming health care through information: case studies*. New York, Dordrecht, Heidelberg, London: Springer.
Giddens, A. (1984). *The constitution of society*. Berkeley: University of California Press.
Grunig, L. A., Grunig, J. E., & Dozier, D. M. (2002). *Excellent public relations and effective organizations. A study of communication management in three countries*. Mahwah, NY: Lawrence Erlbaum Associates, Inc.
Ludwig, A. (2008). *Unternehmenskommunikation. Frauen und Führung*. München: Grin Verlag.
Mast, C. (2010). *Unternehmenskommunikation* (4th ed.). Stuttgart: Lucius & Lucius Verlag.
Nelke-Mayenknecht, A. (2008). Das Intranet als Kommunikationsstruktur im organisationalen Informations- und Wissensmanagement. Am Beispiel der Deutschen Lufthansa AG. Dissertation published as FU Dissertation online. http://www.diss.fuberlin.de/diss/receive/FUDISS_thesis_000000004989. Accessed 10 May 2011.
Nelke, A., Sievert, H., & Tipon, B. (2013). Karrierewege als Thema der Internen Kommunikation. Befragungen der Beschäftigten und Inhaltsanalyse der internen Medien im Auswärtigen Amt. Wiesbaden, Springer US.
Picot, A., Reichwald, R., & Wigang, R. T. (2008). *Die grenzenlose Unternehmung. Die grenzenlose Unternehmung. Lehrbuch. Information, Organisation und Management. Unternehmensführung im Informationszeitalter*. Wiesbaden: Gabler.
Rommert, F.-M. (2005). *Hoffnungsträger Intranet. Charakteristika und Aufgaben eines neuen Mediums in der internen Kommunikation* (2nd ed.). München: Verlag Reinhard Fischer.
Schick, S. (2010). *Interne Unternehmenskommunikation. Strategien entwickeln, Strukturen schaffen, Prozesse steuern* (4th ed.). Stuttgart: Schäfer-Poeschel Verlag.
School for communication and management, DPRG und prmagazin (2010). *Trendmonitor Interne Kommunikation 2010*.
Short, J., Williams, E., & Christie, B. (1976). *The social psychology of telecommunication*. London: Wiley.
Sievert, H., & Westermann, A. (2009). 'It's the People, Stupid!'—Why general managers and communication professionals often do not understand each other—e.g. in change processes. In: Invernizzi, E., Muzi Falconi, T. & Romenti, S. (eds.). *Institutionalising PR and corporate communication, proceedings of the Euprera 2008 Milan congress*. p. 1109–1129.
Smith, L., & Mounter, P. (2008). *Effective internal communication* (2nd ed.). London: CIPR.
Thielke, S. (2009). *Instrumente der internen Unternehmenskommunikation. Ein Vergleich der klassischen Instrumente mit den Instrumenten der neuen elektronischen Medien in Bezug auf die Einsetzbarkeit in Unternehmen unterschiedlicher Größe. Research paper*. München: Grin Verlag.

Employees' Conceptions of How Management Can Operationalize Employee Involvement

Stavros Georgiades

This is an inductive study of change in a media organization to understand how employees think about the way management can achieve employee involvement, highlighting the importance of the recruitment process and the achievement of employee creation, innovation and confidence that their involvement is true and valid.

The global recession and its subsequent negative consequences have led managers of media organizations consider changes to the way they manage their organizations, aiming for greater efficiency and effectiveness. One of the changes considered was the achievement of employee involvement towards organizational decisions and operations.

Despite long-standing recognition on the importance of gaining employee involvement for implementing change successfully, we know almost nothing about how employees think about the way management can work to gain employee involvement. The purpose of this research is to eliminate this lacuna.

From a theoretical perspective, there has been a great deal of literature on the importance of gaining employee involvement in order to implement change. Academics have looked at organizational arrangements provided by management when aiming to achieve and manage an organizational change and as a result provide employees with more influence. These theories suggest that management needs to gain the support of both employees and managers (Delaney and Sockell 1990), use empowerment practices (Conger and Kanungo 1988), motivate employees, and finally ensure that any problems likely to arise are solved without delay (McHugh 1997).

Even though these theoretical views are helpful, outstanding issues remain. Although there is a great deal of literature about the importance of gaining employee involvement in order to implement change, the existing theoretical

---

S. Georgiades (✉)
Frederick University, Lefkosia, Cyprus
e-mail: bus.gs@frederick.ac.cy

views have not dealt adequately with how the employees think about the way management can work to achieve employee involvement. Also, there is little empirically grounded theoretical account of how employees think about how management can operationalize employee involvement.

In order to address this gap this study explores how employees think about the way management can operationalize employee involvement. As a result this research contributes towards a richer theory on the process behind the implementation of employee involvement, highlighting the importance of the recruitment process and the achievement of employee creation, innovation and confidence that their involvement is true and valid.

1 Theoretical Background

According to Hrebiniak (1974) various experiments and other empirical studies have suggested that increased worker participation in decision making increases organizational effectiveness, while positively affecting satisfaction, trust, involvement and other work related attitudes (Argyris 1973; Coch and French 1948; Likert 1961; Patchen 1970; Porter and Lawler 1968; Morse and Reimer 1956; Tannenbaum 1961; White and Lippitt 1960).

However, Tannenbaum (1954), French et al. (1958) and Vroom (1959) suggest that the response to participation is conditioned by the individual's personality, interpersonal skills and expectations. According to Ruh et al. (1975) personal background, values and job characteristics all influence job involvement. The characteristics of the immediate job situation may also exert considerable influence on job involvement that is related to the characteristics of the situation as well as background factors (Ruh et al. 1975).

Participation can be effective to the extent that participants perceive the opportunity to participate as legitimate or relevant to their work (French et al. 1958). Abdel-Halim and Rowland (1976) considered that personality characteristics and participation should be examined in combination with the degree of personal autonomy or structure in the work environment, which are reflective of the superior–subordinate relationship or the nature of the task to be performed. When tasks are non-repetitive, participative decision making will have a positive effect on job satisfaction and performance regardless of the subordinate's predisposition towards independence or autonomy (Ahmed Abdel Halim 1983). Job autonomy is defined as the authority connected with the job, the opportunity for independent thought and action in the job, the opportunity to participate in the setting of goals and the determination of methods and procedures (Maurer 1967).

Prior research considers the benefits of employee involvement and whether organizational democracy can enhance an organization's competitive advantage. According to Kerr (2004) this will depend of the activities performed by the firm and the types of products or services it sells to customers and clients. The benefits of participation will be greater where the work requires more innovative and creative input from employees and democracy's relative advantage will be proportional to the amount of decision making that actually occurs in a given setting (Kerr 2004).

More specifically, if the organization aims to respond to demand via innovative original products, this diversity of output will require a coordinated diversity of input that can be best achieved via open, collaborative, participative management processes. This leads towards respect and trust in individual and nurturance of talent and creativity. In addition the emphasis must be on the individual initiative rather than bureaucracy. Democratic practices and competitive advantage also depend on the nature of the organization's workforce, the ability and motivation of the workforce to participate in the flow of information and the decisions. Where employees bring specialized or proprietary knowledge to the organization the competitive effect of democratic process is likely to be greater than where the knowledge of employees is homogenous. Also, democratic processes will be most valuable where the workforce possesses unique capabilities and attributes like talent and commitment (Kerr 2004).

It is thus important to consider the organizational climate and structure most encouraging to the emergence of creativity. A creative organization should have a small degree of formalization of relationships among the organizational positions, not over-specify the human resources needed for a specific task, create a flexible power-authority-influence structure, healthy amounts of participation and autonomy, broad spans of control (no management by direction and control), and a performance evaluation based on long time spans. The organization should focus on the idea generation function, open communication, a reward system of intrinsic character via self-selection of tasks, broadly defined constraints, increased freedom of work scheduling and autonomy concerning work methods and enhanced opportunities for professional growth (Cummings 1965).

In addition, information privacy is important to be assured as it signals safety and reduces fears concerning close monitoring and critical scrutiny of time use and behavior that may discourage employees from generating new and useful ideas (Alge et al. 2006; George and Zhou 2001; Pedersen 1997; Westin 1967). Information privacy also contributes to feelings of psychological empowerment which is positively associated with creativity. High-quality relations between supervisors and subordinates and supervisor support have long been recognized as important contributors to creativity (Shalley et al. 2004). Displaying interactional justice and being trustworthy are important ways in which supervisors can provide a supportive work environment for creativity. Also, network characteristics (weak network ties) that promote the sharing and spreading of heterogeneous information and perspectives promote creativity (George 2007).

Prior research has also considered the characteristics of creative people. More specifically, Elsbach and Kramer (2003) suggest that creative people have several handicaps during an interview like appearing to be dull, being unpolished, untrained and anxious. In addition, they make obscure references, lack sophistication and experience, are passionate about their ideas and committed to their projects, possess a naivete which is associated with freshness and originality and focus on their job as a creative art form and not business. On the other hand, uncreative people are too slick (try too hard, not believe in their ideas), appear too desperate, work too hard, get all dressed up and give a laundry (too many) list of ideas which means that they are not passionate and creative as they cannot be for all ideas on their list. Also a creative person is a person that during an interview engages you as well and makes you feel excited about their ideas and you even contribute your own creative idea thus establishing a perception of high engagement, is responsive to the interviewer's ideas/suggestions and does not feel more expert or knowledgeable about the industry than the interviewer (Elsbach and Kramer 2003).

Prior research also offers a general perspective into the concept of employee involvement, highlighting group support and acceptance.

Vroom and Yetton's famous participation model (Vroom 1973) suggests how much decision-making power managers should share with subordinates under certain conditions, noting that one of the major factors influencing this decision should be the acceptance and commitment on the part of subordinates to execute the decision effectively.

The leader-member (manager–employee) relationship also affects the manager's, his group's, and the organization's performance according to Fiedler's contingency model (Fiedler 1972) because group support, trust, respect and acceptance by subordinates affect the favorableness of the situation a manager has to face.

The path goal theory suggests that the task may have an overriding effect on the relationship between participation and subordinate responses, and that individual predispositions or personality characteristics of subordinates have an effect only under some tasks (House and Mitchell 1974).

Several other academics have looked at specific organizational arrangements provided by management when aiming to achieve and manage an organizational change, and have come up with several notions relating to the provision of influence to employees.

In the management literature is appears that management aims to gain the support of both employees and managers (Cobb et al. 1995; Delaney and Sockell 1990; Tesluk et al. 1999), uses empowerment practices towards employees either by regularly expressing confidence in them (Conger and Kanungo 1988; Conger 1986; Bandura 1986) or via the provision of employee development (Tierney 1999; Conger and Kanungo 1988; Neubert and Cady 2001; Rusaw 2000; Block 1987; Kanter; 1979; Oldham 1976; Strauss 1977) and operational freedom (Schwochau and Delaney 1997; Rusaw 2000; Conger and Kanungo 1988; Tierney 1999; Nord et al. 1993) and ensures employees are motivated via the use of several motivational methods (Neubert and Cady 2001; Black and Margulies 1989; Schwochau and Delaney 1997; McHugh 1997) and that any problems likely to arise are solved without delay (Clayton and Gregory 2000; McHugh 1997; Gill 1996).

So, what do employees think about the way management can gain employee involvement?

This question suggests that extant views need to be linked to employee involvement. This observation coupled with the limited research on employee involvement led to the inductive research described in this research.

2 Research Methods

The study used a multiple case design that allowed a replication logic, where a series of cases (interviews) is treated as a series of experiments, each case serving to confirm or disconfirm the inferences drawn from the others (Yin 2003). The study also employed an embedded design, that is multiple levels of analysis, focusing at 3 levels: (1) high level employees (2) low level employees (3) provision of organizational arrangements. Although an embedded design is complex, it permits induction of rich and reliable models (Yin 2003).

The setting is a US online media organization whose mission is to help create and empower an artistic middle class through the use of innovative technology, ensuring that any band from any genre anywhere in the world can find and connect with any type of music promoter, licensor or broadcaster—easily, effectively, and quickly. Due to the internet, this business has made it possible for just about any entrepreneurial artist to meaningfully connect with an audience and build a music career without the traditional backing of a major recording label.

2.1 Data Collection

To obtain multiple perspectives, 19 in-depth interviews were conducted over a period of 6 months with the founder/owner, and 6 higher and lower level employees of the organization from different areas. There were three data sources: (1) initial interview with the founder/owner of the organization (2) semi-structured interviews with the six employees (3) secondary sources.

2.1.1 Founder/Owner
An entry interview, using a semi-structured format was conducted with the founder of the organization who gave some general information about the organization and its mission, and more specifically its aim to achieve employee innovation and creativeness via their involvement and contributions towards organizational decisions and operations.

2.1.2 Six Employee Interviews
After the initial interview with the founder of the firm, semi-structured interviews with the six employees were conducted. Initial interviews involved questions about the department and the decision making process. The second and third set of interviews became more structured and questions during these interviews involved specific organizational arrangements provided by management including several issues on creativeness and innovation. Fourteen matters were discussed in total (Appendix). Following an approach to inductive research, these questions were supplemented with ones that seemed fruitful to pursue during the interview.

2.1.3 Secondary Source and Other Data
Internal documents were examined as available.

2.2 Data Analysis

The data were analyzed as follows. The qualitative responses were combined using the descriptions each employee had given. Once preliminary analyses had been developed from the respective data sets, the analyses and induced propositions were combined using methods for building theory from case studies (Eisenhardt 1989; Glaser and Strauss 1967).

3 Results

3.1 Organizational Support

First, the current study has insights relating to the issue of management gaining the support of employees, their unions and of managers at different levels in order to achieve employee involvement. In this study the employees' opinion is that management must aim to gain employee involvement and contributions during the recruitment process. The employees interviewed believe that management can do so by communicating to new employees the need to create and innovate, leading to higher profits, thus prove their worth and find ways to generate value.

In addition, employees stressed that during the recruitment process management needs also explain how decisions made must follow the organization's formalized path (procedures). This way, employees would be able to vocalize better why they think the path is approved or not for the decisions they make. Although there is a general path laid out for minor decisions, employees are not fully entrusted to make decisions for major issues which would not follow the general organizational path (i.e. pay promoters' procedure). If they do their ideas and suggestions are not heard or even worse they are left out of the decision making process. The employees explained that when they make decisions that fall outside the formal organizational procedures management will ask why the decision was made and talk about it as a first warning. This top-down approach with many priorities and requests from top level leads to lack of execution on other projects and lack of analysis of decisions that have been made, affecting negatively team morale and encouragement.

Proposition 1. *The employees' opinion is that management can encourage and enable employees to get involved in the decision making process by gaining the support of employees and of managers at different levels.*

3.2 Empowerment Practices

Regarding empowerment practices previous literature suggests that regular expressions of confidence and the provision of employee development and operational freedom can encourage and enable employees to get involved and contribute.

The employees interviewed suggested that there are cases when management expresses confidence but there are times when guidance turns into telling them what to do, right down to a detail like what an email should say, which makes them question management's confidence in them. Consequently, it is the employees' view that management should aim to gain their involvement via the way they are evaluated, and more specifically by tying their performance and compensation to revenues and profits generated as a result of creativity and innovation, and that this should also be communicated clearly during the recruitment process. What managers should not do, according to the employees, is to confuse them by not being happy when employees try to innovate and as a result lose track of their individual jobs and criticize them for not trying enough new stuff when they try to focus on the task on hand.

In addition, the employees expressed their views relating to the importance of their development via training. The employees interviewed mentioned that the business offered training to them focusing on the organization's mission, objectives, goals and operations, giving them the opportunity to attend related conferences and providing them with related books and training materials. In the past according to some employees, management used to offer external training as well. However, the organization does not offer any specific training on how to be creative and innovative, something they consider important. Management aims to achieve creativeness and innovation on-the-job by giving employees tasks to solve and coaching them along the way. In addition, management verbally expects and gives employees freedom to execute certain tasks and employees are asked to do so creatively, given guidance with the ideas they have and being challenged on these ideas. Management encourages employees to come up with solutions on their own and try things, not just asking for answers.

The employees interviewed expressed the view that training is essential to develop their skills and knowledge but that initiative only goes as far as the priorities of the company let people take it. Conversations from a company strategy/management perspective for example are handled by leadership exclusively. What is important to note is that employees believe that having to innovate and create and thus accomplish something new is what keeps them going. If they did not have the opportunity to use their talents they would leave their jobs. More specifically, several expressed the view that media makes a meaningful impact on both their individual life and on a greater societal level and that they work to improve other's lives. As a result they enjoy coming up with new ideas and executing them, enabling themselves to live a life from a socially responsible perspective.

Employees also considered the idea of job autonomy and operational freedom. According to the employees interviewed, management allows employees the ability to provide value how and where they feel they are most impactful, as long as they remain focused on the company mission, objectives and strategies and provides them with authority when it relates to their department and its objectives. Personal schedules are generally flexible making employees feel more accountable. However, there are cases when success and reaching preset goals feels out of their hands and thus they do not get a sense of accomplishment and accountability. In addition, there are cases where initiatives for improving their work are not treated like a priority by management and even cases where a decision or a process employees made a million times comes into question by management, making them feel like they are not trusted. Consequently, according to the employees, there is operational freedom and authority provided it lies within the predetermined organizational path. This can explain the employee' opinion that when they look to build something new they can make a contribution by throwing out a lot of ideas which will be trimmed down via a fairly structured process that will satisfy management if it is practical, sellable and creative.

Proposition 2. *The employees' opinion is that management can encourage employees to get involved in the decision making process by providing empowerment practices like regular expressions of confidence, employee development and operational freedom.*

3.3 Employee Motivation

The employees also expressed their thoughts on the way management can motivate them and thus encourage them to get involved. Employees expressed the view that management expects them to be creative in their involvement and contributions towards organizational decisions and operations. This is done via observation and communication on what the employee does, expecting the decisions to line-up with the organizational and departmental goals, and thus by checking return on investment on pre-set goals for team members that require both innovation and creativity.

In addition, employees expressed the opinion that management communicates the final decisions made and gives feedback on how management has come to that decision which is reflected in the final result. Most employees however expressed the view that in order to motivate them to innovate and create management needs to do so via both monetary and non-monetary methods. Personal development, growth potential, a prize for the best idea, being called out in a meeting, added accountability and recognition are all non-monetary methods employees suggest would motivate them to get involved. In addition, there are employees who are self-motivated and their incentive comes from knowing they are making someone's life better and working towards a cause.

In terms of monetary motivation management first shows employees the profit from their creation and innovation, and explains to them how their innovation achieved the specific profit, which is also educational for them. Management then ties salary increases to profits from innovation, offers stock options, revenue-based goals and quarterly bonuses where achieving goals is tied to innovation. Employees feel motivated if they are encouraged to innovate and create new products that can be sold to revenue goals. Showing and explaining these tangible results to employees helps them understand the importance of creation and innovation, gives a real indicator of what innovations paid off and why, and enables employees to do more of the things that were successful.

Proposition 3. *The employees' opinion is that management can motivate employees to get involved in the decision making process by ensuring that their involvement leads to valued outcomes.*

3.4 Disclosure and Solution of Problems

Finally, the study has insights on the disclosure and subsequent solution of any problems arising in relation to the process behind the implementation of employee involvement. The employees interviewed considered that what is important in relation to the process behind the implementation of employee involvement is the employees' relationships with managers because they always affect the latter's willingness to include them in decision-making as an employee must be trusted for a manager to include in a meaningful way. Managers who trust their employees are also affected when they prioritize their thoughts and ideas. According to one employee, it takes a good deal of pro-activity, innovation and proving yourself to be in a position where your feedback is heard.

Another major issue mentioned is that of management encouraging open-door communication, collaboration and team work. An open team environment that fosters this kind of initiative results on the employees' willingness to try to contribute. In addition, the fact that there is no major inter-office politicking or backbiting also encourages employees to get involved. Some employees expressed the view that although open-door environment is important for management to achieve it is hard to get time from the managers to collaborate on everything.

One employee explained the importance of this initiative by expressing the view that is his area it has been tough to get these lines open. The employee explained that when they feel things are moving forward they definitely want to be involved. However, when they are told that things are moving forward but do not see much movement, or when they are told to sit tight on things that need movement its disheartening. Also when they feel they are communicating, collaborating and working together but are not able to get the priority from the rest of the company its also disheartening. Finally, this kind of approach helps individuals who are new or not necessarily visible to leadership to be engaged immediately, gives them an opportunity to prove themselves and gain visibility and puts them in a great position to be heard and included in decision making.

Proposition 4. *The employees' opinion is that management can encourage and enable employees to get involved in the decision making process by ensuring that any problems arising are disclosed and solved via regular management-employee dialogue.*

4 Discussion and Theoretical Implications

4.1 Toward a New Theory on the Process Behind the Implementation of Employee Involvement

Based on the employees' thoughts, this study also contributes into a richer theory on the process behind the implementation of employee involvement.

4.2 Recruitment Method

Several of the propositions focus on how the recruitment method can be used by management aiming to achieve employee involvement.

Management aims to gain the support of employees and managers at different levels (Proposition 1) and the recruitment process can assist management in this effort. More specifically, management needs to explain to employees that they are expected to create and innovate according to the organizational path, leading towards an increase in the organization's profits. The recruitment method can also assist management when aiming to empower employees (Proposition 2). Employees must be encouraged to innovate and create, evaluated accordingly, and the method of evaluation should be clearly communicated to them during the recruitment process. Finally, management needs to ensure that employees are motivated to get involved and contribute (Proposition 3). Due to the fact that there are several employees who are self-motivated, and their incentives come from knowing that they make peoples' lives better by working towards a cause, management should aim to identify and thus recruit those self-motivated to get involved and contribute new employees. In this view interesting research questions could center on how management can identify and thus recruit self-motivated employees.

The emergent perspective thus considers the recruitment method used by the management of a media organization crucial in achieving employee involvement and contributions towards organizational decisions and operations. Others (Tannenbaum 1954; French et al. 1958; Vroom 1959) have argued that recruitment can help identify suitable candidates for an organization. The view here, in agreement with Elsbach and Kramer (2003), is that the recruitment process can also help management to both identify new recruits motivated to get involved and contribute and assist them to create and innovate according to the organization's needs.

4.3 Employee Creation and Innovation

Second, several of the propositions describe how management aiming to achieve employee involvement needs also focus on employee creativeness and innovation.

The management's effort to promote employee creativeness and innovation can be assisted by the provision of empowerment practices like employee training

(Proposition 2) which should specifically and directly relate to different ways employees can become creative and innovative in line with the company's mission, objectives, goals and operations. Management can also train employees on the job via coaching, challenging and encouragement, and not constrain them based on specific pre-determined organizational priorities. Management can also motivate employees to get involved and contribute (Proposition 3) by using several motivational methods aiming to promote employee creativeness and innovation. Management can check return on investment on pre-set goals for team members required to create and innovate and also offer opportunities for their development and growth by tying promotions, stock options and bonuses to profits resulting from employee creativeness and innovation.

This emergent view thus emphasizes the importance of motivating employees to get involved and contribute (Neubert and Cady 2001; Black and Margulies 1989; Schwochau and Delaney 1997).

The results of this research suggest that this view is limited when dealing with a media organization because in order to get involved and contribute media employees should first be able to create and innovate. This should thus be the initial aim of management.

4.4 Employee Involvement True and Valid

Several propositions also highlight the importance of demonstrating to employees that their involvement is true and valid.

One way of doing so is via the provision of empowerment practices like expressions of confidence, job autonomy and decision making authority (Proposition 2). However, expressions of confidence should not turn into telling them what to do in detail because this lack of confidence will have a negative effect. Also, management must allow employees to set their own goals and treat their initiatives as priorities, rather than trim them down via a pre-determined management process.

Another way of showing employees that their involvement is true and valid is via the use of several motivational methods (Proposition 3). Management should communicate the final management decisions to employees and give them feedback on how they are made. In addition, management needs to show employees the profit from their creation/involvement, explain how it was achieved, and as a result indicate clearly the effect of their involvement.

A final way is to ensure any problems arising in relation to employee involvement are disclosed and solved via regular dialogue and without any delay (Proposition 4). Management should aim to promote open-door communication with all employees and not only those that have achieved the management's trust, should ensure communication only relates to employee problems concerning their involvement and not inter-office politics, and demonstrate to employees that their concerns are given priority and solved without delay.

This emergent view thus highlights the importance of management commitment towards the process of employee involvement. The articles (Argyris 1973; Conger and Kanungo 1988; Morgan and Zeffane 2003; Ketokivi and Castaner 2004) indicate that employee confidence and trust are key factors affecting employee involvement in organizational decisions and operations. Similarly, this study suggests that to encourage and enable employees, management needs to both ensure and demonstrate to them that the process of employee involvement is true and valid.

Appendix: List of Matters Discussed During the Interviews

Description of department
1. Operations, structure, number of people, positions
2. Decision making process

Arrangement provided by management to encourage and enable you to get involved in the decision making process
3. Does management express confidence in you?
4. Does management provide training to help you get involved in decisions?
5. Does management provide operational freedom and job autonomy? Does this make you feel responsible and accountable?
6. Does management provide you with authority in your job?
7. Do managers show you the final management decisions made and explain how you affected the final management decision?
8. Would you say that the employee-manager and employee–employee relationships in your team/department and group climate, social structures and interactions affect your involvement in the decisions made in your department? How and why?
9. Do you feel that management trust your creativeness by encouraging open-door communication, collaboration, team work? Does this make you want to get involved and create?

Creativeness and innovation
10. Do they expect your decisions to lead to innovation and creativeness? How do they check you achieve this?
11. How can you create something in media? How do you respond to social needs? What process do you follow to achieve this?
12. Incentives: How do they motivate you to innovate and to create? Is it via money or/and other methods? Which methods?
13. Should they show you the profits from your creation and innovation and explain how and what you achieved in terms of profits? Is this an encouragement to make creative and innovative decisions?
14. Would you say that you like to work in media because they push you to create and innovate?

References

Abdel-Halim, A. A. (1983). Effects of task and personality characteristics on subordinate responses to participative decision making. *Academy of Management Journal, 26*(3), p477–484.
Abdel-Halim, A. A., & Rowland, K. M. (1976). Some personality determinants of the effects of participation: a further investigation. *Personnel Psychology, 29*(1), p41–55.
Alge, B. J., Ballinger, G. A., Tangirala, S., & Oakely, J. L. (2006). Information privacy in organizations: Empowering creative and extrarole performance. *Journal of Applied Psychology, 9*, 221–232.
Argyris, C. (1973). Personality and organization theory revisited. *Administrative Science Quarterly, 18*, 141–167.
Bandura, A. (1986). *Social foundations of thought and action: A social cognitive view*. Englewood Cliffs, NJ: Prentice-Hall.
Black, S., & Margulies, N. (1989). An ideological perspective on participation: a case for integration. *Journal of Organizational Change Management, 2*, 13–35.
Block, P. (1987). *The empowered manager*. San Francisco: Jossey–Bass.
Clayton, J., & Gregory, W. J. (2000). Reflections on critical systems thinking and the management of change in rule-bound systems. *Journal of Organizational Change Management, 13*, 140–161.
Cobb, A. T., Folger, R., & Wooten, K. (1995). The role justice plays in organizational change. *Public Administration Quarterly, 19*, 135–152.
Coch, L., & French, J. R. P., Jr. (1948). Overcoming resistance to change. *Human Relations, 4*, 512–533.
Conger, J. A. (1986). *Empowering leadership*. Montreal: McGill University. Working Paper.
Conger, J. A., & Kanungo, R. N. (1988). The empowerment process: Integrating theory and practice. *Academy of Management Review, 13*, 471–482.
Cummings, L. (1965). Organizational climates for creativity. *Academy of Management Journal, 8*(3), 220–227.
Delaney, J. T., & Sockell, D. (1990). Employee involvement programs, unionization and organizational flexibility. *Academy of Management Best Paper Proceedings, 1990*, 264–269.
Eisenhardt, K. M. (1989). Building theory from case study research. *Academy of Management Review, 14*, 532–550.
Elsbach, K. D., & Kramer, R. M. (2003). Assessing creativity in Hollywood pitch meetings: Evidence for a dual-process model of creativity judgments. *Academy of Management Journal, 46*(3), p283–301.
Fiedler, F. E. (1972). The effects of leadership training and experience: A contingency model interpretation. *Administrative Science Quarterly, 17*, 453–470.
French, J. R. P., Israel, J., & Aas, D. (1958). An experiment in participation in a Norwegian factory. *Human Relations, 13*, 3–19.
George, J. M. (2007). Creativity in organizations. *Academy of Management Annals, 1*, p439–477.
George, J. M., & Zhou, J. (2001). When openness to experience and conscientiousness are related to creative behavior: An interactional approach. *Journal of Applied Psychology, 86*, 513–524.
Gill, J. (1996). Communication—Is it really that simple? An analysis of a communication exercise in a case study. *Personnel Review, 25*, 23–37.
Glaser, B., & Strauss, A. (1967). *The discovery of grounded theory: Strategies for qualitative research*. London: Wiedenfeld and Nicholson.
House, R. J., & Mitchell, T. R. (1974). Path-goal theory of leadership. *Journal of Contemporary Business, 3*, 81–98.
Hrebiniak, L. G. (1974). Effects of job level and participation on employee attitudes and perceptions of influence. *Academy of Management Journal, 17*(4), p649–662.
Kanter, R. M. (1979). Power failure in management circuits. *Harvard Business Review, 57*(4), 65–75.

Kerr, J. L. (2004). The limits of organizational democracy. *The Academy of Management Executive, 18*(3), 81–95.
Ketokivi, M., & Castaner, X. (2004). Strategic planning as an integrating device. *Administrative Science Quarterly, 49,* 337–365.
Likert, R. (1961). *New patterns of management.* New York: McGraw-Hill.
Maurer, J. G., (1967) The relationship of work role involvement to job characteristics with higher-order need potential. Ph.D. dissertation, Michigan State University.
McHugh, M. (1997). The stress factor: Another item for the change management agenda? *Journal of Organizational Change Management, 10,* 345–362.
Morgan, D. E., & Zeffane, R. (2003). Employee involvement, organizational change and trust in management. *International Journal of Human Resource Management, 14,* 55–75.
Morse, N., & Reimer, E. (1956). The experimental change of a major organizational variable. *Journal of Abnormal and Social Psychology, 52,* 120–129.
Neubert, M. J., & Cady, S. H. (2001). Program commitment: A multi-study longitudinal field investigation of its impact and antecedents. *Personnel Psychology, 54,* 421–449.
Nord, W. R., Rosenblatt, Z., & Rogers, K. (1993). Toward a political framework for flexible management of decline. *Organization Science, 4,* 76–91.
Oldham, G. R. (1976). The motivational strategies used by supervisors' relationships to effectiveness indicators. *Organizational Behavior and Human Performance, 15,* 66–86.
Patchen, M. (1970). *Participation, achievement, and involvement on the job.* Englewood Cliffs, NJ: Prentice-Hall.
Pedersen, D. M. (1997). Psychological functions of privacy. *Journal of Environmental Psychology, 17,* 147–156.
Porter, L. W., & Lawler, E. E. (1968). *Managerial attitudes and performance.* Homewood, IL.: Irwin.
Ruh, R. A., White, J. K., & Wood, R. R. (1975). Job involvement, values, personal background, participation in decision making and job attitudes. *Academy of Management Journal, 18*(2), 300–312.
Rusaw, C. A. (2000). Uncovering training resistance—A critical theory perspective. *Journal of Organizational Change Management, 13,* 249–263.
Schwochau, S., & Delaney, J. (1997). Employee participation and assessments of support for organizational policy changes. *Journal of Labor Research, 18,* 379–402.
Shalley, C. E., Zhou, J., & Oldham, G. R. (2004). Effects of personal and contextual characteristics on creativity: Where should we go from here? *Journal of Management, 30,* 933–958.
Straus, G. (1977). Managerial practices. In J. R. Hackman & L. J. Suttle (Eds.), *Improving life at work: Behavioral science approaches to organizational change* (pp. 297–363). Santa Monica, CA: Goodyear.
Tannenbaum, A. S. (1954). The relationship between personality and group structure Unpublished PhD thesis, Syracuse University.
Tannenbaum, A. S. (1961). Control and effectiveness in a voluntary organization. *The American Journal of Sociology, 67,* 33–46.
Tesluk, P. E., Vance, R. J., & Mathieu, J. E. (1999). Examining employee involvement in the context of participative work environments. *Group and Organization Management, 24,* 271–300.
Tierney, P. (1999). Work relations as a precursor to a psychological climate for change. *Journal of Organizational Change Management, 12,* 120–135.
Vroom, V. H. (1959). Some personality determinants of the effects of participation. *Journal of Abnormal and Social Psychology, 59,* 322–27.
Vroom, V. H. (1973). A new look at managerial decision making. *Organizational Dynamics, 1,* 66–80.
Westin, A. F. (1967). *Privacy and freedom.* New York: Atheneum.
White, R., & Lippitt, R. (1960). *Autocracy and democracy: An experimental inquiry.* New York: Harper.
Yin, R. K. (2003). *Case study research—Design and methods* (3rd ed.). Thousand Oaks, CA: Sage.

Book Industry Business, Concentration, Internet and Social Media of Management and Marketing

Paulo Faustino

1 Introduction

From Gutenberg to the present, books and everything that surrounds them have suffered numerous evolutions and transformations, from the literary style itself, which expanded with each new author from the last centuries, to the designers, the marketing formulas and, no doubt, to the publishers and their broad market, which has been developing and modernizing in recent decades. The main driver of this industry will continue to be the growing number of readers; thus, it is important to note the increase in the reading habits over the course of decades. This increase in readers reflects, all over the world, the maturing of the publishing industry itself, which since the revolution driven by Gutenberg has known an exponential growth. Although in some cases, over the past 2 years, the industry has come to denote fails, it is important to stress that this activity has suffered a smaller impact due to the economic crisis when compared to other businesses and creative products.

A classic question that emerges recurrently is: *does the book business have a future?* Sometimes we see pessimistic perspectives which consider the digital age has made books redundant; nevertheless, the concept of book does not seem to be disappearing. In fact, there has been a growing trend in the number of new titles published, although with a tendency for shorter runs. Some experts such as Darnton (2009) demonstrate that traditional books still have many practical advantages, particularly because they are portable and accessible, and they do not require batteries to operate. They have proved their durability, while the tools we have today to store data will be true dinosaurs tomorrow. A new technology does not always substitute a less recent technology; the printed page is not yet about to disappear. Therefore, reading remains a mystery, in spite of the debates that abound in what concerns the production, conservation and interpretation of texts.

P. Faustino (✉)
Nova University Porto, Porto, Portugal
e-mail: faustino.paulo@gmail.com

The practice of reading changes with each generation and there seems to be no evidence suggesting the diminution of its importance in a digital world.

The uncertainties about the future of the book are immense, as are also infinite the opportunities that new technologies present to generate new ways of reaching the readers, especially due to the impact of the Information and Communication Technologies (ICT) and the creation of new applications. As it happens with other media products (radio, television and press), the ICT, especially the Internet, are a driver of change in the publishing activity too, with impacts throughout the whole value chain, from production to marketing, communication and distribution. In this sense, it can be said that the ICT have introduced several disruptive elements in the publishing activity, enhancing the possibilities of new settings in the business models of book publishers. From the business perspective, book publishers have already started to interiorize the idea that the business is not to sell paper (in the sense of selling just the contents in paper books), but it is instead to sell the contents regardless of the medium considered more adequate to reach its customers, even if it is necessary to adopt dematerialization procedures and to reach the readers through digital media.

In the book industry there is a ubiquitous joke which tells that the second book made in Gutenberg's press was about the death of the publishing business. And the concerns of publishers about Amazon are reminiscent of the concerns they had when Barnes & Noble, in the eighties, began producing its own books, causing much disquiet in the editorial world, although with no great harm to the business. However, unlike Barnes & Noble, Amazon generates more than half of its profits—which are close to 25 billion dollars per year (Amazon.com 2009)—with products other than books. Many publishers believe that Amazon sees books only as a mere commodity to be sold as cheap as possible and that it considers publishers to be dispensable. We cannot forget that Jeffrey Bezos (founder of Amazon) declared physical books and bookshops to be dead (*Newsweek*, 2007). Like other successful companies in the Internet, Amazon grew over the trust that readers placed in the firm. Part of the allure for readers was the low price; Amazon sold many books, in particular bestsellers, at substantially lower prices.

This paper's centrality lies on the identification of some disruptive elements and on the analysis of some trends, particularly from the business strategy point of view, including the business concentration movements, as well the changes operated in the value chain and in the impact from Internet and Social Media in book business model, management and marketing. In this context, the paper is divided in three parts: the first is centered in the description and justification of the methodology and its research techniques. On the other hand, the second part focuses transversely on some of the dynamics and trends of the book industry, paying special attention to the movements of business concentration and to the transformations in the value chain and in the business models of book publishers. Finally, some conclusions are presented about the explanatory factors and which represent the centrality of the changes and dynamics observed in the book sector; also, in a more systematic way, some reflections are presented about the implications of technologies in the future of books and of possible business models associated to them.

2 Methodological Strategy and Quantitative Models Applied

As suggested before, the two main research questions which underpin the elaboration of this paper are: **RQ.1:** Is it possible to identify trends and characterize the business tendencies in the book sector, including the business concentration? **RQ.2:** Which are the main challenges and disruptive elements that publishers have to face in terms of their corporate governance and business models? With this aim, the research methodology was largely based on documentary research, namely scientific articles, press articles, books on the sector, industry reports, etc. Taking into account that one of this paper's authors is an editor and a partner of a book publishing company, participant observation was also applied. In this context, the results of this research are presented in four main points: (a) literature review; (b) management, trends and market; (c) value chain and business model; and (d) conclusions and challenges for the industry.

To address the issue of business concentration, and beyond the analysis and description of the objectives normally associated with these strategies, the author also made use of quantitative methodologies, in order to identify objectively the Portuguese situation in terms of concentration in the publishing industry. For this purpose, different information was gathered, allowing the constitution of some indicators, using economical and financial data, official statistics and yearbooks on the publishing markets. The information was collected in order to sustain the creation of three different types of concentration indicators, namely: (a) CR4 (Concentration ratio of the four largest companies), (b) HHI (Herfindahl–Hirschman Index), and (c) Noam Index. The first (CR4) focuses on the weight of the dominant players, gathering the percentage of market share of the four largest companies in an industry. The second index (HHI) is the sum of the squares of the market shares of all the participants in the market. This index has been used worldwide by antitrust authorities considering all the participants in the market, counting nevertheless to the level of asymmetry between participants. The antitrust guidelines of the United States Department of Justice classify the levels of market concentration as follows:

– HHI < 1,000: Not concentrated
– 1,000 < HHI < 1,800: Moderately concentrated
– 1,800 < HHI: Highly concentrated

The comparison between these two indexes reveals that both have advantages and disadvantages in relation to one another. On the other hand, it shows that the HHI verifies a set of consistency requirements that we would like to be checked by a "good" concentration index and it also derives from an axiomatic form as a proportional measure of the market power, which does not happen with the concentration index CR4. In spite of that, the latter concentration index is frequently used because it is relatively easy to calculate as it requires only the information on the largest companies. In addition, there is in reality a high correlation between these two indexes, which suggests that the loss of information in the CR4 index in relation to the HHI is not very significant. However, in case of doubt it is safer to use the HHI. Finally, the third concentration index (Noam Index) was specifically developed for the case of the media industries, normalizing the HHI in order to take into account the number of voices available. Thus, the application of the referred indexes corresponds to the most common approaches in the study of the levels of media concentration. The concentration index CR4, which compares the sum of the results of the four largest companies in the sector with the total of the industry, considers that if the sum CR4 is equal or superior to 50 %, then the market is significantly concentrated, which can be translated in the following formula:

$$CR4 = \sum_{ji}^{4} Sij$$

Where Si = share of companies i within industry j, with companies sorted by their individual size in the industry.
CR4 greater than or equal to 50 %: high concentration
CR4 between 40 % and 50 %: moderate concentration
CR4 between 35 % and 40 %: low concentration
CR4 of 20–35 %: lack of concentration
CR4 less than 20 %: atomistic

Conversely, the Herfindahl–Hirschman Index (HHI) is another instrument which measures the concentration levels of a market. More elaborate than the previous one and more widely used, this index is calculated adding the squares of the market shares of the companies in a given industry. The index ranges between 0 and 1, and the closer it is to 1, the higher is the level of concentration (Albarran and Mierzejewska 2004).

$$HHI = \sum_{i=1}^{f} (s_i)^2$$

Where f = number of participant companies in the industry, Si = share of each company within the industry.
HHI less than 1,000: low concentration
HHI between 1,000 and 1,800: moderate concentration
HHI greater than 1,800: high concentration

The two concentration indexes referred are used (both individually and together) to allow the quantification of the concentration levels and, thus, contribute to clarify the debate on the issue of media concentration in the Portuguese market, which sometimes lacks solid foundations because there are missing rigorous indicators and hard data.

3 Literature Review and Trends in the Book Sector

3.1 Trends, Industry Issues and Technological Impacts

From a business perspective, the study of the publishing sector, including that of the book, is frequently seen in the context of the media and content industries, since the book can be a creative, informative, educational and entertainment product, amongst other possible functions that can be identified. The interest (Albarran 2009) in the study and application of economical principles in the communication industry (which has been creating its own scientific space, designated as media economics and management) has been growing through the combination of several factors, namely the emergence of technological, regulatory, social and global forces that are affecting media companies and their functions as economic institutions.[1] Since the 1920s until the early twenty-first century, the media have been encouraging the development of several lines of research that tend to specialize more and more, without evading an integrated perspective of the social, political, economical and technological phenomena that influence this activity. According to Doyle and Frith (Albarran et al. 2006), for nearly two decades the research in media economics and management has been growing significantly. There are several reasons for this, namely:

1. The digital revolution is transforming the media business and accelerating the convergence and globalization processes.
2. The increase in the deregulation of national media industries, a fact that has caused a greater attention from governments and academics.
3. The growth in the importance of the media as business, which favored the integration of professional managers with MBAs (Master Business Administration) in this industry.

Hence, these changes, as a whole, have boosted new demands and interests in the fields of education and research, focused on specific problems of media economics and management, which includes the book industry. As Pimentel (2007) suggests, the activity of publishing books always represents a microcosm of society, reflecting its trends and manufacturing to some extent its ideas which constitute its interest; also according to this author, the publishing industry has seen important changes in the twenty-first century: in this period book publishing has shifted from its true nature and adopted a business attitude alike to any other industry, under unfavorable market conditions. This has caused many difficulties, since the book industry is not a conventional business and, therefore, it has specific aspects not only in terms of product but also in terms of management and corporate strategies.

The technological changes that have affected the most the dominant companies are neither radically new nor difficult to identify, but they present important characteristics; for example, to Christensen (1997), in the first place, they typically

---

[1] *In Comunicación y Sociedad*, p. 8, 1999, University of Navarra.

have a package that in the beginning is not valued by the existing consumers. On the other hand, the performance attributes that consumers value increase in such a way that they invade the existing markets. Only then consumers want the technology, after a period of some internalization. New technologies have the capacity to introduce new media combinations, to provoke the erosion of the existing revenue models and to force the content companies to elaborate new models for business and for relating with consumers. Thus, it can be said that the book is going through a profound paradigm shift, particularly visible in the change in consumer behavior—that is, if it is true that technologies have contributed to that shift on the consumer's part, it is also true that the book sector is "forced" to change. The protagonists of the book sector consider that these new technologies—mobile application, for example—are one of the most fundamental elements to the current development of the publishing industry.[2] In this sense, it is necessary to add other developments in a sector where integration and concentration of ownership are of increasing importance as a competitive factor.

In fact, and from the perspective of the impact in the business model (and its value chain), the Internet (and the World Wide Web) constitute the most significant technologies of the last decade, having contributed to the emergence of disintermediation processes and also to the reduction of distribution costs, thereby establishing direct relationships between the content owners and the consumers, connecting users with hundreds of thousands of content sources around the world.[3] New technologies have facilitated the work of editing, pre-printing and printing, assisting in the editor's work. The Internet, with its interactive nature, the ability to contact directly with the consumer and the possibility of establishing a relationship with him, has already caused major transformations: for example, it transformed the production and distribution of content, allowing the entrance of new players and it threatens to weaken the relationships between established

---

[2] However, and despite this growing appreciation, it's important to consider this aspect on the basis of each market's situation. For instance, in the Portuguese market, that importance is not clearly visible yet. And even in the case of more mature markets, it is not a certainty yet, because the weight of the new platforms, the e-books, is still much reduced, regarding the investment and the return. In Portugal, the digital book market, in what concerns the production and commercialization of contents, is still in an embryonic phase: there are only testing investments by Leya (with the digital books sold through Mediabooks), through an excessively closed platform, and a few "adventures" from small-sized publishers. Even Porto Editora did not invest seriously in the e-book yet, giving preference to scholar books, DVD (or other platforms) multimedia projects, on which this publisher bets for decades. But the impact already exerts an influence on the printed book distribution, to which the Internet has already found its spot, mainly with Wook and Mediabooks.

[3] In terms of distribution policy, a critical success factor is the choice of the distribution channels, which, in turn, influences the promotion policy that is also related to the profitability generated by the channel chosen. In the book sector, this meant that, for example, the rise in online distribution of some publishers has been a very slow process. The choice of distribution channel is decided in the book sector also by the presence in the market and the total return of the publishing house.

companies and their audiences—the readers.[4] In this wave of new technologies we see the coexistence of printed books versus digital books; initially the digital edition raised controversy and fears: there were authors who did not accept the idea of electronic books and others who questioned if they should be called like that.

We witness the competition between publishers; about this, Pimentel (2007) considers that local publishers can compete in equal terms with publishers based in big cities. These innovations lead to the arising of, for example, audiobooks,[5] e-books and innovative ways of promoting new releases, presentations, book fairs—that is, new ways to promote, to captivate the public and to sell. And the sales orientation constitutes a greater demand in the major publishing groups, since the investors require an adequate return. Conversely, the e-books are growing, raising the question: will this new technology eliminate the paper books? Even though the book is still a difficult object to dematerialize and the paper books are not replaceable, the trend seems to be to prefer an e-book rather than a physical book[6]: for example, Amazon was able to put two authors in the top of best-selling e-books: Janet Evanovich, author of the series *Stephanie Plume,* and Kathryn Stockett, who wrote *The Help.* These names join other authors, such as Stieg Larson, James Patterson, Nora Roberts, Suzanne Collins, Michael Connelly, Charlaine Harris, Lee Child and John Locke, who have also reached the sales podium at Amazon. The authors of classical books are already in the public domain and gain size on Amazon's sales. According to a press release from Amazon, this form of commerce (digital) is revolutionizing the market—and at the moment, the share of sales of digitalized books reaches a significant number (over 50 %) of the total sales, on Amazon. Nowadays, we do not see a book for sale only on paper, there is always the e-book format as well (however, in some markets, as the

---

[4] However, in the case of some publishers, more proactive and more oriented towards new technologies, the Internet is not weakening the relationship between companies and readers, but instead it brought them definitely closer, as was never possible before.

[5] In reality, and despite its popularization during the last decade, it can be said that audiobooks are much previous in relation to the e-books; they have existed for at least 40 years, since the creation of the CD.

[6] In fact, (a) it was not yet possible to identify any trend, in any market, of people's preference for the paper book instead of the e-book. The existing data on digital books sales in a relevant amount are almost exclusively from Amazon and the Anglo-Saxon markets. Amazon never reveals information in an objective way and uses it, indeed, to promote its store and Kindle. These are not generalizable data, and they must be treated carefully; and (b) these authors were, in first place, bestsellers in the paper edition, who sold—and earned—much more than the digital editions. It remains to be seen whether some successes in the digital versions of bestsellers are due to the fact that, first, they have gained reputation and audience in the so called "traditional" market, with the exception of John Locke, who is one of the rare examples of authors who have sold several author's editions in digital format via Amazon and succeeded.

Portuguese one, there are only few books published on paper and e-book simultaneously).

The Project Gutenberg was the pioneer in the digital book format, founded by the late Michael S. Hart[7]; who in 1971 scanned the Declaration of Independence of the United States, thus starting the Project Gutenberg. Today there are already more than 30,000 books digitalized that can be downloaded for free. With this technological revolution, and if the death of the book is imminent as some suggest (Marshall McLuhan[8] already predicted the death of the book in 1980 with the advent of sound and image through radio and television), it is also true that the classical book has resisted. About this issue, Pimentel (2007) argues that the book has a future and also considers that the editor's role will always be fundamental, adapting to new times, although we are still far from achieving a perfect medium. On the other hand, audiobooks, a new format of production and commercialization of books, have not been able to stand on their own: people still buy old books from bookshops. Despite the progressive impact of technology on the book production and commercialization, until the present day there is no evidence that new formats will replace paper books.

The eighties was the age of computers and the nineties the age of Internet. The late twentieth century and the early twenty-first century coincide in the same principle: content editors in paper media can do nothing against the digital universe; on the contrary, they must harness the potentials of these media to enlarge their base of sales and content distribution. In fact, some experts considered that the generation educated with audiovisual media and videogames would never be fascinated by the book, having the technological world in front of them; however, there have been situations of young people (from the digital generation) running to bookshops to buy books, frequently promoted through online advertising[9]—thus creating bestsellers like, for example, Harry Potter. Given this, Pimentel (2007) considers the book to be in good health, the book remains alive and well; he continues to believe in this livelihood of the book because it can be seen as a collection item, since the Web is more easily pirated by millions of people, as it happens in the music industry. It follows that there's a threat to publishers, which is the new way of

---

[7] Michael Stern Hart (8th March 1947—6th September 2011) was an American author who became known for the creation of the Project Gutenberg. The initial digitalizations were made by him, with the aim of promoting the creation and distribution of e-books. His works are also available on Gutenberg.

[8] Communication theorist, literary critic and one of the founding pillars of the study of media theory.

[9] In any case, after some time and experiences following the emergence of this concept, we can say that the term "digital generation" is, to some extent, diffuse, and the theorization of "digital natives" has received different interpretations, in that the earlier contact with technology does not either form or deform—or guarantee—the speed of acquisition, formation or reformation of knowledge, nor the proximity of the new ICT affects the interaction with previous technologies or encourages a more suitable utilization, particularly in the relationship with variables such as age, education, geographic location, social inclusion, economic power, etc.

accessing books: digital books that are downloaded electronically and that can easily step ahead of the traditional book (as exemplified above with the e-books that conquered a place on the top of the sales list), since they weights less, they are easily transported and can be read on a sofa, similarly to what happens with the traditional ones, with cover and pages of text.[10] Nevertheless, the main advantage of the e-books is their storage capacity in a single device. For its part, it is also true that the printed book is at least as comfortable as the digital book—it can be read in a sofa or taken anywhere, it's much cheaper, it's not vulnerable to damage if it falls to the floor, it's not easily replaced by new technological versions and it doesn't become obsolete (something inevitable with the e-book readers and their formats—ePub, Mobi, pdf, etc.). Hence, it becomes easy to build a library—simply downloading and archiving. Yet the essence of reading a book is lost in this format, and for that reason, Pimentel (2007) is convinced that the book has a future. And, as argued by Epstein (2001), the e-books deprive us of the pleasure of going to a bookstore to see the new releases, a ritual act that many readers, surely, will not let go of; other readers will start doing it in a digital library—something they already do largely all over the world, trough Amazon. In fact, going to a bookshop constitutes an experience and it remains to know to what extent the public will value this intangible dimension associated with the search of the book.

In any case, it is undeniable that the Internet constitutes the primary setting of some of the new (and main) trends used by the book market, both in terms of production and distribution (e-book, print-on-demand, etc.) and in terms of marketing and communication (for example, the importance of social media marketing today in the promotion of a work). Using online platforms, such as Facebook, LinkedIn, Youtube, Twitter or blogs, publishers and authors can promote their books increasingly closer to the people, extending their range of customers to a much wider group. Through this new trend there is also greater proximity between publishers, authors and readers, for example, through an author's page on Facebook; there are also bookstores that write weekly in a blog, or even promote books through a video posted on Youtube. Thus, the readers can communicate or follow the author, his works in progress and the new products on the market, released by various publishers. Hence, the Internet can promote a visit to the bookshop without leaving home, exempting the customer from the physical experience. Nowadays, we know not only what new works are published, but also, through reviews, what is their content. The book market took advantage of the

---

[10] However, the current reality is that printed books continue to sell more and to represent much higher revenues when compared to digital books, even in mature markets such as the USA and Germany. Clearly, there is a trend and publishers no longer sell products (books), but contents (in formats adapted to their intended markets, or in several formats for the segments that sell already in different ways); but there is no market where the digital version sells more than the printed one.

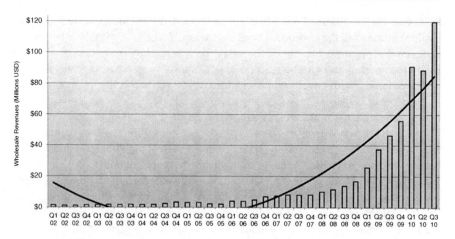

Fig. 1 Evolution of the total sales of electronic books in the USA. *Source*: International Digital Publishing Forum

internet to "enter" people's homes, remaining thereby constantly present in their lives. Following the innovations in society, the book also begun to present itself in digital format, while the market of printed books remains equally dynamic.[11]

From the customer's point of view, e-books present themselves as very tempting, because, if not free, their price will be much lower than that of a normal book. The fact that it is digital means the production and marketing costs are not high, as is the case of printing and distribution. In addition, there will be no shipping costs for having the book sent directly through the Internet, thus presenting another advantage. The e-book represents also a new revolution for any author who is unable to see his works published by an editor, since he can sell or offer directly his story, through the Internet, to anyone who is interested. People who want to buy a digital book can receive it immediately, not having to go out to buy it or to wait until it gets there. Moreover, the e-book offers a great facility of transport, since it is in digital format, and thus can be stored in a CD, pen drive, or even in a computer or e-reader. Figure 1 shows objective data about the significant evolution in the sales of electronic books in the period between 2002 and the third quarter of 2010, where the steady increase in e-books' sales can be perceived.

In the last years, the book market has proved not to be static, and has managed to reinvent itself and to be much closer to the audience, offering a wider choice range and new formats of books. The audience is increasingly broad and the book industry has been feeling the need to respond by extending its markets and innovating processes and products. Not only books have proliferated but also the number of

---

[11] In spite of being available for more than a decade now, the digital book, or e-book, was ignored by most people until 2007, when Amazon released Kindle, a device to read digital books. After that, Sony followed, then Barnes & Noble with Nook, and in 2010 Apple launched the iPad. All these devices serve one purpose, to read e-books, though now it is also possible to read newspapers and blogs. However, we have to take into account that iPad is much more than a simple e-book reader, as well as the new Kindle generation.

authors has increased. On the other hand, as previously mentioned, another trend reappeared strongly in the past years; although it is not a new idea, the fact is that the paperback books have brought a new dynamic to the book market.[12] Costing about half the price and fitting the palm of a hand, paperback books are a good example of how marketing in this business is more alive than ever. The offer of this type of book is well visible at gas stations and airports, for example. For the convenience in transporting it, for the practical way of reading and for the lower price, the demand for paperback books has increased. There are also vending machines that sell these small works, in the subway; some websites from bookshops even have pages fully dedicated to these books, showing the significance they have obtained.

3.2 Business Strategies and Concentration in the Book Industry

Some authors (Pimentel 2007; Thompson 2010) suggest that today's uncertainties can be certainties tomorrow. For that reason, it is important to identify some of the key trends that characterize the current editorial universe, namely (a) a tendency for concentration in large groups, (b) the pressure to increase the rates of return, (c) an increase in the editions of paperback books, (d) the obsession over bestsellers to save the balance, (e) the need for high-rotation books, (f) the maximization of the potentials of the technological revolution, (g) the dynamics of the market of copyright, (h) having trends and authors that are truly global (i) a growing interest in specialized niches and (j) book releases in a multimedia logic. Despite these trends and the changes that are taking place in the publishing business, editors publish more than ever and there is even a super-abundance of new titles. In this context, one of the most visible trends that deserves a highlight in this paper is the concentration in the publishing sector. We are witnessing today a growing agglomeration of small publishers in one, in order to strengthen their capacities of negotiation, marketing and funding, as for example with the publishers who joined the group Leya and also with the publishing house Porto Editora, in the Portuguese case. For example, in addition to the Portuguese market (analyzed and quantified in the final part of this section), in the French market there are six major groups that control the distribution of books, namely: Group la Cite, Hachette, Gallimard, Flammarion, Albin Michel and Le Seuil. The holding Grupe de la Cite, founded in 1988, is the result of the fusion between Presses de la cite and the group Larousse-Nathan and is currently among the top ten book publishers in the world. Besides being the second best in France after Hachette, the group is becoming a

---

[12] The distinction between the paperback book and the hard cover book consists in the difference existent in terms of product configuration, price and target audience. The paperback book is currently characterized by titles with many editions, low prices, paper cover and a homogeneous image in what concerns series. The paperback book has long been the classical form of the second or third publication in the chain of added value of the licenses of books.

leader in education and general knowledge books for all age groups. In Germany, the Bertelsmann group also gathers several publishers and occupies now a leading position worldwide.

Besides of the eventual reduction of pluralism in genres and authors, one of the fears associated with business concentration lies in the possible limitations in the distribution of books. Distribution has become the "Achilles heel" of the entire editorial system, as in the Portuguese case, where small publishers have difficulty accessing major bookstores and chains. The concentration in editorial groups and in large bookstores chains is removing the importance of the traditional territorial distributors, favoring instead centralized retail, where the commercial management is kept while the logistic services are left to third parties. However, this new distribution model penalizes small publishers who cannot access the centralized buyers because their logistics model is less accessible in financial terms, and thus small publishers have less power to negotiate—indeed, it is very difficult to see their works for sale in large stores, and even if they can do it the conditions of sale for the editor are greatly unfavorable, since diverse fees are required, not only in terms of space occupation, but also in terms of marketing and other services that are supposed to be provided.[13]

Some experts (Noam 2009; Faustino 2010; Picard 2002) refer the economic gains as one of the main reasons for the operations of acquisition and business concentration. Nevertheless, they generally ignore the existence of internal pressures. Despite that, there are other reasons that may induce a process of business concentration, namely the fact that the growth strategies of media companies and the concentration processes of the industry can generate the following advantages: (a) Power and prestige for owners and managers; (b) Synergies between several media from each company; (c) Dominant market position; (d) Sharing of knowledge between companies, (e) Diversification of business risk; (f) Increased possibilities for innovation; (g) Career opportunities for employees; (h) Increased bargaining power towards suppliers and authors; and (i) Growing professionalization of the human resources.

In this context, Thompson (2010, p. 111) states that "the process of consolidation in the printing business has been underway since the early 60's, but the world of the publishing trade in the beginning of the twenty-first century is different from that which began to emerge with the first business acquisitions in 1960 and 1970". In another work (Thompson 2010), he states that the major international publishers have some competitive advantages, including: economies of scale, adoption of technologies, marketing knowledge, experience and practices. This author also notes that (1) the growing concentration of resources in the book publishing industry is part of a broader process of concentration and conglomeration that has

---

[13] For example, the author of this paper accessed to the contract of a small publishing house that put books for sale on a large surface and realized that the contractual demands were extremely high. That is, the entire risk of the business was transferred to the editor, including the payment for services of questionable added value, such as marketing and administrative support, for instance.

characterized the media, information and entertainment industry as a whole, (2) the process of consolidation of the book publishing industry tends to involve the strategic restructuring of the editorial activities and (3) the consolidation strategy has become increasingly more international.

According to the study "Book Publishing and Commercialization" (2008), prepared by the Observatory of Cultural Activities (Observatório das Actividades Culturais—OAC), the book publishers have had a turnover of about 400 million Euros, although a GFK study states a turnover of 380 million Euros (this latter will be taken into account). Given the difficulty of an extensive analysis of the numerous small book companies,[14] this study is based on the eight major companies. However, as the considered turnover stands at 380 million Euros, this sample represents about 50 % of the book publishing industry. This analysis is based on the publishers Porto Editora, Lda. and Leya, S.A., which are mainly responsible for the sector business, representing about 50 % of the turnover of the revenues of the total publishing market. Unlike other media markets, Portuguese book publishers are not integrated in large media groups but consist of autonomous book publishing companies. The foreign presence has been decreasing (although Bertelsmann acquired Círculo de Leitores), especially after Porto Editora acquired Bertrand (which core business is the book retail); Leya is the only Portuguese book publisher partially owned by national and foreign companies (with links to Nicolas Berggruen, CEO of North American Liberty Acquisition Holdings who also controls Prisa after 2010). The total turnover here represented by seven publishers shows an increase during this period. The publishers Porto Editora, Lda. and Leya, S.A. are primarily responsible for this fact, followed by Círculo de Leitores, S.A. (bought by Porto Editora in 2011) and Editora Planeta de Agostini, S.A. (Table 1).

Considering a universe of seven publishers, the C4 was 91.29 % in 2010—a high value, due to the significant turnover of one of the companies included. Despite the variations from year to year, the C4 index shows a high concentration degree (C4 > 50 %) of the four main publishers in the market. From 2008 to 2010, HHI grew, justified by the sector's increasing concentration; in 2010, for a universe of seven publishers, HHI was 3,255.59; while in 2008, for the same universe, it was 2,705.40. The Noam Index was 1,022.55 in 2008 and 1,230.50 in 2010, for the same universe of seven publishers.

In summary, the C4 in the book publishing market has increased and is even expected to become a consolidated trend as a result of very recent movements in the market which are not yet fully expressed in the data presented. In 2008, Leya group was formed—the first publishing group to organize itself as a holding company that incorporated several of the most prestigious Portuguese publishers (D. Quixote, Asa, Oficina do Livro, Teorema, among others). The market then experienced its first editorial revolution, showing that books can be attractive products and their massification had been little explored in the country. After the purchase of Editora

---

[14] There are about 250 publishers, according to the Portuguese Association of Publishers and Booksellers.

Table 1 Turnover of the main publishers—2008 to 2010

	2008		2009		2010	
Company	Revenue (Euros)	%	Revenue (Euros)	%	Revenue (Euros)	%
Editorial Presença	8,521,591	4.42	7,735,185	4.09	8,118,019	4.18
Leya	41,878,706	21.75	51,014,616	26.94	56,173,063	28.94
Porto Editora	83,023,906	43.11	87,097,071	46.00	92,743,376	47.79
Coimbra Editora	4,006,012	2.08	4,339,461	2.29	4,242,367	2.19
Gradiva—Publicações	4,899,600	2.54	4,234,838	2.24	4,547,804	2.34
Planeta de Agostini	22,695,516	11.78	16,453,965	8.69	13,291,869	6.85
Círculo de Leitores, S.A.	27,560,136	14.31	18,462,749	9.75	14,953,805	7.71
Total	**192,585,467**	**100**	**189,337,885**	**100**	**194,070,302**	**100**
Indexes						
C4	90.95 %		91.39 %		91.29 %	
HHI	2,705.40		3,039.60		3,255.59	
Noam	1,022.55		1,148.86		1,230.50	

Source: Elaborated by the author based on data obtained from annual reports

Magalhães' (a publisher with a long history), another publishing group emerged: Babel (recently acquired by the Ongoing Group IN 2011), which spans the publishers Arcádia, Ulisseia and Verbo, among others. During the last decade, there was an entry of foreign capital in the Portuguese publishing market for the first time. In 2006, the German group Bertelsmann, which already owned Círculo de Leitores, acquired Bertrand and its associated businesses: publishing, retail trade and distribution. However, the foreign capital in the national book market is not expressive today. The main foreign player is Santillana (from Prisa Group/Spain), which operates with Planeta Agostini Publishing. Among the analyzed players, Planeta Agostini is the only foreign-owned one; on the other hand, there are other foreign-owned players (as Santillana, for instance) excluded from this analysis for not being among the main ones. At the end of 2010, Porto Editora, the publishing industry's leader, whose base has been scholar books and dictionaries' publishing, being a consolidated leader in online sales through the website Wook, definitely fights for the market supremacy and reinforces its leading position acquiring Bertrand's universe, bringing it back to the national capital. With this acquisition, that is still occurring and about which there are no conclusions yet, Porto Editora adds its scholar books business to a library network (in 2008, with the opening of Wook store in the North region, followed by an opening in the South, Porto Editora had already begun a new stage in the retail, distinguishing these stores from the existing ones using their publisher's name), editorial seals to add to its catalog, the distributor and a different form of distribution, Círculo de Leitores. For further research, it would be interesting to evaluate the impact of this acquisition. The main national editorial groups have been developing businesses in Portuguese-speaking countries, such as Angola, Mozambique and Brazil. The concentration and consolidation strategies are also part of a business objective to achieve economies of scale in order to reach more competitive positions in these Lusophone markets.

4 Business Models, Management, Marketing Internet and Social Media Impacts

4.1 Business Models, Value Chain and Book Product Management

A major difference between the strategies adopted by publishers in the recent past and the strategies followed in the present has to do with the greater or lesser market orientation—that is, a few years ago the first decision an editor had to take was to identify which product to launch in the market and what catalog to build and deliver, and now the decision of the editors is determined by what the market wants. Of course each market has its rules and specificities and even a targeted marketing. The new virtual marketplace generates new opportunities for publishers that know how to adapt to the new scenario, including small publishers.[15] For example, an academic publishing segment like the legal segment, conservative by nature, has been adapting its strategies and found on the Internet a way to reconfigure its business and value creation models, including the possibility of updating the works easily and quickly. In general, the university segment is developing in the same direction, and the next step is probably the production of monographs in e-book format for the new emerging markets, for example.[16] The Internet has enhanced the large-scale fragmentation of the market, both in the supply and in the demand.

The new market model, without eliminating the traditional mass market, made of bestsellers, invests simultaneously in the hyper-fragmentation and specialization market—here small publishers can also have their place in the competition. Hence, there is the emergence of a niche culture which consists of a market segment with a small number of consumers with homogeneous characteristics and easily identifiable needs. Due to their small size (including the volume of return), niche markets are often neglected by large companies, constituting, therefore, excellent opportunities for small companies that in this context can escape the dominance

---

[15] Today it is possible for small publishing houses to specialize in a niche and position themselves in the international market. For example, Media XXI (publisher specialized in books on the fields of communication, media and the creative industries), based in Portugal, has made partnerships with various physical and virtual book stores, including Amazon and its own online store, and publishes books in many languages and for various markets, possessing representatives only in some international markets, namely in Brazil, USA and Angola.

[16] Indeed, in some scientific areas (molecular biology, neuroscience, etc.) monographs were already totally replaced by digital documents, due to the ease of access and research, readability, content's hypertextualization, price (substantially lower) and image and video insertion allowed by the e-books.

of big firms and achieve a leadership position by presenting a very specific offer, tailored to the characteristics and needs of the consumers that form a certain niche. As suggested by Anderson (2006) in his Long Tail theory applied to the book sector,[17] the niche is transforming the social landscape, people are regrouped into thousands of groups with a particular cultural interest, connected by common interests, instead of by proximity or work.

Numerous changes can be observed in the sector with impacts on the business models of book publishers. There are various definitions of business model; in a simplified way, it can be understood as the set of activities a company performs, how it performs them and when with the final aim of creating and adding value to the client (e.g. low-cost or differentiation and high quality products) and positions itself for the appropriate value (Afuah 2003, p. 35).[18] As it happens in other economy sectors, the business model of a publishing company is continually subject to external forces; this includes changes in terms of market, law, regulations, social factors, technology, and changes in customer's requirements, for example. In this context, one of the main tasks of managers (or of the main supervisors) of publishing companies is to adjust and adapt their business models through timely feedback, or even the anticipation of external forces to the new market dynamics. On the other hand, the expression *business models* is sometimes confused with strategy—in the sense of corporate strategy, product strategies, market strategies and pricing strategies. In fact, strategies are decisions, reflections and options used by companies to guide their activities towards a set of pre defined objectives, but not only in terms of business models. Magretta (2004) considers that the business model represents a set of assumptions about how organizations operate in order to create value for all entities (stakeholders) they depend on, especially for customers, but not only.

A good business model should therefore be concerned with diverse aspects and not only with profit, incorporating a wider view of the industry, and it must be

---

[17] Original concept used by Anderson to describe a change occurred in the media industry, notably in the book sector. It is a passage from the sale of a small number of successful products in large quantities to sell a large number of niche content, each sold in small quantities. For Chris Anderson, there are three economic circumstances that gave rise to this Long Tail Phenomenon in the media industry: (1) democratization of production tools: decreasing costs of technology gave people access to instruments that years ago were prohibitively expensive, (2) Democratization of distribution: the Internet popularized the distribution of digital content, dramatically lowered the costs of inventory, communication and transaction, opening new markets for niche products, and (3) falling costs of research allow the connection between supply and demand: the real challenge of selling niche contents is to find interested buyers. This became easier thanks to search engines and recommendation tools, to ratings given by users and to communities of interest. In general, many sporadical sales can produce aggregate income equivalent, or even higher than the income produced by a focus on the most successful products. For this author, the new or additional value proposition aims to target a large number of niche customer segments, historically less profitable—which, at the aggregate level, are profitable. Improvements in information technology and operations management allows better value offers, at low-costs, and tailored to a very large number of new customers.

[18] Less comprehensive than the concept of GRP (generation, compensation and sharing) used by Verstraete and Jouison-Laffitte (2009).

constantly tested by the market. The business models are the conceptual basis in which business activities are developed; they explain and organize the relationship between business architecture, funding sources and resources. Business models represent actions and tactics to assist managers in answering questions related with the company's business, products and services, and its respective revenue streams. In addition, business models describe the various activities and functions, including potential benefits to the various stakeholders. For publishers, the definition and identification of the target audience constitutes one of the most important steps when building a business model, since the audience/reader determines the characteristics of the editorial products offered. Therefore, the analysis of business models of book publishers is essential to the objectives of this paper, in the sense that their understanding will allow us to link corporate strategies with catalog management strategies and the corresponding management and marketing practices. To internalize better the concept of business model, it is also necessary to have a good understanding of the value chains—that is, the concept of value chain cannot be dissociated from the concept of business model; the analysis of both is crucial for the comprehension of the company's business and for the definition of the strategies to adopt.

According to Osterwalder and Pigneur (2010), a business model can be described through nine basic principles which demonstrate the logic of how a company intends to make money. These elements cover the four main areas of business: customers, supply, infrastructure and financial viability. The business model can be seen as a schematic overview of a strategy to be implemented through structures, processes, people, money and organizational systems. The nine basic elements of a business model are: customer segments, value propositions, channels, customer relationship; return value; key features, key activities, key partnerships, and cost structure. These authors (Osterwalder and Pigneur 2010), referring precisely to business models of the book sector—distinguishing the old model from the new model—consider that the new business model is based on a selection process through which editors analyze many authors (and manuscripts), selecting those that are likely to reach a minimum sales goal. The authors that are commercially less promising are rejected, because it would not be profitable to edit, design, print and promote books that sell little. The editors are interested in books that can be printed in large quantities to sell to large audiences, generating economies of scale in printing to reduce the unit cost of each copy. On the other hand, the new business model is exemplified with the case of Lulu.com, which is based on helping niche and amateur authors to place their work in the market. It eliminates the traditional entry barriers by giving writers tools to design, print and distribute their work in an online market. The more authors Lulu.com attracts, the more success it has, because the authors become customers. It is a multilateral platform that provides services and connects authors and readers with a Long Tail of niche content generated by users. The books are printed only in response to effective orders. If a title does not sell, that is irrelevant to Lulu.com, because there are no additional costs.

The concept of value chain was developed by Porter (1985), who also described in detail the various stages of the value added process, from creation to use; this

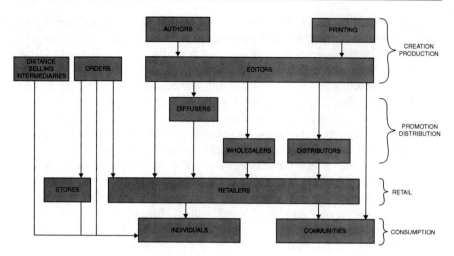

Fig. 2 Book market circuit. *Source*: Gaymard (2009)

author focused in the need to create a competitive advantage. In this sense, it is important to understand each company as a system and be able to identify sequences of events for the various activities, as well as the processes of production of added value. Also according to Porter (1989), the concept of competitive advantage can only be understood if the company is seen as a whole. Competitive advantage is generated by several distinct activities developed by the company within the scope of its production, marketing, transmission and support project for the product. Each activity can help reduce costs and provide a basis for differentiation. The competitive advantage or disadvantage can be seen through any of the five primary activities or any of the four secondary activities[19]; altogether, these activities constitute the value chain of all companies. In Fig. 2, the whole usual business circuit of books can be observed, as well as the synthesis of the main phases in which value can be added, namely: Creation/Production; Promotion/Distribution; Retail/Stores; and Consumer/Reader.

It can be argued that business models—and value chains—reflect the systematic thinking that characterizes management. In recent decades, science and technology have advanced a lot; their impact on the business of publishing companies has been equally rapid. The concept and practices associated with a business model of development and management must be integrated into the holistic view of production processes, which represent the stages of design, funding and implementation of the business model. Business models must evolve from conception to implementation, where the design reflects the strategy of the project, which should be financed

---

[19] According to Porter's (1985) concept of value chain, the primary activities include: inbound logistics, operations, outbound logistics, marketing and sales, and service; while the secondary activities consist of: procurement, technology development, human resource management and infrastructure.

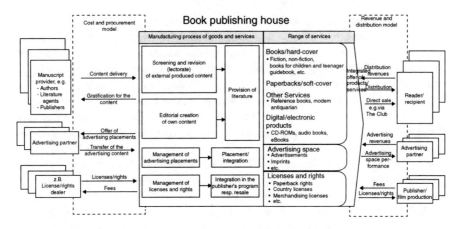

Fig. 3 Business model of a book publishing house. *Source*: Wirtz (2011)

by internal and external funds, and finally implemented in a real company. Naturally, business strategies and business models are directly related; they include similar elements, although they have different perspectives: business models incorporate the strategy with the aim of making profit. In other words, the point of view and strategy of the company are translated into value propositions, customer relationships and value chains. From a more objective point-of-view of business management, it can be stated that one of the most important contributions given to business models is to identify and systematize the company's dynamics. Moreover, the business model approach allows companies to react faster to changes. Finally, business models improve the strategic alignment, organization and technology of business. Figure 3 shows some critical success factors of the business models of the book.

Consequently, when a company decides to adopt a new business model or to change an existing one, identification and visualization of the model will improve the planning, implementation and changes needed. It is easier to go from one point to another when we are really able to understand and show what elements will change. On this subject, Linder and Cantrell (2000) report that the changes in the business model reflect a transformation in the core logic of the company, in order to stay profitable within a dynamic environment. On the other hand, the derivation on business model is centered on the concept of "open business models" (Chesbrough 2003). This author argues that in an open business model, unlike in the traditional one, the company realizes that the useful knowledge is disclosed, engages extensively and deeply with the knowledge network and the external communities, seeks information from external sources and shares resources with competitors, in a logic of *coopetition* (so to avoid a position of competitive disadvantage), and is open to new ideas, even if they come from various sources. Following this dynamic, the business model evolves progressively.

Models of open innovation and open business models are two terms coined by Chesbrough (2003), which refer to the openness of the research process of a company to external partners. In a world characterized by a distributed knowledge, organizations can create more value and exploit better their own research if they integrate knowledge, intellectual property and external products in their process of innovation. Chesbrough (2003) shows that products, technologies, knowledge and intellectual property that are not being used in the company can be monetized, becoming available to external partners through licensing, joint ventures or spin-offs. This author draws a distinction between innovation from the outside (which occurs when an organization brings external ideas, technologies or intellectual property to its processes of development and marketing), and innovation from the inside out (which happens when organizations sell or license their intellectual property or their technologies, particularly assets that are not in use).

Whatever strategy a book publisher follows, the customer should always be at the heart of any business model. Without (profitable) customers, no company can survive long. To better satisfy them, a company may group them into different segments with common needs, behaviors and other attributes. A business model can define one or several, large or small, customer segments, and organizations must decide which of these segments will stay and which will be ignored. After this decision is made, a business model can be carefully planned around a strong understanding of customers' specific needs. Returning to the particular case of publishers, to better understand the book business, some examples of customer segments/markets can be identified, namely: mass market, market niches, and targeted segments. Hence, the above examples also apply to the book sector and to the positioning of publishing companies: large bookstores are more oriented to mass markets (bestsellers), medium-size publishers focus on segments, and small publishers work mostly with niches specialized in a particular area—for example, Media XXI has specialized in publishing books on communication, media and creative industries. Each of these strategies (positioning) is associated with a particular business and funding model. To get a better idea of the book sector, including of the financing aspect of its business model, the following table summarizes the various possibilities of obtaining additional revenues to the traditional model (Table 2).

Therefore, like other media, book publishers also have been making an effort to identify and diversify revenue sources in order to make business models more viable and adapted to the characteristics and capabilities of each publisher. As Picard (2002) suggests, the publishing industry normally consists of companies with national characteristics (such as in Portugal, where two of the three main groups have investors with greater national capital) but they increasingly tend to operate at a regional or global level. Table 3 summarizes some of the features of the book business.

Still according to Picard (2002, p. 13), there are many specific aspects of publishing companies that should be identified and characterized to understand the modern circumstances and problems they have to face:
1. Most publishers fall into the category of small and medium enterprises (SMEs). There is only a small number of truly great publishers, and they typically operate at both regional and global levels.

Table 2 Possible sources of additional revenues to publishing companies

Subscription Users pay a fee to access the content for a certain period of time	**Advertising—sponsorship** Free access to content supported by advertising or sponsorships
Aggregate products Access to online content is included in the purchase of the printed product	**Mobile phones** Content is delivered via wireless devices, with revenue sharing with the mobile operator
Electronic commerce Physical product or services are sold through an online channel	**Electronic commerce** Contents are sold piece by piece basis for online or offline access

Source: Elaborated by the author

Table 3 Market, financial and operational characteristics of the book business

Market characteristics	Financial characteristics/costs	Operational characteristics
Language-based market	Low capital requirements	Few large multinational companies, many small and medium size enterprises
Long term products	Low fixed costs	Intensive labour
Low barriers to enter	High production costs	Dependents on employment contracts
High level of direct competition	High distribution costs	Most of the contents are acquired
Mostly retail sales	Moderate marketing costs	Foreign production is typical
Small participation from the public sector	High design costs	Moderately complex logistics
Few threats from new technologies	Moderate variable costs	Most costs are not related to the core business
	Fast decreasing average total costs	Moderate/very cyclical financial performance
		Many possible product strategies
		High paper waste, moderate chemical waste

Source: Picard (2002)

2. Entry barriers are relatively weak in the publishing industry of magazines, yearbooks and books, but higher in the newspaper industry.
3. Most of the printed products have relatively short life cycles, although it can be said that some books can prolong their life cycle through reprints and editions in other formats, for example, paperback books, digital books, deluxe editions, editions in other languages, etc.
4. Sophisticated logistics and transportation systems, specifically designed for the publishing industry, play an important role in the distribution of products to consumers.
5. Traditional publishers face growing threats and opportunities due to the development of electronic publications. The threats arise primarily because they fail to respond to the opportunities.

6. The protection of intellectual property and collection rights in the fields of electronic information, information, and knowledge production and distribution is not as well developed, which prevents the growth of the electronic publishing sector.

In addition to the features of the book business, it should also be noted that the editorial activity is based essentially on five areas that characterize this industry and that are associated with its business models, namely: (a) sales (bottom of the catalog—backlist; new catalog—frontlist; hardcover, and paper cover—paperback), (b) subsidiary rights (various revenue sources, including translation and international rights); (c) digital publications (e-books, multi-platform); (d) developing models (subscription, pay per view, bundled, mobile, advertising). On the other hand, we are witnessing a tendency to maximize the sales channels, namely: Traditional Retail, Wholesale Trade, Mass Merchandisers, Book Clubs, Online and Internet; Schools and Libraries, Special Sales, Export Sales in other Languages; Premium Sales; Sales in Trading Fairs (and disposal of leftovers). From the standpoint of the business cycle, a book can have more than one life cycle, such as: hardcover; change the paper, mass market, large print/quality; audiobook, digital book, paperback, etc. Moreover, and although these are not a breakthrough in terms of business models for publishers, there is, as already mentioned, a new faith in these formats to expand the market. Traditionally, paperback books were published only when the title ended its cycle in bookstores but now the tendency is to accelerate the production and sale, so it is increasingly common to find these formats in bookstores and other additional distribution points, such as gas stations and airports, for example. In fact, there are new dynamics and critical success factors in this business, including different revenue and cost factors to consider: (1) Develop and introduce digital content in the market, (2) Content Management Systems, (3) Interface with consumers; (4) Consumer Marketing.

4.2 Business Management, Marketing and Social Media Promotion Approaches

As already mentioned, from a business management perspective, publishing companies in general, and especially the larger ones, have been directing increasingly to the market and risking on bestsellers,[20] which is one of the most visible dimensions of this strategy, that also assumes the adoption of aggressive marketing and communication practices. Therefore, we can see a proliferation of bestsellers, which results from a logic of market analysis focused on the response to the demand, matching what the reader likes to read and enabling simultaneously the high speed that bookstores deeply value. In turn, small publishers do not have this obsession with bestsellers; however, they can become profitable with titles targeted

---

[20] A bestseller is a book that is regarded as extremely popular and sought after, in a massive way, by readers and that is inserted into the bestseller list.

at specific market segments or smaller niches. Indeed, in this perspective, small publishers end up taking less risk, compared with the major publishers (since to have a market strategy oriented to bestsellers, it is also necessary to have the capacity to invest in long runs, which success is not guaranteed). In spite of that, the risk can be minimized especially when it comes to global works and authors, whose success has been tested in other markets or eventually popular journalists who have the advantage of having access to public space to promote themselves. Thus, the obsession with bestsellers may have high costs (due to high print runs) and the overall strategy of the major publishers is to concentrate a smaller number of titles with highest runs to optimize production and promotion costs—that is, for example, major publishing companies seek economies of scale visible primarily in the printing runs—the more copies are printed, the lower the unit cost becomes. Also in terms of promotion, the costs of the design and creation of advertising campaigns can be recycled to use in other locations—markets. However, the most common strategy also consists of concentrating as much as possible high print runs in order to optimize the costs of promotion and production, but also to justify the structures of the major publishing groups. That is the reason why there is an overproduction of books, all of them printed in exaggerated print runs.

There is no magic rule to know where to find the next bestseller. In any case, the heavy dependence on the bestseller constitutes a "weakness" of which small and medium-sized publishers can benefit by investing in new authors and entering other segments that can be equally profitable but in a longseller logic (few sales at a time, but many sales in an extended period of time). For example, the case of Harry Potter or The Da Vinci Code demonstrate how small or medium-sized publishers can achieve great successes—in the case of Harry Potter, the book actually became the fusion between the best of both worlds: success as a bestseller and, simultaneously, as a longseller. In fact, it should be considered that if on the one hand, it is true that a bestseller can make a lot of money for an editor, on the other hand, it is a mistake to believe that it can keep the title for a long time in the sales top. It is inevitable that 1 day the bestseller stops selling and drops out of the top. So if the company does not have a good backlist, and the theme of the book is not good, it will not sell and the company will have compromised all the investment made. Fundamentally, the bestseller works as an analgesic (aspirin)—that is, when its effects wears off (when it no longer sells), the headache comes back (difficult to sell and generate revenue). Finally, to some extent, it can be said that, many times, finding a bestseller is like playing a lottery: it is done by trial and it can occur at any time, but there are never any certainties of the author and the time in which it can happen.[21]

---

[21] Of course there are strategies to reduce or circumvent the dependence on bestsellers—and the associated financial risk—as, for example, the one used by Juan Grijaldo, a Catalan exile in Mexico who created a publisher and maintained a curious book catalog which alternated Marxist works with bestsellers, that he justified as being a very simple criterion of choice. He saw in Publisher Weekly (http://www.publishersweekly.com/pw/reviews/) the ten best-selling titles, dismissed the former for being, as he estimated, very expensive, and hired the third and the fourth. With such a simple method, he has achieved many sales.

However, another aspect should be emphasized that shows the interest in risking on bestselling books: these books are perceived as high-speed because they easily and quickly return the funds that generally come slowly.[22] Today's editorial phenomena are increasingly ephemeral, the books that over a period of time dominate editorial sales—and that over time get lost on the shelves of bookstores—rapidly become unknown books. However, these books are nonetheless extremely important to the market, since they allow their publishers to generate fast revenue that ensures the continuity of their publishing activity. In this sense, a sound business (and publishing) strategy is to create a catalog where books that are publishing successes in the short term coexist with works that perpetuate this success and that guarantee its long-term sustainability.[23] Surely the orientation for bestsellers is associated with a greater aggressiveness and sensitivity to the importance and adoption of marketing and communication practices, that is, the marketing and communication of the publishers—and also of the bestsellers—it is essentially done through retail bookselling. We do not see often a direct communication between publisher and consumer, although there are some exceptions to this, as suggested below.

The promotion campaigns and the book or author highlights are negotiated with each retailer, allowing the communication to be made according to the audience's specificities. Therefore, a campaign or highlight taking place at Fnac or Bertrand (the main book store chains in Portugal), for instance, doesn't have the same outlines as a campaign or highlight from the same publisher occurring in a hypermarket. In general, the audiences from these two types of distributor are different targets, both as regards the type of product acquired and as regards the way they understand or perceive the campaigns. In this sense, the main supports used for promotion are usually negotiated by the retailers and the publishers together, in order to communicate an understandable message to the target consumer; of course the media and the new media (including social networks) also can—and should—be part of the book marketing and communication plan.

The emergence of social networks has, nowadays, a fundamental role in what concerns the promotion of publishers and their products (books); however, social networks also contributed to the fact that the advertising and marketing message is no longer controlled by companies and entities. That is, consumers have acquired a

---

[22] In the book market, the distribution and communication policies play an important role to create bestsellers, helping to reinforce the trends that already exist in terms of best-selling books—that is, there are increasing and decreasing trends, according to the competitive level of the publisher in each of the factors mentioned (communication and distribution).

[23] Still on the subject of the bestseller, Portugal has witnessed recently a curious phenomenon: people with professions other than writers, but with some media coverage, whose books become real bestsellers in the publishing field. The phenomenon has even greater preponderance when it is noted that many of these successes are by authors whose main profession is journalism. There are already many names that we can point to as editorial successes: Miguel Sousa Tavares, José Rodrigues dos Santos and Júlio Magalhães are recognized journalists that, having their main field of action on television, have become authors of real bestsellers.

new power which is conferred on them by the information and communication technologies, leveraging a Web 2.0 revolution with a boom in social networks. Thus, it is possible to expand the brand, the product and the news of publishers on a global and local scale. The brands—publishers—that resort to this way of communicating, through social networks, are subjected to criticism, but simultaneously they can obtain advantages, whether they are small or large publishers. Today there are more than 20 active social networks in the Internet, some of them more open to criticism and others with a more exclusive character.[24] Being in a social network enables to communicate a product at a global level and the costs can be reduced when compared with other classic advertising and promotion supports.

Through the Web, products are available 24 h a day and, thus, they can compose an important platform to conduct online marketing campaigns. Besides the communications and the direct relationship between editor/author and reader/consumer boosted by the social networks, it is possible to disseminate a wide range of promotional messages about the editorial product, for example, informing a broad database about an event and suggesting the invitation of a friend, which facilitates the divulgation of that activity and the product promotion, not directly by experts but through the Web 2.0.

Taking into account that one of the marketing communication's objectives is to create and boost campaigns, the Web contributes as a fundamental platform to the customer relationship management (CRM). The technological evolution provided the necessary tools for the CRM, and with the emergence of social networks the so called "Social CRM" is arising.

Therefore, the social networks are forcing the companies (publishers) to reinforce the customer's primacy. Today publishers use the social networks to publicize events, promotions, editorial novelties, etc. On the other hand, social networks can help attract new talents, disseminate artists' works and their ability to reach out to their fans, thus constituting an excellent tool for the relationship marketing in the industry. From the perspective of promotion and public relations with the media, social networks also facilitate the communication between publishers and journalists.[25] Nowadays, the information reaches the communication professionals through social networks, while until recently the email was the preferential option. Drawing on a study carried out, in 2009, by George Washington University, it can be concluded that the majority of publishers and reporters use the social networks as working sources: 89 % of them research blogs, 65 % social networks and 52 %

---

[24] For instance, in Portugal about 3.5 million people have already acceded to social networks, which represent 88 % of the universe of Portuguese internet users. The year 2009 brought deep changes to Portugal, and the Portuguese language is nowadays the second most spoken language in microblogging networks, according to the North American blog "Text Wise".

[25] For example, Press Officers and Public Relation Agents gathered in Palm Springs at the PRSA Conference. One of the panels was about media and their needs in today's Web 2.0 world. After hearing that the press release is dead, it became necessary to discuss the matter, and the conclusion was that it most certainly is not dead—in fact reporters need information from public relations agents more than ever.

micro-blogging services. In the same way, digital subscriptions increased more than 300 % in 1 year.

Therefore, the use of social networks is increasingly frequent—and fundamental—in terms of divulgation of authors, editors, books and events. By their turn, journalists are changing their practices: 98 % of them start by searching news on Google. Today, sending one press release is no longer enough to promote a publisher's activities, so that it must be complemented with other approaches, being that social networks are assuming an increasing centrality in the practice of marketing communication. It is also noteworthy that, from the economical point of view, the use of social networks as communication and marketing platforms does not demand substantial investments, which allows the small publishers to develop promotion strategies for their authors and books, whether in a local or in a global perspective.

To a certain extent, one can also affirm that social networks, in conjunction with other ways of communication below-the-line (sponsorship, patronage, direct marketing, events, telemarketing, public relations, etc.), withdrew, on one hand, the exclusivity from the traditional media in terms of creation and promotion of brands. And, on the other hand, they allowed the democratic practices in marketing communications for small publishers, in that, in the recent past, investment in marketing was made largely through the use of traditional media, which required a high investment, only affordable for publishers with greater economic and financial capacity and with considerable business dimension.

In the book market, the marketing and branding strategy is also very attached to the catalog and brand(s) that the publishing company owns.[26] The tendency is to communicate an image through an author or a collection, rather than the seal that represents it. One of the exceptions to this communication strategy are book fairs; in these cases, the strategy is to directly communicate the brand image to the consumers—from television advertising campaigns taken up by the authors themselves, to changes in the structure of the stands in book fairs, where the activities are constant and where the consumer has the possibility to directly contact with the authors, and also, more broadly, with the editorial world. It should also be mentioned the extension of marketing and communication practices of the books by author (or self-made editions), especially facilitated in the digital world, where authors publish without editors. It is therefore imperative that publishers prove daily their value in front of authors and demonstrate the relevance of their brands. Good publishing companies find and cultivate good writers, some of which do not

---

[26] Branding plays an important role in the marketing management of a publishing firm. To this end, the brand is targeted at different levels or audiences. The publisher's brand indicates a certain competence regarding the topic and the subject of the content. This can be supplemented, if necessary, with different sub-brands for particular series, so that it is possible to have an orientation adapted to the customer. In addition to that, the best known authors also have a brand nature, as they offer to consumers identification, confidence and experience. All brands have to be combined in character and in message, so that there are no contradictions in customer orientation.

seem to be, initially, commercial promises, but that, sometimes, can have an interesting and even surprising performance. Some publishers (especially those with the greatest financial capacity and size), also advance rights, without which most non-fiction writers would hardly be able to do research for new books; advances on rights constitute, in many cases, a high spending to a publisher. Although critics argue that with publication of traditional book too much money is earned with the authors, in fact, the profits earned (by the relatively small percentage of authors whose books make money) are directed primarily to the aid of less known and less commercially profitable writers. The system is inefficient, but relies on a class of professional writers that could not exist otherwise: in the publishing business it applies, to a certain extent, the 80/20 rule, where only 20 % of the books generate return which allows the funding of 80 % of the publications that are not profitable.[27]

Using increasingly more aggressive marketing strategies, publishing companies are not limited to selling their products exclusively in the conventional places—the bookstores. Today, in addition to bookstores, there are also other selling points of books such as newsagents, gas stations and airports, among others. On the other hand, book publishers often make agreements with newspapers or magazines editors to launch offers of book collections with the purchase of a given publication. From the viewpoint of the editors of newspapers or magazines, these practices consist in marketing activities to their own publications in order to increase their circulation and audiences (and sometimes act as additional source of revenue), also serving as promotion for the book itself.[28] In this type of promotions the book is sold at a lower cost than in the market, fostering an increase in demand.[29] There is also the Internet, which began to gain more and more space in the book market, which is visible particularly in the U.S. market (and which growth in Europe and in other locations is slower) and in the growth evidenced by Amazon. Conversely, the book, before being published, will also have the attention of the department of

---

[27] The Law of Pareto (also known as the 80-20 rule) was created in 1887 by the Italian economist Vilfredo Pareto (1848–1923). This rule states that 80 % of the consequences emerge from 20 % of causes. According to Pareto, 80 % the world richness is owned by 20 % of people, 80 % of the pollution is caused by 20 % of the countries and 80 % of a company's revenues come from 20 % of its clients. The percentages may vary between 85/15 or 75/25, depending on the issue, but they hardly escape this proportion.

[28] Sometimes, books distributed with newspapers and magazines reach large runs; some books reach millions of copies. In turn, this practice adopted by publishers will support the distribution and, eventually, improve the rotation of the works in stock.

[29] The Portuguese Association of Publishers and Booksellers—APEL—even states that the majority of the Portuguese people—about 66 %—buy their books in bookstores and newsagents. The super-and hyper-markets have also become a prime selling point, where 28.6 % of the Portuguese people stock up on books. Because they are not the place to buy books par excellence, in supermarkets the works are placed strategically in a passage, attracting the attention of potential buyers. In turn, book fairs gather the attention of only 19 % of Portuguese people, which might be explained by the fact that it is a very specific fair and that, for that reason, attracts few people; they are only attended by potential buyers, unlike what happens, for example, in hyper-markets.

design, marketing, spelling and grammar correction done by the publisher's employees, and of course, printing and distribution of which the publishing company is in charge, personally or through outsourcing to other companies—that is, marketing is present in all stages of the value chain of the book.

A key issue for the definition of the marketing strategy is the planned combination of product and market. On the basis of the selection of the respective market area there are four basic possible strategies, which can be applied in accordance with the combination between product and market, as suggests Ansoff (1984), taking as main general assumptions (1) take advantage of the experience, (2) promote economies of scale, (3) foster innovation on the product and (4) encourage the search for new customers, including through internationalization strategies. Thus, the decision for one of the four scenarios considered in the Ansoff matrix cannot, in any way, exclude other possible options; in many cases, the different components of a company are interconnected. The starting point of the marketing strategy of the company is market penetration, which consists of promoting the current product in the market place today. Nevertheless, in the development of the existing market, the current product must be adapted to new markets. If, instead of entering new markets, new products are placed in the current market, there is a product development. The diversification strategy is common and it differentiates itself by its effects, depending on the distance of the new market and if the new product is removed from the market approach or from the product currently in force. Despite the fact that it was conceived around five decades ago, the Ansoff matrix seems more current (and appropriate) than ever to the book business. This matrix supports strategic decisions and it also provides a basis in case of disinvestment and of retraction of corporate areas and individual markets. In the following table, one can see, in a more objective way, the assumptions and scenarios of the matrix applied specifically to the book business, and one of the main conclusions taken is that the Internet is not only improving the expansion of the book's life cycle and market, but also of its marketing channels (Table 4).

Amazon has had a profound impact on the publishing business, creating a place where readers can find, with confidence, books that are no longer for sale in physical stores. As already suggested, long-run books—those that sell over time—are vital to the publishers: for example, at Random House, more than 50 % of the total revenue is generated by books such as *The Prophet* and *The Art Mastering of French Cooking*, which provide constant profits, allowing publishers to invest on new books. Even on Amazon, people can find backlist books; many books sold by this virtual bookshop are no longer available in classical bookstores. In turn, e-books have clear advantages for publishers, in that there will be no returns, storage fees, printing costs or shipping costs; the elimination or reduction of these costs—which are high—may even constitute a decisive factor in enabling the activity of some publishers. One of the obstacles to the affirmation of the digital book has been the difficulty in finding a functional form of reading, although we are moving in that direction with the new generation of e-readers. In fact, computer monitors have not been sufficiently portable and, for many readers (especially the less young), mobile phone screens are still too small. Thus, initially the electronic

Table 4 Ansoff matrix applied to the book business

Markets	Products Current	New
New	Current products for new markets; *Market development* (E.g.: **Internalization and exploitation of new locations; books sold with newspapers and magazines**)	New products for new markets; *Product diversification* (E.g.: **Books and other functions associated to the digital book, film adaptation**)
Current	Current products for current markets; *Market penetration* (E.g.: **Paperback books and deluxe editions; orders and services on demand**)	New products for current markets; *Product development* (E.g.: **Sale of book chapters, audiobooks, or CDs attached to the book with additional contents**)

Source: Ansoff (1984)

books were a niche market, often overlooked by major publishers (though these begin to be increasingly more attentive to e-book business). There are now about four million Kindle in use and Amazon lists more than 450,000 electronic books, and if the same book is available in print and electronic version, Amazon says that about 40 % of customers order the electronic version.[30]

5   Conclusions, Trends Systematization and Challenges for the Book Industry

The purpose of this study was to attempt to answer two main research questions: *RQ.1: Is it possible to identify trends and characterize the business tendencies in the book sector, including the business concentration? RQ.2: Which are the main challenges and disruptive elements that publishers have to face in terms of their corporate governance and business models?* In a more comprehensive way, these questions were answered and contextualized in the approach and analysis of the major transformations and strategies observed in the book market in an international perspective, but also including approaches and a case study on the Portuguese market. Due to new technologies and to the digital age, the book market is presently a market in revolution and looking for new audiences and business models.

---

[30] Some publishers recognize several similarities between Amazon's strategy and the one used by iTunes. The strategy of Jeffrey Bezos's, such as the one of Steve Jobs before him, is to acquire the device and from 80 % to 90 % of the distribution for the device, ensuring in this way the business model; but the analogy with the business of music can only go so far. What iTunes did was to replace the CD as the basic unit of commerce; instead of having to buy an entire album to get the song that really matters, it is possible to buy just that track. But no one, with the possible exception of students, wants to buy a single chapter of most books. The real concern of publishers is that the low price of digital books will destroy bookshops, which are their primary customers. Burdened with space rentals and operating expenses, physical stores are unable to lower prices in order to compete with online sellers.

Everyday international news record the profitability of digital books, as well as their reading supports, and the fall of large chains of bookstores such as Borders (in England and the USA). Conversely, the majority of European consumers—as indeed happens in Portugal—have not yet adhered to the e-book completely, but this is already a product whose sales results are starting to develop. This is where publishers are beginning to invest more evidently, in order to follow the trends observed in international markets and publishers. Be it the adverse current economic situation—which is felt more intensely in the U.S. and EU—or be it the threat of electronic books, publishing firms, in general, are feeling the need to innovate and seek new markets and audiences. Apart from the investment in commercializing e-books, to help counteract the decreasing tendency of the traditional market, the largest international publishing groups are now focusing on internationalization,[31] with the emerging markets as a priority.

Faced with a world in constant change and modernization, the book, as it is today, encounters some risks of becoming a rarity in the future, but that is not necessarily a threat to the industry or to the readers. Even if you believe in the longevity of the book, the Internet, with its frequent offers, and the new digital age created conditions to introduce disruptive elements in this activity (from production to marketing), creating a new paradigm for the publishing industry. If it is true that the industry faces a crisis, it is also timely to question: *will the next years represent further threats or opportunities for this activity, for both traditional and new operators?* For example, Barnes & Noble is an excellent example of creating opportunities for traditional companies; following side by side the new trends, it launched in the market its own e-book reader and took advantage of its space on the Internet to continue doing what it always did: sell books, whether in normal or in digital format. However, with all this technological innovation, the big question remains: *what will be ultimately the future of the traditional book and, on that, what will happen to libraries, which are, in certain markets,*[32] *the main customers of the book industry?* It seems obvious that they will have to be modernized, incorporating the latest trends and taking advantage of the best that the digital age has to offer. For example, the variety of books in a library could become much wider, and without any lack of space, as sometimes happens[33] with physical libraries where space is a scarce and expensive resource. As suggested by Darnton (2009), with modernization, libraries will also increase their functions, leaving their role of simple silent spaces for reading, and investing more on cultural events, instead of letting themselves be destroyed just for the simple fact that there are digital books; on the

---

[31] For example, in the Portuguese case the main groups (Porto Editora, Leya and Babel) are moving to the Portuguese-speaking countries, especially Brazil, Angola and Mozambique.

[32] In Portugal, on the contrary, libraries buy little or even nothing—they get everything for free due to legal obligations (take the example of the compulsory legal deposit and the State's divestment on the Directorate General of Books and Libraries—DGLB).

[33] And it would be expected that there is also a huge reduction in government expenditure in public libraries, to the extent that digital books are far less expensive.

contrary, they should take advantage of their appearance. Indeed, as it happens in other industries, in the book sector the economics and marketing of experiences can be more and more relevant, providing experiences to their current or potential users, instead of releases in libraries or in other spaces.[34]

The publishing industry has also, besides the old complexities, new challenges for a future that is constantly uncertain and increasingly unpredictable. Despite the fact that new actors and scenarios appear in the world of books resulting from the impact of the Internet (and of the ICT), it is still difficult to foresee what the true scope and influence of technology in setting up a possible new market and business model, though these start to become visible. In any case, publishers have reasons to hope and create new revenue streams, for example, the recession has contributed to change the way of thinking on the part of Silicon Valley companies, including media companies, questioning their reliance on advertising as their only source of revenue. Conversely, YouTube started charging for the viewing of some independent films in an effort to compete with Netflix and its managers know that to be successful they must produce content in a professional manner, so that advertisers—and consumers—pay. As digital companies begin to charge for the access to their contents, the traditional media companies look for ways to change what—and how—they produce. In this context, the incentives for traditional media and new media to form partnerships seem to constitute a critical factor of success,[35] exploring the advantages and disadvantages of each type of media. In the case of the book, the table below presents a summary of the advantages of the electronic book compared to the physical book (Table 5).

For centuries, the book evolved, including in its physical part, in terms of paper, cover and calligraphy. With these new developments, we believe the book has its future and will not end just because the new technologies seem to be taking its

---

[34] For example, some books published by Media XXI, previously mentioned in this paper, which had a public presentation generated more revenue than the sales from traditional bookstores. Of course the amount of sales is also dependent on the ability of the author and of the publisher to mobilize people to attend the launch: marketing communication is essential, including social networks. Even if the author does not have a good network or even if he is not well known, there are alternatives: for example, to join a conference or convention related to the content of the book. Either way, launching a book can be a rewarding experience for the author, not only to discuss the work but also for a mere necessity of socialization, including being with friends which, in some cases, constitutes a good argument and rare opportunity. This publishing company has also made presentations of books in streaming, providing the experience with an international logic, as was the case with the book "Value Creation and the Future of News Organizations" by Robert Picard, who traveled to Lisbon to make the presentation, which was discussed and debated by local experts.

[35] These partnerships involve the recognition of the added value that each partner can provide, for example, Apple is in the business of the device and not in the content business. Steve Jobs (who passed away in November 2011) aimed to ensure that those who produced content were his partners. In fact, it has to be noted that in mid-2010 Steve Jobs met in separate meetings with executives of The New York Times and Time Inc. to demonstrate precisely the potential of the iPad to generate money for newspapers and magazines.

Table 5 Advantages and disadvantages of the electronic book

Advantages	Disadvantages
– Reduction of transaction and production costs	– Requires complex electronic devices
– Increased accessibility for all bookstores	– The devices are expensive to use
– The text is searchable and storable	– Less portability than printed books[a]
– Transformation of the content, easiness for updating	– Reduced quality on the screen[b]
– Low production and distribution costs	– Multiple standards of competition
– Increased durability of contents	– Uncertain business models
– More publishing opportunities for writers	– Difficulties in managing copyright
– More availability of older publications	– Exploitation problems with the authors
– Reduction of the costs in bookshops functions	
– Reduction of the weight of bags with books	

Source: Elaborated by the author

[a]However, this disadvantage is vanishing with the new e-readers; one can transport thousands of books in a Kindle

[b]This disadvantage tends to be suppressed with the increasing progress; for instance, the second version of Kindle and the first version of iPad allow a quite reasonable display quality

place. The book assumes nowadays a great importance in society, despite all the new technologies that continue to arise, and therefore it does not seem questionable—at least in the medium term, in the next 10–15 years—that books in traditional formats cease to be part of people's lives. It is unthinkable to live without books of easy reading, about cooking, children's stories, comics, etc., because people are an integral part of all these experiences and their use. It will be impossible to live without books, without all the knowledge we gained through them over several centuries. We can see and believe in the importance of books and especially understand how they get to our hands: here the technology can be more additive than substitutive (in the sense that it does not replace but only adds new forms of marketing). The purchase and sale of books, using aggressive marketing practices, constitute undoubtedly an integral part of the strategies that contribute to spread more culture and knowledge—that is, we cannot forget that book marketing helps to convey information to everyone and it is accessible to all, after going through the publisher, distributor, retail outlet, finally reaching the end customer—the reader.

Thus, the book world lives—and will always live—from the relationships between publishers, distributors, readers, but it also seems to be clear that the success of a publishing firm depends on its capacity to adapt to the constant challenges—that is, to innovate in terms of product, marketing and distribution, and to make it reach all the possible locations—this is increasingly seen as a critical success factor. In this context, it is also necessary to conduct an analysis and reflection on some fundamental questions, namely: (a) *Which technologies are changing the concept of book?* (b) *Traditional book publishers are more threatened by Internet technologies than new operators in this field?* Evidently, the answers are not easy to give. However, on the one hand, traditional publishers have the advantage of knowledge and of brand reputation; on the other hand, new entrants may find it easier to (re)create business models suited to the competences that technologies allow, not only in what concerns production but also commercialization. In any case, and although there are many uncertainties, as always, it seems clear that the success of a book publisher also implies to (1) identify various types of approach to profitability, (2) reduce the dependence on bestsellers, (3) create brands and marketing for the publisher and author, (4) differentiation of mass and niche strategies, and (5) the existence of a dynamic backlist.

In fact, it can be said that the e-book is already revolutionizing the publishing industry and its way of functioning. According to the Association of American Publishers (AAP), sales of digital books in the United States reached the 313 million dollars in 2009, a 177 % increase over 2008,[36] and in 2010 this trend was maintained, as it can be seen in the most recent data published by the AAP. For its part, Amazon has managed to conquer most of the book market, launching Kindle, selling on its website not only digital books, but also physical books at lower price. Similarly to what occurred in France[37] and England,[38] in Germany[39] this company (Kindle) also became a leader in the book sector.[40] In fact, there is little doubt that the world of books is going through its most profound structural change since Gutenberg. In 1999, right in the *dot.com* boom, a question was much debated: *will the book be superseded by electronic technology?* About a decade later it is still discussed if the devices—Kindle, iPad, Nook, etc.—can replace books. Nonetheless, this debate needs to be refocused on the following reflection: even if we continue to read books in their traditional format, in a few decades, the impact of the Internet—which causes a profound creative disruption in the publishing industry—the challenges in terms of the transformation of the core business and the new developments, are as real and urgent as in any other sector. The book industry is an interesting case study as it was among the first to experience the shift to online transactions of physical goods; we can observe here one of the key

---

[36] Miller and Washington (2009, Chapter 11).

[37] Datamonitor report—Book Industry Profile: France, p. 15.

[38] Datamonitor report—Book Industry Profile United Kingdom, p. 15.

[39] Datamonitor report—Book Industry Profile: Germany, p. 15.

[40] Kindle is for sale on Amazon for a price of about 170€ and it stores more than 1,500 books. These can be acquired from a set of more than 400,000 books, which only take 60 s to load. Similarly to Kindle, also Nook from Barnes & Noble presents a light e-book reader with a broad array of books at the customer's disposal. In this context, the following question emerges: *is it possible to compete with e-book?* Despite some criticism of the e-book from people who prefer the classic format, it can have some advantages. First of all, the e-book responds to the growing concern about the environmental issues (an aspect that should not be devalued); if the book printing wastes lots of paper, which leads to the tree-cutting, the digital book seems not to raise that problem—this might be the publishing industry's key to change. On the other hand, and although the e-book doesn't cause waste of paper, it drives to a huge waste of electric and electronic devices, due to the fast changes in these products, a mandatory characteristic of these markets (Apple launches a new iPad once a year as part of a business model that depends on those constant launches, for instance).

moments of creative rupture (disruption) caused by Amazon[41]; in a second moment emerged the possibility of accessing books in form of e-books.

In less than a decade, the Internet has gone from a niche to a mass-commerce platform; it is now clearly the largest channel for book sales in the U.S. In addition, the super and hypermarkets appeared, with growth levels, competing with traditional bookstores, and with goal of selling large volumes of few titles at greatly reduced prices. Therefore, we see, in short, the existence of various market changes that impact the business model of the book, of which we can highlight:

1. Tendency to economies of global scale. Internationally, the editors had to get used to dealing with customers on a global scale, along with pressures to achieve higher growth rates and ambitions for achieving results, not just for libraries but also for the largest retailers in the world.
2. Tendency to accept less big hits and wait for their long-term sales—long tail effect. A shift has occurred in the book market and in what the public is buying. Amazon offers infinite shelf space, and is easier than ever for small publishers to have titles there and to get good audiences. At the same time, due to the fact that supermarkets sell large volumes of few titles with great discounts, the best-selling books still account for an increasing proportion of total sales.[42]
3. Tendency to the decrease in the importance of retailers—traditional bookstores; and an exponential growth of online bookshops and of large stores especially dedicated to books with great sales potential, in which we can highlight, besides novels and fiction, the segments of cooking, juvenile, fantastic and self-help books.

As other activities of the media industry, the book sector was also greatly affected by the impacts of the Internet, even creating a mechanism for disruption in its business model. As already suggested, not all large companies with the best resources were—or have been—those that have taken more from the potential benefits of the Internet. For book publishers, using the Internet in the book trade produced, initially, a great uncertainty—which still remains in some publishers. In general, it can be said that new technologies were initially faced by book publishers as a threat, but that attitude became gradually relative and new

---

[41] In this context, and in a simpler way, it can be said that disruption is associated with a radical change that completely alters the way in which a certain economic activity is conducted. From the perspective of firms and their business models, this concept, rebuilt in 1997 by Clayton Christensen in his book "*Innovator Dilemma*", can be understood as the impact of new technologies in the existence of a company. On the other hand, this concept is closely related to a classical theory by Joseph Schumpeter, Austrian-American economist, addressed in his book "*Capitalism, Socialism and Democracy*" (1942), in which the author considers that companies and other forms of productive organizations should become competitive through new goods, new technologies, new sources of supply, new types of organization—competition drives a decisive advantage in cost or quality and not reach the hem of the profits and of the outputs of existing firms, but their foundations and their own lives.

[42] The result was an increasing focus on the big hits—biographies of celebrities, cooking books and great fiction franchises (Harry Potter, Twilight)—as the medium authors saw their income decline when retailers started reducing orders.

technologies were even turned into opportunities, fostering the creation of new commercial channels, through electronic distribution and new combinations of products. In this context, one of the challenges of publishers, including from a marketing perspective, consists in adjusting and extending the structure of traditional distribution to new media and digital applications; this duality or multiplicity of channels can even coexist—or add value—to classical distribution channels. On the other hand, sometimes the reconciliation of these elements may increase the concentration trends, to the extent that companies with more resources have been forced to acquire companies with other complementary skills, including in terms of digital distribution, which means it is necessary to monitor situations of ownership concentration that could lead to situations of distortion of competition or adoption of other predatory management practices that, ultimately, harm consumers in the access to more choices of literary genres.

Because consumers have now several ways to purchase books through different devices and shops (and even to receive recommendations from friends on social networks rather than just reading reviews in the press), it is necessary to continually challenge previous assumptions about the profile and behavior of the 'book-buying public', increasingly critical and with alternative sources of recommendation and prescription rather than the traditional media. In this sense, it is essential that publishers look beyond the simple digital replication of their books to new display formats, in order to promote more synergies in the publishing market.[43] The experience of the business world and of publishers (including that of scientific nature) suggests that it is possible to create value in the move to the digital, creating tools to streamline workflow, effectively taking advantage of content based on the printing and using digital technology to create something much more useful to readers. In this context of market transformation and digital convergence, the following table systematizes some critical aspects resulting from the impact of technology and convergence, including in terms of revenue models in the book industry (Table 6).

Therefore, over the years, the traditional book business has undergone various competitive pressures in order to challenge its profit margins, as we can see: (a) first came the bookstore chains; (b) then the number of readers begun decreasing, (c) more recently, Amazon introduced the process of disintermediation of sale and (d) finally, we have the possibility of digital downloads in various applications.

---

[43] For example, the editor in chief of the Canadian Harlequin, a publisher of novels with annual sales of 500 million U.S. dollars, indicates that the digital world makes allows a number of opportunities to obtain more content, in more ways, to more women. In 2009 the bill for the digital activity was around 6 % of global sales, so it was already ahead of the market. In 2012, the publishing company believes to be about 15–20 %. Harlequin first started using e-readers to provide stories only in digital format that would not have the chance to be printed: erotic literature in a small format, priced at 2.99 dollars each. But Harlequin is also developing new formats. In Japan, for example, its novels in English are first translated to Japanese, then converted by a manga artist to BD for printing. These are then scanned, originally for mobile phones in Japan, but find also new functions as iPhone applications.

Table 6 Convergence challenges and possible revenue models of the e-book

Technological convergence
– PC monitors with low resolution, and lack of portable reading devices to compete with the book
– Problems with GDD, lack of standards, and potential solutions; sub technologies of pixel display
– Electronic ink technology, and little content progress in terms of design

Possible revenue models
– The primary model is paid for download: publishers sell electronic versions of printed books to online intermediaries such as Barnesandnoble.com and Amazon.com
– The second model involves fully licensed electronic bookstores: like a subscription model, with a monthly or yearly quota, large institutions typical for consumers, bookshops
– Advertising-supported model: distributor (e.g. Google) provides the rights to show the book, audience and revenue with publishers

Source: Elaborated by the author

On the other hand, the analysis of trends and challenges in the book sector must be contextualized in the transformations that occur in the media industry—that is, the book sector also enters in a great competition with other media products to the extent that there is a large common denominator in terms of competitive factor: the capacity to capture the attention of content consumers.[44] In fact, we live in an economy of attention (a resource that is scarce and increasingly difficult to conquer), which is characterized by its growing diversity and fragmentation. In summary, on the one hand, there are more and more options for consumers, especially in terms of: TV channels, web sites, newspapers, magazines, radio stations, and other activities that absorb time, including e-mail, social networks, as well as other cultural and leisure activities. On the other hand, among other trends described above, the following, which characterize transversally the most visible changes in the book industry, can be highlighted: (1) the shift in the nature of the book market, (2) the increased concentration of resources from major publishers, (3) the growth of internationalization strategies in the book market and (4) the greater importance and impact of information and communication technologies.

References

AAP—Association of American Publishers [Internet]. Disponível em http://publisherlookup.org/ 10th July.
Afuah, A. (2003). *Business models: A strategic management approach*. New York: Irwin/McGraw-Hill.
Albarran, A. (2009). *The handbook of Spanish language media* (pp. 278–292). New York: Routledge.
Albarran, A. B., & Mierzejewska, B. I. (2004, May). *Media concentration in the U.S. and European Union: A comparative analysis*. Paper presented at the 6th World Media Economics Conference, Montreal, Canada.

---

[44] On this topic, the reading of Schmitt (1999): "Experiential Marketing" is suggested; the concept is presented and described in the context of the new trends in marketing and consumer behavior.

Albarran, A., Chan-Olmsted, S. M., & Wirth, M. O. (2006). *Handbook of media management and economics*. Mahwah, NJ: Lawrence Erlbaum.

Amazon Annual Reports and Proxies [Internet]. Disponível em http://phx.corporate-ir.net/phoenix.zhtml?c=97664&p=irol-reportsAnnual 11th July.

Anderson, C. (2006). *The long tail: Why the future of the business is selling less of more*. New York: Hyperion.

Ansoff, H. I. (1984). *Implanting strategic management*. Englewood Cliffs, NJ: Prentice-Hall International.

Chesbrough, H. (2003). *Open innovation: The new imperative for creating and profiting from technology*. Boston: Harvard Business School Press.

Christensen, C. M. (1997). *The innovator's dilemma*. Cambridge: Harvard Business School Press.

Darnton, R. (2009). *The case for books—Past, present, and future*. New York: PublicAffairs.

Epstein, J. L. (2001). *School, family, and community partnerships: Preparing educators and improving schools*. Boulder, CO: Westview Press.

Faustino, P. (2009). The potential of content industry in Iberian American & African Countries. In A. Albarran (Ed.), *The handbook of Spanish language media* (pp. 278–292). New York: Routledge.

Faustino, P. (2010). *Estudo Prospectivo sobre os Media em Portugal*. Lisboa: Colecção Media XXI/Formalpress.

Gaymard, H. (2009). *Pour le libre – Rapport sur l'économie du libre et son avenir*. Paris: Galimard.

International Digital Publishing Forum [Internet]. Disponível em http://www.idpf.org/ 10th July.

Linder, J., & Cantrell, S. (2000). *Changing business models*. Chicago, EUA: Institute for Strategic Change, Accenture.

Magretta, J. (2004). *O Que é a Gestão – Como Funciona e Porque Interessa a Todos*. Lisboa: Actual Editora.

Miller, R. K., & Washington, K. (2009) *The 2011 entertainment, media & advertising market research handbook* (p. 5).

Noam, E. (2009). *Media ownership and concentration in America*. Oxford: Oxford University Press.

Osterwalder, A., & Pigneur, Y. (2010). *The business models generation*. Hoboken, NJ: Willey.

Picard, R. (2002). *The economics and financing of media companies*. New York: Fordham University Press.

Pimentel, M. (2007). *Manual del Editor – Cómo Funciona la Moderna Industria Editorial*. Madrid: Berenice.

Porter, M. (1985). *Competitive advantage: Creating and sustaining superior performance*. New York: Free Press.

Porter, M. (1989). *Vantagem Competitiva*. São Paulo: Editora Campus.

Schmitt, B. (1999). *Experiential marketing—How to get customers to sense, feel, think, act and relate to your company and brands*. New York: The Free Press.

Thompson, J. (2010). *Merchants of culture—The publishing business in the twenty-first century*. Malden, MA: Polity Press.

Verstraete, T., & Jouison-Laffitte, E. (2009). *Business Model pour Entreprendre, le Modèle G.R.P.* Bruxelas: Editions De BOECK Université.

Wirtz, B. (2011). *Media and Internet management*. Alemanha: Gabler.

New Venture Creation in Social Media Platform; Towards a Framework for Media Entrepreneurship

Datis Khajeheian

Entrepreneurship is the main engine of economic growth and prosperity (Dutta et al. 2009), and is a complex and multifaceted phenomenon (Faltin 2001). Most of previous research has explored many different aspects of factors that make individuals more likely to be entrepreneurs and the policies that foster entrepreneurial activity. But influence of media on entrepreneurship has been widely neglected (Hang and van Weezle 2007). Media is one of the most important agency of influence on minds and is a powerful tool for (Khajeheian 2012). It also plays an important role in influencing the entrepreneurship phenomenon, by creating a discourse that transmits values and images ascribed to entrepreneurship, by providing a career promoting entrepreneurial practices, and by encouraging an entrepreneurial spirit in the society (Hang and van Weezle 2007). Dutta et al. (2009) argue that a free press might Promotes entrepreneurial Activities because it increases the flow of ideas and information, leading to both more new discoveries as well as an easier ability for entrepreneurs to market and sell new products and innovations.

Entrepreneurship is the process of exploring the opportunities in the market place and arranging resources required to exploit these opportunities for long term gain. It is the process of planning, organizing, opportunities and assuming. Thus it is a risk of business enterprise (Wikipedia n.d.; Entrepreneurship).

Shane (2003) defines entrepreneur as "one who undertakes innovations, finance and business acumen in an effort to transform innovations into economic goods". He argues that entrepreneurship may result in new organizations or may be part of revitalizing mature organizations in response to a perceived opportunity. The most obvious form of entrepreneurship is that of starting new businesses.

The Chapter has written upon a research project on Iranian media entrepreneurs' digital innovations commercialization. Using a mix method, both qualitative and quantitative approaches used to investigate the subject. The framework results from the study have

---

D. Khajeheian (✉)
University of Tehran, Tehran, Iran
e-mail: datiskh@ut.ac.ir

operated on social media context to offer a better knowledge about the entrepreneurial activity a developing economy and its differences and contingencies.

1 Media and Entrepreneurship; A Reciprocal Impact

"As a scientific field of research, entrepreneurship has strong relevance to media. On the one hand, the entrepreneurship phenomenon heavily impact media industries as long as they, in their very nature, fall into the culture and creativity-related businesses. The essential characteristics of the entrepreneurial activities such as creation, innovation and novel ways of thinking are critical in building media business success. On the other hand, media also Plays an important role in influencing the entrepreneurship phenomenon, by creating a discourse that transmits values and images ascribed to entrepreneurship, by providing a carrier promoting entrepreneurial practices, and by encouraging an entrepreneurial spirit in the society. Through these means, media and entrepreneurship have a reciprocal impact" (Hang and van weezle 2007). On the Other Hand, The characteristics of the media products are very much aligned to the dimensions of the entrepreneurial process, i.e. autonomy, innovativeness, risk taking, proactiveness, and competitive aggressiveness. These dimensions represent the *entrepreneurial orientation* of the firm, which can be defined as the processes, practices, and decision making activities that lead firms to decide to enter a new market or launch a new product (cited by Lumpkin and Dess). Media companies are urged to be particularly risk taking and innovative. The entrepreneurial approach they have to develop is without doubt extremely important (Hang and Van Weezle 2007).

The goal of studying media entrepreneurship must be to build a bridge between the general discipline of entrepreneurship and the specificities of the media industry and media organizations (Achtenhagen 2008, p. 126).

2 Literature Review on Media Entrepreneurship

Most media management research to date focuses on larger, established firms. In comparison, very little is known about entrepreneurial activities of independent start-up companies in the different media industries (Achtenhagen 2008, p. 124). A small number corresponded to studies of the impact of media on entrepreneurship (Hang and Van Weezle 2007). Also despite this increasing interest in media entrepreneurship, very few research articles have been published so far on this topic (Achtenhagen 2008, p. 124).

Khajeheian and Arbatani (2011) investigate Media Entrepreneurship in Recession. They argue that global recession caused some serious negative effects on media industry, mostly referred to decrease in advertising income, and downturn in many media products sale. However recession, like any other Phenomenon in the world, had another face which is growth of entrepreneurial activities in media. Recession caused media entrepreneurship to raise as a suitable option for unemployed technical personnel. The interesting side of this phenomenon consists of low barriers to enter, low capital requirements, more specialization of media production in digital sector and encourage people to enter the media entrepreneurial activities. In fact digital media entrepreneurship plays a crucial role for economics to prevent the expansion of recession in general level. This needs little resources, but offers considerable results, which in economic terms means less unemployment, more national and domestic Production, and offering more services. Media Entrepreneurship also emits some unnecessary costly processes, like prevention from many physical processes to reach a product, is a facilitator for economy to get power and ready to jump up again.

Achtenhagen (2008, pp. 138–139) articulates Media entrepreneurs role as change agents in any society, by five functions. Firstly by adopting a mission to create and sustain some kind of artistic, cultural and/or societal value (not just economic value), secondly, recognizing and relentlessly pursuing new opportunities to serve that mission, thirdly, engaging in a process of continuous innovation, adaptation, and learning, fourthly by acting boldly without being limited by resources currently in hand, and finally by exhibiting a heightened sense of accountability to the constituencies served and for the outcomes created.

3   Media Entrepreneurship Definition

As the area of media entrepreneurship is still a young and underdevelopment field, this phenomenon is poorly understood (Achtenhagen 2008, p. 124.) for better knowledge about media entrepreneurship we should have a concise definition about the concept to know what is media entrepreneurship and who is media entrepreneur. For this reason we start with few definitions that have found in literature review to reach the best definition.

Hoag and Seo (2005, p. 3), define media entrepreneurship as "the creation and ownership of a small enterprise or organization whose activity adds at least one voice or innovation to the media marketplace". But this definition has some lacks, as Achtenhagen (2008, p. 126) critics, any person starting a blog would be covered by it, as this would be a new voice in the media marketplace, so the definition is somewhat problematic.

Achtenhagen, herself, based on Davidsson (2004) defines media entrepreneurship as "how new ventures aimed at bringing into existence future media goods and services are initially conceived of and subsequently developed, by whom, and with what consequences" (p. 126).

Khajeheian and Arbatani (2011) define the Media Entrepreneurship as "using limited available resources of small firm to pursue opportunities recognized to gaining profit from a specific niche market".

To reach an extended and pervasive definition for Media Entrepreneurship, I used a mix method to reach the best possible one. Firstly I collected all definitions from literature review, and then asked from some academics in media management and entrepreneurship area to define it. After collecting all elements and factors which articulated in responses, an elementary Extracted to select the sample for research and conducting interviews. In next step I asked from each of them to define a media entrepreneur themselves, as Real practitioners. This considers as a test for definition. In conclusion, the Concise definition of Media Entrepreneurship offered as following: "Individual or small firms which use their own or others' resources to create value by extracting opportunities via offering a service or product consist of any innovation in each of *product/service characteristics*, *process*, *distribution channel or place*, *or different innovative usage*, to media market, or any other market which media is its main channel of interaction."

4 Media Markets and their Requirements

There is a narrow consideration which highly effects on media entrepreneurship success in social media and digital media at all Which is type of innovation.

Ireland et al. (2003, p. 981) introduce two types on innovation in which firms can engage—disruptive and sustaining. In general, disruptive innovation produces revolutionary change in markets while sustaining innovation leads to incremental change (Tushman & O'Reilly, cited in Ireland et al. 2003). Incremental or sustaining innovation is the product of learning how to better exploit existing capabilities that contribute to competitive advantages. In contrast, radical or disruptive innovation is derived from identifying and exploiting entrepreneurial opportunities through new combinations of resources to create new capabilities that lead to competitive advantages. They believe that through effective Strategic Entrepreneurship, firms are able to engage in both disruptive and sustaining innovation. However, there is another type on innovation which should be considered precisely, especially in developing economies, referred as imitative innovations (Khajeheian 2012). He shows that Disruptive innovations mostly flourish in developed economies with media markets established, While in developing economies, Imitative innovations have a great deal of chance to yield. This type of innovation plays a major role on structure of media entrepreneurship activities in developing countries. We should notice that Hindle and Klyver (2007) literature review reveals that societies stressing different cultural values will experience different levels of innovation and entrepreneurship. Relationship between culture and entrepreneurship is not causal, but that cultural values impact entrepreneurship through the agency of economic freedom national cultures influences individuals' capacities to interpret and respond to strategic issues. One consequence might results an impact on the levels of innovation and entrepreneurial participation displayed by a population. According to this conclusion, Imitative innovations arise from cultural values of developing countries beside the insufficient infrastructures which prevent for disruptive innovations or make it inappropriate.

Another influencing factor on media entrepreneurship activity, which is deeply incorporates with degree of economic development, is Media Market Efficiency (Capitalized E). Media Market structure plays a crucial role in flourishing media entrepreneurships. Some Media markets provide the opportunities to commercialization of innovations while incomplete ones, will prevent from its flourishing. An efficient media market should provide diversity of options for media entrepreneurs to market their innovations. Any media market, regardless of its development and efficiency, consists following Actors: Large media companies, which joys from resource and operational competitive advantage; Small and Entrepreneur media companies, which their innovation

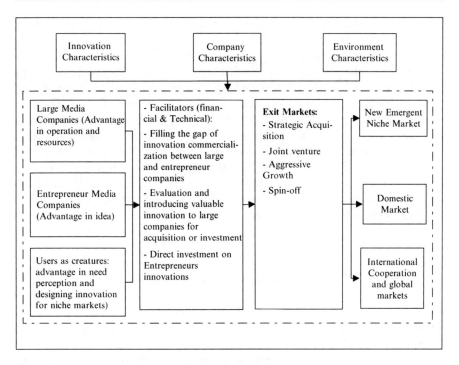

Fig. 1 Structure and elements of an efficient Media Market

and new ideas are their strength; and media users, which help the media to cover more extensive area than its natural power of coverage, by their feedbacks—whether technical or practical—and content generation. Strength of Media Entrepreneurs is exactly in the weak point of media (uncapitalized m) large companies. Media entrepreneurs generally rely on their innovative and risky ideas, which commonly not covered by large ones. Generally large media companies concentrate on idea which is applicable in huge markets and critical mass. This can cover the costs and cause deeper penetration. Media entrepreneurs rely on small pieces of resources.

Beside these three sections which shape major players of any media market, there are some financial and technical facilitators, which their performance is one of the most important determiners of the media markets efficiency. Financials consist of venture capitals and institutions which invest or lend for commercialization of new innovations, and technical are generally small and large non-media companies which offer third party services in commercialization. These facilitators evaluate and filter best innovations offered by media entrepreneurs, and introduce them to larger media companies to buy innovations, or acquisition of small firm, or other options like joint ventures. Efficient market provides an exit market for media entrepreneurs to select their strategy: sell innovation and start new other one, sell the company and work as part of larger company, or aggressively continue to act as an independent firm which aims to grow. Especially in this later strategy venture capital will play a crucial role by financing the project. In such conclusion, Eliasson and Eliasson (2005) stress on the role of venture capitals in fill the gap between operational competitive advantage and innovation advantage. Figure 1 illustrates an efficient media market to promote entrepreneurship:

Quantitative phase of project reveals that Iranian media market suffers from some inefficiency. This lacks major elements such as large private media companies and Venture capitals and many intermediary elements, like third parties and marginal markets facilitators, especially financial institutions interested on investment on media enterprises. Lack of exit markets, technical third parties, and venture capitals force media entrepreneurs to carry the process of commercialization of an innovation from A to Z, which practically is impossible and inefficient and results heavy pressure. The insufficiency in Iranian media market caused the unpleasant results. Despite huge opportunities and interesting niche markets, there is little success stories, and there is not even a famous brand belongs to any media entrepreneur.

5   Social Media and Change in Value Chain

Blackshaw (cited in Xiang and Gretzel 2010) defines Social Media as Internet-based applications that carry consumer-generated content which encompasses "media impressions created by consumers, typically informed by relevant experience, and archived or shared online for easy access by other impressionable consumers". Social media tools cultivate the internal discussions that improve quality, lower costs, and enable the creation of customer and partner communities that offer new opportunities for coordination, marketing, advertising, and customer support. These networks contain information that has significant business value by exposing participants in the business network who play critical and unique roles (Hansen et al. 2011, p. 4). In contrast, to content provided by marketers and suppliers, social media are produced by consumers to be shared among themselves (Xiang and Gretzel 2010). Social media exist in a variety of forms and serve numerous purposes. Consumer-generated content supported through social media is a mixture of fact and opinion, impression and sentiment, founded and unfounded tidbits, experiences, and even rumor (Blackshaw and Nazzaro 2006, p. 4).

In recent years and after emergence of Web2.0, Social Media becomes more popular and now it is the dominant form of internet usage. The growth in Social Media use is not limited to teenagers, either; members of Generation X, now 35–44 years old, increasingly populate the ranks of joiners, spectators, and critics. It is therefore reasonable to say that Social Media represent a revolutionary new trend that should be of interest to companies operating in online space, or any space, for that matter (Kaplan and Haenlein 2010).

According to what Aris and Bughin (2005) suggested, there are four core processes in media industry which shape Value chain: Content Generation, Content Delivery, Advertising sales, and End-customer interaction. They describe the content generation process as heart of media business and argue that the most important step in this process is the generation of rights. In second step this determines that how the value is divided between the creatives and media companies, when the rights are bought and sold. Packaging the individual pieces of content into an integrated offering and be core competence of most media companies, and Pricing the products for end consumers is another part of this process.

They describe Content delivery as the process of turning a right into product and ensuring the product's distribution. They argue that this process usually looked upon as a cost, not as a value-creating activity. The focus is very much on optimizing efficiency and effectiveness, while remaining within the quality boundaries set by the content departments.

Media advertising sales forces are managed like traditional B2B sales forces and they often organized by customer size and region. Te regional aspect is driven by the desire to better interact with the media agencies, which play an important middleman role in all media sectors. The sales approach is mostly push, i.e. the sales force tries to sell the available inventory as effectively as possible, with little room left for the advertiser to shape the inventory.

Efficiently acquiring, developing and retaining end consumers is a core activity for subscriptions-based businesses (p. 18).

The abovementioned value chain in mass media has a clear border, but in Social media the borders fades and are ambiguous: "Web 2.0 applications such as blogs and social networking allow the audience to more fully interact with the original content provider, share comments of content with friends, provide updates, and even vote on the popularity of a piece of content. Therefore, content created by the production team does not end the moment it is published by a media firm. Audience members take the topic and continue the production process through interacting with others ranging from the original creator to other individuals interested in the topic. Comments or notes that audience members post on anchors' Facebook, MySpace or Twitter accounts can end up being aired in the actual programs" (Pitts and Zeng 2010). Media entrepreneurship is an emerging–fast growing trend which thanks to advances in communication technologies has disseminate around the world. Many small firms or even individuals in many different fields are managing media enterprises, which offer very diverse services. Dramatic reduction in media production and distribution in digital platform made it possible to enter the media industry by very lower investment than before.

6 Social Media and Media Entrepreneurship

New Emergent Niche Markets are the wining card for media entrepreneurs in their competition to get market share via Social media. Before the technological advances, media companies ignore small market segments, because many of them were too small to be profitable for media companies. Maybe this is one of the main reasons that mass media directed to folks, and not pleased elites and thinkers of society. Mass audiences consist of folks, who they are profitable for mass, while many niche markets are too small to be profitable, and should ignored (Khajeheian and Arbatani, 2011). Social Media platform has changed the circumstance. Thanks to digital technologies, production cost has reduced and by this low cost of media activity, many of those niche markets become profitable. Now media entrepreneurs, who according to their nature use resources efficiently and have not major sunk costs, are able to cover niche markets, even as dominant player, not a rival, because in many of them there is no competition at all. This is a trend which can reshape media markets fundamentally different from what we experienced before. Coverage of an event can be very different, according to needs and perspective of target market media concentrate to.

As Khajeheian and Arbatani (2011) Argues, this trend plays even more important role in recession period. In recession some market segments will potent for more profitability. In fact recession is an opportunity to re-navigation of society and recount markets. While some profitable segments fall into recession, we face with especial segments, for example retired elders, which based on their characteristics and lifestyle and needs, provide a profitable niche market. In recent recession we mention many efforts to get some share from this special market, for example by designing more convenient and bigger and simpler mobile phones, for this segment.

Social Media Platform investigated with such characteristics: very low barriers for entry ($M = 1.40, SD = 0.5$). This confirms that Social Media offer a suitable context for entrepreneurial activities. The barriers recognized very low, because of costs, the regulations, and market opportunities. This seems the same in different economies, because of intrinsic characteristics of digital and social media. In reverse, Exit Markets are deeply depends on national media markets and economics. Exit markets, becomes a market for strategic acquisitions, offering a supply of radically new innovations embodied in "small new firms", the innovations having been moved beyond the entrepreneurial stage by venture capitalists, who now supply the exit market with strategic investment opportunities (Eliasson and Eliasson 2005, p. 102). Khajeheian (2012) suggests exit market is a necessary element for an efficient media market. The entrepreneurs recognize exit markets as a major drawback in developing economy ($M = 1.89, SD = 0.7$). Another characteristic measured for the study were level of competition and profitability. Competition perceived in medium level, ($M = 3.47$) compare to very competitive markets in global arena, shows the potential of the domestic market for more entrepreneurial activities. The disappointing result reached in profitability. Despite the profitability of media industry, especially in digital sector, media entrepreneurs express low to medium profitability rate ($M = 2.80$). The results show that media entrepreneurship in Iranian market in a very potential market.

7   Framework for Media Entrepreneurship in Social Media Context

Developing Countries have their own opportunities and challenges, and certainly media entrepreneurship in these economies influence on these situations. According to these contextual situations this seems reasonable to consider every country as a unique case and investigate the subject exclusively. As media entrepreneurship studies are fewer than enough to borrow any research framework from them, So I had to design a research from scratch to get a big picture about media entrepreneurship in a developing country and compare it with what literature review offered, which completely operated in developed economies.

Basically, this should be considered that the research not aims to design a model, but tries to offer a framework. The fact is that models offers for commercialization of high tech products and development of technological ventures have been criticized. Moreau (2006) has articulated the disadvantages of these models. He argues these models as: "they are not representative; they are inadequate and imprecise; they either wrongly define or argue a stochastic-non sequential-development. Other models have been criticized as impractical because of the diversity of definitions used and their difficulty. These models have also been criticized for being under conceptualized due to a lack of underlying theoretical analysis" (Moreau 2006, p. 144). A deep study of models shows this is reasonable to ignore designing a model, as the process is, in addition to all above mentioned disadvantages, in its nature contingency and context based. So this seems better to focus on offer the framework instead of a universal model for Media Entrepreneurship. This framework just offer the necessary elements should be mention in Media Entrepreneurship and development of digital media product by these ventures, and ignore about the relationships among them and how they should implement by media entrepreneurs. This framework may provide cornerstone for future researches in development of media entrepreneurship in social media and digital media sphere.

This framework, may reach by a deliberated blend of qualitative and quantitative methods. Researcher designed a qualitative–quantitative and then again qualitative approach to develop the intended framework for media entrepreneurship in developing countries, focused on case of Iranian media market. In first Qualitative phase, observation of environment and screening the media market structure and behavior offers a perception from media entrepreneurship in country. In the next step using internet search engines and online articles, a list of successful global media entrepreneurs provided, according to different criteria of success, like income, market share, growth rate or rank in Google page ranking and Alexa. Their story of success has been studied to know the effective factors for their success.

Concluding the findings, the elementary qualitative phase accomplished and quantitative phase began. A questionnaire has been designed; consist of various scales, from likret to multi choices and short answer. This questionnaire conducted as a mean to perceive the characteristics of Iranian media markets in features like barriers to entry, profitability, etc. the results describe nature and unique characteristics of Iranian digital media market.

The main phase of study, built on the base of descriptive findings. A sample of 15 Media Entrepreneurs has been selected, to study the development of digital media product by entrepreneurial ventures. The criteria to mention as media entrepreneur based on definition Khajeheian (2012) provides, and their activities ranged from internet retailers, to online games; and interactive advertisers to android market developers. Deep interviews conducted and asked them to narrate the way they paved from made idea to product and the problems and challenges they faced with. After conducting any interview, the researcher analyzed the content by theoretical coding, and then interpreted them to make theory. Findings of any interview, developed the theory, and the process continues until the theoretical saturation has been reached. The resulted framework then offered to panel of experts; consist of academics in related fields and practitioners. By their modifications, the final framework resulted and confirmed.

The framework consists five categories which should be mention by media entrepreneur to a successful Commercialization of its innovations to Social Media context. The Categorizes include Resource-Related Factors, Product-Related Factors, Strategy-Related Factors, Enterprise-Related Factors and Finally Infrastructure-Related Factors. Each of them articulated as following:

8 Resource-Related Factors

Resource Related Factors include three major classifications. Most important of them is Competitive advantage, accompanied with Internal Organizational Resources and External Resources. Competitive Advantage as cornerstone of success has mentioned by many of entrepreneurs. However, competitive advantage in social media is very temporary and should be maintained carefully and reinforce during the time. The fast changing nature of digital technology, made competitive advantage unstable in time and any successful enterprise should mention the rivals to know how its advantages are under attack and may destroyed. The interviews analysis reveals that there is two dimensions in competitive advantage, intense and duration. Sometimes advantage is so intensive which rivals cannot threat the enterprise, as this needs high level of knowledge, specific resources, severe support, or any other hard gained resources. Enterprises which offer any kind of radical innovation, joy from intensive competitive advantage, which are usually durable too. Entrepreneurs who offer incremental innovations, or the needs to approach them is easy to gain for rivals, are mostly faced with severe competition and possibility to lose the advantage. However, regardless to the type and context-competitive advantage has mentioned as critical success factor for media entrepreneurs in digital and social media, but they should care about this by different approaches, some using timing to offer innovations and some suggest different protective methods. But most of them imply on Team and Social Capital as the most important tools to exploit competitive advantage. Team, especially technical staff explored as major concern for almost all interviewers. Scarcity of professional technician made it even as competitive advantage for some enterprises. One of the entrepreneurs differs from professional and educated technicians. He implies that educated ones, need to gain experience and learn how to behave professionally, while professional ones are trustable in actions, and they can be progressive factor for enterprise. A lot of educated programmers and IT managers and practitioners are graduated from institutes and universities, but they need to learn and experience in market, which made them rare.

Outsourcing is another skill needed for media entrepreneurs. As described in media market, technical third parties are one of necessary actors of media market. Media enterprises by their nature are limited in staff and resources to operate every activity inside, so outsourcing is a major routine in media enterprise. however this process is not as simple as it seems, especially in inefficient markets. almost half of media entrepreneurs explained their failures on selection of third parties. Part of the problem was lack of skills and other part was about how to arrange the contract.

As one of entrepreneurs argues, there are not enough professional human resources. We have educated, but not professional. Contracting is also another problem. Of course the factors seems obvious, but considering the fact that many media entrepreneurs are youth with academic educations and few market experience, we will see that factors are not so simple as seems in the first look.

9 Product-Related Factors

In proposed framework, three factors consisting Product-related category. The first is Product Idea. This not surprising that opportunity recognition is basis for a good idea. Business idea should be concentrated on a market need, regardless of the size, but attending to profitability. Idea should be fit to competitive advantage of enterprise too, or media entrepreneur should try to build and gain the advantage needed to exploit the opportunity via business idea.

New Product Development mentioned as core competency of a entrepreneur, and of course a major determiner of media product quality. Mostly this part operated by technical departments in companies, but in media entrepreneurs, rarely this department exists. Mostly media entrepreneur rely on his/her technical abilities, or using others ability tries to do some modifications on product design and develop it according to market needs. As explained before, Media Entrepreneurs in developing countries mostly pursue imitative innovations, which not required to research and development activities and mostly use an original innovative product in host context. So new product development activities summarized in minor changes through given product to adapt it with host market needs and preferences.

Timing plays a more important role in entrepreneur success. Some media entrepreneurs believe that innovation should reveal once, to shock market and show enterprise as an innovative entity. Some others believe that innovation should be timely offered. This allowed enterprise to offers a new product in market often. Also this prevents rivals to copy the competencies, as this is prepared for next phase of offering via new product. However this is not our concern. This is critical for media entrepreneur to know timing importance in their plan to market innovations.

10 Strategy-Related Factors

Strategy-related factors imply on the Business managing skills any entrepreneur expect to meet, for successful leading of enterprise. Most of technological entrepreneurs in the study lack the abilities expected in this category, as they mention as total business management skills. This category consists of four factors include: Market and customer needs, Competitive Strategy, Outlook, and Revenue Model.

Competitive Strategy imply on different strategies types, but in study we focused on three Porter Strategy; Cost leadership, Differentiation and Focus (Market segmentation). Most of the entrepreneurs explained focus strategy as most suitable one to reach the capacity of niche market. Basically media entrepreneurs access to limited resources and their size not allow them to cover a great range of costumers and markets. Thus focus on a market segment, allow them to extract maximum potential of the segment, and more productive use of the resources. In our sample six entrepreneurs explain that focus on a market segment let them to better perception of the customers' needs and response them more effectively. Geographical segmentation mostly chased by retailers on social media, to better coverage of the area for delivery and interaction. Also geographical segmentation usually covers people in a specific cultural and income group, and makes it easier to know your costumers. Online Game Entrepreneurs focus on different kind of segmentation; age or income. However we are not in the place to prescribe a specific strategy, but to imply the important role of competitive strategy, in media strategy making. Competitive strategy in social media is under influence of severe competition, because media entrepreneur have to compete not only with domestic rivals, but with global competitors, as the costumers have access to any other enterprises which offer the product in global arena, and if innovations be imitative, the original innovator has a major preference. This is the point that strategy is determiner of success, because focus on some specific local characteristics can lead the enterprise against the rivals. Revenue model is associated with competitive strategy.

11 Enterprise-Related Factors

This category consists of two classifications: Entrepreneurial behaviors and Business knowledge. In literature review Entrepreneurial Behaviors cover a range of characteristics and actions to face with challenges ahead of business. Among very different behaviors, the entrepreneurs imply on agility and organizational learning as two major and influencing factors in success of enterprise. Agility allow the enterprise to quickly reaction to fast changing environment, such as instability of regulations, changes in preferences, emergence of new technologies, etc. agility is not only in size, but in properties. Media entrepreneurs imply on importance of "resource control" instead of "resource ownership". Control means the ability to exploit the resources under ownership of others, by different means, like partnership, rent, lease, etc. agility allows enterprise to quickly change the process, product, distribution channel and any other needed actions to respond the market changes. So enterprise should be so agile in size, personnel, processes, properties which able it to use any recognized opportunity fast, and react to any challenge face with.

Entrepreneurship style is also one of the other influencing factors in design and managing the enterprise. Serial Entrepreneurs aim to establish a chain of firms, while opportunistic entrepreneur focus on an opportunity to gain profit, maybe sustainable or not. Social Entrepreneurs attend to value for society, while Technical entrepreneurs mostly focus on product functions. The criterion for success of enterprise is how the media entrepreneur reach to his/her goal. The style also determines the strategy of enterprise. Growth, acquisition, joint venture, sale of enterprise and etc. are the possible strategies media entrepreneur may select for their enterprise. Business Knowledge and SME management is the main skill media entrepreneurs require to manage enterprise towards the success. Many of entrepreneurs involved in research, explain the lack of business knowledge as their main shortcoming in success, in first phases of their venture creation. Most of them were technical peoples who estimated they will succeed as media entrepreneurs just because of their technical skills, but when they enter to business, mentioned the necessity of strategic management, marketing knowledge, and communication and planning skills to success in market. Some of them even had to change the business model and structure of the enterprise to adapt it to what market required them.

12   Infrastructure-Related Factors

So far explained factors were under control of Entrepreneur, Thus the art and Skill of him/her to mention and arrange them, shape the business. But like any other social phenomenon, nothing is in vacuum. Media enterprise acts with environment, thus should mention all environmental issues to reach its goals. The important and distinguishable characteristic of these factors is that they are uncontrollable by entrepreneur, so he/she have to accept them, as is and try to interact with them, so that leverage the enterprise. Media Entrepreneurs name these environmental issues mostly as infrastructural issues, so we name them so. In our analysis these infrastructure divided to five specific parts: Internet/Network infrastructure, E-Banking/E-Payment Infrastructure, Market Information Infrastructure, Regulations and Distribution System Infrastructure. These five highly depend on host country enterprise operate in. Media Entrepreneurs, Especially in Social Media context should mention this category very precisely to prevent from any unpredicted event which may cause failure.

Internet/Network access is the main determiner. Of course the foundation of social media is on network access, and without it, the Social media will not exist. The factor is important in media entrepreneurs which operate in developing country by unstable internet access. This is interesting that some of entrepreneurs express tricks to solve the problem of sudden interruption in network. One of them which engage on retail sale in social media was named his business and website upon the business phone number, so even in lack on network access, every customer know that may contact 2938 by phone to take order. Entrepreneur expresses this as a solution for unstable internet infrastructure. One other declared that the enterprise is in regular contact with its customers by various tools like Mobile Text Messages, Phone Contacts, postal catalogues, and even phone services, which let him to not miss its customers. The solutions they describe show that media entrepreneurs always face with uncertainty, so they are ready to find some way to do their job and reach the goal.

Entrepreneurship activities in social media severely depend on E-Payment, but in many developing countries E-Banking and E-payment infrastructures are not established and pervasive enough to count on. Distribution System, like Postal services is another important factor which in relation with payment shapes the infrastructure for an e-commerce, especially when a physical commodity is the subject of trade. Media Entrepreneurs explain some solutions again, some innovative ways consist of running a virtual account to save a certain amount of money by customers, running a specific private credit account until a certain amount according to credibility estimate of customers, using some assets as guaranties of credit, and etc. some have established a transportation system to deliver orders and take money. However the media entrepreneurs try to find a way to fit the gaps in infrastructures.

Regulations issue is great challenge against media entrepreneurs, maybe in many places of the world. Nature of media entrepreneurship ties with flexibility, agility, fast changing, changes in staff and personnel, and in almost many entrepreneurial activities. Regulations, in contrast, are slow-changing and worn out, so often not suitable for business needs in social media platform. this is not controllable by media entrepreneurs, just they should mention it and be aware about it.

Market Information system can be mention as a distinguish factor of developed and developing economy and efficient media market. Most of entrepreneurs explain lack of market information as one of their serious problems in strategy making and selection of target markets. So they have to prepare an information system for themselves, which is more expensive and incomplete.

13 Big Picture: Metaphor of Wheel on the Road

The framework extracted from research may exemplify to a wheel on a road, while wheel consist of four controllable categories by entrepreneur, and road consists from uncontrollable, infrastructural factors. Let's take a look on Fig. 1 which illustrates the metaphor.

As we see in Fig. 2, successful commercialization of media entrepreneurs innovations consist of deliberately consideration of four categories in business planning. Media entrepreneur enter to the market by an innovation, but to market it as a product, should notice to many different factors. Firstly He/She should collect the resources required for extract the idea. This is based on his/her Competitive advantage, which could risen from idea, entrepreneur, opportunity, geographical location, restrictions, or any other source of competitive advantage.

What makes this framework different from many other models for commercialization is a balanced perspective towards all factor influence on success of innovation commercialization. Although the framework ignores to explains the relationship between factors and success—and no framework aims it naturally—but this provides media entrepreneurs a concise roadmap to pave in the way to success. It seems that any kind of entrepreneurship in social media context will follow the elements which investigate in the framework. Indeed they will play different roles in different enterprise, for different products and in different economies, but any of them is necessary element should be mention by media entrepreneur.

The study conducted in a developing economy, with inefficient, but very potential media market. The special situation of this market, rise a lot of entrepreneurial opportunities, which many entrepreneurs extract them successfully, but lack of business knowledge, prevent from more progress.

New Venture Creation in Social Media Platform; Towards a Framework for Media... 139

Fig. 2 Framework for Commercialization of Innovations in Digital Media

14 A Formula for Developing Digital Media Entrepreneurship

As framework proposed, the next step may be exploring the relationship among the consisting elements, which should be done by future researchers aim to develop a model. However, I tried to go ahead and open a window to start developing model, by suggestion of a preliminary formula for new venture creation by media entrepreneurs. In this formula I concerned severely to contingency nature of such formula, and avoid from any universal and pervasive approach. The only purpose for this formula is to approach future developments of the framework by weighting the elements according to their importance to developing digital media products.

Panel of experts, consist of media entrepreneurs participated in interviews, asked to rank importance of any element in proposed framework. I ignore about the details of the process, but focus on the results. The final formula proposed as the following:

```
Success = IS * (3[5CA ((Fe+Pe+Se) +OR)] *5TM) *3(ES+SME)
*[2[3 √(2*Idea)*PD*MS] + Market])
  Where SME=5T*2OL*3ER*5BK
  And MS=4CS* 2RM
  And IS= IA * (3PE + D + 3R)
  Where: 1<IA, CA, Fe, Pe, Se, OR<5
  For: 0<IA<5
       0<PE<5
```
If all variables equal or greater than zero[1]

Each of the elements mentioned in the context of domestic digital media market and located in formula according to the importance and determinant role of them in developing media entrepreneurship. As the formula explains, internet access (communication infrastructure) not available, social media not existed at all, so the formula results to zero. This is obvious, as the access to network is most critical element in social media and no social participation and interaction will occur without access to network. We imply on internet access, because the media entrepreneurs involved in the sample all operate in Internet and none operate in mobile networks, so this is better to just refer to internet, instead of network as a more pervasive term. We see also that Business Knowledge, Team and Competitive Advantage are the most important elements in media entrepreneurship in social media context.

Development of the formula, and going ahead towards the contingency models for media entrepreneurship in social media and digital sphere may approached in future studies. What explained here was just an opening to the media entrepreneurship to be developed as field of interest. Both framework and formula are potent for more development and expansion, in different contexts. The study conducted in a developing economy which introduces digital technology as a platform for entrepreneurial activities within its young and educated population. However, the country is paving its first steps in media entrepreneurship and needs more studies and experiences to flourish its digital potential. This seems that story is same for many other developing countries. Media entrepreneurship will open a new window for youth living in developing economies to exploit the media markets opportunities, using the least of resources, and just rely on knowledge.

15 Conclusion

As investigated in the paper, Media Markets face with some evolutionary changes. Emergence of Media entrepreneurs is the major trend of new media markets, because they offer micro-innovations, which maybe in its own term not significant, but in aggregation shape a very niche-conscious media products, and more important, is that they shape a platform for detailed innovations for future. Media entrepreneurship, also has mentioned as a pathway to face with economics crisis, like unemployment and recession.

Developing Countries may use social media as an opportunity for economic growth and employment, but firstly they need to foster media entrepreneurship as attitude and believe, and secondly they should treat it a learnable practice. Doing entrepreneurial actions in new Media Markets and Social Media platforms requires preparing potential entrepreneurs for successful commercialization of their innovations. Lack of business management knowledge perceived as one of the most mentioned difficulties in some developing countries, which have risen from the gap between academics and practitioners, and sometimes underestimating need to managerial issue, against technological issues. The Framework proposed in the article implies on a balance needed to successful managing of innovation. This suggested for media entrepreneurs to mention about necessary factors, and at the same time, considering the specific contingencies of idea. Almost for any kind of media products, the four category of Resource, Product, Strategy and Enterprise, should be managed carefully.

This research can be viewed as cornerstone for development of theories in media entrepreneurship and a base for conducting some experimental researches to measure the phenomena of media entrepreneurship and models to successful commercialization of innovations to exploit opportunities in developing countries.

References

Achtenhagen, L. (2008). Understanding entrepreneurship in traditional media. *Journal of Media Business Studies*, 5(1), 123–142.
Aris, A., & Bughin, J. (2005). *Managing media companies; Harnessing creative value*. New York: Wiley.
Blackshaw, P., & Nazzaro, M. (2006). Word of mouth in the age of the web-fortified consumer. In *Consumer-generated media (CGM) 101*. New York: Nielsen.
Davidsson, P. (2004). Researching Entrepreneurship. Berlin: Springer
Dutta, N., Roy, S., & Sobel, R. (2009). *Does a free press nurture entrepreneurship?* Morgantown, WV: Department of Economics, West Virginia University.
Eliasson, G., & Eliasson, Å. (2005). The theory of the firm and the markets for strategic acquisitions. In U. Cantner, E. Dinopoulos, & R. F. Lanzillotti (Eds.), *Entrepreneurships, the new economy and public policy* (pp. 91–115). Berlin: Springer.
Faltin, G. (2001). Creating a culture of innovative entrepreneurship. *Journal of International Business And Economy*, 2, 123–140.
Hang, M., & Van Weezle, A. (2007). Media and entrepreneurship: A survey of the literature relating both concepts. *Journal of Media Business Studies*, 4(1), 51–70.
Hansen, D. L., Shneiderman, B., & Smith, M. A. (2011). *Analysing social media networks with NODEXL; Insights from a connected world*. Amsterdam: Elsevier.
Hindle, K., & Klyver, K. (2007). Exploring the relationship between media coverage and participation in entrepreneurship: Initial global evidence and research implications. *International Entrepreneurship Management Journal*, 3, 217–242.
Hoag, A., & Seo, S. (2005, April). Media entrepreneurship: Definition, theory and context. *NCTA Academic Seminar*, San Francisco.
Ireland, R. D., Hitt, M. A., & Sirmon, D. (2003). A model of strategic entrepreneurship: The construct and its dimensions. *Journal of Management*, 29(6), 963–989.
Kaplan, A. M., & Haenlein, M. (2010). Users of the world, unite! The challenges and opportunities of Social Media. *Business Horizons*, 53, 59–68.
Khajeheian, D. (2012). *Preparing a framework for commercialization of media entrepreneurships' digital innovations* (Dissertation for PhD degree in media management). University of Tehran, Tehran.

Khajeheian, D., & Roshandel Arbatani, T. (2011). *Remediation of media markets toward media entrepreneurship, how recession reconstructed media industry*. Paper presented at the meeting of European Media Management education Association Conference, Moscow.

Moreau, F. (2006). Strategy development processes. In M. Bernasconi, S. Harris, & M. Moensted (Eds.), *High-tech entrepreneurship; Managing innovation, variety and uncertainty* (pp. 144–157). London: Routledge.

Pitts, M. J., & Zeng, L. (2010). Media management: The changing media industry and adaptability. In J. A. Hendricks (Ed.), *The twenty first century media industry; Economic and managerial implications in the age of new media*. Lanham, MD: Lexington Books.

Shane, S. (2003). *A general theory of entrepreneurship: The individual-opportunity nexus*. Cheltenham: Edward Elgar.

Wikipedia. (n.d.). *Entrepreneur*. Retrieved January 14, 2012 from http://en.wikipedia.org/wiki/Entrepreneur

Xiang, Z., & Gretzel, U. (2010). Role of social media in online travel information search. *Tourism Management, 31*, 179–188.

New Marketing Communication in Social Media Business

Wolfgang Mühl-Benninghaus

New marketing communication in social media business is currently considered to be one of the big challenges in all of the branches of economy because networks and their corresponding software products are progressively becoming cross-section technologies. Consequently, people are increasingly feeling a certain necessity to actually use these kinds of networks. At the same time the question arises what actually is *new* in marketing in social media business. This answer can only be given when you sketch out which factors caused marketing to change in the past, what was the status quo in the year 2000, and which factors apart from digitalization have also contributed to these changes. The structure of this essay follows this basic understanding. The essay begins with a short historical overview to point out which factors influenced marketing in the past and which were the conditions linked to the changes that came up. The second chapter describes the changes in consumption and the changes in the way how media were used within the last 15 years, provided they have influenced and are still influencing marketing. In this regard it becomes apparent that media have to be considered as networks. This implies that the changes of communication in general and particularly in the marketing sector are always recognizable in several or even in all types of media in one way or another. The last chapter is dedicated to new marketing communication. I will illustrate the historical constants of marketing as well as the basic changes of the last years that came along with the development of the Web 2.0.

1 Historical Overview

With regard to theoretical reflections, the history of marketing began with the attempt to add the variables product quality and distribution to the dominating price theory, which until then principally focused on the price and volume of

---

W. Mühl-Benninghaus (✉)
Humboldt Media Business School, Berlin, Germany
e-mail: wolfgang.muehl-benninghaus@culture.hu-berlin.de

products. The reason why this idea came up lies in the fact that already before 1900 many products were being produced that could facilitate or improve customers' lives without the target groups even knowing of their existence.

At this point early mass advertising was introduced. In order for advertising to be effective the target groups for the corresponding products had first to be found. To guarantee and, if possible, optimize target group coverage, the advertising industry and its potential carrier media, in mutual interest for both of them, kept on searching for new possibilities and methods to thoroughly link the aimed target group with the offered media contents. At first marketing was regarded solely in terms of sales. That is why pricing and addressing the corresponding target groups coined not only advertising, but also affected the branching out into different submarkets.

While due to the development of a homogeneous sellers' market the range for pricing kept shrinking, the relation between addressing target groups and the development of different media submarkets, each depending on its context, became increasingly evident. Therefore, in the second half of the nineteenth century, in Germany the printed press market emerged because due to the rising volume of ads the prices of press products dropped substantially in comparison to other products. Apart from this general development the advertising industry also directly influenced the emergence and make-up of specific press products. With regard to statistics the variety of media contents, which had been co-financed by marketing campaigns was mainly dependent on how the development of unit costs for a certain media product related to the demand of the market. It was due to this variety that before 1900 so-called "*Generalanzeiger*" ("general gazettes")[1] came into being and one of the best-known liberal German newspapers of before 1933, the *Berliner Tageblatt*, was founded. Not only the wide-coverage newspapers of big and medium-sized German cities owe their emergence to the increase in advertising around the 1900s. Also the existence of many of the small newspapers with a lesser circulation would have been unimaginable without the advertising industry and its search for a matching target audience. The same phenomenon holds true for the rapid growth of new popular magazines at the turn of the century.[2] The last 150 years clearly show that the economic competition in the media sector funded by advertising—or in other words the struggle for still higher advertising revenues—influenced the media market much more than journalistic rivalry in this sector. With regard to their contents, primarily the entertainment sections made up the part that decisively influenced economic competition in the media sector. Above all, media contents with emotional components were the ones that companies and ad agencies used to build up, maintain and strengthen customer relations. To varying degrees a "one-to-many-communication" aimed at building confidence among potential buyers regarding the products, services and other goods on offer. This especially holds true for the field of market communication. Against this background

---

[1] Translator's note: independent and mostly regional press products of mass appeal that also included advertisements.

[2] For more details see: Mühl-Benninghaus and Friedrichsen (2012, 129 ff.).

corporate communication predominantly focused for decades, up until the early 1960s, on the distribution of products.

In the course of the so-called "economic miracle" the satisfaction of people's essential needs lost its social relevance and marketing became more sales-oriented. At the same time the cost-per-unit of media products with a high variety of contents co-financed by marketing campaigns increasingly lost its significance. Much more important became how demand and supply with regard to their target groups correlated with each other. The reason for this development was the calculation of the advertising industry's costs according to the cost-per-mille-price. This calculation procedure implies—for the purpose of this approach—that the costs for placing ads and the advertising effect are widely decoupled from each other. To keep divergence loss in the advertising industry as low as possible many comprehensive market studies are, even until the present day, an important basis for companies to make their decisions concerning the advertising of a certain product: Which product will be advertised? Which medium will be used? What will the budget be? By this procedure the advertising industry tries to make sure that the target group is addressed as precisely as possible and that marketing objectives and communication objectives are reached as closely as possible within a certain limited advertising budget.

The transition from a product-oriented to a sales-oriented form of marketing coincided with the end of political social milieus. At the same time social milieus developed whose members still had a similar view of the world and a similar outlook and way of life, but now lacked the rigid boundaries those milieus used to have before. Moreover, the variety of values and lifestyles also increased. From the 1970s up to the year 2000 this development virtually gave the magazine market its initial spark. On the one hand this was due to the increasing pluralistic image of the world and the individual needs shaping society, and on the other hand to a change in the understanding of marketing. In the last third of the twentieth century the understanding of marketing was characterized by a stronger segmentation of the markets and an increasing specialization on individual needs.

New establishments of media products relevant for the advertising sector such as magazines, and a transition within corporate communication coincided as they had already done 80 years before for the first time. In about 1900 the market became increasingly anonymous and forced companies to communicate with their potential customers above all by the means of printed ads. This pressure was the basis for the dramatic expansion of the newspaper market. By the 1970s corporate communication followed a marketing mix of changed product advertising and changed pricing procedures and distribution procedures to be able to better satisfy the needs of individuals and organizations. The obsolete distribution-oriented policy was replaced by a new communication policy because satisfying essential customer needs meant lesser effort and its realization became cheaper. New topics were treated reflecting the upcoming segmentation of the market and an increasing specialization on individual needs. Advertising and the rising branch of media, which generated advertising, were trying to adapt to the changing target groups with their new manifestation of social segmentation. With regard to this daily

Werbemarktentwicklung

Monetäre Medienanteile am Werbemarkt in %

Werbeträger	2000	2002	2004	2006	2008	2009	2010
Tageszeitungen	28	25	23	22	21	20	19
Fernsehen	20	20	20	20	20	20	21
Werbung per Post	15	17	17	16	16	17	16
Publikumszeitschriften	10	10	9	9	8	8	8
Anzeigenblätter	8	8	9	10	10	11	11
Verzeichnis-Medien	5	6	6	6	6	6	6
Fachzeitschriften	5	5	4	5	5	5	5
Außenwerbung	3	4	4	4	4	4	4
Hörfunk	3	3	3	3	3	4	4
Wochen-/Sonntagszeitungen	1	1	1	1	1	1	1
Online-Angebote	-	1	1	2	4	4	5
Filmtheater	1	1	1	<1	<1	<1	<1
Zeitungssupplements	-	-	-	<1	<1	<1	<1

Quelle: ZAW: Werbung in Deutschland 2010 & 2011, S. 17

Prof. Dr. Wolfgang Mühl-Benninghaus

Fig. 1 Development of the German advertising market between 2000 & 2010

newspapers profited from the strong confidence that recipients had in their contents. Based on this confidence they were able to accumulate a substantial monetary advertising volume far beyond the turn of the twenty-first century. At the same time they formed an important basis for an active corporate communication.

The increasing saturation of the market and the ongoing differentiation of society and markets in the 1980s evoked a form of marketing, which was mainly focused on underlining the uniqueness of their goods. Their contents did not only focus on client transactions any more. Instead customer relations gained importance. The new aim was to reinforce the relation with their customers and to enhance customer loyalty. Thus, the companies' need for communication grew substantially. This process implied that also within the companies the idea of a market-oriented corporate management gained importance.

The increase of social segmentation and the growth of market saturation required a stronger focus on communicative processes. Thus, when the dual broadcasting system was formed and when the expansion of the Internet started in the 1990s, the same process repeated itself that had already happened in 1900 within the newspaper market and that was already recognizable in the magazine market in the 1970s. The variety of national, regional and sometimes also local commercial broadcasting programs that in the late 1990s was at every household's disposal in Germany was only possible because marketing generated an increasing need in communication, which again refinanced this variety. In just a short period of time television became the medium where companies spend most in advertising and it has maintained this role until today. Even the immense growth in Internet advertising during the last years could not change this fact.

In specific terms the German advertising market between 2000 and 2010 developed as follows (Fig. 1).

This table also shows that currently everyone is exposed to advertising numerous times a day. The Institute for Marketing and Communication found out that every consumer in Germany is exposed to advertising about 6,000 times per day including outdoor advertising. However, consumers manage to only remember about three of these instances within a period of 24 h. The target groups are not able and not willing to receive advertising in this abundance.[3] That is why a high percentage of advertising expenditures are spent without reaching the desired goal or effect. According to current estimates more than 75 % of advertising does not reach the customer.[4] There are only two possible approaches to solve this problem: either the companies invest more financial resources in advertising to penetrate the markets with their own messages or they try to look for new ways and new contents to reach their target groups.

2 New Consumer Habits and Changes in the Usage of Media

Until the end of the twentieth century the sellers' market prevailed. This meant that the consumer behavior of conventional, quite consistent consumers was influenced crucially by their target group structure. This structure is mostly based on a certain milieu an individual person belongs to or is assigned to. As media reception is part of the general consumer behavior, one could assume that, particularly in the different media submarkets such as the magazine market or the television market, media usage and the actual material consumption match quite precisely. Furthermore, both media usage and material consumption showed a high level of habitualization with regard to recipients' or consumers' behavior. Those assumptions and results were the basis for the belief that advertising actually reached its marketing and communication objectives in the past, namely to attract its target groups.

At least since the turn of the century basic changes in the global and regional markets have been detected. In the 1990s many markets were already saturated in many consumption areas. This saturation process continued permanently and spread across an increasing number of market segments. In the wake of this development the outdated sellers' markets gradually became buyers' markets thus turning the former push markets into pull markets. At the same time the bonding force of social milieus abated and was increasingly replaced by individuals who now determined their own consumer behavior according to the great variety offered. Both of these developments were the reason why the consistency of media and consumer behavior began to fall apart, especially with regard to subsequent age cohorts. Suddenly, in this new market situation, much more often than before, consumer cultures of individuals that partly even

---

[3] Groß (2011).
[4] Langner (2009, p. 14).

opposed each other existed side to side within the same markets and media submarkets. Particularly in the media submarkets such as digital media and even more on the Internet, users do not follow strict habitual patterns, but act much more on an as-needed case-by-case basis.[5] These basic elementary changes in consumer behavior and in media usage make it increasingly difficult to predict the future consumer behavior of different populations.

These circumstances will inevitably have a great impact on the traditional marketing and communication objectives of advertising. Especially those fields are affected where necessary decisions concerning advertising are made, for example booking strategies or selecting advertising material. Providers of information nowadays have to analyze their target groups much more precisely than they used to. They have to consider much more carefully than in the past which fields of interest to build upon or to serve, and which events they want to use to reach their target groups. Moreover, they need to consider how these processes can be implemented accordingly. With this in mind it has also to be mentioned that in the past recipients developed more and more strategies to evade advertising. Consumers who usually possess longtime media experience have embarked on a strategy of selective perception: they perceive only what they want to perceive. This attitude can be regarded as a form of advertising resistance, which media are trying to handle by adopting different measures. Private broadcasting corporations, for example, pursue the so-called "opting-out"-tactic, which means using a split-screen when commercials are aired. On the Internet "pop-ups" fulfill the task of attracting the necessary attention to commercial messages. Several magazines assist the readers' effort in evading advertisements to a certain degree by using a quick finder layout. However, it remains to be seen whether the advertising industry is going to accept this policy when applied permanently.

The suggested elementary changes in the markets and in the marketing sector correspond with significant changes in media development. In the 1990s primarily television, radio broadcasting, films, cinema, CDs/DVDs, and press products met the demand for entertainment and information. Around 2000 developments began to change this situation fundamentally. For great parts of the population the Internet gained more and more importance. However, with regard to the total population receiving this new medium, the time people used other media such as radio broadcasting and television was not significantly affected. Nevertheless, the continuous and sometimes dramatic increase of Internet usage showed that fundamental changes in media usage were about to set in (Table 2).

These figures show that television currently undisputedly holds the number one spot with regard to both coverage and—as the following table illustrates—the average usage per day (Table 1).

---

[5] Allensbach Institute for Public Opinion Research/Infosys Limited (2011, p. 4).

Table 1 Media coverage between 1995 and 2010 for persons over 14 years of age (Mon.–Sun., 5.00 a.m.–12 a.m., data shown as percentages)

	1995	2000	2005	2010
Television	83	85	89	86
Radio Broadcasting	75	85	84	79
Daily Newspaper	65	54	51	44
Internet	–	10	28	43
CD/LP/MC/MP3	16	21	28	25
Book	21	18	23	21
Magazine	22	16	17	11
Video/DVD	4	5	4	4

Source: Long-term study in mass communication as executed by ARD/ZDF

Table 2 Media usage per day between 1995 and 2010 (Mon.–Sun., 5.00 a.m.–12.00 a.m. (entire FRG), persons over 14 years of age, in min. per day)

	1995	2000	2005	2010
Television	158	185	220	220
Radio Broadcasting	162	206	221	187
Daily Newspaper	30	30	28	23
Internet		13	44	83
CD/LP/MC/MP3	14	36	45	35
Book	14	18	25	22
Magazine	11	10	12	6
Video/DVD	3	4	5	5

Source: Long-term study in mass communication as executed by ARD/ZDF

According to these figures even in the twenty-first century the vast majority of viewers still prefer a linear program. When radio broadcasting is also included—referring to the total population in Germany—the lean-back-usage of the programs offered still dominates the whole field of media usage quite evidently.

These figures illustrating coverage and time of usage seem to be quite explicit. However, they are blurring the dramatic changes in user behavior that are already at hand today. As is true for all historical changes in media usage, the figures emanate from subsequent age cohorts because they were the ones who have shaped future media behavior for the society as a whole in the last decades.[6] Accordingly, these changes deserve special attention.

Currently, almost 100 % of Germany's teenagers and young adults under 30 years of age are using the Internet on a regular basis. This means that their time of usage is significantly above the average usage time of the total population. Unlike older age cohorts the increased Internet usage of teenagers and young adults affects

---

[6] See. i.a.: Meredith and Schewe (2002).

Table 3 Media coverage of 14- to 29-year-olds between 2000 and 2010 (Mon.–Sun., 5.00 a.m.–12.00 a.m., data shown in percentages)

	2000	2005	2010
Television	83	83	77
Radio Broadcasting	80	78	68
Daily Newspaper	36	31	26
Internet	17	46	73
CD/LP/MC/MP3	41	54	53
Book	18	22	22
Magazine	12	12	7
Video/DVD	9	8	6

Source: Long-term study in mass communication as executed by ARD/ZDF

Table 4 Media usage time of 14- to 29-year-olds between 2000 and 2010 (Mon.–Sun., 5.00 a.m.–12.00 a.m. (entire FRG), in min. per day)

	2000	2005	2010
Television	180	190	151
Radio Broadcasting	173	164	136
Daily Newspaper	16	13	10
Internet	25	79	144
CD/LP/MC/MP3	73	101	80
Book	22	29	30
Magazine	6	7	4
Video/DVD	8	12	8

Source: Long-term study in mass communication as executed by ARD/ZDF

not only the markets of press products, sound carriers and cinema, but also the television and radio broadcasting market. This thesis is to be verified by the coverage in the corresponding age groups (Table 3).

These changes detectable on the basis of media coverage have already been provoking significant changes in the usage time of traditional media amongst subsequent age cohorts for more than one decade (Table 4).

The present data convincingly indicate a general media change for subsequent age cohorts. This process cannot be halted because the availability of new access technologies will increase even more in the future, transmission speed will continually rise, and the costs of digital communication are most likely to drop. Accordingly, the reason why the great dimensional change in media usage in reference to the total population of Germany is only partly noticeable seems to be the onion-like structure of the demographic development.

Due to the rise of the Internet the digitalization of contents expanded in the first decade of the twenty-first century and led to an enormous multiplication of media offerings and contents. This development coincided with a dramatic surge in different storage devices and its associated multiplication of various playing devices. Young audiences always had a penchant for storage devices such as records, tape recorders, cassette recorders or walkmans. Eventually, an entire age cohort was influenced by MP3 players. The possibility to download and store music or video files on a PC, cell phone, or laptop and to subsequently play them everywhere and as often as desired, changed media usage and accelerated the processes that were already changing. The last table does indeed show that the reception of "canned goods" declined after 2005, but nevertheless in 2010 50 % of young adults between 14 and 29 years of age actually used music on their own storage devices on a daily basis. The reception of own resources has had a great influence on the decline of the listening time of radio broadcasting. The visible changes in media usage amongst young age cohorts also changed the expectations placed on the design of audio-visual media.

The rapid development of mobile technologies before, but especially after the year 2000 serves as a good example for this phenomenon. By the end of 2006 the penetration rate of mobile telephony participants had reached already 100 % with regard to the total population of Germany. It shows that mobile telephony participants often use several mobile devices. In parallel to the proliferation of mobile end devices, the drastic surge in call minutes, and the usage intensity of mobile data services, a sustainable progress regarding network-based transmission standards of voice-based and data services for the dissemination of information as well as for interactive communication occurred. The differentiation of reception devices for stationary and mobile services and its associated variety of playing devices for digital contents dramatically increased the number of basic platforms for media usage. Simultaneously, different but also identical contents were available via various access ways. This implies that contents called up via mobile services, the Internet, or other digital storage media are available for everyone and that they accordingly may be put together autonomously for the creation of an individual information and entertainment program. Due to the expansion of the Internet and the various mobile platforms, the lean-back-usage of media contents is increasingly replaced by an active combination of individual media programs. This tendency holds true for the entire usage of media. At a theoretical level there is a difficulty detectable that has been present for years: on the one side there is the increasingly detailed information search spurred by the Internet and mobile applications and—even if only partly—its associated reaction by the media market. On the other side there is the obsolete separation of mass and individual communication, which is still being maintained.

The users' mostly long-term experience with network contents is the basic precondition for users to be able to gather information everywhere. Moreover, motivated by this new infrastructure they are also willing to provide information on the Web.[7] Information about companies and products are data that are often being searched for on a regular basis on the Internet and on mobile services. As the

---

[7] Busemann and Gescheidle (2011, pp. 360–369).

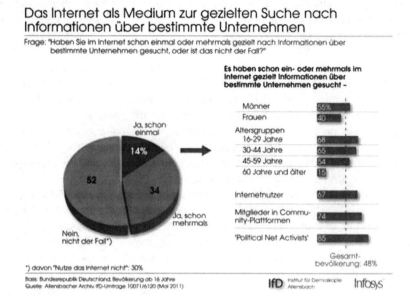

Fig. 2 Search for companies via Internet

following graphic shows, more than half of the German population has already searched for information about companies and institutions utilizing the Web. This tendency applies to the general usage of the Internet and particularly to subsequent age cohorts. Official webpages, however, are in the center of attention independently of age groups. They have been called up by 91 % of Internet users looking for specific information about certain companies. The next most visited webpages were the online lexica Wikipedia and the webpages of media and social network companies. The latter ones were still visited by about 19 % of the users. Sixteen percent of this user group also logged on to forums or groups of social networks.

The search for information on the Internet is mostly focused on company set-ups and fields of activity as well as products and services of companies. Price comparisons, test reports, evaluations, and comments of other users are frequently called up. Forty-two percent of users are also interested in job offers, whereas, for example, the social commitment of companies hardly attracts any attention on the Internet.[8] Therefore, the Internet is the most powerful of all media to form an opinion about companies and their products and services (Fig. 2).

With so many different web offers emerging companies and institutions are losing their interpretation sovereignty over their products and services. That is why they are increasingly being forced to observe more intensively than before how their actual and potential customers are forming their opinions. Accordingly, they have to involve this in their decisions and need to react on trends and statements

---

[8] Allensbach Institute for Public Opinion Research/Infosys Limited (2011, 29 ff.).

respectively. This means that also previous forms of crisis communication need to be rethought because announcements, statements, or other communicative problems may spread at a yet unknown speed. Consequently, new preventive strategies need to be developed. In order to do so, specific contact persons have to be provided for the users. These contact persons who actually have to be available and authorized to make decisions need to be in charge of complaints in terms of services not yet rendered, quality standards of products or other questions users may have about the company.

The reason for this development relates to the fact that via the Internet and mobile devices in a very simple way users are enabled to take on an active role in the production of contents typical for mass media, namely in the form of user-generated content or when chatting. Just like easy to use web applications in the software arena, digital technologies give users the possibility to communicate with each other without having to acquire specific knowledge in how to use the hardware or software. Internet and mobile applications summarized under the term Web 2.0 are the reason why networks are becoming spaces that are formed and designed by their users and that also may influence the public opinion. Accordingly, certain activities that formally were to be evaluated as individual communication such as the membership in Facebook and other social networks or simply clicking the Like button are becoming mass phenomena. Generally, these developments indicate that one-to-many communication is losing its importance, whereas many-to-many communication is gaining significance. Not only the dissolution of obsolete milieus and the emergence of pull markets, but also the synchronously proceeding fundamental changes in media usage are forcing marketing and distribution departments and press offices of companies or organizations to rethink current communication and especially marketing concepts.

3   New Challenges of Marketing

Traditional ways of life are coming to an end, markets are saturated and provoke changes in consumer behavior, individuals are able to use new communication technologies independently from their whereabouts: all of these changes are fostering a tendency of individualization within modern societies. In contrast to how it used to be in the past, today everyone is, with an increasing frequency, responsible for his own status within society. With so many social changes happening and due to the constant accessibility of every individual in many urban spaces, especially in highly developed countries, a "networked individualism"[9] is beginning to take form. This phenomenon is based on the spreading of interlinked individual communities ("personal communities")[10] that has been going on for several years

---

[9] Wellmann (2002).
[10] Kneidinger (2010, p. 56).

now because access to communication networks has become so easy. According to Manuel Castells, who with regard to this development speaks of a network society,[11] new interest communities with varying degrees of bonding are constantly forming and they add to the real physical communities or overlap with them. For Castells the important difference between virtual and real communities is the spatial infinity of virtual community members. In the virtual world predefined social structures and program structures are less frequently existent than in real communities. This is the reason why virtual communities are the ones which most promote the process of individualization. They offer yet unimaginable possibilities for persons to present themselves in every desired role and to fulfill themselves to an almost unlimited degree. The communities that arise from this range of possibilities are more versatile and therefore also smaller than former ones. The diversification of audience interests that is detectable is putting an end to many of the previous forms of the media-evoked bundling of attentiveness and of themes and interests, for example through stars, bestsellers or music charts.

The immediate effects of this development are discernible in the still ongoing decrease in production units and partly also in sales numbers. In the media branch this can best be verified in the sound carrier industry. For quite some years sales numbers of CDs and release numbers of individual tracks have been dropping. In the wake of this overall development the risk for producers increased because due to reduced production units the value compensation between successful and less successful products cannot be performed so easily anymore. Moreover, it has become more difficult to attract the necessary public attention with the offers they have due to the following three causes: First, previous ways of attracting attention do not work anymore. Second, the existing supply with digital contents is constantly growing because the barriers to enter the market with these products have started to become lower long since. This also has caused the information width to surge. Third, previous forms of product storage and product costs as well as the costs for the provision of products are quite low, so that they may be called up for an almost unlimited period of time (long tail). Thus, the surge in the width of information is even complemented by dated contents. The range of this development has to be quantified only in part. It is expressed in the steep upward curve of domains and webpages on the Web. An ending of this process is not yet visible.

4 Total Sites Across All Domains

The steep upward curves also indicate that traditional information brands and possibilities are complemented by the vast variety of online offerings, which are now spreading faster than analog media contents and which are, due to search engines and the variety of existing platforms, also more tangible and visible for

---

[11] Castells (2001, 408 ff.).

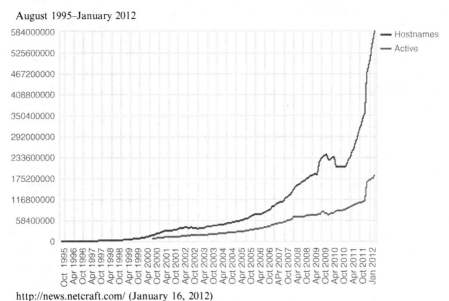

http://news.netcraft.com/ (January 16, 2012)

Fig. 3 Total Sites across All Domains

everyone (Fig. 3). This fact does not only influence the provision of information and search options, but also the role of previous gatekeepers for public opinion-forming such as television commercials or journalists. They are actually losing their former function because they increasingly have to compete with other orientation opportunities of users such as search engines or links on the Web.

Hence, outdated communication hierarchies are increasingly replaced by the numerous possibilities to participate in communication that the Internet and especially the Web 2.0 offers to its users. Accordingly, with the support of these offerings small, network-like spaces that are partially public are developing and undermining the communicative power companies, institutions and other product providers used to have. An important basis for this is the higher credibility of independent opinions that the majority of recipients assigns to the users. According to the market research institute *DSaF* this applies to 56 % of the interviewees.[12] The influence seems to be particularly high when official opinions about products and services are recognizably given by experts who have already suffered from partial damage. This influence I mentioned is even intensified by the possibility of individual users to team up to get their interests or concerns pushed through. On the Web in general and in social networks in particular, communication is turning into a valuable currency that may spread at a yet unknown speed. It is, however, narrowed

---

[12] Schengber (2011).

down by the limited time of users. This holds true for both criticism and the willingness to contribute to user-generated content. Moreover, different user profiles can undeniably be found on the Web. They appear in all different nuances from creators, the ones who put their own content on the Internet, up to inactive users, who do not pay any attention to the social web. With regard to this, Nielsen elaborated the "90-9-1-rule." According to this rule 90 % of users are listeners ("lurkers"), nine percent contribute content sporadically and only one percent of users participates and publishes content on the Web on a regular basis.[13]

In spite of the mentioned limitations this process implies that companies and all other traditional gatekeepers of information are increasingly losing control over the communicative messages they are disseminating as soon as they are placed on the Internet. The reason for this development is based on the conversational communication on the Web where all participants are equal. So, within the Web community this situation limits the possibilities for information providers to influence information according to their own interests or as originally intended. This fact means that products, services, and companies or institutions are generally exposed more intensely to the public. The growing loss of control over contents challenges them to take preventive measures for crisis communication, which too has to follow the conversational pattern typically used on the Web. The general loss of control over their own information leads to the situation that companies are not willing to take the supposed risk of conversational communication.[14] However, what they do not realize is that the discussions are taking place anyway whether directly or indirectly affected parties participate in them or not.

It may become problematic for product providers that contents published online usually do not disappear and may therefore be associated with the companies at all times. This also applies to users and customers. Accordingly, this gives the advertising industry the chance to use this gained knowledge to specifically address customers. As a side effect of the digital communication on the Internet basically it can be said that the Web serves as an archive. Even if users' rights are still underdeveloped on a worldwide basis, the Web has the power to make companies and also users more transparent.

It has already been pointed out that the conventional advertising and marketing measures are currently losing their significance because customers are confronted with thousands of advertising messages every day. This situation is unsatisfying for all parties. One solution may be viral marketing as a strategic means of communication within an interlinked public. As a result of this changing process towards new communication technologies, conventional marketing is transforming into individual marketing making use of the great variety of digital channels with an individual and specifically target-group-oriented appeal. That way viral marketing

---

[13] Nielsen (2006).

[14] Fink and Fuchs (2011).

is reconstructing the communicative processes that can generally be observed in modern societies. The precondition of these changing processes is that products reflecting individual needs correspond with the individually designed communication demands of marketing. Here, just like marketing in the age of analog technology, emotionalized contents have a particularly important strategic role to play. Longtime recipient loyalty towards certain media or successful marketing campaigns was and still is almost always linked to emotionalized contents. A new development, however, is that viral marketing allows individual users or recipients to share their insights and findings with a community of interested participants. That way online content may be utilized by a great number of consumers and affected companies. Consumers may be more interested in user-related questions whereas companies may use the comments as suggestions for how to improve their offerings. In order for users to take interest in the topics presented on the Web, communities are required to provide social gratifications regarding the contents placed online.[15]

This fact significantly influences the nature of media networks and its associated value-added process. In the past the boundaries in media production and their relations to media markets were clearly structured and usually comprehensible from the outside. In the wake of digitalization the traditional added value is changing. "Company boundaries are becoming blurred. The interface of companies and markets, the clear differentiation between the inside and the outside is fading. Instead joint organizational forms of companies and markets are becoming more frequent, for example network organizations, cooperation networks, virtual organization structures, or telecollaborations. They have resulted from the reactions to new market and competition conditions and the possibilities offered by new information and communication technologies. (...) Consequently, rather solid production technologies, long-term organizational forms, and management structures are giving way to more flexible forms that may be adapted to new conditions more rapidly."[16]

This results in an open space for all kinds of possible solutions when new offerings are in the process of being developed. This space may then be filled up with ideas by cooperative and voluntary collaborations between producers and customers as well as users and companies. However, this trend is not only due to new technologies and its associated communication possibilities. The process of individualization that is now visible and the changing structure of needs that comes along with it are increasingly preventing companies from solely fulfilling all their customers' wishes.

As the individualization increasingly influences the strategy of added value, also the requirements of marketing have to be designed accordingly. Of course,

---

[15] Stafford (2004, pp. 259–288).
[16] Reichwald and Piller (2009, p. 32).

conventional forms of advertising will still be in use as well as those forms that are already being used and cultivated in the various media networks. Nevertheless, it is inevitable to keep introducing new strategies, contents, or forms of addressing customers in order to reach different networks. As pointed out by Charlene Li et al. important preconditions to reach this goal are clear definitions of market relevant company objectives as well as respective planning processes, a precise determination of target groups, and ultimately a strategy taking into account technologies and their progressions.[17]

Conclusion

The numerous factors that have to be taken into account to arrange marketing campaigns in social media are also inevitably changing the way how these campaigns are implemented. In the analog era companies focused all their attention in advance on how marketing activities and commercial spots were constructed regarding their precisely elaborated contents, designs, and dramaturgy not least because once the campaigns were initiated there communicative and creative/dramaturgic contents could hardly be changed any more. However, this fact is currently changing. Outdoor advertising and other forms of advertising, for example, are now mainly serving the purpose to call attention to the corresponding Internet addresses prompting users to visit them. That means that advertisers have the chance to save money because the costs for Web campaigns are much lesser than for campaigns in other advertising carriers such as daily newspapers, general interest magazines, or television. Advertisers may also use this fact to interlink their target groups by utilizing the networks and to influence opinion forming in favor of their own added value.

When potential target groups are regarded from this point of view, you may conclude that all communicative activities within networks are inevitably constructed as long-term arrangements that require time-intensive counseling. Accordingly, the costs that have been saved from waiving the production of traditional commercials can now be invested in personnel costs. The variety of information provided on the Internet has already shown that marketing can build a reputation only to a limited degree. However, there are exceptions, above all the activities that are initiated in the networks themselves. With this in mind, communication contents and activities may be tested until surveys and all other forms of purposeful media monitoring, also including coverage measurements, show that the intended target group and the implicated communication objectives are being reached. For this purpose various parameters may be used to indicate how a company's image on the Internet actually is. There are numerous computer programs that can be applied to collect data. The most important key figure is the traffic that is reached within a certain period of

---

[17] Li and Bernoff (2009, 75 ff.). The authors use the acronym "POST" (people, objectives, strategy, and technology) to refer to the described planning process.

time because it indicates how much attention users are paying to the subject. Furthermore, there are also "authority" and "influence." Adequate measurement parameters are the numbers of incoming links regarding the contents placed online as well as the increasing number of feed-subscribers, followers, or fans. Further important factors also are the participation rate, conversion rate, transactions, and the sustainability. The latter ones can be measured according to the participation numbers in blogs. With regard to this, as a general rule it can be stated: The longer the users' commitment endures, the more successful the initiated campaign is. [18]

By and large it can be stated that communication has always been a central category when individuals, companies, institutions etc. operated on the markets. Since the middle of the nineteenth century one-to-many-communication that was dominating the era of analog media has shifted the dominance of contents on all levels of marketing more and more towards the side of the communicators. When asked about what they remember about a brand or when they purchased a product, the only option left for recipients was usually to just react to these activities. Presently, one-to-many-communication is beginning to give way to many-to-many-communication. In the course of this development, marketing is now confronted with active consumers on the Web who have their own demands. If companies do not want to lose control over their own contents they need to react on this development in terms of marketing contents and in a wider sense also in terms of products and services. However, this also implies that all participants will be confronted with higher security risks not only with regard to data protection, harmful software or spyware.

It is equally problematic that no user rights for networks have been defined by the legislator for either side. This is a deficit that will inevitably affect the acceptance and economy of digital communication within networks in general and of marketing in particular. This is also the reason why the legislator is required to fill this legal vacuum. This conclusion is not only due to the fact that a growing number of companies must be open to flexible data availability in all of the different networks and platforms because Web 2.0 applications are spreading at an obviously unstoppable speed, especially among young adult users. It will also be the only way for companies to secure their marketing activities in the long run, thus creating the basis for a successful added value. The short history of the Internet has already clearly shown that the professional and private usage of the Web is beneficial for both parties. Therefore, the total added value will suffer when users in their domestic environments face up to the further development of networks only in part. However, they will only face up to those requirements voluntarily when their security is guaranteed for a permanent and efficient network usage and when they know who exactly has access to their data and who may see into their activities on the Web.

---

[18] Weinberg (2010, 338 ff.).

References

Allensbach Institute for Public Opinion Research; Infosys Limited. (2011). *Social Media, IT & Society 2011.* Frankfurt/M.
Busemann, K., & Gescheidle, C. (2011). Web 2.0: Aktive Mitwirkung verbleibt auf niedrigem Niveau. *Media Perspektiven, 7–8,* 360–369.
Castells, M. (2001). *Der Aufstieg der Netzwerkgesellschaft. Teil 1 der Trilogie Das Informationszeitalter.* Opladen: Leske.
Fink & Fuchs. (2011). *Social media governance 2011. Kompetenzen, Strukturen und Strategien von Unternehmen, Behörden und Non-Profit-Organisationen für die online-Kommunikation im Social Web.* Retrieved Febraury 26, 2012 from http://www.ffpr.de/de/news/studien/social_media_governance_2011.html
Groß, W. (2011). *Erfolgsfaktoren und Weiterempfehlungsanreize bei viralen Spots.* Retrieved February 26, 2012 from http://www.mediadesign.de/blog/erfolgsfaktoren-und-weiterempfehlungsanreize-bei-viralen-spots
Kneidinger, B. (2010). *Facebook und Co.: Eine soziologische Analyse von Interaktionsformen in Online Social Networks.* Wiesbaden: VS Verlag Für Sozialw.
Langner, S. (2009). *Viral marketing. Wie Sie Mundpropaganda gezielt auslösen und Gewinn bringend nutzen.* Wiesbaden: Gabler.
Li, C., & Bernoff, J. (2009). *Facebook, YouTube, XING und Co. – Gewinnen mit Social Technologies.* Munich: Carl Hanser.
Meredith, G., & Schewe, C. (2002). *Defining markets, defining moments: America's 7 generational cohorts, their shared experiences, and why businesses should care.* New York: Wiley.
Mühl-Benninghaus, W., & Friedrichsen, M. (2012). *Geschichte der Medienökonomie. Eine Einführung in die traditionelle Medienwirtschaft von 1750 bis 2000.* Baden-Baden: Nomos.
Nielsen, J. (2006). *Participation inequality: Encouraging more users to contribute.* Retrieved February 26, 2012 from http://www.useit.com/alertbox/participation_inequality.html
Reichwald, R., & Piller, F. (2009). *Interaktive Wertschöpfung.* Wiesbaden: Gabler.
Schengber, R. (2011). *Social media: Einfluss auf das Kaufverhalten im Internet. Eine Studie.* Retrieved February 26, 2012 from http://www.dsaf.de/downloads/Studie_-_Social_Media_Einfluss_auf_das_Kaufverhalten_im_Internet.pdf
Stafford, T. S. (2004). Determining uses and gratifications for the Internet. *Decision Sciences, 35,* 259–288. doi:10.1111/j.00117315.2004.02524.x/full.
Weinberg, T. (2010). *Social media marketing.* Köln: Strategien für Twitter, Facebook & Co.
Wellmann, B. (2002). *Little boxes, globalization, and networked individualism.* Retrieved Febraury 26, 2012 from http://homes.chass.utoronto.ca/~wellman/publications/littleboxes/littlebox.PDF

Social Networks as Marketing Tools for Media Companies

Alfonso Sánchez-Tabernero, Julián Villanueva, and José Luis Orihuela

1 From Web 1.0 to Web 2.0

The first era of the Web as a platform enabling access to digital information linked via hypertext was bookended by the launch of *Mosaic*, the first online graphic web browser, in 1993 and the publication of Tim O'Reilly's groundbreaking article, "What Is Web 2.0: Design Patterns and Business Models for the Next Generation of Software", in 2005.

Initially by means of the manual index *Yahoo*! and later through the algorithmic internet search engine *Google*, users of the Web in its original form accessed contents made available by companies and experts that drew on the technical knowledge and skills required to encode information in HTML format and, via file transfer protocols such as FTP, upload contents to web servers.

The radical transformation of the Web began when the content management tool *Blogger* went into operation in August 1999: the Internet gradually changed from a platform enabling consultation into a platform facilitating participation and conversation (Orihuela 2006).

The emerging panorama of the social Web or Web 2.0 was shaped by the launch of the collaborative global encyclopedia *Wikipedia* (2001), by the proliferation of services that enable the uploading and sharing of contents and links (*Delicious*, 2003), images (*Flickr*, 2004), videos (*YouTube*, 2005), and—in particular—by the appearance of general purpose social networks (Facebook, 2004) and the microblogging platform *Twitter* (2006). Inspired by the *Cluetrain Manifesto* (1999), the defining metaphor for Web 2.0 is "conversation".

A. Sánchez-Tabernero (✉) • J.L. Orihuela
School of Communication, University of Navarra, Spain
e-mail: astabernero@unav.es

J. Villanueva
IESE, University of Navarra, Navarra, Spain

The first thesis of the *Manifesto* written by Rick Levine, Christopher Locke, Doc Searls and David Weinberger states that "markets are conversations", thus structuring a paradigm of relations between companies and clients on the Web based on the model framed by traditional markets in which buyers and sellers agree on prices and conclude transactions by means of intercommunication.

2 Online Social Networks

As virtual spaces of social interaction, social networks transfer "conversation" to a public and global field where transparency is the preeminent cultural value, a development noted by Scoble and Israel in *Naked Conversations* (2006), which carries the apt subtitle, "How blogs are changing the way business talk with customers".

Given that social media grant individuals a public voice that can be communicated globally without the need for the traditional media intermediaries, corporate communication strategies, as well as political communication processes and journalistic procedures, have had to adapt in relation to models of audience interaction.

The evolution of web users in the field of public communication, whom Rosen refers to as "The People Formerly Known as the Audience", has transformed social networks into a new information arena where centralized agenda-setting procedures give way to distributed trending topics, and the professional mediation enacted by 'gatekeepers' is reconfigured as a socially-based prescription system of 'friends'.

3 Changing Media Attitudes Towards Social Networks

From the first online editions of traditional media in 1994 or so to the popularization of social networks that may function as platforms for political mobilization (the "Arab Spring" in 2010) onwards, the communication media as companies and journalism as an institution have gradually refined their view of the significance and impact of web-user participation in social media.

The Iraq War (2003) disclosed the extent to which the voice of a single citizen of Baghdad, a blogger, could alter perceptions of the conflict worldwide. The work of Salam Pax, the pseudonym of the architect who published his letters to his friend Raed Jagger as *Where is Raed?* on *Blogger*, was a milestone on the road that was to lead to Julien Assange and *Wikileaks*, via Yoani Sánchez in *Generación Y*, and on to the thousands of demonstrators marching in streets throughout the world, prompting *Time* magazine to name "the protestor" as its Person of the Year, 2011.

The earthquakes in Haiti (2010), Chile (2010) and Japan (2011) as recounted on social networks in real time by witnesses and victims also modified the attitudes of media, broadcasters and journalists to the potential of social networks as sources of information.

The media have gradually included weblogs and microblogs in the catalogue of information contents they provide, using social networks to communicate their output more effectively and to enhance their interaction with sources, experts and the audience.

4 From Mass Media to Social Media

The incorporation of social networks into the public communication space and the need to voice the presence of communication media in emerging fields of participation and conversation have prompted media companies (from 2009 onwards) to define the role of "community manager" as a social media editor and/or participation coordinator. At the same time, online editions have begun in a general way to draw on the "social layer", whereby users participate in the task of sharing news contents on their favorite social networks.

The values linked to the culture of social networking sites, such as transparency, conversation, participation and community, call into question the hierarchical, centralized and unilateral model of traditional media and call for a paradigm shift that may bring them closer to the new culture of their audiences.

Insofar as they are aware of the fact that social networks comprise the new market of news contents, the mass media become social media. News-stories are rated, shared, commented on and go viral in virtual spaces of participation, and network-users take on the increasingly important role of social advisor in relation to information contents.

Although the prestige of news-titles as brands in social environments may function as a distinguishing feature and seal of quality on the information provided, there is a growing demand among web-users for a more conversational approach in the media, as well as a sharp critique of the top-down uses made of social platforms.

5 Social Networks and Marketing

Social networks disrupt the unilateral flow from content providers (heretofore professional suppliers) to users (who were not organized, remained relatively uncritical and adopted a basically passive attitude). At the same time, moreover, such networks restructure the relationship between companies and institutions that need to publicize their products and target audiences: in this functional field, too, the old paradigm, which might be described as an imposed monologue, gives way to the notion of sharing information and taking a range of perspectives into account—in short, rendering individuals more powerful (Whitlock and Micek 2008).

Media companies began to realize that social networks comprised both a threat and an opportunity for their commercial communication strategies: a threat, because dissatisfied audiences might undermine even the most ambitions communication campaigns based on the purchase of advertising times and spaces; and an opportunity, because a new tool has emerged which, used correctly, might enable the company to reach its target audiences in a very effective way.

Besides, Facebook, Twitter, YouTube, LinkedIn, Orkut, Flickr and other similar networking sites afford excellent opportunities to acquire detailed knowledge of the market; users leave a trail of information across the Internet regarding their interests, preferences, opinions and consumer habits. Hence, their behavior may be predicted in relation to changes in price, product design and service provision, distribution channel and the emergence of new competitors (Kozinets 2002; Cooke and Buckley 2007).

Our research project explores how Spanish companies are using social networks as part of their marketing plans. Data has been gathered from 681 management personnel, 42 of whom work in the communications sector. The information presented below discloses the existence of certain trends in this regard, but also a series of unknowns in relation to the development potential of social networks as marketing tools. So as to draw on a larger sample and to trace differences between media companies and other types of business in general, it was decided not to analyze media companies in isolation.

6 The Survey

The survey was designed by the authors and shown to a group of six leading executives from a variety of firms in different sectors. The survey was then re-designed: some questions were deleted, others were added, and a number were slightly revised. A pre-test was carried out with 15 participants, to test the length of the survey and the comprehensibility of each question. A final survey was then designed and administered.

The study was conducted via email with a sample comprising IESE alumni registered in the IESE alumni database on 15 October 2011 as currently working in Spain and holding one of the following job titles: CEO (all types), Board Director (all types), Director of Communications or Director of Marketing. Furthermore, the following key words were used to narrow the search: Marketing, *Marquetin*, Communication, *Comunicación*, *Mercado*, and *Mercadotecnia*. IESE is the business school of the University of Navarra; it is based in Barcelona and has a strong international profile.

The initial email announcing the survey was sent on Thursday, 17 November 2011 at 10:00, and a follow-up reminder was sent one week later on Wednesday, 24 November 2011 at 16:00. Upon receipt, participants were allowed and encouraged to forward the survey to the appropriate contact within their organization. The survey was closed on 1 December 2011 at 20:00. The original survey was sent to 5,489 contacts; 681 responses were generated (12 % response rate), from which a more limited group of media companies (42) was selected.

The management personnel who responded to the survey may be categorized as follows: 200 work for international corporations; 101 for large Spanish corporations; 292 for SMEs; 76 for other companies; while 12 did not specify the type of firm. The most frequently cited sectors were consumer goods companies (16 %), technology and telecommunications (13.1 %), raw materials, industry and construction (12.2 %), financial and real estate services (8.5 %), media companies (6.1 %) and consumer services (5.9 %).

The management positions were as follows: CEO, 49.9 %; Director of Marketing, 17.5 %; Brand Manager, 3.2 %; Director of Communications, 2.2 %; Consultant, 2.2 %; while 6.9 % did not specify the position, and 18 % ticked other positions. As regards company size, 353 had fewer than 100 employees; 199, between 100 and 1,000 employees; 76, between 1,000 and 10,000 employees in Spain (staff numbers for other countries were not included); 20, more than 10,000 employees; and 33 did not specify the number of employees working for the company.

The categorization of companies encompassed by the survey in relation to marketing budgets (including above-the-line, below-the-line and other marketing expenditure) was as follows: 155 invested less than €10,000 per year in the promotion of products and services in Spain; 200 companies invested between €10,000 and €100,000; 96, between €1m and €10m; 53, between €10m and €100m; 22, more than €100m; and 29 did not cite their marketing budget figures.

7 Initial Experiences

62.7 % of the 681 management personnel surveyed said that social media are included in their marketing plans, as compared with 35.1 % that do not use them (the remaining 2.2 % either did not know or did not respond). However, the percentages for media companies as a sector are markedly different. 85.7 % of media management personnel responded that their companies make active use of social networks, whereas 14.3 % do not do so. Such differences, which are mirrored in the responses to other questions, suggest that media companies are early adopters in the use of social networks, most likely due to the specific training of management staff in that field, as compared with equivalent personnel in other sectors.

Indeed, trends in the use of social networks by media companies are a reliable indicator of the increasing significance of social networking as a tool in the marketing mix of any organization. Social networks transform the way in which the relationship between company and target market may be understood. According to Tapscott and Williams (2006), the new commercial panorama is shaped by "mass collaboration", a trend showing that, as Pérez-Latre et al. (2010) aver, "message control by hierarchical management structures is increasingly under attack": the success of Wikipedia is emblematic in this regard.

A further significant result is that some managers (specifically, 7.1 % of the panel of experts who responded) said that their companies had used social media in their marketing plans at one time but ceased doing so. The reasons given for this decision were as follows: they did not have or had to let go people skilled in the professional management of social networks; difficulty with the measurement of results; the expected increase in sales was not achieved; and budget cutbacks. In all cases, the problems involved were circumstantial, relating both to difficulties with using social networks effectively as marketing tools and to the crisis affecting the advertising sector in general.

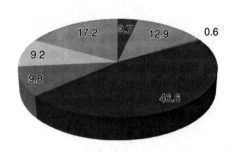

Fig. 1 Why are social networks not yet included in the marketing plan? (valid percent)

The initial experiences of social network use imply that they are not overestimated as marketing tools, nor do they amount to a fleeting fashion, nor is their usefulness limited only to a specific set of commercial sectors. As the information set out in Fig. 1 suggests, management personnel not yet using social networks in an ongoing way (179 of the 681 surveyed) tend to respond with a "wait and see" attitude, rather than with outright rejection.

If this data is compared with that for management responses in the communications sector, no managers in the latter see social networks as too risky, regard them as unnecessary, or lack the right talent in their companies; rather, two managers acknowledged that they do not yet use social networks because the budget does not cover them, and two others stated that they do not know how to use them well.

8 Usefulness of Social Media

Marketing actions have two basic objectives: to increase sales and to strengthen the company's reputation (De Mooij 2009); these two objectives are compatible with one another; and indeed, advertising campaigns frequently bring about an increase in the consumption of the advertised product or service, while simultaneously enhancing company recognition and reputation. Nevertheless, in each case, marketing teams pursue a particular set of priorities.

For instance, if a substance toxic to consumer health is discovered in a mineral water bottling plant, the marketing objective will be to restore the company's damaged reputation rather than to try to increase sales; and if an advertiser's goal is to increase trade volume, the objective will be to ensure persuasive messages reach the target market, not simply to sponsor a concert or sporting event.

The usefulness and effects of every part of the marketing mix used by different companies have been validated by a great deal of empirical evidence. Many researchers have studied years of business practice across a wide range of markets,

Social Networks as Marketing Tools for Media Companies

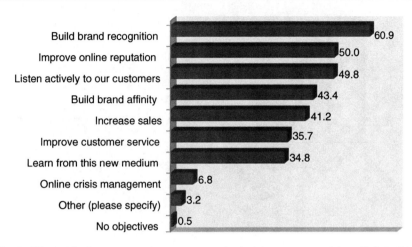

Fig. 2 What objectives prompted your company's decision to use social media? (multiple response) (valid percent)

thus disclosing that in a given competitive context each marketing tool may have a bearing on sales and/or corporate image (Trusov et al. 2009).

In contrast, however, the relative novelty of social media means that enabling analysis of their actual usefulness remains to be done. Figure 2 summarizes the responses of the experts surveyed in this regard. Of the total number involved, only 442 of the management personnel responded to this question, 36 of whom work in the communications sector. (Naturally, managers that do not use social networks as part of their media strategies did not respond to the question.) The data is presented in terms of multiple response because, as noted above, a marketing tool may pursue a variety of objectives at the same time.

The opinions recorded in Fig. 2 imply that social networks are more commonly used to strengthen brand image than to increase sales figures. The former goal involves the protection of the company's future, encompassing the following objectives: "improve online reputation", "listen actively to our customers", "build brand affinity", "build brand recognition" and "online crisis management" (normally crises relating to brand reputation). Almost all of these objectives generate a high response rate. At the same time, however, the response figures regarding sales results in the short term are also noteworthy: "increase sales", "improve customer service" and use social networks "as a promotional channel".

Social networks are also used frequently for purposes other than "external" marketing as such—that is, "as a corporate communication channel", as well as to learn from new media (Holzner 2009). However, the highest response figures, for all managers in general and management personnel in the communications sector in particular, relate to two specific objectives: "build brand recognition" and "improve online reputation".

Figure 3 presents the target interest groups that companies aim to reach by means of social networks. Above all, most companies endeavor to communicate with their

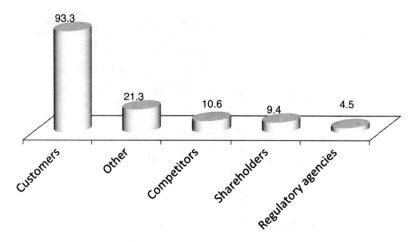

Fig. 3 In social media, what is your target interest group? (multiple response) (valid percent)

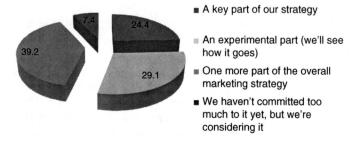

Fig. 4 How important are social media as part of your marketing plan? (valid percent)

customers, although the proportion (around 10 %) seeking to engage with their shareholders and competitors is likewise notable.

The importance of social networks as part of company marketing plans is also of significant interest in this regard. In other words, it is worth inquiring into whether the use of social media is still at an experimental stage, if its role is complementary, or if indeed it has already begun to play a leading part in corporate communication strategies. The managerial responses regarding this issue are presented in Fig. 4 above.

Two conclusions may be drawn from a reading of this data. First, the most common response is that social networks are already another element in the overall marketing plan; in a limited number of cases, they are a "key part" of such strategy, but they are also rarely regarded as a merely "experimental part". And second, a comparison of the figures for companies in general with the responses for media companies discloses that the latter attribute more importance to social networks than the former: only 11.1 % of media managers hold that social networks amount to a simply experimental part of their marketing plans.

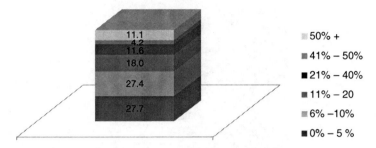

Fig. 5 What is the online marketing budget figure as a percentage of the marketing budget as a whole? (valid percent)

9 The Management of Social Media

As is the case for any marketing tool, the effectiveness of social networks may depend as much on how closely it is attuned to the intended objective (that is, whether or not it is an efficient way of achieving a particular business goal) as on correct management (Li and Bernoff 2008). Deficiencies in the use of a given tool may prompt the conclusion that the tool itself is defective, whereas in fact the problem may lie in the failure to use it correctly.

One way of managing social networks more effectively—or, at least, of attempting to limit the frequency of failure—is to learn from the experience of pioneering users. Some organizations have succeeded in enhancing corporate prestige and recognition through only quite moderate investment in social media. The opposite phenomenon may also be observed: other organizations have invested large sums in traditional advertising only to see sales figures stall and their reputation sink into decline as dissatisfied customers voice their discontent via social networks (Ojeda-Zapata 2008; Shih 2009).

Successful management of such media requires, first of all, that social network use be aligned with the company's overall commercial and marketing strategy. Those responsible for handling online communication must see their role as part of a corporate project and understand that their job is to influence the content and tone of virtual conversations, so as to support—or, at least, not to neutralize—the messages communicated via other channels. Hence, the management of social media involves a vision of the company as a whole, a coherent approach as regards general marketing plans, and a refined capacity to engage with other management personnel in the corporation itself.

Second, the correct level of investment and the selection of the most effective means of reaching a particular target audience must be decided on. As the figures in Fig. 5 show, 44.9 % of Spanish companies represented by respondents to the survey spend more than 10 % of their marketing budgets on online communication. This figure rises to 55.6 % for the communications sector. The number of companies investing more than half of their budgets in online marketing is also noteworthy in this regard.

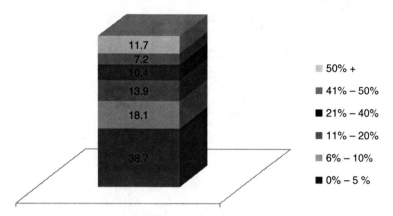

Fig. 6 What is the social media marketing budget figure as a percentage of the online marketing budget as a whole? (valid percent)

As a proportion of the expenditure on online marketing, the resources devoted to social networks is likewise increasing. The data in Fig. 6 shows that almost 30 % of the companies represented by managerial respondents to the survey spend more than 20 % of their online marketing budget on social networks. This figure rises to more than 40 % for companies in the communications sector.

The increasing importance of social networks prompted the definition of the position of "community manager", whose role is to manage the company's online presence and listen to customers, experts, suppliers, distributors, shareholders, regulators and competitors. The community manager role is different to the traditional activity of directors of marketing and sales, whose tasks were to convince the market, relate key product qualities and sell what had already been made. In marked contrast, the community manager is sensitive to opinions, dispenses with the monologue form of conventional advertisements, and aims to ensure that the company changes and improves through dialogue with critical voices expressed on the Internet.

This new vision of marketing makes customers partners or members of a community, whose ties to a company or product are stronger than that afforded merely by 'value-for-money'. One of the first significant instances of this kind in the political sphere was effected by Barack Obama's team, whose intelligent use of social networks rendered the 2008 election campaign a "citizens' movement" (Harfoush 2009). Likewise, many people feel a similar affinity for brands such as Apple, Google, Harley-Davidson, Starbucks, etc., leading them to see themselves as something more than mere customers. An equivalent phenomenon may be discerned as regards universities, sports teams and other bodies, which both enact particular sets of values and make active and effective use of social networks.

49.1 % of the companies surveyed have filled the role of community manager. The figure rises to 61.1 % for the communications sector. As the data presented in Fig. 7 shows, the most common tasks of the community manager comprise

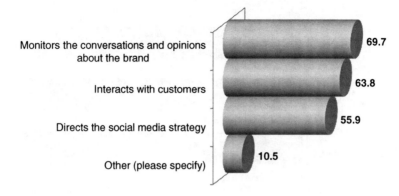

Fig. 7 What does the Community Manager do in your company? (multiple response) (valid percent)

channeling opinions about the company's brand(s), interacting with customers (answering queries, registering complaints, providing information that may more clearly explain controversial decisions, etc.) and, in general, managing the corporate strategy in relation to social media. In this regard, no significant differences emerge between the communications industry and other business sectors.

In practice, many organizations are learning to manage their presence on social networks by means of the traditional process of trial–error–correction. However, there must be clear communication between those responsible for the online marketing strategy and other management personnel at the company if this approach is to be successful. If online communication is regarded as a separate activity, to which only those directly responsible have access, the learning process is likely to be both slower and more costly.

10 Measuring Effectiveness

"Half the money I spend on advertising is wasted; the trouble is I don't know which half"; this celebrated phrase is attributed to John Wanamaker, a US businessman and one of the fathers of modern advertising. Whether or not this perplexing view was expressed by Wanamaker or by one of his confreres 100 years ago, that the overall goal of the advertising industry over the course of the last century has been to establish effective measurement systems for commercial communication tools is unquestionable.

In practice, the media that have garnered most expenditure (both above-the-line and below-the-line) are those that can give advertisers clear indications of the profitability of such investment. This accounts for the success of direct marketing, for instance, where the rate of positive responses may be measured in relation to product- and market-type. In contrast, however, it seems more difficult to assess the degree to which company reputation may be enhanced by sponsoring a concert or sporting event.

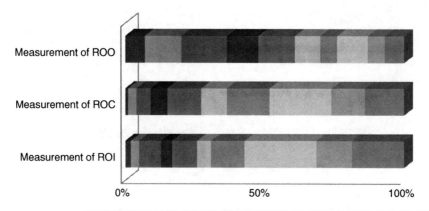

	Measurement of ROI	Measurement of ROC	Measurement of ROO
1 Very easy	2%	1%	7%
2	3%	3%	13%
3	8%	5%	16%
4	4%	6%	11%
5	9%	12%	13%
6	5%	9%	9%
7	12%	15%	6%
8	26%	22%	11%
9	13%	12%	6%
10 Very difficult	19%	14%	7%

Fig. 8 What do you think of the following measurement systems for social media effectiveness?

Therefore, the question of whether social networks are to be part of the set of marketing tools whose effectiveness is difficult to measure (such as sponsorship), and thus are not given priority in the company's communications budget, or if, on the other hand, their effectiveness may in fact be measured in quantitative terms, thus generating major investment by advertisers (Luan 2010), is of significant interest. In other words, if managers are able to measure their usefulness, social networks may play a leading role in communications strategies.

The managers consulted for this research project were surveyed as regards their opinion of three systems that measure the effectiveness of investment in social networks (Fig. 8): ROI (return on investment in social media communication), ROC (return on customer, quantified in terms of greater user affinity for the brand) and ROO (return on objectives, defined in advance as number of followers, responses, tweets, etc.). Most managers favor the latter measurement system, and regard both ROI and ROC as difficult to use. In this regard, the figures for media company managers correspond to those for other sectors, although they do tend to register fewer difficulties with measurement than other managers.

To offer a more detailed analysis of ROO, the measurement system favored by most managers, respondents were also asked to state what they saw as the best indicators of success in the use of social networks. The data on this issue is

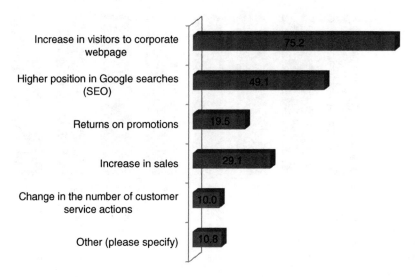

Fig. 9 What indicators do you use to measure the success of social media? (multiple response) (valid percent)

presented in Fig. 9 above. The most frequently cited objectives are to reach a high number of friends or followers and to increase the number of visitors to the corporate webpage; the third most common goal is to improve visibility on Google (SEO), although media company managers tend to regard the latter aim as less important.

The commitment to effectiveness prompts different kinds of presence on different social networks. The most common kind of activity is to open an account or profile, above all on Facebook or Twitter. Other companies, however, engage in debates through comment features on webpages and social networks, report the existence of fake webpages, or simply listen in on other online conversations.

Figure 10 below comprises information relating to the activity of the companies surveyed on the most popular social networks; participation in more general resources such as consumer blogs, which may become advisory sites or professional blogs normally hosted by news websites and portals, is also included. In order of popularity, Facebook, Twitter and Youtube are the most commonly used social networks. Such activity—especially on Twitter, Facebook and professional blogs—is higher for media companies than for companies in other sectors.

11 A Revolution in Marketing

A comprehensive account of the future of social networks as marketing tools must take into consideration their extraordinary rate of development over a very short time period. Despite the failure of a number of preliminary undertakings, such as SixDegrees, the first successful social networks were firmly established by 2002.

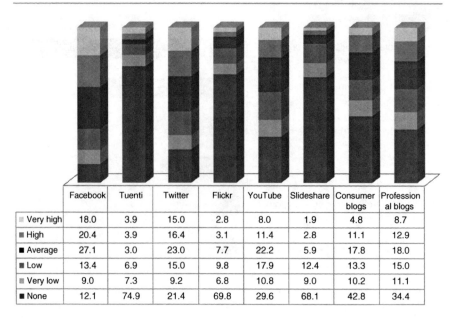

Fig. 10 What level of activity does your main brand achieve on each of these social media platforms? (valid percent)

In 2010, 6 years after its launch, Facebook had more than 500 million registered users. Likewise in 2010, Twitter (launched in 2006) reached a figure of 100 million users. These phenomena ground what Jenkings (2006) referred to as the culture of convergence and participation: a multiple flow across different platforms is produced, aggregating contents at successive stages, which makes it very difficult for any single organization to control the communication of messages.

Companies have begun to realize that audiences are no longer prepared to accept the old marketing paradigm, which was based on the unilateral communication of information (Whitlock and Micek 2008). Individuals have decided to use the power afforded by technology to ensure that their voices are heard. Managers have spent almost 10 years learning to accept the new rules of the game, which are shaped by participation and spontaneity. The first social networks were set up in 1997, but at the time few companies could see that a new marketing tool had emerged.

As the data in Fig. 11 makes plain, Spanish companies paid little or no attention to the new social media until 2007. Nevertheless, a dramatic revolution took place in the commercial sector thereafter: the early successes of pioneering organizations prompted a significant number of imitation strategies. A few companies saw the complementary effectiveness of social networks for their marketing plans, whereas other companies may only have taken action so as not to be left behind by their competitors; whatever the line of reasoning, most companies began to engage from then on in the conversations that arise on social networks.

Companies using this new commercial tool often follow procedures or set objectives according to the criteria of traditional advertising rather than social

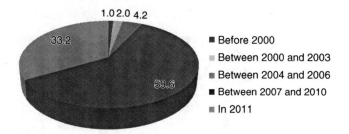

Fig. 11 In what year did you begin actively to devote resources to social media? (valid percent)

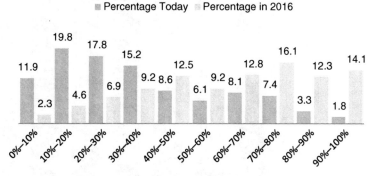

Fig. 12 What is the coverage or reach (% of potential customers) you think your brands may reach using a social media communications strategy?

networks. Little by little, they are learning from their mistakes; in recent years, they have learnt to effect better content management in such key areas as more successful persuasive resources, as well as the tone, frequency and length of messages.

The commercial power of social networks also depends on their popularity. Figure 12 summarizes managerial opinions regarding the reach of such media in the Spanish market as the situation stands and in a 5-year forecast. Even in 2016, a significant proportion of people may not belong to any social networks: 35.6 % of the managers surveyed felt that by 2016 social networks might function as a marketing tool capable of reaching less than half of the total population. However, network users offer advertisers a more attractive profile; and the growing spread of social networks is now beyond question (although the rate of growth may still be a matter of some debate).

Spanish managers appear to be convinced that target markets can be reached more economically via social networks than through traditional advertising actions: 81 % of those surveyed were more in agreement (scores from 6 to 10) than in disagreement (scores from 1 to 5) with the statement (see Fig. 13). In their view, too, social networks are also more effective than traditional advertising in relation to improving customer service and building brand recognition and brand affinity. However, social media are regarded as being less useful in increasing sales.

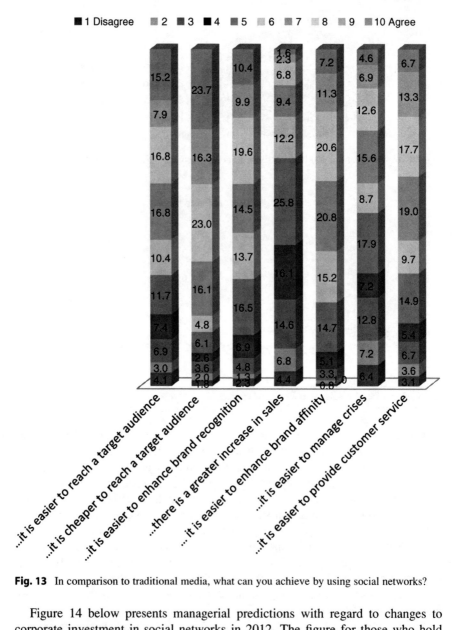

Fig. 13 In comparison to traditional media, what can you achieve by using social networks?

Figure 14 below presents managerial predictions with regard to changes to corporate investment in social networks in 2012. The figure for those who hold that such investment will be increased is almost exactly matched by the result for those who believe it will be decreased. This outcome may be attributed to two contradictory phenomena: managers have begun to acquire a much more refined understanding of the potential of social networks as marketing tools; at the same time, however, this realization is dawning in an extremely negative market context: the economy is in recession, the unemployment rate has reached 22 % of the active

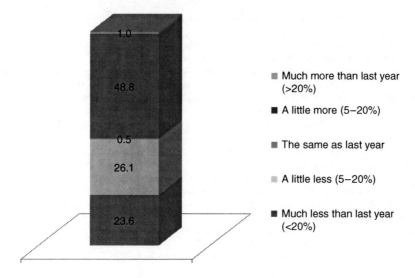

Fig. 14 Do you plan to invest more time and resources in social media this year? (valid percent)

population, financial institutions are weak, and there was 2.3 % fall in advertising expenditure in 2011. These circumstances have led experts in Spain to revise investment figures downwards to 1999 levels (Zenith 2012).

The research results discussed here would seem to suggest that the use of social networks as part of a company's marketing mix is now generally established. The main function of such media is to complement the role of traditional advertising, which tends to be more unilateral and focus on immediate increases in sales. Social networks are especially effective means of listening to consumers and improving customer services, so as to create a sense of belonging or community that may, in turn, strengthen brand values.

A growing number of individuals take part in the conversations that arise on social networking platforms. Such consumers, who tend to be well-informed and more demanding (because they know how to compare products and prices), are more likely to be suspicious of top-down messages that allow of neither response nor debate. Social networks will not replace older marketing tools, but they will complement their effectiveness.

References

Cooke, M., & Buckley, N. (2007). Web 2.0, social networks and the future of market research. *International Journal of Market Research, 50*(2), 267–291.

De Mooij, M. (2009). *Global marketing and advertising: Understanding cultural paradoxes.* London: Sage.

Harfoush, R. (2009). *Yes, we did. An inside look at how social medias built the Obama Brand.* Berkeley, CA: New Riders.

Holzner, S. (2009). *Facebook marketing: Leverage social media to grow your business*. Indianapolis: Que Publishing.

Rosen, J (2006) *The people formerly known as the audience*: Press Think, June 27 http://archive.pressthink.org/2006/06/27/ppl_frmr.html. Retrieved December 26, 2011

O'Reilly, T (2005) *Design patterns and Business models for the next generation of software*. Sep. 30 http://oreilly.com/web2/archive/what-is-web-20.html. Retrieved December 26, 2011

Locke, C., Searls, D., & Weinberged, D. (1999) The Cluetrain Manifesto http://www.cluetrain.com/. Retrieved December 26, 2011

Person (2011) The Protester http://www.time.com/time/person-of-the-year/2011/. Retrieved December 26, 2011

Jenkings, H. (2006). *Convergence culture: Where old and new media collide*. New York: New York University Press.

Kozinets, R. V. (2002). The field behind the screen: Using netnography for marketing research in online communities. *Journal of Marketing Research, 39*, 61–72.

Li, C., & Bernoff, J. (2008). *Groundswell: Winning in a world transformed by social technologies*. Boston: Harvard Business Press.

Luan, Y. J. (2010). Forecasting marketing-mix responsiveness for new products. *Journal of Marketing Research, 47*(3), 444–457.

Ojeda-Zapata, J. (2008). *Twitter means business: How microblogging can help or hurt your company*. Silicon Valley: Happy About.

Orihuela, J. L. (2006). *La revolución de los blogs*. Madrid: La Esfera de los Libros.

Pax, S. (2003). *The Baghdad Blog*. London: Guardian Books.

Pérez-Latre, F. J., Portilla, I., & Sánchez-Blanco, C. (2010). Social networks, media and audiences: A literature review. *Comunicación y Sociedad, 24*(1), 63–74.

Scoble, R., & Israel, S. (2006). *Naked conversations*. New York: Wiley.

Shih, C. (2009). *The Facebook era: Tapping online social networks to build better products, reach new audiences, and sell more*. Boston: Prentice Hall.

Tapscott, D., & Williams, A. D. (2006). *Wikinomics: How mass collaboration changes everything*. New York: Portfolio.

Trusov, M., Bucklin, R. E., & Pawels, K. (2009). Effects of word-of mouth versus traditional marketing: Findings from an internet social networking site. *Journal of Marketing, 73*(5), 90–102.

Whitlock, W., & Micek, D. (2008). *Twitter revolution: How social media and mobile marketing is changing the way we do business & marketing online*. Las Vegas: Xeno Press.

Zenith Media. (2012). *La inversion publicitaria en España*. Madrid: Zenith Media.

Managing New(s) Conversations: The Role of Social Media in News Provision and Participation

François Nel and Oscar Westlund

1 Introduction

News organisations had for most of the twentieth century produced and distributed news to largely passive audiences. Direct responses were limited to occasional letters or phone calls and monitored indirectly through periodic reports on circulation and readership, supplemented by intermittent market research. For newsrooms, feedback and other information about audiences were deemed important to gauge the popularity of the editorial outputs in order to ensure relevance and reputation. For boardrooms, audience metrics were principally important to gauge the commercial opportunities the journalism products offered to advertisers in order to ensure financial reward. For both, "audiences" or "publics" tended to abstractions (Bolin 2012) conceived as, amongst others, "recipients" and "products" (e.g. Ang 1991). As that century drew to a close, those perspectives were increasingly tested by the advent of the World Wide Web and other networked digital technologies.

These technologies are seen not only to have impacted on the sweep of news producers' activities—such as the platforms for news, production processes, news products and places of distribution—but also on their interactivity with news users (e.g. Fidler 1997). At the start of this Millennium, a key challenge for news publishers is how to profit from digital clicks and online conversations both editorially—and commercially.

F. Nel (✉)
University of Central Lancashire, Preston, UK
e-mail: FPNel@uclan.ac.uk

O. Westlund
University of Gothenburg, Vasastan, Sweden

IT University of Copenhagen, Copenhagen, Denmark

2 Changes in News Production

Scholars examining developing and preferred forms of journalistic practices have noted the opportunities that arise from greater openness to cooperation, co-creation and conversations (e.g. Bruns 2008, 2010; Singer et al. 2011), which is becoming increasingly associated with social media (Nel and Westlund 2012).

Woven through these discussions are notions about the benefits derived from harnessing the collective intelligence and contributions of the population (Lévy 1997), which have also come to be associated with the plethora of collaborative, social sharing initiatives that express the conceptualization of Web 2.0 (O'Reilly 2007). Many prominent organisations in the contemporary digital habitat (e.g. Google, Amazon, eBay) have been built on structures that enable and encourage user participation—in stark contrast to traditional occupational journalistic logic of professional control (Lewis 2012). Following from this thrust, and more generally, there are studies suggesting that there has been a power shift from journalists to users (Heinonen and Domingo 2008; Deuze and Fortunati 2010), which has not been universally welcomed by journalists (Quandt and Singer 2009) because, as Raviola (2010) argued, this change challenges long-held perceptions about what journalistic work includes and excludes. Other scholars who have explored these tensions suggest that journalists have resisted embracing the more participatory logic that drives social media. However, the picture that is emerging is multifaceted. Some journalist have held audiences at bay by steadfastly adhering to traditional practices, while others have ensured the inclusion performance of their audiences kow-tow to these traditional norms (e.g. Williams et al. 2011; Westlund 2011, 2012a, Domingo et al. 2008; Lasorsa et al. 2011; Lowrey 2011). Ultimately, journalists have been seen to resist relinquishing their professional control, which has been attributed to their traditional journalistic culture, even though user participation has become almost a mythical ideal (Domingo 2008; Knight 2012). Nevertheless, the new digital and social media landscape that is emerging is one in which both the participatory logic, conceptualized as Web 2.0 (e.g. O'Reilly 2007), and traditional logics of "professional" journalism are converging for the production and consumption of contemporary journalism. Ultimately, there is a transforming tension between journalists as producers, and the changing faces of their audiences (e.g. Westlund 2012b).

3 Changes in News Consumption

In relation to other modes of accessing news, the role of traditional news media has also transformed over time. While navigational usage patterns of the web (based on recommendations by media producers), were dominant in the formative years of the World Wide Web in the 1990s, there has been an orientation towards search practices since the start of the 2000s. More recently, patterns of news accessing have changed. These changes are partly caused by third-party actors such as Pulse Reader and Flipboard, who are functioning as technologically led hijackers of the RSS feeds of content newspapers and others have made available to facilitate audience access. Some publishers strive to lock out such third parties, as their content is published beyond their control and ways of profiting. Others appreciate the extended reach of their journalism, which they see as enhancing brand awareness and creating additional opportunities for audiences to discover their content.

Social media and sharing are also shaping the way audiences are accessing and interacting with news. In one sense, this marks a return to navigational usage patterns, but with the difference that ordinary citizens have become those recommending links and news content, stimulating and facilitating conversations. For example, in May 2008 Facebook launched the so-called Facebook Connect, which has made possible for users to easily share or like an article provided on a news site by a news organisation, making it accessible on their own Facebook profile and thereby visible to all their friends (Morin 2008). Facebook, and also Twitter, have become increasingly important for news accessing, hence the rise of mediated social discovery of the news (Newman 2011). With the number of redirections to news articles from social networking sites (SNS) growing, it makes sense for publishers keen on growing audiences to facilitate such activities. As result, news organisations are increasingly engaged in social media optimization (SMO). Furthermore, these new and powerful SNS have become inexorably linked to the sites of traditional news media providers. SNS are paving way for the virtual coffee house, in which conversations about, or at least recommendations of, news articles can take place. This is evidenced by, for instance, the partnerships of old media with social media, such as the creation of Facebook applications by *Washington Post* and the *Guardian,* in which users are functioning as social editors of news articles by their mere usage of news, which is being exposed to their peers. The applications proved to be immensely popular with audiences and The Guardian reported more than 4 million downloads of their Facebook app within the first two months of its launch (Arthur 2011), but the business case for such social media initiatives for news is still to be proven.

4 Changes in News Publishers' Position, Profits

Undeniably contemporary news publishers who aim to exploit social media need great dexterity to juggle the various conceptions of audiences simultaneously at play throughout the journalism organisation. The shaping of social media demands investment in appropriate technology (audience as recipient), sensitivity to new and lost business opportunities (audience as product), and equipping of journalists with new skills and attitudes to facilitate interactivity (audience as empowered network). Despite these hurdles, media executives around the world see social media as an important business opportunity, as reported in an annual industry survey by the World Association of Newspapers and News Publishers (Stone et al. 2010). There are clearly both opportunities and threats for news publishers when it comes to social media. A disadvantage involves that legacy media gradually have lost their monopolies of the old media world, in favour of a new media world in which news is both produced and distributed beyond their proprietary platforms. On the other hand, social media enable publishers to move closer to those inclined to access and discuss their news reporting. However, at the forefront of social media are new powerful global actors, such as Facebook, Twitter and Google, who do not only grant more power to " the people formerly were known as the audience" (Rosen 2006), but also become intermediaries in commercial relations.

Against this background, this chapter analyses how social media facilitates the editorial and commercial relationships between journalism and audiences by examining three aspects of inclusion performance. Firstly, the *audience performance for inclusion* is analysed, involving three modes of accesses news: direct accessing (i.e. browsing and bookmarks), accessing via search sites, and accessing via social media. This inquiry draws on 2009–2011 UK industry news audience data from Experian Hitwise and from the Audit Bureau of Circulation. Secondly, the social media interactivity *performance for inclusion among journalism institutions* is analysed, drawing on all three role conceptions of audiences. This investigation draws on data from a robust annual audit of the digital activities of U.K newspapers over the same period. These datasets provide unique and empirically-based insights to contemporary practices and perceptions of social media business by newspapers that operate in a vigorous media market with high ICT-diffusion. Hence the third area analyses, the implications of these two aspects of inclusion for the emergent business of social media. The study expands the thematic gaze of research into journalism, business and technology in a digital era.

5 The Role of Social Media in the Inclusion Performance Practices of Journalism and Audiences

The transforming tensions between journalists and audience have been of interest to a growing number of scholars. The starting point is typically the traditional polarised view that put journalistic producers on the one side and recipients on the other (Berman et al. 2007). As the mediascape have evolved from a first phase (in which it was deemed to be insufficient) to a second (web 2.0) or even third (web squared) phase (e.g. O'Reilly 2007; O'Reilly and Battelle 2009), these tensions between news producers and news audiences have been seen to be re-negotiated and re-defined (e.g. Nel et al. 2006; Westlund 2011; Lewis 2012). Scholars have noted a transition into a so-called convergence culture (Jenkins and Deuze 2008). Many in industry and academia have (normatively) pre-scribed rather cyberoptimistic, even technologically deterministic, views on how the future will and should be shaped. Such sentiments have often been found in discussions on the "potential" of networked digital media and led to conclusions that imply traditional newspapers have yet to explore its "full potential". Though these notions have not been universally welcomed by the journalism community, it is clear that the view that digital media is being shaped by the emerging social architecture has gained traction in many influential circles.

Some have suggested that there has been a power shift from journalists to users (e.g. Deuze and Fortunati 2010). The rise of social media and its capacity to enable audiences to engage through, for instance, "participatory journalism" (e.g. Singer et al. 2011) or "produsage" (e.g. Bruns 2010, 2012), has been seen to come down to more power being exerted by users and less by journalists. Perhaps unsurprisingly, research has found instances in which the loss of the traditional power of journalists has caused journalists to battle against user involvement in journalism (Singer 2005; Domingo et al. 2008). While it seems as if journalists are becoming more positive to user involvement, partly through social media, this mostly involves activities that do not threaten the traditional role and tasks of journalists (Steensen 2011). Based on their cross-cultural investigation of editorial managers, a team of researchers conclude: "Despite a myriad of ways for audiences to take part in the news, we found that journalists retained control over the stages of identifying, gathering, filtering, producing and distributing news" (Hermida et al. 2011, p. 16). They further argue that the conception of "active recipients" were framed by the newspaper representatives as people who could contribute with observations and ideas on newsworthy stories for journalists to write, as well as commenting on the stories they did write. Audiences were, however, not conceived of as producers of articles in their own right (Hermida et al. 2011). Ultimately, the inclusion of audiences is often limited to more peripheral ways. So, while being more interactive with audiences has served as an almost mythical ideal and has put pressure on the journalistic community, it has frequently been resisted because of their established professional culture (Domingo 2008). Thus, whereas digital technology startups situate themselves within an ideology of open participation that welcomes collaborative innovation, legacy media seem to conform to the old journalistic logic of professional control (Lewis 2012).

Against this backdrop, the analysis of the relationship between journalists and audiences in this chapter draws upon Loosen and Schmidt's (2012) heuristic model of audience inclusion in journalism, which builds on social inclusion theory, and also Nel's (2011) four-part model of digital news interactivity, which draws from communication, journalism and informatics theory.

Loosen and Schmidt (2012) treat journalism as a social system that continuously scrutinizes and reports on society; as such, journalism has a performance role in relation to those who take up an audience role. The researchers argue that audiences can be perceived in three different ways: as "recipients" or receivers of journalism; as "products" with commercial value to advertisers and others; and, increasingly, as "empowered networks" in which, enabled by networked technologies, the distinction between journalists as senders and audiences as receivers is seen as blurred. Loosen and Schmidt posit that the long-term decline of newspaper circulations (in the industrialised world) is evidence that legacy news media are struggling to include the audience through traditional approaches and are increasingly being pressured to include audiences through more channels with a wider array of interactive features. In their heuristic model of audience inclusion in journalism, Loosen and Schmidt make use of some key concepts, first and foremost *inclusion performance* and *inclusion expectations*. The first involves practices and results, while the latter predominantly subsumes a cognitive dimension involving attitudes and perceptions. Each of the two is analysed for journalism and audience, respectively, and also in relation to each other, since they are inexorably intertwined. The relationship between inclusion performance of journalism and audience is conceptualized as *inclusion level, focusing the* degree of (in-) congruence between the two. In a similar fashion, inclusion performance of journalism and audience is conceptualized as *inclusion distance*. Their model comprises the enduring asymmetry and tensions between producers and users, and also lays forward a way for empirically investigate transformations between the two in an era of digital media and augmented participation. It makes an analytical framework to systematize the performance and expectations of journalists and audiences (Loosen and Schmidt 2012).

While these researchers encourage investigating both inclusion performance and inclusion expectations to explore symmetries and asymmetries, this chapter will be focusing principally on inclusion performance by considering, in particular, on the role social media plays in the relationship between journalism and audiences. Furthermore, we will consider how inclusion performance relates to business performance.

More precisely, the chapter will explore in some detail how the communicative architecture of journalism enables the interactivity that is a prerequisite for audience inclusion whether conceived as recipients, empowered networks or products. In doing so, the chapter consider Nel's (2011) four-part model of digital news interactivity, which argues for the need to distinguish between the interactive agents (humans and computers) and the direction and control of the communication. The next section presents some notes on the two methods and data sets utilized for the study of social media inclusion performance among the journalists and the audience respectively. Thereafter follows sections on the inclusion performance of the audience, the inclusion performance of journalism and on how these activities might contribute to enhance commercial performance of journalism enterprises. Each of these sections firstly continues to discuss the operationalization of the theoretical measurements used, thereafter the data is analysed and conclusions drawn. The chapter closes with a discussion focusing on the implications for the business of social media.

6   Three Longitudinal Datasets Have Been Employed

There are many methods, such as surveys and focus groups, which can be used to generate valid responses on different aspects of social inclusion performance. In this chapter, we build our discussion on three different longitudinal datasets that cover the period from 2009 to 2011. The discussion on inclusion performance of audiences is built on both newspaper circulation and website visit data supplied by the Audit Bureau of Circulations and on data called Clickstream, collected by Experian Hitwise. This company, which has local operations on five continents, has one of the largest samples of online consumer behaviour data. Their dataset, which makes it possible to analyse how 25 million Internet users worldwide interact with more than one million Web sites, has here been used to primarily to explore the interplay between social media and news sites in the U.K. Their data, made available for this book chapter, measures the performance of audience and news accessing in terms of three categories. The measurement of audience performance has been categorized into accessing of newspapers news sites in three ways: *via social media*, *via search sites*, and *via direct accessing* (i.e. browsing, bookmarks etc.). The dataset open for analysis transforming patterns over time, making possible to determine whether social media has gained traction for the ways people access news online. The strength of the dataset is that it make possible to measure audiences more general patterns of including social media into their news accessing. A shortcoming regards that it does not explore the plethora of ways and nuances in which this comes into play.

The inclusion performance of journalism has been analysed by drawing primarily on quantitative findings from a longitudinal data audit of metropolitan newspapers in the United Kingdom. The purposive sample was constructed from the 66 UK cities listed on the website UKCities.com. Details of newspapers in England (50 cities), Scotland (6) and Wales (5) were taken from the Newspaper Society database (nsdatabase.co.uk), while the Audit Bureau of Circulation data was used to identify the newspapers in the five cities of Northern Ireland. The 66 newspapers in the research sample were owned by 16 publishers with the top four publishers—Trinity Mirror, Johnston Press, Newsquest[1] and Northcliffe—owning 51 (77 %) of the titles audited. Paid newspapers with the highest circulation for each city were prioritised in the audit, but when there was not a paid newspaper the highest circulating free paper or newspaper that covered the city was audited. Data on the newspapers' websites and then, where apparent, the concomitant mobile sites, smartphone and tablet applications was collected in June and July each year of 2009, 2010 and 2011 by two coders, who followed standard quality assurance procedures. The audit measured the social media and social sharing features of the newspapers' digital activities, conceived of more broadly as different forms of interactivity.

7 Audience Inclusion Performance

The World Wide Web emerged in the early nineties as a more user-friendly interface for information and communication through the Internet. The ways in which people access news and information through the Internet, described amongst "participatory practices" of audiences (Loosen and Schmidt 2012), has evolved in three important ways since the advent of the Web: (1) direct accessing, (2) search accessing, and (3) social media accessing. With each addition, there has been displacing effects (i.e. partial replacements) to the ways make use of the Web, while it is important to acknowledge that these three ways all co-exist.

During the nineties people explored sites mainly through direct traffic, that is, using bookmarks or inserting web addresses manually, as well as using hyperlinks to redirect from an email or from another website. These patterns of information discovery were in other words much influenced by the links offered by websites, often established institutions, in combination with the routines formed through bookmarking. Throughout the nineties different portals served as gateways to the web. In terms of conceptions of audiences, the browsing experience can be seen as one in which audiences are principally treated as recipients. While there obviously was a degree of activity, their usage for most part involved reacting on information and links pushed forward by established institutions. In the context of journalism, access to news sites was characterized by audiences in principle being only receivers of journalists output.

During the end of the nineties search engines were gaining traction. This is exemplified by the formation of the Google corporation in 1998, which has emerged from an academic project at Stanford called Backrub (which was initiated in 1996). At the start of the twenty-first century, Google has become the global leader for accumulating web traffic. Widespread use of search engines transformed the dynamics of the web, empowering people to access information and journalism on a more individualistic and active level. Considering the uptake of search, it has obviously had a displacing effect on Web- and news usage via direct accessing. Search engines not only enable users to navigate news specific news articles based on the results generated via search queries, but also by personalising search engines such as Google to extract and deliver news stories that are presented on a Web site or through various mobile applications (Westlund 2013). The rise of social media has triggered a third phase, which has seen direct and search navigation complemented by social discovery, that is, Web access directed by recommendations through social media that greatly advance the social sharing options that previously had only been possible through email forwarding. Both the roles of e-mail forwarding and social media will be scrutinized in this chapter.

In practice, the platforms making possible for sharing the article one reads, and what one thinks of these, has shaped new roles for producers and receivers of journalism. These platforms make possible for people to act as recipients of news in one instance, while also reacting to what others recommend and share, while in the next instance utilizing sharing and commenting functionalities in ways which make them editors of news content more or less on behalf of their friends and followers. As discussed by Loosen and Schmidt (2012), audiences in that instance can be seen as empowered networks. Also the conceptualization of produsage by Bruns (e.g. 2008, 2010, 2012) encapsulates the essence of the mixed roles people nowadays take.

Figure 1 shows a three-year decline of 31 % in print circulation and a concomitant 247 % rise in website traffic, confirming that the inclusion performances of the UK regional news audiences in this study are in line with trends seen elsewhere in the developed economies. It is clear from Fig. 1 (above) and Figs. 2, 3 and 4 (below) that digital media, in general, and social media, in particular, occupy increasingly prominent places in the UK mediascape. The Experian Hitwise analysis[1] notes 1.3 billion UK visits to UK News and Media sites, a category which includes websites of newspapers, magazines, broadcast, and other media providers such as e-zines of a general nature, covering a variety of subjects. This is about 21 visits for every resident given a population of about 62,036,000.[2] Compare this to 4.4 billion in the US (or 14 visits per person based on a population estimate of 312,858,000) and 445 million in Australia (or 19 visits per person based on a population estimate of 22,268,000).

By contrast, in December 2011 there were twice[3] (2.6 billion) as many UK visits to social media websites, a category in which Experian Hitwise includes websites that facilitate online communication and networking via profile pages. This can include

---

[1] The figures only include traffic from UK Internet users not visits from outside of the UK. The same is true for the US and Australian data.

[2] *Source for population estimates*: Population Division of the Department of Economic and Social Affairs of the United Nations Secretariat, *World Population Prospects: The 2010 Revision*, http://esa.un.org/unpd/wpp/index.htm, accessed 12/01/2012.

[3] In the US there was 2.75 times the number of visits to social media sites than there was to news and media sites; in Australia, it was 2.5 times.

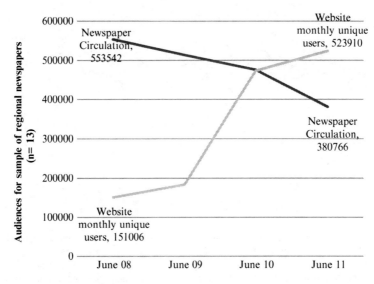

Fig. 1 Daily circulation and web visitors for a sample of UK regional newspapers. *Source*: Audit Bureau of Circulations. *Comment*: Only data from newspapers in our sample that had both verified circulation (ABC) and website traffic data (ABCe) was used ($n = 13$)

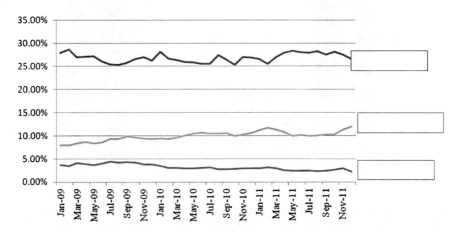

Fig. 2 Monthly traffic *to* news and media *from* social media and search in the from 2009 to 2011 (percent). *Source*: Experian Hitwise 2009–2011. *Comment*: Monthly upstream traffic percentage for 'news and media' through computers and Internet in the U.K. Upstream traffic flow to news sites from social media takes place as audiences click on an article in social media and are redirected to the news site. The article may be shared by their friends as well as distributed through the pages or people they subscribe to

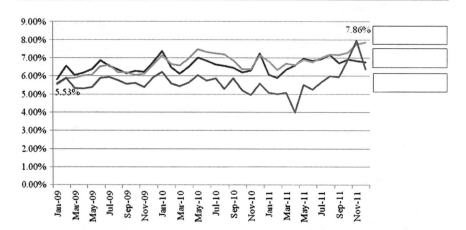

Fig. 3 Monthly traffic from news and media to social media, search and e-mail in the U.K. from 2009 to 2011 (percent). *Source*: Experian Hitwise 2009–2011. *Comment*: Monthly downstream traffic percentage for 'news and media' through computers and Internet based on U.K. Downstream traffic flow from news sites to social media, such as using Facebook connect to share an article read

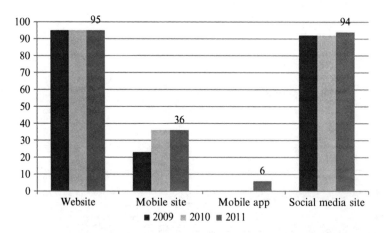

Fig. 4 UK regional newspapers initiatives to engage with digital audiences as recipients 2009–2011. *Source*: Audit of regional U.K newspapers 2009–2011. *Comment*: While both their websites and social media sites are widely used by the newspapers to include audiences, they have been considerable more cautious in their use of mobile sites and apps

sites where users are linked through regional/social groups or specific interests, as well as more general online networks. This category also features forums. Closer scrutiny of the data sheds light on the social media inclusion performance of the audience as recipient and also of the audience as empowered network. Figure 2 shows the evolving traffic to news and media from email, search and social media and search, respectively, from Jan 2009 to Dec 2011.

Different forms of direct accessing have not been included in the analysis presented, but can obviously be expected to represent most of the traffic coming to news and media sites. Figure 2 makes it clear that while search engines remain the most important route of audience visits to news and media sites among the three, traffic from social media is steadily increasing while there is a small decline for traffic generated by e-mails. More than a quarter of all visits came from search engines, while the proportion generated by social media rose almost 60 % over the last three years—growing from about 7.5 % in 2008 to almost 12 % in Dec 2011. Over the same period, the number of visits from free email[4] accounts (such as Hotmail, Gmail and Yahoo mail) declined from nearly 4 % to just over 2 %. All in all, these results suggest that over 40 % of all traffic to news and media is accumulated from the recommendation of search engines and empowered networks of friends through social media. Following from that, it is reasonable to ask what the opposite relationship is.

When it comes to streams of traffic from news and media to social media, as reported on in Fig. 3, is comprised by actions such as when users actively decide to share a news article etc. through social media. For instance, utilizing Facebook connect, hitting the "share" button will redirect the user to their Facebook account, encouraging them to post a comment that supplements the publishing of a link to the news article on their private Facebook wall. Also various other forms of social media redirections are included in this measurement. The data shows the monthly share of such traffic to news sites grew from 5.5 % in 2009, which was less than for that for search, to nearly 8 % at the end of 2011, when it surpassed search traffic. In this context, search is represented by traffic direct from search engines, such as Google, Bing and Yahoo.

The fact that there is more traffic travelling to news and media from social media and search, than in the opposite direction indicates that audiences only pass along/share a fraction of the information they access. Ultimately, however, it is also clear that, despite declining print circulations, news and media publish content that is relevant to people who, in ever larger numbers, seek it out online directly and via search engines, and who also find, share and discuss it through email on social media.

8 Journalism Inclusion Performance

The inclusion performance of journalism, as Loosen and Schmidt (2012) point out, can be assessed through various indicators and aspects of interactivity. However, while the notion of interactivity has been central to many discussions about shifts in journalistic logic, there is a lack of consensus on the meaning of the concept. Rafaeli, for instance, maintains that "interactivity is a widely used term with an intuitive appeal, but it is an

---

[4] This Experian Hitwise category features all free e-mail services, including those that provide web-based accounts and mail forwarding services. It excludes email sent from and opened on proprietary servers.

under-defined concept. As a way of thinking about communication, it has high face validity, but only narrowly based explication, little consensus on meaning, and only recently emerging empirical verification of actual role" (Rafaeli 1988, p. 110). As such, this section briefly introduces and on reflects on relevant discussions and models for interactivity, in order to lay the ground for an empirical measurement valid to the study of inclusion performance of journalism.

There are those who consider whether interactivity is best conceived as a process or as a perceptual variable (e.g. McMillan 2002; Bucy 2004), measureable through attitudinal and emotional scales. Though the value of insights from studies of interactivity-as-process and interactivity-as-perception is not disputed, this chapter recognises that an understanding of the evolution of communication architecture is an essential antecedent to further exploration into the process and outcomes of interactions. McMillan (2002) points out that much of the feature-based research grows out of Heeter's (1989) conceptual definition of interactivity. She suggested that interactivity resided in the processes, or features, of a communication medium. Massey and Levy (1999) operationalised Heeter's conceptual definition, and examined websites for interactivity based on the presence of functional features such as email links, feedback forms and chat rooms. A number of researchers, (e.g. McMillan 1998; Ha and James 1998; Thurman 2011) have expanded Massey and Levy's list of website features that may be considered interactive to include bulletin boards, search engines, forms for registration, online ordering, curiosity-arousal devices, games, user choice and surveys. Nel and Westlund (2012) expanded the investigation from websites to explore mobile news services.

Nel (2011) has further argued for the need not only to distinguish between various form of interactivity, but also the importance of identifying the direction and control of communication, as well as whether the interactive agent is human or computer.[5] In an attempt to understand who is interacting with whom, consideration in the first instance is given not only given to the interactivity between traditional news producers and the news audiences, but also to interactivity between users.

In addition to these collective and individual human agents, Nel consider whether technologies are simply channels, as generally conceived in communication literature since Laswell (1948), or if there are features that compel us to consider technologies as agents of interactivity in their own right. In so doing, his four-part model of news interactivity not only considers computer-mediated communication, but also human-to-computer interactivity and vice versa.

In particular, it considers *personalisation*, which is seen as a form of human-to-computer interactivity (HCI) that relies on technological features to adapt the content, delivery, and arrangement of a communication to individual users' explicitly articulated preferences; *customisation*, view as the site's technological response to the user-based on his or her explicit or implicit actions and therefore a form of computer-to-human interactivity (CHI). Two further forms of interactivity were also identified: *allocution* or dialogical communication where, though limited feedback channels may exist, the

---

[5] Here the term *agent* is used in the general sense of something or someone that produces an effect.

significant consumer activity is pure reception; and *conversation*, which occurs when information is produced and owned by the information consumers who also control distribution. This is a case of traditional two-way communication. Nel (2011) argues that there are instances of conversation between human agents or Computer Mediated Communication (CMC) and between computer agents, Computer to Computer (C2C), such as in the case of geo-located news that is updated as a result of an ongoing 'conversation' between a smartphone and a publisher's server.

With this in mind, this chapter empirically explores in detail the social media features in the communication architecture that journalism uses to include audiences. The operationalization utilizes the three conceptions of audiences, conceived as recipients, empowered networks or products (Loosen and Schmidt 2012) and also scrutinizes whether the interactive agents are humans or machines. This section emphasises the findings which are summarised in the tables below.

9 Interactivity Features of Journalism Institutions that Enable Audiences as Recipients

As the summary of the findings in Appendix 1 show, the UK newspaper publishers have widely adopted a variety of digital channels to enable interactivity with audiences as recipients of news and information. In 2011, 64 of the 66 newspapers in this study had individually-branded companion websites; the content of three others were included in portal site in 2009 and 2010 and were therefore excluded from the study in those years (i.e. n = 63), though one of those newspapers had established its own site by 2011 and was then added in (i.e. n = 64). Propriety mobile news sites were first audited in 2009 at which time 15 (23 % of the total number of websites audited) specific mobile sites where identified, with the number rising to 23(38 %) in 2010. No additions were noted at the time of the 2011 audit (June-July).

Software applications (apps) for mobile devices were offered by five of the 66 newspapers audited in 2011[6] which, while still a relatively small percentage, was a marked increase from the previous year when only two apps, both only available for iPhones, was noted. The six apps, from four different publishing companies, varied significantly in structure, content, features and costs, indicating diversity of both editorial and commercial logics. Firstly, both "Web apps" and "Native apps" were noted. In the context of this discussion, the distinction is important as native apps are designed for specific platforms (apps for iPhones run only on iOS) and, typically, downloads content from the media's server onto the user's device where it can be consumed offline. A web app, however, is typically coded in a browser-rendered language such as HTML combined with JavaScript and relies on real-time connectivity to deliver content.

---

[6] The Manchester Evening News' app was launched in October 2009 (after the 2009 audit was completed), making it the first of all UK regional newspapers to do so. The London Evening Standard followed in May 2010.

While these lines are increasingly blurred, it is recognised that without real-time web connectivity the options of, in particular, conversational interactivity is curtailed.

The vast majority of the publishers in this audit had included some type of social media channel in their communication architecture, with the use of Facebook and Twitter the most widespread. In 2009, 86 % of the sites audited had Facebook pages and by 2011 that number had climbed to 92 %. In 2009, 71 % of the sites had Twitter feeds and the number continued to increase in 2010 (88 %) and 2011 (92 %). There was also a steady rise in the number of newspapers with branded channels on YouTube, which rose from 14 % in 2009 to 43 % in 2010 and 63 % in 2011. On the other hand, in 2009 only 23 % of sites had channels on the photo sharing site Flicker. That number rose to 24 % in 2010 and dropped slightly to 23 % in 2011. The first paper to create a Google Group (Southern Daily Echo in Southampton) was noted in 2011.

Not only did the newspapers differ in the variety of communication channels they adopted, but the manner and extent to which those spaces enabled interactivity with audiences as empowered networks varied greatly and will be examined next.

10   Interactivity Features than Enable Relationships Between Journalism with Audiences as Empowered Networks

While the incorporation of social sharing features (such as email forwarding) and social media channels (such as Facebook) are now almost ubiquitous, the channel use varied as closer scrutiny of the use of Twitter will show. For example, the 2011 audit revealed that one of the new entrants (Lichfield Mercury) had signed up but never tweeted, while 6 other titles (owned by different publishers) appeared to have stopped. Specifically themed feeds (e.g. entertainment or sport) rose from 8 % to 35 % in 2009 and appeared to drop in 2010 when examples from only 25 % of the news sites were noted. In 2011, 28 % of newspapers had specific feeds, most notably sport (25 %), entertainment (8 %) and business (6 %). but also including one each of events and culture, politics, race for life, sail Solent, heritage, websites and magazines, and the Beatles. Interestingly, although a myriad of individual journalists have their own Twitter feeds, only 3 % advertised the Twitter presence of individual journalists on their newspaper website. In 2011 there was an average of 3,317 followers for each site with a Twitter presence.

In 2008, 32 % of the 63 sites audited had a Facebook presence. By 2009, the number had risen to 87 % before dipping slightly in 2010 (83 %) and increasing in 2011 to 92 %. The extent of interactivity varied significantly. In 2011, a number of titles (14 %) merely had an information page that readers could "like" whereas the more interactive sites averaged 1,811 readers who either "liked" them or were their "friend", with the Belfast Telegraph and Yorkshire Evening Post having 9,904 and 14,570 readers liking them respectively. Significantly, where features that enabled sharing from mobile sites were noted, Facebook and Twitter were the only social network site options.

Overall, the largest number of interactivity features was those that aimed at enabling audiences conceived as empowered networks to explicitly personalise their social media experiences (HCI) and which triggered an automated customisation response, or CHI, from the journalism institution.

The examination of the features that facilitate either allocation or conversation resulted in three key findings. The first was that while features such as comments on stories may be seen as facilitating asymmetrical communication between users and the media, it also enables symmetrical communication amongst users. Secondly, newspapers have rapidly incorporated features that enable social sharing through email forwarding as well as third party channels, such as Twitter, and on social network sites, such as Facebook. The third notable finding was that symmetrical communication occurred both between human and computer agents, challenging long-held views such as that conversational interactivity would remain principally in the interpersonal domain (e.g. Fidler 1997; Table 1).

11 Interactivity Features than Enable Relationships Between Journalism with Audiences as Products

Commerce is a key driving force of many technological developments and that is also the case in the news industry (Deuze and Fortunati 2010). However, though they have been exploring digital technologies since the 1970s, newspaper companies have struggled to make significant profits from their online ventures and that has not changed much over the course of the first decade of the twenty-first century (Mitchelstein and Boczkowski 2009; Nel 2010). Advances in interactive technologies have brought renewed optimism about the commercial prospects of digital. However, while increasing social media interactivity has resource implications for publishers, it is not yet clear if there is a direct relationship between greater customer interactivity and increased business performance. In fact, a survey of 54 news executives attending a global industry conference found no evidence to support such assumptions, which the researcher notes "is, undoubtedly, an unexpected result because customer interaction is usually accepted as a badly needed characteristic of the new media firms" (Van Weezel 2009, p. 129).

As such, perhaps it would be prudent to start off by pointing out that, as Table 2 shows, this study has identified a number of potential revenue streams that flow directly and indirectly from such inclusion performance. While determining the richness of those veins goes beyond the scope of this study, it is clear that social media and social sharing are significant sources of traffic to websites. Proprietary social media features also allow the media (and, by extension, their advertisers) to gain valuable understanding of the behaviour and preferences of audiences. Almost all of the newspapers (98 %) collect data during various registration processes.

While mobile platforms provides significant opportunities for conversational interactivity between and amongst users and publishers through, for example,

Table 1 UK regional newspapers initiatives to engage with audience as empowered networks 2009–2011 (per cent)

		2009	2010	2011				2009	2010	2011
Personalisation: human to computer interactivity (HCI)						**Customisation**: computer to human interactivity (CHI)				
Website	Search facility	*	*	100			Personalized home page	2	3	3
	Registration for web content	95	98	98			Aggregated content filters	83	84	91
	Personal home page	2	3	3			Contextual recommendations	38	50	28
	Aggregated content filter	83	84	91			Email newsletters	86	63	63
	Games and curiosity devices	63	52	41			Twitter	70	88	94
Website	Registration for email newsletters	86	63	63	W		Games and curiosity devices	63	52	41
	RSS	92	95	92			Social Networking sites	92	92	94
	SMS alerts	22	2	0	M		Location-based services	*	*	0
	Twitter				App		IP-based services	*	*	17
Mobile sites	Content personalisation			7			User device filters	*	*	0
	Search box			17						
Apps	Search	*	*	0						
	Personalisation settings	*	*	4						
	Personalisation categories	*	*	5						
	Aggregated content filter	*	*	1						
	Link to web browser	*	*	1						
Allocation: features that facilitate asymmetrical two-way dialogue between journalism and audiences, as well as amongst audiences (C2C, CMC)						**Conversation**: features that facilitate symmetrical, two-way communication between journalism and audiences, as well as amongst audiences (C2C, CMC)				
Websites	Newsroom contact	98	98	98		Websites	User device filter	*	*	*
	Comments on stories	88	91	89			Location-based services	*	*	*
	Live blogs/chats	11	14	28			Comments on articles	88	91	89
	UGC	*	*	78			Email forwarding	94	95	94
	Twitter	*	*	44			Live blogs/chats	11	14	28
	Surveys & polls	59	50	47			User blogs	64	61	48

(continued)

Table 1 (continued)

		2009	2010	2011			2009	2010	2011
Mobile	Contact newsroom	2	2	57	Apps	Email forwarding	0	0	22
	Rating of stories	*	*	26		Twitter	*	*	4
	Share via email	0	0	22		Facebook	*	*	4
	UGC via email	*	*	52	Third Party Sites	Email forwarding	*	*	67
	Peer promotion	*	*	26		Twitter sharing	*	*	67
	Polls & surveys	*	*	9		Facebook sharing	*	*	67
Apps	Contact newsroom	*	*	17		Facebook	86	83	64
	Share via SNS	*	*	67		MySpace	13	14	9
	Comments on stories	*	*	33		LinkedIn	0	8	42
	Rating of stories	*	*	17		Bebo	31	6	6
TPS	Sharing via social networking sites	*	*	67		Flickr	13	25	23
						Twitter	70	88	94

Source: Audit of regional U.K newspapers 2009–2011
*signifies that this issue was not audited that year
Comment: This summary of the interactivity features on websites, mobile sites, apps and third-party social media sites clearly shows that journalism primarily includes audiences in asymmetrical communication, while aiming to facilitate symmetrical communication amongst audiences

features that enable real-time, geo-located news and information,[7] there is no evidence as yet that newspapers are making use of these features.

However, it is also apparent that publishers need to contemplate the potential risks. Key amongst these are the implications of greater reliance on interactivity facilitated by third party social network services, such as Twitter (used by 91 % & of the papers) and Facebook (64 %), and the potential displacement effects of making their content available by such social media sites as well as via news aggregators such as HuffingtonPost.co.uk, which lists 30 UK regional newspapers amongst its 58 sources including 14 titles in this study sample (21 %).

---

[7] Geolocation social networks draw on user-submitted location data or geo-location techniques to connect and coordinate users with local people or events that match their interests. On web-based social network services geolocation can be IP-based or use hotspot trilateration (both C2C). For mobile social networks, texted location information (HCI) or mobile phone tracking (C2C) can enable location-based services to enrich social networking.

Table 2 UK regional newspapers initiatives to engage with audience as products 2009–2011 (per cent)

		2009	2010	2011			2009	2010	2011
Revenue streams associated with *personalisation*, in addition to general advertising and/or subscriptions					**Revenue streams associated with *customisation*, in addition to general advertising and/or subscriptions**				
Website, mobile sites, apps	Data generation	95	98	98	W	Advertising or sponsorship n email newsletters	23	55	45
	Targeted advertising	*	*	*	W, M	Targeted advertising by location	*	*	*
	Targeted offers	*	*	*	W, M	Targeted advertising by device	*	*	*
	Content sales	98	94	94	W, M, A	Content sales	*	*	*
SNS	Promotion	*	*	*	W, M	Offers	95	98	98
	Audience recruitment	*	*	*					
Revenue streams associated with *allocution*, in addition to general advertising and/or subscriptions					**Revenue streams associated with *conversation*, in addition to general advertising and/or subscriptions**				
	Data on consumers	95	98	98		Promotion	*	*	*
	Subscriptions	39	56	42		Additional users	*	*	*
						Additional inventory for ads	64	61	48
						Higher value advertising	*	*	*

Source: Audit of regional U.K newspapers 2009–2011
*signifies that this issue was not audited that year
Comment: This table summarises those revenue streams that, in additional to regular advertising or subscriptions, might be associated with audience interactivity features on websites, mobile sites, apps and third-party social media sites. At the time of the audits, only one of the sites charged for access to any of the sites or apps (Belfast Telegraph).

Conclusions

This book chapter bear witness to an increasing level of inclusion performance for participation among both journalism and audiences. While news has always been coupled with a social dimension, such as discussing the news in coffee houses, digital media have enabled new forms for such social activity. This chapter has analysed the role of social media, as an enabler of mediated socialness that have come to influence patterns of news accessing. Utilizing three robust datasets generalizable for the U.K, it has scrutinized inclusion performance in the relationships between journalism and audiences, as well as amongst audiences.

When it comes to audience inclusion performance, the analysis showed that while audiences' participation in newspapers is in decline, there is a steady rise in audiences' inclusion in journalism through various digital platforms, including search and social media. As such, both search engine optimisation (SEO) and social media optimisation (SMO) become important practices for contemporary newspapers to consider.

However, closer scrutiny of the data indicated that while search, social media and e-mail forwarding channel significant numbers of users to news and media institutions, far less traffic flows in the opposite direction. This is generally in line with observations that underpin the so-called "90/9/1" principle or 1 % power law (Huba and McConnell 2006) of online content creation communities (e.g. Wikis), which note that a very low percentage of active participants (i.e. 1 %) typically account for a disproportionately large amount of the content; a slighter higher (i.e. 9 %) number make a small or indirect contribution; and, finally, that a vast majority (i.e. 90 %) are passive recipients or consumers of the content. And though the findings in this study question the actual proportions in the "1 % power law", there are indications that the audiences themselves prefer to be included as largely-passive recipients in in relationships *with* journalism and that they reserve active participation *about* journalism for third-party social network sites. The fact that journalism institutions are encouraging exactly that may, therefore, not simply be because they are resisting audience participation and are striving to normalise the participatory logic by keeping it peripheral to the core of journalism (e.g. Domingo et al. 2008; Lasorsa et al. 2011). Instead, these approaches may well also be in line with the expectations of audiences who are, in the main, satisfied with receiving the fruits of professional journalistic endeavour rather than needing to actively participate in its co-creation. And that they prefer to engage about journalism with each other on their "own" social media network sites, rather than to engage in journalism with journalists on journalism sites.

This suggests that the enduring levels of journalism control may indeed be slowly dissolving in the wake of a plethora of contesters who recontextualize news articles by employing either machine-led personalisation or user-empowered selection and sharing. But that as these transforming tensions are shaping a hybrid logic that comprises increasing levels of participation *with* journalism as well as *about* journalism on and through various forms of social media. As such, it challenges the normative perspectives of those media scholars and commenters that posit that the extent to which audiences actively contribute to news products is a key indicator of success of journalism 2.0 (e.g. Harrison 2010). This would also offer a cautionary note to news executives who endeavour to host news conversations primarily on their own proprietary platforms.

Finally, the increased use of social media is not only reshaping power relations between journalism and audiences, but also between institutions of journalism and the practitioners of journalism. This is because journalists increasingly rely on their personalised channels, such as Twitter, to engage directly with audiences rather than only with sources, as was traditionally the case. The implications came under the spotlight recently when the BBC's then political correspondent, Laura

Kuenssberg, took around 60,000 followers with her as she moved to be business editor at ITV News. She changed her Twitter name from @BBCLauraK to @ITVLauraK, sparking a fierce debate about whether her rights to her followers were vested in her as an individual or as a BBC reporter (Booth 2011). This is also likely to be tested in the courts, after the US company PhoneDog decided to sue ex-employee Noah Kravitz for U$340,000 (£217,000), saying his 17,000 followers on Twitter constitutes a customer database (ibid).

In addition, journalism institutions themselves are increasingly working to participate through intermediaries (e.g. Facebook Pages) who not only have their own separate relationships with audiences, but also with the advertisers on whom much of the business of both mainstream media and social media sites depend. As such, while greater reliance on third-party social network sites to facilitate dialogue and conversation with and amongst audiences might enhance inclusion performance overall, there is no evidence that this would ultimately lead directly to enhanced business performance of media companies. Indeed, the possible displacement effect on proprietary journalism sites of increased reliance on third-party social network sites warrants greater scrutiny.

Acknowledgements The authors would like to acknowledge the most valuable contributions made to this study by Experian Hitwise Marketing Research Analyst James Murray and the support of the Centre for Research-Informed Teaching at the University of Central Lancashire, which funded the Undergraduate Summer Internship Programme that enabled Patrick McGee, Michael Brightman, Jake Hooson and Aunurag Chandok to contribute to the study.

References

Ang, I. (1991). *Desperately seeking the audience*. London/New York: Routledge.
Arthur, C. (2011). Guardian's Facebook app installed by more than 4 million users. Retrieved November 30, 2011, from http://www.guardian.co.uk/media/pda/2011/nov/30/guardian-facebook-app. Accessed 12/01/2012.
Berman, S. J., Abraham, S., Battino, B., Shipnuck, L., & Neus, A. (2007). New business models for the new media world. *Strategy and Leadership, 35*(4), 23–30.
Bolin, G. (2012). The labour of media use: The two active audiences. *Information, Communication & Society*. In O. Westlund (Ed.), Special issue: Transforming tensions: legacy media towards participation and collaboration, *15*(6), 796–814.
Booth, R. (2011, December 27). Company sues ex-employee for his Twitter followers. http://www.guardian.co.uk, http://www.guardian.co.uk/technology/2011/dec/27/company-sues-ex-employee-twitter. Accessed 12/01/2012.
Bruns, A. (2008). The active audience: Transforming journalism from gatekeeping to gatewatching. In C. A. Paterson & D. Domingo (Eds.), *Making online news: The ethnography of new media production* (pp. 171–184). New York: Peter Lang.
Bruns, A. (2010). News produsage in a pro-am mediasphere: Why citizen journalism matters. In G. Meikle & G. Redden (Eds.), *News online: Transformations and continuities* (pp. 132–147). London: Palgrave Macmillan.
Bruns, A. (2012). Reconciling community and commerce? Collaboration between produsage communities and commercial operators. *Information, Communication & Society*. In O. Westlund (Ed.), Special issue: Transforming tensions: legacy media towards participation and collaboration, *15*(6), 815–835.

Bucy, E. (2004). Second generation net news: Interactivity and information accessibility in the online environment. *International Journal on Media Management, 6*(1 & 2), 102–113.

Deuze, M., & Fortunati, L. (2010). Journalism without journalists: On the powershift from journalists to employers and audiences. In G. Meikle & G. Redden (Eds.), *News online – Transformations and continuities* (pp. 164–177). London: Palgrave Macmillan.

Domingo, D. (2008). Interactivity in the daily routines of online newsrooms: Dealing with an uncomfortable myth. *Journal of Computer-Mediated Communication, 13*(3), 680–704.

Domingo, D., Quandt, T., Heinonen, A., Paulussen, S., Singer, J. B., & Vujnovic, M. (2008). Participatory journalism practices in the media and beyond. *Journalism Practice, 2*(3), 326–42.

Fidler, R. (1997). *Mediamorphosis – Understanding new media*. London: Sage.

Ha, J., & James, E. L. (1998). Interactivity re-examined: A Baseline analysis of early business Web sites. *Journal of Broadcasting and Electronic Media, 42*(4), 457–474.

Harrison, J. (2010). UGC and gatekeeping at the BBC Hub. *Journalism Studies, 11*(2), 243–256.

Heeter, C. (1989). Implications of new interactive technologies for conceptualizing communication. In J. L. Salvaggio & J. Bryant (Eds.), *Media use in the information age: Emerging patterns of adoption and computer use* (pp. 217–235). Hillsdale, NJ: Lawrence Erlbaum Associates.

Heinonen, A., & Domingo, D. (2008). Weblogs and journalism: A typology to explore the blurring boundaries. *Nordicom Review, 29*(1), 3–15.

Hermida, A., Domingo, D., Heinonen, A., Paulussen, S., Quandt, T., Reich, Z., et al. (2011, April). *The active recipient: Participatory journalism through the lens of the Dewey-Lippmann debate*. Paper presented to International Symposium on Online Journalism 2011, University of Texas, Austin, Austin.

Huba, J., & McConnell, J. (2006). Citizen marketers: When people are the message. Posted at http://customerevangelists.typepad.com/blog/2006/05/charting_wiki_p.html (04/05/2006). Accessed 12/01/2012.

Jenkins, H., & Deuze, M. (2008). Editorial: Convergence culture. *Convergence, 14*(5), 5–12.

Knight, M. (2011). *The origin of stories: How journalists find and create news in an age of social media, competition and churnalism*. Presented at the Future of Journalism Conference, 8–9 September 2011, Cardiff University, Wales, UK.

Lasswell, H. D. (1948). The structure and function of communication in society. In L. Bryson (Ed.), *The communication of ideas* (pp. 37–51). New York: Harper & Brothers.

Lasorsa, D. L., Lewis, S. C., & Holton, A. E. (2011). Normalizing twitter: Journalism practice in an emerging communication space. *Journalism Studies, 13*(1), 19–36.

Lévy, P. (1997). *Collective intelligence: Mankind's emerging world in cyberspace*. Cambridge, MA: Perseus Books.

Lewis, S. C. (2012). The tension between professional control and open participation: journalism and its boundaries. *Information, Communication & Society*. In O. Westlund (Ed.), Special issue: Transforming tensions: legacy media towards participation and collaboration, *15*(6), 836–866.

Loosen, W., & Schmidt, J. (2012). (Re-)Discovering the audience. The relationship between journalism and audience in networked digital media. *Information, Communication & Society*. In O. Westlund (Ed.), Special issue: Transforming tensions: legacy media towards participation and collaboration, *15*(6), 867–887.

Lowrey, W. (2011). Institutionalism, news organizations and innovation. *Journalism Studies, 12*(1), 64–79.

Massey, B., & Levy, M. (1999). Interactivity, online journalism, and English-language web newspapers in Asia. *Journalism & Mass Communication Quarterly, 76*(1), 138–151.

McMillan, S.J. (1998). Who pays for content? Funding interactive news media. *Journal of computer-mediated communication, 4*(1). http://jcmc.indiana.edu/vol4/issue1/mcmillan.html

McMillan, S. (2002). A four-part model of cyber-interactivity: Some cyber-places are more interactive than others. *New Media and Society, 4*(2), 271–291.

Mitchelstein, E., & Boczkowski, P. (2009). Between tradition and change: A review of recent research on online news production. *Journalism: Theory, Practice & Criticism, 10*(5), 562–568.

Morin, D. (2008). Announcing Facebook Connect. Blog post May 9th, 2011. Retrieved from https://developers.facebook.com/blog/post/108/. Accessed 6 December 2011.

Nel, F. (2010). Where else is the money? *Journalism Practice, 4*(3), 360–372.

Nel, F., Ward, M., & Rawlinson, A. (2006). The future of online journalism. In P. J. Anderson & G. Ward (Eds.), *The future of journalism in the advanced democracies*. Aldershot: Ashgate.

Nel, F. (2011). *Control shift & returns: The tactics and tools local newspapers use to maintain relationships with users online and on mobile*. Presented at the Future of Journalism Conference, 8–9 September 2011, Cardiff University, Wales, UK.

Nel, F., & Westlund, O. (2012). The 4C's of mobile news – Channels, conversation, content and commerce. *Journalism Practice, 6*(5), 395–415. http://dx.doi.org/10.1080/17512786.2012.667278.

Newman, N. (2011). *Mainstream media and the distribution of news in the age of social discovery: How social media are changing the production, distribution and discovery of news and further disrupting the business models of mainstream media companies*. RISJ report. Oxford: Reuters Institute for the Study of Journalism, University of Oxford.

O'Reilly, T. (2007). What is web 2.0: Design patterns and business models for the next generation of software. *Communications & Strategies, 65*(1), 17–37.

O'Reilly, T., & Battelle, J. (2009). *Web Squared: Web 2.0 Five Years On*. Web 2.0 Summit Special Report. Accessible at http://assets.en.oreilly.com/1/event/28/web2009_websquared-white paper.pdf. Accessed 9 December 2011.

Quandt, T., & Singer, J. B. (2009). Convergence and cross-platform content production. In K. Wahl-Jorgensen & T. Hanitzsch (Eds.), *Handbook of journalism studies* (ICA handbook series, pp. 130–146). Philadelphia, PA: Lawrence Erlbaum.

Rafaeli, S. (1988). Interactivity. From new media to communication. In R. P. Hawkins, J. M. Wiemann, & S. Pingree (Eds.), *Advancing communication science: Merging mass and interpersonal processes*. Newbury Park, CA: Sage.

Raviola, E. (2010). *Paper meets web – How the institution of news production works on paper and online*. JIBS Dissertation Series No. 065, Jönköping International Business School, Jönköping, Sweden.

Rosen, J. (2006). The people formerly known as the audience. PressThink. http://archive.pressthink.org/2006/06/27/ppl_frmr.html. Accessed 12/01/2012.

Singer, J. B. (2005). The political j-blogger: "Normalizing" a new media form to fit old norms and practices. *Journalism, 6*(2), 173–198.

Singer, J. B., Hermida, A., Domingo, D., Heinonen, A., Paulussen, S., Quandt, T., Reich, Z., & Vujnovic, M. (2011). *Participatory journalism: Guarding open gates at online newspapers*. New York: Wiley-Blackwell.

Steensen, S. (2011). Online journalism and promises of new technology. *Journalism Studies, 12*(3), 311–327.

Stone, M., Nel, F., & Wilberg, E. (2010). *World news future and change study 2010*. Paris, France: World Association of Newspapers and News Publishers (WAN-IFRA).

Thurman, N. (2011, May). Making 'The Daily Me': Technology, economics and habit in the mainstream assimilation of personalized news. *Journalism: Theory, Practice & Criticism, 12*(4).

Van Weezel, A. (2009). *Entrepreneurial strategy-making mode and performance: A study of the Newspaper industry*. Jonkoping: JIBS Dissertation Series 55.

Westlund, O. (2011). *Cross-media News Work – Sensemaking of the Mobile Media (R)evolution*. JMG Book Series no. 64, University of Gothenburg.

Westlund, O. (2012a). Producer-centric vs. participation-centric: On the shaping of mobile media. *Northern Lights, 10*(1), 107–121.

Westlund, O. (2012b). Guest editorial: Transforming tensions – Legacy media towards participation and collaboration. *Information, Communication & Society*. In O. Westlund (Ed.), Special issue of *Information, Communication and Society, 15*(6), 789–795.

Westlund, O. (2013). Mobile news: a review and model of journalism in an age of mobile media, *Digital Journalism, 1*(1), 6–26.

Williams, A., Wardle, C., & Wahl-Jorgensen, K. (2011). "Have they got news for us?" Audience revolution or business as usual at the BBC? *Journalism Practice, 5*(1), 85–99.

Social Media: Managerial and Economic Opportunities and Challenges

Francisco J. Pérez-Latrel and George Tsourvakas

1 Introduction

A twenty-first century phenomenon, the brave new world of social media or social networking, as it is also known, has captured the attention and interests of consumers, marketers, advertisers, businesses, and scholars around the world, which has led to the publication of a number of works about Twitter, Facebook YouTube and the like. Most of these books and articles are practical and industry-based in nature and do not try to explain in-depth the social media impact in audiences and communication strategies. Nevertheless, the vitality of the editorial market underlines the research relevance than social media and social networks are acquiring.

In the last 5 years, Social Media have become key venues for interaction. They allow media companies to nurture and develop conversations with audiences, improving levels of trust; understand their implicit and explicit demands, thus increasing their accountability; sense environmental and societal concerns, assess risks, and, in general, be part of the public debate. Thus provide an opportunity to engage in socially-responsible programs that help to accomplish media's broad social responsibility and increase their ability to create value.

While the number of social media users changes literally by the hour, it is clear that millions of people are using these sites on a regular basis around the world. Social media had its beginnings with the popular web site MySpace, which debuted in 2003 and allowed users to post profiles consisting of photos, updates, and the sharing of music and video files. Facebook appeared in 2004, at first limited to just college students, but later opened up to anyone who wanted to have a Facebook page, including businesses. Other popular social media sites include LinkedIn,

---

F.J. Pérez-Latrel (✉)
University of Navarra, Navarra, Spain

G. Tsourvakas
University of Thessaloniki, Thessaloniki, Greece

Twitter, Flickr, and YouTube. Globally, a number of popular social media sites have emerged in native languages, but Facebook remains the leader with 900 million users as of May 2012.

Young demographics are among the heaviest users of social networks. Young people are heading towards universal adoption of social networking usage while more than four in five adults in the United States are using social media at least once a month. Because of the vast numbers of users, social networking has been of huge interest to businesses. BIGresearch (2009) conducted a study to learn more about the habits and demographics of social media users, and determined they are more likely to use more than one platform. Social media users tend to skew towards females, younger than the general population and statistically have a slightly higher income. In terms of demographics, social media usage indexes high across different ethnic groups on most social media sites.

Baker (2009) reports friendships have changed as a result of the rise in social networking sites. Sites such as Facebook have yet to take off as an advertising platform because visitors tend to pay more attention to friends and socializing than the ads on the page. However, advertisers are attempting to analyze these linkages among friends because they recognize that friends are more likely to be influenced by other friends and use the same types of goods and services.

The popularity of Facebook has negatively impacted MySpace. MySpace's new executive team is attempting to re-invent their brand because users are rapidly abandoning their site. The goal is to refocus the site in order to make it more entertainment based, as a place for users to connect with their friends over content like music and TV. Moving to a strategic position as an entertainment site puts MySpace in direct competition with other popular video sites such as Hulu and YouTube.

Twitter debuted in 2006, and brought in a new era of social media as users were limited to posting "tweets" that consist of no more than 140 characters. While many users and businesses were unsure how to utilize Twitter, others quickly gravitated to the new site and realized its potential for "broadcasting" to followers who wanted the latest updated information. Soon news organizations and all types of business and industry recognized the value of using Twitter as both a tool to send information and a way to expand marketing efforts.

Forrester Research is predicting that by 2013, an estimated 2.2 billion people worldwide will be online. Social networking sites are hesitant to charge fees for their users, instead focusing on making as much money as possible via advertising on the sites. Facebook is now experimenting with different ad formats in order to gain better control over their advertising on the sites. Forrester suggests Twitter should charge corporate users in order to offer premium services as well as generate a profit for the site itself.

As the previous discussion illustrates, business and industry see immense value and economic potential in social media not only for the massive numbers that use the platforms, but for advertising and marketing purposes as well. Social media has also been embraced for its many possible research opportunities by the academic community, with a number of books already in print along with scholarly investigations starting to emerge in journals, edited volumes, and at conference venues. The academic literature on social media is discussed in the next section of the paper. Many of the studies have limited their samples to college-age students found on one campus, and most studies lack much sample diversity in terms of ethnicity.

2 Literature Review on Social Media

Boyd and Ellison (2008) have summarized recent research and social network history. The authors, Berkeley and Michigan State professors, consider social Networks as increasingly attractive for researchers, fascinated for their usefulness, audience size and market research potential. They define social networks as "web-based services that allow users to build a public or semi-public within a system; articulate a user list with shared relationships; and observe the list of relationships of those persons with other people within the system" (Boyd and Ellison 2008). Boyd and Ellison also explain that SixDegrees (1997) was chronologically the first social network but disappeared in 2000. The most important current social networks were established after 2002: Fotolog (2002), LinkedIn (2003), MySpace (2003), Last.FM (2003), Hi5 (2003), Orkut (2004), Flickr (2004), Facebook (2004), YouTube (2005), Bebo (2005), Ning (2005) and Twitter (2006).

From 2003 on social networks reach the mainstream, and start producing audience figures we could consider "massive". Their audience growth has been explosive. In April 2009, Facebook had 200 million users worldwide: in March 2010 it had reached 400 million. Only 30 % of the users are in the United States: we are facing a genuinely global phenomenon. Twitter shows more modest audience figures (19 million in March 2009; 75 million in March 2010), and more than 44 % of users are in the United States (Qualman 2009). Nevertheless, the figures speak by themselves and might well give Facebook and Twitter a place in the history of communications.

The scholarly literature regarding social media is limited in size and scope due to the relatively short time that these sites have existed. The majority of academic studies have focused on the uses and gratifications of social networking, but some other examinations exist that look at the uses of social media as part of a broader investigation of Internet usage. Uses and gratifications is a communication theory that focuses on how individuals use media and other forms of communication to fulfil social and psychological needs. This theory proposes that people select and use media based on specific motivations. In the past, gratifications were often delayed due to the lack of interactivity with traditional media. However, social networking sites allow individuals to play an active role, changing the traditional effects of mass media (Valenzuela et al. 2009).

In one of the first studies involving social media, Lampe et al. (2006) surveyed first-year students at Michigan State University and found the students were using Facebook as a means to "social search" and investigate people with whom they share an offline connection. Students were less likely to engage in "social browsing" to meet new people online to then create an offline relationship. In a series of related studies, the same researchers examined Facebook users among college students to identify relationships between social media website and the formation and maintenance of individual social capital (Ellison et al. 2007a). The authors found that people were mainly using Facebook as means to keep in touch with individuals with whom they already shared an offline connection. Other findings indicated that the relationship between Facebook use and bridging social capital varied based upon the degree of self-esteem and satisfaction with their life.

Steinfield et al. (2008) conducted two more surveys 1 year apart to determine how Facebook use changes over time among a college population. Between the years of 2006 and 2007, users reported time spent per day on Facebook was significantly higher, increasing by over 1 h per day, while the average number of "friends" also increased by 50 %. Findings also indicated that students with lower self-esteem had a higher relationship in regards to the lagged intensity of Facebook use and bridging social capital, while those with high self-esteem the effect was reversed.

Some papers have concentrated on the "management of impressions" by the audience: how users introduce themselves, and the quality of relationships that are generated in this context. Marwick (2005) has analysed the degree of authenticity of user's profiles. Looking into their different roles Kumar, Novak and Tomkins divide users have been divided among different groups: passive, and "connectors", that participate fully in the networks' social evolution (Kumar et al. 2006, pp. 611–617).

Most available research suggests that the majority of social networks serve a need to reinforce existing relationships. We could say that they cater to a need: building bridges between the online and offline worlds. Some suggest that Facebook is used to strengthen "offline" friendships more than to meet new people (Ellison et al. 2007b). Such relationships could be thin, but often there are previous links, like sharing college.

Another key research thread deals with issues of privacy and intimacy generated by social networks. Sometimes the need for a safe environment for children and adolescents is stressed, like in works by George (2006), or Kornblum and Marklein (2006). It might be especially valuable to study what Barnes (2006) defines as "privacy paradox". Acquisti and Gross (2006, pp. 36–58) describe the "disconnect" between the goal of protecting users' privacy and their social network behaviour (increasingly narcissistic, to say the least), also described in Stutzman's research (2006, pp. 10–18).

Narcissism has been explored by Twenge and Campbell (2009). Their book includes survey data from 37,000 college students. In this sample population, narcissistic personality traits rose from the 1980s to the present, and the shift was especially pronounced in women. The rise in narcissistic traits has accelerated with each decade since the data began to be collected. The authors assemble evidence to show that these trends are generalizable to other age groups, not simply confined to the sample's college students in their opinion, writes Kheriaty (2010), it symptoms of narcissism are vanity; materialism; an inflated sense of one's own specialness or importance; antisocial behaviour; little interest in emotionally close or unselfish relationships, along with a lack of empathy; exaggerated overconfidence; and a strong sense of entitlement" (Kheriaty 2010).

Dwyer et al. (2007) explain that Facebook beat MySpace, for its better capacity to deal with privacy. Researchers agree that the most serious crisis faced by social networks have been related to privacy and personal data protection. MySpace's audience decrease and Friendster's decline have been related to this by scientific literature.

Social networks might also be a tool for audience and market segmentation and the analysis of specific or "niche" audiences. Different authors have studied their use by audiences defined by gender (Geidner et al. 2007), ethnicity (Gajjala 2007, pp. 257–276), or religion (Nyland and Near 2007). Specifically, ethnicity has often been researched in the U.S., as some of the better established social networks are used to connect ethnic minority targets. Such is the case of AsianAvenue, AsianAve today (established in 1999), BlackPlanet (1999), and MiGente (2000). Some other authors study the role of social networks in different cultures, which opens up a very interesting field for research (Herring et al. 2007). It is indeed worthwhile to find out whether social networks are more successful in some cultures or countries, or the rationale for local versus global social networks.

The possibility of segmentation is also interesting for market researchers. They have developed new ways to obtain information from the net that are also applicable in social networks. Social networks have also been considered in market research as a new tool for collecting information.

There are also a number of issues related to education. Some authors have researched students' reaction to educators' presence in Facebook (Hewitt and Forte 2006) and how student–Faculty relationships are influenced (Mazer et al. 2007). Students are typically ahead of Faculty in social media terms, like Kalamas et al. (2009) have shown. This new landscape is a source for relevant educational challenges, like those explored by Caravella, Ekachai, Jaeger and Zahay, in their research about education in advertising (Caravella et al. 2009).

Researchers have also been looking ahead, trying to find out what will be social networks' life cycle. Along these lines, Boyd studied the rise and decline of Friendster, a social network born to compete with match.com in 2002 (Boyd 2006). Somewhat paradoxically, its popularity increased technological and social disruptions that caused an erosion of users' trust with the site. As the market in the US fell, Friendster was winning popularity in Asia (especially Philippines, Singapore, Malaysia and Indonesia), where it still was a relevant social network in 2007 (Goldberg 2007). Friendster's case is interesting to see what the future of social networks might be, and what kind of mistakes might be lethal for their future.

3 Research Questions

Based on the theory of human behaviour on social media, we tried to answer some questions in depth:

1. Which is the profile or those people who use the social networks?
2. Why do they use Internet to communicate and how use it in order to accomplish social and individual needs?

Besides, we try to make some clusters with common characteristics according to different levels of social network usage, and according to the influence they have on the users. Our results seem to be useful both to build some theoretical ground, and for companies and institutions that relate to social media.

4 Methodology

In order to investigate Internet users' attitudes to Social Media and its consequences to the market, society and culture in general, two quantitative telephone surveys, using the tool of structured questionnaire, took place December 2008 and October 2010 in Greece. The research sample was composed of 701 internet users that utilized internet services and applications at least once per month in the first survey and 1.022 in the second. Samples were chosen according to random stratified sampling from MRB Hellas S.A. Company for the Institute of Communication of Greece and in cooperation with Panteion University and Economic University of Athens.[1]

In the present research we analyze parts of those two studies based on the previous theoretical analysis. Regarding its demographic characteristics, a majority of the research sample was composed of male respondents. The total sample was 61.2 % men, and 38.8 % women between 15 and 64 years old from all over the country, both urban and rural areas in Greece.

5 Empirical Evidence

Firstly, were investigated knowledge and use of the term "Social Media". The majority of people of the sample (77.9 %) didn't know about this term before, and only 22.1 % was familiar the term "social media" in 2008. According to demographic characteristics, men (23.3 %) are more familiar with the term than women (20.3 %). Young people (25–30 years) had the highest percentage of knowledge (25 %), especially college students (25.7 %), but also people living to the two major cities of Greece, Athens (30 %) and Thessaloniki (23 %) (Table 1).

The above results indicate that a large proportion of respondents (48.8 %), those that know the term (48.6 %), but also those that don't (48.9 %) believe that Social Media are all the media involved in society (internet, print, TV). Internet

---

[1] Research results are presented in the following web addresses: http://dl.dropbox.com/u/14714405/Presentations_ioc09/IoC_social_media_Research_180208.pdf and http://www.instofcom.gr/tools/download_file.php?which_file=../media/download_items/ioc10_socialmedia_surveydamsm.pdf

Table 1 What to do you believe is "social media"?

	People who use the Internet N = 701	People who know the term social media N = 153	People who don't know the term social media N = 548
Internet applications used to develop of cooperation, exchange and interaction between users (such as blogs, site, photo sharing, etc.)	33.2 %	39.1 %	31.6 %
All services offered by the Internet	15.2 %	12.3 %	16.0 %
All media involved in Society	48.8 %	48.6 %	48.9 %
Other	0.2 %	–	0.2 %
I don't know	2.6 %	–	3.3 %

Table 2 Internet users activity N = 701

Share files with friends	63.1 %
To visit/read blogs	57.2 %
Visit the site of a friend via a social network	50.2 %
Voting or post a video	38.6 %
Update profiles on social networks	36.2 %
Download a podcast	34.2 %
Comment on blogs	33.3 %
Participation in a forum	25.7 %
RSS reader	22.6 %
Subscription at RSS feed	15.0 %
Create their own blog	8.9 %
Upload music	3.1 %

applications that are used to develop cooperation, exchange and interaction between users (such as blogs, sites, photo sharing, etc.) follow with a total percentage of 33.2 %. Finally, some believe that Social Media are all Internet applications in general (15.2 %) (Table 2).

Regarding internet user activity, the majority of internet users access it to share files with friends (63.1 %), visit or read blogs (57.2 %). Users like to comment on blogs (33.3 %) but only 8.9 % like to create their own blog (Table 3).

Favourite topics for blogs are music (26.3 %), politics (20 %), everyday news (16.1 %), and breaking news (14.2 %) (Table 4).

While visiting other blogs, they like to read news (40.3 %), politics (35 %), and music (32.6 %). Celebrities and business issues are at the bottom of the rankings both in terms of visits (3.8 and 3.7 %) and leaving comments (0.4 % and 1 %, respectively). Favourite sites to leave comments are politics/society (14.1 %), sports (12.4 %), music (11.3 %) and news (9.4 %). Sports attract great interest: users like to read sports (26.8 %) and comment (12.4 %) about sports to other blogs, but only a small percentage like to create a blog about sports (8.9 %) or post comments in their own site (Table 5).

Table 3 What do you write about on your own the blogs? N = 58

Music blog	26.3 %
Politics/society	20 %
Daily news	16.1 %
Breaking news	14.2 %
Personal diary	13.8 %
Employment news	10.5 %
Sports	8.9 %
Blog for family or friends	4 %
Holidays	4 %
Sciences	2.9 %
Technology	2.6 %
Opinions for brands and products	2.3 %
Gaming	2.1 %
Business	1.5 %
Gossips	0.6 %
Any other topic (culture, education, photography, entertainment, interactivity)	25.3 %

Table 4 What kind of blog contents do you read or comment about? N = 405 and N = 218

Content	Reading	Commenting
Breaking news	40.3 %	9.4 %
Politics/society	35 %	14.1 %
Music blog	32.6 %	11.3 %
Sports	*26.8 %*	*12.4 %*
Daily news	20.2 %	6.6 %
Movies/television	17.7 %	4.3 %
Technology	12.6 %	3.1 %
Employment news	10.7 %	3.8 %
Sciences	9.7 %	2.8 %
Holidays	8.1 %	2.0 %
Computers	7.2 %	1.7 %
Blog for the family or friends	6.6 %	2.5 %
Personal dairy	6.4 %	3.4 %
Opinions for brands and products	4.7 %	1.2 %
Gaming	4.4 %	1.3 %
Gossip	3.8 %	0.4 %
Business	3.7 %	1 %
Other	7.6 %	1.4 %

In our survey 36.2 % of users like to use social networks. Facebook is at the top of the preferences (81.1 %), with a great distance to the second (Hi5, 23.9 %). MySpace (15.1 %) and YouTube (9.7 %) followed. Twitter has developed in Greece in the last 2 years and we might lack the necessary perspective. Therefore we have no significant results for 2008. 61.2 % of Facebook users (182 people) visit

Table 5 Which social network do you prefer? N = 222

Facebook	81.1 %
Hi5	23.9 %
Myspace	15.1 %
Youtube	9.7 %
Zoo.gr	3.5 %
Blogger	1.4 %
Second life	0.6 %
Linkedin	0.6 %
Wordpress	0.4 %
Other	8.9 %

Table 6 What are your favourite activities in social networks? N = 222

Sending messages to friends	82.2 %
Upload photos	51.8 %
Searching old friends	50.6 %
Visit friend's sites and I post on it	48.4 %
Put music video	45.9 %
Chat	45.0 %
Read websites	41.5 %
Send emails	41.0 %
I am looking for my friends	33.1 %
I am searching to add in a group	30.6 %
I put a video	30.4 %
I use apps	29.8 %
I add apps	25.6 %
Online games	24.7 %
I am writing comments	23.8 %
To meet new people	19.6 %
To share my favour music group	10.7 %
To make a relationship	10.1 %
Other	0.6 %

their profile page every day or almost every day; 12 % visit it 4–5 times per week; 12.3 % 2–3 times per week; 7.7 once per week; and 5.9 once per month, and 0.8 % less often.

According to Table 6 the favourite activity of social network's users is sending messages to friends (82.2 %). Publish photos (51.8 %), sharing music (45.9 %), and instant messaging (45 %) come next. But social networking also brings people closer; users find people they knew in the past (50.6 %), or meet new people either for making friendships (33.1 %), or, in a smaller percentage, relationships (10.1 %).

A cluster analysis indicates that from a sample 701 Internet users, 56.5 % are active users and 11.6 % are "inactive". 20.5 % are simple viewers and 11.2 % creators. *Active users* are mainly between 25 and 34 years old from Thessaloniki

Table 7 Activities by "content creators", "active users" and "simple viewers" N=701

Activities	Content creators	Active users	Simple viewers
Share files with friends	88.9 %	73.2 %	57.6 %
Create their own blog	80.2 %		
Visit the site of a friend via a social network	79.2 %	60.1 %	35.9 %
Read a blog	78.7 %	67.6 %	49.6 %
Update the profile on social network	70.1 %	50.2 %	
Comments on blogs	62.0 %	46.6 %	
Participation in a forum	58.1 %	34.0 %	
Voting or post a video	57.0 %	57.0 %	
Download a podcast	55.8 %	39.7 %	26.9 %
RSS reader	54.2 %	29.2 %	
Subscription at RSS feed	30.1 %	18.1 %	6.4 %
Upload music	27.4 %		

and a small percentage of the rest cities of Greece, with higher education and having a job. On the other hand, *inactive* users with low activity are typically people between 45 and 64 years old and women between 35 and 44 years old without a job. Students have the higher activity between 15 and 24 years old; they *create content* more often, and live mainly in Athens (Table 7).

Content creators prefer to share files with their friends (88.9 %) and to create their own blog (80.2 %). This figure can be compared with the 73.2 % of active users who share files with friends, and the 67.6 % who read a blog. Finally, a majority of "simple viewers" share files too (57.6 %), and 49.6 % read a blog. Active users believe that social media offer firstly information (50.1 %), and then communication (25.9 %) and entertainment (23 %). Asking active users to characterize Social Media with a word that fit more to them usability comes first (67.5 %). Collaboration (60.2 %), freedom (59.8 %) and creativity (59.1 %) are the words that follow. The last is trust (13.7 %).

Active users took seriously information from social networks for products and services. They choose products according to recommendations they found in them and spent more time on social networks. The two last behaviours are similar with "creators". The only significant difference is that "creators" spend more time in social networks, reducing the time that they spend on TV and the social networks are part of their daily life. For "simple viewers" social networks are information sources, but very valuable to influence their choices.

Concerning the impact of social media on people's behaviour, our research suggests that from 2008 to 2010 the percentage of people who have heard the term Social Media has increased dramatically (from 22 % to 74 %). In 2010, the picture was completely different. The social media landscape might well be characterised by three words: richness, diversity and fragmentation. There is a symbiosis between three main types of media: owned media (subscription sites, mobile phones, pay TV, internet TV), paid media (public and private TV channels, radio stations, print media and portals), and earned media (Facebook, YouTube, twitter, Linkedin, Technorati, Myspace.com, Digg, Flickr) (Table 8).

Table 8 Habits replaced by social media

Watch less tv	45 %	25–34 years old
Read less newspapers	26 %	Male 35–54
Read less magazines	24 %	35–54
Talking less on the phone	23 %	
Relatives	14 %	
Got to movies less	13 %	
Exercise less	11 %	Male 35–44
Listen to less radio	10 %	
Go out less	8 %	
None of the above	29 %	

Table 9 Why are people involved with social media?

Keep in touch with friends who are away	72 %
Keep in touch with people I do not see often	65 %
Learn things about society in general and current affairs	46 %
It's a way to speak out and hear others' opinions	38 %
Feel closer to my friends making comments, jokes, an so on	37 %
It's a way to decompress from everyday life	35 %
I love the gossip about other people's lives	24 %
It helps my professional life	14 %
Everybody is part of it and I can't be an exception	11 %

Table 10 Involvement on political and social issues through social media

Looked for further content in social media	75 %
Made comments on social media about what was being said	53 %
Promoted/uploaded on social media part of what was being watched	38 %

In our survey, 71 % of respondents have changed their behaviour since they became active in Social Media: 45 % watch less television; 26 % read less the newspaper; and 23 % talk less on the phone with their friends. Also, an 11 % exercise less (Table 9).

As reported above, people use social networking firstly as a way to come closer with friends who live far (72 %), and in general to keep in touch with people (65 %). Its informational role follows (46 %); a 38 % finds social networking as a public forum to express freely opinions and views (Table 10).

Regarding political content, the results of the survey showed that while watching TV news, shows or political and social debates, social media users tend to interact by simultaneously looking for further information and posting comments (53 %). Males tend to do this more often. People found out about news from Egypt from TV (71 %), but 73 % were informed by online newspapers and online magazines and posts in Facebook, YouTube, Twitter, blogs, or other social media, from newspapers (24 %), from radio (20 %) and from magazines (2 %). Almost half

Table 11 Involvement on entertainment thorough social media

Looked for further content in social media	60 %
Made comments on social media about what was happening	47 %
Became friend of the show and started following all posts and comments for the specific show	40 %
Promoted/uploaded on social media part of what was being watched	24 %

Table 12 How do you complain about products and services?

Telephone	46 %
Via the official webpage of the product, company or service	37 %
Forum/blog/Facebook, Twitter or any other social media	35 %
Post	6 %
No Complaints	22 %

Table 13 What is the most effective way to complain about companies, products or services?

Forum/blog/Facebook, Twitter or any other social media	31 %
Via phone directly to the company	25 %
Via the official webpage of the product or service	21 %
TV channel	14 %
Directly to friends, relatives, word of mouth	5 %
Newspaper or magazine	2 %

the audience considers social media as an official source of information (43 %), with blogs playing the most significant role. Additionally, a 53 % of social media active users (especially men) who are active in Social Media have made some kind of comment regarding the Greek economic crisis in them (Table 11).

Regarding entertainment content, a 45 % of the audience tends to interact within Social Media while watching popular programs, especially women. That increases the effect of the shows by creating content outside the medium (TV) (Table 12).

It seems that the relationship between consumers and products has been increased as a result of social media use: 45 % of users make now comments on products and services; shop less from shops and more online (25 %) and upload material related to products and services (14 %). There are several ways of complaining about a product or a service it appears above that the favourite one is telephone (46 %). Online complains have also high percentages, via the official webpage of the product, company or service (37 %), and also via forums, blogs, or social networks or any other social media (36 %).

However, according to Table 13, it appears that complaining through the Social Media is considered the most impactful way to complain about products, companies and services (31 %).

The most active users making their purchases online where working men between 24 and 54 years old from the rest of Greece who bought a product/service through internet within the last 3 months (52 %).

6 Concluding Remarks

Based on the theory and the specific empirical results the term "Media for Social connections" is a combination between electronic media, especially internet, as a place to express and to share publicly personal opinions and files, and the social connection that means interactions among people, groups and so on. It is similar to this definition: "Social means the ability of one agent to connect to and interpret information generated by other agents, and to communicate in turn; and network means that there are specific connections technological enabled and not an abstract group" (Potts et al. 2008, p. 172).

The main characteristic of social media is that are an electronic place for social communication, personal communication and social relations. The importance of them as medium to communicate, to link and to come in touch each other people, friends, companies and others was already shown in most other research evidence (see, for example, Taylor et al. 2011). Secondly, social media are a place to find information and express opinions. They promote dialogue, accountability and a loyalty among people. Thirdly, social media is also place for fun and entertainment most of the people connected with events, with common activities and there is a feedback from the people who attended some events. Finally, social media is an easy way for people to come in touch quickly and reliably with large companies, knowing that companies will answer.

7 Implications, Limitations and Areas for Future Research

In terms of managerial and economic implications, we first consider what this study means for advertisers and marketers. In an evolving and rapidly changing media environment, advertisers have been shifting more and more resources from traditional media to new media platforms. If companies are not including social media as a part of their marketing strategy, they are potentially missing a huge growing segment of the market.

From an economic standpoint, it is hard to imagine that social media sites won't benefit from significant growth in advertising revenues over the next decade. In this sample, the average amount of time spent with social media on a daily basis was just below 90 min. Social media access will be facilitated as more and more of the world's population replaces their mobile phones with smart phones, enabling easier access through applications devoted to social media.

From an audience research perspective, Baker (2009) points out a number of research companies are just now starting to analyze networks of "friends" and "followers" on social media sites. As these research efforts come to fruition, marketers and advertisers will identify more efficient and targeted ways to reach their audiences through social media sites than through other forms of advertising. The relationship among friends and peers has long been established in the mass communication literature as influential in forming opinions, referrals, and recommendations.

From the standpoint of businesses and media companies, this study offers some additional considerations for engaging social media. Firms will need to recognize that their social media presence needs to consist of more than just creating "fan" pages. While these pages can be part of a strategy, much more must be considered. Social media sites must be updated regularly with relevant information, and can become a great tool to capture opinions and attitudes towards specific programs, services, and products. Social media can be leveraged as a working research tool to constantly receive feedback from potential audiences.

Firms also need to actively recruit followers for all of their social media sites, especially services like Twitter. While a lot of Twitter users may not be sending "tweets" as this study illustrates, many more are using the medium to follow individuals and companies. Followers can receive the latest information on content, promotions, advertising incentives (such as sending coupons directly to customers at the point of sale), and other tools to engage audiences in this highly fragmented competitive environment.

This study also illustrates the higher usage and gratifications associated with sharing music and video content. Companies involved in content creation and distribution should be aware of this key aspect of the data. While many companies are debating the merits of offering content for free versus a paid basis, it is clear that social media sites can be a driver of different types of media content to share with friends. This makes social media a critical platform moving forward for sharing content, not necessarily as complete programs, but through trailers and snippets to attract users and their friends. The study also points out that social media is yet another way to disseminate news and information, and that Facebook and Twitter are perceived as more useful in this area than MySpace.

Research suggests some differences between social media and the rest of "online media". Social media call for a new audience relationship framework. Some rules seem to be emerging for environments shaped by such audiences: authenticity, participation, transparency and relevance. There seems to be a premium in avoiding commercial interruptions. Communications between individuals that are potentially always connected to the Internet, and often on the move, will be an area of growing interest for researchers.

Although their audience growth has been spectacular, there are still significant business model doubts in social media. Their early life has been fostered by crucial bets by investors. But this market situation will not last forever. Therefore, research about advertising effectiveness will be crucial. We have already some indications about the low level of click-through rates for banners in social media. How are going to be the most interesting advertising messages in a social media environment? What is it going to be effective? Advertising is a key source of income for social media survival but interruption-based models are unlikely to work.

Nevertheless, researchers will still be looking to understand better not as much the ever-changing technology, but audience relationships. Markets have become conversations and the consequences are far-reaching. It is interesting to see to what extent we go back to the beginning. From mass communication media the flow of messages goes back to person-to-person communication, as Lazarsfeld explains in his classic work "Personal Influence" (1955). When Lasswell defined mass media rules, he was indicating that a radio station or a newspaper could be compared with persons communicating messages. But now the emphasis is again in person-to-person communication and it is increasingly clear that an individual that reads something and discusses it with others can't be considered only as a social entity, analogue to a newspaper or magazine: it needs to be studied in its double capacity as communicator and contact point in the mass communication network (Lazarsfeld 1955, p. 1).

The need for human contact and interaction is a constant that always finds new ways to express itself. Some could argue that the present passion for social media will give way to some scepticism. But we seem to be witnessing more than an ephemeral passion. Qualman (2009) already describes a "social media revolution". In any case, and paraphrasing Lazarsfeld, we have person-to-person communication back again at the very core of media, communications strategies, and academic conversations.

References

Acquisti, A., & Gross, R. (2006). Imagined communities: Awareness, information sharing, and privacy on the Facebook. In P. Golle & G. Danezis (Eds.), *Proceedings of 6th Workshop on Privacy Enhancing Technologies* (pp. 36–58). Cambridge, UK: Robinson College.

Baker, S. (2009, June 1). What's a friend worth? *BusinessWeek*, 32–36.

Barnes, S. (2006). A privacy paradox: Social networking in the United States. *First Monday, 11*(9). Retrieved from http://www.firstmonday.org/issues/issue11_9/barnes/index.html.

BIGresearch. (2009, August 13). *BIGresearch profiles social media users.* Retrieved from http://www.rbr.com/media-news/research/16395.html.

Boyd, D. (2006). Friendster lost steam. Is MySpace just a fad? *Apophenia Blog.* Retrieved from http://www.danah.org/papers/FriendsterMySpaceEssay.html.

Boyd, D.M., & Ellison, N. (2008). Social network sites: Definition, history and scholarship. *Journal of Computer-Mediated Communication, 13*, 210–230.

Caravella, M., Ekachai, D., Jaeger, G., & Zahay, D. (2009). Web 2.0 opportunities and challenges for advertising educators. *Journal of Advertising Education, 13*(1), 58–63.

Collins, T. (2009). *The little book of twitter: Get tweetwise.* London: Michael O'Mara Books.

Dwyer, C., Hiltz, S.R., & Passerini, K. (2007), *Trust and privacy concern within social networking sites: A comparison of Facebook and MySpace.* Paper presented at the Proceedings of AMCIS 2007, Keystone, CO. Retrieved from http://csis.pace.edu/-dwyer/research/DwyerAMCIS2007.pdf

Ellison, N., Steinfield, C., & Lampe, C. (2007a). The benefits of Facebook friends: Exploring the relationship between college students' use of online social networks and social capital. *Journal of Computer-Mediated Communication, 12*(3).

Ellison, N., Steinfield, C., & Lampe, C. (2007b). The benefits of Facebook "friends:" Social Capital and college students' use of online social network sites. *Journal of Computer-Mediated Communication, 12*(4), 1143–1168.

Gajjala, R. (2007). Shifting frame: Race, ethnicity, and intercultural communications in online social networking and virtual work. In M. B. Hinner (Ed.), *The role of communication in business transactions and relationships* (pp. 257–276). New York: Peter Lang.

Geidner, N.W., Flook, C. A., & Bell, M.W. (2007). Masculinity and online social networks: Male self-identification on Facebook.com. *Eastern Communication Association 98th Annual Meeting*, Providence, RI.

George, A. (2006, September). Living online: The end of privacy? *New Scientist*, 2569. Retrieved from http://www.newscientist.com/channel/tech/mg19125691.700-living-online-the-end-of-privacy.html

Goldberg, S. (2007, May 13). Analysis: Friendster is doing just fine. Digital Media Wire. Retrieved from http://www.dmwmedia.com/news/2007/05/14/analysis-friendster-is-doing-just-fine

Herring, S.C., Paolilllo, J.C., Ramos Vielba, I., Kouper, I., Wright E., Stoerger, S., Scheidt, L. A., & Clark. B. (2007). Language Networks on LiveJournal. *Proceedings of Fortieth Hawai'I International Conference on System Science*. Los Alamitos, AC: IEEE Press.

Hewitt, A., & Forte, A. (2006).*Crossing boundaries: Identity management and student/faculty relationships on the Facebook*. Banff, AB: CSCW.

Kalamas, M., Mitchell, T., & Lester, D. (2009). Modeling social media use: Bridging the gap in higher education. *Journal of Advertising Education, 13*(1), 44–57.

Kheriaty, A. (2010, February). The era of the Narcissist. *First Things*. Retrieved May 2010 from http://www.firstthings.com/onthesquare/2010/02/the-era-of-the-narcissist

Kornblum, J., & Marklein M. B. (2006, March 8).What you say online could haunt you. *USA Today*. Retrieved from http://www.usatoday.com/tech/news/internetprivacy/2006-03-08-facebook-myspace_x.htm

Kumar. R., Novak, J., & Tomkins, A. (2006). Structure and evolution of online social networks. In *Proceedings of 12th International Conference of Knowledge Discovery in Data Mining* (pp. 611–617). New York: ACM Press.

Lampe, C., Ellison, N. B., & Steinfield, C. (2006). A Face(book) in the crowd: Social searching vs. social browsing. In *Proceedings of the 2006 20th Anniversary Conference on Computer Supported Cooperative Work* (pp. 167–170). New York: ACM Press.

Lazarsfeld, P. (1955). *Personal influence: The part played by people in the flow of mass communications*. New York: Free Press.

Marwick, A. (2005, October). I am a lot more interesting than a Friendster profile. Identity presentation, authenticity and power in social networking services. *Internet Research 6.0*, Chicago, IL.

Mazer, J. P., Murphy, R. E., & Simonds, C. J. (2007). I'll see you on Facebook: The effects of computer-mediated teacher self-disclosure on student motivation, affective learning, and classroom climate. Communication Education, 56 (1), 1–17

Nyland, R., & Near, C. (2007, Febraury). Jesus is my friend: Religiosity as a mediating factor in Internet social networking use. *AEJMC Midwinter Conference*, Reno, NV.

Potts, J., Cunningham, S., Hartley, J., & Ormerod, J. (2008). Social network markets: A new definition of the creative industries. *Journal of Cultural Economics, 32*, 167–185.

Qualman, E. (2009). *Socialnomics: How social media transforms the way we live and do business*. New York: Wiley.

Steinfield, C., Ellison, N. B., & Lampe, C. (2008). Social capital, self-esteem, and use of online social network sites: A longitudinal analysis. *Journal of Applied Developmental Psychology, 29*(6), 434–445.

Stutzman, F. (2006). An evaluation of identity-sharing behavior in social network communities. *Journal of the International Digital Media and Arts Association, 3*(1), 10–18.

Taylor, D., Lewin, J., & Strutton, D. (2011). Friends, fans, and followers: Do ads work on Social Networks? How gender and age shape receptivity. *Journal of Advertising Research, 51*(1), 258-275.

Twenge, J. M., & Campbell, W. K. (2009). *The Narcissism epidemic: Living in the age of entitlement*. New York: Free Press.

Valenzuela, S., Park, N., & Kee, K. F. (2009). Is there social capital in a social network?: Facebook use and college students' life satisfaction, trust, and participation. *Journal of Computer-Mediated Communication, 14*, 875–901.

Part III
New Value Chain with Social Media

Social Media, Aggregation and the Refashioning of Media Business Models

Charles Brown

1 Introduction

It is more than a decade now since John Ellis, writing in the journal *Media, Culture and Society* posed the question of whether scheduling was 'the last creative act in television?' Ellis' essay focused attention on an issue that had been somewhat downplayed by the majority of European media academics (Ellis 2000).

Raymond Williams had addressed the issue in his 1974 work, *Television: Technology and Cultural Form* in which he introduced the notion of 'flow'—the piecing together of programming, advertising and interstitial material into a seamless whole—as the defining characteristic of the television (Williams 2003). Nonetheless, compared to the United States, such concerns had been largely ignored.

Much of the debate concerning the changing nature of the media (and the power enjoyed by media firms) has focused on either content creation or its distribution. Such discussions were often framed by models derived from Michael Porter's work on the nature of the value chain in creating competitive advantage (Porter 1985). Porter's model has been highly fruitful in analysing how organisations can create efficiencies (reducing costs) or optimise activities to help create high-value products. They also used the chain to describe how *positioning* in the value chain can enable organisations to play a dominant role. One example is the use of conditional access systems by pay-TV and distribution platform operators to control upstream value chain functions (Brown and Goodwin 2010).

Surprisingly, here too, aggregation has been relatively overlooked. Surprising because in value chain terms, aggregation is arguably *the* defining function of mass media models.

In traditional media and content industries, aggregation has involved the integration of multiple content elements into packages or collections in order to rationalise

---

C. Brown (✉)
University of Westminster, UK
e-mail: brownch@westminster.ac.uk

M. Friedrichsen and W. Mühl-Benninghaus (eds.), *Handbook of Social Media Management*, Media Business and Innovation, DOI 10.1007/978-3-642-28897-5_13,
© Springer-Verlag Berlin Heidelberg 2013

the process of distribution and to underpin the functioning of business models. In the attention economy, where consumers are easily distracted, attracting ears and eyeballs is eased by having a compendium of attractive content with which to lure them. By combining dozens of stories within each issue newspapers and magazines provide a powerful incentive to purchase—or in the case of freesheets, pick up at distribution points—an issue.

Traditional media systems have been also been shaped by the economics of scarcity. Occupancy of scarce analogue spectrum or ownership of costly production and distribution infrastructure created barriers to entry and reinforced existing value chain dominance. To properly understand the process of aggregation one has to see it not as a unitary process but as a number of related functions, linked to other processes in the upstream and downstream in the value chain.

Porter himself stresses not only the fact that these stages are linked together, but also the significance of the *manner* in which value creating and transforming capabilities are linked together (Porter 1985: 48–52). In industries like television, development and production are often conducted relatively autonomously and for some broadcasters, independent producers are allowed considerable scope for developing their own projects.

This was the case in the early years of UK public service broadcaster, Channel 4. Channel 4 pioneered a publisher-broadcaster model in which a large population of independent producers pitched programme ideas to commissioning editors who used those ideas to create an often varied and innovative schedule (see Maggie Brown 2007). Although far from passive, the role of such commissioners could be argued to be more one of filtering and selection rather than the pro-active commissioning and design of schedules. However, as Brown and others have argued, over time Channel 4's programme strategy became precisely that; a proactive approach in which the channel sought to build an audience that attempted (sometimes successfully, sometimes not) to strike a balance between the objectives of meeting its public service remit and delivering a commercially attractive schedule. The demands of aggregation—in this case, scheduling—informs the content development strategy and in turn helps shape the supply chain, encouraging the emergence of more commercially-adept and market sensitive production companies and perhaps discouraging or marginalising the smaller, cultural and minority-focused entities. The function of aggregation is itself influenced by inputs from marketing. Market research provides insight into the performance of programming and user data ('the measured audience') forms, as Napoli has argued, the core of the 'audience product' that is sold to advertisers (Napoli 2003: 22–24). Such insights also inform forward planning. At the same time, aggregation, branding and marketing communications are also intimately connected.

2 Modes of Aggregation

Industry deliberations concerning aggregation tend to be confined to the agglomeration and manipulation of content. However, in its wider sense, aggregation provides a useful term for conceptualising the central operational mechanism of traditional media models, and for examining the threats posed to them by new technologies and modes of behaviour.

At both industrial and organisational levels, forms of aggregation have underpinned activities at discrete stages in media and content value chains.

The era of traditional media was characterised by a variety of emblematic packaging and integration functions which facilitated the consumption of media content. In many respects these functions were interdependent and were underwritten by their own constitutive techniques. Scheduling, service packaging on basic and premium cable and satellites systems, publishing, page design, magazine and newspaper editing; all of these techniques serve to engage the audience or individual viewer or listener more closely.[1]

It is not simply content that is aggregated. In mass media, audiences are also aggregated and delivered, either as direct customers for content (through subscriptions, the purchase of individual items of content (CDs, DVDs, books, magazines, newspapers, cinema tickets) or as recipients of advertising and marketing messages. The aggregation of audiences thus, in turn, facilitates the aggregation of revenues, essential to the financing of new production.

Onscreen design, logos and idents, mastheads, page layout and design elements, jingles and 'stings' and the character and quality of the content gathered on any particular media service add other dimensions to the aggregation process—the expression and communication of a media firm's brand. By extension, it might also be argued that media organisations are also aggregators of reputation or trust: reputation for the ability to deliver a certain type of content, or content which may be *trusted* to a greater or lesser degree by the public at large (or a specific segment of the audience). Reputation and trust are, for media organisations, key intangible assets.

Such qualities can manifest themselves in a wide variety of ways. At one extreme, an independent producer of low-budget exploitation movies like Troma Entertainment has a clear brand and audience, although its reputation may extend (and have purchase) with a loyal and comparatively small audience compared to that enjoyed—in another field—by say, *The Economist*.[2]

---

[1] Of course, there is considerable variation in the character of these functions and way in which they are deployed. Publishers have played a *filtering* function and through their lists, assert a status of arbiters of quality. For some publishers (for example, the feminist publisher, Virago Press) they indicate a certain type of book. Others may be associated with specific genre, but for most, the brand is the individual book or author.

[2] The importance of trust, particularly in the news media, is highlighted and discussed at length in Baumüller (2012).

3 Aggregation, the Internet and Social Media

The old world of limited network capacity and user choice is rapidly disappearing. Infrastructure bottlenecks remain and broadband suppliers frequently overstate their networks' capabilities. However, the end of scarcity is in sight and with it significant challenges for all the traditional players.

And scarcity is not the only challenge. The old model in which value chain and aggregation functions were tightly bound together has been eroding for some considerable time, driven by tools designed to enable the disaggregation and syndication of content and the emergence of both new producers and new intermediaries.

These changes have impacts on both physical and digital media. Indeed, the arrival of consumer codecs from the mid-1990s enabled consumers and entrepreneurs to start ripping individual tracks out of their packaged form (the long-playing CD) and distributing them across the web. For the newspaper publishing industry the first inroads were made by unauthorised deep-linking from sites, followed by the aggregation of headlines on portals and search engines, news syndication using Web 2.0 standards like RSS and Atom, and now, the repackaging of news content with sophisticated tablet and phone-based reader applications like flipboard.

Publishers acted quickly to adopt syndication technologies like RSS to head off the threat of stories being disassociated from advertising messages (and thereby any cutting of potential sources of income). In many respects, the embrace of RSS marked a turning of the corner by the press as publishers sought to prevent readers and rivals alike from harvesting their pages for news and information. What followed was a series of attempts to co-opt emerging technologies and thereby and re-forge the relationship with the reader.

3.1 Disintermediation/Reintermediation

Content owners' embrace of social media and increasing willingness to work with key platform owners and intermediaries—facebook, YouTube, twitter—stands in stark contrast with the previous attitudes over redistribution of content via third parties, portals and first generation news aggregators like Google News.

News Corporation has been the most vocal in its opposition. In 2009, Rupert Murdoch attacked Google News's 'kleptomania', arguing that in gathering links to its content it was acting as a 'parasite.' (Johnson 2009). In television, executives like All3Media, chief executive described Google as 'cowboys', taking revenues from paid search to his company's content (Campbell 2010). Such responses amplified existing concerns over unauthorised exploitation of content by peer-to-peer networks, the swapping and free redistribution of copyrighted materials by users, and the prospect that commissioners and distributors would be disintermediated.

There has also been a tendency to see the breakdown of traditional methods of aggregation as the disappearance of aggregation *per se*. In reality, total disintermediation, collapsing the distance between content producer and the point of consumption, is comparatively rare. Even where content is being produced by non-professionals and exchanged free of charge with others, such exchanges are frequently mediated by intermediary platforms and services which apply new kinds of aggregation technique.

In reality, the story of the past decade has been one of the emergence of new intermediaries, a process not of disintermediation but of *re*intermediation. Aggregation does not necessarily take the form it once did, rather it has adopted new forms. Indeed, different means of signposting, linking, collecting and arranging of content are likely to form crucial components of sustainable, stable media business models.

4 A Hierarchy of Aggregation and Channelling Functions

In traditional media, aggregation was a discrete process albeit one linked systemically to other value creating functions. On the internet aggregation is intimately connected to adjoining processes of promotion, engagement, signposting and filtering. Again, much has been made, in the past, about the 'parasitic' nature of much social media, with even amateur blogs being seen as being predominantly providers of comment (and at best, analysis) of news stories researched and reported by others.

Today, many newspapers and television news organisations encourage commentary and blogging, and provide the tools necessary to share content. Even so, many editors and publishers remain ambivalent towards such practices. Shortly before stepping down from the role of executive editor at *The New York Times*, executive editor Bill Keller reflected on the nature of content aggregation: "'Aggregation' can mean smart people sharing their reading lists, plugging one another into the bounty of the information universe. It kind of describes what I do as an editor. But too often it amounts to taking words written by other people, packaging them on your own Web site and harvesting revenue that might otherwise be directed to the originators of the material. In Somalia this would be called piracy. In the mediasphere, it is a respected business model (Keller 2011)."

Frédéric Filloux, general manager of France's ePresse consortium and co-author of the newsletter, Monday Note, distinguishes between good aggregators and what he terms, the 'looters' (Filloux 2010). Filloux and Keller are both critical of the approach adopted by one of the leading media aggregators, *The Huffington Post*. *The Huffington Post* does commission and produce its own material. However, it has, from the outset, been highly reliant upon the aggregation of third-party content, user generated content and increasingly, social media functions.

The root of the criticisms levelled at the *Post* is that it summarises and aggregates content within its pages rather than simply aggregating (and adding to) links, which drive the user to the original source of the content. The précised story may contain links but the summary is so extensive it makes going to the original almost superfluous.

Nevertheless, many media organisations are taking a far more relaxed view of the role of linking and recommendation. Indeed, increasingly they do all they can to encourage it. In addition to their own online distribution platforms, like the BBC's iPlayer and the US networks Hulu platform, most now incorporate social sharing functions into their online sites. From permalinks onwards, such tools enable sharing not only through facebook, YouTube and twitter but also via a host of other services from stumbleupon to del.icio.us.

For online jukeboxes and digital distribution services like iTunes and Netflix (and for the legitimate content they host) social media functions enable a form of 'superdistribution' in which one's recommendations direct friends and contacts to items of content, potentially generating new streams of revenue. Endorsements also indicate popular content, alerting the general community to content that is 'trending' and worthy of investigation.

5   Platforms, Apps and Signposting

For the platform operators recommendation and sharing functions play a pivotal role, and sharing (and signposting) via these platforms is becoming increasingly important for traditional media organisations. This was highlighted when in February 2012, the UK newspaper, The Guardian, received more traffic from Facebook than it did from Google. Facebook now accounts for more than 30 % of its referral traffic (Cordrey 2012).

It is not simply that platforms are where users share, swap and link to content resident on other sites (like the Guardian). Platforms are also manoeuvring so as to position themselves as *the* infrastructure upon which media content and applications *reside*. In September 2011, facebook founder and CEO, Mark Zuckerberg outlined his ambition for facebook to become an entertainment hub, representing users' lives and enabling not only sharing and recommendation but also consumption (Halliday 2011).

In doing so it is in competition with other major players, among them Google, Amazon, Apple and increasingly, Twitter, each of which is aiming, in different ways, to provide the infrastructure for digital distribution. The development of standard application programming interfaces (or APIs) is a key element in the development of platforms, providing a standardised way of developing applications so that they can work across an entire platform (and its related technologies).

Social platform recommendation based on users' real-time consumption also provides an important source of traffic for subscription video distributors like Netflix and cloud and peer-to-peer, ad-supported and subscription music services such as Spotify. Such services are accessed via software applications (apps), utilising the facebook APIs. Many of these operators are also opening their platforms and APIs, providing an increasing number of routes towards audiovisual content.

Media and content companies are looking to these technologies as a means of developing more sophisticated, integrated offerings and enabling companies to leverage one another's brand strength and customer bases to driver traffic and thereby revenues. In principle, APIs enable companies to create new offerings, drawing upon existing, interoperable media services. For example, the *Guardian* links its reviews and features to music via Spotify.

Other products and services have entered the arena, bringing together content from a wide variety of sources, functioning as new intermediaries and reaggregators. Apps like Flipboard, Zeebox and Zite enable users to integrate content on smartphones, tablets, PCs and can be expected, in some cases, to extend onto other platforms including games systems and broadband-connected Smart TVs.

These applications also connect to platforms like twitter and facebook, either using the platforms as sources of content or providing social networking functions for viewers and readers of mainstream content services.

Flipboard describes itself as a 'social magazine'. The application takes feeds from newspaper and magazine sites, RSS feeds, twitter and facebook and reformats them into an attractive format that accentuates the visual appeal and readability of content for the devices on which it is used. Flipboard also allows users to share their reading with friends via social networks (and to receive recommendations). By recasting the original content into a new format, Flipboard breaks out of the original content providers' formats. This might seem to radically undermine the content owners' own aggregation efforts (and its revenue stream). However, Flipboard works with publishers (initially with Conde Nast) to insert advertising into its application (particularly on the larger format PC and tablet versions) and in the long term, analyse user behaviour in order to direct targeted adverts at individuals and groups.

Other applications seek to transform media consumption into a social process. Zeebox is a mobile, PC or tablet based application which can be integrated with some PVRs and set-top boxes to enable it to function as a software-based remote control. Zeebox combines attributes of an electronic programme guide with social networking software, straddling the worlds of the traditional and the social and opens up the way for the exploitation of new revenue streams.[3]

Zeebox's cloud-based service spiders live television feeds and adds metatags (zeetags) which can link to information (Wikipedia entries for example) or to products (allowing the tags to be resold in the same way that search terms are auctioned via Google's AdWords system and providing a 'click to buy' functionality. It is also introducing song recognition so that users can buy music that they here on programmes.

The electronic programme guide can be linked to television sets via certain set top boxes, enabling the application to act as a Smart remote. Tweet streams around each chosen programme allow users to discuss programmes with friends and other viewers of individual programmes. Zeebox has also published its APIs so that

---

[3] Applications like Zeebox have also been described as 'co-viewing' apps. Networks have also developed their own co-viewing apps. ABC was an early entrant with its co-viewing app for the mockumentary series, My Generation.

broadcasters, content producers, and multiple system operators can build it into their applications and services (Sky has taken a 10 % stake in the company).

6   From Channels to Apps

In the words of Zeebox co-founder (and former chief technical officer for the BBC iPlayer) Anthony Rose, the aim of social app like Zeebox is to "make TV clickable" (Rose 2012). In such a model, the application serves as social glue, improving the television consumption experience and making channels less vulnerable to erosion by social media competitors.

This model is coming into conflict with other models and ways of inserting social media into television. While Zeebox *organises* channels and provide links to social media, apps can be seen as channels (or channel bundlers in their own right).

Smart TV manufacturers (like Apple) and developers of next generation set top boxes (like the UK's YouView) are seeking to emulate Apple's success with mobile devices and the App Store.

Rather than simply providing content, apps allow the addition of interactive functionality and enable content owners to design and control the user experience, and differentiate themselves from rivals. Indeed, in application design it is possible to discern the emergence of techniques that are analogous to the practices of scheduling, onscreen promotion and editorial design adopted by the broadcasting and publishing industries.

Even more importantly, apps return control to the content owners. Within the 'envelope' of the app, owners are able to dictate—to a degree—where advertising appears (or to charge for the use of their applications). Although it would be foolish to dismiss the emergence of technologies capable of parsing applications and disaggregating content, at present they provide a means of protecting business models.[4]

While some apps are used as exclusive channels by content brands, others serve as platforms for a range of professional and amateur content providers. In 2011 YouTube adopted the kind of channels model used by broadcasters. This might seem to be a retrograde step, running in the face of the on-demand logic of the online environment. However, as an aggregator of other peoples' content, Google/YouTube felt it necessary in order to aid content discovery and enable commercial content partners to brand their content and consolidate their revenue models. Google has also invested over $100 million in its own professionally produced content.

YouTube's adoption of a channels model anticipates the growth of Smart TV and 'over the top' technologies in which television sets are connected directly to the web. It recognises the relatively more passive, 'lean back' nature of user

---

[4] Relatively crude methods such as 'screen scraping' are possible.

interactions and helps viewers navigate the expanded range of choices available via the web.

It is by no means clear which approach will prove to be successful. As News Corporation's chief digital officer, Jon Miller has said; "The question that hasn't yet been answered is whether television viewing will consist of a single app that mimics the pay- TV bundle or a series of different apps that together form a content experience. (Wingfield 2012)."

A battle is emerging between advocates of multiple applications (an approach advanced by smart TV manufacturers) and others who question whether users will be prepared to engage with multiple platforms. Zeebox (perhaps understandably, given its own model) suggests that applications are better suited for 'second screen' devices, possessing the kind of interactive affordances. Initially enthusiasts for smart TV, Zeebox is arguing that televisions will become "beautiful but dumb hi-res panel [s]," which do what the smartphone or tablet tells them. In effect, the site of aggregation becomes the second-screen device (Johnson 2012).

Such a model has worrying implications for traditional aggregators like broadcasters and publishers. App providers begin to wrest control of content away from traditional aggregators, forming relationships with producers and content consumers, reducing the role played by media companies. Rights owners have begun to challenge new aggregators, particularly those which repackage content. Flipboard has sought to work with publishers and initially had success in forming commercial relationships. Leading journals like Wired and the New Yorker pulled their advertising and said they would no longer serve Flipboard with optimised versions of their articles (Indivik 2012). Zite (now owned by CNN) met with a more robust reaction from publishers. Like Flipboard, Zite enables content to be reworked into forms suited to mobile devices. It combines this approach with a recommendation engine that learns from users' preferences. Zite found itself in receipt of multiple cease-and-desist notices from irate publishers and was forced to take down content.

Recent surveys suggest that streaming platforms are the most popular applications on smart TVs. A 2012 Harris poll cited Netflix and YouTube as the applications most US users want to access, followed by Amazon Instant Video, facebook and internet radio aggregator, Pandora (Harris Interactive, 2012).

Whether smart TV and device manufacturers will continue to work collaboratively with application operators is less clear. Competition seems likely to intensify over the control of the aggregation function (and the relationship with the user) this antagonism can already be seen in developments such as Apple's decision to no longer bundle YouTube with its iPhones and iPads once the new operating system, iOS 6 is introduced. The control of application distribution systems (and back end support systems) also places considerable power in the hands of platform operators. Apple is able to dictate which companies are allowed into the App Store and conflicts have broken out between Apple and content partners (especially publishers) over the percentage of download and subscription income payable to Apple. This has resulted in some publishers such as the Financial Times, leaving the App Store and offering their own applications directly.

7 Aggregation and Control

Content aggregation and the business models erected around it have been predicated upon certain organisations retaining control over the process and being able to dictate what content is acquired, how it is assembled together, how it is distributed and how it is consumed. Social media, whether in the form of user generated content, content sharing or the reworking and repackaging of content, entails the ceding of control to other actors. Initially, media companies sought to limit this erosion of control, through technological means or by exercising their legal rights. Now, an increasing number of organisations are recognising the necessity of working with users and other aggregators in order to deepen engagement or extend reach.

The UK newspaper, *The Guardian,* has put considerable resources into the development of its Open Journalism strategy and in developing its online engagement activities. *The Guardian* has worked with its readers on key stories, most notably the scandal of Member of Parliaments' expenses. Lacking the resources to go through thousands of pages of expense submissions, *The Guardian* introduced an app to enable readers to log information gleaned, and thereby help build the investigation. Editor-in-chief, Alan Rusbridger, has gone further, articulating a policy of 'mutualisation' at the Guardian. Historically, Rusbridger argued, journalists found themselves in positions of authority: "We had the information and the access; you didn't. You trusted us to filter news and information and to prioritise it—and to pass it on accurately, fairly, readably and quickly. ….. That state of affairs is now in tension with a world in which many (but not all) readers want to have the ability to make their own judgments; express their own priorities; create their own content; articulate their own views; learn from peers as much as from traditional sources of authority (Guardian 2010)." He went on to outline ten provisional principles including the encouragement of participation, the ending of 'us and them' publishing and importantly, "It is open to the web and is part of it. It links to, and collaborates with, other material (**including services**) on the web." (emphasis added).

In this model, control—particularly over the aggregation and design of content areas—remains with the publisher, but others are taking further risks. UK commercially-funded public service broadcaster, Channel 4, allows users to make an online scrapbook of their favourite shows and Channel 4 content (http://scrapbook.channel4.com/). It went further still, however, with the launch of digital channel, 4Seven. Although designed as a platform for re-running Channel 4 programmes, its selection of programmes to repeat is driven by a number of factors including critical reception in newspapers and the levels of discussion on Twitter and Facebook.

Most of these models assume that aggregation is always exercised in a conscious fashion. However, the storing and sharing of content on sites is based, in an increasing number of cases, on 'frictionless sharing'. Standalone apps and apps tied into networks such as facebook may track users' content consumption and share that information with their friends and other extended networks. Rather than having to actively like or score content, users' preferences are broadcast to these wider circles automatically. *The Guardian's* facebook app, for example, indicates in continually updated sidebar, which stories friends are reading.

Commentators have questioned the desirability and ethical nature of automatically sharing such information. The appeal is clear. Popular stories and content items can be promoted quickly. Recommendations by friends are regarded by marketers and content companies as more effective than other forms of promotion. From resisting sharing, some media companies have embraced such forms of promotion (and by extension, distribution). Indeed, for music services like Spotify, frictionless models appear to have the potential to deliver the kind of superdistribution functionality promised but never delivered by digital rights management technologies.[5]

Evidence regarding the success of frictionless sharing is mixed. Although adoption appeared to cause an early spike in content recommendation and sharing, some users seem to be resisting or abandoning frictionless apps or disabling the frictionless sharing functions. Many Spotify users choose *not* to share their tastes. Privacy is one of the principle reasons cited for such actions—many users many not wish for their friends, families or employers to know what stories they are reading and content they are consuming.

8 Restructuring of the Model

The arrival of new aggregation technologies and operators does not, of course, abolish the traditional model. Traditional publishers and broadcasters remain powerful, if not dominant, players within the media economy. While newspaper models, in western media markets, are seeing declining readership and profitability, newspaper publishing remains relatively buoyant in many markets in the global south and east. The consumption of linear television, meanwhile, continues to grow, although on-demand, timeshifting and other consumption models are eating in to network broadcast.

As we have argued, aggregation has a number of attributes which extend beyond the simple aggregation of content. Content aggregation is a key activity but it is concomitant with other functions (Fig. 1). Content attracts attention which is in turn underpinned by trust on the part of content consumers and commercial customers (advertisers). Content creation, is in turn, dependent on the income aggregated further down the line (although they may have access to other sources of income such as grants, subsidies and tax incentives from national and transnational bodies. Porter highlighted linkages between value chain functions, stressing the importance

---

[5] In superdistribution models, content is typically encoded and made publicly available. Individuals can pass content between themselves as the content is only usable on payment or compliance with a specified condition (e.g. registration or, within closed systems, entering a password.

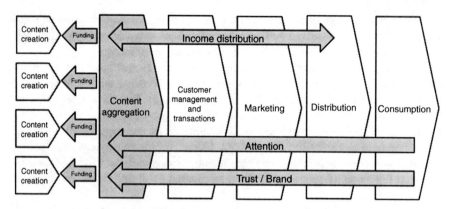

Fig. 1 Aggregation attributes and the value chain

of optimisation and coordination activities in ensuring efficiency and differentiation (Porter 1985).

In the new models discussed in this chapter, integrated value chains are beginning to fragment and the centralised functions of aggregation are being, to a greater or lesser extent, distributed across networks.

Figure 2 illustrates, albeit in schematic form, the way in which this process is changing. It would be wrong to suggest that major media and content companies are being *immediately* and *fully* destabilised. The challenges to existing media are certainly serious (especially for newspapers) but there are dangers in completely discounting the strengths of established models.

Broadcasting models, for instance, remain highly effective ways of reaching large audiences, especially around 'event programming'. Nonetheless, legitimate and illicit subsidiary aggregation functions are beginning to play an important role in channelling audiences to content. The aggregation function now takes the form of a network of relationships. Some of these re-aggregators—Google-YouTube, Amazon—are injecting *some* money into content production (and thereby sustaining professional content producers). However, total sums are relatively small compared to those of traditional media players, particularly in fields such as television and film production. It should also be noted that the boundary of the aggregation function is more permeable, open to individuals engaged the generation of user generated content and in what Axel Bruns has termed, produsage ("the collaborative and continuous building and extending of existing content in pursuit of further improvement" (Bruns 2007). Not all users are engaged in active production but many are engaged in reworking and sharing, even if that is confined to activity on platforms such as facebook.

Not all aggregators are equal. Aggregators with lock in—for example, closed satellite and cable networks, protected by conditional access systems—will still be able to bundle together channel bouquets. Bruised by battles over wholesale fees some cable programmers may decide to risk going the a la carte route, using TV apps as means of accessing audiences without being held to ransom. For those

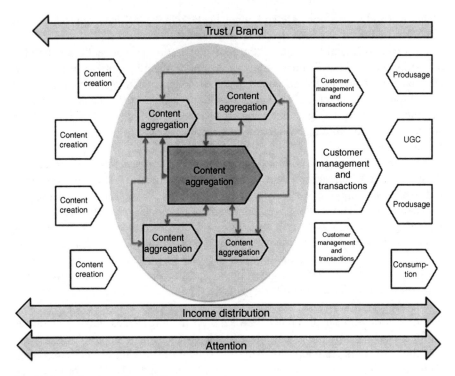

Fig. 2 Reconfiguring value creation

without lock in or exclusive content the environment will undoubtedly prove savagely competitive, placing a premium on execution and the containment of delivery costs.

Just as content production and aggregation is distributed across the network, networks and operators from which they are constituted will be expected to exhibit the attributes formerly exhibited by centralised business models.

9 Trust and Branding

The success of content producers and aggregators is dependent, in large part, upon the degree of confidence they inspire in content consumers (and other members of networks of exchange and redistribution). The strength of individual nodes within these networks (producers and aggregators) is similarly dependent on the degree to which they are trusted and/or the strength of their brands.

For news organisation, trust in reporting and analysis is an important intangible asset. With the growth of citizen journalism and blogging, trust has become contested with a wider range of sources analysing and critiquing mainstream news sources or increasingly, breaking stories of their own. The proliferation of professional and amateur news sites and blogs has also placed the mainstream media under greater scrutiny. Reporting scandals such as the Jayson Blair plagiarism and fabrication case and phone hacking in the UK have led to a decline in the trust enjoyed by sections of the news media.

However, as Baumüller argues, "the construct of trust has not yet been defined in a broadly accepted way" and a variety of discipline-specific approaches have been adopted from fields including communication science, sociology, economics and psychology (Baumüller 2012). For Baumüller, trust is an important market in helping consumers navigate information sources and simplify decision-making when it comes to deciding which news sources to follow and to—at least partly—believe.

Trust is also important in underpinning emerging business models, particularly those involving commercial and information exchanges. Online intermediaries today play an important part in recommending goods and services and even in facilitating transactions. Trust is important for such models, providing reassurance regarding likely outcomes and the ability of commercial actors to meet their promises. Trust in this sense does not mean just credibility. Instead, it extends to the confidence users have in the way that they will be treated, the manner in which their actions are recorded and acted upon, and the way that this information is exposed to the wider community. Again, frictionless applications are particularly problematic in this respect.

There is a significant difference between users trusting friends and acquaintances and trusting *platforms*. A recent study by Harris Interactive suggested that while two thirds of users are happy for Amazon to target them with offers, based upon their purchasing history, this drops to 41 % for Google and only 33 % for Facebook (Heine 2012). Privacy and issues relating to the use of data have become increasingly contentious, seconded only by those regarding security (particularly where the interests of children are concerned). This was highlighted by the pressure to close down the chat areas of UK-based online community, Habbo Hotel, when it was revealed that adults were targeting the site for the purpose of sexual grooming (Walker 2012).

Despite user unease over issues such as frictionless sharing some companies continue to press for an easing of regulatory constraints. Netflix, in particular, has been agitating for a change to US law to allow the sharing of information about video consumption. Similarly, Pinterest has been accused of adding tracking codes enabling it to follow users' consumption patterns and generating income from their transactions.

Trust is not a simple function of organisational culture or behaviour. On the contrary, trust is highly dependent on the relationship with the audience and the organisation's ability to engage with them. Fox News and CNN may both be trusted by their respective audiences but few loyalists, of either channel, would imagine that they shared identical news values. They are trusted either because they conform with viewers' existing values or because they are able to succeed in attracting them to the operator's position.

Is the issue of trust relevant principally for news and commerce sites? As we have already suggested, trust is yet to be satisfactorily defined. Content providers' ability to meet user expectations, time and time again, is certainly important.

More complex is the question of how such reliability is communicated. It is here that branding enters the frame.

Brand acts as an important means of differentiating a content product and enabling users to find content that meets their needs, whether that takes the form of 'simple' consumption or more active engagement. Media brands can take a wide variety of forms, from corporate brands (Disney) to individual brands (Madonna, Jay-Z, Dizzee Rascal). This prompts a further question—which brands will come to the fore in this increasingly distributed, networked environment. Will it be traditional media brands like the BBC, NBC, ARD, Der Spiegel or will new players come to the fore—intermediaries like Zeebox or entirely new players, perhaps consumer brands or technology companies like Sony or Samsung.

Expanding choice is, in some respects, making finding content harder, not easier. Branding and social-connections are two ways in which it is becoming easier. This need not happen through large networks, instead smaller, more focused networks can perform better for engaging with end users, delivering the *right* audiences to advertisers rather than audiences that are larger, but of lower quality.

10 Income Distribution

As aggregation decentralises it is inevitable that to a greater or lesser extent, income distribution will also have to be distributed across the network with new players entering into networks to help fund production. Fragmentation of audiences and increasing pressures on budgets meant that by the 1980s high budget programmes were already having to find supplementary sources of funding, typically through co-production or co-finance.

The disaggregation of content by third-party aggregators and re-aggregators places pressure on existing income streams both through competition and by undermining traditional revenue models. Google does not simply compete. Ad Words is preferred by many clients because it is perceived as more effective than much traditional display or classified advertising and with something at least simulating demonstrable RI or return on investment. Social channels are even less receptive to display advertising.

Instead, the currency of social applications and services is user data and the building of relationships with users, enabling the targeting of messages and promotional offers.

This is likely to have serious implications for the funding of production—particularly in high-risk areas like film and television production. Uncertainty over advertising revenues has already led broadcasters around the world to opt for safer forms of programming, especially format-based shows or event-programming (including sports) which encourage contemporaneous viewing.

A number of social funding media models *are* emerging and others have been proposed to offset the destabilising effects of fragmentation and decentralisation. Social models enabling the containment and reduction of costs are also being explored.

Crowdfunding models such as Crowdfunder (http://www.crowdfunder.co.uk/) draw upon hundreds of investors (often fans) to cashflow low-budget feature film production. At a policy level, a variety of models have been explored to encourage different forms of production, from regional newshub models for the local newspaper industry to compulsory licensing and levies upon companies like Google, for television, music and other sectors disrupted by the search giant.

Again, this doesn't mean that the traditional players are obsolescent. Many will continue to have substantial incomes and will serve as repositories of expertise in piecing together financial packages. Public service broadcasters will have an important role in underwriting diversity and plurality, as will—it is likely—trusts, public institutions and charities.

Other income streams are likely to emerge from the unique characteristics of various devices. Lokast networks, for example, may enable the development of new local advertising models.

11 Constructing Value Networks

As the diagrams above indicate, conventional value chain models are of limited use in describing complex services, particularly those residing on digital networks. The first notable challenge to Porter's approach was that of Richard Normann and Rafael Ramírez. For Normann and Ramírez, the understanding of value it embodied was, "as outmoded as the old assembly line it represents" (Normann and Ramírez 1993). Instead of focusing on value addition, Normann and Ramírez's value network engages with, "the value creating system itself, within which different economic actors—suppliers, business partners, allies, customers—work together to *co-produce* value" (Normann and Ramírez 1993: 66).

Whether addressed through the metaphors of networks, webs or constellations, network-based value creation models proliferated in the 1990s and 2000s, and were seized upon by theorists and practitioners engaging with the challenges posed by the internet, mobile networks and more broadly, digital convergence.

As well as co-creation or co-production a number of features have come to characterise value analyses (Ramírez 1999):

- Rather than being linear, value networks are characterised by two-way interactions and feedback loops.
- Value networks are characterised by relationships between network actors.
- Rather than being tightly integrated, value-adding agents and entities may be loosely coupled to one another.
- Value networks are essentially financial in nature with the focus upon cost-saving and value addition. Value networks involve other forms of exchange, not just financial. Transactions and flows within the network may be based around exchanges of information, knowledge, contacts, the building of reputation.
- Benefits to users may be highly intangible (emotional, reputational, for example).

- Rather than being linear and time-based, value networks are 'synchronic'.
- Consumers are themselves assets (and networks typically increase in value with the addition of new members).
- User-focus rather than product focus.

Others highlighted the importance of peer production, most notably Benkler (2002) Further work by Chesbrough and Rosenbloom (2002) and Chesbrough et al. (2008) have extended this model to address open innovation models in which customers (as well as other external parties) are included in new product and service development.

In the models discussed in this chapter, user interactions contribute to the populating and the use-value of the services. The degree to which the operator or the user contributes to this process may very considerably but the locus has undoubtedly shifted from within the media firm.

There is also considerable variation in the nature of value exchanges within these models. Some models are free but others charge a subscription (for example, Netflix) or use a 'freemium' model (Spotify), where consumption is free at the point of use (supported by advertising) but a premium subscription version, with a wider variety of content and functionality is also available, should the user wish to upgrade.

In the new models that are emerging the borders of the aggregation process are becoming increasingly porous with aggregation shared with user-producers. Naturally, some users prefer to simply visit sites and consume content.

As illustrated in Fig. 3, in the majority of services, high-level aggregation (control over the broad functionality of applications) remains in the hands of the proprietor or prime mover in the service creation process with users aggregating and/or producing content within pre-defined templates and formats. In some instances, such as gaming environments, users may have considerable scope to introduce new characters or artefacts to the environment. Other contributors may include commercial content partners (producers or brand-owners).

Other high-level functions may well be retained by the proprietor, such as moderation and customer and transaction management (for example, advertising and subscription sales). However, even some of these functions (most notably moderation) may also be delegated. Users can also play an important role in functions such as content ingestion and the tagging of content (images, stories, clips).

Newspapers and broadcasters may provide the vast majority of original content on services. The balance in the case of services like Wikipedia and online classifieds service Craigslist shifts almost entirely towards the user-producer.

Proprietors may also provide the underlying infrastructure through their server farms. Increasingly, however, such infrastructure is being outsourced to cloud services.

Revenues in such models may reside with the operator (some, like Wikipedia may be non-profit and reliant on donations). Some revenue sharing may take place with professional or amateur content providers.

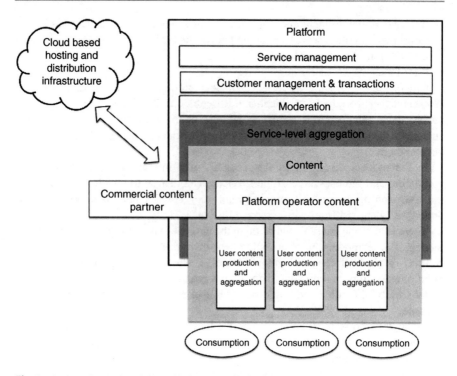

Fig. 3 Aggregation and social applications and platforms

In many instances, the value to the end user is the service itself, although willingness to tolerate such terms can prove to be limited. Huffington Post was able to rely on hundreds of unpaid contributors until its lucrative sale to AOL at which point many former contributors sought legal recourse and their share of the value realised in the AOL transaction. Their lack of success in such cases does not negate the fact that the relationships between proprietor and content providers are not particularly robust and can easily break down.

Of course, services and applications exist within wider networks that are becoming increasingly open with few opportunities for gatekeeping or exclusivity. Application and service operators that are able to aggregate unique content and protect that content are better positioned to become strong nodes within the wider network. Moreover, by placing interactions and sharing within a controlled space, services like facebook are able, to a certain extent, to hive off users from the wider web. Others seek to use technological or platform advantage to assume a dominant position. D'Arma (2011) has highlighted the ability of "hardware and software facilitators like Apple, Google and manufacturers of new Internet-enabled TV sets to push traditional content operators back along the vertical chain into content creation-related activities and forcing them to enter into revenue-sharing deals."

12 Implications

As we have argued, prior to the arrival of the web, aggregation was driven by the desire to control the value chain or, as Murray has noted, discussing broadcast scheduling, by Weberian logics of rationalisation (Murray 2012: 2). Network logics and on-demand technologies and consumption modes challenge established techniques. Counter-programming and 'hammocking' (scheduling new programmes between viewer favourites) are no longer so useful when any show can be watched in catch up mode. But this does not mean that aggregation techniques are disappearing, simply that they are changing. Social television technologies and applications may yet prove to make successful content brands *more* sticky than they have been in the past, introducing counter-incentives to channel surfing.

At the same time, however, it is undeniable that the aggregation activities of media proprietors takes place in an increasingly fragmented and diffuse network. For both broadcasters and newspaper proprietors, time constraints (the schedule or the edition deadline) have become less important in what Castells has termed 'the space of flows' (Castells 2000: 440).

Fragmentation of consumption and revenues pose significant challenges, suggesting that greater levels of collaboration may be required, particularly where production is costly or risky (feature film production, for example). Such pressures may also create a need for new funding models from governmental and intergovernmental agencies, and generate opportunities for commercial funding intermediaries (investors).

The challenge for media organisations in this new environment is to use these new aggregation techniques to reinforce their positions within these diffuse networks, creating and strengthening path dependencies, developing relationships with users and partners, and increasing their ability to route and channel traffic and revenues. Such strategies imply a recognition that they are unlikely to enjoy the levels of dominance and control they have enjoyed in the past, but nor are they simply victims of technological and behavioural changes that are beyond their control.

References

Baumüller, I. (2012, February 10–11). *News media and their challenge to manage recipients' trust European Media Management Education Association Conference*. Budapest.
Benkler, Y. (2002). Coases penguin, or, Linux and the nature of the firm. *Yale Law Journal, 112*, 2002.
Brown, M. (2007). *A licence to be different: The story of Channel 4*. London: British Film Institute.
Brown, C., & Goodwin, P. (2010). Constructing Public Service Media at the BBC. In G. Lowe (Ed.), *The public in public service media*. Gothenburg: Nordicom.
Bruns, A. (2007). *Produsage: A working definition*. Available from http://produsage.org/node/9. Accessed 6 May 2012.
Campbell, L. (2010, September 28). All3Media boss slams Google. *Broadcast*.
Castells, M. (2000). *The rise of the network society: Volume 1: The information age*. Oxford: Blackwell Publishers.

Chesbrough, H., & Rosenbloom, R. S. (2002). The role of the business model in capturing value from innovation: Evidence from Xerox Corporation's technology spin-off companies. *Industrial and Corporate Change, 11*(3), 529–555.

Chesbrough, H. (2008). *Open innovation: Researching a new paradigm.* Oxford: Oxford University Press.

Cordrey, T. speech presented by Tanya Cordrey, director of digital development, Guardian News & Media, at the Guardian Changing Media Summit, London. 21 March, 2012. http://www.guardian.co.uk/gnm-press-office/changing-media-summit-tanya-cordrey Accessed 23 March 2012.

D'Arma, A. (2011). Content aggregation in the age of online video: An analysis of the impact of Internet distribution on the television business. *Journal of Media Business Studies, 8*(3).

Dredge, S. (2012). Google TV YouTube app gets discovery-focused update. Guardian Apps Blog. Available from http://www.guardian.co.uk/technology/appsblog/2012/feb/13/google-tv-youtube-app-update. Accessed 13 February 2012.

Ellis, J. (2000). Scheduling: The last creative act in television. *Media, Culture and Society, 22*, 25–38.

Filloux, F. (2010, September 19) Aggregators: The good ones vs. the looters. The Monday Note.

Halliday, J. (2011, September 22). Facebook to transform into an entertainment hub. *The Guardian.*

Harris Interactive. (2012). *Netflix and YouTube are must have apps for Smart TV owners.* Available from http://www.harrisinteractive.com/NewsRoom/HarrisPolls/tabid/447/mid/1508/articleId/1048/ctl/ReadCustom%20Default/Default.aspx. Accessed 19 July 2012.

Heine, C. (2012, July 20). Amazon recommending offers? Cool. Facebook? No thanks. *Adweek.*

Indivik. (2012). Publishers begin pulling advertising from Flipboard. Mashable. Available from http://mashable.com/2012/06/25/flipboard-new-yorker-wired-advertising/. Accessed 25 June 2012.

Johnson, B. (2009, November 9). Murdoch could block Google searches entirely. *The Guardian.*

Johnson, B. (2012). Zeebox boss says smart TV is a dumb idea. GigaOM. Available from http://gigaom.com/2012/04/02/zeebox-boss-says-smart-tv-is-a-dumb-idea/. Accessed 5 April 2012.

Keller, B. (2011, March 10). All the aggregation that's fit to aggregate. *The New York Times.*

Murray, A. M. (2012, February 10–11). *Rationalising public service: Scheduling as a tool of management in RTE television.* Paper European Media Management Education Association Conference. Budapest.

Napoli, P. M. (2003). *Audience economics: Media institutions and the audience marketplace.* New York, NY: Columbia University Press.

Normann, R., & Ramírez, R. (1993, July–August). From value chain to value constellation: Designing interactive strategy. *Harvard Business Review*, 65–77.

Porter, M. (1985). *Competitive advantage.* New York, NY: Free Press.

Ramirez, R. (1999). Value co-production: Intellectual origins and implications for practice and research. *Strategic Management Journal, 20*, 49–65.

Rose, A. (2012, June 17). Interview. TechCrunch TV. Available from http://techcrunch.com/2012/06/17/zeebox-tctv-demo/. Accessed 24 June 2012.

The Guardian. (2010, July 6). Leading the way through mutualisation. *The Guardian.*

Walker. (2012, June 14). Habbo Hotel: NSPCC urges government and technology industry to act. *The Guardian.*

Williams, R. (2003). *Television: Technology and cultural form.* London: Routledge Classics.

Wingfield, N. (2012, April 27). In search of apps for television. *New York Times.*

How Media Companies Should Create Value: Innovation Centered Business Models and Dynamic Capabilities

Hans van Kranenburg and Gerrit Willem Ziggers

1 Introduction

Globalization, deregulation, technological innovation and the convergence of previously separated industries such as media, entertainment, information, and consumer electronics industries, have changed the media landscape into a turbulent environment. As a consequence of these developments, many media firms are experiencing severe challenges, as content proliferates, audiences change behaviors, advertising revenue erodes, and new competitors emerge. Digital technology is eroding the benefits of scale to media companies, in particular traditional media companies: as print circulation declines and cost savings generated from centralized production and distribution decline. Media firms operating in this rapidly changing environment have to make adequate adaptations to these fast moving changes and respond quickly to create or to sustain their competitive advantage. They are generally confronted with the fact that existing resources and capabilities are no longer sufficient to deal with the new demands and requirements (Oh 1996). In order to adjust to the new environment, the media companies need to obtain, integrate, and reconfigure resources and capabilities in order to adjust to the new environment (Kranenburg et al. 2001). An interesting development is that it is no longer necessary for media firms to make the 'three pronged investments' (Chandler 1990):

- Manufacturing Production facilities to exploit the advantages of scale and scope;
- Marketing and distribution networks: to keep up the pace with mass production;
- Management to govern the enlarged complex business activities: Managerial hierarchies and technological skills.

These firms instead simply build capacity to manage a customer responsive network. Such a network can constitute a viable organizational form in today's media environment. A group of researchers has called such firms 'network firms' and

---

H. van Kranenburg (✉) • G.W. Ziggers
Radboud University Nijmegen, Nijmegen School of Management, The Netherlands
e-mail: h.vankranenburg@fm.ru.nl

suggests that they may constitute a new organizational form with new business model concepts (Teece 1993). These companies have undoubtedly been successful. Flexible specialization and contracting may today yield greater advantages than economies of scale and scope generated internally. These kind of firms are distinctly non-Chandleresque. Hence, media firms have to rethink their traditional manner of revenue generation, the structure of the organization, the core competencies of the organization and the way of creating value through new opportunities. The companies should therefore redesign their business models. These models describe the rationale of how the organization creates, delivers, and captures value (Osterwalder and Pigneur 2010). Present systems, governance structures and established institutions are not capable to provide adequate solutions since they were created in a bygone area. Media companies act more and more in projects, value-chains and networks. New and often innovative forms of collaboration are emerging. This requires new concepts, new ideas and new managerial approaches. Two important questions that arise are what kind of business model do media companies need to maintain their competitive advantages and how should the media company simultaneously benefit from the old business models and introduce new innovative business models to create value in the rapidly changing media landscape. In this paper, we present the main characteristics of the new innovative business models for media companies and how media companies should transform themselves into more flexible networked organizations enabling them to gain and create sustainable competitive advantages. The likelihood to develop a multiple business model system successfully within their own organization will be enhanced by embracing ambidexterity. We will also discuss the importance for media companies to develop dynamic capabilities (Eisenhardt and Martin 2000; Teece et al. 1997) within a strategic network context (Dyer and Singh 1998) in acquiring and retaining a sustainable competitive position for the firm.

The structure of the paper is as follows. The next section discusses the business models and introduces the innovation centered business model. Section 3 discusses the mechanisms (i.e. organizational rigidities and tardily reactions) that restrain the ability of media firms to adequately react and introduce the innovation centered business model. Section 4 presents the ambidextrous strategy as a solution to overcome the rigidities and tardily reactions. Section 5 addresses and explains the required dynamic capabilities that companies should develop to become an ambidextrous organization enabling the adoption of the innovation centered business model a prerequisite to obtain sustainable competitive advantage. Section 6 presents how a media company can focus on exploitation of existing businesses but also be innovative. The closing section presents some conclusions that can be drawn from this contribution.

2 Innovation Centered Business Models

For media companies confronted with business turbulence caused by technological progress a salient issue becomes the way it chooses to position itself against competitors in the industry and what business model to adopt. The business models

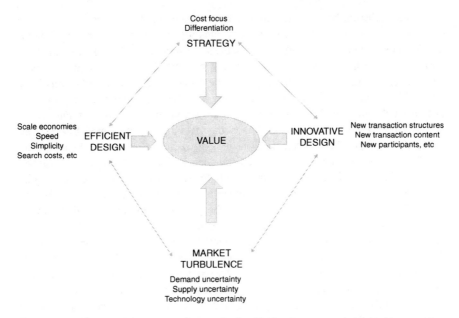

Fig. 1 The business model concept: value creation by aligning strategy, market & business structure

reflect the company's product market strategy and entails those decisions that affect the main drivers of customer demand: price, quality, and timing. A firm can leverage these drivers by answering two fundamental strategic questions, namely what type of product market positioning approach to adopt, i.e. cost leadership and/or product/service differentiation (Porter 1985); and when to enter the market (Lieberman and Montgomery 1988). The answers to these questions are central to the understanding of how companies and their business models that operate in competitive product markets create and appropriate value. The design choice for a certain business model relates to its product market positioning and can be characterized as either being innovation or efficiency centered. Both design types are not mutually exclusive as several design choices may be present in any given business model (Geoffrion and Krishnan 2003; Zott and Amit 2007, 2008). The business model itself represents the structural template that captures the focal company's transactions with external partners to create value (Fig. 1).

It has to be noticed that a business model is often considered as being similar as a model for generating revenues. However to avoid confusion and misconception a revenue model refers to the specific modes in which a business model enables revenue generation. Media firms generate revenues through subscription fees, advertising, and transactional income (i.e. including fixed transaction fees, referral fees, commissions). These revenue generating modes are often used in combination. Derived from the provided definitions, the business model and the revenue model are complementary but distinct concepts. A business model refers primarily to value creation whereas a revenue model is primarily concerned with value appropriation (Zott and Amit 2008).

As the media market is a turbulent market, media companies are confronted with a need to adapt their business models to stay synchronized. Therefore, companies should develop innovation-centered business models to sustain or improve their competitive positions. Innovation-centered business models refer to new ways of conducting business exchanges among various participants. The conceptualization and adoption of new ways of conducting business transactions can be achieved by connecting previously unconnected parties or by designing new transaction mechanisms. The innovation-centered business model construct builds on several ideas promoted by the main theoretical frameworks of strategic management. It is consistent with Schumpeter's (1942) idea of innovation as an act of 'creative destruction'. Innovation in the perspective of the business model refers not only to products, production processes, distribution channels and markets, but also to the exchange mechanisms and transaction designs. Innovation centered business models have the potential to disrupt existing industry structures and thereby pose a serious threat to incumbents. The innovation centered business model construct also draws on arguments that are central to the value chain framework (Porter 1985) by emphasizing that processes and multiple sources of value matter. This includes the processes that are centered on product flows and those processes that enable transactions. In line with this it builds on strategic network theory (e.g. Burt 1992; Coleman 1990) posing that there is a link between the network configuration and value creation and that the locus of value creation may be the network rather than the firm. It encompasses suppliers, intermediates and customers with which the firm has to cooperate or to compete. It is the unique combinations of inter-firm cooperative arrangements, such as strategic alliances or joint ventures that allow for value creation (Dyer and Singh 1998). It also builds on transaction cost economics (Williamson 1975) as it addresses efficient governance mechanisms that mediate transactions that contribute to efficiency enhancements. Lastly, the innovation centered business model builds on the dynamic capability view (Helfat et al. 2007; Teece 2009) as it reflects the firm's ability to purposefully create, extend, or modify the resource base enabling a firm's organizational fitness as well as help shaping the environment advantageously. The value embedded in the business model increases as the bundle of resources and capabilities it encompasses becomes more difficult to imitate, less transferable, less substitutable, and more complementary. The innovation centered business model perspective therefore should take into consideration the ways in which resources can be valuable and how a firm can stay synchronized with market changes.

3 Drivers of Market Turbulence and Inhibitors of Adaptability

Both business to business markets and business to consumer markets are confronted with increasing market turbulence caused by fragmentation of markets, proliferating digital media and rapidly growing number of customer touch points and channels. Illustrative is the mobile phone market. Ten years ago there were only three demographic segments served by wireless carriers, now over twenty value based segments are distinguished. The number of the offerings has increased into the hundreds, with a variety of calling and messaging plans, telephones with a variety of devices, and operating systems becoming a major differentiator. The number of distribution channels has increased from three to over more than ten, including company stores, shared and exclusive dealers, telemarketing agents and related partners. Pricing point exceeding 500.000 due to tailored pricing plans. Variants of the same story of fragmenting markets segments, proliferating digital media, and rapidly growing number of customer touch points and channels are found in both business to business and business to consumer markets (Day 2011). Consequently, changes in customer search and choice, the fragmentation into micro-segments, the convergence of industries intensifying competition, and growing power of channels is increasing (Hagel et al. 2009). The drivers are the enormous falling costs of band-with, storage, and computing, as well as easier wireless connectivity, promoting the use of digital and internet technologies (i.e. detailed customer tracking systems, digital sources like websites, social media and the like). The result is that many mass markets are becoming a mass of niches (Anderson 2006) providing opportunities for value creation and profit (Day 2011). It illustrates the fast moving developments in the media landscape and the opportunities it provides for media companies, but also the need to introduce an innovation centered business model. However, most media companies have difficulties to grasp these new opportunities and find it even more difficult to embrace and introduce the innovation centered business model concept to reposition themselves and regain competitiveness. The innovation centered business model requires new capabilities and strategic and resource alignment well beyond the companies (Day 2011; Dyer and Singh 1998).

The underlying mechanisms that restrain the ability to adequately react and introduce the innovation centered business model are organizational rigidities and tardily reactions. *Organizational rigidities* When an organization has mastered a capability it is likely to keep doing it long past the point of obsolescence. As a capability emerges from series of path dependent learning experiences, successful experiences are reinforced and repeated. This eventually limits other possible approaches and may lock the company into a dominant approach (Day 2011). The selection of a capability (e.g. creating a community platform) requires that it works in a replicable and reliable way in a variety of contexts. This often hampers the adaptation to new circumstances as it crowds out the necessary sensing, experimentation, and exploration which is the essence of a dynamic capability (Helfat et al. 2007; March 1991). Also there are scale economies to capability building. A lack of intra-organizational exchange of information and cooperation may inhibit the development of deep expertise in next-generation capabilities. Despite the benefits of specialization and focus, a media company with independent operational units limits the sort of cross-functional dialogue and learning that creates novel ideas, and thus reduces adaptation (Aaker 2009). *Tardily reactions.* Even if a media company can overcome the organizational rigidities it takes time to absorb new information, interpret its meaning, and then mobilize it to act. Traditional decision processes are slow and by the time a new marketing initiative is launched the market has moved forward to a new state. Meanwhile the pace of technology has not slowed. Any feedback from the initiative is lagging behind and difficult to interpret (Day 2011).

4   The Strategy of Ambidexterity

Today's reality is that media firms should adapt to the fast changing technological, market and demand developments to build a competitive advantage that is sustainable because market dynamics make existing capabilities obsolete tomorrow. Instead of trying to create stability, media firms must actively work to disrupt their own advantages and the advantages of competitors by continuously challenge existing capabilities. It implies a tension of how to both exploit existing businesses and to explore new ones. This distinction between exploitation and exploration has long been addressed as structures designed for efficiency and those designed for innovations (D'Aveni 1994; He and Wong 2004). The former involves continuous search for improvement along a fixed production function, while the latter requires discontinuous shifts from one production function to another that is more profitable. Both capture a number of fundamental differences in media firm behavior and strategy that have significant consequences for performance (March 1991). On the one hand, adaptation to existing market demands may foster structural slowness and reduces media firm's capacity to adapt to future environmental changes and new opportunities (Hannan and Freeman 1984). It implies a media firm which is only incrementally adapting its existing business model emphasizing process efficiency and effectiveness. On the other hand, experimenting with new alternatives reduces the speed at which existing capabilities are improved and refined (March 1991). It may disrupt successful routines in a media firm's existing markets to the point that it cannot compensate for the loss in the existing business (Mitchell and Singh 1993). The challenge for media firms is to develop and to incorporate new business models, such as the innovation centered business model, to fulfill the new requirements and demands. This approach enables the media firm to be really innovative and to develop new capabilities and resources to sustain their competitive position.

Consequently, media firms should transform themselves into ambidextrous organizations. With the ambidextrous structure media firms develop a capability to both compete in mature markets, (emphasizing costs, efficiency, and incremental innovations) and develop new products/services for emerging markets (emphasizing experimentation, speed, and flexibility (O'Reilly and Tushman 2004). The potential of ambidexterity is supported by empirical findings of He and Wong (2004), although their findings also suggest that there are limits to ambidexterity. Because both exploration and exploitation compete for scarce resources and require different strategies and structures trade-offs have to be made (Smith et al. 2010). Inherently this implies tensions and ambidexterity may become unmanageable when pushed to extreme limits. However, this tension may apply to an individual media company, in a business model and network context conflicts over mindsets and organizational routines become non-issues when considered as either loosely connected or connected via standardized/modular interfaces. Ambidexterity in this context becomes an issue of where to dedicate exploration and exploitation. In other words some firms may be specialized in exploration while others in exploitation. A balance is achieved via inter organizational relationships. Such a strategy is likely to be effective if (1) the firms involved control mutually complementary resources, (2) the domains represent both dynamic and stable environments ensuring a persistent need for exploration and exploitation (Gupta et al. 2006), and (3) a governance structure ensuring that each get compensated adequately for its contribution.

5 Required Capabilities

To become an ambidextrous organization, to introduce the innovation centered business model, and to obtain sustainable competitive advantage, dynamic capabilities are required that create, adjust, and keep relevant stock of capabilities. The dynamic capability is the company's ability to purposefully create, extend, or modify its resource base (Helfat et al. 2007; Teece et al. 1997; Eisenhardt and Martin 2000). A dynamic capability is a deeply embedded set of skills and knowledge exercised through a process enabling a company to stay synchronized with market changes and to stay ahead of competitors. It entails the capabilities that enable organizational fitness (Winter 2005) as well as help to shape the environment advantageously (Day 2011). Its main function are (1) sensing environmental changes that could be threats or opportunities, by scanning, searching and exploring across markets and technologies; (2) responding to the changes by combining and transforming available resources through partnerships or acquisition. The first type of dynamic capabilities are known as market sensing capabilities and the latter type are known as the relational capabilities. These dynamic capabilities will help the media companies to select the business model configuration for delivering value and capturing revenues.

5.1 Market Sensing: Handling Volatile and Unpredictable Markets

Dynamic capabilities in market sensing comprise the function of marketing intelligence and coordination of internal business processes to act quickly and effectively in response to information gathered from customers and other external stakeholders (Kohli and Jaworski 1990; Narver and Slater 1990). It entails a behavioral shift from a reactive to a sense-and-respond approach amplified with emerging technologies for seeking patterns and sharing insights quickly. But how can media companies learn to make sense out of an increasingly volatile and unpredictable market? Drawing on complexity literature and organizational mindfulness literature may provide an answer. Complexity theory demonstrates that all successful adapting systems transform apparent noise into meaning faster than the apparent noise comes to them (Haeckel 1999). This means, these companies have mastered a vigilant market sensing capability that helps to discover sooner. Literature on organizational mindfulness (Fiol and O'Connor 2003; Levinthal and Rerup 2006) has addressed the capability of early sensing. Mindfulness is a heightened state of awareness, characterized by curiosity, alertness, and a willingness to act on partial information. Media companies that have developed a robust market sensing capability differ from their counterparts in various ways. They have developed an orientation towards the market and by means of multiple inquiry methods ambiguous signals are thoroughly analyzed to learn more about promising patterns and new opportunities. They use scenario thinking to consider multiple possible futures and a high tolerance for ambiguity along with the ability to pose the right questions to identify what they do not know. Also these companies have a transparent organization avoiding organizational filters and allowing them to notice threats or opportunities detected by someone deep in the organization or the network of partners. Media companies with a market sensing capability work hard to bring together different perspectives on an issue to avoid the coerciveness of group thinking allowing to jump to most convenient conclusion and seeking evidence that confirms the consideration (Day 2011).

To develop a market sensing capability requires learning, which entails a willingness to focus on (1) past, present en prospective customers and observe how they process data and respond to social networking and social media space without a biased view; (2) an open minded approach to latent needs; and (3) an ability to sense and act on weak signals from the business environment. It is the difference between testing copy versions with controlled experiments and continuously scanning the market for ideas concepts and formulations that are working or failing (Day 2011). This learning from markets is not fully effectuated until the findings are accurately interpreted an adequately shared throughout the organization as well as business partners. Similar to ambidexterity, developing a market sensing capability is problematic. Managers may misinterpret what they see in favor of what they want to see or ignore the results that challenge prevailed knowledge, and/or do not share information with their business partners. As a consequence it may lead to failures of new market initiatives.

The same technologies that cause market turbulence can be applied to strengthen this learning capability. Particular promising are advances in (social) networks enabling intra- and inter-organizational learning. For example media companies can detect and share nowadays in an early stage shifts in buying patterns or emerging micro markets by tracking trend data, market data and derived studies by the use of search-engines (Day 2011).

5.2 Relational Capabilities: Managing Collaboration

Responding to market turbulence urges media companies to collaborate with network partners. This puts a premium on relational capabilities that extend the company's resource base beyond firm boundaries and enable access to partners' resources (Dyer and Singh 1998) and to compete more effectively in the marketplace (Day 1995; Ziggers and Tjemkes 2010). A company that possesses relational capabilities places a high priority on present and prospective inter-organizational relationships and has advanced several skills. First, it possess the skills to monitor and identify partnering opportunities. Those skill represent a deliberate and conscious investment to monitor the business environment that allow firms to have a more precise view on the kind of partners or resources to generate revenues from and to form partner relationships with them (Dyer and Singh 1998; Gulati 1999). Second, it is able to systematically integrate strategies, to synchronize activities and to disseminate knowledge across their network of partners. To leverage the uniqueness of their network, to combine the respective resources available, and to generate new capabilities that may be required, coordination skills become critical (Kandemir et al. 2006). If done properly the company can exploit its competitive advantages more completely (e.g. Anderson and Narus 1990; Ziggers and Tjemkes 2010). Third, the ability to handle unforeseen contingencies in partner interactions, requires partnering learning skills. That is a firm's internalisation of its direct experiences, successes, and failures when collaborating with other firms (Kale and Singh 2007) and diffusion of learning effects across its network of partners (Kandemir et al. 2006). For example to organize inter-organizational team meetings to exchange information about the progress and problems with regard to the collaboration. Finally, a company has to put emphasis on the development of capable alliance managers, that understand and are capable to manage the key activities at every stage of the partnering life-cycle (e.g. Day 1995; Kale and Singh 2007; Lambe et al. 2002). It requires a deliberate and conscious investment in training and educating alliance managers. If done properly, these managers will be able to broker partner relationships such that partners develop and transfer knowledge that facilitates the pursuit of commercial opportunities (Simonin 1999).

Nevertheless, the effective management of inter-organizational relationships is a complex endeavour. The main reason is the huge control and coordination problems that have to be dealt with when managing a network of businesses, including monitoring, accountability, and conflicts of interests. Relational capabilities enable the effective management of such networks. As they are difficult to learn and far more difficult to copy, they can contribute to gain advantage over competitors (e.g. Dyer and Singh 1998; Kandemir et al. 2006; Ziggers and Tjemkes 2010). Therefore, media companies who have the right conditions and commitment grab the best partners and will succeed.

6   Towards Adaptive Organizations and Business Models

While all markets are subject to greater complexity at higher velocities, the urgency to respond and to adapt will differ depending on whether a firm serves mass markets with millions of customers or sells complex systems to small number of customers (Moore 2006). Also media companies will face difficult choices when deciding how to build a capability for responding more adaptively. An enthusiastic approach of pursuing many diverse uncoordinated opportunities will end-up in escalating complexity, coordination costs, dissipating scale economies and the like. A more ambitious approach will therefore be to become and to build an organization that embraces ambidexterity. This challenge requires changes in a company's culture, structures and business model. Compelling leadership and commitment and the ability to develop essential capabilities are prerequisites for developing adaptive organizations and innovation centred business models. It will lead companies to determine what key-issues it faces in their business environment and to decide on a course of action that will create sustainable competitive advantage. What the right choice will be will depend on a company's circumstances and its competitive analysis. The strategy must respond, in some form, to the following questions: Which markets will we target? What is the value proposition that distinguishes us?, What key processes give us competitive advantage?, What are the (human capital) capabilities required to excel at these key processes?, What are the technology enablers of the strategy?, What are the organizational and network enablers required for the strategy?

The likelihood of a successful transformation or to become more adaptive will increase sharply when senior management is committed and takes accountability along with a compelling vision, relentlessly communicated. It requires executives who have the ability to understand and be sensitive to the needs of very different kinds of businesses. Combining the attributes of exploration and exploitation, i.e. cost efficiency and free-thinking entrepreneurship, while maintaining objectivity required to make difficult trade-offs are essential.

The ability to develop essential capabilities is a continuous learning process that requires clear objectives and relentless monitoring to determine whether the capabilities are improving. The emphasis should be on designing metrics to assess the progress from different initiatives. Tools like a balanced scorecard management system (Kaplan and Norton 2008), can provide support in aligning the business and the ability to respond adaptively. In the case of market initiatives the chosen set of metrics should reveal what target markets think and what they actually do, and should reveal actual delivered value. In the case of collaborative initiatives the chosen set of metrics should reveal how the partnership is lived, focusing on strategic, operational and relational fit. The key is to combine measures of ultimate success with intermediate diagnostic metrics that can be used to identify successes and problems and to transfer learning effects within the organization and across the network of partners. Figure 2 presents the generic simplified business model strategy map. It visualises a media company's strategy as a chain of cause-and-effect relationships to effectuate strategic objectives based on the principles of the balanced scorecard (Kaplan and Norton 2008). It starts with the company's long term performance objectives which are related to objectives and value propositions for the market From there it links to goals related to internal and external processes. Finally, it is related to the organizational climate and culture and market and relational capabilities required for successful business model development and execution.

Conclusions

Most managers will acknowledge the uncertainty about how to navigate in the reality of technological and market turbulence. It raises classic questions of "What business are we in?", "Who is our customer?", "What does our customer value?" But also fundamental questions as "Which activities are performed by the company?", "What is the economic logic that explains how these activities deliver value?", and "How do we make profit of it?". It is all about how media companies can reposition themselves to regain competitiveness. It requires strategic and resource alignment well beyond the companies' boundaries.

However most companies have difficulties to cope with it. Market turbulence demands companies for tailored programs, mass customization, multimedia optimization, and adaptive and innovation centered business models with a set of capabilities appropriate to deal with them. Today's reality is that no media firm

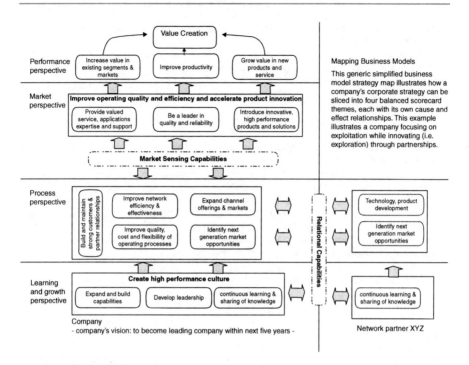

Fig. 2 Mapping business models

can maintain its competitive advantages based on existing capabilities and their existing business model. To retain and sustain their competitive advantages, media firms should be innovative and may have to disrupt their own existing advantages by continuously challenging existing capabilities.

Media firms can only do this when they use the existing businesses as cash cow to finance innovative and explorative businesses. This implies that the media firm should develop and use different types of business models simultaneously. An innovation centered business model will increase the media firm's capacity to adapt to future environmental changes and new opportunities. The likelihood to develop a multiple business model system successfully within their own organization will be enhanced by embracing ambidexterity. Backed up by an organizational climate and culture and dynamic capabilities for successful business model development and execution.

References

Aaker, D. A. (2009). *Spanning silos*. Boston: Harvard Business School Press.
Anderson, C. (2006). *The long tail: Why the future of business is selling less of more*. New York: Hyperion.
Anderson, J. C., & Narus, J. A. (1990). A model of the distributor's firm and manufacturer firm working partnerships. *Journal of Marketing, 54*, 42–58.

Burt, R. S. (1992). *Structural holes: The social structure of competition.* Cambridge: Harvard University Press.
Chandler, A. D., Jr. (1990). *Scale and scope: The dynamics of industrial capitalism.* Cambridge, MA: The Belknap Press of the Harvard University Press.
Coleman, J. S. (1990). *Foundations of social theory.* Cambridge: Harvard University Press.
D'Aveni, R. (1994). *Hypercompetition: Managing the dynamics of strategic maneuvering.* New York: Free Press.
Day, G. S. (1995). Advantageous alliances. *Journal of the Academy of Marketing Science, 23*(4), 297–300.
Day, G. S. (2011). Closing the marketing capabilities gap. *Journal of Marketing, 75*(4), 183–195.
Dyer, J. H., & Singh, H. (1998). The relational view: Cooperative strategy and sources of interorganizational competitive advantage. *Academy of Management Review, 23*(4), 660–679.
Eisenhardt, K. M., & Martin, J. A. (2000). Dynamic capabilities: What are they? *Strategic Management Journal, 21,* 1105–1121.
Fiol, C. M., & O'Connor, E. J. (2003). Waking up! Mindfulness in the face of bandwagons. *The Academy of Management Review, 28*(1), 54–70.
Geoffrion, A. M., & Krishnan, R. (2003). E-business and management science: Mutual impacts (part 1 of 2). *Management Science, 49*(10), 1275–1286.
Gulati, R. (1999). Network location and learning: The influence of network resources and firm capabilities on alliance formation. *Strategic Management Journal, 20*(5), 397–420.
Gupta, A. K., Smith, K. G., & Shalley, C. E. (2006). The interplay between exploration and exploitation. *Academy of Management Journal, 49,* 693–706.
Haeckel, S. H. (1999). Winning in smart markets. *Sloan Management Review, 41*(1), 7–8.
Hagel, J., Brown, J. S., & Davison, L. (2009). The big shift measuring the forces of change. *Harvard Business Review, 87*(7–8), 86–89.
Hannan, M. T., & Freeman, J. (1984). Structural inertia and organizational-change. *American Sociological Review, 49*(2), 149–164.
He, Z. L., & Wong, P. K. (2004). Exploration vs. exploitation: An empirical test of the ambidexterity hypothesis. *Organization Science, 15*(4), 481–494.
Helfat, C. E., Finkelstein, S., Mitchell, W., Peteraf, M. A., Singh, H., & Winter, S. G. (2007). *Dynamic capabilities: Understanding strategic change in organizations.* Oxford: Blackwell.
Kale, P., & Singh, H. (2007). Building firm capabilities through learning: The role of the alliance learning process in alliance capability and firm-level alliance success. *Strategic Management Journal, 28*(10), 981–1000.
Kandemir, D., Yaprak, A., & Cavusgil, S. T. (2006). Alliance orientation: Conceptualization, measurement, and impact on market performance. *Academy of Marketing Science, 34*(3), 324–340.
Kaplan, R. S., & Norton, D. P. (2008). Mastering the management system. *Harvard Business Review, 86*(1), 62–77.
Kohli, A. K., & Jaworski, B. J. (1990). Market orientation – The construct, research propositions, and managerial implications. *Journal of Marketing, 54*(2), 1–18.
Lambe, C. J., Spekman, R. E., & Hunt, S. D. (2002). Alliance competence, resources, and alliance success: Conceptualization, measurement, and initial test. *Journal of the Academy of Marketing Science, 30*(2), 141–158.
Levinthal, D., & Rerup, C. (2006). Crossing an apparent chasm: Bridging mindful and less-mindful perspectives on organizational learning. *Organization Science, 17*(4), 502–513.
Lieberman, M. B., & Montgomery, D. B. (1988). 1st-mover advantages. *Strategic Management Journal, 9,* 41–58.
March, J. G. (1991). Exploration and exploitation in organizational learning. *Organization Science, 2*(1), 71–78.
Mitchell, W., & Singh, K. (1993). Detach of the lethargic – Effects of expansion into new technical subfields on performance in a firm base business. *Organization Science, 4*(2), 152–180.

Moore, G. (2006). *Dealing with Darwin: How great companies innovate at every state of their evolution*. New York: Penguin Portfolio.

Narver, J. C., & Slater, S. F. (1990). The effect of a market orientation on business profitability. *Journal of Marketing, 54*(4), 20–35.

O'Reilly, C. A., & Tushman, M. L. (2004). The ambidextrous organisation. *Harvard Business Review, 82*(4), 74–81.

Oh, J. (1996). Global strategic alliances in the telecommunications industry. *Telecommunications Policy, 20*(9), 713–720.

Osterwalder, A., & Pigneur, Y. (2010). *Business model generation: A handbook for visionaries, game changers, and challengers* (Wiley Desktop Editions Series). New York: Wiley.

Porter, M. E. (1985). *Competitive advantage*. New York: Free Press.

Schumpeter, J. A. (1942). *Capitalism, socialism, and democracy*. New York: Harper.

Simonin, B. L. (1999). Ambiguity and the process of knowledge transfer in strategic alliances. *Strategic Management Journal, 20*(7), 595–623.

Smith, W. K., Binns, A., & Tushman, M. L. (2010). Complex business models: Managing strategic paradoxes simultaneously. *Long Range Planning, 43*(2–3), 448–461.

Teece, D. J. (1993). The dynamics of industrial capitalism: Perspectives on Alfred Chandler's scale and scope. *Journal of Economic Literature, 31*, 199–225.

Teece, D. J. (2009). *Dynamic capabilities and strategic management*. Oxford: Oxford University Press.

Teece, D. J., Pisano, G., & Shuen, A. (1997). Dynamic capabilities and strategic management. *Strategic Management Journal, 18*(7), 509–533.

Van Kranenburg, H. L., Clood, M., & Hagedoorn, J. (2001). An exploratory study of recent trends in the diversification of Dutch publishing companies in the multimedia and information industries. *International Studies of Management and Organization, 31*(1), 64–86.

Williamson, O. E. (1975). *Markets and hierarchies: Analysis and antitrust implications*. New York: Free Press.

Winter, S. G. (2005). *On fitness and the survival of the fittest*. Working paper, University of Pennsylvania.

Ziggers, G. W., & Tjemkes, B. V. (2010). Dynamics in inter-firm collaboration: The impact of alliance capabilities on performance. *Journal of Food System Dynamics, 1*(2), 151–166.

Zott, C., & Amit, R. (2007). Business model design and the performance of entrepreneurial firms. *Organization Science, 18*(2), 181–199.

Zott, C., & Amit, R. (2008). The fit between product market strategy and business model: Implications for firm performance. *Strategic Management Journal, 29*(1), 1–26.

Media Management and Social Media Business: New Forms of Value Creation in the Context of Increasingly Interconnected Media Applications

Reinhard Kunz and Stefan Werning

1 Introduction

Media companies are facing the problem of modelling the increasingly volatile and complex forms of emergent media use and of channelling it through their services in order to create a sustainable business model. Thus, media usage processes increasingly constitute a core aspect of value creation for emerging media companies. From that angle, virtually all types of media can and should be considered "social" in the sense that they trigger socially structured forms of usage; recent developments such as "collective viewing", which are gradually gaining scholarly attention, illustrate this point (Xu and Yan 2011). Anticipating patterns of media use and converting them into stable forms of use allows for companies to identify new ways of value creation. Since different disciplines have different understandings of the concept of value, we will primarily distinguish between the terms "value creation" (economics) and "value conception" (media studies).

Porter (1985) introduced the concept of value creation and particularly the notion of the "value chain" into management studies. Based on Thompson's (1967) "organizational technologies", Stabell and Fjeldstad (1998) added the "value shop" and the "value network" as two additional configurations for services. Although it has hardly been used with regard to media yet in on-topic literature, we especially consider the value network to be relevant for analyzing media-specific value creation. In times of digitization, convergence, and social networks media companies and services become increasingly dependent on strategic co-operations in networks and alliances regarding production and marketing. Moreover, the consumers become an active part in value creation as "prosumers" (Toffler 1980). Network-based value creation and the consumers being a part of the production

R. Kunz (✉) • S. Werning
University of Bayreuth, Bayreuth, Germany
e-mail: reinhard.kunz@uni-bayreuth.de

processes themselves coincides as well with the idea of "value in context" in service-dominant logic in marketing (Vargo and Lusch 2008).

This chapter aims at investigating the manifold points of contact between media use and corresponding concepts of value creation, which, as will be elaborated using concrete examples, challenge existing scholarly models. For that purpose, we develop a systematic and comparative perspective on the sprawling field of start-ups, which focus on a central online platform or a web-based application. Albeit growing rapidly, sometimes even into multi-billion dollar businesses, these companies are essentially very flexible—starting small and often exchanging data or revenue with competitors in order to define their market quickly—and usually revolve around one software product or platform. Therefore, we will label this type of company, which increasingly shapes the media landscape and the ways in which media are being used, micro business models (MBMs).

From a media studies perspective, these usage scenarios are primarily being discussed within the context of software studies (Fuller 2008). The most applicable body of research within this field is the notion of web studies, which analyzes the specific functionality and emergent practices of web technologies (Rogers 2009). This rather technology-centric field could be productively complemented with a fan studies perspective which maps motivations of users investing in a given media property and more or less actively social usage behaviour (Mittell 2009).

Drawing on this body of research, this chapter shall focus especially on the interplay of media technological and management rationalities, which is characteristic of MBMs following the aforementioned definition but has only cursorily been approached within the on-topic literature. Moreover, existing approaches usually cover the biggest and most visible examples such as *Facebook* or *Twitter*. Inversely, we propose the thesis that dynamic constellations of smaller, interconnected applications and companies designed to monetize them constitute an increasingly relevant phenomenon within the contemporary media economy.

2 Concepts of Value Creation

The creation of value by an enterprise generally refers to using different resources such as materials or the employees' skills and knowledge (input) in order to produce goods and services (output). It is assumed that the output of the company's processes is more valuable than the input. In consequence, the company yields profits that can be distributed to stakeholders such as shareholders, employees, banks, etc. (Gläser 2008). In management and marketing literature different concepts of value creation exist. These will be addressed in this section in order to find a suitable concept describing the value creation activities of contemporary media enterprises in general and media micro business models in particular.

2.1 Value Chain

Porter (1985) introduced the term "value creation"—a term formerly used in economics—to the management theory and thus created the "value chain". The value chain represents a strategic instrument for the analysis and planning of corporate activities. As a matter of principle these activities can be assigned to two different levels, namely the primary and the secondary level. Primary activities are directly involved in the value creation process, while secondary activities indirectly facilitate and support the value creation. Support activities are generally differentiated between procurement, firm infrastructure, technology development and human resource management.

With the conception of the value chain, Porter applied the logic of a transformational process as it is typically used in industrial enterprises and produced goods (Porter 1985; Woratschek et al. 2002): production factors are put in the enterprise (inbound logistics), are being transformed, edited and combined to products (production operations), then stored and kept at hand for sale (outbound logistics), subsequently they are advertised, sold and distributed (marketing and sales). Following, customer questions are being solved and warranty activities realized (customer services).

On that note, the highly vertically integrated Hollywood studio model, which has been studied in great detail within media studies discourse, basically corresponds to the general form of the value chain, since the major studios attempted to combine as many primary and support activities, including production of film stock and control over the movie theatres, as possible. This development, which differs dramatically from the film industry during the early years of the twentieth century, has thus been appropriately understood as an "industrialization" process (Bakker 2003).

Current developments in the media sector—most notably processes of digitization—have led to the emergence of numerous modifications and re-configurations of medial value chains, for example (dis-)intermediation as well as the integration and networking of value chains (Gläser 2008). Former independent business segments (print, radio, television, Internet) are becoming more and more interdependent as well as difficult to be separated. Media enterprises frequently rely on co-operations in strategic partnerships, networks and alliances; others merge with other media enterprises or with companies from adjacent industries. Especially online media combine diverse possibilities of networking and integration. They represent a good example of growing convergence. Exclusively focusing on the value chain as logic of value creation is insufficient in this context.

Based on Thompson's (1967) "organizations in action", Stabell and Fjeldstad (1998) amended the value chain with two further logics of value creation which are especially suitable for complex services (Woratschek et al. 2002): the value shop and the value network. The primary activities differ from value chains whereas the support activities basically remain the same.

2.2   Value Shop

Enterprises, whose primary activities follow the logic of a "value shop", provide a problem-solving-function (Stabell and Fjeldstad 1998). First, customers are acquired via marketing activities (acquisition); these customers have to deal with certain problems which need to be captured and later solved (problem-finding).

After the reconsideration of different solution possibilities (problem-solving), an alternative needs to be chosen (decision) and measurements, which support the problem-solving, need to be realized (execution). Finally, the process has to be controlled and documented (evaluation) in order to learn from experience and gather knowledge for future and refined solutions. Value creation activities of value shops do not operate in a linear and sequential manner like value chains but cyclically and iteratively. A typical example for this phenomenon is a business consultancy (Woratschek et al. 2002). Within the media system such a problem-solving-function is accredited to airtime marketers and media agencies that attempt to optimally position brands and advertising messages of enterprises among suitable media and in an appropriate context of media contents in order to selectively reach specific target groups.

2.3 Value Network

"Value networks" such as telecommunication service providers primarily occupy an intermediary function; they establish and maintain contacts between different participants in the market. The value creation activities of mediation occur simultaneously. Primary activities of value networks comprise the network infrastructure operation, the network promotion and contract management as well as the service provisioning within networks (Stabell and Fjeldstad 1998; Woratschek et al. 2002). A platform among which people and organizations can get in touch with each other needs to be established. Therefore, an exchange of information, agreements on certain standards and a guarantee of compatibility have to be established. The infrastructure of the network needs to be controlled and fostered constantly (infrastructure operation). The attraction of the network has to be communicated in order to interest and convince potential partners to participate (promotion). Besides the promotion of the network, contracts between the network participants need to be initiated and concluded (contract management). The participants of the network have to be offered certain benefits or added value by the network legitimating the participation in the network. In this context the quality and size of the network is of high importance. Core services of the focal network enterprise are the management of contacts and the distribution of commonly created values between all network partners (service provisioning).

The logic of value networks also means that each network participant concentrates on their core competences resulting in an effective division of labour within the network. Relations between the different network participants seem to be highly complex; however, this complexity can be reduced with an effective network management. Besides suppliers, distribution partners and the service provider, consumers themselves become more and more productive in terms of "prosumers" (Toffler 1980) who actively participate in the network and its value creation activities. In this sense, values are "co-created" (Grönroos 2009) in an interactive process between different partners. Such logic of value creation can generally be applied to social networks and other forms of media which generate value by the pooling and management of different partners.

2.4 Value-in-Context

"Value-in-context" is another concept, which is also in concordance with the idea of value networks. It was introduced by Vargo et al. (2008) and Vargo and Lusch (2008) in service-dominant logic (SDL).With SDL (Vargo and Lusch 2004) the understanding of marketing in general has fundamentally changed. Service is considered as the core of value creation of every enterprise: "All economies are service economies" (Vargo and Lusch 2008, p. 4). Tangible assets merely represent appliances to adduce services. Service is defined as "the application of specialized competences (knowledge and skills) through deeds, processes, and performances for the benefit of another entity or the entity itself" (Vargo and Lusch 2004, p. 2). Marketing is developing "from a goods-dominant view, in which tangible output and discrete transactions were central, to a service-dominant view, in which intangibility, exchange processes and relationships are central" (Vargo and Lusch 2004, p. 2).

In terms of SDL customers contribute to the value creation themselves as co-creators. The value of a service is always measured in consideration of the "value-in-use". The value-in-use is the value which is created in interactive processes between the enterprise and the customers; the value is the co-created result of an integration of resources as well as the application of competences of both parties which is actually realized by the claiming of the service. In their recent publications Vargo and Lusch additionally indicated the "value-in-context". Besides the enterprise and the customers, other important network participants as well as context factors contribute to the value co-creation of service. All protagonists contributing to the process of value creation—including customers—are so called "resource integrators" (Lusch and Vargo 2006) who co-create value and mutually provide benefits. "Ultimately, value is phenomenologically and contextually derived [...] by the service beneficiary (i.e. customer). In other words, value is not created until the beneficiary of the service, often the customer, integrates and applies the resources of the service provider with other resources, in the context of its own, specific, available resources, including those from other service systems" (Vargo and Akaka 2009, p. 36).

In coherence with the "value-in-context", not only the providing enterprise but also different other network participants and frame conditions such as economic, social, cultural and environmental factors play an important role. Value creation depends on the respectable situation and different external conditions. Context-specific factors such as resources or circumstances, however, constantly influence the process of value creation. "[T]he context of value creation is as important to the creation of value as the competences of the participating parties" (Vargo et al. 2008, p. 150).

3 Networks of Micro Business Models

In this section, we will attempt to provide examples and identify a number of characteristics of Micro Business Models (MBMs) as defined in the introduction, putting special emphasis on how they are organized into business networks and how they operate internally, i.e. which mechanisms are required to successfully catalyze and channel media use in order to ensure long-term profitability.

3.1 Media Business Models

The business activities of an enterprise can be described by a business model. Business models principally aim at value creation. Thus, the presented concepts of value creation help us understanding business models. "A business model depicts the content, structure, and governance of transactions designed so as to create value through the exploitation of business opportunities" (Amit and Zott 2001, p. 511). Business models link a company's management, production, marketing, and provision of service. Wirtz (2011) differentiates business models in several sub-models: a market, procurement, production, provision, distribution and finance model. The revenue sources of an enterprise can be described by revenue models. "A revenue model refers to the specific modes in which a business model enables revenue generation" (Amit and Zott 2001, p. 515). Eventually, the mode of revenue generation determines the long term success of an enterprise in the market.

Regarding different types of business models of media enterprises providing audio-visual contents television can be differentiated basically in public broadcasting, private free TV and pay TV. These can be distinguished by their objectives (non-profit vs. profit maximization) and their primary revenue generation (broadcasting fees vs. advertisement vs. direct payments from subscriptions).

Internet business models can be categorized by the "4 C-net" (Wirtz and Kleineicken 2000; Wirtz 2011): Content, Commerce, Context and Connection. But only the first business model (content), emphasizes the provision of media content such as the *LIGA total!* Channel by *Telekom Entertain* in Germany (IPTV) or web-based video-on-demand by *Eurosport* in Europe (Web TV). The collection, composition, systematization and provision of digital media contents are core activities of value creation of content-based online business models. Commerce refers to the electronic commerce, e.g. practiced by online enterprises such as *eBay* or *Amazon*. Context providers are search engines such as *Google* or *Yahoo*. *T-Online* and *Vodafone* for example provide access to the Internet and electronic communications enterprises such as *Hotmail* or *Web.de* provide email services (connection). Sigler (2010) differentiates the last business model regarding current developments in terms of web 2.0 and introduces a fifth model for social networks such as *Twitter* or *Facebook*: community.

The 4 C- or 5 C-models can also be applied to mobile media. Mobile devices are supposed to be the most common devices worldwide to access the Internet in the near future (Walsh 2010). Regarding mobile services nowadays especially concerns numerous applications ("apps") based on mobile Internet. These apps that are used via different kinds of devices are the starting point for MBMs.

3.2 Characteristics of Interconnected Micro Business Models

In order to carve out a niche for themselves and to remain competitive, the smaller companies that we focus on in this approach need to form dynamic networks in order to secure a sufficiently large user base and well-defined functionality to survive. For example, Levy (2011) illustrates the shift from large companies to more flexible, highly interconnected business entities with reference to the social music business, outlining some of the key features of competitors such as *spotify, earbits, turntable. fm, rhapsody, MOG, Grooveshark, iheartradio, last.fm, Pandora, rdio*. This form of business model has been formalized for example by entrepreneur and author Eric Ries as the "lean startup" model, which similarly emphasizes modularity, flexibility and frictionless modifiability as key virtues for media start-ups (Ries 2011). Moreover, revisiting the aforementioned 4C- or 5C taxonomies for business models, MBMs often seem to defy these categories and constitute hybrid models, deriving their value proposition from novel re-combinations of heterogeneous business portfolios. We will attempt to point out some of these hybrids in the examples below.

As a by-product of emerging networks of MBMs, the functions of larger companies change in the process as well. Especially in the digital games industry, established companies tentatively re-organize to take advantage of new developments such as crowd-funding (Crossley 2011) and established developers or producers occasionally part ways to create their own company, often working as sub-contractors for their former employers. Moreover, as Levy (2011) indicates with regard to *Facebook*, major companies do not necessarily monopolize all aspects of the production process any more but instead often act as catalysts for smaller companies, providing visibility, marketing momentum and access to a large user base of potential customers.

3.3 Micro Business Models as Socio-Technical Systems

Judging from this corpus, practices of media use appear even less stable than before but instead are highly dynamic and interdependent. For example, Canniford (2011) outlines how "consumer tribes", i.e. more or less organized groups of active consumers need to be maintained and how they interact with each other to produce emergent forms of behaviour.

The micro-blogging service *Twitter* is a particularly rich source of emergent behaviour. Originally designed to send short status updates at irregular intervals for business communication, *Twitter*'s core appeal arguably lies in the novel and occasionally even subversive forms of conversation and collaboration that emerged quickly from the user communities (Honeycutt and Herring 2009). One such example is the #FollowFriday phenomenon, with which the community fixed a problem that had compromised *Twitter*'s usefulness for many users, i.e. knowing which people to follow (Baldwin 2009). Using the hashtag #FollowFriday, Twitter users began to recommend one or two of their favourite accounts to others every Friday, thus rapidly increasingly the number of mutual subscriptions and the density of the *Twitter* community fabric.

A number of factors were relevant for the system to work. First, the imposed regularity encouraged many users to integrate #FollowFriday into their weekly schedule. Second, the simple rules and little time required made #FollowFriday easily accessible. Third, it had a community-building impact without requiring users to be too actively involved. This mode of organizing user interaction has been employed more and more thoroughly in digital games and could be termed "passive multiplayer"; for example, widely popular games that allow for players to co-operate or compete asynchronously without direct contact include *The Nethernet, Demon's Souls* and *Battlefield 1943*.

Following the work of Niederer and van Dijck (2010) on *Wikipedia*, one potentially fruitful analytical approach would be to understand *Twitter* and other MBMs as a socio-technical system, which operates based on a number of interlocking, regulatory mechanisms. In the case of *Wikipedia*, two core mechanisms are the internal bot network and the reputation system, which distributes users' editing rights based on peer review as well as the level of activity. Most notably, by ensuring an expectable level of quality, the system simultaneously optimizes the value creation process. While *Wikipedia* is a non-commercial service, the model can arguably be applied to MBMs as well; in that case, economic aspects such as modes of monetization, revenue sharing or distribution can be regarded as (or be part of) mechanisms that drive the socio-technical system. Thus, user communities increasingly carry the potential to structure themselves, fuelled by a combination of technological provisions but also motivational factors. Anticipating these patterns and converting them into stable forms of use allows for companies to identify new ways of value creation.

One way to do this would be to enable but intrinsically constrain "subversion" by users. This approach draws on existing studies on how brand subversion, as long as it stays within predictable boundaries, can add to the value creation process. For example, Arnhold (2010) delineates how user-generated content is being integrated into marketing campaigns, which poses the challenge of creating an authorial frame that accommodates unpredictable layers of content while maintaining a coherent core narrative. Following up on the *Twitter* example, the same principle appears applicable to the functionality of media applications as well.

4 Strategic Implications for the Management of Value Creation in Media Networks

Observing recurrent patterns of media use in the context of micro business models can yield a number of strategically relevant aspects, some of which will be elaborated upon below.

4.1 Value Creation of Media Enterprises

Considering the primary value creation activities of media enterprises, it is notable that these activities generally comprise the conception, procurement, selection, production, editing, bundling and distribution of media contents in terms of a content value creation process. In times of convergence of media and other industries as well as fragmentation of audiences the target group-specific segmentation of media recipients and users is central (Siegert 2001; Siegert and Rademacher 2007). The establishment and the disposition of contacts to these target groups also become central elements of the value creation of media enterprises. Within networks of different participants media enterprises have an intermediary function. As a consequence, the value creation of media enterprises especially includes the management of contacts to different participants of a media value network (Kunz 2013). They establish and maintain a platform (infrastructure) enabling the interaction of their partners, they select suitable network participants (promotion), and they additionally offer an added value by providing contacts, contents and other media goods (services). In order to generate revenue media enterprises use certain contents to bring different customers, who are willing to pay, together: recipients/users, advertising companies, telecommunication service providers and/or content providers such as production enterprises. The consumers themselves become increasingly active respectively productive; media consumers in terms of "prosumers" thus influence the network and participate in value creation, e.g. by creating user generated content.

Following up on the hypothesis that—particularly with regard to social media—emergent patterns of media use noticeably frame corresponding models of value creation, one such pattern is the shift towards creating social systems of media use rather than providing an isolated but thoroughly curated media experience. The prototypical example of the latter category would be the Hollywood studio system and the mode of film reception it co-created. As an example of the former category, the *Wikipedia* reputation system shall be briefly revisited. The system characteristically employs a small set of highly interconnected rules that, in combination, produce a self-sustaining system. For instance, it differentiates between pre-set types of users with different functions and privileges. This has the dual advantage of (a) structuring the community and making it more tangible to the individual users and (b) ensuring accountability by giving contributions and modifications of different levels of authority. Arguably, this shift towards a network model exhibits a similar rationality as the shift from the value chain model towards configurations such as the value network.

4.2 Shift of Value Creation from Companies to Company Networks

Most basically, value creation in the context of MBMs or social media businesses in general does not primarily originate from a company itself but from continually reshaping networks of companies, i.e. networks of value networks.

For that reason, enabling symbiotic forms of usage in combination with other services becomes a valid mode of value creation; this can either entail a formal cooperation or a unidirectional approach, e.g. most basically by offering layers of social use. For example, *Paypal* originally positioned itself as a way of "beaming money between Palm pilots" (Sisinni 2011); however, the company dramatically increased its relevance, which had been questioned after the acquisition through *eBay* in 2002, by offering an API-based interface and acting as a monetization partner for small businesses (Roth 2010). In the process, external developers used the interface to create novel payment solutions and, for instance, to implement more and more granular micro payments; simultaneously, this opened up the technology to a more mainstream audience and lead to new value creation opportunities. An example of an MBM that ties into this setup is *movieclips.com*, a service that offers iconic, seconds-long sections of movies, selling both the clips via content providers as well as related merchandise and monetizing the emerging community. As a result, since users can now buy very specific movie scenes, corresponding practices of media use emerge which, in turn, lead to new value conceptions. For instance, the official *movieclips.com* website suggests using the service as a plug-in for e-mail or instant messaging applications so that users can seamlessly embed movie clips into their regular online communication, either to create or to connote a statement.

4.3 Frictionless and Rapid Modifiability as a Key Virtue

As a consequence of the previous consideration, the friction-less and almost real-time modifiability of a company's value configuration becomes a primary virtue and allows for adapting to changes in the network. The most pressing reason for this strategy is the fact that every new, innovative type of MBM—the social shopping service *Groupon* being a prominent example—quickly spawns numerous imitators (Feng 2011). These usually fall into two categories and either (a) extend or streamline the functionality of the original application, or (b) cater to a regionally differentiated, more defined target audience. A third case which is becoming more and more occurs when major players such as *Google* or *Facebook* integrate new functionality, field-tested by dedicated MBMs into their core applications. This happened for example in the case of *Foursquare*, a company that originally positioned itself as a location-based social network. After location awareness gained traction and *Facebook Places* as well as *Google Places* opened up their APIs to the general public, *Foursquare* needed to quickly adapt its basic value configuration, de-emphasizing the social network aspect and exporting its check-in and gamification features by becoming a technology partner for self-improvement MBMs such as *RunKeeper* or *Health Month* (Weigert 2010a).

4.4 Shifts of Value Conception from Products to Processes

Apart from the fact that the locus of value creation shifts from the company to a network of smaller, interrelated business entities, the characteristics of value creation arguably shifts from products to processes and, thus, service (following the value-in-context terminology). For example, considering the case of the music industry, Stöckler (2009) argues that the traditional product form of music is altered due to technological contingencies, i.e. digital downloads, as well as changes in the distribution and pricing of music. These changes are not neutral and re-considering earlier, structurally similar transformations can point to those epistemological aspects, which are often only observable in retrospect (Kusek and Leonhard 2005). For instance, the shift from vinyl to the CD provided a more durable carrier media and, thus, led to more casual, carefree handling of the objects of music delivery; at the same time, CDs were easier to carry around and facilitated listening to one's music in new locations. In order to encourage users to re-purchase music they already owned, compilations were sold which had the added effect of putting familiar songs in new contexts and "linking" to other, potentially interesting music, a mechanism all too familiar for contemporary social media users.

However, while music as a product is becoming hard to sell, the examples from Stöckler (2009) indicate that new forms of value creation can arise from considering music as a process (or, in other words, as a service). One such example is the use of music as a "giveaway" (p. 267), e.g. by offering download codes for *iTunes* tracks as part of a bonus system or directly as an "add-on" to a completely unrelated product. Again, these forms of distribution produce emergent patterns of media use (e.g. trading or collecting cards with download codes). Thus, creating cyclical, self-sustaining systems of usage becomes more important than creating a good product. Tying into Stöckler's argument, it appears important to add that the product form is still being maintained and applied but rather as a metaphor, for example in the way music websites adopt the aesthetics of traditional record stores. This is especially relevant because it frames the users' value conception with regard to music, which changes much slower than the technological conditions.

4.5 Complementary Support Processes of Micro Business Models

In addition to the aforementioned strategies, focusing on emergent media use and networks of companies also yields more practical rationales. For instance, MBMs as well as social media businesses in general can often mutually act as support processes within the respective value configurations. Thus, through the added flexibility, common support processes can occasionally be omitted or transferred to other elements of the MBM network.

For example, the service *brandslisten* acts as a mediator that integrates users into customer support and customer relations functions, opening up the traditional forum-based communication to the entire user base of a company (Weigert 2010b). The basic infrastructure for every *brandslisten* partner is a wiki; users can easily synthesize new and verifiably relevant knowledge for the wiki from related questions and answers they read via the *brandslisten* service. Another common support function is the provision of server capacity; this is especially problematic from the planning side since specific events (marketing campaigns, themed sales etc.) cause usage peaks, which are difficult to accommodate and cause negative backlash in the case of technical problems. While earlier, companies had to maintain their own servers, web services such as the *Amazon Elastic Compute Cloud* (2006) have started to flexibilize this increasingly important support process further. On top of that, however, MBMs such as *SpotCloud* again introduce a different approach by characteristically creating a marketplace for server capacity that any company can buy or sell server capacity on (Trowbridge 2011). Thereby, *SpotCloud* uses market forces to establish temporary, context-sensitive MBM networks, which allow for optimizing the value configuration by decentralizing the server capacity problem. In other words, MBMs employ a combination of technological and economic rationales, which is applicable to other common support functions as well.

4.6 Networks as Simulations of Novel Value Creation Models

From a macro perspective, the dynamic networks of business models arguably simulate conceivable forms of media use as well as prospective value creation. Eric Ries argues that rapid prototyping, as an approach towards production, should be adopted for the entire management process. Related notions such as determining the "minimum viable product (MVP)" (Widman et al. 2010), i.e. the product stage with the minimal set of features required to acquire real customer feedback, illustrate this approach. While the MVP can be understood as a form of simulating media products, the same arguably can be applied to simulating media companies by starting with only the elements required to offer and communicate a unique value proposition. From that angle, constant re-evaluation and iterative adaptation of the business model become indispensable aspects of media management in the content of MBMs.

The simulation hypothesis is further validated by the fact that the major players retroactively implement many "simulated" models of emergent value creation as well, after the financial viability has been proven by a number of MBMs and the corresponding usage practices have been established within a large enough target audience. For example, while coupons have already been employed since the late nineteenth century and spawned a number of coupon-related cultural practices, *Groupon* was among the first widely successful companies to re-invent this economic model (Schwartz 2010) after it had continually declined for years and lay the foundation for social shopping as an amalgam of media use and economic activity. With reference to the 5 C-model, *Groupon* combines aspects of commerce (temporary deals), context (embedding each deal into a meta game with an arbitrary time limit and other rules) and community (fostering social interaction between users with shared purchase intentions) into a value proposition greater than the appeal of related offers such as bonus programs or paper-based coupons. Even though *Groupon* still dominates the field, major players such as *Google* (*Google Offers*), *Twitter* (the *@earlybird* account) and others have adopted that type of functionality and increasingly integrate it with their own characteristic strengths, thereby creating new value conceptions that *Groupon* has to adapt to over time (Marsden 2011). For instance, the *Google Offers* personalization quiz (Hijleh 2011) capitalizes on *Google's* existing extensive data sources and quickly introduced personalized deals into the users' value conception.

An example of a seemingly counter-intuitive value creation strategy, which, however, has been successfully "simulated" in a number of cases already is the notion of MBMs charging money for functionality that had previously been available via free, albeit more generalized and ad-funded services. Clive Thompson describes current "freemium" models (i.e. applications with a free basic version which charge extra for added functionality) and ad-based services as "cynical designs that work against what people want" (Thompson 2011), i.e. business cases in which the genuine user and company interests only marginally converge or, often, are even diametrically opposed. Instead, MBMs such as *Pinboard.in*, *Instapaper* or *Ning* provide a "pure", ad-free experience which enough users valorize to make these services profitable. Borrowing the concept of remediation with which Bolter and Grusin (2000) characterize the emulation of older media paradigms within new media forms, theses companies similarly "remediate" older, pre-digital business models while adjusting them to benefit from the current level of technology.

Conclusion

The emerging networks of media businesses or MBMs outlined above noticeably challenge both traditional models of value creation as well as the corresponding value conceptions from the users' point of view. One important aspect in this context is the increasingly intricate conflation of media technological and economic rationalities. New technologies are often designed to support pre-existing economic rationales and, inversely, new economic developments such as crowd-funding or in-app purchases are often closely modelled after the technological framework they require in order to become workable. MBMs such as the aforementioned *SpotCloud* or *Fiverr* illustrate this principle; reflecting the technological outline of peer-to-peer networks, these businesses create value by self-sustaining peer-to-peer economies, designed to solve certain problems or channel emergent behaviour (Clark 2003).

A broader media historical perspective shows that similar patterns emerged during earlier transformative periods. For example, Gitelman (2004) points out that the amusement phonograph had initially been built for recording speech in the office. Yet, the device was emergently used primarily for playback of pre-produced music, so that, in the process, later iterations of the hardware evolved around this pattern of media use. With regard to social media and MBM networks, combining technologically and economically driven value propositions all the more becomes a key to successful value creation.

To conclude, within the scope of this chapter, we pointed out current phenomena in the online media business and derived theoretical implications for future media management using an interdisciplinary approach. It is designed as a road map and theoretical foundation for a broader research project within the "Media Culture and Media Economy" program (http://mekuwi.uni-bayreuth.de) at the University of Bayreuth (Germany), which enables work across disciplines such as media studies, media management and marketing, history, law and computer studies. The chapter at hand is a starting point and further publications in this context will follow.

Acknowledgements We would like to thank Prof. Dr. Jürgen E. Müller (Media Studies, University of Bayreuth) for setting up the initiative "Networks in Media Culture and Media Economy" as a valuable and fruitful platform of trans-disciplinary research, which inspired us to write this paper.

References

Amit, R., & Zott, C. (2001). Value creation in E-business. *Strategic Management Journal, 22*(6/7), 493–520.

Arnhold, U. (2010). *User-generated branding. Integrating User generated content into brand management*. Wiesbaden: Gabler.

Bakker, G. (2003). Entertainment industrialized: The emergence of the international film industry, 1890-1940. *Enterprise and Society, 4*(4), 579–85.

Baldwin, M. (2009). #Followfriday: The anatomy of a Twitter trend. *Mashable*. http://mashable.com/2009/03/06/twitter-followfriday/

Bolter, J. D., & Grusin, R. (2000). *Remediation. Understanding new media*. Cambridge, MA: MIT Press.

Canniford, R. (2011). How to manage consumer tribes. *Journal of Strategic Marketing, 19*(7), 591–606.

Clark, D. D. (2003). Economics and the design of open systems. *IEEE Internet Computing, 7*(2), 96–95.

Crossley, R. (2011). Crowd-fund plan could transform Triple-A. *Develop*. http://www.develop-online.net/news/38858/New-crowd-fund-initiative-could-transform-triple-A

Feng, X. (2011, August). *A comparative study of online group-coupon sale in USA and China*. Paper presented in Artificial Intelligence, Management Science and Electronic Commerce (AIMSEC), 2011, 2nd International Conference

Fuller, M. (2008). *Software studies: A lexicon*. Cambridge, MA: MIT Press.

Gitelman, L. (2004). How users define new media: A history of the amusement phonograph. In D. Thornburn, H. Jenkins, & B. Seawell (Eds.), *Rethinking media change: The aesthetics of transition* (pp. 61–80). Cambridge, MA: MIT Press.

Gläser, M. (2008). *Medienmanagement*. München: Vahlen.

Grönroos, C. (2009). *Towards service logic: The unique contribution of value co-creation*. Working Papers – 544, heruntergeladen am 19. Helsinki: Hanken School of Economics. https://helda.helsinki.fi/handle/10227/499

Hijleh, A. (2011). What is the importance of the new personalization quiz in Google offers for marketers? *Search Engine Journal*.

Honeycutt, C., & Herring, S. C. (2009). *Beyond Microblogging: Conversation and collaboration via Twitter*. 42nd Hawaii International Conference on System Sciences.

Kunz, R. (2013). Neue Medien im Sport. In H. Woratschek & T. Ströbel (Eds.), *Sportmanagement*. Stuttgart: Kohlhammer.

Kusek, D., & Leonhard, G. (2005). *The future of music: Manifesto for the digital music revolution*. Boston, MA: Berkeley Press.

Levy, S. (2011). The second coming. *Wired Magazine, 19*(11), 200–207.

Lusch, R. F., & Vargo, S. L. (2006). Service-dominant logic: Reactions, reflections and refinements. *Marketing Theory, 6*(3), 281–288.

Marsden, P. (2011). In E. Theobald & P. T. Haisch (Eds.), *Ebranding and social commerce* (pp. 357–372). Wiesbaden: Springer.

Mittell, J. (2009). Sites of participation: Wiki Fandom and the case of Lostpedia. *Transformative Works and Cultures, 3*.

Niederer, S., and van Dijck, J. (2010). Wisdom of the crowd or technicity of content? Wikipedia as a sociotechnical system. *New Media & Society, 12.8*, 1368–1387.

Porter, M. E. (1985). *Competitive advantage*. New York: Free Press.

Ries, E. (2011). *How today's entrepreneurs use continuous innovation to create radically successful businesses.* New York, NY: Crown Business.
Rogers, R. (2009). *The end of the virtual: Digital methods.* Amsterdam: Amsterdam University Press.
Roth, D. (2010). The future of money. *Wired Magazine, 18.3*, 70–76.
Schwartz, M. (2010). The Coupon Rebellion. *Wired Magazine, 18.12*, 188–193, 222–224.
Siegert, G. (2001). Medien, Marken, Management – Relevanz, Spezifika und Implikationen einer medienökonomischen Profilierungsstrategie.
Siegert, G., & Rademacher, P. (2007). Sportmedienmanagement. In T. Schierl (Ed.), *Handbuch Medien, Kommunikation und Sport, Beiträge zur Lehre und Forschung im Sport* (pp. 256–273). Schorndorf: Hofmann.
Sigler, C. (2010). *Online-Medienmanagement: Grundlagen - Konzepte - Herausforderungen ; mit Praxisbeispielen und Fallstudien*, Wiesbaden.
Sisinni, F. (2011). Dispatch from Ctia: What is the future of money? in: PayPal Blog.
Stabell, C. B., & Fjeldstad, Ø. D. (1998). Configuring value for competitive advantage: On chains, shops and networks. *Strategic Management Journal, 19*, 413–437.
Stöckler, E. M. (2009). 'Produkt Musik'. Eine Musikwissenschaftliche Annäherung. In G. Gensch, E. M. Stöckler, & P. Tschmuck (Eds.), *Musikrezeption, Musikdistribution und Musikproduktion. Der Wandel des Wertschöpfungsnetzwerks in der Musikwirtschaft* (pp. 267–292). Wiesbaden: Gabler.
Thompson, J. D. (1967). *Organizations in action.* New York: McGraw-Hill.
Thompson, C. (2011). Clive Thompson on the Problem with Online Ads. *Wired Magazine* http://www.wired.com/magazine/2011/08/st_thompson_onlineads/
Toffler, A. (1980). *The third wave–The classic study of tomorrow.* New York: Bantam Books.
Trowbridge, B. (2011). *Cloud sourcing the corporation.* Austin, TX: Live Oak Book Company.
Vargo, S. L., & Akaka, M. A. (2009). Service-dominant logic as a foundation for service science. *Service Science, 1*(1), 32–41.
Vargo, S. L., & Lusch, R. F. (2004). Evolving to a new dominant logic for marketing. *Journal of Marketing, 68*(1), 1–17.
Vargo, S. L., & Lusch, R. F. (2008). Service-dominant logic: Continuing the evolution. *Journal of the Academy of Marketing Science, 36*(1), 1–10.
Vargo, S. L., Maglio, P. P., & Akaka, M. A. (2008). On value and value co-creation: A service systems and service logic perspective. *European Management Journal, 26*(3), 145–152.
Walsh, M. (2010, January). Gartner: Mobile to Outpace Desktop Web by 2013. *Online Media Daily.*
Weigert, M. (2010a, September). *Vom Location-Service Zum Manager Für Das Reale Leben.* Netzwertig. http://netzwertig.com/2010/09/24/foursquare-vom-location-service-zum-manager-fuer-das-reale-leben/
Weigert, M. (2010b, June). *Brandslisten: Wenn Kunden Den Besseren Support Leisten.* Netzwertig. http://netzwertig.com/2010/10/06/brandslisten-wenn-kunden-den-besseren-support-leisten/
Widman, J., Hua, S. Y., & Ross, S. C. (2010). Applying lean principles in software development processes - A case study. *Issues in Information Systems, XI.1*, 635–639
Wirtz, B. W. (2011). *Medien- und Internetmanagement*, 7. Auflage. Wiesbaden: Gabler, Betriebswirt.-Vlg.
Wirtz, B. W., & Kleineicken, A. (2000). Geschäftsmodelltypologien im Internet. *WiSt – Wirtschaftswissenschaftliches Studium, 29.11*, 628–635.
Woratschek, H., Roth, S., & Pastowski, S. (2002). Geschäftsmodelle und Wertschöpfungskonfigurationen im Internet. *Marketing ZFP, Spezialausgabe E-Marketing, 24*, 57–72.
Xu, H., & Yan, R.-N. (2011). Feeling connected via television viewing: Exploring the scale and its correlates. *Communication Studies, 62*(2), 186–206.

Managing Social Media Value Networks: From Publisher (Broadcast) to User-Centric (Broadband-Narrowcast) Business Models

Zvezdan Vukanovic

1 Introduction

When Web 2.0 applications emerged in 2005–2006, cultural theorist Henry Jenkins (2006, p. 24) was one of the first to notice a definite paradigm shift in the way social media content is produced and circulated: 'Audiences, empowered by these new technologies, occupying a space at the intersection between old and new media, are demanding the right to participate within the culture.' The result, according to Jenkins, was a participatory culture which increasingly demands room for ordinary citizens to wield media technologies—technologies that were once the privilege of capital-intensive industries—to express themselves and distribute those creations as they seem fit (van Dijck 2011). When 'old media' still reigned, media recipients had little direct power to shape media content and faced enormous barriers to enter the marketplace, whereas 'the new digital environment expands the scope and reach of consumer activities' (Jenkins 2006, p. 215). The technological opportunities seized by grassroots movements and individuals increase their creativity and provide a diverse palette of voices (Deuze 2007). Moreover, with the emergence of Web 2.0 applications, most prominently UGC-platforms, the qualification of 'user' has gradually entered the common parlance of media theorists (Livingstone 2004). Users are generally referred to as active Internet-contributors, who put in a 'certain amount of creative effort' which is 'created outside of professional routines and platforms' (van Dijck 2011). Since the 1980s, the term 'prosumer' has been deployed by various academics to denote how user's agency hovers between the bipolar categories of producer versus consumer, and of professional versus consumer. New hybrid terms such as 'produser' and 'co-creator' have meanwhile entered academic discourse to accentuate user's increased production prowess (Bruns 2007).

Z. Vukanovic (✉)
University of Donja Gorica, Podgorica, Montenegro
e-mail: zvezdanv@t-com.me

The ubiquity of Web 2.0 services has transformed the landscape of online content consumption (Szabo and Huberman 2010). With the Web, content producers can reach an audience in numbers inconceivable through conventional channels. Examples of services that have made the exchange between producer and consumer possible on a global scale include video, photo, and music sharing, blogs, wikis, social bookmarking, collaborative portals, and news aggregators, whereby content is submitted, perused, rated, and discussed by the user community. Portals often rank and categorize content based on past popularity and user appeal, especially for aggregators, where the "wisdom of the crowd" provides collaborative filtering to select submissions favored by as many visitors as possible. Over the last few years the Web 2.0, now uniformly tagged as social media has fundamentally shifted towards user-driven technologies such as blogs, social networks and video-sharing platforms (Smith 2009).

Social media focus on both global and personal topics demonstrating how the future of content will be increasingly bottom up and consumer driven (Smith 2009). Characteristics of user generated reviews and reviewers can affect ecommerce demand, feedback in blogs can affect firms' pricing policies and the nature of competition, the attributes of user-generated search queries can affect the performance of search engine advertising and the content of customer support dialogues can affect product design (Ghose and Ipeirotis 2009).

2   Literature Review

In order to substantiate the main hypothesis the author has consulted most important international academic research papers published between 2004 and 2010 in the field of business and technology of web media. These research papers are examined via the largest international research database—EBSCO and include following journals: Communications of the ACM, Journal of Information Science, Harvard Business Review, Journal of Media Business Studies, Journal of Revenue and Pricing Management, Multimedia Systems, Journal of Interactive Advertising, Management Information Systems, International Journal of Market Research, International Journal of Cultural Studies, European Journal of Communication, Journal of Computer-Mediated Communication. Furthermore, the author cites a relevant European and North American literature in the field of social media (Benecchi and Colapinto 2011; Qualman 2010; Bakos and Brynjolfsson 2000; Jenkins 2006; van Dijck 2011; Livingstone 2004; Vizjak and Ringlstetter 2003; Doyle 2002; Anderson 2008) which dominantly substantiate the paper's main principles.

3 Main Objectives of Research

The main objective of this conceptual, exploratory and longitudinal research paper is to provide a framework and contribution to the strategic media restructuring caused by recent economic recession and decline of financial revenues of traditional media sector such as newspaper publishing, radio and free-to-air broadcasting.

In the main hypothesis of the paper, the author argues that the economic shakeout of media firms and economic downturn of media markets is dominantly evident in traditional media industries (TV, print and radio) whereas in new media (web, internet, digital, network and online media) the profit has been relatively stable. So, the author argues that a real media crisis did begin a decade before the global recession that officially started in September 2008 as a result of the

1. Emergence and subsequent convergence of digital media
2. Falling costs of computing and online (internet-web) distribution
3. Exponential growth of internet and broadband adoption
4. Media market deregulation.

In addition, the author argues that in order to attain the sustainable competitive advantage media executives and companies are required to strategically adopt, implement and utilize following technological, economic and managerial concepts and strategies:

1. Advanced financial and revenue models: micropayments
2. New advertising and marketing models: nicheization of media market, VoD—Video-on-demand and PPV—Payment-Per View mode, B2B and C2C Marketing
3. Innovative distribution models, solutions and applications: 3D TV, sharing and usability of media content, global convergence, mass personalization (customization) including more interactive, on-demand, ambient, pervasive, augmented, immersive media as well as wireless and mobile user interfaces
4. New economic, market and consumer strategies: long tail economics, tipping point, crowd sourcing, mesh company strategy
5. Innovative and high quality social and web media content production: media content repurposing, cross-media content and UGC—User Generated Content (question–answer databases, digital video, blogging, podcasting, mobile phone photography and wikis).

4 Economic, Market and Consumer Paradigm Shifts

4.1 Long Tail Economics

As the cost of reaching consumers via social and web media drops dramatically, our markets are shifting from a one-size-fits-all model of mass appeal to one of unlimited variety for unique tastes (Anderson 2008). Social media's ability to offer vast choice is changing the media market and causing corporations and consumers to rethink where profitable markets lie and how to get to them.

Unlimited selection is revealing truths about the nature of media consumerism that ranges from selling DVDs, accessing internet video over computers and mobile phones, to advertising on Google. Accordingly, social and web media create an entirely new economic model for business—"The Long Tail". With the proliferation of niche sites and communities on the Internet, it's becoming increasingly important to target long tail search terms and cast a wide net. After a century of obsessing over the few products at the head of the demand curve, the new economics of distribution ("The Long Tail") allow consumers and corporations to turn their focus to the many more products in the tail, which collectively can create a new and more innovative market. Thus, "The Long Tail" is a powerful new force in digital and information economy characterizing the rise of the niche. The Long Tail is essentially about the economics of abundance. New efficiencies in distribution, manufacturing, and marketing are essentially resetting the definition of what's commercially viable across the board (Anderson 2008).

4.2 Tipping Point Strategy

It is advisable to point out that the efficient usage of the long tail economic strategy leads to the reaching of the Tipping Point. Tipping points are "the levels at which the momentum for change becomes unstoppable" (Gladwell 2002). Furthermore, it is defined as "the precise moment of critical mass, the threshold, the boiling point when a trend becomes a trend" (Gladwell 2002). In economics, the tipping point represents the point at which a dominant technology or player defines the standard for an industry-resulting in "winner-take-all" economies of scale and scope.

An excellent example of the application of the tipping point strategy in social media is the launch of three well established international social networking and UGC generated websites: Facebook, You Tube and Twitter. The business and market growth of each of these companies is subsequently analyzed.

4.2.1 Facebook

Facebook positions itself as leader of interactive, participant-based online media, or Web 2.0, the descriptor for websites based on user-generated content that create value from the sharing of information between participants (Hoegg et al. 2006). With the advent of new social technologies, users no longer have to rely on an individual's self-composed emails, chat statements, or personal web pages to garner impressions about a subject. Communication technology has evolved beyond the means by which senders had more or less complete control over the impression-related information that receivers could observe (Tom Tong et al. 2008, p. 531) (Table 1).

Between August 2008 and September 2011 (Table 2) the number of Facebook users increased eight times (from 100 to 800 million). If Facebook were a country it would be the world's 3th largest between India and the United States. In addition, the revenue of Facebook company increased from 52 million dollars in 2006 to 2 billion dollars in 2010. Based on traffic data from Alexa and Google Trends in

Table 1 Facebook revenues (estimated, in millions US$)

Year	Revenue	Growth
2006	$52	—
2007	$150	188 %
2008	$280	87 %
2009	$775	177 %
2010	$2,000	158 %
2011	$4,270	114 %
2012	$5,780 (expected)	

Source: TechCrunch (2010) and Bloomberg L.P. (September, 2011)

Table 2 Facebook total active users

Date	Users (in millions)	Monthly growth
August 26, 2008	100	178.38 %
April 8, 2009	200	13.33 %
September 15, 2009	300	10 %
February 5, 2010	400	6.99 %
July 21, 2010	500	4.52 %
January 5, 2011	600	3.57 %
May 30, 2011	700	3.45 %
July 2011	750	4.16 %
September 22, 2011	800	3.73 %

Source: Bloomberg L.P. (September, 2011)

June 2011 Facebook was the most popular social network in 119 out of 134 countries. Moreover, it was the most popular social network in the U.S., followed by Twitter and LinkedIn. More than 50 % of active users log on to Facebook in any given day.

The overall display marketplace in the U.S. is expected to be $12.33 billion this year and $14.82 billion the next. Facebook will have a 16.3 % share of the U.S. display market this year, followed by Yahoo at 13.1 %, Google at 9.3 %, MSN at 4.9 %, and AOL at 4.2 %. Collectively, those top five display leaders have 47.9 % of the display space in the U.S. That means there's a lot of territory still to conquer amid an otherwise fractured market.

Twenty five billion tweets are sent on Twitter in 2010. Thirty billion pieces of content (links, notes, photos, etc.) are shared on Facebook per month. Thirty six billion of photos are uploaded to Facebook per year. These numbers although appear to be very impressive should not surprise the researchers as Facebook currently has about 550,000 different applications. Such a large number of applications creates the personalization of web and media content on Facebook profiles both effective and efficient.

Table 3 You Tube video views per day

Date	Users (in millions)
December 2005	8
July 2006	100
October 2009	1,000
May 2010	2,000

Source: Online Marketing Trends (2010)

4.2.2 You Tube

You Tube serves 2 billion views per day making up 13 % of global mobile data bandwidth and covering 10 % of the Internet Traffic. An average Internet user spends around 15 min every day on YouTube. It is forecasted by eMarKeter, a New York based digital marketing, media and commerce company that YouTube revenue reached in 2010—$825 million and could exceed $1.3 billion in 2011 and rise to almost $1.7 billion in 2012. In December 2010 online video advertising forecast from eMarketer pegged the whole online video industry's ad revenue at $1.97 billion in 2011, meaning YouTube alone could account for approximately 65 % of the entire industry's revenue. The increasing growth of You Tube usage is particularly evident in the fact that between December 2005 and May 2010 the number of video views per day has increased approximately 250 times (from 8 million to 2 billion). This number nearly doubles the prime-time audience of all three major U.S. broadcast networks. More video is uploaded to You Tube in two moths than all three major U.S. networks created in 60 years. In addition, partner ad revenue more than tripled in 2009. At the same time, the number of advertisers using display ads on You Tube increased 10-fold in 2009. Fifty one language versions of You Tube services are available through user interface (Table 3).

4.3 Twitter

Twitter is a website, which offers a social networking and microblogging service, enabling its users to send and read messages called tweets. Tweets are text-based posts of up to 140 characters displayed on the user's profile page. It has been described as "the SMS of the Internet Innovative and high quantity of registered Twitter applications have made Twitter services very popular". Thus, between August 2010 and August 2011 the number of Twitter applications has increased from 150,000 to more than one million. There are currently approximately 300 million Twitter users worldwide and their number is growing at an average of 15 million per month or 500,000 a day. The number of Twitter mobile users over the past year has increased for 182 %. The number of employees at Twitter has increased from 8 in January 2008 to 600 in December 2011. eMarketer expects Twitter to earn $150 million in revenues this year, the vast majority ($140 million) of which will come from the US. This represents a substantial increase over the company's 2010 revenues of $45 million. eMarketer forecasts that by 2012, Twitter

Table 4 Number of Twitter employees

Date	The numbers of employees
January 2008	8
January 2009	29
January 2010	130
January 2011	350
March 2011	400
December 2011	600

Table 5 Twitter advertising revenues

Date	Revenue (in millions US$)
2010 (USA)	$45
2011 (USA)	$140
2011 (International)	$11
2011 (Worldwide)	$151
2012 (USA)	$225
2012 (International)	$25
2012 (Worldwide)	$250

Source: eMarketing (January, 2011)

Table 6 Twitter market valuation 2009–2012

Date	Market valuation (in millions US$)
February, 2009	$250
September, 2009	$1,000
December 2010	$3,700
January, 2011	$4,000
March, 2011	$7,700
July, 2011	$8,000
September, 2011	$10,700

revenues will reach $250 million, passing MySpace in revenue generated. As such, Twitter advertising revenues between 2010 and 2012 are expected to grow for 405 % in the U.S. and 456 % in the worldwide market (Tables 4, 5, and 6).

4.4 Crowd Sourcing Strategy

In order to expand markets, social media such as Wikipedia use Crowd sourcing strategy. Such strategies function as reward programs and are only likely to grow more important, especially as the Web reaches into corners of the world where it never benefited from the frisson of a social movement (Dokoupil and Wu 2010). In 2009, Google launched successfully the Kiswahili Wikipedia Challenge to grow the number of Swahili-language Wikipedia entries in parts of Eastern Africa by tying them to the chance to win modems, cell phones, and a laptop (Dokoupil and Wu 2010). Jeff Howe (2009), the author of Crowd sourcing: Why the Power of the Crowd Is Driving the Future of Business predicted in 2006 that the winners in the social-media world would be "those that figure out a formula for making their users feel amply compensated." Moreover, it is advisable to point out that with more than a million entries, hundreds of thousands of contributors, and tens of millions of fully recorded article revisions, Wikipedia's freely available database/online encyclopedia has also made it possible to study how human knowledge is recorded and organized through an open collaborative process (Spinellis and Louridas 2008).

In this new world of Social networks, the blogosphere, online communities, the ever-growing notion of crowd sourcing ("collective wisdom"), factual information of the masses provides the "true statements and facts" by testing a wide range of users with vastly different opinions (Edwards 2009). It is expected that eventually the truth will be solidified.

4.4.1 Mesh Companies Strategy

Unlike the traditional businesses which follow a simple formula: create a product or service, sell it and collect money, in the last few years a fundamentally innovative business model has taken root-one in which consumers have more choices, more tools, more information, and more peer-to-peer power. Organizations that use social media, wireless networks, and data crunched from every available source to provide people with goods and services at the exact moment they need them, without the burden and expense of owning them outright are called "Mesh companies" (Gansky 2010). This strategy can be profitable as it creates trusted brands and build strong communities by helping customers to buy less but use more products and services. Mesh strategy s successful if aligned with the peer-to-peer power of social media networks as it can inspire customers in a highly competitive world where access trumps ownership (Gansky 2010).

4.5 Strategic Shifts in Marketing and Value Chain

Marketing is experiencing a profound paradigm shift. In the old paradigm, marketers controlled the conversation with consumers through commissionable media—television, radio, newspapers and magazines (Qualman 2010). In the new paradigm, marketers risk is being marginalized in the electronic dialogue now taking place real-time. The solution is to adopt efficiently new technologies (e.g., weblogs, RSS, wikis) which together with the diffusion of broadband Internet allow companies to interact effectively with media consumers (Lacy and Bauer 2006) and massively integrate consumers into the production process at all levels of the value chain. Each step of the traditional value chain of media production—from concepts, know-how, and technology to content production, packaging, marketing and distribution—has a user-generated equivalent (Schaedel and Clement 2010). This strategy allows social media to considerably increase market share and generate exponential returns for consumers and businesses. Those returns could vary for media business from sales, brand awareness, customer service. A subset of this is that in the future we will no longer search for products and services, rather they will find us via social media. Because of the speed in which social media enables communication, word of mouth now becomes world of mouth. Nielsen Global Online Consumer Survey "Trust, Value and Engagement in Advertising" in July 2009 shows positive influence of social media on consumer trust as 78 % of consumers trust peer recommendations, while only 14 % trust advertisements.

4.6 Micropayment and, Nicheization of Media Market

Industry and market structure of the social media industry will be niche-oriented. If the twentieth century was about hits, the twenty-first will be equally about niches (Anderson 2006). On demand media and particularly VoD—Video on Demand will considerably gain more importance. As such, long tail economics will become more prevalent in capturing the fragmented media market. In terms of advertising and marketing revenue, it is advisable to point out that online and interactive advertising as well as micropayment strategies will be increasingly important. Micropayment will provide potential consumers with immediate transaction processing and will increase VoD—Video-on-demand and PPV—Payment-Per View models. It is argued that micropayment is in the process of becoming web's new currency and will be especially useful in purchasing electronic books, online articles, music, video and film files. The case of micropayment strategy is additionally supported by the exponential growth of the Internet during the past decade. Thus, between 2000 and 2010 the number of internet users worldwide increased for 445 %.

Micropayment strategy is widely becoming an alternative to subscriptions as it moves content creators closer to consumers. The competitive advantage of micropayments can potentially provide consumers with a payment model in which content can be unbundled and further sold via B2C channel. On the other hand, cloud computing will be especially important in terms of B2B marketing as many international companies will hire another firms to manage their data via the Internet in private spaces, rather than those companies using their own servers, in an effort to gain storage space and, rather than those companies using their own servers. The increasing development of social media, web, personal computing devices (PCs, mobile phones and portable media players) made possible the wide dissemination of various online contents over the consumer-to-consumer (C2C) channel.

4.7 Media Distribution Strategies

From a technological and distribution viewpoint, the usage of different applications for mobile, wireless and network media will become more dominant. The most important technology trends in the future are sharing and usability including more interactive, immersive, wireless and mobile media as well as user interface. Mobile TV is an effective media technology that allows to leverage and customize (personalize) the content of UGC and distribution of the social (web) media services (Blanco-Fernández et al. 2009).

In addition, the distribution of web media will migrate from broadcast to unicast. This means that web media will dominantly operate as a multimedia platform integrating variety of different media TV, video, radio, internet, telephony. Moreover, 3DTV is increasingly considered a viable option to the traditional LCD and plasma full HD TV sets. The original feature of 3D TV presents the option of more immersive watching experience by potential viewers. However, the lack of universal technological standard as well as unease about wearing 3D glasses could postpone more intensive consumers' adoption. Web media have now become an on-demand, participatory, non-linear means of communication in which viewers will be able to control the type of content they watch as well as its timing.

4.8 User-Generated Content as a Promoter of Collaborative Information Services

User generated content is characterized as 'Conversational Media', as opposed to the 'Packaged Goods Media' of the past century. The former is a two-way process in contrast to the one-way distribution of the latter. Conversational or two-way media is a key characteristic of so-called Web 2.0 which encourages the publishing of one's own content and commenting on other people's. UGC can be twofold and include both personal and collaborative publishing. The personal publishing consists of weblog, podcast, photo, whereas the collaborative publishing consists of internet forum, wiki. Thus, consumer becomes Prosumer—both producer and consumer of information goods. The proliferation of UGC has made a strong impact on consumers, media suppliers, and marketing professionals while necessitating research in order to understand both the short and long-term implications of this media content (Daugherty et al. 2008).

One of the main competitive advantage of the conversational media is that within the UGC, all digital media technologies are included, such as question–answer databases, digital video, blogging, podcasting, mobile phone photography and wikis. In addition to these technologies, user generated content may also employ a combination of open source, free software, and flexible licensing or related agreements to further reduce the barriers to collaboration, skill-building and discovery. As the consumption, creation, and distribution of UGC continues to evolve, content aggregation tools and Web 2.0 applications built on Really Simple Syndication (RSS) technology will become more usable and accessible to consumers, helping create a manageable information space that is both customized and relevant (Daugherty et al. 2008).

User-generated content is a part of the development of collaborative information services and the usage of folksonomies. Folksonomies represents collection of tags. The term folksonomy is a portmanteau of the words folk (or folks) and taxonomy that specifically refers to subject indexing systems created within Internet communities (Snuderl 2008). Folksonomy has little to do with taxonomy—the latter refers to an ontological, hierarchical way of categorizing, while folksonomy establishes categories (each tag is a category) that are theoretically "equal" to each other (Snuderl 2008). Folksonomies turn the classification system from criteria-centric into a resource-centric approach (Peters 2009, p. 3).

On the other hand, Tags are a "bottom-up" type of classification, compared to hierarchies, which are "top-down" (Snuderl 2008). Tags are keywords, entered as additional metadata to each uploaded file—words that describe the content according to author's opinion and experiences (Snuderl 2008). So tagging is a method of categorizing information in a collaborative and decentralized way. Tagging, or using keywords to add metadata to shared content, is gaining much popularity in recent years (Cattuto et al. 2007; Golder and Huberman 2006; Marlow et al. 2006). Tags are used to annotate various types of content, including images, videos, bookmarks, and blogs, through web-based systems such as Flickr, YouTube, del.icio.us, and Technorati, respectively. The popularity of tagging is attributed, at least in part, to the benefits users gain from effective sharing and from organization of very large amounts of information (Ames and Naaman 2007; Cattuto et al. 2007). Due to the fact that user participation is critical to the sustainability of content sharing communities, as a collaborative tagging system cannot succeed without higher level of user contribution (Nov and Ye 2010; Koh et al. 2007).

4.9 Content Re-purposing, Cross-Media Content and Global Convergence

Content re-purposing is particularly important because in the future, only media companies focusing on selling content and services in maximum quantities will manage to maintain a profitable position in this highly volatile market (Vizjak and Ringlstetter 2003, p. 17). Moreover, the strategic management of cross-media content and platform is important because of two dominant reasons: (1) It increases the number of media distribution platforms and services, and (2) it diversifies firms' corporate portfolios while reducing financial risk in highly volatile global markets.

The concept of cross-media content will integrate both the hypermedia and multimedia models. Cross-media and on-demand content offer the enormous content base (linear and nonlinear) as a part of web and social media content. In addition, on-demand web and social media services are able to promote premium, niche, and user generated content. As such, innovative services are based on convergent technological architecture (Bakos and Brynjolfsson 2000). Due to the faster product life cycles, volatile markets, and increased competition, future cross-media services will be more interactive, dynamic, enhanced, and flexible. This enhanced technological and content integration will more efficiently stimulate the economies of aggregation that, in turn, will bring value added services to the media business and industry. The future of web media strategies including media re-purposing and UGC looks very bright. It was recently estimated by Mark Selby, Vice President of Nokia Multimedia, that the mixing up of media content will increase a multimedia content by 25 % by 2012.

Globalization and convergence have created additional possibilities and incentives to repackage or to repurpose media content into as many different formats as is technically and commercially feasible (books, magazine serializations, television programs and formats, videos, etc.) and to sell those products through as many distribution channels, outlets, or windows in as many geographic markets and to as many paying consumers as possible (Doyle 2002, p. 22). Accordingly, repurposing represents the joint emphasis of media firms on both the content and distribution.

5 The Increasing Influence of New and Social Media

The increasing influence of social media is well documented in the fact that five among ten most visited global websites belong to the category of social media that favor the creation of UGC—User Generated Content (Facebook # 2, You Tube # 3, Blogger.com # 5, Wikipedia # 8 and Twitter # 9). The importance of social media is further exemplified by the fact that 75 % of search results for the world's top 20 largest brands are links to user-generated content. The Nielsen Research found that in April 2010 most popular global brands online are: Google, MSN/WindowsLive/Bing, Facebook, Yahoo!, Microsoft, YouTube, Wikipedia, AOL Media Network, eBay, Apple. This research shows that the highest percentage of Social Networking/Blog Sites users are to be found in Brazil, Italy, Spain, Japan, United States, United Kingdom, France, Australia, Germany, Switzerland. Furthermore, total worldwide social media advertising revenues are projected to reach more than $8 billion by 2012, with the lions share going to Facebook, which is projected to generate $5.78 billion that year.

The increasing usage of social media is additionally supported by present and future demographic trends. As such, it is estimated that over 50 % of the world population is under 30 years old. Accordingly, in 2010 generation Y outnumbered Baby Boomers. In addition, it is the generation Y that in 96 % of cases have joined social network. More than 80 % of Twitter users are less than 30 years old. In November 2010 CBS reported that the number of social media users age 65 and older grew 100 % throughout 2010, so that one in four people in that age group are now part of a social networking site.

Erik Qualman, the author of "Socialnomics: How Social Media Transforms the Way We Live and Do Business" lists several empirical and quantitative facts/data that prove the increase of social media usage in the global media business:
- By 2010 Gen Y outnumbered Baby Boomers which is evident in the fact that 96 % of them have joined a social network
- comScore, Inc. digital marketing intelligence research company indicates that Russia has the most engage social media audience with visitors spending 6.6 h

and viewing 1,307 pages per visitor per month—Vkontakte.ru is the #1 social network
- The fastest growing segment on Facebook is 55–65 year-old females
- Generation Y and Z consider e-mail passé. The number of social media and UGC users (Facebook, You Tube) exceeds the number of e mail users.
- A 107 trillion of emails are sent on the Internet in 2010.
- 24 of the 25 largest U.S. newspapers are experiencing record declines in circulation because we no longer search for the news, the news finds us.
- In the near future the consumers will no longer search for products and services as they will find them via social media
- Successful and profitable companies in social media follow two primary rules of (1) listening first, selling second and (2) acting more like party planners, aggregators, and content providers than traditional advertiser.

6 Reasons for Corporate Embrace of Social Media

Today's media companies must embrace social media for three reasons. First, they provide a low-cost platform on which to build consumer personal brand. Second, they allow consumers and corporate executives and managers to engage rapidly and simultaneously with peers, employees, customers, and the broader public, especially younger generations, in the same transparent and direct way they expect from everyone in their lives. Third, they give users and prospective business clients an opportunity to learn from instant information and unvarnished feedback. (Dutta 2010, p. 128).

It's no secret that social media—global, open, transparent, non-hierarchical, interactive, and real time—are changing consumer behavior and workplace expectations. As a result, the best businesses are creating comprehensive strategies in this area to support their goals. However, my research on the organizational implications of social media and consulting work with dozens of companies in America, Europe, and Asia suggest that it is taking longer for corporate leaders to consider what the new paradigm means for them personally. As such, it is advisable to take into consideration the world's leading CEOs as a sample. According to data from Fisheye Analytics, the top 50 chief executives (as identified by Morten T. Hansen, Herminia Ibarra, and Urs Peyer in "The Best-Performing CEOs in the World," HBR January–February 2010) are increasingly discussed in online venues, but few are using social media to spread their own messages: Only 19 were on Facebook, only six had a LinkedIn page, and only two—Google CEO Eric Schmidt and former Norilsk Nickel CEO Mikhail Prokhorov—were tweeting or blogging (although some used their corporate pages for blogs) (Dutta 2010, p. 128).

Furthermore, social media provide advantage to the media corporations in terms of
1. Reducing distribution and advertising costs
2. Prolonging the business cycle of media products and service through UGC and media content repurposing
3. Managing more effective target marketing.

Moreover, recent studies in social networking sites have found a positive relationship between certain kinds of Facebook use and the maintenance and creation of social capital (Ellison et al. 2007). Accordingly, Facebook appears to play an important role in the process by which its users form and maintain social capital. The findings in this research demonstrate a robust connection between Facebook usage and indicators of social capital, especially of the bridging type (Ellison et al. 2007). It is advisable to point out that Internet use alone did not predict social capital accumulation, but intensive use of Facebook did. Boyd and Ellison (2007) define three main characteristics of SNS: such sites allow users to "(1) construct a public or semi-public profile within a bounded system, (2) articulate a list of other users with whom they share a connection, and (3) view and traverse their list of connections and those made by others within the system."

7 Business Benefits of Using Facebook's and Other Social Network Sites

As it relates to social networking in the corporate business, there is no one-size-fits-all approach. Benefits of social networking platforms are based on platform type, features and the corporation itself. Social networking platforms may allow organizations to improve communication and productivity by disseminating information among different corporate groups of employees in a more efficient manner, resulting in increased productivity. Contemporary academic research in the field of business and social studies (Utz 2009; Subramani and Rajagopalan 2003; Stelzner 2011, p. 16) points out that social networking sites provide benefits in business as they

- Increase Customer Loyalty And Trust
- Build and enhance corporate reputation
- Assess corporate markets in real time
- Facilitate open communication, leading to enhanced information discovery and delivery
- Allow employees to discuss ideas, post news, ask questions and share links.
- Provide an opportunity to widen business contacts
- Target a wide audience, making it a useful and effective recruitment tool
- Generate, enhance, increase and improve brand awareness, business reputation management and client base with minimal use of advertising
- Expand market research, implements marketing campaigns, delivers communications and directs interested people to specific web sites.
- Entice consumer engagement
- Act as a portal point for driving traffic to corporate site and other online properties

- Provide an opportunity and an efficient feedback mechanism to acquire new segments of customers and consumers by targeting specific vertical markets with specific business objectives.
- Provide another potential interception point to build the relationship with corporate consumers and increase client retention.
- Effectively and efficiently access the inherent value of the different consumer segments
- Bring more Traffic and subscribers to Website by increasing Email Marketing Capability and Viral Syndication of Content
- Understand consumer behavior based on the sharing of content and commentary on the social networking site
- Generate qualified lead
- Improve sales and search rankings
- Generate exposure for corporate business
- Reduce overall marketing expenses.

8 Trends of Global IP Traffic Growth

The Cisco Visual Networking Index 2009–2014 white paper "Hyperconnectivity and the Approaching Zettabyte Era" forecasts that global IP traffic will quadruple from 2009 to 2014 (176 to 767 exabytes). Overall, IP traffic will grow at a compound annual growth rate (CAGR) of 34 %. In 2014, the Internet will be four times larger than it was in 2009. Advanced Internet video (3D and HD) will increase 23-fold between 2009 and 2014. Cisco's research shows that by 2014, 3D and HD Internet video will comprise 46 % of consumer Internet video traffic. Video-on-demand (VoD) traffic will double every 2½ years through 2014. Consumer IPTV and CATV traffic will grow at a 33 % CAGR between 2009 and 2014.

Globally, mobile data traffic will double every year through 2014, increasing 39 times between 2009 and 2014. Mobile data traffic will grow at a CAGR of 108 % between 2009 and 2014, reaching 3.5 exabytes per month by 2014. Almost 66 % of the world's mobile data traffic will be video by 2014. Mobile video will grow at a CAGR of 131 % between 2009 and 2014. Business IP traffic will grow at a CAGR of 21 % from 2009 to 2014. Business video conferencing will grow 10-fold over the forecast period. Business videoconferencing traffic is growing almost three times as fast as overall business IP traffic, at a CAGR of 57 % from 2009 to 2014. Web-based video conferencing will grow 180-fold from 2009 to 2014. Web-based video conferencing is the fastest growing subcategory (183 % CAGR from 2009 to 2014) within the business portion of the Cisco VNI Forecast at this time. HD video conferencing will account for over half (57 %) of business video conferencing traffic in 2014, up from 31 % in 2009. Increasing broadband speed: the average global residential Internet connection download speed is 35 times faster in 2010 (4.4 megabits per second) than 2000 (127 kilobits per second).

9 The Decreasing Influence of Old Media

The decreasing economic and social influence of traditional media (print, radio and TV) is particularly evident in the statistical data which show that radio needed 38 years in order to reach 50 million users. TV needed 13 years to reach the same number of users, Internet 4 years, IPOD—3 years; while Facebook added 100 million users in less than 9 months. Moreover, iPod application downloads hit 1 billion in 9 month. On the other hand, global internet company such as Google in 2009 has increased the value of their brand for 25 %.

Simultaneously, all the trend lines were downwards for the newspaper business. Global newspaper advertising revenues fell −17 % in 2009; North American newspapers lost a quarter of their advertising revenues. Ad spend was also down in Western Europe −13.7 %, Central and Eastern Europe −18.7 %, Asia 9.6 %, Latin America −2.9 % and was stable in the Middle East and Africa. Between 2004 and 2009, the US newspaper industry lost 34 % of its readers; the UK industry lost 22 %.

> The research of the Newspaper Association of America shows that daily newspaper print ad has been constantly decreasing since 2005. Furthermore, in the USA The Wall Street Journal is the only newspapers in 2010 to gain in circulation among the top 25 newspapers. The importance as well as the market expansion of digital media is evident in the bookseller Barnes & Noble assertion that the company in 2010 sells more digital books than physical books on its Web site. Accordingly, Forrester Research expects U.S. e-book sales to total $2.8 billion in 2015, up from nearly $1 billion in 2010. The research firm projects the number of e-readers and tablets in the U.S. will soar from more than 15 million in 2010 to nearly 60 million in 2015.

10 Main Competitive Advantage of New/Social Media Over Old/Traditional Media

Although, both the old/traditional and new/social media can reach small or large audiences, there are many fundamental differences in terms of the competitive advantage in distribution, production, technology, market targeting that favor new/social media over old/traditional media (Table 7).

> **Conclusion**
> Today social media represent an important segment of ICT industry that together represent the fastest growing sector of modern economies. Moreover, this industry sector is undergoing a massive metamorphosis and a profound change. This rapid change includes the digitization of information, digital convergence, cross-media content management, the emergence of the internet, Web 2.0, Web 3.0, Web 4.0, Web X.0, dramatic increases in computing power and bandwidth capacity, IPTV,

Table 7 Differences between old and new media consumption patterns

Old/traditional media	New/social, Web and UGC media
Industrial media dominantly produced by large multinational corporations	Personal media primarily produced by internet users
Top-down content production	Bottom-up content production
Centralized framework for organization, production, and dissemination of media	Decentralized (network and on-demand) based media
One to many content distribution	Many to many content distribution
Linear, One-way media communication	Interactive and immersive media communication
Reaching the audience	Connecting the audience
Passive users—Users as Recipients	Active users—Users as participants
Static media	Mobile media
Economies of scale	Economies of scope (Long tail Economics)
Content is the king	User is the king
One-sided platform distribution	More diversified multi-platform (hypermedia and multimedia) distribution, less hierarchical, and distinguished by multiple points of production and utility
Less available and accessible to the public, distribution costs and viewing is more expensive	Generally available and accessible to the public at little or no cost
The time lag between communications produced by industrial media can be long (days, weeks, or even months)	Capable of virtually instantaneous responses; only the participants determine any delay in response
Once created content, it cannot be altered (once a magazine article is printed and distributed changes cannot be made to that same article)	Easily altered content by almost instantaneously editing and writing comments
Less creative content creation	More creative content creation
Storage capacity for media content is relatively low	Storage capacity for media content is very high Acts as an online database
Low level of content categorization and sharing	High level of content categorization, annotation and sharing: Widgets, collaborative tagging, social classification, social indexing, and social tagging, folksonomy
Less peer-to-peer power Publisher-Centric	More peer-to-peer power User-Centric Model UGC—User generated content
Analogue	Digital media Digital convergence Mobile and wireless media Ambient media Augmented media Widget(ized) media Tagged media Folksonomy
Two-dimensional media	3D media
Traditional market targeting (B2C and B2B marketing)	Better and more efficient market and consumer marketing (B2C and C2C) Nicheization Social network and online communities

Internet TV, Mobile TV, Cable TV. Accordingly, this process requires new mechanisms to create more innovative and profitable media content and viewers' experiences. Effective application of content repurposing will help media and ICT companies to reach a wider and more varied audience. With new internet and mobile TV technologies (UGC, media content repurposing) companies have an opportunity to stretch the life of the same content across platforms and audiences.

> Looking from a macro economic perspective, it is advisable to point out that the digital/social (web) media revolution corresponds with the decreasing economic and industrial influence of the leading western countries such as the USA. Thus, the market capitalization growth of the American market in 1970. Represented 66 % of the global market capitalization, while in 2001 the American market capitalization represented 47 %. It is estimated that by 2020, the USA market capitalization growth will be reduced to 27 % of the global market capitalization.
>
> The future of television goes through the interactive services (IPTV, Web TV, Cable TV) such as income tax statement, taxes payment, medical services, shopping. With all these changes, media companies are not any more companies that only deliver contents. Media managers have to set departments of marketing, retailing, and stores, or to signed agreements with external firms. Whereas traditional, centralized, old media favorized communication and content distribution from one to many, new, social, web media produces and distributes content and services from many to many. In old media environment the content was the king. However, in social media, the user becomes new king. In an increasingly converged and global digital media landscape it is easier than ever to reach a large audience, but it is harder than ever to effectively connect with it. Therefore, old media traditional preoccupation was to reach the audience, however, in the age of digital media globalization, new media companies have a twofold task to reach and connect the audience.

In summary, the twenty-first century media is apparently becoming increasingly interactive, immersive, ubiquitous and digital. Furthermore the future of the media appears to be specifically oriented towards the establishment of, networked, 3D, on-demand, broadband and unicast as well as multimedia and hypermedia models of distribution, communication and content creation. Therefore, it is becoming very common that social media is regarded among scholars and media businessmen as a fundamental communication, marketing, content production and distribution, shift in which successful social media companies will have to act more as corporate planners, aggregators, and content providers than traditional advertiser.

References

Ames, M., & Naaman, M. (2007). *Why we tag: Motivations for annotation in mobile and online media*. Proceedings of the ACM SIGCHI Conference on Human Factors in Computing Systems, San Jose, CA.

Anderson, C. (2006). *The long tail: Why the future of business is selling less of more*. London: Random House Business Books.

Anderson, C. (2008). *The long tail: Why the future of business is selling less of more*. New York: Hyperion.

Bakos, Y., & Brynjolfsson, E. (2000). Bundling and competition of information goods on the Internet. *Marketing Science, 19*, 63–82.

Benecchi, E., & Colapinto, C. (2011). Television and social media in the era of convergence and participation. In Z. Vukanovic & P. Faustino (Eds.), *Managing media economy, media content and technology in the age of digital convergence*. Lisbon: Media XXI.

Blanco-Fernández, Y., Pazos-Arias, J. J., Gil-Solla, A., Ramos-Cabrer, M., & López-Nores, M. (2009). Broadcasting and personalization of user-generated contents in DVB-H mobile networks. *Multimedia Systems, 15*, 173–185.

Bloomberg L.P. (September, 2011) Womack, Brian (September 20, 2011). "Facebook Revenue Will Reach $4.27 Billion". Bloomberg.com. Retrieved September 25, 2011 http://www.bloomberg.com/news/2011-09-20/facebook-revenue-will-reach-4-27-billion-emarketer-says-1-.html.

Boyd, D. M., & Ellison, N. B. (2007). Social network sites: Definition, history, and scholarship. *Journal of Computer-Mediated Communication, 13*(1), 210–230.

Bruns, A. (2007, June). *Produsage: Towards a broader framework for user-led content creation*. Proceedings of the 6th ACM SIGCHI conference on Creativity & Cognition, Washington, DC, USA (consulted April 23, 2007) http://snurb.info/node/720

Cattuto, C., Loreto, V., & Pietronero, L. (2007). Semiotic dynamics and collaborative tagging. *Proceedings of the National Academy of Sciences, 104*(5), 1461.

Cisco Visual Networking Index 2009-2014 white paper "Hyperconnectivity and the Approaching Zettabyte Era."

Daugherty, T., Eastin, M. S., & Bright, L. (2008). Exploring consumer motivations for creating user-generated content. *Journal of Interactive Advertising, 8*(2), 1–24.

Deuze, M. (2007). Convergence culture in the creative industries. *International Journal of Cultural Studies, 10*(2), 243–263.

Dokoupil, T., & Wu, A. (2010). Take this Blog and shove it! *Newsweek, 156*(7), 42.

Doyle, G. (2002). *Understanding media economics*. New York: Sage.

Dutta, S. (2010, November). What's your personal media strategy. *Harvard Business Review*, 127–130.

Edwards, T. (2009). *User-generated content* (pp. 18–19). April/May: MultiLingual.

Ellison, N. B., Steinfield, C., & Lampe, C. (2007). The benefits of Facebook "friends": Social capital and college students' use of online social network sites. *Journal of Computer-Mediated Communication, 12*(4).

eMarketing, January 2011 Facebook Now Has 800 Million Users, Adam Ostrow, September 22, 2011 http://mashable.com/2011/09/22/facebook-800-million-users/.

Facebook Now Has 800 Million Users, Ostrow, A. (2011, September 22). http://mashable.com/2011/09/22/facebook-800-million-users/

Gansky, L. (2010). *The mesh: Why the future of business is sharing*. London: Penguin Group.

Ghose, A., & Ipeirotis, P. (2009). The Econo Mining project at NYU: Studying the economic value of user-generated content on the Internet. *Journal of Revenue and Pricing Management, 8*(2/3), 241–246.

Gladwell, M. (2002). *The tipping point: How little things can make a big difference*. New York: Little, Brown & Company.

Golder, S., & Huberman, B. (2006). Usage patterns of collaborative tagging systems. *Journal of Information Science, 32*(2), 198–208.

Hoegg, R., Martignoni, R., Meckel, M., & Stanoevska-Slabeva, K. (2006). *Overview of business models for Web 2.0 communities*. Proceedings of GeNeMe - Gemeinschaften in Neuen Medien, Technische Universität Dresden.

Howe, J. (2009). *Crowdsourcing: Why the power of the crowd is driving the future of business.* New York: Crown Publishing Group.

Jenkins, H. (2006). *Convergence culture. Where old and new media collide.* Cambridge: MIT Press.

Koh, J., Kim, Y., Butler, B., & Bock, G. (2007). Encouraging participation in virtual communities. *Communications of the ACM, 50*(2), 68–73.

Lacy, S., & Bauer, J. (2006). In A. Albarran, S. Chan-Olmsted, & M. Wirth (Eds.), *Handbook of media management and economics.* Mahwah, NJ: Lawrence Erlbaum Associates.

Livingstone, S. (2004). The challenge of changing audiences. *European Journal of Communication, 19*(1), 75–86.

Marlow, C., Naaman, M., Davis, M., & Boyd, D. (2006). *Tagging paper, taxonomy, Flickr.* Proceedings of the 17th ACM Conference on Hypertext and Hypermedia, Odense, Denmark.

Nielsen Global Online Consumer Survey. (2009, July). *Trust, value and engagement in advertising.* Nielsen Consumer Research, New York.

Nov, O., & Ye, C. (2010). Why do people tag?: Motivations for photo tagging. *Communications of the ACM, 53*(7), 128–131.

Online Marketing Trends, 2010 YouTube Reaches 4 Bilion Views Per Day, Sarah Perez, January 23, 2012 http://techcrunch.com/2012/01/23/youtube-reaches-4-billion-views-per-day/.

Peters, I. (2009). *Folksonomies.* Berlin: De Gruyter Saur.

Qualman, E. (2010). *Socialnomics: How social media transforms the way we live and do business.* New York: Wiley.

Schaedel, U., & Clement, M. (2010). Managing the online crowd: Motivations for engagement in user-generated content. *Journal of Media Business Studies, 7*(3), 17–36.

Smith, T. (2009). The social media revolution. *International Journal of Market Research, 51*(4), 559–561.

Snuderl, K. (2008). Tagging: Can user-generated content improve our services? *Statistical Journal of the IAOS, 25,* 125–132.

Spinellis, D., & Louridas, P. (2008). The collaborative organization of knowledge. *Communications of the ACM, 51*(8), 68–73.

Stelzner, M. A. (2011, April). *Social media marketing report. How marketers are using social media to grow their business.* Social Media Examiner.

Subramani, M. R., & Rajagopalan, B. (2003). Knowledge-sharing and influence in online social networks via viral marketing. *Communications of the ACM, 46*(12), 300–307.

Szabo, G., & Huberman, B. A. (2010). Predicting the popularity of online content. *Communications of the ACM, 53*(8), 80–88.

TechCrunch (2010) and Bloomberg L.P. (September, 2011) http://blog.twitter.com/2011/03/numbers.html.

Tom Tong, S., Van Der Heide, B., Langwell, L., & Walther, J. B. (2008). Too much of a good thing? The relationship between number of friends and interpersonal impressions on Facebook. *Journal of Computer-Mediated Communication, 13,* 531–549.

Utz, S. (2009). The (potential) benefits of campaigning via social network sites. *Journal of Computer-Mediated Communication, 14*(2), 221–243.

van Dijck, J. (2011). *"You" as in "You Tube": Defining user agency in social media platforms, in ... and Paulo Faustino, Managing media economy, media content and technology in the age of digital convergence.* Lisbon: Media XXI.

Vizjak, A., & Ringlstetter, M. (2003). *Media management: Leveraging content for profitable growth.* New York: Springer.

Womack, B. (2011, September 20). *Facebook revenue will reach $4.27 billion.* Bloomberg.com. Retrieved September 25, 2011, from http://www.bloomberg.com/news/2011-09-20/facebook-revenue-will-reach-4-27-billion-emarketer-says-1-.html

YouTube Reaches 4 Billion Views Per Day, Perez, S. (2012, January 23). http://techcrunch.com/2012/01/23/youtube-reaches-4-billion-views-per-day/

http://blog.twitter.com/2011/03/numbers.html

Two Faces of Growth: Linking Customer Engagement to Revenue Streams

Biser Zlatanov

1   Introduction

When it comes to evaluate growth perspectives and business model of social media networks I often refer to the story of the fortune-teller who asserted that she can revive the death people for a friendly talk, but in the same time ridiculed the people's superstition of parallel worlds. In the last few months after LinkedIn IPO in May 2011 many analysts and investors are wondering whether the rest of the social media expected to go public are capable to build competetive advantage. It is strange, however, that many of them are sceptical towards LinkedIn and in the same time are eulogizing Facebook foretelling the latter a prosperous future.

This paper studies the elusive nature of social media growth and the key drivers for their expansion. The LinkedIn IPO data is used predominantly here since we have more reliable and raw data that could be employed in the analysis, while value is understood in its intrinsic aspects. The analysis, however, is limited and could not be taken for investment decision or for any other purposes outside the theoretical framework. Inevitably, the introduction of social media metrics supports the understanding and social biases towards media, dependant on the fashion of consumption and the exaggerated media coverage of the issues related to the social media.

In mixing the facts with fiction media are conspicuously enthusiastic, but it is not something new that we have not witnessed. The history of speculative bubbles mingles with the ability to disseminate information in large quantities and at long distances. Some analysts even see a correlation between the (large) scale of bubbles and the advent of different media—starting with the advent of newspapers (Shiller 2005:85).

We can not rely too much on the stock markets and media since they are too volatile and affected by the investment gurus or analysts' predictions. The fundamentals of the company are what we have to rely, but the upscale of the next

---

B. Zlatanov (✉)
Sofia University, Sofia, Bulgaria
e-mail: biserz@yahoo.com

growth metaphor wave can change our perception of risk and thus can turn natural inclination of risk aversion to risk seeking and vice versa. It has already happened while the "new era" metaphor conceived the dot-com bubble in the Y2K euphoria.

Calling the 2011 technology IPOs success the next "irrational exuberance" or Bubble 2.0, however, has to share our inability to make distinction between the dot-coms and the social networks and to search shallow analogies between then and now. If we recall dot-coms and their business model, if we can call it so, it was focused on creating network externalities, which is demand side view on the value creation and few of the IPOs like Amazon were engaged with the supply side issues. Value creation, whether online or offline, is a two sided process, where enterprise should unite the demand side (consumer growth and satisfaction) with supply side (shareholder value and investor satisfaction). In the social network context, linking network externalities that create engagement to the revenue streams is a key question.

One of the major differences between the social media buzz today and the dot-coms mania is in the way the enterprises perceive the value creation and business models. The obvious distinction is that before going public social media networks has proved that they are capable at least to make a profit. However, this poses the question of their valuation and their ability to create and deliver value.

2   Disruptive Innovations and Growth

There are different ways to diagnose the process of value creation in companies. It has often been somehow associated with growth, which is a natural inclination of prosperous companies to explore the limits of the market. Usually, we intuitively consider that growth, especially market size growth, is related to innovation and prosperity. However, our intuition often goes in a wrong direction. We can take for instance the market for corporate control, where companies fairly easy grow in terms of market power and market share and often use it so as to substitute the need of internal innovation (Hitt et al. 1996).

Social media on the other hand are an emanation of the need for innovation and the constant internal innovation in media sector. Conceived after the burst of the dot-com bubble these media has incorporated in their strategies the lessons learned from the dot-com companies. However, learning from the past is not a sufficient argument when we speculate about the future, in this case—the historical growth (Damodaran 2002; Copeland et al. 2000).

In the time of technological changes and disruption in media the efforts were directed to fill the gap between productivity growth measures and innovation. In Schumpeter's seminal work "Business cycles" (1939) innovation is broadly defined and in some respects derived with reference to the cost. An evidence of innovation is the ability of enterprise to produce a given quantity of output with less cost, if the prices of factors are constant or has not fallen (Schumpeter 1939:85). This view of innovation was embodied in the waves of media restructuring and integration in the 1980s and 1990s, when companies were competing for gaining competitive advantages through increasing its production capacity and delivery process, reducing the diagnostic tools of innovation to the level of the cost analysis. However, cost advantage is not sustainable to build competitive advantage in industry sectors where profitability is driven by the application of innovation. Schumpeterian view of innovation process has solely partially to do with this notion.

The business mantra of scale and scope economies and synergies has produced a race for gaining larger market share, due to the uncertainty that technological change has produced. The dot-com companies bearing the idea of cost advantages and gaining share on the basis of network externalities has become very popular. Finally, in the peak of the dot-com bubble and thereafter it turned out that cost perspective of innovation has its disadvantages. External innovation process is correlated to internal innovation and vice versa. Additionally, there were also costs that growing in size companies during the dot-com mania have underestimated and that have nothing to do with production—the transaction costs (Coase 1937).

The transaction costs in growing business entities are connected with the price paid to gather, to process and to interpret information before and after transaction and for the failure to do so. The costs that often are miscalculated are related to the impact of introducing innovative processes or substituting them through acquisitions—ex ante and ex post transaction costs (Willamson 1985). This in turn relates the question of how well we manage the information stream and which interpretation framework we choose—the financial framework or the strategic framework. The former captures the financial measures and indicators which are the guidelines in the way we interpret the company's ability to create and/or introduce innovation and consequently experience growth. The latter is more intuitive and put more value on the understanding of how company creates and delivers value for participants in the exchange process—customers, shareholders, managers and employees.

With the advent of social media hype and media buzz financial framework has its proponents, while the enterprises and investors community are more focused on ratios that consists of earnings. The ability of the company to make and grow its profits is used as evidence that it is able to create value, to build and to sustain competitive advantage.

We can not understand the fragmented financial data we have for social media if our knowledge does not penetrate to the depths of how they work and what intrinsic value they deliver. For instance, earnings, used in price-earnings ratio are loved by the investor community, but it is also a question of how those earnings are calculated and if they indicate higher earning capability or are taken as accounting entries. It is hard to find fast growing innovative media company, heavily investing in R&D that has reported substantial earnings in their financial reports. In the same time there are companies that are in the last stage of their life cycle that could pump the earnings selling property that creates extraordinary, one-time cash flow or just by cutting their capital expenditures.

2.1 Growth and Its Limits

Due to restraints of financial reporting bottom line earnings could give distorted view of the company performance. Identifying growth companies and the growth assets could be further restrained from the phenomenon of controlled information.

Damodaran (2002) raised the question of managed reporting of financial information by the companies' boards. Copeland, Koller and Murrin (2001) asserted that it is essential to understand how and why business achieves its results. The expectation treadmill (Dobbs and Koller 1998) discusses the problem of accelerating the expectations of the market—the better managers perform, the better results market expects from them and this causes the treadmill of expectations to move faster. It is quite probable social media to have problems with rising expectations, which any achievements could not support.

The successful IPOs and blue chip companies are challenged by the questions of how to control the phenomenon of rising expectation and to outperform them. The pursuit of beating the analyst expectations was a pattern modeled by Microsoft and Intel in the 1990s and perfected by the social media lately. In the case of social media in pre-IPO period public impression is filtered and guided since the information we receive is fragmented and in most cases comes from questionable sources. The lack of necessary information leaves a room for intense media coverage which mixes facts with personal comments.

The stage of the life cycle of the firm is another question when analyzing growth assets in firms that need new investments and/or diversification strategy (Mueller 1972). Product life-cycle and specific assets are also a topic in evaluating the determinants of media diversification (Chan-Olmsted and Chang 2003). In general, the growth rate expected from mature versus young companies and from larger versus smaller companies is quite different. The smaller firm effect is used as an explanation for higher returns and expected growth from smaller companies (Dimson and Marsh 1986; Chan et al. 1991). In the same vein, the risk associated with smaller firms is greater and many of them do not survive after few years of existence (Knaup and Piazza 2007).

The problem of introducing innovation influences the growth perspectives of the media. It has been argued that major shifts in innovation are unlikely to come from well-established companies (Clayton Christensen 1997). A study of the global media conglomerates has introduced the same position, adding that relatively big companies embracing market power strategies in the sake of market efficiency hampered the innovation process (Zlatanov, B. (2008). Unpublished papers). The relationship between innovation and its diffusion in the advertisers and audience markets creates another topic of concern since the two markets show differing patterns and stages of innovation adoption. The declining market of news media with post-recession effects could hardly expect growth relying on traditional products and services.

3   Questions and Method

The questions raised in the current social media growth wave are connected with the ability of the companies to introduce viable business model that links the demand side measures of growth with supply side measures. The linkage between customer engagement and revenues, in particular, has its qualitative and quantitative implications.

Customer engagement analyzes two questions—how we define the social network customers and what is their engagement with one another and with the organization. Behavioural approach to engagement values the growth in demand of the social networks and perceives it as user involvement with the media or network. Quantitative aspects of the engagement with the user network are illustrated by the measures of his consumption—duration and/or money spent, clicks and page views, recency and frequency of visits. Qualitative aspects represent attitudinal approach and encompass the attitude toward the network—how the user perceives the value he derives from the network.

The supply side view of the social networks introduces the enterprises objectives and addresses the monetization issues—the financial results of consumption. In most cases reported earnings are preferred as a valuable indicator for the performance of the company, its ability to create value to its shareholders. However, accounting earnings bear at least two disadvantages. First, they are not a stable indicator to analyze performance and growth. Second, the estimate is contingent on the accounting policy adopted by the company management (Damodaran 2006).

The growth of social networks has different dimensions and analyzing the linkage between the customer engagement metrics and the revenue streams provide us with analytical tools to study these dimensions. The adopted approaches to measure the network value in terms of length (number of member nodes) and depth (the customer engagement) need to focus on the quality of the diagnostic tools used.

The data of LinkedIn is used here to study how the customer engagement is translated in the company profitability. In the current case the social network performance is viewed from the standpoint of the strategic performance. This paper uses the data from LinkedIn annual reports from 2006 to 2011 (Security Registration Statement) and Q-10 reports for the first three quarters of 2011.

Since the company invests intensively in product development these expenses are capitalized using a three years straight line amortization, which is the average period for the companies in the Internet. Accordingly, earnings from the statements are adjusted and so are the implied cost and expenses. The revenues are preferred metric for growth since the probability to give biased results is limited.

So as to evaluate the linkage between network length growth and customer engagement metrics and revenue streams this paper uses cross ratio values that indicate the relation between membership growth and various indicators. The first part of the indicators measure how membership growth influences consumption of the social network and encourages engagement—page views per member and monthly unique visitors per member.

The linkage between customer engagement and revenues could be measured through their correlation with members and unique visitors. The study measured revenue per member and respectively unique visitor and cost per member and per unique visitors. Since members are the "assets" for the network to increase in value they could be valued as an average number of members registered during the fiscal year. In a similar manner could be calculated average unique visitors. I assume that the membership growth and unique visitor growth have a positive correlation.

The study applied industry structure analysis by Porter (2008) and Coyne and Subramaniam (1996) strategy model that proposed several refinements of the Porter model. The models are used to provide strategic scope of the forces that could affect profitability in the social media business. LinkedIn data is used, because it is the only social network that provided necessary financial and other data, so as to perform the current analysis.

It is reasonable to point out that not all of the cost and expenses and the revenues respectively could be associated with the membership growth, but since the growth of network value is contingent on the membership base I valued them on per member base. LinkedIn Corporation (2011a) has declared members as its prime objective and it is used as a growth measure here. Membership growth influences customer recruitment and retention and the growth of customers for hiring solutions and advertising (marketing solutions) is correlated with it.

4 Determine the Demand Side of Growth

Business models and business model design in social media put an extreme emphasis on the demand side of the media product—value of the media is becoming a function of its network valuation dependant on the number and the perceived value of its users. While Facebook has reached approximately 800 million monthly active users (as of September 2011), LinkedIn reached 135 million members—as of the 3d of November 2011.

All these numbers are here to convince us in the ability of the social media to build competitive advantage which we could translate in terms of demand side economy as building customer engagement. However, the numbers of consumption alone still do not posses the quality to engage consumers, though examples in the opposite exist.

The ability of social media and LinkedIn in particular, to build competitive advantage is contingent on the structure of the media market and the expectations of the consumer network. The open source strategy that company has applied is a customer-centered with prime focus to build the so-called critical mass—the minimum required number of users in a network, so as to enjoy the network externalities.

The value and the nature of the network externalities however are contingent on the links between the nodes in the network, not just the numbers of consumption. The valuation of network, as Economides (1996) pointed out, seems counterintuitive, since the value gained through consumption rises with the units consumed or sold. What is essential for the networks are the ownership and the nature of the externality—if the network creates direct or indirect externalities, the availability of substitute and complementary components or links.

The nature of the externalities is connected with the complementarity issue (Economides 1996)—the network value for the customer is a question of the added value of the network complements. The externality value and respectively the nodes in the network grow exponentially when there are interconnection, compatibility, interoperability and coordination of quality of services between two or more network owners. Proprietary rights that are used for foreclosure of competitors and influenced economic development (North 1981) here have different meaning. It is not the exclusivity of property rights to foreclose other competitors from the source, but because of the nature of the externalities users and owners derive more value through granting an access and through forming alliances or coalitions to better utilize the effects of the network. In the media industry the value and the profit gained through cooperation is often greater than the gains from competition (Daidj, Grazia & Hammoudi 2010). Thus, Nash equilibrium is often stable, because it is value and profit maximizing.

4.1 Customer Engagement

The core value and central point of the network and loyalty business models from the perspective of the demand side externalities is the customer engagement. As a response to the changing economic environment social media are including new features that correspond to the growing bargaining power of customers and reaffirming that prosumer behaviour is becoming major "value" driver.

The motives behind social media consumption are various and might be related to the rise of citizen journalism. The question of change in the social paradigm and counter-power (Castels 2007) has caused the increase in social networks consumption. According to a survey among business journalists the overall attraction to the power of new media and citizen journalism could be considered a "fad" (Arketi 2009). The motives that lie behind social media consumption are still not quite clear and does not have stable pattern even in the context of Facebook hegemony. The important issue here is the perceived value user gains through using social media platform. To make the question more complicated the results of the surveys are controversial and do not support the intuition of social media hegemony online.

In the social media management and marketing context two approaches are used for measuring customer engagement and to determine value—behavioural and attitudinal (Godson 2009). While the behavioural approach brings us at the surface of raw data—time spend, number of clicks/impressions/views, number of purchases, the attitudinal approach gives us in-depth analysis of the incentives and emotions that drive social media consumption. However, attitudinal approach in social media analysis is rarely applied.

If we adopt the behavioural perspective the results sound optimistic. Social networks are competing hard and in some respects are outperforming search engines and Internet portals for unique visitors and page views. Social networking is the most engaging in terms of time spent and unique visitor online activity with over 82 % of online population and almost every one out of five minutes in Internet are spent in the social networks (comScore 2011).

In contrast, if we apply the qualitative approach that measures attitudes we can reveal another perspective of the social media and social networks, in particular. A study of American Consumer Satisfaction Index (Foresee 2011) presented results that deconstruct the media image, underpinning the high perceived value of the

Table 1 American Customer Satisfaction Index

Aggregate scores	2010	2011	Points change	Change 2011/2010	Change 2011/2000
E-business sector	73.5	75.4	1.9	2.6 %	19.7 %
Social media	70	70	0.0	0.0 %	0.0 %
Portals & search engines	77	80	3.0	3.9 %	27 %
Online news	74	73	−1.0	−1.4 %	0.0 %

Source: ASCI

social networks. The ACSI measured more than 240 companies across 47 industries, and social media are among the least satisfying consumers. The only underperformers ranked after the social media are merely airlines, cable television, and print newspapers. While LinkedIn score was included in the aggregate social media score (70), the score of the leader Facebook was under the average level for a second consecutive year (66).[1]

In comparison with other e-business categories, social media—and in particular, social networks—are the least capable to meet their customers needs. Table 1 above presents the data from ACSI.

The social networks are the lowest-scoring among other social media—content sharing sites like YouTube and the social media leader the non-profit Wikipedia. However, the survey does not answer what is the purpose of social media consumption and why so many people are using it so often.

The tarnished image of the social networks looks better when applying quantitative measures of behavioural approach. Both social networks and blogs are the top destination online. It has been calculated that the monthly visits globally in Facebook are over 730 millions, while professional social network site LinkedIn.com reached more than 84 million visitors in June 2011 (comScore 2011). The females, who are targeted by advertisers, make up the majority of visits in social networks, according to Nielsen & NM Incite (2011), while the most active age group of social networkers was 18-to-34-year-olds.

When we apply the demography of consumers to the purpose of consumption it has revealed that most of the social network users in U.S. and ten other major markets are using it for social purposes—to keep in touch with their reference groups (family and friends) and to find new friends. Entertainment features, as well as practical issues to be informed or release information about products and services share the second cluster of social media consumption drivers. Accordingly, it includes entertainment and creative outlet, read about products or provide a feedback. Not surprisingly, business purposes and career networking are other reasons that generate traffic.

It is interesting that except for information regarding products, users in this category add also getting coupons and promotions (Nielsen & NM Incite 2011). In the same vein over half of the Facebook users that have clicked "Like" button of a

---

[1] According to the Index the maximum score is 100 (the highest), while 1 is the lowest.

brand or product expect corresponding return. It is indicative that Facebook liker expects both access to exclusive content, events or sales, and discounts or promotions (Exact Target 2011). In similar manner the above denotes the intuition that "Like" should be understood as a personal devotion to the company that user has become fan or advocate. The usage of "Like" has different meanings depending on to whom it is related—company or individual, and the expertise and characteristics of the online visitor who uses it.

Clicking "Like" could not be considered as a permission to initiate advertising or other marketing activity and similar is the implication for the usage of LinkedIn "Share" button. However, in terms of Internet usage "Share" has less strong meaning than "Like" and "Recommend", though the volatility of meanings of those terms should be adjusted according to the demographics, expertise and psychographics of the social networker. It could give us some guidelines regarding the motives that lie behind the social networks consumption.

Regarding social plug-ins that measure engagement there is a clear cooperation and interoperability between content sharing social media and community and engagement media like LinkedIn. One of the purposes of social plug-ins or bookmarks such as "Like Box" or "Share" is to drive traffic back to the site, but in the same time it sends the IP address information of all visitors to the social network. Although it is controversial and raises important privacy issues this feature adds value for several reasons—it is used to build social authority, to popularize the network (the buttons are used in many sites, including online websites of the traditional media) and to register customer engagement quantitatively.

Not less controversial are the problems connected with permission marketing and customer relationship management. In the light of the recency, frequency and monetary (RFM) approach, used in data mining and direct marketing it is a debatable question how often companies to communicate via social networks. Recent research suggests almost equal preferences—28 % of the respondents said that this could be done once a month or even less, while another part (26 %) expect it to happen once a week (ROI Research 2011).

Even though it is debatable that we understand the consumption drivers, their application in customer engagement strategies and their limits arising across customer satisfaction issues, it is important how consumption transforms in revenues. Rising demand for social network services could be driven, because of the free access, which generates growth in traffic, in membership, but it is not indicative for the quality of the service and the customer perceived value. Quality of services and long term growth even with respect to traffic and membership depends not only on the satisfaction and engagement, but on the ability of the service provider to generate revenue.

5 Supply Side of Growth: Advertisers

One of the challenges of the online business is that consumption level outperforms the desire to pay for the services. Public good delivered by the social media implicitly assumes variant of the free-rider problem, where eventually everyone could benefit from the service, but fewer are likely to pay for it. The problem introduced by technological change is either the lack of dominant design or its fragility and the relatively low rate of adoption on the market where media derive their revenues.

The leading controversy in the business models of online media and social networks in particular stems from the differing stages of innovation diffusion on the two main markets where media operate—audience and advertising. The overwhelming results on the audience markets are still not correspondingly absorbed and transformed by the advertising markets. Online advertising on a global base is outperformed by TV, print (both newspapers and magazines) and newspapers alone (MagnaGlobal 2011). It seems that it is the advertisers who interpret the process of technological change and impact the key definitions of dominant design in social media.

Not less important than customer engagement is the question of how are interpreted the characteristics of innovation that affect diffusion—relative advantage, compatibility, complexity, trialability and observability (Rogers 2003). The recent hype of social media marketing and advertising is focused on the relative advantages that technological change offers. However, current studies raise questions about compatibility and observability directly linked with the dominant standards of gathering and measuring results of marketing communication and ROI for advertisers.

The relationship of the social media with avertisers and other paying customers has a quite short history, since media needed critical mass and data first to turn it in a promise for successful marketing strategy. The majority of the marketers included in a survey conducted by Technorati (2011) responded that they use social media on behalf of their clients for not more than two years.

However, the rise of permission marketing, the social media influence on the purchasing behaviour and high consumption levels elevated the probable long term gains to a more immediate profit maximizing opportunity for advertisers. After search engine optimization social media are the second most cited destination where marketers are going to raise the investments of their clients (Marketing Sherpa 2011).

It is a predominantly shared notion that search marketers who integrate social media improve conversion rate. An important feature of the social media content is the rankings, which determine the frequency and the relevance of the content by the people who engage—unique visitors who like, comment and share. The more Edge Rank and other social media rankings are driven by relevance, the more this creates credibility, which is the main reason for conversions.

One of the most valuable aspects of social media consumption for advertisers is that it creates trust and allows better targeting possibilities. Since most of the social media are used to connect with friends and to review products or learn about them they are targeted channel to promote brand. Behavioral advertising and viral marketing are easily used, because social media data give more details how the advertiser could engage with the audience. Social media are used to predict the target audience behavior and ease brand personification (Stone 2010).

About six in ten (59 %) online shoppers say user-generated customer product reviews have a significant or good impact on their buying behavior, (e-tailing Group and Power Reviews 2011). In terms of the decision making people inform themselves more likely from the social network sites than from shopping or deal sites for the products, but majority usually use shopping sites when they start searching for the product or right before making the purchase. Consequently, it has been revealed that according to the number of buying decisions the more desired target audience for social shopping is men than women—men are more likely to conduct social shopping activities than women (Performics 2011).

The impact of social media has influenced the traditional marketing funnel—awareness-consideration-preference-action-loyalty. It is questionable at this stage of social media research to assert whether social media has changed the purchase process itself, but they added value to the decision making through word-of-mouth communication and reviews. This has led social media marketers to speak about the power of engagement advertisements and earned media—the ability of advertising from display-paid ad to transform in a social media conversation, becoming part of the user's news feed and creating viral marketing effect.

Not less important are the growth drivers that stay behind the social media advertising market—the budgets of small and medium sized enterprises (SMEs). As long as technology produces fragmentation of audiences across content it is increasingly effective to target niche audiences. Although brand-based advertising is currently a key to long-term growth both for advertisers and social media, the small budgets and respectively SMEs advertisers are the key segment for growth in the market. And this conclusion is correspondingly shared not only for social media, but for online advertising as a whole (Marketing Sherpa 2011; MagnaGlobal 2011).

Though seemingly easy to predict, the bright future of social media advertising has some foreseeable limits that are related to the common standards of advertising effectiveness measurement—low click-through rates. Thus, social media marketing is more inclined to enforce adoption of currently obscure customer engagement measures as "liking" behaviour of users and engagement ads. However, this raises controversies about the ambiguity of the social meaning of "Like". It is probably this reason why most of the marketers prefer to value, than to measure brand sentiment. In terms of measurability of the social media traffic volume slightly more than a half (53 %) of marketers measures it (Marketing Sherpa 2011).

6 How Social Networks Manage Growth: LinkedIn

LinkedIn IPO raised many questions regarding the commonly held beliefs of the social media future. Undoubtedly, social media are able to generate traffic volume sustainable to provoke advertising and direct selling activity. The question still unanswered is how social media are able to transform customer engagement they pretend creating to measurable results and most importantly to a viable business model. An interesting answer is related to LinkedIn, since this professional network differs in many respects from the rest of the community and engagement social media.

LinkedIn IPO was successful example of making an impressive public offering which has raised the initial price more than twice after the first day of trading. What has become notoriously known afterwards as a small float strategy has rocketed the share price from pre-IPO $45 to the closing price of $94.25 after the first day of trading on 19 of May 2011. In the first day peak level the price almost tripled the initial valuation, which raised the question of the overvaluation of the social network from the market.

The media coverage changed from optimistic and positive attitude towards the social media to negative to the LinkedIn IPO and its ability to create shareholder value. The wave of negative feedback has raised controversial questions for the following social media IPOs drawing analogies between them and the dot-coms. Consequently, the LinkedIn share price has been driven by volatility, not only because of the overall stock exchange volatility, but because of the uncertainty and lack of understanding of this "new and unproven market" (LinkedIn 2011a), where social media operate.

During the current study 377 articles appeared in the Wall Street Journal has been analyzed using the keyword LinkedIn and covering a period of two calendar years—18 December 2009 to 18 December 2011. The media attention to the company shifted three times focusing on different thematic areas (thematic shifts) and there has been two main shifts of media sentiment (thematic sentiment). It is worth noting that before the intentions to launch IPO had been made public most of the articles, containing the keyword LinkedIn, referred to the social networks or social media as a whole. All over the whole period of two years the interest in Facebook dominates and the company received the most exaggerated attention.

The first thematic shift, though there has not been clear chronological pattern and order, occurred after the middle of 2010. Until then the company was predominantly described as a member of the social media and the overall sentiment was positive, while articles sound optimistic. The most powerful keywords were "talent" and "friends" relating to the opportunities that social media create with respect to the advertising in the social circles and to the professionals. The newspaper has published a featured experience of a computer engineer hired by LinkedIn.

Another article revealed that success is dependant on your network, while most jobs come from second- and third-degree contacts (Garone 2010). There has been a comment of Josef Schuster, founder of Schuster LLC, a financial-services firm specializing in IPO products, who said that he likes social networking, because it could be a new industry segment having the characteristics like "successful Internet companies" (Cowan 2009).

After the thematic shift occurred the focus changed and the journalistic interest moved to the business model of social media. The talent question continued to be mentioned in relation with the network effect benefits. The major interest is how social media can "translate" the benefits in a viable business model. However, the main players that media commented and praised are Twitter and Facebook, while LinkedIn has been somehow attached to them. There has not been shift in sentiment towards social networks.

The second thematic shift occurred after the intentions of LinkedIn to launch its own IPO had been made public. It is worth noting that the professional network has not received any approval remarks while the sentiment changed and sounded more neutral. From January to the middle of May The Wall Street Journal covered the issues connected to the valuation of the IPO. Information was reported to correct the major changes in valuation even though for less than a day the media revealed two different probable values of the LinkedIn shares in The Wall Street Deal Journal. In the first article the offering has expected to "value LinkedIn in the ballpark of $2 billion" by unnamed source (Ovide and Das 2011). On the second day the value of the company was three billion according to the SharesPost estimate (Ovide 2011).

The third thematic shift happened after the IPO launch which revealed the successful small float strategy and poor valuation. The afterthought in the post-IPO period that the price had been exaggerated gradually shifted the sentiment towards the company to negative. The LinkedIn share price and company ability to grow earnings was questioned. One of the articles cited an analyst who concluded the observation "good company—bad price" (Russolillo and Conway 2011).

6.1 The LinkedIn Business Model

The IPO pricing and current share price volatility is not an evidence for the viability of the business model. The professional network has crossed the earnings line before going public with an after-tax net income of $15.3 million (accounting measure) or adjusted after-tax net income of $58.7 million.[2] In 2010 the company is on the second stage of the life cycle after more than 7 years of existence. It is an important fact since previous studies show that only about one fourth of start-ups in information industry in the US survived more than 7 years. However, this is not evidence whether the social network is capable to cross the earnings line with sustainable profits in future.

The shifts of the institutional and individual investor sentiment and the overall economic turbulence had an impact on the stock exchange volatility and the company shares. Table 2 presents the calculated average share price (on the basis of closing price), the standard deviation and the average volume of traded shares on NYSE for the period to December 16th, 2011:

Table 2 LinkedIn share price (in U.S. $)

Average share price	Standard deviation of the shares	Average volume
81.67	11.05322	1,423,778

---

[2] The after-tax net income is accounting measure of performance taken from LinkedIn Income Statement (LinkedIn 2011a), while the adjusted after-tax net income is author's calculation after capitalization of R&D and other items that influence intrinsic value.

The business where the company operates characterizes with considerable network effects, intensive competition, switching barriers to customers, price sensitivity and lower barriers of entry, alternative products and technology-driven changes in content creation and delivery, complementary products. Key value driver for the company market success is its ability to create benefits for its members and to encourage prosumer behaviour through the usage of the online professional network. Most of the members are passive professionals that could utilize the dynamic network where their social equity and career prospects are determined not only by their expertise and skills, but also through their contacts. The network externalities create complementary benefits for professionals, enterprises and professional organizations worldwide. The existence of the network allows identifying and acquiring specific talent within the global network, to promote the organization or talent, to enhance knowledge and expertise and eventually build social equity in the community.

The company has three diversified revenue streams—hiring solutions, marketing solutions and premium subscription. Hiring solutions revenues are derived primarily from hiring services to corporate customers—number of over 7,300 enterprises (as of 30th September 2011) and professional organizations—and job postings. Marketing revenues (solutions) are fees from advertising—display, text ads, including self-service advertising. Premium subscriptions are derived from monthly and annual subscription and are primarily online sales. The share of the third stream is constantly decreasing since 2006.

Key factor that influences industry profitability is related to the access to new technology, ability to engage customers and translate engagement into revenues. The revenue streams of the company are related to Internet advertising, staffing and talent acquisition services.

The staffing and talent acquisition policies are critical for the know-how intensive industries, where competitive advantage is dependant more on inimitable knowledge-based competences, than on property-based resources. This market is expected to expand especially in the mature industries in developed economies, where the talent is going to be critical resource. The worldwide professional population in 2010 was approximately 640 million and the worldwide labor force was approximately 3.3 billion. According to International Data Corporation (IDC), the worldwide market for staffing and talent acquisition services for 2010 totaled $85 billion (LinkedIn 2011a). The forecast is the market to expand to $121 billion in 2012, estimated in previous IDC report issued in 2008.

On the hiring market LinkedIn faces competition from two directions—recruiting services organizations and online professional networks. There is a growing number and scope of established online and offline recruiting companies such as Monster Worldwide, Career Builder and talent management companies, such as Taleo. Online professional networks are growing their membership base, however with a slower pace and include companies that operate internationally, such as Xing (11 million) in Germany and Viadeo (40 million) in France, that provide online professional networking solutions, as well as Internet companies in the customer relationship management market, such as Salesforce.com. The first signs for more intensive competition and consolidation in a strategic alliances are coming from Europe, where Viadeo entered a joint venture with a Russian subsidiary of the publisher Sanoma Qyj (Chao 2011). Simultaneously, the penetration of LinkedIn at the Chinese market is insignificant, where the first professional networks are established.

Entry barriers that are primarily related to technology are easy to surmount by technologically advanced companies such as Facebook, Google, Microsoft and Twitter, capable to develop substitutes or other competing solutions. However, the business environment at the emerging growth market of social networks and the need of widely adopted dominant design favours strategic alliances formation and co-opetition.

The Internet advertising in 2010 totaled $63 billion and in 2011 is estimated to be $70.9 billion according to Magna Global (2011). Online advertising is usually viewed as a complement of the TV advertising and is used from brand-based advertisers. The compounded growth rate of the Internet advertising globally is expected to be 10.6 % to the 2016, while the largest segment is paid search and most of the advertising is display-related. The growth in this market is mainly associated with the increase in the budgets of SMEs. There is also a major shift in the habits of the advertisers from content media to ad networks, which suggests advantages for community and engagement media to target the growing segment.

The premium subscription market is hard to define since the social media competes with other networks, where professionals build their identity. Broadly defined these are other networks with free of charge content or paid premium content such as Facebook, Twitter, Toolbox. Competitors are professional networks mentioned above such as Xing, Viadeo and recruiter services organizations—Monster Worldwide, Career Builder.

According to LinkedIn (2011a) considerations the immediately addressable market for hiring solutions is approximately $27.3 billion, while the marketing solutions, serving primarily business-to-business advertisers, are approximately $25.4 billion. From 2009 to 2010 LinkedIn marketing solutions doubled (107 %) and were used by more than 33,000 customers, while the average advertising budget is decreasing (Alexa Rankings 2011). This indicates the rising prominence of the small budgets and expected further efforts to integrate small budget advertising in the business model. Simultaneously LinkedIn corporate customers for hiring solutions are expected to double until the end of the 2011.

Company has built online and field operations units that facilitate the advertising and hiring services and integrate the diversified revenue streams. The primary focus of field sales organization is business-to-business services for the two largest revenue streams—hiring solutions and marketing solutions. In comparison with the online operations the field sales has a longer product sale cycle, but in the same time more engaged customers with lower rate of cancellation. Additionally, field sales have higher selling prices, higher associated expenses and a longer cash collection cycle.

In contrast the online sales, introducing automated self-service system characterizes with shorter sale life cycle, lower operation costs and lower selling prices, while the rate of cancellations is higher (LinkedIn 2011a).

The company is strongly positioned in United States and United Kingdom, developing position in some parts of Europe, North America, Latin America and Asia-Pacific, while weakly positioned in China, where it has not started operations officially.

6.2 Customer Engagement Key Metrics

Main advantage of networks such as LinkedIn is the ability to build social equity for users through their network affiliation and gaining recognition in professional network. One of the reasons social networkers to value the LinkedIn account most is the ability to build and manage their professional identity and receive better career prospects. According to a survey of 2,997 active social networkers, about 6 out of 10 of the respondents said it is important to have a LinkedIn account, more than any other social network, including Facebook and Twitter (ROI Research 2011; Performics 2011).

The above study revealed that the respondents with an active LinkedIn account, 50 % visit the site at least weekly and 20 % visit the site at least daily. However, the frequency of LinkedIn visits is decreasing since 2010—67 % weekly and 22 % daily visits. Table 3 shows the growth of page views and registered members during years from 2009. Company members, unique visitors and page views are taken from the LinkedIn Key Metrics (LinkedIn 2011b).

Table 3 LinkedIn key metrics

Company metrics	FY 2009 Q4	FY 2010 Q4	FY 2011 Q4	CAGR 2009–2011
Average members (MM)	45.6	76.75	123.375	64 %
%y/y	71 %	64 %	60 %	
Unique visitors (MM) (comScore)	30.3	52.175	84.15	67 %
% y/y	n/a	52.2	84.1	
Unique Visitors (incl. non-members)/members	0.66	0.68	0.68	
Page views (BN)	2.8	4.5	7.35	62 %
%y/y	n/a	18.1	29.4	
Page views/members (Page views per member)	n/a	58.63	59.57	
Page views/unique visitors(incl. non-members)	n/a	86.25	87.34	
LinkedIn Corporate Solutions customers	1,242.25	2,711.75	6862	135 %
%y/y		144 %	139 %	
Corp. Sol. customers/members in (MM)	27.24	35.33	55.62	

Since I apply the asset perspective on the membership base the membership number was averaged for the whole year and so are other indicators. This is used for cross reference purposes.

The results show that LinkedIn has achieved substantial growth in absolute numbers—membership base, unique visitor, page views and corporate solutions customers. LinkedIn succeeded to acquire stable results or grow, though slightly, when relative values of engagement are applied - cross indicators on per member/per unique visitor base. Until the second quarter of 2011 the company succeeded to accelerate the growth of all presented indicators, including the cross indicators introduced by the current research—unique visitors/members, page views per member and corporate solutions customers per million members. In the second quarter of 2011 and thereafter the cross indicators, representing per member values are constantly decreasing. Thus, the drop in indicators, revealing quantitative and behavioural aspects of customer engagement coincide with the IPO launch.

The corporate solutions customers per million members is the only cross indicator constantly rising. However, the correlation of the corporate solutions customers and members is weaker and depends on various reasons, including the performance of the field operations.

The United States is the major market that generates about a third of the LinkedIn unique visitors according to Alexa Rankings. By U.S. market shares of visits LinkedIn share represents 0.63 % of the total social networks and forums in November 2011 (Experian Hitwise 2011). The market share of visits percentage does not include traffic for all sub-domains of certain websites that could be reported on separately. According to US social network users who follow company or brand in social media, 3 % of respondents preferred to connect with brands through LinkedIn, while the leader Facebook engaged 80 % (Edison Research and Arbitron 2011). Men enter the professional network (at least once a month) substantially more frequently than women—20 % of men and 16 % women visit it at least monthly.

The time spent by users in LinkedIn is 325.6 million minutes in April 2011 (Nielsen). This is far from the rest of the online media such as Facebook (53 billion), Yahoo (17 billion), Google (12.5 billion) and a modest result for a social network.

Not less important is the quality of the leads that serve the advertising and hiring services objectives and transform the customer engagement into revenue streams. The members of the network are professionals, with high level of household income, half of them senior levels of management. More than two million companies have Company Page, while 75 of the Fortune 100 have used its services for hiring (LinkedIn 2011c).

6.3 Linking Customer Engagement to Revenue Streams

The dynamics of revenue streams shows that the share of hiring solutions rises in the sake of subscription revenues. The advertising revenues are a relatively stable cash stream, which until 2010 has performed growth rate as the whole company. The compounded growth rate of the total revenue is 75.6 % for the period from 2008 to 2010. Revenues increased from $78.8 to $243.1 million, respectively. In 2011 the company has maintained the growth it experienced in previous years and even accelerated it. The compounded growth rate in the first three quarters of 2011 provided better results compared to the corresponding quarters or periods in the previous 2009 and 2010 years—measured by quarter to quarter or extended to three quarters or a year (December–September).

Even though the company beat the average analyst estimate of $127.6 million in third quarter with net revenues of $139.5 million the positive effect on the LinkedIn share price was weak. The prices after the company made public its results in November 2011 fell, due to various reasons—among them debt crisis and overall drop of the exchange indexes, negative expectations after the end of the lock-up period for LinkedIn shares, the expectation treadmill effect and the initial market overreaction to the IPO launching in May.

Since the company continued to invest in product development and started to broaden its field operation activities it realized small profits and thus, received critical remarks. There are, however, decrease in the product development investments and substantial increase in marketing and sales expenses, measured as a share of the relevant entries in the reports, including costs associated with field sales. This shows that currently company perceive the diversification on geographic markets and field operations, as well as building brand identity, as a priority.

The product development is a capital expenditure which is aimed to attract and facilitate the professional network members, unique viewers and page views and to generate revenues in multiple periods. The indicative metric for LinkedIn potential to create and deliver value to its customers and shareholders is its ability to generate revenues through the repeat consumption of its customers. Table 4 presents how members' growth correlates to the revenues and cost and expenses growth. The data shows revenues and acquisition costs per member linking customer engagement growth to revenues growth. It represents the fiscal year values from 2009 to 2011.

The revenue per member and per unique visitor has increased during the years, though the growth pattern is not stable year by year. The company experienced increase in all per member and per unique visitor measures. The compounded annual growth rate of revenues for the period of 2009–2011 is over 26 % per member and over 25 % per unique visitor. There is a pronounced growth of hiring solutions stream over the years, which is noticeable even in the company financial statement. There is also an evident decrease in the freemium subscription segment year by year.

The combined metrics prove that company was able to efficiently grow revenue per acquired member from $2.63 in 2009 to $4.23 in 2011, while simultaneously LinkedIn new members grew in 2011 by 60 %.

Cost and expenses increased with a lower compounded growth rate which shows that LinkedIn was able to lower its cost per member relative to its revenue per member, although slightly. Total cost and expenses per member increased from $2.7 to $4, but the cost and expenses in the table are accounting measures that do not take into account the fact that some expenses are investments able to create revenue streams in multiple periods. The adjusted cost here represents the cost per member or unique visitor after capitalization of R&D and operating leases. Even after adjusting it, the cost and expenses however include special and one time charges which are incurred during and after the IPO.

It could be expected the company to increase per member revenues, due to better value proposition, growth of the market for professional hiring solutions and

Table 4 Revenues and cost per member or unique visitor on average

	Per member 2009	Per member 2010	Per member 2011	Per un. vis. 2009	Per un. vis. 2010	Per un. vis. 2011
Revenues:						
Hiring solutions	0.79	1.33	2.11	1.19	1.95	3.10
Marketing solutions	0.84	1.03	1.26	1.26	1.52	1.85
Premium subscription	1.0	0.81	0.85	1.51	1.19	1.25
Total	2.63	3.17	4.23	3.96	4.66	6.20
Cost and expenses:						
Cost of revenue	0.57	0.58	0.66	0.85	0.86	0.97
Sales and marketing	0.59	0.77	1.34	0.89	1.13	1.97
Product development	0.87	0.85	1.07	1.30	1.25	1.58
G&A	0.43	0.46	0.61	0.64	0.67	0.90
Depreciation and amortization	0.26	0.25	0.35	0.39	0.37	0.52
Total costs and expenses	2.71	2.9	4.02	4.08	4.28	5.94
Adjusted cost	2.14	2.41	3.30	3.21	3.34	4.87
Total average members (MM)	45.6	76.8	123.4			
Total average unique visitors (MM)				30.3[a]	52.2	83.6

[a] The unique visitor data is available for the fourth quarter of 2009 and is calculated, assuming that the compounded growth of visitors quarter by quarter is 13.45 %. It is possible the compounded growth to be a little bit higher from Q1 to Q3 in 2009

international diversification. Additionally, in future it is expected the company to be able to relatively reduce its cost and expenses, due to economies of scope and scale.

It is worth noting that comparing revenues with cost and expenses in LinkedIn case bears the disadvantage of time discrepancy related to the value creation and delivery. In many cases cost reporting is onward looking—some costs are incurred in the current period, but deliver value in future periods and thus, customers pay for the value of services in future periods, as it is usual. The opposite holds true regarding the subscription revenue stream.

Conclusion

The growth of social networks, measured through customer engagement metrics and financial metrics has many controversial aspects. It is debatable that we understand the consumption drivers, their application in customer engagement strategies and their limits arising across customer satisfaction issues.

The social networks in terms of customer engagement metrics approaches two key aspects of growth. The first one that uses the level of consumption as a self-satisfying prophecy for value creation is built primarily through quantitative measures and explores behavioural aspects of consumption. The second one understands value and customer engagement as a function of the perceived relative value.

Simultaneously social networks growth in revenues is contingent on the innovation diffusion and adoption on the advertising market and other markets, where companies derive their revenues. The growth of paying customers also reflects the growth of the membership base, but however, there are many details that membership growth does not encompass. This metric together with unique visitors and page views give us some details of the engagement of the members and perceived value of the network services. The revenue growth independently contains another detail. Combination of these metrics give better idea of the growth.

LinkedIn data presented here shows that social networks need better and adjusted metrics and indicators that should be evaluated. However, this raises controversial questions and need better diagnostic tools. Social networks need not only members and "Like" or "Share" buttons, but also proper idea of the value delivered to customers and value paid from the customers.

The repeated consumption in social networks does not necessarily measure the engagement and satisfaction and are not an evidence for the perceived value. Facebook, the online social networks leader according to customer engagement metrics, exhibits low customer satisfaction level. LinkedIn provides us with another perspective.

This paper confirms that key LinkedIn metrics of growth in consumption are supported by the relatively high value that customers perceive of the social network services among other social networks. The company key objective, namely membership growth, has increased in the past years and continues to grow every quarter of 2011 with compounded growth rate of 13.7 %. The cross indicator values show that through membership growth company achieves to experience similar growth in other customer engagement metrics such as unique visitors and page views.

Further metrics of revenues and cost and expenses per average member or unique visitor analyze LinkedIn ability to transform user consumption into revenues. There is a correlation between membership and unique visitor growth and revenue growth. In per member or unique visitor numbers the analysis shows that there is a link between customer engagement growth and revenue growth. The cost and expenses present a similar pattern of growth just like revenues. However, the data is not sufficient to make more detailed analysis of the past growth pattern and the links between indicators.

The difference between LinkedIn adjusted cost and expenses and revenue demonstrate its ability to realize earnings, which was major investor concern regarding social media. However, in future the social network has to prove its ability to reduce cost and increase revenues, due to economies of scale and scope.

One of the biggest threats to LinkedIn future is its growth and ability to manage it. Ironically or naturally, the professional network that promotes professionals engagement recruited more than half of its staff in less than a year, as of March 2011. The engagement of the staff with the company objectives and the integration in the organization here is a key question for the company to survive and sustain. Currently, the principal-agent paradox has a considerable impact on the growing in size, less efficient internal control systems. This question, however, relates the subject to the motivation strategies of the company and the performance-rewarding correlation.

References

Arketi. (2009). A PR professional guide to understanding Web 2.0 and new media. Available from http://www.arketi.com/.
Castels, M. (2007). Communication, power and counter-power. *International Journal of Communication, 1*(1), 238–66.
Chan, L., Hamao, Y., & Lakonishok, J. (1991). Fundamentals and stock returns in Japan. *Journal of Finance, 46*, 1739–1789.
Chan-Olmsted, S., & Chang, B. (2003). Diversification strategy of global media conglomerates: Examining its patterns and determinants. *Journal of Media Economics, 16*(4), 213–233.
Chao, L. (2011, December 13). Viadeo in venture with Russian unit of Sanoma. *The Wall Street Journal.* Retrieved from, http://www.online.wsj.com.
Christensen, C. M. (1997). *The innovator's dilemma: When new technologies cause great firms to fail.* Boston, MA: Harvard Business.
Coase, R. (1937). The nature of the firm. *Economica, 4*(6). Available from http://onlinelibrary.wiley.com.
comScore. (2011, December 21). It's social world. Available from http://www.comscore.com/layout/set/popup/request/Presentations.
Copeland, T., Koller, T., & Murrin, J. (2000). *Valuation: Measuring and managing value of companies* (3rd ed.). Wiley: New York.
Cowan, L. (2009, December 27). IPOs in 2010: More and more diverse. *The Wall Street Journal.* Available from www.online.wsj.com.
Coyne, K., & Subramaniam, S. (1996). Bringing discipline to strategy. *McKinsey Quarterly, 4*, 14–25.
Daidj, N., Grazia, C., & Hammoudi, A. (2010). Introduction to the non-cooperative approach to coalition formation: The case of the Blu-Ray/HD-DVD standards' war. *Journal of Media Economics, 23*(4), 192–215.
Damodaran, A. (2002). *Investment valuation.* New Jersey: Wiley.
Damodaran, A. (2006). *Damodaran on valuation: Security analysis for investment and corporate finance.* New Jersey: Wiley.
Dimson, E., & Marsh, P. (1986). Event studies and the size effect: The case of UK press recommendations. *Journal of Financial Economics, 17*, 113–142.
Dobbs, R., & Koller, T. (1998). The expectation treadmill. *McKinsey Quarterly, N3*, 32–43.
Economides, N. (1996). The economics of networks. *International Journal of Industrial Organization, N16*, 673–699.

Edison Research & Arbitron. (2011). The social habit II: the Edison research/arbitron internet and multimedia study 2011. Retrieved from http://www.hubspot.com.
e-Tailing group and power reviews (2011). The 2011 social shopping study.
Exact Target. (2011) The meaning of Like. Available from www.exacttarget.com.
Experian Hitwise. (2011). Top 10 social-networking websites and forums. Available from http://www.marketingcharts.com.
Freed, L. (2011) Foresee Results – Annual e-business report for American Customer Satisfaction Index. Available from www.foreseeresults.com.
Garone, E. (2010, March 5). Promoting yourself on LinkedIn. *The Wall Street Journal*. Available from www.online.wsj.com.
Godson, M. (2009). *Relationship marketing*. Oxford: Butterworth-Heineman.
Hitt, M., et al. (1996). The market for corporate control and firm innovation. *Academy of Management Journal, 39*(N5), 1084–1119.
Knaup, A., & Piazza, M. (2007). Business employment dynamics data: Survival and longevity. *Monthly Labor Review, 130*, 3–10.
LinkedIn. (2011a). Form S-1/A (Securities Registration Statement). Available from http://www.linkedin.com.
LinkedIn. (2011b). Analyst metrics 2011 Q3. Available from http://www.linkedin.com.
LinkedIn. (2011c). Form 10-Q (Quarterly Report), 2011 Q3 report. Available from http://www.linkedin.com.
MagnaGlobal. (2011). 2011 Advertising forecast. Retrieved from http://www.magnaglobal.com.
Marketing Sherpa. (2011). Search marketing benchmark survey. Available from www.marketingsherpa.com.
Mueller, D. (1972). A life cycle theory of the firm. *The Journal of Industrial Economics, 20*(N3), 199–219.
Nielsen, & NM Incite. (2011). State of the social media: Social media report Q3 2011. Available from http://blog.nielsen.com/nielsenwire/social/.
North, D. (1981). *Structure and change in economic history*. New York: Norton.
Ovide, S. & Das, A. (2011, January 27). LinkedIn IPO: It's here! *The Wall Street Journal*. Retrieved from http://www.online.wsj.com.
Ovide, S. (2011, January 28). Is LinkedIn worth $3 billion? *The Wall Street Journal*. Retrieved from http://www.online.wsj.com.
Performics. (2011, October 26). Social shopping summary.
Porter, M. (2008). The five competitive forces that shape strategy. *Harvard Business Review*, 86–104.
Russolillo, S. & Conway, B. (2011, November 2). Short Sellers Seize on LinkedIn Ahead of Earnings. *The Wall Street Journal*. Available from www.online.wsj.com.
Rogers, E. (2003). *Diffusion of innovations*. New York: Free Press.
ROI Research. (2011, June). S-Net: A study in social media usage & behaviour. Sponsored by Performics.
Schumpeter, J. (1939). *Business cycles: A theoretical, historical and statistical analysis of capitalist process*. New York: McGraw-Hill.
Shiller, R. (2005). *Irrational exuberance*. Princeton, NJ: Princeton University Press.
Stone, B. (2010, September 22). Facebook sells your friends. *Businessweek*. Available from http://www.Businessweek.com/magazine/content.
Technorati. (2011). The state of the blogosphere. Available from http://technorati.com/blogging/.
Willamson, O. (1985). *The economic institutions of capitalism* (pp. 55–60). New York: The Free Press.

Keys to Monetize Social Media in the Audiovisual Business

Mónica Herrero and Mercedes Medina

1 Introduction

Television companies have started to pay attention to social media. For years, they have been the audience leaders, so they have got enough advertising revenue to be profitable. However, they are nowadays struggling due to the competition from the Internet, social media and new electronic devices. The 30-s spot continues to lose relevancy and effectiveness (Greenberg 2010).

Some articles of doom from periodicals have proclaimed the threat posed by new media to the traditional ones. For example, one of the covers of *The Economist* in 2006 was devoted to the subject under the title of "Who killed the newspaper?" and *Advertising Age* published in 2011 the article "Is social media killing TV?" by Patel and Slutsky. They try to reflect and question the current mission of traditional media and the threat posed by social and online media.

In the audiovisual landscape, most television companies have reacted to this threat developing online strategies to experiment with new media. For example, some television shows have first been launched in the Internet through social media, and then on the screen; that is the case of *Zombies* from TNT. News programmes have incorporated content generated by viewers, news coming from citizens. Some shows, for example *Lost*, have reached their finale with a last episode widely advertised through social media; others have been specifically produced for online media and have their own YouTube channel. There is an interesting case called

---

This chapter forms part of the subsidized research project "New Consumption Habits in Audiovisual Contents: Impact of Digitalization on the European Media Diet", financed by the Spanish Ministry of Education and Culture for the period 2011–2013 (CSO2010-20122).

M. Herrero (✉) • M. Medina
University of Navarra, Pamplona, Spain
e-mail: moherrero@unav.es; mmedina@unav.es

Private, produced by Sony and sponsored in Spain by the firm Neutrogena and the retailer El Corte Inglés. Some quiz shows, such as *American Idol* or *Pop Stars*, try to promote audience participation through social media.

In terms of revenue, not all the examples were successful; most of them did not get any extra revenue. What it seems is that the question of where revenues stem from is not an easy one (Picard 2009; Pérez-Latre et al. 2011). How to monetize these actions is the key question for media managers, since new media have different business models than traditional ones. Therefore, these experiments may become an innovative source of income, different from traditional audience ratings and thirty-second spots.

Boyd and Ellison (2008, p. 211) define social media as "web-based services that allow users to build a public or semi-public profile within a system; articulate a user list with shared relationships; and view the list of relationships of those persons with other people within the system". Consequently we would like to reflect what we understand by "profitability" in this new context; because it may be that profitability has more to do with nearness, identification, satisfaction, entertainment experience and branding than with massive audiences and large revenues.

Social media are characterised by peer collaboration, transparency, audience participation, segmentation and globalisation (Tapscott and Williams 2006; Kozinets 2006). Some of these features are complementary to broadcast media, so they can enrich their potential. However, new difficulties arise, such as piracy and copyright control, and media companies have to develop tools in order to avoid them or make the most of them (Li and Bernoff 2008).

In this chapter, we will first review, from a theoretical perspective, the existent literature on monetizing social media in the audiovisual business. Although our focus will be the broadcasters' business in relation to social media, it will be helpful to look briefly at the added value and business models of social media themselves. Secondly, two main Spanish broadcasters, which have integrated social media with television shows, will be analysed in depth; in addition, other relevant examples where social media have been developed along with television programmes will be mentioned. And finally, the key indicators of efficient use of social media in television shows in terms of profitability will be outlined, and a conclusion will be raised about the new meanings of profitability for media companies.

2 The Economics of Broadcasting Products in Relation to Social Media

When attempting to lay the foundations of the economics of broadcast products in relation to social media, it is helpful to look at the main economic characteristics of audiovisual products, which have allowed broadcasters to develop Internet strategies and, therefore, to integrate social media as part of their activities.

This requires going back to the very nature of media products as public goods. A public good is independent of the number of people that consume it, that is to say, the available amount of the commodity is not reduced by an increase in the number of consumers (Picard 1989, p. 18). From this we can deduce that consumers find themselves in a non-rivalry situation in terms of their enjoyment of the same commodity (Hoskins et al. 1997, p. 31; Herrero 2009a).

Given the nature of audiovisual products as public goods, a series of consequences arise that condition managerial decisions in the television industry. The high costs and the almost null marginal cost are the reasons why scale economies operate strongly in the audiovisual industry (Picard 1989, p. 62). Programme producers try to distribute their products among the largest possible audience, so the cost-per-viewer can be reduced. That results, for example, in distribution strategies or *windowing*, which intend to achieve the maximum economic profit of a single product by distributing it in different windows and at different times (Owen and Wildman 1992, pp. 26–38). These repetition strategies prove that the value of a television product does not come to an end with its first broadcasting (Dunnet 1990, p. 39; Medina 2007).

The traditional activity of broadcasters reflects the dependence of programming in relation to the time factor. As Dematté and Perreti point out, the television activity is represented by the composition of a sequence of audiovisual programmes according to the quantitative and qualitative forecast of public's demand (Dematté and Perretti 1997, p. 7). The logic behind the organisation of the schedule may be a question of either maximising audiences in some cases, or of reaching certain segments in others, as well as a matter of carrying out the principles of a public service.

As Frith assesses, "by and large radio/television culture is (like the Internet, but unlike publishing) based on the expectation that programmes are generally accessible and not subject to price restriction" (Frith 2000, p. 47). Furthermore, the nature as a public-good of television programming hinders effective price discrimination, due to the uncertainty of the demand and the virtually nonexistent marginal costs. The television industry could be said to be in a situation of lack of cost competition, as occurs in other cultural sectors. Until the advent of pay television, the audience had never had to consider cost when it came to choosing a particular channel or programme and enjoyed a certain free-of-charge feeling as far as television programming was concerned (Nieto 1984, p. 85; Nieto 2000).

Most of these characteristics of the audiovisual products are taken to the full in the case of their diffusion through the Internet. Their nature as public goods is reinforced, given the flexibility and universality of the Internet as a means of distribution, as well as the absence of geographical and legal barriers. The marginal cost is null, making it possible to develop economies of scale and windowing strategies in a more efficient way than ever before. Furthermore, apart from a free access to the Internet, a culture of free enjoyment of products was established since the very beginning, even more firmly for the Internet than for the television industry. Moreover, regarding audiovisual products, some important limits of the television industry, such as the dependence of time, are overcome by the Internet.

This explains that broadcasters have seen the strategic importance of the Internet, since television and the Internet develop a symbiotic relationship with significant financial implications. As Chan-Olmsted and Ha pointed out in 2003, the Internet was first used to enhance the core product of the established business

(Chan-Olmsted and Ha 2003, p. 597). However, and following Doyle, the big question for broadcasters to answer is: "Is the migration to multi-platform enabling television companies to use their resources more effectively than before?" (Doyle 2010, p. 432). And taking a step further, we would ask: are the complementarities between broadcasters and social media strong enough to be monetized and make the broadcasters' businesses more profitable?

The basic economic characteristics that have been outlined in previous paragraphs are at the root of the likely (or not) profitable use of social media by broadcasters. The difficulty of charging for content lies in the nature as public goods of media products, and following Hayes and Graybeal, "by not charging for content, media providers have created a completely price elastic market for content" (Hayes and Graybeal 2011, p. 29). In such a market, substitution of products is highly predominant, and also the possibility of sharing content among users without cost. Aware of the potential of sharing content and the impossibility of stopping this practice, Hayes and Graybeal suggest a micropayment model which lies in the concept of sharing. In such a model, "sharing content with a friend would be exactly what the media provider would want consumers to do" (Hayes and Graybeal 2011, p. 34). And that is exactly what social media encourage users to do.

As a consequence of the windowing strategies, the Internet makes it possible to spread audiovisual products, to repeat their consumption and to increase the audience's knowledge of them. Programmes distributed in this way have already been broadcast on television, and so have become a new type of rerun, but using different media (mobile phones, portable media players), and usually sooner than before. The Internet avoids the constraints of the traditional grid, not only by making it more flexible, depending on the wishes of the user, but also by rendering the media more flexible in terms of time and place (Herrero 2009b, p. 48). From the broadcasters' point of view, complex windowing techniques will play an increasingly important role in the exploitation of television content assets (Doyle 2010, p. 445).

Those windowing techniques will require for the broadcasting industry and other industries to converge. Complementarities refer to the degree to which a bundle of goods provides more value than the separate consumption of those goods (Brandenburger and Nalebuff 1996). Convergence between different new media technologies can be viewed from this notion of complements. Dowling et al. (1998) propose that, in a "complementary convergence" situation, additional synergistic products may emerge to form a larger market (a complement view). We could assert that the traditional economies of scope go beyond the broadcasting industry.

In that sense, many Internet-related opportunities will require the integration of skills and capabilities residing outside a traditional media company. This, in turn, will lead to structural changes in the media sector which may involve market boundaries. That explains the increase in mergers and acquisitions among large media companies as a consequence of the emergence of the Internet (Sullivan and Jiang 2010, pp. 23–27).

Following this idea, Chan-Olmsted, Lee and Kin, regarding the convergence with mobile phones, assert: "The broadcasters, with a keen appreciation of the mobility and personalization value provided by the mobile platform and of its compatibility and complementarity with their current offerings, focus on enhancing mobile television content, finding ways to monetize the content beyond advertising revenues, and integrating the strategic value of mobile and fixed television to make their overall product portfolio more competitive" (Chan-Olmsted et al. 2011, p. 88). In the same line, and looking for ways to monetize within a "free" culture, Hayes and Graybeal point out: "the mobile environment offers micropayment a clean sleight. Smart phones have ushered in a culture of paying, in fact, micropaying, for apps and games where the Internet fostered a 'free' culture" (Hayes and Graybeal 2011, p. 39).

Convergence of industries and complementarities of products are very much linked to the brand communication of the broadcasters themselves and their products. Branding and engagement of audiences are also linked.

3   Social Media Added Value and Business Models

The Internet allows for a stable relationship between content creators and consumers, especially through social media, to an extent undreamt of not long ago. We consider social media as part of what is called web 3.0, that is to say, the possibility to share, comment, send, choose and participate in content. Most of these possibilities are not new on television; however, what it is new is the use and the integration of these actions with television content thanks to the Internet.

Technology allows enthusiasts to develop activities that go beyond viewing again or following the programmes in television magazines. If fan or enthusiast activity came before the Internet, the web provides new means of participation. Sharing is one of the keys of social media (Guerrero 2011). Apart from visiting the official websites, the enthusiasts have created new sites, and visit those of other fans. The community feeling that arises from these relationships between people who had not met before, shows the possibilities of engagement of audiovisual products. In this sense, not only has the product spread to other media, but the way in which members of the audience understand this product has significantly changed as well.

Obviously, some audiovisual contents are more likely to engage with the audience and, therefore, more suitable to develop social media strategies. Stefanone, Lackaff and Rosen talk about the popularity of the so-called 'reality television' and the concomitant adoption of social networking sites (SNSs). In fact, their study links the consumption of a specific television genre with specific behavioural outcomes in new media (Stefanone et al. 2010, pp. 508–525). According to Godlewski and Perse, reality television could be defined as follows: "unscripted programs that record real people as they live out events in their lives, as these events occur (...) Moreover, for some of these programs, audience participation is a central agent to the shared experience or lived reality of the program" (Godlewski and Perse 2010, p. 149).

As television programmes develop to allow more interaction between them and their audiences, more interactive forms of reality television encouraging heightened audience activity will be developed. Television series, especially soap operas, are also likely to engage greatly with the audience. The series go beyond their broadcast time not only in reference to the real world of the individual but also in the relationships with other followers. Some media products, such as drama, seem more compatible with the value of SNS and consumer engagement (Diego and Herrero 2010).

Although audience participation gives the channels certain amount of power, Siapera believes that the broadcasters' activity on the Internet through the official websites gives them even more power, as they can in this way control their fans' activity, know their preferences, promote the creation of communities, and so strengthen audience loyalty for the following *off line* broadcasts (Siapera 2004, p. 164).

Moreover, other studies show the importance of using social media for news programmes and how SNSs help to promote their on-air programmes, escalate viewership, and boost popularity among viewers. Since modern viewers go online for their communication experiences, SNS characteristics provide television networks with great brand management and relationship development opportunities. According to Lin and Peña, "through the use of socioemotional messages, television network brands can facilitate optimized selfpresentation, favourable conversations about the brands, and valuable relationships with consumers at both individual and collective levels" (Lin and Peña 2011, pp. 17–29).

The use of social media linked to programmes is also very adequate for television events. Such events result in an increased willingness to twit. For example, *Super Bowl* XLV produced more than 4,000 tweets per second during the final moments of the game (Patel and Slutsky 2011). According to data used by Patel and Slutsky (2011), some of the top programmes in social media—such as Twitter, Facebook and other social networks—are not necessarily the top audience rating programmes. Only in week April 4–10 2011 was there a programme that reached number one in both lists: *American Idol*.

According to AMETIC (2011, p. 116), thanks to the free access to social media the main business model followed by social networks is *advertising*. The main added value of social networks lies in the number of users, and the time spent on them. These parameters are essential for advertisers to decide on what social network their campaigns will be launched. According to several studies, the primary social network is Facebook. It could surpass in advertising revenue Internet giants like Google or Yahoo. Facebook's display advertising revenue will grow from $1,800 million in 2010 to $3,500 million expected in 2011. Meanwhile, Google (and dependent pages like YouTube) expected $2,600 million in 2011, compared to a $2,000 million revenue in 2010 (Enders Analysis 2011). Google has launched Google +, a social network of similar characteristics, to compete against Facebook, but it is not being too successful (O'Neil 2010).

Another business model being used by social media is the *payment for the purchase* of virtual objects. In April 2010 Facebook launched *Facebook Credits*, a virtual currency for financial transactions made in the network. These Facebook Credits are purchased with real money (through credit card or Paypal) and can be used in more than 60 applications including the social network. It is, therefore, a replica of Freemium, used mainly in the gaming industry. Revenues from this model represent 10 % of total Facebook revenues.

The third model is *subscription or premium payment* for services. In the case of LinkedIn, premium accounts give users access to more information about searched profiles, knowledge about other premium users, etc. LinkedIn has several types of Premium accounts with subscriptions from $19.95/month to $74.95/month. According to company figures, in the first 9 months of 2010 revenues from this business model accounted for 27 % of total revenues of the social network (Parr 2011).

However, which of these is the most profitable business model is still not clear. As an example, for the Spanish company Antena 3, which will be described later, income from SMS, webs and mobiles declined from 2009 to 2010, because of the use of social media. In 2010 the firm got €26 million from "other income", €23 million less than in 2009. However, traffic is the variable that has increased: 50 million video streams were downloaded in the first 9 months of 2011 from Antena 3 sites, in comparison with 26 million in 2010. Its site got 6.5 million of unique users in 2011 and 4.8 in the same period of 2010.

4 The Use of Social Media by Spanish Broadcasters

Most television companies have reacted developing online strategies to experiment with new media. The number of examples and the variety of initiatives are huge. Therefore we will focus especially on two Spanish broadcasters, the commercial one, Antena 3, and the public one, Radio Televisión Española (RTVE), though we will show some other examples to enrich the research.

As it is known, YouTube is the biggest video-streaming website and therefore most television channels opened a channel in YouTube (*The Economist* 2011, p. 5). The advantage of the YouTube channel is that the streaming is quicker than in the site of the television channel, but you need to subscribe to access it; however, there is not much more activity there than in the site. In fact, there are many suggestions in the YouTube channel to go to the company site.

RTVE created its own channel on YouTube in 2006. In October 2009, it had 13,784 subscribers. RTVE uses YouTube to enable previews of some of its most popular series, including the 90-min long ones.

Other examples related to social media are blog creation and participation in social networks. Blogs are a good example of the closeness between RTVE professionals and the corporation's users. In October 2009, there were 17 blogs related to cinema and television, 22 on music, on radio, 21 on sports, 33 on current affairs, and 22 from the international correspondents. Viewer responses help to know their tastes, although this has not yet been systematised.

In 2006, the ombudsperson's online programme was created to deal with complaints and comments from radio, television, and web users. Once a month, the "ombudsperson" has a television programme, *RTVE responde*, where he/she talks about the complaints, recommendations, and suggestions from the public. In 2008, the ombudsperson received 4,954 inputs.

RTVE also signed agreements with Facebook and MySpace, although the latter was terminated at the beginning of 2009. With Facebook, RTVE implemented some unique ways of participation never seen before on a public broadcasting company, creating real interactivity between web users or television audience and the programme hosts. With MySpace, for two consecutive years, they organised the presentation and pre-selection of candidates to the Eurovision Song Contest.

TVE a la Carta is a catch-up service and enables viewers to watch streaming content. The availability limit is seven days. The most viewed content on TVE are series, *Muchachada Nui*, sporting events, both pre-recorded and live coverage of certain topics, radio sites and blogs. RTVE's website had six million visits in May 2008, and in 2009 it reached about nine million. In May 2008, the average connection time was about 6 min 40 s; this rose to 13 min 35 s a year later.

Moreover, the drama *Cuéntame* created its own community Fly Bar (http://www.flybar.es) to participate in the culture of the eighties where the series is set. It is like an avatar game where users have to choose their own avatar to play a role and to listen to their favourite music. This example is a copy of American initiatives such as *Glee* or *True Blood*.

The other most innovative television company in Spain has been Antena 3. In order to stay ahead with new technologies, the Antena 3 group put great effort into their multimedia development and in 2007 it launched different online services (Moreno 2008). In February it launched *Tuclip.com*, a platform for videos sent by viewers, and it got an average of 400,000 viewed pages and 300,000 videos a month. Antena 3 was the first television company in Spain—second in Europe after the BBC—to launch a channel in *YouTube*. The number of Antena 3 video clip downloads was 3.4 million from March 2006 to April 2009. On 9 December 2011, the site had 66,649 subscribers and 301,855,804 video streams.

In April 2007, they developed a channel called *tucanaltv*, composed of the finest videos of Antena 3, such as news, humour and entertainment. In addition, partners were incorporated with a revenue model that represents new revenue for those companies, while for Antena 3 is a way to increase traffic. It represented a way to provide an access to all the audiovisual material available online.

Nowadays, all these services can be found in the new site of Antena 3, launched in June 2010, http://www.antena3.com, where it is possible to find live television and the mode "salón" (sitting room) to watch whole chapters of the most popular television programmes. Antena 3 includes advertising before the chapter and between the six parts into which the chapter is divided. Many advertisers only invest in the Internet. According to the company's General Manager, income from multimedia in 2010 was €7 million. They are studying the option to pay per view the content through micro-payments. The GM thinks that online services are a very useful tool for most popular programmes to catch and involve viewers, and they help to develop the fan phenomenon that it is a good tool for merchandising (Bardají 2011). Apart from this generalist site, they have launched sites specialised in news (http://www.antena3noticias.com) and others that depend on the company's radio channels (http://www.ondacero.es and http://www.europafm.com).

Since 2009, they have developed a strategy 3.0, delivering content through three different platforms: television, the Internet and mobile devices. With this strategy, they tried to show the viewers that they were not only a television channel but a multimedia company, and therefore interactivity and cross consuming were developed. In some cases television was the first window, but sometimes they first launched a programme online and afterwards on television.

Antena 3 has also produced online series, such as *Desalmados*, or *Diarios de la webcam*. The latter was so successful in the Internet that, after that, it was broadcast in one of the new DTT channels, Neox.

Social media have also become a new tool to interact with the audience. Through Facebook (more than 250,000 followers), Windows Life, Tuenti (more than 93,000 fans) and Twitter (more than 20,000 followers), it is possible to send comments to the channel or to share contents with other users. To go into these networks, registration is needed through a tool called *Zona 3*.

The company has also developed several blogs on its own channel, the audiovisual industry (http://www.antena3.com/objetivotv/) or different general topics such as fashion, current affairs, and sports. To increase interactivity and audience participation, *video-meetings* were created to chat with actors, singers or writers, and to play online games related to the programmes. For example, the game related to the series *Hispania* got 150,000 registered users. In addition, they created vertical portals, such us *Celebrities*, where it is possible to find news, rankings and gossips about stars worldwide. Furthermore, Antena 3 created its own room in the second-life site *Haboo*. In 2010 the company incorporated a *Community Manager* to manage all these sites and content.

In June 2007, they launched a new project of IPTV called *teleporlared* with the logos of the digital television channels Antena 3 and the new ones Neox, Nova and Nitro. However, all of them are nowadays integrated in the site antena3.com.

In a study coordinated by Ha and Ganahl on the development of webcasting in different countries around the world in 2005, the Spanish analysis showed interesting findings for broadcasters. Among the ten largest Spanish webcasters, selected by a roster of experts, were the commercial television companies http://www.telecinco.es and http://www.antena3.com. They can be described as *clicks-and-bricks*, as they offer free content and e-commerce operations. As for off-line market, advertising was also the most important source for the financing of this emerging market (Herrero and Sádaba 2006).

In the following Table 1 we find the top Spanish online media in October 2011, according to official sources. RTVE is in 8th position and Antena 3 in 11th position, just behind http://www.rtve.es and http://www.telecinco.es, although the average time spent by the audience on the Antena 3 website is longer than that spent on Telecinco's website.

According to Antena 3, during the first 9 months of 2011 the number of unique users increased by 36 % to reach 8.5 million, while video streams doubled, reaching 59,900 videos per month (Vara 2011). The number of visited pages was 90 million. In Table 2 it is possible to see the evolution of unique users and video streams of Antena 3 sites.

Table 1 Unique users of Spanish online media (October 2011)

Web	Users (avg)	Duration (avg)
Softonic.com	4,489,422	2:23
MSN	3,418,770	20:52
El Mundo	1,913,466	11:00
Marca.com	2,864,802	14:13
20Minutos.es	745,670	5:53
Euroresidentes	561,301	4:27
ABC.es	717,568	11:01
RTVE.es	787,423	32:32
Terra.es	779,114	4:33
Telecinco.es	671,253	3:56
Antena3.com	624,284	7:29
El Tiempo.es	644,188	1:28

Source: OJD Interactiva

Table 2 Antena 3 Internet division (in millions)

	2009	2010	2011
Unique users	3.9	4.8	8.5
Video streams	13.4	26.3	59.9

Monthly average
Source: OJD/Nielsen Market Intelligence/Smartadserver

There are some paradigmatic cases which cannot be ignored. The BBC has been a pioneer during the past years, and it is also an innovator in web-apps (Medina and Ojer 2011). It has also made alliances with different online social communities such as YouTube, Facebook, and MySpace. For example, it is possible to find in MySpace classic BBC programmes such as *Doctor Who*, *The Mighty Boosh*, *Attenborough*, *Robin Hood*, and others. However, after some years many of these alliances do not continue. In fact, BBC has launched a new project called "YouView" that allows the user to access all channels that offer content through the Internet at any time and free. Just a YouView box and broadband Internet are needed. YouView is a joint venture by some of UK's television and broadband companies.

The BBC website, as that of many other television companies, is very much oriented not only toward information but also toward the provision of a useful service to users. For example, in the section "Get Involved" in Sports, there is information about the nearest court to play tennis in England, Wales, and Scotland. Moreover, in the BBC shop online, one can get DVDs, audios, books, magazines, and children's products. There is also the possibility of being part of the charity *Children in need*, whose mission is to make a positive change to the lives of disadvantaged children and young people across the UK.

All these services give the BBC the opportunity to be in contact with the British citizens, who finance the public corporation and, thanks to the *iPlayer*, also receive audiovisual content. Through it, British citizens can freely download programmes, while the international audience pays for them. This archive system has had a great impact on other public bodies such as RTVE. On the one hand, it allows access to a valuable historical content and, on the other hand, it generates a new source of funds, whose income will be reinvested in public service quality content.

iPlayer was launched in December 2007, and in March 2008 it got 42 million downloads of BBC programmes. From December 2007 to March 2009 it had over 360 million visitors, and an average of 1.1 million unique users per week in 2008 (BBC 2007, p. 31). This initiative won a Prix Italia for *Best Cross Media Public Service*. As Tapscott (2008, p. 192) outlines, the BBC hopes that web services develop innovative offerings and new revenue sources, especially with its archives for international audiences. Through *iPlayer* children can access children content, but there is also a system to facilitate parental control. The *CBeebies iPlayer* puts parents in control of their children's viewing by enabling them to choose what they watch and when. It is designed to provide a safe, dedicated area for children, where they can view content intended for them and which restricts inadvertent access to non-children's programming. In the children section there are many entertaining and educational games and quizzes.

Finally, and going back to the Spanish broadcasting industry, there are two examples which help to understand the various and multiple roles that social media can play within this industry.

A very interesting use of social media to foster film production is the Spanish project called "El Cosmonauta". This was a project plan launched through the web in 2009. In 2011 it got 54 % of funding (€462,340). At present it counts with 502 investors that have contributed with amounts ranging from €100 to €50,000, and more than 3,700 producers that have contributed with an average of €6.9. To encourage contributions from investors the project has used social networks, where users have been very active. By November 2011, the movie had already been shot.

On the other hand, social media are starting to be a very efficient tool to denounce advertising campaigns and television content. Two recent cases in Spain are described next. In September 2011, an interesting case appeared in Twitter as a complementary tool of the Spanish Advertising self-regulation body, Autocontrol. Donette, one of the products of the well-known Spanish bread company Panrico, had to put an end to its campaign because of the audience's reaction in Twitter. The company had received some tweets against the slogan "Do not touch my Donettes", because some members of the public felt offended by one of its possible meanings. The company reacted immediately, answering on Twitter and removing its campaign. In November 2011, a campaign was launched in the social media against a television show called "La Noria", broadcast in Tele 5, because the mother of a person condemned for covering up the murderer of a young woman had been invited to the programme (Díaz 2011).

5 Keys to Monetize and the Search for Profitability: Final Considerations

As we have seen both in the literature and in the examples, social media have proved useful means of establishing contact with the audience and fostering emotional engagement and brand loyalty. There is no doubt that they are both very valuable intangible assets for broadcasters.

In this line, some authors use the term "social capital" (Burt 2005), which can be useful for our final considerations. Social capital is described as "the benefits individuals derive from their social relationship and interactions: resources such as emotional support, exposure to diverse ideas, and access to non-redundant information" (Ellison et al. 2010, p. 873).

However, social capital is very difficult to monetize, even from users. What social media provide for media companies, rather than revenues, is traffic to their sites; as for other companies, social media are a very efficient decision-making prescriber about their products. In 2010, the number of social network users worldwide would have reached 1,000 million with a penetration of 19 % of the total population, 7 points more than in 2009. Spain had in 2010 10.1 million social network users, which is a penetration of approximately 43 %. Over 80 % of Spanish Internet users are social network users, and 20 % use at least three networks (Fundación Orange 2011).

The potential to provide traffic to broadcasters' sites may attract advertising, which is the traditional way to monetize in the broadcasting industry. The more audience, the more advertising expenditure; which should also mean: the more traffic, the more advertising expenditure in social media. However, advertising expenditure is not at its best. Looking at the Spanish industry we find the following data:

Media ad spending decreased from 2007 to 2009 by 27 %. Media earned in 2009 over €2,300 million less than in 2007, as shown in Table 3. Television is among the media that have lost more advertising. In recent years, the television channels' advertising revenue has decreased by 33 %. Although in 2008 a slight recovery was seen, investment is still less than in 2005. Moreover, in 2010 there were more television channels. However, television is still considered the most attractive medium for advertising investment. In 2010, 43 % of advertising expenditure went to television.

Only advertising investment on the Internet has increased: from €162 million in 2005 to €748 million in 2010. Online advertising was 2.4 % of the advertising pie in 2005, to become 12 % in 2010. As it was shown in Table 1, most of the top web sites in Spain are media sites. So, there are reasons to believe that advertising investment will move from traditional media (analogue and paper) to online ones, but that it will still mainly remain within the Spanish media companies. In fact, according to IAB (2011), in 2010 36.14 % of online advertising investment went to media; 37.64 % to portals, 9.4 % to emailing; 5.8 % to social networks in Spain and 3 % to online sales.

Table 3 Media investment evolution in Spain 2005–2010 (€ million)

Media	2005	2006	2007	2008	2009	2010
Television	2,951	3,188	3,468	3,082	2,368	2,516
Newspapers	1,666	1,791	1,894	1,507	1,174	1,141
Magazines	674	688	721	617	401	175
Radio	610	636	678	641	537	538
Outdoor	493	529	568	518	401	415
Sunday supplements	119	123	133	103	68	293
Internet[a]	162	310	482	610	654	748
Cinema	43	40	38	21	15	24
TOTAL	6,721	7,309	7,985	7,102	5,621	5,851

[a]Computers and mobile devices
Source: Infoadex 2010

We would like now to reflect on what we understand by profitability in this new context. At the moment, profitability may have more to do with nearness, identification, satisfaction, entertainment experience and branding, than with massive audiences and big revenues. As Picard (2009) outlines, social media help to interact, but it is necessary to understand why interaction is needed and how benefits are going to be measured. The posts, the click-ins and the mentions in the different social media can be measured, but the difficult part is to monetize them. Benefits can be measured not only in monetary terms, but in terms of popularity and brand.

Therefore, and following the economic foundations previously outlined, social media represent for the broadcasters the most evolved step of the windowing strategies. Whereas in the previous steps these strategies allow profits to be maximised through different prices and time slots, social media increase engagement with and knowledge of the product, based on the concept of sharing which has its roots in the nature of the product as public good.

Following Lin and Peña, "the economic advantages usually generated from strong brand relationships (Fournier 1998) imply that it is important for television network brands to determine not only SNS distribution strength but also the degree and type of involvement that consumers experience through SNS" (Lin and Peña 2011, p. 25).

It seems clear that from a media economics perspective, there are reasons enough to believe in the multiple synergies between broadcasters and social media. Engagement and branding seem to be the most valuable benefits which have to be monetized; they are the real 'social capital'. Where there are opportunities for additional consumption and additional audience value (Doyle 2010, p. 444) there are ways to monetize. In the end, what is more important for broadcasters is to create popular content and try to facilitate their consumption in the highest possible number of platforms, so tagging is an important task to increase the visibility through search engine.

References

AMETIC. (2011). *Informe sobre la Industria de contenidos digitales*. Ametic. http://www.ametic.es/media/Ou80/File/Informe_ContenidosDigitales2011.pdf
Antena 3 de televisión, s.a. (2010). Annual report 2010. http://www.grupoantena3.com/nuevaa3tv/doc/Cuentas.pdf
Bardají, J. (2011, December 8). General Manager of Antena 3. Personal interview.
BBC (2007) BBC Annual Report and Accounts. London: BBC.
Boyd, D., & Ellison, N. (2008). Social network sites: Definition, history and scholarship. *Journal of Computer-Mediated Communication, 13*, 210–230.
Brandenburger, A. M., & Nalebuff, B. J. (1996). *Coopetition*. New York: Doubleday.
Burt, R. S. (2005). *Brokerage and closure: An introduction to social capital*. Oxford: Oxford University Press.
Chan-Olmsted, S., & Ha, L. S. (2003). Internet business models for broadcasters. How television stations perceive and integrate the Internet. *Journal of Broadcasting & Electronic Media, 47*(4), 597–617.
Chan-Olmsted, S., Lee, S., & Kim, H. (2011). Competitive strategies in Korean mobile television markets: A comparative analysis of mobile operators and television broadcasters. *International Journal on Media Management, 6*(1), 77–93.
Dematté, C., & Perretti, F. (1997). *L´impresa televisiva*. Milan: Etaslibri.
Díaz, I. (2011). Convocan por redes sociales un 'apagón' de Telecinco en protesta por la entrevista a la madre de 'el Cuco'. *El Mundo*, 2011/11/12. http://www.elmundo.es/elmundo/2011/11/11/comunicacion/1321027921.html
Diego, P., & Herrero, M. (2010). Desarrollo de series online producidas por el usuario final: el caso del videoblog de ficción. *Palabra Clave, 13*(2), 325–336.
Dowling, M., Lechner, C., & Thielman, B. (1998). Convergence – Innovation and change of market structures between television and online services. *Electronic Markets, 8*(4), 31–35.
Doyle, G. (2010). From television to multi-platform: Less form more or more from less? *Convergence, 16*(4), 431–449.
Dunnet, P. (1990). *World television industry. An economic analysis*. London: Routledge.
El Cosmonauta. http://elcosmonauta.es/
El Mundo. (2011). Donettes retira una campaña por la presión de Twitter. 2011-10-01. http://www.elmundo.es/elmundo/2011/09/30/valencia/1317365823.html, http://twitter.com/#!/donettes
Ellison, N., Steinfield, C., & Lampe, C. (2010). Connection strategies: Social capital implications of Facebook-enabled communication practices. *New Media & Society, 13*(6), 873–892.
Enders Analysis. (2011, May). Facebook's threat to Google. http://www.endersanalysis.com/category/key-companies/facebook Retrieved November 17, 2011.
Fournier, S. (1998). Consumers and their brands: Developing relationship theory in consumer research. *Journal of Consumer Research, 24*(4), 343–373.
Frith, S. (2000). The black box: The value of television and the future of television research. *Screen, 41*(1), 33–50.
Fundación Orange. (2011). *Informe eEspaña*. Fundación Orange, Madrid http://www.informeeespana.es/docs/eE2011.pdf
Godlewski, L. R., & Perse, E. M. (2010). Audience activity and reality television: Identification, online activity, and satisfaction. *Communication Quarterly, 58*(2), 148–169.
Greenberg, B. (2010, May 3). *MediaWeek, 20*(18), 37.
Guerrero, E. (2011). El ecosistema multiplataforma de los grupos televisivos españoles: los formatos de entretenimiento. *Comunicación y Hombre, 7*, 85–103.
Hayes, J., & Graybeal, G. (2011). Synergizing traditional media and the Social Web for monetization: A modified media micropayment model. *Journal of Media Business Studies, 8*(2), 19–44.
Herrero, M. (2009a). La economía del producto audiovisual en el mercado de la comunicación. *Comunicación y Sociedad, 22*(1), 7–31.

Herrero, M. (2009b). The economics of series of audiovisual entertainment products. In M. Medina (Ed.), *Creating, producing and selling TV shows* (pp. 31–52). Lisbon: Formal Press.

Herrero, M., & Sádaba, C. (2006). Spain: An emerging market still giving its first steps. In L. Ha & R. Ganahl (Eds.), *Webcasting worldwide: Business models of an emerging global medium* (pp. 155–170). Mahwah, NJ: Lawrence Erlbaum.

Hoskins, C., McFadyen, S., & Finn, A. (1997). *Global television and film. An Introduction to the Economics of the Business*. New York: Oxford University Press.

IAB Europe. (2011). European online advertising expenditure, IAB, UK. http://www.iabspain.net/ver.php?mod=descargas&id_categoria=4,14,40,17

Kozinets, R. V. (2006). Click to connect: Netnography and tribal advertising. *Journal of Advertising Research, 46*, 279–288.

Li, C., & Bernoff, J. (2008). *Groundswell: Winning in a world transformed by social technologies.* Boston: Harvard Business Press.

Lin, J.-S., & Peña, J. (2011). Are you following me? A content analysis of TV networks' brand communication on Twitter. *Journal of Interactive Advertising, 12*(1), 17–29.

Medina, M. (2007). Explotación económica de las series familiares de televisión. *Comunicación y Sociedad, 20*(1), 51–85.

Medina, M., & Ojer, T. (2011). The transformation of Public TV Companies into Digital Services at the BBC and RTVE. *Comunicar, 36,* 87–94.

Moreno, J. (2008, January 13). Multimedia Contents Management, Antena 3, Conference at Universidad de Navarra.

Nieto, A. (1984). *La prensa gratuita.* Pamplona: Eunsa.

Nieto, A. (2000). *Time and the information market: The case of Spain.* Pamplona: Eunsa.

O'Neil, N. (2010, September 23). Facebook could generate $300 million in credits revenue next year. *All Facebook.* http://www.allfacebook.com/facebook-could-generate-300-million-in-credits-revenue-next-year-2010-09

Owen, B. M., & Wildman, S. S. (1992). *Video economics.* Cambridge: Harvard University Press.

Parr, B. (2011, January 28). LinkedIn's IPO: An overview. *Mashable Business.* http://mashable.com/2011/01/28/linkedins-ipo-an-overview/ Retrieved 11/17/11.

Patel, K., & Slutsky, I. (2011). Is social media killing TV?. *Advertising Age*, 4/18/2011, *82*(16), 4.

Pérez-Latre, F. J., Blanco, I. P., & Sánchez, C. (2011). Social networks, media and audiences: A literature review. *Comunicación y Sociedad, 24*(1), 63–74.

Picard, R. (1989). *Media economics.* London: Sage.

Picard, R. (2009). Blogs, Tweets, Social Media, and the News Business. *Nieman Reports,* Fall, 10–12.

Siapera, E. (2004). From coach potatoes to cybernauts? The expanding notion of the audience on TV channels' websites. *New Media & Society, 6,* 155–172.

Stefanone, M. A., Lackaff, D., & Rosen, D. (2010). The relationship between traditional mass media and 'Social Media': Reality television as a model for social network site behavior. *Journal of Broadcasting & Electronic Media, 54*(3), 508–525.

Sullivan, D., & Jiang, Y. (2010). Media convergence and the impact of the Internet on the M&A activity of large media companies. *Journal of Media Business Studies, 7*(4), 21–40.

Tapscott, D., & Williams, A. (2006). *Wikinomics: How mass collaboration changes everything.* New York: Portfolio Trade.

Tapscott, D. (2008). *Wikinomics: How mass collaboration changes everything.* New York: Portfolio.

The Economist. (2011, May 1). A special report on television. 16 pp.

Vara, R. (2011). Multimedia Marketing Manager, e-mail 1st December.

YouView. http://www.youview.com/

Digital Hollywood: How Internet and Social Media Are Changing the Movie Business

Alejandro Pardo

1 Introduction

The history of Hollywood runs in tandem with the history of technological development. The inclusion of sound, followed by that of color, along with the need to adapt to new audiovisual media (first television and then video), are milestones in the history of the largest entertainment factory in the world. Each of these forms of technological development in turn marked a growing pain or turning point at the time of its invention, by which the Hollywood industry was ultimately strengthened. However, the changes over the last decade have been both more fast-paced and more far-reaching than anything that came before. The digital revolution and globalization have transformed the film and TV industry in ways that could never have been foreseen. The big Hollywood studios have been forced to respond to the uncertainty—and potential for profit—prompted by the popularity of the Internet and the success of new digital platforms, especially among young people.

This chapter is an attempt to trace the recent evolution of the present and future challenges the Hollywood industry is facing up in this paradigm shift—from analogical to digital. In order to respond to the complex nature of this phenomenon, I will try to cover, in an exploratory way, a different set of topics, going from the change in consumption habits and the emergence of new virtual markets to the clash of management mentalities, the search for the right business model and a summary of some of the key transformations the entertainment industry is experiencing.

The literature at this respect is quite abundant. On the one hand, some authors have studied the economics of the media and entertainment industries as a whole (Ulin 2009; Vogel 2010) or in the particular case of Hollywood (De Vany 2004; Epstein 2010), not to mention those who have emphasized the impact of globalization and digitalization (Hoskins et al. 1997; Miller et al. 2005; Holt and Perren 2009). On the other, some

---

A. Pardo (✉)
University of Navarra, Pamplona, Spain
e-mail: alexpardo@unav.es

experts have approached the issue of media convergence and new technologies in general (Jenkins 2006; Pavlik and McIntosh 2011) or focused on the consumer (Tapscott 2009) and on the market (Anderson 2006, 2009). On the specific case of the relationship between Hollywood and the Internet, we can also find a series of books published along the last decade, which represent a critical account of the different attitudes the majors studios have had towards new media (Geirland and Sonesh-Kedar 1999; Dekom and Sealey 2003; Lasica 2005; Tryon 2009). On top of that, I am especially relying of the researches done by some scholars on how Internet and the digital economy are changing the current business models and management strategies in the media industry (Stöber 2004; McPhillips and Merlo 2008; Clemons 2009; Vukanovic 2009; Artero 2010) and more particularly in the case of the Hollywood studios (Currah 2006; Perren 2010; Iordanova and Cunningham 2012). Lastly, I am including numerous news and data from trade papers like *Screen Digest*, *Screen Daily* and *Variety*.

What follows is a step forward from previous researches already published (Pardo 2009, 2012).[1] First, I will examine the defining features of the emerging consumer profile and address the most significant elements of the new digital economy, epitomized by the 'long tail market' model. Secondly, I will describe the Hollywood reaction to this new digital scenario and discuss on the business models adopted by major American studios in relation to the online audiovisual market. Thirdly, I will summarize some of the most significant transformations Hollywood is undergoing. Finally I will draw some concluding remarks, which will be necessarily open due to the permanent state of change, innovation and tentativeness of this digital scenario.

2   Being or Not Being Digital

In mid-1990s, Nicholas Negroponte announced in his famous book *Being Digital*: "I am convinced that by the year 2005 Americans will spend more hours on the Internet (o whatever is called) than watching network television" (Negroponte 1995, p. 98). Although this prediction has not yet been fulfilled to the letter, the truth of what he argued is likely to be confirmed in the near future. Effectively, as *Newsweek* graphically illustrated in July 2010 under the provocative title of "How the Digital Revolution Changed Our World", the daily time spent in the Internet by the average US citizen has growth from 2.7 h per week to 18 h in the last decade. In addition, the amount of downloads for entertainment content on iTunes surpasses the ten billion figure (*Newsweek* 2010).

Something is changing in our planet. To get just a glimpse of it, let's take a look at the rapid expansion of the 'Apple ecosystem'. Since 2001, the late Steve Jobs'

---

[1] A preliminary and shorter version of this text was published under the title of "Hollywood and the Digital Revolution: New Consumers, New Markets, New Business Models", in Tribulations numériques du Cinéma et de l'Audiovisuel à l'amorce du 21e siècle, monográfico de Mise Au Point, Cahiers de l'Association Française des Enseignants Chercheurs en Cinéma et Audiovisuel (AFECCAV) [on line], n. 4, 2012. URL: http://map.revues.org/246

company has sold more than 140 million of iPods. Equally, the success of the iPhone first and of the iPad latter has no precedent. The company surpassed the figure of 100 million units sold in the whole world by the end of 2012 in the case of both devices which amount to more than 50 % and 20 % of the company's annual income respectively. As a result, following the market-launch of the iTunes Music Store, the Apple brand has commercialized more than 16 billion songs, over 3 million feature films, and approximately 100 million TV shows since October 2005. On top of that, at the beginning of 2013, Apple Store announced that customers have downloaded over 40 billion apps, with nearly 20 billion in 2012 alone. Despite of being mainly a hardware company, Apple has now over 435 million iTunes accounts with credit cards attached (McBride 2006; Fritz 2007; Screen Digest 2007, 2012; Grover 2008; Hesseldahl 2008a, b; Apple Press Info 2013). This 'iPod/iPhone/iPad generation' epitomizes the new peer group of users whose audiovisual experience is based on all sorts of media platforms and whose profile to a large extent mirrors that of the cinema-going public and those who play videogames. For that very reason, Apple competitors (Microsoft, Samsung, Sony, Google, Amazon, etc.) are trying to catch up the train of the present-and-future technology and to come up with the right business model.

"How will all this revolution affect to the movie business? Some recent market indicators show there is no reason to be worried about. According to Screen Digest, consumer expense on online movies and TV shows in USA doubled from 200 to 400 million dollars between 2008 and 2010—being rental more solid than retail—and reached the 900 million figure at the end of 2011 (ScreenDigest 2009, 2010a, b, 2011c, 2012c). Similarly, revenues from the European online video market were worth of 350 million Euros at the end of 2011, a substantial growth in regard to previous year (ScreenDigest 2011a, 2012b). On top of that, the total online revenues for international territories (outside the US) increased to more than 276 million US dollars in 2010, a 117.5 % rise over 2009 (*Screen Digest* 2011b). Finally, according to the last Deloitte's *State of the Media Democracy* global report (including data for 2011), the number of people opting to stream movies (42 %) is getting closer with those who watch them on DVD, Blu-ray or VHS (51 %). Whereas DVD viewership has scaled down two points over the past 2 years, the number of people who cited streaming as their favorite way to watch a movie increased from 4 to 14 % (Morris 2012a).

Thus, Hollywood is standing at a new digital (and global) crossroad, charted by two basic movements: on one hand, the emergence of a new market for the commercialization of audiovisual products (Internet, digital reproduction devices, smart phones, smart TVs), initially framed under 'the long tail market' tag; and, on the other, the emergence of new type of consumer, known collectively as 'the iPod-' or "the Net-generation" (Tapscott 2009). The two, linked questions set out below sum up the challenges facing the major studios in Hollywood: What new consumer habits define this emerging viewer/audience profile? And, as a consequence, what business model will define the network of relations on the Internet with regard to the commercial practices of the film and TV series industry? Or, in other words, what are the rules governing this new market? These two questions are closely bound up together; the response to one conditions any response to the other.

3   'The Martini Culture' Meets 'The Long Tail' Markets

> The Internet is the most liberating of all mass media developed to date. It is participatory, like swapping stories around a campfire or attending a Renaissance fair. It is not meant solely to push content, in one direction, to a captive audience, the way movies or traditional network television have done. It provides the greatest array of entertainment and information, on any subject, with any degree of formality, on demand. And it is the best and the most trusted source of commercial product information on cost, selection, availability, and suitability, using community content, professional reviews, and peer reviews. (Clemons 2009, p. 17)

This description of the new virtual world drawn by the expansion of the Net reveals a complete new scenario to play the business of entertainment game. The rules have changed as well as the number of key players. Within this game-board, Hollywood studios are trying to make sensible moves.

The Internet has brought with it a new peer group of 'digital natives'. Marketing experts are convinced that this generation of new technology users has now reached a critical mass in numerical terms, and their consumer behavior is markedly different to that which went before. Among others, the following features should be remarked: (a) a more participative and active attitude with respect to audiovisual and entertainment contents (user generated contents); (b) multi-tasking skills; (c) new forms of socializing through virtual communities; (d) a preference for versatility and portability over quality in consumer use ("platform agnostics", in the words of David Denby, the renowned film critic at *The New Yorker* (Denby 2006)); (e) new consumer behavior as a catalyst for the creation of new market niches (low demand, personalized and individually tailored consumption); and (f) unconventional understanding of the free circulation of audiovisual material (piracy).

This matrix of aspects has been distilled into the well-known slogan taken as the motto for the new media scene: "*What* you want, *when* you want, *where* you want and *how* you want". Or, as Michael Gubbins—editor of *Screen Daily*—calls it remembering an iconic advertisement of the 1970s, this is the ultimate expression of 'the Martini culture' in our "ubiquitous leisure society". In regard to this term, he explains:

> It is the sexier big sister of the more prosaic term ICE (information, communication and entertainment) coined in India during the dotcom boom to denote a marriage of information technology and entertainment. And to an extent, both dreams have come true. It is barely impossible to walk 100m in a city in any developed country without seeing the distinctive white earphones of an iPod. Mobile gaming is expanding quickly and telephones have lost their dowdy role as a means of speaking to people, to become portable electronic leisure centers. (Gubbins 2008)

The following question inevitably arises in this context: What rules govern business in this new window of commercial opportunity? Chris Anderson, editor of *Wired*, christened this recently discovered 'gold mine' with the name 'the long tail', a term that has since become common currency (Anderson 2004, 2006). His argument, which soon drew on empirical evidence from an analysis of several companies in the retail sector, runs as follows: commercialization on the Internet is not a marginal market; rather, it is an emerging market whose value is increasing all the time. This argument for Internet commercialization defers to three reasons: (a) the Internet brings together a dispersed and fragmented audience which, as a whole, constitutes a significant market; (b) distribution costs are eliminated and product consumption becomes more personalized and attuned to the demands of these 'digital natives'; and (c) popularity is no longer the key factor in market value; in fact, the Internet is especially apt (and profitable) for the sale of relatively unknown or minority interest products (Anderson 2004, pp. 174–177).

Thus, the emergence of this new virtual market undermines one of the classical laws of consumer goods economics—20 % of products account for 80 % of sales (the Pareto principle). Having analyzed the online services of companies such as Amazon, Netflix and Walmart, Anderson concluded that the proportion of products that contribute to overall profitability in virtual markets might be as high as 98 %. This conclusion does not mean that the most successful titles in conventional distribution channels cease to be so in the virtual world; however, less well-known or minority interest products also become more easily available and are acquired by the fragmented audience(s) of which the virtual market is composed. As a result, a specific catalogue of audiovisual goods may repay on the outlay involved in their production, and marginal profits may rise.

Finally, Anderson outlines three rules to govern this new business model, entirely focused on the consumer's leading role and singularity: (1) availability of a wide range of titles ("make everything available"); (2) competitive pricing in comparison with other distribution channels ("cut the price in half; now lower it"); and (3) personalized consumption ("help me find...") (Anderson 2004, pp. 174–177). And he concludes: "The companies that will prosper will be those that switch out of lowest-common-denominator mode and figure out how to address niches" (ibid., p. 177).

However, this theory has been criticized by some well-known scholars. Anita Elberse (Harvard Business School), for example, based on her own empirical research, states that the tail may be long but is equally flat in terms of benefits. In addition, she affirms that compared with heavy users, light users have a disproportionately strong preference for the more popular offerings, while both groups appreciate hit products more than they like those in the tail. As she concludes:

> It is therefore highly disputable that much money can be made in the tail. In sales of both videos and recorded music—in many ways the perfect products to test the long-tail theory—we see that hits are and probably will remain dominant. That is the reality that should inform retailers as they struggle to offer their customers a satisfying assortment cost-efficiently. And it's the unavoidable challenge to producers. The companies that will prosper are the ones most capable of capitalizing on individual best sellers. (Elberse 2008, p. 96)

In my view, both interpretations can be compatible. On the one hand, it is clear that Internet has widened the commercial exploitation for all sorts of products and, therefore, has given opportunity to those considered "marginal" or "obscure"—with no chance of commercial exposure through the conventional windows. On the other, hits will always be hits. They will continue to act as the locomotive for entertainment consumption and will therefore remain as the hard core of the business.

In this regard, after some false starts, a number of the changes to business strategies adopted by Hollywood studios in recent times have attempted to take those principles mentioned above into account. For any key player in the entertainment industry aimed at a ubiquitous leisure society, the challenge is to understand this new scenario, where 'the Martini culture' meets 'the long tail' markets.

4 Hollywood at the Digital Crossroad: A Management Clash?

Contrary to what it could be assumed, Hollywood has been quite reluctant for many years to face up these profound changes. Two insiders as Peter Dekom and Peter Sealy asked in 2003:

> How has Hollywood responded to the huge changes afoot? Unfortunately, no very well so far. First, Hollywood has ignored the facts both inside and outside the industry... [It] has fought to put the technological genie back in the bottle. The Hollywood approach: change must be legislated o litigated to a stop. (Dekom and Sealey 2003, pp. 2–3)

Another expert analyst as Joseph D. Lasica, pointing out at this resistance from the Hollywood majors, assessed in 2005:

> Media companies need to learn to let go. Successful entertainment companies will create new products and pricing schemes, embrace fair use by giving customers flexibility in choosing how they want to view or listen to a work, and give outside innovators the freedom to tinker with and improved existing products. Media companies should embrace their digital destiny, even as their business models suffer short-term dislocation. (Lasica 2005, p. 265)

From inside Hollywood, opposite voices can be heard. Although the majority of studio executives assume the need for change, others get despaired at the slow rhythm of the decision-making process within the huge and bureaucratic corporations. This is the case, for example, of David Wertheimer, former Paramount Digital Entertainment Head and current President of Digital Fox. Few years after abandoning the former studio, he assessed:

> In the studios... you end up doing things that are slow and incredibly safe... In order to move quickly enough, you have to think like a startup—and that means you have to *be* a startup and run like a startup. The studios are always going to be followers rather than leaders. (in Rose 2000)

Why does this fear to change exist? Someone as significant as George Lucas points it out in a very clear way:

> The consortium of rich corporations that used to control this entire medium are now doomed... In some ways we're moving to a world without borders. We are seeing a paradigm change in how movies get made, how they get distributed, and the Internet has pretty much wiped out those borders. Now you can get people around the world to see your film. (in *Screen Daily* 2010)

In other words, what is at stake is the current Hollywood *status quo* as unbeatable oligopoly of production and distribution of branded entertainment content. Executives at the major studios acknowledge that the existing commercial models are in terminal decline. Box-office takings in mid 2000s amounted between 10 and 15 % of total income. The other 85–90 % was generated through the sale of audiovisual products designed for use at home and/or in an individualized way (DVD sales and pay-per-view television). Nevertheless, the digital revolution is also likely to radically transform the market in this regard. The physical copy of the audiovisual product is disappearing, and the existing distribution channels along with it. According to *Screen Digest*, traditional physical rental video spending fell from 51 to 36 % in the United States in 2010, whereas subscription video spending reached as much as 42 %—thanks to Netflix, among others (*Screen Digest* 2011a). Nevertheless, the industry response to this prospect ought to be measured.

Hollywood studio executives have now taken careful note of the rules detailed above. Having been initially resistant—if not openly hostile—to the development of television and video, and thus slow to adapt these new media to their existing business model, the response of such executives to the emergence of new technologies has been markedly different. Nowadays, there is no one reluctant about it—"We have to adapt", said some years ago Barry Meyer, former Chairman and CEO of Warner Bros. Entertainment, "or we'll become dinosaurs" (Denby 2006). And more recently, Mike Dunn, president of Twentieth Century Fox Home Entertainment, stated: "The opportunity in front of us is bigger than it's ever been. We're looking at a renaissance here" (Marich, 2013). However, prudence must rule the progressive incorporation of new business models. As Bob Iger, CEO of The Walt Disney Company and one of the most committed defenders of digital change in Hollywood, explains:

> I have tried to keep two obvious philosophies. First, that our current business not get in the way of adopting new technologies, and, second, that our business belongs to these new platforms. (Swisher 2010)

In other words, the *quid* of the question is how incorporate new business models without killing the most profitable window—home entertainment, which includes DVD, Pay TV and different forms of online video-on-demand (iVoD).

If the Hollywood reaction to the digital scenario shows anything, this is a sort of management clash: the new and challenging versus the old and conservative; or, in other terms, the 'digital' mentality versus the 'analogical' one. This is one of the conclusions deducted by Andrew Currah (2006) after interviewing 150 Hollywood executives. In particular, he summarizes three concluding remarks. First, Hollywood's strategy has been one of preserving the current sequence of commercial windows, rather than exploiting the disruptive power of new technologies (protectionism from oligopoly). In his words, "this has been the case of the collision between Hollywood (a mature oligopoly overseen by six studios) and the Internet (a decentralized P2P [peer-to-peer] architecture)" (Currah 2006, p. 463). Similarly, Frank Rose, editor of *Wire*, pointed out at the turn of the century: "Hollywood exists to feed the proven bottom line, not to invent the next one" (Rose 2000).

Secondly, we should understand at the same time the main reasons argued by Hollywood executives for their hesitancy. On the one hand, the risk of DVD cannibalization—killing the most profitable window—and the subsequent pressure exercised by big retailers' like Walmart or Blockbuster (until recently, DVD accounted for 55 % of total income). On the other hand, the cost of clearing rights for the Internet (Currah 2006, pp. 455–463).

Thirdly, despite of the fears and reluctances, there is no doubt the future of Internet as window depends on Hollywood involvement (ibid., p. 463). As *Variety* stated at the beginning of this decade,

> Hollywood is suspicious of technology. It always has been. But when it comes to the World Wide Web, it turns out that Hollywood is actually taken over the reigns of Internet entertainment—it just hasn't done it the way everyone thought it would. (Graser 2000, p. 22)

What lies behind this Hollywood management clash, in Michael Gubbins' words, is the collision between two opposing discourses. One is that "the current technology trends are no more than the 'digitisation' of the existing business; just another big step in a series of evolutionary changes in the history of cinema" (Gubbins 2012, p. 70). This approach acknowledges the disruptive power of digitisation in the short term, but understands the immediate future just in terms of replacements or upgrades of existing standards and processes. The other is that "digital represents a wholesale change in consumer attitudes and even taste, based on interactivity and a democratisation of the process of film-making" (ibid., p. 71). This second perspective aims at the real core of the digital revolution, as stated along these pages.

In summary, the new digital scenario is demanding a change of business and management mentality: the old assumptions of limits on creation and access, typical of an economy of content scarcity must open way to the new value drivers of free access, almost infinite variety of products, customized consumption, content aggregators and search engines, typical of an economy of abundance—although with time and expense restrictions.

The move from analogical to digital has been slow and extended in time. At the beginning of the new millennium, the alliance between Hollywood and Silicon Valley became more intense. Technological companies were looking to create Hollywood relationships and a number of industry players moved to 'dot-com' companies. Nevertheless, and it was stated at the moment, "Hollywood's new Web-friendly stance and new deals don't necessarily mean Hollywood understands the ways of the Web" (Graser 2000). In fact, it was more a question of using Internet as a testing laboratory for commercial exploitation or being the first to show (Graser 2000; DiOrio 2000). This attitude towards new markets is quite typical in the case of oligopolistic industries, as Currah explains:

> The commercial developments of new markets and technologies often takes place in a bifurcated fashion, particularly in oligopolies. Specifically, it is possible to make a broad distinction between processes of *exploration* and *exploitation* (Tushman & Anderson, 2004). First, the exploration of emerging markets tends to be pioneered by smaller firms, outside the orbit of incumbent firms... Second, a tipping point occurs when emerging markets obtain a critical mass, attracting the interest of incumbents. In a few cases, this process of exploitation might lead to the displacement of incumbents and the ascendance of innovative 'first movers'... In most cases, however, the growth of a new market actually depends upon incumbents given their assets and market power. Generally innovators are more likely to 'sell out' rather than challenge the ruling oligopoly. (Currah 2006, p. 463)

Effectively, the never-ending strategic movements of mergers, acquisitions and alliances that have taken place along this decade exemplify this dynamic: Fox + MySpace, Disney + Pixar + Apple, Blockbuster + MovieLink vs. Walmart + Netflix, Google + YouTube vs. Hulu, Amazon-Unibox + TiVo, etc. These strategic initiatives provide ample evidence of the determination of Hollywood studios not to miss the boat on so-called *gear-media*. The alliance between Hollywood and Silicon Valley is becoming tighter, like the recent appointment of Bob Iger (CEO of Disney) as new member of Apple's board exemplifies (Lawson 2007; Wallenstein 2011a).

5 Business Models: What Did Go Wrong, What Should Be Right

For the Hollywood studios—as well as for the rest of the key players in the entertainment industry—the search for the right business model in Internet has become as harder and crucial as the quest for the Philosopher's Stone. As one industry expert assesses,

> Once upon a time... the movie business was about making movies. Nowadays, it is about creating intellectual property that can be licensed in a raft of different markets... The [Hollywood] studios stand to gain even more from huge audience willing to pay to download movies from their libraries... [Therefore], the real issue for Hollywood studios is how they can dig into this potential gold mine without undermining their existing revenue streams. (Epstein 2005)

Apparently, the theoretical principles have been always clear, but reality has widely demonstrated that this new market—this new consumer—has its own rules. Back in 2001, a *Variety* expert stated,

> Advertising, development, syndication and subscription. The seeds have been planted for profitability, but all these business plans are facing a dot-comeuppance. The basic problem? Nobody can quantify or define the type of content people are willing to pay for... Netizens are willing to pay for content if they get something in return that facilitates their Internet experience, and this realization is starting to dawn on traditional entertainment outlets. (Donahue 2001, p. 18)

More recently, some scholars like Eric Clemons explains how the majority of attempts to date to monetize Internet applications targeted at individuals have been based on natural extensions of traditional media or traditional retailing—in particular, some form of consumer-focused advertising and/or of consumer-focused e-commerce. Nevertheless Internet "is far more powerful than traditional media on one hand, and far more liberating and thus inappropriate as an alternative to traditional media on the other" (Clemons 2009, p. 15). Apart from those business models based on advertising, the two others with more potential are "those that sell some product, experience, content, or service and earn revenues from the sale, and those that provide access to consumers and charge for access" (ibid.). In summary, "selling real things, selling virtual things and selling access" (ibid., p. 19). In this regard, Hollywood studios, as content and service providers, are potentially at the pole position in this new digital scenario.

In addition, other authors like Simon McPhillips and Omar Merlo assess that,

> [t]he fundamental principles of the industry's business model are not changing. It will still centre on mutually advantageous relationship between media owners, consumers and advertisers. However, what is also evident is that the dynamics contained within the model are radically changing. (McPhillips and Merlo 2008, p. 251)

For this very reason, as a number of industry analysts have pointed out, the future of the film and TV online business model will be dependent on a hybrid financing structure, involving a combination of direct (pay-per-view and subscription) and indirect (advertising and sponsorship) funding (Fritz 2007). The three current business model to consolidate are: (a) *Transactional*: consumers can buy a permanent download ('download-to-own', DTO), rent a temporary download or buy temporary access to a stream (VoD rental); (b) *Subscription*: consumers can subscribe to an 'all-you-can-eat' rental service offering temporary downloads or streams in return for a single monthly fee (SVoD); and (c) *Ad-supported*: consumers can download or stream titles for free in return for watching video ads within the content (FVoD) (*Screen Digest* 2007, pp. 270–271; Perren 2010, p. 73). Which one would be the most significant in terms of income, is still an open question. Paying for contents and services will experience the most significant growth according to some experts (Clemons 2009, p. 33). Nevertheless, ad-supported formulas will be remain if they can find ways of being unaggressive and naturally embedded in the audiovisual content (McPhillips and Merlo 2008, pp. 250–251).

Surprising though it may seem, Hollywood took a long and hard way to learn the lesson. In fact, the failure of the first business models adopted by the studios in response to the commercial potential of new technologies—CinemaNow, MovieLink and MovieBeam (Disney), the three first websites for downloading movies, launched in 1999, 2002 and 2005 respectively—was attributed to an error at the level of basic principles: if the Internet is to be a new entertainment platform capable of competing with the conventional media (DVD rental and pay-per-view TV) then either the audiovisual experience it offers should be more attractive and user-friendly, and thus sold at a correspondingly higher price, or its products should be sold at prices considerably lower than those of the existing media. Nevertheless, the reality was quite the contrary: high prices for a limited (library) and not very satisfying (downloading problems) viewing experience (Pardo 2009, pp. 77–79). With a wisdom based on common sense, *Billboard* analyst Michael Greeson wrote

an article prophetically titled "Movie Downloads: Why This Model Won't Work"...
(Greeson 2006). Effectively, the three of them ceased operations few years later,
after being sold out and merged. Only the emergence of the iTunes model—first for
music (2001), then for any sort of audiovisual contents (2005)—marked a turning
point (Pardo 2009, pp. 81–82). Since then, the iTunes formula of buying a wide
variety of music, films and TV shows on a single basis, at a reasonable price and in a
very user-friendly way has been an continuous success. According to Clemons,

> Apple's iTunes is the most successful at charging for content, perhaps because the price for
> an individual song is low enough and the prospects of litigation are now daunting enough to
> discourage piracy (Clemons 2009, p. 33)

Some *Screen Digest* data illustrate this level of hegemony: Apple reached 63 %
of the online movie market share in the first half of 2011, followed in the distance
by Microsoft (17 %), Vudu-Walmart (6 %), Amazon (5 %) and Sony-PlayStation
(4 %) (*Screen Digest* 2011c).

Nevertheless, there are still some contrasting attitudes inside the Hollywood
system. In a very suggesting article, Alisa Perren points out the different strategies
the film and TV divisions of media conglomerates have employed in circulating
their properties on line. In this regard, she assesses:

> In general, the television divisions... of the media conglomerates (especially the Big Seven
> [Hollywood studios]) have reacted in a far more proactive manner in terms of their online
> distribution efforts than have the theatrical motion picture divisions of these same
> companies (Perren 2010, p. 73)

To illustrate this point, she mentions two productions from the same media
conglomerate, News Corporation-20th Century Fox: the TV show *Glee* and the
feature film *Wolverine*, both of them released at same time of the year (May 2009).
Whereas in the case of the TV show, Fox network used Internet to distribute and
promote the program as wide as possible (Fox.com, MySpace, Hulu, iTunes), the
film division tried to prevent any circulation of the movie online without success—
it was illegally leaked online months before the theatrical release and downloaded
more than four million times worldwide, causing a estimated loss of 30 million US
dollars in ticket sales (ibid.).

This same author offers some reasons to justify this different mentality. Regarding
TV divisions, Internet has a promotional value attached; it helps viewers to stay up;
and it enables to compile more precise measurement figures for viewership on multiple
platforms (ibid., pp. 73–74). In summary, "placing the content online following a
program's initial broadcast marks an effort by the networks to combat viewer erosion"
(ibid., p. 73). In the case of the conglomerates film divisions, apart from the piracy
risks, their reluctance to place movies online is based on the theater owners' opposition
to make any changes in the existing windows sequence; the nature of the film text—its
value is somehow diminished; and some others cultural and economic reasons—the
cinema going experience and the need to keep the enhanced theatrical standards in the
case of blockbuster franchises (ibid., pp. 75–76). As a consequence, until now,

"the first content made available online is mass appeal broadcast fare and highly niche-oriented feature films" (ibid., p. 76).

Among her arguments, Perren doesn't mention the risk of 'cannibalization', although it represents one of the greatest fears for the Hollywood executives, as seen before. Nevertheless, there are some examples that contradict that threat. Perren offers one of them. The movie *Flawles* (2007), a crime drama starring Demi Moore and Michael Kane, coproduced by Magnolia Pictures, earned 1.2 million US dollars at the box office and more than 2 million through video on demand (Perren 2010, p. 76). And even more clear, when *Iron Man* became available on iTunes in September 2008, it sold more than 1 million US dollars in 2.99 US dollars downloads in its first seven days of release—almost pure profit, because of the low cost of delivery. Nevertheless when the same movie was released in DVD, it achieved the 140 million US dollars revenue figure in its first week (Barnes 2008). A similar case was Clint Eastwood's *Gran Torino*, which earned 60 million US dollars from VoD and downloads, against a total box office take of 148 million US dollars (Gubbins 2012, p. 82).

6 Towards Digital Consensus?

In fact, it seems that Hollywood has finally come to terms. One revealing fact, for instance, is its corporate presence in one of the most important new technologies forum for the entertainment industry, the Consumer Electronics Show (CES) at Las Vegas, source of big events and important announcements every year. There, the Hollywood studios and other entertainment companies meet hardware and software manufacturers as well as any sort of state-of-the-art technology companies, looking for the latest digital delivery platforms for content distribution and even for potential franchise ideas. And not only the studios are doing so, but also well-known celebrities like Tom Hanks, Justin Timberlake, Barry Sonnenfeld or Will Smith (Graser 2012b; Stanley 2012).

In the 2010 CES edition, a consortium of the major Hollywood studios, retailers, cable operators, hardware manufacturers and rental services (with the exception of Disney and Apple) known as Digital Entertainment Content Ecosystem (DECE), announced the launching of UltraViolet, an online content locker that stores and plays movies and TV shows on a variety of devices.[2] This platform is intended to enable consumers to purchase a film from any provider and store it online in order

---

[2] DECE is made up of more than 75 members, which pretty much covers most major entertainment suppliers and device manufacturers. Founding members include Best Buy, Netflix, Comcast, Cox Communications, BSkyB, Intel, Microsoft, Cisco, Dell, IBM, HP, Toshiba, Samsung, LG, Nokia, Motorola, Dolby, Adobe and Sonic Solutions. While Fox, Warner Bros., Paramount, Lionsgate and NBC Universal are supporters, Disney is focusing on its similar Disney Studio All Access offering. Apple is also holding out from joining the organization, although it's likely that DECE's companies will create apps that will play UltraViolet content on devices like the iPod, iPhone and iPad.

to view it using any device with Internet connection—computers, smart TVs, cable set-top boxes, Blu-ray players, videogame consoles, smart phones and tablets.

The most significant change is that this new online device really meets the consumption habits and demands of the 'digital natives'. Every single household can create an account for six family members to access their movies and TV shows, and later music, books and other digital content, from retailers, cable operators and streaming services. Up to 12 different devices can be registered—to cover most of the hardware options on the market, being possible up to three streams at a single time. In addition, content can be downloaded and transferred onto physical media, like recordable DVDs, SD cards and flash memory drives.

In words of Mitch Singer, DECE president and chief technology officer of Sony Pictures Entertainment.

> We've tried to emulate consistent consumer behavior [in developing this service]... What we found was that consumers were getting content from the Internet for free and burning DVDs for friends or playing it across every device. We looked at what consumers are currently doing and gave them that with UltraViolet (Graser 2011b).

On his part, Thomas Gewecke, president of Warner Brothers Digital Distribution confirms:

> We believe that UltraViolet will provide consumers with an easy-to-use way to buy and watch digital entertainment across multiple devices... Making interoperability possible meets a key consumer need and fundamentally improves the digital video experience. With UltraViolet, consumers will be able to purchase a title once and enjoy it anywhere and anytime they wish (Graser 2010).

Three years since its launch, UltraViolet is still at the takeoff phase. On the one hand, it is still only available in a few English-speaking countries (US, UK and Canada, and hopefully it will reach Ireland, Australia and New Zealand in 2013). On the other, its title library is still limited. On top of that, the process of loading films is still less than optimal and the promise of being able to watch your film on any device is one that hasn't completely been fulfilled yet due to different DRM formats. Those early-stage problems have led some analysts to remain skeptical about this digital locker's long-term success. One strategic innovation consultant assesses.

> I'm not convinced UltraViolet is the silver bullet studios are looking for. At the end of the day, a customer is looking to purchase a piece of content and have it run right out of the gate on virtually any device.... Studios, to their credit, are intent on embracing the digital revolution, but they need to be as flexible as possible and keep it as simple as possible. From the customer's perspective, convenience and comfort win (Morris 2013).

In any case, Hollywood is ready for UltraViolet service to go mainstream. By the end of 2012, this platform had achieved nearly 9 million accounts, according to the Digital Entertainment Group. Nevertheless, home entertainment executives at the studios calculate it would need at least 20 million accounts to be considered consolidated (ibid).

Meanwhile, Disney—the only self-excluded studio in this venture—, after some false starts (Disney Studio All Access, Disney Movies Online) is developing its own online window named Disney Movies Anywhere (Graser 2012a). In addition, the Mouse firm announced a new rental deal with YouTube. The Google-owned video online platform offers Disney films for rental on its website, ranging from 1 to 4 US dollars depending on whether they are library titles or releases timed day and date with the home-video window. This rental deal is just a step forward in the increasing cooperation between the two companies, whose strategic plans include a co-branded channel with original programming that would reside both on YouTube and Disney. com (Kaufman 2012; Wallenstein 2011b). On its part, Apple is also out of UltraViolet, confident is its power as leader in the online movie market so far. As these two cases illustrates, the dilemma here is whether joining efforts in a single-platform and dilute your own brand power or betting for a different platform trusting in the your brand market appeal. The *quid* of the question, of course, relies on the consumers' acceptance of a variety of digital lockers to access the entertainment contents they want.

Finally, it is worthy of mention the support that some Hollywood big stars are granting to some online initiatives. This is the case of Tom Hanks and Justin Timberlake—to name just two examples. The former attended the 2012 CES edition to present his upcoming digital production, *Electric City*, a 20-episode animated series, coproduced by his company Playtone together with Reliance Entertainment and Yahoo (Wallenstein 2012). Also in this same CES edition, singer and actor Justin Timberlake, one of the MySpace's investors, announced the teaming between Panasonic and MySpace for the rollout of the social network's new social TV experiment (Morris 2012b).

7 The Future Is Now: Movie Business in Digital Hollywood

The previous pages reveal the profound transformation the Hollywood industry is undergoing due to the digital revolution. Some of the authors I have been quoting offer right diagnoses and make thoughtful propositions in this regard. McPhillips & Merlo, for instance, underline how value chain is decoupling, new strategies must be consumer-centric, and business models more 'equitable' between consumer's and advertisers' interests (2008, pp. 251–252). On his part, Clemons, concluding his research on how to monetize Internet and websites, assesses that "community content recommendations, social search, and contextual mobile advertising" provide "value for users, as long as they are trusted". And he adds: "the greater the monetization of each, the less trusted it may become, and the more subject it may be to deliberate manipulation" (2009, p. 33). In his study about strategic management of new media, Vukanovic analyze the five most successful international conglomerates—four of them including Hollywood studios—and identifies six factors to explain the successful growth of them: cross-media content distribution leveraging and repurposing, innovation management, vertical integration, vertical expansion, media diversification, and large number of shareholders (2009, pp. 82–87). Finally, after offering a comparative study of Hulu's and Youtube's business models, Artero warns that "the corner stone will lie with the capacity of these new models to contribute not just traffic, relevance or users, but revenue" (2010, p. 122).

Taking into account all these contributions, as well as the challenges mentioned in the previous sections of this chapter, I would like to summarize in five points some of the most significant transformations the Hollywood studios are facing to get adapted to the new digital scenario:

1. *Customized consumption*: As explained before, the new generation of tech savvy consumers (the 'digital natives') demands a personalized way to enjoy online entertainment contents—music, movies, TV shows, videogames—which means complete freedom of choice, flexibility and portability. This 'Martini Culture' meeting the 'long tail' markets requires the right targeting, pricing and technological infrastructure (broadband) strategies. In other words, "media convergence has empowered consumers... the imperative is to develop consumer-centric strategies and keep innovating" (McPhillips and Merlo 2008, p. 251). Initiatives like Ultra-Violet show a change of mentality by the Hollywood studios, in their effort to accommodated to these new consumption habits. One question to be determined here is how to keep the competitive market power of the different brands whereas using common digital platforms (either the mentioned UltraViolet, iTunes or Amazon).

2. *Redefining the windows sequence*: This profound transformation in consuming entertainment—consumers' new habits and disappearance of the physical copy— is definitely changing the current sequence of commercial windows. On the one hand, the time period of exclusivity is narrowing in order to avoid market competition and piracy effects; on the other, customized consumption obliges to design simultaneous release strategies—product availability in several windows at the same time with price discrimination (Ulin 2009, pp. 33–36). Recent examples are *Margin Call*, simultaneously released on theatrical and VoD, and *Abduction*, released at the same time on DVD and social networks—both Lionsgate productions (Goldsmith 2012a). As a consequence, the distribution sector as we know it is condemned to disappear or be dramatically transformed—into online content aggregators, for instance. Physical copies will be soon no longer existing, and 'virtual markets' will end up as the preferred option—as the iCloud option launched by Apple and Google (Morris 2011). Nevertheless, it must be remarked, as some industry analysts do, that cloud computing ecosystems will demand "new behaviors and attitudes about ownership, discovery, value of storage, offline media use, joint ownership, commoditization of services, competing with freemium business models, and licensing of content across blossoming new platforms..." (Johnson 2012, p. 2).

3. *Content is still king but needs adaptation*: "Paying for content and services may be the area that experiences the most growth" (Clemons 2009, p. 33). Despite recent advances in technology, creativity is still the cornerstone of the audiovisual industry. No matter how fast technology is evolving or how dramatically distribution is changing, "if you have a great story to tell, it will work on any delivery system", affirmed Michael Eisner few years ago (in Tartaglione-Vialatte 2008). Nevertheless, this new market physiognomy is leading to a polarization of entertainment contents:

on the one hand, the big-budget Hollywood blockbusters, with high production values, especially design for a 3D cinema experience; on the other, the small and target-specific niche films, aimed directly at home entertainment. This polarization also explains the need to create 'event-movies' based on franchises and brand-entertainment content in order to feed a regular market (Ulin 2009, pp. 18–29; Finney 2010, pp. 15–16). Finally, fiction and entertainment contents must be developed since its first stage for a multimedia and interactive consumption. From this perspective, the keys to develop successful contents are related to its capability to be multiplatform distributed and customized by the consumer—i.e., interactive options, potential to create a prestigious brand and capacity to tell an original 'transmedia' story (Jenkins 2006).

4. *In search for the right business model*: After many failures and few successes, the search for the right online business model—how to monetize the power of Internet and of social networks—is still a pending issue. What remains clear is that it will include the combination of hybrid formulas, including direct payment, paid subscription and advertising or sponsorship. The successful business model should guarantee two key issues: first, the possibility of customized consumption; second, competitive prices—good price-quality (or consumer's experience) relation (McPhillips and Merlo 2008; Clemons 2009; Pardo 2009). If some of the latest initiatives launched by Hollywood studios (UltraViolet) really address the first demand, other decisions may be probably wrong. Whereas some experts in online markets defend the predominance of free content and looking for alternative ways of making money out of internet exposure (Anderson 2009), Hollywood studios are thinking in offering select films to rent for 30 US dollars around 60 days after their theatrical release (Graser 2011a). So far, consumers prefer subscription VoD (such as Netflix), where movie deals are a relatively low-profit proposition for studios—It's estimated that profit for major studio movies is seven times higher in transactional VoD 25 times higher in electronic sell-through. It seems that Hollywood is again coming to terms. "What we learned from all our consumer research is that the product needs to be in hi-def[ignition] and under 15 US dollars to be relevant", says Mike Dunn, president of Twentieth Century Fox Home Entertainment (Marich 2013).

5. *Internet and social networks have become the key 'agora' of our time*: Viral marketing and the need to feed the vast array of fandom 'cyber-initiatives' are key tools in creating awareness about any movie or TV show nowadays. 'Digital natives' have a high participatory attitude as well as a self-conscience of peer group. We are living in an era of personalized services and recommendations, where social networks (MySpace, Facebook, Twitter) have become the most efficient forums to promote any sort of product or event (Gubbins 2012, pp. 74–75). Hollywood has been much more diligent at this point, taking advantage of these virtual and social marketing mechanisms, not only for building up franchise power (*Lord of the Rings*, *Harry Potter* or any adaptation of comic superheroes), but also to transform low budget independent movies (*The Blair Witch Project*, *Cloverfield* or *Paranormal Activity*) into worldwide blockbusters (Mueller 2007; Wessels 2011; Kaplan and Haenlein 2011). Social networks have become the most efficient forums to

promote any sort of product or event. And even more, they are being tested as a window per se for commercial exploitation, as the recent case of *Abduction*, released by Lionsgate via Facebook, exemplifies (Goldsmith 2012a).

Conclusion: From Reluctance to Prudent Embrace

The previous pages shows how Hollywood has progressively gone from a reluctant attitude to a prudent embrace of new technologies. Nevertheless, as some authors state,

> there will be no revolution or "industry stampede", as many observers have predicted. Rather, the industry will experience an evolution as the old and new models first learn to co-exist, until they ultimately converge. (McPhillips and Merlo 2008, p. 237)

Effectively, 'convergence' is a fashionable word in this new environment (Jenkins 2006; Pavlik and McIntosh 2011), and somehow marks the aim of this last Hollywood evolution. If anything is clear at the present moment, is that this paradigm shift has no way back. According to McPhillips and Merlo (2008), following Stöber's theory about what defines media evolution (2004), there are three stages to be gradually covered: *invention, innovation* and *institutionalization*:

> Media convergence is driving the evolution, and the change will prove profound and permanent. The invention and innovation phases of the transition are complete. We now appear to be in the institutionalization phase... Inevitably, there will be a period of adjustment as large players consolidate and specialist firms define their niches. (McPhillips and Merlo 2008, p. 251)

Unquestionably, Hollywood majors belong to those "large players". Their executives are therefore facing the most challenging transformation in the whole history of the entertainment industry. The digital revolution is shaking the traditional-conservative business models (analogical) and new options are emerging with unavoidable impetus (the online ones). The discussion is open: access vs. content, franchises over distribution channel, free vs. pay/premium content (or mixed ones), user-generated-content vs. professional works, etc.

There are some hopeful facts. Firstly, the consolidation of an emerging market—consumer expense on online movies & TV series has doubled in the last year both in USA and in Western Europe, and it is steadily increasing in the whole world. Secondly, the consensus achieved by most of the Hollywood studios, to create a consumer-centered platform (UltraViolet), much more in the lines of the iTunes model. And finally, the entry of new players and new forms of synergies and competition—Hollywood alliances with Google-You Tube, Hulu, Apple TV, TiVo, Walmart-Vudu, Amazon-Unibox, MySpace-Panasonic, etc.; the transformation of distributors into search engines or content aggregators; of retailers into 'e-tailers' (Netflix, Blockbuster, Amazon, Best Buy or Walmart) and even beyond—into pay TV channels, like Netflix, or movie studios, like Amazon (Cohen 2010).

At the same time, uncertainties are still there. Hollywood studios won't abandon their reluctance to widely license their content to online services in the short term. As said, they may be willing to embrace new technologies but without 'cannibalizing' their so far most profitable windows (cable TV and

DVD). Nevertheless, as main content providers, they own the key for the digital change. Recent ups-and-downs of successful online platforms like Netflix and Hulu, together with their strategic moves, show up to what point content is still king (Goldsmith 2012b, c; Wallenstein 2011c). Paraphrasing *Screen Digest*:

> If the movie industry is to build an online business, major content owners must emulate their counterparts in TV by loosening their grip on content and experimenting with services and business models. Until they do, online services will continue to represent a nominal revenue stream for the movie business. (*Screen Digest* 2010a)

As it can be noticed, the Hollywood studios are still taking positions on the digital game board, but no one exactly knows which rules will be definitely applied and who will success in offering the golden formula to win the consumer's confidence. And meanwhile, the grounds the Hollywood majors are walking on are far from being solid, as one *Variety* analyst points out:

> To say the digital distribution industry is in flux would be an understatement. As a result of this instability, roles shift, allies become competitors and competitors join forces... In an environment of brands competing to build out their platforms, competition is likely to win out over cooperation in the near term. (Kaufman 2012)

For this very reason, studio executives are not going to sit idly anymore. As one industry consultant from Price-Waterhouse-Coopers stated after attending the 2013 CES edition, I've seen a lot more willingness to try different business models in the past year alone than in the previous five years. The studios are starting to move faster and experiment. And that's key (Marich, 2013).

Welcome to Digital Hollywood.

References

Anderson, C. (2004, October). The long tail. *Wired*, pp. 170–177.
Anderson, C. (2006). *The long tail: Why the future of business is selling less of more*. New York: Hyperion.
Anderson, C. (2009). *Free: The future of a radical price*. New York, NY: Hyperion.
Apple Press Info. (2013). App store tops 40 billion downloads with almost half in 2012. Retrieved from http://www.apple.com/pr/library/2013/01/07App-Store-Tops-40-Billion-Downloads-with-Almost-Half-in-2012.html
Artero, J. P. (2010). Online video business models: YouTube vs. Hulu. *Palabra Clave, 13*(1), 111–123.
Barnes, B. (2008, November 23). Movie theaters look keep the streak alive. *The International Herald Tribune*. Retrieved from http://www.iht.com
Clemons, E. K. (2009). Business models for monetizing internet applications and web sites: Experience, theory, and predictions. *Journal of Management Information Systems, 26*(2), 15–41.
Cohen, D. S. (2010, November 16). Amazon.com gets into development business. *Variety*. Retrieved from http://www.variety.com/article/VR1118027595
Currah, A. (2006). Hollywood versus the Internet: The media and entertainment industries in a digital and networked economy. *Journal of Economic Geography, 6*, 439–468.

De Vany, A. (2004). *Hollywood economics: How extreme uncertainty shapes the film industry.* New York: Routledge.

Dekom, P. J., & Sealey, P. (2003). *Not on my watch... Hollywood vs. the future.* Beverly Hills, CA: New Millennium.

Denby, D. (2006, December 25). Big Pictures: Hollywood looks for a future. *The New Yorker.* Retrieved from http://www.newyorker.com

DiOrio, C. (2000, December). New Hollywood Heavies. *Variety, Entertainment and the Digital Economy,* pp. 26, 28.

Donahue, A. (2001, January). Pay here, get content. *Variety, Entertainment and the Digital Economy,* pp. 18–19.

Elberse, A. (2008). Should you invest in the long tail? *Harvard Business Review,* pp. 88–96.

Epstein, E. J. (2005, November 28). Downloading for dollars. *Slate.* Retrieved from http://www.slate.com

Epstein, E. J. (2010). *The Hollywood economist: The hidden financial reality behind the movies.* Brooklyn, NY: Melville House.

Finney, A. (2010). *The international film business: A market guide beyond hollywood.* London: Routledge.

Geirland, J., & Sonesh-Kedar, E. (1999). *Digital babylon: How the geeks, the suits and the ponytails fought to bring Hollywood to the internet.* New York: Arcade.

Goldsmith, J. (2012a, January 17). 'Abduction' in day and date Facebook release. *Variety.* Retrieved from http://www.variety.com/article/VR1118048738

Goldsmith, J. (2012b, January 12). Hulu revenue rises sharply. *Variety.* Retrieved from http://www.variety.com/article/VR1118048537

Goldsmith, J. (2012c, January 4). Netflix stock up on deal talk. *Variety.* Retrieved from http://www.variety.com/article/VR1118048122

Graser, M. (2000, October). The new studios. *Variety, Entertainment and the Digital Economy,* pp. 22, 24, 32.

Graser, M. (2010, July 19). DECE unveils UltraViolet platform. *Variety.* Retrieved from http://www.variety.com

Graser, M. (2011a, July 8). Biz redefines PVOD plan. *Variety.* Retrieved from http://www.variety.com/article/VR1118039574?refcatid=13

Graser, M. (2012a, November 19). Disney shutting its digital locker. Variety. Retrieved from http://www.variety.com/article/VR1118062412/

Graser, M. (2012b, January 6). Hollywood heavyweights head to CES. *Variety.* Retrieved from http://www.variety.com/article/VR1118048271?refcatid=1009

Greeson, M. (2006, April 22). Movie downloads: Why this model won't work. *Billboard, 118,* 4.

Grover, R. (2008, January 7). Apple Closes In on Hollywood. *Business Week.* Retrieved from http://www.businessweek.com/technology/content/jan2008/tc2008016_825385.htm?chan=search

Gubbins, M. (2008, April 18). Film in an 'anytime, any place anywhere' Martini culture. *ScreenDaily.* Retrieved from http://www.Screen Daily.com/Screen DailyArticle.aspx?intStoryID=38291

Gubbins, M. (2012). Digital revolution: Active audiences and fragmented consumption. In D. Iordanova & S. Cunningham (Eds.), *Digital disruption: Cinema moves on-line* (pp. 67–100). St Andrews, UK: St Andrews Film Studies.

Hesseldahl, A. (2008a, March 28). How iTunes subscriptions Could succeed. *Business Week.* Retrieved from http://www.businessweek.com/technology/content/mar2008/tc20080327_462730.htm?campaign_id=technology_AK

Hesseldahl, A. (2008b, March 20). Unlimited tunes from Apple? Not so fast. *Business Week.* Retrieved from http://www.businessweek.com/technology/content/mar2008/tc20080319_503917.htm?campaign_id=technology_AK

Holt, J., & Perren, A. (Eds.). (2009). *Media industries: History, theory, and method.* Hoboken, NJ: Wiley-Blackwell.

Hoskins, C., McFadyen, S., & Finn, A. (1997). *Global television and film: An introduction to the economics of the business.* New York: Oxford University Press.

Iordanova, D., & Cunningham, S. (Eds.). (2012). *Digital disruption: Cinema moves on-line.* St Andrews, UK: St Andrews Film Studies.

Jenkins, H. (2006). *Convergence culture: Where old and new media collide.* New York: New York University Press.

Johnson, G. (2012). *Opening Pandora's digital box: Shifting metaphors and media storage to the Cloud* (Digital media transition series). Los Angeles, CA: Maremel Institute.

Kaplan, A. M., & Haenlein, M. (2011). Two hearts in three-quarter time: How to waltz the social media/viral marketing dance. *Business Horizons, 54*(3), 253–263.

Kaufman, D. (2012, January 11). Turf war puts bucks in flux. *Variety.* Retrieved from http://www.variety.com/article/VR1118048340?refcatid=3866

Lasica, J. D. (2005). *Darknet: Hollywood's war against the digital generation.* Hoboken, NJ: Wiley.

Lawson, S. (2007, March 20). Hollywood and Silicon Valley – Online allies? *InfoWorld.* Retrieved from http://www.infoworld.com

Marich, R. (2013, January 9). "Opportunity locks". *Variety.* Retrieved from http://www.variety.com/article/VR1118064279/

McBride, S. (2006, March 4). Movie debut: Films for sale by download. *The Wall Street Journal,* p. B1. Retrieved from http://www.wsj.com

McPhillips, S., & Merlo, O. (2008). Media convergence and the evolving media business model: An overview of strategic opportunities. *The Marketing Review, 8*(3), 237–253.

Miller, T., Govil, N., McMurria, J., Maxwell, R., & Wang, T. (2005). *Global Hollywood 2* (2nd ed.). London: BFI.

Morris, C. (2011, May 31). Apple confirms iCloud. *Variety.* Retrieved from http://www.variety.com/article/VR1118037790?refcatid=1009

Morris, C. (2012a, January 9). CES: Digital audiences rapidly growing. *Variety.* Retrieved from http://www.variety.com/article/VR1118048357?refcatid=1009

Morris, C. (2012b, January 9). Panasonic, MySpace team for TV experiment. *Variety.* Retrieved from http://www.variety.com/article/VR1118048350?refcatid=1009

Morris, C. (2013, January 9). "Future hue of homevid?" *Variety.* Retrieved from http://www.variety.com/article/VR1118064273/

Mueller, M. (2007, December 14). Marketing: The social revolution. *Screen Daily.* Retrieved from http://www.ScreenDaily.com/ScreenDailyArticle.aspx?intStoryID=36313

Negroponte, N. (1995). *Being digital.* New York: Alfred A. Knopf.

Newsweek. (2010, July 21). How the digital revolution changed our world. Retrieved from http://www.newsweek.com/feature/2010/by-the-numbers-how-the-digital-revolution-changed-our-world.html

Pardo, A. (2009). Hollywood at the digital crossroad: New challenges, new opportunities. In A. Albarran, P. Faustino, & R. Santos (Eds.), *The media as a driver of the information society: Economics, management, policies and technologies* (pp. 67–97). Lisbon: MediaXXI-Formalpress and Universidade Católica Editora.

Pardo, A. (2012). Hollywood and the digital revolution: New Consumers, new markets, new business models. Mise Au Point, Cahiers de l'Association Française des Enseignants Chercheurs en Cinéma et Audiovisuel (AFECCAV), Tribulations numériques du Cinéma et de l'Audiovisuel à l'amorce du 21e siècle (4). Retrieved from http://map.revues.org/246

Pavlik, J. V., & McIntosh, S. (2011). *Converging media: A new introduction to mass communication.* New York: Oxford University Press.

Perren, A. (2010). Business as unusual: Conglomerate-sized challenges for film and television in the digital arena. *Journal of Popular Film and Television, 38*(2), 72–78 (Special issue: Mixed-up confusion: Television in the twenty-first century).

Rose, F. (2000, June). You Oughtta Be in HTML. *Wired,* 8.06. Retrieved from http://www.wired.com/wired/archive/8.06/hollyweb.html

Screen Daily. (2010, May 18). George Lucas Q&A. Retrieved from http://www.ScreenDaily.com/home/interview/george-lucas-qa/5014082.article
Screen Digest. (2007, September). Internet selling of online movies, pp. 269–276.
Screen Digest. (2009, February). Movie download market fragments, p. 44.
Screen Digest. (2010a, April). Online film spending near doubled, p. 105.
Screen Digest. (2010b, October). Online movies market value doubles, p. 292.
Screen Digest. (2011a, January). Subscriptions lead video spending, p. 3.
Screen Digest. (2011b, June). Online movies in international markets, pp. 173–180.
Screen Digest. (2011c, October). US online movie market up 25 per cent, p. 294.
Screen Digest. (2012a, October). Apple's new iphone launch, p. 115.
Screen Digest. (2012b, August). European video market overview 2011, pp. 127–130.
Screen Digest. (2012c, January). Trends in US Entertainment Spending, pp. 15–18.
Stanley, T. L. (2012, January 12). Vegas meets H'wood. *Variety*. Retrieved from http://www.variety.com/article/VR1118048559?refcatid=1009
Stöber, R. (2004). What media evolution is: A theoretical approach to the history of new media. *European Journal of Communication, 19*(4), 483–505.
Swisher, K. (2010, October 9). When you wish upon two (web) stars: CEO Bob Iger talks about the next digital direction for. *All Things Digital*. Retrieved from http://kara.allthingsd.com/20101004/when-you-wish-upon-two-web-stars-ceo-bob-iger-talks-about-the-next-digital-direction-for-disney/
Tapscott, D. (2009). *Grown up digital: How the Net generation is changing your world*. New York: McGraw-Hill.
Tartaglione-Vialatte, N. (2008, October 14). Content remains king, Michael Eisner tells MIPCOM. *Screen Daily*. Retrieved from http://www.ScreenDaily.com/ScreenDailyArticle.aspx?intStoryID=41380
Tryon, C. (2009). *Reinventing cinema: Movies in the age of media convergence*. New Brunswick, NJ: Rutgers University Press.
Tushman, M. L., & Anderson, P. (Eds.). (2004). *Managing strategic innovation and change: A collection of readings*. Oxford: Oxford University Press.
Ulin, J. (2009). *The business of media distribution: Monetizing film, TV, and video content* (2nd ed.). Burlington, MA: Focal.
Vogel, H. L. (2010). *Entertainment industry economics: A guide for financial analysis* (8th ed.). New York: Cambridge University Press.
Vukanovic, Z. (2009). Global paradigm shift: strategic management of new and digital media in new and digital economics. *International Journal on Media Management, 11*(2), 81–90.
Wallenstein, A. (2011a, November 15). Bob Iger joins the board of Apple. *Variety*. Retrieved from http://www.variety.com/article/VR1118046171
Wallenstein, A. (2011b, November 23). Disney, YouTube in movie deal (electronic version). *Variety*. Retrieved November 30, 2011, from http://www.variety.com/article/VR1118046548
Wallenstein, A. (2011c, November 30). Sale may be still be in Hulu's future (electronic version). *Variety*. Retrieved November 30, 2011, http://www.variety.com/article/VR1118046834
Wallenstein, A. (2012, January 10). Tom Hanks hits CES to tubthump Yahoo show. *Variety*. Retrieved from http://www.variety.com/article/VR1118048434?refcatid=1009
Wessels, E. (2011). 'Where were you when the monster hit?' Media convergence, branded security citizenship, and the trans-media phenomenon of *Cloverfield*. *Convergence: The International Journal of Research into New Media Technologies, 17*(1), 69–83.

Distributing Audiovisual Contents in the New Digital Scenario: Multiplatform Strategies of the Main Spanish TV Networks

Enrique Guerrero, Patricia Diego, and Alejandro Pardo

1 Introduction

Technology and entertainment have followed parallel paths along history. The advent of television first, video-recorders later (both VHS and DVD formats), and nowadays the Internet represent some crucial landmarks in this evolution. Each one of these stages brought with them new opportunities for the creators, producers and distributors of movies and TV shows.

In particular, digitization is propelling the entertainment industry towards limits never imagined before. Media companies are trying to face up the challenges of this emerging scenario, were new consumers and new markets are pushing to transform traditional business models into innovative digital ones. As a consequence, the players on this game-board are moving strategically and the whole audiovisual product's value chain will be readjust.

In the case of the TV industry, Internet has become the perfect ally—new concept of home entertainment—as well as threatening enemy—competing for consumers'-viewers' time and budget. 'Convergence' is a fashionable word in this new environment, as the European project for the connected TV—Hybrid Broadcast Broadband Television (Hbb TV)—shows. TV executives are facing the most challenging transformation in the whole history of this industry. This huge turmoil is shaking the traditional and conservative business models (analogical) and new options are emerging with unavoidable impetus (the digital ones). The discussion is open: access vs content, franchises over distribution channel, free vs pay/premium content (or mixed ones), user-generated-content vs professional works, etc.

The multiplatform environment has also transformed the very notion of television: its links to the TV set and particular channels or networks have disappeared. The brand identity of the television product in itself has surpassed that of the

E. Guerrero (✉) • P. Diego • A. Pardo
University of Navarra, Pamplona, Navarra, Spain
e-mail: eguerrero@unav.es

channel on which it is distributed. At the same time, television viewing based on the schedule programmed by the network has likewise been substituted by personalized user access. However, the television channel continues to occupy a prevalent position with respect to other platforms, thanks to its enhanced brand identity, regarded as high-quality or premium products.

In this context, fiction and entertainment contents must be developed since its first stage for a multimedia and interactive consumption in order to be enjoyed by the audience on a wide range of platforms. From this perspective, the keys to develop successful contents are related to its capability to be multiplatform distributed and customized by the consumer—i.e., interactive options, potential to create a prestigious brand and capacity to tell an original 'transmedia' story.

The uncertainty of this new scenario has led the TV networks in some countries to adopt a 'wait-and-see' attitude, compatible with the launching of some online platforms. In the case of Spain, for instance, TV networks have tried to transform themselves into a new model of home and mobile entertainment, with mixed results. This chapter analyses with some detail the multiplatform strategies of the main Spanish TV networks, including the public broadcasting service, Televisión Española (TVE), and the biggest private companies, Mediaset España (Telecinco and Cuatro) and Antena 3 Group (Antena 3 and La Sexta)—these two last operators merged in 2012[1]—together with their relationships with independent producers.

2   Literature Review, Research Questions and Methodology

The literature about the impact of digitalization on the audiovisual industry is abundant. To begin with, some authors have offered a detailed overview of these changes taking into account the whole media and entertainment industries (Pavlik 1996; Hoskins et al. 1997; Ulin 2009; Vogel 2011). Others have focused on the business of television (Forrester 2000; Griffiths 2003; Blumenthal and Goodenough 2006). There are also several authors who have directly approached the relationship between television and new media—Internet in particular (Palmer 2006; Adams 2009; Vukanovic 2009; Doyle 2010; Gunter 2010). In addition, some experts have studied the emergence of a new digital culture and its consequences on media and entertainment consumption (Jenkins 2006; Ytreberg 2009; Pavlik and McIntosh 2011). Finally, this topic has been also addressed from the generic perspective of media economics and/or media management (Vizjak and Ringlstetter 2003; Hoskins et al. 2004; Gershon 2009).

To the previous references, we should add some authors who have specifically studied from different perspectives the convergence of television and new media in the Spanish case, like Cebrián (2003), Medina and Ojer (2011), Guerrero (2008,

---

[1] Until very recently, there were four private commercial TV networks in Spain (Antena 3, Telecinco, Cuatro and La Sexta). In 2010, the Mediaset Group (owner of Telecinco) bought Cuatro. In 2012, the merger between Antena 3 and La Sexta was completed.

2011), Arrojo (2010), Álvarez Monzoncillo and Menor (2010), and Francés et al. (2010) among others.

After analysing the most significant contributions made by this vast array of authors, a number of preliminary research questions arises. To mention some of them: Are the different screens complementary or mutually exclusive? Is every type of product equally appropriate in form and content for every type of screen? How does the multiplatform model affect modes of production and distribution? What would be the best business model to recoup investment? Are audiences prepared to pay to access contents? Does the possibility of shaping a personalized television schedule constitute a threat to the continued existence of linear programming channels? Will interactivity be generalized as such or be retained as an additional option available to users?

This chapter does not pretend by any means to respond to all these questions—among other reasons, because each question may prompt a range of responses. However, a number of observations may be made to shed some light on this crucial period in the history of television and home entertainment.

In particular, this text analyses the most innovative trends in production, distribution and commercialization of multi-platform contents in the case of the main TV networks in Spain, together with their relationships with independent producers. In this sense, we are presenting a comparative analysis of their different multiplatform strategies following a two-step methodology: first, a descriptive study of their respective websites, online players and apps (mobile, television and computer); second, this comparative analysis is completed with questionnaires answered by the multimedia managers of these networks, together with some personal interviews.

Before going in depth with the analysis of the multiplatform strategies of the main Spanish TV networks, it is necessary to describe with some detail the transformation of television as medium and as business, propelled by the digital revolution and, more particularly, by its marriage with Internet.

3 The Changing Pattern of 'Television': From the TV Set to the Multiplatform Experience

3.1 'The Multiplatform Ecosystem': When Internet Meets the TV

The notion of multiplatform television involves nothing other than the distribution of contents through a variety of devices. However, the simplicity of this statement occludes the complexity of what it implies for both the television industry and the audience. Rather than replacing the experience of watching television in one's living-room, the possibility of watching such contents on other devices enriches the experience (Adams 2009, p. 3). As far back as 1995, experts such as Nicholas Negroponte had begun to speak of the gradual replacement of *prime time* with *my time*, the trend among users to shape a personalized schedule of contents by means of on-demand television that is available at any time, anywhere (*time-shifting* and *place-shifting*) (Negroponte 1995, p. 172).

In addition, another common viewing habit discloses the existence of the multitasking viewer (Tapscott 2009; Arrojo 2010) or *double dipper* (Gunter 2010). That is, users who watch television and surf the Internet, commenting on or sharing contents via social networking sites at the same time. For example, according to the 2010 Nielsen figures (2010), 13 % of viewers watching the Oscars in that year were also online. Furthermore, in 2011, 70 % of smartphone and tablet owners confirmed that they used these devices at the same time they were watching television (Nielsen 2011).

In Spain, according to the Televidente 2.0 study (2010), 35 % of viewers acknowledge having commented on television contents via social networking sites during the broadcast often or from time to time. The latter figure rose to 50 % when viewers were consulted regarding comments made about entertainment shows, series and films, outside the scheduled broadcast time. That trending topics on social networks like Twitter during prime time are directly related to prime time television broadcasts should come as no surprise; nor, likewise, the emergence of television-specific social networking sites such as Miso. In fact, in 2010, almost 56 % of Spanish Internet users had at least one active profile in a social network (ONTSI 2011). In the end, *my time* and prime time would appear to overlap, revealing a symbiotic relationship between TV and the Internet through which the role of each medium is mutually reinforced, especially when young audiences are involved.

A reading of the user ratings suggests that TV and the Internet are complementary as platforms. However, this comparison may be rendered obsolete when convergence between the two media is complete thanks to the development of projects such as Hbb TV, in which television is connected to the Internet. For example, in Spain, Telefónica, Radio Televisión Española (RTVE) and Mediaset signed an agreement in order to test interactive contents (Alonso 2011).

Despite growing consumption of online contents, the audience figures for conventional television, rather than falling, have likewise risen to a record average of 192 min per person per day in 2009 globally (Létang 2010). In Europe, in spite of some ups and downs, the TV consumption keeps being high, especially in some countries like Italy and Spain (Fig. 1).

In relation to the issue of whether or not digital media are siphoning viewers away from television, Gunter (2010, p. XIII) holds that the Internet plays a twofold role: on the one hand, it competes with television in terms of available user time; on the other, however, it also functions as an alternative platform for the distribution of television contents. Gunter argues that the question of whether or not the Internet and television are in direct competition is preceded by other considerations: Do both media meet the same needs? And that being the case, how successfully do they do so? (Gunter 2010, p. 67). Rather than coming to a firm conclusion in this regard, Gunter reflects on the issue, reasoning that the Internet cannot be regarded merely as a competitor; rather, it enriches other media, offering a new platform by means of which the audience may be engaged (Gunter 2010, pp. 31–33). As discussed in

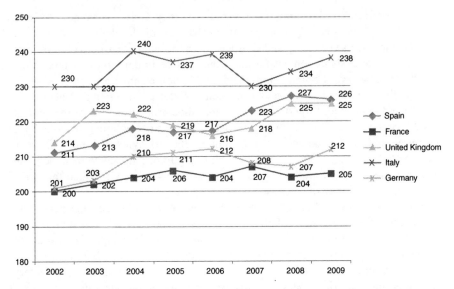

Fig. 1 TV consumption in the main European markets (2002–2009). *Source*: 2010 Yearbook issued by the European Audiovisual Observatory using data from Eurodata TV Worldwide. Figures in minutes

greater detail below, this is the position adopted by the main Spanish television operators. Given the difficulties involved in trying to compete with as global, powerful and flexible a medium as the Internet, such companies have opted to distribute their contents via online platforms.

3.2 Content Distribution Strategies

Another key question relating to the challenges facing the audiovisual industry in the context of emerging technologies may be raised in this regard: What kinds of content are to be distributed? The focus here is on professionally produced contents, the real dynamo of digital business, although the importance of 'user generated content' should not thereby be overlooked. The best example is YouTube, a video-sharing website focused on amateur content since its beginning, which is increasingly offering more professional premium content, such as its movie-rental service (Halliday 2011).

Doyle (2010, p. 433) argues that a television operator may avail of the following options in designing a multiplatform strategy:
(a) Distribute the contents produced for conventional television broadcasting on other platforms.
(b) Alter and adapt existing contents to the defining features of other platforms, adding new 'layers' that update and enrich them.
(c) Create original contents for online platforms to complement the programming range on offer via linear television channels.

These options are not mutually exclusive: they may be combined in a multiplatform strategy. Nevertheless, given that one of the defining features of digital content is its versatility and ability to cross the boundaries between different media, the debate about content-format should not be limited to the nature of the distribution platform. Content-format and distribution channel are rendered separate by digitalization (Vizjak and Ringlstetter 2003, p. 5). Digital contents are flexible and malleable: 'liquid'. Hence, format should be a function of the content as such, and not bound up with any particular platform. A number of terms have been used to describe such contents, including '360º' (Doyle 2010, pp. 432–433), 'transmedia' (Jenkins 2006, p. 93) and 'multiplatform'; however their defining characteristic is that, from the very beginning, they have been designed for distribution on a wide range of screens.

Before going any further, a more refined account of two of these concepts should be provided: the terms 'multiplatform' and 'transmedia' are not synonymous. As defined above, the former refers only to the distribution of contents via a variety of media. In contrast, transmedia connotes further development in relation to production: the content is designed to be broadcast on a range of mutual-complementary platforms, thus offering users an enhanced and interactive viewing experience. Bolin (2010, p. 82) draws a distinction between multiplatform productions and the narration of transmedia stories. To his mind, all transmedia stories are multiplatform because they involve the production of contents that enrich storytelling on all screens. On the other hand, not all multiplatform projects are transmedia: the distribution of contents via a number of different media need not in itself amount to a further contribution to the narrative process as such.

Clearly, not only is the nature of such contents and the way they are viewed conditioned by the design of a multiplatform operation and distribution strategy. Its influence also extends to the process of content production itself. As Doyle (2010, pp. 339–340) has pointed out, multiplatform distribution involves multiple production—with the exception of simulcasting. In other words, the creation of a range of contents under a single heading or brand, which enrich each another and are amenable to delivery on a variety of screens. Thus, given that it involves a greater number of contents, multiplatform production may be described as more expensive in absolute terms. However, in relative terms, the cost-benefit ratio is lower: by increasing the number of distribution channels, risks are diversified, a greater operating potential is generated and the commercial life of the product is extended via market strategies such as 'the long tail' (Anderson 2006, p. 10). In short, given the synergies in the production and distribution processes, a small additional investment yields a much more 'commercialisable' audiovisual product. For instance, the cost of acquisition rights for a particular format would be much more appealing if such rights encompassed more platforms, rather than being limited to a single medium (Vizjak and Ringlstetter 2003, pp. 8–9).

3.3 Looking for the Right Business Model

The next question that arises in this regard is how the extra cost of multiplatform production and multi-channel content distribution may be recouped. The sustainability of this model depends on the ability to transform the higher audience figures engaged via online media into greater financial income (Doyle 2010). Despite successful audience figures for different kinds of content, pioneering initiatives such as YouTube, which draws on user generated content, and Hulu, which focuses on professionally produced content, have thus far largely failed to establish a profitable business model (Artero 2010, p. 121). Moreover, the market system based on 'the long tail' strategy has yet to produce significant financial yields.

The issue of the influence of the multiplatform audiovisual model on production is inextricably bound up with the question of the business models that may enable a recouping of the costs involved. A key aspect of the design of any business model is the identification of revenue streams. In reality, the only viable options are as follows:

1. Advertising
2. A pay-per-view system: subscription to a service for a period of time or payment for specific contents (rental or purchase)
3. Subsidisation

Only the first two options—advertising or payment—are of any real interest from a commercial point of view. In relation to advertising, the model conforms to the established pattern: the audience views an audiovisual product punctuated with advertisements, which may be video commercials or superimposed on other images. However, it does have some added value that is not available in the traditional model: advertising may be interactive on the Internet and, to a certain extent, personalized to individual taste. In addition, branded entertainment is becoming more and more common as a means to integrate advertising messages within audiovisual contents as such: the advertiser funds the production of content in which its brand plays a starring role, forming a key part of the story being told (Arrojo 2010).

While it may be true to say that the online environment promises great potential in relation to the pay-per-view model, it is no less true that significant obstacles remain to be overcome. The Internet has fostered the development of free-access culture, a "cybernetic utopia of completely free access" (Álvarez Monzoncillo and Menor 2010). A great many users feel that by paying to access the Internet they have earned the right to enjoy all available contents for free. This scheme of things has been reinforced by the introduction of unpopular legal measures such as the digital levy, as well as the failure of audiovisual companies to address the massive boom in video contents on the Internet from the very beginning, by making their contents freely available online with advertising or at attractive prices, in case such initiatives would damage the traditional business model. For example, the homepages of television channels in Spain only began to function as multimedia portals in the 2007–2008 season, but without offering all their contents. Other

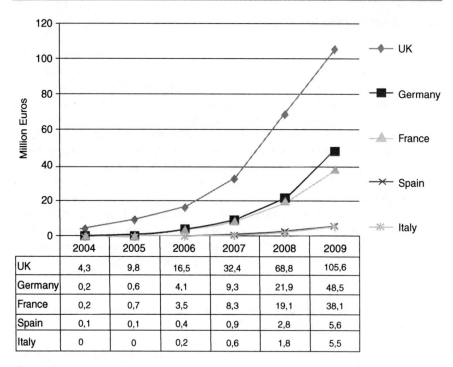

Fig. 2 Revenue from online TV in the main European markets (2004–2009). *Source*: 2010 Yearbook issued by the European Audiovisual Observatory using data from *Screen Digest*. Income from the main business models is included: digital renting and sales, subscriptions and advertising

barriers to pay models are defensive and non-creative systems such as DRM (Digital Rights Management) and 'geoblocking', making legal products less attractive and difficult to access.

The online business results generated by the audiovisual sector in Europe are very revealing in this regard, disclosing a very low rate of implementation of the pay-per-view model as Fig. 2 shows.

Although mobile television is at an early stage in its evolution throughout Europe, a steady growth in subscribers may be observed year-on-year, with notable exceptions such as Italy (see Fig. 3).

A shift from offering linear programming channels and video clips to *catch-up TV* services comprising long-running on-demand contents is the prevalent trend among mobile television services in most European countries. Nevertheless, the consolidation of a particular business model remains remote, as does the threshold of profitability (Gaten 2010, p. 227).

No discussion of business models can be limited to the nature of audiovisual content in itself. The core of the question may not lie in the purchase or rental of such contents; rather, the key may consist in offering related added-value services and in managing the business of content access (Leonhard 2010, p. 8). Contents can

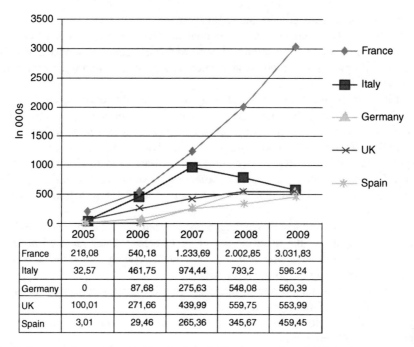

Fig. 3 Payments for mobile television in the main European markets (2005–2009). *Source*: 2010 Yearbook issued by the European Audiovisual Observatory using data from *Screen Digest*. Figures in thousands

be copied; access cannot. A number of researchers have described an economy of access and connectivity (Cerezo 2010), by which they mean access to a range of contents that is always available in *cloud content* (an image of the Internet), as distinct from physical download and storage. The number of content access-points has increased due to technological progress (Ulin 2009, pp. 222–224), and the more numerous such access-points, the more opportunities for doing business emerge. The economy of access is best illustrated by the boom in applications for mobile devices and by the business model most closely associated with it: *freemium*. Furthermore, when connected television (Hybrid TV) becomes popular, the app business will rise sharply thanks to the interactive TV set.

According to figures published by *Screen Digest*, 6,700 million applications were downloaded in 2010, of which 92 % were free of charge. Apple is the market leader by far: its Appstore for iPhone, iPod Touch and iPad—launched in July 2008—processed 4,900 million applications and generated more than 1,000 million of euros in 2010 (Kent 2010, p. 369). Although a stable business model has not yet been established, free app downloads have begun to generate significant amounts of revenue. The *freemium* (free + premium) model may account for this development. In general terms, *freemium* involves the free download of an application, a content access-point or service portal, so as to generate real financial returns through it later. A free application may yield real income in a number of different ways:

1. By advertising bundled with the application.
2. By offering the purchase of premium contents/services via the application.
3. By providing a free application that comprises basic contents/services, with the option of upgrading to more sophisticated, pay-per-view premium contents and services.

At its most basic, therefore, the strategy underlying this business model is the age-old craft of baiting the hook: providing free contents/services to attract a certain number of users, and then selling other contents/services and/or incorporating advertising. Thus, the "payment threshold" involved in business strategies that require an initial outlay may be overcome. By contrast, user loyalty is first earned in the *freemium* model, and only thereafter may revenue be generated. In other words, interaction with audience precedes any financial transaction (Leonhard 2010, p. 6).

The approach outlined above has been adopted by most of the television operators in Spain, as discussed in greater detail below. The audience may avail of free applications that enable live and on-demand viewing so that operators may achieve the following purposes (Kent 2010, p. 371):

- To strengthen the relationship with the audience by offering contents that may be accessed at any time, from anywhere.
- To establish a closer relationship with the audience via interactive services relating to TV programs.
- To improve brand-identity by producing attractive applications.
- To increase audience ratings and participation in ways that would be impossible on other platforms.
- To generate additional revenue via download payments, subscription costs, service packages and advertising.

The discussion above makes plain that digital technology and the Internet have revolutionized the audiovisual industry, in general, and the television sector, in particular. This revolution has been so dramatic that changes have been registered at every level: production, distribution, programming, business model, content, consumer habits, audience ratings, etc.

3.4 Setting Up Multiplatform Strategies

The following may be listed among the consequences brought about by digitalisation and the convergence of television and the Internet: the fragmentation of the programming range on offer; the proliferation of multiplatform contents and transmedia; the emergence of a more active audience; and a more personalized consumption of audiovisual products.

The multiplatform context has also transformed the very notion of television: its links to the television set and particular channels or networks have been broken. The brand identity of the television product in itself has begun to eclipse that of the channel on which it is distributed. User loyalty is to the content, not the channel. At the same time, television viewing based on the schedule programmed by the network has likewise lost ground to personalized user access, except for major live television broadcasts such as important sporting events.

However, the television channel continues to occupy a prevalent position with respect to other platforms; contents offered under its logo are enhanced by the brand identity, regarded as high-quality or premium products. The channel's brand image and contents are rolled out on the other platforms (Englert and Bürger 2003, p. 178), thus transferring the audience and retaining its loyalty. The multiplatform approach to viewer transfer and loyalty mirrors the programming strategy followed in conventional television, as described by Raymond Williams in the 'flow theory' (1974, p. 177). The difference lies in the fact that the flow of contents distributed as part of shared brand occurs across a range of platforms, rather than over a single television schedule.

In general, there are only two real options when a television network sets out a strategy to build its brand: to build a new brand or to expand the existing one (Ulin 2009, pp. 39–40). Thus, just as television networks often opt to create new contents under new brands linked to their main channel, so the network brand is linked to new platforms such as the Internet in order to take advantage of emerging synergies and facilitate the transition of an already loyal audience.

4   The Spanish Case: Multiplatform Strategies of the Main TV Networks

The Spanish digital content industry billed more than 9,000 million euros in 2010, 44 % of it coming from the audiovisual sector (ONTSI 2011). According to the Spanish National Institute of Statistics (INE), that year, 42.2 % of Internet users in Spain between the ages of 16 and 74 log on to the web to watch television or listen to the radio. This figure is 53 % for users between the ages of 16 and 24, which indicates that younger users are more likely to access audiovisual contents online (INE 2010). According to information supplied by Antena 3, at the beginning of 2011, the profile of the average user accessing the Internet to view television contents may be summarized as follows: young or young-adult, between 25 and 35 years old, members of the middle or upper-middle classes. In spite of growing consumption of online contents, the audience figures for conventional television, rather than falling, have likewise risen to an average of 234 min per person per day in 2010 (Fig. 4), reaching a new record in 2012 with 246 min.

A shared assumption among television operators in Spain is that the multiplication of distribution platforms will tend to reinforce brand identity. According to the Deputy Director of Antena 3 Multimedia, the emergence of new distribution modes does not in any way weaken or dissipate the brand; rather, it impacts "very positively" on brand identity; and he observed that "the creation of the 3.0 brand to represent Antena 3's visibility on every platform has significantly enhanced our image" (Personal Interview, Madrid, 11/02/2011). Similarly, the executive in charge of Telecinco.es avers that the overall purpose of multiplatform strategy is to "enrich" brand image and provide the network with "added value". She also acknowledges

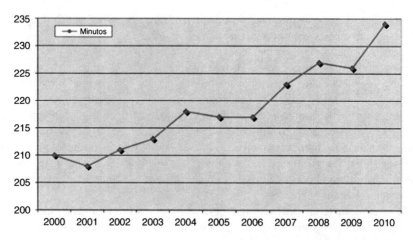

Fig. 4 Growth in TV consumption in Spain (2000–2010). *Source*: Kantar Media, SGAE and Barlovento Comunicación

that "there is a new way of watching TV", and television groups and their websites "should not be left out of this" (Personal Interview, Madrid, 11/02/2011).

However, this Antena 3 executive noted that the objective during the initial stages of the multiplatform strategy at his company was "to create a brand rather than generate revenue, whereas nowadays the main goal is to make money" (Personal Interview, Madrid, 11/02/2011). Television networks already regard new platforms such as the Internet as real business prospects, not merely as space in which a certain level of visibility is required. Although the early motivation for television networks to move onto the Internet may have been defensive (Doyle 2010), to prevent third parties illegally uploading their contents and thus depriving the channel of profits, the strategy soon became more proactive. Indeed, a further form of motivation also underlay this shift: to establish—or maintain—audience loyalty across all media, creating a sense of community that might later be monetized.

Nevertheless, despite the progress in this regard, networks are still very aware of the threat of illegal downloads. For the Antena 3 representative, "fighting illegal viewing is very important. The channel has to give the audience a simple, quick and accessible content, in order to avoid the audience watching it in other illegal websites" (Personal Interview, Madrid, 11/02/2011).

Survey responses completed by the main operators disclose that all of them regard the multiplatform distribution of contents as either significant or very significant. Figure 5 below presents the strategy being pursued by each network in the beginnings of 2012.[2]

---

[2] During the rest of the year 2012, more changes transformed the multiplatform scene, but they are not included in this chapter because occurred after the time of closing these lines.

	TVE	Mediaset (Mitele)	Antena 3	La Sexta (On)
Free Contents	•	•	•	•
Pay Contents		•	•	
Advertising		•	•	•
Live Broadcasting	•	•	•	•
TV on Demand / Catch Up TV	•	•	•	•
In-House Produced Content	•	•	•	•
Acquired Contents	•	•	•	•
Fiction Series	•	•	•	•
Entertainment TV Shows	•	•	•	•
Exclusive Online Content		•	•	
Social Networking	•	•	•	•
Interactive Services	•	•	•	•
Apps for Mobile Devices	•		•	•

Fig. 5 Mutiplatform strategies of the main television networks in Spain in the beginnings of 2012. *Source*: Own elaboration

4.1 Online Strategies

All the online multi-platform players mentioned here—RTVE a la carta, Mitele (result of the merging of Telecinco a la carta and Play Cuatro, both of them managed by Mediaset España), Antena 3 and La Sexta On (as mentioned before, these two networks merged in 2012, therefore their online players joint together in just one, named Modo Salón) -offer free contents made by foreign production companies—generally fiction series, but also some entertainment TV shows—the range is relatively limited because the operator rarely owns the distribution rights across all platforms (Guerrero 2011a, p. 94). For instance, in the case of La Sexta On—previously called Misexta TV—only some episodes are available online given that the channel does not have permanent distribution rights to such products. Finally, because they are generally based on (internal or external) in-house production formulae, entertainment programs are offered whole or in sections, and for unlimited periods of time.

In all cases, too, contents are accessible via streaming, in both live broadcast and *catch-up TV* modes. There are not download options similar to those allowed by the BBC iPlayer. The linear programming schedule broadcast via the conventional television signal is available live, such as La 1, the 24 Horas channel and Teledeporte from TVE. Mitele (Mediaset), Antena 3 and La Sexta do not offer 24-h online programming; rather, certain time-slots are broadcast live, either because of limited on-air commercial rights to outsourced contents or because agreements have not been reached with production companies. If the channel's complete programming range cannot be provided, the standard approach is to offer entertainment and news programs live. The treatment of fiction contents is different, with notable exceptions such as *Aída* (Telecinco) on Mitele, although the live provision of such products might be expected to rise in future. Moreover, 'geoblocking' (Palmer 2006) is now a common industry practice, whereby only some of the contents available online may be accessed from outside Spain, for example.

Most of the on-demand television products available are contents that have already been broadcast on conventional television. In general, episodes are posted in the online player immediately after on-air broadcast. Most of such contents are in-house productions. Outsourced contents are not yet commercialized in a global way. This is especially true of the most popular products, productions made in Hollywood, an industry player that has been rocked to its foundations by the digital revolution (Pardo 2009, p. 68). The explanation for this situation is that the negotiation of rights to on-air television broadcasts is based on sales in local markets and windows. International distribution is also of vital importance to the major American studios, which have opted to risk the illegal online consumption of their products rather than launch a global online business model that would enable legal access to their contents. Although this strategy may generate some additional income, it may also undermine the even more lucrative market for international rights (Guerrero 2008, p. 307; Artero 2010, p. 121).

Besides, when the major Hollywood production companies agree to sell Internet broadcasting rights to TV networks, they require a minimum guarantee, regardless of whether they win or lose money through online distribution. Therefore the commercialization of foreign contents online is still not profitable, and it is only feasible in the case of a "marketing strategy", according to Antena 3 Multimedia Deputy Director (Personal Interview, Madrid, 11/02/2011).

Thus, almost all of the contents available online are in-house productions, and television networks tend to see the Internet as another mode of distribution/commercialisation, Telecinco.es Supervisor explains that "Telecinco.es offers for free almost all its whole contents, fiction series and entertainment programs, in addition to the live broadcast of some of them". Despite this fact, she stresses that "the web is not simply a reflection of what is offered on TV", but another channel of the media group (Personal Interview, Madrid, 11/02/2011). However, few audiovisual contents have been produced specifically for online broadcast: Telecinco's series *Becarios* and program *Adopta un famoso*, which was later switched to La Siete, and Antena 3's *El Sótano* (webseries) are examples in this regard. These contents are available to users for free.

Adopta un famoso was not the first audiovisual product to originate on the Internet before transferring later to the conventional television programming schedule; *Qué vida más triste* on La Sexta set an interesting precedent (Diego and Herrero 2010, pp. 328, 333–334). This phenomenon suggests another area of potential afforded by the Internet: the online environment may function as a test-site where contents made to meet lower (web-based) production standards may later be remade with higher production values for on-air television broadcast. Hence, the objective is to form a fan club around the online product and, once it has been established, to transfer such audience loyalty to the conventional television channel. This approach has proven especially effective with young audiences, and is a strategy that is frequently implemented by such channels as MTV (Doyle 2010, p. 436).

Another increasingly common practice is to produce content linked to a television brand. For instance, filming the making of a show, promotional events reports and live video-chats with actors and presenters. Then these videoclips, produced exclusively for new platforms, are offered online and on mobile devices. According to the Antena 3 Multimedia representative "is trying to produce more content for the web such as making of, interviews and reports about social events related to Antena 3's TV shows" (Personal Interview, Madrid, 11/02/2011).

In the same direction, the responsible of Telecinco.es acknowledges that "[our website], although it's based on the TV programming, is much more than a network website. We produce our own content, we don't just offer videos previously aired on TV. For example, we invite the audience to participate in surveys and in interactive games. Besides, these initiatives for the web influence the content broadcast on TV and its production" (Personal Interview, Madrid, 11/02/2011).

In any case, as recognized by the Antena 3 Multimedia executive, "eighty percent of our online success is due to the content produced for television. Most of our revenues are generated by the viewing of whole episodes, where advertisers want to be and what attracts a larger number of users. However, given that the audience comes to our web to watch an episode, for instance *Los protegidos*, we also try to hook them up with online exclusive contents. This is the strategy, because it's very difficult to attract users only with extra TV contents produced by the multimedia division" (Personal Interview, Madrid, 11/02/2011).

With regard to the business model involved, the main revenue stream is advertising, which is used on all platforms except TVE, the public service operator. This point is confirmed by the Antena 3 executive, who highlights that revenues mainly come from advertising. "We try to reach the maximum audience possible to offer it to advertisers. We have alternative and complementary revenue sources such as online games and premium previews of our TV shows, but our main business model is based on advertising" (Personal Interview, Madrid, 11/02/2011).

The online business results generated by the audiovisual sector in Spain are very revealing, disclosing a very low rate of implementation of the pay-per-view model: in 2009, 99 % of income generated by online television came from advertising, as compared with 1 % from the pay-per-view strategy. Of the total advertising revenue available, 41.4 % was secured by the major television operators (Bloowfield 2010, p. 204). These figures do not compare well with equivalent outcomes in other European countries as seen in Fig. 2.

Because they can draw on extensive catalogues of audiovisual products and have established agreements regarding access to premium contents, the online television market in Spain is dominated by the main national television networks: TVE, Mediaset (mainly Telecinco and Cuatro) and Antena 3 (including La Sexta and other minor channels). Moreover, these groups also benefit from stable commercial relationships with leading advertisers. Although all these operators do offer a significant proportion of their contents online and on-demand, the initial delay in implementing this approach has significantly hampered the development of the multiplatform television model in Spain (Bloowfield 2010, p. 204).

In 2012, the pay-per-view model appeared to be very limited. Users were encouraged to purchase via text messages or sales calls, although there was a more integrated approach to such promotion. For instance, Antena 3 enabled viewers to purchase contents using PayPal. That year only Mediaset and Antena 3 had pay-per-view services to watch premium contents. Besides, Antena 3 offered a subscription service called *Modo Salón premium* to access without restrictions to a wide catalogue of more than 1,000 episodes of in-house produced TV fiction series.

In fact, contents were offered through pay model services for the following main reasons: users may have pay-per-view access to episodes of Spanish-made fiction series prior to broadcast on the television channel (premier); to added-value versions of such episodes following broadcast (in HD format, for instance, without commercial breaks); to the original language version in the case of acquired fiction series; or finally to have access to a wide library of contents. In short, therefore, payment is due for privileged access to audiovisual contents before they are broadcast, for a better viewing experience or for unlimited access.

This practice also has implications in the production process; for example, in contracts between networks and producers. The Antena 3 Multimedia Deputy Director explains that "a few time ago, contracts said that every episode could be in the network even on the same day it was released. However, now, Antena 3 has a new business line offering online premieres, so we need to receive episodes 48 hours in advance" (Personal Interview, Madrid, 11/02/2011).

4.2 Mobile TV and Apps

Television operators may avail themselves of several options in relation to the provision of audiovisual contents on mobile platforms. The first one is to develop and push de Digital Terrestrial Television (DTT)—broadcasting. Due to its technical and legal complexity, another alternative is distributing contents via the mobile network through agreements with telecommunication companies—'unicasting'. However, the easiest way is the online mobile television. In this case, there are two possibilities: adapting online players to the distinctive features of mobile devices such as smartphones and tablets, thus enabling access via the Internet and the web (wep-apps); or to design applications specifically for such platforms (Guerrero 2011b, pp. 247–248).

With the exception of Mediaset, all the television operators discussed here offer applications for mobile devices at the beginning of 2012 (later this year, Mediaset launched a mobile application for Mitele, its online player, with the same features that the ones described here). In all cases, the application is free to the user and functions as an access-point to contents produced for the television channel and online media player. Thus far, no content has been produced specifically for viewing on mobile devices, nor is access to independently-produced contents generally available. According to the Antena 3 Multimedia executive, "right now, what we do for mobile devices is the same that we do for the Internet" (Personal Interview, Madrid, 11/02/2011).

The content is available via on-demand streaming, by complete episode or edited in parts to facilitate the viewing experience. In addition to on-demand contents, a number of channels broadcast by the public service operator TVE, including La 1, the 24 Horas channel and Teledeporte, are available live and 24 h a day, including major sporting events. When limited commercial rights preclude the provision of some programs, as is often the case with the applications offered by private television networks, users may access a pared-down schedule of news and in-house entertainment programs.

TVE's, Antena 3's and La Sexta's apps work as mobile online players (La Sexta's app was discontinued after the merger with Antena 3 in 2012). In addition to the audiovisual contents themselves, applications often include added-value services such as breaking news alerts, games and promotional materials. A significant example in this context is Clan TVE, the children's channel broadcast by TVE, which offers educational contents as well as games, including cartoon series in English. In general, applications are not designed for particular programs; rather, they are devised for the television channel or network as a whole.

Given that they are supplied free of charge, the main revenue stream is advertising which is folded into the application or contents—TVE is an exception in this regard. A former Telecinco's application was more closely focused on the pay-per-view model. The application was provided free together with a limited number of contents, which function as both samples and 'hooks'. The goal was to encourage to users to buy additional contents via the application. Telecinco also offered a rental service for its in-house fiction series, enabling viewers to access episodes or whole seasons for a period of 60 days. There was a cost increase if the product selected had not yet been broadcast on the conventional television channel. Prices varied according to the kind of contents and their date of production. Nevertheless, this strategy failed and the app was discontinued in 2010.

Mobile TV applications, besides function as a window to access a world of contents and interactive services related to television brands, also work as a small second screen that complements and enriches the TV viewing experience in a bigger one—second screen phenomenon (Tsekleves et al. 2011). For instance, Ant 3.0 is a app that offers live interactive contents related to those being broadcast at he same time on TV. Moreover, similar applications will be available on the television set once the convergence process ends and the connected TV arrives to almost every living-room.

4.3 TV and Social Media

In like of the need to create user communities and to build audience loyalty across all available platforms, all the television networks discussed here have established a certain level of visibility on social networking sites such as Facebook and Twitter, targeting younger viewers, in particular. Furthermore, blogs are also used to give more relevance to contents. Unlike the strategy adopted in relation to mobile applications in the Spanish TV market—most of the apps are channel based instead of content based, TV shows, presenters, actors and characters may have profiles on such social networks, in addition to the television group and channels. Besides, specialized social networking sites on TV, such as Miso or Qvemos, are getting more popular.

Moreover, the versatility of these means of social interaction enables their inclusion in online multi-platform players and mobile applications; thus, rather than functioning as separate platforms as such, they enrich and complement existing ones. According to the Telecinco.es Supervisor, "it is amazing the user response to contents through social networks in real-time. And, at the same time, this feedback is used to generate new content for the TV show" (Personal Interview, Madrid, 11/02/2011). This assertion implies that audience participation has a direct impact on content. This data is confirmed by the questionnaire answered by the main Spanish television networks, whose managers recognize that users' feedback influence the production process. In this sense, the passive audience has become an active group of users.

It may be concluded, therefore, that the promotion of interactivity, facilitating relationships with and among fans, and between producers, actors, hosts and those fans, is a key component of any multiplatform strategy and in the development of transmedia narratives. Besides, social networking sites function as very important tools with regard to viral videos and marketing strategies, and even more to measure audience engagement—the audience is measured in positive or negative tweets.

5 Adapting Multiplatform Contents

In light of the industry context outlined above, television is now one more among a number of content-distribution channels, although it remains the main medium by which large audiences may be reached, with add-on activity effected via the Internet and mobile devices. However, any entertainment format that is designed ambitiously to become a killer format must escape the confines of the programming schedule and expand across all available media. A killer format is an audiovisual product capable of generating high viewer ratings and committed audience loyalty, spreading its success across the programming schedule and other commercialization platforms (GECA 2004, pp. 81–82).

The contents with most potential in this new business are transversal—that is, they supersede the boundaries of television as a medium and may be developed, from the very beginning, on all media platforms in parallel yet independent ways.

The challenge goes beyond simply adapting contents to the requirements of different screens or devising integrated promotion campaigns; rather, the goal is to conceptualize multimedia formats as such with the market strength needed to build a brand and win viewer loyalty. Such formats give rise to a range of spin-off and interconnected products, which may still function independently of one another, becoming a franchise.

The greater the users' engagement with different platforms (television, the Internet, online games, social networks, merchandising, mobile apps, etc.), the more committed their participation in the narrative of the television series or game show, although multiplatform engagement need not be an indispensable requirement of viewing as such. Thus, television programmes no longer come with an inbuilt expiry date based on a single broadcast; rather, they are long-life products (Sánchez-Tabernero 2008, p. 274), extra-televisual experiences in which the user may play a key part, whose commercial value and durability depends on their inherent quality and capacity to foster audience loyalty (Guerrero 2008, pp. 307–308).

5.1 TV Shows

Over the course of the last decade, the reality game-show multiplatform format has played a pioneering role in this regard (Ytreberg 2009, p. 470). The genre first appeared on Spanish television in 2000 (*Big Brother* on Telecinco), sparking some controversy. However, at the same time, its introduction brought about significant changes in terms of production, distribution and audience participation. Also notable in this context are talent-spotting programs such as *Operación Triunfo*, following the same formula as international formats like *Pop Idol*, which are designed to encourage viewer participation and to be commercialized via a multimedia strategy (Cebrián Herreros 2003).

Given that contents must be developed for all available screens, separately for each or adaptable to all, a multiplatform program requires greater effort in production terms. For instance, in reality game-shows, production may run 24 h a day. The CEO of Telecinco when *Big Brother* was first broadcast summed up the impact of the format as follows: "For the very first time, a program can be broadcast on a theme-based channel on pay-per-view television, on an Internet website, on free-to-air television, in a magazine show or debate program. This type of program can avail of many more windows than other formats" (Saló 2003, p. 107).

The use of a range of different platforms in the development of a coherent, multimedia, interactive narrative also has a significant bearing on scriptwriting: to a certain extent, the dramatic structure of the script mirrors that of a serialized fiction program. Multimedia entertainment formats are marked by such distinctive features of fiction contents as plots, characters, conflicts, cliffhangers, dramatic catalysts, etc. The coherence of such a diverse audiovisual product may be effected by building a brand identity capable of generating audience loyalty, ultimately acquiring value in itself that may be further commercialized through merchandizing, for example, and used to tap new revenue streams through royalties. Moreover, a recognizable brand identity facilitates user migration from one platform to another, whereby script devices may function as "junction points" that encourage the audience to switch medium so as to access new contents (Ytreberg 2009, pp. 472, 479).

Multiplatform formats require very detailed strategy design in terms of content programming and distribution so as to ensure both that contents on the same platform are not competing with one another and that the range on offer can compete successfully with company rivals. The main objective of multimedia contents management is to generate audience loyalty on all platforms, thus enabling intensive commercialization to facilitate profitability. Therefore, the content distribution strategy is very closely bound up with a business model that can combine the provision of free contents funded by advertising with the pay-per-view approach, as the distinctive features of different media may require.

Interactivity plays a key role in multiplatform formats, especially in shows which are broadcast live and presented as major television events so as to capture a large audience share. Interactivity reinforces both the sense of immediacy and viewer commitment to the content, and may even have an influence on narrative development. However, interactive features are not limited to live broadcasts; they may also be availed of in contents pre-recorded for later broadcast, albeit produced to mirror a live event (Ytreberg 2009, p. 478). The main forms of interactivity include online and telephone contributions (in the case of pre-recorded programs, no reference is made to information available at the time of broadcast), as well as online games linked to the content of the format and social networking sites, which enable ongoing contact with the audience and function as a very useful tool in the creation of user communities and fan clubs.

An illustrative example in this regard is the game show *Atrapa un millón*, which is based on the Endemol format *One Million Drop*, produced in Spain by Gestmusic and broadcast on Antena 3 in 2011: an online game runs in parallel with the television broadcast. Given this real-time play option, viewers may watch the program and take part at the same time, as though they too were contestants, although they cannot win the prize. In addition to this interactive game, the original version of the program on Channel 4 in the UK, which was broadcast live, unlike its pre-recorded Spanish counterpart, tapped the potential of social networks such as Facebook and Twitter to make contact with future contestants as part of the casting process.

5.2 TV Series

In the case of TV series, Spanish TV networks post the episodes on line after their broadcast and make pay-per-view showings. They also create new contents and cross-platform events related with the series, in order to expand their commercial cycle and strengthen ties with loyal audiences (fandom). This strategy has been developed, for instance, by Globomedia, one of the leader independent production companies in Spain. Among its most famous multiplatform series are *El internado* (2007–2010) and *El barco* (2011–) produced for Antena 3; and *Aguila Roja* (2009–) for TVE1.

As in the case of the entertainment formats, the multiplatform development of a TV series is designed by the TV network and the production company from the very beginning and includes online games, books, musical groups, contests for fans, video-chats with characters, characters' profiles in social networks (Facebook or Tuenti) and *twitsodes* (mini-episodes for Twitter). Their goals are to attract young audiences, increment advertising income and create a strong brand related with the series (franchise). For example, the popularity of *Piratas* (2011), produced by Mandarina and Tele 5, grew substantially during the broadcast of the first episode because the main actress become a 'trending topic' on Twitter in Spain this night (*El Mundo* 2011).

The cross-platform possibilities of TV fictions formats are numerous and creative talents explore new ways every day. In the case of the mystery series *El internado*, for instance, the production company (Globomedia) and the TV network (Antena 3) produced for the first time in Spain an Alternative Reality Game (ARG). Its title was *¿Dónde está Yago?* (*Where is Yago?*—one of the characters). The story departed from a plot included in one episode, where one of the students at the school suddenly disappears. In the game, the audience had to figure out what have happened to him. This production was very expensive and complicated, but they got sponsorship from Coca Cola.

In the case of another successful TV series, *Aguila Roja*, Globomedia and TVE decided to produced the big screen version. The movie was recently released with a disappointing results (only 262,000 viewers and 1,600,000 euros at box office, for a budget of 7 million euros).

This effort for developing cross-platform TV series requires a bigger understanding between networks and independent production companies. On the one hand, screenwriters must widen the narrative universe of the story and the characters' backgrounds. On the other, cast members must be more available for social networking. In addition, deadlines for episode delivery are tighter since the TV network needs at least a 48 h margin to release in advance the episode on line (prior to the conventional broadcast release). In any case, the common goal is teamwork and being able to produce a good and profitable multiplatform TV series (Diego 2010).

Concluding Remarks

The multiplatform media environment offers TV networks and TV production companies a range of attractive opportunities. However, neither the multiplicity of content access-points nor the introduction of interactive services is any guarantee of success. Despite recent advances in technology, creativity is still the cornerstone of the audiovisual industry. Thus, ongoing investment in format development is crucial, furthermore if it is taken into account that in-house produced contents are dominant in new platforms.

Nevertheless, the development of multiplatform contents is not only a question of creativity. Every format must be based on a business model that draws on a number of revenue streams so as to ensure its financial viability. This is the overall goal of the main commercial television operators in Spain: to cross the threshold of profitability with their products by marketing and distributing contents intensively on different platforms. The Internet is no longer regarded as a TV accessory, nor as a rival to television; rather, it is seen as a medium that lies at the heart of the television industry, the provision of audiovisual entertainment, whose business model remains to be consolidated. Moreover, television and the Internet are in an advance process of convergence (connected TV).

The audience is another significant factor in this regard. Users of audiovisual media have become more active, not only playing a part in programming contents, but also taking on a role in production and promotion campaigns via social networking sites. Developing closer ties to fan clubs and taking their suggestions into consideration during the content-design phase are tasks that no production company can afford to ignore.

In light of the foregoing discussion, the delineation of a multiplatform strategy must be seen as a key element in the early stages of the overall development process of entertainment formats, not as an afterthought or add-on activity. Furthermore, the multiplatform strategy has a bearing on each and every stage in the value chain of the audiovisual industry, from production and distribution to the commercialization of contents and services. Content is still the king, although will be not longer linked to a distribution system.

Spanish TV networks had adopted in the beginning a 'wait-and-see' attitude in regard to the Internet, trying to avoid any possible 'cannibalization' of their traditional business model. They finally launched the first version of their online platforms in the 2007/08 season due to defensive reasons—previously, they offered just a website with information and some videos. Since then, they have been updating and improving their websites until converting them in proper interactive multi-platform players (catch up TV). At this moment, networks already regard these new platforms as a real business prospect, although they are not generating revenue yet via the Internet. The main income stream continues to be advertising, given the very low rate of implementation of the pay-per-view model.

Before a real convergence is achieved, this multiplatform strategy is mainly based on three connected windows: the television set, the Internet and mobile devices. The trend consists of offering via the online player the whole TV content in streaming, mainly shows produced in-house, given that there is still a lack of content produced by foreign production companies such us the Hollywood majors. Networks are also producing some exclusive content for the Internet, most of which is related to pre-existing TV shows, with the exception of some brand new formats such as *Becarios* and *Adopta un famoso* (Telecinco). These shows were transferred to the conventional programming schedule after their relative success on the Internet had been tested. In contrast, networks are not offering exclusive content for mobile devices. Instead, they are just moving the content from the online media player to the mobile one, mainly through free applications that function as a content access-point and as a second screen implement.

At present, the interviews with executives reveal that designing an effective multiplatform strategy is also important in order to strengthen their brand identity and to cultivate audience loyalty. In this regard, it is specially outstanding establishing a certain level of visibility on social networking sites such us Facebook or Twitter, whose interactive tools allow receiving permanent feedback from the audience, which really influences the most important part of the value chain: the content production.

Acknowledgments This chapter forms part of two subsidized research projects: *New Consumption Habits in Audiovisual Contents: Impact of Digitalization on the European Media Diet*, financed by the Spanish Ministry of Education and Culture for the period 2011–13 (CSO2010-20122); and *The Impact of Digitalization on the Spanish Audiovisual Industry* (2011–13), financed by the University of (PIUNA).

References

Adams, M. (2009). Bullpen: Implementing multiplatform TV. *Communications Technology, 26*(12), 3.
Alonso, J. F. [online] (2011, July16). RTV E, Telecinco y Telefónica ensayan la futura "television conectada". *ABC*. Available at: http://www.abc.es/20110716/television/abcp-rtve-telecinco-telefonica-ensayan-20110716.html
Álvarez Monzoncillo, J. M., & Menor, J. (2010). Previsiones sobre los recursos del audiovisual. La televisión, entre la gratuidad y el pago. *Telos, 85*, 36–44.
Anderson, C. (2006). *The long tail: Why the future of business is selling less of more*. New York: Hyperion.
Arrojo, M. J. (2010). Nuevas estrategias para rentabilizar los contenidos. Distribución y financiación de formatos audiovisuales en Internet. *Telos, 85*, 117–128.
Artero, J. P. (2010). Online video business models: YouTube vs. Hulu. *Palabra Clave, 13*(1), 111–123.
Bloowfiald, M. (2010, July). Slow start for Spanish Online TV. *Screen Digest*, p. 204.
Blumenthal, H. J. & Goodenough, O. R. (2006). *This business of television*. New York: BillBoard Books.
Bolin, G. (2010). Digitization, multiplatform texts, and audience reception. *Popular Communication, 8*(1), 72–83.
Cebrián, M. (2003). *Estrategia multimedia de la televisión en Operación Triunfo*. Madrid: Editorial Ciencia 3 Distribución.
Cerezo, J. M. (2010). Smartphone. Toda la información al alcance de tu mano. *Telos, 83*, 97–99.
Diego, P. (2010). *La ficción en la pequeña pantalla. Cincuenta años de series en España*. Pamplona: Eunsa.
Diego, P., & Herrero, M. (2010). Desarrollo de series online producidas por el usuario final: el caso del videoblog de ficción. *Palabra Clave, 13*(2), 325–336.
Doyle, G. (2010). From television to multi-platform: Less from more or more for less? *Convergence, 16*(4), 431–449. ISSN 1354-8565.
El Mundo. [online] (2011, February 11). Los piratas de Pilar Rubio abordan la red. Available at: http://www.elmundo.es/elmundo/2011/05/10/television/1305021405.html

Englert, M., & Bürger, B. (2003). KirchMedia – Synergies by maintaining cross-media balance. In A. Vizjak & M. J. Ringlstetter (Eds.), *Media management: Leveraging content for profitable growth*. Berlin: Springer.
European Audiovisual Observatory. (2010). *Yearbook 2010. Film, television, video and multimedia in Europe*. Strasburg: Council of Europe.
Forrester, C. (2000). *The business of digital television*. Boston: Focal.
Francés, M., Gavaldá, J., Llorca, G., & Peris, A. (2010). *La calidad de los contenidos audiovisuals en la multidifusión digital*. Barcelona: Editorial UOC.
Gaten, T. (2010, August). Better conditions for mobile video. *Screen Digest*, p. 227. ISSN 1475-017.
GECA. (2004). *El anuario de la televisión 2004*. Madrid: GECA.
Gershon, R. A. (2009). *Telecommunications and business strategy*. New York: Routledge.
Griffiths, A. (2003). *Digital television strategies: Business challenges and opportunities*. Hampshire: Palgrave Macmillan.
Guerrero, E. (2008). En busca del elixir de la alquimia televisiva: el contenido transversal y las alianzas estratégicas como claves del negocio. *La televisión en España. Informe 2008 (UTECA)* (pp. 295–309). Barcelona: Ediciones Deusto.
Guerrero, E. (2011a). El ecosistema de los grupos televisivos españoles: los formatos de entretenimiento. *Comunicación y Hombre, 7*, 85–103.
Guerrero, E. (2011b). Aplicaciones móviles para la televisión multiplataforma. *La televisión en España. Informe 2011 (UTECA)* (pp. 237–254). Madrid: CIEC.
Gunter, B. (2010). *Television versus the Internet: Will TV prosper or perish as the world movies online?* Oxford: Chandos.
Halliday, J. [online] (2011, May). YouTube to expand movie-rental service. *The Guardian*. Available at: http://www.guardian.co.uk/technology/2011/may/10/youtube-movie-rental-itunes
Hoskins, C., McFadyen, S., & Finn, A. (1997). *Global television and film: An introduction to the economics of the business*. Oxford: Oxford University Press.
Hoskins, C., McFadyen, S., & Finn, A. (2004). *Media economics: Applying economics to new and traditional media*. Thousand Oaks: Sage.
Instituto Nacional de Estadísitca. (2010). *Encuesta sobre equipamiento y uso de tecnologías de la información y comunicación en los hogares 2010*.
Jenkins, H. (2006). *Convergence culture: Where old and new media collide*. New York: New York University Press.
Kent, J. (2010, December). Free content drives mobile apps. *Screen Digest*, pp. 369–372.
Leonhard, G. (2010, August). The future of content in a connected economy. *Ideas Magazine*, pp. 5–8.
Létang, V. (2010, July). TV viewing still growing globally. *Screen Digest*, p. 195.
Medina, M. & Ojer, T. (2011). La transformación de las televisiones públicas en servicio digitales en la BBC y RTVE. *Comunicar, 36*, 87–94
Negroponte, N. (1995). *Being digital*. New York: Knopf.
Nielsen. [online] (2010, March 16). *Facebook, Google and Yahoo! are top sites while watching big TV events*. Available at: http://blog.nielsen.com/nielsenwire/online_mobile/facebook-google-and-yahoo-are-top-sites-while-watching-big-tv-events/
Nielsen. [online] (2011, May 19). *In the U.S., Tablets are TV Buddies while eReaders Make Great*. Available at: http://blog.nielsen.com/nielsenwire/?p=27702
ONTSI. [online] (2011). *Informe anual de los contenidos digitales en España*. Madrid: red.es. Available at: http://www.red.es/media/registrados/2011-11/1322643299698.pdf?aceptacion=90137b79eeab82bead3056cf098f3558
Palmer, S. (2006). *Television disrupted: The transition from network to networked TV*. Amsterdam: Focal.
Pardo, A. (2009). Hollywood at the digital crossroad: New challenges, new opportunities. In A. Albarran, P. Faustino, & R. Santos (Eds.), *The media as a driver of the information*

society: Economics, management, policies and technologies (pp. 67–97). Lisbon: MediaXXI/ Formalpress and Universidade Católica Editora, Unipessoal Lda.
Pavlik, J. V. (1996). New media technology: Cultural and commercial perspectives. Boston: Allyn & Bacon.
Pavlik, J. V., & McIntosh, S. (2011). Converging media: A new introduction to mass communication. New York: Oxford University Press.
Saló, G. (2003). ¿Qué es eso del formato? Cómo nace y se desarrolla un programa de televisión. Barcelona: Gedisa.
Sánchez-Tabernero, A. (2008). Los contenidos de los medios de comunicación. Calidad, rentabilidad y competencia. Barcelona: Ediciones Deusto.
Tapscott, D. (2009). Grown up digital: How the net generation is changing your world. New York: MacGraw-Hill.
The Cocktail Analysis. (2010, June). Televidente 2.0.
Tsekleves, E., Whitham, R., Kondo, K., & Hill, A. (2011). Investigating media use and the television user experience in the home. Entertainment Computing, 2(3), 151–161.
Ulin, J. C. (2009). The business of media distribution: Monetizing film, TV and video content in an online world. Burlington: Focal.
Vizjak, A., & Ringlstetter, M. J. (2003). Media management: Leveraging content for profitable growth. Berlin: Springer.
Vogel, H. (2011). Entertainment industry economics: A guide for financial analysis (8th ed.). New York: Cambridge University Press.
Vukanovic, Z. (2009). Television and digital media in the 21st century: New business, economic and technological paradigm. Novi Sad: Media Art Service International.
Williams, R. (1974). Television: Technology and cultural form. London: Fontana-Collins.
Ytreberg, E. (2009). Extended liveness and eventfulness in multiplatform reality formats. New Media Society, 11(4), 467–485.

Other Resources

Interview with Jesús Moreno, Deputy Director of Antena 3 Multimedia, 11/02/2011.
Interview with Sandra Vicente, Supervisor of Telecinco.es, 11/02/2011.
Questionnaire completed by the multimedia managers at TVE, Antena 3, Telecinco, Cuatro and La Sexta in November 2010.

Facebook: A Business Perspective on the Power of Intelligent Networking and Social Media

Richard A. Gershon

1 Introduction

Facebook is the world's largest social network, with more than one billion active users around the world. Approximately 80 % of those users are outside the United States. In a few short years, Facebook has become one of the principal giants of the digital age challenging companies like Google and Amazon with its vision of the Internet tied together by personal relationships and recommendations, rather than by search algorithms. The Facebook experience is built around the people you know. Facebook users flood the social network with their thoughts, commentaries and photos on a daily basis. Facebook is available in over 70 languages. Analysts estimate that Facebook users post more than 30 billion pieces of information every month.

While Facebook is first and foremost a social medium, it has also become an important business tool. Facebook has proven to be an essential communication and marketing strategy for those organizations that wish to operate in today's digital media environment. Central to this idea is that social media like Facebook provide a low cost platform with which to market and promote a company's brand. Secondly, it provides an excellent way to recommend products, services and ideas based on advice and support coming from someone the user knows. This chapter provides a case study analysis of Facebook with special attention given to the power of intelligent networking and social media.

1.1 Facebook Today

Today, Facebook claims an international work force of over 3,500 employees. In December 2011, Facebook moved into a new corporate space in Menlo Park,

---

R.A. Gershon (✉)
Western Michigan University, Kalamazoo, MI, USA
e-mail: Richard.Gershon@wmich.edu

California. The 57 acre campus formerly belonged to Sun Microsystems. The new Facebook headquarters building is set up very openly, reflecting their core philosophy of sharing and openness. There are no private offices or cubicles to divide coworkers. Instead, software designers and engineers occupy rows of shared desk space. Even CEO Mark Zuckerberg has a desk off to the side. The first of 10 planned structures, now house some 2,000 Facebook employees and includes an array of features, including glass-paneled conference rooms and hallways lined with chalkboard. The new style of office space has been described as "hacker style."

> Workers roam with laptops, meet on sofas and scribble on walls at Facebook Inc.'s new Silicon Valley headquarters, where rusted steel beams, exposed heating ducts and plywood-covered corridors are part of the decor. The office campus in Menlo Park, California, was renovated for $250 million in a "hacker" style intended to express the culture of the world's largest social-networking company ("Facebook's Cool Space" 2011).

Facebook has become one of the most sought-after high-tech companies to work for in Silicon Valley. The company's international headquarters opened in October 2009 and is based in Dublin, Ireland. It should be noted that Dublin is a popular location for many other high-tech companies including Google and Amazon. From a simple Boston dorm room at Harvard, Facebook has dramatically grown into a worldwide presence.

2 Historical Overview

The story of Facebook begins with Mark Zuckerberg who launched his Web 2.0 venture from a Harvard dorm room. Prior to its launch, the prodigy programmer coded multiple websites including *CourseMatch* and *Facemash*. CourseMatch was a simple online tool used by students at Harvard that recommended which courses to take based on what their friends were enrolled in. Zuckerberg's second and more controversial software program, Facemash, was a rating system that evaluated Harvard female co-eds based on their relative attractiveness (Vargas 2010). According to the *Harvard Crimson*, Facemash, used photos compiled from the Facebook network of nine residence houses, co-locating two women next to each other at a time and asked the user to choose the "hotter person."

To accomplish this, Zuckerberg hacked into the protected areas of Harvard's computer network and copied the houses' private dormitory ID images. The idea of rating one's classmates quickly proved to be a viral sensation and quickly spread among friends and classmates. Zuckerberg's creation achieved 20,000 page views from over 400 visitors around campus and was reported to have crashed Harvard's computer network. The site was promptly shut down and Zuckerberg was reprimanded by Harvard's senior administration. The university was initially prepared to file charges against Zuckerberg for infiltrating the university's online campus directory and for privacy invasion. The charges were later dropped (Vargas 2010). Shortly thereafter, Harvard classmates Cameron and Tyler Winklevoss brought Zuckerberg in to help finish a new social networking project they were working on. Instead of completing the project, Zuckerberg started a separate website called Thefacebook.com. He registered the domain name in January and launched the website on February 4, 2004. Kirkpatrick (2010) makes the argument that Facebook's ultimate success owes a lot to the fact that it began in a college setting where student social networks are densest and where they generally socialize more vigorously than at any other time in their lives. Facebook's origins on the campus of Harvard also lent the project an elitist aura that gave it a unique status for early users.

Facebook's initial launch captured the interest of venture capitalist Peter Thiel, the co-founder of PayPal, who provided a beginning investment of $500,000 in the summer of 2004. Zuckerberg had also made friends with Sean Parker, an entrepreneur, who co-founded Napster. Zuckerberg eventually dropped out of Harvard and made the decision to move the company to Palo Alto, California (Kirkpatrick 2010). This region of the U.S., better known as Silicon Valley, was home to such companies as Apple, Hewlett Packard and Intel to name only a few.

The year 2005 proved to be an important period of growth for the young fledgling network. By year's end, Facebook supported over 800 college networks and was now accessible internationally. The Facebook Photos application was implemented as well, quickly becoming one of the most popular photo sharing services on the Internet. The company gained $12.7 million in additional funding and ended the year with 5.5 million active users. Facebook's meteoric rise gained the attention of some very large media companies. First, in March 2006, there were negotiations with Viacom's MTV Networks for a $750 million acquisition. Zuckerberg declined, stating that he wanted $2 billion. Later, in September, search engine giant Yahoo! offered $1 billion for Facebook, which Zuckerberg also turned down. According to then Yahoo CEO, Terry Semel,

> I'd never met anyone—forget his age, twenty-two then ... who would walk away from a billion dollars. But he said, 'It's not about the price. This is my baby, and I want to keep running it, I want to keep growing it.' I couldn't believe it. One bidder that was able to successfully partner with Facebook was Microsoft which purchased a 1.6% share in the company for $240 million (Vargas 2010).

2.1 Worldwide Active Users

By 2008, Facebook was able to claim over 100 million users. In 2010, that figure grew to over 600 million users worldwide. Today (as of this writing), Facebook reaches more than one billion active users around the world (Facebook, Company Timeline 2012). Facebook's sudden and dramatic growth rate can be seen in Table 1.

The success of Facebook was evidenced when Time magazine selected Facebook founder, Mark Zuckerberg, as *Time* Magazine's 2010 person of the

Table 1 Facebook: number of worldwide active users

August 26, 2008	100 million
April 8, 2009	200 million
September 15, 2009	300 million
February 5, 2010	400 million
July 21, 2010	500 million
January 5, 2011	600 million
May 30, 2011	700 million
March 25, 2012	845 million
May 1, 2012	900 million
October 1, 2012	1 billion

Source: Facebook Company Timeline

year. Zuckerberg's selection was the result of his having established the world's largest social network.

> For connecting more than half a billion people and mapping their social relations among them (something that has never been done before); for creating a new system of exchanging information that has become both indispensable and sometimes a little scary; and finally for changing how we all live our lives in ways that are innovative and even optimistic... (Stengel 2010, p. 43.)

3 The Facebook Business Model and the Power of Intelligent Networking

Facebook is an example of an intelligent network. An intelligent network can be described as any system of communication that organizes, transmits and displays information with the goal of providing information and/or entertainment. Intelligent networks are also responsible for providing decision support capability. What gives a network its unique intelligence are the people and users of the system and the value added contributions they make via critical gateway points (e.g., desktop/laptop computers, smart phones, electronic readers etc.). What do we mean by value-added contributions? They represent the kind of hardware and software contributions that add to the overall system design of the network (Gershon 2011).

A second assumption is that intelligent networks do not operate in a vacuum. Rather, the use of intelligent networks are an integral part of any human or organizational decision-making process or initiative (Gershon 2011; Monge and Contractor 2003). As Berners-Lee (1999) points out, the Internet is as much a social creation as it is a technical one. This is particularly true for Facebook which harnesses the power of the Internet to help advance an innately human activity: the desire to socialize with one's friends, family, colleagues and acquaintants. Hence the term, social networking. Facebook, first and foremost, is the world's leading social networking site. A social networking site allow individuals to present themselves and maintain connections with others. Facebook has been described by its founder and CEO, Mark Zuckerberg, as a "mathematical construct that maps the real-life connections between people. Each person is a node radiating links to other people they know ("Most Innovative Companies" 2007)."

As friends and acquaintances join Facebook, they become part of a larger social grid that matters to the individual. It creates value to the individual by adding to one's social capital (Ellison et al. 2007). Since that person's friends are connected to other friends on the network, there is the opportunity to virtually expand one's circle of friends and acquaintances (Grossman 2010). Each new person and extended link adds value and dynamism to the overall network. The Facebook network has grown exponentially over time and become greater than the sum of its parts. Researchers like Gershon (2011) and Monge et al. (2008) refer to this as the principle of network evolution. Facebook's mission, according to the company's profile page, is "to give people the power to share and make the world more open and connected" (Facebook company time line 2012).

3.1 Facebook Tools

The user's profile page starts with a photo of the user (or a substitute image) located in the upper left hand corner of the user's homepage. A thumbnail version of the profile picture appears each time the user interacts with others, such as posting comments or sending messages. The same profile image appears on the friends list of anyone who is part of the user's social grid of contacts. The category listing known as "information" provides a brief biographical sketch about the individual. It contains information pertaining to education, professional work and affiliations, personal interests and contact information. Also featured on the profile page is the "user's wall." It acts as a public bulletin board where any of the user's listed friends can write short public messages. These comments can be viewed by anyone with access to the user's profile (Taylor 2011).

The "Photos" feature is a second important Facebook tool which enables the user to post photos to a general photos location. The posting of photos is a particularly attractive feature when it comes to travel or the celebrating of a special event. They are part of the user's personal narrative; albeit visually. Within the Photos application, there is a useful Tag function which allows anyone to identify and attach their friends to pictures. Once someone is Tagged in a picture, the picture will be linked to that person's profile for easy sharing. Videos function in much the same way as photos. They can be tagged and shared as well.

Facebook provides a number of additional software tools such as status updates, news feeds, opinions and commentary postings, chat (instant messaging), likes and dislikes external links as well as electronic mail. The various Facebook tools share the common goal of enabling the user to maintain a virtual, real-time conversation with those individuals who comprise the user's list of friends. Being part of a social network, allows individuals to present themselves and maintain connections with others. It is the electronic equivalent of the modern day café. As the user's social grid increases, so does the power of information (Taylor 2011). This, in turn, forms the basis for the Facebook's business model; the more people are willing to share personal information, (and by extension provide demographic data), the more advertisers are willing to pay for such direct access and capability.

3.2 A Business Perspective on the Use of Social Media

Social media represents a category of Internet based activity where a virtual community of users share information through the use of individual profiles, contact information, personal messages, blogs and commentary, and videos. The operative word is "social" since it involves the reaching out and sharing of one's ideas, thoughts and experiences to a common community of users. Simply put, social media is about relationship building. Some of the more notable examples of social media, include Facebook, Linked-In Twitter and You Tube. The use of social media satisfy five important communication goals. First, they provide a low cost platform with which to market and promote a company's brand. Social media provides a creative way to extend brand awareness and help facilitate long-term relationships with prospective customers. Consider, for example, that one in four ads. purchased by automobile giant, Ford, are digital media ads. According to Ford, 60 % of the people who "like" Ford on Facebook eventually purchase a Ford automobile. ("How Powerful is a Facebook Like" 2012).

Second, social media allows for instantaneous communication between and among one's customers, employees and peers (Vukanovic 2011). The power of intelligent networking makes it possible to communicate in real time regardless of time zones, geographical borders and physical space (Gershon 2011; Tapscott 1996). It creates a virtual community of users. Third, social media allows individuals to meet new people (and potential clients) as well as strengthening existing relationships (Piskorski 2011). To that end, one of the important features of social media is the ability to add friends and acquaintances to one's contact list. Both Facebook and Linked-In use a specialized algorithm that generates a list of potential friends using a friend-of a-friend reference matrix (i.e., common index naming points) based on three or more sites.

Fourth, social media provides an excellent way to recommend products, services and ideas based on advice and support coming from someone the user knows. Facebook Chief Operating Officer Sheryl Sandberg makes the point that marketers are always looking for the person who's not just going to buy a certain product, but will likewise spread the word to their friends ("How Powerful is a Facebook Like" 2012). This is word-of-mouth advertising in its purest form. Fifth, social media provides fast and immediate feedback in terms of user/customer reaction. One of the major distinguishing points between having an Internet presence and being located on Facebook is the level of interactivity. Nothing is more powerful than a product launch or special event gathering that goes viral on the Internet and Facebook in particular.

3.3 Facebook as a Business Strategy

Facebook exhibits a kind of dual identify. On the one hand, Facebook is a highly engaging medium of communication for personal expression. On the other, Facebook is a for profit business that is advertiser driven. Facebook's claim that it has one billion active users is an impressive number. It has gained the attention of major companies around the world. There is a clear recognition that most businesses need to have a social media strategy even if they don't fully understand how it works. While many such companies have succeeded in generating lots of friends and followers on *Facebook, Linked-In* and *Twitter*, few fully understand the potential of social media as a business strategy.

From the very beginning, Facebook strategists understood that advertising was going to play a central role in any business strategy going forward. The attraction to advertisers is obvious. Facebook users willingly volunteer enormous amounts of personal data that can eventually be leveraged into targeted advertisements toward the individual user. By "liking" a certain advertisement, the user is giving their personal endorsement for a product or service that may appear in a friend or colleagues' news feed. As Grossman (2010) points out,

> Looked at one way, when a friend likes a product it's just more sharing, more data changing hands. Looked at another way, it's your personal relationship being monetized by a third party (p. 58).

Early on, the challenge for Facebook was how to introduce advertising into the social networking mix without being overly intrusive and, thereby, destabilize the social network's growing momentum. The concern was that highly intrusive ads. would compromise the user experience. The decision was made to scale back the size and location of banner ads.

By opening up one's user profile, what becomes immediately observable are the advertisements that sometimes appear along the right side of the screen. The placement of ads. is based on the principle of micromarketing where the ads. correspond to the stated interests of the user on his/her profile page. The Facebook computer server is designed to track the regular posting history and status updates of the user. It utilizes a set of highly sophisticated data mining algorithms (Han and Kamber 2006). Facebook ads. are designed not to be overly intrusive. The user is invited to give a thumbs up or thumbs down to the ad. The thumbs down will permanently remove the ad. from future viewing. Alternatively, a thumbs up (or stated like preference) can change the ad. from a simple billboard display into a casual buzz inside the user's news feed and, thereby, into the newsfeed of the user's friends. A stated like preference becomes part of the conversation between friends, colleagues and family members. Says Zuckerberg, "The whole premise of Facebook is that everything is more valuable when you have a context about what your friends are doing...That's true for ads. as well." ("Sell Your Friends" 2010).

From a marketing standpoint, the goal isn't necessarily for the user to go out and immediately buy the advertisers' product or to click through to their website. Rather, the goal is to quietly locate the advertisers message into the users thinking and elicit a future purchase. Marketers like this approach. It costs them nothing to build a long term relationship with the user via his/her news feed once the user has indicated a preference for a certain product or service. ("Sell Your Friends" 2010). According to Jim Cuene, Director of Interactive Marketing, for General Mills foods:

> For what could be considered the cost of a 30 second spot, you have a year's worth of conversation with people who love the brand... If someone likes Betty Crocker and they tell that to 150 other people, they are helping us to market our brand. In some ways, it's a more credible message to the community. (p. 68).

The advertiser's goal should be to find creative ways to extend brand awareness and help facilitate long-term relationships with prospective customers. They should quietly become part of the social conversation. It can and often becomes the catalyst for a future purchasing decision or mobilizing a group of people to action.

4 Facebook's Financial Performance and Estimated Valuation

Facebook has experienced a progressive increase in annual revenues since the time of the company's formation. While the company is privately held, estimates suggest that the company achieved revenues of $4.2 billion in 2011. Estimated revenues for the year's 2006–2012 can be seen in Table 2.

4.1 The 2012 Facebook Initial Public Offering

Another important consideration is the company's current valuation. In May 2012, Facebook completed a highly anticipated initial public offering (IPO) that was expected to place the company's valuation at more than $100 billion. Facebook hoped to raise 15 billion from its IPO. At $100 billion, Facebook would rank second only to Google in terms of Internet company valuation. The 2012 IPO offering, however, proved to be a spectacular failure. While the offering reached a first day high of $38 dollars per share, the stock closed flat after the first day of trading. Both investors and the media began to speculate whether Facebook's initial offering price was too high. Others argued that part of the first day's momentum was damaged by Nasdaq's technical difficulties, which delayed buying by a half hour as well as mistakes executing purchase orders at the correct price.

Reuters later reported that Morgan Stanley, the lead underwriter on Facebook's public offering, told its top clients most likely to place large orders for Facebook stock that the bank's analysts were cutting their revenue forecasts for the company just days before the IPO. That may have contributed to a lessening in demand for Facebook stock which proved a lot weaker than was originally expected ("Facebook lessons" 2012). In the three months that followed, Facebook investors saw the value of their shares drop nearly in half, wiping out some $50 billion in

Table 2 Facebook estimated yearly revenues

Year	Revenue
2006	$52 million
2007	$150 million
2008	$280 million
2009	$775 million
2010	$2 billion
2011	$4.2 billion
2012	$5.4 billion est.

Sources: TechCrunch and Bloomberg

shareholder value. The IPO was supposed to be a shining moment for Facebook and its major investors. Instead, between trading glitches on the NASDAQ exchange, accusations of selective disclosure favoring select Facebook's bankers, and the subsequent decline in the company's stock value, the 2012 IPO became a debacle of epic proportions.

5 Privacy Concerns

Privacy worries have been a source of major concern for Facebook since the company's very beginning. The problem is understandable. In order to have a true social network, the user must be willing to share select details of one's personal life. If there is a single quality or feature that separates young people in their teens and 20's from previous generations, it is a willingness to broadcast the details of their private lives to the general public. The give and take exchange between Facebook and its users over privacy is gaining importance as the company's growth continues unabated. From Chicago, USA to sub-Saharan Africa, Facebook's one billion worldwide users vary in their degree of knowledge about what it means to be a part of a social network.

Facebook's policies, more than those of any other company, are helping to define privacy standards in the Internet age. The issues vary in size and complexity from personal, demographic data being shared with third party advertisers to the use of facial recognition technology to identify people in photographs. Implicit in these discussions are the challenges brought on by the company's success. Facebook has struggled to find the right balance between giving users too little privacy control versus giving them too much and the risk that such individuals won't be forthcoming in the information that they share. In August 2011, Facebook introduced a set of changes designed to help user privacy. Every time a Facebook user makes a comment, adds a picture, or initiates any other change to their profile page, the user can specify who can see the information whether it's specific Facebook friends or anyone who has access to the Internet. Icons now replace the previous, more complicated padlock menu ("New Control Over Privacy" 2011).

5.1 Settlement with the F.T.C.

On November 29, 2011, the U.S. Federal Trade Commission (FTC) announced a proposed settlement with Facebook. The company had been accused of unfair and deceptive trade practices. Facebook is now required to obtain a users' consent before making changes to privacy settings, and to subject itself to an independent audit on consumer privacy for the next 20 years. The strongly worded order, announced by the Federal Trade Commission in Washington, stems in large part from changes that Facebook made to its users' privacy protocols in December 2009. As part of its complaint, the FTC alleged that Facebook routinely made private information publicly available without warning the user or obtaining consent beforehand. The complaint also stated that Facebook allowed advertisers to have access to personally identifiable information each time a user clicked an ad. on the Facebook site. The FTC's eight-count complaint against Facebook is part of the agency's ongoing effort to make sure companies live up to the privacy promises they make to American consumers ("Federal Trade Commission" 2011).

5.2 Additional Legal Issues

Privacy is not Zuckerberg's only problem. Both Zuckerberg and Facebook have been the target of several intellectual property disputes since the company's inception The 2010 Academy nominated film *The Social Network* dramatized these events. The film suggests that Zuckerberg had stolen the original idea of Facebook from Harvard classmates, Cameron and Tyler Winklevoss. The Winklevoss brothers had brought Zuckerberg in to help finish a new social networking project that they were working on. Instead of completing the project, Zuckerberg started a separate website called Thefacebook.com. Before the Winklevoss brothers could take action, Facebook had already been launched and become an overnight sensation. The brothers filed a lawsuit against Facebook accusing Zuckerberg of using their idea from their project (Kirkpatrick 2010). Eventually, an out of court settlement was reached for a reported $65 million.

In addition to the Winklevoss lawsuit, Mark Zuckerberg had a falling out with co-founder Eduardo Saverin, his former college friend. Saverin originally served as Facebook's Chief Financial Officer and business manager until internal differences of opinion caused the company to reduce his stake in the company from 34 % to less than one percent. Saverin sued Facebook and the case was settled out of court for an undisclosed amount. As part of the settlement, Saverin's name was returned to the official Facebook founder's page.

6 Political Activism and the Power of Social Media

If Facebook was a country, it would have the third largest population in the world, trailing only China and India. Facebook's estimated users suggest that one out of every eight people around the world has a Facebook profile. That figure reached the one billion person mark in October 2012. The challenge, of course, is that not all countries, and by extension—political power structures—are equally enamored by Facebook's grassroots mobilizing capability. Quite the opposite. The lessons from the 2011 Arab spring in Tunisia, Egypt and Yemen demonstrated the important role that social media like Facebook and Twitter, played in helping to mobilize street demonstrations. While Facebook did not create the revolutions that took place in these countries, it did play a major role in helping to organize large public demonstrations. Facebook in combination with cell phones, video cameras, blog posts as well as traditional media outlets like Al Jazeera, set into motion a flood of inflammatory information and images.

Facebook provided a common space where people were able to watch shocking pictures and sometimes gruesome videos of fellow protesters being brutalized by police and military authorities. Facebook and its numerous special interest sites provided a political platform for people to express their solidarity, both within the country and with others in the region and beyond. Egyptians heard about Tunisia from Tunisian citizens instead of the national news media. Such images and commentary proved highly incendiary and mobilized people to rebel.

Many of those same Facebook sites provided basic logistical information for protesters in terms of where to go and when to show up. The power of instantaneous communication made it possible to mobilize large numbers of people in just days and sometimes hours—simply because someone knew someone on Facebook, and the word spread from there. This became grassroots, collective mobilization in its purest form. It is not surprising, therefore, that countries like China see Facebook as a major threat to preserving political stability. In 2008, Facebook established a presence in China gaining a small number of users. The Chinese government, soon thereafter, made the determination that Facebook was an undesirable site. Today, Facebook operates outside the country's strictly guarded network known euphemistically as "The Great Firewall." Says Facebook's Zuckerberg,. "How can you connect the whole world if you leave out 1.6 billion people?" (Caulfield 2010).

Facebook is not alone. Two other major Internet companies; most notably, Google and Twitter, face similar issues when dealing with authoritarian regimes in places like China, Russia, and Iran. As revolution sweeps through the Middle East and elsewhere, these three companies find themselves playing a central role given the power of social media to mobilize large numbers of people to act. Google, Facebook, and Twitter are confronting a myriad of political and ethical problems that most business start-ups try to avoid. There are no easy solutions.

Google, thus far, is the most willing to take a political and business stand against authoritarianism. A good example can be seen by the company's willingness to pull out of the China market rather than accede to government demands for search results information of its citizens as well as participating in censorship. Likewise, Google lent its support to one of its employees Wael Ghonim who played a major role in the Egyptian uprising. Google's senior management made it known that it respected Ghonim's efforts and that it would welcome him back to his old job.

In addition, You Tube (owned by Google) also created a hub to promote videos from protestors in Tahrir Square (Weisberg 2011).

While Facebook has proven to be a remarkable organizing tool, the company itself, seems to be very ambivalent in terms of whether to embrace political and social causes. There is no question that Facebook (and its numerous special interest sites) played a critical role in bringing about the downfall of Egyptian prime minister, Hosni Mubarak. It was Wael Ghonim's Facebook page "We Are All Khaled" created to memorialize a young Tunisian businessman who died in police custody that became the epicenter of the revolution. After Ghonim was released from Egyptian police custody after 11 days of captivity, he spoke to CNN about the role of social media in the Egyptian revolution (Weisberg 2011).

> I want to meet Mark Zuckerberg one day and thank him... I'm talking on behalf of Egypt. This revolution started online. This revolution started on Facebook. This revolution started in June 2010 when hundreds of thousands of Egyptians started collaborating content. We would post a video on Facebook that would be shared by 60,000 people on their walls within a few hours.
>
> I always said that if you want to liberate a society just give them the Internet... The reason why is the Internet will help you fight a media war, which is something the Egyptian government regime played very well in 1970, 1980, 1990, and when the Internet came along they couldn't play it ("Freed Google Exec." 2011).

With Facebook playing a major role in the events that led to the downfall of the Tunisian and Egyptian governments (including the personal endorsement of Google's Wael Ghonim) it might be expected that Facebook's senior management would have used this opportunity to highlight its role as being a major catalyst for democratic change. Instead, the company stays silent on the topic. At issue, is the fact that Facebook is trying to balance competing pressures from both activist groups as well as host nations that it seeks to do business with. Facebook does not want to be seen as picking sides for fear that countries like China, Russia and Saudi Arabia will impose restrictions or closely monitor their activities. Simply put, political revolution is bad for business. A related problem is that Facebook does not want to alter its stated policy of requiring users to sign up with their real identity. In principle, Facebook does this in order to protect its users from fraud and misrepresentation. Various human rights groups, however, take issue with this argument. They point out that the listing of one's true identity puts some people at risk from governments looking to target political dissenters. According to Susannah Vila, the Director of Content and Outreach for Movements.org "people are going to be using this platform for political mobilization, which only underscores the importance of ensuring their safety." (Preston 2011)

Ironically, one of the protest pages that Facebook shut down was that of Wal Ghonim, the very same person who previously thanked Zuckerberg and Facebook for their support of the Egyptian revolution. Apparently, Wal Ghonim used a pseudonym to create a profile as one of the administrators of the page, which was in clear violation of Facebook's terms of service. To be sure, Facebook hasn't come to terms with its business values as an organization nor its role as a political organizing force. Whereas, Google voluntarily chose to withdraw from China,

Facebook, is trying to find a way to enter it. For now, Facebook's overriding objective is to expand geographically and build market share. This presupposes building good relations with foreign governments; even one's that are politically authoritarian.

7   The Future of Search: Discussion

Facebook and Google are on a collision course with each other. Though fundamentally different, Google and Facebook overlap in a few crucial areas, including how people search for information. Google is the world's preeminent Internet search company. Google's principle advantage is its ability to collect and analyze vast amounts of data. The company's highly sophisticated search algorithm calls up a set of web pages out of the known universe of possibilities in terms of what is most appropriate to the user's query. Google researchers and staffers have steadily improved the search engine's capability adding a variety of enhanced features, including the Google Directory, expanded language versions, key word searches G-mail and Google Image. What information management tools the company lacks, it has acquired over time, including Picasa, photo management; Double Click, web ads. and Keyhole Corporation, later to become Google Earth. In 2006, Google paid $1.65 billion in stock for YouTube, the video-sharing phenomenon that has given breadth and depth to the company's multiple Web. initiatives (Auletta 2009).

In contrast, Facebook is the world's preeminent social network. The company's primary focus is on making social connections between Internet users. But in the process, Facebook has created a platform that knows the identity, activities and general interests of more than one billion users worldwide. Both Google and Facebook are jockeying for position in terms of controlling the future of Internet search. Both companies want to be the user's first destination point. The stakes are very high. By becoming the principal gatekeeper of people's on-line experience and information search, both Google and Facebook expect to lay claim to an expanding market share of loyal users who will rely on them not only to help navigate the Internet but to utilize them for trusted advice and guidance. Both companies hope to influence the user's web browsing and viewing experience.

Equally important, both Google and Facebook are well positioned to capitalize on various kinds of advertising opportunities. The launch of Google's keyword search advertising program in 2001 provides the basic business model that propels the company forward as a major communications company. Keyword search, also known as contextual advertising, involves text-based ads. and links that appear next to a search engine result (Gershon 2009). Alternatively, Facebook's approach relies more on making the connections between potential advertisers and what it knows about the user's background and general likes. Facebook's increasing sophistication allows it to know with greater certainty what its customers are really interested in. The challenge for Facebook, however, is walking the fine line between providing a service to its members as well as providing a platform for advertisers. With each software advance that Facebook develops, that line keeps moving. In

2012, Facebook introduced a new service called *Timeline*. According to Facebook, Timeline is simply a new way to tell your story and share your content. Timeline provides the user with an expanded set of formatting tools to provide a more detailed narrative of one's personal history. This includes both important personal moments as well as daily living occurrences. The potential addition of Timeline moves Facebook one step further in the direction of search capability by providing real-time linkages between people and their activities on the web. In practical terms, Facebook continues to expand the definition of what it means to be part of a social network.

References

Auletta, K. (2009). *Googled: The end of the world as we know it*. New York: Penguin Press.
Berners-Lee, T. (1999). *Weaving the web*. New York: Harper Collins.
Caulfield, P. (2010, December 20). *New York Daily News*. Facebook's Mark Zuckerberg kicks off trip to China. Available from http://articles.nydailynews.com/2010-12-20/news/27084933_1_baidu-kaiser-kuo-robin-li
Ellison, N., Steinfield, C., & Lampe, C. (2007). The benefits of Facebook friends: Social capital and college students' use of online social network sites. *Journal of Computer Mediated Communication, 12*(4). Available from http://jcmc.indiana.edu/vol12/issue4/
Facebook company time line. Key Facts. (2012, May 17). Available from http://newsroom.fb.com/content/default.aspx?NewsAreaId=22
Facebook lessons: What not to do when planning an IPO. (2012, May 24). *Reuters*. Available from http://www.reuters.com/article/2012/05/24/facebook-lessons-idUSL1E8GOEI220120524
Facebook's cool space' campus points to the future of office growth. (2011, December 22). *Bloomberg*. Available from http://www.bloomberg.com/news/2011-12-20/facebook-s-cool-space-campus-points-to-future-of-office-growth.html
Federal Trade Commission. (2011, November 29). Facebook settles FTC charges that it deceived consumers by failing to keep privacy promises. Available from http://ftc.gov/opa/2011/11/privacysettlement.shtm
Freed Google exec Ghonim thanks Facebook for role in Egyptian revolution. (2011, February 11). *The Inquisitr*. Available from http://www.inquisitr.com/98197/wael-ghonim-thanks-facebook/
Gershon, R. (2009). *Telecommunications & business strategy*. New York: Routledge.
Gershon, R. (2011). *Intelligent networks and international business communication: A systems theory interpretation* (Media Markets Monographs, No. 12). Pamplona, Spain: Universidad de Navarra Press.
Grossman, L. (2010, December 27). Person of the year, Mark Zuckerberg. *Time*, 44–75.
Han, J., & Kamber, M. (2006). *Data mining: Concepts and techniques*. San Francisco, CA: Elsevier.
How Powerful is a Facebook Like for Advertisers? (2012, May 17). *CBS News*. Available from http://www.cbsnews.com/8301-505268_162-57436041/how-powerful-is-a-facebook-like-for-advertisers/
Kirkpatrick, D. (2010). *The Facebook effect*. New York: Simon & Schuster.
Monge, P., & Contractor, N. (2003). *Theories of communication networks*. New York: Oxford Press.
Monge, P., Heiss, B., & Magolin, D. (2008). Communication network evolution in organizational communities. *Communication Theory, 18*(5), 449–477.
Most innovative companies. (2007, May 14). *Business Week*, 60.

New control over privacy on Facebook. (2011, August 23). *New York Times*. Available from http://www.nytimes.com/2011/08/24/technology/facebook-aims-to-simplify-its-privacy-settings.html

Piskorski, H. (2011, November). Social strategies that work. *Harvard Business Review*, 117–122.

Preston, J. (2011, February 14). Facebook officials keep quiet on its role in Revolts. Available from http://www.nytimes.com/2011/02/15/business/media/15facebook.html

Sell your friends. (2010, September 27). *Bloomberg*, 63–72.

Stengel, R. (2010, December 27). The 2010 person of the year. *Time*, 43.

Tapscott, D. (1996). *The digital economy: Promise and peril in the age of networked intelligence*. New York: McGraw-Hill.

Taylor, T. (2011, April 11). *Facebook: A case study analysis of telecommunications and business strategy*. Paper presented at the 2011 ITERA Conference, Indianapolis, IN.

Vargas, J. A. (2010, September 20). The face of Facebook. *The New Yorker*, 54.

Vukanovic, Z. (2011). New media business model in social and web media. *Journal of Media Business Studies*, (8)3, 51–67.

Weisberg, J. (2011, February 24). Tech revolutionaries. *Slate*. Available from http://www.slate.com/articles/news_and_politics/the_big_idea/2011/02/tech_evolutionaries.html

Multimedia Strategies for FM Radio Stations in Moscow

Elena Vartanova, Mikhail Makeenko, and Andrei Vyrkovsky

1 Introduction

The process of introducing multimedia technologies into the practical activities of mass media and shaping a convergent medium wherein mass media exist and develop has long become obvious to workers and theorists in the field of mass communication (Gillmor 2004; Feldman 1996; Flew 2005; Kung et al. 2008; Lukina 2010).

The development of digital technologies enables mass media to provide numerous types of content (audio, video, textual, photographic and infographic) on a single platform (normally, an internet-resource) and distribute this content by means of various digital devices. This phenomenon significantly increases the audience for mass media by giving it additional opportunities to both get information and perceive it (Kolodzy 2006; Meikle and Redden 2010; Quinn and Filak 2005; Wilson 2009).

Convergence of different types of content, made possible by the digital revolution, has generated an altogether "non-technological" effect, that of a change in the methods and forms of dealing with information: different departments of an editorial office (and sometimes whole companies) work together at shaping the agenda and creating materials, and also "multiprofile" journalists able to work with various types of content become involved (Allan 2006; Deuze 2007).

In addition, digitization gives an opportunity to engage a huge army of media product consumers, which makes it possible to increase not only the quantity but also the quality of the information provided (so long as it is appropriately processed) (Vartanova 2010b; Vartanova and Smirnov 2010; Doctor 2010).

These processes, which drastically change the life and work of mass media, occur in every sector of the media market (Baranova 2011). They are equally important for radio, in particular, for FM radio stations, which attract special attention because of both objective (specific features of consumption of radio as a mass medium) and

E. Vartanova (✉) • M. Makeenko • A. Vyrkovsky
Department of Journalism, Lomonosov Moscow State University, Russia
e-mail: evarta@mail.ru; mikhail.makeenko@gmail.com; a.v.vyrkovsky@gmail.com

subjective characteristics (an extremely high level of competition among FM stations in Moscow).

Among radio professionals, there is an obviously growing interest in the issues of creating and implementing multimedia strategies on the basis of radio stations (Vartanova 2010a), which enables them to shape a convergent medium: a universal system for content generation, aggregation and distribution.

In order to realize the general tendencies in the convergent medium of the market for FM radio stations in Moscow, the authors have conducted a quantitative (a study of types and forms of the multimedia information radio offers) and qualitative (a study of experts' opinions and a quality content analysis) research into multimedia activity of the participants of the market.

The article focuses on the analysis of multimedia strategies adopted by a number of Moscow radio stations and used for very different purposes ranging from image improvement to enlargement of the audience. In addition, we have surveyed a number of media managers to get an idea of the prospects for the multimediatization process.

The data obtained enable us to conclude: there is a considerable growth of interest in the issues of development of the convergent medium, which is manifested in a drastic reorganization of activities of online-resources and a more intensive use of online technologies, notably under the conditions of unpredictability of economic benefits.

2   The Moscow Market for FM Broadcasting and the Convergent Competitive Medium

In the experience of Russian and world practice, today there are several major reasons for radio stations to set up their own office on the Internet and develop their network presence in every possible direction.

The first reason may be linked with the marketing strategies of the station itself. In such a case, creation of a website, cooperation with social platforms and the like are regarded as important tools for promoting the station, attracting the audience to terrestrial broadcasting, and cross-promotion of terrestrial products and projects (Vartanova 2010a; Baranova 2011; Vartanova and Smirnov 2010).

Another reason may consist in the appeal of business development on the online basis. On the Internet, it is possible to sell opportunities related to internet advertising and marketing of all kinds, to raise revenues from pay services for ultimate consumers/listeners (subscription, selling content, joint projects, and so on), to develop cross-sales of terrestrial and online advertising. In this case the competitive medium will consist of both players in the internet broadcasting market and all the media and non-media RUnet projects rendering similar services (Vartanova and Smirnov 2010; Vartanova 2010b; Rosenholm et al. 2010).

The third reason is a natural tendency to follow the development of modern media landscape, which, in response to digital technologies, is gradually turning into a universal convergent/multimedia competitive space. Under these circumstances, any project/product of a radio station as well as of any other content creator has to make use of the opportunities of convergent production/distribution.

By "convergence" the authors of this article mean the opportunity to create a media product/project based on the integration of multimedia and social elements, things that are almost incompatible in offline and analog reality, and to distribute them through a large number of channels by digital means.

Further we shall briefly analyze the reasons and strategic prospects of Moscow FM radio stations in seeking to set up their online offices.

Competition in the market for FM broadcasting. Even among the largest metropolitan cities of the world, the Moscow market for FM broadcasting is one of the most saturated.

In the mid-2010 there were 54 stations in the market competing for the audience and advertisers. 10 management companies are represented in the market, the largest, in terms of the coverage area, being VKPM, Russkaya media gruppa, Yevropeyskaya media gruppa, VGTRK, and Gazprom-Media. In such groups they most often tend to separate stations from one another in terms of format and use the opportunities for packet advertising sales. The remaining 13 station are either part of the group of independent players ("Radio Shanson", "Megapolis FM" and "Serebryaniy Dosht") or affiliated with the companies for which radio is not their profile business. The number of private stations in the capital is 43 (*Radio Broadcasting in Russia* 2010, pp. 9–12).

As of July–September, 2010, according to TNS Rossiya, an average daily audience was about 9.5 million people listening to 2.5 stations on average. More than one million people showed preference for the top five stations in the market (with a figure exceeding 400 thousand people a station is likely to enter TOP20), the other stations had a smaller audience. The cumulative share of the ten leaders has been going down: in 2010 it dropped from 51 % to 46 %. This is indicative of sharpening competition: smaller players "drain" the audience from the leaders.

Competition for listeners' time and attention and advertisers' money in the Moscow market is really high, and radio stations have to resort to a wide range of marketing tools for interacting with the audience.

From this viewpoint, setting up one's own website and stream broadcasting on the Internet are absolutely essential today in the framework of promotion strategy. The benefits from online setting-up in the form of podcasts or stream transmissions are obvious for the already popular programmes and those that are yet to come. With their help, additional audiences can be created among both those listeners who try to make up for the missed episodes and those who are not keen on traditional terrestrial radio but become interested in a programme on the Net. In the world experience, many of them turn to terrestrial stations, and these online listeners are often found to be more active and more interactive. And, which is very important for radio, they are younger, often aged under 30. A circumspect use of podcasts, ideally, accompanied by video, and video clips on the website and across the Net, those coming from talk shows and even news programmes, is an important part of the multichannel strategy. Notably, the effect the Internet has on listening to terrestrial radio is opposite to what is going on in the print media. In the latter case, the effect is destructive: the Internet "drains" readers and advertising (especially in recent years). In the case of radio or television, the relations are more complicated. The main point here is to create a product, on the basis of a website, which would turn an internet user into a listener of traditional terrestrial radio.

A special task may consist in making online presence into an independent field of activity able to generate original products and services being in demand in the online and convergent medium.

For radio stations an online media business could take the form of stream broadcasting (terrestrial broadcasting + original channels) or setting up a portal/social platform which supports broadcasting with an original offer of products and services. Both require considerable human, temporal and financial resources. And it is doubtful whether such investments will prove financially rewarding.

Managing content and the audience on the Internet, at least today, cannot be limited to a certain resource, and, consequently, to a particular brand. Coverage of a wide audience on the Net is carried out through maximally open distribution, through setting up partnership networks wherein stream audio of "Ekho Moskvi" or "Serebryaniy Dosht", for example, becomes available on dozens and hundreds of platforms, while not so much the audience as advertising sales are limited to the basic websites. Unfortunately, the Russian market fails to supply sufficient data enabling us to make a conclusion about the traffic level of stream broadcasting of leading Moscow terrestrial radio stations. American and European experience indicates that even with successful stations and holdings, the figures do not exceed 5, maximally 10 % of the cumulative terrestrial audience. It should be noted, however, that competitors in internet broadcasting will include not only terrestrial colleagues but also dozens and hundreds of purely online stations.

For example, according to radiorating.ru, TOP20 of internet broadcasters includes only one terrestrial player, Love Radio Moskva, occupying a modest place in the middle of the list. Moreover, in Russia sales of advertising opportunities around internet radio broadcasting, both media and contextual ones, are at an early stage of development.

As far as the Russian market for internet advertising in general is concerned, it should be remembered that both in Russia and worldwide this advertising segment is characterized by a very high level of concentration (*Internet in Russia*, 2010, p. 54). For example, in 2009 the Yandex company, RUnet's leader in traffic and revenues, controlled 50 % of its total advertising turnover and in the market of contextual advertising about 75 %. The total share of Mail.ru and some other players in the segment of internet advertising amounts to 15–20 %. As a result, hundreds of other pretenders including projects of radio stations are left with the money which may seem big only at first sight.

Therefore, the opportunity to create financially independent projects based on internet presence is certainly important, but at present it is really available for a limited number of players in each media sector, including Russian radio stations.

Along with this, the development of digital technologies and the global trend towards shaping multimedia/convergent news and entertainment space are making the convergent strategy inevitable. Nowadays, any project on the levels of content creation, promotion and distribution implies this or that degree of using convergence opportunities.

Because of these, the project reaches a certain stage of completeness and makes use of opportunities for promotion and monetization.

3 Multimedia Technologies in Moscow FM Stations

To analyze multimedia strategies, we selected the following FM radio stations: "Biznes FM", "Vesti FM", "Russkays sluzhba novostey", "Ekho Moskvi" and "Serebryaniy Dosht". All of them (except for "Serebryaniy Dosht" mostly focusing on musical content) represent the so-called news/talk format. Such a preference for information and analytical broadcasting was deliberate, the aim of the research being to analyze convergent strategies with regard to radio, which attracts the most "serious" and economically and socially active audience. The research was made in the late 2010.

The most popular platform for distributing different types of content is a website, which can serve as a platform for audio, video, photographic, textual and infographic elements.

The website analysis showed that all the radio stations at hand (and, apparently, most of the stations present in the market) at least partially make use of multimedia opportunities for distributing different types of information.

Leaving aside the issues of posting textual content we shall consider the volume and form of audio and video materials here.

All the radio stations at hand, in this form or another, post audio content on their websites (see Table 1).

As it follows from the above information, all radio stations provide their listeners with an opportunity to listen to the audio stream. Not all of them post their podcasts on the website, and still fewer make downloading possible.

Therefore, it is obvious that the multimedia strand in the work of radio stations started to develop as just one more way of delivering content to the listener, i.e. terrestrial broadcasting came to be "diluted" with a non-terrestrial way of getting the same information. Podcasts, which suggest repeated listening and subsequently a deeper exposure to information, appear to be the second step. And lastly, downloading files, i.e. being able to "share" content with the audience, is the last stage.

Video content is one more type of multimedia information which can be represented on the websites of radio stations. Delivery can also take place in various forms (see Table 2). An important aspect is the origin of information. If audio content is always an original product of a radio station, video content may be either original or borrowed from other providers.

As one can see from the table, the attitude at the websites of radio stations to video content is different as compared to audio content. Some radio stations ("Biznes FM", "Vesti FM") do not operate with video at all. Others (for instance, "Ekho Moskvi") have worked out a wide range of videos—recordings of broadcasts, interviews, speeches, some of which are transmitted live. According to Yuri Fedutinov, general director of "Ekho Moskvi", every day the radio station produces from 4 to 5 h of video content. At the time of the research, "Ekho Moskvi" was planning to abandon WebCams and switch over to transmission from a special studio equipped with professional cameras, which was supposed to improve the quality of the materials. However, "Ekho Moskvi" does not have its own video archive as the radio station cooperates with RuTube, and the expenditure on storage is too high.

Table 1 Forms of providing audio content on the websites of radio stations

Radio station	Website	Type of audio content		
		Stream broadcasting	Podcast	Archive (file for downloading)
Serebryaniy Dosht	http://www.silver.ru/	+	+[a]	−
Russkays sluzhba novostey	http://www.rusnovosti.ru	+	+	+
Biznes FM[b]	http://radio.bfm.ru	+	−	−
Vesti FM	http://radio.vesti.ru/fm/	+	+	+
Ekho Moskvi	http://www.echo.msk.ru/	+	+	+

Source: data obtained from radio stations, our own analysis
[a]The "Peremotka" programme
[b]The research focuses on the radio station's website proper—http://radio.bfm.ru, but not on the resource http://www.bfm.ru, which is an independent information product, though it is part of the same media group

Table 2 Forms of providing video content and its origin on the websites of radio stations

Radio station	Website	Type of video content			Origin
		Stream broadcasting	Video podcast	Archive (file for downloading)	
Serebryaniy Dosht	http://www.silver.ru/	−	+	−	Outside provider[a]
Russkays sluzhba novostey	http://www.rusnovosti.ru	+[b]	+[c]	−	Outside provider
Biznes FM	http://radio.bfm.ru	−	−	−	−
Vesti FM	http://radio.vesti.ru/fm/	−	−	−	−
Ekho Moskvi	http://www.echo.msk.ru/	+[d]	+	−	Original product
					Outside provider

Source: data obtained from radio stations and our own analysis
[a]For the most part, the website demonstrates b-rolls made by a specially hired video studio
[b]Video transmission from the studio of "Russkays sluzhba novostey"
[c]Video blog of RSN
[d]Live transmission is not always there

A wide-scale mastering of the video space by "Ekho Moskvi" and total disregard for video content by "Biznes FM" and "Vesti FM" are two extremes. There are many in-between cases, however. For example, "Russkays sluzhba novostey" has introduces only certain types of presenting video materials: the radio station transmits live from its studio. It also has a special video blog with a slicing of topical items borrowed from outside sources. B- rolls about the life of the radio station are posted on the website of "Serebryaniy Dosht".

Textual materials represented on the websites of the radio stations at hand are also heterogeneous. "Serebryaniy Dosht" counts on reports about its events, the newsreel is also quite intense. The texts are original, they are written by the copy desk.

The main body of texts with "Russkays sluzhba novostey" consists in original news about current events, provided by the news service of RSN. The situation with "Biznes FM" is about the same: its website is the newsreel of the radio station.

The radio station "Vesti FM" normally confines itself to posting on its website transcriptions of its broadcasts and the news that has been on air.

The structure of the text body on the website of "Ekho Moskvi" is more complicated. Apart from the newsreel, the website includes transcriptions of original broadcasts, texts of interviews and a large number of blogs. As the editor-in-chief Nargiz Asadova put it, "We deliberately overload the first page of the website to facilitate our user's vision of the picture of the day. We assume that our users would choose to see the full picture without extra clicks. We have a small news block. The news is renewed every 30 minutes, simultaneously with newscasts coming out on the radio station."

Concluding the brief analysis of content typology represented on the websites of radio stations it should be noted that there is a direct dependence of content diversity from the position of the website in the general development strategy of the radio station. The website of "Ekho Moskvi" was initially designed as an appendix to the air, but now it is an independent media outlet living its own life. This is why it provides consumers with the widest possible spectrum of types of multimedia content.

By comparison, the website of "Biznes FM" is in fact a replica of the radio station's air while the role of multimedia information provider was taken upon by the website http://www.bfm.ru, an independent structure unrelated to terrestrial radio broadcasting. The current version of the website of "Vesti FM" is not viewed by the executive management of the company as an independent and valuable resource, while "Serebryaniy Dosht" and "Russkays sluzhba novostey" appear to be somewhere in between.

Interaction with the audience: the growth strategy. The specific character of interaction between the radio stations at hand and multimedia information consumers is also determined by the position of the online-resource in the radio station's development strategy.

"Ekho Moskvi" enjoys the largest audience among the five websites under consideration. According to Mail.ru, in October 2010 it was visited 38.2 million times, while the number of unique visitors amounted to 3.5 million. By comparison, the website of "Serebryaniy Dosht" is visited 20 000 times a day, "Vesti FM" has from 17,000 to 20,000 unique visitors a day. In spite of the discrepancies arising from heterogeneity of the data provided by the radio stations, it is obvious that the audience for "Ekho Moskvi" is many times larger.

The structure of the audience is determined by the position of the radio station and its online resource and, subsequently, by the types of content and its themes. For instance, in the case of the entertainment and information website of "Serebryaniy Dosht", the audience is divided into two almost equal parts between men and women (see Fig. 1), nearly half of them aged from 25 to 34, the most active section of the population.

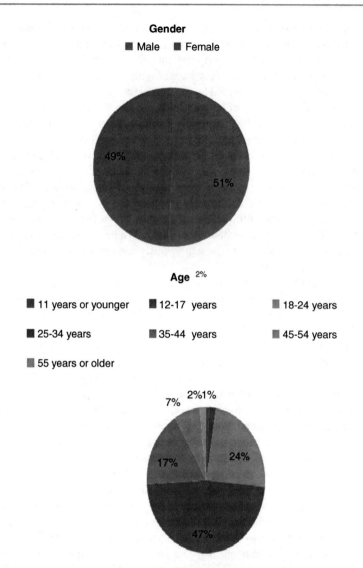

Fig. 1 Demographic characteristics of the audience for the website "Serebryaniy Dosht"

With a more analytical website "Ekho Moskvi", the audience is rather "masculine" and much more "elderly": the proportion of people aged over 36 amounts to 45 % (see Fig. 2).

The other radio stations at hand could be compared along the same lines, but is already obvious: a website develops in accordance with the development strategy for the terrestrial radio station, and the audience is also shaped in accordance with it.

It is equally obvious that the audience for the websites of the radio stations focusing on purposefully working with content is growing.

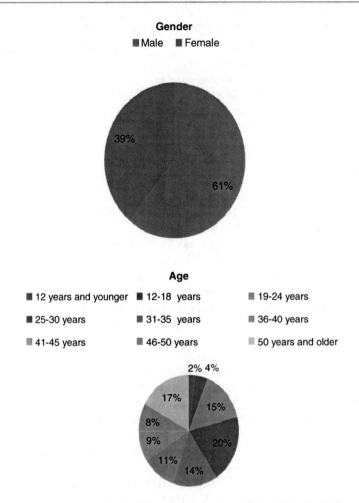

Fig. 2 Demographic characteristics of the audience for the website "Ekho Moskvi"

Thus, the number of visits to the website of "Serebryaniy Dosht", according to the data obtained by the company, has grown over the past year by 21 %. And the number of unique visitors to the website of "Ekho Moskvi" over the past 3 years has increased 3.5 times.

As Nargiz Asadova puts it, "it is the blog project that has become the engine (of audience growth). Plus social networks links with which have made the audience two or three times larger."

Blogs and elements of social media have traditionally been regarded as a part of the convergent medium. We have analyzed them for this paper because they represent user generated content.

In fact, all the five websites under analysis tend to use this method in order to both attract new readers (viewers, listeners) and generate new content (see Table 3).

Table 3 The use of blogs and their origin on the websites of radio stations

Radio station	Website	By its own authors[a]	By outside authors[a]
Serebryaniy Dosht	http://www.silver.ru	+	–
Russkays sluzhba novostey	http://www.rusnovosti.ru	+	+
Biznes FM[b]	http://radio.bfm.ru	–[b]	–[b]
Vesti FM	http://radio.vesti.ru/fm/	–	–
Ekho Moskvi	http://www.echo.msk.ru/	+	+

[a]Including those published for the second time (repostings)
[b]The radio station "Biznes FM" has a joint project with the portal BFM.RU: "Nadya Grosheva's portfolio". The so-named programme exists on the radio and, in the form of a blog, on the portal

As it becomes clear from the above table, there are websites which have no blogs; this, however, is true of those resources which are not strategically important for the media companies ("Biznes FM" and "Vesti FM").

By contrast, "Ekho Moskvi" has made its blogs into a major tool for attracting the audience; here the share of diaries carried over from some other platforms is rather large. Among the authors there are famous and even emblematic figures, such as politicians Boris Nemtsov and Irina Hakamada.

Presence in social networks is another element of the convergent medium. We have already mentioned that links with social networks (VKontakte, Facebook, Twitter, and "Moy Mir") have increased its audience two or three times. "Russkaya sluzhba novostey" has set up an office in the network of microblogs Twitter. "Serebryaniy Dosht" is represented in VKontakte as well as in Twitter and Facebook.

"Vesti FM" and "Biznes FM" meanwhile do without their offices in social networks.

Another point to consider is radio stations providing content for other than an online resource platforms, i.e. mobile telephones (particularly, iPhones) and pocket PCs.

The radio station "Ekho Moskvi" distributes its content by means of mobile telephony: a special supplement is being worked out for iPhone containing specific forms and types of interactive communication with the audience. The website of "Serebryaniy Dosht" reserves an option for subscribing to sms-memos signalling the beginning of selected programmes. In addition, radio programmes can be listened to on the mobile phone.

A similar service is offered by "Russkays sluzhba novostey", whose latest newscast can be listened to on the phone at any time. In addition, listeners using iPhones and iPods have an opportunity to listen to their radio station with the help of supplements Radio TimeMachine and iRusRadio, the free version included.

"Vesti FM" and "Biznes FM" have not got any special forms of content distribution through alternative devices and platforms so far (except for the Internet).

Changes in the work of editorial offices in response to convergence. The last element of convergence is applying its principles to work organization in the editorial office. In particular, we mean the use of the system referred to as "joint editorial office" and "joint staff meetings", a system implying that members of different departments work together at creating various types of content and shape the agenda distributing tasks among correspondents. We also mean the activities of "multiprofile" correspondents able to produce different types of content: texts, audios, videos, and photographic materials.

Our analysis has shown that editorial offices are eager to engage in "joint staff meetings", where journalists from different departments (in particular, radio and internet editions) work in a team at covering events but they hardly ever make use of "multiprofile" journalists' work. What is important for radio stations here is not saving on journalists' labour but achieving consensus among the departments and the rate of submitting materials.

Concluding our brief analysis of the convergent activity of FM radio stations, it should be noted that the levels of development of multimedia platforms in radio stations vary considerably, which is manifested in the variety of types of content, in the forms and ways of communicating with the audience, and in the selection of platforms for content distribution.

It is evident that the development of multimedia platforms is far from being a **spontaneous** process; it is a **strategic** process depending on the decisions made by the executive management of a radio station with regard to the prospects for development of its website and mastering new ways of interacting with the audience, information and staff. The more attention the management of a radio station give to the development of its online resource, the higher is the level of convergence. Notably, a large part of the audience turns to the website **only because of the multimedia elements that are used**. Thus, only about 40 % of visits to the website of "Ekho Moskvi" are accounted for by interest in terrestrial materials, and as many as 60 % by interest in blogs, repostings and videos.[1]

4   The Strategies for the Convergent Medium Development on the Basis of Radio

Development of online platforms. This chapter is a description and analysis of the strategies for the convergent medium development as radio stations themselves formulate them.

So far the radio stations we have studied do not have any documented strategies for the multimedia development as they are not planning their actions step-by-step (the only exception is business plans).

It is notable, however, that most managers surveyed (3 in 5) voiced their plans to make considerable changes to the website and, subsequently, to the media platform as it is. The character of changes depends on the position of the online resource in the structure of the company or holding.

Now we shall analyze the plans of the radio stations in greater detail.

"Originally, the website was set up as a reflection of the air, a kind of its appendix, for no commercial purposes. By now, it has grown into an enterprise. Our policies have changed...We engage professionals, who analyze the website in order to understand which direction we should move in. We also commission and post on the website

---

[1] The data obtained from the companies.

monthly statistical researches", says Nargiz Asadova from "Ekho Moskvi". In the near future (spring 2011) they are planning to launch a new version of the website. One of its important peculiarities will be elements of social networks: users' personal pages and subscription to bloggers' texts. In "Ekho Moskvi" these changes are driven by a strategic purpose: to form a community of people around the internet resource who will feel a kind of belonging to agenda formation.

As we pointed out above, by means of new equipment "Ekho Moskvi" is planning to secure higher quality of content on the website and to create new supplements to its mobile version.

The website of "Vesti FM" is faced with a prospect of more radical changes. In the early 2011 plans were announced to launch a drastically different version of the website. Unlike today's website, the new one is likely to attract a large audience. The target audience for the new website will be the so-called "premium sector" of users, in particular, the age cluster of 30–50, whose members are most active economically.

In spite of the fact that most original materials on this new website will continue to duplicate the air, this resource is likely to become an independent networked structure relying in the first place on the interactive work with the audience. In particular, user generated content is to be widely used. In addition, the new website will have its mobile version and integrate with Russian and foreign social networks.

"Biznes FM" has somewhat different plans. As the radio station is part of the holding "Objedinyonnye media" along with the popular portal of business information http://www.bfm.ru, which is a media outlet historically independent from radio, an independent powerful portal of the radio station with original content would become a strong competitor to the already existing resource.

For this reason, the main task of "Biznes FM" is to set up an independent page on the portal http://www.bfm.ru as soon as possible. However, the radio station is not planning to offer a wide range of media products on this page: the chief aim is to regulate the structure and sort out texts in terms of genre, priority and so on. Radio will remain the primary source of content; it will provide materials for the website for further, minor adaptation.

As it becomes clear from the above materials, the changes in the operation of the websites of the radio stations at hand are quite profound and touch upon various aspects of their work and of the volume of multimedia materials represented on them. In spite of the considerable differences in the programmes described, they prove that multimedia technologies are used in the work of FM radio stations more and more actively and that the convergent medium expands.

Financial efficiency. An important element of the further development of multimedia technologies on the basis of Moscow FM radio stations is their financial efficiency.

We surveyed some managers from the radio stations at hand to find out how financially rewarding their multimedia technologies are.
- "Ekho Moskvi" claims that the radio station pays off and has a very good potential.
- The profits from the website gained by "Serebryaniy Dosht" are too insignificant to speak about.

- The website of "Biznes FM" contributes more to the image of the company than to its incomes, and there is not much hope for the future.
- The financial benefits from the website of the radio station "Vesti FM" are low but the future version of the site seems to be promising.

Conclusion

The process of transformation of mass media activities in response to digitization is fast and irreversible. The radio market is not an exception to this general rule.

The research we have made reveals drastic differences in the level of development of multimedia platforms in Moscow FM radio stations. These differences are manifested in the variety of types of content, in the forms of communicating with the audience and in the selection of platforms for content distribution.

There is every reason to believe that the use of multimedia platforms enables radio stations to increase the audience for the website and perhaps the audience for the radio station itself. A change in the social and demographic characteristics of the audience and its loyalty is also possible. Combined with the formation of a specific community around a multimedia project this may contribute to its monetization.

Another conclusion to be made is that members of the professional multimedia community realize the importance of multimedia development and engage in forming strategic plans. Normally, these plans are concerned with widening the range of multimedia products, more intense interactive work with the audience and changes in the system of managing the website content.

Implementing multimedia strategies are very likely to have a positive commercial effect, a fact supported by the data obtained from the radio stations and online-resources. But in shaping and implementing multimedia strategies, however, monetization remains a less important matter giving way to such "non-material" characteristics as shaping a loyal and creative community and creating a positive image of the radio station.

In spite of objective difficulties involved in implementing multimedia strategies we believe that in the nearest future the use of multimedia platforms on the basis of radio stations will be increasingly active.

References

Allan, S. (2006). *Online news: Journalism and the Internet*. Maidenhead: Open University Press.
Baranova, E. (2011). Mass media convergence through the eyes of Russian journalists. In E. Vartanova (Ed.), *World of media 2011 yearbook of Russian media and journalism studies*. Moscow: Faculty of Journalism, Lomonosov Moscow State University, MediaMir.
Deuze, M. (2007). *Media work*. Cambridge: Polity.
Doctor, K. (2010). *Newsonomics. Twelve new trends that will shape the news you get*. New York: St. Martin's Press.
Feldman, T. (1996). *An introduction to digital media*. London and New York: Routledge.
Flew, T. (2005). *New media. An introduction*. Oxford: Oxford University Press.

Gillmor, D. (2004). *We the media. Grassroots journalism by the people, for the people.* Sebastopol, CA: O'Reilly Media.

Kolodzy, J. (2006). *Convergence journalism. Writing and reporting across the news media.* Lanham, MD: Rowman & Littlefield.

Kung, L., Picard, R., & Towse, R. (2008). *The Internet and the mass media.* London: Sage.

Lebedev, P., Pautina, L., Barabanov, V., Khudolei A., Makarova, A., Sidorenko, A. (2010). Internet in Russia. Current state, trends and prospects for development. Retrieved from http://www.fapmc.ru/

Meikle, G., & Redden, G. (Eds.). (2010). *News online. Transformations and continuities.* Basingstoke: Palgrave Macmillan.

Quinn, S., & Filak, V. F. (Eds.). (2005). *Convergent journalism: An introduction.* Burlington, MA: Elsevier, Focal Press.

Radio Broadcasting in Russia. (2010). Current state, trends and prospects for development. Retrieved from http://www.fapmc.ru/

Vartanova, E. (2010a). Konvergenz und Medien. In M. Friedrichsen, J. Wendland, & G. Woronenkowa (Eds.), *Medienwandel durch Digitalisierung und Krise* (pp. 95–103). Baden-Baden: Nomos.

Vartanova, E. (2010b). Media industry and convergence [In Russian: Mediaindustriya I Convergencia]. In M. Lukina (Ed.), *Internet and mass media. Theory and practice [In Russian: Internet-SMI. Teoriya i praktika]* (pp. 40–62). Moscow: Aspekt.

Vartanova, E., & Smirnov, S. (2010). Contemporary structure of the Russian media industry. In A. Rosenholm, K. Nordenstreng, & E. Trubina (Eds.), *Russian mass media and changing values* (pp. 21–40). Routledge: London.

Wilson, T. (2009). *Understanding media users. From theory to practice.* Chichester: Wiley-Blackwell.

Social Media in Russia: Its Features and Business Models

Marianna Blinova

Social Media. Is it fashion and passion or the greatest communication breakthrough since the technological revolution times? Or is it an innovation management instrument, which helps companies and clients to stay in equal positions to affect the goods and services? It is phenomenon of social interaction or wikinomics—the innovation economical model, stated on the global collaboration people all over the world, isn't it? Everyone of these questions could be positive answered.

Audience became not only the consumer of information but the producer and distributor at the same time. This communication model attracts the business society as a channel of communication with consumers and as an independent business model, which could be profitable.

We know many different forms of social media, but in general we can divide them into two big groups: general interest (global) social media and niche social media or web-sites for special interests. General interest social media tries to combine as big Internet audience as possible and become a kind of base of Internet users contacts. The niche social media are devoted to special interest. Both models have preferences and lacks as for users as for owners of those resources.

Today users from all over the world integrated on the social media. In the middle of 2010 the global audience of social media showed 72.5 % of the whole number of Internet users.

Russia has the most engaged social networking audience worldwide. According to official data, 34.5 million of Russian users (74.5 % from the whole number of Internet users in Russia) are members of at least one of social media in 2010. In 2010, Russians spent on average twice the amount of time within social networks as their global counterparts, racking up about 9.8 h per month. The second place takes

M. Blinova (✉)
National Research University – Higher School of Economics, Moscow, Russia
e-mail: mblinova@hse.ru

Table 1 Top three Russian social media ranked by the audience among the biggest social networks in Russia (000) (2010).

		Total unique visitors (000)[a]
1	Vkontakte	25,500
2	Odnoklassniki	19,900
3	MoiMir@Mail.ru	6,655
	Total Internet Audience	**44,027**[b]

[a] http://www.liveinternet.ru/rating/ru/meeting/day.html
[b] comScore Media Metrix
http://www.comscore.com/Press_Events/Press_Releases/2010/10/Russia_Has_Most_Engaged_Social_Networking_Audience_Worldwide

Israel (9.2 h), third is Turkey (7.6 h).[1] According to unofficial data, the social media audience coincides with 98 % of general Runet audience—more than 44 million Web users.

This research is focused on Russian social media, especially: Vkontakte, Odnoklassniki and MoiMir@Mail.ru, which are the first ones on Russian social media market and the most popular in Russia (Table 1). It is very important to explore features and to show business models and monetization of those web-sites. These three social media belongs to the one media holding Mail.ru Group, which holds 100 % Mail.ru (MoiMir), ICQ, Odnoklassniki, 97 % Headhunter, 32.5 % Vkontakte, 25.1 % Qiwi, 30 % Liveinternet, 30 % Mamba, 2.4 % Facebook, 1.47 % Zynga, 5.13 % Groupon, etc.

В КОНТАКТЕ

The leader of Russian social networks is **Vkontakte**. It is also the most popular resource in Ukraine. According to TNS Gallup's data, *Vkontakte* is one of the most popular Social resource with more than 100 million registered users, but just about 25.5 million really access the web.[2] Of all the unique users *Vkontakte* 70 % are from Russia, including 15 % Muscovites and 12 % users from Saint Petersburg.[3]

Vkontakte.ru means "In touch" or "keeping contact". You can get the profile on *Vkontakte* just being invited by some of your friends—user of *Vkontakte*. The platform was founded in October, 2006 as Company Limited.

Vkontakte was created upon the model of Facebook. And now it looks very much like Facebook, although with less functionality. Just like Facebook, *Vkontakte* users can create profiles with their content, connect with friends, create and join groups. Groups have more or less the same functionality as Facebook groups, i.e. publish

---

[1] http://www.comscore.com/Press_Events/Press_Releases/2010/10/Russia_Has_Most_Engaged_Social_Networking_Audience_Worldwide

[2] http://vkontakte.ru/help.php?page=about

[3] http://www.liveinternet.ru/rating/ru/meeting/day.html

Fig. 1 VKontakte Sources of Profit

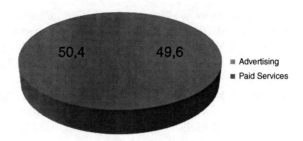

links, posts, videos and photos on the wall. *Vkontakte* group pages can be programmed, rebuilt and optimized. With a good knowledge of *Vkontakte* internal programming language one can develop subpages and navigation menus, add banners and links to external websites, etc.

VKontakte offers additional possibilities such as opening two accounts "Rubles" and "Golosa" (voices). These accounts could be recharged via SMS, online banking and money transfer systems, paying terminals outside Russia. "Golosa"—is universal currency for paying off for all the applications. "Golosa" could be also used for rates definition and gift cost definition.

"Rubles" was crated for payment for any payable services in website: advertisement, online shopping, and other services. But the system of electronic currency "Rubles" was cut off in July 2011, because it was incompatible with the Russian Federation Law about paid system. According to the Law signed by Dmitry Medvedev in July 2011 only the lending agencies are allowed to work with imitation of the electronic currency.

Vkontakte also has similar to Facebook advertisement program with similar targeting options. *Vkontakte* started advertisement in June 2008. Thus they signed a contract with company Media Plus—the European Media group sales house, one of the leaders in broadcasting advertising sales.

The basic trend of advertising activity in *Vkontakte* is contextual advertising, targeted with demographic location, browsers and user's platform.

The advertising is the main profit source for *VKontakte*, but, as in two other social media, not the only one income item of the company. Though the information about overall profit is closed (Fig. 1).

Odnoklassniki.ru (The analog of English Classmates.com)—is the second popular social platform in Russia searching for classmates, schoolmates, alumnies, colleagues, friends, etc. This media society combines Russian speaking users from all over the world. According to TNS Gallup's data, has about 20,000,000 users.

Odnoklassniki.ru started in March 2006 as a social net. Initially this project started as a hobby with a sole business model as a little mark in one advertising agency as a new platform for advertising placement. In November 2006 this web site has had 1.5 million registered members. Founder decided to inaugurate website. The users were multiplying in arithmetical progression.

The search on *Odnoklassniki.ru* is organized by name, location, university / school name, year of graduation, place and year or army service, etc. Every person signing up creates a profile and can connect with friends, publish photos, update status and join groups. Neither profiles nor group pages are public (i.e. are not open for search engines). There is no such thing as a fan page. There is no possibility to search for groups.

Every user can see the guest's name who visited user's profile. Besides, all user public actions (forum messages, photo uploading, adding friends, etc.) are visible on a line activity. Quite recently, they implemented paid service named "Invisible". The user with this service being rambling on other's profiles will be indicated as invisible with neither name and profile photo, nor any profile's information.

Since October 2008 it is possible to register account only with limited functionality. This version does not allow to send the messages, upload and estimate pictures, leave comments on forums, visit other profiles. To obtain all functions listed above is necessary to send paid SMS message. Moreover this social media portal offers a wide range of payable services such as: more space for photo placement, erase negative photo estimation and remain positive estimation, switching off indicator user is online, a lot of emoticons and more other useful and fun functions.

In addition the web-site allows several paid services: space for additional pictures, deleting rates and good marks for your own pictures, shutdown the message that user is online, a wide range of choice the emoticons.

Since the 23rd January 2009 there is a new service which allows to delete all uninvited quests from the viewed quests list. It is also possible now to lock profile for all users except friends.

Since April 2010 they implemented payable online game service where users can pay off the service through SMS message or e-money (Fig. 2).

Banned link list. There is a rigid taboo in this social media platform for the links of one significant competitor—*Odnoklassniki*—*Vkontakte*. The links with content "vkontakte.ru" do not work, moreover user receives message "your message contains inadmissible words or phrase", the phrase "vkontakte" automatically distorted on "vkontakte". It should be noted that the competitor—*Vkontakte.ru*—has no similar restrictions on the links.

Odnoklassniki.ru is prize-winner of "Runet Awards" in 2006 and 2007, "Russian Entertainment Awards" in nomination "Website Of The Year" in 2007, National

Fig. 2 Odnoklassniki.ru Sources of Profit

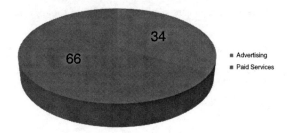

top-ten of Runet in 2008, winner of grand prize in competition of "Master of Brandbuilding" in 2008, grand prize winner in professional competition Rotor 2008 and Rotor ++ in nomination "Influence on Offline".

Recently *Odnoklassniki* started new social project Glavmarket. This project is based on the most popular worldwide online marketing. Online marketplace is a new option in this social media, that makes unique online marketing project.

During a month there were placing more than 600,000 items, created 180 online stores such as: ozon.ru, holodilnik.ru, pleer.ru, svyaznoy.ru, eldorado.ru, tehnosila.ru, darom.ru, etc.

There are several motives of a fast growth popularity online marketing among advertisers: possibility to offer the items to all Runet online audience and social media audience, the method to place online stores on given platform which is easy, fast and convenient, and the last but not least—simple and transparent model pay off.

The rates of online stores are constructed solely on the basis of user's assessments. The rates are available to user's friends, there is also available feedback, hint, purchasing list. These options allow to make item selection and purchasing consciously and purposefully.

After the merger of two biggest players of the Russian Internet market Port.ru and NetBridge, Mail.ru started up at the end of 2001 with free email service and with the time turned into Russia's second largest portal and a major search engine (although they have not used their own search algorithm until recently, relying on those of Google and Yandex).

In May 2007 Mail.ru started social media—*MoiMir* (My world) with lots of services for communication, searching new friends, share the information—blogs, photos, video, music, etc. Distinctive feature is the possibility to download the special application for communication from mobile phone or laptop (ICQ analog). Today *MoiMir@Mail.ru* is the third most popular social media in Russia with about 6.7 million active users.

Table 2 Common and distinctive features of Russian social media

Social media	Options Vkontakte	Odnoklassniki	MoiMir@Mail.ru
Creating profile	+	+	+
Creating and joining groups	+	+	−
Video, photo, music sharing	+	+	+
Online games	+	+	+
Advertising	+	+	+
"Like"	+	+	+
Searching for person	+	+	+
Searching for group	+	+	−
Switching off indicator user is online	−	+	+
Space for additional pictures	+	+	+
Deleting rates for your own pictures	+	+	−
Visible guests	−	+	+

During a long period banner advertising of *Mail.ru* was without a rival. That is why there was a notion that banner advertising is the basic source of the company revenue. But recently online games became one of the important part of *Mail.ru* business model. All games are free-to-play, but for the extra advantages you have to pay: armour, weapons, promptings. According to Forbes[4] online games bring about 47 % revenue. Within planning IPO in Summer 2010, owners of *Mail.ru* decided to merge with social media *Odnoklassniki*. During the first 6 months the income of advertisement brought just 26 %. The rest of networks implemented additional services such as virtual gifts which users pay off via sms-service *(Table 2)*.

Odnoklassniki is the last social media among largest in Russia who launched online games in 2010.

On the first half of a year 2010 they charged 167,000 users per month for usual multiuser online games, and 564,000 users were charged for the games in social media. The most popular online games are: "Perfect World" adapted for Runet, "Legacy of the Dragons" and "Allods Online" designed by *Mail.ru*. For these two games they charge 103,000 users per month. The top-three games of social media: "Lovely Farm", "Legacy of the Dragons" and "SuperCity", 329,000 users monthly pay for these games.

Recently *Mail.ru* announced creation of their new ad platform, which will serve ads in their social network *MoiMir*.

MoiMir@Mail.ru was completely monitizated in 2010 (Fig. 3).

---

[4] http://www.forbes.ru/tehno/internet-i-telekommunikatsii/59084-glavnyi-istochnik-dohodov-mailru-onlain-igry

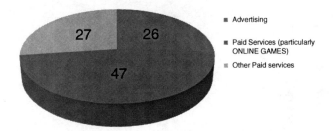

Fig. 3 MoiMir@Mail.ru Sources of Profit

1 Russia's Representation in International Social Media

It is impossible to imagine life of modern person without Internet. Global Net is one of the most popular and demanded communication channel in the world.

Russian Internet market is recognized as one of the fastest developed in the world.

When *Odnoklassniki* and *Vkontakte* were started the international-known Facebook and Classmates did not have Russian version. Today we can say that these two Russian social media are made very similar to their international rivals. The owners and management of international and foreign social media saw that they lost a lot not starting Russian version as well, but it was too late. So Facebook and some other international social platforms are popular in Russia but not that much as their Russian "analogues".

As we noted before Russia is the leader of social media users and there are many international social media which are popular among Russians. For comparison: In Russia, Twitter has managed to avoid the initial user fall-off that the platform suffers from in the United States — roughly 60 % of Russians update their profile daily according to Yandex, the preeminent search provider in Russia.

Worldwide Twitter has over 50,000,000 users, which produce 4,000,000 tweets every day. In Russia they've got only 76,000 Twitter users and approximately 50,000 tweets per day.[5]

Russian President Dmitry Medvedev is one of those prolific tweeters (he has more than half a million followers on his four accounts). Medvedev has engaged on social platforms such as Twitter with an often refreshing and surprisingly candid approach.

Although Twitter and microblogs are not that popular among Russians as Russian social media.

---

[5] http://www.russiansearchtips.com/category/social-media-in-russia/

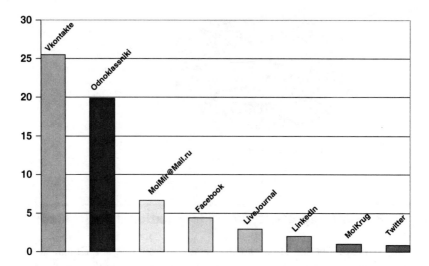

Fig. 4 Total Russian social media audience ranked by unique visitors (000)

Facebook officially launched its site in Russia in April 2010 and only ranks about No. 4 with 4.4 million now.[6]

Odnoklassniki.ru has become the domain of the older generation, and VKontakte the hangout of young middle- and lower-class Russians, Facebook is the network of choice for the urban and the urbane. Facebook's Russian users are generally of the wealthier, well-traveled, cosmopolitan variety, have foreign friends and tend to live in Moscow and St. Petersburg.

In June, 2011 LinkedIn has launched new versions of its website, particularly in Russian, Romanian and Turkish. According to the company, the English version of the website already had 400,000 users from Russia and over 1,000 groups related to Russia, a website covering IT and telecom issues.

The IT and telecom sectors provide the largest number of registered Russian users, LinkedIn representatives told ComNews.ru. Among the leading Russian employers represented on the website are oil joint venture TNK BP, mobile operator MTS and search engine Yandex.

MoiKrug.ru (means "My Circle") is the largest Russian social network for professionals.

As for June, 2011, there is about 31,773 million accounts exist on LiveJournal. LJ is one of the largest Internet community on the Runet with about 12 % of global share (Fig. 4).

International social media are popular mostly among young generation in Russia. Basically it is rather high social status people, mostly 25–50 years old

---

[6] http://www.socialbakers.com/facebook-statistics/russia

Table 3 Total Internet Audience Russia

	Total Internet audience	Total unique visitors 44,027,000 Among them	Reach (%) 100
1.	Vkontakte	25,500,000	57.9
2.	Odnoklassniki	19,900,000	45.2
3.	MoiMir@Mail.ru	6,655,000	15.1
4.	Facebook	4,400,000	10.0
5.	LiveJournal	874,785	2.0
6.	LinkedIn	630,000	1.4
7.	MoiKrug (Yandex.ru)	400,000	0.9
8.	Twitter	76,000	0.2

[a]Based on different sources, 2011

high education audience, who know foreign languages and have real interest to global problems (Table 3).

2 Monetization of Social Media: Advertising as One of the Income Sources

Social media is more often used for placing advertising, because social nets are the most active distributor of media content. Thus today we can talk about new type of advertising communications—**SMM** (Social Media Marketing). This strategy could be very efficient for advertising goods and services for the primary audience. Social media is a possibility for dynamical dialog with audience for interactivity and cooperation.

The advertising market of Runet grows intensively. In spite of crisis influence online advertising sector is developing very fast and this trend increases from year to year. For the most part of social media advertising still the only one method of getting profit. Although the business model in niche social media advertising works rather effectively than the model of general interest web-sites, in spite of less audience.

The share of Mail.ru grows as well. Especially in the first quarter of 2011 the advertising of Mail.ru Group increased by 77 % with $ 25.4 million and by 66.7 % for media and contextual advertising accordingly.

Though there is some limitation of advertising as a source of profit, in spite of rapid growth of Internet advertising. Here is an appreciable tendency that major part of advertising budgets flows into the social media, but will never flowed there entirely. Thereby there is every day establishing brand new internet projects with advertising business model oriented.

According to the Rose Creative Strategy agency's data there is about 58 % Russian Internet users watch online advertising, especially brands, about 28 % search information about brands in social media before effecting a purchase and

Table 4 Top three Russian social media monetization (2010)

	2010 million dollars	Share (%)	Source of profit
Vkontakte[a]	47.3	50.4	Advertising
	46.5	49.6	Paid services
	93.8	100	TOTAL
Odnoklassniki[b]	23.2	33.7	Advertising
	45.7	66.3	Paid services
	68.9	100	Total
MoiMir@Mail.ru[c]	16.9	26	Advertising
	30.6	47	Paid services (particularly ONLINE GAMES)
	17.5	27	Other paid services
	65.0	100	TOTAL

[a]http://isocialnetwork.ru/2011/04/29/financial-report-vkontakte-odnoklassniki.html
[b]http://www.lenta.ru/news/2011/03/28/kontakte/
[c]http://www.forbes.ru/tehno/internet-i-telekommunikatsii/59084-glavnyi-istochnik-dohodov-mailru-onlain-igry

even subscribe for brands, their groups, webs and blogs on social media. The first Top 10 brands on *VKontakte* in average gets more than 41 thousand followers. Every fourth Russian Internet user suppose, that information found on social media, had an influence on their decision of purchasing.[7]

There are several growing tendencies of Russian advertising market. We can see the erasing distinction between contextual advertising and media advertising. Now the media advertising could be targeted on specific particular consumer, while contextual advertising is getting media features.

Simultaneously is developing new formats video advertisement alike. One of the important goal of internet advertising is approximation to TV advertising visualization level. Internet platforms such as Mail.ru Group with the same scale level audience as Federal TV channels, will plan the approximate same budget as Federal TV channels. Video advertisement as a new format is also developing.

The most efficient business model among social media is to give both: free and paid online services. It is very simple, free online services combine wide audience, paid services bring the profit. From this point of view the big global networks became a hostage of their own business model. As far as users join not by interests, it is extremely difficult to segment them. Advertisers often refuse to spend their money on advertising for abstract, inappropriate audience, who will never buy their goods. That is why many global social media are concerned in searching new models and ways of content and traffic monetization.

Subject social media—is community, which join people by interests. We can say that just subject social media bring unexpected profit. Thereby creation and

---

[7] http://www.cossa.ru

supporting subject resources do not require extra expenditure. Niche social media segmenting the audience by categories, it is allowing to hypertargetting campaigns (Table 4).

Conclusions

Although social media in Russia are young enough, Russia is one of the fast growing social media markets in Europe and in the world. More than 30 % of population in Russia (141.8 million people[8]) are engaged on Internet. About half of the total number of Russian users use the mobile telephones for logging on Internet, in particular more than 30 %—for logging on social media. Russians are embracing social and digital media in ways deeper and more impactful than other countries around the world.

Russians prefer Russian social media more than international ones, although the Russian representation on international web-sites is considerable.

The business model of Russian social media is based on free and paid services, especially advertising and online games which bring significant income to the holder.

The advertising market in Russia and especially of Runet grows intensively. Its share is about 10.3 % of Russian advertising market.[9] Though the clear distinction between contextual advertising and media advertising is erasing, the contextual advertising is still more popular than media ads. According to our research the advertising revenue on three most popular Russian social media is from 26 to more than 50 % of total income. Online games generate another half of revenue for Russian social media. It is important to remember that the most part of Russian Internet users watch online advertising, search information about brands in social media before effecting a purchase and even subscribe for brands on social media.

---

[8] http://demoscope.ru/weekly/2011/0455/barom01.php
[9] http://www.akarussia.ru/knowledge/market_size/id457

China's Media Industry: Landscape and Development

Min Hang

1 Introduction

As a country with 1.3 billion people moving fast forward into the information age, China features a rich media landscape. The media industry in China is characterized by a fast transformation from a government owned structure into new models, from traditional press into new media and innovative forms of news making. This chapter will introduce the development of China's media industry and portray the landscape of different media sectors in China.

China's media industry is composed by traditional media sectors and new media sectors. The total industry revenue was 580 billion RMB in the year of 2010, a 17.8 % growth from the previous year. The following paragraphs will present China's media development according to ten major sectors, including radio, TV broadcasting, newspaper, book publishing, magazine, movie, audio visual, online news, ISP and search engineer sectors.

1.1 Radio Broadcasting Sector

Before 1978, there existed no advertising market in China—there was no business in broadcasting or publishing advertisements in newspapers, on magazines, by radio or television. Only after the opening up of China did the broadcasting stations start to receive revenues from advertising. The 1980s was a time when every station began to play advertisement, but with many restrictions.

Through the continual opening up of China, especially during the 1990s when the market economy mechanism was established in China and began to develop, radio stations started to rely more on the advertisement fees. The limited funds,

M. Hang (✉)
Tsinghua University, Beijing, China
e-mail: hangmin@tsinghua.edu.cn

allocated from the government, could not satisfy the quick development of media. By the year 2000, China's advertisement revenue had already broke through 1.5 billion RMB Yuan, while it topped 3 billion Yuan in 2004 and surpassed 7 billion Yuan in 2008. The advertisement market continued to expand in the past few years (China Radio and TV Development Annual Report 2002–2009).

In China, the radio broadcasting market consists of China National Radio (CNR), China Radio International (CRI) and stations at the provincial, prefectural and county levels, all of which form a "tripod" state. But in a market with three portions, the local radio stations are increasingly becoming more competitive. Even in first-tier cities like Beijing, Shanghai or Guangzhou where markets are very saturated, stations of "localized" traits control the local market.

While the competition in radio broadcasting market is developing fast, CNR has the largest market share in China. For CNR, one of its major advantages is that it broadcasts around the whole country, securely occupying first in the nation for the single frequency market. Among the top ten stations with the largest number of listeners in cities across the country are CNR's *Sounds of China*, *Music Radio* and *Business Radio*, which also rank the top three and account for 10 % of the total market share.

Even though radio broadcast in China has remained in a state of growth, economic and local development is entwined. At places where the economic situation is well off, the proportion of investments takes up a large share of the amount invested in advertisements nationwide. The advertisement business at economically developed regions is more advanced than that of those regions lagging behind. However, it is different from the unique television advertisement of "China Central Television (CCTV)." Radio stations at the provincial level have higher volumes of advertisement sales.

In the wave of digitalization and the surge of networks, radio broadcasting firms have greatly changed by merging traditional broadcasting with digital broadcasting. Through the wide use and spread of DAB, CMMB and other new technologies, a new trend appears in the industry. The proportion of listeners listening outdoors at some given periods of time are much higher than those people who listen to radio at home. In addition, people's expenditure on listening to radio outdoors has reached around 30 %, especially in Beijing, where it has passed 40 %. Listening to radio outdoors because of the increase of vehicles and wide coverage in public transportation is another reason why mobile listeners skyrocketed (National and Provincial Radio and Television Income Report 2000–2008).

The radio broadcasting market is fragmented in China with local radio stations playing major roles in their respective areas. A research conducted by the author on China's media concentration shows a declining HHI in the radio broadcasting sector, the HHI figures changed from 334 in year 1992 to 1993 in year 2008. This indicates a decentralized market structure in the radio sector.

1.2 TV Broadcasting Sector

The revenue sources for TV broadcasting include cable subscription and advertisement, with advertisement as the major source for TV companies in China. China Central Television (CCTV) dominates the advertising market, while some provincial TV companies attract large advertising revenue because of their popular satellite TV channels, such as Hunan Satellite TV, Jiangsu Satellite TV, etc.

There were 354 TV stations in China in 2010, broadcasting a total number of 1,206 channels. Through the process of TV companies merging, the number of TV stations in the country decreased to 296 in 2007, while the total number of channels increased to 2,984, offering diverse media content to audiences.

Since the new millennium, China formally launched its plan of transforming from analog TV to digital TV. The number of digital TV subscribers surpassed 50 million in 2011, and the country is expected to switch off the analog signal nationwide in 2015.

The other trend affecting the TV broadcasting arena is the spread of internet usage for TV content. The development of webcasting makes it possible for audiences to view TV programs online. The current trend is for TV companies to move online, offering program from their websites.

CCTV is the dominant player in the broadcasting sector. It has 16 national channels, most of them airing 24 h a day. It is considered one of the big three media outlets in China, along with the People's Daily newspaper and Xinhua News Agency. The CCTV New Year's Gala is a Chinese New Year special produced by China Central Television, broadcast on the eve of Chinese New Year on its flagship CCTV-1. The broadcast has a yearly viewership of over 1 billion viewers, making it one of the premiere television events of Mainland China.

Shanghai Media Group (SMG) is the second largest player in the TV market. SMG has widely diversified its media business in recent years, attracting large advertisement revenue. Next to SMG are media groups at the provincial level, including Hunan Provincial Media Group, Anhui Provincial Media Group, etc.

If measured company wise, China's TV broadcasting market is concentrated by major players including CCTV and SMG. However, if measured channel wise, there is less concentration in the TV broadcasting sector. Usually, Chinese viewers have more than 60 different channels to choose from, and the development of digital TV provides more channel selections for the audiences. An increasing competition can be seemed among different TV channels in the country.

1.3 Newspaper Sector

China's newspaper industry continued to operate during the planned economy and the opening phase of China. In the closed economy era, many cities had a "single large newspaper" structure. The industry was a monopoly with no competition, so traditional media continually gained economic benefits. After the opening of China, the industry transformed through different developmental stages, mainly concentrating on the distribution of the business system, less on the operation of how news is covered and edited, and even less on macro-management aspects.

China's newspaper industry mainly earns revenue from distribution, advertisements, and diverse operations, among which advertisement is the major revenue source. During the market economy, the country gradually decreased allocated funds to newspapers. Thus, newspaper companies became more commercialized to create income and followed the trend of the economy to become collectivized firms. The development of internet pressured the newspapers, with many companies launching their own websites to avoid being eliminated, beginning a phase of merging media.

Although in 1992, the market economic regulations of China added the domain of newspapers, many were financially independent, but had yet to be commercialized completely. By then, newspaper firms were small, dispersed with a low level of marketization. So when China entered the WTO, the market faced more pressure from international competition. Media companies began to expand, forming conglomerates playing their roles well. The formation of conglomerates has the opportunity to earn more profits, and was not just an economic process after 1996.

There have been more newly formed newspaper conglomerates at both national and local level these recent years. The author used newspaper circulation data published by the State Administration of Press and Publication to measure the market concentration in the newspaper sector, the result indicates a declining concentration in the newspaper market, HHI figures dropped from 2,104 in year 1992, to 1,393 in year 2007. The recent years have witnessed this trend of decentralization in the newspaper sector in China.

1.4 Book Publishing Sector

Along with the news publishing industry, computers, internet, wireless communication, e-commerce, and other new technology sped up mergers. The carrier format, technological skills, format of broadcast, method of sales, idea of management, and the way the firm is managed are all in the process of reform. News publishing firms are entering into a period of large transformations, adjustments, and developments in China.

Currently, the monopolization of the news publishing industry is lower than others and in China a monopoly has yet to occur. The largest and most comprehensive publishing company in terms of economic scale is Jiangsu's Phoenix Publishing & Media. In 2009, the firm had revenue of 6.81 billion Yuan (China Publishing Yearbook 1995–2008), only 11 % of the 2008 revenue of Pearson Group in the UK, and EBIT of 1.21 billion Yuan, only 12.4 % compared to Pearson Group. This accurately reflects the situation of news publishing firms, which is "large but weak" and "small but scattered." The economic strength of key enterprises or corporations is unobvious and not prominent. When compared to international standards, there is a large gap and monopolization is far from forming (National Press and Publication Statistics Network).

There is another characteristic of China's publishing industry, which is the profit of the firms heavily relying on teaching materials. The top ten central and local publishing companies all depend on main and supplementary teaching materials to profit. The other types of books from the publishing firms only take up a small percentage of the market.

The media concentration study conducted by the author shows very fragmented market structure in the book publishing sector. According to the statistics from the State Administration of Press, the HHI figures of both local and central book publishing markets are lower than 100, indicating a very low concentration rate in the book publishing market in China.

1.5 Periodicals and Magazines Sector

Since the reform and opening up of China, the country's periodical industry experienced a transition. The various journals increased greatly and the scale of the market continued to expand. From the perspective of periodical advertisement development, the total advertisement sales was 3.1 billion Yuan in 2008, 286 times more than the 1,978 amount, far more than the increase of the kinds and total amount of periodicals. However, compared to other developed countries, China's amount is much less. The size of the market is small, and has not fully developed, with a large gap for advancement.

The concentration of periodical advertisement is low; this would be considered diffuse competition with small changes in concentration. There are no drastic fluctuations in this market, so it is more stable compared to others. The variations in periodical advertisement market share are not that obvious, the greatest difference of share is only around three times between the top ten. Compared with other large media, the competition of the periodical advertisement market is much dispersed. No strong periodical can get a complete monopoly in the market. Overall, the periodical advertisement market is a scattered competitive market structure, so it is currently in the state of diffused competition. The market lacks a large and powerful corporation, which is a great disadvantage if Chinese periodicals want to compete in the international market.

The concentration of the periodical advertisement market is much lower due to the direct reason of the market structure and indirect reason of issues with the media system. The concentration of the market and the periodical circulation are correlated positively. Compared with the concentration of the periodical advertisement market, the concentration of the circulation market is much lower. This is the more direct reason for lower concentration in the periodical market.

From the perspective of the whole nation, China's periodical circulation market does not have the power to have a monopoly and is in a state of diffused competition. The disperse competition of the circulation of periodicals directly causes the lower concentration of the advertisement market. Currently cross-region operations have many restrictions, affecting the possibility of a periodical becoming big and strong, ultimately lowering the concentration of the periodical advertisement market.

1.6 Film Sector

From the aspect of film production, investments, scale, experience, government intervention, and others are the main factors for barrier to entry. During the screening process, the barrier to entry is lower. On June 1, 2002, the Chinese cinema officially launched under the encouragement of the government and has been developing for almost ten years.

Through continuous integration, there are currently 34 mainstream cinemas (China Film Yearbook 1994–2008) in Chinese cities. Through cross-region reorganizations, the top six cinemas have a clear advantage. These are then roughly divided into two types: newly constructed cinemas and traditional film studio cinemas. Newly constructed cinemas include Wanda Cinemas, China Film Stellar Theater, and G Z. JinYiZhuJiang Movie. Traditional cinemas include Shanghai United Circuit, China Film South Cinema Circuit, and New Film Association. These cinemas take up almost 66.6 % of the market shares nationwide (China Film Development Annual Report 1994–2008).

The study of market concentration shows that the film production market is moderately concentrated between 1992 and 2005. While in 2008, because of the industry restructuring, the concentration index steeply increased to above 5,000. The cinema market is less concentrated, and the HHI is lower than 1,000 in most years. The year 2008 is also a turning point for Chinese cinemas, box office revenues increased dramatically in that year due to successful release of a number of blockbusters.

2 Audiovisual Sector

In China, the whole audiovisual industry has a small aggregate capital. There are less than ten audiovisual publishers where their capital is in the hundred millions. Firms with more than ten million in assets are just a bit more than the previous, while most companies are small and have around a few thousand to a few million Yuan in capital. When compared to any single record company from the big four international labels, whether it be size of assets or gross sales, surpasses China's overall audiovisual industry many times.

The industry also has a chaotic internal competition. During the early development phase of the audiovisual industry, every region, every industry, especially the three individual systems of culture, publishing, and broadcasting did its own thing, missing the best opportunity to join forces and become a conglomerate. At the same time, they lost a standard market behavior and the chance to foster a consumer group.

Thus, the overall traits of the industry shown are: (1) the lack of a powerhouse, (2) many small and weak firms making up most of the market triggering price wars with fierce competition, messing up the market, and (3) law breakers and rampant piracy not prohibited.

The actual scale of the audiovisual industry is 15–20 billion Yuan, however, genuine audiovisual only account for about 10 %. Means of survival and most of the market is swallowed by illegal audiovisual products.

2.1 Internet Service Providers (ISP)

Overall, in China there are ten large ISPs, namely CHINANET, CSTNET, CERNET, CHINAGBN, UNINET, CNCNET, CMNET, CIETNET, CGWNET, and CSNET. Among them, CSTNET, CERNET, and CGWNET are non-profit networks (China Telecommunication Yearbook 2000–2008). CIETNET is the only one in China that specifically caters to business companies and institutions not competing on the market. The providers that compete on the market are China Mobile, China Telecom, China Unicom, China Jitong, China Netcom, China Railcom, ChinaSat, and CRNet that joined later.

What needs to be emphasized is that China has a certain amount of Metropolitan Area Network (MAN) present. The scope of these MAN is smaller and need to connect through the abovementioned backbone networks in order to connect to the internet. Thus, from the perspective of the MAN market around the country, there is little competition because of the restrictions placed by the operations of ISPs. Entering the Chinese ISP market is mainly through these nationwide operators, however after 2000, China's telecommunication industry experienced frequent reorganizations. The above listed providers also underwent a transformation when they competed in the market where one provider merged with another.

Most of the backbone networks of China's internet were mostly developed or officially established in 2000. In addition, the true opening of the internet was not until December 20, 2001 when the ten backbone networks signed an agreement. Thus, when analyzing the market of China's ISP, there is limited information. Only data between years 2004 and 2008 are available, and in which period, there is a high rate of concentration in the market, with the HHI figures higher than 3,000.

2.2 Online News Media Sector

China's online news market is mainly dominated by four leading companies: Sina, Sohu, Net Ease and Tencent. Sina was founded in 1998 and listed in NASDAQ in 2000. As a website that mainly caters to the Chinese population around the globe, SINA.com has about 230 million registered users and three billion page views every day. The company also has other business lines including Sina Mobile, Sina Online and Sina.net. Sohu was founded and listed in the same year as Sina did, and it is competing with Sina as one of the leading internet companies. Sohu and its subsidiaries offer online news, advertising, on-line multiplayer gaming and other services.

Net Ease and Tencent were founded 1 year earlier than Sohu and Sina. Net Ease is famous for its online news services, mail service and online gaming business; its mail service attracts more than 200 million users. Tencent was developed from instant message service: OICQ, and now its social network software QQ has the largest population of users in China.

The four leading companies attract more than half of the total traffic on the online news sites. Other popular internet news sites include the online portals of the traditional media companies; for example, renmin.com of People's Daily newspaper and xinhua.net of Xinhua News Agency. Although there have been increasing number of online news sites emerging in recent years, the concentration level is still high, as most advertisement revenue flew to the leading companies.

The study on market structure indicates a sharp decrease of concentration for online news media in 2008, because the Olympic Game held in Beijing that year pushed a large stream of revenue to the online sport media sites, which scattered the concentration level. Right after 2008, the concentration level climbed up to new heights.

2.3 Search Engine Sector

Since the twenty-first century, the search engine market can be divided into three stages of development in China, and currently the country is in the third stages of rapid development. Due to Baidu becoming listed, Chinese search engines have plans to go global. As the propeller of internet sales, search engines have successfully developed their search services, keyword advertisements, hit rankings and others, which have become the highlight of the Chinese internet industry.

At the third stage, the essence of China's search engine market has entered into a period of fierce competition (I-Research China Online Search Annual Report 2003–2009). This is when strong rivals compete with each other on the market. Every mainstream business has solid financial power, technical strength, and strong market share. The current powerhouse may not be the future one, so changes in the market are hard to forecast. This results in competition at all levels, with not a single element, so the inevitable trend is a three-dimensional competition and product homogenization.

In the area of Chinese search engines, Yahoo was the market leader in 2003, while Google stayed in second for most years. Now the market leader is Baidu, taking over 60 % of market shares. In recent years, many other Chinese firms are attempting to innovate their searches. For the next few years, vertical search hits will have better opportunities and greater room for development. As Baidu and Google are becoming successful on the internet in these few years, tycoons and entrepreneurs will already entered or start entering into the wireless search field.

There are many features in the rapid development of China's search hit industry. First, the further step of China's internet to generalization and marketing-effect realization will gradually permeate. Second, the quick development of e-commerce constituted the increase of rigid demand for search marketing. From the perspective of the competitive market, the Google Incident of 2010 hastened the spur of operators such as Soso, Sougou, Etao, Youdao, and others, resulting in the possibility of a diversified competition in the future.

3 Summary

China's major media corporations include China Central Television, China National Radio, Southern Daily Press Group, The People's Daily Newspaper Group, Xinhua News Agency, Guangzhou Daily Newspaper Group, and others. But overall, there is still a big gap between China's media corporations with western ones: first is that they are smaller in size and resource. Second is a lower profit. Third is not yet able to make good use of economies of scale and the scope economic effect. From the developmental history of western media firms, collectivization is an inevitable process, from a single media company into a media corporation that is inter-regional, cross-media, and cross-space, is the only way to become a successful media corporation.

Currently, there is still regional market segmentation in China. In the early stages of the industry's development, local markets showed explosive growth with shortcomings yet to appear. However, once regional media industry become more mature, the industry must shift from extensive to intensive growth, otherwise the problems of market segmentation will emerge.

This will not guarantee leading media companies "to survive in competition," which would impair the formation of a strong media group. Under these conditions, many media companies can only operate in certain provinces or urban areas. Established media companies and brands are constrained by the market without enough room to grow, while poorly run businesses can continue to survive with low profit margins or even losses because of local government support. Media companies will not be able to further develop, while poor media companies are not eliminated due to market mechanisms. It will lead to a situation where competitive media corporations are restricted from healthily developing into a true media group that is able to compete with large international firms.

The media industry is growing in such a distorted way in many regional markets that normal development is jeopardized. Competition is a required factor and only under this condition will the media industry continue to thrive rapidly. China's media industry has proved that in areas where competition is relatively high, are the areas where the media grows into relatively mature and influential businesses. For example, Guangdong Province is the most competitive market. For newspapers alone, there are four groups, Southern Daily Group, Guangzhou Daily Newspaper Group, Yangcheng Evening News Group, and Shenzhen Press Group. In television, there are numerous TV stations from Hong Kong and Macau in Guangdong. As a result of fierce competition, Guangdong Province's media industry has made tremendous progress through mutual learning. In addition, the media market of Shenzhen, Dongguan, and Foshan has also gained considerable ground in the recent years.

In China, the developments of different types of media are highly uneven. Before the wireless and cable stations merged, the television industry was a duopoly market. In the press, government maintains a monopoly. Different from government oligopolies, the marketization of newspapers in metropolitan areas is a fierce competition for a monopoly.

In today's metropolitan media market, there are many newspapers to compete with. Although the positioning of these papers is similar, there are still many differences in their content, distribution channels, readers, advertisers, and many other aspects. Despite the competition due to the low barriers to entry and exit, many new media firms subsequently enter the market.

Newspapers, radio, television, Internet, and other media of various structures develop in different way. According to the market, aside from cable television, the TV market is an oligopoly market, which exhibits a high market concentration structure and greater homogeneity or differences. The newspaper market with high barriers to entry and exit is a monopolistic competitive market with a low concentration market structure, and product differentiation.

The television production market that produces television shows has a low barrier to entry and exit that is almost a completely competitive market. Internet media is almost a perfect competition, which is the lowest monopolized media. Cable TV has the characteristic of a regionalized monopoly so it is classified as a more concentrated market. This is because cable television networks require a lot of pre-laid fiber optic cables, which will requires huge investments. In order to reduce costs and duplication, the government may only allow a single cable network operator to exist, or have their own monopoly.

In the new media sphere, the internet media combines the functions and advantages of traditional media. It also has its own unique traits that greatly affect the development of traditional media. In China, the appearance of the internet media does not restrict the development of traditional media, but as both grow, they search for a balance. Right when the internet media is developing, it prompts the transformation of traditional media to survive and develop in the new structure of China.

The thriving progress of internet media in computer science results in traditional media integrating through media convergence to jointly deal with the changing environment. During this process, the change of media market structure can fittingly reflect the operations of media firms and the improvements and changes in strategy of media companies in China.

Data Sources and References

China Film Yearbook 1994–2008, published by China Film Press.
China Film Development Annual Report 1994–2008, published by China Film Press.
China Publishing Yearbook 1995–2008, published by the General Administration of Press and Publication.
China Radio, Film and TV Development Annual Report 2002–2009, retrieved from the site of the State Administration of Radio, Film and Television (SARFT).
China Telecommunication Yearbook 2000–2008, Published by China Telecom.
I-Research China Online Search Annual Report (2003–2009), published by I-Research.
National Press and Publication Statistics Network, published by the General Administration of Press and Publication.
National and Provincial Radio and Television Income Report 2000–2008, retrieved from the official site of the State Administration of Radio, Film and Television (SARFT).

Part IV
Forms and Content of Social Media

Social Media Strategies and Practices of Integrated Media Companies

Piet Bakker, Sanne Hille, and Marco van Kerkhoven

1 Introduction

Media are not social. People are social. People can use media to be social beyond face-to-face contacts and carry on conversations beyond time and space. Letter writing, talking over the telephone, and exchanging e-mails expanded the possibility of people to be social, although we never called letters, phones or computers 'social media'. These 'simple' ways of being social were initially limited to private and one-to-one conversations. The possibilities of text messages and emails, however, went beyond that. Not only could we reach more people with one message, also organizations and companies could use them.

Media now can be 'social' by engaging in conversations. Newsletters and text-alerts still resembled a sender-receiver model of communication. Services like Twitter, Facebook, Google+ and LinkedIn combine the conversation-mode with group-message options. Media can send one message to many users, receive feedback, react on messages, see how their message is passed along different users and ask for interactions. Interactions between users—questions, answers, comments, likes, retweets, clicks on links, shared photos and video's—create a valuable element of social media: the community, at least in theory. Media that integrate online efforts with their traditional print and broadcast offerings will therefore do more than just move content to a different platform—they will move from a content-creating company to content-conversation operation.

P. Bakker (✉) • S. Hille • M. van Kerkhoven
Research Centre for Communication and Journalism at Hogeschool Utrecht,
University of Applied Sciences, Amsterdam, Netherlands
e-mail: Piet.Bakker@uva.nl

2 The Social Media Community

An audience, consisting of receivers of messages, is a passive concept. A community, on the other hand, is a living organism, active beyond the input of one central source of information. The community not only distributes information, it also creates content by commenting and enriching items, adding value to the original product.

It is not hard to see why media embrace this model. The potential audience could grow effortless, content could be created for free, traffic to websites would rise and online revenues would increase. This would be a dream come true as traditional print and broadcast audiences shrink and online revenues are still lagging behind.

In theory the model is a dream—in practice it can be more difficult. Creating or 'building' a community and have this community work for you is not something that can be attained without effort. It needs a careful construction of the technical infrastructure, training and instruction of personal, continuous monitoring of traffic and participation from company staff as well.

3 Communities

Communities come in different flavors. The concept is rather fuzzy as friends and families, neighbors and neighborhoods, colleagues and alumni, but also faint acquaintances and complete strangers can belong to a community. All people who are active on social media are—to start with—the center of their own unique community: their friends on Facebook, their followers on Twitter, their connections on LinkedIn, their circles in Google+. Users actively construct these communities. On the other hand, there is 'passive' community-formation when people belong to communities because others follow them; add them to circles or 'like' their posts.

Media are mostly interested in people who actively connect with their brand or with content they create. They want people to become a fan on Facebook, to like, recommend or share posts—or to react to posts, either by using their Facebook account to comment on the website of the medium or to post that comment on their own Facebook profile. When users are on Twitter, they are hoped to follow the medium, re-tweet content, or react to the content (preferably in positive ways).

In all these cases media expect users to use their own personal and unique community and spread content from the media-community. Not all communities have the same value and not all users are equal. Facebook users with many 'real' friends have value. Twitter users who follow many people don't have much value, in contrast to users with many followers. At Google+ users can be added to circles without consent, meaning that usually only people that are in the 'inner circles' (friends, family, colleagues) usually are of value, as are the people connected to brand pages. The professional with many followers on LinkedIn is mostly interesting when he or she is active in groups and discussions. For media this means that simply introducing a Facebook page or start Twittering is not enough. Every social medium has its own dynamics, with some features having distinctively more content-creating and content-distributing value than others. All platforms offer the option for media to create their own page (Facebook), account

	Personal, active	Added, passive	Media, active
Facebook	Friends	Likes	Friends
Twitter	Following	Followers	Followers
Google+	Own circles	Added to circles	Brand pages
LinkedIn	Connections		Groups/discussions

Fig. 1 Communities on Facebook, Twitter, Google+ and LinkedIn

(Twitter), brand page (Google+) or company page (LinkedIn). Twitter and Facebook differ, however, when it comes to the relations users are having, in Facebook the number of friends is important, in Twitter the number of followers and the follower/following ratio (Fig. 1).

Although the use of social media can be passive, active contribution from media can spark discussions, result in more active use and more active users. It is hard to envision that others actively engage in distribution and discussion while the source can limit its activity to just creating and distributing content, without actively engaging with users.

4 Information Control

Using "the people formerly known as the audience" (Rosen, 2006, in Deuze 2008, p. 107) to distribute and create content, however, can have serious consequences for the control media have over information. Bordewijk and Van Kaam's (1986) model shows that moving from traditional 'allocation' to registration, consultation and conversation, means that individual 'receivers' control much more when information is 'consumed' but also that traditional receivers start to act as sources (Fig. 2). For traditional media this is a fundamental change in the way they communicate.

5 Drivers for Digitalization and Integration

Notwithstanding possible drawbacks, there are strong drivers towards producing more content with less staff on more platforms, meaning that using social media could be a welcome contribution. For journalists the use of social media platforms can be a challenge, as they will encounter new ways of communication with audiences. They will enter into direct communication, which could be awarding but also threatening. For owners and management new platforms offer different opportunities. As customers move online, costs of technology rise and traditional revenues drop, they will introduce organization change—including multi-skilling of staff—to counter these issues. Integrating journalistic operations to one newsroom catering different platforms (Bechmann Petersen 2008; García Avilés et al. 2009; Gimbert 2009;

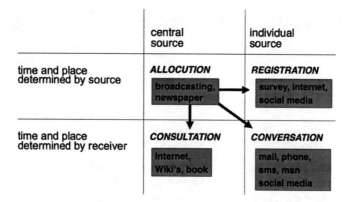

Fig. 2 Communication modes, based on Bordewijk and Van Kaam (1986)

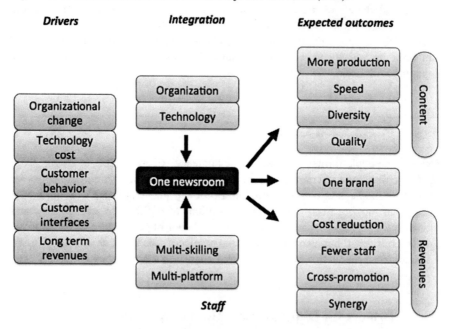

Fig. 3 Drivers of media integration, based on Bakker and Küng (2012)

Smyrnaios and Bousquet 2011; Tameling 2008) is expected to result in cost reduction and producing more output or distributing the output to more platforms (Fig. 3).

From a management perspective the fact that content by users is 'free' or produced at lower costs and may lead to more website traffic and consequently to more advertising revenue is extremely appealing. For journalists, user-generated content could contain possible leads for news stories, and more transparency because of interactions with users (Fig. 4).

Fig. 4 Expected benefits of user-generated content (Bakker 2012)

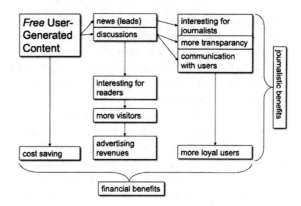

6 Social Media Expectations

Management and journalists may have rather different expectations when it comes to inviting users to participate in newsgathering and distribution. For management it is most of all a business opportunity, involving issues like building platforms and training staff members. For journalists it may have more profound consequences, as the relation with audiences and sources will change and the control over how the final product is consumed, distributed and discussed, is now in the hand of the users.

Employing social media is a step beyond inviting users to send in tips, photo's or video's and to ad content by blogging or commenting. This 'traditional' user-generated content usually takes place on the digital platform of the medium itself or on alternative media platforms (Bowman and Willis 2003; Gillmor 2004). With the use of Twitter, Facebook, Google+ or LinkedIn, users can be active with media content on their own platform, outside the reach of the original content producer.

Experiences with 'traditional' user-generated content, however, have been mixed. Users are reluctant to send in material and when they do, the quality is often disappointing. Also the moderation costs of user-generated content can be substantial (Bergström 2008; García-Avilés 2010; Hermida and Thurman 2008; Pantti and Bakker 2009; Paulussen and Ugille 2008; Rebillard and Touboul 2011). These experiences, however, have also sparked interest in using the new 'social media' options as there are less platform and moderation costs and media are expected to use existing communities instead of building communities themselves.

7 Design of Study

In this chapter we investigate how Dutch media employ and incorporate social media. What is their strategy when using these media, and how successful are these efforts. Do users like and follow media, how is content distributed and how much activities do media and their journalists employ on these platforms?

One part of the research concerns the use of Facebook as a way to distribute content. The service is the most popular Dutch social media platform with six million users (almost 40 % of the population) in the beginning of 2012. One of the most promising features of Facebook is that it can drive traffic to the website if links in liked articles are clicked upon. Another advantage is that comments on articles are never anonymous and don't need moderation.

Research by the American PEW Institute showed that 51 % of users of social networks receives news on the network while 23 % said they got news on their social networks from specific media or journalists (Purcell et al. 2010). The Facebook activities can take place on three levels: on the website of the medium (liking, sharing or recommending, commenting with Facebook or becoming a fan of a medium), on the Facebook 'page' of a medium (like, comment, share) or on the users' personal Facebook 'profile' (like, share, comment and having the media content on the personal 'wall' after becoming friends with the medium). We expect media to introduce at least some of these features in their online offerings.

In 2011 64 media were analyzed to access how they use Facebook. Do they have a Facebook fanpage? Can you 'like' articles, share of recommend them? How many fans do media have? Detailed analysis on ten media was later done with the commercial service Allfacebookstats. For nine regional newspapers, the Facebook and Twitter activities (accounts, followers, fans, post) were analyzed during 2011 and the beginning of 2012.

8   Results

Of the 64 media researched, 59 did have a Facebook 'page', the professional version of the personal Facebook profile. Strangely enough, only 39 media had a "Find us on Facebook" or "Become our fan on Facebook" on their homepage. The Share, Like and Recommend buttons (Fig. 5) perform more or less the similar functions, *recommending* and *liking* result in placing a news article on "the wall" of the user, sharing—the first 'social plug-in' option Facebook offered—gives the default option of adding a comment and also places a bigger part of the original item, often with a picture, on wall of the user. Buttons can show the number of people who liked the item and show the pictures of the people who liked the story. News organizations often prefer recommendations over likes as it sounds more neutral; 'liking' a news item on a disaster for instance does not sound right. Likes and recommendations also offer opportunities for websites to get information on the people who connect with the website in that way (see Thurman and Schifferes 2012).

Only 18 websites contained a Like button, a third of the websites (22) had a Recommend button; the Share button was most popular (found on 38 websites). The order seems logical as Recommend is more suited to news websites and Sharing offers more options for interactions (Fig. 6).

The number of websites with only one or two buttons, however, is still substantial, meaning they miss opportunities to have their page or content promoted on Facebook. There is a relation between the number of followers and the number of

Fig. 5 Facebook buttons

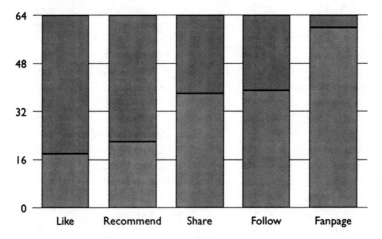

Fig. 6 Facebook Fanpages, and buttons used on media website

buttons news media use on their website. The media with many fans more often use three or four buttons, the media with fewer fans use no, one or only two buttons. The relation, however, is not linear while it is most visible for the online websites of newspapers (Table 1).

There is not a direct relation between the number of fans and the off-line presence of media. The newspaper with the highest circulation, *De Telegraaf*, is only fourth after smaller papers like *AD*, *de Volkskrant* and *nrc.next*. The position of the last paper is interesting because it only has a circulation of 70,000—against 200,000 or more for the other papers in the top-5. The smallest free newspaper *De Pers* has more followers than *Metro* and *Spits* who are twice as big. Regional newspapers often perform poorly, except of *Het Parool*, *Leeuwarder Courant* and *Dagblad van het Noorden*—all three of them medium-size newspapers doing better on Facebook than the papers with the highest circulation. The smallest (counting circulation) magazine *Groene Amsterdammer* has more fans than larger magazines.

The most popular TV-news programs *NOS* and *RTL* are on positions 4 and 7 in the table. The daily human-interest program *Hart van Nederland* has the highest number of fans; weekly investigative journalism programs *Tegenlicht* and *Zembla*—both have substantial lower viewer ratings than the daily news programs—are second and third. The third investigate journalism program on the list, *Reporter*, has only eight fans. Regional broadcasters—all 13 are included in the research—perform rather differently,

Table 1 Media, number of Facebook fans and number of Facebook options

Print			Non print		
	Fans	Buttons		Fans	Buttons
Newspapers			*Radio*		
AD	37,000	3	BNR Nieuwsradio	913	3
nrc.next	13,731	3	Argos[a]	0	0
de Volkskrant	10,534	4			
De Telegraaf	9,523	2	*Television*		
NRC Handelsblad	7,049	3	Hart van Nederland	6,873	2
Parool	2,907	2	Tegenlicht	4,098	3
De Pers	1,791	2	Zembla	3,525	2
Leeuwarder Courant	1,445	3	RTL Nieuws	2,817	3
Metro	1,443	3	RTV Rijnmond	2,207	1
Dagblad van het Noorden	1,372	3	EenVandaag	1,575	2
Eindhovens Dagblad	405	2	NOS	1,510	0
Brabants Dagblad	368	2	RTV Noord	1,494	2
TC/Tubantia	363	2	Omroep Gelderland	1,047	3
Haarlems Dagblad	278	1	Omroep Fryslan	1,009	2
De Gelderlander	275	1	Omroep Brabant	798	3
Trouw	230	3	Omroep Zeeland	729	2
Reformatorisch Dagblad	194	2	L1	716	2
BN/de Stem	157	3	RTV Noord	467	2
Gooi- & Eemlander	129	2	Buitenhof[a]	356	0
Financieele Dagblad	82	1	RTV Noord Holland	325	1
Stentor	30	1	Brandpunt	309	3
Nederlands Dagblad	23	2	Nieuwsuur	266	0
Noordhollands Dagblad	21	1	RTV Oost	266	2
Dagblad de Limburger	13	1	Omroep West	253	2
Leidsch Dagblad	9	1	RTV Utrecht	243	1
Friesch Dagblad	4	0	Omroep Flevoland	202	2
Barneveldse Krant	2	1	RTV Drenthe	42	1
PZC[a]	0	1	Reporter	8	2
Spits[a]	0	1			
			Online		
Magazines			Nu.nl	25,625	2
Groene Amsterdammer	3,741	2	Fok.nl	3,819	2
Elsevier	1,862	2	Geenstijl.nl	289	1
Vrij Nederland	1,838	2	Sargasso.nl	29	3
HP/de Tijd	71	2	nieuws.nl[a]	0	1

[a] No Facebook Page

with *RTV Rijnmond* (Rotterdam) having more than 2,000 fans and another (*RTV Drenthe*) less than 50.

Online news website nu.nl—the most popular news website in the country—has 25,000 fans. As the site already has millions of daily users and ample opportunities

Table 2 Fans, weekly average number of posts, comments per post, likes per posts and activities on 10 Dutch media sites, December 2011

	Fans	Posts	Comments	Likes	Activities p. 1,000 fans
Hart van Nederland	6.873	71	6	6	1.7
Volkskrant	10.534	36	6	13	1.9
RTV Rijnmond	2.207	19	3	8	5.0
EénVandaag	1.575	18	1	2	1.7
AD	37.000	19	26	45	1.9
Nu.nl	25.625	19	18	37	2.2
Groene Amsterdammer	3.741	12	1	6	1.8
Nrc.next	13.731	17	2	9	0.8
VPRO Tegenlicht	4.098	2	1	6	1.8
Trouw	230	0	0	1	–

Activities is the sum of comments and likes divided by the number of fans *1,000

for interaction, one could ask why it should invest in running a parallel Facebook platform at the same time. Apparently the organization is so web-savvy that seizing all opportunities is part of their daily habit. The second place in 'online' is occupied by fok.nl—actually a community itself. But the site has more fans than 24 of the 29 newspaper websites. The very popular weblog *GeenStijl* is clearly lagging behind with just over 300 fans. Crucial is that almost all commenters on the *GeenStijl* website want to stay anonymous, something that is virtual impossible at Facebook.

Ten websites were analyzed more in depth. It shows that *Hart van Nederland* really makes an effort on Facebook, resulting in a high number of fans. All websites—except for *Tegenlicht* and Trouw—post regularly. A high number of followers results in more comments and more likes. When the number of activities (comments and likes together) per 1,000 fans is considered, the users of local TV-channel *RTV Rijnmond* are by far the most active with five comments or likes. But is still means that only one in 200 fans actually performs any activity—if the activities are performed by different users. Other media show only two weekly activities per 1,000 users, with more 'likes' than 'comments'—less than one user out of a thousand bothers to comment on a post (Table 2).

In the research on how regional newspapers use Twitter and Facebook, the main result seems to be that Twitter is far more popular than Facebook. Six newspapers don't post any news on Facebook or don't even have an official page. Only one title—*TC Tubantia*—posts more than one story a day (Table 3). This low number is somewhat puzzling as content can be automatically published on Facebook.

Using Twitter seems logical as this service is mainly used for news updates. Eight out of nine papers had a Twitter account—often more than one—while seven had more than 1,000 followers, two of them even more than 5,000. When looking at the content, virtually all papers only automatically post headlines from the website. Twitter is seldom used for interaction, relatively few other accounts are followed, there are almost no reply's or retweets. Human interference is incidental. The account with the highest number of followers—*Dagblad van het Noorden*—even stopped its total Twitter activity during 3 months because of a technical issue. Also on the sub-accounts

Table 3 Twitter followers and Facebook activities, Dutch regional newspapers

	Twitter followers (main account)	Facebook (posts)
Gooi- en Eemlander	1,600	Every other day
Dagblad van het Noorden	9,300	One daily
Brabants Dagblad	3,000	Company info
Barneveldse Krant	1,500	Company info
AD/Utrechts Nieuwsblad	–	–
Noordhollands Dagblad	1,400	Empty
Dagblad de Limburger/LD	600	Empty
TC Tubantia	6,800	3 a day
Provinciale Zeeuwse Courant	4,300	Empty

Number of followers: early 2012. Facebook activities: 2011

(sports, local, events) the dominant mode is tweeting headlines with a link. There are, however, also individual journalists who Twitter—these accounts were not included in the research.

9 Discussion

The expectation was that integrated media—traditional print and broadcast media that expand online—would incorporate social media because it offered a quick and easy way to drive traffic to the media website and resolved the problem of costly moderation. It could also offer journalistic benefits.

What we see, however, is something different. There is no clear aggressive strategy of media companies to employ social media. With Twitter they go for automatic posting headlines without using the interactive features of the service—actually going for underperformance. The reason is that using social media is not cheap and easy at all. People have to be trained and more important, they have to be given dedicated tasks to manage social media. Wolthuizen (2012) asked Dutch media why they did not use humans on their Twitter account—as these would probably generate more traffic and interactivity—and got almost the same answer everywhere: lack of journalists who feel the urge to employ social media and lack of money to train staff or hire new staff.

Facebook use is also underdeveloped. A third of the media with a specific 'fanpage' on Facebook does not offer users to directly become a fan by clicking on the button below articles. There is also no clear strategy when it comes to use the different Facebook buttons. The number of fans is quite low, 40 media—usually with hundreds of thousands of readers, viewers or listeners—have less than a 1,000 fans. Also the activities are not impressive. The detailed analysis of ten media showed that only one medium generated more than one comment per posting. Liking an item is easier and is therefore done more often, although half of the media get less than one 'like' on average per posting. The absolute number of activities per 1,000 users is still very low. Facebook is definitely not an automatic webtraffic machine.

The second analysis of regional newspapers showed that almost all media do have a Facebook page but don't really use the page, not even for automatic posting of news items. Interviews with managers and journalists of regional media showed that there was a big gap between the managers and journalists. Managers formulate broad strategies of online presence and activities, often in a rather abstract and general way. Implementing these strategies, however, is often halfhearted while training, investments and facilities are often inadequate (Van Kerkhoven 2011).

When looking closer at the Facebook followers and activities of 64 media, it is clear that the biggest newspapers, the magazines with most readers, and the best-viewed programs, don't necessarily have the most followers. On the contrary, many smaller media perform much better than their bigger brothers and sisters. One possible explanation is that they try harder—instead of only launching the platform, working on the platform, interacting with users. Going beyond automatic posting needs dedication, skills and support from owners and management as well.

Further research should focus more on the actual activities media and users perform, track discussions and the distribution of content. Also different expectation by management and journalist need further investigation. Most of all, however, the obvious underperformance of social media by most media should be analyzed. Why do media have a Facebook page but don't direct users to that page? Or have a Facebook page without posting any content? Why do some media only one or two buttons to engage users while using more options leads to more traffic? Why do media rely so much on automatic postings on Twitter and Facebook? How could human interaction boost traffic and lead to more interaction between informed users and media?

The rhetoric of online strategies is very clear in most cases. In December 2011 and January 2012 the two largest publishers in the Netherlands, De Telegraaf Media Group (TMG) and Wegener/MGL (owned by UK-based publisher Mecom) both published new strategies in which the online activities were getting special emphasis. Implementing these strategies and making the transition to a truly integrated news organization a much more difficult task.

References

Bakker, P. (2012). Expectations, experiences & exceptions; Promises and realities of participation on PBS and commercial media websites. In G. F. Lowe & J. Steemers (Eds.), *Regaining the initiative for public service media* (pp. 237–251). Stockholm: Nordicom.

Bakker, P. & Küng, L. (2012). *Newsroom integration – Deconstructing the prevailing logic*. Paper presented at the 10th World Media Economics & Management Conference, Thessaloniki, 23–27 May 2012.

Bechmann Petersen, A. (2008). *Cross media as innovation strategy: Digital media challenges in the Danish Broadcasting Corporation*. Paper presented at RIPE@2008 Conference Public Service Media in the 21st Century: Participation, Partnership and Media Development. Mainz, Germany.

Bergström, A. (2008). The reluctant audience: online participation in the Swedish journalistic context. *Westminster Papers in Communication and Culture*, 5(2), 60–80.

Bordewijk, J. L., & Van Kaam, B. V. (1986). Towards a new classification of tele-information services. *InterMedia*, 14(1), 16–21.

Bowman, S. & Willis, C. (2003). *We media: How audiences are shaping the future of news and information*. The Media Center at the American Press Institute. Found at http://www.hypergene.net/wemedia. Accessed May 23, 2008.

Deuze, M. (2008). The professional identity of journalists in the context of convergence culture. *Observatorio (OBS*), 7*, 103–117.

García Avilés, J. A., Meier, K., Kaltenbrunner, A., Carvajal, M., & Kraus, D. (2009). Newsroom integration in Austria, Spain and Germany models of media convergence. *Journalism Practice*, iFirst Article, 1–19.

García-Avilés, J. (2010). "Citizen journalism" in European television websites: lights and shadows of user generated content. *Observatorio (OBS*) Journal, 4*, 251–263.

Gillmor, D. (2004). *We the media: Grassroots journalism by the people, for the people.* Sebastopol: O'Reilly Media Inc.

Gimbert, C. (2009). *Les Nouveaux Medias Du Groupe Bollore: Des Rédactions a L'epreuve Du Modèle Industriel.* Paper presented conference New media & information; convergences & divergences, Athens, 6–9 May 2009.

Hermida, A., & Thurman, N. (2008). A clash of cultures: The integration of user-generated content within professional journalistic frameworks at British newspaper websites. *Journalism Practice, 2*(3), 343–356.

Pantti, M., & Bakker, P. (2009). Misfortunes, memories and sunsets; Non-professional images in Dutch news media. *International Journal of Cultural Studies, 12*(5), 471–489.

Paulussen, S., & Ugille, P. (2008). User generated content in the newsroom: Professional and organisational constraints on participatory journalism. *Westminster Papers in Communication and Culture, 5*(2), 24–41.

Purcell, K., Rainie, L., Mitchell, A., Rosential, T., & Olmstead, K. (2010). Understanding the participatory news consumer, pew internet and American life project. http://www.pewinternet.org/Reports/2010/Online-News.aspx. Accessed November 29, 2011.

Rebillard, F., & Touboul, A. (2011). Promises unfulfilled? 'Journalism 2.0', user participation and editorial policy on newspaper websites. *Media Culture Society, 32*, 323–334.

Smyrnaios, N., & Bousquet, F. (2011). The development of local online journalism in South-Western France: The case of 'La Dépêche du Midi'. In R. Salaverría (Ed.), *Diversity of journalisms. Proceedings of the ECREA Journalism Studies Section and 26th International Conference of Communication (CICOM)* at University of Navarra, Pamplona, 4–5 July 2011.

Tameling, K. (2008). http://WWW.CONVERGENTIE.NOS; Mediaconvergentie binnen NOS Nieuws - Van beleid tot praktijk (Thesis University Groningen).

Thurman, N., & Schifferes, S. (2012). The future of personalization at news websites; lessons for a longitudinal study. *Journalism Studies*, 13(5). iFirst-article, 1–18.

Van Kerkhoven, M. (2011). *Convergence practice. Strategy and digital future of regional news media.* Paper presented at conference Diversity of Journalisms, 4–5 July, Pamplona.

Wolthuizen, J. (2012, January 26). Geen tijd en geld voor Twitterredacteuren. *De Nieuwe Reporter.* http://www.denieuwereporter.nl/2012/01/geen-tijd-en-geld-voor-twitterredacteuren/

"Telekom hilft": Customer Service in the Social Web

Andreas H. Bock

"Telekom hilft" (which means "Telekom cares") is a social media program initiated by Sales & Service at Telekom Deutschland GmbH. It has been exploring new service channels on Twitter and Facebook since 2010. Customer service on the social web aims to reassure, enthuse and retain customers. But the support offered to the general public also serves as communication and community management for the company's reputation—turning service teams into editors, moderators and crisis managers who face a steady stream of entirely new challenges.

1 Deutsche Telekom

Deutsche Telekom's vision is "to become an international market leader for 'connected life and work'" with the corresponding aspiration "to become the most highly regarded service company in our industry". The "Telekom hilft" program pursues this mission.

Telekom's brand vision incorporates three brand values:
- Innovation: We set standards and drive social networking.
- Simplicity: A basic need of our customers. We make complex things simple so that our customers can concentrate on what matters.
- Competence: Focus on a few things that we're really good at. Networks, services, content management and our relationship with our customers are at the heart of everything we do.

These brand values were translated into the concept behind "Telekom hilft":
- Innovation: We give customers the chance to communicate with us about service issues using popular, growing platforms and to work with us on improving these offerings.

A.H. Bock (✉)
Telekom, Bonn, Germany
e-mail: AndreasHBock@voss-publishing.net

- Simplicity: We make it easy for customers who use the Internet and social media, such as Facebook, Twitter and blogs, to communicate via these new services with our dedicated teams.
- Competence: "Telekom hilft" allows our staff to learn how to communicate with connected customers and to manage user-generated content.

The structure of our new customer contact points for social consumers is aligned with our defined brand personality:
- **Sociable**
- **Authentic**, honest, natural, relaxed
- **Approachable**, open, eye to eye
- **Inspiring**, enriching life, vitality, enjoying
- **Reliable**, strong

These attributes were incorporated into the "Telekom hilft" service design by presenting the frontline social media team in the interaction design of the social media accounts as a team, showing a photo of each team member and their forename and initials, but also by the definition of the communication guidelines.

2   Objectives

The "Telekom hilft" program was buoyed by another simultaneous initiative dealing with corporate culture. Many areas within the company had already set up Web 2.0 projects, and in 2009 an informal working group "Enterprise 2.0" was formed to serve as an in-house, cross-functional forum for social business projects at Telekom. This effort was initiated by HR and Corporate Communications. The forum evolved into a program sponsored by Deutsche Telekom Board members René Obermann and Thomas Sattelberger. This initiative for a cultural shift within Telekom generated considerable momentum for social media projects and a company-wide platform for exchanging ideas and opinions. "Telekom hilft" is a flagship project in the Enterprise 2.0 program, and is intended to be a shining beacon and role model for future projects.

While designing "Telekom hilft", we established a support line "social media management" function within the Internet Sales & Service Germany area, thus creating a specific entity for continuous development of the program. The following objectives were agreed upon (see also Bock 2010, p. 449f.):
- Innovation: Position ourselves as a category leader in the telco market to explore new customer touch points and new forms of communication; support a positive image as an innovator in line with Telekom's vision of becoming "the most highly regarded service company in our sector"
- Service: Increase customer satisfaction and loyalty, reduce costs by disseminating information virally, support the production and distribution of user-generated content and promote customer self-care offerings

- Sales: Boost sales through on-top revenues, cross-selling and up-selling
- Management: Specify and evaluate key performance indicators (KPIs) to make new processes traceable and permit profitability analyses.

In line with its purpose and objectives, the program was supported at an organizational level by three additional success factors:

- The "Telekom hilft" program management team was asked to work across divisions and combine their various fields of expertise. Different perspectives, multifaceted empirical knowledge and multi-layer problem solving concepts were core prerequisites for launching the project, as well as directly promoting transparency and thus acceptance.
- From a management perspective, the goal was to collect experience quickly and comprehensively and to report on this in full and complete detail to compile findings for the next steps in planning. This "agile exploration" approach massively increased the speed at which the program was implemented.
- However, empowerment and enthusiasm were the critical factors in its success. A small project team was granted the necessary decision making authority, developed the requisite trust-based relationships with each other and, through a shared will to innovate, evolved into a close-knit team.

3   General Conditions

The need for action in developing customer service in the social web was initially identified from the observation that customer communication behavior is changing. A study by Ovum (Dawson 2009, p. 4) showed that 15–25 year olds in the US are spending more and more time during the week on social networking than on SMS, e-mail, mobile phones and fixed line communication. The conclusion drawn is that companies need to adapt to this ever-changing communication behavior to stay in touch with their customers.

A 2011 ARD-ZDF online study also showed shifts in electronic means of communication in favor of Web 2.0 in Germany:

> Web 2.0 offerings are still used most often by youth (aged 14 to 29). Teenagers generally use private communities more than e-mail, whereas all other age groups see e-mail as the most important online communication application. (Busemann and Gscheidle 2011, p. 360)

A study by Edelman Digital surveyed 8,095 people from the "millennial generation"—those born between 1970 and 1990, who grew up with digital media and who, according to Edelman, currently represent the most influential trendsetter group. In response to a question about their primary source of customer service information, the majority of people stated clearly that social networks were their preferred source over traditional call centers:

Company website	50 %
Search engine	46 %
Store location	45 %
Friends	30 %
Family	22 %
Social networks	20 %
Call customer service	<1 %

(Edelman Digital 2010, p. 23)

As well as their communication behavior, social consumers are also altering their decision-making processes for buying. The classic AIDA funnel (attention-interest-desire-action) is no longer suitable for describing the consumer world and understanding the market. Connected and self-publishing customers now have completely new opportunities for finding information about products, services and brands, influencing purchase decisions through word-of-mouth, and offering each other mutual support through crowd-sourcing customer service.

McKinsey proposed a successor to the AIDA model, the customer decision journey, where consumers move through loops of research, purchase and product experience. (Court et al. 2009). Forrester's successor marketing funnel model uses the customer life cycle: "Customers' relationships with a brand as they continue to discover new options, explore their needs, make purchases, and engage with the product experience and their peers" (Noble 2010).

These new models are characterized by the following key features:
- More attention is paid to the existing customer base, customer retention and loyalty, and how these interact
- Existing customers are identified as potential advocates, ambassadors, fans, and above all recommenders of brands, products and services, who can positively or negatively influence interested prospects.

Social media as a contact channel is on the rise. Detecon (2010, p. 6) surveyed 78 experts in customer service, CRM, marketing and corporate management about the key customer service trends of the future:
- 80 % of respondents believe that customer service needs to head in a new direction.
- 85 % see a trend toward greater automation and an increasing share of self-services.
- 70 % believe there is a trend toward social media as a future service channel.

Detecon expects that "by 2015, companies in German-speaking areas across all sectors will map and manage around 25% of their total service contact volume using automated web self-services and social media" (Detecon 2010, p. 40).

4   Theoretical Framework

Social CRM (social customer relationship management) serves as a theoretical approach to strategic concept design for "Telefom hilft". Paul Greenberg offers the following definition:

> Social CRM is a philosophy and a business strategy, supported by a technology platform, business rules, processes and social characteristics, designed to engage the customer in a collaborative conversation in order to provide mutually beneficial value in a trusted and transparent business environment. It's the company's response to the customer's ownership of the conversation. (Greenberg 2010, position 1064)

For Greenberg, social CRM is the next step up from CRM. Traditional CRM makes available internal company processes to allow for efficient customer management. Social CRM expands on classic CRM. As well as new methods of integrating and analyzing customer-related data from the social web, it primarily involves focusing all business activities in marketing, sales, service, innovation/ product management on boosting commitment with regard to "social customers". As well as a radical focus on customers, Greenberg sees customer experience management (CEM) as a component of social CRM.

According to Schmitt and Mangold (2004), customer experience management is "the process of strategically managing a customer's experience with a brand via all touch points" (Schmitt and Mangold 2004, p. 21). That experience is shaped by the contact or communication situation between customer and company. Depending on how this situation develops, various "moments of truth" emerge that are relevant to the customer's behavior (Carlzon 1995):

> 'Moments of truth' refers to those moments and situations in which customers turn to a company concerning a matter which is of great importance to them.
>
> Typical examples: complaints, questions about inconsistent offers via various distribution channels, the provision of a new product requiring explanation, or a malfunction that needs to be corrected on location.
>
> If not handled properly, such critical customer contacts can have a detrimental effect on customer loyalty or even lead to termination by the customer.
>
> (Detecon 2009, p. 4)

Developing the roadmap for the "Telekom hilft" program was based on the 18 use cases for social CRM as proposed by the Altimeter Group. For customer service the three use cases are as follows:

1. Generate **social support insights** through monitoring, listening and analysis of the opportunities and risks inherent in the social web.
2. Build a **rapid social response** by reacting to customer queries and feedback, which means establishing customer contact points and contact channels in the social web.
3. Enable **peer-to-peer (P2P) unpaid armies (SP3)** to activate advocates for your own brand and allow for collective support in cooperation with company employees and dedicated customers.

(Wang and Owyang 2010, p. 14f.; see also Metz 2012, p. 93ff.)

5 Service Design

We first designed the strategic concept: What are the objectives? What is the environment like? What best practices and best cases are already in place? What approach is effective? How should the roadmap be structured, and what associated projects should be included? What roles and resources are needed? What technology is needed and what techniques have to be learned? What elementary organizational prerequisites must be met? Which service staff should be assigned to customer service on the social web?

In terms of choosing social media platforms for the new service touch points, we decided to apply one basic principle: Go where our customers are. And to make it efficient: Follow the masses and the growth! At the end of 2009, Facebook and Twitter were already growth candidates whereas the German "VZ Netzwerke" were starting to stagnate. As well as Facebook and Twitter, we also planned a blog to (a) create more space for in-depth information and (b) use additional methods of content distribution: trackbacks and pingbacks for networking as well as search-engine-friendly content.

Of course, "Telekom hilft" was intended to be excellent. But what does that mean for a customer service design project? In DIN SPEC 77224, service excellence is defined as a management system. This system should enable a company to systematically develop excellent services that do not just satisfy customers, but delight them. One of the seven components of service excellence is "Achieving customer delight through service innovations". For our Support 2.0 service design, the first important step was to explore the differences between it and traditional customer service, to help identify what is innovative.

- In the social web communication is individual and context-specific—not automated as in customer self-care systems, voice response systems, or semantics-driven text module distribution. The Cluetrain manifesto states: "Conversations among human beings sound human. They are conducted in a human voice" (Weinberger et al. 2009).
- Customer service in the social web means that service staff communicate individually but in public, not in screened face-to-face communication via telephone, e-mail, or chat.
- Service communication can turn a two-person conversation into a multi-way collaboration between many people, which can be synchronous or asynchronous.
- A customer conversation between many people can include customer service staff and employees from other business units, customers, potential buyers, non-customers, staff from partner companies or competitors and even third parties.
- Since service communication takes place in a public forum, it is easier to make service communication a part of communication itself, turning customer dialog into a social object.
- Service communication is stored so that it is publicly accessible. Every statement can be read in real-time, and is also indexed by search engines for future research and review.

- Real-time service communication and stored service communication can be distributed, edited, aggregated and evaluated by customers or third parties using social technologies.

We rejected the idea of outsourcing the frontline customer service team to a call center provider, in order to ensure that know-how is accumulated in-house and to allow for flexible reactions to unexpected events. We selected the Kiel Competence Center as a location because it possesses highly trained personnel who have a broad and deep range of experience. The team was recruited through an internal effort in cooperation with the HR department and the local works council. Four FTEs (full-time equivalents) were available when we launched on Twitter; we created eight FTEs for the Facebook start date and the total number rose to 13 FTEs in 2011. These FTEs were allocated to several people, since the team members were also deployed to other tasks and areas.

One key element in this innovation is the type and form of communication: the human, personal interaction between service staff and their communication partners. These staff really do "show" what they are made of: one outstanding visual design element of both the Twitter account and Facebook page is the team members' profile pictures. These photos are "signed" with the team member's first name, and each individual tweet and post is flagged with the team member's forename and initials. This gives customers a completely personal impression of the person they are talking to.

Above all, the conduct guidelines emphasize a human, empathetic and polite tone:
- All conversations are individual, no text elements or automated responses are used.
- For German customers, it is permitted to use the informal form of address if your conversation partner uses it first or requests it of you. In all other cases, the formal tone of address is required.
- A "greeting tweet" may be posted at the start of every day, and the team may sign off at the end of the day and at the weekend.
- Service staff acknowledge and say thank you for every reaction including praise, recognition, or positive feedback. If the situation seems appropriate, the communication partner is asked to pass on their recommendation to others and is sent a note containing a hyperlink to Telekom's recommend-a-friend page.

The mission statement for the first project incorporates the vision:

Perfect service in 140 characters

Our @Telekom_hilft account is Telekom's central point of contact on Twitter for all private consumer customer inquiries relating to fixed line and mobile phone issues.

Service-relevant news and information are published through the Telekom_hilft account. On a case-by-case basis, notes about sales campaigns can be communicated by tweet. However, the primary purpose of the service account must not be diluted as a result.

The team actively seeks out contact with other Twitter users who are having problems with Telekom products and services and make these public via Twitter. The aim is to resolve the problem collaboratively.

The general job description for the team's day-to-day work is as follows:

- Publish information
- Detect tweets that refer to Telekom to identify service cases
- Openly address Twitter users who have announced problems they are having with Telekom products or services, who have made negative statements, or who simply have questions
- Respond to questions from customers and interested parties
- Link to Telekom service offerings and functions.

Since customer service on the social web is also a PR activity, we developed a set of editorial guidelines:

- Reliability: Information must be reliable. Quality assurance is in place, e.g., everything is reviewed by two separate people.
- Credibility: Be genuine, write and communicate authentically.
- Confidentiality: Do not reveal any sensitive information and urge customers not to reveal any of their own data.
- Novelty: Regularly communicate interesting information, e.g., new offers.
- Value: Information must be valuable and aimed at the target group, e.g., offer a resolution to a problem.
- Dialog: Having a conversation means listening, answering questions and commenting on tweets.
- Multiplication: Disseminate useful information, e.g., re-tweet relevant information from other Twitter users.

Incoming queries are classified as either passive or active dialog. For these dialogs, Twitter is used to monitor whether any negative statements about Telekom have been made. If so, and it is clearly a service case, the service team actively tweets the person who published the complaint. These unexpected offers of support generate an incredibly positive experience for everyone involved. When Twitter users tweet their followers or third parties about problems with Telekom products or services and are then offered, and actually receive, unexpected help from the service team, they turn into the most satisfied and most enthusiastic customers. It also gives the service staff a positive and motivating experience to take away from each "moment of truth".

6   Previous Milestones

The service innovation "Telekom hilft" certainly arrived with a bang. News about the existence of the Telekom_hilft Twitter account spread virally online within hours. A variety of tweets, posts, messages, reports, analyses, tests, and comments appeared within days after the launch—with not a single official press release or conference.

> **Milestones for the Program and Associated Projects* at the Time of Going to Press.**
> May 2010: Twitter service channel "Telekom_hilft" launched
> July 2010: First appearance of Telekom service staff as official contacts in external forums, e.g., onlinekosten.de
> September 2010: Facebook service channel "Telekom hilft" launched
> October 2010: "Service Notes" blog launched
> October 2010: Facebook campaign "Windows Phone 7 Test Pilots" launched
> November 2010: Recommend-a-friend on Facebook in "Telekom hilft" section
> December 2010: Telekom.de service video published on Facebook in "Telekom hilft" section
> January 2011: Service forum expanded to cover mobile phone topics
> Spring/summer 2011: Sales campaigns launched via "Telekom hilft" on Facebook
> June 2011: First use of URL shortener with domain dt.de
> August 2011: Sales campaigns launched for Telekom shops using location-specific services Facebook Places and Foursquare
> *This overview also lists associated projects that are linked with the "Telekom hilft" program through synergies or interactions. Telekom's service forum has been available for more than 10 years. In the past, the forum focused on content relating to fixed line, Internet and IP TV. At the beginning of 2011, the requisite resources and processes were put in place to present and deal with mobile phone topics in the forum.

7 Lessons Learned

By the end of 2011, "Telekom hilft" had sent more than 60,000 tweets and had 17,000 followers, receiving almost 28,000 Likes on Facebook. The rate of interaction on Twitter has stalled, apparently because Twitter is not yet part of mainstream Internet use in Germany. It is a different story for Facebook, where interactivity is growing organically and continuously. We are very pleased by the high customer satisfaction values, even though these are subject to confirmation due to limitations in how the data was collected and the low number of cases.

Customer service in the social web works. The social web is a public space for dialog between citizens and consumers about organizations, brands, products and services. Tools are easily accessible and intuitive to use, from five-star ratings in shops and review portals, through spontaneous opinions expressed in blog posts and comments, to high-end, in-depth hobbyist reviews in visual, audio and written form. In this world of do-it-yourself advice, a heartfelt and serious offer of consumer dialog from a company will be immediately accepted if there is value added for existing customers and interested parties. Customer service on the social web adds value.

Selling, in the sense of traditional commodities, via Facebook does not work. At least not for telecommunications contracts. Randomly organized teams of social consumers immediately tear into the heart of gimmicky sales campaigns with superficial, attention-grabbing slogans, subjecting them to more or less sound peer comparisons with differentiated representation of the sales arguments. And all this on the company's own Facebook page.

Being able to offer innovation and positively influence Telekom's image was the biggest surprise outcome of this project, in a good way. Communicators and influencers in particular subjected "Telekom hilft" to a comprehensive function test and the majority gave it a good score. As a result, many posts, features and book articles appeared presenting "Telekom hilft" as a best practice for customer service in the social web. The media resonance for "Telekom hilft", as well as its profile as a reference for customer service on the social web in articles and text books, is made abundantly clear with a basic search engine query. One year after launch, an internal resonance analysis (data compiled March 1 to October 15, 2011) found that "Telekom hilft" is still having a significant impact on the perception of Telekom as a service-oriented company. (Telekom 2011)

Amassing practical experience was an absolute goal during this initiative and we are still experiencing new things every day. This includes a variety of unexpected incidents in service communication, both positive and negative. One of the viral waves was very welcome. The scheduled soft launch involving no PR effort whatsoever did not work at all, since customers, users, influencers and communicators discovered the new support channel within a few hours, tested it, rated it, enjoyed it and then put it on the agenda for various new and old media. Sudden rushes of negativity soon set the alarm bells ringing, with customers leveraging the reach of their personal networks to put pressure on an organization and trigger a round of "mud-slinging" ("shitstorm" is a neologism in Germany). These surges of negative energy are usually easy to spot and calm because we have a specialist task force and "handlers" in place—our social media customer service team.

We have had both good and bad experiences with parodies as well. Since customer service is now a PR activity, "Telekom hilft" itself is also a PR activity that has varying outcomes. One Twitter parody had little to no resonance and was interesting only to the program management team because it targeted "Telekom hilft". In contrast, a hobby publicist created a deliberately fake Telekom_hilft account to respond to tweets from customers. Some were happy with the results, but it did confuse customers and frustrated efforts by the real service team to the extent that they were forced to take appropriate action. The fake Twitter account was shut down.

When influencers and celebrities receive help and then thank and express their appreciation for both the team and the brand publicly, those are the motivating highlights that stick in the memories of the service staff and company. For example,

Tagesschau host Jens Riewa posted a complaint on his Facebook page. Once the "Telekom hilft" team had resolved the problem, they received both praise and recognition: "From now on, I'm adding a '!' to the end of your page's name. Thanks to Ulli and everyone else working behind the scenes."

Nevertheless, the best experiences come when support is provided by the service team during day-to-day activities and in crisis situations, as demonstrated by (a) customers who enjoy using the program and offer their own helpful advice and (b) staff from other areas who identify with their company's innovative offering and also support the social media team. Customers and staff are increasingly getting together in the "Telekom hilft" community, creating a large interest group. One good example of support from customers comes from October 2010, when 80 test devices were given away to existing customers for testing, review and rating, as part of the "Windows Phone 7 Test Pilots" promotion.

> **Facebook user A:** What a load of garbage, you have to be a Telekom customer to take part! You complete ***. That's just typical Telekom, what a load of ****. This is another shining example.
>
> **Facebook user B:** What do you mean load of ****? I think it's the only fair way…it's called customer retention, a benefit of being a Telekom customer… :-)
> Any other provider would do the same … xD
>
> **Facebook user C:** I think it's a real shame that people post stuff like that here just because they hate Telekom! I've got 3 T-Mobile contracts and am a fixed line Entertain VDSL customer! 100% satisfied…so a big thank you to Telekom for launching campaigns like this to say thanks to their customers once in a while, which IMO is what they're doing here.
>
> **Facebook user D:** Yeah, I'll admit that I really like Telekom. Otherwise I wouldn't have been a completely satisfied customer for 8 years. Both fixed line and mobile…

8 Outlook

Diving into customer service in the social web brings with it a need to continuously develop processes, resources, competencies, roles, tools and KPIs. Given the dynamic nature of the Internet, there's no end in sight for the "Telekom hilft" program. However, we do predict a new role for service staff in Support 2.0. The social web requires much more than outstanding social, communication and problem solving competencies. It demands a group of multimedia-producing, multichannel-savvy service editors and community moderators who are constantly discovering new ways to network with social consumers and to cultivate an excellent customer service program.

References

Bock, A. H. (2010). Telekom_hilft: Erste Erfahrungen mit Twitter als neuem Service-Kanal. In M. Bentele, N. Gronau, P. Schütt, & M. Weber (Eds.), *Mit Wissensmanagement Innovationen vorantreiben!* (pp. 449–454). Congress documentation for KnowTech 2010; 12th congress on IT-assisted knowledge management in companies and organizations. Bad Homburg: Bitkom.

Busemann, K., & Gscheidle, C. (2011). Web 2.0: Aktive Mitwirkung verbleibt auf niedrigem Niveau Ergebnisse der ARD/ZDF-Onlinestudie 2011. In: Media Perspektiven, No. 7–8.

Carlzon, J. (1995). *Alles für den Kunden. Jan Carlzon revolutioniert ein Unternehmen.* Munich: Heyne.

Court, D., Elzinga, D., Mulder, S., & Vetvik, O. J. (2009, June). The consumer decision journey. http://www.mckinseyquarterly.com/The_consumer_decision_journey_2373 (called up on: October 18, 2011).

Dawson, J. (2009, June 1). The Social Telco. London: Ovum.

Detecon. (2009). Customer experience management: Managing customer experience profitably, Bonn.

Detecon. (2010). Kundenservice der Zukunft. Mit Social Media und Self Services zur neuen Autonomie des Kunden: Empirical study: Trends und Herausforderungen des Kundenservice-Managements, Bonn.

Edelman Digital. (2010). The 8095 Exchange: Millennials, their actions surrounding brands and the dynamics of reverberation. http://www.slideshare.net/EdelmanDigital/8095-white-paper (called up on: October 19, 2011).

Greenberg, P. (2010). *CRM at the speed of light, fourth edition: Social CRM strategies, tools and techniques for engaging your customers.* New York: McGraw-Hill (Amazon Kindle Edition).

Metz, A. (2012). *The social customer: How brands can use social CRM to acquire, monetize and retain fans, friends and followers.* New York: McGraw-Hill.

Noble, S. (2010). It's time to bury the marketing funnel. http://www.forrester.com/rb/Research/time_to_bury_marketing_funnel/q/id/57495/t/2 (called up on: October 19, 2011).

Schmitt, B. H., & Mangold, M. (2004). *Kundenerlebnis als Wettbewerbsvorteil: Mit Customer Experience Management Marken und Märkte Gewinn bringend gestalten.* Wiesbaden: Gabler.

Telekom. (2011, October 15). *Social Media: Engagement und Resonanz: Deutsche Telekom & Wettbewerb.* Bonn: Telekom Marketing Communications Strategy & Media.

Wang, R., & Owyang, J. (2010). *Social CRM: The new rules of relationship management: 18 Use cases that show business how to finally put customers first.* San Mateo: Altimeter.

Weinberger, D., Locke, C., Levine, R., & McKee, J. (2009). *The Cluetrain Manifesto: 10th anniversary edition.* New York: Basic Books.

Online Radio: A Social Media Business?

Paul Dwyer

As marketers and media companies struggle to make sense of their role in this transformed media landscape, the idea that media might "go viral"... has emerged as a popular cultural logic... The promise is simple if deceptive- create a media virus and watch it infect the public (Joshua and Jenkins 2011, p114)

1 Introduction

Digitisation and the internet have enabled the emergence of free digital music streaming services, like Last.fm, Spotify and We-7, and online-only radio services like Mixcloud, which disintermediate the traditional broadcast radio station's role as a gatekeeper between the music industry and the listener (Wiechmann 2009). UK radio broadcasters have responded to these challengers with their own webcasting and with a platform—Radioplayer—created by a unique collaboration between BBC and commercial radio stations. Although online listening is still small compared to broadcast audiences, the potential exists for social media to transform the way audiences listen to music online and on mobile devices (Ofcom 2011).

This chapter proposes a new analytical framework to analyse the different services offered by traditional and digital radio and music services and to evaluate their performance, from an audience perspective. Having differentiated the various services within a competitive field, the chapter gives a more detailed examination to two innovative companies—Radioplayer and Mixcloud—which are attempting to redefine radio services online, on mobile and on social media. The particular focus of the final part of the chapter is in applying the analytical framework to analyse and evaluate the performance of the social media applications implemented by these companies, in comparison with a key competitor, Spotify.

P. Dwyer (✉)
University of Westminster, London, UK
e-mail: p.dwyer@westminster.ac.uk

2 Analytical Framework

Digital media present audiences with a wide array of new choices, and pose significant challenges to existing media management practices. For radio producers and broadcasters, the challenges are such that many academic commentators now argue that the concept of radio is itself obsolete. Digital production and distribution of audio content via the internet has enabled the development of new services which are clearly not technically 'radio' (they do not use radio waves) and which some academics have argued are 'radiogenic' (Tacchi 2000:292), or 'radioesque' (Berry 2006:155; Jones 2002:226) or 'radio-style' (Coyle 2000:59). However, the persistence with which media managers (and audiences) describe these services as radio demonstrates that they are using some of the thinking from the broadcast era to navigate a path through the emerging digital landscape.

This definitional debate highlights a fundamental problem facing practitioners, audiences and researchers in attempting to understand the changes (and continuities) in management, production and cultural practices which have followed the emergence of digital and online media alongside traditional broadcast media. As digital and online media have emerged, an array of new terms and concepts has arisen to describe and analyse their operation, which differ significantly from their broadcast counterparts. Concepts like schedules, programming and formatting, for example, are central to broadcasting but can become marginal or even redundant in the online space (Lotz 2007).

This chapter attempts to deal with this conceptual problem by creating an analytical framework using concepts from the digital space to enable better description and comparison of the practices of the broadcast and online arenas. Four central concepts drawn from the online world—linear streaming, on-demand, aggregation and curation—are defined as the extremes of two continua. As Fig. 1 shows, linear streaming and on-demand are opposite poles of a continuum of *user interaction* with a music/radio service; aggregation and curation are opposite ends of a continuum of practices of *content creation, selection and scheduling* (see Fig. 1).

Linear Streaming and **On-Demand**: This distinction goes to the heart of the definitional debate about 'radio'. Because the difference between on-demand *downloading* and on-demand *streaming* of music tracks is, for the listener, relatively small, the music industry demands significantly higher copyright payments from services which allow on-demand streaming (see IPO 2007 and below). Copyright bodies tend to accept that music services are not competing with downloading services to the extent that they are 'radio-like', that is that the stream of music is controllable by the listener only to the extent that they can in using the dial on the traditional radio receiver. Thus, broadcast radio can be considered to have similar features to streamed, minimally-interactive internet music services.

Curation and **Aggregation**: Museum and gallery curators are subject-matter experts who collect and literally "take care of" valuable art and artefacts. The size of and diversity of the content of most collections means that curators have to identify the most relevant or important pieces to be acquired and/or displayed in exhibition (Proctor 2010). This recognition of the importance of selecting and

Fig. 1 Analytical framework for music radio services

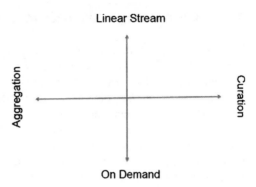

presenting content has produced the neologism 'curation' to describe the work done by (among others) journalists and film-makers in the online world (Jarvis 2011; Rosenbaum 2011). Bhargava (2009) defined content curation as "the act of finding, grouping, organizing or sharing the best and most relevant content on a specific issue".

Digitisation enables the aggregation of content in databases across the internet. As Bhargava (2011) notes, aggregation is at the opposite end of a continuum of practices of content curation; "the act of curating the most relevant information about a particular topic into a single location... you still may have hundreds of pieces of source material—but just the fact that it is in a single location and not millions of pieces of information has a high value for people interested in a particular topic."

The matrix framework in Fig. 1. will be used to compare and contrast the management practices of broadcast and online music and radio services and identify the key differences between the main players in this sector in the UK. The matrix enables evaluation of these services from an audience's point of view in terms of four related concepts: audience responsiveness, ease of use, relevance of music recommendation and diversity of content A key additional concept—*barriers to entry*—is used to explain how technology first created, and then gradually removed, barriers to practitioners in operating along the dimensions shown in the matrix (see Demsetz 1982).

Using this 'online' conceptual framework to compare broadcast and online practices will inevitably simplify some of the traditional practices of radio station/network management, and focus attention on some areas at the expense of others. The hope is that losses in detail will be more than compensated by the gains in clarity in identifying the key similarities and differences between services developed during the broadcast and online eras.

Having identified the differing *modi operandi* of the main UK broadcast and online players, it will be possible to analyse the contrasting approaches to, and results of social media strategies undertaken by two case study radio companies. The first of these—Radioplayer—operates as a bridge between online and broadcast radio. The second—Mixcloud—is online only in its conception and operation.

3 Methodology: Radio Connected

This chapter is the first publication from an 18-month R&D project—'Radio Connected', which has drawn together the major UK broadcasters, online radio channels, independent radio producers and digital technology companies to conduct R&D on the evolution of radio on connected devices. As a member of the steering committee of the project I have participated in all the key meetings and had the opportunity to interview the key participants. I have also been allowed privileged access to documentary evidence relating to the performance of the participant media organisations. As an academic member of the project, part of my role has been to develop a conceptual framework to conduct a comparative assessment of music and radio services and make an evaluation, from an audience perspective, of the strengths and weaknesses of these services. The four concepts can be used to evaluate the costs and benefits to the audience of the different approaches.

As a first step in the publication and dissemination of results, this chapter outlines the conceptual framework and briefly reports the comparative assessment and the evaluation. The second section of the chapter reports the findings from the experience of two of the project participants—Radioplayer and Mixcloud in developing social media applications to promote their brands and recommend content. In particular, this section reports on the success of their integration of their online offerings with Facebook.

4 Linear Streaming

Broadcasters distribute content in a linear stream to radio receivers. The number of hours of streaming (transmission) is determined by factors including the costs (per hour) of production and the size of the available audience (and thus revenue) at different hours of the day, within a geographic area (Briggs 1985). The techniques of radio station management derived from the barriers to entry created by scarcity of radio spectrum and audio production and distribution technologies (see Coase 1950). Constraints of spectrum space (available frequencies) and the costs of broadcast technology limited the number of channels which could transmit radio content in any geographical area, and costs of production technology limited the number of content producers and thus the volume and range (within and across genres) of radio content available (Briggs 1985).

5 'Genre Knowledge' Curation

These barriers to entry tended to give broadcasters have monopoly/oligopolistic control over the distribution of content across a geographical area for a given period of time (Coase 1950). The number of channels/stations and their hours of streaming created a limit on the hours of content which could be distributed by radio waves. Broadcast management, producers and presenters developed complicated processes for selecting which content to create or acquire and to stream. The traditional metaphor used in media studies is the gatekeeper (or sometimes 'cultural intermediary', see Hennion and Meadel 1986) and so the typical radio professional has been described as "a gatekeeper determining popular taste" (Rothenbuhler and McCourt 1992:101).

The model of selection was based on the genre knowledge of producers and presenters or DJs. This practice can best be illustrated by reference to the studies of the doyenne of such curators in pop music radio in the UK, John Peel, who broadcast on Radio 1 from its inception in 1967 until his death in 2004. The success of Peel's curatorial approach was partly defined by his ability to identify new artists or sounds (in the 1960s The Doors, Love and Judy Collins in the eighties and The Fall and Pulp) which would be liked by a wider audience.

But as Peel recognised, curation cannot be reduced to accuracy in selecting innovative content which would be successful: "that's one of the things I like, the fact that you're so often proven wrong. A lot of the stuff I used to play, in the early 1970s in particular—James Taylor and stuff like that—I now find agonizingly embarrassing" (cited in Long 2006). Almost as important as the music selected is the context genre experts can provide audiences for the music selected. Taylor (2003), recalling his time as a DJ at Xfm, noted "the concern for the DJ is that... the individual listener will turn off if a less obvious selection is made. It is vital therefore that the listener is aware of a distinctive context surrounding such a selection". Thus for Taylor, the role of the DJ is "constantly discovering new music and contextualising older music within an ever developing canon" it is "a vocation which requires an historical, cultural and aesthetic knowledge of music, who is qualified to make selections determine the context of those selections". Peel's particular values and rules were his love of the amateurism and ordinariness of many pop groups and "his rejection of the glamour, unmerited privilege and self-obsession of the pop world" (Long 2006).

Hendy (2000a) shows that in the mid-1990s this approach to curation became the convention at Radio 1. "Many long-standing and familiar presenters left, to be replaced by presenters who were unknown by mainstream radio audiences, but better known in the clubs and specialist music shows of London regional radio stations." But, as Hendy continues, "selection is in itself only the first stage of music programming: next comes the process of distributing those selected records across the time map of output—the scheduling of each particular record within each programme and across each day and each week." Hendy shows that since the 1930s, BBC scheduling practices were such that "specialist musics, representing a series of minority tastes, were equated with evening broadcasting, while more familiar and less demanding musics were served before the larger—and therefore more diverse—daytime audiences."

6   Evaluation of Genre Knowledge Curation

For 90 years, UK broadcasters have provided reliable, high quality, linear streamed music services which are exceptionally easy to use. From an audience perspective, the principle criticism of genre knowledge curation is that control of content selection and scheduling is exercised by an elite which may be unrepresentative of, or indifferent to, audience demand. The 'gatekeeper' concept was imported from social research into media analysis to highlight the necessarily partial representation by media channels of culture, politics or society (Lewin 1947; Breed 1955; Glasgow Media Group 1976). This critique was particularly effective when applied to Public Service media where much of 'popular' culture was defined by a small elite (many of the most celebrated BBC radio 1 DJs, including Peel, were educated at elite private schools, see Farsides 2011). From an audience perspective we can see that this is essentially a critique of the limited relevance of the content recommendations produced by this form of curation, or what critics of Peel have called "the amount of gristle in his shows, his soft-headedness in the face of mediocrity" (Stubbs 2004).

7 Curation by Formats

The main alternative to genre knowledge as a basis for curation is some calculation of audience demand. For many years broadcasters curated content to meet the demands of an imagined 'typical' audience member (Alhkvist 2001). In this model, the DJs or presenters are not involved in music curation but are 'emotive' personality-presenters, more inclined to talk about themselves or other topics which make for companionable listening (Crisell 1994; Montgomery 1991). This 'typical-audience-member' approach has been criticised for its reliance on unscientific, solipsistic or stereotypical assumptions about audiences (Ang 1991; Mitchell 2000).

Technological change reduced the barriers to entry created by spectrum scarcity and production costs and the licensing of advertising funded ('commercial') radio in the UK 1973 was followed by significant waves of market entry (see Lister et al. 2009).

As deregulation removed ownership barriers radio companies sought to limit competition for audiences and advertisers, and achieve efficiencies, by creating networks of stations. Radio networks achieved economies of scale by spreading costs (including curation) across stations in different markets. Thus commercial radio networks developed a centralized system of curation based on audience research methods (Ahlkvist and Faulkner 2002).

Radio advertising sales were based on audience research organisations' measurements of unduplicated audience members listening to a station in any quarter hour segment. "The logic of commercial radio is against discrete programmes (which stop and therefore cue stopping listening) and more in favour of 'flow'" (Deegan 2011). Radio networks replaced scheduling—of discrete, curated 'programmes' or 'shows'—with curation of the linear stream by formats based on radio 'clocks'—quarter hourly repetitions of content elements (such as news, weather, travel and station identifications). Rather than scheduling a range of content genres throughout the day, networks filled the entire stream with a single form of content (either a musical genre or genre 'mix' or various forms of news and talk content). Channel/station managers identified a target audience based on potential advertising revenue and local competition, tried to predict which genre(s) would be most relevant to this audience and adopted or developed a format of music or speech which would deliver this on a consistent basis throughout the linear stream. To communicate these formats, channels developed brand identities which audiences would recognise and recall, when searching for content. In 2005 Graham Bryce, MD of the UK's Capital Radio Group stations observed that "listeners by and large choose 'radio stations, not programmes'" (cited in Berry 2006).

8 Curation by Playlist

Formats replace the scheduling aspect of genre-knowledge curation and assure audiences of the predictability of the content throughout the linear stream. The weekly playlists of songs replaces the genre-knowledge selection of individual music tracks and thus provides the variety. Playlists still involve selection from musical genres, but guided by audience research and music industry sales lists and ranking systems, rather than the uncertainty, risk (and creativity) of genre knowledge.

Hesbacher et al. (1975) define a radio playlist as "25–40 rank-ordered recordings currently presumed to be popular and one to eight 'pick hits' chosen from among recent new releases". As Taylor (2003) noted of his time at Xfm "playlists became the key programming tool and output was carefully controlled to ensure the brand identity of the product was not undermined..." The presenter was given "a scheduled list of the tracks... together with specific instructions concerning the ... duration and basic content of each speech break." Taylor also describes how Selector, a software system common in the US, has been used in the UK to determine the proximity of tracks "due to their style, pace, instrumentation or vocal timbre" and thus to automate curation. This form of algorithm-based music selection prefigured the forms of automated curation and smart aggregation discussed below.

Curation based on enduring formats and changing playlists has proved a more predictable and cost-efficient way of delivering target audience demographics (and therefore advertising revenues) than the uncertainties and risks of 'genre knowledge'. This competitive advantage (greater revenue potential and lower costs) has enabled the most popular formats to succeed at the expense of those commercial stations and small networks which persisted with 'genre knowledge' or adopted less-popular formats (see Lister et al. 2009). Globally, some of the most successful formats are—Top 40 or All Hit Radio (CHR), Country, Album Oriented Rock (AOR), Adult Contemporary (AC), and Urban (Ahlkvist and Fisher 2000). Figure 2 compares the BBC genre knowledge approach to the format/playlist approach of the largest UK commercial radio group, Global Radio, in its Capital Radio network.

Fig. 2 Music and radio services compared

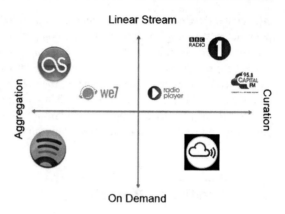

9 Evaluation of Curation by Format

From an audience perspective, the problem with curation by format is the severe limits to the diversity of the formats and—within formats—of the length of the playlists. Much research suggests market entry and deregulation have produced playlists which are shorter and more similar to other stations (Ahlkvist and Fisher 2000). Deegan (2010) has shown that in a given week, Capital played 89 different tracks, compared with BBC Radio 1's 443. "Capital's playlist isn't designed to help discovery of the music long-tail" (Deegan 2011). In fact, as the Radio 1 Controller Matthew Bannister, argued in the mid-1990s "A combination of demographics and economics is driving commercial radio towards the middle-aged, middle-class. And, in a sweeping generalization, what those middle-aged, middle-class listeners want is comfort—music they already know or that sounds like something they already know ... [commercial stations] are moving towards the middle ground, playing more established classic hits and taking fewer and fewer risks with new music and artists" (cited in Garfield 1998:92–93).

10 Aggregation and On-Demand

Digitisation further removes technological barriers to entry to music curation and streaming and, in enabling aggregation, in theory, solves the problems identified with both methods of curation discussed—the scarcity of the schedule or playlist is replaced by the abundance of the catalogue. Crucially, digitisation enables audiences to interact with the stream, and so take control over curation- each audience member can select and schedule his/her own music stream 'on-demand'. Elite curation and commercial curation of standardised formats with limited playlists for mass audiences are replaced by 'mass, customisation' of individual playlists using huge aggregations of diverse content (see Pine 1993). Spotify, for example, is a UK-based music service offering streaming of around 15 million tracks, on-demand (either free with advertising or for a subscription) from a range of major and independent record labels. Music can be searched and browsed by title, artist, album, record label, genre or playlist. Figure 2 shows the relationship between Spotify and BBC and commercial radio.

11 Evaluation of Aggregation and On-Demand

One of the key advantages of Spotify—for users and the music companies—is its ease of use. Music companies have negotiated copyright agreements with Spotify because they hope audiences will find Spotify easier to use than illegal sites (Greely 2011). But for the audience, sheer aggregation of content can create the 'paradox of choice' (Schwartz 2005). By removing curation from the process, the listener has no guide to which parts of the extensive 'long tail' are worth 'customizing'. Most aggregators try to help users customise playlists by providing "smart aggregation" systems which replicate some of the processes of curation (Celma 2010). Music recommendation engines are designed to anticipate a user's musical desires by correlating expressed user preferences with 'inherent' qualities of the music or sound file (content-based approaches), aggregating user ratings (collaborative filtering), or a combination of these methods. Many recommendation systems are based on collaborative filtering—the system identifies similar users based on data collected from their previous consumption/listening choices, and then recommends content popular with these users to new, similar users—Amazon is one such system (Celma 2010).

12 Aggregation and Linear Streaming

Content aggregation strategies depend on the willingness of the content owners—the music companies—to allow their content to be aggregated. The music companies clearly hope that people will choose services like Spotify—which do provide a (very modest) return, rather than using pirated digital music sharing services (Greely 2011).

But the music companies face a dilemma because, from a user experience perspective, the differences between 'on-demand streaming' and 'download' are slight. For practical purposes the definition of 'radio' in an online context centres on the degree of interactivity, the degree to which the service "enables the user to influence the playlist" (IPO 2007). US copyright bodies treat linear broadcast and internet music streams as equivalent subject to the same copyright rules (see Arista vs Launch Media 2009). In the UK, the copyright bodies drew a distinction between internet music streams and broadcast streams, based on the degree of interactivity (IPO 2007). So streamed radio broadcasters pay the same low copyright fees for real-time internet 'simulcasts' of their live broadcast output, because these are treated as non-interactive. Copyright charges for internet-only radio stations—like last.fm and We-7 (and including some Radioplayer stations like totallyradio.

com)—are a third more expensive and are most expensive for on-demand services like Spotify. The BBC was the only UK broadcaster with an agreement to make music programmes available on-demand, until Mixcloud made its own agreement with the copyright body PRS.

13 Last.fm

Last.fm (UK) has aggregated more than 12 million songs, but ended its on-demand service in 2010 (Last.fm 2010). The service does not allow streaming of individual songs 'on-demand' but although the stream is linear, the scope for audiences to indicate their demands is clearly greater than in broadcast radio. Content is selected and scheduled not by 'curation' but by what Foremski (2010) and others have called 'smart aggregation' (see Fig. 2.). Last.fm's 'smart aggregation' is based on a collaborative filtering, recommendation system—the "Audioscrobbler"- which collects data about listening habits on a computer, ipod or other media players. Listeners can also influence ('customise') the stream ('tag radio') manually using folksonomies, tagging, "love" and "ban" buttons. These two smart aggregation systems enable Last.fm to generate a stream of music which is tagged as similar to the user's profile or preferences. Users can skip recommended tracks which are not relevant but cannot pause the stream. Martin Stiskel, one of the co-founders of Last.fm argued that the linear streaming and smart aggregation aspects of the service gave it an advantage over on-demand services like Spotify; "Last.fm always had an emphasis on making you discover new music. On demand is not about discovery" (cited in Moscote Freire 2007). In making this argument, Stiskel is drawing attention to the 'paradox of choice' problem of on-demand aggregation, and arguing that users prefer smart aggregation.

14 We-7

Steve Purdham, CEO of We7, another UK based music service, has pointed to empirical evidence from the development of this music service which supports Stiskel's view. We7 attempted a number of service models including free and subscription on-demand music services before, largely because of the copyright fees for on-demand music, it began to operate as an internet radio station in January 2010 (Youngs 2010). When he discovered that more than 55 % of tracks on the site were being accessed through the radio feature rather than on-demand, Purdham concluded; "I thought the ultimate music service was one where you get to choose… Actually, users are saying, 'I can't be bothered, just entertain me'." (Andrews 2010)

15 Evaluation of Linear Streamed Aggregation

Services based on linear streaming and aggregation attempt to solve the 'paradox of choice' by using 'smart aggregation' systems to replicate the processes of curation. However there are a number of problems associated with music recommendation systems (see Celma 2010) which have led some commentators to conclude that curation processes can outperform automated processes in recommending relevant content to audiences (Foremski 2010).

16 Mixcloud: On Demand User Curated Content

Further barriers to entry to curation and distribution of music shows were removed with the arrival of production tools like Audacity, ProTools, Adobe Audition, and CoolEdit which enabled recording and internet distribution of music shows via peer-to-peer networks or linear streaming (Priestman 2002). The user curated content which has emerged is described by Mixcloud's founder, Nikhil Shah; "Lots of DJs host their own shows on file-sharing services—currently they put their shows on zshare and send out a link—on e mail or on twitter—to that individually hosted show" (Shah 2010). These 'user curators' work in a similar way, and constitute a similar population to the group of genre knowledge DJs, discussed above, recruited by BBC Radio 1 in the mid-1990s. Gavin Handley, presenter, NTS Radion, says "most music comes to me through long term relationships with producers and labels", Julien, a DJ for Laid Back Radio adds "a lot of our music comes from trusted contacts on Facebook and twitter, and emails from labels we like" (cited in Shah 2011).

These user curators also apply the 'typical audience member' approach, described above, learning about audience demand through DJ-ing in clubs. "As for ideas, you just have to know your audience and think a lot. And play a bit too, lots of ideas come from playing!" DJ, RarFM (cited in Shah 2011).

From an audience perspective, user curation may be more responsive to individual demand because unlike radio stations, user curators do not have oligopolistic control over the production and distribution of music shows—if their recommendations are not relevant, the audience can choose other providers. However, many of these services are not easy for audiences to access. The technical difficulty of finding such online services limits the degree to which this form of curation provides a solution either to problems of elite or format curation in traditional radio or the 'paradox of choice' created by on-demand services. Furthermore, as these platforms enable music listening and even downloading without payment of music copyright, they operate illegally, without the permission of copyright owners.

17 Aggregation

Mixcloud is a platform which tries to solve the problems identified with existing music services by enabling on-demand access to user curated music, without the ease of use and copyright problems which were associated with this content. Founder Nikhil Shah identified the problem as follows: "On demand content and independent radio content DJ mixes are very distributed across the internet". Mixcloud uses smart aggregation and ease of on-demand access to try "to build the definitive platform to promote that content to a big audience. We want to replace the individually hosted show with a page on Mixcloud... like YouTube for audio content" (Shah and Perez 2009). Mixcloud enables greater ease of use of this form of content by attaching metadata to the user curated playlists/mixtapes to improve the listener's ability to search, navigate and inter-relate them.

A crucial part of Mixcloud's strategy is its agreement with the copyright owners to allow on-demand listening, but not downloading, of tracks, on the basis that it provides a legal alternative to piracy. Rather than DJs sharing their playlists on sites which allow the music content to be illegally downloaded, Mixcloud offers a platform, like Spotify, where audiences can access this music but can't illegally download/own it. "Not offering downloads has been a challenge for us in terms of persuading the content creators (i.e. DJs) to use a platform like ours. What we have to get around for listeners is the idea that they can't own the file but the experience of listening and streaming on Mixcloud is superior. So it's very similar to the Spotify model. Spotify's competitor is illegal downloading and they are trying to cannibalise illegal downloading by offering a streaming-only and superior alternative." (Shah 2010)

Mixcloud has also negotiated agreements with other content producers, to increase the aggregation of content on the website, and the platform's content now comes from an increasing variety of curators, across a range of genres, in addition to music DJs. Independent podcasters, (e.g. 'Answer Me This' (comedy); 'Hospitality' (music)) speech radio production companies producing syndicated radio shows (e.g. 'Somethin' Else'; 'The Radio Department'; 'Wise Buddah') radio stations (student, community, hospital, and internet radio stations) and other content creating organisations (such as *The Guardian* newspaper and the Royal Society for the Arts).

18 Radioplayer: On-Demand Aggregated Curated Linear Stream

This chapter has identified the limited diversity of content curated in linear broadcast streams as a key problem with broadcast radio. A second problem, in the digital context, is ease of use. Whilst many broadcasters have been 'simulcasting' their broadcast streams online for years (see Priestman 2002) switching between these streams is much more difficult than on a traditional radio receiver and so broadcast radio has been harder to use than other music services on digital platforms.

A number of companies have launched 'third party' applications designed to improve the ability find and switch between stations, TuneIn being one of the oldest and most widespread (Dredge 2012).

Radioplayer is a partnership between the BBC, the UK's main commercial networks (Global Radio, GMG Radio and Absolute) and the industry body the Radio Centre. Radioplayer attempts to solve the diversity and usability problems of broadcast radio on digital platforms. The platform enables traditional radio stations to compete with other music services, and also third party aggregators like Tun3r and TuneIn, by being the definitive aggregator for UK radio. It address the useability problem by integrating the Radioplayer platform with the digital products of UK radio stations.

By developing an open application interface and a simple 'DIY' tool-kit for stations to create their own bespoke player, Radioplayer aims to make it easy for smaller radio stations to develop an online presence. When the platform was launched in Spring 2011 it announced its intention to aggregate the 400 Ofcom-licensed, linear curated UK radio stations on the platform within a year, to create 'UK Radio in one place'. The BBC's Tim Davie argued "Successful aggregation of content can only happen when a platform is truly open like Radioplayer is and it has all of the major content partners on board—which this does." (Barnett 2011). Currently Radioplayer aggregates streams from 300-stations. By enabling smaller local or community stations to go online and by making online-only stations accessible to a wider audience via a single platform, Radioplayer has increased the diversity of linear curated radio available to audiences.

Copyright conditions limit the amount of on-demand music content traditional broadcasters can offer through Radioplayer—except from the BBC, which has an individual license agreement. But listeners can customise their own stream by combining the broadcast stream with on-demand speech-podcasts by their favourite presenters.

Like other aggregators aware of 'paradox of choice' problems, Radioplayer uses smart aggregation techniques. The online Radioplayer is also a downloadable 'app' designed to make it easier to find and listen to UK linear streamed curated radio online using a single, standard, pop-up player. The app enables users to find online radio streams using features (such as 'presets') similar to those on a traditional radio receiver. The app installs this 'radio' on the user's computer, puts an icon in their 'Start' menu (and at the top of Google's 'Chrome' browser) and launches the Radioplayer with one click, opening at the 'last station listened to'. Listeners can personalise the player, saving their favourite stations using the presets function. But Radioplayer also aggregates metadata from the stations, to enable audiences to search for curated radio streams by brand/station, genre/format, presenter; artists-regularly-played, location, presenter or topic. The player then produces a ranked list of stations which fit the search criteria, and helps listeners find curated radio which is relevant. "If you like Rihanna and One-Direction it will help you find Capital Radio" (Deegan 2011). There is some evidence this strategy is bringing audiences to streamed radio online—the latest figures, from August 2011, showed Radioplayer attracted around 6.7 million unique users a month (Hill 2012).

Figure 2. illustrates the different approaches of Radioplayer and Mixcloud to online radio. Mixcloud provides on-demand access to user curated, 'long tail', niche content; Radioplayer enables access to linear streams of professionally curated mass media content.

19   Social Media Curation and Aggregation

The creation of social media sites, and in particular Facebook, removed many of the final 'barriers to entry' to the curation and distribution of content (Rosenbaum 2011). While the web enabled sophisticated users, like the Mixcloud DJs, who learned HTML and devoted considerable time to the task, to distribute content, it was Facebook (and its predecessors), which enabled 'anyone' to become a content curator. Users could select content (images, videos, articles, audio, podcasts) by pressing the "Like" button add context by adding a line in a drop down comment box, and publish to their Facebook page.

As well as enabling social curation, social media create 'network effects' as users share content with friends who may share the same content with other friends. This has reduced the power of 'elite' genre and format curators of the broadcast era—and significantly increased the power of 'users'—to influence popular culture. As Gehl (2011) noted "web 2.0 sites such as Facebook, MySpace, Twitter... have enabled... constant production of content by...users... (who) now have unprecedented power over popular trends on the Web". The classic case of this power is the 'viral distribution' of the Susan Boyle video (see Joshua and Jenkins, 2011). Viral marketing has been the subject of huge interest (see for example Shuen 2008) as brands see the potential for social media to drive online audience metrics (visits, return visits, time on site, sales conversions etc.) and provide market research data.

On-demand music services have clearly recognised the potential for social curation to help solve the 'paradox of choice'—likes or comments by friends may offer an even more reliable guide to music recommendation than a genre expert or format DJ. Spotify's early social networking tools included the ability for users to share playlists (hugely longer than anything a radio station could have) with friends who had Spotify accounts.

As we have seen, Mixcloud is built on a process of curation which is more social (because 'user generated') than many other platforms. Communities of expert DJs interact with audiences to find new music content, contextual information and presentation ideas. Mixcloud is thus building on existing 'network effects' rather than seeking to create them through viral marketing. As Shah says "our users were our marketing arm, we didn't have to pay for traffic". However, as business funded by a advertising (and to a much lesser extent e-commerce) the company has developed a marketing team which interacts with users on via e mail as well as on social media platforms to promote the content and the platform. The team have developed their own practical experience about how to optimise social media to bring traffic to the platform. "Be funny, be humourous and ask questions because people will respond. We have a team which is looking for positive actions (great things people should be sharing) but also things which shouldn't be on the platform—like single tracks and spammy behaviour. They can take certain actions, like deleting posts, but we always explain why we've taken an action, so people don't disengage with the service" (Shah 2011).

"Facebook is the most important, and then Twitter. You can talk to people you wouldn't normally—engage with big DJs, the biggest content brands in the world via Twitter. But ultimately you have to talk—to cement that relationship. Twitter was amazing at the launch stage—when we (Mixcloud) were in private BETA—people sharing their content and links even though the system was in BETA" (Shah 2010).

Many of Radioplayer's partner stations have fan pages and group pages on Facebook and some of their presenters have large numbers of followers on Twitter. The role of the presenter as an entertainer (rather than music curator) in the speech elements of radio content is well suited to social media interaction, as Tony Moorey, Absolute Radio Content Director makes clear "There have always been some people who have wanted to interact with a radio station. It started with letters and postcards, then phone, then texts and e-mails, etc.—Terry Wogan was the biggest and most successful broadcaster in the UK by reading out letters and cards" (Moorey 2011).

However there is clearly a potential conflict between social media curation and the genre knowledge or format curation represented on Radioplayer. As Matt Deegan (2011) of Radioplayer explains, the link between the linear stream, audience measurement and curation by format and playlist is still paramount: "Commercial radio is about listener hours, not audience reach. It does best out of its P1s—10 % of its audience account for 50 % of listener hours". Encouraging participation and social curation could lose these key listeners or reduce their listening hours "there's a danger that radio could be infected by Twitter, that participation could ruin your station. There is a tendency to keep the live stream and social media separate—so presenters on Radioplayer stations can get audiences to chat on Facebook messenger" (see Arbitron 2000).

The ability for social curation—'tags' and 'likes'—to generate 'network' effects for linear streamed radio is limited compared to on-demand. "Radio stations are live. How do you jump back to that point (in the stream) or just upload that segment of the output?" (Deegan 2011).

20 Aggregated, Linear Streamed Social Curation

In 2011 Facebook announced 'deeper integration' enabling users to access music services including Spotify, within Facebook (Constine 2011). As Facebook's design strategist Eric Fisher (2011) explains, this is based on a strategy of 'social design' which tries to improve recommendations to users by enabling "frictionless" sharing or social curation. Facebook's Open Graph Protocol means music services can include Open Graph tags (title, type, image, url, and the Like button) on their sites effectively turning them into Facebook pages. When a user clicks a Like button on the website, this appears in the "Likes and Interests" section of the user's

Fig. 3 Social media strategies compared

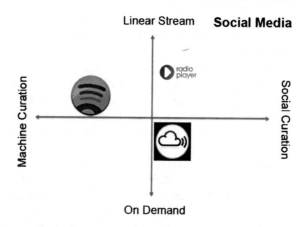

profile. This effectively automates social curation—everything the user listens to on Spotify is automatically shared to friends who have also authorised the app. This 'builds-in' network effects, moving social curation in the direction of aggregation, aggregating media and social media use and sending it to users' Facebook sites in a linear stream. Thus, Spotify's deep integration with Facebook turns user listening habits into a socially curated virtual radio station. Figure 3. shows how Spotify's Facebook application favours streaming and automated curation rather than social curation.

There is evidence that the integration created network effects which did increase Spotify's user's significantly (Constine 2011). But there is also evidence that, in automating the process of social curation, frictionless sharing has reduced the relevance of the recommendations significantly. Many users have echoed Loukides (2011) comment "It is meaningful if I tell you that I really like the avant-garde music by Olivier Messiaen. It's also meaningful to confess that I sometimes relax by listening to Pink Floyd. But if this kind of communication is replaced by a constant pipeline of what's queued up in Spotify, it all becomes meaningless... There's something about the friction, the need to work, the one-on-one contact, that makes the sharing real."

From an audience point of view, frictionless sharing does improve the 'ease of use' of social curation, but it does so by removing the actual processes of selection and contextualisation which we have described as fundamental to the value of curation. In so doing, users like Loukides (2011) have found that the value of the recommendations has reduced considerably.

Radioplayer's initial strategy aimed to use the app to make linear radio easier to use online by embedding it within Facebook. A key problem identified with social media use by most of its radio station partners was that the stations had FB pages which cost money to maintain, but which didn't enable users to listen to the station (Hill 2012). The Facebook app combines the metadata collected from radio stations, and additional information from Media UK, with Facebook's social graph to create a personalised radio app enabling users to search for and listen to

UK Radio stations within Facebook, to recommend/share their favourite stations and programmes with their friends via their wall and to see what their friends are listening to.

This approach to Facebook integration demonstrates first, the potential for social media to build brands. It is estimated that 80% of Radioplayer users access the player via the station website, rather than the website (Hill 2011). This reflects the strategy of building usage by making online listening more easy to use -with Radioplayer as a 'plain vanilla' brand providing services. In developing the Facebook app, the aim is partly to build the Radioplayer brand. In its current state of development, Radioplayer's partner stations/brands are embedding the player on their corporate Facebook pages. Listeners who want to play the station within Facebook authorise the Radioplayer App for their Facebook pages and are then made aware of their friends' use of the app to listen to other stations.

As Matt Deegan (2011) explains, in developing the App he was "faced with a question about how much to push sharing or virality. Wall posts are quite intrusive—not so much in terms of privacy, more in terms of the user's Facebook experience". Figure 3 represents this as a choice between social and 'machine' curation. "Radioplayer started with a Spotify-esque experience—publishing each track change to your wall/sharing as an opt-out rather than opt-in. It was a bit 'spammy' to give it a kick start" (Deegan 2011)

Radioplayer's initial experience demonstrates the problems with using 'machine' curation, particularly for linear streamed radio. The App was pushed to the closest network (around 200) of Radioplayer enthusiasts and their followers. But after 2 days, Facebook informed Radioplayer that their systems had identified undesirable patterns of usage and so, briefly, the system shut down the automated message posting (Deegan 2011) The reasons for this brief imprisonment in 'Facebook gaol' were revealed in the user analytics (Hill 2012). The data suggested users were not 'opting out' of frictionless sharing and so every track they listened to was published to their friends'. When these friends identified these automated posts as largely irrelevant recommendation information they clicked "hide" to stop receiving these posts. Facebook's 'quality control' algorithms identified this as an unwanted pattern of usage, largely because—without a history of use of the App—the sudden surge in posts was identified as unusual. The relatively high percentage of people choosing to hide the posts caused FB to classify a large percentage of them as spam. Unfortunately for Radioplayer, at that time Facebook was taking 48 hours to provide its partners' analytic data, so this pattern of use wasn't apparent until they were informed that frictionless sharing had already been shut down.

Once Radioplayer had received these data they were in a position to evaluate the app. "The system was creating 'boilerplate' messages and posting them to people's walls—clearly this was a dumb listening experience. So virality alone is not a success" (Deegan 2011). In fact, the users' tendency to hide these posts suggests that the app may not actually have achieved significant network effects (in terms of new users and increased listening) even if frictionless sharing had not been suspended.

The second generation of the Radioplayer app was developed to try to encourage greater social curation and less machine curation. The aim was still to achieve 'viral' promotion of the stations but more through positive comments about the listening experience than by machine curation and frictionless sharing. The App is also useful for brand awareness and recall "it's more about reminding people to listen to Radioplayer or individual stations. So it works well for smaller or digital only stations. You may know and like lots of digital stations but you may not remember them all (Deegan 2010).

Mixcloud has had close links with Facebook since it launched its Facebook sign-up app in 2011. Now of 85 % Mixcloud users are connected via Facebook and 85 % of new users sign up via Facebook. As a founder partner in Facebook's deep integration, Mixcloud's Facebook app also publishes all a user's actions automatically to their friend's pages. However, Mixcloud's experience suggests that frictionless sharing, machine curation, is more relevant to long-form, on-demand content and to content which already involves a degree of social curation. When a user starts to listen to a podcast, the app generates one automated post, even though the podcast may contain 20 or more tracks. Rather than receiving 20 individual automated posts, their friends will receive one post showing that they are listening to the podcast. The system also deletes a post after a few seconds if the user quickly switches to another podcast.

As a service which was already largely based in Facebook, Mixcloud did not achieve a significant growth in new users following the introduction of the app (Shah 2012). However, the network effects generated by curation have been significant. Mixcloud has found users curate content in three main ways. Two are social, manual, curation—either from an external site or by copying and pasting a link into Facebook. The other is the machine curated post. Although they have had little negative reaction to machine curation, it is clear that the greater network effects are produced by manual social curation. Each machine curated post, on average, produces 0.8 clicks back to the Mixcloud site. Each manual post produces, on average, 6.1 clicks back—and this is higher if the post includes a comment (Shah 2012).

Because most content is on-demand there is no currently no potential conflict between social media interaction and the content playlist, as there is in live, streamed radio. On Mixcloud the two are always separate. For Mixcloud the question currently is whether the platform should inform the creator about social media conversations about their content, so that they can participate too. This might become more significant as Mixcloud has noticed a trend to live streaming—where presenter/DJs stream their playlists live as they mix them. At present, however the niche audience status means that increased social participation in this form of live stream is unlikely to have the impact it would on mass audience broadcast radio.

Conclusions

This chapter has proposed a new analytical framework to compare digital music services and traditional radio services and evaluate their performance from an audience perspective. The framework has enabled a systematic comparison of the strengths and weaknesses of the main music and radio services in the UK, as barriers to entry have been removed over time. This analysis has made it possible to situate the social media strategies of radio broadcasters and a music service like Spotify within an overall understanding of how social media, and Facebook in particular, may or may not build on the strengths of these services. The chapter has suggested that the 'machine curation' of Facebook's frictionless sharing may enable better recommendations for long-form, on-demand content, but may undermine social curation processes if applied to streamed content.

Green and Jenkins (2011) have argued that the "virus" metaphor routinely applied to social media suggests that "network effects" are more 'automatic' than is the case. And this may produce strategies which do not adequately reflect the role of audiences as gatekeepers, deciding which content will be distributed. It is possible that Facebook's approach to 'frictionless sharing' was influenced by the 'viral' analysis of social media and thus that this approach led integration partners, like Spotify and Radioplayer to adopt social media policies which, initially at least, caused adverse audience reaction by creating a stream of irrelevant content recommendations. Both companies learned quickly that this 'machine curation' had less value to users than social curation.

On the other hand, the smaller scale, on-demand nature of Mixcloud, and its pre-existing base in Facebook meant that frictionless sharing was perceived as relevant. However Mixcloud's analysis of the network effects generated by Facebook usage demonstrated that social curation outperformed machine curation by a factor of more than six to one.

As Green and Jenkins observe: "Choosing to spread media involves a series of socially embedded decisions; that the content is worth watching... that the content might interest specific people we know; that the best way to spread that content is through a specific channel of communication; and often that the content should be circulated with a particular message attached" (Green and Jenkins 2011:113–114).

References

Ahlkvist, J., & Faulkner, R. (2002). Will this record work for us? *Qualitative Sociology, 25*(2), 189–215.
Ahlkvist, J., & Fisher, G. (2000). And the hits just keep on coming. *Poetics, 27*(5–6), 301–325.
Alhkvist, J. A. (2001). Programming philosophies and the rationalization of music radio. *Media Culture & Society, 23*(3), 339–358.
Andrews, R. (2010) We7 Repositions. *PaidContent.* Retrieved September 1, 2012, from http://paidcontent.co.uk/article/419
Ang, I. (1991). *Desperately seeking the audience*. London: Routledge.
Arbitron (2000) Where do my P1 listeners go? Retrieved September 1, 2012, from http://www.arbitron.com/study/where_listeners_go.asp

Arista Records LLC BMG RCA LLC Umg V. Launch Media Inc. (2009). US Court of Appeals, Docket No. 07-2576-CV. Retrieved September 1, 2012, from http://caselaw.findlaw.com/us-2nd-circuit/1362489.html

Barnett, E. (2011, March 31) Radioplayer: Radio's digital future. *Daily Telegraph.*

Berry. (2006). Will the iPod kill the radio star? *Convergence, 12*(2), 143–162.

Bhargava, R. (2009). Manifesto for the content curator. Retrieved September 1, 2012, from http://www.rohitbhargava.com/

Bhargava, R. (2011). The 5 models of content curation. Retrieved September 1, 2012, from http://www.rohitbhargava.com

Breed, W. (1955). Social control in the newsroom. *Social Forces, 33*(4), 326–335.

Briggs, A. (1985). *The BBC—The first fifty years.* Oxford: Oxford University Press.

Bryce, G. (2005, June 24). Hearing the i-Pod Hype. *Broadcast, 16.*

Celma, O. (2010). *Music recommendation and discovery in the long tail.* Berlin: Springer.

Coase, R. (1950). *British broadcasting: A study in monopoly.* Cambridge: Harvard University Press.

Constine, J. (2011) Spotify gains 1 million new Facebook users following f8. *Inside Facebook.* Retrieved September 12, 2012, from http://www.insidefacebook.com/2011/09/26

Coyle, R. (2000). Digitising the wireless. *Convergence, 6*(3), 57–75.

Crisell, A. (1994). *Understanding radio* (2nd ed.). London: Routledge.

Deegan, M. (2010). Comparing Radio 1 and Capital's Music. Retrieved September 1, 2012, from http://www.mattdeegan.com/2010/10/24/comparing-radio-1-and-capitals-music/

Deegan, M. (2011) Interview with the author 14/12/2011

Demsetz, H. (1982). Barriers to entry. *The American Economic Review., 72*(1), 47–57.

Dredge, S. (2012, Thursday 5 January) Tunein radio talks ... *The Guardian.*

Farsides, A. (2011) A social history of the british music industry since 1945 Unpublished Paper, University of Westminster February 2011.

Fisher, E. (2011) *Social design: A definition.* Retrieved September 1, 2012, from developers.facebook.com/attachment/SocialDesign.pdf.

Foremski, T. (2010). Curation versus aggregation. Retrieved September 1, 2012, from http://www.zdnet.com/blog/foremski

Garfield, S. (1998). *The nation's favourite: The true adventures of Radio 1.* London: Faber & Faber.

Gehl, R. W. (2011). The archive and the processor: The internal logic of Web 2.0. *New Media & Society, 13*(8), 1228–1244.

Glasgow Media Group. (1976). *Bad news.* London: Routledge.

Greely, B. (2011, July 14). Spotify's Ek wins over music pirates with labels' Approval. *Bloomberg News.* Retrieved September 1, 2012, from http://www.bloomberg.com/news/2011-07-14/spotify-wins-over-music-pirates-with-labels-approval-correct-html

Green, J., & Jenkins, H. (2011). Spreadable media. In V. Nightingale (Ed.), *Handbook of media audiences.* Oxford: Wiley–Blackwell.

Hendy, D. (2000a). Pop music radio in the public service. *Media, Culture & Society, 22*(6), 743–761.

Hendy, D. (2000b). *Radio in the global age.* Cambridge: Polity Press.

Hennion, A., & Meadel, C. (1986). Programming music: Radio as mediator. *Media Culture & Society, 8*, 281.

Hesbacher, P., et al. (1975). Record Roulette. *Journal of Communication, 25*, 74–85.

Hill, M. (2011, June) Report to Radio Connected Steering Group,

Hill, M. (2012, January) Report to Radio Connected Steering Group.

IPO. (2007). Copyright tribunal: In the matter of a reference under the Copyright, Designs and Patents Act 1988, 19/07/2007, CT84-90/05. Retrieved September 1, 2012, from www.ipo.gov.uk/ctribunaldownloadingdecision.pdf.

Jarvis, J. (2011). *What would Google do?* New York: Harper Collins.

Jones, S. (2002). Music that moves. *Cultural Studies, 16*(2), 213–232.
Last.fm (2010) http://blog.last.fm/2010/04/12/yes-it-does
Lewin, K. (1947). Frontiers in group dynamics. *Human Relations., 1*(2), 5–41.
Lister, B. et al. (2009) *Managing radio*. Sound Concepts (online) available at www.soundconcepts.ltd.uk/managingradio/
Long, P. (2006). The primary code. *The Radio Journal: International Studies in Broadcast and Audio Media, 4*, 25–48.
Lotz, A. (2007). *The television will be revolutionized*. New York: New York University Press.
Loukides, M. (2011) The end of social. Retrieved September 1, 2012, from http://radar.oreilly.com/2011/12/the-end-of-social.html
Mitchell, C. (2000). *Women and radio*. London: Routledge.
Montgomery, M. (1991). Our tune: A study of a discourse genre. In P. Scannell (Ed.), *Broadcast talk*. London: Sage.
Moorey, A. (2011). Social media in radio, panel discussion at the Radio Academy. Retrieved September 1, 2012, from http://www.radioacademy.org/events/london-events/social-media-in-radio/
Moscote Freire, A. (2007). Remediating radio. *The Radio Journal: International Studies in Broadcast and Audio Media, 5*(2&3), 97–1125.
Ofcom (2011, July). The communications market. Digital Radio Report (Ofcom).
Pine, J. B. (1993). *Mass customisation*. Cambridge: Harvard Business Press.
Priestman, C. (2002). *Web Radio*. London: Focal Press.
Proctor, N. (2010). Digital: Museum as platform, curator as champion. *Curator: The Museum Journal., 53*(1), 35–43.
Rosenbaum, S. (2011). *Curation nation*. New York: McGraw-Hill.
Rothenbuhler, E., & McCourt, T. (1992). Commercial radio and popular music. In J. Lull (Ed.), *Popular music and communication*. Newbury Park: Sage.
Schwartz, B. (2005). *The paradox of choice: Why more is less*. New York: HarperCollins.
Shah, N. (2010). Mixcloud interview. Retrieved September 1, 2012, from http://www.youtube.com/watch?v=xAKMdoUpuOw
Shah, N. (2011, June) Report to Radio Connected Steering Group.
Shah, N. (2012, January) Report to Radio Connected Steering Group.
Shah, N., Perez, N. (2009). Mixcloud interview. Retrieved September 1, 2012, from http://intruders.tv/en-tech/
Shuen, A. (2008). *Web 2.0: A strategy guide*. Sebastopol: Reilly Media.
Stubbs, D. (2004, December). JP:RIP. *The Wire*. 250.
Tacchi, J. (2000). The need for radio theory in the digital age. *International Journal of Culture, 3*(2), 290–8.
Taylor, S. (2003). I am what I play. In A. Beck (Ed.), *Cultural work*. London: Routledge.
Wiechmann, D. (2009). *The impact of online music services on the music recording industry*. Munich: Grin.
Youngs, I. (2010). We7 relaunch pins hopes on web radio. Retrieved September 1, 2012, from http://www.bbc.co.uk/news/entertainment-arts-11708924

Platform Leadership in Online Broadcasting Markets

Tom Evens

1 Introduction

For decades, the main television business model seemed relatively stable and simple. Television channels acquired content further up the value chain, relied on their own transmission infrastructure or managed to agree distribution deals with satellite and cable operators for passing on the programmes to the viewers, and sold these viewers to interested advertisers. In recent years, however, the broadcasting industry has undergone a fundamental reform as a result of political, economic, social and technological developments. Whereas market liberalisation allowed new competitors entering the production and distribution stage of the industry, digitisation created a window of opportunities for innovative broadcasting services and disruptive business models (Rangone and Turconi 2003). The widespread manifestation of the Internet as a global distribution network, driven by convergence between media, telecommunications and informatics, facilitated the provision of content over converged networks and dissolved the traditional linkage between content and carriage technology (Küng et al. 1999). Consequently, the digital context of television production, distribution and consumption has dramatically altered, increasing the sources of uncertainty and the level of risks for all the players involved in broadcasting (Chalaby and Segell 1999; Christophers 2008). Hence, the traditional configurations of power and control in the industry are in large part influenced by the pace of technological progress, creating opportunities for new entrants to gain dominant position in the near future. In turn, these opportunities are shaped or even blocked by pre-existing social formations and incumbents' foreclosing strategies.

One of the most prominent changes in today's industry is the far-reaching integration between traditional broadcast content with broadband delivery

T. Evens (✉)
iMinds-MICT, Ghent University, Ghent, Belgium
e-mail: Tom.Evens@UGent.be

platforms. Television broadcasting no longer relies on over-the-air transmission infrastructure only, but increasingly reaches the audience via converged broadband networks spreading content across multiple platforms and end user devices. Over-the-top television (OTT) services allow companies to go directly to consumers, bypassing traditional network gatekeepers and access providers. In addition, the intermediary role broadcasters used to fulfil is pressured by content owners' opportunity to directly target consumers (Chan-Olmsted and Kang 2003). This scenario of disintermediation, eliminating entire industry branches and making traditional retail activities in the value chain obsolete, was widely debated at the peak of the dot.com bubble (Kelly 1998) and is now becoming highly relevant to the broadband television industry. Indeed, one of the major strategic issues currently at stake in broadcasting is either the risk of losing or the opportunity of establishing a direct customer relationship, which is essential in developing audience intelligence and building relationships of trust and loyalty. Because of the increasing strategic value of a genuine user experience, companies with direct access to customer information and relationship may create a competitive advantage over rivals, may derive bargaining power vis-à-vis competitors and may position themselves favourably in the value network (Picard 2011). In this context, social media outlets provide companies with popular and often freely available instruments to engage with audiences, and are regarded extremely valuable information gateways for marketers and product developers.

As a result of the integration between broadband and broadcasting, traditional value chains and business models become destabilised and bottlenecks may need to be re-invented in order to regain competitive advantage in the broadband television market environment. Traditional operators, such as broadcasters and distributors, may need innovative business strategies in their attempt to leverage the rising popularity of broadband Internet and to counter online video initiatives deployed by newcomers arising out of convergence processes in distribution networks, online services and end user device manufacturing. Since all these converged players attempt to take the most favourable position in the broadband television value network and control the user interface, this article studies how different players deal with OTT broadband television services and what strategies they employ in achieving platform leadership in this market. It is argued that television incumbents try to leverage controlling points and employ foreclosing strategies hindering new entrants to directly target consumers. But once settled, new entrants that benefited from this technological abundance may be willing to create scarcity to preserve their stakes as well.

Addressing the issues of power and control in broadband television markets, the article would like to make a valuable contribution to the future analysis of converged broadcasting markets. First, this article is topical since OTT services are a burgeoning market and may have radical potential for the existing configurations of power and control in the television business in the mid-long term. Albeit prevalent in technology and telecommunications markets, such analysis of power and control related to the latest evolutions in broadcasting industries is rather scarce. Following a mainly qualitative approach, the article provides a theoretical, conceptual and empirical exploration of the struggle for platform leadership in Internet television markets. Complementing concepts from strategic management, political economy and innovation theory, the analysis is built upon a more integrated and interdisciplinary approach than mostly used in communications research.

The article is structured as follows. Section 2 comprises a literature overview, introducing theoretical concepts related to the analysis of power, control and competitive advantage that are applied to broadcasting markets. In Section 3, several OTT scenarios for the main industry players and the key resources for achieving platform leadership are discussed. Section 4 contains a case-by-case overview of OTT platform initiatives deployed both by incumbent companies and new entrants in this market. In the final section, the results are summarised and concluding remarks are made.

2 Issues of Power and Control

2.1 Scarcity and Abundance

The fusion between broadband and broadcasting technologies may have a disruptive potential to existing market structures and even though OTT services are still in their infancy, they could pressure the institutionalised distribution of power and control in the industry (De Boever and De Grooff 2010). In short, the Internet is widely regarded as producing the conditions that may reduce the intermediary role and power of traditional gatekeepers and access providers in the broadcasting industry. In this context, broadband could fuel the process of 'creative destruction', i.e. a period in which radical innovations and new technological combinations destroy 'old' economic structures and create 'new' ones (Schumpeter 1942). New pervasive technologies may provoke industrial transformations and bring economic growth to those companies and industries that adopt them. Incumbent firms are challenged by entrepreneurial, new entrants to adopt changes in the external environment through institutional innovation and avoid the scenario of being 'destructed'. However, this adaptability of incumbent firms may not be underestimated since the impact of technological innovation can be accelerated or decelerated by pre-existing social formations and structures of power. Hence, complex technological systems are subject to institutional design and deeply rooted in established structures of power (Koppenjan and Groenewegen 2005). Since the widespread diffusion and sustainable implementation of a new technology largely depends on how this technology is shaped by existing patterns, the interplay between social, economic and political interests and powers offers a valuable framework for assessing the likely impact of technology on these structures. Developing within a complex set of definitions and institutions, new communications technologies, which present social processes and structures, may reproduce existing patterns of use and sustain existing power relations (Williams 2003). Winston (1998) widely illustrates how the regulatory framework and communication technology industries have repeatedly suppressed the radical potential of new television technologies in order to prevent them from disrupting established economic interests. By integrating satellite and cable businesses in the 1970s, which had the potential of reallocating power and control within the US communications industry, incumbent broadcasting and telecommunication firms absorbed these emerging competitors in the established institutional structures. Although this period of transition created great institutional instability, the US television industry was able to reinvent its industrial practices to compete in the digital era (Lotz 2007). Similarly, telecommunications operators have maintained hegemonic power over Internet protocol television (IPTV) systems as an aggressive attempt to counter the cable industry and develop appropriate business strategies (Kim 2009).

A growing body of literature, mainly stemming from a more critical political economy tradition, acknowledges that, in contrast to more idealistic and techno-optimistic views on the Internet, the new electronic environment is not immune to forces of corporate power, monopolisation and market dominance. Wasko et al. (2011, p. 5), for example, claim that 'digital media appear not as a primary lever of change but as a new field of struggle dominated by long-standing battles and incumbents'. This may be true for the broadband television developments, which are increasingly colonised by established traditional and dot.com intermediaries that manifest themselves to compete for platform leadership, and become and control an 'ecosystem of innovation' in which third parties are encouraged to develop complementary products and services (Gawer and Cusumano 2008). Ballon and Van Heesvelde (2011) have contended that such multi-sided platforms could operate as gatekeepers of control and value around bottleneck functionalities that platform owners employ. Bottlenecks refer to scarce and critical resources that create competitive advantage to firms and enable them leverage market power vis-à-vis complementary innovators in particular markets (see Poel and Hawkins 2001). According to Mansell (1997, p. 975), 'incumbents historically have controlled the development of the communication infrastructure and have defined the architecture of new services' as a way of controlling the key points in communication infrastructure and service markets. This dialectic interplay between technological innovation leading to abundance and innovative strategies for maintaining scarcity is a long-run trend towards new media markets (Mansell 1999). Katz (2004) suggests that with the advent of broadband television services, technological bottlenecks have been replaced by commercial bottlenecks due to monopoly control. This fully supports Garnham's (1987) early call for investigating processes of scarcity and thus the allocation of critical resources across companies in cultural industry analysis. In the rest of this article, it is argued and illustrated that established players in television industries try to leverage controlling points and deploy foreclosing strategies to prevent new entrants in broadband television markets from establishing a direct customer relationship.

2.2 Customer Intimacy and Competitive Advantage

Porter's (1985) concept of the value chain serves as a valuable instrument for identifying competitive bottlenecks in the broadcasting industry. This framework has been widely applied for the strategic analysis of all contributing partners in the value creation process within the broadcasting industry. Basically, the approach of Porter maps the position these stakeholders occupy in the flow of value-adding activities. Whereas the model was originally used to assess the performance of individual companies, it became increasingly applied to represent the processes of production and distribution within the total industry. In this model, value is created as a sequential flow of stages in which upstream suppliers add value and pass their output downstream until the product or service is finally consumed by the end-customer. Firms may acquire a competitive advantage by occupying a crucial stake in this sequence of activities. Hence, this system of value creation ultimately leads to strategies aimed at controlling and monopolising bottlenecks in the chain. This monopolistic control over competitive bottlenecks may raise serious barriers to entry for new firms entering the market (Wirtz 1999). Focusing on why newcomers often tend to fail, Teece (1986) contends that incumbents possessing critical assets may foreclose new entrants even if the latter has a potential technological superiority. In broadcasting and pay-television markets, such competitive bottlenecks no longer relate to access to essential network facilities only, but increasingly to complementary end-user services (Cowie and Marsden 1999). More in particular, access to (premium) content is regarded a major bottleneck for alternative service providers as first-moving platforms exclusively contract (premium) rights holders (Nicita and Rossi 2008). In addition to distribution and content bottlenecks, the establishment of a direct relationship between producers and end customers is regarded an important parameter of control in the value network (Ballon 2007).

In strategic management theory, the idea that the exclusive control over bottlenecks gives the owner of scarce and critical resources a competitive advantage over a rivalling company refers to the resource-based theory of the firm (Barney 1991). This theory holds that a firm may obtain a sustained competitive advantage based on the properties or resources it owns or controls. Resources should be valuable, rare, costly to imitate and without strategic substitutes to bestow the firm with a sustained competitive advantage, which can be eliminated only by a process of creative destruction (Barney 1997). As the ultimate goal of firms should be creating significant customer value, firms could consider a strong customer orientation to create competitive advantage. In this context, Rowe and Barnes (1998) have identified that the development and maintenance of customer relationship management could generate a sustained competitive advantage and could contribute to long-term profitability. Treacy and Wiersema (1993) propose 'customer intimacy', i.e., the establishment of an intimate relationship between service provider and consumer aimed at translating consumer data into smarter products or services, and compelling user experiences, as a general strategy for creating competitive advantage. Since success in today's experience economy demands a deep understanding of consumers' needs and expectations, this strategy is currently pursued by a growing amount of consumer electronics and connected home providers (Anderson et al. 2011).

Customer intimacy, however, implies a fundamental shift from the traditional manufacturer-consumer relationship towards a mutual partnership whereby customers gain by increasing intimacy. Such approach requires a more dynamic framework for analysing the processes of value creation and extraction that recognises horizontal inter-firm relationships and strategic alliances (Normann and Ramírez 1993; Stabell and Fjeldstad 1998). Hence, value is co-created by a series of partnerships and relationships in a value network, in which different stakeholders—suppliers, partners, allies and consumers—join forces, innovate and co-produce value (Chesbrough 2003). Consumers are encouraged and empowered to co-create value within this ecosystem of interconnected firms and become active agents in the process of developing, designing and refining products.[1] Firms that better capture and analyse the data generated by end-user communities may create competitive advantage helping them to play the first fiddle in the media innovation ecosystem (Prahalad and Ramaswamy 2004). Hence, all firms in the television business ecosystem strive for closer access to the end customer and are keen to develop enhanced customer services in an attempt to achieve platform leadership.

3 Broadband Television Ecosystem

3.1 Players and Key Resources

Regardless of whether broadband Internet represents an enemy or ally to established broadcasting firms, managing the impact of the Internet on existing business models remains one of the major strategic issues for such a conservative industry (Küng 2008). For new players, the integration of broadcast programming and broadband connections creates the ability for providing direct-to-consumer relationships and could destroy the value 'old' media companies derive from scarcity in content provision and distribution capacity. Several forces drive this evolution towards 'next-generation television' on the supply and demand side. On the supply side, the growing penetration of broadband Internet, smart consumer electronics and cloud services induce a multiplatform environment whereas the growing consumer preferences for on-demand video consumption are giving more

---

[1] One of the topical questions, however, is whether and to what extent consumers capture value from their involvement in the product development process. Increasingly, co-creation is regarded as exploitation of unpaid labour and creativity. Through these processes of user involvement, consumers are said to relieve manufacturers from performing activities along the value chain and reduce development costs not only for the time and effort, but also for deploying skills and knowledge (e.g. Cohen 2008; Ritzer and Jurgenson 2010).

Table 1 Companies, key resources and risk in the broadband television ecosystem (own elaboration)

	Content	Network	Cloud	Device
Key resources	Content rights	Network capacity	Find, play and share	User experience
	Brand name	Customer base	Global reach	Customer data
Main risk	Piracy	Bit pipe	Throttling	Alliances
Companies	Disney, Fox, BBC, Mediaset, HBO	Cablevision, AT&T, BSkyB, BT, Orange	Google, Netflix, Facebook, Yahoo	Samsung, Apple, Sony, Microsoft

choice and control to the viewers.[2] From a business outlook, hybrid revenue models may further drive the industry towards the provision of a multi-screen viewing experience monetised through traditional advertising and subscription models (e.g., Meadows 2010). Owing to these forces, the supply and consumption of broadcast content over IP networks may radically reshape the market conditions for every player and reconfigure existing power relationships within the television ecosystem. Confronted with the risk of losing market power, established companies may create competitive bottlenecks by limiting access points.

As convergence has paved the way for companies from outside the industry to enter, the relationships between all firms in this television ecosystem have become more complex than ever. What once were separate sectors and strictly defined roles have now been transformed into a converged ecosystem and cross-sector competition. Roughly speaking, four groups of companies, each with their own sources of competitive advantage in the value network, are now competing for a significant stake in this expanding market (see Table 1). Firstly, content creators (film studios, sports rights holders, programming producers, etc.) and content aggregators including television broadcasters have been important stakeholders since the management of exclusive rights windows granted them a powerful position in the value chain. Reaping the fruits of their widely reputed brand names, these players are eager to strengthen this position. In the OTT environment, however, content aggregators face being disintermediated by content creators in relationships with viewers (Meadows 2010). Privileged access to content thus becomes an extremely valuable asset in the ecosystem, but may induce piracy as well. The widespread but illegal availability of content on the Internet may reduce scarcity, reduce the economic value of original content and therefore weaken the market position of content creators. Secondly, network operators and content distributors including telecom operators and cable companies are another important group of companies that are keen to take leadership in the online market. Companies like AT&T, Deutsche Telekom and BT own critical network infrastructure and operate as gatekeeper for

---

[2] One could argue here that the Internet provides more of the same and that the emergence of OTT models is only increasing the physical accessibility of existing content instead of bringing more diversity in terms of new and original content. Regardless of this discussion, OTT services may widen consumers' freedom, especially in terms of time- and place-shifting.

accessing mass audiences. Distributors allow direct access to consumers and help third party providers to reach audiences. However, they have fear of cord-cutting according to which especially younger viewers tend to drop cable subscriptions and directly connect with online platforms for watching videos. As the television service is the main cash flow generator of these carriers, they become disintermediated and become a 'dumb pipe' making money by offering broadband access and voice. Hence, network operators need to develop a continuous stream of value-added services delivered on multiple platforms (Liu et al. 2008). Thirdly, traditional broadcast companies face competition from web-based distribution platforms such as YouTube and Netflix that could expand into global on-demand video libraries. While granting consumers unlimited access to often freely available video content via the unmanaged Internet, these platforms directly compete with broadcasters for advertising income. These platforms therefore not only risk to become blocked by main content providers, but also risk being charged by carriers for the traffic they generate referring to the much-debated issue of net neutrality (Marsden 2007). Finally, consumer electronics companies including software developers and equipment providers, have the opportunity to become access gatekeepers and develop walled gardens to host content services and interactive applications. Connected television manufacturers like Apple and Sony are building an ecosystem by providing a hard-to-replicate user experience based on customer insights. To spur its widespread adoption, OTT technology is ideally based upon open standards allowing video productions to be streamed on all devices. These open standards, however, do not prevent OTT service providers from creating points of control and locking in customers and partners, which are not always eager to transfer power and control to these vendors. Hence, the real challenge for these vendors is in establishing industry-wide cooperation and partnering with all stakeholders in the value network. Rather than a highly concentrated market characterised by the appearance of only a few vertically integrated multinational conglomerates, this suggests that network effects may induce a business architecture with several consortia and alliances competing for becoming the leading ecosystem in the broadband television market.

3.2 Alliances and Platform Leadership

In the broadband television industry, the traditional sources of competitive advantages become questioned. Proprietary and vertically integrated distribution networks are being challenged by the open broadband architecture whereas the multitude of platforms is eroding classic rights windows, which granted owners a monopoly over quality content (Venturini 2011). Although these sources are still valuable, OTT business models may benefit from horizontal partnerships in the ecosystem rather than vertical integration in the value chain. Building solid partnerships with companies owning complementary resources is considered to create competitive advantage in this broadband television environment. Strategic alliances are seen as a way to gain quick and relative cheap access to new markets and opportunities, and to share distinctive resources and competences (Liu and Chan-Olmsted 2003). Any OTT operator without network infrastructure or media content portfolio may need to partner with multichannel providers to ensure the provision of content on television sets, smart phones, tablets, game consoles, etc. Consumer electronics manufacturer Samsung, for example, has announced key partnerships with leading players Time Warner Cable, Comcast and DirectTV allowing them to compete more effectively with a growing number of OTT players such as Netflix or Hulu that are also becoming available on connected devices. In addition, dot.com firms like Google and Amazon are partnering with hardware manufacturers. By purchasing Motorola, a mobile device manufacturer but also a leading provider of cable set-top boxes, Google got a stake in the cable business. Consequently, the firm is able to implement its Android operating system and control the future design of these devices.

The abovementioned examples may illustrate that all industry players, both old and new, are involved in an intense platform competition and deploy strategies for controlling the future platform for online video delivery and consumption. All these companies want to play a leading role in tomorrow's television industry and are thus pursuing platform leadership. Essentially, companies secure access to controlling points via alliances and gain bargaining power vis-à-vis competitors. Platform leadership therefore crucially depends on taking a central place in the value network and partnering with complementary innovators (Gawer and Cusumano 2008). Rather than a battlefield, the struggle for leadership in broadband television markets may resemble a chessboard, 'where alliances, partnerships and commercial collaborations across different players will become key imperatives for success' (Venturini 2011, p. 12). Although the outcome is highly uncertain, several likely OTT scenarios could pop up. Rather than technology, content may drive this OTT ecosystem. Following the 'content rights are king' adage, content rights owners may be in a comfortable bargaining position for developing multi-screen strategies and establish direct-to-consumer relationships. With their large customer bases, bandwidth capacity and service bundling, telecoms and cable operators may be well positioned to participate in the OTT environment. In such an operator-centric scenario, these companies serve as the single point of access controlling a common user interface to the consumer over any connected device. As worldwide players, device manufacturers could derive market power by building up closed ecosystem and manage global content acquisition deals to optimise this ecosystem. Hence, all players may employ their own strategies for achieving platform leadership.

4 Incumbents' and New Entrants' Strategies

4.1 Broadcasters

Whether content providers, network operators, device manufacturers or dot.com companies control this business ecosystem mainly depends on these players' strategies for creating scarcity in the market. As mentioned, rights holders and broadcasters may benefit from a genuine multi-screen strategy responding to changing video consumption patterns. With the BBC iPlayer, the UK public service broadcaster started its own Internet radio and television service already in 2008. The platform is an on-demand video aggregator providing access to original and archive television content (including shows, comedies, news, documentaries and concerts), but also allows viewers to watch live streaming. To UK viewers the service is freely available as part of the BBC's public service remit, while international users may need to subscribe for £73/year. The service is available on PC, mobile devices and platforms, game consoles and connected TV sets. Faced with capacity problems due to the overwhelming success of the iPlayer, network operators (both mobile and fixed) have called the BBC to help pay for the rising costs in network capacity that is needed to allow for services like the BBC iPlayer. In response, the BBC argued that the iPlayer was driving demand for broadband subscriptions. Since the BBC partnered telecom operators BT and Talk Talk for bringing the iPlayer to the regular TV screen in the YouView project, multichannel and pay-television providers become challenged as they need to deploy strategies for protecting their revenues from subscription services and building a multi-tenant platform. Hence, BSkyB and Virgin Media have complained that this YouView project will severely restrict competition and innovation in the IPTV business. In a similar way, US television networks ABC, NBC and Fox launched the Hulu platform as a high-quality counterweight to YouTube and similar initiatives deployed by multichannel operators (e.g., TV Everywhere). In contrast to YouTube, television networks can run their full-length series and programmes, sell advertisements and share revenues. The premium Hulu Plus service also allows streaming shows and movies across four screens—PC, TV, mobile and tablets—for $7.99/month. These initiatives can be regarded good practices of how broadcasters can position themselves in the middle of the broadband television ecosystem.

4.2 Network Operators

Under the umbrella of 'TV Everywhere', US cable operators, satellite companies and IPTV providers have started to tackle these online offerings of programmers. Broadcast content is brought online at no additional cost, but access to this content is restricted to those users who are also authenticated as pay-television subscribers. Additionally, the service can only be used on the network of that particular multiservice operator and is not supported by other operators' networks. The underlying strategy behind TV Everywhere is to ensure that consumers do not cancel their TV subscription and switch to OTT offerings. In December 2009, Comcast became the first company to launch its TV Everywhere product, under the brand XFINITY TV. Dual-play subscribers (cable and high-speed Internet) are able to access content from partner networks like ABC, HBO and Cinemax. An app is also available for iOS and Android devices allowing users to watch videos, schedule their digital video recorder when they are away from home and use their smartphones as remote control. In January 2011, the merger between television network NBC and cable company Comcast raised conflicts of interest as the Hulu video platform owned by NBC would directly compete Comcast's cable business. Whereas there were rumours that Comcast would withdraw NBC content from Hulu, the FCC ruled that Comcast/NBC will continue to provide content to Hulu, which had a semi-exclusive deal with the broadcast network owners. Now Comcast has to share its content with other competing video platforms like Netflix and iTunes that need popular movies and shows to lure viewers. However, to sabotage competing these competing video services, Comcast has considered to block access to Netflix unless Level 3, an Internet backbone company that supports Netflix and iTunes, pays new tolls. By violating these fundamental net neutrality principles, Comcast can price competitors out of the market and ensure that its online video platform remains the only choice for consumers.

4.3 Cloud Platforms

Albeit being threatened by network operators' extensive control over data traffic management, OTT models are mainly pushed by 'webcos' that are driving the offerings of online services. Originally launched as a video-sharing website for amateur productions, Google-owned YouTube announced it will start offering professionally-produced original programming to vastly improve the quality of its content. The aim is to provide full-length programming including live broadcast streams and on-demand content, and construct an online challenge to the television experience. So far, the number one global video platform has failed to find a viable business model with user-generated content. Therefore, YouTube leverages its massive user base of over 800 million monthly viewers to enter into licensing deals with rights owners. In November 2011, Google announced that it would invest more than $100 million in launching over 100 channels to the YouTube platform, categorized by theme and populated with original content from partner contributors like Disney, Reuters and the Wall Street Journal. Earlier, YouTube managed distribution deals with major Hollywood studios like Warner Bros and Universal to launch a subscription service for movies similar to Netflix and Amazon. YouTube also announced talks with major sports leagues to show live games. YouTube regards live sports broadcasting as a way to keep viewers on its site for longer periods of time, increasing its value to advertisers. Another part of Google's strategy of becoming a next-generation television provider is Google TV. This smart TV platform integrates the Android operating system and the Google Chrome web browser to create an interactive overlay of existing video websites to add a common user interface. Consumer can access content from third party providers (HBO, Amazon, Netflix, etc.) through the browser although major US networks ABC, CBS and NBC have blocked Google TV enabled devices from accessing (free) web content. Like multichannel operators, Google should be able to provide advanced demographic and audience behavior data in order to bring these networks aboard. The acquisition of Motorola also earned Google more arm strength for pursuing its strategic agenda in the consumer electronics market.

4.4 Device Manufacturers

Now that consumer electronics equipment start to provide Internet-based video access, device manufacturers are ambitious for conquering the living room as well. Set-top box and game console manufacturers like Roku or Microsoft allow direct access to the Internet and video platforms. Microsoft entered into partnerships with more than 40 parties including telecom operators (AT&T, Verizon), pay-television companies (BSkyB, Canal+), broadcasters (ESPN, BBC), VOD providers (Lovefilm, CinemaNow) and online firms (YouTube, Facebook). Consumers will have access to stream and download shows, music videos and movies from these associated providers. Verizon also provides live broadcast streams so that the Xbox increasingly functions as set-top box. Microsoft will also integrate search engine Bing, voice controller Kinect and voice-over-Internet application Skype to build an entire ecosystem. Roku, a US-based consumer electronics company, has launched a portable Internet video streaming receiver box and closed partnerships with Hulu, Netflix, Amazon and HBO. Traditional hardware manufacturers become also involved in this connected TV market. Major companies like Sony and LG have started to include smart and social applications in their classic TV sets. Under its Bravia brand, Sony released connected television devices including streaming partners like Amazon, YouTube, Yahoo!, Netflix and Sony's video platform Qriosity. Because Sony has major stakes in entertainment production and also runs its own video website Qriosity, US network operators are reluctant to support Sony's operations. At its turn, Sony was not keen to give an opportunity to these operators, of which most have TV Everywhere offerings, for strengthening their position in the online video market.

Conclusion

The integration of broadband and broadcast content, and the advent of OTT services could have far-reaching implications for established companies in the television business and have the potential to trigger off a process of creative destruction. According to such a disruptive scenario, the traditional gatekeeper role of broadcasters and especially content distributors would erode and eventually be destroyed by global players outside the business. Albeit such a disruptive scenario is still not under way and new technologies mostly provoke incremental change because of the complex institutions in which they are rooted, consumer electronics providers and online video aggregators are manoeuvring themselves in this market and are competing for a share of this burgeoning online video environment. One of the major strategic challenges for all players involved in this business, is the establishment of a direct-to-consumer gateway so that companies can bypass traditional gatekeepers and start building relationships of trust and loyalty with their customers. Since controlling the user interface, owning the customer relationship and securing proximity to consumer wallets enable companies to create a sustained competitive advantage, it has become the major site of struggle in this market.

Although the outcome of these mainly technology-driven market developments is highly uncertain, it becomes clear that all players—content providers, network operators, cloud services and device manufacturers—pursue for platform leadership and explore strategies to position themselves in the centre of this market. Rather than embedding in existing ecosystems, both incumbents and new entrants attempt to build and control their own OTT ecosystems that are emerging as complex webs of partnerships, alliances and joint ventures. In such strategic chess games, platform leaders deploy a 'conquer and divide strategy' and benefit from partners' complementary assets. Hence, all companies are creating controlling points on which third parties rely to enter the business. Although hardware manufacturers and cloud service operators benefit from a mostly global reach and technology ownership, local-based television companies have re-invented bottlenecks in order to maintain their historically leading position in the television market. In a similar way, they attempt to counter newcomers' online video platforms and leverage the rising popularity of and demand for broadband television. Whereas content rights holders and broadcasters have control over the content, network operators dominate the conditions for access to their network infrastructure (except for must-carry legislation). Techno-optimists may herald the abundance of the future television business, but established players are willing to create scarcity and employ pre-emptive strategies for dominating future television ecosystems and stabilising existing patterns of power and control. But also newcomers, which benefited from abundance to enter the market, are concerned with strategies of scarcity. Hence, this struggle for platform leadership is characterised by managing scarcity and controlling bottlenecks as main business strategy.

Since the OTT market is still very immature and expected only to boost within a couple of years, it is impossible to predict which protagonists have the winning cards and will succeed in this struggle for platform leadership. Aside from this battle for power and control in the industry, one could question whether the viewer will be the undeniable winner of the evolution towards OTT services. Thanks to cross-platform offerings and on-demand viewing opportunities, the consumer could be able to access an unlimited array of content via a set of connected devices. In the end, more control could be with tomorrow's television viewer since online and mobile on-demand consumption allows control of programming schedules, advertisement skipping and fast-forwarding. But, this growing pattern of interactive viewing and the erosion of advertising-based revenue models could also lead to a situation in which the viewer is charged more for watching television content. In a worst-case scenario, service providers will preserve popular content behind closed walls and migrate to a 'premium rate culture' (see Goggin and Spurgeon 2007, p. 755). Such an environment, in which the free lunch of content is an anachronism, only the elite can afford full access and control of audiovisual content in the digital broadcasting world. These forces of digitisation and convergence may thus threaten television's key values of non-excludability and universality, which could raise concerns about digital exclusion. Hence, this radical transformation of the television business, which urges the need for more innovative business models adapted to the future television business architecture, may also trigger off issue of policy intervention to ensure that socially and culturally valued broadcasting content remains universally, equally and freely available to the citizen-consumer.

References

Anderson, B., Burnett, S., & Dao, W. (2011). *The road to customer intimacy. Leveraging investments in customer insight to maximize returns*. New York: IBM Corporation.

Ballon, P. (2007). Business modelling revisited: The configuration of control and value. *Info: The Journal of Policy, Regulation and Strategy for Telecommunications, Information and Media, 9*(5), 6–19.

Ballon, P., & Van Heesvelde, E. (2011). ICT platforms and regulatory concerns in Europe. *Telecommunications Policy, 35*(8), 702–714.

Barney, J. (1991). Firm resources and sustained competitive advantage. *Journal of Management, 17*(1), 99–120.

Barney, J. (1997). *Gaining and sustaining competitive advantage*. Reading: Addison-Wesley.

Chalaby, J. K., & Segell, G. (1999). The broadcasting media in the age of risk: The advent of digital television. *New Media & Society, 1*(3), 351–368.

Chan-Olmsted, S. M., & Kang, J.-W. (2003). Theorizing the strategic architecture of a broadband television industry. *Journal of Media Economics, 16*(1), 3–21.

Chesbrough, H. W. (2003). *Open innovation: The new imperative for creating and profiting from technology*. Boston: Harvard Business School Press.

Christophers, B. (2008). Television's power relations in the transition to digital: The case of the United Kingdom. *Television & New Media, 9*(3), 239–257.

Cohen, N. S. (2008). The valorization of surveillance: Towards a political economy of Facebook. *Democratic Communiqué, 22*(1), 5–22.

Cowie, C., & Marsden, C. T. (1999). Convergence: Navigating bottlenecks in digital pay-tv. *Info: The Journal of Policy, Regulation and Strategy for Telecommunications, Information and Media, 1*(1), 53–67.

De Boever, J., & De Grooff, D. (2010). Peer-to-peer content distribution and over-the-top TV: An Analysis of value networks. In X. Shen, H. Yu, J. Buford, & M. Akon (Eds.), *Handbook of peer-to-peer networking* (pp. 961–983). Berlin: Springer.

Garnham, N. (1987). Concepts of culture - public policy and the cultural industries. *Cultural Studies, 1*(1), 23–37.

Gawer, A., & Cusumano, M. A. (2008). How companies become platform leaders. *MIT Sloan Management Review, 49*(2), 28–35.

Goggin, G., & Spurgeon, C. (2007). Premium rate culture: The new business of mobile interactivity. *New Media & Society, 9*(5), 753–770.

Katz, M. L. (2004). Industry structure and competition absent distribution bottlenecks. In E. Noam, J. Groebel, & D. Gerbarg (Eds.), *Internet Television* (pp. 31–60). Mahwah: Lawrence Erlbaum Associates.

Kelly, K. (1998). *New rules for the new economy*. New York: Penguin.

Kim, P. (2009). Internet protocol TV in perspective: A matrix of continuity and innovation. *Television & New Media, 10*(6), 536–545.

Koppenjan, J., & Groenewegen, J. (2005). Institutional design for complex technological systems. *International Journal of Technology, Policy and Management, 5*(3), 240–257.

Küng, L. (2008). *Strategic management in the media: Theory to practice*. Thousand Oakes: Sage.

Küng, L., Kröll, A.-M., Ripken, B., & Walker, M. (1999). Impact of the digital revolution on the media and communications industries. Javnost—the Public, 6(3), 29–48.

Liu, F., & Chan-Olmsted, S. (2003). Partnerships between the old and the new: Examining the strategic alliances between broadcast television networks and internet firms in the context of convergence. *International Journal on Media Management,* 5(1), 47–56.

Liu, K., Gill, A., & Berendt, A. (2008). IPTV: The entertainment game has changed. *IEEE Communications Magazine,* 46(8), 88–89.

Lotz, A. D. (2007). *The television will be revolutionized.* New York: New York University Press.

Mansell, R. (1997). Strategies for maintaining market power in the face of rapidly changing technologies. *Journal of Economic Issues,* 31(4), 969–989.

Mansell, R. (1999). New media competition and access. *The scarcity-abundance dialectic. New Media & Society,* 1(2), 155–182.

Marsden, C. (2007). Net neutrality and consumer access to content. *Script-ed,* 4(4), 407–435.

Meadows, J. (2010). Broadcast and cable on the third screen: Moving television content to mobile devices. In J. A. Hendricks (Ed.), *The twenty-first century media industry. Economic and managerial implications in the age of new media* (pp. 173–189). Lanham: Lexington Books.

Nicita, A., & Rossi, M. A. (2008). Access to audio-visual contents, exclusivity and anticommons in new media markets. *Communications and Strategies,* 71(3), 79–101.

Normann, R., & Ramírez, R. (1993). From value chain to value constellation: Designing interactive strategy. *Harvard Business Review,* 71(7–8), 65–77.

Picard, R. (2011). *The economics and financing of media companies.* New York: Fordham University Press.

Poel, M., & Hawkins, R. (2001). The evolution of access bottlenecks in Europe: Re-locating the regulatory issues. *Communications and Strategies,* 44(4), 71–101.

Porter, M. (1985). *Competitive advantage. Creating and sustaining superior performance.* New York: The Free Press.

Prahalad, C. K., & Ramaswamy, V. (2004). *The future of competition: Co-creating unique value with customers.* Boston: Harvard Business School Press.

Rangone, A., & Turconi, A. (2003). The television (r)evolution within the multimedia convergence: A strategic reference framework. *Management Decision,* 41(1), 48–71.

Ritzer, G., & Jurgenson, N. (2010). Production, consumption, prosumption: The nature of capitalism in the age of the digital 'prosumer'. *Journal of Consumer Culture,* 10(1), 13–36.

Rowe, W. G., & Barnes, J. G. (1998). Relationship marketing and sustained competitive advantage. *Journal of Market-Focused Management,* 2(3), 281–297.

Schumpeter, J. (1942). *Capitalism, socialism and democracy.* New York: Harper.

Stabell, C. B., & Fjeldstad, Ø. D. (1998). Configuring value for competitive advantage: On chains, shops, and networks. *Strategic Management Journal,* 19(5), 413–437.

Teece, D. J. (1986). Profiting from technological innovation: Implications for integration, collaboration, licensing and public policy. *Research Policy,* 15(6), 285–305.

Treacy, M., & Wiersema, F. (1993). Customer intimacy and other value disciplines. *Harvard Business Review,* 71(1), 84–93.

Venturini, F. (2011). *The race to dominate the future of TV.* New York: Accenture.

Wasko, J., Murdock, G., & Sousa, H. (2011). Introduction: The political economy of communications. Core concerns and issues. In J. Wasko, G. Murdock, & H. Sousa (Eds.), *The handbook of political economy of communications* (pp. 1–10). West Sussex: Blackwell.

Willams, R. (2003). *Television: Technology and cultural form.* New York: Routledge.

Winston, B. (1998). *Media technology and society. A history: From the telegraph to the Internet.* London: Routledge.

Wirtz, B. W. (1999). Convergence processes, value constellations and integration strategies in the multimedia business. *International Journal on Media Management,* 1(1), 14–22.

Ad Addressability and Personalized Content in IPTV Markets

Christoph Fritsch

1 Introduction

The formation of internet based TV channels denotes an elementary change in media markets. By combination of traditional broadcasting and interactive networks, television can be transformed from a mass medium into a customized service. In view of virtually unlimited channel capacity and addressable audiences, content will increasingly be adjusted to viewer preferences. Traditional channels compete with new entrants for audience shares by improving viewer satisfaction. The emergence of theme specific channels in digital TV as well as the growing supply of time independent programming in IPTV indicates the development of customized content provision. The consecutive extension of content choice alters consumer behavior. Viewers in IPTV markets become more active in a way that content is selected according to individual preferences and higher quality is being requested.

For ad-financed networks IPTV furthermore represents an opportunity to provide targeted ads to viewers. If consumer preferences can entirely be identified by a channel, appropriate ads can be allocated to each viewer. Accordingly, individual ad-aversion is diminished, because no irrelevant information has to be consumed anymore. Further the advertising effect gets stronger due to the fact, that uninterested viewers are fully excluded from the reception of these ads. Ad addressability therefore enhances the networks optimal ad level and advertisers' profits. In our analysis, the implications of ad addressability and personalized content on optimal ad levels are discussed in a two-sided market framework with ad-averse viewers. Each IPTV network chooses ad levels according to the magnitude of cross-group externalities and in regard of the rival's behavior. The market equilibrium is derived for a monopoly channel as well as in the duopoly case. It is

---

C. Fritsch (✉)
University of Cologne, Cologne, Germany
e-mail: Ch.Fritsch@uni-koeln.de

shown that customization of IPTV services is a source of additional network revenues. In both settings ad addressability enhances equilibrium advertising levels and increases channels profits.

With ad-averse audiences, higher ad levels impose some disutility on viewers that decrease audience shares of a network. On the other hand, a larger audience attracts more advertisers and increases their willingness to pay (Kind et al. 2007). The network's ad level decision is therefore a problem of balancing cross group externalities between the two market sides, a network interacts with.

In classical TV markets viewer loyalty is mainly achieved by strategic program location (Kind et al. 2007, p. 217 and Barros et al. 2004, p. 6) and the extension of program quality[1] (Armstrong 2005, p. 296). In IPTV markets, networks obtain additional options in order to control viewer satisfaction. Via ad addressability and personalized content, networks can diminish ad-aversion and improve preference compatible program supply. The analysis of enhanced program supply options is based on the theory of two-sided markets.[2] These models address particular problems of markets, where two or more different market sides interact with each other via an intermediary platform. Unlike traditional models of two-sided markets such as Rochet and Tirole (2003), Caillaud and Jullien (2003) and Armstrong (2006), advertisements are a negative externality for viewer's program satisfaction, while increasing audience rates are a positive externality for advertisers. The crucial point of two-sidedness is that a platform coordinates the different groups by internalizing cross-group externalities via prices. The platforms general attempt is to get all market sides 'on board' (Rochet and Tirole 2003, p. 1013).

Ad-financed TV programs are an example for two-sided markets. The network acts as the intermediary platform. Its assignment is to balance cross-group externalities between viewer and advertiser demand. As will be shown later, its only true decision parameter is the ad level. Advertisers' willingness to pay increases in audience shares with diminishing returns to scale, while viewer demand decreases with the ad level. Thus a networks profit maximizing ad level is attained if the marginal loss of viewer demand equals the marginal gain of an additional advertisement. The analysis is organized as follows. In the next section the bench mark case of a monopoly platform in a classical TV market is derived. In Sect. 3 the impact of individualized program schemes is discussed. Section 4 introduces network competition and in Sect. 5 individualization is analyzed for the duopoly case. Section 6 concludes.

2 Optimal Ad Levels in a Classical TV Monopoly Market

In an ad-financed TV market with z viewers and w advertisers, a monopolistic TV platform maximizes revenues by choosing its optimal advertising level. The case of a classical TV market with a linear program design is derived as a benchmark for

---

[1] Quality is measured as per viewer satisfaction.
[2] For an overview see Peitz (2006).

customized IPTV services. Thereby, the impact of personalized advertising and individualized programming is measured. Viewers are ad-averse and maximize utility. Advertisements decrease each viewer's net utility by a constant factor $\alpha > 0$. The outside option for viewers is set to 0. In case of a negative program utility, viewers prefer the outside option. With heterogeneous program preferences the viewers demand function n_z is decreasing in the ad level n_w.

2.1 Viewers

A simple approach to describe heterogeneous viewer preferences is the Hotelling-Model (Hotelling 1929). It assumes that viewers are uniformly distributed on the spectrum of program preferences. With the purchasing decision of content, a network chooses its position S on the spectrum (Fritsch and Lucas 2009, p. 5; Noam 1987, p. 167). The program satisfaction of viewer z is then described by the distance between its individual preference x_z and the networks location S on the preference spectrum. A larger distance indicates a lower satisfaction level for viewer z. If the monopolistic network is for instance specialized on sporting contests, a viewer with a pronounced preference for classical music will have a low appreciation for the program. The difference $|S-x_z|$, as well as increasing ad levels n_w have a negative impact on the viewers net utility (Anderson and Gabszewicz 2006, p. 583). Accordingly, the utility function of viewer z is:

$$u_z = q - \tau \cdot |S - x_z| - \alpha \cdot n_w. \qquad (1)$$

The parameter q indicates viewer's maximum satisfaction level. This parameter can also be interpreted as the general preference for TV consumption. The maximum satisfaction level can only be reached in the absence of commercial breaks, if the individual viewer preference is fully satisfied. Otherwise the disutility of non optimal programming $(\tau \cdot |S - x_z|)$ and the opportunity costs of advertising $(\alpha \cdot n_w)$ must be subtracted from q. The parameter $\tau > 0$ denotes the viewer aversion to non-requested content.[3] A lower preference satisfaction level implies a higher switch off probability for the viewer. It follows that the viewer's demand function n_z is decreasing in the ad level n_w. With a given outside option of zero utility, a viewer z chooses to attend the monopolistic TV network, if the program provides a weakly positive net-utility:

$$u_z \geq 0 \quad \Leftrightarrow \quad \frac{q - \alpha \cdot n_w}{\tau} \geq |S - x_z|$$

---

[3] In a model extension with heterogeneous aversion to non requested content (τ_i) it can be shown that networks with a superior number of passive viewers choose higher ad levels then networks with a large share of active viewers.

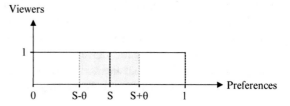

Fig. 1 Program location of a monopolistic TV network

$$\Leftrightarrow \quad S - \theta \leq x_z \leq S + \theta \quad \text{with} \quad \theta \equiv \frac{q - \alpha \cdot n_w}{\tau}. \tag{2}$$

The network position is shown in Fig. 1. Viewers are uniformly distributed on the spectrum of program preferences. For simplification, this spectrum is limited to the unit interval.

A larger distance between the program location S and a viewer z indicates a lower satisfaction level. Therefore, only a fraction of viewers who derive a positive net utility form the program, choose to attend the network. These viewers are located within the acceptance range $[S-\theta, S+\theta]$.

As is shown in Eq. (2), the amplitude of this acceptance range decreases with larger ad levels. However, with a large general preference for TV consumption (q), the acceptance range might exceed the unit interval. In that case, all viewers are within the acceptance range and an audience share of 1 is realized. This corresponds to a situation, where the role of TV consumption is so superior to a society, that each viewer will attend the program independently of its own preference. Usually, this case can be excluded for a monopolistic network, hence very low opportunity costs need to be presumed. With an acceptance range below 1, the TV network locates somewhere in the middle of the unit interval to ensure a maximum of viewers. For an ad-financed network, this is the precondition for profit maximization. The audience share is calculated as the integral of the network's acceptance range:

$$n_z = \int_{S-\theta}^{S+\theta} f(z)dz = [z]_{S-\theta}^{S+\theta} = 2\theta = 2\frac{q - \alpha n_w}{\tau}. \tag{3}$$

2.2 Advertisers

Viewers constitute a positive externality for advertisers. Accordingly, the demand for ad time is increasing in the audience share n_z. In our model, advertisers only use informative ads (Bagwell 2007, p. 1705) and ad prices are assumed to be equal for all products. Viewers correspond with buyers of the advertised consumption goods. On the consumer demand side, there is uncertainty about the product attributes such as price or quality. By means of advertising this uncertainty can be solved for all viewers that attend the program. For this fraction the likelihood of purchasing the good increases by an exogenous factor $\beta > 0$ (Anderson and Gabszewicz 2006, p. 584). The parameter β therefore describes the advertising effect of the network. It is assumed to be homogenous for all advertisers and independent from the advertising level of the network. Although research on advertising effects shows that viewer awareness is diminished with the length of commercial breaks and the number of received ads (Tacheny 1989, p. 301), these intergroup externalities are excluded from the analysis by assuming β as an exogenous and constant factor. However, endogenizing β might enhance the analysis. Advertising costs other than the networks advertising price p are abandoned. The advertisers profit is

$$r_w = \beta \cdot n_z - p. \tag{4}$$

We assume excess demand for advertising time, so that the monopoly network can skim the whole producer surplus on the market for advertising. In order to maximize profit, it will set the advertising price according to the advertiser's willingness to pay. Due to homogenous valuations for ad space, an equilibrium advertising price of

$$p = \beta \cdot n_z \quad \Leftrightarrow \quad r_w = 0 \tag{5}$$

is established. The monopolistic network is thus faced with a perfectly elastic demand on the market for advertising time. This outcome stands in line with earlier models of ad-financed networks (e.g. Gabszewicz et al. 2001; Spence and Owen 1977).

2.3 Network

The monopolistic network generates its entire profits out of ad revenues:

$$\pi = p \cdot n_w. \tag{6}$$

Inserting Eq. (5) into Eq. (6) yields the networks objective function:

$$\pi = \beta \cdot n_z(n_w) \cdot n_w. \tag{7}$$

This expression reveals the cross-group externalities of the two-sided market. Network profits consist of ad sales, which depend on the amount of viewers. Viewer demand on the other hand is a dependent variable of the ad level. Accordingly, the optimization problem for the network is:

$$\max_{n_w} \pi = \max_{n_w} (\beta \cdot n_z(n_w) \cdot n_w). \tag{8}$$

The first order condition is:

$$\frac{\partial \pi}{\partial n_w} = \beta \cdot n_z(n_w) + \beta \cdot \frac{\partial n_z(n_w)}{\partial n_w} \cdot n_w = 0. \quad (9)$$

The optimality condition for the ad level is derived by inserting Eq. (3) and solving for n_w:

$$2\beta \cdot \left(\frac{q - \alpha n_w}{\tau}\right) = 2\beta \cdot \frac{\alpha n_w}{\tau} \Leftrightarrow n_w^* = \frac{q}{2\alpha}. \quad (10)$$

Larger ad-aversion decreases the optimal ad level while a higher maximum satisfaction level increases it. Surprisingly, the magnitude of viewer aversion to inappropriate content (τ) has no influence on the optimal ad level in Eq. (10). This is due to the fact that τ only influences the amplitude of the acceptance range. From Eq. (9) it follows that[4]:

$$\beta \cdot n_z(n_w) + \beta \cdot \frac{\partial n_z(n_w)}{\partial n_w} \cdot n_w = 0 \Leftrightarrow \frac{\partial n_z(n_w)}{\partial n_w} \cdot \frac{n_w}{n_z(n_w)} = \eta_{n_z, n_w} = -1$$

$$\text{with } \eta_{n_z, n_w} \equiv \frac{\partial n_z(u_z)}{\partial n_w} \cdot \frac{n_w}{n_z}. \quad (11)$$

The general optimality condition states that the demand elasticity equals -1. This elasticity is independent of τ and thus τ cannot be a parameter of the optimal ad level in Eq. (10). The according audience share is derived by inserting the optimal ad level into Eq. (3):

$$n_z^* = 2 \frac{q - \alpha\left(\frac{q}{2\alpha}\right)}{\tau} = \frac{q}{\tau}. \quad (12)$$

The networks profits are derived from Eq. (7):

$$\pi^* = p \cdot n_w^* = \frac{\beta}{\alpha} \frac{q^2}{2\tau}. \quad (13)$$

The exceptional case, where the acceptance range exceeds the unit interval, is abandoned for the rest of the paper. It is generally assumed that $2\theta \leq 1$. From Eq. (13) follows that the advertising effect and the general preference for TV consumption contribute to network profits, while ad-aversion and disutility of inappropriate program supply lower profits. In the short run these parameters are

---

[4] It has to be considered that the derivative of n_z is strictly negative.

predetermined, but in the advent of IPTV markets, some parameters can be influenced by the network. Due to bipolar transmission techniques in internet based TV networks attain control over the advertising effect and viewers ad-aversion.

3 Optimal Ad Levels in an Individualized TV Monopoly Market

In this section two ways of individualization are analysed, that are eligible to foster ad-financed program schemes in internet based TV markets. Advertisers' willingness to pay is generally determined by the amount of additional sales due to advertising. Accordingly, the network profit per advertisement depends on the audience share and viewers purchasing probability. Therefore a network will always try to improve audience shares and ad awareness. With bipolar transmission techniques, these parameters can be influenced by the network. Through ad addressability, commercial breaks can be restricted to a relevant subset of ads for each viewer, provided that individual consumption preferences can be identified by the network. Augmenting the relevance of ads shown to viewers, decreases viewers ad-aversion (α) and simultaneously enhances the advertising effect (β) (Gomes 2006; Kim and Wildman 2006). Furthermore, personalized content increases the satisfaction level of viewers, which allows for higher ad levels.

3.1 Ad Addressability

We assume that there are two types of consumers. One half of the viewers are left-handed (LH) and the other half is right-handed (RH). LH-types only consume LH-products and RH- types only consume RH-products (Kim and Wildman 2006, p. 58). LH- and RH-viewers are therefore disjunctive groups in terms of consumption. However, in terms of program preferences, both types are uniformly distributed on the unit interval. The advertising effect of LH- [RH-] products is 0 for RH-[LH-] viewers. The utility function for a type $i = LH, RH$ is:

$$u_z^i = q - \tau \cdot |S - x_z| - \alpha^i \cdot n_w^i \tag{14}$$

Ad addressability lowers viewers' ad-aversion but does not solve it completely. We assume $0 < \alpha^{RH} = \alpha^{LH} < \alpha$. With a given outside option of zero utility, viewer demand is given by:

$$n_z^i = \int_{S-\theta}^{S+\theta} \left(\frac{1}{2} f(z^i) \right) dz^i = \theta^i \equiv \frac{q - \alpha^i \cdot n_w^i}{\tau} \tag{15}$$

In comparison to the classical TV market Eq. (3) the demand function has a lower intercept and a smaller slope. This is due to the fact that ad addressability segments the audience into homogeneous types. The advertiser's profit function is:

$$r_w^i = \beta^i \cdot n_z^i - p^i. \tag{16}$$

Ad addressability augments the effect of advertising ($0 < \beta < \beta^{RH} = \beta^{LH}$), because ads are solely shown to the relevant group. Accordingly, ad prices in classical TV markets contain a reduction to the extent of the probability, that a viewer from the other group receives the ad. We still assume that the monopoly network can skim the whole producer surplus ($r_w^i = 0$). Therefore the ad price is:

$$p^i = \beta^i \cdot n_z^i. \tag{17}$$

The network's profit consists of the advertising revenues from each group:

$$\pi = \beta^{LH} \cdot n_z^{LH} \cdot n_w^{LH} + \beta^{RH} \cdot n_z^{RH} \cdot n_w^{RH}. \tag{18}$$

Inserting Eqs. (15) and (17) into Eq. (18) and differentiating with respect to n_w^{LH}, n_w^{RH} yields:

$$\max_{n_w^{LH}, n_w^{RH}} \pi = \max_{n_w^{LH}, n_w^{RH}} \left(\beta^{LH} \cdot \frac{q - \alpha^{LH} \cdot n_w^{LH}}{\tau} \cdot n_w^{LH} + \beta^{RH} \cdot \frac{q - \alpha^{RH} \cdot n_w^{RH}}{\tau} \cdot n_w^{RH} \right)$$

$$\Rightarrow \frac{\partial \pi}{\partial n_w^{LH}} = \beta^{LH} \cdot \frac{q - \alpha^{LH} \cdot n_w^{LH}}{\tau} - \beta^{LH} \cdot \frac{\alpha^{LH} \cdot n_w^{LH}}{\tau} = 0 \text{ and}$$

$$\frac{\partial \pi}{\partial n_w^{RH}} = \beta^{RH} \cdot \frac{q - \alpha^{RH} \cdot n_w^{RH}}{\tau} - \beta^{RH} \cdot \frac{\alpha^{RH} \cdot n_w^{RH}}{\tau} = 0 \tag{19}$$

$$\Leftrightarrow n_w^{LH*} = \frac{q}{2 \alpha^{LH}} \text{ and } n_w^{RH*} = \frac{q}{2 \alpha^{RH}}.$$

Ad addressability increases the equilibrium ad level by the scale of reduced ad-aversion. The corresponding audience share is derived by inserting Eq. (19) into Eq. (15):

$$n_Z^{LH*} = \frac{q}{2\tau} \quad \text{and} \quad n_Z^{RH*} = \frac{q}{2\tau}. \tag{20}$$

The aggregate audience share is equal to the classical TV market equilibrium:

$$n_Z^{LH*} + n_Z^{RH*} = \frac{q}{\tau} \tag{21}$$

The network profit is:

$$\pi = \beta^{LH} \cdot \frac{q}{2\tau} \cdot \frac{q}{2\alpha^{LH}} + \beta^{RH} \cdot \frac{q}{2\tau} \cdot \frac{q}{2\alpha^{RH}} = \frac{q^2}{4\tau} \left(\frac{\beta^{LH}}{\alpha^{LH}} + \frac{\beta^{RH}}{\alpha^{RH}} \right). \tag{22}$$

It can easily be shown that the network has a strong incentive to introduce ad addressability. Profits strictly increase with targeted advertising:

$$\frac{q^2}{4\tau}\left(\frac{\beta^{LH}}{\alpha^{LH}}+\frac{\beta^{RH}}{\alpha^{RH}}\right) > \frac{\beta}{\alpha}\frac{q^2}{2\tau} \Leftrightarrow \frac{\beta^{LH}}{\alpha^{LH}}+\frac{\beta^{RH}}{\alpha^{RH}} > 2\frac{\beta}{\alpha}. \tag{23}$$

This inequality holds, since $\beta^{RH} = \beta^{LH} > \beta$ and $\alpha^{RH} = \alpha^{LH} < \alpha$. The profit increase simply results from a more efficient allocation of commercials. In a classical TV market every viewer is exposed to all commercials. With ad addressability, irrelevant ads are replaced by relevant ads for each viewer (Kim and Wildman 2006, p. 77). In our model the inefficiency is completely eliminated by solely transmitting LH-ads to LH-viewers and RH-ads to RH-viewers. In reality there are no completely disjunctive groups like LH- and RH-viewers. Therefore, the critical condition for ad addressability is sufficient information about viewer's consumption preferences.

Another efficiency enhancing effect of ad addressability is caused by indivisibilities in classical linear program schemes. While each commercial is exposed to the complete audience share in classical TV markets, ad addressability allows to restrict exposure to a small target group. Thereby TV advertising becomes more attractive for advertisers with niche products, because addressability prevents them from paying for irrelevant viewer contacts:

$$p^{classical\ ads} = \beta \cdot n_z, \quad p^{i\ targeted\ ads} = \beta^i \cdot n_z^i. \tag{24}$$

The smaller their target group i, the more inefficient is advertising in the classical TV market. Instead of paying ad prices for the whole audience share n_z, addressability enables networks to only charge ad exposure to the relevant group n_z^i. Thus, the advertising demand can be extended by niche producers such as luxury goods suppliers, local companies, etc.

3.2 Personalized Content

A second way to increase equilibrium ad levels is to improve viewer satisfaction. By customizing content to individual preferences, a network can raise its audience's program satisfaction. With complete customization, each viewer receives its preference optimal program mix. In order to analyze the impact of higher satisfaction levels, the original advertising scheme of non targeted commercials is assumed here. In order to assure preference optimal program supply for each viewer it is further assumed that the network has free access to the whole range of contents.

Preference adequate programming changes the utility function. Each viewer receives its optimal program mix, so that deviations from network position and viewer preference are ruled out. The network adapts its program design to the particular preference of each viewer. Noam (1995, p. 3) describes this as the

"Me-Channel". In terms of the model this is equal to minimizing the distance between individual preference x_z and networks location S on the preference spectrum ($|S-x_z| \to 0$). Personalization of content thus modifies the utility function of viewers:

$$u_z^p = q - \alpha \cdot n_w^p. \tag{25}$$

A viewer attends the monopolistic network, if non negative net utility can be derived from it ($u_z^p \geq 0$). For viewer demand it follows that:

$$n_z^p = \begin{cases} 1, n_w^p \leq \frac{q}{\alpha} \\ 0, n_w^p > \frac{q}{\alpha} \end{cases}. \tag{26}$$

For personalized content demand is perfectly elastic due to the fact that each viewer derives an equally high gross utility (q) from the program. Accordingly, willingness to pay is identical for all viewers and the network can capture all consumer surplus by adjusting its ad level. The ad price is derived from the advertisers revenue function:

$$r_w^p = \beta\, n_z^p - p^p \quad \Rightarrow \quad p^p|_{r_w^p=0} = \beta\, n_z^p. \tag{27}$$

The networks profit function is:

$$\pi^p = p^p \cdot n_w^p = \beta\, n_z^p \cdot n_w^p. \tag{28}$$

Profit maximizing behavior is to increase ad levels until marginal ad revenue equals marginal loss in audience shares. Due to perfect demand elasticity the ad level can be extended as long as viewers derive a weakly positive utility from the program. The maximum ad level is thus given by:

$$n_w^{p*} = \frac{q}{\alpha}. \tag{29}$$

Overstepping this value causes all viewers to switch off simultaneously and yields zero profits for the network. Below this value, increasing the ad level ever pays off. In equilibrium all viewers join the network

$$n_z^{p*} = 1 \tag{30}$$

and the network profit is:

$$\pi^{p*} = \beta \cdot n_w^{p*} = \frac{\beta}{\alpha} q \tag{31}$$

Personalized program content enables the monopolistic network to serve the whole market by maximizing the individual satisfaction level. Thereby ad levels are doubled from $q/(2\,\alpha)$ in the classical TV market Eq. (10) to q/α. Network profits are at least doubled.[5] This increase is driven by two effects. First, with personalized content the outside option becomes relatively less attractive to viewers and second, the responsiveness to increasing ad levels is harmonized across viewers. The network has a strong incentive to personalize content, since it can fully capture the viewers increased program valuation by adjusting ad levels. In the next section the analysis is extended by the duopoly case. Analogous to the monopoly case, the classical TV market is derived as the benchmark to analyze the impact of individualization.

4 Optimal Ad Levels in a Classical TV Duopoly Market

With two competing networks program location becomes a strategic decision. While the monopoly network chooses program location in order to realize the possible audience share, location in the duopoly market determines the degree of competition. The closer the programs are located, the bigger is the overlapping region of their acceptance ranges. It is in line with program choice literature to assume that viewers single home (Steiner 1952; Beebe 1977; Noam 1987). In our model, viewers will always choose the network that optimizes net utility or select the outside option. Thus, viewers in the overlap region are split between the networks. A higher overlap causes lower audience shares for each network. However, since the length of the acceptance range depends on the networks ad level, rivals audience shares can be conquered by lowering the ad level. A viewer will only choose a network with an inferior program location, if he is compensated by a lower ad level.

In the duopoly case each network has two substitutive decision parameters, program location and the ad level. We assume that networks act simultaneously. In the first step they decide for a program location on the preference spectrum and ad levels are chosen afterwards. The two networks S_j with $j = 1, 2$ can only differ in program location and ad level. The viewer's utility function is:

$$u_{zj} = q - \tau |S_j - x_z| - \alpha \cdot n_{wj}. \tag{32}$$

Viewers consume a program if $u_{zj} \geq 0$ holds for some j. The acceptance range can be derived from Eq. (32):

$$S_j - \theta_j \leq x_z \leq S_j + \theta_j, \quad \text{with} \quad \theta_j \equiv \frac{q - \alpha \cdot n_{wj}}{\tau} \tag{33}$$

---

[5] With the assumption $2\,\theta \leq 1$ it is ensured that (31) exceeds 13 at least by the factor 2.

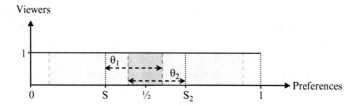

Fig. 2 Program location in a duopoly TV market

For simplicity we assume $S_1 < S_2$. On the unit interval network 1 is located to the left of network 2. If $u_{zj} \geq 0$ applies to both networks, then viewer z will choose S_1 if:

$$q - \tau|S_1 - x_z| - \alpha \cdot n_{w1} - \tau|S_2 - x_z| - \alpha \cdot n_{w2} \Leftrightarrow$$

$$\frac{\alpha \cdot n_{w2} - \alpha \cdot n_{w1}}{\tau} > |S_1 - x_z| - |S_2 - x_z| = \begin{cases} S_1 - S_2, x_z \leq S_1 \\ 2x - (S_1 + S_2), S_1 < x_z \leq S_2 \\ S_2 - S_1, x_z > S_2 \end{cases} \quad (34)$$

The duopoly market is displayed in Fig. 2. The dark-shaded area indicates the overlapping region of the networks acceptance ranges θ_1 and θ_2. Viewers in this area will ceteris paribus choose the network which is located nearest to their preference. Accordingly, these viewers will be split equally among networks. The networks in Fig. 2 have an incentive to depart from each other to minimize the overlap region. This is profitable for a network, as long as additional viewers can be attracted in the fringe of the distribution. A marginal shift to the border of the distribution causes a marginal increase of viewers that is two times higher than the accompanying marginal loss of viewers in the overlap area. Once the acceptance range reaches the edge of the distribution, no further shift towards the periphery is profitable, since this only causes additional losses in the overlap region without attracting new viewers.

The extent of network competition is determined by ad levels. In general, two cases are possible. If ad levels are sufficiently high that is $2(\theta_1 + \theta_2) < 1$, acceptance ranges do not overlap and networks will coexist without competition. This trivial case is excluded from the further discussion. For smaller ad levels with $2(\theta_1 + \theta_2) > 1$, acceptance ranges overlap and competition occurs. Since the preference spectrum is limited to the unit interval, the networks location is constrained to the condition $S_1, S_2 \in [0, 1]$. As is shown in Fig. 2, networks have an incentive to depart from each other. Optimal network locations are therefore determined by the acceptance ranges. S_1 optimally locates at θ_1 and S_2 locates at $(1 - \theta_2)$. The corresponding audience shares are calculated, as the integrals of the networks acceptance ranges. With $S_1 < S_2$ this is:

$$n_{z1} = \int_0^{\frac{S_1+S_2+\theta_1-\theta_2}{2}} f(z)dz = \frac{S_1 + S_2 + \theta_1 - \theta_2}{2}$$

$$n_{z2} = \int_{\frac{S_1+S_2+\theta_1-\theta_2}{2}}^{1} f(z)dz = 1 - \frac{S_1+S_2+\theta_1-\theta_2}{2}. \quad (35)$$

The interior limit of integration depicts the median of the overlapping range. Viewers with a preference below that value choose network S_1 and vice versa. By inserting the optimal network locations $S_1 = \theta_1$ and $S_2 = (1-\theta_2)$, we obtain:

$$n_{z1} = \frac{1}{2} + \theta_1 - \theta_2 = \frac{1}{2} + \frac{\alpha}{\tau}(n_{w2} - n_{w1})$$

$$n_{z2} = \frac{1}{2} + \theta_2 - \theta_1 = \frac{1}{2} + \frac{\alpha}{\tau}(n_{w1} - n_{w2}). \quad (36)$$

The advertisers' revenues are:

$$r_{wj} = \beta \cdot n_{zj} - p_j. \quad (37)$$

Unlike the viewers, advertisers can multi home in the way that they advertise on both networks (Anderson and Gabszewicz 2006, p. 585). Independently from this, excess demand for advertising time is still assumed and networks skim the whole producer surplus on the market for advertising:

$$r_{wj} = 0 \quad \Leftrightarrow \quad p_j = \beta \cdot n_{zj}. \quad (38)$$

The networks objective functions are detected by inserting Eqs. (35) and (38) into the general profit function:

$$\pi_1 = p_1 \cdot n_{w1} = \beta \cdot n_{z1} \cdot n_{w1} = \beta \left[\frac{1}{2} + \frac{\alpha}{\tau}(n_{w2} - n_{w1})\right] \cdot n_{w1}$$

and

$$\pi_2 = p_2 \cdot n_{w2} = \beta \cdot n_{z2} \cdot n_{w2} = \beta \left[\frac{1}{2} + \frac{\alpha}{\tau}(n_{w1} - n_{w2})\right] \cdot n_{w2}. \quad (39)$$

Differentiating with respect to n_{wj} yields the first order conditions:

$$\frac{\partial \pi_1}{\partial n_{w1}} = \beta \cdot \left(\frac{1}{2} + \frac{\alpha}{\tau}(n_{w2} - n_{w1})\right) - \beta \frac{\alpha \cdot n_{w1}}{\tau} = 0 \quad \Leftrightarrow \quad n_{w1}^* = \frac{\tau}{4\alpha} + \frac{n_{w2}}{2}$$

and

$$\frac{\partial \pi_2}{\partial n_{w2}} = \beta \cdot \left(\frac{1}{2} + \frac{\alpha}{\tau}(n_{w1} - n_{w2})\right) - \beta \frac{\alpha \cdot n_{w2}}{\tau} = 0 \quad \Leftrightarrow \quad n_{w2}^* = \frac{\tau}{4\alpha} + \frac{n_{w1}}{2}. \quad (40)$$

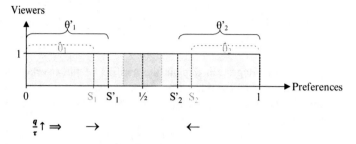

Fig. 3 Relocation with increasing acceptance ranges

The competitive character of the networks decisions become apparent in these conditions, since the optimum ad levels n_{w1}^* and n_{w2}^* depend on each other. The equilibrium ad levels are derived by mutually insertion of the first order conditions:

$$n_{w1}^* = \frac{\tau}{2\,\alpha} \quad \text{and} \quad n_{w2}^* = \frac{\tau}{2\,\alpha}. \tag{41}$$

Equilibrium ad levels are equal and therefore acceptance ranges have the same amplitude, so that networks locate symmetrically around the median:

$$S_1^* = \theta_1 = \frac{q}{\tau} - \frac{1}{2} \quad \text{and} \quad S_2^* = (1 - \theta_2) = \frac{3}{2} - \frac{q}{\tau}. \tag{42}$$

The corresponding audience shares are:

$$n_{z1}^* = \frac{1}{2} \quad \text{and} \quad n_{z2}^* = \frac{1}{2}. \tag{43}$$

Thus, we obtain a symmetrically Nash-equilibrium with the network payoffs:

$$\pi_1^* = \beta \cdot n_{z1} \cdot n_{w1} = \frac{\beta}{\alpha}\frac{\tau}{4} \quad \text{and} \quad \pi_2^* = \beta \cdot n_{z2} \cdot n_{w2} = \frac{\beta}{\alpha}\frac{\tau}{4}. \tag{44}$$

Unlike the monopoly case, the optimal satisfaction level (q) does not affect network profits anymore. This is due to the fact that the side condition $2(\theta_1 + \theta_2) > 1$ ensures full audience participation. Furthermore, the impact of τ changes. In the duopoly case a higher τ diminishes the overlap region θ_j. This causes higher network profits, as competition is reduced (see Fig. 3). With the side conditions $S_1 < S_2$ and $2(\theta_1 + \theta_2) > 1$ the Nash-equilibrium is defined for $\frac{q}{\tau} \in \,]\frac{3}{4}, 1\,[$.

In equilibrium, acceptance ranges are determined by the exogenous parameters q and τ. A higher general preference for TV (q) and a lower aversion against non preferred program content (τ) extend the acceptance range. A general implication of this result is that passive viewer behavior leads to a higher elasticity of substitution for competing networks. This is shown in Fig. 3. An increase in q/τ brings the networks to relocate towards the median of the distribution. Hence, networks program mixes become more homogenous and the elasticity of substitution rises. This result is in line with Noam (1987) and Fritsch and Lucas (2009) who show for normally distributed audiences, that higher acceptance ranges diminish the networks incentive to differentiate their programs. In the next section we analyze the impact of individualization for the duopoly case.

5 Optimal Ad Levels in an Individualized TV Duopoly Market

Information goods such as TV programs are appropriate for customization since copy costs are very low (Shapiro and Varian 1998, p. 22). Until today, individualization in IPTV markets mainly consists of time shifting and versioning. Growing competition will lead IPTV networks to improve their customization strategies in future as will be shown for ad addressability and personalized content.

5.1 Ad Addressability

According to the analysis of a monopolistic TV market, it is assumed that there are two disjunctive consumption types among viewers, namely LH- and RH-types. Program preferences are uniformly distributed on the unit interval (Kim and Wildman 2006). For the duopoly case with $i = LH, RH$ and $j = 1, 2$ viewer utility is described as:

$$u^i_{zj} = q - \tau \cdot |S_j - x_z| - \alpha^i \cdot n^i_{wj}. \qquad (45)$$

Ad addressability reduces ad-aversion according to $0 < \alpha^{LH} = \alpha^{RH} < \alpha$. A viewer z of type i chooses network 1 if:

$$q - \tau|S_1 - x_z| - \alpha^i \cdot n^i_{w1} > q - \tau|S_2 - x_z| - \alpha^i \cdot n^i_{w2}. \qquad (46)$$

With the optimal network locations[6]:

$$S_1 = \theta^i_1 \quad \text{and} \quad S_2 = (1 - \theta^i_2), \quad \text{with} \quad \theta^i_j \equiv \frac{q - \alpha^i \cdot n^i_{wj}}{\tau} \qquad (47)$$

---

[6] According to Sect. 4.

the corresponding audience shares are:

$$n_{z1}^i = \int_0^{\frac{S_1+S_2+\theta_1^i-\theta_2^i}{2}} f(z)dz = \frac{S_1+S_2+\theta_1^i-\theta_2^i}{2} = \frac{1}{4} + \frac{\alpha^i}{2\tau} \cdot (n_{w2}^i - n_{w1}^i)$$

$$n_{z2}^i = \int_{\frac{S_1+S_2+\theta_1^i-\theta_2^i}{2}}^1 f(z)dz = 1 - \frac{S_1+S_2+\theta_1^i-\theta_2^i}{2} = \frac{1}{4} + \frac{\alpha^i}{2\tau} \cdot (n_{w1}^i - n_{w2}^i). \quad (48)$$

Network profits are:

$$\pi_1 = \beta^{LH} \cdot n_{z1}^{LH} \cdot n_{w1}^{LH} + \beta^{RH} \cdot n_{z1}^{RH} \cdot n_{w1}^{RH} \Leftrightarrow \quad (49)$$

$$\pi_1 = \beta^{LH} \cdot \left[\frac{1}{4} + \frac{\alpha^{LH}}{2\tau} \cdot (n_{w2}^{LH} - n_{w1}^{LH})\right] \cdot n_{w1}^{LH} + \beta^{RH} \cdot \left[\frac{1}{4} + \frac{\alpha^{RH}}{2\tau} \cdot (n_{w2}^{RH} - n_{w1}^{RH})\right] \cdot n_{w1}^{RH}$$

and

$$\pi_2 = \beta^{LH} \cdot n_{z2}^{LH} \cdot n_{w2}^{LH} + \beta^{RH} \cdot n_{z2}^{RH} \cdot n_{w2}^{RH} \Leftrightarrow \quad (50)$$

$$\pi_2 = \beta^{LH} \cdot \left[\frac{1}{4} + \frac{\alpha^{LH}}{2\tau} \cdot (n_{w1}^{LH} - n_{w2}^{LH})\right] \cdot n_{w2}^{LH} + \beta^{RH} \cdot \left[\frac{1}{4} + \frac{\alpha^{RH}}{2\tau} \cdot (n_{w1}^{RH} - n_{w2}^{RH})\right] \cdot n_{w2}^{RH}.$$

Ad addressability causes segmentation of the audience and augments the advertising effect ($0 < \beta < \beta^{RH} = \beta^{LH}$). For the network's profit maximization $r_w^i = 0$ is assumed. The first order conditions are:

$$\frac{\partial \pi_1}{\partial n_{w1}^{LH}} = 0 \Leftrightarrow n_{w1}^{LH} = \frac{\tau}{4\alpha^{LH}} + \frac{1}{2} \cdot n_{w2}^{LH}, \quad \frac{\partial \pi_1}{\partial n_{w1}^{RH}} = 0 \Leftrightarrow$$

$$n_{w1}^{RH} = \frac{\tau}{4\alpha^{RH}} + \frac{1}{2} \cdot n_{w2}^{RH} \quad (51)$$

and

$$\frac{\partial \pi_2}{\partial n_{w2}^{LH}} = 0 \Leftrightarrow n_{w2}^{LH} = \frac{\tau}{4\alpha^{LH}} + \frac{1}{2} \cdot n_{w1}^{LH},$$

$$\frac{\partial \pi_2}{\partial n_{w2}^{RH}} = 0 \Leftrightarrow n_{w2}^{RH} = \frac{\tau}{4\alpha^{RH}} + \frac{1}{2} \cdot n_{w1}^{RH}. \quad (52)$$

The corresponding equilibrium ad levels are:

$$n_{w1}^{LH*} = \frac{\tau}{2\alpha^{LH}}, \quad n_{w1}^{RH*} = \frac{\tau}{2\alpha^{RH}}, \quad n_{w2}^{LH*} = \frac{\tau}{2\alpha^{LH}}, \quad n_{w2}^{RH*} = \frac{\tau}{2\alpha^{RH}}. \quad (53)$$

Both networks choose equal ad levels for LH- and RH-types.[7] The network's location decision is not affected by ad addressability (see Eq. (42)):

$$S_1^* = \theta_1^i = \frac{q}{\tau} - \frac{1}{2} \quad \text{and} \quad S_2^* = (1 - \theta_2^i) = \frac{3}{2} - \frac{q}{\tau}. \tag{54}$$

Reduced ad-aversion increases acceptance ranges ceteris paribus. In equilibrium, networks fully compensate this increase by adjusting the ad level. Optimal ad levels and corresponding network profits are:

$$n_{z1}^* = n_{z1}^{LH*} + n_{z1}^{RH*} = \frac{1}{2} \quad \text{and} \quad n_{z2}^* = n_{z2}^{LH*} + n_{z2}^{RH*} = \frac{1}{2}.$$

$$\pi_1^* = \beta^i \cdot n_{z1}^* \cdot n_{w1}^{i*} = \frac{\beta^i}{\alpha^i} \frac{\tau}{4} \quad \text{and} \quad \pi_2^* = \beta^i \cdot n_{z2}^* \cdot n_{w2}^{i*} = \frac{\beta^i}{\alpha^i} \frac{\tau}{4}. \tag{55}$$

The Nash-equilibrium is again defined for $\frac{q}{\tau} \in \,]\frac{3}{4}, 1\,[$. In comparison to the duopoly benchmark case, profits increase:

$$\pi_2^{*\,classical\ ads} = \frac{\beta}{\alpha} \frac{\tau}{4} < \frac{\beta^i}{\alpha^i} \frac{\tau}{4} = \pi_j^{*\,targeted\ ads} \quad \text{with} \quad \alpha^i < \alpha \quad \text{and} \quad \beta^i > \beta \tag{56}$$

5.2 Personalized Content

In the duopoly case, content customization can be used to compete for audiences. Viewers select the net utility maximizing program. Since program differentiation is not feasible in a personalized program market ($|S_j - x_z| = 0$), the network with the lowest ad level attracts all viewers. According to Eq. (26) a viewer selects S_1 if $n_{w1} \leq \frac{q}{\alpha}$ and $u_{z1}^p > u_{z2}^p$. The corresponding demand functions are:

$$n_{z1}^p = \begin{cases} 0, & n_{w1}^p > \min\left[\frac{q}{\alpha}; n_{w2}^p\right] \\ 1, & n_{w1}^p < \min\left[\frac{q}{\alpha}; n_{w2}^p\right] \end{cases} \quad \text{and} \quad n_{z2}^p = \begin{cases} 0, & n_{w2}^p > \min\left[\frac{q}{\alpha}; n_{w1}^p\right] \\ 1, & n_{w2}^p < \min\left[\frac{q}{\alpha}; n_{w1}^p\right] \end{cases} \tag{57}$$

Network profits are:

$$\pi_j^p = \beta^p \cdot n_{zj}^p \cdot n_{wj}^p \tag{58}$$

---

[7] If viewers differ in income, consumption time, activity level or ad aversion, asymmetric equilibria might result.

Table 1 Equilibrium outcomes of ad-financed IPTV services

Monopoly case	Network profit (π)	Audience share (n_z)	Ad level (n_w)
Monopoly case			
Classical	$\frac{\beta}{\alpha} \cdot \frac{q}{2} \cdot \frac{q}{\tau}$	$\frac{q}{\tau}$	$\frac{q}{2\alpha}$
Targeted ads	$\left[\frac{\beta^{LH}}{2\,\alpha^{LH}} + \frac{\beta^{RH}}{2\,\alpha^{RH}}\right] \cdot \frac{q}{2} \cdot \frac{q}{\tau}$	$\frac{q}{\tau}$	$\frac{q}{2\,\alpha^i}$
Personalized content	$\frac{\beta}{\alpha} \cdot q$	1	$\frac{q}{\alpha}$
Duopoly case			
Classical	$\frac{\beta}{\alpha} \cdot \frac{\tau}{4}$	$\frac{1}{2}$	$\frac{\tau}{2\alpha}$
Targeted ads	$\frac{\beta^i}{\alpha^i} \cdot \frac{\tau}{4}$	$\frac{1}{2}$	$\frac{\tau}{2\,\alpha^i}$
Personalized content	0	0	0

Assumption: $2\theta \leq 1$

With content customization networks lack the opportunity to choose different program locations. The only remaining competition parameter is the ad level. This leads to Bertrand competition, where networks underbid each other until profits are zero. The market collapses since zero profits imply the absence of commercial breaks.

Conclusion

In the monopoly case network profits increase with targeted ads and personalized content. Furthermore program personalization enables the network to serve the whole viewer market, as is shown in Table 1.

In the duopoly case network profits increase with targeted ads while program customization causes the market to collapse. This is due to the loss of differentiation. If networks can provide full customization, program supply becomes homogenous for viewers. Therefore the only remaining parameter to attract additional viewers is the advertising level. Ad addressability appears to be a profit increasing tool for IPTV providers. Customized content on the other hand leads to a more severe competition in advertising levels. An essential question for the future development of IPTV markets is therefore, to what extend channels can differentiate their program with exclusive broadcasting rights.

References

Anderson, S. P., & Gabszewicz, J. J. (2006). The media and advertising: A tale of two sided markets. In V. A. Ginsburgh & D. Throsby (Eds.), *Handbook of the economics of art and culture* (pp. 567–614). Amsterdam: Elsevier.

Armstrong, M. (2005). Public service broadcasting. *Fiscal Studies, 26*, 282–299.
Armstrong, M. (2006). Competition in two-sided markets. *The RAND Journal of Economics, 37*, 668–691.
Bagwell, K. (2007). The Economic Analysis of Advertising. In M. Armstrong & R. Porter (Eds.), *Handbook of industrial organization* (pp. 1708–1725). New York: Elsevier.
Barros, P. P., Kind, H. J., Nilssen, T., & Sørgard, L. (2004). Media competition on the internet. *Topics in Economic Analysis & Policy, 4*, 1–18.
Beebe, J. H. (1977). Institutional structure and program choices in television markets. *Quarterly Journal of Economics, 91*, 15–37.
Caillaud, B., & Jullien, B. (2003). Chicken and egg; competing matchmakers. *The Rand Journal of Economics, 34*, 309–328.
Fritsch C., & Lucas J (2009) program choice revisited (forthcoming).
Gabszewicz, J. J., Laussel, D., & Sonnac, N. (2001). Press advertising and the ascent of the Pensée unique? *European Economic Review, 45*, 645–651.
Gomes, O. (2006). The dynamics of television advertising with boundedly rational consumers. *Munic Personal RePEc Archive*, 1–30.
Hotelling, H. (1929). Stability in competition. *The Economic Journal, 39*, 41–57.
Kim, E., & Wildman, S. S. (2006). A deeper look at the economics of advertiser support for television—The implications of consumption-differentiated viewers and ad addressability. *Journal of Media Economics, 19*, 55–79.
Kind, H. J., Nilssen, T., & Sørgard, L. (2007). Competition for viewers and advertisers in a TV oligopoly. *Journal of Media Economics, 20*, 211–233.
Noam, E. M. (1987). A public and private-choice model of broadcasting. *Public Choice, 55*, 163–187.
Noam, E. M. (1995). *Towards the third revolution of television* (pp. 1–17). Bertelsmann Foundation: Gütersloh.
Peitz, M, (2006). Marktplätze und indirekte Netzwerkeffekte. *Perspektiven der Wirtschaftspolitik 7*, 317–333.
Rochet, J. C., & Tirole, J. (2003). Platform competition in two-sided markets. *Journal of the European Economic Association, 1*, 990–1029.
Shapiro, C., & Varian, H. R. (1998). *Information rules*. Boston: Harvard Business School Press.
Spence, M., & Owen, B. M. (1977). Television programming. Monopolistic competition and welfare. *Quarterly Journal of Economics, 91*, 103–126.
Steiner, P. O. (1952). Program patterns and preferences, and the workability of competition in radio broadcasting. *Journal of Economics, 66*, 194–223.
Tacheny, T. (1989). Observation and measurement of audience viewing habits: Zapping. In European Society for Opinion and Marketing Research (Ed.), *Seminar on broadcasting research: experiences and strategies Paris (France), 25th-27th January* (pp. 259–315). Amsterdam: ESOMR.

The Social Media War: Is Google+ the David to Facebook's Goliath?

Richard Ganahl

1 Introduction

By all measures, Google+, the newest entrant in the already dominated social media category, should be dead in the water.

Just consider some of the dimensions of absolute dominance reached by the privately held Facebook, which was launched from a Harvard dorm room in 2004. With over 800 million current users, it is the world's most visited website with more than 1.8 billion visits during an average week. Over 400 million users post every day more than 2 billion likes and comments in 70 languages.

More than 45 % of Facebook's 18–34 years old users check the site when they wakeup, and more than 30 % of this group checks in before "even getting out of bed!" This stand-alone, walled-garden's $4.3 billion in sales is valued at an incredible $82.9 billion for a 41.5 sales to value ratio.

So then, is Google+ the David to Facebook's Goliath?

Launched in July 2011 as an invitation-only social network site, Google+ quickly jumped to third place as the U.S.'s most popular social media site by September 2011 when it became an open-access site with more than 40 million members. Published by publicly owned Google, it joins a stable of more than 105 companies that are among the top category leaders in search, email, image-search and Internet browsers. Google's more than $35 billion in revenue and $192 billion valuation dwarfs Facebook.

Additionally, Android, launched by Google in 2007 as an open source OS, leads the cell phone industry with a 42 % market share. And, Google's aggressive $12.5 billion cash offer in August 2011 for third ranked cell phone manufacturer Motorola may present serious obstacles for Facebook's mobile strategies.

R. Ganahl (✉)
Bloomsburg University, Bloomsburg, PA, USA
e-mail: rganahl@gmail.com

This chapter explores as a case study the long-term potential of Google+ and analyzes its ultimate viability as a full social media competitor rather than a niche player. This study is based on a complete review of the current literature; a thorough analysis of real world indicators including site metrics, market shares, revenue and valuations; a comparative analysis of the sites' formats and features; several small-sized focus groups with dedicated users of the social media sites, and analysis of several individual Facebook, Twitter and Google+ accounts.

2   Brief History of Social Media

Media researcher Dana Boyd defines social media as, "as web-based services that allow individuals to (1) construct a public or semi-public profile within a bounded system, (2) articulate a list of other users with whom they share a connection, and (3) view and traverse their list of connections and those made by others within the system."[1]

Web-based applications supported within these 'bounded systems' are extremely varied and include forums, wikis, podcasts, blogging, microblogging, music, photographs, video, messaging, ratings, social bookmarking, calendars, and document sharing among others. Most social media sites are free, and most seek to build a business model based on leveraging the user-generated content (UGC) to attract a sufficient number of users to support various forms of advertising.

Much has happened in the world of computer-mediated social connectivity since the sending of the world's first email in 1971. While the exact words of the first email are forgotten, the initial test message "QUERTYIOP" lives on. Most social media historians mark the Bulletin Board System (BBS) in the late 1970s as the beginning of social networking or social media. Early BBS systems where managed by computer hobbyists and enabled individual computer users to share common interests and messages through modems connected by fixed copper telephone lines.

GeoCities, one of the first social networking sites, launched in 1994 and hosted free, personal web sites originally organized into six communities labeled with various addresses including Hollywood, WallStreet and SunsetStrip. The initial intention was to group individual personal web pages by common interests. The site offered chat, bulletin boards and experimented with advertising as it became one of the most visited websites in 1999. Yahoo! purchased GeoCities in 1999 for more than $3.5 billion in stock and closed it to new members in 2009.

Blogging, an integral part of today's social connectivity tools, gained increasing acceptance in the late 1990s as freely hosted blog sites were started. These early blog sites offered online diary and reader comment, and include LiveJournal, Open Diary and Blogger launched by Pyra Labs in 1999. Google purchased Blogger for an undisclosed amount in 2003. Today's blogging community is global, immense

---

[1] Boyd and Ellison (2007).

and diversified. Sites host both the hobbyist and the professional, and range from micro-blogging sites to multi-platform sites.

A plethora of social media sites were launched in early 2000. Friendster, recognized as the original social media site, launched in 2002 and gained immediate popularity by offering photo, video, message and comment sharing between one's online profile and its network of friends. The privately owned company refused Google's 2003 purchase offer of $30 million and was soon overtaken by newcomer MySpace. Today, Friendster is an Asian-based social gaming and entertainment site.

MySpace launched in 2003 and quickly surpassed Friendster's dominance because it allowed individual's more freedom to customize their personal sites and enforced fewer restrictions on content. MySpace was purchased by Rupert Murdoch's News Corporation for $580 million in 2005 and remained the most popular social media website until Facebook overtook it in 2008. Today, Facebook remains the overwhelming favorite among all social media sites. A detailed discussion about Facebook follows.

YouTube pioneered video sharing with its launch in 2005. The site quickly became one of the Internet's fastest growing sites, and it beat MySpace's rate of growth as it climbed in popularity. Google purchased YouTube in 2006 for $1.65 billion in stock. It remains one of the Internet's most popular sites.

Twitter introduced micro-blogging on the heels of Google's purchase of YouTube in 2006. This shortened form of blogging has been described as a network-based, web-delivered SMS application because it limits individual comments, or Tweets, to 140 characters. These tweets can be archived, analyzed, searched, broadcast to the network whole or to individual users using simple character additions. Twitter has gained widespread popularity in a very short time and is especially useful in promoting individual celebrities and editorial content.

The newest social media site Google+ launched as an invitation-only beta site in July 2011, and became an open-access site in September 2011. A detailed discussion about Google+ follows. Table 1 labeled The Top 10 American Social Networking Sites and Forums in November 2011 depicts the dominance of Facebook and the emergence of Google+ into the top ten sites.[2]

While Facebook has the dominant market share of almost 64 % among the U.S. social media sites, it's worth noting in Table 2 labeled Top U.S. Web Sites by Unique Traffic in November 2011 that combined Google sites lead the U.S. in the total number of unique visitors with 186.7 million, and that Google's total traffic led Facebook's total traffic by almost 25 %.[3]

---

[2] Kallas (2011).
[3] ComScore (2011a).

Table 1 Top ten U.S. social networking sites and forums in November 2011

Facebook	63.80 % market share
YouTube	20.83 % market share
Twitter	1.47 % market share
Yahoo! Answers	0.99 % market share
LinkedIn	0.63 % market share
Tagged	0.74 % market share
MySpace	0.53 % market share
MyYearbook	0.40 % market share
Google+	0.33 % market share
Yelp	0.30 % market share

Dreamgrow: social media marketing resources, November 2011

Table 2 Top U.S. web sites by unique traffic in November 2011

Total internet audience	220,995,000
Google sites	186,659,000
Microsoft sites	175,499,000
Yahoo! sites	174,481,000
Facebook.com	166,007,000
Amazon sites	112,878,000

comScore Media Metrix ranks top 50 U.S. web properties for November 2011

3 Social Media Today

"Social networking is the most popular online activity worldwide," concludes comScore in its January 2012 report *It's a Social World: Top 10 Need-to-Knows About Social Networking and Where It's Headed*.[4] comScore estimates that nearly 1.2 billion, or 82 % of the global online population, spend on average 19 % of their Internet time engaging with 100's of social networking sites, an increase of more than 300 % in just 5 years, or 2006 when social media sites accounted for just 6 % of online activities.

The report concludes the world's high level of penetration and intense engagement in social media sites is pervasive across genders, all ages and almost all countries. Of the 43 countries studied by comScore, all but 2 have a penetration level of 85 % or more. China reports only a 53 % penetration level along with some politically closed areas of the Middle East. While the 84.4 % penetration level among those 15–24 years old is the highest, social media use among those 55 and older is growing the fastest, at almost 10 % in the last year, for an 80 % penetration level.

Females 15–24 years old are the world's most engaged social media users averaging 8.6 h per month, while females 55 and older average just under 5 h a

---

[4] Ibid., p. 7.

month using social media. Males across all ages are somewhat less engaged as males 15–24 years old average 7.5 h per month, and males 55 and older average 2.7 h per month on social media sites.

The American-based sites Facebook and Twitter dominate the world's social media category. Facebook leads the world in every measure, and accounts for 75 % of every minute spent worldwide on a social media site. It has the largest market share in all but seven measured countries, and is in the top five sites in all but one of those seven countries. Recently launched Twitter grew 59 % last year and is among the top five social media sites in all but eight measured countries. Its rapid growth underscores the increasing popularity of microblogging, or short form blogging. Twitter's role in globe-changing events like the Middle East's Arab Spring in 2011 suggests social media have powers to mobilize large numbers of people instantaneously.

Both comScore and Nielsen document the users' growing reliance on mobile access to engage social media sites. In its *State of the Media: The Social Media Report Q32011* Nielsen concludes "nearly 2 in 5, or 37 %, social media users access these services from their mobile phone."[5] The Nielsen study reports that 47 % rate social networking as the second 'most valued' mobile utility, just after downloading and playing music, which is rated at 49 %.

comScore says that on a worldwide basis, "mobile devices represent the future of social networking as they provide the means for users to connect on-the-go, facilitating real-time interaction."[6] It reports a wide range of personal engagement through mobile-based social activities including 80 % that read friends' posts, 70 % that update their own status, 54 % that read posts from institutions or brands, 45 % that read celebrity or public figure posts, and 34 % that receive coupons or other purchase deals.[7]

The Pew Internet & American Life Project says, "the pace with which new users (in the U.S.) have flocked to social networking sites has been staggering; when we first asked about social networking sites in...2005, just 8 % of internet users—or 5 % of all adults—said they used them."[8] Moreover, the most common response of social media users was "good" when Pew asked them to describe their experiences with social media sites. "Overall, positive responses far outweighed the negative or neutral words (and) users repeatedly described their experiences as fun, great, interesting and convenient."[9]

Table 3 summarizes Pew's findings regarding who uses social networking sites in the U.S.

---

[5] Nielsen (2011).
[6] ComScore, p. 20.
[7] ComScore, p. 23.
[8] Pew Internet & American Life Project (2011).
[9] Ibid., p. 7.

Table 3 Who uses social networking sites in the U.S.

All internet users	65 %
Men	60 %
Women[a]	69 %
Age	
18–29 years old[a]	83 %
30–49 years old[a]	70 %
50–64 years old[a]	51 %
65+ years old	33 %
Education	
Less than high school	68 %
High school grad	61 %
Some college	65 %
College+	67 %
Geographical location	
Urban	67 %
Suburban	65 %
Rural	61 %

The Pew Research Center, May 2011
[a]Statistically Significant

Of course, all this posting, friending, tweeting, sharing, rating, liking, commenting, poking, voting, etc. doesn't happen in a vacuum. Many social media sites, most notably Facebook, insist they 'own' their users' freely contributed content. The sites then leverage this user-generated content against the vast number of user-created social networks to sell highly targeted advertising campaigns. This user-generated, social network-driven content forms the basis of many potentially very productive business models.

comScore notes that social networking, "strongly leads all content categories in the number of display ads delivered, accounting for more than 1 in 4 U.S. display ad impressions, or 28 %, in October 2011." It further states that the social networking category has a "significant lead over other categories…even outpacing Portals."[10] It speculates that as the popularity of social media grows, so will its preeminence in delivering online advertising.

In addition to delivering highly targeted advertising, the social media content has become an integral part of the marketing mix as brands, events, media, celebrities and public figures create 'fan pages' or social media accounts, build their own fan or supporter-based networks, and then deliver multi-media marketing campaigns to their own social networks.

For example, rock star Lady Gaga is very sophisticated in her use of social media to build her brand as 'Mother Monster'. Daily she shares provocative pictures of herself, her music, her videos, tours and social causes to her more than 43.3 million

---

[10] ComScore, p. 151.

Table 4 Social media followers of selected U.S. notables: 12.11

Name	Facebook	Twitter	Google+
Celebrities or public figures			
Lady Gaga	46,309,966	17,901,090	396
Bill Gates	779,717	5,055,365	1,860
Oprah Winfry	6,525,369	8,795,320	None
Media companies			
CNN	3,177,380	3,513,803	7,957
FOX	2,376,470	1,219,944	24,268
New York TMS	1,924,045	4,265,232	194,307
WSHNGTN Post	4,900,000[a]	781,598	12,389
Journalists or TV commentators			
Andrs Cooper	644,540	1,949,583	170,240
Bill O'Reilly	503,205	125,112	None
Katie Couric	67,916	347,158	None
Media researchers			
Jeff Jarvis	43,706	87,602	424,689
Dan Gillmor	None	18,336	374,841
Jay Rosen	None	74,534	28,721
Dana Boyd	None	54,887	52,501

[a]WP = reader app unpublished research by author, January 2012

Facebook fans and more than 17.9 million Twitter followers. In December 2011 she posted more than 60 times to her Facebook page, and shared with her 'Little Monsters' almost 70 Tweets on Twitter. Her Facebook page hosts numerous promotional photos, provides a link to her website and offers updates through SMS and RSS.[11]

How successful is her social media marketing? At midnight on New Years Eve 2012 Lady Gaga posted her resolution "Never be afraid to be kicked in the teeth. Let the blood and the bruises define your legacy"[12] to her Facebook page. And, the results? More than 116,428 fans 'liked' the post and shared Lady Gaga's resolution on their personal wall, while more than 10,262 fans made specific comments to the post. Certainly, the network effect is working for Lady Gaga.

Table 4 depicts the utilization in the U.S. of the social media sites Facebook, Twitter and Google+ by several categories including celebrities, media companies, journalists and media researchers. Each category appears to use social media for different purposes: celebrities build brands and market share; media companies and journalists break stories and build circulation; and media researchers share insights and foster dialogue. These network-based, symbiotic, market-driven relationships among the various entities and social media are the genesis of sustainable business models for the emerging social media industry.

---

[11] Ganahl (2011a).
[12] Ibid.

The future of social media is captured in one word: explosive. The network effect is powerful enough to drive increased utilization and deeper user engagement on a global scale. No longer is social media something just for the 'digital native' or the young people. The intoxication of network-enabled, socially shared, multi-platform communication in real-time is quickly supplanting the status quo. Post offices are closing, emails go unanswered and instant messaging is not instant or broad enough.

comScore concludes:

> the next disrupters have yet to be decided...reflecting the inherent volatility... in an industry that thrives on the power of the network effect. Just as Facebook (is now) the nearly universal social network (so could) new social networks...emerge and disrupt the existing fabric of social networking as we currently know it.[13]

4   The Facebook Story

> To give people the power to share and make the world more open and connected.

If you believe all tech-blockbusters are created by young, college dropouts (think Bill Gates and Steve Jobs), on a laptop (think Shawn Fanning and Pierre Omidyar) in garages or other youth hangouts (think Hewlett-Packard and Apple), then Facebook's founding follows this script. Truly, Facebook was launched in 2004 by college dropout Mark Zuckerberg in his Harvard dorm room. This is the basic storyline followed in the popular 2010 film drama *The Social Network*. While Zuckerberg claims director David Fincher's film distorts the truth, popular culture accepts much of the film as an accurate portrayal.[14]

Facebook initially limited user participation to Harvard students, but gradually broadened membership in stages from Ivy League schools to students with college emails until it was completely opened to anyone 13 years or older with a valid email address in September 2006. Zuckerberg and his team didn't create social networking software (remember Friendster and MySpace?), and its market share languished behind MySpace until April 2008 when Facebook became the most trafficked social media site in the U.S.

Throughout its short history, Facebook has been parodied and criticized for its alleged inanity and violation of privacy. A 2007 comical op-ed piece contributed to *The New York Times* by Alice Mathias titled 'The Fakebook Generation' said it was a "time chugging Web site" that was more like an "online community theatre" that delivered a constant "soliloquy to our anonymous audience...It's all comedy".[15]

---

[13] ComScore, p. 17.
[14] IMBd (2010).
[15] Mathias (2007).

Table 5 Top U.S. social network and blog sites by time spent per month

Facebook	53.5 billion
YouTube (owned by Google)	9.1 billion
Blogger (owned by Google)	724 million
Tumblr	624 million
Twitter	565 million
LinkedIn	326 million

Nielsen: social media report: Q32011

Recently, *The New York Times* noted that the visitor growth rate in the U.S. had declined to a 10 % annual increase compared to the previous year's 56 % rate of growth citing, "some who steer clear of the site say it can have the...effect of making them feel more, not less, alienated."[16] The article labeled these holdouts "Facebook Resisters."

In spite of its critics, Facebook's performance is stunning. And today, the privately owned, walled-garden, stand-alone is the world's most visited website. American Internet users spend more time on Facebook than any other website according to Nielsen's "The Social Media Report," spending 53.5 billion minutes a month. This compares to the 9.1 billion minutes a month spent on YouTube and the 723 million minutes a month spent on Blogger. Google owns both YouTube and Blogger. Table 5 lists the top six U.S. social networks and blogs by total minutes spent on them per month according to Nielsen.

Facebook reports that more than 50 % of its 800 million global users log on daily, install more than 20 million apps and upload more than 250 million photographs each day. The site is available in more than 70 languages, and 3 out of 4 Facebook users are outside the U.S. The average Facebook user has 130 friends and is 'connected' to at least 80 event, group or community pages.[17]

For most of the Internet's users, Facebook is seen as that place "where we reach out when life happens."[18] And where does 'life happen' for Facebook users? It happens up close, at the personal level including one's daily doings, personal relationships, and major life events like marriage, birth and death. Life also happens at the global level including everything from Japan's spring 2011 tsunami to Osama Bin Laden's May 2011 death. Hitwise says that Facebook, "is a form of (a) digital biography of our lives...a digital home," and that traffic visits related to one's personal life, "peak(s) on Saturday and Sunday," whereas other, "peaks in traffic...tend to correlate with major news events."[19]

---

[16] Worthham (2011).
[17] Facebook (2011).
[18] Dougherty (2011a).
[19] Ibid.

Facebook seems relentless in its pursuit to enhance its interface for increased user engagement. Most are familiar with its typical tools of engagement including privacy settings, profile, status, friends, networks, posts, pokes, walls, chat, messaging, photo sharing, likes, etc. As one media analyst says in an article in *The New York Times*, "(Facebook is) likely more worried about the novelty factor wearing off...That's a continual problem that they're solving, and there are no permanent solutions."[20]

Most recently it announced a number of changes at its F8 2011 developer conference including Timeline and content sharing partnerships with Spotify, Netflix, Rhapsody and Hulu. Timeline is designed to be a more graphic 'scrapbook of your life' or a 'digital autobiography' in that it allows you to build a personal history extending as far back as your birth (!) through your posts, photos and apps. The new sharing partnerships will "let users see what songs and albums their friends are listening to in real time...(and) every movie you watch (will) appear in your Ticker."[21]

Sound more engaging? A survey of comments made on news sites after F8 2011 were generally critical and included 'information overload, over-engineered, and irrelevant nonsense pushed in our face.'[22] Selected responses to a Facebook-based survey conducted by the author are similar in tone:

> (it's) extremely overwhelming. It isn't as easy to find content on my own page anymore...it is great. I basically like it cause it is a cool design and keeps things in order...don't have too much extra time to dedicate to it. Plus I do most of my Facebooking from my phone...as long as I can avoid it, I'm going to :)...the two columns of timelines (are) extremely confusing but most important, I don't want all my older posts and conversations, which have been posted years ago, to be that available and attainable...I don't use my timeline so much, I'm not adding all my life there. :)[23]

However, user engagement seems unmitigated, and perhaps as one writer surmises, "because people see Facebook as so personal, they are shocked when Facebook tries to leverage their personal information and they get upset when the interface changes with new features."[24]

Facebook's revenue increased more than 125 % in 2011 to $4.27 billion from the 2010 total revenue of $2 billion according to EMarketer,[25] Almost 90 %, or $3.8 billion, of the 2011 revenue is from advertising, an increase of 104 % from the 2010 total of $1.86 billion. Because of its relationship with Microsoft, Facebook only serves advertisements from Microsoft's inventory. It is expected that Facebook will surpass Yahoo! and rank first in 2011 for the selling of display advertisements in the

---

[20] Ibid., NYT #15 http://mediadecoder.blogs.nytimes.com/2011/12/14/online-sharing-the-how-what-and-when-of-2011/?scp=3&sq=facebook%20vs%20google%20+&st=cse

[21] Burnham (2011).

[22] Ganahl (2011b).

[23] Ibid.

[24] Caruso (2011).

[25] Womack (2011).

U.S., while Yahoo! and Google ranks second and third respectively. Facebook is expected to generate $1 billion in profit in 2011.

Facebook remains privately owned. However, an initial public offering (IPO) is expected in April 2012. Zuckerberg is Facebook's largest shareholder with 24 %, and Microsoft owns 1.3 % through its October 2007 investment of $240 million. The SEC may soon require public disclosure of Facebook's financial information because its number of shareholders is expected to be at least 500 by the end of 2011. Facebook expects to raise $10 billion through the IPO, placing its valuation over $100 billion. Based on the 2011 projected revenue of $4.27.[26]

Bloomberg News estimates that Facebook's expected $100 billion valuation, "would be worth 23 times projected revenue (while) Google trades at 6.4 times...revenue...Apple Inc. (at) 2.5 times sales, while the multiple for Microsoft Corp. is 2.8."[27] Of course some analysts question Facebook's debut at such a high valuation pointing to the recent lackluster Internet IPO's including Groupon, Zynga and LinkedIn. The *MercuryNews.com* reporting on Zynga's December IPO said, "Zynga's (an online gaming company) disappointing debut indicates that the market's interest in shares of startup Internet companies is waning."[28] Notwithstanding the critics, most analysts expect a robust IPO.

Nearly 44 %, or 350 million Facebook users interact via mobile phone. Also, because Google and Apple operate the two major smartphone operating systems, and neither has any incentive to develop an OS to accommodate Facebook, a mobile strategy is extremely important for the social media giant. So, what does it have planned?

Over the last 12 months or so, there has been speculation about Facebook's plan to have telephone maker HTC manufacture a 'Facebook' phone. Allegedly the project is code-named 'Buffy,' after TV's vampire slayer. Needing to offer more than the button dedicated to Facebook that is already-available on several models, the phone is expected, "to run on a modified version of Android that Facebook has tweaked heavily to deeply integrate its services, as well as to support HTML5 as a platform for applications."[29] Some fear that the 12–18 month roll out cycle for the phone maybe 'too little too late' to make much difference for Facebook.

---

[26] Raice (2011).

[27] MacMillan and Womack (2011).

[28] Wolverton (2011).

[29] Gannes and Fried (2011).

5 The Google Story

> To organize the world's information and make it universally accessible and useful.

While Google's founding doesn't involve a college dropout (both founders have a Master of Science from Stanford University), it does involve a garage which the company website lists as 'Susan Wojcicki's garage at 232 Santa Margarita, Menlo Park,' complete with a Google Map link to its location and picture. Founders Larry Page and Sergey Brin met as Ph.D. candidates at Stanford University. The two developed a web crawler called BackRub that converted a web page's backlink data into a measure of the page's relative importance. The initial version of Google launched in August 1996 on a Stanford University server, and moved to 'Susan's garage' in August 1998 as the officially incorporated Google. The name Google is a play on the mathematical term googol which refers to the number 1 followed by 100 zeros.

Google today includes more than 100 individual products, has over 32,000 employees, and its expected annual revenues in 2011 is over $35 billion that will generate more than $10 billion in profit. Revenue grew 24 % in 2010 and averaged over 30 % growth through Q3 of 2011. Advertising, primarily key word search ads, is 96 % of revenue, and 66 % of the total advertising is generated on Google websites. The company had $42.6 billion in cash and cash equivalents at the end of Q3 2011.[30] The personal wealth of the two founders in 2011 is estimated to be over $16 billion each.

Table 2 demonstrates that the combined Google sites rank number one in the U.S. with total Internet traffic of 186.7 million unique visitors a month. Among its product stable are some of the world's most well known Internet brands including YouTube, Blogger, Google Search, Gmail, AdSense, Google Maps, Chrome, Google Analytics, Google Docs, Reader and Android. Moreover, these products are unique, and category leaders in traffic and innovation. Consider these specific stories in addition to YouTube and Blogger:

- Google Search is the linchpin of the Google empire and is the platform for the company's search advertising revenue, which generates most of the company's revenue. Launched in 1998, it is the global search engine leader with over 91 % market share.[31]
- Gmail launched in 2004 and is available on mobile phones and integrates Google Docs directly through Gmail. Free voice telephone was added in 2009. While the various email services do not provide uniform information, Hitwise ranks it number 1 or 2 as 'most popular' among Yahoo!, and Hotmail.[32]
- Google Chrome launched in 2008 and now a large section of the web browser's source code has been released as open source. In December 2011 it became the

---

[30] Google (2011).
[31] StatCounter (2012).
[32] Brownlow (2011).

Table 6 U.S. mobile phone industry

No. of mobile device users	234 million
No. of smartphone users	38 % market share: 90 million
Market share of U.S. mobile device manufacturers	
Samsung/Android	25.5 %
LG/Android	20.6 %
Motorola/Android	13.6 %
Apple/iOS	10.8 %
Blackberry/RIM	6.6 %
Market share of U.S. smartphone device platforms	
Google/Android	46.3 %
Apple/iOS	28.1 %
Blackberry/RIM	17.2 %
Microsoft	5.4 %

comScore: U.S. mobile subscriber market share

most used browser worldwide with a 24 % market share, while it ranks second in the U.S., with a 27 % market share to IE's 39 % market share.[33]
- Google Maps is a free map service with no advertising that was launched in 2005. It offers directions in 4 modes of travel plus street, aerial, geological and satellite views. It is the leading map service with 13.2 % market share while MapQuest owned by AOL is second with a 5.3 % share.[34]
- Android was purchased by Google in 2005, then released in 2007 as an open sourced operating system for mobile devices along with the founding of the Open Handset Alliance dedicated to promoting open standards for mobile and tablet devices. Android leads the smartphone market with 47 % share to Apple's 29 %.[35]

It's hard to overestimate Google's mobile phone industry footprint. In August 2011 it announced it would acquire Motorola Mobility in a cash deal for $12.5 billion, or 63 % more than the closing price the day before the announcement. Motorola holds over 17,000 patents, and is the world's third largest mobile device producer with 14 % market share. Its phones run on Google's mobile phone platform Android.[36]

The purchase solidifies Google's dominance in the mobile industry as Android is the OS for 44 % of the mobile phones manufactured by 39 OEMs. The Android OS has a 52 % market share in smartphone. Table 6 depicts this dominance.

Google was no stranger to the social media industry prior to launching Google+ in June 2011 as an invite-only beta version. In addition to its current social media

---

[33] StatCounter (2011).
[34] Experian Hitwise (2011).
[35] ComScore (2011b).
[36] Rusli and Miller (2011).

successes YouTube, which it purchased in 2006, and Blogger which it purchased in 2003, Google's offer to purchase Friendster at social media's inception in 2003 was unsuccessful. Other social media experiments include Orkut: launched in 2004 and now the most visited website in Brazil and India; Buzz: launched in 2010 as a built-in messenger to Gmail closed in 2011; and Wave: closed in 2010 after 1 year as a 'real time messaging platform.'

Google+ traffic spiked at 15 million per week and it became the third most visited social media site when it opened access to all Internet users in September 2011. Hitwise reported Google+ traffic, "jumped 55 % (to) more than 49 million total U.S. visits in December."[37] Paul Allen (the founder of Ancestry.com and not Microsoft) says, "it may be the holidays, the TV commercials, the Android 4 signups, celebrity and brand appeal, or positive word of mouth (but at) this rate of new signups (625 k daily)...I predict...Google+ will end next year (2012) with more than 400 million users."[38] Allen, who bases his projections on traffic studies conducted by Ancestry.com, is often quoted by writers on Google+ growth.

The synergy among Google products helps build Google+ traffic as Hitwise notes that, "among the top 10 referral sources, 8 are Google properties and accounted for 73 % of all upstream traffic."[39] Some of these Google referral sites and their referral percentage include Google Search (45 %), Gmail (17 %), YouTube (6 %), Google Maps (2 %), and Google docs (2 %). Also, a possible significant source of future Google+ users is the more than 3.5 million Android mobile devices that are activated each week.

Most social media junkies have explored Google+. Its interface has plenty of white space, incorporating the simplicity that graphically unifies Google's other products. Google+ incorporates many social media features with its own clearly unique twists. For example, Circles organizes connections by interest or intimacy...your choice: simply 'drag and drop'. One can also message and video chat through Circles and a new Hangout feature. The navigation bar at the top of page is consistent across all products, displays notifications, and is a portal to other products.

Data liberation makes it easy to export your data...it's your data! A tiny YouTube tab triggers a simple 'what would you like to play?' query. Google+ supports games, brand pages and a nifty 'send feedback' button. Most significantly, Google+ recently added social searching to its flagship search engine. This feature serves up searches with relevant ties to links, photos, and posts of one's friends or noteworthy individuals provided their privacy settings allow.

Does Google+ offer enough clearly distinct features that add value to the social media ecosystem? Some argue that it doesn't matter. "Can Google gain number one, or at least a number two market share of social media users? Will your parents,

---

[37] Albanesius (2012).
[38] Allen (2011).
[39] Dougherty (2011b).

non social media marketing friends and average Facebook users REALLY switch to anything?" asks Bundlepost founder Robert M. Caruso.[40]

On the other hand there seems to be something qualitatively distinct about the Google+ experience. It does support conversations or dialogues about issues through threads, or posts, that are quantitatively different from the several word comments on Facebook. For example, the media researchers Jeff Jarvis and Dan Gillmor listed in Table 4 regularly engage in multi-user discussions through 50–100 word paragraphs about innovations and ideas.[41]

6   Discussion

One could argue that with a worldwide penetration level of 85 %, the 'staggering' days of growth in new users of social media are over. Last year the growth in new users of social media declined to 10 % in the U.S. A slowdown in the penetration growth at the global level is next. Today, Internet users are convinced about the value of social media: they know it's useful and entertaining. The category is established, and the low hanging fruit have all been picked: now it's time for brand building and product differentiation.

Most of the engaged social media users have largely built their social networks, and these individual networks are portable. With a little ingenuity the engaged social media user can take her network to the 'next big thing.'

Is Google+ the next big thing?

Facebook enjoys the status of frontrunner, and it overwhelmingly dominates the category in every metric: number of users, time spent on site, revenue, number of likes, photos, comments, etc. It's huge, but is it invincible?

First, consider its size. Facebook is big but not crushing when its $4.3 billion in revenue is compared to Yahoo!'s $6.3 billion, Ebay's $9.2 billion, Apple's $28.3 billion, Amazon's $34.2 billion, Google's $35 billion and Microsoft's $69.9 billion. Its $1 billion in profits is about one month's profit at Google, and its 3,000 employees are less than 10 % of Google's 35,000 global workforce. And Google's $46 billion cash reserves is more than 4 times what Facebook may raise through its IPO.

Next, consider its product mix. One could argue that Facebook is a one trick pony. Admittedly, it's one heck of a trick and it's playing to a huge global audience of 700 million users, but aside from changing one's status, commenting on a friend's post or photo, liking someone else's content and sending a few private messages, how essential is Facebook anyway? How easily could one live without it? Could the 'novelty factor' fade over time?

---

[40] Caruso (2011).
[41] Ganahl (2011c).

And what about the Facebook brand: what does it really mean to its users? How loyal are they, and how deeply do they trust Facebook? What are the users' real concerns about privacy, and the decisions Facebook may ultimately make regarding the monetization of their personal information? Remember how Jesse Eisenberg portrayed Mark Zuckerberg in the movie *The Social Network*? Did you empathize with that character? How likely is it that Mark Zuckerberg will become a cultural icon on par with Steve Jobs?

Finally, how important is the coming mobile revolution to the social media category? If 30 % of all social media engagement is mobile-driven now, what role will mobile play in 2 years? 5 years? How ready is Facebook for this platform transformation, and how will Timeline look on the third screen? Does the mobile Apple iOS depend on Facebook? Does Android's Ice Cream Sandwich depend on Facebook? Will Buffy slay the two vampires?

But is Google+ positioned to be David to Facebook's Goliath?

First, consider the many advantages Google has: its size, its depth and its product diversity. It's a corporate giant: large in revenue, deep in profits, dominate in market share. But does its size inhibit its entrepreneurial energy? Has it become too big to be innovative, or can it match the nimbleness of its much smaller, hungrier competitors? Has the corporate model of consensus and collaboration dulled its fighting instincts? Is it so focused on the big picture that it can't catch a glimpse of an epiphany's moment of emergence?

Of course, Google has many successful web-based products (over 100!) including a browser, a search engine, an email system, maps, video and photo hosting, and blogging. But, are all these products necessarily essential to a social media franchise? Do they constitute a genuine synergy, or do they keep Google from concentrating on the essential parts? Is it really connecting the dots, or, are the dots just taking Google all over the page?

And is the Google brand any warmer, any more trustworthy than the Facebook brand? What kind of personality does the iconic interface of Google search have anyway? Does it seem sort of *logarithm-tic*? Do we have more affinity for a company that wants to, "organize the world's information and make it universally accessible and useful," than we do for a company that wants, "to give people the power to share and make the world more open and connected?" How do we feel about its founders Larry Page and Sergey Brin? Do we even know them?

Finally, Google does seem better poised to ride the coming wave of the mobile revolution. Not only is it riding the wave, it's helping create the wave. When Google released the Android OS as an open sourced operating system for mobile devices it dedicated itself to promoting open standards among the mobile device manufacturers. Today, the Android OS platform powers almost 50 % of the U.S. mobile devices. But, does managing the Android OS make Google any more ready to be a mobile device manufacturer? Is Google the search engine company ready to be Google the phone maker? And, what does it all mean to Google+ anyway?

After Facebook launched in 2004 it took more than 4 years to reach over 100 million unique visitors and surpass the 5 year-old social media leader MySpace in April 2008. The real irony of this Facebook milestone is that the majority of its growth was in international users and less than 33 % of its users were domestic! In April 2008 MySpace still led Facebook in U.S. visitors. TechCrunch reports, "MySpace still dominates Facebook in the U.S. market with 72 million monthly uniques. Facebook has 36 million monthly uniques...at this rate it will take 4+ years for Facebook to catch up to MySpace in the U.S. market."[42]

Fast-forward to today's Facebook and Google+ social media war. If history is prelude to the present, might Google+ lead Facebook in December 2015? Possibly. War's window can be lengthy and more than a matter of months. There is room for both websites in the social media war. It's not necessarily a zero-sum game where one company wins and the other looses. Technology companies can be remarkably resilient, and their markets can be extraordinarily flexible. Remember how defeated Apple seemed just a few years ago?

But this is the age of 'staggering' change: it's the age of social media. Most likely its next iteration is being written right now in a dorm room or in a rented garage by some young visionary on her laptop: "the next disrupters have yet to be decided...reflecting the inherent volatility... in an industry that thrives on the power of the network effect."[43]

References

Albanesius, C. (2012). Google+ traffic jumps 55 percent in December. *PC Magazine*. Retrieved January 5, 2012, from http://www.pcmag.com/article2/0,2817,2398300,00.asp

Allen, P. (2011). *Google+ growth accelerating*. Paul Allen Google+ Personal Page. Retrieved January 5, 2012, from https://plus.google.com/u/0/117388252776312694644/posts

Arrington, M. (2008). *Facebook no longer the second largest social network*. TechCrunch. Retrieved January 2, 2012, from http://techcrunch.com/2008/06/12/facebook-no-longer-the-second-largest-social-network/

Boyd, D. M., & Ellison, N. B. (2007). Social networksites: Definition, history, and scholarship. *Journal of Computer-Mediated Communication*. Retrieved November 15, 2011, from http://www.comscore.com/Press_Events/Press_Releases/2011/12/comScore_Media_Metrix_Ranks_Top_50_U.S._Web_Properties_for_November_2011

Brownlow, M. (2011). *Email and webmail statistics*. Email Marketing Reports. Retrieved November 15, 2011, from http://www.email-marketing-reports.com/metrics/email-statistics.htm

Burnham, K. (2011). *Recap: Facebook's biggest F8 announcements*. CIO Blogs. Retrieved October 15, 2011, from http://blogs.cio.com/web-20/16520/recap-facebooks-biggest-f8-announcements

Caruso, J. (2011). *Facebook* vs. *Google+* vs. *Twitter* vs. *LinkedIn*. NetWorkWorld. Retrieved November 15, 2011, from http://www.networkworld.com/news/2011/102111-tech-argument-google-facebook-twitter-linnkedin-252279.html

Caruso, R. M. (2011). *Business is about market share—Google+ brand pages*. Bundlepost. Retrieved December 15, 2011, from http://bundlepost.wordpress.com/2011/11/09/business-is-about-market-share-google-plus-brand-pages/

---

[42] Arrington (2008).
[43] ComScore, p. 17.

ComScore. (2011a). *It's a social world: Top 10 need-to-knows*. ComScore. Retrieved January 10, 2011, from http://www.comscore.com/Press_Events/Presentations_Whitepapers/2011/it_is_a_social_world_top_10_need-to-knows_about_social_networking

ComScore. (2011b). *ComScore reports November 2011 U.S. mobile subscriber market share*. ComScore. Retrieved December 15, 2011, from http://www.comscore.com/Press_Events/Press_Releases/2011/12/comScore_Reports_November_2011_U.S._Mobile_Subscriber_Market_Share

Dougherty, H. (2011a). *Where we reach out when life happens*. Experian Hitwise. Retrieved October 15, 2011, from http://weblogs.hitwise.com/heather-dougherty/2011/09/facebook_where_we_reach_out_wh.html

Dougherty, H. (2011b). *Google+ records 3rd biggest week since launch*. Experian Hitwise. Retrieved December 15, 2011, from http://weblogs.hitwise.com/heather-dougherty/2011/11/google_records_3rd_biggest_wee_1.html

Experian Hitwise. (2011). *Top 10 websites*. Experian Hitwise. Retrieved December 15, 2011, from http://www.hitwise.com/us/datacenter/main/dashboard-10133.html

Facebook. (2011). *Company statistics*. Facebook. Retrieved November 15, 2011, from http://www.facebook.com/press/info.php?statistics

Ganahl, R. J. (2011a). [Lady Gaga's use of social media]. Unpublished raw data.

Ganahl, R. J. (2011b). [User comments following Timeline release]. Unpublished raw data.

Ganahl, R. J. (2011c). [Analysis of Google+ comment pages]. Unpublished raw data.

Gannes, L., & Fried, I. (2011). *The Facebook phone: It's finally real and its name is buffy*. All Things D. Retrieved December 15, 2011, from http://allthingsd.com/20111121/the-facebook-phone-its-finally-real-and-its-name-is-buffy/

Google. (2011). *2011 financial tables*. Google. Retrieved November 15, 2011, from http://investor.google.com/financial/tables.html

IMBd. (2010).*The social network*. IMBd. Retrieved December 1, 2011, from http://www.imdb.com/title/tt1285016/

Kallas, P. (2011). *Top 10 social networking sites & forums*. Retrieved December 15, 2011, from http://www.dreamgrow.com/top-10-social-networking-sites-by-market-share-of-visits-and-google-november-2011/

MacMillan, D., & Womack, B. (2011). *Facebook said to plan IPO at a $100B valuation*. Bloomberg. Retrieved December 1, 2011, from http://www.bloomberg.com/news/2011-11-29/facebook-said-to-plan-10-billion-ipo-with-100-billion-of-social-network.html

Mathias, A. (2007).The Fakebook generation. *The New York Times*. Retrieved October 22, 2011, from http://www.nytimes.com/2007/10/06/opinion/06mathias.html

Nielsen. (2011). *State of the Media: The Social Media Report Q32011*. Nielsen. Retrieved December 15, 2011.http://blog.nielsen.com/nielsenwire/social/

Pew Internet & American Life Project. (2011). *65 % of online adults use social networking sites*. Pew Research Center. Retrieved December 1, 2011, from http://www.pewinternet.org/~/media//Files/Reports/2011/PIP-SNS-Update-2011.pdf

Raice, S. (2011). Facebook targets huge IPO. *Wall Street Journal*. Retrieved December 1, 2011, from http://online.wsj.com/article/SB10001424052970203935604577066773790883672.html

Rusli, E. M., & Miller, C. C. (2011). Google to buy Motorola mobility for 412.5 billion. *The New York Times*. Retrieved November 15, 2011, from http://dealbook.nytimes.com/2011/08/15/google-to-buy-motorola-mobility/

StatCounter. (2011) *Chrome 15 becomes world's most popular browser*. StatCounter. Retrieved January 5, 2012, from http://gs.statcounter.com/press/chrome-15-becomes-worlds-most-popular-browser

StatCounter. (2012). *StatCounter global stats*. StatCounter. Retrieved January 5, 2012, from http://www.dreamgrow.com/wp-content/uploads/2011/12/top-10-social-networking-sites-by-market-share-of-visits-november-2011.pdf

Wolverton, T. (2011). *Zynga rakes in $1 billion in IPO, then sees stock fall in market deput.* MercuryNews.com. Retrieved December 28, 2011, from http://www.mercurynews.com/venture-capital/ci_19561894

Womack, B. (2011). *Facebook revenue will reach $4.27 billion.* Bloomberg. Retrieved October 15, 2011, from http://www.bloomberg.com/news/2011-09-20/facebook-revenue-will-reach-4-27-billion-emarketer-says-1-.html

Worthham, J. (2011).The Facebook resisters. *The New York Times.* Retrieved December 15, 2011, from http://learning.blogs.nytimes.com/2011/12/15/would-you-consider-deleting-your-facebook-account/?scp=6&sq=facebook&st=cse

Applications for the Media Sector to Leverage Content in Social Networks

Jochen Spangenberg and Birgit Gray

1 Business Challenges

1.1 Social Media as a Content Resource

The continued growth of Social Media has led to a significant increase in user-created content within social networking sites. This is not only the case in terms of volume, but also concerns diversity, media types, quality and societal relevance of contributions. User-created content that is found in Social Media now also originates from professional or semi-professional sources. These include: media companies, public relations agencies, governments, news organisations, media professionals, photographers, political activists or citizen journalists. In addition, there is the traditional Social Media material related to peoples' everyday lives and opinions, which can contribute to various types of media output, audience interaction, interactive programming and new forms of journalistic storytelling.

As a result, but to varying degrees, journalists are now actively sourcing background information and content items such as photos or videos from Social Media. Initially, the priority was on breaking news and regions or events difficult to access due to political constraints or because of natural disasters. This has continuously expanded. The content from social networking sites is nowadays also used for wider journalistic application areas and the development of new forms of content. The concept of Social Journalism describes these new tendencies and opportunities (see Sect. 2).

J. Spangenberg (✉) • B. Gray
Deutsche Welle (DW), Berlin, Germany
e-mail: Jochen-Spangenberg@edu.du

1.2 Issues for the Media Sector

The situation outlined above represents new business challenges for content producers in the electronic media sector. Journalists require dedicated tools in order to effectively access, view, assess, harvest and use content (which may imply its purchase) in social networking sites.

One problem is the sheer volume of content that journalists have to deal with across major social networks such as Twitter, Facebook, YouTube or Flickr. This is illustrated by the following figures:

- The number of tweets posted on Twitter rose from one billion in November 2008 to ten billion in March 2010.[1] In February 2011, an average of 140 million tweets were posted daily, and it took all users merely 1 week to post one billion tweets.[2] Top events in the year 2011 achieved more than 7,000 tweets per second (e.g. the MTV Music Awards on 28 August 2011 reaching 8,668 tweets per second, and the death of Steve Jobs being tweeted on average at a rate of about 6,049 times per second on 6 October 2011).[3]
- At the end of 2011, Facebook had more than 800 million active users, according to the company's own statistics. More than 50 per cent of these active users log into the social network on a daily basis, so the Palo Alto-based company claims. On average, more than 250 million photos are uploaded to Facebook every day.[4]
- According to official YouTube figures of early January 2012, 48 h of video were uploaded to YouTube per minute. That equals 8 years of content uploaded every day or 240,000 full-length films every week.[5]
- In 2008, Flickr had 27.5 million monthly visitors. By the end of that year, a total of three billion images had been uploaded. According to Flickr, by mid September 2010 the photo sharing site had increased the number of hosted images to more than five billion. With regard to the total Flickr user base this implies that, on average, Flickr members are uploading more than 3,000 images per minute to the site.[6]

The above figures clearly illustrate that significant volumes of data and information are added to social networking sites on a daily basis. This represents a vast

---

[1] See Mashable.com (http://on.mash.to/9yWbSI: *Twitter hits 10 billion tweets*, by Ben Parr, dated 5 March 2010—last accessed on 29 May 2012).

[2] Based on information on the Twitter blog (http://bit.ly/hqStPu—last accessed on 29 May 2012).

[3] See http://yearinreview.twitter.com/en/tps.html. The "hottest topics" of the year 2011 can be found on http://yearinreview.twitter.com/en/hottopics.html (both sites were last accessed on 29 May 2012).

[4] Based on information provided by Facebook (see http://on.fb.me/a4QL5X—last accessed on 3 January 2012).

[5] Based on information provided on the YouTube blog (see http://bit.ly/gzYBVx—last accessed on 2 January 2012).

[6] See scribd.com (http://scr.bi/FneRj—last accessed on 2 January 2012) and information provided on the Flickr blog (http://bit.ly/do1VUC—last accessed on 2 January 2012).

potential resource for journalists and media organisations. Consequently, further business challenges related to what we term Social Journalism are the verification of media items, the clearing of intellectual property rights and the assessment of reliability of both content and social networking users, to name but a few of those new tasks that have to be addressed by media outlets today. Journalists also need to detect content related to events as they unfold.

The array of social media tools currently available can support processes such as social media management, search, mashups or publishing. However, they are usually not specifically designed for journalists and do not serve their particular workflows and processes. Given tools are usually related to a particular social network (the most popular being Twitter), rather than providing access across relevant networks in a seamless, integrated way, also functioning in a content or topic-centric way.[7]

1.3 Towards a Solution with SocIoS

At present, journalistic research and newsgathering across social networks is a cumbersome and time consuming task that often has to be abandoned due to budget or time constraints.

With this as a baseline, Germany's international broadcaster Deutsche Welle developed a use case in the EC co-funded project SocIoS, which aims to address some of the business challenges mentioned above (for more details see also Sect. 5). It leverages the opportunities provided by the SocIoS platform that is to be developed. SocIoS aims to provide easy access to content across several social networking sites for both professional and non-professional web users. This includes non-technical end users in the networked media industry such as journalists and other media professionals. SocIoS is based on the notion of service composition in a service oriented architecture, allowing for fast and simple application development, also by non-professional end users.

---

[7] Most auxiliary analysis tools have been designed for Twitter, e.g. Twiangulate (http://www.twiangulate.com) for analysing various Twitter accounts, Monitter (http://www.monitter.com) a real-time search and trending topic tool, Tweet Grader for measuring account holders' influence across the Twitter universe (http://tweet.grader.com) or Trendsmap (http://trendsmap.com/) a tool for real-time mapping and visualisation of Twitter trends across the world. One of the most popular auxiliary tools that works across individual networks is Tweetdeck (http://www.tweedeck.com), a dashboard-like system acquired by Twitter in 2011. It functions like a Social Media Content Management System for Twitter and other social networks. Hootsuite is a web-based system that allows the monitoring and posting to multiple social networks, including Facebook and Twitter, using the HootSuite dashboard (see http://www.hootsuite.com). All sites mentioned were last accessed on 8 January 2012.

Note: Readers who are interested in obtaining a list of further tools that are suitable for social network management and analysis can do so by contacting the authors of this paper.

Based on Deutsche Welle's user requirements in the context of Social Journalism, the SocIoS project develops a specific SocIoS application for Deutsche Welle and the media sector. Another commercial use case in the project will demonstrate the use of the platform for the production of television commercials, with a focus on casting and location scouting.[8]

In the sections that follow, key aspects related to Deutsche Welle's use case in the SocIoS project are described.[9] This includes the market context of Social Journalism (Sect. 2), respective requirements of journalists and those working in the media business (Sect. 3) and social media applications available in the market today (Sect. 4). Section 5 presents the SocIoS project, the planned SocIoS platform and key activities that journalists are to conduct with the planned SocIoS application for the media sector.

2 Social Journalism

The digital age is transforming the media industry in almost every aspect. This includes workflows and new forms of content related to *original* journalism, which is based on independent fact finding rather than content aggregation. In particular news media are changing rapidly with regard to digital sourcing, reporting, aggregation, distribution and sharing. One of the changes in news media has been coined by the phrase: "We no longer search for the news—the news finds us."[10]

2.1 A New Form of Journalism

Digital Journalism or Online Journalism are now common concepts and well established in producer media organisations. An emerging concept is Social Journalism, referring to both sourcing from and publishing in social networking sites.

---

[8] The second use case in the SocIoS Project is managed by Stefi Productions S.A., based in Athens, Greece.

[9] Although the use case and requirements that have been formulated and developed as part of the SocIoS project are based largely on the particular situation that exists at Deutsche Welle, much is also valid for other media organisations. (As part of the project work, the DW project team conducted interviews with Deutsche Welle staff, freelance journalists and employees of other media organisations such as SWR, ZDF, BBC and DR).

[10] This quote is often attributed to Jeff Jarvis, Professor at New York's City University, author of the blog buzzmachine (http://www.buzzmachine.com/) and the book "What would Google do?", published by Harper Collins, New York, 2009.

Someone who has written extensively on the subject of news and Social Media, paired with practical experience is Nic Newman. Nic is a founding member of the BBC News Website and played an important part in the development of social media strategies and guidelines for the wider BBC. He is currently (early 2012) a Visiting Fellow at the Reuters Institute for the Study of Journalism. See for example his contribution "How the news finds you..." on http://bbc.in/q6f05j (last accessed on 29 May 2012) and Newman (2011).

The borders between these two areas become increasingly blurred as more new forms of sourcing, reporting, storytelling and publishing emerge.

Social Journalism addresses the popularity of social networks, their increasing societal relevance, the ever growing volumes of content within them and the social graphs created by their members. The societal and hence journalistic relevance of content in social networking sites has recently been highlighted by the revolutions in Iran, Egypt and Tunisia, as well as the earthquakes in Haiti and Japan, or the unrests in Syria. Media reports about these events entailed significant proportions of user generated content from social networking sites. Media companies often relied on users' videos and images, as access on the ground was often limited or at least difficult.

2.2 Sourcing in Social Networks

A key aspect of Social Journalism is related to research and newsgathering (the process of 'sourcing'). It entails:
- Researching and cross-checking facts;
- Finding images and audiovisual material;
- Establishing networks of peers/trusted sources;
- Contacting (eye)witnesses or experts;
- Discovering trends for further investigation;
- Assessing particular moods or sentiments.

The challenge for journalists is to find, access, filter, verify and clear the information of relevance in particular situations and for particular tasks.

More and more traditional media companies have integrated Social Media into their day-to-day operations, or are in the process of doing so.[11] The British Broadcasting Corporation (BBC), was one of the first media organisations to establish a unit that deals primarily with user-generated content, named appropriately "User-Generated-Content Hub". Originally launched on a trial basis in 2005 by a small team, it continuously rose in importance. Nowadays, it is an essential (and central) part of the BBC's news operations. A key task of the unit is to find, filter and verify content that is published in social networking sites for use in BBC journalism.[12] A statement made by Peter Horrocks shortly after he took over as

---

[11] An interesting insight including case studies that outline how German media organisations ARD and ZDF, the British BBC and the German newspaper "Rhein-Zeitung" deal with Social Media in their daily journalistic routine is provided in Bouhs (2011).

[12] For an observational study on how the BBC deals with user-generated content (UGC) see Harrison (2010). An insight interview of Jonathan Stray/Nieman Journalism Lab with Silvia Costeloe of the BBC's UGC Hub can be found at http://www.niemanlab.org/2010/05/drawing-out-the-audience-inside-bbc%E2%80%99s-user-generated-content-hub/ (*Drawing out the audience: Inside BBC's User-Generated Content Hub*, by Jonathan Stray, dated 5 May 2010. Last accessed on 29 May 2012. See also Wardle and Williams (2008). Part of the assessments made here are also based on interviews Jochen Spangenberg conducted with staff of the BBC's UGC Hub in December 2011, in particular its Head Chris Hamilton.

Director of BBC Global News in early 2010 shows how important content from social networks is for Britain's public service broadcaster. In the BBC's in-house magazine Ariel, he told BBC staff to use social media as a primary source of information. "This isn't just a kind of fad from someone who's an enthusiast of technology. I'm afraid you're not doing your job if you can't do those things. It's not discretionary."[13]

When it comes to sourcing content from Social Networks, Twitter has been used by journalists for some time now. Growing usage tendencies can be observed, with more and more journalists discovering Twitter's usefulness as an alternative source in the information gathering process, often the first one and particularly relevant for eye-witness material. Facebook is becoming more relevant for similar purposes, but seems to be more useful for the better understanding of public opinion. Ian Shapira, staff writer at The Washington Post, describes the role of Facebook as follows: "Facebook has dramatically transformed the way journalists do their jobs. It's become an essential tool, making our jobs far more efficient."[14]

2.3 Publishing in Social Networks

Social networks are equally used by journalists for creation and publishing purposes. They enable near real-time publishing, new forms of content, interactive programming, deeper audience engagement, co-produced programming, as well as new forms of storytelling. Most media organisations and many individual journalists publish in Twitter, Facebook and YouTube, to name but a few. This includes both traditional content and specific services for social media platforms. An increasing proportion of media output now has a social aspect, component or context. This is driven further by emerging two-screen applications and formats, as well as participatory programming concepts with a social media focus.

Some news media organisations have dedicated online services that are co-produced with users and largely contain user-generated content. Examples are CNN's "iReport"[15] or France 24's "Les Observateurs".[16] These offerings provide material that can otherwise be difficult to obtain. Such offers also enhance user engagement and tie users more closely to the media brand.

---

[13] Peter Horrocks quoted in The Guardian on 10 February 2010 (*BBC tells news staff to embrace social media*. Available on http://bit.ly/9GVfPQ). An interview of The Guardian with Peter Horrocks can be found on http://bit.ly/cZpEsV (*Q&A: BBC World Service director Peter Horrocks on social media and news.*) Both links were last accessed on 29 May 2012.

[14] Ian Shapira quoted on mashable.com: *Facebook's growing role in Social Journalism* by Vadim Lavrusek, dated 27 February 2011. (See http://on.mash.to/hLKMzy—last accessed on 29 May 2012.)

[15] See http://ireport.cnn.com/ (last accessed on 7 January 2012).

[16] See http://observers.france24.com/ (last accessed on 7 January 2012).

In April 2011, the international television channel Al Jazeera launched a new service called "The Stream".[17] The service actively uses content from its audience that is contributed via Twitter, Facebook and YouTube posts, and encourages viewers to interact live with the show while it is broadcast, as well as before and after the screening, via Al Jazeera's website.

"The Stream" is created with Storify,[18] a new tool that is also used by the Washington Post, National Public Radio (NPR) and other companies. Storify can support digital interactive storytelling, including content from social networks. According to Andy Carvin, senior strategist on NPR's social media desk: "There's a big need for tools that allow people to collect bits of social media context and organise them in some fashion."[19]

3 User Requirements

Developments in Social Media and the specific context of Social Journalism result in a number of business challenges and respective requirements for producer media companies. Journalists need dedicated tools such as web applications and services to better conduct activities that are currently subject to a number of process barriers. These activities include finding, assessing, filtering, verifying and rights-clearing of content in social networks.

3.1 A Vision for 2014

As part of its work in the SocIoS project and with regard to business analysis purposes, a team at Deutsche Welle's Innovation Projects Department (New Media) analysed and defined user requirements related to a scenario entitled "research and newsgathering in social networks". This was performed on the basis of primary and secondary research, including a literary review, desk research and interviews with about 20 journalists from different media organisations, as well as freelancers. The resulting list of user stories and service requirements enabled the creation of an overall "vision" for the SocIoS project. For the technical project partners, this vision illustrated what kind of situations journalists encounter in 2010/11 and what they would like to achieve and have at their disposal by 2014, ideally using platforms such as the one planned by the SocIoS project team.

---

[17] See http://stream.aljazeera.com/ (last accessed on 7 January 2012).
[18] See http://storify.com/ (last accessed on 7 January 2012).
[19] Andy Carvin quoted in the New York Times of 24 April 2011 (see http://nyti.ms/g7f7UT: *Filtering the Social Web to Present News Items*, by Claire Cain Miller, dated 24 April 2011—last accessed on 29 May 2012).

3.2 Issues Encountered by Journalists

At present, journalists are facing a range of problems associated with the use of content in social networks. There is a lack of tools to find the right content for a specific topic or research area in a fast and user-friendly way. Further, journalists often do not have access to tools that structure, aggregate and filter the content found according to their requirements. There are continued questions over general reliability, compared to standard sources for journalists. It takes too long to separate "rubbish" and "gossip" from other relevant contributions. Dealing with the constant repetition of content is also a major problem. The time required to deal with intellectual property issues in social networks is also not satisfactory. For journalists it takes too long to pay content owners for their content items. It is often difficult to relate a content item to a source and, as a result, it often cannot be used. Further, it is often difficult to verify whether a content item is authentic.

3.3 Areas for Support

The user requirements identified by Deutsche Welle were grouped into the following areas, for which journalists require support:
- General time saving functions;
- Integration of existing web applications;
- Searching for specific content for a task;
- Translation of content found;
- Analyzing links within content;
- Assessing the reliability of content found;
- Verifying content found (authenticity);
- Handling IPR issues and IPR payment;
- Creating updates/versions of a story.

They relate to the following workflows: finding content, selecting content, clearing content with regards to intellectual property rights and using content for various products/services.

A fully automated solution is less important, as media organisations will always conduct "human" verification and quality control prior to publishing. However, they require the utmost technological support in a variety of tasks along the value chain.

3.4 Journalistic Needs

A keyword search across social networks (not related to "people/groups") is difficult to achieve. Journalists need dedicated search solutions across networks that focus on real-world events, eye witnesses, topics (keywords), selected relevant social networking users, geographic parameters, original content (items first published), sources/authors and image/video quality.

Due to the specific nature and origin of content in social networks, verification and reliability are also major concerns for journalists. It is important to separate fact from opinion, to assess the reliability of content/users and to verify the authenticity of content items (in particular photos and videos).

Once a suitable content item has been found the IPR status has to be identified and, ideally, IPR payment can be made in near real-time.

Other important aspects are the monitoring of topics/stories over time in order to create updates or versions of a story.

Media companies also need to consider a range of legal issues that are encountered when dealing with content from individuals in social networking sites. The three main areas for consideration are: (1) privacy and data protection, (2) intellectual property rights and (3) issues regarding liability for the user-generated content.[20]

Key sources for journalists are major social networking sites such as Twitter, Facebook, Flickr and YouTube, but also other regional networks such as Orkut or more focused sites such as Vimeo. Content types include among others tweets, posts, comments, profiles, links, images, videos and audios.

4 Tools Available Today

Today, journalists can choose from an array of web-based Social Media tools and applications provided outside the context of social networking sites. In addition, there are applications within Social Media platforms. These web-based applications differ in both complexity and usefulness. They can support both research and publishing in social networks. However, such tools have been designed for web and Social Media users rather than professional journalists. Although useful for some aspects of their work they lack specific journalistic functions and usually relate almost exclusively to Twitter or Facebook.

Currently available tools fall into three main groups: General Social Media tools, Twitter tools and Facebook tools. The majority of tools is related to the social networking site Twitter, comparatively few to Facebook. Some of the Social Media tools enable functions across networks (see also footnote 7).

Social Media tools are largely applied for social network management (e.g. Tweetdeck), social media browsing (e.g. Flock—discontinued in April 2011), link-shortening (e.g. Bit.ly) and Social Media search and publishing (e.g. Storify).

Specific Twitter tools support users in
- Posting tweets;
- Finding content (search);
- Geographic linking of tweets/users across maps;
- Listing of trending topics;

---

[20] The three legal areas for consideration in the SocIoS project context have been identified by the SocIoS partner responsible for legal issues: Katholieke Universiteit Leuven (Belgium).

- User ranking, rating and analysis;
- Content publishing; and
- Image/video posting.

Facebook tools are primarily focused on open profile search and trending topics.

5 The SocIoS Project

The EC co-funded R&D project SocIoS[21] that started in September 2010 aims to develop a platform that enables the building of business applications which leverage user-created content and the social graph of users in social networks. During the project it is planned to deploy *SocIoS Applications* on top of the following social networking sites: Twitter, Facebook, YouTube, DailyMotion, Flickr and sites supporting OpenSocial (e.g. MySpace, Hi5, or LinkedIn). After project completion in 2013 further networks could be added to extend the capabilities of the platform.

The following section covers research related activities that journalists might be able to conduct with a *SocIoS Application* focused on Social Journalism. This application is to be developed in the SocIoS project as a proof-of-concept prototype. The application will be using the technology components provided by the SocIoS platform such as the *SocIoS Software Services* and the *SocIoS API*, which are described in Sect. 5.2.

5.1 The Planned SocIoS Application

At the end of 2012/early 2013 SocIoS aims to deliver implemented applications to its two user partners in the form of a proof-of-concept. *SocIoS End Users* are the consumers of the *SocIoS Applications* for different business purposes. Journalists (e.g. at Deutsche Welle) are to use a SocIoS application, which is designed and built during the project to satisfy their requirements. These are likely to also apply to other producing media companies.

The SocIoS platform requires end users such a journalists to create an account and to log into the SocIoS platform. The "journalism" application will be managed with a specifically created Graphical User Interface (GUI).

During the research project the following activities will be considered for experimentation and—if feasible—for realisation within the SocIos "journalism" application.

---

[21] SocIoS is an EC co-funded 7th Framework Programme project (Project number: 257774. Call identifier FP7-ICT-2009.1.2; Internet of Services, Software and Virtualization), running from 1 Sept 2010 to 28 Feb 2013. For more information see the project homepage on http://www.sociosproject.eu/.

5.1.1 Media Item Search
- Searching by keywords for media items such as photos, videos, audios or text (tweets/posts) across social networking sites;
- Location-specific searching by generic location names or specific longitude and latitude information;
- Previewing related metadata for multimedia items;
- Reviewing multimedia items in full detail (seeing full resolution images, playing video or reading full text) in the respective social networking sites where they were found (as SocIoS only stores metadata);
- Filtering results based on any relevant element from the metadata stored in SocIoS;
- Filtering by unique media items, i.e. exclude re-tweets, re-posts or the same videos;
- Contacting users in case they are the provider of a selected media item;
- Purchasing media items via an effective payment service to be developed (named "FlexiPrice"[22]);
- Requesting media items in the best existing resolution;
- Requesting the translation of a selected media item.

5.1.2 User Search
- Searching for social networking users by providing their username or a generic keyword that is related to the user;
- Grouping social networking users by assigning tags to them, so as to categorise them to a topic;
- Monitoring the latest activities of social networking users (such as status, tweets, photos or videos);
- Requesting profile information of selected social networking users;
- Requesting the "reputation" of a social networking user or view reputation-related information.

5.1.3 Event Detection
- Listing (and ranking) social networking users who are particularly active related to a defined topic in which the end user is interested;
- Monitoring topics in order to detect events related to the topic (unusual or intense social activity);
- Viewing event-related activities (e.g. tweets, photos or status);
- Ordering event-related activities by originality (the first tweet, video or status posted);
- Setting up crowd sourcing games in order to request activities from social networking users related to an event (e.g. eyewitness accounts or images).

---

[22] FlexiPrice is a service/model that is being developed by the University of Haifa (Department of Information and Knowledge Management), Israel, as part of the project work. For further information on prediction markets see also Geifman et al. (2011).

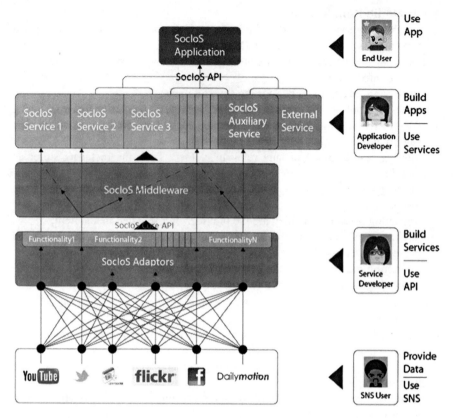

Fig. 1 The SocIoS platform concept

5.2 The SocIoS Platform

The SocIoS platform entails the following key components, which are related to four different user types (social networking users, service developers, application developers and SocIos end users such as journalists) (Fig. 1):
- SocIoS API;
- SocIoS Middleware;
- SocIoS Services;
- SocIoS Applications;
- SocIoS Auxiliary Services.

SocIos API: This is an aggregation of the methods that are provided by the underlying APIs of social networking services such as Twitter, Facebook or Flickr. The SocIoS ontology identifies conceptually common entities and functionalities. The *SocIoS API* allows *SocIoS Developers* to initiate multiple instances of the same functionality to various social networking services by a single call.

SocIoS Middleware: This is the service hosting, provisioning and management environment. SocIoS functionalities at the *SocIoS API* level are being leveraged to a web service level and tools are provided to manage these services.

SocIoS Services: These are the "core" services within the SocIoS platform, which result from the *SocIoS API* functionalities being delivered as a service on the basis of standard web service technologies. They are hosted on the *SocIoS Middleware*. These core services can be used as they are, or by combination.

SocIoS Applications: This is a combined set of *SocIoS Services* to create business-oriented applications to be consumed by commercial end users. These applications utilise user-generated content and social graph information from social networking services. They may combine services external to the *SocIoS Middleware*.

SocIoS Auxiliary Services: These services are more complex and built by combining the core *SocIoS Services* with extra functionalities. Examples are reputation and recommendation services as well as business support services. The aim is to support the larger workflows of the *SocIoS applications*. They are also hosted in the *SocIoS Middleware*.

Conclusion

Today 'Social' Journalism is being discussed as a distinctive aspect of journalism. In a few years time, this is unlikely to be the case. The same happened with 'Online' Journalism which is no longer unusual nor exotic for most journalists and media companies. In the near future both specialised and general journalists will have to use supporting applications in order to address the complex issues presented by Social Journalism, and to successfully source content from Social Media via search, discovery, automatic detection, sentiment-analysis or sharing. These applications will complement and/or replace the array of web-based tools that are available today for general Social Media users. Such applications require complex underlying technological systems, such as the SocIoS platform described in Sects. 1.3 and 5. Eventually, these applications will have to be integrated with advanced content management systems and also entail (near) real-time publishing solutions. Sourcing, aggregation and publishing processes will increasingly converge and happen in (near) real-time. As a result, social and user-generated content is becoming a standard component of many forms of journalistic output.

Higher volumes of relevant and timely content from Social Media sources will not only improve traditional output, but also enable socially oriented material, two-screen applications, participatory social formats, new forms of storytelling and user co-produced services. The latter is central to maintaining existing audiences, gaining new socially oriented audiences and ensuring the media sector's role in a rapidly changing digital media world and the emerging Future Media Internet.

Today, most media companies are establishing new organisational structures and workflows in order to address the challenges presented by Social Journalism. This process will further continue with the deployment of novel tools into existing systems and workflow processes.

Following our analysis of Social Media content development and the *specific* requirements of journalists for the process of research and newsgathering in social networks, we highlight a number of key findings related to the journalistic context at media organsiations that provide news and information services:

- Primarily journalists need tools that enable research and newsgathering *across* major (and other) social networks, with results being displayed on one screen/list.
- Journalists are interested to search, discover and detect information or media items by *topic*, rather than by social network user, group or account parameters. With regard to their given topic journalists need to be able to group the feeds from selected (relevant) social network users/accounts from different social networks.
- New tools have to be *tailored* for the process of research and newsgathering in social networks and designed to meet the specific needs of journalistic workflows and search parameters/approaches.
- Given the time constraints faced by most journalists, these tools/interfaces need to be not only easy to use, but also *priority driven*. These priorities need to be flexible according to the task at hand and defined from a journalistic perspective (e.g. latest status updates first, only items with Creative Commons Licence, only items with high resolution, etc.).
- The most relevant or timely media item found in social networks remains useless unless intellectual property terms, authenticity and veracity can be easily—and for breaking news quickly—established. Journalists need particular support in order to ensure that media items or Social Media accounts are *IPR-cleared, authentic and/or verified*. In the context of IPR-clearing, media organisations are also presented with the challenge to purchase media items from global Social Media sources within a short timeframe.

Acknowledgements This work is supported by the EC co-funded FP 7 project SocIoS (project number: 257774. Call Identifier FP7 ICT 2009.1.2: Internet of Services, Software and Virtualisation. Project duration: 1 September 2010 until 28 February 2013. For more information about the project and its partners see http://www.sociosproject.eu).

The technical descriptions in Sect. 5, in particular the description of the SocIoS platform components, are summarised from and entirely based on project documents written by Dr. Konstantinos Tserpes of the National Technical University of Athens (NTUA), who also acts as project co-ordinator.

Disclosure

The views and findings presented here are those of the named authors. They are not necessarily identical with those of Deutsche Welle, the European Commission or other SocIoS project partner organisations.

References[23]

Bouhs, D. (2011). *Soziale Netzwerke für Nachrichtenjournalisten*. Hamburg: tredition Verlag (ed.: dapd).
Geifman, D., Raban, D. R., & Rafaeli, S. (2011, July 4). P-mart: Towards a classification of online prediction markets. First Monday, 16(7). Available on http://bit.ly/nWICHu – last accessed 29 May 2012.
Harrison, J. (2010). User-generated content and gatekeeping at the BBC. Journalism Studies, *11* (2), 243–256.
Jarvis, J. (2009). *What would Google do?* New York: Harper Collins.
Newman, N. (2011). *Mainstream media and the distribution of news in the age of social discovery*. Oxford: Reuters Institute for the Study of Journalism. Available on http://bit.ly/rbERRJ – last accessed on 29 May 2012.
Wardle, C., & Williams, A. (2008): *UGC@theBBC. Understanding its impact upon contributors, non-contributors and BBC News*. Cardiff University, School of Journalism, Media and Cultural Studies. Available on http://bbc.in/gy9mK – last accessed on 29 May 2012.

---

[23] Please note: Online sources are not listed here. References are given in the respective footnotes.

Star Management of Talent Agencies and Social Media in Korea

Moonhaeng Lee

1 Introduction

In the early 2000s, Korean Wave (hallyu),[1] which refers to a phenomenon of Korean pop culture being all the rage abroad, was characterized by scenes of middle-aged housewives from East Asian countries chasing after Korean actors whom they were enamored of from watching television. Now, Korean pop music, or K-pop, has become the centerpiece of the Korean Wave, and it is largely enjoyed by teenagers around the World, not just in Asia (Noh 2011).

In 2008, Korea's biggest K-pop export TVXQ (Tohoshinki) made it in the Guinness World Records[2] for having the world's largest official fan club. *Cassiopeia*, the band's official fan club, has more than 800,000 official members just in South Korea, more than 200,000 official members in Japan (BigEast) and more than 200,000 international

---

[1] The Korean Wave, also known as the Hallyu, refers to the spread of South Korean culture around the world. The term was coined in China in mid-1999 by Beijing journalists surprised by the fast growing popularity of Korean entertainment and culture in China. Since the late 1990s, hallyu (Korean Wave) has become one of the most frequently used terms in both the popular culture industry and the related academic fields in Asia. The Korean wave is responsible for achieving over one billion dollars in revenue annually for South Korea through cultural exports (Kim, Sue-young, 2008). For further explanation on hallyu, see Chua Beng Huat and Koichi Iwabuchi, "Introduction: East Asian TV Dramas: Identifications, Sentiments and Effects," in East Asian Pop Culture: Analyzing the Korean Wave, ed. Chua Beng Huat and Koichi Iwabuchi (Hong Kong: Hong Kong University Press, 2008), 1–12.

[2] Guinness World Records, known until 2000 as The Guinness Book of Records (and in previous U.S. editions as The Guinness Book of World Records), is a reference book published annually, containing a collection of world records, both human achievements and the extremes of the natural world. The book itself holds a world record, as the best-selling copyrighted book series of all time. It is also one of the most frequently stolen books from public libraries in the United States (Wikipedia).

M. Lee (✉)
University of Suwon, Hwaseong, Gyeonggi Province, South Korea
e-mail: moonhlee@suwon.ac.kr

fans (iCassies). They also made the Guinness World Records a second time in 2009. Aside from having the world's largest fan club, the group was also listed as the most photographed celebrities in the world. From the day of their debut to March 19, 2009, the five members are estimated to have been photographed about 500 million times in magazines, albums jackets, and commercials, etc. The total figure includes individual photos as well as group pictures (KBS World. March 24, 2009; Noh 2011).

Recently, Korean mass media report a series of noticeable phenomena of Korean Wave in relation to K-pop music: the success of SM Entertainment's Paris Tour (Lee, Jong-hoon and Kang, Eun-ji 2011); international Flash mobs in LA, New York, and Buenos Aires to demand K-pop artists' tour (Yonhap 2011a; Kim Won-kyeom 2011a; Yonhap 2011c; NewEn 2011); US K-pop fans visit Korea (Yonhap 20116); and Soshified, the US fan group of Girls' Generation, celebrate the fourth anniversary of Girls' Generation's debut through a huge electronic board in LA (Kim, Won-kyeom 2011b). Among them, one article indicates that YouTube has contributed to the diffusion of K-pop and the construction of fan communities of K-pop idols (Shin, Nari 2011).

This new stage of Korean Wave, transnational diffusion of K-pop, is partly an outcome of socio-technological turns, including YouTube. The rise of new technology such as file-sharing and VOD (video on demand) almost outdated compact disk-based media usage in the last decade. Some research reveals also that social network service such as twitter has also contributed to the exposure of K-pop to international popular music fans (Noh 2011).

2   K-POP and YouTube[3]

Korean pop music, referred to as K-pop (an abbreviation of Korean pop), has become a large part of the Korean Wave (Heo 2011; Pravattiyagul 2011). In recent years, Korean entertainment companies have started to recognize YouTube as a key

---

[3] The two key factors empower the current K-pop phenomenon that exemplifies the rapid transformation of the global cultural market and industry landscape. On June 10 and 11, 2011, "SM Town Live in Paris" was held at Le Zenith de Paris concert hall in France. Five K-pop bands from SM stable (TVXQ, SNSD, Super Junior, f(x), and SHINee) held their first concert in a European city and attracted more than 14,000 fans from across Europe. While initially only scheduling one show on June 10, SM were forced to add another after the tickets to the first concert sold out in 15 min, and hundreds of French fans responded in protest via performing a dance flashmob in front of the Louvre Museum. In my earlier studies, I mentioned that K-pop is still marginalized and "it is still very rare to experience Korean popular culture on an everyday basis in any single city outside Asia." This comment is still true to some degree, the situation is somewhat different in June 2011. The successful SM Town Live in Paris concerts suggest how the global pop market landscape is changing dramatically, and K-pop may cross the cultural borders (between East and West) with ease. Many media commentators have observed how the European fans at the concert were able to sing along to the K-pop songs even though they have not been officially released in Europe. The leader of Super Junior, Lee Teuk, stated, "I think K-pop is gaining popularity thanks to SM's global system, foreign composers and choreographers, and the singers' appearances ... it was also

component to the international spread of Korean culture (Yoon 2011). According to Bernie Cho, president of a Seoul-based agency specializing in the marketing of international K-pop acts, the entertainment companies are "aggressively steering their efforts to go international via the Internet" (Yoon 2010).

With its slogan Broadcast Yourself, YouTube, created in February 2005, was considered an embodiment of digital empowerment of the individual. When the American newsmagazine Time lauded 'You' for its annual 'Person of the Year' issue at the end of 2006, it addressed YouTube as an exemplary element in the democratic digital revolution, emphasizing its grassroots origin and participatory culture (Grossman 2006). Receiving hundreds of millions of views a day, YouTube is ranked as the third most visited website on the Internet, only behind Google and Facebook (Alexa 2010). As such, YouTube has become one of the most important sub-cultural centers of today's new media age.

After Google bought YouTube in November 2006, however, media corporations have become official YouTube users, being able to showcase their content directly to individual users through their YouTube channels. They also make good use of YouTube's social networking services so that their channel subscribers post message and get alert for new music videos (Browers 2008). YouTube's global reach and easy access also led major talent agencies/recording labels in Korea including SM entertainment (SM, hereafter) and YG entertainment (YG, hereafter) launch their channels on YouTube to advertise their artistes globally. This commercial infiltration is a strategic move for the media corporations to incorporate the participatory practices of active fans. With their enthusiastic dedication, close textual readings and growing numbers due to easier access to YouTube, active audiences are recognized as significant fan base. In the end, these active fans become 'agents of consecration' (Bourdieu 1993) who show loyalty to and possess particular knowledge of their stars (Noh 2011).

Since opening in August 2006, SM's official YouTube channel has recorded more than 502 million for the number of music video views and more than 14.8 million for the number of channel visits until 5 August 2011 (YouTube 2011). According to an executive of YG, 'YouTube is important in disseminating K-Pop. Especially, YouTube has an advantage in providing realtime responses' (Ko 2010). Recently, many international news media report that the Internet and video-sharing websites such as YouTube have facilitated the global spread of K-pop fandom (Jeong 2011a; Ramstad 2011; Yoon 2010). Tables 1 and 2 below show the global composition of YouTube users who have seen 923 K-pop music videos uploaded by the three major Korean talent agencies, i.e., SM, JYP, and YG, in the period of

---

helped by social networking sites, such as YouTube." As Lee Teuk clearly identifies here, the globalization and chogukjeok strategies of the Korean entertainment sector and the development of new media technologies have enabled the increasing global circulation of K-pop (Jung 2011).

Late last year, when a major Korean television station MBC (Munhwa Broadcasting Company) initiated a new talent search show, it made a strategic alliance with YouTube. In this sense, it seems that media corporations continue to hold a dominant position into the new media age by having collaboration with active fans (NOH Kwang Woo 2011).

Table 1 Views of K-pop music videos on YouTube (by continent)

Continent	Views	Continent	Views
Asia	566,273,899	Middle East	15,197,593
North America	123,475,976	Oceania	10,738,793
Europe	55,374,142	Africa	1,924,480
South America	20,589,095	South Pole	27

Source: Jeong (2011b) and Noh (2011)

Table 2 Views of K-pop music videos on YouTube (by country)

Country	Views	Country	Views
Japan	113,543,684	Saudi Arabia	10,312,005
Thailand	99,514,297	France	9,707,334
USA	94,876,024	Australia	9,358,642
Taiwan	73,160,633	UK	8,278,441
Korea	57,281,182	Brazil	6,049,920
Vietnam	56,770,902	Germany	5,588,687
Philippines	38,833,639	Russia	1,287,345
Canada	20,859,251	Egypt	630,000

Source: Jeong (2011b) and Noh (2011)

2010. Registered users have to upload their own personal information onto the YouTube database.

As shown in the tables above compiled by the Joong-Ang Daily (Jeong 2011b), the total number of views of K-pop videos by the netizens in 229 countries was around 793.5 million. As noted, the reach of K-pop fandom is not restricted to Asia. What is noteworthy is that non-Asian countries such as USA, Canada, Saudi Arabia and France are ranked among top ten countries of K-pop video views on YouTube (Noh 2011).

3   Talent agencies in Korea: Case of SM Entertainment

With spreading of Korean popular music (K-POP) around the whole Asia and in Europe, the idol star management of Korean talent agencies has become the center of focus. In fact, it is because the agencies play a major role in developing and spreading of Korean wave.

S.M. is an independent Korean record label, talent agency, producer, and publisher of pop music, founded by Lee Soo-man in South Korea. Initially, "SM" was an abbreviation of the agency founder's name, but now stands for "Star Museum." Once the home to top-selling groups such as H.O.T., S.E.S., and Shinhwa, its current roster of recording artists include top selling artists in Korean entertainment like BoA, f(x), Girls' Generation, The Grace, Kangta, Shinee, Super Junior, TRAX, TVXQ and Zhang Liyin. SM Entertainment also co-publishes Avex Trax releases for Japanese artists such as Ayumi Hamasaki, Namie Amuro, and Koda Kumi, as well as Johnny's Entertainment acts like Arashi and KAT-TUN.

3.1 Major Time Line

In February 1995, SM Entertainment set up its capital fund at ₩50,000,000. In January 1996, SM Entertainment purchased land for a recording site and manufactured its contents for broadcasting companies like KBS, SBS, HBS, KMTV, M-NET. In mid-2000, the company was approved and listed in KOSDAQ.[4] Late that year, SM Entertainment and Avex Trax signed a contract for music licensing and an Asia agency.

In January 2001, SM Entertainment established an overseas joint-venture corporation as SM Entertainment Japan Co., Ltd. They are also preparing to establish a new headquarters in Beijing, China. SM Entertainment will also set up its Asian headquarters in Hong Kong. In May of the same year, SM Entertainment spent 10 billion won to organize its first joint-venture investment fund in the music industry. In 2003, it established its affiliation with the Starlight Corporation Ltd and was awarded a prize for the best music contents in Korea. On October 21, 2008, the company announced its plans to debut BoA in the United States under SM's new subsidiary label, SM Entertainment USA.

Last March 2010, KMP Holdings was established via a joint venture between S.M., YG, JYP, Star Empire, and other companies like Medialine, Ken Entertainment and Music Factory. KMP is the official distributor of releases from these companies. KMP stands for Korean Music Power. The firm's first distributed release from SM was Super Junior's fifth studio album, *Mr. Simple* and since this release, SM is not self-distributed any longer.

In 2010, SM Entertainment, YG Entertainment, JYP Entertainment, KeyEast, AMENT and Star J Entertainment will be joining forces to create a huge Asian management agency named 'United Asia Management'. This joint investment corporate body was created in an effort to develop an industry that will push 'Hallyu' to 'Asianlyu'. United Asia Management aims to pioneer a global market, and all artists under the six agencies will be under a database system that manages intellectual property rights. A new contents production system will be utilized as well for movies, dramas, and other media. UAM will also be acting as the global agency for artists planning to advance, or currently promoting, overseas. UAM was officially established as of April 2011.

On August 16, 2011, SM has established their first international joint venture with Thai media company True Visions Group called "SM True". This joint venture will help effectively distribute SM's contents.

4 Idol star in Korea: Popularity in Asia and Globalization

The founding of South Korea's largest talent agency, S.M. Entertainment, in 1995 by Korean entrepreneur Lee Soo Man led to the first K-pop girl groups and boy bands. By the late 1990s, YG Entertainment, DSP Entertainment, and JYP Entertainment

---

[4] KOSDAQ is an electronic stock market, just like NASDAQ.

had burst onto the scene and were producing talent as quickly as the public could consume it (TIME 2011).

Groups such as, S.E.S., Fin.K.L, H.O.T, Sechs Kies, G.o.d., Fly to the Sky and Shinhwa had huge success in the 1990s, not only in South Korea, but also outside of the country as well. Especially, artists such as H.O.T, Kim Wan-Sun, Clon, Baby V.O.X, NRG saw a huge success in China and Taiwan in the mid-1990s. Also during this period was the emergence of hip hop and R&B music in Korea, leading to the success of artists including Drunken Tiger.

Many of K-pop's biggest idol groups and solo acts, including BoA, TVXQ, Super Junior, SS501, BIGBANG, KARA, Girls' Generation, SHINee, 2PM, BEAST, After School, Brown Eyed Girls, Se7en, IU, Infinite, U-KISS, T-ara, 4Minute, Secret, MBLAQ, Rain and 2NE1 began targeting the Japanese market. The group members conduct interviews and sing in Japanese (Matsutani 2011).

By 2011, K-Pop has become the mainstream genre in most East and South East Asia, including Japan, Malaysia, Mongolia, the Philippines, Indonesia, Thailand, Taiwan, Singapore, China, Vietnam (Cerojano 2011). Through the internet, recently, K-pop started to expand to the rest of the world as well, but it yet has not become well known enough to be mainstream in those countries.

K-pop is steadily gaining influence in foreign markets outside of Asia, however, most notably in the United States, Canada, and Australia. In 2001, Nicholas Kim became the first Korean singer to place on the U.S. Billboard Hot 100 chart with his single, "Hello Goodbye Hello" (Korea Times 2007-11-10). In 2009, Wonder Girls, one of Asia's most successful music artists who sold millions of singles including the international #1 songs "Tell Me", "So Hot" and "Nobody", debuted on the Billboard Hot 100 singles chart (Access Hollywood). In a push to further globalize the genre, K-pop artists are increasingly working with talent outside of Korea. In the United States, Korean artists are touring with groups such as the Jonas Brothers and collaborating with well-known producers including Kanye West, Teddy Riley, Diplo, Rodney Jerkins, Ludacris, and will.i.am.

In 2011, Billboard, one of music industry's most acclaimed music charts, implemented the K-Pop Hot 100 Chart, showing the growing influence and popularity of K-Pop within the Americas and Europe.

5   Girls' Generation, the Most Globally Famous K-Pop Musicians

The nine-member girl band, Girls' Generation (also known as So Nyuh Shi Dae, SNSD, SoShi) was formed by a Korean music label giant SM Entertainment in 2007. Their popularity in Asia was such that they attracted more than 24,000 attendees at their 2-day concerts in Taiwan in 2010. About that time, their single Genie reached the number two spot on the Japanese weekly Oricon Chart, a record for non-Japanese musicians to achieve for the first time in 30 years. Girls' Generation's popularity is not limited to Asia that it is reported that their USA-based fan club Soshified boasts of 120,000 members (Jeong 2011a). For information, Soshified is a coined term by combining 'SoShi' and 'Satisfied.' As such, Girls' Generation has countless fan clubs scattered around the world, with SM-sanctioned official fan club called S♡NE (reads: 'So One'). 'S♡NE' symbolizes fans' desire to be 'so one' with SNSD, by changing 'o o' in 'so one' into '♡.' 'So one' is also an English literation of SNSD's Korean single 'So-one'.

Among their releases, Gee in early 2009 is considered the most successful hit single home and abroad. It ranked at the number one spot for 9 weeks in a row at the KBS Music Bank chart in Korea and for 6 weeks in a row at a major Thai music chart (Hwang 2009; Kim 2009a). Since spring 2009 when SM Entertainment uploaded the music video of Gee on its official YouTube channel, 48,488,555 page views have been recorded and 92,540 comments posted until 2 August 2011. Gee's success is comparable to American pop sensation Lady Gaga's Poker Face (95,939,707 page views and 84,868 comments on its official YouTube channel as of 2 August 2011). In addition to the Gee music video on SM's account, we can find more than 50 video clips of Girls Generation's various performances of Gee at TV music shows, their domestic and international lives, and music award ceremonies on YouTube. We can also find many fan-made video clips of dance covers and music covers with their own musical instruments. Considering some YouTube accounts were already suspended and their video clips erased due to the copyright infringement, it is almost impossible to count the exact number of Gee clips (Noh 2011).

6   Making Process of Idol Star: Training System

6.1   Mode of Trainee Selection

Talent agencies select their trainees by auditions, a systematic process (60 %), street castings (30 %) and through TV programs (10 %) (Fig. 1).

Every members of HOT, the Korean idol group in early 2000, was selected through "street castings". Some casting managers say that when they select trainees, they interview more than 1,000 in the whole nation. They also select apprentices by occasional auditions. In 2006, JYP Entertainment, one of the three major talent agencies in Korea, selected trainees from TV audition program. Currently in 2012, the three major agencies which are SM, JYP and YG are selecting together their trainees on TV audition program, *K-Pop Star* on SBS. Recently, SM Entertainment held auditions even abroad: more than 1,100 have applied to "global audition" hosted by SM Entertainment in Kazakstan in July 2011 (Joongang daily, 2011.7.16).

6.2   Apprenticeship: Idol Star Creation System

Today, apprenticeship is the universal strategy for nurturing girl groups, boy bands, and solo artists in the K-pop industry. To guarantee the high probability of success of new talent, talent agencies fully subsidize and oversee the professional lives and careers of trainees, often spending in excess of $400,000 to train and launch a new

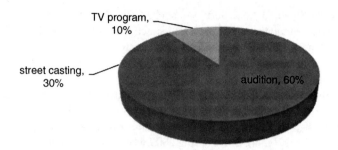

Fig. 1 Mode of selection of talents agencies (*Source*: Joongang daily, 2011)

Table 3 Length of training

Length	Frequency (N)	Percentage (%)
Less than 1 year	19	13.2
1–2 years	24	16.6
2–years	49	34.0
3–years	29	20.1
More than 5 year	23	16.2
Total	144	100

Source: Kim, Hyunji (2011)

artist (TIME 2011). Through this practice of apprenticeship, which often lasts 2 years or more, trainees hone their voices, learn professional choreography, sculpt and shape their bodies through exercise, and study multiple languages all the while attending school (Korea.net 2010-10-28).

Idol star creation systems in Korea has been characterized by drastic discipline due to intensive and long training. According to the table below, more than 1/3 apprentices spend at least 3 years for just training (Table 3).

Average training period for Girls Generation was 9 years, a leading girl group of SM Entertainment, 3 years for Super Junior—a boy group of SM Entertainment, 4.5 years for Big Bang of YG Entertainment (SBS CNBC, 2011-08-03). In other words, idol groups must pass through apprentice program at least 2 or 3 years before their debut. After school, they have to endure intensive vocal and dance trainings until late night. Even though all trainees must go through those drastic training, less than half of them release an album in an occasion of creation of new group. After their debut, they have to practice even more to survive in the competitive music market.

Korean apprentices' distinguished skills in many fields, which they acquired through trainings for singing, dancing, acting, entertaining skill, verbal skill, being able to speak different foreign languages and learning global manners have been appealed to be unique to all over the world. These are the main factors for Kpop's continual popularity even though problems arise (SBS CNBC 2011).

6.3 Controversies

6.3.1 Thirteen-Year 'Slave Contracts'

In late July 2009, three of the TVXQ members; Hero, Micky and Xiah, submitted an application to the Seoul Central District Court to determine the validity of their contract with SM Entertainment (The Korea Time 2009-08-02; KBS World 2009-08-03). Through their lawyers, the members stated that the 13-year contract was excessively long and that the group's earnings were not fairly distributed to the members (The Korea Times 2009-08-03). Early termination penalty of their contract will cost them two times the profit that the group is estimated to earn for the rest of the contract period (over ₩11 billion, or around US$9.2 million)[5] (Thomson Reuters, Forbes.com. 2009. August 3, 2009). The news was enough to cause SM Entertainment's stock price to drop over 10 % on the KOSPI.[6]

The Seoul Central District Court ruled in favor of the three members. They have claimed that the contract was unfair and the members were left out of proper profit distribution (KBS World 2009-10-28). In response, SM called a press conference and claimed that the lawsuit was a fraud, stating that the lawsuit was not about unfair contracts or human rights but a scam motivated by the three members' greed over their cosmetics business. The three members remained silent except to say through their lawyers that they hoped SM would respect the court's decision.

In response to the lawsuit, 120,000 members of TVXQ fan club, Cassiopeia, filed a petition against SM Entertainment's long-term contracts with the Seoul District Court (KBS World 2009-08-21). Cassiopeia also filed for compensation from SM for the canceled SM Town Live Concert, as both SM and TVXQ initially stated that the concert would go on as planned; the concert was canceled a week before its scheduled date (KBS World 2009-09-03). It was later announced in early May 2010 that the three members of TVXQ (Jaejoong, Yoochun and Junsu) will return to the stage as a sub-group. Their group is called JYJ representing the first letter of each of their names.

On December 21, 2009, 5 months after the three TVXQ members filed, Han Geng of Super Junior followed suit. The following day, December 22, 2009, Han Geng's lawyer released the reasons for the contract termination: it contained provisions in SM's favor, the 13-year contract length was unlawful, it would take an unfair sum of money to end the contract, he was not allowed to request to revise his contract, he was forced to do things that were not in his contract, he was forced to do things against his will, he was fined if he disobeyed the company, missed any events or was late, and

---

[5] 1USD = 1,200 Wons

[6] The Korea Composite Stock Price Index or KOSPI is the index of all common stocks traded on the Stock Market Division—previously, Korea Stock Exchange—of the Korea Exchange. It's the representative stock market index of South Korea, like the Dow Jones Industrial Average or S&P 500 in the U.S.

KOSPI was introduced in 1983 with the base value of 100 as of January 4, 1980. It's calculated based on market capitalization. As of 2007, KOSPI's daily volume is hundreds of millions of shares or (trillions of won) (Wikipedia).

there was unfair profit distribution. Along with this, it was disclosed that because of SM Entertainment's refusal to give him a day off in over 2 years, he had developed gastritis and kidney disease.

Han Geng's best friend and now current manager, Sun Le, also submitted a statement to the Korean courts citing SM's violation of Han Geng's rights. This statement was later leaked to the public via the Internet. Though many suspected the statement to be fan-created, it was later confirmed as true (Beijing Youth Weekly Magazine). Sun Le's statement contended that: Han Geng was forced to wear a mask due to SM's ill handling of the visa issue, SM purposely discriminated against Han Geng and his family, including financially, SM refused to cooperate or listen to any of Han Geng's suggestions, SM purposely turned down individual activities for Han Geng (including Ariel Lin's "Fireflies" music video, which later starred two other Super Junior members,) and SM Entertainment treated Han Geng's potential endorsers poorly (Sohu.com).

6.3.2 Fair Trade Commission revisions

SM has released an official statement regarding the contract revisions demanded by the Fair Trade Commission. SME officials clarified on the 23rd, "The FTC only ordered us to revise the contract of one of our trainees by removing the 3 years added onto his contract. We complied, thus making every contract under our agency to date as 'fair.' BoA, TVXQ, Super Junior, SNSD, SHINee, The Trax, and other celebrities under our agency have already been acknowledged as fair contracts by the FTC."

They continued, "As leaders of the industry, we have been cooperating closely with the National Assembly and other related bureaucracies in order to protect the rights and interests of our celebrities, and to aid in the advancement of Korea's entertainment industry and the Hallyu wave." After numerous discussions with the FTC, SME drafted a new contract earlier this year with the changed terms mentioned in the previous article. All artists re-contracted with the agency under the new terms, which were acknowledged by the FTC to be fair. The representative continued, "We fully complied with the recent request by the FTC regarding our contract with a trainee. With the help of the FTC, we will be developing better contracts for the progression of Korean culture and contract customs."

7 Creation of Idol Group: Image Making and Member Casting

When SM makes an idol group, they first think of 'an image of new group' and select suitable members among apprentices. Particularly, talent agencies consider harmony in members as the most important thing when making groups. Each member has to have a unique characteristic and a talent that standout among their members. For example, a symbol of a group 'Girl's Generation' is Yuna; Taeyeon is a main vocal; Seoheon with innocent image. Different images of each member can appeal to diverse audience.

Fig. 2 Personal details report of Korean idol star (Source: Joong-ang Daily, 2010.7.14)

As for references, Korean idols have characteristics as seen in the data below according to their personal details report (report reflects average of 11 idol groups). In other words, their talents as singer, dancer, entertainer and actor with good body type are all necessary in order to become an idol in Korea. Furthermore, they have to be fluent in foreign languages and know well about global manners. Actual phenomena of K-POP proves that Korean talent agencies are competent makers of idols in "dream factory". Today, many Asian teenagers are waiting and trying for auditions of Korean talent agencies. Buildings of the three major talent agencies became one of the most popular tourist sites. It is obvious that the future of Korean wave driven by K-POP will test their capacity (Fig. 2).

8 Global Vision, Knowledge of Multiple Languages

Particularly, Lee Suman, the CEO of SM Entertainment, emphasizes to have a global vision. Regular Camp training is one of his nurturing methods of idols. In this occasion, apprentices learn and develop in foreign languages and global manners.

As for global market entrances, Lee Suman, has pushed into the Chinese market when JYP, another major agency tried to make inroad into American market. He has believed the potential of Chinese market for a long time. However, due to Chinese copy (a private edition) he entered to Japanese market first (Sisa In, 2011). As expected, it a huge success and experiences in Japanese market has provided "penetration model" into Chinese market.

Starting with BOA, leading single idol in early 2000, Japanese market became the test bed to enter foreign market for every idols in the company. Idol groups survived from this process have played the role of locomotive for Korean Wave. Particularly, a song called 'Sorry, sorry' by Super Junior of SM Entertainment ranked the first in Taiwan for 33 weeks continuously. Recently, Japanese Magazine Aera reported that K-POP has been settled in Japanese like British groups Duran-duran or Culture Club under the title 'Korean Invasion' (Joongang Daily, 2010,7,15).

9 Global Music, Global Musician

Talent agencies make an elaborate plan, aiming for global market. They work with foreign composers and choreographers to appeal to young generation around the world. The melody line of repeated chorus of Girls' Generation, called 'hook song' is originated from songs of northern Europe. In fact, Girls' Generation's song was composed by Norwegian composer in Japan.

10 Star Management of Talent Agencies in Korea

After vigorous training, idol groups are managed drastically by the talent agency.

10.1 ACE Strategy

The most notable characteristic of Korean idol groups is that the ace of a member leads the group. Then, as the aces gain popularity, the rest of the members as well as the groups' names get popularized. Regarding fields of area where they can show their talents, they play roles in TV dramas, variety shows, movies and musicals. The diverse activities of idol groups are one of the radical strategies of agencies. Particularly, vigorous training systems and drastic managements that follow after an acceptance from auditions that continue even after their debut have known to be the key strategies of Korean agencies have in making the K-POP stars to be world known stars.

10.2 Career Development

According to the analysis on careers of idols (Lee 2011), they evolve systematically: step 1 is appearance on TV entertainment programs; step 2 be in the highly ranked Music programs; step 3 is appearance on commercials; step 4 is free movement in sectors like acting in TV dramas, films and in musicals, etc. During last 3 years, frequency of 11 idol groups having careers in different fields was 408. Among them, Commercials were ranked first (142 times) and Appearances on TV programs were 100 times (Table 4).

Particularly, a career on commercials has done after their popularity. Even though there is lower frequency for acting in musical compared to other careers, shows that idol stars are very competent and thus are in many areas. In reality, members of Big Bang, Super junior and SS501 have been praised for their excellence after acting in musicals. Their career in a different field is not limited only in music and this makes new audience. Acting on TV drama also gives a change for idol stars to show their talents. So far, 11 idol groups have performed on 26 TV series.

Idols trained in acting and dancing skills as well as their fashionable styles have performed well in different entertainment fields (Sports Seoul 2011). Popularity of

Table 4 Frequency of career

Career	Frequency
TV entertainment programs	100
Commercials	142
Acting in TV drama	26
Releasing album	88
Highly ranked TV music programs	37
Acting in film	7
Acting in musical	8

idols attracted diverse audience in musicals; TV dramas performed by idols earned high ratings and had a huge impact on exports. It is obvious that some easygoing dramas with just casting of idols have turned viewer's back.

In brief, way of management of idols by talent agencies is in series of a chain: through training, harmony in composition of members with distinct roles and characteristics, a relay leading by ace member, etc. Appearance on commercials is a fruit of their popularity. Usually, all members perform together even though differences in the popularity exist between them. Regarding YG, another major talent agency, it is the custom for the most popular group to appear on music video of unpopular groups.

Conclusion

This paper examined how idols of K-pop have been nurtured and managed by talent agencies. First, talent agencies train their apprentices vigorously: vocal training, dancing, acting, and personal skills. Second, they build up experiences of trainees in foreign market through camp training and to acquire different many languages.[7]

Second, idols have been managed systematically to acquire popularity: key factor in the development of careers is a chain of movement from their appearances in TV programs to commercials to effect synergy. Ace strategies of popular member to aware a group and to lead other members have been also one of the characteristics of Korean star management system.

Third, idols are not only limited to be singer but are also prepared to perform in diverse entertainment sectors. Particularly, Korean idols gain popularity not only from teenagers but also from all generations. It has been explained that they appear

---

[7] In many interviews of research done by Jung (2011), most K-pop artists who have been attempting to enter the global (mainly the English-speaking US) market have confessed that the language barrier is the most difficult part of crossing cultural borders. It appears that the language barrier is an unavoidable obstacle for these marginalized pop products to enter the mainstream. In today's global market many different languages are spoken, and some find intercultural communication and exchange to present severe difficulties. Breaking the language barrier does not necessarily mean mastering other people's languages and/or speaking them fluently. From her perspective, breaking the language barrier means accepting BoA's accented English and engaging a range of different subtitled interpretations of Boys over Flowers. It is obvious that advanced digital media technology accelerates the minimization (if not the outright breaking) of such barriers, which enhances the transcultural flows of the once marginalized pop cultural form, K-pop.

on TV entertainment programs targeting all generations. They do not perform just for marketing of releasing albums while ancient singers did it to advertise their albums.

Movement sector is to develop careers and to be more competent. Being as singers, they prepare for other possibilities in career fields since pop dance singers tend to have short careers. Today, some well-known idol stars of 10 years ago are still active in entertainment fields like being show host of TV programs, actor of TV dramas or films, musical singers, etc. It is obvious that movement in different fields came from a plan of talent agencies.

Regarding to distribution strategies, for a goal of entering into global market, talent agencies co-work with globally competent musicians, composers, choreographers, etc. Characteristics of K-POP such as repeated melody line, so called 'hook song' and dynamic dancing styles are successful examples of Korean talent agencies working globally.

According to an executive of YG, YouTube is important in disseminating K-Pop. Especially, YouTube gives an advantage of providing real time responses (Ko 2010). Recently, many international news media reports through Internet including video-sharing websites such as YouTube have facilitated spread of K-pop fandom globally. Therefore, the three major talent agencies open their channels on YouTube and manage them thoroughly.

In brief, way of nurturing and managing idol groups by talent agencies seems to be considered positively in domestic and global market. It is proven that K-POP's phenomena have been spread around the world. However, media commentators have criticized vigorous apprenticeships for a long time continuously. In fact, quite a few idol groups broke up after short career and in some cases, members of group changed.

Korean apprenticeship and management style face challenges continuously. It is crucial to examine the problems and plan more carefully on a long term basis for continual success of Korean Wave.

References

Alexa. (2010). YouTube.com. Retrieved December 30, 2010. http://www.alexa.com/siteinfo/youtube.com

Brouwers, J. (2008). YouTube vs. O-Tube: Negotiating a YouTube identity. *Cultures of Arts, Science and Technology, 1* (1), pp. 107–120.

Bourdieu, P. (1993). *The field of cultural production: Essays on art and literature (R. Johnson, Ed. & Trans.).* New York, NY: Columbia University Press.

Cerojano, T. (2011, September 25). (Associated Press) "K-pop's slick productions win fans across Asia", *Japan Times*, p. 9.

Grossman, L. (2006, December 13). Time's Person of the Year: You, Time. Retrieved Jan 20, 2011. http://www.time.com/time/magazine/article/0,9171,1569514,00.html

Heo, Jeong-yun (2011, February 25). Contents industry shows strong growth with exports of us $3.8 billion. *etnews.co.kr*. Electronic Times Internet. http://english.etnews.co.kr/news/detail.html?id=201102250008

Heo, Y. S. Breakthrough from being Heo Young Saeng, the ballad singer (in Korean). *Sports Seoul*. 15 May 2011.

Hwang, Y. (2009, March 23). Girls generation fever in Thailand: Gee, the number one for six weeks in a row. Retrieved Dec 29, 2010, from http://news.kukinews.com/article/view.asp?page=1&gCode=ent&arcid=1237831198&cp=nv

Is TVXQ headed for breakup?. *KBS World*. 2009-08-03.

Jung, S. (2011a). *Korean masculinities and transcultural consumption: Yonsama, Rain, Oldboy* (p. 5). K-Pop idols. Hong Kong: Hong Kong University Press. ISBN 978988802867.

Jung, S. (2011b). *Korean masculinities and transcultural consumption: Yonsama, Rain, Oldboy, K-Pop idols*. Hong Kong: Hong Kong University Press. ISBN 978988802867.

Jeong, G. (2011a, January 16). Every nine-member of girls' generation is beyonce. *The Joong-Ang Daily*. Retrieved Feb 6, 2011 from, http://article.joinsmsn.com/news/article/article.asp?total_id=4932745&cloc=olink|article|default

Jeong, G. (2011b, January 16). K-pop music videos on YouTube, viewed for more than 800 million time in 229 countries', *The Joong-Ang Daily*. Retrieved 6 Feburary 2011, from http://pds.joinsmsn.com/news/component/htmlphoto_mmdata/201101/17/htm_2 0110117005404c000c010-002.GIF

Kim, Sue-young (2008, May 5). Korean Wave 'Hallyu' Abroad Waning. *The Korea Times*. The Korea Times. http://www.koreatimes.co.kr/www/news/special/2008/05/180_23641.html

Kim, H. (2009, March 13). New history: Girls generation's Gee, no. one for nine weeks in a row. Retrieved Dec 29, 2010, from http://star.mt.co.kr/view/stview.php?no=2009031318410269666&type=1&outlink=1

Kim, W. (2011a, July 7). The boom of flash mob for K-pop concert in USA and UK. *The Dong-A Ilbo*. Retrieved August 2, 2011, from http://news.donga.com/3/all/20110709/38665475/5

Kim, W. (2011b, July 28). International fans introduce girls generation through a huge electronic board in LA. *The Dong-A Ilbo*. Retrieved from August 2, 2011, from http://news.donga.com/3/all/20110727/39131102/5

Korean Group Ranks 2nd in Billboard Chart. Korea Times (2007-11-10). http://www.koreatimes.co.kr/www/news/art/art_view.asp?newsIdx=1998&categoryCode=143

Korean Pop, with online help, goes global. *Time*. http://www.time.com/time/world/article/0,8599,2013227,00.html

Lee, J. and Kang, E. (2011, June 13). The magic of K-pop fascinated a weekend night in Paris. *The Dong-A Ilbo*. Retrieved Aug 2, 2011, from http://news.donga.com/3/all/20110613/37976653/1

Matsutani, M. (2011, August 30). Girls' generation on YouTube.

Matsutani, M. (2011, August 30). K-pop striking chord with the young. *Japan Times*: p. 3. http://search.japantimes.co.jp/cgi-bin/nn20110830i1.html

Noh, K. (2011 August, 17). A study on the transnational circulation of K-pop through Youtube. Journalism and Communication studies Special seminar, Korean Society for Journalism and Communication Studies.

NewsEn. Retrieved February 6, 2011, from http://www.newsen.com/news_view.php?uid=201009150923491001

Pravattiyagul, O. (2011, March 16). K-pop mega gig demands stamina. *Bangkok Post*. The Post Publishing. http://www.bangkokpost.com/arts-and-culture/music/226935/k-pop-mega-gig-demands-stamina

Ramstad, E. (2011 January, 14). YouTube helps South Korean band branch out. *Wall Street Journal*. Retrieved Feb 6, 2011, from http://online.wsj.com/article/SB10001424052748704458204576073663148914264.html

SBS CNBC. (2011, August 3). '*Korea report: K-pop fever*' Sisa In, 2011 August, 6 'Establishment of drama fund between Korea & Japan'.

Shin, N. (2011, June 13). K-pop reaches to Central and Southern America and Africa through YouTube. *The Dong-A Ilbo*. Retrieved Aug 2, 2011, from http://news.donga.com/3/all/20110613/37976513/1

Thomson Reuters. Korea Hot Stocks—Hankook Tire, S.M. Ent, Ssangyong Motor. Forbes.com. August 3, 2009.
TIME Magazine. Korean Pop—Flying Too High? 2011-02-20.
TIME Magazine: Korean Pop—Show Me the Money, 2011-02-20.
TVXQ Fan Club files for compensation for cancelled concert. *KBS World*. 2009-09-03.
TVXQ feuds with SM entertainment. *The Korea Time*. 2009-08-02.
TVXQ in Guinness World Record. KBS World. March 24, 2009. http://world.kbs.co.kr/english/entertainment/enter_chart_detail.htm?No=9374
TVXQ to stick together despite legal dispute. *The Korea Times*. 2009-08-03.
TVXQ vs. SM entertainment trial begins. *KBS World*. 2009-08-21.
Will TVXQ stay together?. *KBS World*. 2009-10-28.
Yonhap News, (2011a, July 7). Flash mob to call on Korean wave tour in LA and New York. *The Dong-A Ilbo*. Retrieved Aug 2, 2011, from http://news.donga.com/3/all/20110707/38638187/1
Yonhap News, (2011b, July 19). 103 US citizens visit to Korea with the schedule of five nights six days to see K-pop. *The Dong-A Ilbo*. Retrieved from Aug 2, 2011. http://news.donga.com/3/all/20110718/38881565/1
Yonhap News, (2011c, July 19). K-pop Flash Mob in South America. *The Dong-A Ilbo*. Retrieved from Aug 2, 2011. http://news.donga.com/3/all/20110719/38900975/1
Yoon, Ja-young (2011, February 8). "YouTube taking 'hallyu' on international ride". *The Korea Times*. The Korea Times.
Yoon, L. (2010), 'Korean pop, with online help, goes global, time. Retrieved October 14, 2010. http://www.time.com/time/world/article/0,8599,2013227,00.html?xid=rss-world-huffpo

Predicting the Future of Investor Sentiment with Social Media in Stock Exchange Investments: A Basic Framework for the DAX Performance Index

Artur Lugmayr

1 Introduction

Today, social media are emerging as a new platform for information exchange, discussions, and as a source of news. Many companies utilize social media platforms as marketing tools or for promotional purposes as a part of a marketing mix. Today, also online brokers provide online discussion forums, blogs, networking tools, educational material, or networking platforms as part of their marketing mix in order to directly reach the end consumer. Thus, today, social networks provide a pool of collaborative knowledge, which also allows the understanding of collaborative pricing behavior on stock markets. This includes e.g. specialized platforms providing collaborative knowledge around the topic of stock exchange trading via blogs, wikis, or communities. It's obvious that social media therefore provide insights into market sentiments and investing behavior, due to the collaborative knowledge and 'shared mind' of many investors. Social media therefore might act as a market sentiment indicator far beyond the currently existing sentiments based e.g. on questionnaires or quantitative consumer spending indexes. The analysis of the content can provide more insights into behavioral finance on stock markets and might lead to more real-time and accurate sentiments. Existing examples show the relation e.g. between discussions on social media and movie sales. It's obvious that social media based sentiment analysis provides new insights into the relation between stock exchange pricing and investors' sentiments and eventually into new behavior financing models. Example services, as e.g. StockTwits demonstrate the efficiency of social media as a tool (StockTwits, n.d.).

Currently the trend of social media attempts to measure brand value, or market sentiments of movies or products. However, their impact as sentiment measurement

---

A. Lugmayr (✉)
Entertainment and Media Management Lab. (EMMi. Lab.), Tampere University of Technology (TUT), Tampere, Finland
e-mail: artur.lugmayr@tut.fi; lartur@acm.org

tool for stock exchange trading is rather poorly researched or leads to completely irrational conclusions that twitter feeds can predict the stock market with an accuracy of 87 % (Bollen et al. 2011), a prediction success rate which even the most experienced analysts are dreaming of. Within the scope of this chapter, the potentials of social media as a tool for measuring investor sentiment are analyzed. However, within this text, *investor sentiment* is defined as "belief about future cash flows and investment risks that are not justified by the facts" (Baker and Wurgler 2007). Therefore a model of measuring sentiment should include variables for describing financial facts, perception of risk, and perception of potential future returns.

1.1 Potentials and Application Scenarios

The aim of this paper is to provide a framework for the potentials of applying social media to the wider scope of the stock exchange. It provides insights into how social media can be utilized as sentiment indicators to determine stock exchange pricing and price changes—and which models might exist to determine stock exchange behavior. The paper provides an overview of tools, methods, and implications in the potential usage of social media within the financial sector far beyond the currently existing probabilistic models assisting investors in their decision making process. In Fig. 1 the potentials of the usage of social media in conducts around financial markets is shown. The application of social media can be clustered into four distinct application areas: marketing and promotion; surveillance, monitoring, and analysis; investment support and visualization; and technical indicator for investment decisions. In the following section these application scenarios are enlisted. Many of the below mentioned scenarios have are mentioned in (Lombardi et al. 2011), but the list below is a more comprehensive list of possible application scenarios:

- **Marketing, Customer Management, and Promotion**
    - *Marketing and promotion* of services from investors, brokers, or financial institutions to end-consumer or professionals;
    - *Customer analysis and evaluation* of products, services, and offers and effectiveness of marketing, sales, and provided information services;
- **Market Surveillance, Monitoring, and Analysis (Lombardi et al.** 2011)
    - *Market surveillance and analysis* to gather insights, trends, forecasts, equity prices, volumes, money flows, and information;
    - *Detections of events and happenings* impacting portfolios, investment decisions, and financial strategies;
    - *Risk management and monitoring of reputational risk* to secure investments and monitor insider trading, anomalies, market habits, business relationships, and self-assessment;
- **Investment Support, Management, and Visualization (Lombardi et al.** 2011)
    - *Market monitoring and investment support tool* for portfolio management, in-depth analysis, and crowed sourced knowledge not available otherwise;
    - *Answering of investors questions or queries* to gain knowledge and information about securities, market, scenario development, trends, and background;

Fig. 1 Social media applied for the financial market [extended list from (Lombardi et al. 2011)]

- *Data visualization of textual data* existing on the web to gain easily access to crowed sourced information and knowledge;
- **Technical Indicator for Investment Decisions**
  - *Sentiment indicators* for stock exchange trading and investments identifying market events, market turns, correlations with equity prices, sentiment values, and portfolio management [extended from (Lombardi et al. 2011)]

1.2 Chapter Structure

This book chapter is divided into four sections. The first section "*The Stock Exchange Environment Market Theories*" gives a general overview of market theories especially focusing on behavioral economics. Theories in behavioral economics seem to match with the phenomenon of social media. The section also gives an outline of market theories, the general stock exchange environment, and key-measures of market valuation. The second section "*Sentiment Analysis and Indicators on the Stock Exchange*" explores sentiment indicators that are currently used for measuring investor sentiment on the stock exchange. The third section "*Framework for Social Media in the Context of Stock Exchange Investments*" provides an overview of social media, and introduces a very basic framework for applying social media at the stock exchange. It also shows the potentials and possibilities of social media for sentiment analysis. The fourth section, "*Analyzing

Social Media and Creating a Social Media Sentiment Indicator Platform" gives a more technical description of potential methods, algorithms, and other implementation details. The last section of the book "Discussion—How can Social Media Predict the Stock Market?" is a round-up chapter, which revises the potentials of social media. It includes also a discussion of the potential of social media under the aspect of how social media can be utilized to predict the stock market.

2 The Stock Exchange Environment and Market Theories

For many decades academic and investment theories focused on the meaningful predictability of stock exchange market prices to increase the probability of correct investment decisions—simply which models can be established to predict the stock market price? An outline of the development of these theories can be found in Fig. 2.

2.1 A Brief History of Theories to Explain the Stock Exchange

A very good and brief explanation for the history of theories explaining stock exchange behavior and its scholars can be found in (Lawrence et al. 2007), upon which this chapter and its references is based on. The introduction section of this article compiles in a few lines the most important scholars, theories, and thoughts. This section of the book chapter extends the basic description of (Lawrence et al. 2007) and provides a wider context. Before the 1950s many researchers believed in models that were capable of predicting stock markets, and in the fact that the market moves gradually, rather than immediately. One of the classical models describes the macroeconomic level of markets as (Keynes 2008), in which business cycles with over-production and under-production lead either to over-employment and under-employment—attempting to equilibrate the market and eventually requiring additional market intervention (Keynes 2008). Nevertheless, these theories describe a market on macroeconomic level and are of little help for specific decisions in stock exchange investments.

Between the 1950s and 1960s these theories were challenged. The believe was strengthened that stock market changes are random and behave in a more immediate way to new information and analysis. Main scholars during these time-period including Mandelbrot (1966) or Samuelson (1965). Fama (Fama and French 1988a; Fama 1970) introduced the *Efficient Market Theory (EMT)*, which basically notes that stock market prices act according to rational behavior of investors. The EMT claims, that the prices of a stock exchange fully reflect the available market information at a certain point in time. The market is efficient and underlays rational principles. This theory was supported by other scholars such as Jensen (1978), Thaler (1999) and Malkiel (2012) argued with this statement. However, the theory was not long lasting and started to be scrutinized from the 1980s onwards, when scholars started to show that stock markets are by far less rational expected,

Fig. 2 History of stock exchange theories

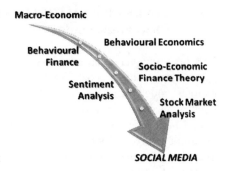

especially when considering stock volatility, reactions on new information, market crashes, or under/overreactions on the stock exchange (Lawrence et al. 2007).

A few of the phenomena, that the stock exchange is by far not reacting rationally have been researched and are compiled in the following [as referenced and listed in (Lawrence et al. 2007)]:

- Extreme losers outperform extreme winners after their low period (Bondt and Thaler 1985);
- Under-reaction to news (Rouwenhorst 1998);
- Overreactions to long streams of news in bullish/bearish direction (Fama and French 1988b);
- Dividend yields predict the performance and variance (Fama and French 1988b);
- Low price/earnings and/or price/book ratios outperform returns (Campbell and Shiller 1998);
- Investors trade to market noise rather than hard facts (Black 1986);
- Cognition and perception influence pricing (Neal and Wheatley 1998);
- An increase/decrease in consumer confidence lead to bullish/bearish investments (Fisher and Statman 2002);
- Theoretical explanations for anomalies as e.g. high trading volumes, bubbles, and volatility (Thaler 1999);
- ...

Thus, stock exchange prices seemed to follow other principles as well. In contrast to what pure rational pricing theorists were trying to underpin. Their research works lead to the emergence of behavioral finance theory, providing new insights into the way of thinking of how stock exchange prices react. Thus, market sentiment and individual emotions seem to play a more crucial role in the development of models describing the behavior of stock exchange prices.

As all the scholars mentioned above have stated, investor sentiment is a driving force in describing stock exchange anomalies and either individual or market emotions and biases. Thus sentiment based stock pricing seems to provide an answer especially to stock exchange anomalies as high volume, bursting bubbles, or volatility (Lawrence et al. 2007). However, even today very specific and probability based models assist investors in their decision making process. And one of the tools to explore the dependence between investor sentiment and the stock exchange are social media.

2.2 Revising the Year 2011 on the Example of the DAX Performance Index

This book chapter is based on examples of the DAX Performance Index 2011, which shows a major stock exchange crash in summer, with a loss of about 1/3 of its total value. Macroeconomic indicators, the financial crisis in Europe, and the Fukushima natural disaster in Japan are only partial explanations for the loss on such a high level. Thus, such a severe crash is not only explained by 'rational' investors, who identify realistic investment risks and realistic valuation of equities. Therefore also emotional decision making, and irrational investors led to such a sever stock exchange crash (Zouaoui et al. 2010)—the investor's sentiment as an explanation for irrational behavior on investment decisions are not fully based on facts (De Long et al. 1990). However the notion that it's better to follow the herd than going against the flow might cause high losses (Shleifer and Vishny 1997) maintains a self-proficiency—or a closed circuit. A decrease of sentiment seems to result into an eventually unjustified magnified decrease of returns, while an increase in sentiment is leading to an eventually unjustified magnified increase of returns.

The year 2011 represented a black year for several stock exchanges worldwide. Three events and crises led to a major crash of several stock exchanges in summer 2011, followed by another crash due to computerized trading systems. The following three major crises dominated the year: the explosion of the nuclear power plant Fukushima in Japan followed by a natural disaster; the European debt crisis caused by an almost default of Greece; and the debt crisis in the USA. Figure 3 illustrates the DAX 30 Performance Index in the year 2011 as a candle stick chart. It shows several events within the scope of its chart patterns: Fukushima in March 2011 and the stock exchange crash in late July/early August due to the European debt crisis that almost led to a Greek default. Within the charts several events are associated with high trading volumes.

Trading volumes represents the simplest indicator for investor sentiment, as it reflects the emotional involvement of market participants: buyers and sellers of stocks commit to their investment actions, either as losers or as winners of a trade. This correlation is described in Elder (1993). From a chart technical perspective high volumes indicate trend confirmations or potential retesting of market lows. Shrinking volumes indicate market turns of the current trends (Elder 1993). Extraordinary changes in volume can easily be spotted in Fig. 3: Fukushima showed high trading volumes, as the crash in summer 2011 does. However, the turn of the market at the end of 2011 is indicated with very low trading volumes, which is partially also due to the low investor activities during the Christmas season. Figure 3 as well shows the DAX 30 returns for the year 2011, and shows major losses in the range of almost up to 6 % on one trading day.

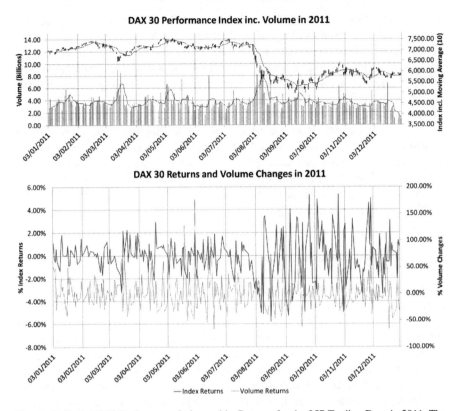

Fig. 3 Daily DAX 30 Performance Index and its Returns for the 257 Trading Days in 2011. The DAX 30 Performance Index is depicted with its Moving Average (Period 10) as Candlestick Graph. The Figure includes the Trading Volume in Billions together with a Moving Average for a period of 5 to indicate Volume Trends. The Figure below the DAX 30 Performance Index presents the Return Series of the Performance Index, and the Changes of Trading Volume Series in Percentages

3   Sentiment Analysis and Indicators on the Stock Exchange

A general distinction can be made between explicit and implicit sentiment indicators to evaluate the expectations of the stock market. Explicit sentiment indicators imply a direct sentiment measurement e.g. via questionnaires or polls conducted on market participants. These measurements allow direct insights into investor's sentiment and their current market behaviour. Examples are polls to gain insight knowledge on the current sentiment conducted by the stock exchange or economic research institutes as e.g. the Deutsche Börse (Boerse-Frankfurt, n.d.) or the *Centre for European Economic Research (CEER)* (Centre for European Economic Research, n.d.a). However, implicit sentiment indicators are indicators whereas other measurements or proxies lead to conclusions on the current market behaviour or sentiment. Methods deriving from statistics, technical chart analysis, or other economic methods allow to estimate and explain the current market behaviour. A prominent example of implicit sentiment is the volatility (Baker and Wurgler 2007). Volatility reveals information of the current possible price changes on the stock market. A high volatility indicates a highly uncertain investor environment, as e.g. a high volume ratio of short selling vs. long selling on the derivate market (Elder 1993).

However, the introduction of social media requires a benchmark or measurement of how potential social media indicators perform. Within the scope of this chapter several indicators combined with index metrics can be considered as an option for benchmarking eventual social media sentiment indicators. The total set of indicators can be seen as a list of sentiment indicators for the DAX 30. Table 1 compiles several indicators [extended from the indicators listed in Baker & Wurgler (2007) and Zouaoui et al. (2010)].

3.1 Explicit Sentiment Indicators

Finding a suitable quantitative measurement for investor sentiment over time is a rather tricky task. Market sentiment data is difficult to obtain, and fluctuation happens rapidly based on emerging news, daily happenings and long-term perspectives changes. Let's consider signals from rating agencies, such as Fitch, Moodies, and S&P which have direct impact on immediate changes in equity prices and the attitude of investors in buying and selling. There are also many other examples for potential sentiment indicator proxies, as e.g. the retail investor sentiment. It is clear that each new event causes a chain of reactions on stock exchanges worldwide—starting with the first stock exchange that opens with the Nikkei in Japan. There are many examples for such a chain reaction in 2011, like the catastrophe in Fukushima, after which stock exchanges worldwide crashed. We might consider stock exchange returns as measurement for investor's sentiment—however, as we would like to identify factors that impact on stock exchange returns, it's a poor measurement for this purpose. Even though returns might be an easy quantifiable measure, they underlay also other principles and factors such as company performance. Returns reflect sentiment as outcome of investor sentiment and are a direct impact from changes in sentiment. Therefore it's a rather poor indicator for stock exchange sentiment changes. Also common indicators such as surveys or market analysis from investment companies might not lead to an objective sentiment analysis, due to the fact, that this data is not sufficiently representative as well as biases and certain agendas can't be ruled out.

However, a previous research work (Baker and Wurgler 2007) evaluated a set of possible proxies for measuring investor sentiment and developed a sentiment index based on the consideration of the following possible sentiment indexes [extended and excerpted from (Baker and Wurgler 2007)] and adapted to specific DAX Performance Index variables):

- *Surveys and Questionnaires:* there are many examples for questionnaires and surveys on consumer, investor, and economic levels based on market surveys. These give insights into various market aspects, such as consumer sentiment,

Table 1 Potential variables for analysing sentiment [extended and adapted set of indicators from Baker and Wurgler (2007) and Zouaoui et al. (2010) to suit the DAX 30 performance index]

Abbreviation	Variable	Description	Frequency
Macroeconomic sentiment indicators			
MA_INT	Interest rate	European interest rates (e.g. EURIBOR) published by the European Central Bank (ECB)	Monthly
MA_INF	Inflation	Inflation rates	Monthly
MA_DCE	Domestic credit	Domestic credit	Monthly
MA_TES	Term spread	Spreads	Monthly
MA_IPR	Industrial production	Production outlook	Monthly/yearly
MA_GRD	Growth durable goods	Growth of durable goods	Monthly/yearly
MA_GDP	GDP	GDP	Monthly/yearly
Implicit sentiment indicators (II) and technical indicators (TI)			
TI_VOA	Volatility	Volatility indicator	Per tick or trading window
TI_VOL	Volume	Trading volume	Per tick or trading window
TI_RSI	Relative Strength Indicator (RSI)	Acceleration deceleration of price movements (0–100)	Per tick or trading window
TI_ARMS	Ratio between advancing/declining items in relation to volume	Indicator for overbought/oversold markets	Per tick or trading window
TI_CCI	Commodity Channel Index (CCI)	Indicator for overbought/oversold markets	Per tick or trading window
II_CPV	Call/Put Volume Ratio	Ratio between options/futures calls/puts	Per tick or trading window
TI_TUR	Market turnover	Turnover of an equity noted on the stock exchange	Per tick or trading window
II_OPI	Open interest	Indicator for the pessimism and optimism on the stock exchange	
II_IPV	Initial Public Offerings (IPO)	Amount/volume of IPOs within a certain period	Time period
II_IPR	Initial Public Offerings (IPO) first day returns	First day returns of IPOs	Multiple
II_MFF	Mutual fund flows	Mutual fund flows between security forms	Daily/weekly/monthly

(continued)

Table 1 (continued)

Abbreviation	Variable	Description	Frequency
Others TIs	Other potential technical indicators	High-Low Index, Net New Highs, Bullish Percentage Index,...	Per tick or trading window
Explicit sentiment indicators			
Börse Frankfurt Sentiment Index	Investment climax	Survey of DAXs' future development	Weekly
Economic Sentiment Index (ESI):	–	General market sentiment evaluated by EUROSTAT	Multiple
ZEW Indicator	–	Survey of experts on economic sentiment outlook	Monthly
Ifo Business Climate Index	–	Survey of experts on economic sentiment outlooks	Monthly

investor sentiment, or retail sentiment. For the German market the following indicators are of relevancy:

- *Börse Frankfurt Sentiment Index:* an example for this type of index is the sentiment analysis contracted by the Börse Frankfurt, Xetra (Boerse-Frankfurt, n.d.). The index is collected on a weekly basis by Cognitrend (n.d.), and shall predict if DAX or TecDAX increases, decreases, or is neutral during the following 30 days based on the sentiment of 150 professional investors. It reflects the ratio of optimists (bulls) and pessimists (bears) on the stock exchange.
- *Economic Sentiment Index (ESI):* an index representing sentiment from an economic perspective is the *Economic Sentiment Index (ESI)* published by Eurostat (n.d.), composed of indicators for consumer, industrial, service, construction, and retail sentiments. This index reveals a rather general view towards market sentiment, however, does not indicate the direct impacts on stock exchange prices.
- *ZEW Indicator:* another important index for sentiment analysis is published by the *Centre for European Economic Research (CEER)* (Centre for European Economic Research, n.d.a) entitled ZEW Indicator for Economic Development (Centre for European Economic Research, n.d.b). The index is evaluated on a monthly basis by surveying 350 financial experts about the economy in Germany, total Europe, Japan, Great Britain, and the USA resulting into a ratio between optimists and pessimists as economic sentiment outlook for the next 6 months.
- *Ifo Business Climate Index:* the Ifo (CESifo GmbH, n.d.) publishes a series of sentiment indexes, where the most significant is the Ifo Business Climate Index published on a monthly basis. However, the institute as well publishes a wide range of other indicators relevant for the German market (e.g. employment barometer, credit constraint indicators, investment surveys, manager survey) or indicators for the global market.

- *Newsletters and Market Journalist Opinion:* there is a wide range of specialized media, newsletters, email distributors, or online forums that reflect current investor sentiment [see e.g. finanzen.net, (n.d.)]. However, professional investors argue that journalistic opinion on sentiment is rather ambiguous, as journalists ought to provide true insights requiring a high degree of interpretation. Also turns in opinion follow rather slowly in trend changing markets (Elder 1993).
- *Endogenous Sentiment Indexes:* endogenous sentiments relate to events not directly related to market data which might impact the performance of investors such as football game results, seasons, or urban legends about the behaviour of stock exchanges at a certain constellation. It has been e.g. shown by (Edmans et al. 2007) that there might be an impact on stock exchange performance; however, the impact of these sentiment indicators can be considered as rather questionable. They might only be considered with a very low weight in the calculation of the total sentiment of investors or rather be ignored due to their statistical insignificance.

3.2 Implicit Sentiment Indicators

There is a wide set of tools available to measure implicit sentiment through proxies and technical analysis. Implicit sentiment variables are proxies that reflect the current investor sentiment and are based on measurements, chart analysis, and macroeconomic indicators among other quantifiable metrics. In the following the most prominent indicators are enlisted. The description of technical indicator is based on Stockcharts (n.d.), which is also an excellent resource for further investigation of technical indicators on the stock exchange.
- *Volatility:* The most prominent indicator for sentiment on the stock exchange is the volatility indicator—the investor's "panic gauge" (Elder 1993). In the case of Germany the VDAX-New is the volatility index for the DAX performance index. Volatility gives information on how risky the current market is for investments and moves inverse to the current stock market prices. A high volatility indicates a bearish and risky market, whereas a low volatility indicates a bullish market. However, volatility extremes often indicate excessive sentiments (Stockcharts n.d.). Figure 4 shows the VDAX-New for the year 2011 nicely reflecting the risk attitude at the stock market in summer 2011, and its recovery period in fall.
- *Call/Put Volume Ratio:* The call/put (or long/short) (Scoach n.d.; Baker and Wurgler 2007; Stockcharts, n.d.) volume ratio of options and derivatives is a good indicator for market sentiment. A high amount of put (short) options indicate a declining market, whereas a high amount of call (long) options indicate an increasing market. The ratio is calculated by dividing "market optimism" (volume of buying calls plus sales of puts) through "market pessimism" (volume of buying puts plus sales of calls). Thus, the higher the number over 0.5, the more bullish market sentiment; whereas the lower the number under

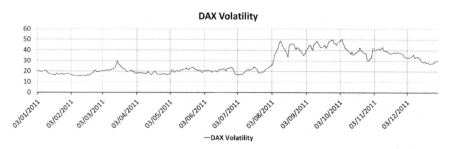

Fig. 4 DAX volatility index for 2011

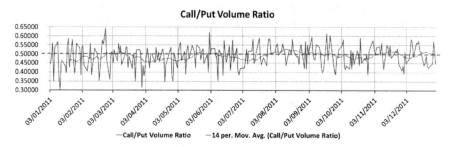

Fig. 5 Call/Put Volume Ratio as published by Scoach for 2011 (Scoach, n.d.)

0.5, the more bearish market sentiment. The indicator measures market emotions, as it reflects if investors fear a declining market by hedging their positions by puts to protect their equities, or if they speculate on a declining market. Figure 5 illustrates the call/put ratio for the year 2011, as published by Scoach on a daily basis (Scoach, n.d.) and shows the low call/put ratio especially during summer 2011 and an increasing number during the recovery period.

- *Trading Volume:* Trading volume (Elder 1993) is a rather simple sentiment indicator reflecting investor emotions—depending on the market scenario, high or low volume indicates a change or continuation of a trend. From the investor sentiment point of view volume always reflects the "emotion" of the market as it represents a market action of buying or selling. Thus the money is transferred between winners and losers of the specific interaction (Elder 1993). Figure 3 shows e.g. nicely extraordinary high volumes indicating panic sales during the natural disaster in Japan and during the stock exchange crash in summer 2011.
- *Technical Indicators:* There are several technical indicators deriving from chart analysis that indicate the current market state (thus either bull, bear, or neutral market). There is a wide range of further technical indicators that can be utilized as implicit sentiment indicators to indicate investor's sentiment, as there is a wide range of further implicit sentiment proxies. However, this chapter contains the most utilized ones in studies. An excellent resource for exploring technical

indicators can be found on (Stockcharts, n.d.), which acted as resource to explain these within the scope of this book chapter. The most prominent indicators utilized in research works examining sentiment are ARMS and RSI:

- *ARMS (TRIN) Indicator*: the ARMS (or Short-term TRading INdex) was developed by Richard Arms in 1967. It is a very simple indicator that represents the relationship between the ratio of advancing/declining equity's and the ratio of traded volume of advancers/decliners. The indicator reflects an inverse market movement. Values above 1 show a market decline and values below 1 indicate a rising of the market. Above or below equity specific thresholds the indicator reflects an overbought or oversold equity price [as defined in (Stockcharts, n.d.)].
- *Relative Strength Indicator (RSI):* The RSI was developed by Welles Wilder in 1978 and measures the acceleration or deceleration of price movements. It ranges from 0 to 100 and a value above or below a certain threshold indicates an overbought or oversold equity price. Per default these values are set at above 70 and below 30 and the indicator is calculated for 14 periods. However, the threshold is as well equity specific, and can be utilized to reduce or increase the number of trading signals [as defined in (Stockcharts, n.d.)].
- *Other Market Indicators:* There is a wide set of other market indicators that allow identifying a market trend that could be utilized: *Commodity Channel Indicator (CCI)*, High-Low Index, Net New Highs, or the Bullish Percentage Index. As their description would go beyond the scope of this book chapter, it is referred to (Stockcharts, n.d.) for further investigation.

- *Market Turnover and Return:* another well-suited sentiment indicator is the market return, describing daily returns on the stock exchange, as e.g. presented in Fig. 3. Market returns indicate the change of a stock exchange index, thus its performance. The turnover on a stock exchange indicates the total price of the total shares traded within a certain period. The turnover ratio gives information how many times equities are exchanged within a certain period (Sheu et al. 2009).
- *Open Interest:* open interest (Eurex n.d.; Stockcharts, n.d.) is an indicator for the number of put and calls positions of options or futures expressed in the number of contracts or total price. The ratio between puts and calls is a well suited indicator for investor sentiment—the higher the amounts of puts, the more pessimistic investors are. Open interests are directly proportional to the level of interest in an option or future. Historical data is e.g. available at Eurex (n.d.).
- *Initial Public Offerings (IPO):* the amount of IPOs (thus companies entering the stock market) (Baker and Wurgler 2007), and their first day returns are well suited sentiment indicators, as first day returns show the level of interest of investors in a particular equity. The interest level can be interpreted as directly proportional to the sentiment of investors (Baker and Wurgler 2007). Statistical data of IPOs in Germany is e.g. available at (Deutsche Boerse Group, n.d.). An excellent example for a failed IPO is Facebook, reflecting a negative sentiment towards the underlying asset.

- *Mutual Fund Flows:* mutual fund flows (Baker and Wurgler 2007) are an indicator where investors are allocating their capital. A sentiment indicator based on mutual fund flows allows visualizing where capital is currently allocated and gives insights in which asset classes investors believe (Baker and Wurgler 2007).

3.3 Macroeconomic Sentiment Indicators

A further category of sentiment proxies are macroeconomic sentiment indicators. However, a full enumeration of these indicators would be beyond the scope of this book chapter. The most prominent indicators are: interest rate [as published by the ECB (European Central Bank, n.d.)], inflation, domestic credit, GDP, term spread, industrial investments, industrial production, growth of durable goods, etc.

4 Framework for Social Media in the Context of Stock Exchange Investments

The role of social media in stock exchange trading is based on theories of behavioural finance, and the investor's sentiment reflected in social media. Figure 6 gives a general overview of the relationship for a framework including social media in stock exchange trading.

4.1 Social Media as Marketing Tool

The application of Social Media for online brokers and financial firms shows similarities to other market segments, especially when focusing on social media as a tool for marketing and promotion and the application of social media as a customer analysis tool. Social Media have increased influence on the consumer, especially on the young generation in their decision making in buying products. This is also valid for applying social media in the context of investments. Brokers can actively use social media market channels for branding, providing product advertisements, and getting in touch with the consumer. Thus the three main reasons to deploy social media tools can be compiled as follows (Vukanovic 2011):
- Reduced costs for advertising, distribution of information, and targeted offers;
- Low-cost possibility for brand building, consumer engagement, and communication;
- Active and rapid engagement with peers, consumers, and the public;
- Building knowledge, learning professional knowledge, and instant information.

While these application areas are currently under heavy investigation, another opportunity for the application of social media in the context of stock exchange pricing is provided—merging social media with the theories of behavioral finance.

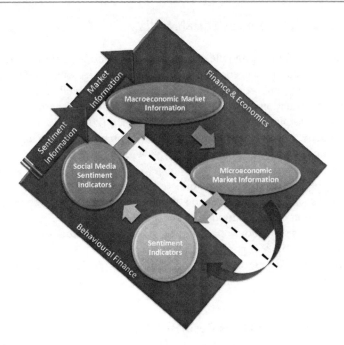

Fig. 6 Social media as support tool for stock exchange investments

4.2 Behavioral Finance and Social Media

Social media as sentiment indicator allow providing new insights into investor's behavior, especially from a behavioral finance viewpoint. As the market is seen to reflect the real value of securities, the direct impact of social media based sentiment analysis of investors has to consider several variables. To establish the connection between stock exchange prices and the sentiment of investors a correlation to stock exchange prices has to be established. The following stock market behaviors and indicators can be utilized as basic measures:

- *General market knowledge:* consumer confidence indicators (e.g., consumer indices), expected market or market segment growth rates, market environment, chart analysis and backtracking theories, and general investment principles;
- *Principle market state:* bull market (increasing), bear market (decreasing), neutral market (equilibrium);
- *Anomalies:* stock market bubbles, stock market crashes, unusual trading volumes, increased or high volatility;
- *Market perception and reaction:* reactions of the market on news, new information, rumors, general believe, current market perception, filtering of news, and discussions;
- *Equity price:* future cash flows, growth rate, discount rate, company data and their interpretation, investment risk rate, and fluctuation of these parameters over time.

4.3 Potential Forms of Social Media

As content source for the principle data analysis exist various different social media genres that adapted to the needs of investors and traders. A wide variety of tools is available either to support marketing and promotion, as well as they can act as source for the evaluation of market sentiments. The following enumeration gives an overview and was published in Lietsala & Sirkkunen (2008):
- *Collaborative networks and content creation*: common creation and publishing of information, and knowledge (e.g. blogs, wikis, podcasts, twitter);
- *Content sharing and knowledge exchange:* sharing of information with similar minded people on dedicated networks (e.g. Flickr);
- *Dedicated social networks:* creation of community, exchanging knowledge, and communication of information (e.g. Facebook);
- *Virtual worlds:* creation of a digital simulated environment for common specialized activities (e.g. virtual trading rooms);
- *Features and add-ons:* usage of social media in dedicated environments for specific purposes (e.g. mobile applications).

4.4 Sentiment Analysis Results

As sentiment analysis deals with the analysis of "an attitude, thought, or judgment prompted by feeling[s]" (Merriam-Webster, n.d.) and is most commonly based on textual analysis techniques. Thus, the key idea is the analysis of social media data either in (1) real-time to gain more knowledge about the sentiment of the status of the market at a specific time; (2) as assisting tool to evaluate the current market state on a longer time-scale; (3) obtaining specific pieces of knowledge and information concerning actual issues; or (4) sentiment towards future events, such as IPOs, performance, or political event. These four possible directions have been analyzed within the scope of the IST project FIRST (Lombardi et al. 2011). Thus, sentiment analysis can be performed based on qualitative methods as e.g.:
- *Dimensions of mood:* categorized representations of the current state of social media sentiments (e.g. calm, angry, pessimistic);
- *Predictors for stock indicators:* quantitative predictors for stock pricing with associated probabilities and reliabilities;
- *Qualitative indicators:* acquisition of knowledge and information about successful investment strategies and future trading behavior.

4.5 Additional Framework Requirements and Impact Factors

The previous sections discussed many aspects of applying social media around financial services. Within the scope of this section, other considerations that have not been discussed as far are mentioned. It shall give an overview of research works and framework requirements and additional impact factors:

- *Semantic data framework:* semantic data framework for describing social media and investment data and knowledge mining as e.g. based on methods from the semantic web (e.g. ontologies) as evaluated in (Lombardi et al. 2011);
- *Sentiment impact and causalities:* impact and causalities between sentiment and stock market returns under various market scenarios and causalities between different sentiment indicators. E.g. (Sheu et al. 2009) showed, that the "causal relationships between sentiment indicators and returns are mixed, if the market scenario is not classified according to investors' sentiments", which is supported by other studies [e.g. (Zouaoui et al. 2010)].
- *Networking and social media propagation:* measurement and propagation models of social media information and how online communities diffuse information (Garg et al. 2011);
- *Stock exchange networks:* based on the thought that social media propagate differently across online communities, the European stock exchange structure might impact on sentiment, as there might be correlations on how news and sentiment spread (Sakalyte 2009);
- *Benchmarking of social media sentiment indicators:* social media sentiment indicators require a benchmarking with existing quantitative market data or other sentiment indicator to validate their reliability;
- *Data source quality and weighting:* one of the major issue is the quality of social media data, as well as weighting source data according potential impact;
- *Predictive investment model:* models and algorithms for predicting the future behavior of the stock exchange considering social media information;
- *Financial decision support:* integration of the social media framework into existing financial management systems and investment support systems;
- *Model for sentiment impact on various equity types:* different forms of equities react differently on sentiment changes. A theoretical model describing different equities under first different market scenarios [e.g. Sheu et al. (2009)]; and second relating these to different equity types [e.g. Baker and Wurgler (2007)];

5 Analysing Social Media and Creating a Social Media Sentiment Indicator Platform

Most of existing sentiment analysis on stock exchanges is based on qualitative evaluation methods as e.g. questionnaires as e.g. performed by Xetra, Börse Frankfurt [see Cognitrend (n.d.); Boerse-Frankfurt, (n.d.)]. The analysis is addressed to professional investors and financial institutions, and gives insights into the attitude if they believe in a downward (bear) or upward (bull) trend of the DAX performance index. However, this method has several major drawbacks:
- Information is not gathered and analyzed in real-time and provided to the consumer;
- It reflects a general trend of the stock market, rather than current happenings;
- Poor illustration of the correlation between current sentiment and stock prices;
- The too scarce updates do not provide sufficient information for guiding daily investments.

Fig. 7 Principle workflow for performing a social media data analysis based on social media input data

Within the scope of this section very briefly existing sentiment analysis techniques and methods are discussed. Existing works already show the importance and application of social media in industries, as e.g. the work of (Asur and Huberman 2010) which demonstrates the effect of social media on motion industries. It analyses sentiments extracted from social media platforms and demonstrates how these sentiments predict real-world outcomes, as e.g. movie sales in this particular example. Existing experiments show e.g. a direct correlation between sentiments extracted from Twitter messages and stock market prices. The accuracy of predicting basic bull and bear markets is obtained via an accuracy of 86.7 % (Bollen et al. 2011).

For individual trading decisions a higher granularity is required to place correct investments. Other research e.g. focused on the analysis and effect of events such as sport events on stock exchange prices, demonstrating that the result of sport events has an effect on stock returns and the impact of investors' mood (Edmans et al. 2006). Other research focuses on the impact of the 'weekend effect' on the stock exchange, and how stock pricing is affected by investors' sentiment (French 1980).

However, neither of these studies will help to make concrete investment decisions. They are only showing some sort of statistical correlation rather than concrete issues. Within the scope of this chapter, a principle workflow based on social media input data is presented in Fig. 7. The key-component of this workflow is taking place in the steps *semantic annotation*, in which sentiment extraction is taking place; and within the step *knowledge mining*, in which e.g. correlations between social media data and stock exchange data are performed. A more technical view for the utilization of social media information on the stock exchange is presented in Fig. 8. The presented architecture is extended from the principal architecture in (Lombardi et al. 2011).

5.1 Sentiment Dictionary

The central component of a social media based sentiment analysis is a sentiment dictionary. There are many English language based dictionaries. German language dictionaries that could be utilized for sentiment analysis for stock exchange sentiment analysis are rather scares. However e.g. SentiWS (Remus et al. 2010) provides a solution for general data sets and input formats with an extensive set of approximately 16.000 positive and negative word forms weighted within the interval $[-1;1]$. As the dictionary solely provides general words, an extension of the dictionary with stock exchange words and their weight is essential.

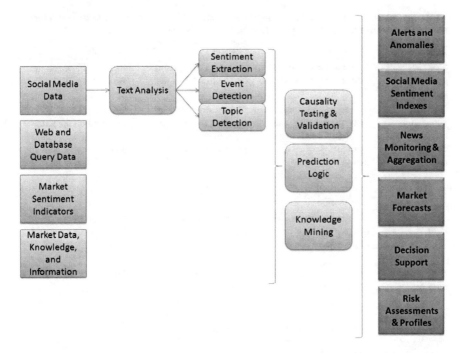

Fig. 8 Principal architectural blocks for a system for analysis of social media data as investor support system [extended and generalized from the architecture presented in (Lombardi et al. 2011)]

5.2 Data Sources and Acquisition

The data source and acquisition part has been well described by the IST project FIRST (Lombardi et al. 2011): in addition to real-time data streams containing the actual market information (e.g. equity quotes) social and online data streams have to be aggregated. These data feeds containing information on the web, proprietary resources, or social media are provided in a certain timeframe (e.g. real-time, daily, weekly) and range from simple RSS based web-feeds up to complex web conversations taking place in e.g. discussion forums or blogs. Thus, in principle we can distinguish between structured or unstructured data formats. Structured data follows certain syntax and encoding, and enables easy machine readable processing. Unstructured data such as conversations or other textual data requires much higher efforts in gaining the desired results. However, different data sources impact equity prices in a different level—a simple blog entry has rather no or minor effects on the equity market. But central bank interest changes, credit ratings from rating agencies, unemployment data from governmental institutions, or events such as natural disasters can be considered as having high impact on equity valuation. Therefore it is useful to attribute data sources with certain relevancy information (e.g. *very high*, *high*, *neutral*, *low and very low*) (Lombardi et al. 2011). An overview of potential data sources is given in Table 2.

Table 2 Overview of web and social media data sources suitable for gaining sentiment information [widely extended from the ideas in Lombardi et al. (2011)]

Type	Description	Content	Examples
News services and news aggregators	External news feeds from information provider	Structured data from news provider in real-time	Reuters, Finanzen.net, Bloomberg, Yahoo! news,…
Queries, knowledge mining, and database mining	Specific web-query analysis and analytics, mining of databases or available data sets, company internal information, portfolios, or proprietary information	Mostly structured data from database queries from internal or proprietary sources	Google queries, information source queries, web query analysis, customer portfolio analysis, trading strategy analysis,…
Conversational data	Data from forums, blogs, discussions on blogs, social media discussions, etc.	Unstructured textual data from online sources	Blog comments, Facebook discussions, Twitter, …
Professional data feeds	Subscription based or professional data feeds	Quantitative or qualitative structured or unstructured data	Equity price data streams (e.g. DataStream)
Online informational services or news aggregators	Articles, newsletters, websites, dedicated to provide stock exchange information and strategies	Qualitative, mostly unstructured data containing trading information	Newsletters, market predictions, online analysis of equities,…
Policy makers and Advocates	Newsfeeds from policy makers such as central banks, rating agencies, or governmental agencies	Quantitative or qualitative structured or unstructured data with a high impact on stock exchange performance and sentiment	S&P, Moodies, Fitch, European Central Bank (ECB),…

5.3 Analysis Methods and Techniques

To provide an insight into the total set of analysis methods and techniques is a rather complex task. However, the three major techniques for the analysis of social media data are based on financial economic analysis; statistical methods; and the core method for social media data analysis is natural language processing.

5.3.1 Text Mining and Natural Language Processing

The core of the analysis of social media data streams is textual analysis of mostly unstructured data, especially tools for *Natural Language Processing (NLP)*. There is a wide variety of methods and techniques to perform this task, which have been e.g. revised in (Pang and Lee 2008). Textual information is the data source to obtain information on investor sentiment. Thus textual input from various social media platforms is analysed, and by the application of probabilistic models or analysis software additional insight and support about investment decisions can be gained (e.g. via advanced software such as recommendation systems, information extractions tools, summarization, etc.) (Pang and Lee 2008). Examples for such models are e.g. Facebook APIs, or more sophisticated *Probabilistic Latent Semantic Analysis (PLSA)*.

5.3.2 Effect of Sentiment on Investors' Equity Valuation

One of the major concerns in modelling a sentiment based investment system is how sentiment affects equity prices. Sentiment changes have different effects on equities. As discussed in (Baker and Wurgler 2007), the valuation level of equities is dependent on the level of speculation of specific equities (e.g. high sentiment lead to high valuation levels of highly speculative equities). However, to obtain a more general model it can be useful to cluster sentiment according equities representing company types (e.g. medicals, consumables). As has been especially seen in the DAX crash in 2011, sentiment impacts equity prices differently. Whereas e.g. the valuation level of shares of consumables is higher in market turbulences than the one of production industry.

5.3.3 Benchmarking and Correlation of Social Media Sentiment

Another issue is the evaluation and benchmarking of social media sentiment indicators and especially finding the variables that correlate to allow predictions and other more advanced models. Benchmarking and correlation analysis evolves according three different modalities:
- Causality of social media sentiment indicators and live-market data;
- Causality between social media sentiments and other sentiment indicators;
- Prediction methods for explaining the impact of social media on market returns.

In (Sheu et al. 2009) a method for benchmarking sentiment indicators such as put/call volumes, put/call opened interest ratio, volatility, and a technical indicator as e.g. ARMS in various market scenarios is introduced. This method has high potential in describing the causality of social media sentiment indicators and their statistical relevancy. Other methods based on the selection of market variables and non-social media related sentiment data are presented in (Chen et al. 2010).

5.3.4 Creating a Social Media Sentiment Index

To create a sentiment index reflecting the current social media sentiment is a far more complex task. Simple models exist on the market, as e.g. *Thomson Reuter's Social Pulse* (Thomson Reuters, n.d.) providing sentiment indexes for single equities together with additional market information based on social media. The main challenge in providing a social media sentiment index is to find the correct variables influencing equity sentiment but there are many examples for methods how a social media sentiment index can be calculated based on sentiment index calculation methods for other sentiment indexes [e.g. (Baker and Wurgler 2007)].

5.3.5 Stock-Exchange Predication Models

The development of statistically valid predictive models for the stock exchange is rather tricky. Similar to benchmarking social media sentiment, a prediction model

requires the selection of correct correlating variables. The underlying questions therefore are:
- Which variables correlate with social media data?
- Can liquidity and volume be forecasted?
- What is the correlation between volatility and sentiment?
- What is the relation between noise (sentiment) trading and correct valuation?
- How can the overreaction to news be forecasted?
- Can the rational/irrational behaviour of investors be predicted?
- How can influences from markets be removed from sentiment indicators?

However, there are a few approaches that are based on indirect crowd sourcing models as e.g. web-search engine queries (Bordino et al. 2011). The study examines the relation between the volume of web queries for a specific equity and its trading volume. The study also demonstrates that web queries can be utilized as early warning system for changes of investment sentiment. Another interesting study determines that sentiment has high impact on volatility forecasting (Sheu and Wei 2011). An additional aspect is that market changes imply a change in sentiment indicators. Thus the power of sentiment indicators to predict the market can be increased by purifying sentiment indicators from such influences, as shown in (Aronson and Wolberg 2009). Thus a purification of social media sentiment indicators impacts also the predictive power these.

6 Discussion: How Can Social Media Predict the Stock Market?

Social media affect the stock market as e.g. discussed by (Eler 2011) and first communities are created [e.g. StockTwits, (n.d.)]. Many brokers already offer online service portals that include social media features such as blogs, wikis, podcasts, and discussion forums—many of these even free of charge. The main aim of these forums is the creation of a community to sell the products associated with the current discussions and trends. Still, one thing is very obvious—social media will definitely not be able to predict the stock price with 100 % accuracy. Also in social media, the social media customer is not always right (Read 2011). Customers complain, and especially when investors loose, it's easy to shift a failure trade to wrong information online platforms and published trading aids. This implicates clear advices for consumers that investments cannot be predicted as many would believe and a clearer communication method with consumers to avoid misunderstandings. Especially inexperienced private investors might take discussions and advices as granted facts rather than guides.

However, what this publication definitely was presenting was a wide set of application scenarios of social media in investment. Especially the application of social media in marketing of financial products will gain of importance with the advent of online brokerage and opening of the market to everyday consumers (Weinhardt et al. 2000). For the professional trader social media are already considered as serious form of media in investment decisions, as social media platforms as e.g. StockTwits (n.d.) show.

But there still one major question remains: *Can social media predict the stock market?* Since decades people attempt to develop models to explain stock market behaviour. Many of these have been listed within this publication. From the current point of view the answer to this question is rather simple: *no*. Social media sentiment analyses are just one additional tool to assist investors in their decision process. Especially financial management and investment support systems will benefit from the analysis of social media data as an additional data source for various purposes as e.g. risk management, event detection, or to assist in forecasting markets. Social media are simply another analysis tool to help increasing performance together with traditional investment analysis tools. For everyday consumer social media allow to gain access to information, which was as far solely in the hands of professional. It empowers the consumer, to understand the markets, and it assist in risk management and give an edge to survive on the market. Only together with traditional investment analysis tools social media will help in increasing performance.

Social media are a tool especially reflecting market crowd psychology, and existing applications of social media in other domains demonstrate the power of the crowd. Also in investments, social media will show their power, and be a major factor in decision making. Social media as sentiment indicator could act as tool for fundamental and technical analysis. Eventually new indicators assisting investors are emerging. However, as for many indicators, also this indicator will lose its power or trading secret, as many other indicators did, when they have been revealed to a large community. But they will give new insights and potential new possibility to bet on the right investment, thus stay on the market longer. The field is still rather unexplored, and new indicators might emerge rather quickly and are part of professional analysis software packages.

For event-, topic-, and current news detection social media is already proven to be efficient in many domains. Thus it can be predicted that social media will also show its powers and strength as financial support tool. Also in rating and gaining additional information about equities social media will definitely be a very helpful tool to gain additional knowledge and information.

However, this research work is on-going, and has been arising many new questions requiring a more thorough examination and research. As a next step a series of social media data will be examined and causalities on predictability tested.

Acknowledgments With many thanks to Martin A. for his discussions and insights!

References

Aronson, D. R., & Wolberg, J. R. (2009). Purified sentiment indicators for the stock market. *Journal of Technical Analysis, 66*, 7–27.

Asur, S., & Huberman, B. A. (2010). Predicting the future with social media. *CoRR*, abs/1003.5699.

Baker, M., & Wurgler, J. (2007). Investor sentiment in the stock market. *Journal of Economic Perspectives, 21*(2), 129–151.
Black, F. (1986). Noise. *Journal of Finance, 41*(3), 529–543.
Boerse-Frankfurt (n.d.) *DAX Sentiment.* http://www.boerse-frankfurt.de/DE/index.aspx?pageID=44&NewsID=6417.
Bollen, J., Mao, H., & Zeng, X. (2011). Twitter mood predicts the stock market. *Journal of Computational Science, 2*(1), 1–8.
Bondt, W. F. M. D., & Thaler, R. (1985). Does the stock market overreact? *Finance, 40*(3), 793–805.
Bordino, I., Battiston, S., Caldarelli, G., Cristelli, M., Ukkonen, A., & Weber, I. (2011). Web search queries can predict stock market volumes. *Arxiv preprint arXiv11104784v1*, 22.
Campbell, J. Y., & Shiller, R. J. (1998). Valuation ratios and the long-run stock market outlook. *The Journal of Portfolio Management, 24*(2), 11–26.
Centre for European Economic Research (n.d.a). http://www.zew.de.
Centre for European Economic Research (n.d.b). *ZEW Indicator of European Sentiment.* http://www.zew.de/en/publikationen/Konjunkturerwartungen/Konjunkturerwartungen.php3.
CESifo GmbH (n.d.). *Ifo Surveys.* http://www.cesifo-group.de/portal/page/portal/ifoHome/a-winfo/d1index/10indexgsk.
Chen, H., Chong, T. T.-L., Duan, X., et al. (2010). A principal-component approach to measuring investor sentiment. *Quantitative Finance, 10*(4), 339–347.
Cognitrend (n.d.). http://www.cognitrend.de/de/index.php.
De Long, J. B., Shleifer, A., Lawrence, H. S., & Waldmann, R. (1990). Noise trader risk in financial markets. *Journal of Political Economy, 98*(4), 703–38.
Deutsche Boerse Group (n.d.). http://www.dax-indices.com/.
Edmans, A., Garcia, D., & Norli, O. (2006). Sports sentiment and stock returns. *Sixteenth Annual Utah Winter Finance Conference; EFA 2005 Moscow Meetings.* May.
Edmans, A., García, D., Norli, Ø., et al. (2007). Sports sentiment and stock returns. *Journal of Finance, 62*(4), 1967–1998.
Elder, A. (1993). *Trading for a living: psychology, trading tactics, money management.* Wiley Finance: Wiley.
Eler, A. (2011 December). *How Social Media Is Changing the Stock Market.* http://bx.businessweek.com/social-media-marketing/view/?url=http%3A%2F%2Fwww.readwriteweb.com%2Farchives%2Fhow_social_media_is_changing_the_stock_market.php%3Futm_source%3Dfeedburner%26utm_medium%3Dfeed%26utm_campaign%3DFeed%253A%2BreadwriteWeb%2B%2528ReadWriteWeb%2529.
Eurex (n.d.). http://www.eurexchange.com/.
European Central Bank (ECB) (n.d.). http://www.ecb.int/.
Eurostat (n.d.). *Selected principal European Economic Indicators.* http://epp.eurostat.ec.europa.eu/portal/page/portal/euroindicators/peeis.
Fama, E. F. (1970). Efficient capital markets: a review of theory and empirical work. *Journal of Finance, 25*(2), 383–417.
Fama, E. F., & French, K. R. (1988). Dividend yields and expected stock returns. *Journal of Financial Economics, 22*(1), 3–25.
finanzen.net (n.d.). http://www.finanzen.net.
Fisher, K. L., & Statman, M. (2002). Consumer confidence and stock returns. *Journal of Empirical Finance, 18*, 225–236.
French, K. R. (1980). Stock returns and the weekend effect. *Journal of Financial Economics, 8*, 55–69.
Garg, R., Smith, M. D., & Telang, R. (2011). Measuring information diffusion in an online community. *Journal of Management Information Systems, 28*(2), 11–38.
Jensen, M. C. (1978). Some anomalous evidence regarding market efficiency. *Journal of Financial Economics, 6*(2–3), 95–101.

Keynes, J. M. (2008). *The general theory of employment, interest and money.* New Delhi: Atlantic Publishers and Distributors Pvt. Ltd.
Lawrence, E. R., McCabe, G., & Prakash, A. (2007). Answering financial anomalies: sentiment-based stock pricing. *The Journal of Behavioural Finance, 8*(3), 161–171.
Lietsala, K., & Sirkkunen, E. (2008). *Social media. Introduction to the tools and processes of participatory economy.* Hypermedia Laboratory Net Series, no. 17. Tampere, Finland: Tampere University Press.
Lombardi, P., Aprile, G., Gsell, M., Winter, A., Reinhardt, M., & Queck, S. (2011). *Definition of market surveillance, risk management, and retail brokerage usecases.* Report D1.1. FIRST—Large scale information extraction and integration infrastructure for supporting financial decision making (IST STREP).
Malkiel, B. G. (2012). *A random walk down wall street: The time-tested strategy for successful investing.* Norton.
Mandelbrot, B. (1966). Forecasts of future prices, unbiased markets, and "Martingale" models. *The Journal of Business, 39*(1), 242–255.
Merriam-Webster (n.d.). *Merriam-Webster Online Dictionary.* http://www.merriam-webster.com/dictionary/.
Neal, R., & Wheatley, S. M. (1998). Do measures of investor sentiment predict returns? *Journal of Financial and Quantitative Analysis, 33*(4), 523–547.
Pang, B., & Lee, L. (2008). Opinion mining and sentiment analysis. *Foundations and Trends in Information Retrieval, 2*(2), 1–135.
Read, B. (2011 June). *The (Social) Customer Isn't Always Right.* http://blog.tmcnet.com/call-center-crm/call_center_crm/the-social-customer-isnt-always-right.asp.
Remus, R., Quasthoff, U., & Heyer, G. (2010). SentiWS—A publicly available German-language resource for sentiment analysis (pp 1168–1171). European Language Resources Association (ELRA).
Rouwenhorst, K. G. (1998). International momentum strategies. *Journal of Finance, 53*(1), 267–284.
Sakalyte, J. (2009). European stock exchange networks: connections, structure and complexity. *Applied Economics: Systematic Research, 3*(2), 31–39.
Samuelson, P. (1965). Proof that properly anticipated prices fluctuate randomly. *Industrial Management Review, 6*(2), 41–48.
Scoach (n.d.). http://www.scoach.de.
Sheu, H.-J., Lu, Y.-C., & Wei, Y.-C. (2009). Causalities between the sentiment indicators and stock market returns under different market scenarios. *International Journal of Business and Finance Research, 4*(1), 159–172.
Sheu, H.-J., & Wei, Y.-C. (2011). Options trading based on the forecasting of volatility direction with the incorporation of investor sentiment. *Emerging Markets Finance and Trade, 47*(2), 31–47.
Shleifer, A., & Vishny, R. W. (1997). The limits of arbitrage. *Journal of Finance, 52*(1), 35–55.
Stockcharts (n.d.). http://stockcharts.com.
StockTwits (n.d.). http://wwwstocktwits.com/.
Thaler, R. H. (1999). The end of behavioral finance. *Financial Analysts Journal, 56*(6), 12–17.
Thomson Reuters (n.d.). *Social pulse.* http://www.reuters.com/social.
Vukanovic, Z. (2011). New media business models in social and Web media. *Journal of Media Business Stud, 8*(3), 51–67.
Weinhardt, C., Gomber, P., & Holtmann, C. (2000). Online brokerage: transforming markets from professional to retail trading. *ECIS 2000 Proceedings*, 826–832 ST – Online–Brokerage – Transforming Mark.
Zouaoui, M., Nouyrigat, G., & Beer, F. (2010). How does investor sentiment affect stock market crises? Evidence from panel data. *Recherche, 46*, 723–747.

Branding with Social Media at RTS

Stéphane Matteo, Giulia Spolaor, and Cinzia Dal Zotto

1 Introduction

The aim of this paper is to describe branding oriented actions undertaken by media firms faced with challenges brought by social media. In particular, the study focuses on the creation of a new job position: the Digital Corporate Communication Manager[1] (DCM).

As social media and especially social networks (SN) are playing a crucial role in our civil society—increasing access and diffusion of information—changes in the media industry are to be observed. Even if this evolution is true for most type of organizations, information and entertainment industries are subject to important concerns since the object of change, content production, is their core business. SNs bring both new competitions in the market as well as greater content diffusion possibilities. Thus, it appears necessary to observe and understand branding strategies that media firms could implement to cope with the new variables in the equation such as interactivity.

The literature on social media strategies is rising but still remains very restricted if considered for the media industry specifically or from a branding perspective only. This is true even though the literature on corporate branding is vast and studies about media management numerous. That is why this work aims at investigating media-specific branding issues in the era of social media. We focus on describing and understanding the tasks of the new position of DCM from a brand strategy perspective, the brand building activities employed and the implications derived from the use of those activities.

Furthermore, with the support of a case study we examine the critical aspects of the social media presence for a public service media.

---

[1] Different titles are commonly used to describe similar tasks, e.g. social media manager, social media strategist, community manager or online communication manager among others.

S. Matteo (✉) • G. Spolaor • C.D. Zotto
Université de Neuchâtel, Neuchâtel, Switzerland

2 Literature Review

2.1 Branding and Media Branding

A brand is more than a product, or a packaging, a sign or a logo. It is all those elements plus all the emotional values and feelings as well as intangible attributes consumers link to a given brand. One of the scopes of branding is naming products and making them distinguishable, underlining their unique features and transmitting signal of quality (Chan-Olmsted 2006).

The recent emergence of research in the field of media branding might be induced by the peculiarities provided by media companies. As Picard (2005) mentioned, media products differ significantly among themselves and operate in economic environments with business dynamics that most other products and services do not encounter. Nevertheless, what makes media companies atypical in many regards does not prevent them to be subject to major economic and managerial laws and forces (Picard 2005). According to Chan-Olmsted (2006), branding is considered less applicable to media than to other industries, because of the intrinsic characteristics of content as a product. Media brand communication has to deal with the fact that every communication is addressed to two markets: a business-to-consumers (B2C) and business-to-business (B2B) market. Anyway, it is worth noting that in the case of public service media the B2B market has a lower impact than in the case of commercial broadcasters.

Media firms adopted brand management over 20 years ago (McDowell 2006), even though, its practice is considered more promotional rather than strategic. Moreover, great focus was put on brand extension in order to run the right way in case of market expansion (Chan-Olmsted 2006). Since media brand management is a relatively new discipline in general, there is a need to increment the literature concerning this topic in particular with the recent web 2.0 trends and the increasing number of competitors, media organizations, private bloggers and citizen journalists. Indeed, Shaver and Shaver (2008) recently identified three levels of competition for traditional media firms, which are: competition with other traditional media firms; competition with content aggregators; and competition from non-conventional information sites.

Rieseboz (2003) suggests two main objectives of branding for media companies: first, it helps consumers (a) to remember products by differentiating them from those of competitors, and (b) to choose among different products. Secondly, the brand delivers added value and benefits associated with the brand itself. According to Ots (2008), media organizations employ brand management in an attempt to create and exploit long-term relationships with their audience.

In the case of news organizations, the importance of branding has been increasing since firms are investing in building long-term relationship with stakeholders. Moreover, the high degree of competition within the news media market makes more difficult for companies to attract viewers, listeners and readers merely basing their attempt on the content of the offer (Chan-Olmsted and Cha 2007). Chan-Olmsted (2006) argues that because of information-overload as well as the great number of competitors in the market, consumers are more willing to select those brands which they are more familiar with, avoiding the search and selection of new and unknown brands and products.

When brand management is related to public services, which are for their nature non-profit organizations as suggested by Chan-Olmsted and Kim (2002), the efforts are to be made towards the source of brand equity more than the outcomes.

In literature, it is pivotal the concept of brand personality, which is described as "the set of human characteristic associated with a brand" (Aaker 1997, p. 347). In the field of media branding, this notion it is even more significant, because it helps consumers in the identification of human traits in media brands who delivery news. The five brand personality dimensions which are sincerity, excitement, competence, sophistication and ruggedness can be applied to all products and industries. Chan-Olmsted and Cha (2007) add three more personality dimensions that are more suitable for news media; they are: competence, timeliness, and dynamism.

Moreover, exploiting the fact that usually media organizations are identified by their anchors, the personalities of their anchors are usually associated with the brand itself and there is space for a media firm to "cultivate brand personality" (Chan-Olmsted and Cha 2007). Furthermore, McDowell (2006) claims that the personality of a broadcaster is strictly linked with the personality of the programme hosts.

Another crucial concept is brand identity to defining branding strategies among all the industries. Among the definition that many scholars provide about brand identity, the concept usually refers to the soul of a brand. Thus, it is worth looking at how media managers intend the idea of media brand identity and which the factual implications for media companies are.

In order to create a straight link between a media firm and its brand identity there should be the condition as suggest by Siegert, Gerth and Rademacher (2011, p. 59) "only when the quality is deeply grounded in the brand identity and actively sustained inside media companies can it survive as a core element of the news coverage". Again, Siegert et al. (2011) underline the fact that when it is applied to media firms, brand identity allows making considerations regarding two indivisible aspects for this industry, which are the economic and journalistic dimensions. Moreover, they also introduce a relevant consideration concerning the two levels of branding: corporate and product. Within the context of media organizations there are two groups responsible for the brand strategy adopted (Siegert et al. 2011) which are the group in charge of the editorial creativity and the one in charge of the management operations (journalistic dimensions vs. economic dimensions).

Finally, it worth adding the idea of brand image referred to media companies. It can be defined as the idea that consumers have about a given media brand and it is strictly linked to the media brand reputation. As a consequence, companies should make efforts in order to constantly monitor their brand image and reputation both offline and online.

2.2 Branding with Social Media

Given the rapid evolution of the field, studies on how social media actually influence the branding process emerge. Companies currently evolve in a trial and error environment and corporate managers have to deal with new circumstances. They adapt and rethink their corporate reputation, branding management practices and communication strategies (Jones et al. 2009). Digital communication has impacted corporate brands, from e-commerce to viral marketing campaigns. Social media not only affect marketing management but also branding strategies.

A decade ago, Aaker (2002) stated that firms need to be able to operate outside the traditional media channels in order to build brand awareness successfully. As we have entered the digital age, it would appears clear to the author that the strong brands would be those that best utilize the web as a brand building tool. Consequently redrawing the rules of branding is now necessary (Jones et al. 2009). Currently the interest throughout all industries focuses on SNs. This is especially true in the media sector, where the new media stimulates great effervescence.

Most organizations already incorporate new media possibilities into their promotional mix (Mangold and Faulds 2009). However, even if social media allow a better market segmentation of target groups, they are clearly not only about advertising and selling, but play an important role in participation, content sharing and collaboration activities (Kaplan and Haenlein 2010).

Both promotional and social exchange enhancing characteristics of social media help building branding strategies, therefore adding new media in the promotional mix helps develop stronger brands (Veloutsou and Moutinho 2009) and has the advantages to develop brand relationships. Indeed, experience and engagement are new components already used to build brands online and offline (Awata 2010). Accordingly in their study Tynan et al. (2010) clearly suggest that branding is going toward individual consumer experience.

Social media help building groups around brands, products, companies or specific interests. The active participation of users can create a kind of "we" feeling amongst participants and develop further social relationships among them. From a corporate perspective this engagement could lead to a stronger emotional tie and loyalty toward what is being offered or proposed.

Social media practices like the Facebook groups or fan's page act in a way as customer clubs do. Like in the clubs described by Aaker (2002) firm engagement in SNs demonstrate that they care about their clients. Furthermore, both clubs and SNs groups share elements of sympathy toward the group and amongst members, giving the possibility to experience the brand in relationship with other brand enthusiasts. Building communities (online or offline) move customers closer to the organization. The branding benefits of such connections are mentioned by various researchers (Kotler and Keller 2008; Muniz and O'Guinn 2001). Hence, well executed online conversations can help companies build their presence, reputation and brand image (Jones et al. 2009). As Aaker (2002) explains, strong brands do not limit themselves to product attributes but build relationships with customers. Social media facilitate those interpersonal relationships between brands and customers, through brand experience and emotional benefits.

Thus, brands in general can be considered as aggregators of customers communities (Aaker 2002). Through SNs, not only the firm can interact with its customers and vice versa but also customers can interact with one another. This many-to-many kind of interaction happens beyond the firm's control (Thorson and Rodgers 2006; Mangold and Faulds 2009).

Corporate brands represent the organization and what stands behind what is offered. Aaker (2004) explains that they play an important role in our time of brand proliferation. Besides differentiation corporate brand also provide credibility (Aaker 2004). Even if less at threat to critics than specific products brands—they become always more property of a broader community (Pitt et al. 2006). Brands have reached what Pitt et al. (2006) call the open-source era of branding, where corporate brands have reached a final stage of openness. According to the authors, this evolution of corporate branding, toward a concrete loss of control in terms of content, experience and meaning, leads to the co-creation of those elements where the creators of the firm and the customer communities. The changes undergone by brands help understand the emergence of new managing roles within organizations that act as a single interacting entity in the social media dialogue and represent the brand far away from the pre-existent broadcast media monologues.

3 Method

We develop the study focusing on corporate branding related to media companies in the public service. A case study methodology was employed. RTS, the Radio Television Suisse was selected in order to investigate its approach to social media branding. Focus was given on how the company strategically and operationally deals with social media imperatives when branding online.

The case focuses on the following research question: what are the brand building activities in which RTS invests online (social presence) and what are the reasons for those choices?

The research is descriptive but intends also to understand the reasons for conducting specific brand activities, in a theory building perspective.

The case is built on interviews, observations and document analysis. They were used in triangulation to corroborate and augment evidence from other sources as suggested by Yin (2009). The interviews were either focus or in-depth, semi-structured interviews conducted with the Head of Corporate Communication, the TSR and Multimedia RTS Promotion Manager, General Secretary of the Direction, Resources and Development department, and the DCM. They lasted at least 1 h and were tape-recorded on June and July 2011. The other material employed was in part gathered from interviews with RTS managers. Administrative documents (organizational charts, job description, public and internal documentation or presentations), corporate website and SNs content plus news clippings were used.

RTS was selected as object of study due to its advanced position with regards to social media in Switzerland. This is testified by the recently created Digital Communication Manager position started in October 2010. The method based only on one case is justified by its uniqueness in the Swiss French media market. Exploring implications of SNs for media companies, the case seeks to develop new insights into management activities for public service media companies to build further knowledge.

4 The Case: Digital Communication Manager @RTS

The Radio Television Suisse (RTS) is a business unit of SSR SRG, the national Swiss public broadcaster. The entity is a newly converged media company, primarily dedicated to serving the French speaking part of Switzerland. It is composed by four radio channels, two television channels and various interactive platforms. Approximately 1,600 employees work at RTS, mostly situated in Geneva and Lausanne, the two historical headquarters of radio and television. Regional offices are situated in the French speaking cantons covered by the SSR entity plus Zurich, Bern, Lugano and major capital cities abroad.

With an annual budget of 380 million Swiss Francs, RTS is the market leader in its sector with respectively 58.9 % and 28.6 % market share for its radio and television channels. The penetration is of 833,000 (radio) and 921,000 viewers (television) within its 1.7 million audience market (Facts and Figures 2010/2011). In line with its public service mandate, RTS provides programmes with a scope of information, entertainment and education.

4.1 RTS Online Presence

The main channels of Corporate Communication online are the website, a Facebook (FB) page and a Twitter account. Of course RTS is not only visible through its corporate presence. A repertory of RTS's SN accounts is visible on the corporate fan's page. In it there are 63 FB fan's pages, 15 Twitter accounts and one YouTube channel. Most of them concern various RTS channels and programmes and totalize around 100,000 fans altogether.

Despite the inventory, the social presence of the company is not limited to channels and programmes. In fact, social media are mostly about people. Radio and television employees are by definition also highly visible by nature and are thus inclined to resonate on SNs. Indeed, given the architecture of the brand, we not only find the social media channels for the various business unit and respective programmes, but also the SN feeds of journalists, presenters as well as managers of the company. This holds true on the two main SNs considered. As a consequence, the online presence of RTS results very fragmented. For instance, a list of RTS Twitter accounts curated by the Head of Multimedia Operations News Department TV Unit enlists 67 Twitters feeds. In it, around 60 journalists and presenters and half a dozen special activities accounts are to be found. Yet, none of the above mentioned lists seems to be exhaustive. As an example, other RTS employees such as trainees were found in the micro-blogging network but not enlisted. We also found official YouTube and DailyMotion channels for TV programmes where RTS videos are available but remain unlisted because of uncertainty about their future. Channels and programmes officially appear on the corporate FB page, whereas personal profiles of journalists and presenters do not. In the moving environment of social media presence, RTS seems to push channels and programmes more than persons, with few exceptions, like the key anchor presenter of the evening news show. Quite interestingly though, the news presenter operates on the second most followed channel RTS owns (21,000 likes, right after the youth radio channel Couleur3 that reaches almost 40,000 fans) (Facebook.com/rts.ch, 2011). It has to be mentioned that RTS is not focusing on quantity (only 1,700 likes for the Corporate FB fan's page), but is more interested in interacting and building quality discussions with the audience and opinion leaders. The dialogue is established with micro-communities around key programmes and persons.[2] This infatuation for people leads toward high fragmentation in term of discourse, which explains the necessity for RTS as other media brands to actively manage their presence on SNs.

4.2 Genesis of the Digital Communication Manager

In 2010, radio and television at RTS began a process of convergence. The newly created enterprise involved modifications in terms of content production and management. The organizational charts were redesigned with the advent of the new merged entity. Since then, the chart of the Corporate Communication Department is made up of four units. Besides managers in charge of Internal Communication, Media Relations and Public Relations, RTS institutionalized a new position in charge of Online Relations, the Digital Communication Manager (DCM).

According to the Head of Corporate Communication[3] the creation of this new position is both due to external and internal factors. The main exogenous variables influencing this decision were those concerning the contextual situation. Internet and above all the SNs are considered tools to be strategically managed and from which to take competitive advantages. Through its presence in the SNs, the firm has both an active and proactive role. RTS operates actively when it publishes content and interacts with the audience, whereas it acts pro-actively when it performs all those activities of monitoring and interception of audience' needs and comments with regards to the company itself. The activity of production as well as the activity of monitoring are continuous and are the base of strategic decision making.

With regards to the endogenous factors, the settlement of the DCM was derived from the need to better express and define RTS presence on SNs. There was a necessity to define the institutional presence of the company online and mostly into SNs and to reorganize the online activities already existing by providing common rules and guidelines for the whole company.

Moreover, since the typology of language commonly used within SNs is different from other kinds of written communication as well as the technique of diffusion, it seems strategically imperative to hire a person with specific skills in charge of those tasks among others. This figure transmits and educates other employees to reach a higher degree of coherence and to respect the corporate brand identity.

---

[2] Yan Luong, June 24, 2011.
[3] Manon Romerio, June 24, 2011.

Furthermore, with regards to public media service, the focus on the brand image and brand identity is even more stressed because of the role that the company itself plays to satisfy the essential values in this kind of organization, such as: integrity, coherence and professionalism.[4] It is also worth adding that the online presence of the firm implies its ability to respond properly and by using the most suitable instruments to protect and defend promptly the company's reputation.

Finally, the need of a DCM is also justified by the fact that the linear radio consumption is decreasing among youngsters. However, thanks to podcasts and radio on demand RTS was able to invert this trend (Public Service 2009). On this perspective, developing an efficient and focused web strategy on SNs is intended to play a strategic role in attracting audience and in building lasting brand awareness.

4.3 The Role of the Digital Communication Manager

The DCM is in charge of the e-reputation of RTS and works under the direct supervision of the Head of Corporate Communication. He monitors the web, relies on specific tools and concentrates on sentiment analysis for the corporate brand. Trusted for his expertise and targeted knowledge, the manager also works as an internal adviser. In reality, he is a very autonomous figure and benefits from great flexibility of action and decision power.

He is responsible for the RTS use of social networking and helps building the firm's social media strategy. This strategy relies on the company's will to engage users on websites where they are already present and active by generating discussions, on the corporate website or outside. Besides, SNs allow RTS to reach a broader range of population, who might be less inclined to access RTS content trough traditional distribution channels[5] and make this portion of the population consume and engage more with RTS content. The presence on SNs gives the audience alternative possibilities to access content allowing them to interact with RTS.

The DCM is active engaging online communities. In particular, the DCM is in charge of the relations with key stakeholders on internet and manages the corporate brand content on the different RTS platforms. The figure represents the company on the web. He works both as the internal voice of the company outside and represents the external voices inside.

However, his tasks cover more than the mere presence. The position is cross-section by essence. In fact, the DCM also acts as an internal consultant and works in close relationship with the Marketing and Promotion Department as with journalists and program producers directly. He does not take active responsibility in terms of content for the program pages and accounts, but he advices, supports and follows up social media strategies and tactics for programs and channels. Typical examples are the

---

[4] Serge Gremion, July 1, 2011. According to Manon Romerio, the above mentioned values are followed, however the official values are: open-mindedness, creativity, proximity, independence and responsibility, May 26, 2012.

[5] For TV channels 15–29 years old target penetration is 2.5 times lower than for 30–49 target.

supervision for the creation of a new account or active coaching in case of crisis within a SN. The sub-brands instead are managed, but not defined, by the Marketing and Promotion Department. The brand responsibilities are divided by media type. There is a person in charge of the television and a person in charge of each radio channel. Then, every producer is responsible for the content of its own programs online, according to the framework set by the DCM. He works as guidance for social media related issues in the company, calling himself an evangelist.[6] In fact, in his duty, the DCM will notably play the role of integrator in many departments from Human Resources to the newsrooms. That is mainly why in his specifications, the DCM had to build specific guidelines for employees and content producers on how to use and behave on social media platforms. This implies the development of an overall strategy in terms of brand, programs and persons for the RTS official online presence. In order to build it, he brings back feelings of stakeholders, anomalies. patterns and trends to the company's executive team.

5   Results and Discussion

The main competitive advantages in having a DCM within a public service broadcaster are the following. He collaborates to the definition of a media corporate strategy both internally and externally. Indeed, by involving employees it is possible to guarantee high level of coherence and transparency, as expected by the public service. At the moment of our research, as argued by the General Secretary of the Direction, Resources and Development department (GS), official guidelines concerning the social media behavior for RTS employees do not formally exist yet. Instead, there is an unwritten code of conduct according to which people using SNs are entirely responsible for the posts and twits they make. The company, through the DCM, is involved in raising awareness and responsibility among the organizational members in order to ward and to protect the image of independence and neutrality of the organization itself. However, even though the boundary between public and private sphere is to be found, the firm allows the employees at every level (journalist, managers and collaborators) to use SNs, trusting in their proper code of conduct. Indeed, according to the GS, the tacit rule is "do not post online what you would not say on air".[7]

The ability to use a proper code of communication is pivotal to perform an efficient communication and be attractive, from a marketing point of view; an undesired way to engage the audience could provoke damages to the company.

However, the introduction of this new figure and the consequences of his social media plans could create problems. For instance extra work needs be carried out by organizational members to exploit the social media strategy. Furthermore, since the job position is cross-section, some issues deriving from the integration within the corporate structure

---

[6] Yan Luong, June 24, 2011.
[7] Serge Gremion, July 1, 2011.

could emerge. We actually have not found such a problem at RTS, probably thanks to the small and regional dimension of the broadcaster. Finally, a concrete challenge, at least to public service broadcasters, is the separation between public and private spheres, also because employees (journalists, presenters) are publicly visible and are used to express opinions and comments. SNs give them exposure outside the traditional channels and set questions around their rights and obligations. This has certainly impacts on how to establish new sets of brand guidelines to be used with new platforms such as SNs.RTS is using its social media presence to listen to what is said and establish a dialogue with the audience on the new platforms. RTS approach also demonstrates the growing need within media firms to professionally and strategically manage the content produced on social media. By monitoring the content produced by external stakeholders or providing guidance for the content released from company's members, the current company's practices demonstrate ways to handle the loss of control over brands that can arise within SN interactions, from both inside and outside RTS. The DCM has brought expertise at many levels and helps the company facing challenges that go beyond its established management resources and capabilities, setting priorities and boundaries.

At the time of our research RTS was using SNs mostly to monitor and protect the brand. According to the managers interviewed, the company will be aiming at stronger brand building activities online with the channels rebranding beginning in spring 2012. SNs will be used to accompany the operations, in building awareness, community and identification around the new channels, creating dialogue with the customers, strengthening the newly created sub-brands.

Conclusion

Social media and social networks are still a field of experimentation in many regards mostly from a branding perspective. As a consequence, limited amount of respective literature so far impedes proper comparison with industry practices. Our findings suggest that public service media companies have to take the lead in term of online content production policies given their peculiar employees profiles as their brand will otherwise be affected. Indeed, the necessity to develop guidelines for social media is already mentioned by Kaplan and Haenlein (2010), as it is considered to reduce risks affecting the corporate credibility. Public service media firms defend specific values and have to cope with third parties owned SNs, playing according to their own rules. A lack of consistency within corporate mission or of coherence with the third party platforms might induce brand damages. Therefore, a specific person having a more relevant role and greater power monitoring and analyzing SNs information will be determinant in a time of transition, where experience and reference points still lack.

The definition and integration of a Digital Communication Manager position has a role to play in making individuals inside the company aware of SNs branding implications and has high potential in generating the firm competitive advantage.

5.1 Limitations of the Study

Given that, the research focuses solely on a public radio-television broadcaster, the findings will certainly be applicable to media companies in the broadcasting sector. Since the case regards a firm with a public service mission discrepancies might appear concerning private media companies, considering their different institutional objectives. Generalization concerns will be less linked with the narrow sub-national area researched given the global worthiness of SNs rather than to the size of the firm investigated and its organizational implications. We believe analyzing RTS—a business unit of SSR SRG—allows salient and heuristic extrapolations of branding implications in similar contexts.

5.2 Implications

Further research should focus on models to measure, quantify and evaluate the contribution of the presence of media companies within SNs in terms of success and brand equity. Moreover, it may be worth analyzing how to integrate the figure of the DCM within media firms from an organizational point of view.

Some concerns emerge with regards to being present on an existing social media application and benefit from its popularity and user base (Kaplan and Haenlein 2010), or create an own. As Kaplan and Haenlein (2010) explains, it is a usual make-or-buy decision. However the presence on third parties platforms, could lead to conflicting visions between a commercial company and the public service mission.

In order to build a consistent brand identity in those interactive times a direction has to be provided with the scope to integrate all the factors influencing the brand online. This paradigm shift implies a pro-active use of technology and clear guidance, putting brand imperatives, deontology and network usages components into the balance, driving back credit to the master brand.

References

Aaker, J. L. (1997). Dimensions of brand personality. *Journal of Marketing Research, 34*(3), 347.
Aaker, D. A. (2002). *Building strong brands*. New York: The Free Press.
Aaker, D. A. (2004). Leveraging the corporate brand. *California Management Review, 46*(1), 6–18.
Awata, K. (2010). *An exploration of the impact of social media on branding strategies*. Retrieved from http://kentarohawata.com/blog/wp-content/uploads/2010/11/Social-Media-and-Brand.pdf
Chan-Olmsted, S. M. (2006). *Competitive strategy for media firms—Strategic and brand management in changing media markets*. Mahwah, NJ: Lawrence Erlbaum Associates.
Chan-Olmsted, S. M., & Cha, J. (2007). Branding television news in a multichannel environment: An exploratory study of network news brand personality. *The International Journal on Media Management, 9*(4), 135–150.
Chan-Olmsted, S. M., & Kim, Y. (2002). The PBS brand versus cable brands: Assessing the brand equity of public television in a multi-channel environment. *Journal of Broadcasting & Electronic Media, 46*(2), 300–320.

Couleur3. (ca. 2011). In Facebook [Fan page]. Retrieved July 18, 2011, from http://www.facebook.com/rsr.couleur3
Facts and Figures 2010/2011 (2011). Retrieved from http://www.srgssr.ch/en/publications/facts-and-figures/
Jones, B., Temperley, J., & Lima, A. (2009). Corporate reputation in the era of web 2.0: The case of Primark. *Journal of Marketing Management, 25*(9), 927–939.
Kaplan, A. M., & Haenlein, M. (2010). Users of the world, unite! The challenges and opportunities of SocialMedia. *Business Horizons, 53*(1), 59–68.
Kotler, P., & Keller, K. (2008). *Marketing Management*. Upper Saddle River: Prentice-Hall.
Mangold, W. G., & Faulds, D. J. (2009). Social media: The new hybrid element of the promotion mix. *Business Horizons, 52*(4), 357–365.
McDowell, W. S. (2006). Issues in marketing and branding. In A. B. Albarran, S. M. Chan-Olmsted, & M. O. Wirth (Eds.), *Handbook of media management and economics*. New Jersey: Lawrence Erlbaum Associates.
Muniz, A., & O'Guinn, T. (2001). Brand community. *Journal of Consumer Research, 27*, 412–432.
Ots, M. (Ed.). (2008). *Media brands and branding*. Jönköping: Media Management and Transformation Centre, Jönköping International Business School.
Picard, R. G. (2005). Unique characteristics and business dynamics of media products. *Journal of Media Business Studies, 2*(2), 61–69.
Pitt, L. F., Watson, R. T., Berthon, P., Wynn, D., & Zinkhan, G. (2006). The penguin's window: Corporate brands from an open-source perspective. *Journal of the Academy of Marketing Science, 34*(2), 115–27.
Public Service - Broadcast Your Benefit. (2009). Retrieved from http://www.srgssr.ch/en/publications/public-service/
Radio Television Suisse (RTS) (ca. 2011). In Facebook.com/rts.ch [Fan page]. Retrieved July 18, 2011, from http://www.facebook.com/rts.ch
Rieseboz, R. (2003). *Brand management*. New Jersey: Prentice Hall.
Shaver, D., & Shaver, M. A. (2008). Generating audience loyalty to internet news providers. In M. Ots (Ed.), *Media brands and branding*. Jönköping: Media Management and Transformation Centre, Jönköping International Business School.
Siegert, G., Gerth, M. A., & Rademacher, P. (2011). Brand identity-driven decision making by journalists and media managers—The MBAC model as a theoretical framework. *International Journal on Media Management, 13*(1), 53–70.
Thorson, K., & Rodgers, S. (2006). Relationships between Blogs as eWOM and interactivity, perceived interactivity, and parasocial interaction. *Journal of Interactive Advertising, 6*(2), 39–50.
Tynan, C., McKechnie, S., & Chhuon, C. (2010). Co-creating value for luxury brands. *Journal of Business Research, 63*(11), 1156–1163.
Veloutsou, C., & Moutinho, L. (2009). Brand relationships through brand reputation and brand tribalism. *Journal of Business Research, 62*(3), 314–322.
Yin, R. K. (2009). *Case study research: Design and methods* (4th ed.). Los Angeles: Sage.

Social Television, Creative Collaboration and Television Production: The Case of the BBC's 'The Virtual Revolution'

Nicholas Nicoli

1 Introduction

Social media have forced organisations to reconfigure strategies pertaining to how they communicate with their stakeholders (Burnett et al. 2009; Qualman 2011), as well as to how stakeholders communicate back (Kaplan and Haenlein 2010; Correa et al. 2010). Depending on the nature of the organisation, the exact amount of commitment devoted to reconfiguring these strategies varies. In the field of television, social media have had a profound effect. Online users discuss plotlines, characters, narratives and other issues depending on the genre of the programme. Users for example, might start discussions on Arsenal Football Club's #*Arsenal* twitter feed while the team is playing. At the same time, various other twitter feeds from users that the team cannot control might also be discussing the game; these might come from Arsenal blogs, injured players (teams possibly have some control in this case), opposing team blogs and others. Within the audiovisual sector such examples are part of a growing phenomenon known as social television. Social television is how online users/audiences, as well as programme developers (these might include the station, presenters, producers, actors et cetera), make use of social media to create a richer television experience. Almost certainly, the more the internet and television converge, the more central a role social television will have. It would be foolish of Arsenal FC (or any televised event, programme et cetera), not to have its own presence therefore.

In academia, studies on social television are still very much at an early stage of social media studies (which itself as an academic area of research, is still in its infancy); even the industry is only now coming to grips with its potential. The focus of this chapter is to explore the impact social media have before the final version of the programme is aired. In other words, the chapter looks specifically at how social

N. Nicoli (✉)
University of Nicosia, Nicosia, Cyprus
e-mail: nicoli.n@unic.ac.cy

media might affect television production creativity. Although this particular area of study can also be considered social television studies, here too, the field needs to mature further before any labels are attached to it. It is for this reason that this chapter offers only an exploratory account of social media and television production.

Central to this study is the notion of 'creative collaboration'. Both social media and television production have creative collaborations at their core. Creative collaboration has also become significant in how all organisations attempt to stay ahead of competition. The chapter is in five sections. The first offers a contextual and historical account of creative collaboration by attempting to extend the relevant literature of its two components, creativity and collaboration. The second section describes the nature of social media, highlighting those characteristics that overlap with methods of creative collaboration. It distinguishes the definitions of social media that might apply to creative processes. The third section addresses the field of television production. It specifically looks at the different stages of television production and the characteristics of each one. This section also explores the precarious nature of working in television production. The fourth section sheds empirical light on the above theoretical frameworks by exploring the production of the BBC documentary, *The Virtual Revolution*. It examines the unique way in which the four-part documentary was developed and how online collaboration—through social media—played a role in the final version of the programme. Finally, based on the findings of this study, a smaller fifth section offers a possible direction in future television production and social television research. The chapter draws on a wide range of primary and secondary sources. It combines case study exploratory analysis of the programme *The Virtual Revolution* with long-term historical perspectives on television production.

2 Collaboration and Creativity

The *Harvard Business Review* spotlight feature on collaboration (HBR 2011, pp. 67–107) exemplifies its current significance in management studies. The reason behind the attention afforded to collaboration is its ability to stimulate creativity in organisations seeking competitive advantages. This is known as creative collaboration. Creative collaboration is an area of creativity that has been growing for a number of years. Henry (2006) identifies the early 1980s as an important period in the overlapping of the two, since until then creativity was considered an individual process. In the 1950s and 1960s, psychologists focused on reading and mapping the mind, taking images of the brain and seeking answers from 'creative individuals' in order to draw conclusions on creativity. As we entered the 1970s, psychologists began looking at other issues that might affect creativity, albeit not yet at those external to the individual (Sawyer 2007). For example, psychologists began looking at how people with more diverse experiences might make them more creative than those with less. It soon became clear that different parts of the brain, different memories, at different moments (e.g. changes in mood), stimulated people into generating more ideas. In effect, certain areas of the brain were *collaborating* with other areas. While these breakthroughs in creativity studies were important, possibly the most significant shift in the field occurred during the mid-1990s. Psychologists during this period began to understand that if collaboration *within* the mind allows us to generate ideas, then the environment, external networks, and collaboration between people were also significant variables.

Teresa Amabile's *Creativity in Context* (1996) and Mihaly Csikszentmihalyi's *Creativity: Flow and the Psychology of Discovery and Invention* (1997) became highly influential in shedding light on the collaborative nature of creativity. Together, they helped a number of other disciplines familiarize themselves with creative collaboration. Amabile has since continued her work on organisational creativity at Harvard Business School, whereas Csikszentmihalyi's social-system model is possibly the most applied theoretical framework used to study creativity (it is therefore used extensively in this study). It is based on three mechanisms: the *domain*, the *field* and the *person*. Each of the three mechanisms plays a significant role in the creative process. The *domain* consists of a set of rules, such as mathematics, music, television production. The *field* consists of all the gatekeepers in the domain. The *person*, or creator, uses the symbols of the domain to create a novel idea that is analysed by the field before its members decide whether or not to include it as part of that same domain. Therefore according to Csikszentmihalyi, the definition of creativity is *(p. 28)*:

> Any act, idea, or product that changes an existing domain or that transforms an existing domain into a new one.

As mentioned, in the 1990s interest in creative collaboration grew in other academic areas. Both business studies and the social sciences began looking closer at the effects of creativity, collaboration and the environment.[1] Richard Florida's account of the creative class (2002) led the way forward in how societies thought about acting more creatively. Based on the work of Ikujiro Nonaka and Hirotaka Takeuchi (1995), organisations began looking at how creative collaboration could occur in working environments through the use of technologies that better managed knowledge (see Mesquita 2011 for a more recent perspective of technology for creativity). A subsequent surge in social digital technologies occurred in organisations that wanted to share and create knowledge.

As the use of social digital technologies spread, it became apparent that creative collaboration through technology would be more effective if it were closer in design with face-to-face communication. Sonnenburg (2004) has coined the term 'creaplex', defining it as, 'a specific kind of communication system from which collaborative creativity emerges' (p. 255). Creaplex success depends on the different forms of communication platforms it happens on. The ones Sonnenburg

---

[1] Many of these disciplines had already addressed issues of collaboration (e.g. social network analysis, social capital theory, systems theory), but grounding collaboration with creativity processes was a new approach.

distinguishes are face-to-face interaction, tool-interaction and tool-mediated communication. Significantly, each platform offers different aspects of human communication. These might include leadership, conflict, emotions, culture and others.

Upon closer examination, Sonnenburg's creaplex theory has similarities with 'social presence theory' (Short et al. 1976) which looks at the degree of 'presence' (acoustic, visual, physical, intimacy, immediacy) in each medium. In essence, social presence theory states that communication effectiveness can be based on the 'presence' of the medium. The more enriched it is, the closer to face-to-face collaboration it will be. A similar approach was taken by Coleman and Levine (2008) who pointed to the difficulties required in communicating with other people and the subtleties involved in interpersonal communication (e.g. signs of conflict, managing emotions etc.). Only if these are realized and understood at the interpersonal level of communication can virtual collaboration thrive. As they note, 'if people do not become students of understanding the nuances of how to communicate most effectively in a virtual environment, they will be forced to face the same consequences of ineffective communication as in the physical world' (p. 146). What these studies have in common is that they all stress the limitations of social digital technologies since various communication elements are missing when compared to interpersonal forms.

As the literature on social digital technologies and creative collaboration expanded, various scholars were concurrently looking at best practices of face-to-face creative collaboration without the use of technology. In 2000, almost in unison, *Managing Creativity* (2000) by Howard Davies and Richard Scase in the UK, and *Creative Industries* (2000) by Richard Caves in the USA, presented a perspective of collaboration for creativity that became ubiquitous in both countries. Both volumes emphasised the strength of media management practices in stimulating creativity. As they argued, media managers have always had an implicit motive to manage creativity because creativity has always been a core component of media products. The main tool media managers use to stimulate creativity is to allow specific forms of nonconformist, autonomous and indeterminate collaborations to flourish (Davis and Scase 2000). Caves (2000), drawing on sociologists of culture (e.g. Howard Becker's *Art Worlds* 1982 and Pierre Bourdieu's *The Field of Cultural Production* 1993), called these teams' *motley crews* and noticed that they came from both diverse backgrounds and areas of expertise in order to create high-quality media content.

It soon became accepted that small, diverse teams working on common creative projects similar to those used in media production projects is the most effective way to stimulate creativity (Bilton and Leary 2002; Moultrie and Young 2009). The main focus of subsequent studies was on what happens *inside* these collaborations (Bilton 2007; Sawyer 2007; Coleman and Levine 2008). For example, Keith Sawyer (2007) studied thousands of hours of tape of jazz performances and improvisation theatre for a decade before identifying patterns of successful collaboration, whereas Clydesdale (2006) looked at how competition between those collaborating can either stimulate or stifle creativity depending on various factors.

It is beyond the scope of the chapter to look in detail at what creativity is and where it comes from, but the aggregation of the above studies have certain common themes that are important for this study. Firstly, creativity is not the work of a lone genius but rather a combination of occurrences between the individual and the external environment. Secondly, the most important aspect of the external environment regarding where creativity is found, is collaboration. Thirdly, collaboration is a specific form of communication that works best in small, equal, diverse teams that are given time to create ideas that might work, but might also fail (and this needs to be understood as a possible outcome). Fourthly, social digital technologies are allowing new forms of collaboration to flourish. The more we enhance our understanding of virtual collaboration and realize the limitations of the technology as opposed to face-to-face collaboration, the more we will be able to stimulate creativity. As broadband speeds increase and digital technologies develop into ubiquitous and cheap applications, social creativity will continue to grow on an unprecedented scale.

3 Social Media and Creative Collaboration

Many chapters in this book have put forward noteworthy definitions of social media. Although this chapter does not exactly follow suit, it does wish to ascertain those elements of social media that are relevant to creative collaboration and how they are changing the very essence of creative processes.

Charles Leadbeater's *We Think: Mass Innovation not Mass Production* (2008), Clay Shirkey's *Here Comes Everybody: The Power of Organizing Without Organizations* (2009) and David Gauntlett's *Making is Connecting* (2011) are three examples of the growing number of publications noting how web 2.0 is radically changing creativity. According to these authors, social media is causing mass collaborative forms of creativity that extend beyond small teams formed within organisations. As Leadbeater notes (2009, p. 240).

> The web invites us to think and act with people, rather than for them...The principle that we should think 'with' stands in stark contrast to the kind of outlook, organisation and culture spawned by the mass production and mass consumption of the twentieth century.

Social media is a technological space where online users create their own content and engage with their acquaintances, with similar users as well as with the virtual world as a whole. Kaplan and Haenlein (2010) note, 'user generated content (USG) can be seen as the sum of all ways in which people make use of social media' (p. 61). Furthermore, there are four key enablers of social media similar to those highlighted in creative collaboration studies (Bahnisch and Bruns 2009). These are: low threshold to participation, highly granular participation (gradual socialisation to community), assumption of user equipotentiality (equal potential to become valued), and shared content ownership. When users generate content on social media, the key enablers become a catalyst for creative collaborations. Some are large, others are smaller, but all are significant in that creativity can be achieved.

Consequently, since creative acts can occur through social media, Csikszentmihalyi's social-systems model can be embedded as a theoretical guideline. The *domain* (regardless of what kind) is susceptible to change since through social media anyone can be involved in creating, therefore the rules can change, at any given moment, based on what the field says is acceptable (through for example, online recommendation systems, number of hits, number of downloads etc.). The *field* changes since traditional gatekeepers become disempowered and new ones emerge due to the attributes of the technologies behind social media (e.g. *youtube*).[2] Finally, the *person* or creator might change because since it is a collaborative effort achieved online, it is often difficult to point to one creator (e.g. a computer programme in which many programmers contribute).

As an example of this, according to Csikszentmihalyi's social-system model, gonzo journalism can be seen as a creative act because it transforms the existing domain of journalism. When Hunter S. Thomson began writing in that particular style, a new form of journalism was established since from that moment onwards, a number of journalists started using the same approach (and in so doing giving it a stamp of approval). In the same way, civic journalism can also be considered a creative act, possibly of a larger magnitude than other journalistic creative acts, because not only does it change the domain, it also changes the field and the characteristics of the person (creator) at the same time. Social media therefore can be considered a hugely significant creative collaboration tool because it has the potential to continuously redefine domains, fields and persons using the symbols of that domain.

4 Television Production

According to David Hesmondhalgh (2007), television is the largest of the media industries that 'produces social meaning' (p. 11). Although this can be challenged today by looking at internet-user habits, television arguably plays the most significant role in shaping public opinion and serving the interests of millions of viewers, either as consumers or as citizens; the importance of television production as a field of study therefore, should not be underestimated (Born 2000).

Television production can be broken down into different stages (Ryan 1992; Hesmondhalgh 2007; Randle 2011). This occurs in order to 'discipline the creative process...such that management may set the standards, rate and timing of creation and keep labour costs to a minimum' (Ryan 1992, p. 104). According to Hesmondhalgh (p. 66), television production involves the following stages, *creation*, *reproduction* and *circulation*. The creation stage is divided further into three

---

[2] It should be noted that political economists researching the internet are not yet convinced that gatekeepers have changed (see Fuchs 2011).

parts (pp. 66–69). These are, (1) *conception* (design, realisation, interpretation etc.), (2) *execution* (performance in recording studios, film and TV sets etc.), and (3) *transcription* on to a final master (editing, mixing etc.). Ryan points out that the creation stage, particularly the conception phase, stands out as a complex and different process to others stages. The original idea during this phase is 'held to be a product of the imagination and talents of identifiable individuals and an expression of human experience', and as such the stage 'revolves around collaborative relations and is characterised by discussion, negotiation and compromise' (p. 111). This echoes the work of Caves (2000) aforementioned. The reproduction stage, divided into transcription and duplication, involves a combination of trained technical workers using highly advanced technologies in order to edit, record, mix, film, plate-make etc. (the transcription phase); other 'mechanical' processes such as making copies from a master, printing, pressing, packaging and labelling, binding etc. are part of the duplication phase. Reproduction therefore involves a combination of routinized labour with 'considerable dexterity and a broad knowledge of operational possibilities' (Ryan 1992, p. 113). The circulation stage consists of marketing, advertising and packaging design, publicity, distribution and wholesaling and, significantly, market research. While the circulation stage is a significant component of all sectors of contemporary economies, in television production its role is accentuated due to the rapid deterioration of television programmes once they enter the market.

As aforementioned, from the three stages of production, the creation stage requires the most demanding creative attention, and is therefore often more expensive and more risky to achieve success than the other stages. Consequently, television managers attempt to prolong the life of programmes by using techniques such as episodes and seasons (Barwise and Ehrenberg 1988). This way there is less demand for original content, and as a result less need to get involved in the creation stage. Yet all programmes are based on a certain life-cycle and audiences continuously expect original content. Television producers therefore, are constantly under pressure to create original programmes and to be involved in the creation stage. Küng-Shankleman (2000) notes that in broadcasting there is a '[ ]...pressure for constant product innovation [whereby] each product is effectively a prototype or one-off' (p. 46).

The creation stage of television production has traditionally been a closed and defined subsector of the television industry. Yet signs of it 'opening up' have been occurring for a while now. Due to various socio-economic and political factors, television producers working internally in large, vertically-integrated broadcasting organisations have gradually been forced to work independently either as freelancers or as owners of their own independent production companies. This can be seen positively in that it has given opportunities to new programme-makers, therefore increasing the creativity and diversity of television. At the same time, it has also transformed the field into one that is precarious, whereby those in it often find themselves without work for long periods of time (Randle 2011).

Independent producers create programmes that are commissioned to them from free-to-air broadcasters and increasingly from digital subscription channels, following a sequence of: *proposal* (submission of idea to broadcaster), *development* (finalising the proposal), *approval* (submission of programme proposal and confirmation by commissioning editor) and *contract* (final terms are made, such as prices, rights, net profits share et cetera) (Deakin et al. 2008, pp. 4–5).

Based on the above, television production has increasingly become more complex and competitive. Consequently, despite the growth in television production, it has hitherto remained a relatively difficult field to succeed in. This fact is exacerbated by social media. Younger film and television makers are using social media platforms to promote and establish themselves, in the hope they will be 'discovered' (adding another dimension to social television).

5 The BBC's 'The Virtual Revolution'

Over the years the BBC has proficiently executed the most current management approach of the day (Küng-Shankleman 2000; Born 2004). At a time when creativity management is fast becoming the model that organisations of all sectors are applying, it seems the public service broadcaster is looking to take more of a leadership role in this particular managerial paradigm. Under the management team of Mark Thompson (the Director General at the time of writing this chapter), the BBC aspires to be 'the most creative organisation in the world' (BBC 2006). In order to do so it is forced to take actions that are unique and useful in its domain (originality and value are two characteristics of creativity that all creativity theorists endorse, Amabile 1996). As a result the organisation often attempts to take risks, to change structural norms, and to elevate the benchmark of its television production.

The organisation's confidence in creativity management—albeit its ongoing budget cuts—stems from the fact that as one of the largest and most prestigious cultural institutions, managing creativity is its main undertaking and core function. Furthermore, the BBC has been managing creativity at a high level for longer than most organisations in the world, and today stands as a bastion of excellence in media management. Since Director General Mark Thompson took over at the BBC in 2004, the organisation has adopted many methods stimulating the creativity of the organisation as a whole—but particularly of its television production units (Nicoli 2011). Moreover, as one of the largest public service broadcasters in the world, it is looking to move strongly into the digital age (Iosifidis 2007). Its digital ambitions coupled with its drive to pursue creative ideas in production, is really what incentivised the organisation to pursue a project using social media early in the creation stage. The organisation had been experimenting with social media and television production earlier than the decision to develop *The Virtual Revolution* although none of its previous projects were either as ambitious or as successful (e.g., see BBC's *Signs of Life*). The organisation's perseverance paid off with this production since it drew high ratings and has won a 2010 Digital Emmy Award for Best Digital Programme: Non Fiction, and the 2010 BAFTA television award for New Media.

5.1 What Is The Virtual Revolution

The Virtual Revolution is a technology documentary that aired on BBC Two from January 30th, 2010 until February 20th, 2010. It was broadcast in four weekly episodes that lasted 60-min each. The documentary is a coproduction by the BBC and the Open University. Its main theme is how the World Wide Web, 20 years after its creation, has impacted all aspects of life. Presenting the documentary is a charismatic social media researcher, academic, blogger, and newspaper columnist/podcaster for *the guardian* named Aleks Krotoski. Throughout the series Krotoski meets with, and interviews some of the most influential internet scholars and commentators; the series manages to successfully inform, educate and entertain (what is considered a common 'postmodern' turn in documentary production, see Fursich 2003; as well as the three main pillars of public service broadcasting). Some of the people interviewed in the series are, Tim Berners-Lee, Jeff Bezos, Clay Shirkey, Robin Dunbar, Bill Gates, Al Gore, Susan Greenfield, Chad Hurley, Jimmy Wales, Steve Wozniak, and Mark Zuckerberg.

Each of the four episodes emphasises different aspects of the internet and uses informative graphics that highlight various internet characteristics that in turn, give the interviews more credence. The first episode, *The Great Levelling?*, asks whether the Internet is breaking down traditional hierarchies; the second episode, *Enemy of the State?* looks at how the internet is affecting freedom of speech and democracy; the third episode, *The Cost of Free*, addresses the commercial aspects of the internet and wonders whether all the information available on the internet is actually free, or if there is a covert price to pay; and finally the fourth episode, *Homo Interneticus?*, seeks to understand how the internet is changing how we think, our attention spans and whether it has a negative or positive outcome for society.

5.2 The Making of The Virtual Revolution

The BBC's in-house production unit that developed the documentary already had strong connections with people important in the internet domain; it therefore felt that with the support of the BBC, it was a good time to take advantage of its connections and develop something special to celebrate the web's 20th anniversary. As mentioned, what has made this programme unique is the decision by its programme developers to 'open-up' all phases of the creation stage (see previous section), to online users of social media. The producers felt that because of the subject-matter of the programme, using social media early in its creation would make it a more interesting and possibly more creative production. Senior producer Russell Barnes, writing at the time of production mentioned (2010), 'we don't want to observe bloggers from high; we want to blog ourselves and get feedback and comment on our ideas'. The programme's blog posted the following copy (BBC 2011a):

> The Virtual Revolution looks at how the web is shaping our world...it has been an open and collaborative production, which asked the web audience to debate programme themes, suggest and send questions for interviewees, watch and comment on interview and graphics clips, and download clips for personal use and re-editing.

The documentary therefore, broke new ground by inviting online users, through social media platforms, to take part in a form of creative, crowdsourcing collaboration. Specifically, an attempt was made to use social media at the conception phase, the execution phase, and the transcription phase (all the phases of the creation stage).

5.3 The Conception Phase

At the earliest stage of development, even from before the series directors and other members of the production team joined on, the senior producer and development producer posted twitter feeds announcing the concept of the documentary. To a certain extent, the early responses on twitter shaped the production of the documentary by what one producer phrased as 'spiking' ideas on how to proceed. The next stage of the process was an event organized at the BBC marking the Web's anniversary and kicking-off the production of the documentary. Present at the event were internet VIP's (e.g. Chris Anderson—Editor-In-Chief *Wired Magazine*), and Open University and BBC personnel. Also invited were well-known bloggers and editors of significant online and print media. By inviting them an attempt was made to generate awareness of the programme across the blogosphere. The main event of the launch was the keynote speech given by Tim Berners-Lee. Following the launch, the next task was to mobilize social media users through certain online avenues such as podcasts and facegroup groups. The target again was to generate traffic on the documentary's own twitter page and blog. During these early stages, the production team consciously targeted users with high social network potential hoping they would be active in responding to the posts they were sending out.

One of the most collaborative initiatives the BBC took during the conception phase was to invite users to consider possible names for the title (the production team coined this task 'namestorm'). By doing so, the BBC's efforts focused on engaging with both future audiences (who would watch the programme when it finally aired), and online users (fulfilling in this way, its public service remit, among other things). It posted calls through its blog and through twitter, inviting people to come up with possible names. British actor, writer and blogger Stephen Fry (also an interviewee and internet advocate in the documentary), helped to attract awareness. At the time, on his twitter page (Fry 2011), he posted the following, 'Help name this New DigiRevolution open source BBC doc series!@bbcdigrev I'm being int'ed for it now. http://bit.ly/2CLEfy#bbcnamestorm'. Following this, a list of names was displayed on the blog (what the BBC divided into, 'names that have come close', and 'names that haven't'). The original name given to the series was *The Digital Revolution* but the 'namestorm' initiative led to the producers changing it to *The Virtual Revolution*.

As a discussion opened up between the production team and social media users, user influence and contribution grew. As an experiment, users were even asked to film their own experiences regarding the internet. It was an experiment because the producers were still unsure of how to use the content (as it turns out none of that content was used in the final version). Some of the comments made however, were more useful and a number of them were taken into consideration before the execution phase began. For example, the observation made that more women should be interviewed.

5.4 The Execution Phase

When the execution stage began, the production team had been hoping to use online users more. Some of the team wanted users to send in questions during the shooting of the interviews, but traditional production obstacles made this difficult. For example, if the team were given one hour with Al Gore or Bill Gates, it would be difficult to fit everything within that time restriction. On the other hand, various social media contributions during this stage were more valuable albeit not directly in filming the documentary. For example, the BBC's *lab UK* (BBC 2011b) in collaboration with leading UK academics, initiated a web experiment (*what web personality are you*?), whereby users were invited to take part in order to see, essentially, what kind of thought-processes each user conducting the experiment has (this was done by using animal metaphors). The following tweet illustrates its success in building traffic, (BBCDigRev 2011), '@: I guess a lot of people want to know what web animal they are, BBC's web servers seem to be struggling!! #bbcrevolution'. While it is debatable as to whether the *lab UK* initiative was indeed a 'creative' collaboration, some form of original collaboration undoubtedly did take place. One final effort to draw online users to collaborate in the creative process was made when the production team uploaded early rushes of interviews on the programme blog, again as an experiment, in the hope that users would contribute creatively in the production. Unfortunately, the effort made with the rushes did not manage to make much of an impact, at least creatively for the programme.

5.5 The Transcription Phase

During this last phase of the creation stage, the BBC production team felt it could engage with online users by using the rushes uploaded online in the execution phase. The rushes were allowed to be used by online users to create their own mash-ups and upload them on social media platforms. Consequently, the programme's blog encouraged users to view rushes of interviews and embed their own creative work. The copy posted on the programme blog read (BBC 2011a):

> These rushes sequences are part of our promise to release content from most of our interviews and some general footage, all under a permissive licence for you to embed, or download a non-branded version and re-edit.

Furthermore, twitter was also used to encourage users to utilize the rushes. The following example (BBCDigRev 2011) demonstrates how the professional production team invited users to take part in the process, '@: All content on our site http://bit.ly/bbcvrev is global—rushes of interviews can even be downloaded and reused. ~danb, January 31st'. In this case, twitter was used as a tool to redirect users to the programme blog where they could subsequently use software code to edit the rushes.

5.6 The End Result

From the outset it seems the producers had truly wanted to make this a collaborative effort between themselves and social media users. It just so happened that all the right ingredients were in place. The subject-matter was ideal for the production team, and it was also supported by BBC management. As a result, *The Virtual Revolution* will be remembered, among other things, as a successful example of a production that employed social media early in the creative process of its development. The documentary was well-received by members of the audience, by online users, as well as by the industry itself. Yet for a number of reasons, it seems that similar productions will not be made too often, at least not from traditional broadcasting stations. The programme was more of an experiment and an exception rather than a new production trend we might see more of. The production team came across plenty of obstacles that encumbered them throughout the creation stage. Merely in monitoring the amount of information coming in from online users was in itself cumbersome. How that information could be applied, or more significantly, how it could be used in a creative manner required both human and fiscal resources that were simply not available. Furthermore, keeping the social media platforms active and responding to the inflow of questions and comments was time-consuming to the point that it often got counterproductive. While the team consciously put in a lot of effort in trying to make this project a creative collaboration with social media users, many of these efforts turned out to be interactive communication processes rather than true creative collaborations. In other words, although the production team managed to engage successfully with online users, it is debatable as to whether any major creative decisions were affected on account of social media collaboration. The example of how the rushes were used is a clear case in point. The producers could not find a way to make the most of online user creativity to use the rushes in a way that would affect the creation stage; the rushes were merely used by online users to make mash-ups and upload them back on social media platforms. They essentially became promotional material for the documentary—part of the reproduction and circulation stages, rather than part of the creation stage. It is also the case that as a large and unavoidably bureaucratic organisation, the BBC made it harder for the producers to do things that might have made this production truly a collaborative effort with online users (e.g. restrictions on licenses, policies et cetera).

Finally, by using a simple textual analysis approach to construct meaning from these sites (Markham 2010), it can be concluded that traditional television production hierarchies remained intact as seen on the blog, programme website and twitter account feeds. Phrases such as, '*our* site', 'part of *our* promise', 'permissive licence' are all examples of this. To use Csikszentmihalyi's model, the *field* put up resistances rather than allow the *domain* to change. Social media users picked up on this. For example, some users had concerns with certain issues as shown in this tweet, '@: Is it wrong for BBC to call @BBCDigRev documentary "open source" when their licence is more restrictive than any CC licence?' (BBCDigRev 2011).

The production team's efforts are notable since they did much to accommodate social media users during the creative stage. Despite their efforts however, the team—possibly subconsciously—felt as though this project was 'theirs only' and not theirs *and* the online social media community.

6 Future (Social) Television Production Research

Social television is increasing in importance and will continue to do so due to the convergence of the internet and television. Television producers and audiences will continue to engage with each other through social television; exactly when in the development of programmes this engagement will begin is important to analyse, because by knowing this, programme-makers will be better placed to use social television. Looking at the case of the making of *The Virtual Revolution*, although the producers tried to get online users to take part in the creative stage, it seemed easier using social media as a means to keep users informed of updated news regarding the documentary than in actually generating and using ideas. In other words, social television becomes effective immediately after the creation stage and not necessarily to make a programme more creative. The following tweet (BBCDigRev 2011) posted on the series' twitter page 2 weeks before the show aired is an example of how social media was used as production entered the circulation stage, "BBCDigRev Virtual Revolution, Hot off the press—The Virtual Revolution has been given a broadcast slot—BBC2 on Saturday nights at 8 pm from 30th Jan., January 12".

The reason behind this is that it is likely those working during the creation stage will show resistances vis-à-vis the use of social television—often subconsciously—because they need to apply their energy, skills and creativity elsewhere. Going back to the basics of creative audiovisual programmes, it still remains the case that small, diverse groups of talented and committed individuals is the most appropriate way of developing creative television. Motley crews will continue to function more or less as they have done so hitherto. A possible exception of when social television might be used during the creation stage is when a programme is aired live (during the execution phase). This is so because social television can actually be used in the content of the programme (for example when *X-Factor* audiences are shown what twitter users are saying about Simon Cowell). Generally speaking however, the *domain* of television production is hard to change by using social media since the *field* puts up resistances. The motley crew will strive to remain a motley crew, working in small face-to-face collaborations with people they know can deliver. Consequently, while social television has many benefits for the field of television, it seems that they will more likely be for engaging with users and audiences for promotional purposes rather than collaborate creatively with professional production teams. Social digital technologies have set off seismic changes within organisations and television is no different; but as these technologies continue to fuel the convergence of television and the internet, the actual people working in this industry (and possibly other creative industries that are more accustomed to working in small creative teams), possibly require more time to come to terms with them and find ways to use these technologies to collaborate more creatively. As a result, it is this author's view that social television will surely have a huge impact on the audiovisual sector, but it will affect the stages of television production that are more a part of reproduction and particularly circulation (promotion, market research, audience monitoring et cetera) rather than the creative aspects of production.

References

Amabile, T. (1996). *Creativity in context*. Boulder, CO: Westview.
BBC. (2006). *BBC Annual Report and Accounts 2005/06: The BBC Trust's Review and Assessment* [online]. Accessed June 9, 2009, available from http://www.bbc.co.uk/annualreport/2006/pdfs/bbctrust_eng.pdf
BBC. (2011a). *The virtual revolution: How 20 years of the web has reshaped our lives* [online]. Accessed September 13, 2011, available from http://www.bbc.co.uk/blogs/digitalrevolution/2009/10/rushes-sequences-general-views.shtml
BBC. (2011b). *BBC Lab UK: Take part in groundbreaking science* [online]. Accessed December 3, 2011, available from http://news.bbc.co.uk/2/hi/technology/8144570.stm
BBCDigRev. (2011). Virtual revolution [online: Twitter page]. Accessed December 5, 2011, available from https://twitter.com/#!/BBCDigRev
Bahnisch, M., & Bruns, A. (2009, March). Social media: Tools for user-generated content: Social drivers behind growing consumer participation in user-led content generation. *Smart Services CRC*, Vol. 1 – State of the Art.
Barnes, R. (2010). *Charting the digital revolution* [online]. Accessed August 12, 2011, available from http://news.bbc.co.uk/2/hi/technology/8144570.stm
Barwise, P., & Ehrenberg, A. (1988). *Television and its audience*. London: Sage.
Becker, H. (1982). *Art worlds*. Berkeley, CA: University of California Press.
Bilton, C. (2007). *Management of creativity: From creative industries to creative management*. Oxford: Blackwell.
Bilton, C., & Leary, R. (2002). What can managers do for creativity? Brokering creativity in the creative industries. *International Journal of Cultural Policy, 8*(1), 49–64.
Born, G. (2000). Inside television: Television studies and the sociology of culture. *Screen, 41*(4), 404–424.

Born, G. (2004). *Uncertain vision: Birt, Dyke and the reinvention of the BBC*. London: Secker and Warburg.
Bourdieu, P. (1993). *The field of cultural production*. New York: Columbia University Press.
Burnett, E., Lamm, A., Lucas, J., & Waters, R. (2009). Engaging stakeholders through social networking: How nonprofit organisations are using Facebook. *Public Relations Review, 35*, 102–106.
Caves, R. (2000). *Creative industries: Contracts between art and commerce*. Cambridge, MA: Harvard University Press.
Clydesdale, G. (2006). Creativity and competition: The Beatles. *Creativity Research Journal, 1*(2), 129–140.
Coleman, D., & Levine, S. (2008). *Collaboration 2.0: Technology and best practices for successful collaboration in a Web 2.0 world*. Silicon Valley, CA: Hppy About.
Correa, T., Hinsley, A. W., & De Zuniga, H. G. (2010). Who interacts on the Web?: The intersection of users' personality and social media use. *Computers in Human Behaviour, 26*, 247–253.
Csikszentmihalyi, M. (1997). *Creativity: The flow of psychology of the discovery and invention*. New York: Harper Collins.
Davis, H., & Scase, R. (2000). *Managing creativity*. Buckingham: Open University Press.
Deakin, S., Lourenco, A., & Pratten, S. (2008, March). *No third way for economic organization? Networks and quasi-markets in broadcasting* (Working Paper No. 360). Cambridge: Centre for Business Research, University of Cambridge.
Florida, R. (2002). *The rise of the creative class: And how it's transforming work, leisure community and everyday life*. New York: Basic Books.
Fry, S. (2011). Stephen Fry Twitter Page [online: Twitter page]. Accessed December 5, 2011, available from https://twitter.com/#!/stephenfry
Fuchs, C. (2011). The contemporary world wide web: Social medium or new space of accumulation. In Winseck. D and Yong Jin. D (Eds.), *The political economies of media* (pp. 201–220). London: Bloomsbury.
Fursich, E. (2003). Between credibility and commodification: Nonfiction entertainment as a global media genre. *International Journal of Cultural Studies, 6*(2), 131–153.
Gauntlett, D. (2011). *Making is connecting: The social meaning of creativity, from DIY and knitting to YouTube and Web 2.0*. Cambridge: Polity.
HBR. (2011, July–August). Collaboration: Spotlight feature. *Harvard Business Review*, pp. 67–107.
Henry, J. (2006). *Creative management and development* (3rd ed.). London: Sage.
Hesmondhalgh, D. (2007). *The cultural industries* (2nd ed.). London: Sage.
Iosifidis, P. (2007). *Public television in the digital era: Technological challenges and new strategies for Europe*. London: Palgrave.
Kaplan, A., & Haenlein, M. (2010). Users of the world, unite! The challenges and opportunities of social media. *Business Horizons, 53*, 59–68.
Küng-Shankleman, L. (2000). *Inside the BBC and CNN: Managing media organisations*. London: Routledge.
Leadbeater, C. (2009). *We think*. London: Profile Books.
Markham, A. (2010). Internet research. In D. Silverman (Ed.), *Qualitative research* (3rd ed.). London: Sage.
Mesquita, A. (Ed.). (2011). *Technology for creativity and innovation: Tools, techniques and application*. Hershey, PA: IGI.
Moultrie, J., & Young, A. (2009). Exploratory study of organizational creativity in creative organizations. *Creativity and Innovation Management, 18*(4), 299–314.
Nicoli, N. (2011). Creativity management, technology and the BBC. In A. Mesquita (Ed.), *Technology for creativity and innovation: Tools, techniques and application* (pp. 285–301). Hershey, PA: IGI.

Nonaka, I., & Takeushi, H. (1995). *The knowledge creating company: How the Japanese companies create dynamics*. Oxford: Oxford University Press.
Sawyer, K. (2007). *Group genius: The creative power of collaboration*. New York: Basic Books.
Shirkey, C. (2009). *Here comes everybody: How change happens when people come together*. London: Penguin.
Short, J., Williams, E., & Christie, B. (1976). *The social psychology of telecommunications*. London: Wiley.
Sonnenburg, S. (2004). Creativity in communication: A theoretical framework for collaborative product creation. *Creativity and Innovation Management, 13*(4), 254–262.
Qualman, E. (2011). *Socialnomics: How social media transforms the way we live and do business*. Hoboken, NJ: Wiley.
Randle, K. (2011). The organization of film and television production. In M. Deuze (Ed.), *Managing media work*. Thousand Oaks, CA: Sage.
Ryan, P. (1992). *Making capital from culture: The corporate form of capitalist cultural production*. Sydney: Walter De Gruyter.

Evolution of Strategy and Commercial Relationships for Social Media Platforms: The Case of YouTube

Sonya Yan Song and Steven S. Wildman

1 Introduction

We have long understood that success for most media services depends on their ability to coordinate the interrelated demands of consumers, who may or may not appreciate having advertisements packaged with the content they seek, and advertisers who want access to the audiences the content attracts. This basic insight of the media economics literature was rediscovered, extended and generalized to a variety of other products and services in the more recent economics literature on two-sided markets (or two-sided platforms). In the context of that literature, one can think of a media product or service as a platform used to address and manage tradeoffs involved in serving the linked demands of advertisers and media consumers. While the newer work on two-sided markets has made clear that no simple rule captures the complexities involved even in setting prices for the two sides of a two-sided platform (see, e.g., Armstrong 2006; Parker and Van Alstyne 2005), the problem that must be solved by a traditional media company is still relatively straightforward compared to the challenges of a social media service, which, by its very nature is forced to deal with a much more varied and complicated set of relationships via a platform that typically has more than just two sides.

The added coordination challenges faced by social media services are reflections of the flexibility and capabilities of the Web 2.0 technologies (and their successors) that made these services possible. Furthermore, because their software-defined consumer services facilitate social relationships and practices that can evolve as users experiment with a service, social media services often must reconfigure themselves on the fly to co-evolve with users' demands and expectations. This chapter employs the multi-sided platform lens to examine YouTube, focusing on the relationships it facilitates and how its services and features have evolved since its founding in 2005.

S.Y. Song (✉) • S.S. Wildman
Michigan State University, East Lansing, MI, USA

The chapter is organized as follows. The next section presents data that demonstrates YouTube's prominence among online video services and describes the viewing habits of the YouTube audience. The section that follows describes the heterogeneous mix of users, advertisers and content suppliers who either use or contribute to the set of services offered by YouTube. The next section describes YouTube as a multisided platform that provides a variety of intermediation services to facilitate transactions by and coordination among platform participants. This section also examines the platform's evolution from a relatively simple service that sold advertisers access to web audiences attracted by amateur videos uploaded by other internet users to a service that increasingly features commercial content from a diverse set of sources. The final section summarizes the chapter.

2 A Major Online Video Service Built on Social Media Foundations

Best known as a pioneering online video service featuring-user generated content, YouTube has been social in character from the very beginning: serving as a vehicle for sharing videos among friends and acquaintances, featuring user comments on hosted videos, promoting viral discovery of content, and making traffic statistics on individual videos available to all users. While still a social media service at its core, a significant portion of YouTube's more recent efforts have focused on adding services and features that by themselves are not necessarily social. This strategy of leveraging its social media architecture to diversify its service offerings appears to have paid off. Today it is by many measures the dominant destination for watching video online.

According to comScore measures for the United States during May 2012, Google sites generated just over 17.6 billion streamed video views, which was just over 48 % of the total of approximately 36.6 billion views for all Internet sites (Flosi 2012). A distant second and third by this measure were Hulu and Yahoo! sites, with approximately .89 and .85 billion views respectively. Because YouTube accounts for almost all of the Google sites' video traffic, this is essentially a measure of YouTube's position in the online video marketplace. YouTube's dominance in total views reflects in part the fact that online viewers spend substantially more minutes per month with YouTube and visit it more frequently than most other online video services. But YouTube also towers above competing video sites in total unique viewers, recording 151.7 million unique viewers during May 2012, compared to Yahoo! sites at 57.8 million, and Vevo, Microsoft sites, and Facebook with around 40 million monthly unique viewers each.

By traditional media measures, the rate at which YouTube acquires new content is simply astounding. For instance, at the time this chapter was written IMDb listed 2,219,335 movies and TV episodes produced worldwide since 1880.[1] If we assume

---

[1] We used the "Advanced Title Search" on IMDb and framed our request as anything released between 1800 and 2012. The total number of results accounted for 2,219,335 and the earliest release was *Sallie Gardner at a Gallop* traced back to 1880.

that content units average an hour each, this amounts to 224 continuous years of video. By contrast, 72 h of content is uploaded to YouTube every minute ("*Statistics*" n.d.). At this rate, all of the two million plus films and TV programs listed by IMDb could be uploaded to YouTube in less than a month.

One might expect that viewing patterns for the online short form videos that dominate viewing on YouTube would differ from viewing patterns for traditional television, and this is the case. Some YouTube videos attract many millions of viewers while the vast majority are seen only by the uploader's friends and family. Relative differences in audience size of this magnitude would never be observed on traditional television networks, where programs are intensively pre-screened for audience appeal before being put on the air. Rather, YouTube accepts virtually all uploaded videos that meet their length restrictions (10 min for most users) and don't violate policies governing content deemed offensive.

As with traditional television, the size of YouTube's audience fluctuates substantially during the course of a day and over a typical week, but with differently timed peaks and troughs. For instance, prime time for YouTube is not in the evening. Rather, on a typical day the viewer count begins to rise around 8 am, peaks between 2 pm and 6 pm, and then falls from 7 pm to 7 am; during a week, daily audience starts rising after the weekend, reaches its peak on Wednesday and Thursday, and then declines through Sunday (Gill et al. 2007). On the other hand, even though the range of content types is much broader, the most popular content categories for YouTube are similar to those for traditional TV, with entertainment, music, comedy, and sports being most popular (Cha et al. 2009; Cheng et al. 2008).

3 The Varied Roles of YouTube Participants

For YouTube, as with the vast majority of media services, we can identify three primary sets of activities coordinated by the platform: consumption (in this case viewing), content supply, and advertising. While people who work for companies that supply content to traditional media firms and people who work for advertisers also consume of media content, they constitute such miniscule fractions of the audiences for their content and advertising that for analytical purposes we can think of media consumers, content suppliers and advertisers as three distinct sets of players.

As with other social media services, users are key suppliers of YouTube content, so the neat distinction between users and content suppliers breaks down. For YouTube it is also the case that there are important overlaps between producers and advertisers and between advertisers and users. The mix of participants has become more varied and blended roles have become more important as the platform has evolved. Here we describe YouTube participants who occupy positions on a broad spectrum of roles that includes pure users, pure content suppliers, and pure advertisers and participants who combine the pure roles.

3.1 Pure Users

Because every viewing of a YouTube video is recorded and a views count is reported for every video, every person who watches a YouTube video contributes to YouTube's content. In addition, many people who never upload a video post comments on videos they watch. However, if we think of a content contributor as a person or organization who uploads a video, then only about 2 % of YouTube users are content contributors (Halvey and Keane 2007). By this definition the vast majority of YouTube's audience are pure users.

3.2 User-Contributors

YouTube was founded on the premise that videos freely uploaded by users would attract an audience large enough to build a business. A brief perusal of YouTube videos is sufficient to show that an enormous amount of user-supplied content is contributed by people who have no special expertise in video production, but never-the-less have recorded episodes and events from everyday life that they uploaded to share with family and friends and perhaps, should lightening strike, with a much larger audience. Many of YouTube's most heavily viewed videos have been uploaded by user-contributors of this type. Anyone who has watched "Charlie bit me," which in various versions including remixes has recorded more than a half billion views, can see that this video of two young brothers sitting together when one bites the other's finger was recorded spontaneously without a mass audience in mind. For the remainder of this chapter, we will use the term "shared videos" to refer to videos like this that were uploaded for social sharing and without anticipation of future financial gain.[2] According to Courtois et al. (2012), videos contributed by regular users are more likely to get picked up by the larger YouTube audience if they incorporate elements of pop culture, although, as "Charlie bit me" demonstrates, this is not a prerequisite for mass appeal.

In their study of Flickr users, Angus and Thelwall (2010) found a variety of motives, including sharing with friends, making connections within the photography community, and promoting their work, lead users to upload their photos. YouTube users' motives for uploading videos are undoubtedly similarly diverse.[3] From the nature of their videos' content, it seems clear that for large numbers of

---

[2] The brothers in "Charlie bit me" and their parents live in England. In a newspaper article on the video, Lyall (2012), reports the video was uploaded to YouTube by the boys' father to share with a friend living in the United States in Colorado. It is a good example of how online viral communication can create unexpected hits. Although not uploaded for this purpose, the family has realized significant financial benefits from advertising revenues shared by YouTube and through related merchandise sales (Lyall 2012).

[3] See, for example, Hanson and Haridakis' analysis of what motivates people to watch and share news on YouTube and Lanius' study of commentary on YouTube (Hanson and Haridakis 2008; Lanius 2011).

user-contributors the potentially massive audience available on YouTube is itself an attractant. It would be surprising if some did not see their videos as steppingstones towards careers in some part of the entertainment industry.

To some extent, many of YouTube's more active user-producers resemble the prosumers, people who produce for their own consumption, Toffler (1980) predicted would become increasingly important in post-industrial societies. In his discussion of the implications of prosumers for marketing, Kotler (1986) distinguished between the avid hobbyist, who has an occupation from which she earns a living, but also pursues a major hobby that generates consumable output, and the arch prosumer whose lifestyle and, to a substantial extent livelihood, depends on self-produced goods. Avid hobbyists are an important source of high production-quality videos on YouTube, but we can also identify an increasingly important group of suppliers, many of whom started as simple user-contributors, who now look to YouTube as a major source of income. These home-grown YouTube businesses are one of several types of YouTube video suppliers who provide content to YouTube with the expectation of commercial gain.

3.3 Commercially-Motivated Content Suppliers

From its early beginnings with free user-produced videos, YouTube has expanded its content offerings by adding and promoting videos from a diverse collection of profit-motivated suppliers. Commercially-produced videos may contribute to YouTube profits in two ways: (1) by expanding its audience to include people who either would not visit YouTube if not for the professionally produced content or would visit the site less often, and, (2) by increasing per viewer advertising revenues because advertisers have shown they will pay substantially more for access to the audiences attracted to professionally produced videos (Holahan 2007).

Recognizing that some of its original contributors were attracting substantial audiences, YouTube developed two revenue-sharing programs to encourage them to contribute more high quality videos and to encourage other commercial video producers to contribute content. The Individual Video Program (IVP) is an invitation-only program that identifies popular videos and invites their providers to participate in the revenues they generate ("*What is the Individual*" 2011). The benefit to YouTube of giving individuals who already upload popular videos a share of the advertising revenues their videos generate lies in encouraging them to produce and upload more of the popular fare that commands higher per viewer rates from advertisers (Holahan 2007; Wildman et al. 2012).

A step up from the IVP is the YouTube Partner Program. To become YouTube partners, video providers must demonstrate a sustained capability for creating popular content. YouTube partners range from major entertainment companies such as Universal Music and CBS to individuals who started out as simple user-contributors. In addition to sharing in advertising revenues, YouTube partners enjoy privileges unavailable to other video contributors, including the right to upload videos that exceed the standard 10 min limit on length and the opportunity to post customized thumbnail descriptions next to the titles and links to their videos ("*What is the Individual*" 2011). YouTube "channels" dedicated to their videos also make their content easier to find and to promote. In addition, the opportunity to sell partner-supplied items (e.g., t-shirts with the partner's name or logo) through YouTube's internal merchandise store, which initially was available only to suppliers of music videos, has been extended to all YouTube partners. YouTube even helps its partners find merchandise suppliers and facilitates sales of partner products through links to other online outlets such as iTunes and Amazon.com. YouTube profits from partners' merchandise sales by retaining a small portion of the revenues generated by sales through its merchandise store and by collecting fees from other online sellers to whom it refers sales. YouTube also benefits indirectly from its partners' merchandise sales because their merchandise earnings promote loyalty to YouTube, encourage them to supply more high quality videos, and are an incentive for other high quality video creators to place their content with YouTube.

YouTube has also expanded its video offerings by making commercially-produced films and television programs, including live events like the 2012 Summer Olympics, from major studios and networks available for download or streaming at a price, with both subscriptions for long term access to paid content services and per item prices for one-off purchases of downloads or streamed content. To further increase the amount of high quality, professional content available to its viewers, YouTube recently allocated $150 million to help fund content for new channels, including channels with programming from established television producers using well-known film and television actors. Another $200 million has been allocated to promote the new channels (Efrati 2012).

3.4 Pure Advertisers

As with other media services, for the majority of YouTube's advertisers their dealings with the service are limited to purchasing opportunities to promote their products to audiences attracted by content created by other entities. A long period with little advertising while it built its audience and refined the service was followed by experimentation with alternative ways to present sponsors' ads. Although several ad formats are now available, YouTube has settled on short pre-roll ads placed at the beginnings of videos as their primary vehicle for ad sales. In addition to commercial placements, advertisers have found that they can take advantage of the flexibility and openness of the YouTube platform to create videos designed to both attract viewers and promote their products and advertiser-produced videos are becoming increasingly prominent among YouTube's offerings.

3.5 Advertiser-Producers

Advertiser-supplied videos come in several forms. Some are simply television commercials uploaded unchanged to YouTube. More extravagant, and generally more popular, are "extended" commercials, where a longer video with a more elaborate storyline is built around a 30 s TV commercial. The extended version is built into the advertiser's campaign from the beginning. Extended versions of ESPN "college game day" commercials by major advertisers are popular examples of this commercial form. The extended Game Day Commercial for the Honda CRV featuring Matthew Broderick in an adult reprise of his role in the teen coming-of-age comedy, "Ferris Bueller's Day Off," in which he starred in his youth. (Honda 2012) This video has generated more than 16 million views.

Even though they have evolved into an art form of their own, music videos like those featured on YouTube's most popular channel, Vevo,[4] also promote their artists' recordings and might be considered advertiser-supplied content. Music videos on YouTube also generate substantial revenue for their artists and record companies and for music copyright owners. According to Sandoval (2008), Universal Music has earned "tens of millions" of dollars as a YouTube partner and as a co-owner of Vevo. YouTube pays licensing fees to over 3,000 independent music publishers through the National Music Publishers Association (Perpetua 2011).

Through its promoted videos program, YouTube encourages smaller advertisers to produce videos that promote their products and pay YouTube to place them strategically near complementary content. Because the platform is open, nothing prevents companies from producing videos that promote their products and placing them on YouTube for free. To see examples of this kind of video, type "river rafting" in YouTube's search bar. Most of the videos displayed will be videos of rafting trips that identify in one way or another the commercial rafting companies that organized the excursions. What they lose with this free strategy is the preferred placement they would get if they paid to be part of the promoted videos program. The difference between the videos called up by the search algorithm and those displayed as promoted videos is analogous to the distinction between the organic and paid listings that a search engine displays in response to a search query.

3.6 User-Advertisers

As was mentioned in our earlier discussion of users, some users who create and upload videos are hoping to either attract a commercializable audience and enter the ranks of YouTube Partners be invited to join the Independent Video Program. Others may want to demonstrate their prowess to potential entertainment industry employers (Shankman 2010). From this perspective, these videos are advertisements for their creators, who can be considered user-advertisers. If we accept this broad definition of advertising, we have come full circle returning to users again.

---

[4] Vevo is a music aggregator owned by the major record companies (Stelter 2009). Vevo promotes its owner's videos on its standalone website and partners with YouTube through the Vevo channel.

Fig. 1 The varied roles of YouTube participants

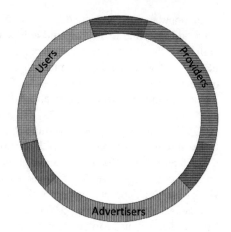

The participants circle in Fig. 1 illustrates the way YouTube participants' roles shade from one into the next.

4 Platform Management

Our discussion of platform management focuses on two distinct sets of activities: (1) managing relationships among the various platform participants, by which we mean defining and giving structure to these relationships and facilitating transactions among platform participants; and (2) guiding the evolution of the platform over time in response to changing technologies, user and customer demands, and market conditions.

4.1 Managing Relationships Among Platform Participants

Evans (2003) describes multi-sided platforms as market organizations that coordinate "the demands of distinct groups of customers who need each other in some way." For example, dating clubs help men and women meet each other. For traditional advertiser-supported media, the two sides are audiences who want content and advertisers looking for audiences. In the case of the YouTube, we must add voluntary suppliers of content who need audiences and, for some, a financial payoff.

Multisided platforms may play any or all of three roles in serving their customers: (1) market makers, (2) audience makers, and (3) demand coordinators (Evans 2003). Market makers make it easier for distinct parties who may benefit from an exchange to find and transact with each other. Shopping malls and eBay are good examples. Audience makers match audiences and advertisers and provide the latter with opportunities to present persuasive messages to the former.

Ad-supported media of all types play this role. Demand coordinators facilitate the development of complementary arrangements among market participants that are less direct than transactions but still mutually beneficial. For example, a computer operating system (OS) establishes standards that make it possible for diverse hardware and software suppliers to independently contribute to the development of a constellation of products that collectively increase market demand for the operating system and, via this feedback process, for the hardware and software products that utilize it. Microsoft and Apple are demand coordinators in their roles as OS suppliers. YouTube's platform serves all three roles. The coordination functions associated with market making and audience making are most visible, but as a software-defined platform it has no choice but to function as a demand coordinator as well when designing the interfaces that govern the interactions among the different types of YouTube participants.

In serving the first two platform roles, YouTube functions as an intermediary making it easier for platform participants to interact with the platform and, through the platform, to transact and coordinate with each other. Audience making itself is a two-sided operation that involves helping video consumers find content they want to watch and then giving advertisers access to the audiences attracted by the content. Note, however, that helping viewers find content is the flip side of helping content suppliers find audiences.

YouTube does a number of things to help users find content. Users can search with keywords, browse across channels, check top 100 charts, review reports on trending videos, and, once they have found videos they like, examine other videos YouTube identifies as similar in content. The names for channels assigned suppliers of popular content also serve as mnemonic devices for finding new videos from favorite producers. More recently YouTube has given registered users tools they can use to customize their first screens to make favored sources of content immediately available. Fu and Sim (2011) found users of an online video aggregation service similar to YouTube were more likely to click the videos that already had high view counts, which suggests that viewers use these counts as indexes of quality. Fu and Sim also found evidence that thumbnail sketches were used to evaluate videos before deciding whether to watch them. Viewer comments posted with videos are probably used in a similar manner. Additionally, YouTube users can now connect their YouTube accounts to other social media, such as Google Plus and Facebook, which makes it easier to use online word-of-mouth to share information, recommendations, and opinions about videos among individuals with similar in social networks (Cheng et al. 2008).

YouTube has a number of mechanisms for matching advertisers with audiences. Advertisers can purchase ad placements directly from YouTube in a manner similar to purchasing ad placements from a television network. Advertiser who purchase ad placements directly from YouTube can target video audiences using demographic and geographic identifiers and by language. YouTube also offers advertisers opportunities for self-managed ad purchases similar to what can be done with AdWords on Google. Key words and video content identifies are both used to trigger the display of ads as viewers search for videos they want to watch.

Advertisers using this service can take advantage of the same analytical tools for optimizing ad strategies as might be used with paid ads on Google. YouTube considers direct ads to be best suited for "a large ad campaign or a major brand marketing initiative", because direct advertising demands "a higher cost commitment with contract requirements and invoicing options" (*"What's the difference between advertising"* 2010).

For small businesses with more limited promotional budgets, YouTube recommends "promoted videos," which are videos produced or commissioned by advertisers to promote their products. As a form of advertising, promoted videos are tied to AdWords and promoted video placements are determined using an auction model similar to those employed by search engines to price paid search ads. Because advertisers are charged per click, the risk of spending heavily on promoted videos that don't connect with viewers is reduced.

YouTube also serves as an intermediary by helping YouTube partners sell their own branded or labeled merchandise to fans and other viewers. It does this by providing an online location where users can find and examine partners' merchandise and make purchases. YouTube distributes the proceeds minus its cut to the partners. YouTube plays a less direct intermediation service by enabling sales by partners to YouTube users through other online merchants like iTunes and Amazon with whom content suppliers have prior arrangements. In this case, YouTube is compensated by the online seller to which the purchaser is directed.

YouTube's various intermediation roles are indicated by directional arrows and the corresponding services are listed in the box in the middle of the participants circle in Fig. 2.

The relationships illustrated in Fig. 2 all require active management to balance the sometimes-conflicting interests of different groups of participants against each other and against YouTube's ultimate interest in maximizing its profits. As with television, viewers prefer fewer ads to more, but ads are the primary source of YouTube revenue. The pricing and placement policies governing the different types of advertising options described above affect the relative payoffs to different advertising strategies and therefore the value of the service to different types of advertisers. Promoted and featured videos clearly start with visibility advantages over videos uploaded by average users. And some users see the Partners Program, the creation of pay-per-view and subscription options for watching commercially-produced content, and YouTube's decision to commit substantial resources to develop and promote professional content unique to YouTube as undesirable departures from YouTube's origins as a simple way to watch short videos created by other users. Managing tradeoffs among different participants' interests in a way that both preserves the value they see in the service while generating profits for YouTube is an ongoing challenge.

Fig. 2 YouTube's roles as intermediary

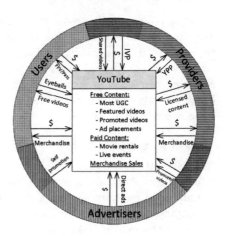

4.2 Guiding Platform Evolution

YouTube today looks very different from the simple platform that allowed Internet users to watch videos uploaded by amateurs like themselves and then sold advertisers access to the audiences they attracted. The challenge was to build a commercially viable business on the foundation created with shared videos without diluting YouTube's appeal to viewers. Viewed as a sequence, each of the changes to YouTube's platform and service offerings seemed to build on a foundation established by the previous set of changes. That YouTube's audience would attract submissions by individuals trying to demonstrate their worth to the larger media marketplace and by commercial enterprises subtly promoting the products and services they sold was inevitable given the open nature of the platform. Promoted videos, the YouTube Partner Program, and the Individual Video Program all helped YouTube to profit from these inherently commercial incentives for contributing content, and the Partner Program became a vehicle for developing a thriving collection of channels featuring professionally-produced content. New channels were then created to feature YouTube-funded content. The strategy of offering partner status and privileges and a share of ad revenues to parties already uploading videos for free only after they had demonstrated their ability to attract an audience was a dramatic departure from traditional television networks' practice of intensively pre-screening potential programs to reduce the risk that those put on air will not appeal to viewers. YouTube's decision to itself fund new channels with original content is a step toward the traditional television model. Whether the two models for content discovery and development can comfortably coexist in the same service remains to be seen.

Each of these changes reflects a strategic choice by YouTube executives. Most were rolled out slowly and could have terminated before causing serious damage had they proven unpopular with viewers. While its social foundations remain, it has also developed into a much more overtly commercial service, increasingly featuring professionally produced content and catering to major advertisers. That YouTube should evolve in this fashion is to be expected for a profit-oriented business. In this regard, its evolutionary path resembles those of other social media services, such as Facebook and Twitter, both of which are constantly exploring new ways to increase their value to advertisers. Examples include the Facebook pages maintained by major consumer goods companies and the sponsored tweets sold by Twitter.

Summary and Conclusions

During its first 7 years YouTube has grown from a simple service selling advertisers access to audiences attracted by short amateur videos to a complex multisided platform serving a diverse mix of users, advertisers and content contributors, many of whom play dual roles. As a multisided platform, YouTube serves as a market maker bringing buyers and sellers together, as an audience maker connecting advertisers with audiences, and as a demand coordinator structuring and facilitating relationships among suppliers of complementary services. In the first two roles YouTube acts as an intermediary supplying a variety of services that make it easier for content contributors to find audiences, for audiences to find content, and for advertisers to present their messages to target audiences. In each of these roles YouTube must strike a balance between the often conflicting interests of different platform participants that both keeps them engaged in the service and allows YouTube to profit from the platform.

YouTube grew by strategically expanding its service offerings to give advertisers more ways to reach viewers and by making the platform more attractive to commercially motivated content suppliers. Three primary strategies were employed to increase the amount of professional quality video available to viewers. First was the development of programs for sharing advertising revenues with video suppliers who demonstrated a sustained ability to attract sizable audiences. A thriving community of YouTube Partners, increasing numbers of which are now able to generate substantial revenues from "channels" they populate with their own content, is a very visible outcome of this strategy. Second, YouTube made itself available as a web outlet where television programs and motion pictures produced primarily for distribution through other media could be watched for a price. Third, and most recent, YouTube has committed substantial resources to support the creation and promotion of professionally-produced content, some from well-known producers and employing recognizable stars, that is original to YouTube. The success of this third strategy, which was only recently implemented, is yet to be determined. The increasing emphasis on professionally produced content is a departure from YouTube's purer social media origins, but its social features remain key components of the service.

References

Angus, E., & Thelwall, M. (2010). *Motivations for image publishing and tagging on Flickr*. Paper presented at the 14th international conference on electronic publishing, Helsinki, Finland.

Armstrong, M. (2006). Competition in two-sided markets. *The RAND Journal of Economics, 37*(3), 668–691.

Cha, M., Kwak, H., Rodriguez, P., Ahn, Y.-Y., & Moon, S. (2009). Analyzing the video popularity characteristics of large-scale user generated content systems. *IEEE/ACM Transactions on Networking, 17*(5), 1357–1370. doi:10.1109/tnet.2008.2011358.

Cheng, X., Dale, C., & Liu, J. (2008). *Statistics and social network of YouTube videos*. Paper presented at the 16th international workshop on quality of service.

Courtois, C., Mechant, P., & Marez, L. D. (2012). Communicating creativity on YouTube: What and for whom? *Cyberpsychology Behavior And Social Networking, 15*(3), 129–134.

Efrati, E. (2012, July 30). YouTube to double down on its 'channel' experiment. *Wall Street Journal*. Retrieved August 16, 2012, from http://online.wsj.com/article/SB10000872396390444840104577549632241258356.html

Evans, D. S. (2003). Some empirical aspects of multi-sided platform industries. *Review of Network Economics, 2*(3). p. 191.

Flosi, S. (2012). Press release: comScore releases May 2012 U.S. Online Video Rankings.

Fu, W. W., & Sim, C. C. (2011). Aggregate bandwagon effect on online videos' viewership: Value uncertainty, popularity cues, and heuristic. *Journal of the American Society for Information Science and Technology, 62*(12), 2382–2395.

Gill, P., Arlitt, M., Li, Z., & Mahanti, A. (2007). *Youtube traffic characterization: A view from the edge*. Paper presented at the proceedings of the 7th ACM SIGCOMM conference on Internet measurement, San Diego, CA.

Halvey, M. J., & Keane, M. T. (2007). *Exploring social dynamics in online media sharing*. Paper presented at the proceedings of the 16th international conference on World Wide Web, Banff, AB.

Hanson, G., & Haridakis, P. (2008). YouTube users watching and sharing the news: A uses and gratifications approach. *The Journal of Electronic Publishing, 11*(3).

Holahan, C. (2007, November 20). Web video: Move over, amateurs. *Business Week*. Retrieved August 20, 2012, from http://www.businessweek.com/stories/2007-11-20/web-video-move-over-amateursbusinessweek-business-news-stock-market-and-financial-advice

Honda. (2012). Official 2012 Honda CR-V Game Day Commercial – "Matthew's Day Off Extended Version". Retrieved August 10, 2012 from http://www.youtube.com/watch?v=VhkDdayA4iA

Kotler, P. (1986). The prosumer movement: A new challenge for marketers. *Advances in Consumer Research, 13*, 510–513.

Lanius, C. (2011). *Working paper on YouTube commentary: Social interaction in online publics*. Department of Anthropology, Columbian College of Arts and Sciences, The George Washington University.

Lyall, S. (2012, February 9). 417.6 Million bites later. *The New York Times*. Retrieved August 19, 2012, from http://www.nytimes.com/2012/02/10/world/europe/charlie-bit-my-finger-video-lifts-family-to-fame.html?pagewanted=all

Parker, G. G., & Van Alstyne, M. W. (2005). Two-sided network effects: A theory of information product design. *Management Science, 51*(10), 1494–1504.

Perpetua, M. (2011). YouTube signs major music licensing deal. Retrieved December 14, 2011, from http://www.rollingstone.com/music/news/youtube-signs-licensing-deal-with-national-music-publishers-association-20110818

Sandoval, G. (2008). Universal Music seeing 'tens of millions' from YouTube. Retrieved December 16, 2011, from http://news.cnet.com/8301-1023_3-10126439-93.html

Shankman, A. (2010). Why social media is the new source of Hollywood talent. *Mashable Social Media*. Retrieved August 20, 2012, from http://mashable.com/2010/06/18/social-media-hollywood-casting/

Statistics. (n.d.). Retrieved June 24, 2012, from http://www.youtube.com/t/press_statistics

Stelter, B. (2009, December 8). Music industry companies opening video site. *The New York Times*, p. B2.

Toffler, A. (1980). *The third wave*. New York: Morrow.

What is the Individual Video Program, and how does it relate to the YouTube Partner Program? (2011). Retrieved December 14, 2011, from http://support.google.com/youtube/bin/answer.py?hl=en&answer=181636

What's the difference between advertising with YouTube directly or using YouTube Promoted Videos? (2010). Retrieved December 14, 2011, from http://support.google.com/youtube/bin/answer.py?hl=en&answer=112958

Wildman, S. S., Lee, S. Y., & Song, S. Y. (2012, May). *How to make money by giving away content you get for free*. Paper presented at the 10th world media economics and management conference, Thessaloniki, Greece.

Part V
Social Media: Impact and Users

Social Media and New Audiences as a New Challenge for Traditional and New Media Industries

Germán Arango-Forero and Sergio Roncallo-Dow

The traditional windows for the audiovisual distribution system have been reshaped by the end of the first decade of the current Century. The digital boom has brought a multimedia transformation characterized by new technological developments, new global media markets and a new audiovisual culture that mixes traditional and new screens consumption (Albarran 2010). As a logical consequence, the new digital revolution has also led to a new configuration on audiences' consumption habits, content preferences and responses, even on emerging and developing media economies like the ones in Latin American, where traditional windows for distribution and exhibition combine with new platforms on a hybrid and eclectic environment. All these changes have configured what might be called a new audience culture that determines new rules for the media business model Haridakis and Whitmore (2006).

Even traditional media such as radio and television, which have played a key role for the media industry, have begun exploring new distribution systems thanks to the boom of digital and convergent communication. Nowadays, audiovisual content is not only available on traditional screens and over the Internet. Gradually, it has been integrated to cell phones, video consoles, and personal digital assistants (PDAs) among others devices. This evolution is easily spotted, and has been amply debated, mainly in developed economies.

Three issues have determined the transition between traditional and new media, mainly in the field of audiovisual industries: (a) Technology: understood as the revolution that allowed new forms in the development of media; (b) Audiences: In the sense that their behavioral changes have determined the establishment of new systems of communication and they have altered the traditional ways of engaging with them; (c) The market: as the outcome of a new relationship between producers, advertisers and consumers, generating in consequence new commercial relationships and new revenue models.

G. Arango-Forero (✉) • S. Roncallo-Dow
University La Sabana, Chía, Cundinamarca, Colombia

1   Technology Beyond a Simple Evolution

Since the last decade of the twentieth century, a new technological development emerged and restructured the communication landscape. It started with the Internet that evolved into social networking; mobile phones that evolved into smartphones; digital recorders and player devices that evolved into Personal Digital Assistant devices (PDAs) which reshaped the personal and individual use and consideration of media messages, as Lindqvist et al. state:

> The Internet and the mobile telephone initiated an informational and social connectivity revolution, and in a decade the media sector has been reshaped by new technologies for creating, editing, publishing, delivering, printing, and sharing information. (Lindqvist et al. 2009, p. 31)

As Lindqvist et al. (2009) confirm, the revolution brought about by the Internet, mobile communications, and Web 2.0, culminates with the appearance of new scenarios that comprise features which make them radically different from what was previously offered: this phenomenon is referred to as the other media, the new media or the multimedia and has, in turn, altered the relationship between producers and consumers.

This technological revolution has been significant in shaping new media, and it has endowed them with three features or aspects that, although not entirely new, could have never being achieved to a full extent without it. Blogs, wikis, texting, VoIP, Social networking, Video on Demand and several other platforms and actions share these features as their main difference with traditional media.

The first inherent technological aspect of new media, which can be considered a significant element of differentiation from traditional media is a phenomenon called convergence. Lindqvist (2009) describes the phenomenon as a result of the attempt made by traditional media to incorporate different formats in their content production.

> As the various providers start offering more and more similar services, their target audiences increasingly overlap with one another. This is a partly because the newspapers are incorporating more and more interactive picture elements, and because 'editorial picture content' has become a new genre for media houses. (Lindqvist et al. 2009, p. 22)

Furthermore, convergence implies a multi-platform, multi-format content available to users, which transcends the physical barriers of traditional media (Marshall 2004). Subsequently, traditional media have become a big part of the convergence phenomenon as well, since they now take advantage of new technologies to cater to the tech savvy audiences and provide them, in addition to the daily print version of the newspaper, or the weekly delivery of the TV show, with an Internet platform in which all the formats (audio, video and text) merge, delivering more relevant contents to the users.

> The former distinctions no longer make sense in terms of the site or physic allocation of media. Printed media blends into other media; visual media is not isolated in its delivery systems of television and film exhibition. The distinctions may still play in how people use media forms, but in terms of the technological forms there is a blurring of the machines of reproduction and dissemination. (Marshall 2004, p. 2)

The importance of convergence lies not only in the mixing of contents, but on the convergence of distribution networks. In the traditional media value chain system, content from studios, media production, personal content, private content, and advertisement came through a series of specific networks based on the type of content (i.e. TV screens, telephones, personal computers, etc.). Nowadays, due to this technological revolution, a system has been established in which all this content is distributed through a single broadband network that, in turn, spreads the content to any number of devices which can display it without distinction.

2 Interactivity as a New Concept

Another aspect that all new media platforms share, enabled by technological development, is interactivity. It is defined as the chance audiences have to manipulate, react and respond in real time to any message consumed. Granted, interactivity is not a new concept, nor is it exclusive to new media. There have been notions of interactivity in previous stages of traditional media, such as fan mail, letters to the editor, calling live radio shows etc... Nonetheless, interactivity as a real time occurrence is something that new media technologies have enabled more than any prior media: Internet, web 2.0, smartphones, PDAs, and tablets are basic examples of user interaction with new media.

> The digitalization of media contents and the normalization in many societies of fast Internet access, whether from fixed points or via mobile devices, means that, in principle, every point in space is connected through mediated communication to every other point; and that connection is always potentially two-way, since either end may be sender or receiver (or both). As a result, one-way senders—specialist media producers/distributors—and one-way receivers—'mere' consumers or audience members—become less common in their pure form, while hybrid sender/receivers, in some form at least, become more common. (Couldry 2009, p. 438)

The main outcome of interactivity is the blurring of the line between producer and consumer. Wikis, Blogs and forums on the social networking environment allow the readers to reply, comment, transform, and co-author contents, in a form of collaborative writing that would have been impossible in traditional media such as newspapers and magazines. The possibility of manipulation is a form of collaboration and co-authoring of the text. Cover (2006) defines the new relationship between author, text and audience as a contest, a fight for control over the medium and the text, in both creation and distribution.

> A digital environment promoting interactivity has fostered a greater capacity and a greater interest by audiences to change, alter and manipulate a text or a textual narrative, to seek co-participation in authorship, and to thus redefine the traditional author-text-audience relationship (...) eroding older technological, policy and conventional models for the 'control' of the text, its narrative sequencing and its distribution. (Cover 2006, p. 140)

3 Produce and Broadcast Yourself

Convergence and interactivity create a media environment in which producers and consumers of media may become one. Besides, professional media content developers and creators of amateur cultural productions are not distant anymore, but closely overlapping "regions of the same vast spectrum" (Couldry 2009, p. 438) and it is through the two first aspects of new media that we come about the third, user generated content (see also Uribe-Jongbloed 2011).

Once again, these characteristics are not absolutes, they are not restrictive to new media and they did not appear overnight. User generated content, just like interactivity, is a concept that has existed long before the invention of the Internet and appearance of the new media, but that came to full potential through these technologies (Uribe-Jongbloed 2011).

> Users' capacity to generate content has been around for quite some time, due to the long-established availability of production technologies such as home video cameras, personal computers, typewriters, and home recording equipment. What is different today is the ability of users to distribute content, to use the Web to circulate their user-generated content (as well as, to media companies' dismay, traditional media content) to an unprecedented extent. (Napoli 2008a, b, p. 13)

As a trend, technology has become more accessible to users, now it is possible to purchase audio and video recording devices that match the output quality of their professional counterparts, and cost but a fraction of their price. This availability means that, today, user generated content might have the same—or nearly the same—technical specifications as professional output, and can be distributed and exhibited online on a leveled playfield with the mainstream media.

> It is important to recognize that the one-to-many dynamic at the core of the meaning of mass communication persists here. It is simply that there are many more instances of it. It is this proliferation of the one-to-many capacity that represents the communication dynamic that was largely absent from previous incarnations of our media system, in which the capacity to mass communicate was technologically constrained to a select few. (Napoli 2008a, b, p. 12)

As to the implications that user generated content has for the media audiences, where some see the end of mass media and mass communications, Napoli (2008a, b) sees the spirit of its model being preserved, only being altered in terms of an increase in the supply of media contents, and in the possibility that those suppliers have acquired to reach masses instead of small audiences within their physical reach. Therefore, the communications dynamics reflected in Web 2.0 applications such as YouTube, Facebook, MySpace, and Flickr are increasingly foregrounding an approach to mass communication in which the individual audience member operates on nearly equal footing with the more traditional institutional communicator (Napoli 2008a, b, p. 12).

The connection between technology and new media is undeniable; however, it would be reductionist to define new media as nothing but a new step of the ladder. Clearly it is more than a series of platforms and characteristics that allow for new forms of interaction with the media content. According to Bermejo (2009), if something new is not simply more recent, but also something which has not been properly digested, tamed or domesticated, both in conceptual and practical terms, then newness has to do with historically situated comparisons and distinctions (p. 134).

These technological developments shape the future of traditional media, but without the changing in media habits and media economics, the landscape would remain the same (Couldry 2009). Convergence, Interactivity, User Generated Content and all the possibilities that come about with new technologies are only relevant when there are audiences willing to interact and participate in their development.

4 The Significance of the New Audience

What does the word audience mean today? The audience can be considered a construct with more than one single signification, which can date back even thousands of years, if one might consider Greek theater attendees as part of the earliest theoretical audiences, and it has evolved and changed from century to century (Piscitelli 1998). But the way to study audiences in the new media environment is through a particular focus; one that should develop a deeper understanding about how these social constructions of media audiences change over time, how technological and institutional forces may affect such change, and how such changes are negotiated and resisted by stakeholders involved in attracting and monetizing media audiences from an economical perspective (Napoli 2011, p. 3).

The definition of audience that assimilates its relationship with the so called new media and the media market could be the one described by Napoli (2011) as the "institutionalized audience". From an economical and managerial point of view, the audience can be defined as socially constructed by media industries, advertisers and associated audience measurement firms. However, audience is not only conceptually created but also manufactured by the actors involved in the media market as an article of trade to sustain the advertising business model (Napoli 2001).

> Thus, ratings firms do not simply 'check to determine' the size and characteristics of the audience, they actually manufacture the audience through a set of measurement procedures that are shaped by both industry dynamics and the technological and usage patterns of the media whose audience is manufactured. (Bermejo 2009, p. 139)

Following Napoli and Bermejo's definition, audiences currently do not behave on a passive way. On the contrary they are able and willing to react to the external changes. Thus it becomes relevant to question how the second instance of the new impact has been determined by the technological developments that have led to new media. The main shift in the new dynamics of the audiences structure can be summarized under two headings as Napoli (2011) describes them: audience fragmentation and autonomy.

As a result of new technological implementations, the proliferation of digital wireless communication channels is spreading the mass audience of yore ever-thinner across hundreds of narrowcast cable and radio channels, thousands of specialized magazines, and millions of computer terminals, video-game consoles, personal digital assistants, and cell-phone screens (Bianco 2004, p. 62).

Similarly to what occurs with interactivity and user generated content, fragmentation is not a trend that comes about exclusively with new media; it had arisen with the broadening of traditional media offers with the coming of subscription television, thematic radio stations and multiplication of specialized print magazines among other developments. However the rate at which the new media have permitted outlet multiplication has meant a significant shift in the traditional "producer-media-audience" paradigm.

> The most obvious cause of fragmentation is a steady growth in the number of media outlets and products competing for public attention. This happens when established media, like television, expand or when newer media, like the Internet, enter the competition. (Webster and Ksiazek 2012, p. 4)

There have been two main streams of outlet multiplication: the first being the use of new technologies by the traditional media, as part of the multi-platform convergence that is inherent to technological development.

> A few programs, sporting events, or clips on YouTube are the stuff of water cooler conversations, which encourages those who want to join the discussion to see what everyone else is talking about. The advent of social media, like Facebook and Twitter, may well extend these conversations to virtual spaces and focus the attention of those networks on what they find noteworthy. (Webster and Ksiazek 2012, p. 19)

The second is due to the new contents and platforms that have come to existence since the development of new media that incorporate interactivity, convergence and user generated content, such as social media platforms. Several social networking services have received the most attention, due to ability and capacity to create entirely new social infrastructures among their networked users (Lindqvist 2009, p. 18).

Altogether the technological aspects and characteristics of the new media that have altered the patterns of the media landscape, regarding audiences, can be put together under a second simple word: autonomy. As of now, the control over media consumption has shifted from the producers to consumers themselves, for it is they who decide how, when, where and what to consume. Now they also have the power to decide over the content they consume, how it will unfold, and the possibility to manipulate it or to generate their own outcomes, being more demanding of the media than ever before.

New media technologies that empower audiences to take control and increased choice over when, where, and how they consume media are transforming the relationship between audiences and the media (Kenyon et al. 2008). At the same time, new technologies for measuring and monitoring audience behavior are revealing aspects of how and why audiences consume media that previously were unknown (Napoli 2008a, b, p. 3).

5 The Meaning-Making of New Audiences

Numbers and statistics about the new fragmented media markets are insufficient to explain the new environment in which new audiences establish a particular relationship with the so called new media, on the broad sense previously analyzed. The perspective that we propose in this chapter relates to the need of rethinking about the audiences and the new media environment from a dense dimension and as a structuring condition of the human status.

From the perspective of the users and their uses, we propose a vision of the subject which oversteps the more traditional idea of decoding, and turns to the problem of cultural practice in order to understand what it means to think about the audiences and their relationship with technology today.

The perspective of decoding proposes a subject inserted in a specific area, a subject possessor of a cultural memory: a subject of preconceptions and particularities. These features pose a framework of competencies that determine the hermeneutic condition of the subjects. This is, no doubt, a perspective of analysis that is quite interesting insofar as it recognizes the subject in its uniqueness, and opens up the possibility of establishing a dialogue with the media text, whose meaning is constructed in a task of continuous negotiation and insertion of the messages within the assumptions raised by everyday life.

From the perspective of decoding, media play an instrumental role in the process. Being in front of a decoding subject, the creation of the sense is given, strictly speaking, on the receiver. There is a strongly autonomous position which suggests the non-interference of media in the search and constructions of the sense and meaning. It is clear that, despite the free and optimistic vision that there is of the individual, the point of view of decoding establishes a split between media and culture (understood here as a way of life) because it suggests the existence of two poles which, apparently, coexist independently of one another.

This idea may appear initially as problematic, mainly because, from a contemporary perspective, independence between sender and receiver seems to have been exceeded. It is said that the two are elements of a communicative process that presents itself as a whole, since there is an active and simultaneous activity of its components. There is, however, an obstacle here. When talking about decoding we think, by definition, of a medium (sender) that presents a text (message) and sends it towards a reader-decoder (receiver): communication here is limited to the analysis in terms of media and sets aside a number of factors that play a leading role in the process of decoding the text.

6 From Media Centrism to the Mediation Process

However, from the perspective of decoding there is awareness of the cultural memory and of the receiver as subject, and it is necessary to go beyond the medium-message-subject relation and to propose the scheme in new terms: subject-subject-media-message-subject-subject. This second perspective leaves aside the media centrism and focuses much more on the relations between subjects that are mediated, inter alia, by media texts.

Understanding the new media communication in developing environments does not mean to undertake only a theoretical and practical analysis of media. In Latin America, Jesús Martín-Barbero, one of the promoters of the mediations theoretical framework makes this point very clear: There is no doubt that if the sole objective of studying communication are the media, it is very difficult for us to think of the authors, subjects and processes (Montoya 1992, p. 24).

Evidently, when we talk about cultural practices, we are carrying out a displacement of the reflection which might represent a return to the origins of communication: its use. Wittgenstein (2009) raised the idea of 'language-games' that immediately made reference to the practices, to the ways of carrying out a certain process: the use of language. Since his proposal, communication is defined by the use, and here it is where the notion of meaning starts making sense. Wittgenstein, who develops the idea of 'language-games', addresses this point.

The concept of language-game is closely related to the abandonment of certain statements of the *Tractatus*, and to the birth of a new way of conceiving language, away from the pretensions of generality and seeking to elucidate the way that language is really used in the actual context, the so-called real world. From this perspective, language is something that has to do with human practice and with the way in which man uses language and communicates: "I shall [...] call the whole, consisting of language and the activities into which it is woven, a "language-game"" (Philosophical investigations, 7).

We have made this digression to Wittgenstein's ideas aimed to remark that if our goal is to achieve a closer understanding of communication and human ways of interaction, it is necessary to understand everything that occurs in the process and then engage in its analysis. Decoding highlights the importance of prejudices in the system of opinions from various individuals. The perspective that can be obtained from cultural practices turns out to be more complex because, by having overcome media-centrism and having gone beyond it, the problem of the construction of the meaning that comes from the use arises.

It is from the practices, i.e., from the *what is (going to be) done with the media messages*, in this case, that the meaning sees the light. This suggests that there is not a hegemonic and unique reading. The meaning is not given as a metaphysical entity. We are not talking about the idea of a unique meaning which reading has to match with and the success of communication lies in this correspondence. The meaning, as the practices, is variable.

From this perspective, the vision of the problem of reception turns out to be very attractive because it opens the door to a concept of a free subject, who autonomously uses reason and his cultural environment to fill with meaning the signs that he perceives. This semiotic process (led by the subject) of everyday life allows for an understanding of the reception and interpretation in more interesting terms. Paraphrasing Jesús Martín-Barbero, the object (proper of the media-centrist conception) gets lost in order to gain the process, *the what and the how* that are immersed in everyday life. Martín-Barbero argues that even though everyday life sometimes is taken as something insignificant from a perspective that focuses on the logics of production, it is clear that it opens the way to new stories, to new visions of the social spectrum (Martín-Barbero 1987, p. 93).

There is, however, a need to clarify. The abandonment of media-centrism does not represent an abandonment of media; when we use the term here, we are referring to a (re) conception of media from a new perspective that goes beyond the instrumentality and the typical conceptions of post-Marxism and structural functionalism according to which media are instruments of power and domination, mainly on developing societies. What arises here is that media are part of an apparatus of power, and that they are there to defend a certain dominant ideology. Media are considered to be part of an ideological arena in which different perspectives of class compete, but within the context of the domain of certain classes (Curran and Gurevitch 1977, pp. 4–5 as cited in Curran et al. 1998, p. 385).

But from the perspective of cultural practices, it is clear that media are presented as much more than power devices: they are builders of the social and the cultural meaning. They give an account of the world that is a world, of the reality that they build and that, at the same time, builds them. Morley's reflection concerning the family and the television consumption could be located in this path. A critical position against media that are consumed is assumed here, and certain rules about the *how* and the *why* of cultural consumption within society are evident, taking as a unit of measurement the family and the various modes of interaction within the given with media, in this case, television (Morley 1992, p. 113).

Returning to the problem of the subject, it is clear that what prevails here is a comprehensive analysis of the process in which parts cannot be seen as completely disconnected. If communication is taken as the summation of several coexisting but independent processes of construction of meaning the result will be headless. It must be understood as a whole: this whole not only includes the sender, the message, and the receiver but also the how, when, where and why in which they collide. It is from this perspective that reception-interpretation is analyzed. García Canclini suggests that it is not only about measuring the distance between messages and their effects, but to build a comprehensive analysis of the consumption, understood as the set of social processes of appropriation of the products (García Canclini 1984, p. 24, quoted by Martín-Barbero 1987, p. 295).

The point of view of decoding is exceeded because in here a text is neither decrypted nor interpreted; a hermeneutics of reality is done as a whole. The change, if wanted, is given in the idea of what is conceived as subject and which poses an abandonment of the 'I' to go in search of a 'we' which is from where the meaning is built. Therefore, we start to develop a view of a subject that is built upon his relationship with others, and under the tacit rules that determine the communicability and give meaning to what is said and done. Belonging to a framework determines the way of life, the culture and, from there, the way of being with the world is conditioned. The perspective of the practices exceeds decoding insofar as it proposes an idea of a construction of sense and meaning, not from a solipsist and personal angle as decoding *might be*, but from the sociality that is displayed as the juxtaposition of a whole series of subjectivities that converge in a form in common.

The subject-receiver is a necessary condition for the existence of communication. How is it possible to think of a successful communication process where there is no reception? However, reception can be seen from multiple perspectives ranging from the idea of the immediate effects on individuals (hypodermic theory, for example) to visions, way more elaborated, of the constructions of sense and meaning coming from media messages. In other words, when we study reception we face a dichotomy between the receiver—subject and the receiver—decoder—re-coder subject who constructs based on what he receives. It is clear that recognition of the subject in these latter terms is far more interesting than the former, because it risks not only its natural ability to understand, but also a range of elements initially extrinsic to its receiver status, but that, ultimately, acquire a key role at the recoding time.

In order to answer or to review the problem of the decoder subject, we will go to some ideas of hermeneutic philosophy that will help us clarify this question. There are, however, a couple of considerations that we need to bear in mind:

First of all we would like to review Raymond Williams' comments, according to which the concept of culture is bifid (Williams 1976). Indeed, on one side it is understood as "a way of life"; the common meanings; and (on the other) to designate the arts and knowledge: the special processes of discovery and creative effort (Williams 1988, p. 4, quoted by Stevenson 1998, p. 33).

The first conception of culture is particularly interesting: as a *modus vivendi*. It is clear that if there is a hallmark in humanity is, precisely, multiculturalism, i.e. the multiplicity of ways of life and constructions of the proper and the common. A non-cultural man is a utopian project impossible to conceive in reality and, to that extent, if we stick to Williams' proposal we would have a cultural subject as a decoder-subject, i.e., an individual with certain specific determinations and as existing by virtue of its belonging to a cultural collective. However, this belonging should not even be considered in terms of an *active presence* within this conglomerate, the point here is that when we talk about the receiver we are facing a subject that shows himself as culturally conditioned, if we could say so.

It is appropriate to emphasize a statement made by Morley, which turns out to be particularly suggestive:

> Thus the meaning of the text must be thought of in terms of which set of discourses it encounters in any particular set of circumstances—and how this encounter may re-structure both the meaning of the text and the discourses which it meets. The meaning of the text will be constructed differently according to the discourses (knowledge, prejudices, resistances) brought to bear on the text by the reader: the crucial factor in the encounter of audience/subject and text will be the range of discourses at the disposal of the audience. (Morley 1992, p. 80)

With Morley's formulation we can see interesting elements emerge from which it is possible to start constructing the subject that decodes. It makes reference to a sense of the text which is constructed according to certain preconditions in the receiver. Morley uses the idea of pre-judgments which give way to a reading from the hermeneutics of this point in particular. When speaking of preconceptions we are in front of a receiver which, in Gadamer's words, has a cultural memory, a set of conditions that determine the interpretation: language, theories, social roots, fundamental myths (2004). All in all what Williams (1988) seems to understand by culture in its broader meaning. Now, how is the interpretation, i.e. the hermeneutics task understood?

We start from the fact that the interpreter is not a tabula rasa; he approaches the text based on his pre-conceptions, and from that point he constructs senses: this implies an essentially active task carried out by the interpreter, but it also supposes a double game in which the text says something and shows us something. What is shown is understood as a *something* that puts in contrast all our system of views in relation to that text, and it is from there that the interpretation is carried out. This is a task that is infinitely constructed step by step with pause. The first interpretation (decoding) constitutes a first construction of sense about the text that is shown as an initial approximation and that, to that extent, is destined to be exceeded by further analysis of the text that will lead to new interpretations from which we will start to collate if the preconceptions are confirmed or crumbled.

Pre-conceptions and culture are revealed as the main conditionings faced by the interpreter, and the double game to which we referred earlier, is based, essentially, on approaching the texts not from the dogma and the barriers that pre-conceptions might cause, but rather based on the understanding of the text in its otherness, and from there start making the construction. Morley is explicit when he presents this tripartite reflection:

(a) The same event can be encoded in more than one way;
(b) The message always contains more than one potential 'reading'. Messages propose and prefer certain readings over others, but they can never become wholly closed around one reading: they remain polysemic.
(c) Understanding the message is also a problematic practice, however transparent and 'natural' it may seem. Messages encoded one way can always be read in a different way (Morley 1992, p. 78).

Thus, it is clear that when we face the media message there is a *culture* between the sender and the receiver that acts as a filter and a mold between the text and the interpretation. It is not about the interpreter-receiver assuming a privileged position: if we are to interpret we must let the text speak, and in this dialogue lies the essence of hermeneutics. What is this essence? The recognition of the presence of pre-conceptions; it is from their effective being that an interpretation of texts can be carried out.

In many cases, in the media message we find texts that contradict our system of opinions and are revealed as a sort of contradiction in the subject. It is from this dialectic that the hermeneutic task can be carried out, a task in which, by acknowledging the otherness of the text, it becomes apparent that both sender and receiver are active, and it is from that mutual recognition that dialogue is achieved. In this point, when we talk about receptors and the consequent decoding, we are talking precisely about dialogue. In order to decode it is necessary that the message has something to say, moreover, something to say to a particular subject. Secondly, decoding presupposes a prior coding which in turn presupposes a range of pre-conceptions in the issuer, i.e.: the whole of the process is transversely crossed, by a cultural mediation.

But let's go back to the receiver-decoder. We already mentioned that the receiver could not be considered as a tabula rasa. That statement can be taken even further because what is shown here is precisely its opposite: a subject full of pre-conceptions, ideas, conjectures and expectations. Here is the reason why the idea of the automatic effect of the message on the receiver is somewhat precarious: it arises from the unawareness of a cultural memory, and takes for granted what has been posed as a utopia: the presence of a non-cultural subject.

The theory of decoding, which is closer to the hermeneutical paradigm, brings back the subject as belonging to a world and as an interacting being with it. It is telling, in the same way, that the information (the mere content) of the media message alone has no sense, it is necessary for the receiver-decoder to transpose what it has in itself, and that based on this transposition the interpretation can be achieved. Therefore, the decoder subject is foremost a cultural subject, and from that point the process is structured, for it is in culture (according to Williams) where the conditions of reading/interpreting rest. Along with this, we have a receiver that must renounce to dogmatism in his reading and that should allow the text to talk to him.

This might be seen as an unorthodox point of view of the receiver's role. However, it is interesting because this perspective of hermeneutic philosophy brings back the idea of the otherness of the text, and recognizes the idea of the cultural subject, i.e., the decoder subject.

However, the problem of the incorporation of technology has been addressed by Ihde (1990), who referred to a certain type of relationship of *hermeneutical* tendency with the technical. It makes reference to certain techniques which lead the world, somehow, to have a level of readability absent in pure perception. Ihde allows us to think that the problem we are posing here, regarding cultural practices and the cultural subject, has to do with a more phenomenological approach to the problem that moving the reflection involves from the transcendental to lifeworld.

7 The Revival of Uses and Gratifications Approach

The incorporation of technology has to do with the way in which lifeworld has been colonized and redefined by technology which, far from being only appliances, becomes a founding element of the contemporary worldview. Perhaps, this can be understood a little better if one accepts that the media landscape has an effect upon our day to day experience; since the massive advent of media, life itself is increasingly rewritten by the presence of the flow of symbolic contents that determine the work, lay down conditions and generate behaviors all across the social framework.

One of the first trends to show this everyday influence was, in fact, the so-called uses and gratifications theory, which fits temporarily between the 1940s and 1950s.[1] Considering everyday life as a situation crossed transversely by the influence of media poses new challenges to communication studies. On one hand, the need to retrieve the subject as a key element of the communicative process becomes evident; on the other, it poses difficulties from the methodological point of view, because the psychological component is too high, and this hinders the investigative approach of the subjects who receive/decode/re-code the media contents.

The first point that must be taken into account is the presence of a subject (cultural, as we already know), of an "I", if wanted, that it is receiving and interpreting the messages that come to him from the media. This perspective demonstrates the fact that media messages **only** make sense if there is a subject that filled them with meaning. The idea that led communication studies at its inception, the postulates of hypodermic theory for

---

[1] There seems to be a kind of divergence on this point. In this regard see Huertas (2002, p. 101) and Mattelart and Mattelart (1997, p. 102).

example, seem to have been overcome in pursuit of the discovery of a reader/re-coder subject and, at the same, time interpreter which from its psychological—social context asks about the uses that can be given to the media content.

The retrieval of the subject carried out by this trend of uses and gratifications raises an overcoming of the informational paradigm; from that perspective, communication is *more* than a just a simple transmission of data: the effectiveness is no longer, as in the case of the cybernetic model of Wiener, by achieving the transition from entropy[2] to information, which was the utopia in the midst of a new community of researchers that bet on the mathematical formalization of information, seeking the possibility of conceiving it as a proper calculable symbol.

The simple transmission of data is no longer the very same essence of communication, because now, playing with new digital media, there is a subject who *uses and manipulates* the media content. But also s/he, interprets it, transforms it and finally obtains a personal gratification out of it. This means that it is necessary that the receiver decides whether the communication process actually occurs (Katz, Blumler and Gurevitch 1985, p. 137).

It is clear that this "rediscovery" of the subject as an essential part of the process involves the idea of an active receptor. To this point, however, it must be added the fact that, from this model of analysis, the receiver/subject has requirements which, in one way or another, s/he seeks to fill from media output: there is an individual who seeks in media; But what is that s/he is looking for using new media?: Specific gratifications.

From this point onwards it is essential to think about the social, cultural and economical conditions that lead to these searches, and which determine and redefine everyday life in terms of inclusion or exclusion of that which is reflected medially. These factors are crucial to understand the hybrid model of media consumption on developing countries. There are certain kinds of shortages that should be filled; after all, the search for a gratification implies the existence of a shortage: meaningless without the presence of it.

Katz et al. (1985, p. 153) propose a series of points found in the form of needs and involving the "media gratifications". Among these needs, closely related to the social situation, we can find: conflicts and tensions, problems that require attention, scarcity of some real opportunities, need to strengthen certain values, expectations of familiarity with certain media messages. These five points, the authors claim, seek to be filled with media, and are a starting point to understand the origin of the projection of the idea of gratification, and the searches undertaken by the receivers.

It seems clear that these needs are socially determined; they are there due to external stimuli set by the environment. This raises the idea of an embedding of media in the individual's everyday life: by being the focal point of their searches,

---

[2] We follow Mattelart and Mattelart to give a clear explanation of the concept of entropy. Entropy, is understood here as a trend which has the nature to destroy what is ordered and to precipitate the biological degradation and social disorder, constitutes the fundamental threat. The information, the machines that treat it and the networks which they weave are the only ones able to combat this trend to the entropy (Mattelart and Mattelart 1997, p. 47).

the day by day experience reformulates in terms of a media experience or, at least, medially mediated.

We can refer an example to explain this in more detail. As mentioned before, in many cases (in most of them), the social environment determines a shortage of real opportunities which can manifest itself from a lack of emotional and aesthetic fulfillment, to many other voids. The absence of actual relationships is met through media in many cases. A relationship of this kind is established with the musicians, actors, anchormen, and movie stars that we see on a daily basis. They, in effect, become part of our lives and are inserted into our everyday life.

However, there are certain moments when the media relationship lost its center and reaches extreme cases, such as the one cited by Thompson (1995, p. 220): When Joanne, a 42 year-old wife, made love to her husband she imagined that she was having sex with Barry Manilow. Each time she finished and realized that she was making love to her husband, and not to the star, she suffered a deep depression. Something similar might occur when in developing societies where media consumers can create and idealistic world (based on societal models provided by international TV series or movies) but once they are confronted with their own social reality might generate a feeling personal and social frustration and anxiety.

Although this limiting cases raise the possibility of a loss of control and a decentring of the outbreak of the relationship, what is clear is that media fill the gaps created by the social environment: in one way or another the active subject, receiver, endorses the symbolic content, re-builds it in some way, and obtains something out of it.

In this way, thinking about the subject supposes the recognition of the presence of media in everyday experience. The retrieval of the subject proposes a conception of media as a leading actor in the experience, but it is precisely from there, from where the subject comes to play its role: to decide how and what will be used out of anything that media puts at its disposal for his own gratification.

8   A Methodological Challenge

The capacity of the receiver for choosing, rethinking and using media messages looking for a specific gratification highlights a body of limitations at the time of conducting a research project based on audiences.

From the quantitative method, a constraint that has to do with the very same form of methodological tools is posed. Huertas (2002, p. 109), following Schroder (1999), argues that most inquiries use questionnaires with closed questions proposing, at the outset, a list of certain gratifications. From this point of view the results of the sample are largely determined.

On the other hand, based on the qualitative method (but related to previous point), the needs can become diametrically different[3] in each individual; this implies an

---

[3] And numerous; a list of closed questions would leave out a whole range of possibilities. This is what we mean by in relation with the previous point.

approximation to the object of study (in this case the receivers) in a nearby and individual manner by the researcher. The subject itself, the receiver, is the one who provides information about his needs and the gratifications he hopes to obtain. This point is problematic because the ethnographic data can have a highly subjective component that could, in a way, debase the reality of the receivers. All the work undertaken in recent research has relied on direct feedback from the public and such statements have been accepted by their apparent validity. Although there was no reason to doubt the validity of such acceptances, it would still be relevant to ask to what extent they relate the whole story (Katz et al. 1985, p. 165).

This point in particular opens up a new question that has to do with the type of receptor that is being investigated. In a case such as the British viewers (Katz et al. 1985, p. 140) it is possible to talk about a particular type of subject, able to understand and articulate its needs. But in the case of an approximation to other viewers, the ones who live in developing societies, this does not seem to be so obvious. Therefore, social, economical and cultural level of the object of study conditions the investigative approach. In other words: the success or failure of the sample depends on the capabilities of the same subjects and that, somehow, imposes conditions on the researcher.

From this methodological perspective one could argue for a **third way** of addressing the question. The study of the subject, based on the uses and gratifications theory, presumes an awareness of cultural heterogeneity posed by the various social systems and by the limitations that they raise. This is an evident challenge that has to be taken in to account in order to conduct accurate analysis that support successful commercial and media strategies considering local, regional and global media markets.

9   The Transforming New Media Markets

The technological impact on the new media environment and its implications for the field of audiences' behavior, habits and responses, in terms of fragmentation and autonomy, also has a notorious impact on the third big issue mentioned on this study: the changing media market, its impact on the traditional advertising model and the responses an reactions of content producers in a new media economical system (Lin 1994).

The implications of technological changes and audience responses can be clearly seen in the reply of the market to these changes. This response to the consumer behavioral changes mediated by technology comes from two actors of the media market, the content producers and the advertisers.

As far as the producer's response to audience is shifting, a clear example could be the response to audience fragmentation through content specialization (Picard 2000). Parallel to audience fragmentation comes what Tewksbury (2005) defines as audience and outlet specialization, the first one refers to the way in which individuals chose their content consumption, according to their particular requirements; the second refers to the outlets capacity to attract different kinds of audiences.

Audience specialization means a significant shift in the behavior of consumers of media, while audiences seem to get smaller; the media are multiplying and specializing to reach those niches of audiences. According to Shaver and Shaver it seems to be a matter of "divide and conquer", where the impact of this fragmentation is felt most heavily by traditional mass media. This, in turn, provides an impetus for industry consolidation, as corporate owners seek larger aggregate audiences by increasing the number of individual outlets under their control, and individual owners are encouraged to sell because of dwindling audience share (Shaver and Shaver 2006, p. 641).

A clear response to the emergence of the new media, in terms of the market behavior, is the development of the long-tail structure that contemplates the amount of products sold vs. the frequency of them being purchased. This model of the long-tail gives a marketing edge to new media firms that produce larger amounts of specific content for specialized audiences (Anderson 2006).

However, traditional media producers have seen also an opportunity in the development of new technologies that harbor new media; they have devised strategies to overcome the limitations of the physicality of their medium and created a link between new and old to be able to remain actual and relevant in the new media landscape.

> Technological advances continue to enable marketers to draw an ever-finer bead on consumers through a variety of media. Already, many publishers—offline as well as on—are able to distribute content tailored to particular households. (Bianco 2004, p. 68)

Not only print media have been able to take advantage of new media technologies to trace the audience's response to content; for television and film new media represent a great possibility to create a more dynamic and interactive relationship with consumers in order to achieve a similar effect to the one that is distinctive of new media.

Fan forums trough Internet and text messaging in reality shows among others feedback resources allow content producers to open an interactive dialogue with their publics and let the audience to get involved in the development of the content. New electronic media technologies offer programmers a source of feedback that goes beyond ratings information. Viewers can respond directly to programs through chat rooms or program Web sites, and decision makers can use these sites to monitor opinions, tastes, and trends (Phallen 2006, p. 634).

Still, the second collective whose actions determine the market dynamics, the advertisers, have seen a significant transformation in the audience, as far as it is manufactured by measuring systems. Advertisers find that the new fragmented audience is difficult to account for, especially when measurement relies on the use of samples. "In addition, the ever-greater control of audiences over the use of broadcasting media has become a threat to audience measurement operations" (Bermejo 2009, p. 143).

This threat described by Bermejo is not only occurring to the broadcasting media. As audiences fragment and move in a larger spectrum of outlets, throughout various platforms, they become harder to measure, and therefore, to reach; at least using the parameters of traditional media measuring. "The media have increasing difficulty in identifying and retaining *"their"* particular audience... Patterns of media use will simply be a part of varied and changing lifestyles" (McQuail 1997, p. 23).

On the other hand, new media such as Internet propose a new model of audience measurement that, even though it is still difficult to interpret, gathers specific characteristics of the audiences, beyond their mere consumption, that help to create a panoramic view of its behavior, activities, affiliations, likes, dislikes, etc.

> Perhaps the most relevant technological peculiarity of the Internet is its ability to generate a trace. A record of online activity is generated routinely and automatically collected as part of the activity itself, and this record can be used to monitor online activity. (Bermejo 2009, p. 144)

Thanks to the technological tools for measurement provided by the new media, it becomes easier to trace ad impact on audiences, and feedback becomes much more relevant for advertisers (Napoli 2010). Here traditional media are losing the battle to new media in the sense they can gather specific information from consumers that tracks their preferences and make the advertisements fit their particular needs, as Bianco states:

> In the competition for ad dollars, the new digital media—especially the Internet—are blessed by two intrinsic advantages over mass media. First, they are interactive. This capability enables marketers to gather reams of invaluable personal information directly from customers and adjust their sales pitch accordingly, in some cases in real time. Second, in part because digital media are interactive they permit a fuller and more precise measuring of advertising's impact. (Bianco 2004, p. 65)

New media technologies allow advertisers to target more specific and specialized audiences, through specific outlets and according to the information gathered in the feedback and the tracking provided by these technologies. Thus, traditional media advertising budgets have shifted to the new interactive and specific audiences' niches offered by the web. However, this changing scenario has turned slower on developing media markets, where traditional media such as radio and television still get the attention of the majority of both audiences and advertisers, while broadband internet access, smart phones and PDA markets tend to grow at a slow yet stable pace.

> High-value customers are less and less reached through specific media packages, in which particular advertising can be placed, and increasingly reached through continuous online tracking which targets them, as they move online, with advertising tailored to their individual online consumption. (Couldry 2009, p. 444)

Finally, the loss of advertising money for traditional media, in favor of the new media, has had a great impact on the traditional media market structure, as Lindqvist (2009) states:

> While the industrial media-sector was built on traditional value-chain thinking and a strong division of tasks between the various media and their consumers, this is different in the new media. Here it is the network models that are gaining a stronger hold. And in the network models, the relationship between companies in the old value chains is changing dramatically. (Lindqvist 2009, p. 24)

10 Towards New Challenges for Media Management on Developing Markets

All this new media environment previously analyzed on the three main issues has pictured a big transformation for the media industries. This transitional phenomenon has turned pretty common on mature media markets and developed societies such us the USA, Western Europe, Far East (Japan) and some Asian countries like China. However, a question remains and that's how the transitional process has looked like on the so called developing economies, in terms of audiences' responses and adaptations to the changing new media environment?

Longitudinal research conducted by the authors on the Colombian media market[4] between 2007 and 2010 showed a transitional but stable penetration of new telecommunication services mainly in the urban areas. There is a growing market on the field of triple play service (fixed telephony, close television and broadband Internet access) and the cell phone industries (Arango Forero et al. 2010).

Statistical analysis also reveals that audiovisual new media consumption tends to rise mainly among adolescents and young audiences. While there is a lack of new media literacy among 40 and older, the audiovisual media young users in Colombia are now becoming multitaskers.

Even though Colombia is a country ranked as a developing media economy, there is a combination between traditional and new media in terms of consumption among the young audiences analyzed.

Television and radio keep their importance among audiences, but their consumption shows the veneer of fragmentation due to an oversupply and undeniable influence, mainly among kids, adolescents and young, from the international offer (LAMAC 2010). Although national private and in some cases public networks still remain on their preferences, International frequencies have become an important part of their daily audiovisual routine.

Traditional industries like radio are progressively losing attention among young audiences, who are slowly moving away from the traditional broadcasting system, and currently are paying more attention to digital media and personal digital assistant devices for entertainment and music listening, mainly among mid and high income levels in the most important urban areas.

Finally, Latin America accounts up to 8 % of the global Internet audience by the end of 2010. Latin American internet audience grew up 23 % in 2009 and Colombia showed the highest growing share with 32 %. While the world wide average of individual internet connection was 22.6 h on February 2010, Latin America as a region got 24.3 h in average (Brazil 26.4, Mexico 25.7, Argentina 22.9).

During 2010 Social networking became in Latin America the second most important function on internet (81.9 %) after search/navigation (85.5 %). E-mail was third (78.9 %), entertainment fourth (78.8 %) and instant messengers were fifth (71 %).

---

[4] Colombia has the second Hispanic largest potential media market after México, considering population, and the third largest in Latin America after México and Brazil (DANE 2007).

Facebook remained as the most popular social network in the region (49.1 %), followed by Windows Live Profile (36.7 %), Orkut (25.4 %), Hi5.com (12.6) and Twitter (10.5). Four out of five internet users in Colombia and Chile were Facebook users in 2010 (Fosk 2010).

In 2009, a study conducted by Professor Alan Albarran (University of North Texas) among young from Argentina, Colombia, Chile, Mexico, USA and Uruguay was aimed to determine similarities and differences regarding social media uses among people between 18 and 25 years old. One thousand five hundred and seven respondents were surveyed and 106 focus groups were conducted.

Based on Uses and Gratifications framework, the study found 68 min per day as an average of social networking use. 94.8 % had a Facebook account; 25.6 % My Space; 17.9 % Twitter and 3.7 % LinkedIn. Social networking use altered the consumption of traditional media such as newspapers and television. México and Colombia showed the lowest levels for reading newspapers.

In average, young Latin Americans use Facebook to keep contact with friends and relatives and exchanging pictures; they use MySpace to share musical files; Twitter for passing time. Finally, regardless of country, young Latin Americans are among the social networking most active users. It means traditional media industries must pursue effective strategies in order to catch the attention of consumers under a social networking environment.

References

Albarran, A. (2010). *The transformation of the media and communication industries*. Pamplona: Ediciones Universidad de Navarra.

Anderson, C. (2006). *The Long Tail: Why the future of business is selling less or more*. New York: Hyperion.

Arango Forero, G., Arango, M. F., Llaña, L., & Serrano, M. C. (2010). Colombian media in the XXI century: The re-conquest by foreign investment. *Palabra Clave, 13*(1), 59–76.

Bermejo, F. (2009). Audience manufacture in historical perspective: From broadcasting to Google. *New Media & Society, 11*(1–2), 133.

Bianco, A. (2004, July 12). The vanishing mass market. *Business Week*, 60–68. Retrieved from http://www.businessweek.com/magazine/content/04_28

Couldry, N. (2009). Does 'the media' have a future? *European Journal of Communication, 24*(437), 437–450. doi:10.1177/0267323109345604.

Cover, R. (2006). Audience inter/active: Interactive media, narrative control and reconceiving audience history. *New Media Society, 8*(139), 139–158.

Curran, J., Morley, D., & Walkerdine, V. (1998). *Estudios culturales y comunicación [Cultural studies and communication]*. Barcelona: Paidós.

DANE, National Statistics Administrative Department. (2007). *Proyecciones nacionales y departamentales de población 2006-2020*. Bogotá: DANE.

Fosk, A. (2010). *Situación de Internet en Latinoamérica*. Retrieved from http://www.slideshare.net/francoalfero/estado-de-internet-en-latinoamrica-comscore-2010

Gadamer, H. G. (2004). *Truth and method*. London: Continuum.

Haridakis, P. M., & Whitmore, E. H. (2006). Understanding electronic media audiences: The pioneering research of Alan m. Rubin. *Journal of Broadcasting & Electronic Media, 50*(4), 766–774.

Huertas, A. (2002). *La audiencia investigada [Audience investigated]*. Barcelona: Gedisa.

Ihde, D. (1990). *Technology and the lifeworld. Form garden to earth.* Indianapolis: Indiana University Press.

Kenyon, A. J., Wood, E. H., & Parsons, A. (2008). Exploring the audience's role: A decoding model for the 21st century. *Journal of Advertising Research, 48*(2), 276–286.

Katz, E., Blumler, J. G., & Gurevitch, M. (1985). Usos y gratificaciones de la comunicación de masas [Uses and gratifications of mass communication]. In M. De Moragas (Ed.), (1992) *Sociología de la comunicación de masas* [*Sociology of mass communication*]. Barcelona: Gustavo Gili.

McQuail, D. (1997). *Audience analysis.* Thousand Oaks, CA: Sage.

LAMAC. (2010). Penetración de TV Paga-Latinoamérica. Retrieved Agosto, 2010, from http://www.lamac.org/Espa%c3%b1ol/Investigaci%c3%b3n/Penetraci%c3%b3n/Penetraci%c3%b3n_de_ TV_de_Paga/Latinoam%c3%a9rica/

Lin, C. A. (1994). Audience fragmentation in a competitive video marketplace. *Journal of Advertising Research, 34*(6), 30–38.

Lindqvist, U., Bjørn-Andersen, N., Kaldalóns, O. S., Krokan, A., & Persson, C. Nordic Innovation Centre (NICe), VTT, SFTI-Packforsk, NTNU, CBS, ICEPRO. (2009). *New business forms in e-business and media, 'e-media'* (Project 06212). Retrieved from http://www.itu.dk/people/rkva/2011-Spring-EB22/readings/E-MediaFinalReportMay09.pdf

Mattelart, M., & Mattelart, A. (1997). *Historia de las teorías de la comunicación [History of communication theories].* Barcelona: Paidós.

Martín-Barbero, J. (1987). *De los medios a las mediaciones. Comunicación, cultura y hegemonía [Communication, culture and hegemony: From the media to the mediations].* Barcelona: Gustavo Gili.

Montoya, M. (1992). *¿Un nuevo modelo de comunicación en América Latina? Conversaciones con nueve estudiosos de los medios y la cultura [A new model of communication in Latin America? Conversations with nine scholars of media and culture].* Ciudad de México: Fundación M. Buendía.

Morley, D. (1992). *Television, audiences and cultural studies.* London: Routledge.

Napoli, P. (2001). The audience product and the new media environment: Implications for the economics of media industries. *The International Journal on Media Management, 3*(II), 66–73. Retrieved from The audience product and the new media environment: Implications for the economics of media industries.

Napoli, P. (2008a). *Revisiting "mass communication" and the "work" of the audience in the new media environment.* Informally published manuscript, The Donald McGannon Communication Research Center, Fordham University, New York, NY. Retrieved from http://www.fordham.edu/images/undergraduate/communications/revisitingmasscommunication.pdf

Napoli, P. (2008b). Toward a model of audience evolution: New technologies and the transformation of media audiences. *McGannon Center Working Paper Series.* Paper 15. Retrieved from http://fordham.bepress.com/mcgannon_working_papers/15

Napoli, P. (2010). Revisiting 'mass communication' and the 'work' of the audience in the new media environment. *Media Culture Society, 32*(505), 505–516. doi:10.1177/0163443710361658.

Napoli, P. (2011). *Audience evolution: New technologies and the transformation of media audiences.* New York: Columbia University Press.

Phallen, P. F. (2006). Audience research and analysis. In A. Albarran, S. Chan-Olmsted, & M. Wirth (Eds.), *Handbook of media management and economics* (pp. 623–636). Mahwah, NJ: Lawrence Erlbaum.

Picard, R. (2000). Audience fragmentation and structural limits on media innovation and diversity. In J. van Cuilenburg & R. van der Wurff (Eds.), *Media and open societies. Cultural, economic and policy foundations for media openness and diversity in East and West* (pp. 180–191). Amsterdam: Het Spinhus.

Piscitelli, A. (1998). *Post Televisión, ecología de los medios en la era de Internet.* Buenos Aires: Paidós.

Shaver, D., & Shaver, M. A. (2006). Directions for media management research in the 21st century. In A. Albarran, S. Chan-Olmsted, & M. Wirth (Eds.), *Handbook of media management and economics* (pp. 639–654). Mahwah, NJ: Lawrence Erlbaum.

Stevenson, N. (1998). *Culturas mediáticas [Media cultures]*. Buenos Aires: Amorrortu.

Tewksbury, D. (2005). The seeds of audience fragmentation: Specialization in the use of online news sites. *Journal of Broadcasting & Electronic Media, 49*(3), 332–348. doi:10.1207/s15506878jobem4903_5.

Thompson, J. B. (1995). *The media and modernity: A social theory of the media*. Stanford, CA: Stanford University Press.

Uribe-Jongbloed, E. (2011). Estudios de medios de comunicación en idiomas minoritarios y la comunicación para el cambio social: diálogo entre Europa y América Latina. *Investigación y Desarrollo, 18*(2), 2–25.

Webster, J., & Ksiazek, T. B. (2012). The dynamics of audience fragmentation: Public attention in an age of digital media. *Journal of Communication, 62*(1), 39–56.

Williams, R. (1976). *Keywords: A vocabulary of culture and society*. London: Fontana.

Wittgenstein, L. (2009). *Philosophical investigations*. Oxford: Blackwell.

Towards a Typology of Strategies for User Involvement

Arne H. Krumsvik

This chapter will propose a typology of four key strategies for user involvement through social media for the news industry. Based on an extensive literature review of international research, and original research in Scandinavia and the US,[1] this contribution will explore the rationale for user involvement, and the strategic use of social media by traditional news media institutions.

Identified rationales for user involvement through social media do, among others, include:

Civic journalism: Technology allows for more user intervention in the communication process. The promise of this new opportunity became linked to the American Civic Journalism movement (also called Public Journalism), aiming to reform print and television journalism. Followers of this movement had used town meetings to involve the public in the journalism process. Now new technology made it possible for more users to participate.

Citizen reporting: The labels of Citizen Journalism and Responsive Journalism are also used in the analysis of the different aspects within the general phenomenon of Participatory Journalism. In dramatic situations this relationship with the users is of obvious value to the news organization.

User loyalty: When asked to rank the top three reasons for promoting participation-based output out of a list of seven, Norwegian executives ranked 'establishing audience loyalty' as the most important reason. The securing of loyalty is seen as a main strategic aim that underlies the various tactics for promoting and shaping participation. As one informant put it: 'interactivity creates loyalty' (Sundet & Ytreberg 2009).

---

[1] This chapter is in part based on original research by the author: Analysis of Scandinavian online newspapers 2011, case study of newspaper production for iPad in Norway 2011, surveys of newspaper executives in Norway 2005, 2007, 2009, and 2011, survey of Danish newspaper executives 2007, surveys of users and producers of online newspapers in 2005 and 2008, case studies of Norwegian Broadcasting Corporation (NRK) and Cable News Network (CNN) 2005–2008.

A.H. Krumsvik (✉)
University of Oslo, Oslo, Norway
e-mail: arne.krumsvik@hioa.no

Enhancement: Consumption of traditional media has gone from being an individual activity, to be an activity where users have the opportunity to interact with others. When participating, users become part of a community and feel socially included. This might also become important for people's identity.

Image: Involvement in social media might be used as part of a strategy for traditional media to improve the contemporary or visionary image of the brand or product.

Promotion and distribution: Sharing of news stories by users in social media becomes an important driver of traffic for online publications by traditional media institutions. This form of social distribution has high impact and is an extremely cost-effective means of digital distribution.

In the following we will discuss how these approaches might be used in systematic strategies to create editorial and economic value for news media corporations. It will be elaborated on the historic development and future potential of four identified strategic types.

First it might be appropriate to introduce the philosophical origin of user involvement in news media, dating back to the 1920s' philosophical debate between John Dewey and Walter Lippmann. The latter asserted that modern life was too complex for the average American to understand, and he advocated governance by a technocratic elite whose actions were transmitted to the public by a press practicing a professional code of objectivity. Dewey responded that democracy's promise could only be kept by reviving the power of the public, by strengthening community life, and by informing and educating the public to this purpose. To Lippmann, the press function was dispensable. To Dewey, the press function was vital to this purpose, and to the survival of democratic society (Bybee 1999; Loomis 2001; McMillan et al. 1996).

The Civic and Citizen journalism journalist movement has redrawn Dewey's links between the ideas of press, democracy and community, and addresses the issue of detachment rooted in professional norms of objectivity and credibility. In this view, traditional detachment has created a "disconnection" between journalists and the communities they cover, with accompanying losses in the public life of those places. The aim of this movement is that user interaction in news production should help people function as political actors and not just as political consumers. These dialogues have the potential to vitalize people by engaging them in a public discussion.

Traditional journalists counter that public journalism's willingness to weaken professional norms of detachment puts news media credibility at risk. Professional norms and issues of brand identity are part of the contemporary debate on user involvement in the production of media content, as are legal and ethical considerations. From an economical point of view, the promise of reduced cost of production and promotion makes active strategies for social media very interesting for traditional media institutions (Krumsvik 2009).

In contrast, however, to the revolution in journalism assumed by many new media researchers after the introduction of hypertext, interactivity and multimedia (Deuze 2001; Engebretsen 2001; Harper 1998; Pavlik 1999), technological assets of new media were for the broader part ignored in online journalism (Domingo 2004; Matheson 2004; Schroeder 2004) or at least implemented at a much slower rate then earlier suggested (Boczkowski 2004). When it comes to audience participation, the online strategy of traditional media tends to replicate the gatekeeper model to user-generated content, filtering and separating it from the news produced by professionals (Hermida and Thurman 2007). However, studies of local media indicate fewer problems with inappropriate user generated content for these outlets compared to their national counterparts (Lindholm 2006; Skogerbø and Winsvold 2007). We will take a closer look at how this affects strategy.

Most online news entities offer some kind of arena for deliberation, and this is the starting point for the first strategic type.

1 The Deliberation Strategy

This strategy is rooted in the traditional newspapers legacy of being an arena for public deliberation, as an important part of their social responsibility.[2] Limited space on paper led to a need for editors carefully to decide which contributions that should be accepted for publishing. Nielsen's (2010) study of Danish newspapers show that local newspaper editors receive 2–5 times as many contributions as there are room for in the designated space and that national newspapers can receive up to 10–50 times the amount they need. The norms and principles dominant in the selection process were perceived news values, textual quality, the relevance to the current news agenda, diversity of views, fairness, and disagreement. Other studies also reveals how the selection of contributions from readers are influenced by editorial attitudes to the writing public (Wahl-Jorgensen 2002a), based on certain selection criteria and narrative genres (Wahl-Jorgensen 2002b), and edited to fit particular purposes (Raeymaeckers 2005).

In the online environment scarcity of place is no longer an issue, and the gatekeeper role might also be different. However, the professional norms and practices of traditional gatekeeping functions, linked to the forces behind what becomes news and why (McCullagh 2002; Shoemaker 1991; Shoemaker and Vos 2009), do also represent an expectation for what is being offered by the media houses, and might be linked to the brand of the news outlet. Without the 'selection, addition, withholding, display, channeling, shaping, manipulation, repetition, timing, localization, integration, disregard, and deletion of information' (Barzilai-Nahon 2008a), unwanted content produced by amateurs is published in the context of professional media.

To secure the quality of this kind of online content, the question of pre or post control has been the subject of extensive debate. The core issue has been whether or not the editor should be held accountable for what users publish, and when editorial control should be applied. The question of pre or post control has divided media professionals and users alike. In my 2008 survey of users and producers of online

---

[2] Literature review on The Deliberation Strategy is in part based on Ihlebæk and Krumsvik (Forthcoming). Online gatekeepers—facilitating participation from ordinary people.

newspapers, 52 % of the journalists and 37 % of the users were positive towards pre-moderation of online debates, while 20 % of the journalists and 29 % of the users were negative. However, among users who regard the online newspaper's discussion forums to be a more important arena than traditional newspapers for exercising freedom of expression, 48 % of users were opposed to pre-moderation, while 33 % were positive (Ottosen and Krumsvik 2010). In general journalists are more sceptical towards the online debates, while the users have a more favourable view, especially those recognising the democratic value of online deliberation.

There has also been a noticeable division between journalists and editors. While the Norwegian Union for Journalists have been arguing for pre-control of user generated content, the Norwegian Association for Editors (NAE) has been advocating that the present guidelines are sufficient. The Code of Ethics set up by the Norwegian Press Association has a paragraph regarding online deliberation, stating that publishers need to inform the users if the discussion is not edited and that the publisher is responsible for deleting improper postings. A suggestion from a revision committee in 2005 to change the practice and to demand the editor's approval of all postings on message boards in media belonging to the Press Association failed to be implemented due to a lack of consensus on the matter. If the majority had pushed the decision through, the major news sites, which have strong economic interests in heavily-used unmoderated and post-moderated forums, would not have complied and this could have put the whole self-regulative system of media ethics in jeopardy (Krumsvik 2005; Lindholm 2006; Ottosen and Krumsvik 2008).

My biennial surveys of Norwegian newspaper executives from 2005 to 2011 do however indicate some reluctance from the editors to adapt the participatory potential of online media, due to issues of giving up control. This willingness to let users take part in public deliberation and feedback opportunities online are linked to both the social responsibility of the industry to provide such arenas, and to the professional norms emphasising of the press' ethical responsibility. A central argument is that users should be able to express themselves in real time without too much interference, adapting to the Internet's open structure and democratic features, where freedom of speech can be exercised. Public journalism advocates stresses the importance of strengthening the relation between users and professional journalists to increase democratic participation (Bruns 2005, 2008; Gillmor 2004; Haas 2007; Ihlebæk 2009; Krumsvik 2009; Rosen 1999, 2000). Participation has also become a central strategy in the media industry to strengthen loyalty bonds and increase revenue (Carpentier and De Cleen 2008; Jenkins 2006; Krumsvik et al. 2013; Küng et al. 2008b).

Bruns (2005, 2008) suggests the term 'gatewatching' to describe how control is executed in the age of participatory media, following public journalism ideals. By gatewatching he means:

> ...(t)he ability of users to decide for themselves what they find interesting and worth noting and sharing with their peers, it harness the tendency of members of interest communities to pass on to their peers those news items which they have found interesting...it is a process of highlighting news, of publicizing rather than publishing information (2008:75).

Table 1 The use of social features in Scandinavian newspapers

Publication	Comments on articles	Debate forums	User blogs	Other (promoted on home page)	Distribution
Aftonbladet (tabloid, SE)	Yes (Facebook)	No	Yes	Live news chat	3
Expressen (tabloid, SE)	Yes	No	Yes		3
Sundsvall Tidning (local, SE)	Yes	No	Yes	User photos What's on	4
Dagens Nyheter (morning, SE)	No	No	No		6
Aftenposten (national, NO)	No[a]	Closed	No		9
Dagbladet (tabloid, NO)	Yes	No	Yes		4
VG (tabloid, NO)	Yes (Facebook)	Yes	Yes	Birthday congratulations	4
Sunnmørsposten (local, NO)	Yes	No	No	User photos What's on	4
Jyllandsposten (morning, DK)	Yes	No	No		346
Politiken (morning, DK)	No	No	No		2

[a]Only on selected stories

Gatewatching presents a shift from the traditional gatekeeping to a more coactive form of editorial decision-making, presuming that control is carried out after the contribution is published, and assuming that the contributors will strive for constructive participation.

Jenkins (2006) is more sceptical, stating that "when people take media into their own hands, the result can be wonderfully creative; they can also be bad news for all involved", while Keen (2007) argue that the trend of participation from ordinary people in media and cultural industries is dangerous, meaningless, and degrading.

Some news organizations separate discussion forums from the editorial content, due to issues of quality and control, while others facilitates debate at the same page as news articles (see Table 1). A third option is to direct users towards social networks like Facebook and Twitter for further discussion, and then mirror this "external" activities on the news site. After the terrorist attack on Oslo in 2011, this option also became an ad hoc solution to deal with issues of anonymity. On the other hand, outsourcing deliberation is an issue of customer relationships (see discussion on the Data Gathering strategy).

User interaction became an important part of early experiments in the online news industry. CNN had gained some online experiences from its relationship with CompuServe since 1993, and identified the global World Wide Web in 1995 as a platform well-suited to expanding their global news operation. Being the first major broadcasting organization to provide breaking news online, CNN became a creator of change in the industry, in the same way as it had 15 years previously when the first 24-h news channel on TV was launched by Ted Turner in Atlanta.

Breaking news attracted users, and feature sections made them stay longer and read more than they did on competing news sites. Message boards and forums were used to facilitate user interaction.

Hence, forums, message boards, and chat rooms became a major part of their offering on the web in the mid 1990s, until the AOL/Time Warner merger and the dot-com downfall in 2001. Then it was decided that their partner AOL would be the party to take responsibility for online forums because of its strength in this field, while CNN.com focused on its core business as a news distributor.

The news professionals did not have any problems with this division of labor, as they found community services and message boards very expensive to manage, in both time and resources, with not much perceived results from them. Relative to their total reach, very few people participated, and they had to be guarded for improper content. Online chat events with correspondents and newsmakers also took a lot of time setting up and moderating, and could have as few as 15–20 participants:

> "Maybe 50 people would sometimes participate in a chat. [...] It's just such a tiny portion for a pretty large expenditure of resources. And sometimes out of that you would get an interesting transcript, but it became pretty intensive to go back through a chat and pull out all these extraneous comments and make it something that was readable." (CNN intervuee, Atlanta, 2005)

In 2005 the Q&A format formerly created from online chat events was extracted from transcripts of interviews on air. The journalist had taken back the position as the interviewer.

According to the CNN staff, the core reason that people come to the CNN site is to read about the news and not necessarily to discuss the news on the site. They may e-mail their friends about it or talk to a co-worker about it, so the interactivity happens around the site and not necessarily on the site:

> "You know, we're a mass market news and information site, our goal is to inform as many people in as many ways as possible ... and we make some of our directional decisions based on how certain initiatives or strategies are going to improve our reach and our overall ability to serve more people, and that's where community as a component of that certainly has a place" (CNN interviewee, Atlanta, 2005)

This implies that the content from users should be edited in such a way as to ensure the professional norms of objectivity and the credibility of the journalist. The citizen is welcome to become a reporter, as long as the same standard applies. However, the issue of detachment may be addressed in the possibility of participation in the newsgathering due to new technology. In dramatic situations this relationship with the users is of obvious value to the news organization (Krumsvik 2009).

2 The Donation Strategy

While the Deliberation strategy have published news stories as the basis for user involvement, the Donation strategy is about involving the public in the journalism process. The 'gatekeeper role' of the journalist in selecting and presenting news the traditional model of media production is transformed to a 'shepherd' role in the process of guiding citizen reporters (Glaser 2004). The professional journalist seeks out voices and encourages submissions, then vetting copy for legal issues and readability issues before publications. This approach has been labeled 'citizen journalism', 'participatory journalism', 'open source journalism' (Bentley et al. 2005), or 'grassroots journalism' (Gillmor 2004). The term 'citizen *reporting*' clarifies the role of the user as a contributor in the input process, while *journalism* is the end result after professional vetting (Krumsvik 2009).

In the CNN case the Deliberation strategy were discontinued by the online department due to professional issues on content quality, scalability, and cost of gatekeeping. Later a Donation strategy was implemented. This time the initiative came from the traditional part of the organization, wanting to expand their newsgathering network.

CNN already had the world's largest newsgathering network through a global web of partner TV channels. At the initiative of the CNN TV operations, this network was extended by introducing the *iReport* in August 2006, a service enabling users carrying cameras or mobile phones to capture and share breaking news. This came about as a result of *ad hoc* initiatives inviting users to contribute images and stories, such as those from major disasters (i.e. the 2004 tsunami, the 2005 London bombings, the 2005 Hurricane Katrina, etc.). A pilot service was included in the CNN Fan Zone as part of the coverage of the 2006 FIFA World Cup in Germany.

CNN's iReport represents the state of the art in utilizing the economics of participatory news production: users provide breaking news video footage for free.[3] The service has further developed from its original intended function to include a "home video" style entertainment show on TV and a separate website for the direct submission of post moderated user-created content (Krumsvik 2009).

At the 2006 and 2007 Online Journalism Awards,[4] CNN.com was a finalist for the Breaking News award in the Large Site category; in 2005 it was honored for its coverage of the *London terrorist bombings*, a story where pictures and videos captured by the public became important in the newsgathering; and in 2006 the coverage of the *Virginia Tech shootings* was honored, a story where *iReport* played an important role in the CNN newsgathering process. At the 2008 Online Journalism Awards, CNN.com won the General Excellence in Online Journalism award in the Large Site category. The jury described CNN.com as:

---

[3] In special cases CNN will pay for exclusive rights.

[4] The Online Journalism Awards, launched in May 2000, honor excellence in digital journalism around the world, and are traditionally awarded at the Online News Association's annual conference.

"... a site that made substantial changes in the past year, making it one of the more dynamic destinations out there; one that takes user content seriously and integrates it into the whole, opening a new era of networked content. One judge predicted, 'Everyone will copy it'." (Online News Awards 2008)

Drawing upon the idea pioneered at OhMyNews in South Korea, newpaper across the world are developing models for reader participation in content production for both new and old media. In California *The Northwest Voice*, published by the *Bakersfield Californian*, used material from the Web edition to revive its shopper edition (Terdiman 2004). "Whereas OhMyNews was intended to compete directly with existing media, the first incarnation of citizen journalism in America was an attempt at synergy" (Bentley et al. 2007) This "umbrella" model of user-generated content (UGC) sees this as a way to enhance the company's products rather than compete with them. MyMissourian was a similar initiative by *The Missourian* (Bentley 2005).

In Oslo the Origo Group provides web upload options birthday congratulations and local event listings for the 50 newspapers of the Norwegian Labour Press, automatically producing hundreds of pages in the paper editions of their properties every day.

The opportunity to create user generated content is presently largest within the areas of popular culture and personal/everyday-life. In many traditional newspapers consumers are provided with little or no opportunity to generate actual news as content (Örnebring 2008).

The values for users to participate in UGC activities are both an issue of self-expression, and group belonging—a dimension of ego-defensive, which means to minimize doubts about one self (Daugherty et al. 2008).

3   The Distribution Strategy

Utilizing person-to-person recommendations is the core of the Distribution Strategy. This viral marketing approach exploits existing social networks by encouraging customers to share news stories with their friends. Studies have shown that social networks affect the adoption of individual innovations and products [see Rogers (1995) and Strang and Soule (1998)]. Word of mouth is a powerful factor influencing consumer decisions. Some of the most spectacular success stories are services used to communicate, as the advertising can be part of the communication. Hotmail spent a minute amount on traditional marketing and still grew from zero to 12 million users in 18 months (Jurvetson 2000). Their user base grew faster than any media company in history by every email sent through them containing an advertisement for the service. By mid-2000, Hotmail had over 66 million users with 270,000 new accounts being established each day (Bronson 1998). Google's Gmail also captured a significant market share in spite of the fact that the only way to sign up for the service was through a referral (Leskovec et al. 2007).

While most products cannot be advertised in such a direct way, online news stories might be an ideal case, as the service are available immediately, usually for free.

In addition to 'share' buttons linked to e-mail and various social networking sites on news stories, integrated social readers have been developed for systematic sharing of consumed news stories. As the user reads a story, it will instantly be shared with friends, creating a socially powered newswire. In the fall of 2011 *Yahoo News*, *The Washington Post*, *The Independent*, and *The Guardian* accumulated millions of readers for their social editions. After a few months of operation, the following numbers were reported (Cohen 2011):

- The *Washington Post Social Reader* allowed users to read and share their own news articles and content from partner media outlets (i.e. Associated Press, Reuters, Mashable, SB Nation, Slate, and The Post Express) within the Facebook ecosystem, as users had the option to, but did not have to, follow shared links to other web sites in order to access content. The app had more than 3.5 million monthly active users, 83 % of which are 35 or younger.
- **Yahoo News**: More than ten million Facebook users activated the social news features, and Yahoo! News experienced a 600 % increase in traffic from the social network.
- *The Independent*: More than one million monthly active users connected their Facebook accounts to the newspaper's social news functions, and long tail effects were observed, as articles from the late 1990s became part of its most-shared and most-views lists.
- *The Guardian*: Four million monthly active users of their Facebook app, and it generated nearly one million page impressions daily, with more than half of its users 24 or younger.

Some news operations also encourage their journalists to share own stories in social networks, and interact with user feedback.

Table 1 indicates a tendency of Distribution as the main strategy for user involvement for major subscription based morning newspapers, while local newspapers and single sold tabloid newspapers tends to utilize a broader portfolio of social components. The latter approach has a potential to be developed into the fourth strategic type.

4 The Data Gathering Strategy

Many news organizations have struggled with establishing single sign-on (SSO) across their offerings of online community and other services demanding a login by the user, often provided by a portfolio of third parties. The idea of allowing users to enter one name and password in order to access multiple services has been around since the launch of Microsoft Passport (later Windows Live ID). Since then numerous single sign-on services has been launched, offering universal registration and login.

Most major social network providers (i.e. Facebook, Google, Microsoft, Twitter, etc.) offer single sign-on capabilities for publishers. These lower the threshold for

logging in to a new service from a news provider. In 2011 the Facebook Connect service gained growing market share, with the following benefits:
- Users can log into sites without the need for registration or authentication
- Quick and simple "One-click login" process
- Publishers gained access to a user's Facebook friend list
- Publishers had the ability to post information back to a Facebook user's news feed
- New users can find other Facebook friends using the news sites very easily
- The publisher also had access to other Facebook platform features

The main hesitation for many publishers is the fact that the primary customer relationship will be to a third party. This does not comply with the newspaper tradition of 'ownership' of customer relationships in dual markets. Newspapers have seen a strategic forte in keeping the relationship to their readers and advertisers.

However, it is possible to combine the advantages of utilizing social media login, and accumulate user data as a basis for future business development. Single sign-on capabilities provided by social networks represents a means of acquiring "customers" and improving customer retention.

The news organization might support multiple single sign-on services, publisher should however understand their user base and select single sign-on partners that matches their marketing targets. Facebook and Google bring additional features and functionality, and a communication link that should be leveraged to extract user information for publisher's own aggregations.

At the same time, the development of a Data Gathering strategy enables the news publisher to deliver targeted advertising in competition with third party social networks, and lay the ground for personification of services, niche offerings, and transaction based business opportunities. In Oslo the Origo Group are a case of such a strategy, providing the 50 newspapers of the Norwegian Labor Press with social tools for publishing and user interaction, enabling login with third party social network single sign-on, while gathering data for future business development.

Conclusion: The Four D's of User Involvement

The four strategic types focus on different parts of the news operation value chain. The Donation strategy includes users in the production of content. The Distribution strategy utilizes viral marketing in order to invite potential users to consume this content, while the Deliberation strategy enables users to react and interact with the produced and distributed content. At last The Data Gathering Strategy accumulate information about users and their interaction in order to better serve the same users and potential advertisers (Fig. 1).

The different strategies do also represent distinct different value propositions for key stakeholders. Participating users will be able to express themselves as a result of both the Donation and the Deliberation strategies. The threshold for participation is however different. Taking part in a discussion has a lower threshold than taking the role as a citizen reporter. The value of these two strategies is also very different for advertisers. Discussions are not a desirable

Fig. 1 The four D's of user involvement

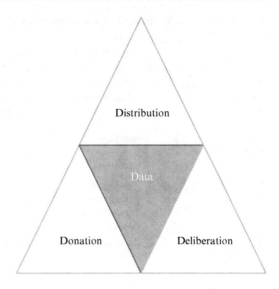

context for advertising due to the high-perceived risk of offending expressions, while other kinds of user created content might represent a neutral proposition for advertisers, given an acceptable level of quality. For advertisers the two other strategies represents a more positive value proposition. The Distribution strategy will have the potential to provide better reach for advertisers, while the Data Gathering strategy will offer more targeted communication opportunities.

For users the lowest threshold of participation is to share news stories with friends through social networks, while the creation of a local profile represents a higher threshold that needs to be met by a clear value proposition for the transaction to be attractive. While more relevant advertising creates a clear value for the user, it is not easy to communicate as a concept. Possibilities for personification of content in general might have a better appeal.

For the news organization the Donation strategy represents free content and creates user loyalty. The loyalty aspect will also be a key part of the Deliberation strategy, probably involving more users, and also contribution to the traditional social responsibility of these kinds of institutions. The distribution strategy represents free marketing and better reach, and the Data Gathering strategy secure ownership of user data and might be a key component in future business development.

See Table 2 for a summary of the thresholds of participation and value for the stakeholders from the four types of strategies.

News organizations might chose to execute several of the strategies in order to create value for users, advertisers, shareholders, and the society. This will especially be relevant if Data Gathering is the main strategic approach. However, observed practices indicates a low strategic awareness of the potential of different approaches, hence higher awareness and clarity on strategic intentions

Table 2 Threshold for participation and value for stakeholder from the four strategic types

Strategic type	Threshold for participation	Value for participating users	Value for advertisers	Value for news organization
The donation strategy	High	Self-expression and group belonging	Indifferent pending acceptable quality	Free content. Loyalty
The deliberation strategy	Medium	Self-expression. Engaging interaction with peers	No-desirable context	Social responsibility. Dynamic content. Loyalty
The data gathering strategy	Medium	More relevant advertising. Personification of content	More relevant targeting.	Ownership of user data, potential for business development
The distribution strategy	Low	Share experiences with friends	Better reach.	Free marketing. Better reach

might contribute to both higher value creation and possibly also reduce some of the professional skepticism to user involvement as part of the online efforts by traditional news organizations.

References

Barzilai-Nahon, K. (2008a). Gatekeeping: a critical review. Pre-Print Draft – February 2008. *Arist-Annual Review of Information Science and Technology*.
Bentley, C. H. (2005). Reconnecting with the audience. *Nieman Reports, 59*(4), 26–28.
Bentley, C., Littau, J., Hamman, B., Meyer, H., Welsh, B., & Watson, B. (2005). *The citizen journalism movement: Mymissourian as a case study, association for education in journalism and mass communication*. TX: San Antonio.
Bentley, C., Hamman, B., Littau, J., Meyer, H., Watson, B., & Welsh, B. (2007). Citizen journalism: A case study. In M. Tremayne (Ed.), *Blogging, citizenship and the future of media* (pp. 239–259). New York: Routledge.
Boczkowski, P. J. (2004). *Digitizing the news: Innovation in online newspapers*. Cambridge, MA: The MIT Press.
Bronson, P. (1998). Hotmale. *Wired Magazine, 6*(12), 166–174.
Bruns, A. (2005). *Gatewatching: Collaborative online news production*. New York: Peter Lang.
Bruns, A. (2008). *Blogs, Wikipedia, Second Life, and Beyond. From Production to Produsage*. New York: Peter Lang.
Bybee, C. (1999). Can democracy survive in the post-factual age? A return to the Lippmann-Dewey debate about the politics of news. *Journalism Communication Monographs, 1*(1), 29–66.
Carpentier, N., & De Cleen, B. (Eds.). (2008). *Participation and media production. Critical reflections on content creation*. Cambridge: Cambridge Scholars Publishers.
Cohen, D. (2011). Facebook 'Social Readers' Amass Millions Of Users. Allfacebook.com

Daugherty, T., Eastin, M. S., & Bright, L. (2008). Exploring consumer motivations for creating user-generated content. *Journal of Interactive Advertising, 8*(2), 16–25.

Deuze, M. (2001). Understanding the impact of the internet: On New Media Profesionalism, Mindsets and Buzzwords. *Ejournalist, 1*(1).

Domingo, D. (2004). *Comparing professional routines and values in online newsrooms: A reflection from a case study.* Paper presented at the IAMCR Conference.

Engebretsen, M. (2001). *Nyheten som hypertekst: Tekstuelle aspekter ved møtet mellom en gammel sjanger og ny teknologi.* Kristiansand: IJ-forlaget.

Gillmor, D. (2004). *We the media. Grassroots journalism, by the people, for the people.* Sebastopol, CA: O'Reilly Media.

Glaser, M. (2004, November 17). The new voices: Hyperlocal citizen media sites want you (to write). *Online Journalism Review,* Los Angeles: USC Annenberg.

Haas, T. (2007). *The pursuit of public journalism. Theory, practice, and criticism.* London: Routledge.

Harper, C. (1998). *And that's the way it will be: News and information in a digital world.* New York: New York University Press.

Hermida, A., & Thurman, N. (2007). *Comments please: How the British news media are struggling with user-generated content.* Paper presented at the International Symposium on Online Journalism. From http://journalism.utexas.edu/onlinejournalism/2007/papers/Hermida.pdf

Ihlebæk, K. A. (2009). Folkejournalistikk i NRK redaksjonelle valg og utøvelse av kontroll. *Norsk Medietidsskrift, 16*(4), 363–378.

Jenkins, H. (2006). *Convergence culture. Where old and new media collide.* NewYork: New York University Press.

Jurvetson, S. (2000). What exactly is viral marketing? *Red Herring, 78,* 110–112.

Keen, A. (2007). *The Cult of the Amateur. How today's internet is killing our culture.* New York: Doubleday/Currency.

Kleis Nielsen, R. (2010). Participation through letters to the editor: Circulation, considerations, and genres in the letters institution. *Journalism, 11*(1), 21–35.

Krumsvik, A. H. (2005). Presse-nei til nettdebatt. Dagens Næringsliv (20.06.05).

Krumsvik, A. H. (2009). *The online news factory: A multi-lens investigation of the strategy, structure, and process of online news production at CNN and NRK.* Ph.D. thesis. Acta Humaniora No 394. Oslo: University of Oslo/Unipub.

Krumsvik, A. H., Skogerbø, E., & Storsul, T. (2013). Size, ownership, and innovations in newspapers. In T. Storsul & A. H. Krumsvik (Eds.), *Media innovations.* Gothenburg: Nordicom.

Küng, L., Leandros, N., Picard, R. G., Shroeder, R., & van der Wurff, R. (2008a). The impact of the internet on media organisation strategies and structures. In L. Küng, R. Picard, & R. Towse (Eds.), *The internet and the mass media.* Los Angeles, CA: SAGE.

Küng, L., Picard, R., & Towse, R. (Eds.). (2008b). *The internet and the mass media.* Los Angeles, CA: SAGE.

Leskovec, J., Adamic, L. A., & Huberman, B. A. (2007). The dynamics of viral marketing. ACM Transactions on the Web, 1, 1 (May 2007).

Lindholm, M. (2006). Maskespill og nettdebatt. *Nytt Norsk Tidsskrift, 23*(4), 357–367.

Loomis, D. (2001). *A tale of two cities: Do small-town dailies practice public journalism without knowing it?* Paper presented at the AEJMC Conference.

Matheson, D. (2004). Weblogs and the epistemology of the news: some trends in online journalism. *New Media and Society, 6*(4), 443–468.

McCullagh, C. (2002). *Media power. A sociological introduction.* Houndmills, Basingstoke, Hampshire: Palgrave.

McMillan, S., Guppy, M., Kunz, B., & Reis, R. A. (1996). *Defining moment: Who says what about public journalism.* Paper presented at the AEJMC Conference.

Örnebring, H. (2008). The consumer as producer of what? User-generated tabloid content in The Sun (UK) and Aftonbladet (Sweden). *Journalism Studies, 9*(5), 771–785.

Ottosen, R., & Krumsvik, A. H. (Eds.). (2008). Journalistikk i en digital hverdag. Kristiansand: IJ-forlaget/Høgskoleforlaget (Norwegian Academic Press).

Ottosen, R., & Krumsvik, A. H. (2010). Digitization and editorial change in online media. Findings from a Norwegian research project. *Nordicom Information, 32*(4), 17–26.
Pavlik, J. (1999). *Journalism and new media*. New York: Colombia University Press.
Raeymaeckers, K. (2005). Letters to the editor: A feedback opportunity turned into a marketing tool. *European Journal of Communication, 2*(20), 199–222.
Rogers, E. M. (1995). *Diffusion of innovations* (4th ed.). New York: Free Press.
Rosen, J. (1999). The action of the idea. In T. Glasser (Ed.), *The idea of public journalism*. New York: The Guilford Press.
Rosen, J. (2000). The essence of public journalism. In J. Strömbäck (Ed.), *Public Journalism på svenska*, SDMI Skrift nr. 3, Demokratiinstitutet.
Schroeder, R. (2004). Online review. *Journalism Studies, 5*(4), 563–570.
Shoemaker, P. (1991). *Communication concepts 3: Gatekeeping*. Newbury Park: Sage.
Shoemaker, P., & Vos, T. (2009). *Gatekeeping theory*. New York: Routledge.
Skogerbø, E., & Winsvold, M. (2007). Lærer seg debatt på nettet. Aftenposten (08.01.07).
Strang, D., & Soule, S. A. (1998). Diffusion in organizations and social movements: From hybrid corn to poison pills. *Annual Review of Sociology, 24*, 265–290.
Sundet, V. S., & Ytreberg, E. (2009). Working notions of active audiences: Further research on the active participant in convergent media industries. *Convergence: The International Journal of Research into New Media Technologies, 15*(4), 383–390.
Terdiman, D. (2004). Open arms for open-source news. *Wired News*. http://www.wired.com/news/culture/0,1284,64285,00.html?tw=wn_tophead_4
Vaage, O. F. (2010). *Norsk mediebarometer*. Oslo: Statistics Norway.
Wahl-Jorgensen, K. (2002a). The construction of the public in letters to the editor. Deliberative democracy and the idiom of insanity. *Journalism, 3*(2), 183–204.
Wahl-Jorgensen, K. (2002b). Understanding the conditions for public discourse: Four rules for selecting letters to the editor. *Journalism Studies, 3*(1), 69–81.

Social Media Monitoring Tools as Instruments of Strategic Issues Management

Johanna Grüblbauer and Peter Haric

1 Strategic Issues Management as a Result of Paradigm-Shifts

Social Media are more than just chit-chat on Facebook. Social Media change the communication regimes[1] (Meyer 2007, p. 16 ff.), the structure of interaction between sender and receiver that has regulated human 1:n communication since the area of mass media started. Beyond the basic face-to-face communication setting in segmentary societies (tribal societies) there has always existed an insurmountable gap between senders and recipients: while only a few were sending and many more could only receive.

The advent of media enabling n:n communication marks a turning point in the history of human communication. The basic configuration of concepts such as 'publicity' and 'the public' itself are changing: today, the many publicly communicate at any time with many others. This development also marks the inception of Issues Management as a branch of corporate communication (Heath 1997, p. 35 ff.).

This conceptual shift—'publicity' used to describe the communicative conjunction between 'publicised' and 'public opinion'—towards a panopticum of continuous discourses also massively affects the 'economy of society' (Luhmann 1988), the structural environment of corporations and organizations: concepts such as mutability, complexity and risk have dominated expert discussions in the field of marketing, strategic management and organizational development for roughly 30 years.

---

[1] Communication Regimes refers especially to the third part of Meyers definition "...a system in which the types of communication are tightly coupled to the production system in which they are embedded."

J. Grüblbauer (✉)
University of Applied Sciences, St. Pölten, Austria
e-mail: JGrueblbauer@fhstp.ac.at

P. Haric
Leading Companies Institute, Vienna, Austria

(cf. Mathe and Zerfaß 2010, p. 108) Some even proclaim the "end of control", i.e. the end of traditional corporate, organization and communication management (Kelly 1997; Hamel and Breen 2008). Breaking the rules appears to be the order of the day (Ridderstrale and Nordström 2000; Foerster and Kreuz 2007; Normann 2001, p. 4ff; Faltin 2008; Jarvis 2009; Cole 2010; Kopp 2011) when faced with the complexity crisis and the resulting crisis of management (Malik 2011, p. 32 ff.).

This development can be traced historically: in management and marketing/communication, the toolkit used to deal with complexity, risk, uncertainty and mutability is growing by the day. One central tool, however, has emerged from the flood of ideas, consolidated and influenced other functional areas of corporations and organizations: Strategic Issues Management.

2 Strategic Issues Management: Recognizing and Observing Connections or Patterns

The term "Issues Management" describes the way organizations (companies, government agencies, parties, collectives, etc.) deal with the demands, concerns and critical topics in their stakeholder environment. In operative terms this means identifying, observing and analyzing social, technological, political and economic forces, trends and topics that could influence the organization.

The goal of Issues Management is to interpret and define topics and trends relevant to the organization, to interpret the consequential implications, and to present a choice of options and implement strategies to deal with these topics, i.e. to influence them on behalf of the organization or to raise topics into the spotlight of public discussion.

The term Issues Management was coined by the American public relations expert Chase (1977, p. 25 f.). The goal of Issues Management was to establish conventional public relations (PR), which Chase saw as nothing more than an accumulation of heterogeneous techniques, as a management function. Grunig and Hunt viewed Issues Management as one of the core functions of public relations (1984, p. 21 ff.). The term was usually used to mean observation and opinion making in topical areas relevant to the organization, via PR.

A more inclusive definition, broadening the view to include strategic foresight techniques on a management level, was proposed by Igor Ansoff, the "father of strategic management". Instead of taking the requirements of PR as his point of departure, Ansoff developed his "Strategic Issues Management" (SIM) from the perspective of Strategic Management (Ansoff 1980, p. 131 ff.). Burmann et al. posited that the increasingly turbulent environment of any given organization could not be mastered by the use of rigid and inflexible planning cycles (cf. Burmann et al. 2005b, S. 551). Faced with such an environment, it is necessary for an organization to recognize "weak signals" indicating potentially disruptive trends early in their development, and to include these considerations in its strategic management (Ansoff 1975, p. 21 ff.). SIM is thus concerned with the analysis of trends and topics with regard to their potential effects on corporate strategy.

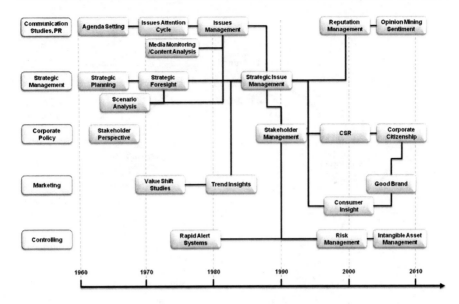

Fig. 1 Conceptual genesis of strategic issues management, in chronological order (based on Liebl 2003)

In recent years, the adoption of the term "Issues Management" and its subsequent integration into the theory of strategic management have yielded an integrated tool for strategic management, combining tools from marketing, organizational development, public relations and other corporate/organizational functions (cf. Burmann et al. 2005a, b). Its primary function is to provide early intelligence of critical topics and threads, in order to afford the management of an organization or company the time and leverage to react accordingly.

From the point of view of strategic management, Issues Management strives to reduce risk and uncertainty, i.e. to avoid surprises or conflicts that might arise from these issues and, conversely, to take advantage of opportunities connected to an issue (cf. Gilad 2004) (Fig. 1).

3 Social Media Analysis in the Context of Strategic Issues Management

There are numerous different ways of identifying trends, such as the popular method of "Genius Forecasting".[2] More sophisticated approaches, however, rely on layered multi-level processes to identify a trend. The process of identifying an issue can be subdivided into three steps: scanning, analysis and monitoring (cf. Heath 1997, p. 88 ff.).

---

[2] Experts define trends based on their own authority and experience.

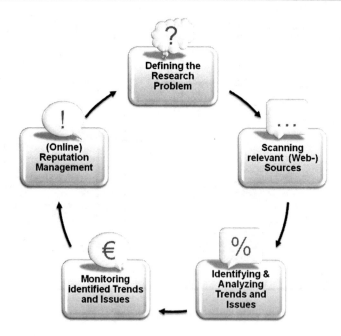

Fig. 2 Trends and issues management using social media monitoring tools

This chart (Fig. 2) illustrates the five circular steps in which trend and issues management proceeds: a research question and the relevant sources have to be defined; on this basis, trends and issues can be identified, analyzed and finally monitored in order to optimize an organization's (online) reputation management, which again necessitates constant adjustments to the original research question, etc.

3.1 Scanning

Scanning is the nondirectional observation of an organization's environment for events, "weak signals" and, in consequence, trends, topics or critical issues likely to affect the organization. The scope of this observation encompasses all events and issues in the organization's area of contact.

Because of this broad spectrum, the scanning process is traditionally rather intuitive and poorly structured. The problem is intrinsic in the act of looking for something without knowing what it is. This is compounded by the multiplicity of data, especially where the Internet is involved. Scanning usually covers mass media as well as content published online and in other sources. So the first stage consists of scanning for trends, i.e. aggregating information by analyzing websites, newsgroups, bulletin boards, weblogs, intra- or extra-corporate personal, verbal or written messages, semi-public sources (manuscripts, surveys, conference papers, newsletters, etc.), professional publications, print media, etc.

One advantage of online data mining is the multitude of (hitherto) different types of media that can be accessed in digitalized form via one common platform; another is the opportunity to observe the reactions of non-journalists,[3] providing an extensive basis for empirical field studies. The research work proper then consists of sorting the abundant data in a target-oriented way, e.g. through text mining, categorizing it accordingly and then presenting it in an appropriate format, e.g. as expressions of consumer sentiment or keyword clusters.

A number of social media monitoring tools and analytical tools, as well as bibliometrical analysis and classical sentiment analysis or media impact analysis, promise solutions to these problems. They are different in many ways, from their choice of data sources to their presentation of the results. Therefore the utility of these tools cannot be assessed on a general scale, but only with regard to specific research questions. Every tool has its strengths in particular fields, so a combination of different analytical tools is likely to yield the best results.

3.2 Identifying and Analyzing Trends and Issues

Once the sources have been accessed, the question arises of how to sort the collected data, i.e. how to pinpoint and connect those data items indicating or comprising a "trend". This can be achieved either through searching for semiotic clues or by checking the selected data items against the market and thus validating them.

Besides content clues, however, the form of the data items and their interconnections must be taken into account. Thus, results can be presented as term relations, as tag clouds, association maps or as semantic networks (StarMaps).[4] The available monitoring tools differ in their depth of analysis, from relying on the mere spatial proximity of terms to identifying types of connections through vector-based pattern recognition.

The issues identified through scanning and semiotic analysis can be validated by comparing them to extant data published by competent institutes, professional magazines or experts in the field, such as consumer surveys, trade sector surveys and analyses of shifting values, etc. However, a lack of correspondence between new and established data cannot be reason enough to ignore the signs of the times. Trends that

---

[3] Consumers, users, critics, etc.

[4] A term relation identifies a number of terms and the correlations among them. Tag clouds indicate the frequency of a term's use by varying the font size or color-coding the terms, thus providing a good overview of relevant topics. For graphic representations in the form of semantic networks the strength of correlation between terms is calculated, thus showing not only the terms themselves but also the varying strength of their interconnections. This is especially relevant for trend analysis when the temporal element is incorporated into the representation, showing the dynamic semantic development of term correlations, i.e. how an issue's pertinency increases or decreases over time.

are recognized only late in their development are now commonly called "wild cards" (e.g. Mendonça et al. 2004; Steinmüller and Steinmüller 2004). They arise from or incorporate unexpected or "disruptive" events, i.e. ignored or underestimated trends in society, technology, politics, lifestyle, the economy, etc. which nevertheless are on the verge of drastically changing our environment.

A survey conducted by the German Fraunhofer Institute in July–September 2010, evaluating 20 Social Media Monitoring Tools used in German-speaking countries, shows that trend analysis and Issues Management are considered the primary application of about 85 % of the tools.

Tonality analysis, also called semantical analysis or sentiment analysis, is generally considered one of the most important functions of monitoring tools. However this is also the field which presents the most obstacles, being one of the few remaining areas in which machines cannot outdo the human mind in terms of exactness. Fully automated analyses may be economical, but they are frequently beset with errors. Tonality analysis makes use of various different methods, some based on complex adaptive algorithms, wordlists containing positively or negatively connoted terms, or simple manual (human) tonality tagging.

3.3 Monitoring identified Trends and Issues

Analysis and monitoring refer to the specific observation of emergent trends, issues and topics. Employed methods include media monitoring, content analysis, interviews and expert discussions. Of these, media monitoring and content analysis are the primary techniques employed by the social media monitoring tools described in this paper, over a field of observation ranging from electronic versions of conventional print media to the so-called "blogosphere" and a multitude of other platforms enabling n:n communication.

Unlike classical (print) media, online media can be integrated into an organization's CRM as a sort of early-warning system, as many issues are discussed early on in the relevant weblogs or bulletin boards. Social Media Monitoring thus facilitates a multi-stage ORM (online reputation management) (e.g. Eck 2008; Amigó et al. 2010): once an organization's reputation has been determined through market and competition analyses, it can be influenced and stabilized through selective issues and crisis management and finally improved through trend analysis and Social CRM (e.g. Greve 2011, p. 261 ff.).

Once trends and issues have been identified it is necessary to name them in order to be able to trace their further development. "Trendy" terminology is frequently non-standardized and can be massively divergent, necessitating the inclusion and specification (often retroactively) of various synonyms. The form and depth of automated monitoring of trends and issues in social media depends on the specific tools provider, as the next chapter will illustrate through the presentation of three case studies.

4 Analyzing and Monitoring the Digital Sociosphere

The Social Media Monitoring Tools presented here were selected on the basis of a sample compiled in a different research context (Harriet et al. 2010). One determining factor was a homogeneous distribution over price segments (costs per year). This paper compares one tool each from the lowest third (€), middle third (€€) and highest third (€€€) of the *price range*. The differences arise from setup costs and work hours necessary for setup as well as the average monthly fee for a tool.

Other parameters relevant to the application of a tool within the framework of Strategic Issues Management include:

(a) *Search queries*: the quality of the results depends on the *search terms* on the one hand and on the *availability of sources* on the other hand. The choice and combination of search terms (connected by Boolean operators[5]) (cf. Zaefferer 2011, p. 98) is contingent on the topic and on the experience of the searcher. For this paper we selected those tools which allow for search queries to be determined by the user/customer, rather than relying on hardwired search queries determined by external advisors (cf. Harriet et al. 2010, p. 22 ff.).

(b) *Full text access*: the *user interfaces* of different tools are also distinguished by whether they present the whole of a retrieved text or only fragments or summaries. Many tools also offer hyperlinks to the original sources. This analysis concentrates on those tools which offer full text access (cf. Harriet et al. 2010, p. 32 ff.).

(c) *Tonality tagging*: different *analytical methods* employ different means of ascribing tonality (or "sentiments"). The ascription of positive, neutral or negative tonality to a given message can either be automated or done manually, or a combination of both. Other criteria for the evaluation of tonality analysis in a monitoring tool are its range of languages and its method for sentiment analysis. Our sample consists exclusively of tools which are at least capable of automated sentiment tagging[6] (cf. Harriet et al. 2010, p. 24 ff.).

Social Media monitoring and analysis tools meeting the above criteria (query input by the customer, full text access and automated tonality tagging) are offered in different price ranges. On this basis, three providers have been selected for analysis in this paper:

- €: Radian6, acquired by Salesforce.com in 2001 and used internationally by more than half of the so-called "Fortune 100" companies[7] to monitor social media (Davey 2012).
- €€: Cogia's Web 2.0-Observer[8]
- €€€: IBM's Corporate Brand and Reputation Analysis (COBRA)

---

[5] The most commonly used operators are "AND", "OR" and "NOT".
[6] To date, automated tagging in Radian6 is only possible for English-language texts.
[7] The world's top 100 companies sorted by gross revenue, including e.g. Kodak, Dell and PepsiCo.
[8] The provider's predecessor company Cogisum Intermedia AG had to file for bankruptcy, but is now back in business as Cogia GmbH.

These tools are presented in the following section, focusing on sources and search method as well as their range of analytical options. Because of the multiplicity of data, the amount of content already digitalized and the resulting possibility of (almost) real-time analysis, this paper will describe and evaluate these tools systematically in order to find out whether they allow for a faster, and maybe even more valid, recognition of topics, issues and trends than traditional methods.

4.1 Radian6

4.1.1 Sources

Radian6 retrieves its sources through the use of spiders/crawlers scanning the Internet for predefined keywords. The quality and relevance of the retrieved sources thus depends on the exact definition of the search query (inclusion and exclusion of terms). Retrieved sources are also supplemented retroactively if the crawlers retrieve additional material. Search terms can be connected by Boolean operators (AND, OR, NOT).

The scope of analysis, focusing on the English-speaking world,[9] includes weblogs, bulletin boards, mainstream news sites, news services and aggregators, picture and video sharing websites (text-based, e.g. YouTube, FlickR), review and retailer sites, Facebook and other social networks, MicroMedia (e.g. Twitter) and comments (on weblogs, news pages and portals). According to the provider, Radian6 is tracking about 150 million sources world-wide.

These sources can be supplemented by the user. The sources supplied by Radian6 cannot be accessed by users. Historical data is also provided; the length of time depends on the date of database creation (usually 30 days before the effective date of the contract) and can be extended back to 2008 for a fee.

4.1.2 Search Queries

Search queries are defined by the user. On a superordinate layer it is possible to choose from global filters for the entire profile: languages, media types, regions, and source filters. The search queries themselves can be configured as keywords or groups of keywords. User fees are calculated according to the monthly volume of retrieved search results. Because of this, both an efficient choice of keywords and the use of the abovementioned global filters is essential to a cost-effective utilization of the product. To facilitate administration, keywords can be assigned to the global categories "brands", "competitors" or "industry". The next step is the definition of desirable content through keywords, context keywords, and exclusion keywords. For groups of keywords it is also possible to define the maximum distance between the keywords in a text.

---

[9] Radian6 is especially strong in the English-speaking world, but it also permanently generates new German-language sources. The provider does not specify the exact number of German-language sources.

4.1.3 Analytical Options

Although the sources provided by Radian6 cannot be accessed, they can be supplemented or suspended manually at will. The options for analysis depend mainly on the keyword configuration and the utilization of the above mentioned filters. Apart from the default filters, sentiment analyses can be implemented by predefining keywords via the configuration menu. Users can also determine the weighting of individual influencers for weblogs, videos/images, MicroMedia and bulletin boards/replies in various categories via slide controls.

A plethora of additional analyses can be implemented directly on the dashboard. As a first step the user creates a New Topic Analysis. The topics are analyzed on the basis of user-defined keywords or predefined topics and filtered by period and media type. Another option that can be selected here is real-time monitoring, with the program adding new content during the analysis.

All results can be displayed as interactive bar or pie charts, showing the results both in per cent and in absolute numbers. The retrieved results can then be processed further, e.g. as River of News, Topic Trends, or tag clouds. Additional segmentation options include Keyword Group, Language, Media Type, Post Tag, Region, Sentiment, Source Tag, and User Assignment.

Open River of News enables a click-through source access on an article basis. Besides media type and publication the dashboard also shows an author's following, number of followers and frequency of updates, as well as the sentiment assigned to that author. Radian6 also supports proactive involvement, i.e. active access to sources and the administration of involvement activities.

Topic Trends displays the development of specific topics over a user-defined period of time. The quality of the results is dependent on the predefined variables, as at this level it is only possible to sort by brands, competitors or industry, or by keywords.[10]

4.1.4 Relevance Analysis

The results can be sorted and segmented according to Classification, Engagement Level, Language, Media Type, Region or User Assignment. The classification figures can also be determined by the user. The default option assigns priority according to the Number of Posts, but Comment Count, View Count, Likes and Votes, Twitter Followers, OnTopic Inbound Links, Total Inbound Links or Unique Source Count can also be used as a basis. In Radian6, relevance can be determined per various criteria as a classification number in the form of the Influencer EQ Weighting.

4.1.5 Demographic and Profiling Analysis

Radian6 offers various meta tags for every media type and displays them both globally over a specified period of time and as a timeline showing their development over that period of time. In Twitter, Following, Followers and Updates are taken into account. For bulletin boards, Forum Thread Size or Comment Count, Unique Commenters,

---

[10] Apart from the interactive quantitative presentation, the program also provides access to the original sources and tag cloud view.

Likes and Votes are displayed. Videos and images are also tagged with a View Count. For mainstream News, Comment Count, Unique Commenters, Likes, Votes and Inbound Links are displayed. Entries from Facebook, MySpace or sites in the category Buy/Sell do not support meta tags.

4.1.6 Tonality Analysis

Sentiment analysis is automated for English-language sources, however the majority of sources is tagged as "neutral". For other languages it is possible to assign or adjust sentiments manually on a five-step scale (positive, somewhat positive, neutral, somewhat negative and negative, as well as "mixed"), but automated sentiment analysis is not supported. Sentiments adjusted by the user are highlighted in blue. The reasons for which an article is classified as positive, negative or neutral are not made explicit.

4.1.7 Integration

Radian6 can be integrated with various other services via API interfaces, e.g. in-house into a Salesforce CRM tool, but also externally with Google Analysis tools, etc.

4.2 Cogia's Web 2.0-Observer

4.2.1 Sources

The Web 2.0-Observer collects articles and posts from weblogs, bulletin boards, social networks and review sites as well as from regular news sources. The starting point for this compilation is a list of sources (URLs) to be included in the survey.[11]

In the second iteration the identified sources are complemented by additional sources retrieved by the crawler/parser.[12] It is possible at a later stage to sort the compilation by different types of sources, either by using preset classifications (e.g. "bulletin boards", "weblogs" or "Twitter") or by configuring user-specific categories.

4.2.2 Search Queries

Cogia's Web 2.0-Observer employs profiles or filters to store relevant terms for every topic as text files and compare them to the retrieved sources in order to determine the relevance of their content.

---

[11] Cogia offers such a list for a fee, however the provider cautions that their list focuses on sources from Germany/the EU.

[12] Crawlers are programs used for searching and indexing the entire content of a website, making it possible for future searches to access additional "historical" data retrieved by the crawler. APIs scan entries in social media platforms such as Twitter, Facebook or YouTube for specific search terms and integrate the results into the search engine circuit. Both sets of data are then refined by an extractor that performs author analyses, creates text information tables, scans blogs and bulletin boards for authors and posts and provides structural information for indexing. Supported file formats are: HTML, TXT, PDF, archive files (ZIP, RAR), PS, PPT, MS Word, and MS Excel files.

The Web 2.0-Observer supports complex search queries through a full database search (not limited to a single topic) using the Boolean operators "AND", "OR" and "NOT". A catalog search function allows for easy correlation of topics in table view and sorted by source types as defined. For this, the Web 2.0-Observer uses cascading categories, i.e. type ascriptions are stored in layers, meaning that e.g. the brand BMW can have a subordinate product group like X1 which will only appear in the search results if it is found in a BMW context.

The retrieved documents are made available as full text, summaries or tag clouds. Besides the document title and a text excerpt, each entry in the list of results also contains additional information such as a running number (sorted by relevance or recency), relevance value (based on mathematical analyses comparing the retrieved document to the search query), source type (weblog, bulletin board, etc.), date of first indexing (not necessarily identical to the creation date), last viewed date, document URL, automated summary (following an author analysis) as well as a clipboard for personal memoranda.

The Options menu also offers a word stem search, i.e. a function that extends the search beyond the exact search term to words sharing the same linguistic stem (e.g. a search for "medium" including "media", "mediated", etc.). The stem search option is based on a Boolean OR connector. It is also possible to set up a list of synonyms (thesaurus function) for the search. Search queries including the topical filters "positive" or "negative" allow for a basic automated tonality analysis.

4.2.3 Analytical Options

For posts in weblogs and bulletin boards, Cogia's Web 2.0-Observer provides automated statistics about the most active posters or blogs, bulletin boards or threads over a given period of time.

The statistical analysis allows for a definition of topic directories and filters as well as of issues and their subcategories. This facilitates trend observation, as the evolution of an issue or the intersection of multiple issues can be displayed over time, presented as quantitative developments in the form of interactive line graphs, either for a single issue (individual analysis) or for two or more issues (intersections). In the graph interface, it is also possible to access the individual sources for each day.

Term correlations can also be displayed as a diagram, ranked by strength of correlation. These are grouped into correlations that appear on a daily basis (regularly) and strong correlations which nevertheless do not appear daily (irregularly). It is also possible to display the results as semantic networks (StarMaps) or tag clouds.

4.2.4 Relevance Analysis

Every document is assigned a relevance value according to the degree of consistence with the search profile. The results can be sorted by relevance or by date. In tag clouds, relevance is denoted by different text colors as well as different font sizes.

4.2.5 Demographic and Profiling Analysis

Weblog and bulletin board profiling is based on an analysis of individual posts performed by automated parsers. Collected meta data include creation date, author's name and thread title, which can be integrated into statistical analyses.

4.2.6 Tonality Analysis

Tonality analysis is supported for German and English-language sources. Sources are assigned positive or negative values on the basis of their consistence with topical filters, i.e. word lists containing a multitude of positively or negatively connotated terms. Because of this, it is possible for a single text to be assigned both a positive and a negative value.

However, automated tonality analyses are not always reliable. For example, the word "idiot" is included among negatively connotated terms, resulting in a negative value assigned to the following text from Worldcarfans.com: "BMW Canada That's CGI, anything who thinks otherwise is an idiot".

4.3 IBM's CCI

IBM's Corporate Brand and Reputation Analysis (COBRA) tool as presented in the Fraunhofer survey has been developed further in the meanwhile and integrated together with other components into the Cognos Consumer Insight tool (CCI).

4.3.1 Sources

IBM includes social media such as Facebook and Twitter as well as Myspace, LinkedIn, FlickR, etc. among its source basis, complemented by weblogs, bulletin boards and newsgroups. The sources are provided by the third-party provider Boardreader rather than by IBM itself. Boardreader is a search engine technology developed by the University of Michigan for the primary task of scanning online bulletin boards, message boards, microblogs, videos and news for keywords. Additional sources can be added or supplemented manually.

CCI's content coverage is growing constantly, encompassing tens of millions of social media sites as well as a historical stock of 80 terabytes of indexed contents. The sources span 40 languages, focusing on those spoken in America, Europe and Asia. Users can group the sources into "Media Sets", deposit keywords and define specific sentiment terms and blockers.

4.3.2 Search Queries

CCI retrieves sources by searching for keywords and groups of keywords and storing data in the form of text fragments ("snippets") from publicly accessible social media websites. Keywords can be interconnected via cross-classification tables. Keyword groups can be defined by connecting keywords through Boolean operators such as AND, OR and NOT, as well as by defining limits for the spatial distance between keywords.

4.3.3 Analytical Options

CCI can represent the results as tables, cross-classification tables, pie charts, bar charts and trend charts. Accessible data includes the Amount of Coverage, Hotword Analysis (i.e. analysis of headwords) as well as Influencer Analysis and Sentiment Analysis. In addition, Evolving Topic Analysis also displays terms not included into the search query itself but frequently used in conjunction with the queried topics.

4.3.4 Relevance Analysis

The Affinity Relationship view shows the degree of connection between keywords/hotwords and other areas of the analysis and displays the relevant snippets retrieved from Facebook, Twitter, weblogs, bulletin boards, etc. The analysis can be displayed on a snippet level or as an affinity index in the form of a table, matrix or network graph. This view also supports the ascription of sentiment analyses to hotwords.

4.3.5 Demographic and Profiling Analysis

IBM's CCI can correlate previously known descriptive and behavioral customer data with interaction data and attitudinal data from social media sources, provided they are shared publicly.

4.3.6 Tonality Analysis

Sentiments can be selected and compared by concepts (a constellation of multiple keywords using Boolean operators), hotwords or media sets. The analysis ascribes positive, negative, neutral or ambivalent tonality to sources, and the results can be displayed in a multi-dimensional parallel diachronic view. In this case, positive and negative ascriptions are not treated as mutually exclusive; an ascription of positive tonality to a source merely indicates that there are more positive than negative sentiments included, or vice versa. An exceptional feature of CCI is that its sentiment analyses do not rely on keywords only, as the program employs a syntax parser to identify syntactic contexts, e.g. to differentiate between the sentiment of a snippet containing "problem" and another containing "solved the problem". The display is clickable and links to the corresponding snippets. "Sentiment blockers" such as the word "idiot" can be removed manually. The displayed sentiments can also be adjusted manually. Tonality analysis is supported for the German, English, French and Spanish languages but can be supplemented by user-defined word lists for other languages.

4.3.7 Integration

Data can be exported directly to SPSS, another IBM tool, for further analysis.

5 Conclusion: Strategic Issues Management Using Social Media Monitoring Tools

Significant drawbacks of the above mentioned Social Media Monitoring Tools include:

- Radian6's sources included in the analysis are not made explicit. The analytical categories for tonality are intransparent: the predefined library of "value judgments" cannot be optimized through human intervention to refine the interpretation of value judgments. German-language sources are excluded from automated sentiment analysis altogether as no library (word lists or syntactic correlations) are provided. As a consequence, the quality of Radian6's tonality analyses depends entirely on the package furnished by the provider.
- Cogia's analytical categories on which the tonality analysis is based are not made explicit. While it is possible to access the library of value judgments,[13] the analysis proceeds exclusively on a lexical rather than a syntactic level. Cogia's Web 2.0-Observer is not an adaptive system, although it can be adapted manually to a given semantic and syntactic area of investigation.

Positive aspects:
- Radian6 offers the greatest range of sources. The source directory for the basic version includes roughly 150 million sources which are constantly updated by crawlers/spiders. This facilitates a valid early recognition of emergent trends and issues, because of the three tools discussed in this paper Radian6 scores the most hits by accessing the largest sample (barring manual user additions to the source basis of other tools).
- In addition to trend validation, CCI also employs keyword co-occurrence analysis to validate its samples by scanning for terms that occur frequently in correlation with the keyword. This facilitates the identification of trends beyond the defined search pattern.
- Contrary to the empirical validity problems in Radian6 and Cogia's Web 2.0-Observer because of their intransparent tonality analysis processes, (cf. Sterne 2011, p. 220 f.) CCI provides an option that is both transparent and adjustable through human intervention. Besides word lists, its library of value judgments also includes syntactic entities and both the classification of individual words and that of syntactic entities can be adjusted manually.
- Radian6's visibility rating is the most exact because of the tools' greater range of sources.
- Both CCI and Radian6 support the addition of sources via API interfaces or the preset integration of other tools.[14] Especially the IBM tool can easily be supplemented by analyses e.g. of conversations from customer relations or behavior and memoranda from customer care[15] and surpasses Radian6 and Cogia's Web 2.0-Observer with its integration of SPSS, enabling complex statistical analysis of the retrieved data.

---

[13] I.e. the terms used to define tonality as positive or negative.

[14] Such as Salesforce and others for Radian6; for IBM's CCI, ERP, data warehousing and deep data mining tools and others.

[15] Customer e-mail, clicks in service portals, memoranda or protocols of call center conversations, etc.

Conclusion: Advantages and Best Practice

The following basic advantages of using social media analytics tools in the context of Strategic Issues Management have been identified in this evaluation:
- Broadening the scope of analysis from the traditional fields of journalism and professional communication to include "opinion media" (social media sources) helps to identify the opinion of a more general "public".[16] This helps to increase the probability of spotting issues, trends and topics early on, sometimes before they appear in traditional media or fall victim to "agenda cutting". It also increases an organization's chance of recognizing and monitoring emergent issues (weak signals) and topics before they become trends.
- Some tools allow for constant optimization of the tools' "semantic intelligence" through manual adjustment and refining of the classification of keywords, semantic entities and statements about products, brands, companies or organizations. Compared to the classical process of media resonance analysis—viz. "black box" code compendia in the hands of the provider—this is a manifest advantage both with regard to the validity of the results and because of the constant optimization by experts in the semantics of the stakeholder: the user knows what is measured and how it is evaluated/analyzed, and user interventions allow for an increasingly close approximation to the stakeholder group's idiosyncratic semantics.

The quality of scanning, analysis and monitoring is of course dependent both on the amount of processed material and on the quality of the analytical method (cf. Bergmann and Pradel 1999, p. 750), but also on the privacy policies of social media platforms, which sometimes differ with different social media analytics tools.

Whereas the observation of public and professional "classic" media used to be sufficient for monitoring issues and topic trends—particularly in corporate communication and marketing—during the "age of mass media", it is possible nowadays to monitor a much greater number and variety of consumer or voter opinions as well as expert and media discourses. A prerequisite for this analysis is the proper technology for scanning the growing sphere of information and communication—and this is the point at which social media analytics tools come into play, with their capability to employ traditional analytical logic over a data space that is immeasurably larger than the classical set of print media. Through this, even "weak" signals can become visible and traceable, significantly lowering the chance of any emergent trend, issue or topic escaping attention. This is the most important contribution of social media analytics tools—at least where text-based formats are concerned.

However, each of the tools presented here has its own particular algorithms and features, i.e. they measure different things and present their results in a different manner. They also differ in how they combine and analyze the retrieved

---

[16] The divergence from classical media resonance analyses is discernible both in the total number of stakeholder communications and in the number of scanned stakeholder groups.

results. Because of this, these tools are subject to the same caveat as the natural sciences: one has to know what exactly it is one wants to measure, and how the results of the measurement can be connected to form meaningful statements and suggestions for action. To adapt a quote from Albert Einstein: Not everything that can be counted is counted, and not everything that counts is measured.

Thus we return to the assumption stated at the beginning of this paper: that the new regime of (online) communication opens up great potential for the early recognition of issues, topics and trends, of corporate risks, market potential and opportunities for innovation, but also for managing employee and stakeholder satisfaction. Katie Pain, a specialist in social media metrics and analysis, views the development of the Web 2.0 as more than an evolution of media: "Social Media isn't about media, it's about the community in which you do business" (Paine 2011, p. 4). It is not merely about media or public relations anymore; the scope has expanded to stakeholder relations and thus to all groups which shape the success or failure of an organization. A closer form of stakeholder contact is only imaginable in the form of direct human contact with the interested parties themselves—which would require considerably more time and effort.

References

Amigó, E., Artiles, J., & Bing, L. (2010). *Weps-3 evaluation campaign: Overview of the online reputation management task*. In: Third Web People Search Evaluation Forum (WePS-3), CLEF 2010. http://clef2010.org/resources/proceedings/clef2010labs_submission_115.pdf

Ansoff, H. I. (1975). Managing strategic surprise by response to weak signals. *California Management Review, 18*(2), 21–33.

Ansoff, H. I. (1980). Strategic issue management. *Strategic Management Journal, 1*, 131–148.

Bergmann, G., & Pradel, M. (1999). Marktforschung als Beitrag für ein lernendes Unternehmen. In W. Pepels (Ed.), *Moderne Marktforschungspraxis. Handbuch für mittelständische Unternehmen* (pp. 749–759). Neuwied: Luchterhand.

Burmann, C., Freiling, J., & Hülsmann, M. (Eds.). (2005a). *Neue Perspektiven des Strategischen Kompetenz-Managements*. Wiesbaden: Gabler.

Burmann, C., Freiling, J., & Hülsmann, M. (Eds.). (2005b). *Management von Ad-hoc-Krisen. Grundlagen - Strategien - Erfolgsfaktoren*. Wiesbaden: Gabler.

Chase, W. H. (1977). Public Issues management: the new science. *Public Relations Journal, 33*(10), 25–26.

Cole, T. (2010). *Unternehmen 2020. Das Internet war erst der Anfang*. München: Carl Hanser.

Davey, N. (2012). *Social-media-strategy*. Retrieved January 27, 2012, http://www.smartinsights.com/social-media-marketing/social-media-strategy/social-media-strategy/

Eck, K. (2008). *Karrierefalle Internet: managen Sie Ihre Online-Reputation, bevor andere es tun!* München: Carl Hanser.

Faltin, G. (2008). *Kopf schlägt Kapital. Die ganz andere Art, ein Unternehmen zu gründen. Von der Lust, ein Entrepreneur zu sein*. München: Carl Hanser.

Foerster, A., & Kreuz, P. (2007). *Different thinking. Creative strategies for developing the innovative business*. London: Kogan Page.

Greve, G. (2011). Social CRM: Zielgruppenorientiertes Kundenmanagement mit Social Media. In C. Bauer, G. Greve, & G. Hopf (Eds.), *Online targeting and controlling. Grundlagen – Anwendungsfelder – Praxisbeispiele* (pp. 261–186). Wiesbaden: Gabler.

Grunig, J., & Hunt, T. (1984). *Managing public relations*. New York: Holt, Rinehart and Winston.

Gilad, B. (2004). *Early warning–using competitive intelligence to anticipate market shifts, control risk, and create powerful strategies.* New York: AMACOM.

Hamel, G., & Breen, B. (2008). *Das Ende des Managements: Unternehmensführung im 21. Jahrhundert.* Berlin: Econ.

Harriet, K., Dausinger, M., Kett, H., & Renner, T. (2010). *Marktstudie. Social Media Monitoring Tools. IT-Lösungen zur Beobachtung und Analyse unternehmensstrategisch relevanter Informationen im Internet. Fraunhofer-Institut für Arbeitswirtschaft und Organisation IAO.* Stuttgart: Fraunhofer.

Heath, R. (1997). *Strategic issues management. Organizations and public policy challenges.* Thousand Oaks, CA: Sage.

Jarvis, J. (2009). *What would Google do?* New York: HarperCollins.

Kelly, K. (1997). *Das Ende der Kontrolle. Die biologische Wende in Wirtschaft, Technik und Gesellschaft.* Mannheim: Bollmann.

Kopp, R. (2011). Enterprise 2.0 als soziodigitales Innovationssystem. In J. Howaldt, R. Kopp, & E. Beerheide (Eds.), *Innovationsmanagement 2.0: Handlungsorientierte Einführung und praxisbasierte Impulse* (pp. 37–66). Wiesbaden: Gabler.

Liebl, F. (2003). Erkennen, abschätzen, Maßnahmen ergreifen: Issues Management auf dem Weg zum integrierten Strategiekonzept. In M. Kuhn, G. Kalt, & A. Kinter (Eds.), *Chefsache Issues Management: Ein Instrument zur strategischen Unternehmensführung – Grundlagen, Praxis, Trends* (pp. 62–73). Frankfurt am Main: FAZ Institut.

Luhmann, N. (1988). *Die Wirtschaft der Gesellschaft.* Suhrkamp: Frankfurt am Main.

Malik, F. (2011). *Strategie. Navigieren in der komplexen Welt.* Frankfurt: Campus.

Mathe, R., & Zerfaß, A. (2010). Medienanalysen als Steuerungs- und Evaluationsinstrument für die Unternehmenskommunikation. In: Pfannenberg, J., & Zerfaß, A. (Eds.), *Wertschöpfung durch Kommunikation. Kommunikations-Controlling in der Unternehmenspraxis* (pp. 98–111). Frankfurt am Main: Frankfurter Allgemeine Buch.

Mendonça, S., Pina e Cunha, M., Kaivo-oja, J., & Ruff, F. (2004). Wild cards, weak signals and organisational improvisation. *Futures, 36*(2), 201–218.

Meyer, E. T. (2007). *Socio-technical perspectives on digital photography: Scientific digital photographie Use by Marine Mammal Researchers.* Dissertation. Indiana University. Information Science.

Normann, R. (2001). *Reframing business: When the map changes the landscape.* London: Wiley.

Paine, K. D. (2011). *Measure what matters. Online tools for understanding customers, social media, engagement, and key relationships.* Hoboken, NJ: Wiley.

Ridderstrale, J., & Nordström, K. (2000). *Funky business: Talent makes capital dance.* Australia: Financial Times Management.

Steinmüller, A., & Steinmüller, K. (2004). *Wild Cards: Wenn das Unwahrscheinliche eintritt* (2nd ed.). Hamburg: Murmann.

Sterne, J. (2011). *Social Media Monitoring. Analyse und Optimierung Ihres Social Media Marketings auf Facebook, Twitter, YouTube und Co..* Heidelberg: Hüthig Jehle Rehm GmbH.

Zaefferer, A. (2011). *Social media research. Social media monitoring in internet-foren.* Norderstedt: Social Media.

Social Networks: The Question on Efficiency Remains

Harald Rau

Discussing networks seems to be an increasingly interdisciplinary task, including technical and technological approaches as well as the ones social sciences are bringing in, namely classical sociology (e.g. Bourdieu 1997; Simmel 1995; cf. Jansen 2006, p. 37) or social anthropology (e.g., Michell 1969), and not to forget advanced economy (Borgatti and Foster 2003; Moran 2005—or closer to a sociological approach: White 1981, 2002). It's still quite a challenge to examine "social" networks using theoretical concepts as the development of medial centered virtual communities (on the web) cannot be described or apprehended easily. The complexity is even increased by economically established measures like efficiency, success, use or value, in particular within a media context. Nevertheless, some authors focusing on network effects in a social context in the past introduced these variables to the debate by using them to "judge" the value or efficiency of growing networks (cf. Mayfield 2003, 2005, p. 116 ff.; Narahari et al. 2010). During the mid 1980s, the research on networks increased steadily within the field of social sciences (cf. Aulinger 2005, p. 205; Strauß and Hollstein 2006, p. 11). Here and in the context of this article, two earlier studies should also be mentioned: Firstly the one undertaken by Stanley Milgram, who 1967 described the "Small World Phenomenon" (Aldrich and Kim 2007, p. 148). And secondly the one by Mark Granovetter (Aldrich and Kim 2007, p. 148), who discussed interpersonal bindings and the strength of weak ties—the title of his most famous article (Granovetter 1973, p. 1360 ff.); later he focused on the term of "embeddedness" of actors (cf. Jansen 2006, p. 19 f.).

To give a short summary: measuring value or efficiency of modern virtualized social networks in the media world will force us to transfer the considerations about media quality (cf. Rau 2007a, b) to discussing the quality of connectivity and ultimately the quality of single connections in the network, depending on a huge set of variables. No one would be able to ignore the core of media

H. Rau (✉)
Ostfalia University of Applied Science, Salzgitter, Germany
e-mail: h.rau@ostfalia.de

economics—which is an economy of attention (cf. Franck 1998). But what is currently happening is a shift from attention to recognition or reputation. Where in a traditional mass medial context 'attention' is the core economic value, 'recognition' or 'reputation' will be the relevant factors in the social media context—and thus one would need an "economy of recognition and reputation" instead of an "economy of attention" (cf. Franck 1998). Once again, a significant shift in judging value(s) in a social media context can be noted. Therefore the economies of social networks will have to be viewed in a completely new way. By the way: All this will not make it easier to measure efficiency—it will make it even more complex.

1 Efficiency: At Least a Question of Quality

Considering the (social) network realities: It is quite easy to present and analyze the number of possible connections and the growth of connectivity in social media driven networks—and assuming every single connection in a network being of similar value or comparable quality, one can describe the total value or the growth of value parallel to the growing connectivity in any given timeframe. As a consequence, all explanatory models that are available (e.g., Reed, Metcalf) start with the growth of links in the network and use different rules and settings to describe the effect of this growth on the network's value. By now we have also come to realize that the approach introducing the group forming networks (introduced by Reed 1999) is very helpful in having a closer look at everything (currently) happening in social media communication. The existence of hubs and "super hubs" should be taken into account in this context, for these aspects offer an explanation in regards to exponentially growing value. Sadly, while all available blueprints—whether they are describing a linear or exponential curve of efficiency growth—are creating valid figures, they are static and inflexible if one also questions quality.

One major task will now be to (again) discuss the concept of quality within a teleological, normative or action based framework for it is a crucial factor: In order to get a true picture of social media value we definitely must not only take connectivity into account; we also have to reflect on the diverging quality of possible connections, and we will have to argue from an individualized point of view. One of the core questions would be: could some of the theoretically driven rules of the pre-web era possibly be applied to social media? For the author future discussion will on the one hand lead back to socio economic approaches, focusing on preferences and individual decisions (consumption of media content, willingness to actively participate, 'collectivized' dimensions of wants or needs addressed by social media). One therefore has to ascertain whether explainable or even measurable preferences are used to generate activity—as this question is of increasing relevance considering the rapidly growing influence of web based communication in society.

Societal communication has phenomenally "moved" (or is moving) from singularized mass media channels into the web sphere—dominated by social media ("Facebook is reality, is real life."—Ehlers 2011). This is the core hypothesis that should form part of the current discussion: one sees the convergence (or better the merger) of mass and individual communication on the same platform, in the same environment. This will lead (as described: cf. Boltze and Rau 2011) to the end of, targeting' in information processes and instead foster the debate around mass media as a culturally driven phenomenon on a new level or layer. Finally, when trying to measure social media value, one will definitely have to question the current approaches on mass communication, on publicity, on public sphere and—furthermore—on journalism. This will bring the academic discussion back to the roots: to questioning the quality of any content offered. By generating a solution (allowing open discussion) to the challenge of measuring media quality, this article will open a new round in interpreting network efficiency from a social media point of view. As from Katz we all know since 1962 (p. 381): "Yet it seems quite clear that the media may also be sought for purposes of strengthening one's position in his immediate network of social relations."—which is probably true today more than ever.

2 No Final Solutions: But Even More to Discuss

To put it simply: this article focuses on the quality of connections in networks without offering a final solution to the problem of how to measure these quality dimensions. Instead it seeks to open up the discussion for further research and approaches. In the context of this article, it will be comparably easy to describe the number of possible connections—and with that to present and analyze the growth of connectivity. With every single connection within the network being of equivalent value or comparable quality, one would measure the total value in parallel to the increasing connectivity. Here one will find various models of explanation, all of which follow the growth of participants in the network and will on this basis display regularities. But what happens if the value or quality of these single connections diverges? For collaboratively generated web offerings this would normally be the case. To sum it up: the attempt to interpret the efficiency of networks will lead to skating on very thin ice.

To be clear: neither will this article be able to offer final solutions for this theoretically based networking challenge. But it will probably clarify the picture in regards to one particular aspect and therefore prepare the topic for future research. The main aim discussed on the following pages will reduce those attempts to absurdity, directly linking the efficiency criteria to measurable growth of the network—as did, for example, Bender (2005, n.p.) from Massachusetts's Institute for Technology. The following pages will use a broader framework or approach to handle a not at all simple construct of social sciences. And network theory, one has to remember, is much older than today's discussion, which (e.g., through the factor virality) reassigns new dimensions to social networks. A core question is: could the theoretically based considerations from the pre-internet age also be used to measure the efficiency of or even to regulate social media platforms like twitter, facebook, youtube, flickr or slideshare? And could they—to go further—explain the reality (and efficiency) of collaboratively created online media content?

The focus on networks will be an ongoing issue for an interdisciplinary discussion, and it will integrate explanatory approaches from engineering, computer sciences, technological development, sociology and economics. The title of this article implies for it to be concerned with "social" networks. This is an undertaking which is exciting and very difficult at the same time—for the development of virtual communities in the internet can hardly be described with theoretical concepts. In fact, it will get even harder by introducing basic economic measurements such as efficiency, performance, success or use—introduced by several authors in the more recent past (cf. Mayfield 2005, p. 116 ff., 2003, n.p.; Reed 2001, 1999, n.p.). These authors are presenting networking effects in a social context and reflect on values by assessing the growing network. For economists, variables that are oriented on value will be of core interest,—for example earnings, uses, or even efficiency. But this mostly business driven perspective needs an equivalent measure—regularly it will be "money". For all (mass) media published in a democratized process, judging has to follow the journalistic perspective—and it therefore has to be separated from single business assessment rules—even more than today, where informatory offerings of journalism produced in real economic environments (like newspapers and private broadcasting) are often forced to fulfill pure business performance criteria.

3 Analog Effects: Democratization and Commercialization

Here it has to be allowed to step back further in order to ascertain the actual starting point for this article. This is the realization that the democratization of media content has similar effects to a growing commercialization or commodification of this content. Especially if one wants to continue the in no way conclusive discussion about quality for democratized and in a nonprofit way produced media, it becomes apparent that the effect of democratization will be as explosive as the examination of economization—or, to be more precise—the commercialization of journalistic content. Both approaches will (with a growing number of participants) facilitate the increasing satisfaction of more and more individual needs; they both will facilitate addressing increasingly narrowed target audiences on the one hand (segmentation up to the level of individuals), and support the smallest common denominator on the other (leveling down to trivialization). Thiel has described this phenomenon for Wikipedia: "Wikipedia organizes the knowledge of the world as a compromise and is with the democratization hazarding the consequence of leveling" (2005, p. 36). Journalism is well known for that: in the academic discourse, growing economization was often equated with an ongoing decrease in quality (and with that a reduced outcome for societal effort). As a consequence the journalistic production would continuously adapt to the putative wants and expectations of those recipients capable of winning a majority (mass taste).

In his mass communication theory, McQuail also describes this paradox of separation and individualization of content on the one hand, and the serving of the smallest common denominator (which with economic activity tends to get smaller and smaller in saturated societies) on the other. He sees the future of mass communication affected either by social fragmentation or unifying (cf. McQuail 2002, Chapter 10). The background for this paradox is easily explained: it is a fact that media content—whether it is commercially produced or created in a democratized process—needs a certain amount of acceptance and attention in order to be classified as mass media in our current understanding.[1] Following that, even non-profit media using the web as a channel to reach their recipients will have to assure market mechanisms are applied in order to ensure a certain degree of attention. This context is particularly relevant considering the branding processes in regards to the Internet. Interesting brands could either arise from highly democratized or highly commercialized environments.[2] In an "apperception economy" labeled this way in the broadest sense, branding processes could be identified which are quite similar to the ones visible in real economic environments with monetized measures purely concerned with earnings. From this point of view Wikipedia is a typical example of such branding processes for media content that is produced using collaborative and democratized structures. These are the prerequisites for branding in the Wikipedia project:

- Unrestricted availability of source codes, totally independent from economic or political power structure.

---

[1] Media supply, also the one with societal mission—like the European public broadcasters ("öffentlich-rechtlich": e.g. BBC in Great Britain or ARD and ZDF in Germany)—follows an economy of attention (cf. Franck 1998), who in addition in the context of the economy of attention created the word of "mental capitalism" (cf. Franck 2005). This supply strives for quota, for recognition, for clicks, for time of recipients—and there will be no difference to a commercially based supply of media content. This may be the reason why—only to choose one research program as an example—the study on news value and newly defines news factors in German television (cf. Ruhrmann et al. 2003) came to the conclusion that in many areas there are be no differences regarding several news factors between private and public broadcasters. The valid news factors for editors of private broadcasters' news programs in German television are mostly the same public broadcasters are referring to for creating their news supply. The core problem of commercialization lies in the pretension inherent in every media supply of efficacy by attention. Adding the aspects (cf. Rau 2007b, p. 47 ff.) of socioeconomically driven separation and socio-culturally motivated collectivization will then open up the entire field of a journalistic oriented media economy. One cannot avoid this magnitude of the research area; one cannot avoid complexity when discussing quality options.

[2] One here would be able to list all the business transactions of the last 10 years. The increasingly Google-centered way of advertising (adsense), the (therefore growing) attraction of blogging and supporting careers by Facebook or Youtube. The potential of "personal economics" shows up in the way musicians drive their careers only by virtualization (e.g. the outstanding global success of Gotye's song "Somebody that I used to know" would in 2011 and 2012 not have been thinkable without YouTube and the astonishing video)—the classical gatekeepers are fairly irrelevant, so to speak.

- Separating facts from comments (i.e. clear distinction between definition and the discussion level—accessible via tabs on the items site).
- Democratized collaborative production processes with total transparency (availability of earlier versions, corrections, changes).
- Attractiveness through socialized services with perceived high value by recipients.

A detailed look at the prerequisites of branding processes in an open web environment and in a non-profit situation shows a high degree of convergence to the quality criteria of modern journalism.[3]

The theoretically driven discussion in this chapter should make the reader aware of the dangers associated with using economic quantities like use, efficiency or even value when measuring and assessing networks. If these networks are based on content that has been created in open and democratized publication processes this might be even more relevant, as in these situations "quality" and therefore "benefits" can only be determined by actively setting standards in a normative way.[4]

4   Social Networks as a Construct of Anthropology

This chapter will advance the value of single connections in networks by another dimension and therefore allow a comprehensive assessment of networks using an old theoretical approach to social networks that was developed long before the internet even existed. More so, this approach is putting the emphasis on the anthropological aspects in measuring network connectivity. The theory of social networks describes social interactions of various kinds. One might be able to find citations using the term "social network" earlier, but by the 1960s at the latest the concept had been firmly established. Elizabeth Bott, for example, used the term extensively—she was the one trying to identify informal factors influencing the division of labor within marriages in England (cf. Bott 1964). The UK-based "Social Anthropology" also used the term—this school included researchers like J. Clyde Mitchell, A. L. Epstein, and Bruce Kapferer (now associated with the Manchester School of Anthropology). Mitchell, for example (cf. 1969), used the definition "social networks" to describe loose self-organized groups of immigrants (connected to different tribes) in industrial towns in the British colonies. He wanted to explain group forming processes that lead to specific group sizes. Mitchell and with him the Manchester School are mentioned here because their research is highly valuable for the interpretation of the social networks all of us are concerned with.

---

[3] To be fair—one has to add that quality in the context of media is always a construct that needs to be discussed. However, this discussion cannot be achieved with this contribution. For ongoing research (cf. Rau 2007a, Chap. 2).

[4] To what extent the journalistic quality process could be rectified by intentional settings is described in detail in Chap. 2 of the "Economy of Journalism" (cf. Rau 2007a: 49 ff.).

The use of a created list of friends in Facebook might follow the same rules, and the group forming processes investigated in the late 1960s could be used as a blueprint. From this point of view and considering the big number of social (and today often virtual) networks the work of the Manchester School will be of highest relevance. In this understanding social networks are not reduced to single aims or a common basis. Instead, the construct allows to easily integrate disparate aims of single actors and groups that are part of the network. This is the secret of this approach—and this makes it valuable for the century of Internet based communication. For the Manchester School faced almost the same problem—to find an analytically precise term for explaining group forming processes that are no longer based on common aims. The very unspecific term "Web 2.0"[5] encompasses a whole lot of different applications, and one also has to act on the assumption that the aims of users will be disparate. Therefore the definition of social networks invented in the 1960s and firmly established in the Manchester School of thought seems an ideal fit for explaining the development of communities in the current online sphere.

5   The "Rule of 150" and the "Rule of Many"

Mitchell (cf. 1969) reflected more than once on the size of social networks. One of his core findings in colonial Africa was that groups will reach an optimum size when they reach 120 members. More often, a similar number is linked to another British anthropologist: Robin Dunbar. He developed the hypothesis that the number of 150 will be representing the maximum number of individuals with whom one member of a group could establish and foster social connections. If the group size was lower than 150, every single member of the group would know every other member in the group—one knows each other, knows who is related to whom and

---

[5] Web 2.0 still is a diffuse term that tries to cover applications based on network effects in the World Wide Web. In Wikipedia, in itself one of these applications, one will find the following definition: The term Web 2.0 is associated with web applications that facilitate participatory information sharing, interoperability, user-centered-design and collaboration on the world wide web. A Web 2.0 site allows users to interact and collaborate with each other in a social media dialogue as creators (prosumers) of user-generated content in a virtual community, in contrast to websites where users (consumers) are limited to the passive viewing of content (media and publishing that was created for them. Examples of Web 2.0 include Social networking, Wiki, Video sharing sites Web service, Web application, Mashup (web application hybrid) and Flosonomy. The term is closely associated with Tim O'Reilly because of the O'Reilly Media Web 2.0 conference in late 2004. Although the term suggests a new version of the World Wide Web, it does not refer to an update to any technical specification, but rather to cumulative changes in the ways software developer and end-user (computer science) use the Web. Whether Web 2.0 is qualitatively different from prior web technologies has been challenged by World Wide Web inventor Tim Berners-Lee, who called the term a "piece of jargon", precisely because he intended the Web in his vision as "a collaborative medium, a place where we [could] all meet and read and write". He called it the "Read/Write Web". (online article at Wikipedia (English version), keyword: Web 2.0, last at January 20th, 2012).

who is friends with whom, is aware of special connections. From the individual's point of view, the transparency of social networks decreases with increasing group size. Dunbar believes that this restriction is predetermined by the neocortex, which in evolutionary terms is the youngest part of the cerebral cortex and can only be found in mammals (cf. Dunbar 1992, 1993). If the group size grows above the number of 150, so Dunbar (1993), the social structure will change. More rules and laws will be established to secure the stability of the community. Following Dunbar, the rule of 150 describes the cognitively limited number of individuals with whom every man could build lasting and stable social and interpersonal relationships.

The rule of 150 is mentioned here as it is often used to describe virtual networks—and in the meantime it has been extended with the rule of many, used for describing democratized web content production. In 2005, Walter Bender of MIT's MediaLab (cf. 2005, n.p.) created—starting with the rule of 150—this rule of many for computer based communication. In doing so, he took the term of efficiency and transferred it to the content put together by active users collaboratively working together in an open network. Alongside the group size (x-axis) he set the (in this case questionable) definition of efficiency on the y-axis.

The rule of many for self-ruling social networks on the web is jointly connected to the concepts of "new convergence" and "being open" ("open source", "open communication", "open knowledge"—meaning the increasingly free use of content of any kind with an unlimited possibility to use or "reuse" sources, informational content and carriers of communication), which is part of the thinking established at the MIT by expanding the "old convergence" of "being digital" (integration of different services like telecommunication, computing, broadcasting) linked to Negroponte (cf. Bender 2005, n.p.). One of the core aspects for this century of new convergence: in media systems dominated by mass communication, only a few will decide about the content offered to large communities. Communication research found plenty of concepts focusing on this aspect Gatekeeping, agenda setting, framing or priming, to mention just a few. As part of the new convergence, media systems are undergoing a period of change as content is more frequently selected, shared, created and commented on by users themselves. In the web environment with its user generated content and content farming, the relationship between producers and consumers has to be newly defined. From this point of view, the concept of mass media itself will have to be questioned. By analyzing the management of entertainment media, in 2011 we predicted the increasing irrelevance of traditional target groups.

As a consequence, mass communication needs to be redefined, and it will probably follow new rules. According to Bender (2005, n.p.), the efficiency of social networks decreases beyond 150 members (following the rule of 150)—but it will increase exponentially with an unlimited number of actively joining members (the effect of freeriders, the problem of passively using the advantages of the network without delivering own contributions, could be ignored if the number of members tends to be infinite). At first sight, this "rule of many" seems to be self-evident. But following a closer look, the factor "efficiency" is an entirely problematic construct, and the approach of the MIT-team can only be deemed positivistic and unreflective. This article already mentioned trivialization, alignment and the risk of adaptation when reflecting on media content. If one believes that this hypothesis could be validated, the factor "efficiency" has to be replaced. Again—and to paint a clearer picture: the very possibility that there is a "smallest common denominator" that is valid for mass communication processes demonstrates the inapplicability of "efficiency" in this understanding of social networks. With the arrival of Web 2.0 and the semantic web at the latest there is a need for a new systematic approach for defining and measuring social networks—depending on their ability to serve diverse functions.

6   Metcalfe's Law and Reed's Law

Another aspect leading the critiques: The rule of many implies an exponentially driven increase of "efficiency" by infinite group size. So let us neutralize "efficiency" to "value", and the discussion will be much easier and can be better linked to existing approaches. Two of these, Metcalfe's law and Reed's law, will be introduced briefly here, for they seem to be fundamental for the research on networks. Metcalf's law describes an easy to follow concept: when building a network in which every member can easily decide to communicate with any other member, the number of potential connections any member can build given a total number of N members is (N-1). The number of possible connections then is $N(N-1)$ or N^2-N. If every single connection is of similar value, then the value of the total network will depend on the total size of the network. The total value of potential connectivity will increase much more than the net itself—according to the aforementioned formula: proportional to N^2.

The total value of a communication network increases squared to the number of connected devices or persons. If "a" was the value of a newly added user, and "b" the value of the possible connection between two users—following Metcalf's square law, this would create a linear growth of value (aN) for measuring net value—for the bigger N, the greater the convergence with the term (bN^2) with aN (linear growth of value) and $aN+bN^2$. This theoretically driven discussion can be extended even further, by using Reed (2006, n.p.). In all networks supporting communicating subgroups, the value of connectivity will increase exponentially with network size. Reed introduces the definition of "Group Forming Networks"—in this context we would now have to introduce the new variable "c" to our term, resulting in ($aN+bN^2+c2N$). C then is the number of possible subgroups in the existing network. In brief: the number of nontrivial subgroups of a network with N members is (2N-N-1), the growth is defined by 2N. A network allowing simple group communication has a potential number of possible subgroups, which is growing exponentially with N. (cf. Reed 1999, n.p.): We can see this scale-driven value shift in the history of the Internet. The earliest usage of the Internet was dominated by its role as a terminal network, allowing many terminals to selectively access a small number of costly timesharing hosts.

"As the Internet grew, much more of the usage and value of the Internet became focused on pair wise exchanges of email messages, files etc. following Metcalfe's law. And as the Internet started to take off in the early '00's, traffic started to be dominated by "newsgroups" (Internet discussion groups), user created mailing lists, special interest websites, etc., following the exponential GFN (group forming networks, t. a.) law. Though the previously dominant functions did not lose value or decline as the scale of the Internet grew, the value and usage of services that scaled by newly dominant scaling laws grew faster. Thus many kinds of transactions and collaboration that had been conducted outside the Internet became absorbed into the growth of the Internet's functions, and this become the new competitive playing field." (Reed 1999/2012, n.p.). What might be interesting for discussing the quality and value of networks focusing on communication processes in the mass or social media world: following Reed, "content is king" in a network dominated by linear connectivity value growth—for in these networks there will be a small number of sources, a small number of publishers or creators of content. In this mass communication environment the sources compete for users based on the value of their content—like news and stories, offered in text, photography, video or podcasted audio. Following Metcalf's law, transactions will be at the core of measuring network value.

Where Reed's law is dominating, this role will change to a process of exchange, and value will be "jointly constructed value" (Reed 1999/2012, n.p.). Coming back to the rule of many—if one replaced "efficiency" with "value" as we did previously, potentially Reed's law with its suggested exponentially driven growth of value in networks would take effect, conceptually allowing subnetworks. However, not for all applications in which media content is created collaboratively this is valid—so finally the rule of many is questionable.

7 Social Networks in the Era of Web 2.0 Need Systemization

The rise of different networking concepts in Web 2.0 at the latest calls for differentiation and systemization. Mayfield (2003, n.p.) is one of those who have already delivered an interesting aspect: he describes an ecosystem of networks, which could be used to explain different networking concepts, making it fit well with the current discussion. His interesting approach: in order to measure different networks, he uses an activity based context and differentiates between a number of different aims:

- "Publishing"—linear, growth of value proportional to the number of members.
- "Communication"—Metcalfe's law takes effect, with the growth of value proportional to the number of possible links.
- "Collaboration"—Reed's law comes into play, with the growth of value reflecting the number of links as well as the number of possible subgroups.

Interesting about this approach: Mayfield (cf. Mayfield 2005, p. 116 ff.) links these principles to different descriptions and group sizes. If the aim is "publishing", one would talk about political networks where one sender addresses plenty of thousands of recipients. If the aim is "communication", Mayfield speaks of "social networks" with an optimal group size of 150. And if the aim is "collaboration", Mayfield defines the network as a "creative network" characterized by groups operating alongside each other (in the group forming network) that are not exceeding 12 members. In order to be more precise, it needs to be defined here that as soon as the exchange in networks is possible not only in a single-tracked way, networks will display a socially effective component and must therefore be classified as social networks which can be analyzed using the available theoretical modules (cf. Stegbaur and Häußling 2010).

Mayfield established his ecosystem of networks by concentrating on weblogs, and in one of his core findings he uses the term of "social capital" to measure the network.[6] This is a denotative step, for now it is implied that the network is of value to society, putting quality into the equation as an evaluating or rating parameter—and this is not trivial. It means losing neutrality and even losing the basis of the discussion. Still—the dilemma of judging the quality of published content is valid (cf. Rau 2007a, 102 ff.) and still forms part of media sciences in the era of the Web 2.0 or the semantic web. The problem remains evident and is still not resolved. Participatory or collaboratively created media content with its possibilities in terms of reaction, commenting, changing versions, etc. is not exempt from the risk of adaptation (Rau 2008) to the lowest common denominator. The "risk of adaptation" could then be another "term of value" that could form part of the described principles—but there will still be the problem of measuring this risk.

8 The Need for Discussing the Value of Social Networks: And With That the Need for a Debate on Values

No one who concentrates on the value of media in a societal context can ignore the discussion of values. This applies to all mass media, even to those produced conjointly in the social community, as at the end of the day even this deliberately created plurality requires attention. Therefore, in order to measure value or efficiency of networks in a media context, we have to bring in the term of "economies of attention" (cf. Franck 1998), and we have to reflect on the individual communication preferences used to guide action. Only by discussing this dimension will we at least be able to measure the generated social capital of Web 2.0. Castells (cf. his trilogy of the information age 2001a, b, 2002, 2003) takes a very differentiating position of sociology to explain how information technology influences culture and the global society in total and thus implies the increasing creation of modern societies around the bipolar dichotomy of net and self. More than 15 years after the first book on the "information age" was published (Castells 1996, cf. 2001a, b), the user still remains stuck in this area of conflict.

---

[6] Again—to recall: In the rule of many Bender (cf. 2005) argued with "efficiency"—here the author changed the term to the much more neutral measure "value".

Future research will need to return to socio-economically based explanatory approaches and here—in particular—some thorough work on preferences and individually motivated decisions (e.g. about the consumption of media content or the willingness to participate). In this context one will have to explain or judge which of the seen preferences are followed by action—for this question is of increasing relevance in the Web 2.0 era. Once again and finally—there will be no way out. The discourse on quality remains open.

References

Aldrich, H. E., & Kim, P. H. (2007). Small worlds, infinite possibilities? *Strategic Entrepreneurship Journal, 1*(1), 147–165.
Aulinger, A. (2005). *Entrepreneurship und soziales Kapital*. Marburg: NetzwerkealsErfolgsfaktorwissensintensiverDienstleistungsunternehmen.
Bender, W. (2005). In: Triangles and curves: The shapes of new media, MIT Media Lab; Contribution to the "International Seminar on Journalism", October 1st, Tampere, Finland
Boltze, A., & Rau, H. (2011). The end of the target group. In J. Müller-Lietzkow (Ed.), *Economy, quality and management of entertainment media—theory and developments in entertainment markets. Row of media economy. Tape 1*. Baden-Baden: Nomos.
Borgatti, S. P., & Foster, P. C. (2003). The network paradigm in organizational research: A review and typology. *Journal of Management, 29*, 991–1013.
Bourdieu, P. (1997). *Zur Soziologie der symbolischen Form*. Suhrkamp: Frankfurt a.M.
Castells, M. (2001). Das Informationszeitalter; Band 1: Der Aufstieg der Netzwerkgesellschaft, Leverkusen: Leske und Budrich Verlag. Original (1996): The Information Age: Economy, Society, and Culture, Volume 1: The Rise of the Network Society. Oxford and Malden, MA: Blackwell
Castells, M. (2001). Das Informationszeitalter; Band 3: Jahrtausendwende; Opladen, Campus Verlag. Original (1998): The Information Age: Economy, Society, and Culture, Volume 3: End of Millennium. Oxford and Malden, MA: Blackwell.
Castells, M. (2002). Das Informationszeitalter, Band 2: Die Macht der Identität; Leverkusen, Leske und Budrich Verlag. Original (1997): The information age: Economy, society, and culture, Volume 2: The power of identity. Oxford and Malden, MA: Blackwell.
Castells, M. (2003). Das Informationszeitalter. Wirtschaft, Gesellschaft, Kultur, Band III, Wiesbaden: Springer VS.
Dunbar, R. (1992). Neocortex size as a constraint on group size in primates. *Journal of Human Evolution, 22*, S469–493.
Dunbar, R. (1993). Coevolution of neocortical size, group size and language in humans. *Behavioral and Brain Sciences, 16*(4), 681–735.
Elizabeth, B. (1964). *Family and social network: Roles, norms, and external relationships in ordinary urban families* (2nd ed.). London: Tavistock.
Franck, G. (1998). *Ökonomie der Aufmerksamkeit*. München: Hanser.
Franck, G. (2005). *Mentaler Kapitalismus*. München: Hanser.
Granovetter, M. S. (1973). The strength of weak ties. *American Journal of Sociology, 78*(6), 1360–1380.
Jansen, D. (2006). *Einführung in die Netzwerkanalyse. Grundlagen, Methoden, Forschungsbeispiele*. Wiesbaden: VS.
Mayfield, R. (2003). The Network Ecosystem Model, verfügbar als Onlinedokument, Stand 11.4.2007. http://radio.weblogs.com/0114726/2003/02/12.html
Mayfield, R. (2005). Social network dynamics and participatory politics. In: Lebowsky, Jon; Ratcliffe, Mitch: *Extreme Democracy*, pp. 116–132.

McQuail, D. (2002). *McQuails Mass Communication Theory*, London.
Michell, J. C. (1969). *Social networks in urban situations: Analyses of personal relationships in Central African towns.* Manchester: University Press.
Moran, P. (2005). Structural vs. relational embeddedness: social capital and managerial performance. *Strategic Management Journal, 26*, 1129–1151.
Narahari, Y., Garg, D., Narayanam, R., & Prakash, H. (2010). *Game theoretic problems in network economics and mechanism design solutions.* Berlin: Springer.
Rau, H. (2007a). *Qualität in einer Ökonomie der Publizistik.* Wiesbaden: VS.
Rau, H. (2007b). Metajournalismus. In H. Rau (Ed.), *Zur Zukunft des Journalismus* (p. 31). Berlin: Peter Lang.
Rau, H. (2008). Journalism between Commercialization and Adaptation in a Today's View. Questioning Quality—from Frankfurt School to Game Theory. Research Paper, presented at ICA's annual conference 2008, Montreal, Canada. Online document available at www.ostfalia.de/imm (last: January 20th, 2012).
Reed, D. P. (1999/2012): That Sneaky Exponential—Beyond Metcalfe's Law to the Power of Community Building. In Context Magazine, n.P., document online available: http://www.reed.com/dpr/, last: 10.5.2012.
Reed, D. P. (1999). That sneaky exponential—Beyond Metcalfe's Law to the power of community building. In: *Context magazine*, Spring 1999.
Reed, D.P. (2001). The law of the pack. In: *Harvard Business Review*. February 2001, pp 23–24
Ruhrmann, G., Woelke, J., Maier, M., Diehlmann, N. (2003). Der Wert von Nachrichtenwerten. Ein Modell zurValidierung von Nachrichtenfaktoren, Opladen. Summary at URL: http://www.lfm-nrw.de/downloads/studie-nachrichtenwert.pdf; Stand: Jan 2012.
Simmel G (1995) Aufsätze und Abhandlungen 1901–1908, 1. Teilband. Band 7 der Georg-Simmel-Gesamtausgabe, herausgegeben von. R. Kramme, A. Rammstedt und O. Rammstedt. Frankfurt a.M., Suhrkamp.
Stegbaur, C., & Häußling, R. (Eds.). (2010). *Handbuch Netzwerkforschung.* VS: Wiesbaden.
Strauß, F., & Hollstein, B. (2006). *Qualitative Netzwerkanalyse: Konzepte, Methoden, Anwendungen.* Wiesbaden: VS.
Thiel, T. (2005). Wir sind Sprengstoff! In: *Frankfurter Allgemeine Zeitung* 7.8.2005, Netzwirtschaft.
White, H. C. (1981). Where do markets come from? *American Journal of Sociology, 87*, 517–547.
White, H. C. (2002). *Markets from networks: Socioeconomic models of production.* Princeton, NJ: Princeton University Press.

How to Engage the Audience? A Study on Using Twitter to Engage Newspaper Readers

Aldo van Weezel and Cristóbal Benavides

1 Introduction

The proliferation of media outlets and audience fragmentation imply media companies have to use all available tools to reach and hopefully engage their audiences (Albarran 1996; FIPP 2010–2011; Price Waterhouse Coopers 2010). The widespread use of social networks is seen by many media companies as a way to promote their brands and ultimately establish a link to the people in the audience. Nevertheless, there is still a lot of experimenting on the most effective ways to approach social networks users to engage them beyond what traditional advertising can do to promote a media brand and its extensions (Johnson and Prijatel 2007). This paper will explore the concept of engagement in order to determine whether a social network is useful for this purpose. A user is engaged if she participates in a conversation with the journalists producing the content, make comments about the content that is distributed via the social network, and help diffuse the media content to other users in her network. Furthermore, this study will assess if different tactics employed by the media firm can increase engagement. The findings are valuable to better understand the concept of engagement when applied to the social networks. Also, the results are helpful for managers who need to use social networks to improve the relation between the media brand and its audience.

The ability to reach a specific niche audience becomes more valuable as the media environment gets saturated of information and stimuli, which end up confusing the audiences (Pew Research Center 2011). Thus advertisers are looking for ways to establish a closer, trustworthy relationship whit their consumers (Kotler & Armstrong 2003). The goal is to position a brand closer to the heart than to the rational mind (Malthouse, Calder & Eady 2003). This is what has been called engagement (Mathwick and Rigdon 2004; Simmons 2009). Page views, unique visitors and

---

A. van Weezel (✉) • C. Benavides
University of the Andes, Santiago, Chile
e-mail: aldo.vanweezel@gmail.com

audience demographics are not enough anymore. What is truly important is the effect of the media and the advertising it carries on the person consuming the media (Moorman 2003).

2   Engagement

The concept of engagement is used in several contexts. For instance, Porter et al. (2011) claim engagement is a set of behaviours reflecting community members' demonstrated willingness to participate and cooperate with others in a way that creates value for themselves and for others (Aaker and Brown 1972). In the business context and from a behavioural perspective, engagement refers to actions by consumers towards a firm going beyond transactions. Cognitive and emotional forces motivate such actions. Therefore, engagement is a positive state of mind that is characterized by high energy, commitment, and loyalty toward a firm (Van Doorn et al. 2010). Also, engagement is about being connected, involved with something. It is the feeling coming from experiencing something beyond what is perceived by someone not familiar with it (Bahary and Fielding 2005).

It is possible to define engagement in as many ways as the variety of experiences between a company and its customers. When it comes to media companies in particular, Marc (1966) argues that asking audiences how much they would miss a media outlet if it ceases to exist assesses the existing level of engagement. The Advertising Research Foundation (2006) states "media engagement is turning on a prospect to a brand idea enhanced by the surrounding context."

Usually consumers are attracted to an engaging experience through entertainment, whether a game, video, or song. As more features define the experience, marketers and agencies have the opportunity to deepen the engagement and relationship with the consumer, thus their offering ultimately takes on the role of a utility (Deighton et al. 1989). Over time, these utilities are perceived as tools and become necessities in the daily routines of the target audience, becoming as common as a toothbrush or mobile device (Martin and Todorov 2010).

Evidence suggests that when consumers are strong admirers of a firm and a firm's brand (Calder and Malthouse 2005), they want to engage with others and the firm directly. Porter et al. (2011) propose a framework illustrating how to increase and sustain engagement through social networking (Fig. 1).

The first step is to understand what are the needs of community and consumers. It is important for the organization to know what people expect from it (Agostini 1964), what motivate consumers to act, and what is the feeling of belonging that the brand, product or service produces in her. Fulfilling social and psychological needs motivates consumers to engage in a variety of social media platforms. That is why this framework is rooted in the notion that consumer engagement is based on the value created when community sponsors help members meet their needs with the social community. "Managers should target their efforts appropriately according to the different needs of community members to accelerate and amplify engagement with the firms' community" (Porter et al. 2011, p. 85).

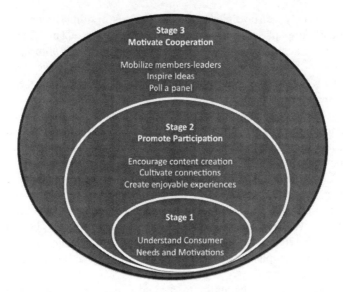

Fig. 1 Three-stage process for engagement. *Source*: Porter et al. (2011)

The second stage focuses on promoting the participation of the members in the community. Encouraging people to create and share the content they produce, working for increasing the quality of what they receive, but also in the content they share with others. At this step the managers should work for cultivating the connections with the contributors but also strength the relation among the users. Another action that managers should do is to create enjoyable experiences. That feeling will generate a repeated action that is useful for the media, as well as rub off others—in a positive way—to participate in the conversation. The authors suggest these actions align with the needs of the members and might increase the engagement with the brand, service or product.

The last stage focuses on motivate cooperation through create leaders in the community that moved others to act. Porter et al. (2011) concluded that when members are motivated to cooperate with a firm when the organization integrates and empower them giving some exclusive access or information that produces engagement feelings, which in turn generates feelings of wanting to cooperate even more than they already do. In a certain way it is close to involving people in the "decision making".

Although these communities can emerge around any brand, new or mature, they are more likely to form around mature brands that have built a strong image with consumers over time (Muniz and O'Guinn 2001).

3 Engaging Consumers

Engagement needs to give consumers a voice, both with another consumer and with a brand, so it enables creating a dialogue. Martin and Todorov (2010) establish five levels of engagement that determine the impact of a brand:

1. The Gag. Usually seen on digital billboards, banners, or simple iPhone applications, gags use a "big-pop" strategy to get attention quickly, disrupt activities, and make the consumer laugh. Essentially, it offers something fun to play with and might even tap into a new behaviour that the consumer did not previously have access to or did not know was available. But gags are very short lived, and consumers' attention quickly moves on to the next thing.
2. Utility. This form of engagement ordinarily comes in the form of a calculator, recommendation engine, price finder, or similar task-oriented feature. With a utility, it is important to leverage available contextual data and thus provide in-the-moment value.
3. Social Connectivity. The organic nature of the engagement helps converting consumers into brand ambassadors. Simply giving them the tools to help leads to spreading the word and influencing community opinions across existing social networks such as Facebook or Twitter. This is critical because they begin to fight for brand bragging rights. The fight might also extend to iPhone apps, websites, online activities (e.g., completing a Shopping experience), digital board short messaging campaigns, etc.
4. Brand Customization. The ability to customize and express individuality builds strong brand affinity and loyalty. Such expressiveness enables the brand to permeate the consumers' psychology and grants personal ownership over the interactions. For maximum impact, customization platforms should be linked to social media to allow users to flaunt their customized products and influence their peers.
5. Brand Lifestyle. The highest engagement level arrives when brands provide everyday services, utilities, customization, and social ecosystems that enable consumers to truly live the brand. The ultimate success comes when the brand can create a movement that unifies the group of consumers around a common goal or feeling.

Martin and Todorov (2010) propose a three-step framework for planning an integrated digital platform:

1. Lead with Human Truths
   - Establish brand objectives and develop personas for the target demographic.
   - Plan to make consumers stakeholders in the brand.
   - Build a "day in the life of" diagram and visualize what target consumers do and where they do it every ever hour of the day.
2. Conduct a Brand Presence and Touchpoint Effectiveness Analysis
   - Where does the brand sit, and where do its competitors sit, in relation to an element of consumers' life? What is the frequency of the communication?
   - Find the untapped opportunities and needs of the consumer.
   - Is the brand maximizing the effectiveness of every touchpoint throughout the day? What is the engagement level?
3. Design Campaigns and Select the Best Digital Platforms
   - Select platforms that best fit with the various touchpoint opportunities and perform best against competitors, always taking into account the location and activity pros and cons.
   - Have competitors saturated the location? Can the touchpoint be made more effective and engaging to overtake those competitors?

- Analyse the environment, noise, and distractions-is the installation going to be affected by the weather (e.g., sunlight, rain)? Is the location too noisy for an offer that relies too much on sound? Is the technology affected by light availability (e.g., cameras)?

The idea of barriers between people and technology is being debunked as marketers seek to integrate more digital platforms into consumers' lifestyles. Naturally, interactions are quickly becoming more intuitive, intelligent, and human. Technologies are starting to seek out consumers, rather than consumers seeking out the technologies. Consumers even have come to expect innovation from their beloved brands, as long as those brands' usage of digital platforms provides them with entertainment value, service, and relevance.

Every brand has the potential to become interwoven into every moment of every day of its consumers' lives (Shepley 1996). The robustness of the platforms, both independently and in an integrated approach, will continue to give marketers new ways to provide greater connectivity between brands and consumers.

4   Engaging the Audience

Studying engagement with media products implies understanding the experiences people in the audience have with the content offered in such products (Cabello 1999; Daly et al. 1997). If managers from digital platforms are able to understand these motivations it is possible to better cater the needs of advertisers to reach specific market segments. That will turn the support in a much influential advertising platform (McQuail 1997).

Calder and Malthouse (2008) identify two approaches to media engagement in relationship to advertising. The traditional approach describes the media as merely a channel to reach the final consumer. This view has evolved and now media are perceived as something more complicated than time (e.g. 30 s for a television ad) or physical space (e.g., an ad in a magazine page). Hence, a modern approach to media engagement recognises the context where the advertising takes place. Context may affect positively or negatively the perception of an ad by a consumer.

Experiences can be classified in many forms. They can be external or internal. The latter ones are based in the innate, organic needs for competence and self-determination. It energises a wide variety of behaviours for which the primary rewards are the experiences of affectance and autonomy (Deci and Ryan, 1985: 32).

Bronner and Neijens (2006) offer a more detailed typology, where experiences can be one of the following types regarding the effect on the individual:
1. Information: Offered something new, gave useful information, taught me about what is going on.
2. Stimulation: Stimulation excited me, made me curious, made me enthusiastic.
3. Negative emotions: Irritated me, was unclear, disturbed me, and made me sad.
4. Transformation: Gave me enjoyment, made me cheerful, made me forget everything for a moment, was relaxing.
5. Pastime: Filled an empty moment.
6. Identification: Recognized myself in it, felt involved, empathized with it.

7. Social: Subject of conversation.
8. Practical use: Useful tips/advice, motivated to do something.

Using this typology, Bronner and Neijens (2006) surveyed audiences to detect any differences in the varied experiences they had with different media and how that experienced was transferred to the relation between the audience and the advertisements. The results showed a strong relationship, likely reinforced because newspapers and magazines were targeted to specific audiences.

Calder and Malthouse (2008) propose engagement generates thirteen different kinds of experiences. Its effects show up as likeness, increase usage, higher degree of attention, and positive feelings regarding advertising. They can be gathered in four major groups: promotion, transportation, rejection, and irritation.

1. Promotion: This experience involves the pursuit of hopes and aspirations. The goal is to gain or attain something.
   (a) Talking About and Sharing Experience
   (b) Utilitarian Experience
   (c) Makes Me Smarter Experience
   (d) Community Connection Experience
   (e) Participation and Socialization Experience
   (f) Inspirational Experience
   (g) Civic Looks Out for My Interests Experience
2. Transportation: Here the consumer's goal is either to be transported into a different state, for instance from bored to happy, or to be transported into taking part in an activity.
   (a) Timeout Experience
   (b) Visual Imagery Experience
   (c) Regular Part of My Day Experience
   (d) Entertainment Experience
3. Rejection: When the goal is extrinsic to the activity, we have the simple case of Rejection. The person wants to have something not happen as a consequence of the activity.
   (a) Overload, Too Much Experience
4. Irritation: When the person wants to avoid the activity itself, we refer to this as Irritation. The person feels forced to perform the activity and is annoyed by this and adverse to it. Irritation experiences are mitigated, but not irrelevant, in the case of media use because consumers generally exercise choice in this area.
   (a) Ad Interference Experience

Calder and Malthouse (2008: 5) propose engagement to be "the sum of motivational experiences consumers have with the media product." Thus, if readers like a magazine and they are engaged to it, then the ad might become part of what they are trying to happen in their lives.

5   Using Twitter to Engage Newspaper Readers

Newspapers worldwide are struggling to keep readers who are drawn away by numerous news websites. As suggested in the previous discussion, media companies wanting to remain as an attractive platform for advertisers must engage their audiences. Therefore, social networks can help media to retain their audiences by engaging them. The problem is social networks are so new no one seems to really understand how to use them to engage audiences. Certainly there are hints on how to do it. Next, we show an engagement experiment carried on during 10 working days (November 21 through December 2, 2011) using a newspaper Twitter account for testing different ways of approaching followers—i.e. readers.

The newspaper is the leading financial newspaper in Chile and publishes from Monday through Friday. The company has been transforming its digital operations during 2011 and after revamping its website, launching an iOS app and starting to charge for some of its online content, the CEO decided to promote the newspaper presence in social networks, particularly Twitter.

The newspaper was already tweeting news headlines with their corresponding links to the story at the moment the experiment started. The scheme employed to tweet during each week was the following:

- Day 1 (week 1): Tweeting all news stories from all sections (8) to find out the most mentioned/retweeted stories.
- Day 2 (week 1): Tweeting differently news from the three most popular sections by retweets and mentions. Also, they were tweeted several times according to the busiest times of day given by users' behaviour.
- Day 3 (week 1): Generating conversations and trying to keep them as long as possible in order to show users they are talking to another person and not to a robot.
- Days 4 and 5 (week 1): Analysis of users behaviour.
- Days 6–10: Repeating previous week.

Figure 2 shows the results of Day 1. The most retweeted and commented sections were Companies, Politics and Finance. On the website, the most visited sections were Finance, Companies and Op-Ed (Figs. 3, 4, 5, 6).

The results show that after trying new ways to connect to users via Tweeter the number of replies, retweets and comments increased. This can be translated into a higher level of engagement between the readers and the newspaper given an increased in "conversation" between both. The reasons are three and are outlined next.

1. Users prefer some sections to others. Thus after identifying them, actions on Twitter were directed towards those sections.
2. An overload of information coming from the newspaper was detected since all news stories were tweeted as they were available. After knowing the preferred hours of users for checking Twitter it was possible to cater better to their information needs.

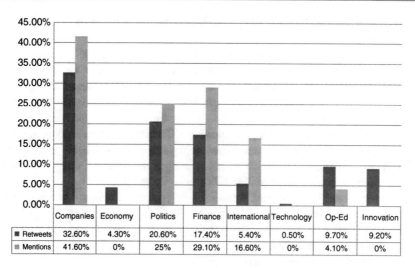

Fig. 2 Audience preferred sections

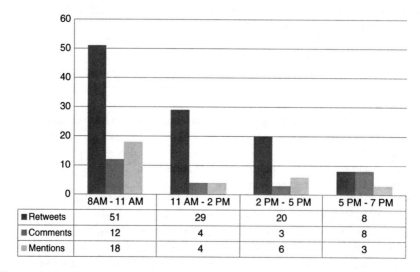

Fig. 3 Distribution of tweets during the day

3. Traditionally, the newspaper was tweeting headlines that did not catch users attention to retweet or reply. Changing the way the tweets were constructed users felt attracted to "engage" in a conversation.

Conclusions

Media companies need to engage their audiences in order to show advertisers they are a still an effective advertising platform. Social networks allow media to foster audience engagement if employed adequately. This engagement process can be seen as promoting a series of conversations with the audience and Twitter

How to Engage the Audience? A Study on Using Twitter to Engage Newspaper Readers   711

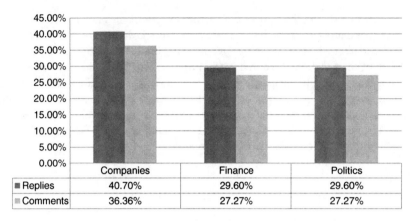

Fig. 4 Replies and comments

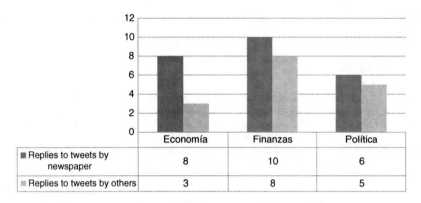

Fig. 5 Interaction

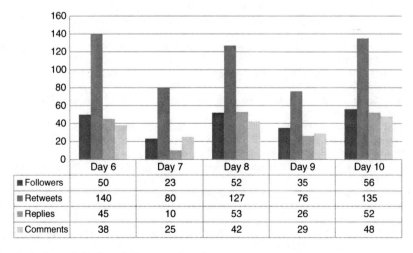

Fig. 6 Audience behaviour during second week

is a tool facilitating this process. Nonetheless, companies need to adapt to how these social tools work. In the case of Twitter, as shown in the experiment, media need to detect which sections are favoured in the social network—which may be different than sections favoured in the print edition. Then, the news need to be tweeted according to the use patterns of the audiences. This can be done studying when during the day users are prone to be checking their timelines. Finally, tweets have to be constructed in a way that promotes establishing a conversation. For instance, asking questions, asking for opinions on a variety of topics, highlighting controversial parts of an interview, and so on.

References

Aaker, D., & Brown, P. (1972). Evaluating vehicle source effects. *Journal of Advertising Research, 12*(4), 11–16.
Advertising Research Foundation (2006). *Engagement*. Retrieved 25 November, 2011, from http://www.thearf.org/research/engagement.html
Agostini, J. M. (1964). The case for direct questions on reading habits. *Journal of Advertising Research, 2*, 28–33.
Albarran, A. (1996). *Media economics: understanding markets, industries, and concepts.* Ames, Iowa: Iowa State University Press, EE.UU.
Bahary J., Fielding R. (2005) Are you experienced? An engagement-based planning approach in print. In: *Worldwide Readership Research Symposium*.
Bronner, F., & Neijens, P. (2006). Audience experiences of media context and embedded advertising. *International Journal of Market Research, 48*(1), 81–100.
Cabello, F. (1999). *El mercado de revistas en España: Concentración Informativa*. Ariel: España.
Calder, B., & Malthouse, E. (2005). Managing media and advertising change with integrated marketing. *Journal of Advertising Research, 45*, 356–361.
Calder, B., & Malthouse, E. (2008). Media engagement and advertising effectiveness. In B. Calder (Ed.), *Kellog on media and advertising* (pp. 1–36). Hoboken, NJ: Wiley.
Daly, C., Henry, P., & Ryder, E. (1997). *The magazine publishing industry*. Boston: Ally and Bacon.
Deci, E., & Ryan, R. (1985). *Intrinsic motivation and self-determination in human Behaviour.* New York: Plenum.
Deighton, J., Romer, D., & McQueen, J. (1989). Using drama to persuade. *Journal of Consumer Research, 16*(3), 335–343.
Johnson, S., & Prijatel, P. (2007). *The magazine from cover to cover*. New York: Oxford University Press.
Kotler, P., & Amstrong, G. (2003). *Fundamentos de Marketing*. Madrid: Pearson Educación.
Malthouse, E., Calder, B., & Eadie, W. (2003). Conceptualizing and measuring magazine reader experiences. *Worldwide Readership Symposium*. England: Ipsos-RSL.
Marc, M. (1966). Using reading quality in magazine selection. *Journal of Advertising Research, 6*(4), 9–13
Martin, K., & Todorov, I. (2010). How will digital platforms be harnessed in 2010, and how will they change the way people interact with brands? *Journal of Interactive Advertising, 10*(2), 61–66.
Mathwick, C., & Rigdon, E. (2004). Play, flow, and the online search experience. *Journal of Consumer Research, 31*(2), 324–332.
McQuail, D. (1997). *Audience analysis*. Thousand Oaks, CA: Sage.

Moorman, M. (2003). *Context considered: The relationship between media environments and advertising effects.* PhD thesis, University of Amsterdam.

Muniz, A., & O'Guinn, T. (2001). Brand community. *Journal of Consumer Research, 27*(4), 412–432.

Pew Research Center's Project for Excellence in Journalism (2011). http://stateofthemedia.org/2011/

Porter, E., Donthu, N., MacElroy, W., & Wydra, D. (2011). How to foster sustain engagement in virtual communities. *California Management Review, 53*(4), 80–110.

Price Waterhouse Coopers (2010). Global Entertainment and Media Outlook: 2010–2014.

Shepley, P. (1996). 52 Moremagazine success stories, Magazine Publisher Association, Nueva York, EE.UU.

Van Doorn, J., Lemon, K., Mittal, V., Nass, S., Pick, D., Pirner, P., & Verhoef, P. (2010). Customer engagement behavior: Theoretical foundations and research directions. *Journal of Service Research, 13*(3), 253–266.

FIPP World Magazine Trends 2010–2011. London, UK.

Blogs and Social Media: The New Word of Mouth and its Impact on the Reputation of Banks and on their Profitability

Eleftheria (Roila) Christakou and George-Michael Klimis

1 Definition of Reputation

People have always been struggling for reputation in an effort to attain social status and mobility among others. For firms (Mailath and Samuelson 2001), reputation can guarantee financial resources such as capital or loans, from banks and markets in general, but also revenue from sales to consumers and lower cost from better relations with suppliers.

The reputation of a company is dependent on many factors. Some of these are the quality of goods, the power of branding and communication, leadership and strategy, the goals and vision of the company, the ability to understand and meet customer needs, the perceived risks, and reliability (Money and Hillenbrand 2006) and also include employees' performance, the impact of the media, and external partners' influence.

According to game theorists such as Sztompka (2000) reputation is the perception, or better phrased, the opinion that other players have about the value of a "player" in a game.

Under the same lens, reputation is based on the record of a player's past actions and thus is an important signaling mechanism in a game, especially when Axelrod's (1984) shadow of the future, i.e. the possibility of repeating the game with the same players, is high.

Following Sztompka's perception of reputation based on past actions, Pizzorno (2004) states that the latter can actually be a record of acts worthy or not worthy of trust. The reputation of one person, like other intangible assets, is particularly valuable if and only if it has been recognized by other "important" persons.

Clearly one should agree with this view of Pizzorno, as it is evident that important factors, familiar faces, other means such as media, political figures, known authors,

---

E. (Roila) Christakou (✉) • G.-M. Klimis
Panteion University of Social and Political Sciences, Athens, Greece
e-mail: Roila1@yahoo.gr

professors and scholars tend to coordinate the public and establish a reputation for a person or an organisation. Nevertheless, one must not forget that the diffusion of information which is often responsible for fame and reputation occurs on a daily basis from contact with everyday people—via word of mouth.

Practitioners also agree on the importance of reputation. In a survey conducted by Paul Dunay (2008) with a sample of financial institution's senior management executives, 53 % of respondents agreed that reputation management is a high priority. A large number of companies seem not only to monitor corporate reputation but also try to enhance it by participating in blogs and social networking sites like Facebook and LinkedIn.

Another important finding from Dunay's research is that more than half of the respondents are not prepared to protect their corporate reputation in a possible crisis in the Internet. This under-researched area, measuring how reputation is affected by online wom, is the focus of this research and the researchers consider the findings vital for any organisations, although, they do not underestimate traditional wom (i.e. this generated in the physical world), which is thought to be influenced partly by its online counterpart, a hypothesis to be developed in another paper.

2 Reputation Measurement

This research started with the assessment of the models—tools that have been, so far, identified in the literature as efficient in recognizing and measuring whether reputation can be influenced by the wom communication and to what extend this might influence a firm's performance.

In their study about reputation measurement, Money and Hillenbrand (2006) conclude on a small number of widely used models, the most prominent of which seem to be variations of Fortune's Most Admired Companies List (MAC), the Reputation Quotient (RQ) and RepTrak Pulse (Reputation Institute), the Corporate Personality Scale (Davies et al. 2003), the Extension of the RQ in Germany by Walsh and Wiedmann (2004) and the Emotion, Feeling, Intention Model (SPIRIT, MacMillan et al. 2004).

Table 1 offers an overview of the above models in relation to "what is measured" in each case/model.

In this paper only a short overview of each of the above models will be offered.

3 Overview of the Models

The MacMillan et al. SPIRIT model (2004) of Reputation, proposes measures in four fields.
1. Stakeholder experience of the communication (listening and informing), service benefits, non-material benefits, material benefits, shared values, keeping commitments, coercion and termination costs experienced by stakeholders
2. Stakeholder experience of outside influences

Table 1 Overview of the reputation measurement models

Measures of reputation	What is measured
Fombrun (1996) Reputation Quotient (RQ)	Vision & Leadership
	Financial Performance
	Social Responsibility
	Products & Services
	Workplace Environment
Rep Trak Pulse, Reputation Institute	Products & Services
	Innovation
	Workplace
	Governance
	Citizenship
	Leadership
	Performance
Davies (2003) Corporate Personality Scale	Judgment of the personality of an organization
Walsh & Wiedmann (2004) Extension of the RQ in Germany	Suggested the development of scales to measure sympathy, transparency, fairness and perceived customer orientation in addition RQ concepts
MacMillan et al. (2004) SPIRIT	Communication, Service Benefits, Non-Material Benefits, Material Benefits, Shared Values, Keeping Commitments, Coercionand Termination Cost

Money and Hillenbrand (2006)

3. Stakeholder emotional support towards a business
4. Stakeholder behavioral support towards a business. This includes stakeholder intentions to behave in certain ways towards the business in the future. Concepts identified and measured include stakeholder advocacy, co-operation, extension, retention and subversion.

One realizes, when examining this particular model, that it is mainly focused on antecedents, the consequences of Reputation, and Reputation as a positive or negative "attitudinal concept" (Money and Hillenbrand 2006).

The Davies Corporate Personality Scale (2003) measures the Reputation of organisations by eliciting stakeholders' comments on their personalities (Davies et al. 2003), therefore simply measuring beliefs.

Berens and Van Riel (2004), review the models used until the publication of their paper which are listed below:

The model provided by Walsh and Wiedmann (2004) is an extension of the RQ, based on a qualitative analysis of Reputation in Germany. Using mainly personal interviews they tried to associate the traits and characteristics of the German public in the context of the German mentality and the RepTrack model creating thus a bespoke German RQ model.

The study suggests that future measures of Reputation should include additional dimensions such as sympathy, transparency, fairness, the organisation's perceived customer orientation and stakeholder feelings of satisfaction and trust. In our study, the additional dimensions are not used.

However, Walsh and Wiedmann's study can provide a useful insight to this research as we share their recommendation that future studies should include measures of stakeholder wom. Following that, in this study, the researchers do not only measure wom, but also examine the effect of wom on the most applicable dimensions of reputation (as these are defined by Fombrun and Van Riel).

Fombrun's Reputation Quotient (RQ) (1996) and its seven dimensional extension, called the RepTrak Pulse, was chosen for the measurement of Corporate Reputation (Money and Hillenbrand 2006). It provides information for the intangible assets within the firm and a measure of beliefs and attitudes of stakeholders. This information can be linked together to enhance strategic decision-making (Money and Hillenbrand 2006). While this model provides an indication of the state of reputation of an organisation, it is not an adequate indicator of how this reputation has been developed or of its consequences.

The strength and flexibility of RepTrak Pulse, suggest a wide range of research applications and many testable hypotheses across a range of stakeholder groups (Vidaver-Cohen 2007).

Taking into consideration research that connects the seven dimensions of the model with their impact on organisations (Vidaver-Cohen 2007), the researchers of this study proceed to examine:

1. How online wom (as defined by that generated by blogs and online social media) affects the reputation of an organisation?
2. To what extend the positive or negative effect of wom can further influence the actual performance of the organisation?

Presented by Fombrun and Van Riel, this tool tracks 23 key performance indicators grouped around seven reputation dimensions that research has proven to be effective in getting stakeholders to support the company. The "beating heart" of the RepTrak™ Model, is considered to be the Pulse. The RepTrak™ Pulse measures the health of a company's overall reputation with consumers. The RepTrak™ Pulse score is based on four statements: the esteem, good feeling, trust, and admiration that consumers feel towards a company. Establishing of a good reputation is not a goal in itself; the ultimate goal is getting stakeholders to support the company. Supportive behaviors can be shown in various areas, such as the willingness to purchase products from a company or to invest in company stock.

In this research the authors borrow the seven indicators offered by this model (namely, Products & Services, Innovation, Workplace, Governance, Citizenship, Leadership, Performance), in order to investigate how wom affects each of them (particularly for banking institutions) and finally, how this overall reputational relation can affect the performance of the organisations under investigation.

Figure 1 demonstrates the correlations of the Rep Trak Pulse.

For the present study we choose the extended form of the Fombrun's Reputation Quotient, i.e. the seven dimensions of reputation offered by the Rep Trak Pulse of the Reputation Institute which provides a standardized framework that has been tested with companies (Helm et al. 2011), enabling managers and researchers to

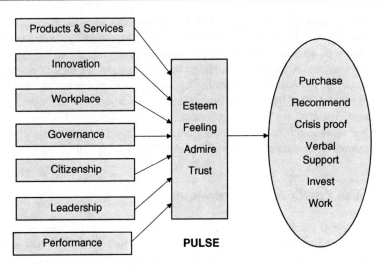

Fig. 1 The correlations of the Rep Track Pulse (Reputation Institute 2012)

identify the factors that drive reputation and benchmark their corporate reputations internationally.

Additionally, in a pilot study we did, the seven dimensions proved to be a robust framework to categorize the content of the social media studied.

4 Word of Mouth

An overview is provided of the literature around wom with the intention of linking it with each one of the seven dimensions of reputation.

Wom is considered to be a powerful marketing tool, and regardless of the fact that internet penetration is high and social networking tools are already an indispensible part of customers' lives, people still spend considerable part of their time offline. Wom can be defined as an ordinary conversation between people that happens face to face, by phone, or electronically. It is a process of exchanging information or opinion. Within the area of the present study, wom is observed as a powerful tool in keeping the offered services/products discussed among public (Keller and Berry 2006). The same authors assert:

> We don't need expensive copywriters, a specially crafted brand voice, and big campaigns to reach customers. We just have to talk with people in our own style, through direct channels—from conference calls and small salon like conferences to blogs and online communities. (Keller and Berry 2006, p. 3)

Wom need not necessarily be brand, product or service-focused. It may also be organisation-focused. Neither need wom be face-to-face, direct, oral or ephemeral. The electronic community, for example, generates virtual wom which is not face-to-face, not direct, not oral, and not ephemeral (Buttle 1998).

There have been a great number of studies about wom since the frequently cited Arndt study (Arndt 1967), although many of these investigations are focused on other constructs, such as satisfaction, and consider wom merely as having behavioral consequences. A recent investigation has emphasized the lack of research on the "antecedents of wom when considering wom as a focal construct." (Mazzarol et al. 2007, p. 1478). Although positive effects of the antecedents of wom, such as satisfaction, loyalty, quality, commitment, trust, and perceived value, are well established in research, there is still a question of how this be practically useful for companies and therefore be incorporated in their strategic decisions.

5 The Power of Word of Mouth

Until the 1940s, marketers assumed that communication was a one-way process flowing from the marketer to consumers. This view, however, was challenged by Lazarsfeld et al. (1948). They brought forth the importance of opinion leaders in distributing the messages, and the role of the followers. According to Lazarsfeld et al. opinion leaders initiate process of influence and they are defined as persons who are asked for advice. People who ask for advice are followers of the opinion leaders. The followers are influenced by the leaders in terms of their decision making processes. In many cases though, Lazarsfeld argues, followers might change their perception and even influence the leaders themselves in a two step model.

Taking it a step forward, in the examination of the e-media Sullivan (2010) refers to the strong impact the internet has on the decision making process of buyers. The internet, and more specifically the blogs and social media, have also opinion leaders and followers.

Although wom is an indispensible factor in consumer decision-making, it is not the dominant factor. Wom alone cannot change attitudes of consumers who have already developed strong brand attitudes (Herr et al. 1991). Moreover, wom is unlikely to change a consumer's attitude if she feels uncertain about a product due to credible negative information.

In terms of negative wom, the Marsha L. Richins study (1984), demonstrates that when a high level of dissatisfaction occurs with regards to a product or a service, then the implications of the wom—negative wom are intense and therefore have to be considered when creating communication strategy.

Mack et al. (2008) examined whether wom created through blogs and social media, namely the e-word of mouth (e-wom), has the same or similar importance—effect on the consumers' buying behavior, with traditional wom (created by the face to face interaction). They conducted an online survey in which they that traditional wom cannot be compared to any other kind of wom in terms of credibility and effectiveness. This includes face to face communication and the direct exchange of opinions. It has been traditionally considered to be a form of communication that can create perceptions and influence decisions (Brown and Reingen 1987). However the assert that we must not discredit the use of blogs in developing integrated communication strategies

Other researchers also agree with the fact that the traditional wom has a powerful influence on behavior, especially on consumers' information search, assessment, and consequent decision making process (Cox 1963; Brown and Reingen 1987; Money et al. 1998; Silverman 2001).

In yet another study Goldsmith and Horowitz (2006) claim that e-wom constitutes a very important factor in the consumer's seeking opinions and moreover to their decision making process. Their survey studies the motivations for opinion seeking online. Their findings are quite interesting. They found that the motivational factors for opinion seeking online, range from basic utilitarian motives such as to get information to a more hedonic motive such as "it's cool". Additionally, some of the factors seem more thoughtful and planned, while other motivations are more impulsive. According to Goldsmith and Horowitz, consumers seek the opinions of others online to reduce their risk, to secure lower prices, to get information easily and finally because others do it.

Concluding, there are certain limitations as to the comparison of the importance and effectiveness of e-wom with traditional wom. Nevertheless the aim of the present study is to examine whether the particular from of wom (e-wom i.e. that facilitated by blogs and online social media) can actually affect the seven dimensions of reputation of a banking institution.

6 Word of Mouth and the Seven Dimensions of Reputation

Table 2 summarizes the research that links the effect of wom on each of the seven dimensions of reputation.

The research concludes the literature review with a table summarizing the literature where the wom was placed in the context of media (traditional as well as online).

7 The Research Model

The analysis of the content of the above table led the authors of the present study to conclude to the fact that the model used by Deephouse (2000) could set the foundation of the research model that needed to be created.

The purpose of Deephouse's research was to examine the influence that the media and especially newspapers, can have on the reputation of a financial institution and to what extend this can influence the financial performance of the particular institution. He studied, therefore, all the newspaper archives that had been published for 1 year in single metropolitan area of the United States, and referred to all the commercial banks of this particular area. The research design integrated quantitative and qualitative methods to test the resource-based view of the firm (Barney 1991; Hall 1992; Sirmon et al. 2007). They characterized each media announcement as either positive negative or neutral and that is how they came up with their quantitate results. By measuring the media reputation of the banking institutions for 1 year,

Table 2 A review of the literature on the effect of wom on the 7 dimensions of reputation

No	Author	Publication title	What was the basic investigation	Methodology info—model	Interesting finding	Relation with wom
Wom effect on seven dimensions of reputation						
Products & Services						
1	Marsha L. Richins	1984 Advances in Consumer Research Volume 11 WORD OF MOUTH COMMUNICATION AS NEGATIVE INFORMATION	Negative word-of-mouth (Nwom) is a consumer response to dissatisfaction	Reviews existing literature	Nwom, quite high and can be extensive, since most consumers tell several others about their dissatisfaction	Strong effect of nwom—dissatisfaction incidents are always reported more than satisfaction ones
2	PAUL M. HERR, FRANK R. KARDES, and JOHN KIM	1991 by JOURNAL OF CONSUMER RESEARCH. Inc. Vol. 1 Effects of Word-of-Mouth and Product-Attribute Information on Persuasion: An Accessibility-Diagnosticity Perspective	Effects of word-of-mouth (Wom) communications and specific attribute information on product evaluations were investigated	Experiment with focus groups—measurement of anecdotal information Accessibility diagnosticity model analysis	Anecdotal information had a stronger impact on brand attitudes when it was presented in a vivid, face-to-face manner as opposed to a pallid, printed format	Strong effect of wom on products and services evaluation this becomes less when memories or strong negative written information is provided
Innovation						
1	Vijay Mahajan and Eitan Muller	1979 The Journal of Marketing Vol. 43, No. 4 Innovation Diffusion and New Product Growth in Marketing	New products diffusion processes	Review of assumptions, applications and diffusion models	Wom influences the speed and rate of innovation diffusion	Wom affects innovation diffusion
2	Nelson P. Repenning	1999, Department of Operations Management, Massachusetts Institute of Technology	A simulation based approach to understanding the dynamics implementation	Commitment Innovation Linkage	Very fast and before having appreciable results spread of innovation information creates negative wom	Fast spread of innovation creates nwom

#	Author	Source	Topic	Method	Findings	Conclusion
3	Sebastiano A. Delre, Wander Jager, and Marco A. Janssen	2007 Journal Computational & Mathematical Organization Theory, June 2007, Diffusion dynamics in small-world networks with heterogeneous consumers (after the Bass model)	Innovation diffusion dynamics that differ according to the social structure that connects their consumers, the strength of social influence and the degree of consumers' heterogeneity about their social susceptibility	Innovation diffusion model cluster	Innovations spread faster via wom when in the groups of consumers there are both many internal relationships and enough external relationships	Relatively indifferent. Shows wom affects diffusion of innovation under certain circumstances

Environment

Social Responsibility

Indifferent

#	Author	Source	Topic	Method	Findings	Conclusion
1	Charles J. Fombrun, Naomi A. Gardberg, and Michael L. Barnett	2000 Business and Society Review; Opportunity Platforms and Safety Nets: Corporate Citizenship and Reputational Risk	(Theoretical overview)	(Theoretical overview)	Companies that do good in CSR will create positive wom by employees and users	Positive CSR affects the creation of positive wom Low CSR will create Reputation Risk
2	C.B. Bhattacharya and Sankar Sen	2004 CALIFORNIA MANAGEMENT REVIEW VOL. 47, NO. 1 FALL Doing Better at Doing Good	When, Why, and How Consumers Respond to Corporate Social Initiatives	Focus groups, in-depth interviews, surveys, and experiments	Positive CSR activities drives consumers' willingness to talk positively about the socially responsible company	Positive CSR affects the creation of positive wom
3	Teresa Tan and Mark D. Uncles	2005 University of New South Wales	To gain insight into CSR as an advertising appeal	Theory of Planned Behaviour (TPB) model questionnaires	For current users of the brand compared to non-users, CSR communication will more positively influence the likelihood of pwom recommendation	CSR communication will positively influence pwom recommendations
4	Xueming Luo and C.B. Bhattacharya	2006, American Marketing Association; Corporate Social Responsibility, Customer Satisfaction, and Market Value	Influence of corporate social responsibility (CSR) on perceived customer responses and how it affects the market value	Conceptual framework based on a large-scale secondary data set	Product If low level of quality and innovativeness and high level of CSR then negative wom	Positive CSR creates nwom (if low level of quality & innovation)

(continued)

Table 2 (continued)

	No	Author	Publication title	What was the basic investigation	Methodology info—model	Interesting finding	Relation with wom
	5	Reputation Institute	2008 Top Socially Responsible Companies	List of American companies that the US public sees as most socially responsible	Corporate Social Responsibility Index (CSRI) based on the RepTrack	The majority would not recommend the companies that are not seen as socially responsible In a time where "word of mouth" recommendations is a top driver of business success CSR is a critical area for companies to improve	**Strong effect of negative wom on companies that are not socially responsible**
	6	Pavlos A. Vlachos & Argiris Tsamakos	2009 Academy of Marketing Science; Corporate social responsibility: attributions, loyalty, and the mediating role of trust	They investigate whether consumers' perceptions of motives influence their evaluation of corporate social responsibility (CSR) efforts	Construct operationalizations—operationalized using multiple-item scales assessed by ten-point semantic differential and Likert scales	Low level of CSR will create (coupled with low quality) will create negative wom	**Strong effect of low CSR on creating nwom**
Governance		*Indifferent*					
Leadership	1	Marsha L. Richins and Teri Root-Shaffer	1988, Advances in Consumer Research Volume 15 THE ROLE OF EVOLVEMENT AND OPINION LEADERSHIP IN CONSUMER WORD-OF-MOUTH: AN IMPLICIT MODEL MADE EXPLICIT	Opinion leadership literature to determine how consumer behavior researchers have viewed opinion leadership at the sender level and identifies the model implicit in their work	Literature review implicit model is expanded and tested empirically	The relationship between opinion leadership and word-of-mouth is strongest for advice-giving, the form of word-of-mouth traditionally linked with opinion leadership	**Strong relationship of wom and opinion leader for advice giving**

	2	David Godes and Dina Mayzlin	2007 Firm-Created Word-of-Mouth Communication: Evidence from a Field Test	The effectiveness of the firm's proactive management of customer-to-customer communication	1. Implemented a large-scale field test in which a national firm created word of mouth through two populations: customers and non-customers 2. Collected data from two laboratory studies	Opinion leadership is associated with higher wom-creation for very loyal customers, it is less true for less-loyal customers	**Strong effect of wom by opinion leaders for loyal users**
Financial Performance	1	Judith Chevalier and Dina Mayzlin	2004, Yale School of Management THE EFFECT OF WORD OF MOUTH ON SALES: ONLINE BOOK REVIEWS	Effect of voluntarily-supplied customer reviews on subsequent sales of books online	Publicly available data from the two leading online booksellers, Amazon.com (Amazon) and BN.comandNoble. com (BN.com), to construct measures of each firm's sales (star ratings) (ENDIAFEROUSA METHODOS)	Improvement in reviews for a book at one site leads to a relative increase in the sales of that book at that site the marginal (negative) impact of 1-star reviews is greater than the (positive) impact of 5-star reviews as buyers suspect that many reviewers are authors or other biased parties	**Relative effect of positive wom in financial performance (online)**
	2	David Godes and Dina Mayzlin	2007 Firm-Created Word-of-Mouth Communication: Evidence from a Field Test	The effectiveness of the firm's proactive management of customer-to-customercommunication	1. Implemented a large-scale field test in which a national firm created word of mouth through two populations: customers and non-customers 2. Collected data from two laboratory studies	Wom that is most effectiveat driving sales is created by less loyal customers, not loyals, and occurs between acquaintances (not friends)	**wom strong effect at driving financial performance**

(continued)

Table 2 (continued)

Media versus wom

No	Author	Publication title	What was the basic investigation	Methodology info—model	Interesting finding	Relation with wom
1	David L. Deephouse Louisiana State University	2000, Vol. 26, No. 6, 1091–1112 Media Reputation as a Strategic Resource: An Integration of Mass Communication and Resource-Based Theories	This paper integrates mass communication theory into past research to develop a concept called media reputation, defined as the overall evaluation of a firm presented in the media	Evaluation of newspaper reports (all letters to editors, all editorials, columns)	Media reputation increases the performance of commercial banks	The newspapers "stories" can be perceived as wom. Favorable media is positively related to performance
2	FRANCIS A. BUTTLE	6:241–254 (1998), JOURNAL OF STRATEGIC MARKETING; Word of mouth: understanding and managing referral marketing	A step forward to: What are the antecedents of wom? What are the consequences of wom	The wom model: 1. Intrapersonal variables: these are states or processes which are associated either with seeking input wom or precipitating output wom 2. Extrapersonal variables: these are contextual conditions which influence the seeking of input wom or the production of output wom	Mass communication is the wom by opinion leaders. Wom is driven by satisfaction. And satisfaction is driven by media messages	Positive wom increases as satisfaction is increased that is driven by media messages. The writer proposes further research on: Which antecedent marketing conditions are most closely associated with wom? In the service sector, which of the 7Ps—product, price, place, promotion, people, process and physical evidence—has the greatest impact on wom? Under what contextual conditions?

3	Masayuki Nakajima in collaboration with Prof. Nihei from Asia University	2007 wom Research Results, Tokyo, Japan, Kokokusha Co., Ltd (Advertizing Agency): "Word of Mouth Research 2007"; Relation between 'Word of Mouth' and Mass Media	TUZUMI Model—Internet Survey	Information sources that generate wom	Two biggest information sources of wom was "words from friends/neighbors" and "TV"	**Media and especially TV coverage generates spread of wom**
4	Yuichi Washida Comparative Media Studies, MIT Department of System Science, the University of Tokyo	April 28, 2007, Hakuhodo Inc., Correlation between Word-of-Mouth Effects and New Media: Simulations of Japanese Media Environment Using Artificial Neural Network	New correlation patterns between word-of-mouth generation and other media effects through a computer simulation model by artificial neural network	Empirical Consumer Survey & computer simulation model by artificial neural network	By observing the simulation results, authors tried to establish a new general pattern of media usages from the viewpoint of marketing practitioners to accelerate word-of-mouth effects	**Wom can be considered as an internal part of the media business**
5	Laurie Sullivan	2010 June 11, Internet Can Drive Word Of Mouth Even Better Than Television	Internet influence on wom	Yahoo Study	The Internet has grown more influential when it comes to informing people through conversations about brands, even more so than TV in certain categories. The study also finds that the best vehicles for influencing wom come from consumers who play in social networks. These "Conversation Catalysts" drive a disproportionately higher percentage of wom activity	**Internet Can Drive Word Of Mouth Even Better Than Television**

(continued)

Table 2 (continued)

No	Author	Publication title	What was the basic investigation	Methodology info—model	Interesting finding	Relation with wom
5	Justin Kirby and Paul Mardsen (Editors)	September 9, 2005; Butterworth-Heinemann, Connected Marketing, the viral, buzz and Word of mouth revolution	Connected Marketing, the viral, buzz and Word of mouth revolution	"Two step flow" Model (marketing communication influence on opinion leaders and followers)	The research found, contrary to what was expected, that the mass-media messages do not directly influence the mass market. In fact, they influence a small minority of individuals (the so called "influencers" or "opinion leaders"), who then influence their peers through word of mouth. This is one of the reasons why word of mouth is so important	**Wom as a result of media messages influence the wider public**
6	Renne Dye	2000, Harvard Business Review; Connected Marketing, the viral, buzz and Word of mouth revolution	Buzz marketing (myths and realities)	Case studies	Buzz evolves according to some basic principles. It is not a random force of nature. Spread of buzz can be created by analyzing how different groups interact and influence one another	**When used either too early or too much the media can squelch wom before it ignites**
7	B.J. Jansen, M. Zhang, K. Sobel, and A. Chowdury	2009 Twitter Power: Tweets as Electronic Word of Mouth, JOURNAL OF THE AMERICAN SOCIETY FOR INFORMATION SCIENCE AND TECHNOLOGY, 60 (11):2169–2188	The possible effect of microblogging via ewom on the brand knowledge and brand relationship	Collected these tweets using the Summize tool. Summize4 is a service for searching tweets and keeping up with emerging trends in Twitter in real time. It counts the sentiment for a given period of time. They manually coded the tweets	19 % of microblogs contain mention of a brand. Of the branding microblogs, nearly 20 % contained some expression of brand sentiments. Of these, more than 50 % were positive and 33 % were critical of the company or product	**Microblogging is an online tool for customer word of mouth**

they actually concluded to the fact that "media reputation may influence the financial performance of such organisations" (Deephouse 2000). The resource-based view of the firm proposed that a favorable reputation is an intangible asset that increases firm performance.

The main finding of Deephouse's research is the following: media reputation may influence performance and this has one central implication for managers: they should seek to cultivate positive evaluations by the media (Deephouse 2000).

Starting from that point and taking as a base the measurement model that was used, the authors of the present study concluded to the following research questions:
1. How e-wom influences each of the seven dimensions of reputation?
2. Is this influence significant for the banking sector?
3. Can e-wom eventually affect the financial performance of a particular banking institution?

To answer the first two questions, the third question is not addressed in this paper, as a first step, all the publications made in blogs and social media were collected, from October 2010 until October 2011, that referred to three major Greek Banking Institutions. The time period chosen, is considered to be one of the most extraordinary periods for the financial sector, with a significance that extends beyond Greece to the Eurozone (Münchau 2010).

Data collection was facilitated by a professional reputation monitoring service, an online tool that monitors all media publications: from television, radio, websites, blogs and social media and also provides the impact rate of each publication in blogs and social media.

For blogs, the impact rate derives from an algorithm, according to the popularity and reproducibility of the blog.

For other social media the impact rate derives from:
- The number of Followers in Twitter
- Number of Friends or Likes in Facebook
- Number of Friends or Likes in Google Plus

In some in social media networks, as the profiles of the users are usually personal, access may not be allowed if the researcher is not connected (is a friend) with the profile user. Therefore, in case of restrictive access, the official average numbers are used, namely:
- 120 friends/likes for every Facebook profile and
- 30 for Google Plus

In terms of the research procedure, the following steps were undertaken:
1. All the data/publications of blogs and social media that referred to the three Banks were collected for the period studied. They amounted to a total of 52,365.
2. All publications were sorted by the "impact rate" of the medium
3. An adequate, clean sample of 6,000 publications was selected from 12,320 publications, sorted by highest influence rate and the degree of relevance to our research subject.
4. A measurement model was created where each publication, after having been thoroughly studied,

Table 3 Coding procedure according to the 7 dimension codes

Dimension	Dimension code
Products & Services	1
Innovation	2
Workplace	3
Governance	4
Corporate Responsibility	5
Leadership	6
Performance	7

Table 4 Rating procedure for the evaluation of each publication

Rating	
+1	POSITIVE (favorable)
0	NEUTRAL
−1	NEGATIVE (unfavorable)

(a) Is categorized to one of the seven dimensions of reputation (Fombrun and Van Riel 2004), and encoded accordingly
(b) Is rated as either positive (favorable to the organisation), neutral or negative (unfavorable to the organisation) (Deephouse 2000), with respect to the influence it exercises to this particular dimension and consequently to the reputation of the organisation.

Tables 3 and 4 describe the rating/coding used.

Each of the 6,000 publications was thoroughly studied and evaluated according to its content and impact and was encoded accordingly.

Results and Conclusions

The actual results of the above mentioned data analysis are presented in Tables 5 and 6:

The attitudes of generators of e-wom towards the Banking Institutions are mostly negative and aggressive rather than positive and favorable. This might be expected, during a major financial crisis, a term applied broadly to a variety of situations in which some financial institutions or assets suddenly lose a large part of their value. Since the nineteenth and early twentieth centuries, many financial crises were associated with banking panics, and many recessions coincided with these panics (Kindleberger and Aliber 2005) that were thought to be facilitated via spreading of rumours and wom. It can therefore be considered normal, when studying the attitudes that appear in a socially open network, that the results will be mostly unfavourable towards the Banks under investigation in periods of crises.

Additionally, upon examination of the results pertaining to the seven Dimensions of Reputation, it is evident that Performance of the organisation is

Table 5 Research Results: number of publications for each of the 7 dimensions

Dimension	No of publications
Products & Services	345
Innovation	94
Workplace	37
Governance	233
Corporate Responsibility	420
Leadership	1,456
Performance	3,415
TOTAL PUBLICATIONS	6,000

Table 6 Research Results: number of positive, neutral, negative publications

Rating	No of publications
+1	1,772
0	1,787
−1	2,441
TOTAL PUBLICATIONS	6,000

the one dimension mostly affected followed by Leadership, while dimensions such as Corporate Responsibility (here measured as publications related to Corporate Social Responsibility) were less prominent in the results. As previous research has shown (Luo and Bhattacharya 2006), consumer reactions to CSR and other similar activities are not that straightforward and evident in terms of the value they add to the organisation. Therefore investment on CSR might not generate a return both in monetary, but as evident here, in reputation terms as well. This, hopefully, could lead to further research to generalize this finding, a task for researchers in Strategic Management and Marketing and also Business Ethics and Communication scholars. Comparative studies could also show if e-wom has a different effect on the seven dimensions than "physical" wom has and, of course, their combined effect.

There is also an opportunity, for researchers, to ascertain to what degree the dominance of negative e-wom is limited to certain sectors, certain periods or both. Banking seems to be an obvious candidate for negative e-wom as our research has shown, and we can hypothesize that due to the nature of the business this sign will not change in different periods. A comparative industry analysis and longitudinal research will be useful towards that direction.

Another suggestion for further research will be to try and connect, causally, e-wom and financial performance of an organisation by using e-wom as an independent variable in a model that measures financial performance. This is ongoing research pursued by the authors of this paper.

Concluding, there is evidence from this research that e-wom might affect specific dimensions of the reputation of an organisation. Even thought this has been proven for financial institutions during the beginning of a crisis period, one can only hope that further research will be able to shed more light and generalize this paper's findings using different organisations and periods.

References

Arndt, J. (1967). Role of product-related conversations in the diffusion of a new product. *Journal of Marketing Research, 4*(3), 291–295. American Marketing Association.
Assael, H. (1992). *Consumer behavior and marketing action.* Boston, MA: PWS-Kent.
Axelrod, R. (1984). *The evolution of cooperation.* New York: Basic Books.
Balter, D. (2008). *The word of mouth manual* (Vol. 2). Boston, MA: BzzAgent.
Barney, J. B. (1991). Firm resources and sustained competitive advantage. *Journal of Management, 17*, 99–120.
Berens, G., & Van Riel, C. (2004). Corporate associations in the academic literature: Three main streams of thought in the reputation measurement literature. *Corporate Reputation Review, 7*(2), 161–178.
Bhattacharya, C. B., & Sen, S. (2004). Doing better at doing good. *California Management Review, 47*(1), 9–24.
Booth, S. A. (1993). *Crisis management strategy.* London: Routledge.
Brown, J. J., & Reingen, P. H. (1987). Social ties and word of mouth referral behavior. *Journal of Consumer Research, 14*, 350–362.
Buttle, F. A. (1998). Word of mouth: Understanding and managing referral marketing. *Journal of Strategic Marketing, 6*, 241–254.
Byrnes, W. J. (1999). *Management and the arts.* Boston, MA: Focal.
Carden, P., & Huntley, B. (1992). *Investing in the West End theatrical productions – How to be an angel.* London: Robert Hale. Congress Cataloging-in-Publication Data.
Cha, M., Mislove, A., & Gummadi, K. P. (2009, April 20–24). A measurement-driven analysis of information propagation in the Flickr Social Network. In J. Quemada, G. León, Y. S. Maarek, & W. Nejdl (Eds.), *Proceedings of the 18th international conference on World Wide Web, WWW 2009, Madrid, Spain* (pp. 721–730). New York: ACM.
Chevalier, J., & Mayzlin, D. (2004). *The effect of word of mouth on sales: Online book reviews.* Yale School of Management.
Cooper, L. G., Tschopik, H., Hannon, E. J., & Cochran, L. (1978). *Selected proceedings of the 1978 UCLA Conference of Professional Arts Managers.* London: UCLA.
Cox, D. F. (1963, December). The audiences as communicators. In S. A. Greyser (Ed.), *Proceedings, American Marketing Association* (pp. 58–72). Chicago: American Marketing Association.
Cross, A. (2006). Nonprofit communications from a corporate communications viewpoint. *Business Communication Quarterly, 69*, 316.
Davies, G., Chun, R., Da Silva, R. V., & Roper, S. (2003). *Corporate reputation and competitiveness.* New York: Routledge.
Deephouse, D. (2000). Communication and resource-based theories. Media reputation as a strategic resource: An integration of mass. *Journal of Management, 26*, 1091.
Delre. S. A., Jager, W., & Janssen, M. A. (2007). Diffusion dynamics in small-world networks with heterogeneous consumers. Springer.
Dunay, P. (2008). *Reputation management for new media survey. How ready are you?* Buzz Marketing for Technology.
Dye, R. (2000). Connected marketing, the viral, buzz and word of mouth revolution. *Harvard Business Review.*

Engel, J. E., Blackwell, R. D., & Kegerreis, R. J. (1969). How information is used to adopt an innovation. *Journal of Marketing Research, 9*, 3–8.
Engel, J. F., Blackwell, R. D., & Miniard, P. W. (1993). *Consumer behavior*. New York: Dreyden.
Engel, J. F., Kollat, D. J., & Blackwell, R. D. (1968). *Consumer behavior*. New York: Holt, Rinehart and Winston.
Fombrun, C. (2007). *TA NEA, MBA*. 15 October press release.
Fombrun, C., & Gardberg, G. (2006). Corporate citizenship: Creating intangible asset across institutional environments. *Academy of Management Review, 31*(2), 329–346.
Fombrun, C. J., Gardberg, N. A., & Barnett, M. L. (2000). Opportunity platforms and safety nets: Corporate citizenship and reputational risk. *Business and Society Review, 105*(1), 85–106.
Fombrun, C. J., & Van Riel, C. B. M. (2004). *Fame & fortune. How successful companies build winning reputations*. Upper Saddle River, NJ: Prentice Hall.
Froelich, K. (1999). Diversification of revenue strategies: Evolving resource dependence in nonprofit organizations. *Non-profit and Voluntary Sector Quarterly, 28*, 246.
Godes, D., & Mayzlin, D. (2008). Firm-created word-of-mouth communication: Evidence from a field test. *Marketing Science, 28*, 721–739.
Goldsmith, R., & Horowitz, D. (2006). Measuring motivations for online opinion seeking. *Journal of Interactive Advertising, 6*(2), 3–14.
Goutzanea, E. (2007). TA NEA. Released Monday, 24 September.
Hall, R. (1992). The strategic analysis of intangible resources. *Strategic Management Journal, 13*, 135–144.
Hayes, D. M. (1998). Crisis, what crisis? – An exploration of crisis management strategies used by arts organisations. *City University – Thesis submitted for the degree of MA in Arts Management*.
Helm, S., Gobbers, K. L., & Storck, C. (2011). *Reputation management*. Heidelberg: Springer.
Herr, P. M., Kardes, F. R., & Kim, J. (1991). Effects of word-of-mouth and product-attribute information on persuasion: An accessibility-diagnosticity perspective. *Journal of Consumer Research, 17*, 454–462.
Hill, E. (1995). *Creative arts marketing*. Musselburgh: Scotprint.
Jansen, B. J., Zhang, M., Sobel, K., & Chowdury, A. (2009). Twitter power: Tweets as electronic word of mouth. *Journal of the American Society for Information Science and Technology, 60*(11), 2169–2188.
Katz, E., & Lazarsfeld, P. (1955). *Personal influence*. New York: Free Press.
Keller, E., & Berry, J. (2006). Word-of-mouth: The real action is offline. Accessed February 2, 2010, available at http://www.kellerfay.com/news/Ad%20Age%2012-4-06.pdf
Keller, K. L., & Staelin, R. (1987). Effects of quality and quantity of information on decision effectiveness. *Journal of Consumer Research, 14*, 200–213.
Kelly, L. (2007). *Beyond buzz: The next generation of word-of-mouth marketing*. New York: AMACOM.
Kirby, J., & Marsden, P. (2005). *Connected marketing: The viral, buzz and word of mouth revolution*. London: Butterworth-Heinemann.
Kindleberger, C. P., & Aliber, R. (2005). *Manias, panics, and crashes: A history of financial crises* (5th ed.). New York: Wiley. ISBN 0-471-46714-6.
Kosmidou, K., & Zopounidis, C. (2005). Evaluating the performance of the Greek banking system. *Operational Research: An International Journal, 5*(2), 319–326.
Kotler, P., & Scheff, J. (1997). *Standing room only*. Boston, MA: Library of School.
Lazarsfeld, P., Berelson, B., & Gaudet, H. (1948). *The people's choice*. New York: Columbia University Press.
Luo, X., & Bhattacharya, C. B. (2006). Corporate social responsibility, customer satisfaction, and market value. *Journal of Marketing, 70*, 1–18.
Mack, R. W., Blose, J. E., & Pan, B. (2008). Believe it or not: The perceived credibility of blogs in tourism. *Journal of Vacation Marketing, 14*(1), 133–142.
MacMillan, K., Money, K., Downing, S., & Hillenbrand, C. (2004). Giving your organisation SPIRIT: An overview and call to action for directors on issues of corporate governance,

corporate reputation and corporate responsibility. *Journal of General Management, 30*(2), 15–42.
Mahajan, V., & Muller, E. (1979). Innovation diffusion and new product growth in marketing. *The Journal of Marketing, 43*(4), 55–68.
Mailath, G. J., & Samuelson, L. (2001). Who wants a good reputation? *Review of Economic Studies, 68*(2), 415–441.
Masayuki Nakajima in collaboration with Prof. Nihei from Asia University. (2007). Relation between word of mouth and mass media. Tokyo: Kokokusha (Advertizing Agency).
Mazzarol, T., Sweeney, J. C., & Soutar, G. N. (2007). Conceptualizing word-of-mouth activity, triggers and conditions: An exploratory study. *European Journal of Marketing, 41*(11/12), 1475–1494.
Money, B., Gilly, M., & Graham, J. (1998). Explorations of national culture and word-of-mouth referral behavior in the purchase of industrial services in the United States and Japan. *Journal of Marketing, 62*(4), 76–87.
Money, K., & Hillenbrand, C. (2006, May 25–28). *Beyond reputation measurement: Placing reputation within a model of value creation by integrating existing measures into a theoretical framework*. Presented 10th anniversary conference on reputation, image, identity and competitiveness, New York, NY.
Münchau, W. (2010, April 25). Greece is Europe's very own subprime crisis. *Financial Times.*
Ostrower, F. (2007). Foundations the relativity of foundation effectiveness: The case of community. *Nonprofit and Voluntary Sector Quarterly, 36*, 521.
Pieczka, M. (2002). Public relations expertise deconstructed. *Media Culture Society, 24*, 301.
Pizzorno, A. (2004). Resources of social capital: Reputation and visibility. *A presentation given at the ECSR Summer School on social capital, Trento, Italy.*
Ploritis, M. (2006). ΤΟ ΒΙΜç. Released on 11.1.2006.
Popely, D. R. (2006). *Nonprofit marketing: Marketing management for charitable and nongovernmental organizations.* Thousand Oaks, CA: Sage.
Prasaad, K., & Raghupathy, R. (2005). A snapshot of a successful public relations strategy. *American Behavioral Scientist, 49*, 629.
Rentschler, R. (2001). Entrepreneurship, marketing and leadership in non-profit performing arts organisations. Deakin University.
Repenning, N. P. (1999). *Understanding fire fighting in new product development*. Department of Operations Management, Massachusetts Institute of Technology.
Reputation Institute. (2012). http://www.reputationinstitute.com
Resnick, P., Zeckhauser, R., Friedman, E., & Kuwabara, K. (2006). Reputation systems: Facilitating trust in internet interactions. *Communications of the ACM, 43*(12), 45–48.
Richins, M. L., & Shaffer, T. R. (1988). The role of enduring involvement and opinion leadership in consumer word-of-mouth: An implicit model made explicit. *Advances in Consumer Research, 15*, 32–36.
Richins, M. L. (1984). Word of mouth communication as negative information. *Advances in Consumer Research, 11*(1), 697–702.
Shapiro, B. (1974). Marketing in nonprofit organizations. *Nonprofit and Voluntary Sector Quarterly, 3*, 1.
Sirmon, D. G., Hitt, M. A., & Ireland, R. D. (2007). Managing firm resources in dynamic environments to create value: Looking inside the black box. *Academy of Management Review, 32*(1), 273–292.
Silverman, D. (2001). *Interpreting qualitative data: Methods for analysing talk, text and interaction* (2nd ed.). London: Sage.
Sullivan, L. (2010). Internet can drive word of mouth even better than television. A Yahoo study. http://www.mediapost.com/publications/article/130014/
Sztompka, P. (2000). *Trust: A sociological theory*. Port Chester, NJ: Cambridge University Press.
Tan, T., & Uncles, M. D. (2005). *To gain insight into CSR as an advertising appeal, theory of planned behaviour (TPB) model questionnaires*. Sydney: University of New South Wales.

Thompson, N. (2003). More companies pay heed to their 'word of mouse' reputation. *New York Times*.
Van Riel, C. (2007). *The annual reputation institute study in the Netherlands 2007*. Reputation Institute, New York; Corporate Communication Centre, RSM Erasmus University Rotterdam.
Vidaver-Cohen, D. (2007). Reputation beyond the rankings: A conceptual framework for business school research. *Corporate Reputation Review, 10*(4), 278–304.
Vlachos, P. A., & Tsamakos, A. (2009). Corporate social responsibility: Attributions, loyalty and the mediating role of trust. *Journal of the Academy of Marketing Science, 37*(2), 170–180.
Walsh, F., & Wiedmann, K. P. (2004). A conceptualization of corporate reputation in Germany: An evaluation and extension of the RQ. *Corporate Reputation Review, 6*(4), 304–312.
Washida, Y. (2007). *Correlation between word-of-mouth effects and new media: Simulations of Japanese media environment using artificial neural network*. Comparative Media Studies, MIT Department of System Science, the University of Tokyo.

Social Networks and Media Brands: Exploring the Effect of Media Brands' Perceived Social Network Usage on Audience Relationship

Sylvia Chan-Olmsted, Moonhee Cho, and Mark Yi-Cheon Yim

1 Introduction

The proliferation of social media such as *Facebook*, *Twitter*, and *YouTube* has brought dramatic changes in consumer's media consumption behavior. With more and more consumers participating in some forms of social media, these platforms have become important means of consumer engagement for many marketers. In a Harvard Business Review survey, almost 80 % of the companies indicated they were using or plan to use social media for business (HBR Analytics Services 2010). Another survey conducted among a sample of American social media users, 93 % of them indicated that a company should have a presence in social media and about 85 % said that a company is required to not only have a presence in social media but also interact with customers through social media (Cone Business in Social Media Research 2008).

Comparing to traditional media which are one-directional, social media allow consumers to actively engage in a communication process not only as information receivers but also as message creators, thus enabling better information sharing and opinion exchanges. From a branding perspective, such a two-way communication mechanism creates viable channels for ongoing dialogues and long-term bonds between companies and customers (Williamson 2009). Tsai (2009) suggests that social media provide an opportunity not only to acquire or distribute information but also to develop relationships; and relationships cultivated through social media are effective in building brand loyalty because they are based on mutual interests

---

S. Chan-Olmsted (✉)
University of Florida, Gainesville, FL, USA
e-mail: chanolmsted@jou.ufl.edu

M. Cho
University of South Florida, Tampa, FL, USA

M.Y.-C. Yim
Canisius College, Buffalo, NY, USA

and mutual gain. Empirical studies have repeatedly found that an investment in customer relationships contributes to not only a brand's consumer-based brand equity (CBBE) but also its profitability by reducing marketing costs and/or increasing net sales (Wang et al. 2009). Thus, the utility of social media as branding tools can be meaningfully understood in the context of brand relationship marketing and brand equity. Among all social media, social networks like *Facebook* is the most utilized platform by both consumers and marketers. There are now more social-networking accounts than there are people in the world (10 billion). It was forecasted that *Facebook*, which passed Google, Yahoo, and Microsoft in user engagement in 2010 with users spending 12.7 % of their time, will have $4 billion in ad revenues worldwide in 2011 (eMarketer 2011).

Social networks' branding potential, especially in the context of relationship building, seems to offer traditional media which were handicapped by the one-way communication mechanism an opportunity to connect with audiences more effectively in an increasingly competitive marketplace. Research has empirically confirmed that branding is more important for services than for physical goods (Brady et al. 2005). Under this premise, the branding utility of social networks is especially important for media brands. Nevertheless, social networks, while can complement and be integrated with traditional media content, to a certain degree, also compete with these same media products for consumers' time and attention. In addition, as media brands are intangible, experience goods that typically possess more ambiguity and volatility in the process of consumer brand evaluation; it is unclear how social networks contribute to the development of brand relationship for this type of products.

The purpose of this study is to verify empirically the contribution of social networks as a branding tool for media products from the relational perspective, considering the traditional media's inherent inability for two-way communication. Specifically, it will investigate if the perceived use of social networks by a media brand plays a role in enhancing its brand equity and in consumer's intention to develop a relationship with the brand. With increasing market competition, importance of audience loyalty, online media popularity, and media brand extensions into other product and service categories, more insight on how social media usage might contribute to consumers' intention to build a reciprocal relationship with the media brands will validate media managers' more long-term branding decisions in the world of Web 2.0.

2 Literature Review

As indicated, among all social media, social network sites (SNSs) like *Facebook*, *MySpace*, and *LinkedIn* are the most utilized platform by both consumers and marketers. There are now more social-networking accounts than there are people in the world. In fact, *Facebook* has overtaken *Google* as the most visited website globally (Tsotsis 2010). The use of SNSs for marketing purposes is becoming a norm for many businesses. Industry analysts estimated that worldwide SNS ad revenues, excluding money that companies spend developing and managing their social network presences, would reach $5.97 billion in 2011, a 71.6 % increase from 2010. Many firms have seen returns on the increased investment for the online platform according to a recent survey (eMarketer 2011).

The use of SNSs and its effectiveness for branding might differ between physical and intangible goods. As indicated, Brady et al. (2005) found that branding is more important for services than for physical goods and that there is a direct relationship between the level of intangibility and the importance of branding. In a sense, intangible products possess more ambiguity and volatility in the process of consumer brand evaluation. Because of the lack of standardized, observable features, brands play a more significant role as a source of differentiation for intangible products (Wang et al. 2009). Studies have shown that intangible products have fewer cues for consumers to evaluate, thus elevating the importance of brand image (Murray and Schlacter 1990; Turley and Moore 1995). The ambiguity in the brand assessment process is especially evident in the case of media content brands which are experience goods that are more likely to be influenced by other's opinions or external information (Reinstein and Snyder 2005). Under this premise, SNSs should be an effective means of branding for media content brands.

2.1 Relationship Marketing and Consumer-Based Brand Equity (CBBE)

Relationship marketing is broadly defined as "marketing activities directed toward establishing, developing, and maintaining successful relational exchanges" (Morgan and Hunt 1994, p. 22). In a world of audience fragmentation and increasing competition, a more long-term relationship with viewers might be the key to developing competitive advantages. The premise of brand relationship is that a brand is considered as a relationship partner of consumers and interdependent with them. That is, a brand is referred to as an active contributing member of relationship dyad rather than passive being of marketing transaction (Fournier 1998). Numerous studies have found constructive outcomes from good relationships with consumers. De Wulf et al. (2001) assert that investment in customer relationship through relationship marketing tactics such as preferential treatment, interpersonal communication, and tangible rewards brings behavioral loyalty. It was further suggested that the quality of relationship, as reflected by trust and satisfaction, can have a direct impact on brand equity (Wang et al. 2009). The effect of brand relationship on brand equity is important as it justifies the marketing investment a brand makes that may not lead directly or explicitly to specific consumption or purchasing behavior. Brand equity refers to the value of a product with its brand name compared with the same product without its brand name, and it is usually considered as marketing effects outcomes (Ailawadi et al. 2003; Keller 2003). Keller and Lehmann (2006) summarized that brand equity can be explained with three distinctive perspectives, customer-based, company-based, and finance-based. Keller (1993) further defines customer-based brand equity (CBBE) as "the differential effect of brand knowledge on customer response to the marketing of the brand" (p. 8). Eventually, better CBBE leads to higher profit potential because the brand might attain increased market share and favorable price structure (Aaker 1991; Keller 2002).

2.2 Perceived Brand Relationship Investment

To better understand the dynamics of the relationship between a company and its customers, some scholars focus on the aspect of reciprocity in a relationship (Bagozzi 1995; De Wulf et al. 2001; Smith and Barclay 1997; Yoon et al. 2008). Smith and Barclay (1997) argued that a company's relational investment such as devotion of time, effort, and resources forms psychological bonds that lead customers to stay in the relationship as well as expect reciprocation. Perceived relationship investment is defined as "a consumer's perception of the extent to which a retailer devotes resources, efforts, and attention aimed at maintaining or enhancing relationships with regular customers that do not have outside value and cannot be recovered if these relationships are terminated" (De Wulf et al. 2001, p. 35). Various studies have affirmed the benefit of customer's perceived relationship investment. Baker et al. (1999) found a positive association between seller's relationship efforts and customers' satisfaction. Some specifically identified a positive influence of perceived relationship investment on relationship quality and behavioral loyalty in the case of online marketing communications (De Wulf et al. 2001; Yoon et al. 2008). However, in the context of media brands where there is often no direct risk in purchasing decisions and ambiguity in brand evaluations, do the potential functions of SNSs in facilitating brand relationship and the importance of customer's perceived relationship investment of a brand still hold true? This study attempts to verify empirically the contribution of SNSs as a branding tool from the relational perspective with the following hypotheses:

▶ H1: Consumer's perceived social network usage of a media brand is positively associated with the perceived relationship investment of that brand.

▶ H2: Consumers' perceived relationship investment of a media brand is positively associated with the brand's consumer-based brand equity (CBBE).

2.3 Relation Intention

As stated above, brand relationship is formed between customers and brands. While it is obvious for a company to want to develop and maintain relationships with customers, customers do not always want to build a relationship with brands. This might be especially true in the case of media content products as the relationship between a media brand and its consumers has been one-directional historically. The popularity of social media, however, offers a new mechanism for media brands to change the dynamics of relationship building between audiences and media. In fact, one might argue that there might be more synergistic effect on relationship development through social networks for media content brands because of the importance of contextual information, connection with casts, and peer opinions in the consumption process.

Given that customers can be influenced to choose a certain brand because of marketing related factors such as low prices, switching costs, convenience, inertia, or current trend, rather than by affinity toward the product or company (Burnham et al. 2003), relationship intention is important in predicting profitability (Kumar et al. 2003). Defined as "an intention of a customer to build a relationship with a firm while buying a product or a service attributed to a firm, a brand, and a channel" (Kumar et al. 2003, p. 669), relationship intention leads a firm's profitability in the long run. In the context of media content brands, relationship intention can translate into willingness to try new content from the same brand and/or active audience engagement with the services/products offered by the brand.

Kumar et al. (2003) suggested five dimensions that form relationship intention in an online communication environment: involvement, expectation, forgivingness, feedback, and fear of relationship loss. In general, involvement is considered as the extent to which a person has willingness to engage in relationship activity. High involvement in brand relationship brings great satisfaction as well as high level of identification with the brand. It also makes a customer feel guilty or uncomfortable when purchasing competitive brands. Expectation is developed when customers purchase a brand. Put another way, a customer who has higher expectations about and care for brand is more inclined to develop a relationship with the brand. As for the dimension of forgiveness, the notion is that a customer having the desire to build relationship with a brand is more tolerant of the brand and more forgiving, meaning that the customer will still give another chance to the brand even though his/her expectations were not met. As for feedback, it was suggested that a customer with high relationship intention is more likely to communicate on expectations to the brand. The customer gives both positive and negative feedback without any reward or paycheck in return. Therefore, a customer who is willing to give his/her opinion to firms without any expected benefits has a high degree of relationship intention. Finally, in terms of fear of relationship loss, a customer concerning about the consequence of losing relationship with a brand typically has high intention to build a relationship with the brand. In a comprehensive typology for consumer switching cost, Burnham et al. (2003) stated that brand relationship loss costs are "the affective losses associated with breaking the bonds of identification that have been formed with the brand or company with which a customer has associated" (p. 112). Kumar et al. (2003) found that brand equity positively influences relationship intention of customer. In other words, if a customer is aware of a brand and holds a positive brand image, he or she is more likely to develop a relationship with the brand. Accordingly, the following hypotheses are proposed.

▶ H3: A media brand's CBBE is positively associated with consumer's intention to develop a relationship with that brand.

▶ H4: There is a direct relationship between a consumer's perceived relationship investment of a media brand and his/her intention to build a relationship with that brand.

3 Method

3.1 Data Collection and Sample

Considering that SNS users rely on Internet connections for the platform and online survey is popular in social science studies with cost-efficiency and wide coverage of geographic areas (Deutskens et al. 2006; Wimmer and Dominick 2006), this study conducted a web-based survey using a national online consumer panel maintained by a leading U.S. market research firm. Two qualifying questions that assessed the panelists' social media usage level and familiarity were used to include only those who have had experience with social media from the 1,600 panelists contacted. A total of 340 responses were utilized for data analysis, yielding the final incident rate of 21 %. The majority of the sample consists of Caucasians (87.9 %), female (65 %), and married (57 %). The sample also reflects a diverse range of demographic backgrounds. Specifically, 5.9 % of the participants were in the age group of 18–24, 21.8 % in 25–34, 20.6 % in 35–44, 25.9 % in 45–54, 19.1 % in 55–64, and 6.8 % in 65 or older. In terms of education, about 18 % of consumers completed high school, 25.9 % held college education, 13.5 % hold a 2-year college degree, 27.6 % attended a 4-year college, and 14.4 % completed graduate or professional degree (see Table 1).

As for the media brands studied, using the list of the top 100 "most social brands" in 2009 that rank ordered over 2,000 consumer brands based on their daily social media activities (Virtrue 2009); five leading media brands, CNN, ABC, NBC, CBS, and ESPN, from the intangible product category of television services were identified. A pre-test was conducted among a group of 25 respondents to refine the survey wordings as well as to select the final media brand pair to be tested. CNN and CBS were chosen for the study because the pair has the most significant variance in brand equity and perceived social media usage in the pre-test.

3.2 Measurement Scales

Yoo and Donthu's (2001) overall brand equity scales were modified to measure brand equity of the media brands tested. Cronbach's alphas for both CNN and CBS were .92. Consumer's evaluation on the perceived relationship investment (PRI) for media brands was measured with three items developed by De Wulf et al. (2001), yielding the Cronbach's reliability coefficient of .94 (CNN) and .95 (CBS). Kumar et al.'s (2003) relationship intention items based on the aforementioned five dimensions were adopted to construct the valid components and test hypotheses related to relationship intention. The scale items were refined to reflect the nature of the media products. A total of 13 items including 1 validation item were tested in the study. Cronbach's alpha coefficients for reliability were .81 (CNN) and .85 (CBS). To measure the perceived SNS usage of media brands, this study asked the respondents to evaluate to what extent they think each brand uses SNSs. All the

Table 1 Demographic analysis of sample

	Age (%)		Education (%)
18–24	5.9	Completed high school	18
25–34	21.8	College education	25.9
35–44	20.6	2-year college degree	13.5
45–54	25.9	4-year college degree	27.6
55–64	19.1	Graduate/professional degree	14.4
65 or older	6.8		

items were measured on 7-point Likert scales with 1 indicating strongly disagree and 7 strongly agree (see Table 2).

3.2.1 Analysis Procedure, Assumption Check, and Reliability/Validity

To test the proposed model as suggested by the specified hypotheses (see Fig. 1), structural equation modeling (SEM) was performed using AMOS 18.0. The procedure consisted of assumption check, testing measurement models, and testing the suggested model, including reliability and validity checks. The suggested hypotheses were confirmed by identifying whether each path coefficient among latent variables is significant. The testing procedure was repeated based on two target media brands—CBS and CNN. This test–retest structure of testing allowed researchers to have more rigorous findings. The basic assumptions for confirmatory factor analysis were tested by examining Kaiser-Meyer-Olkin's measure ($> .50$) and Bartlett's Test of Sphericity index ($p < .001$), which were satisfactory. The sample normality was also satisfactory, indicating that all Skewness ($-.78 <$ Skewness $< .59$) and Kurtosis values ($-.84 <$ Kurtosis $< .32$) were within the range of ± 1.96, and thus, the Maximum Likelihood Estimation method was used in the analysis. The scale reliability was examined based on Cronbach's alpha values, indicating that all the latent variables were beyond .70, which is the suggested guidance (Hair et al. 1998). As for scale validity, both convergent and discriminant validity of each latent variable were tested. Convergent validity was judged based on whether the factor loadings of all the items used in latent variables were significant (Anderson and Gerbing 1988) and whether each construct's average variance extracted (AVE) exceeded the ideal guidance of .50 (Fornell and Larcker 1981). Discriminant validity was confirmed based on whether the AVEs for each latent variable were greater than its squared correlation (ϕ^2) (Lichtenstein et al. 1990). The results showed that the samples used in the final analysis were successful in all validity tests. See Table 2 for all scale items and relevant checks.

3.3 Confirmatory Factor Analysis

Before performing the model estimation, the measurement models of each latent variable were tested using confirmatory factor analysis (CFA). While latent variables of "brand equity" and "perceived relationship investment (PRI)" showed

Table 2 Scale items with reliability and validity

Item	Standardized loading CNN	Standardized loading CBS	AVE CNN	AVE CBS	φ² CNN	φ² CBS
Brand equity (α = .92/.92)						
It makes sense to watch this channel instead of any other channels, even if they are the same	.84	.82	.79	.80	.00–.45	.01–.44
Even if another channel has the same features as this channel, I would prefer to watch this channel	.93	.96				
If there is another channel as good as this channel, I prefer to watch this one	.90	.89				
Perceived relationship investment (PRI) (α = .94/.95)						
This channel makes an effort to increase regular audiences' loyalty	.90	.94	.84	.86	.00–.40	.00–.38
This channel makes an effort to improve its tie with regular audiences	.95	.94				
This channel really cares about keeping regular audiences	.90	.90				
Relationship intention (α = .81/.85)						
I get involved in the process when I watch it	.89	.85	.79	.92	.00–.45	.00–.43
I get a great deal of satisfaction when I watch it	.92	.93				
I like to be identified as its audience	–	.90				
I do not care if the quality of the channel is below normal	.94	.98				
I do not care if the quality of the channel is below that of the competition	.92	.91				
I have my expectations about its content when I watch this channel	.80	.87				
I care about the quality of this channel	.87	.87				
When I think about stop watching this channel, I fear I might lose relationship with it	.90	.93				
When I think about stop watching this channel, I fear I might lose relationships with the people I interact with while watching it	.88	.90				

AVE average variance extracted. ϕ^2 = the squared ϕ correlation
All the coefficient values were significant at $p < .001$
In the reliability reports, the former indicates CNN, while the latter indicates CBS

proper model fits, the measure of relationship intention yielded an inadequate fit. Thus, Modification Indices (MI) were examined to find justifiable re-specification (Bagozzi 1983). Referring to the MI results, two items in "involvement for media brands" of CNN and one item for CBS were freed to estimate, while in both brands, the component of "feedback" consisting of two items were freed. Upon these modifications, goodness-of-fit indices were significantly improved (CNN: $\chi^2 (14) = 45.80, p < .001$, CFI = .98, NFI = .98, RMSEA = .08; CBS: $\chi^2 (21) = 68.67, p < .001$, CFI = .98, NFI = .97, RMSEA = .08).

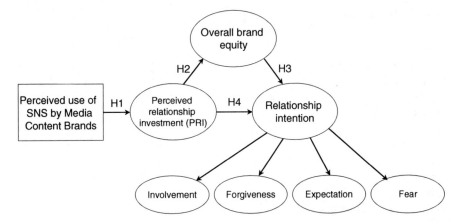

Fig. 1 Proposed model—the influence of perceived SNS use by media content brands

4 Results

Combining the re-specified measurement model, the SEM analysis was executed. All the model estimations based on the samples evaluating CNN and CBS showed goodness-of-fit indices, respectively (CNN: χ^2 (83) = 320.09, $p < .001$, CFI = .94, NFI = .93, RMSEA = .09; CBS: χ^2 (97) = 389.71, $p < .001$, CFI = .94, NFI = .921, RMSEA = .09). The significance of path coefficient values in the model suggested whether the proposed hypotheses were supported or not. The hypotheses testing results were reported in Table 3. As indicated by the SEM results, all the paths were significant as expected. Specifically, perceived use of SNSs significantly affected perceived relationship investment (PRI) in both media brands, supporting H1 ($\beta_{CNN} = .25$, $\beta_{CBS} = .34$) and brand equity served a role as a partial mediator between PRI and relationship intention, supporting H2 ($\beta_{CNN} = .58$, $\beta_{CBS} = .52$), H3 ($\beta_{CNN} = .55$, $\beta_{CBS} = .57$), and H4 ($\beta_{CNN} = .43$, $\beta_{CBS} = .41$). All the paths were significant at $p < .001$ and consistent for both CNN and CBS.

In summary, in the case of media content brands, consumer's perceived social network usage of both CNN and CBS is positively associated with the perceived relationship investment of CNN and CBS. In addition, consumers' perceived relationship investment of CNN and CBS is positively associated with the CBBE of CNN and CBS, which is positively associated with the consumer's intention to develop a relationship with the two brands. Finally, there is a direct relationship between a consumer's perceived relationship investment of CNN and CBS and his/her intention to build a relationship with the brands. One interesting difference between CNN and CBS is in the PRI measure of "forgiveness." While it was a significant component of PRI in CBS ($\beta = .14$, $p < .05$), it was not the case for CNN ($\beta = .07, p = .38$).

Table 3 Hypotheses testing

Hypotheses	Significance CNN	CBS
H1: Perceived use of SNS → PRI	.25***	.34***
H2: PRI → Brand equity	.57***	.52***
H3: Brand equity → Relationship intention	.55***	.57***
H4: PRI → Relationship intention	.43***	.41***
PRI		
→Involvement	.97***	.94***
→Forgiveness	.07	.14*
→Expectation	.88***	.83***
→Fear	.46***	.48***

PRI perceived relationship investment
*Significant at $p < .05$
***Significant at $p < .001$

Discussion and Conclusion

This study aimed to verify empirically the contribution of social networks as a branding tool for media products from the relational perspective. Based on a survey of national consumers in the United States, all four hypotheses about the branding benefits of social networks for media brands were supported. The tested model validated the value of social networks as a brand relationship marketing tool and the importance of brand equity in enhancing "relationship intention" between the viewers and media content brands such as CNN and CBS (CNN: $\beta_{indirect\_effect} = .36, p < .001$; CBS: $\beta_{indirect\_effect} = .31, p < .001$). Specifically, this study suggests a means of developing competitive advantages through an investment in better relationships with audiences utilizing the popular social medial such as social networks. While previous research has emphasized the importance of branding in relationship development and for intangible products, this study provides the first empirical validation on the value of relational branding in the context of media content brands, a product category that is high in ambiguity (in the brand evaluation process) and historically lacking a relational mechanism with its one-directional delivery of products.

Considering the trend toward audience fragmentation and diminishing loyalty, the growth of social media in revolutionizing the capability of media brands to develop relationships with its audiences provides a welcoming new direction for media branding. As the finding suggests, perceived relationship investment of a media brand not only contributes to its brand equity but also the audience's intension to establish a reciprocal relationship with the brand, making the investment a valuable marketing strategy in today's competitive media marketplace. In addition, the positive impact of CBBE on audiences' relationship intention illustrates the importance of media branding and the competitive advantage of established media brands in brand extensions. As suggested, there might even be a valuable synergistic effect in developing brand relationships with audiences via social networks for media content products because of the easy integration between social networks and media contents and the capability of social networks to connect audiences and content/ingredients of content, as well as providing contextual information for better enjoyment of the content.

This study has several limitations. First is its lack of generalizability to all members of the population considering the nature of online panel study. The survey used a panel sample who received small rewards upon their completion of survey, thus the respondents might not be representative of the general social network users and the results might be limited in external validity. Additional research is encouraged to replicate and confirm the findings with a more representative sample. The scale validity about "perceived relationship investment" is somewhat unclear as it produced inconsistent outcome for CNN and CBS for one of its dimensions. Further empirical tests on more media brands are suggested for this measure. The proposed model should also be tested on different media product categories or platforms such as newspapers or cable services. The degree of intangibility or platform specific characteristics might affect the model different. Finally, it is important to note that the effect of branding with social networks here was examined from the perspective of reciprocity and relationship, not variation in the content or design of social networks. In other words, the focus here is on the perceived "efforts" of a brand, not its message or platform variation. Future studies might investigate the effect of social networks or other social media platforms on branding outcomes by examining more media brands concurrently or in different combination, types, and content of social media marketing programs in the context of media brands.

References

Aaker, D. A. (1991). *Managing brand equity*. New York: The Free Press.

Ailawadi, K. L., Lehmann, D. R., & Neslin, A. S. (2003). Revenue premium as an outcome measure of brand equity. *Journal of Marketing, 67*(October), 1–17.

Anderson, J. C., & Gerbing, D. W. (1988). Structural equation modeling in practice: A review and recommended two-step approach. *Psychological Bulletin, 103*(3), 411–423.

Bagozzi, R. P. (1983). Issues in the application of covariance structure analysis: A future comment. *Journal of Consumer Research, 9*(4), 449–450.

Bagozzi, R. P. (1995). Reflections on relationship marketing in consumer markets. *Journal of the Academy of Marketing Science, 23*(4), 272–277.

Baker, T. L., Simpson, P. M., & Siguaw, J. A. (1999). The impact of suppliers' perceptions of reseller market orientation on key relationship constructs. *Journal of the Academy of Marketing Science, 27*, 50–57.

Brady, M. K., Bourdeau, B. L., & Heskel, J. (2005). The importance of brand cues in intangible service industries: An application to investment services. *Journal of Services Marketing, 19*(6), 401–410.

Burnham, T. A., Frels, J. K., & Mahajan, V. (2003). Consumer switching costs: A typology, antecedents, and consequences. *Journal of the Academy of Marketing Science, 31*(2), 109–126.

Cone Business in Social Media Research (September 25, 2008). *Cone finds that Americans expect companies to have a presence in social media.* Retrieved November 10, 2009 from http://www.coneinc.com/content1182.

De Wulf, K., Odekerken-Schroder, G., & Iacobucci, D. (2001). Investments in consumer relationships: A cross-country and cross-industry exploration. *Journal of Marketing, 65*(4), 33–50.

Deutskens, E., Jong, A., Ruyter, K., & Wetzels, M. (2006). Comparing the generalizability of online and mail surveys in cross-national service quality research. *Marketing Letters, 17*(2), 119–136.

eMarketer. (June 24, 2011). *Social media marketing brings new revenues, customers.* Retrieved July 15, 2011, from http://www.emarketer.com/Article.aspx?R=1008459.

Fornell, C., & Larcker, D. F. (1981). Structural equation model with unobservable variables and measurement error: Algebra and statistics. *Journal of Marketing Research, 18*(3), 382–389.

Fournier, S. (1998). Consumers and their brands: developing relationship theory in consumer research. *Journal of Consumer Research, 24*(4), 343–73.

Hair, J. F., Anerson, R. E., Tatham, R. L., & Black, W. C. (1998). *Multivariate data analysis* (5th ed.). Upper Saddle River, NJ: Prentice Hall.

Harvard Business Review Analytics Service Report. (2010). *The new conversation: Taking social media from talk to action.* Boston, MA: Harvard Business Publishing.

Keller, K. L. (1993). Conceptualizing, measuring, and managing customer-based brand equity. *The Journal of Marketing, 57*, 1–22.

Keller, K. L. (2002). Branding and brand equity. In B. Weitz & R. Wensley (Eds.), *Handbook of marketing* (pp. 151–178). London, UK: Sage.

Keller, K. L. (2003). *Measuring, and managing brand equity* (2nd ed.). Upper Saddle River, NJ: Prentice Hall.

Keller, K. L., & Lehmann, D. R. (2006). Brands and branding: Research findings and future priorities. *Marketing Science, 25*(6), 740–759.

Kumar, V., Bohling, T. R., & Ladda, R. N. (2003). Antecedents and consequences of relationship intention: Implications for transaction and relationship marketing. *Industrial Marketing Management, 32*, 667–676.

Lichtenstein, D. R., Netemeyer, R. G., & Burton, S. (1990). Distinguishing coupon proneness from value consciousness: An acquisition-transaction utility theory perspective. *Journal of Marketing, 54*(3), 54–67.

Morgan, R. M., & Hunt, S. D. (1994). The commitment–trust theory of relationship marketing. *Journal of Marketing, 58*, 20–38.

Murray, K. B., & Schlacter, J. L. (1990). The impact of services versus goods on consumer's assessment of perceived risk and variability. *Journal of the Academy of Marketing Science, 18*(1), 51–65.

Reinstein, D. A., & Snyder, C. M. (2005). The influence of expert reviews on consumer demand for experience goods: A case study of movie critics. *The Journal of Industrial Economics, 53*(1), 27–51.

Smith, J. B., & Barclay, D. W. (1997). The effects of organizational differences and trust on the effectiveness of selling partner relationships. *Journal of Marketing, 6*(1), 3–21.

Tsai, J. (2009). Marketing and social media: Everyone's social (Already). *CRM Magazine, 13*(6), 34–38.

Tsotsis, A. (December 29, 2010). *Hitwise: Facebook overtakes google to become most visited website in 2010. Techcrunch.* Retrieved July 15, 2011, from http://techcrunch.com/2010/12/29/hitwise-facebook-overtakes-google-to-become-most-visited-website-in-2010/.

Turley, L. M., & Moore, P. A. (1995). Brand name strategies in the service sector. *Journal of Consumer Marketing, 12*(4), 42–50.

Virtrue (2009). *The virtue 100: Top social brands of 2009*. Retrieved January 10, 2010, from http://vitrue.com/blog/2010/01/04/the-vitrue-100-top-social-brands-of-2009/.
Wang, C.-H., Hsu, L.-C., & Fang, S.-R. (2009). Constructing a relationship-based brand equity model. *Service Business, 3*(3), 275–292.
Williamson, D. A. (November, 2009). PGs and social media: Much more than advertising. *eMarketer*. Retrieved January 6, 2010, from http://www.emarketer.com/Reports/All/Emarketer_2000620.aspx.
Wimmer, R. D., & Dominick, J. R. (2006). *Mass media research: An introduction* (38th ed.). Belmont, CA: Wadsworth.
Yoo, B., & Donthu, N. (2001). Developing and validating a multidimensional consumer-based brand equity scale. *Journal of Business Research, 52*(April), 1–14.
Yoon, D., Choi, S. M., & Sohn, D. (2008). Building customer relationships in an electronic age: The role of interactivity of e-commerce web sites. *Psychology and Marketing, 25*(7), 602–618.

Social Media Involvement Among College Students and General Population: Implications to Media Management

Louisa Ha and Xiao Hu

The past decade witnessed the evolution of social network sites (SNS). From the first recognizably dedicated modern social network site SixDegrees.com established in 1997 (Boyd and Ellison 2007; Chapman 2009; Donath and Boyd 2004) to the rapidly expanding and the most popular SNS Facebook (Hampton et al. 2011), SNS have been constantly improved in terms of new features and applications (apps). However, the rapid development of SNS also accompanies with problems and controversies. The increase of controversial issues, such as privacy (Boyd 2008; Cain 2008; Chew et al. 2008; Huffaker and Calvert 2005; Barnes 2006), online bullying (Boyd 2008), trolling (Ybarra and Mitchell 2008), and other potential misuse, etc., are on a constant rise, along with the debate on sustainable growth in social network services.

SNS have become the most influential online medium and promptly conquered the Internet world. Nearly 1.2 billion people around the world, 82 % of the world's online population, are SNS users. SNS are no longer young people's activity but are attracting all age segments, especially the older people (ComScore 2011). According to Nielsen's (2010) report, Americans spent the most time on SNS among online activities. Moreover, the percentage of time spent on SNS kept increasing by 43 % from 2009 to 2010. Since the dominating power of SNS online and their popularity worldwide, the media industry started to integrate the social media into the TV networks.

1 Social TV, Transmedia and Intermedia

With the birth of the first social TV network, *Youtoo*, the dawn of intermedia is approaching. Social TV is the combination of social media and TV networks that allows viewers to interact with each other about the relevant topics of TV shows in

---

L. Ha (✉) • X. Hu
Bowling Green State University, Bowling Green, OH, USA
e-mail: louisah@bgsu.edu

the context of watching TV shows. To engage their audience in the TV programs, TV networks take advantage of the nature of SNS and combine them with their own TV networks to build up a new compelling platform as social TV network. The successful stories in industry have verified the potential of the new platform. In addition, TV networks are trying to use the social media technology to drive their TV ratings. In this fall, with the help of massive social buzz, Fox's "The X Factor" ranked number one show among the new series in this fall; also, BET's "Born to Dance: Launeann Gibson," ranked the top five which was attributed to the huge social-media response (Dumenco 2011). In addition, the significance of real-time participation when the shows are on the air has been realized. TV producers encourage such audience participation because the social buzz from viewers provides not only quantitative data such as how many fans are watching; but also delivers qualitative data, such as the main concerns of viewers and who are the key influencers around hot topics, to TV networks (Hsia 2010). The real-time participation empowers the audience and makes the interaction between audiences on SNS and TV producers become a transmedia conversation.

Intermedia is the use of social TV and transmedia (Liebling 2011). The intermedia strategy helps TV producers better know the needs of audiences through interaction. Then, the TV producers can create the content in which audiences are interested; and in turn, the interest in content drives the TV ratings and reputations. It seems like a virtuous circle for TV industry. The intermedia strategy has been recognized in industry. Take the recent successful cases for example, ESPN integrates Twitter, Facebook, and YouTube with its NFL32 programming; Spike TV is powering a live feedback loop for *Deadliest Warrior*, in which the audience's interactions with the show's hosts will alter the show's outcome (Liebling 2011).

2   Growth of Social Media

To assess the impact of SNS on the media industry for media managers, it is important to understand the nature of the medium. Scholars have engaged in relevant SNS research from interdisciplinary perspectives, such as psychology (Magnuson and Dundes 2008; Muise et al. 2009), sociology (Lewis and George 2008; Skog 2005), communication (Johnson et al. 2009; Utz 2010; Valkenburg and Peter 2008), and even law (Hodge 2006). Although the wordings of the definition of SNS vary according to different scholars, a consensus emerged that SNS shares these same characteristics: SNS is an online social medium (Boyd and Ellison 2007; Constantinides et al. 2008; Tredinnick 2006) where people can (1) create their personal profiles, (2) contact others, and (3) exchange comments, information, or thoughts (Barker 2009; Boyd and Ellison 2007; Constantinides and Fountain 2008). These three basic features and other newly developed features and apps (e.g. Newsfeed, group, posting apps, and game apps) attract millions of users worldwide. They not only help users to maintain the existing networks, but also facilitate users to initiate new connections among people who have common interests (Boyd and Ellison 2007; Cliff et al. 2006; Donath and Boyd 2004; Ellison et al. 2006, 2007;

Lampe et al. 2007). Although researchers recognize the various features and apps of SNS, they have not critically examined and analyzed strengths and limitations of SNS as a mass medium.

One of the biggest reasons for the scholarly and public interest in SNS is that SNS attracts huge number of users in a short period of time. It has taken Facebook only 6 years to grow into a giant that had 500 million active users in 2010, which is about one person for every 14 in the world (Helft and Wortham 2010). The users of SNS have nearly doubled since 2008 (Keith et al. 2011). And now the active users of Facebook increased by 300 million in only 1 year from 2010 to 2011 (Facebook 2011). Constantinides et al. (2010) differentiated the passive and active users of SNS by the activities they did in SNS. Passive users did fewer activities than the active SNS users or they merely updated their SNS pages. Heavy and light users were distinguished based on their time use (Ellison et al. 2007; Fang and Ha 2011; Pew Research Center 2011). Nevertheless, these studies all categorized SNS users by only a single variable, such as either time use or motivation to participate. In this present book chapter, we conceptualized a new term combining both motivation and time use dimensions to categorize SNS users and examine the behaviors of different types of SNS users based on their involvement level.

3   Purpose of Study

The purpose of the study in this chapter is to bridge the gaps in the examination of SNS use and compare the SNS behaviors of college students (an important group of SNS users) and the general population to shed light on how to attract new audiences and keep existing audience against competition for media management. We began by articulating characteristics of SNS as a mass medium and discussing the attributes and limitations of SNS. Then, based on the motivation and time use dimensions, we proposed a new concept of SNS involvement to measure the degree to which SNS users indulge in social media. Relevant socio-demographic variables, which might predict SNS involvement and help media managers to identify the target audiences in SNS, were tested. Then we compared the SNS activities, other online activities and topic preference of users with different levels of SNS involvement. The implications of different social media consumption behavior of different SNS involvement groups were discussed. Moreover, it is worthy to mention that we employed both college students and general population data when testing these relationships and made comparisons between the two different populations. The extensive data revealed different populations have different social media use behaviors, which have different implications to media management.

4 Strengths and Weaknesses of SNS as Mass Media

Generally, personal profile, friend list, instant messaging, and bulletin boards/postings ("walls") are recognized as main features of SNS. With the development of SNS, new features and apps are developed as new functions of SNS, such as customization of users' profiles, posting, individual private settings, and game apps. We identified five basic attributes of SNS which explains its success as a mass medium:

1. Social networks creation. Dated back to its precursors (e.g. BBS), the original purpose of SNS is let users log on to interact with one another (Chapman 2009). At the early stage, people who interacted with each other on SNS were almost anonymous and created new networks with each other. Even now, through some search channels (e.g. By name, by e-mail address, by school, by city, by interests, by keyword, or just browse without membership to find "friends" one is interested in), people can search "friends" who share the same interests with them, or with whom they want to make friends. Furthermore, one can also create new social networks and make friends with strangers through the common "friends" they both have. Thus, social networks creation is a basic attribute of SNS.
2. Social networks maintenance. Studies have shown that people were not necessarily initiating relationships, or looking for their new friends on SNS. Rather, they primarily maintained their existing relationships with their friends (Boyd and Ellison 2007). A report from Pew Research Center (Keith et al. 2011) revealed that Facebook users seem to have a larger number of close ties than users of other SNS, which means Facebook is maintaining intimacy and networks. According to the report, high school friends are the main type of friends in the social networks on SNS, while only a fraction of friends are strangers or people whom users have never met. Compared to 29 % SNS users who used SNS to contact all their close networks, the number this year increases to 40 %. SNS is more likely to be used to maintain the close social networks. Similarly, scholars argued that the popularity of MySpace depends on how the site assisted social interaction among preexisting friends (Boyd 2008), Young people primarily use social network sites for articulating and developing their existing social relationships (Robards 2010).
3. Expandability. The original features of friend list, personal profile, and instant messaging of SNS, have expanded to include News Feeds, e-mail service, posting apps, game apps, and joining groups. SNS have constantly improved beyond the original functionality to strengthen themselves. We have seen the enormous potential of SNS in adding more features and apps to improve and promote themselves. Such continuing evolution of the SNS is one of the major factors accounting for their success as a mass medium.
4. Sharing. The sharing attribute can also be considered as a unique feature of SNS. Posting, forwarding, and the News Feeds features of SNS are unique sharing features. Users can post whatever they want on their personal wall through the posting feature. The News Feeds feature, launched on Sep 5, 2006 by Facebook,

enabled users to see a start page upon logging in with all acts undertaken by their friends (Boyd 2008). With the help of News Feeds, users can share stuff they want with their friends on SNS. Then, by forwarding the contents posted on SNS by friends, users can spread and share the contents with their own friends on SNS.
5. Identifiability of the user. Although the identifiability of the user varies depending on the types of SNS, in general, users are required to use real names and they were encouraged to upload identifiable photos to represent their profiles on SNS (Gross and Acquisti 2005). Especially, when the mainstream SNS, like Facebook, try to connect the users' profiles with their public identities, the identifiability of users becomes a significant attribute of SNS. The identifiability attribute enables SNS to obtain lots of information about users and their networks, which also raises concerns about privacy issues on SNS. Such attribute also differentiates them from other online media such as online communities or Second Life.

Despite all these attributes of SNS, there are two major limitations of SNS as a mass medium:
1. Privacy divulgation. Privacy violation is the primary focus of scholarship on SNS. Since real names and personal information of users are used in profiles, privacy invasion and public exposure inevitably happened. Scholars (Chew et al. 2008) considered that users' privacy also could be compromised by the following three areas, (1) exposing users' activity to unanticipated audiences, (2) automatically sending linking and e-mails without approval of users, and (3) digging up relative social networks to amalgamate users' social graph. Additionally, many scholars (Barnes 2006; Gross and Acquisti 2005; Livingstone 2008; Lenhart and Madden 2008; Lewis et al. 2008) paid attention to teens' privacy-protection on SNS. These studies examined personal information exposure among teens, from which arose privacy evasion and its potential harm to teens. The increase of abuses such as privacy invasion issues, online bullying, and potential misuse, are also potential limitations of SNS. Fully 32 % of online teens have been contacted by someone with no connection to them or any of their friends, and 7 % of online teens say they have felt scared or uncomfortable as a result of contact by an online stranger (Pew Research Center's Internet and American Life Project 2007) and the potential for online bullying (Boyd 2008). However, some scholars argued that privacy invasion on social network sites is the "privacy paradox" when considering the public nature of SNS (Barnes 2006; Stutzman 2006). Users are worried about their privacy, but at the same time they put detailed personal information on their profiles (Utz and Krämer 2009).
2. Information fragmentation. The attribute of fragmentation of SNS is originated from computer science. Fragmentation refers to a problem in computer storage. Since computers storage is randomly used when users saved some information; such randomness is inefficient and reduces the storage capability, and lowers the performance of computers. In a similar fashion, people received random unclassified information from their friends on SNS, which resulted in information fragmentation of SNS. When the random information is too much to clean, it

will reduce the efficiency of finding the necessary information. Moreover, in a fast-pace society people are more likely to be attracted by the highlighted and short information instead of the long extensive articles. This trend is also demonstrated on SNS, which are full of short updated statuses or highlighted postings. The limitation of Facebook posting to 400 characters and Twitter to 140 characters resulted in more fragmentation. In this case, people's capability of thinking deeply and logically decreases, even if their ability of processing large amounts of information in a short time increases.

5   SNS Involvement

To better understand SNS users, previous research clustered SNS users by the active or passive activities of users on SNS. From a psychological perspective, Alarcón-Del-Amo et al. (2011) classified active and passive users according to their activities on SNS. Likewise, in the study of Constantinides et al. (2010), they believed active SNS users had more activities in SNS, such as updating, communicating, and searching, than the passive users. According to the proportion of different activities on SNS, SNS users were grouped as "beginners," "habitual users," "outstanding users," and "expert users." Also, many studies classified SNS users by time variables (Ellison et al. 2007; Fang and Ha 2011; Pew Research Center 2011). The frequency of updating status decreases from the young to old. In addition, most young people spent nearly 25 % of their time online on SNS (Nielsen 2010). Younger SNS users were more likely to be heavy users because of higher proportion and more time spent on SNS. However, these previous studies examined SNS users only from one aspect, either activities or time variables and not both. We believed a better understanding of SNS users should be based on both motivation and time use. SNS involvement is a concept should be used to categorize the users and measure the impact of SNS because when activities are only used to categorize SNS users, the time spent on SNS was ignored; people who did many SNS activities might be only active users, but we did not know if they were also heavy users who spent much time on SNS as well. Likewise, people who spent much time on SNS only can be counted as heavy users; they might be passive users, who merely viewed postings on their SNS pages without update their own information. Thus, based on this analysis, we employed a new concept of SNS involvement that combined activity and time dimensions together to examine SNS users.

Before we further discuss about social network sites involvement (SNS involvement), we should first clarify the definition of involvement. According to consumer behavior research, involvement refers to "a person's perceived relevance of the object based on their inherent needs, values, and interests" (Zaichkowsky 1985). Since involvement is the motivation to process information (Mithchell 1979), and motivation of information processing can range from inertia to passion (Solomon 2002), so involvement includes many aspects. The first aspect of involvement is "product involvement," which is related to the level of consumers' interests in a particular product. The second one is "message-response involvement," which referred to consumers' reaction to a particular product marketing communications. And the last one denoted differences occurred when buying the same object for different contexts (Solomon 2002). The range from cognitive and mental reaction to behavior reaction clearly marks the different level of involvement. Clancy (1992) argued that, the more an audience was involved with a television show, the more positively s/he would respond to the commercial contained in that show. He indicated involvement in the shows and its commercial spots would exert great influence on his or her purchase intentions and behaviors. Hence highly involved SNS users are those most valuable to advertisers and organizations that use SNS for promotion. We measured SNS involvement in terms of time consumption (behavior variable) and the frequency of respondents' update (motivation variable). We believe frequency of update is a good indicator of how much the individual care about the site and the strength of motivation to use the site. If the individual updates his/her own SNS page very frequently, it means he/she want to share with people immediately on the activities or information and cannot wait for long. But if the person hardly updates the SNS page, he/she does not see the page as a major communication medium between him/her and his/her own social network. SNS are not seen as important to the person.

Additionally, it is important to clarify the difference between SNS use and SNS involvement. As addressed above, SNS involvement does not only include the time spent on SNS, but also embraces SNS users' activities especially how important is the SNS to the user. However, SNS use could refer to an individual just spending time on viewing the content on SNS but posting nothing on SNS or participate in other activities as a passive user.

6 Research Hypotheses

Previous research has demonstrated that socio-demographic variables predict SNS use. Younger people use SNS more than older people (Pfeil et al. 2008). Almost all the young people (18–19) use SNS (95.1 %); while only 37.0 % of people aged more than 30 do so (Salaway et al. 2008). According to data from Pew Research Center's Internet and American Life Project (2005, 2011), social network use among Internet users aged 18–29 grew from 12 % to 86 %, meanwhile aged 50–64 and 65+ grew respectively from 5 % to 47 % and from 5 % to 23 %. Although young adults continue to be the largest group of social network site users, older users are becoming a new point for membership growth. To fully understand the use of SNS, we employed two different populations in collecting the data to test the relationships between socio-demographic variables and SNS involvement. Based on that, we advanced the first hypothesis based on age:

▶ **H1**: The higher the age, the lower the SNS involvement in general population.

Moreover, SNS use varies also by gender, racial, and socioeconomic variables (Cooper and Weaver 2003; DiMaggio et al. 2004; Hargittai 2008b; Junco et al. 2010; Kaiser Family Foundation 2004). Although previous study suggested there were more females using SNS than males (Constantinides et al. 2010; Fang and Ha 2011), some other studies found males spent more time than females on SNS (Aghazamani 2010). We posited that females are likely to have higher SNS involvement because they are usually more emotional and more attached to the medium than males. Such stronger female involvement in SNS should be across different populations.

▶ **H2a:** Females are more likely to have higher SNS involvement than males among college students.

▶ **H2b:** Females are more likely to have higher SNS involvement than males among general population.

Also, from a racial perspective, Hargittai (2008a) found Latino students were less likely to use Facebook than Caucasians; and students whose family were higher educated were more likely to use Facebook than those whose family were lower educated. The finding contradicted with the national study of college students of Ha et al. (2012). They found that minority students significantly used more online videos than non-minority college students because they were not served well in the mainstream media so that they had to look for alternatives online. Fang and Ha's (2011) study of SNS also found high use of SNS by minority college students. In addition, education level may be a useful predictor of SNS use because heavy entertainment media users typically are low education people or students with lower academic performance. A recent study of college students' academic performance and Facebook use controlling prior academic ability show that students with lower grade point averages are more likely to be heavy users (Junco 2012). If SNS is an important entertainment medium, lower education users should be more likely to be involved. Based on previous research, we included ethnicity and education level of the general population as predictors of SNS involvement. But we did not include income as a predictor because none of the previous studies of social media use found income as a significant predictor. So the third and fourth sets of hypotheses were formulated below:

▶ **H3a:** Minority students are more likely to have higher SNS involvement than Caucasians among college students.

▶ **H3b:** Minority populations are more likely to have higher SNS involvement than Caucasians among general population.

▶ **H4:** The higher the education level, the lower the SNS involvement of general population.

In addition, research on Internet use have shown that early Internet adopters are more likely to appreciate the various benefits of Internet than late adopters and more likely to displace the traditional media with the Internet (Ha and Fang 2012). The early adopters of SNS might be more familiar with the utility value of SNS and would probably develop dependency on SNS and increase their involvement in the medium.

▶ **H5a**. The more years of experience in SNS, the higher the SNS involvement of college students.

▶ **H5b**. The more years of experience in SNS, the higher the SNS involvement of general population.

Fang and Ha's (2011) study of college students showed that those who used SNS for socialization gratifications and had higher number of friends were more likely to use SNS. Because social networking is the main function of SNS, those who try to use SNS to expand their social networks rather than maintaining their existing networks should be more involved in SNS.

▶ **H6a**: The higher the number of friends (network size), the higher the SNS involvement of college students.

▶ **H6b**: The higher the number of friends (network size), the higher the SNS involvement of general population.

Moreover, people have social networks both offline and online. Previous research (e.g., Boyd 2008) has shown that social network use is an extension and often a reinforcement of the individual's offline network. People with high community participation have a larger social network size offline and may have a higher need to use social media to keep up with their offline network. Hence we also hypothesized that individual's community participation will positively predict on the SNS involvement of both the students and the general population.

▶ **H7a**. The higher the community participation, the higher the SNS involvement of general population.

▶ **H7b**. The higher the community participation, the higher the SNS involvement of the college students.

Furthermore, one important research topic on SNS is its commercial value. Considering the low cost to reach the vast number of customers, SNS is regarded as a potential powerful marketing tool or platform for both the industry and the academia (Alarcón-del-Amo et al. 2011; Constantinides et al. 2010; Newman 2011; The Economist 2007). A lot of research has demonstrated that the word-of-mouth marketing is more effective and persuasive in affecting purchase intentions and behaviors of costumers, as people are more likely to trust word-of-mouth communication (Katz and Lazarsfeld 1955; Wilson and Sherrell 1993). SNS is really like virtual online community; and the information disseminated on SNS is really like the virtual word-of-mouse. Based on this, users can freely share, edit, and post information about business, product, or service; even they can create online group/community to spread and interact the business information if they would like to. Some scholars tried to study SNS as marketing platform starting from classifying SNS users by their activities on SNS to get insights into market (Alarcón-del-Amo et al. 2011; Constantinides et al. 2010). Therefore, at this point we were considering if SNS users' SNS use activities are related to SNS involvement; we need to know SNS users' other online activities and topic preferences; and their implications to media management. The corresponding research questions were formulated below:

▶ **RQ1.** Are there differences between high and low SNS involvement in the use of SNS, online activities, and topic preference?

▶ **RQ2.** Do these differences exist in both college students and general population?

7 Research Method

7.1 Sampling and Procedure

This study is based on a mail and self-administered survey in Northwest Ohio area from September 15 to November 25, 2011. Respondents could choose to respond to the web version of the survey. There were two sampling frames for this study to cover all spectrums of the population: (1) Northwest Ohio resident database supplied by a local newspaper, and (2) college students in a large Northwest Ohio public university, Bowling Green State University. College students were separate from the general population sample because college students typically are not reachable through regular household addresses but they are a highly desirable target audience for advertisers and heavy users of social media.

For Northwest Ohio residents, a simple random sample selected from the Northwest Ohio residents database (n = 1,500) were sent the questionnaire package with a cover letter, a visually attractive questionnaire booklet, and a stamped reply envelope with a fresh one dollar bill as incentive for participation, following the Tailored Design Method suggested by Dillman (2007). The non-respondents of the first mailing were sent a postcard reminder three weeks from the initial contact. For college students, the student sample was recruited from 32 small size general education classes and three introductory large lecture classes, which ensured wide range of majors and class standings. Students received extra credit for participating in the study. A total 660 responses were received, of which 215 were from Northwest Ohio residents and 445 were from college students.

The survey, which took approximately 15 min to complete, focused on the respondents' use and opinion of various media. There were two types of variables related to this research. The first group of questions measured the media usage variables with specific reference to social media. The second group of questions measured demographic variables such as age, gender, household income, education level, community participation and Internet experience.

7.2 Measures

Socio-demographic Characteristics. Age, gender, ethnicity, and education are four main social-demographic characteristics we examined as predictors of SNS involvement for general population. Age was measured by an open-ended response in which respondents filled out their age in number; gender was measured by a nominal question in which respondents could check the options that applied; likewise, ethnicity was also measured by a nominal question. Education was measured in six different levels from Grade 8 or less to attended or completed graduate school.

SNS Involvement. To measure SNS involvement, the respondents were asked to check how frequently they update their social network page. Seven items were presented in this question: (1) several times an hour; (2) every several hours; (3) everyday; (4) once to several times a week; (5) between once a week and once a month; (6) less than once a month; (7) hardly ever update. We grouped the seven items into three levels—first three items as high level, item four and five as medium level, and the last two items were viewed as low level. SNS involvement was computed as the product of the time spent on social network sites and the update frequency level. Additionally, we took the median of SNS involvement as the cut-off point to determine high and low involvement groups because of the highly skewed distribution of the involvement score.

SNS Activities. We measured users' SNS activities they did on SNS. The respondents were asked if they did anything below on SNS: (1) post news content from other news media; (2) link to other media sites; (3) read news posted on the site; (4) regularly follow Twitter or Facebook newsfeed for breaking news, (5) play game. The activities level was measured by summing up all the activities that respondents checked.

Network Size and Experience in Social Media. The network size was measured by an open-ended question, in which respondents were required to fill out the numbers of their friends on their SNS page. The experience in social media was measured by asking the respondents how many years that they have used SNS.

Topic Preference. Respondents were asked to check the topics that they are interested. A multiple response list of 11 topics were given for them to choose.

Community Participation. Community participation was an 11-item scale. Eight items were based prior research on community participation (Campbell and Kwak 2010) and three additional items including voting in an election, creating awareness of something they care about and reporting a local event to local news media. The

Table 1 Profile of respondents

		College students (N = 445)	General population (N = 215)
Gender	Male	35.6 %	−41.1 %
	Female	64.4 %	−58.9 %
Age	18–25	99.8 %	6.1 %
	26–30	0.2 %	4.1 %
	31–49	N/A	22.5 %
	50+	N/A	−67.3 %
Ethnicity	Caucasian	80.0 %	88.9 %
	African–American	12.8 %	5.3 %
	Hispanic	2.4 %	2.9 %
	Asian	2.1 %	−1.4 %
	Native American	N/A	−1.0 %
	Other	2.6 %	−0.5 %
Annual household income	Under US $ 30,000	58.4 %	28.5 %
	$30,001–$60,000	12.2 %	31.6 %
	$60,001–$90,000	13.9 %	18.1 %
	$90,001–$150,000	10.7 %	16.1 %
	Over $150,000	4.9 %	5.7 %
Time spent on SNS per week (in hour)	Mean (SD)	6.6 (6.3)	2.2 (5.5)
Time spent online per week (in hour)	Mean (SD)	29.8 (33.5)	14.8 (14.3)
Frequency of updating SNS	Several times an hour	4.6 %	1.0 %
	Every several hours	24.3 %	7.6 %
	Once everyday	18.9 %	8.6 %
	Once to several times a week	32.5 %	13.3 %
	Between once a week and once a month	11.4 %	18.1 %
	Less than once a month	2.9 %	8.6 %
	Hardly ever update	5.3 %	42.9 %

Note: Missing data were excluded from the analysis

reliability of the scale was high for both students (Cronbach's alpha = 0.83) and the general population (Cronbach's alpha = 0.81).

8 Results

Respondent Profile. Among 215 cases of general population (a response rate of 18.6 % after excluding the undeliverable mails), 74 (43.8 %) did not use SNS; while for 445 students, only 11 (2.6 %) were not SNS users. The respondent profiles of college students and general population were shown in Table 1. On average, college students spent much more time on the Internet and SNS than general population did,

Table 2 Regression analysis predicting SNS involvement

	College students (N = 365)	General population (N = 116)
	Beta	Beta
Gender	0.070	0.147
Age	–	−0.112
Ethnicity	−0.005	−0.050
Education level	–	−0.043
SNS use experience	0.167*	0.306*
SNS network size	0.153*	−0.060
Community participation	0.064	−0.149
Adjust R^2	0.061	0.151

Note: Missing data were excluded
Significant at the 0.05 level (2-tailed)
*Significant at the 0.01 level (2-tailed)

which is consistent with previous research finding that young people are heavy users of the Internet and SNS. Additionally, college student updated their SNS page more frequently than general population did; nearly half of the general population respondents never update their SNS. The results are reasonable when looking at the age ranges of the general population sample in the table: 67.3 % was comprised by people aged 50 or more.

Predictors of SNS Involvement. To test the hypotheses we advanced, multiple regression analyses were run respectively for the college students and the general population. H1 predicted that the age and SNS involvement of general population were negatively related: older people have lower SNS involvement. A bivariate correlation shows that age indeed negatively predicted SNS involvement ($r = 0.43$, $p < 0.01$). But after controlling the other variables in the regression, the age variable becomes insignificant. Thus, H1 was only supported without controlling the other variables.

H2a posited that females had higher SNS involvement than males did among college students. Table 2 shows that gender had an effect on SNS involvement at 0.05 level in one-tailed test ($t = 1.76$, $p = 0.04$). However, when the gender variable was controlled in the regression, the effect of gender was lowered to an insignificant level. This hypothesis was only supported without controlling the other variables.

H2b tried to found the relationship between gender and SNS involvement corresponding to the general population. The difference between gender was more pronounced in the general population ($t = 3.74$, $p < 0.01$). Females were more likely to have higher SNS involvement than males. However, when the other variables were controlled, the effect of gender attenuated. So H2b was only supported without controlling the other variables.

H3a and H3b predicted the minority had more SNS involvement than the Caucasian. However, the results did not support the two hypotheses in both the student population ($t = 0.31$, n.s.) and the general population ($t = 0.31$, n.s.).

Table 3 SNS activities by SNS involvement

SNS activities	College students (N = 410)		General population (N = 172)	
	Low	High	Low	High
Post news content from other news media	37.8 %	62.2 %*	5.3 %	94.7 %*
Link to other media sites	39.9 %	60.1 %*	13.6 %	86.4 %*
Read news posted on the site	46.7 %	53.3 %	4.2 %	95.8 %*
Play games	40.0 %	60.0 %*	5.6 %	94.4 %*
Follow twitter or Facebook newsfeed for breaking news	39.3 %	60.7 %*	5.9 %	94.1 %*

Note: Missing data were excluded
*Significant at the 0.01 level (2-tailed)

H4 proposed that education level had effect on SNS involvement of the general population. Our result indicated that there was no relation between education level and SNS involvement among the general population ($r = 0.02$, n.s.). Thus, H4 was rejected.

H5a and H5b predicted the effect of SNS use experience on SNS involvement of college students and the general population respectively. The results in Table 2 confirmed the two hypotheses. Both the SNS use experience of college students and the general population is positively related to their SNS involvement when controlling the other variables. Thus, H5a and H5b were strongly supported.

H6a and H6b examined the relationship between network size and SNS involvement correspondingly among the college students and the general population. For H6a, the result indicated that the network size of the college students had a positive effect on their SNS involvement ($r = 0.16$, $p < 0.01$) the hypothesis was supported. Network size also was positively correlated to SNS involvement among the general population ($r = 0.33$, $p < 0.01$). However, network size had no effect on the general population's SNS involvement. So after controlling the other variables, only H6a was supported but H6b was not fully supported.

H7a and H7b examined the relationship between community participation and SNS involvement. To our surprise, community involvement did not significantly predict SNS involvement both in bivarate correlations and in the regression analysis. Notably, community participation even negatively predicted SNS involvement in the general population (beta $= -0.06$, n.s.). Both 7a and 7b were rejected.

The overall prediction of SNS involvement using socio-demographic variables was not high. For college students, only 6 % of the variance can be explained by the variables. The result is better in the general population with 15 % of the variances explained by the socio-demographic variables.

SNS Activities of High and Low SNS Involvement Individuals. The first research question examined whether there were differences between high and low SNS involvement in the use of SNS, online activities, and topic preference. As shown above for the college students in Table 3, the students who had high SNS involvement were average 1.5 times more than those who had low SNS involvement in doing such these SNS activities: (1) posting news content on SNS from other news

Table 4 Online activities by SNS involvement

Online activities (times per month)	College students (N = 410)			General population (N = 172)		
	Mean scores		t	Mean scores		t
	Low	High		Low	High	
Post videos made by myself or people I know	0.31	0.74	−2.317*	0.00	0.28	−2.697**
Post video from other sites	1.96	4.08	−2.306*	0.12	2.26	−1.650
Post pictures taken by myself or people I know	3.05	9.23	−3.544**	0.51	3.45	−4.069**
Post pictures from other sites	1.29	4.32	−1.917***	0.10	2.27	−1.665
Participate in e-mail opinion/poll/ratings or questions	0.45	1.18	1.122	0.41	0.19	0.933
Post product reviews	0.14	0.16	−0.181	0.09	1.51	−1.080
Post comments/suggestions	5.36	20.22	−2.683**	0.25	6.94	−3.204**
Participate in contests	0.22	0.35	−0.973	1.04	0.69	0.434
Add entry to collaborative content sites (e.g. Wikipedia)	0.04	0.10	−1.028	0.00	0.03	−1.426
Forward or discuss online news content to friends via twitter or Facebook, etc.	1.52	5.69	−3.099**	0.12	3.82	−2.135*

Note: Missing data were excluded
*Significant at the 0.05 level (2-tailed)
**Significant at the 0.01 level (2-tailed)
***Significant at the 0.05 level (1-tailed)

media; (2) linking to other media sites; (3) regularly following Twitter or Facebook for breaking news. They also significantly played more games than lower SNS involvement users. The results demonstrated that college students who had high SNS involvement were more likely to do a variety of SNS activities.

The difference is even more pronounced in the general population data in Table 3, we found the same result that people who had high SNS involvement were more likely to have activities on SNS. Moreover, the difference between high SNS involvement in SNS activities among the general population was remarkably larger than that of the college students. The people who had high SNS involvement had many times more than those who had low SNS involvement in SNS activities.

SNS Involvement and Online Activities. According to Table 4, college students with high SNS involvement were more likely to post more video/pictures made/taken by themselves or people they knew than those with low SNS involvement. Moreover, high SNS involvement among college students also posted more video/pictures online from other sites. It should be noted that the difference between high and low SNS involvement in posting pictures from other sites was significant only under one-tailed t tests. Furthermore, students with high SNS involvement were more likely to post more comments/suggestions and discuss and forward more online news content to friends via SNS. There were no differences between high and low SNS involvement in participating in e-mail opinion/polls/ratings or

Table 5 Topic preference by SNS involvement

	College students (N = 410)		General population (N = 172)	
	Low	High	Low	High
Sports	51.1 %	48.9 %	**61.5 %**	**38.5 %**
Humor	46.5 %	53.5 %	55.3 %	44.7 %
Politics	52.7 %	47.3 %	**61.5 %**	**38.5 %**
Human interest	46.4 %	53.6 %	55.4 %	44.6 %
Parenting/education	49.7 %	50.3 %	48.8 %	51.2 %
Music and entertainment	49.1 %	50.9 %	56.3 %	43.7 %
Business	**53.2 %**	**46.8 %**	**66.2 %**	**33.8 %**
Celebrity, lifestyle and fashion	**41.4 %**	**58.6 %**	**38.5 %**	**61.5 %**
Science/technology	**56.2 %**	**43.8 %**	**61.0 %**	**39.0 %**
Health and medicine	52.3 %	47.7 %	59.2 %	40.8 %
Local people/happenings	50.0 %	50.0 %	55.0 %	45.0 %

Note: Missing data were excluded

questions, posting product reviews, participating contests, and adding entry to collaborative sites.

For the general population, people with high SNS involvement posted more video/pictures made/taken by themselves or people they knew than those with low SNS involvement. Similar to college students, people among the general population with high SNS involvement were more likely to post more comments/suggestions and discuss and forward more online news content to friends via SNS. There were no differences between high and low SNS involvement in posting video/pictures from other sites, participating in e-mail opinion/polls/ratings or questions, posting product reviews, participating contests, and adding entry to collaborative sites.

Topic Preference. Comparing the topic preference of college students with high and low SNS involvement, we did not find many significant differences between the two groups as shown in Table 5. However the bigger difference was the preference to celebrity, lifestyle, and fashion between the two groups. College students with high SNS involvement were more likely to prefer media content about celebrity, lifestyle, and fashion than those with low SNS involvement; though, they prefer less on media content about science and politics, than those with low SNS involvement.

The differences between high and low SNS involvement in topic preference among the general population were relatively large, especially in certain topics. People with high SNS involvement have much higher interest than those with low SNS involvement in the content about celebrity, lifestyle, and fashion, which was consistent with the college student data. Additionally, people involved in SNS heavily less prefer about sports, politics, business, and science.

R2 asked whether the differences between high and low SNS involvement in the use of SNS, online activities, and topic preference exist in both college students and general population. In sum, people with high SNS involvement among both college students and general population had more SNS activities than those with low SNS involvement; and both college students and general population with high SNS involvement had more online activities on posting videos and pictures except that general population posted very little of videos of themselves people they know and much less than college students in all kinds of online posting activities even if they were highly involved in SNS; but for topic preference, the differences between high and low SNS involvement among college student were much less than that among general population.

9   Discussion and Implications to Media Management

9.1   Similarities Between College Students and General Population

Our study showed some similarities between college students and the general population. We found both among college students and general population, people with high SNS involvement were more likely to do more SNS activities, such as posting news content from other news media, linking to other media sites, reading news posted on the site, playing games, and following SNS for breaking news. Media industry could promote, distribute, or advertise their products/services through focusing on people with high SNS involvement and sending links or contents to them. In addition, SNS use experience predicted SNS involvement for both college students and general population. This finding also confirmed that the earlier people used SNS, the more knowledge they had about SNS and fully utilized their various features. The early SNS users should be important target audiences for media marketers who want to use SNS to promote their media content. However, the demographic characteristics of these early SNS users should be identified for better promotion.

9.2   Differences Between College Students and General Population

However, there are many more substantial differences between the college students and the general population in the SNS use. College students are much more highly involved in SNS than general population and have much larger social network size. The highly involved SNS users in college students are much more active online and in SNS activities than the highly involved SNS users in general population. Media managers interested in taking advantage of using social media for viral effect type of promotion or cultivating brand loyalty should focus on highly involved SNS users who are most likely college students rather than the general population because the impact will be much higher. TV shows or other media content that target at college students would benefit the most from using social media. The effect might not be well for media content that has an older demographic audience. Nonetheless, the highly involved SNS users in the general population are more likely to post product reviews and participate in contests. So media managers who would like to encourage audiences to post comments or participate in the contests organized by the TV station or newspapers should focus on the general population.

The lack of significant difference in SNS involvement by gender and age after controlling in the other variables such as SNS use experience, network size and community participation shows that past research which showed the gender and age difference in SNS use might be confounded by SNS use experience. The effects of age and gender were suppressed on SNS involvement after a more important variable, SNS use experience, was included among college students. SNS use experience is more important than age to predict SNS involvement.

Another big difference between college students and general population is the different impact of network size. College students' network size on SNS also predicted their SNS involvement. The more friends they had on SNS, the more SNS involvement they had. But this result could not be applied to the general population because there was no relationship between SNS network size and SNS involvement among general population. These results might be explained by the fact that students were more likely to make "friends" and have interactions with their "friends," while among general population, people were more likely to do something by themselves, such as, posting, linking, or forwarding. Media marketers should not ignore either of the two groups. Students who have large SNS network size could be potential word-of-mouth ads for media promotion. People in general population who did not have the advantage of network size also could help media promotion through receiving information.

9.3 Differences Between High and Low SNS Involvement Users

Third, we found that college students with high SNS involvement posted more videos/pictures made/taken by themselves or people they knew, and posted more videos/pictures from other sites. And people with high SNS involvement among general population posted only more videos/pictures made/taken by themselves or people they knew. It means in general population people are more likely to communicate the self-created video/pictures. For online visually interactive websites, such as YouTube, the high SNS involvement users among college students and general population should be their target audiences. For TV networks, which are planning to engage their audiences into their programs/shows, they could use the videos/pictures posted by high involvement SNS users to construct their intermedia strategy. Additionally, we found the differences between high and low SNS involvement users in posting comments/suggestions and forwarding or discussing online news content to friends via SNS among college students and general population were both significant. These results has significant implications for print media, online media, and TV networks. Media managers could get valuable comments and suggestion about their news reports and TV shows through SNS and adjusted their products to the taste of audiences. Also, they could promote their media product and even their brands on SNS because the high SNS involvement users are more likely to forward and discuss news content on SNS.

Lastly, although we did not find significant differences between high and low involvement SNS users in topic preference among college students, the results in general population provided some insights for media managers. In general population, people with low SNS involvement who preferred sports, politics, business, and science were nearly twice than those with high SNS involvement. It seemed that high SNS involvement users were more interested in soft news such as celebrity news for gossip, which did not need to think; while people with low SNS involvement were more concerned about political news and technology, health and medicine which required more deep thoughts. For media managers who consider combining SNS and their own media need to realize the different interests of people with high and low SNS involvement. People with high SNS involvement could be powerful potential marketing tool considering their intense participation in SNS activities and online activities. Meanwhile, people with low SNS involvement suggested they were interested in hard news content. So the critical/informative media such as TV news networks should target at those with low SNS involvement either directly or through the dissemination of those with high SNS involvement.

9.4 Limitations and Suggestions for Future Research

This study was also limited by two factors. First, our sample was biased for both college students and the general population. Also, our general population is not representative because a higher proportion of old women responded to the survey. We did not have sufficient representation from different age ranges and males. Second, to assess SNS content consumption of users, we only summed up all the activities we tested, rather than examined what attitudes the respondents were toward each activity. Their evaluation of each of the activity opportunities on SNS could be an important mediating variable on prediction of SNS involvement to support our hypotheses. The low adjusted R squares for SNS involvement means future research should identify more variables that facilitate SNS involvement.

Finally, because of the notable differences in the results between the general population and the college student data in the study, future research on social media use or social media involvement should be cautious in their findings by not generalizing the results of one type of sample to the other and highlight the limitation of using one type of sample. What works in the general population do not work in the college student population and vice versa as shown in the many differences we found between students and general population. Media managers should note that college students grow up with the Internet and are more homogeneous not just in age and education, but also in media content preference than the general population. SNS are an important part of their life among the highly involved SNS college student users. The reciprocal effect of social media is high in that a user must have friends who use SNS in order to use the medium. Because fewer older people use SNS, the reciprocal value of SNS is lower than college students because older people have fewer friends on SNS. Media managers must realize this limitation of SNS and should expect low effect in using SNS on general population who are mostly lowly involved SNS users.

Acknowledgement The authors would like to acknowledge the funding of this study from the Bowling Green State University Research Capacity Enhancement Grant and the Toledo Blade.

References

Aghazamani, A. (2010). How do university students spend their time on Facebook? An exploratory study. *Journal of American Science, 6*(12), 730–735.
Alarcón-Del-Amo, M. D., Lorenzo-Romero, C., & Gómez-Borja, M. A. (2011). Classifying and profiling social networking site users: A latent segmentation approach. *Cyberpsychology, Behavior, and Social Networking, 14*(9), 547–553.
Barker, V. (2009). Older adolescents' motivations for social network site use: The influence of gender, group identity, and collective self-Esteem. *Cyberpsychology and Behavior, 1*, 5.
Barnes, S. (2006). A privacy paradox: Social networking in the United States. *First Monday, 11*, 9. Retrieved November 5, 2010, from http://firstmonday.org/htbin/cgiwrap/bin/ojs/index.php/fm/article/view/1394/1312
Boyd, D. (2008). Facebook's privacy trainwreck: Exposure, invasion, and social convergence. *Convergence, 14*(1), 13–20.
Boyd, D., & Ellison, N. (2007). Social network sites: Definition, history, and scholarship. *Journal of Computer-Mediated Communication, 13*, 1.
Cain, J. (2008). Online social networking issues within academia and pharmacy education. *American Journal of Pharmaceutical Education, 72*, 1.
Campbell, S. W., & Kwak, N. (2010). Mobile communication and civic life: Linking patterns of use to civic and political engagement. *Journal of Communication, 61*(3), 536–555.
Chapman, C. (2009). The history and evolution of social media. Retrieved November 17, 2010, from http://www.webdesignerdepot.com/2009/10/the-history-and-evolution-of-social-media/
Chew, M., Balfanz, D., & Laurie, B. (2008). Undermining privacy in social networks. *W2SP 2008: Web 2.0 Security and Privacy 2008*. Retrieved October 27, 2011, from http://w2spconf.com/2008/papers/s3p2.pdf
Clancy, K. (1992). CPMs must bow to 'involvement' measurement. *Advertising Age, 63*(3), 26.
Cliff, L., Ellison, N., & Steinfield, C. (2006). A face (book) in the crowd: Social searching vs. social browsing. In *Proceedings of the 2006 20th Anniversary Conference on Computer Supported Cooperative Work*.
ComScore (2011, December 21). *It's a social world: Top 10 need-to-knows about social networking and where it's headed*. Retrieved January 2, 2011 from http://www.comscore.com/Press_Events/Presentations_Whitepapers/2011/it_is_a_social_world_top_10_need-to-knows_about_social_networking
Constantinides, E., Carmen Alarcón del Amo del, M., & Romero, C. L. (2010). Profiles of social networking sites users in the Netherlands. In *18th Annual High Technology Small Firms Conference, HTSF*, 25–28 May 2010, Enschede, The Netherlands.
Constantinides, E., & Fountain, S. (2008). Web 2.0: Conceptual foundations and Marketing Issues. *Journal of Direct, Data and Digital Marketing Practice, 9*(3), 231–244.
Constantinides, E., Lorenzo, C., & Gómez-Borja, M. A. (2008). Social Media: A new frontier for retailers? *European Retail Research, 22*, 1–27.
Cooper, J., & Weaver, K. D. (2003). *Gender and computers: Understanding the digital divide*. Mahwah, NJ: Lawrence Erlbaum.
Dillman, D. A. (2007). *Mail and Internet surveys: The tailored designed method*. Hoboken, NJ: Wiley.

DiMaggio, P., Hargittai, E., Celeste, C., & Shafer, S. (2004). Digital inequality: From unequal access to differentiated use. In K. Neckerman (Ed.), *Social inequality* (pp. 355–400). New York: Russell Sage.

Donath, J., & Boyd, D. (2004). Public displays of connection. *BT Technology Journal, 22*(4), 71–82.

Dumenco, S. (2011, November 4). Fall TV update: Five social-TV successful stories (and one ratings disappointment). Retrieved January 2, 2012, from http://adage.com/article/trending-topics/fox-takes-top-spots-show-social-buzz-ranking/230843/

Ellison, N. B., Heino, R., & Gibbs, J. (2006). Managing impressions online: Self-presentation processes in the online dating environment. *Journal of Computer-Mediated Communication, 11*, 2.

Ellison, N. B., Steinfield, C., & Lampe, C. (2007). The benefits of Facebook "friends:" Social capital and college students' use of online social network sites. *Journal of Computer-Mediated Communication, 12*, 4.

Facebook.com. (2011). Retrieved December 20, 2011, from http://www.facebook.com/press/info.php?statistics

Fang, L., & Ha, L. (2011, August). *Who are the heavy users of social network sites among college students? A study of social network sites and college students.* Paper presented in AEJMC conference, St. Louis, MO.

Gross, R., & Acquisti, A. (2005). Information revelation and privacy in online social networks. Pre-proceedings version. ACM Workshop on Privacy in the Electronic Society (WPES). Retrieved December 21, 2011, from http://www.heinz.cmu.edu/~acquisti/papers/privacy-facebook-gross-acquisti.pdf

Ha, L., & Fang, L. (2012). Internet experience and time displacement of traditional news media use: An application of the theory of the niche. *Telematics and Informatics, 29*, 177–186. doi:10.1016/j.tele.2011.06.001.

Ha, L., Leconte, D., & Savidge, J. (2012). From TV to online to mobile phones: A national study of US college students' multiplatform video use and satisfaction. In F. L. Lee, L. L. Leung, J. L. Qiu, & D. S. C. Chu (Eds.), *Frontiers in new media research* (pp. 278–298). UK: Routledge.

Hampton, K., Goulet, L. S., Rainie, L., & Purcell, K. (2011). Socail networking sites and our lives. Retrieved December 25, 2011, from http://www.pewinternet.org/Reports/2011/Technology-and-social-networks.aspx

Hargittai, E. (2008a). Whose space? Differences among users and non-users of social network sites. *Journal of Computer-Mediated Communication, 13*(1), 276–297.

Hargittai, E. (2008b). The digital reproduction of inequality. In D. Grusky (Ed.), *Social stratification*. Boulder, CO: Westview Press.

Helft, M., & Wortham, J. (2010, August 18). Facebook unveils a service to announce where users are. *The New York Times*. Retrieved from http://www.nytimes.com/2010/08/19/technology/19facebook.html

Hodge, M. J. (2006). The Fourth Amendment and privacy issues on the 'new' Internet: Facebook.com and MySpace.com. *Southern Illinois University Law Journal, 31*, 95.

Hsia, L. (2010, December 10). How social media is changing the business of Television. Retrieved January 2, 2012, from http://mashable.com/2010/12/10/social-media-business-tv/

Huffaker, D. A., & Calvert, S. L. (2005). Gender, identity, and language use in teenage blogs. *Journal of Computer-Mediated Communication, 10*, 2, 1. Retrieved October 25, 2011, from http://jcmc.indiana.edu/vol10/issue2/huffaker.html

Johnson, T. J., Bichard, S. L., & Zhang, W. (2009). Communication communities or 'CyberGhettos?': A path analysis model examining factors that explain selective exposure to blogs. *Journal of Computer-Mediated Communication, 15*(1), 60–82.

Junco, R. (2012). Too much face and not enough books: The relationship between multiple indices of Facebook use and academic performance. *Computers in Human Behavior, 28*(1), 187–198. doi:10.1016/j.chb.2011.08.026.

Junco, R., Merson, D., & Salter, D. W. (2010). The effect of gender, ethnicity, and income on college students' use of communication technologies. *CyberPsychology, Behavior, and Social Networking, 13*(6), 37–53.

Kaiser Family Foundation. (2004). *The digital divide survey snapshot*. Menlo Park, CA: Kaiser Family Foundation. Retrieved December 21, 2011, from. http://www.kff.org/entmedia/loader.cfm?url1/4/commonspot/security/getfile.cfm&PageID1/446366

Katz, E., & Lazarsfeld, P. F. (1955). *Personal influence: The part played by people in the flow of mass communications*. Glencoe, IL: Free Press.

Keith, N. H., Lauren, S. G., Lee, R., & Kristen, P. (2011). Social networking sites and our lives. *Pew Internet and American Life Project*. Retrieved December 19, 2011, from http://www.pewinternet.org/~/media//Files/Reports/2011/PIP%20-%20Social%20networking%20sites%20and%20our%20lives.pdf

Lampe, C., Ellison, N., & Steinfeld, C. (2007, April). *Profile elements as signals in an online social network*. Conference on Human Factors in Computing Systems, San Jose, CA, USA.

Lenhart, A., & Madden, M. (2008). Teens, privacy and online social networks. *Pew Internet and American Life Project*. Retrieved November 18, 2010, from http://www.pewinternet.org/Reports/2007/Teens-Privacy-and-Online-Social-Networks.aspx

Lewis, C. C., & George, J. F. (2008). Cross-cultural deception in social networking sites and face-to-face communication. *Computers in Human Behavior, 24*(6), 2945–2964.

Lewis, K., Kaufman, J., & Christakis, N. (2008). The taste for privacy: An analysis of college student privacy settings in an online social network. *Journal of Computer-Mediated Communication, 14*, 79–100.

Liebling, R. (2011, October 6). Social TV: How content producers can engage their audiences in new ways. Retrieved January 2, 2012 from http://mashable.com/2011/10/06/social-tv-intermedia-strategy/

Livingstone, S. (2008). Taking risky opportunities in youthful content creation: Teenagers' use of social networking sites for intimacy, privacy and self-expression. *New Media and Society, 10*(3), 393–411.

Magnuson, M. J., & Dundes, L. (2008). Gender differences in "social portraits" reflected in MySpace profiles. *CyberPsychology and Behavior, 11*(2), 239–241.

Mithchell, A. (1979). Involvement: A potentially important mediator of consumer behavior. In W. L. Wilkie (Ed.), *Advances in consumer research* (Vol. 6, pp. 191–196). Provo, UT: Association for Consumer Research.

Muise, A., Christofides, E., & Desmarais, S. (2009). More information than you ever wanted: Does Facebook bring out the green-eyed monster of jealousy? *CyberPsychology and Behavior, 12*(4), 441–444.

Newman, A. A. (2011, August 4). Brands now direct their followers to social media. *New York Times*. Retrieved September 12, 2011 from: http://0-web.ebscohost.com.maurice.bgsu.edu/ehost/detail?sid=ce7507d4-cd36-4ad0-94ee-57a9ac4a031e%40sessionmgr11&vid=1&hid=9&bdata=JnNpdGU9ZWhvc3QtbGl2ZSZzY29wZT1zaXRl#db=a9h&AN=63620002

Nielsen Media Research (2010, August 2). What Americans Do Online: Social media and games dominate activity. Retrieved December 17, 2011 from: http://blog.nielsen.com/nielsenwire/online_mobile/what-americans-do-online-social-media-and-games-dominate-activity/

Pew Research Center's Internet & American Life Project. (2005). Retrieved December 21, 2011, from http://www.pewinternet.org/Trend-Data.aspx

Pew Research Center's Internet & American Life Project. (2007). Retrieved December 21, 2011, from http://www.pewinternet.org/Trend-Data.aspx

Pew Research Center's Internet & American Life Project. (2011). Trends in teen communication and social media use. Retrieved December 20, 2011, from http://www.pewinternet.org/Presentations/2011/Feb/PIP-Girl-Scout-Webinar.aspx

Pfeil, U., Arjan, R., & Zaphiris, P. (2008). Age differences in online social networking-A study of user profiles and the social capital divide among teenagers and older users in MySpace. *Computer in Human Behavior, 25*, 643–654.

Robards, B. (2010). Randoms in my bedroom: Negotiating privacy and unsolicited contact on social network sites. *PRism, 7*, 3.

Salaway, G., Caruso, J. B., & Nelson, M. R. (2008).The ECAR study of undergraduate students and information technology. Research Study, 8. Boulder, CO: EDUCAUSE Center for Applied Research. Retrieved December 22, 2011, from http://www.educause.edu/ecar

Skog, D. (2005). Social interaction in virtual communities: The significance of technology. *International Journal of Web Based Communities, 1*(4), 464–474.

Solomon, M. R. (2002). *Consumer behavior buying, having, and being* (5th ed.). Upper Saddle River, NJ: Prentice Hall.

Stutzman, F. (2006). An evaluation of identity-sharing behavior in social network communities. *Journal of the International Digital Media and Arts Association, 3*(1), 10–18.

The Economist. (2007, November 10). Retrieved September 12, 2011, from http://0-web.ebscohost.com.maurice.bgsu.edu/ehost/detail?sid=8fe667fa-a095-4f2b-bf21-5a9142de7215%40sessionmgr15&vid=1&hid=9&bdata=JnNpdGU9ZWhvc3QtbGl2ZSZzY 29wZT1zaXR l#db=a9h&AN=27504860

Tredinnick, L. (2006). Web 2.0 and business: A pointer to the intranets of the future. *Business Information Review, 23*(4), 228–234.

Utz, S. (2010). Show me your friends and I will tell you what type of person you are: How one's profile, number of friends, and type of friends influence impression formation on social network sites. *Journal of Computer-Mediated Communication, 15*(2), 314–335.

Utz, S., & Krämer, N. (2009). The privacy paradox on social network sites revisited: The role of individual characteristics and group norms. *Cyberpsychology, 3*, 2.

Valkenburg, P. M., & Peter, J. (2008). Adolescents' identity experiments on the internet: consequences for social competence and self-concept unity. *Communication Research, 35*(2), 208–231.

Wilson, E. J., & Sherrell, D. L. (1993). Source effects in communication and persuasion research: A meta-analysis of effect size. *Journal of the Academy of Marketing Science, 21*, 101–112.

Ybarra, M. L., & Mitchell, K. J. (2008). How risky are social networking sites? A comparison of places online where youth sexual solicitation and harassment occurs. *Pediatrics, 121*(2), 350–357.

Zaichkowsky, J. L. (1985). Measuring the involvement construct in marketing. *Journal of Consumer Research, 12*, 341–352.

Customer Integration and Web Interactivity. A Literature Review and Analysis of the Role of Transaction Costs in Building Value Webs

Paul Murschetz

1 Introduction

Publishing is facing a variety of profound and disruptive challenges that come to threaten the printed news media industry's race for survival. By offering interactive e-commerce and Web 2.0 applications and services, and thereby actively engaging consumers in communication and transaction processes, publishers increasingly are emphasizing solid and sustainable relationships that may help them achieve improved economic viability and sustainable competitive advantage in the electronic marketplace. As a result, one might expect a rich literature and ample empirical insights into the plethora of issues involved in interactivity and social media which have both broadly impacted the evolution of e-commerce (Wigand et al. 2008).

However, my own review of the literature concludes that a clear picture of the relationship between these broad phenomena is only emerging (Picot et al. 2008; Wigand et al. 2008; Yadav and Varadarajan 2005a). I will address this void and pursue some selected crucial underpinning issues of this wide theoretical canvas. Essentially, I will develop some propositions as first principles of a (yet to be built) conceptual model integrating web interactivity, customer integration, and transaction cost theory.

The concept of interactivity is usually thought of as a key characteristic of new media, notably the Internet, but also mobile telephony and interactive television (Durlak 1987; Carey 1989; Rafaeli 1988; Rafaeli and Sudweeks 1997; Jensen 1998; Kiousis 2002). Web interactivity, on its part, is said allow for multi-directional social interaction and exchange between and among the participants. Web interactivity even allows role changes of the interacting participants. In the extreme case, online end-users may become what Alvin Toffler (1980) named 'prosumers', when

P. Murschetz (✉)
ICT&S Center, Advanced Studies and Research in Information and Communication Technologies and Society, University of Salzburg, Salzburg, Austria
e-mail: paul.murschetz@gmx.net

he predicted that the role of producers and consumers would begin to blur and merge. Customer integration is a fairly new concept emerging from management studies and innovation management research. Broadly, it refers to an interaction process whereby consumers are actively integrated into innovation and products development activities of business firms. Transaction cost theory describes specific types of costs which emerge as possible hindrance factors between the trading partners in order to achieve more frictionless cooperation in these new forms of integrative value creation and exchange.

The overall purpose of this study is to lay a conceptual groundwork for further research into the role of transactions costs in the way web interactivity and customer integration could be related. In fact, transaction cost theory (TCT) can provide a useful research perspective into the relative merits conducting transactions within business firms and between the business firm and the consumer using the market as organizational governance structure (Williamson 1979, 1985, 2005). TCT, as developed primarily by economists Ronald Coase and Oliver Williamson, suggests that economic organizations emerge from cost-minimizing behaviour (including transaction costs) in a world of limited information and opportunism. This means that integrated consumers would, in theory, be able to deliver value contributions to a business firm more cost-efficiently compared to transactions being organized exclusively internally.

Before exploring the concepts at stake more deeply, let me first give you some first notions about how web interactivity, customer integration and transaction costs may be interrelated in an online publishing context. Web interactivity is said to deliver benefits on both sides of an online exchange or transaction in the following ways:

First, publishers may gain competitive advantage, widen their product range through adding interactive features, offer new content channels to audiences, or integrate once passive readers into the content creation processes of media publishing in various ways. This, in return, may leverage consumer trust and loyalty in both the print and online brands of a publishing offering. End-users, on their part, are set to experience higher degrees of involvement and personalization with information products and services offered (Franz and Robey 1986; Hartwick and Barki 1994; McMillan 2002; Tseng and Piller 2003). In turn, this shall again benefit publishers in that personalized content and services can better discriminate among elaborate end-user preferences. Further, as mentioned above, web interactivity encourages the publishing of end-user's own content and commenting on other people's, thus increasing both the content wealth of a website and the rate of end-user engagement on various levels. It is well known that online users do not passively consume content any more, but extensively contribute to its creation. New types of online platforms such as, for instance, Wikipedia, YouTube and Facebook emerged, which are summarized under the term 'social media'. Social media support creation, upload, sharing and collaborative creation of user generated content (Stanoevska-Slabeva 2011). Alternatively, customer integration describes a mode of integrated value creation. Applied to a publishing context, publishers and customers are collectively taking part in both operational and innovational value creating activities which used to be seen as the exclusive domain of the firm. This co-creation builds the basis for a voluntarily cooperation between both actors, which is driven by specific motives of both parties.

Now, this article aims at reviewing and synthesizing selected literature on web interactivity and the management of customer integration with a view to evaluating both concepts against the role of transaction costs involved in social and economic transactions in the electronic marketplace.

As for methodology, this study is exploratory in design and qualitative in nature. Literature reviewing will be applied as prime methodology. This paper proceeds with developing deeper conceptual insights to web interactivity and customer integration. It will then investigate whether transaction cost theory (TCT) has epistemological value to act as background theory for analyzing potential impacts between the two concepts. A conclusion will sum up key findings and critically discuss results.

2 Conceptual Issues

Interactivity was coined as *the* buzzword during the late 1980s and early 1990s when the multimedia euphoria fascinated politicians, economists, and researchers alike. Over the past 20 years, however, there has been little agreement among researchers on how interactivity should be conceptualized (Bucy 2004a; Heeter 2000; Neumann 2008). Therefore, it is difficult to develop concrete knowledge regarding its constituent factors and consequences for computer-mediated communication (CMC) in the electronic marketplace. This makes the prospect of synthesizing and integrating the literature on the business value of interactivity rather elusive (Amit and Zott 2001; Bandulet and Morasch 2005; Bucy 2004b; Chen and Yen 2004; Coyle and Thorson 2001; Jee and Lee 2002; Lee et al. 2000; Lowry et al. 2009; McMillan 1998; Normann and Ramirez 1993; Piller 2002; Rangaswamy and Pal 2003; Reichwald and Piller 2000; Taylor 1911; Tseng and Jiao 2001; Varadarajan and Yadav 2002; von Hippel 1998; Wigand 1997; Williams et al. 1998; Williamson 1996).

2.1 Dominant Views of Interactivity

Academic scholars developed three dominant views alongside the structural characteristics of the phenomenon (Heeter 2000; Jensen 1998; Kiousis 2002; McMillan 2002, 2006; Quiring and Schweiger 2008): *technology, communication process*, and *user perception*. Each of these characteristics locate the reference point of interactivity differently according to the nature of the participants (i.e., active or passive), the level of user or receiver control (i.e., high or low), and the centre of control (i.e., human or computer) (McMillan 2006).

First, the *interactivity-as-technology tradition* sees interaction between humans and the computer itself (or other types of new media systems) as central to new media. Rooted in HCI research (Baecker 1980; Baecker and Buxton 1987; Guedj et al. 1980; Hartson 1998; Nielsen 2000), this tradition defines the interaction between a single human and a single computer as the most elementary form of interactivity (Shaw et al. 1993).

Key underlying constructs of this view of interactivity are: *bi-directionality* (McMillan 2000a, b; Nickerson 1977; Noll 2003), *bandwidth* (indicating the speed at which data are transferred using a particular network medium; Burke and Chidambaram 1999), and *speed of response* (as explained by the *timeliness* construct described further below; Hanssen et al. 1996). In addition, *symmetry*, which refers here to (a) a technology characteristic where speed or data quantity transferred is the same in both directions; measured by down *and* upstream channel or bandwidth capacity by transmit time per mega bytes, and (b) a communication characteristic where the sender and receiver roles becoming virtually indistinguishable in environments such as chat rooms, bulletin boards, etc., as described in Grunig and Grunig's (1989) model of two-way symmetric communication), and *synchronicity* (similar to *speed of response* this construct refers to the extent to which a message exchange occurs in real time or is delayed; Burgoon et al. 2000a, b; Dennis et al. 2008; Dennis and Valacich 1999) come to explain interactivity-as-technology.

The second school of thought identifies interactivity as communication process at the heart of which lies computer-mediated interaction between humans. Rooted within computer-mediated communication (CMC) theory, this view refers to themes of interpersonal interaction, symbolic interaction, and social interaction (Goffman 1967; McMillan 2006). Underlying constructs on this dimension are: *reciprocality of participants* (also discussed as *reciprocity, participation, mutual action, action-reaction,* and *two-way communication*; Ha and James 1998; Gouldner 1960; Johnson et al. 2006), *exchange of (symbolic) messages* (whereby networked interactivity in computer-mediated communication settings goes beyond natural interactivity in that "later messages in any sequence take into account not just messages that preceded them, but also the manner in which previous messages were reactive. In this manner interactivity forms a social reality"; Rafaeli and Sudweeks 1997; para. 8), *active user control* (Rice and Williams 1984), *immediacy of feedback* (tools such as e-mail links that allow the receiver to concurrently communicate with the sender; Dennis and Kinney 1998), and *participation* (defined by Laurel 1991, p. 21, as "how immersed you are in the experience"). CMC theory, in particular, stresses the way by which the communicators process social identity and relational cues (i.e., the capability to convey meanings through cues like body language, voice, tones, that is basically social information) using different media (Fulk et al. 1990; Walther 1992).

And third, interactivity is viewed to have more anthropomorphic properties (Quiring 2009). Here, interactivity refers back to the concept of action in the social sciences, whereby action is presupposed to depend on an active human subject intentionally acting upon an object or another subject. Interaction with objects and the creators of these objects modify their actions and reactions due to the actions by their interaction partner(s) (Jaeckel 1995). Seen this way, interactivity is understood as a subjective mode of perception and cognition and, as interpreted from a communication theory perspective, focuses on how a receiver actively interprets and uses mass and new media messages. In the CMC literature, two key themes have emerged under this rubric: individual experiential processes of interactivity (McMillan and Hwang 2002; McMillan 2000a, b; Downes and McMillan 2000), and perceptions of individual control over both presentation and content (Bezjian-Avery et al. 1998; Hanssen et al. 1996). *Self-awareness* (i.e., the psychological factor that impacts on social interaction as mediated by CMC), *responsiveness* (the degree to which a user perceives a system as reacting quickly and iteratively to user input; Rafaeli 1988), a *sense of presence* (discoursed as virtual experience made by humans when they interact with media and simulation technologies; Lee 2004; Lombard and Ditton 1997; Short 1974; Short et al. 1976; Steuer 1992), *involvement* (defined as perceived sensory and cognitive affiliation with product and content; Fortin and Dholakia 2005; Franz and Robey 1986; McMillan 2000a, b; Zaichkowsky 1986), and *perceived user control* are further constituent psychological activities on this level of discussion (Robey 1979).

2.2 Interactivity and Economic Theory

The idea that business value and thus profit is co-created and enhanced through the producers' interaction with their customers is as old as Frederic W. Taylor who developed the concept of scientific management in 1911. Taylor's concept contains aspects on the division of labor being relevant to the theory and practice for improving efficiency of existing business processes and thus making non-value adding work obsolete. Secondly, modern organization theory around Chester Barnard (1948), the author of pioneering work in management theory and organizational sociology, has originated the idea of *relationship marketing* whereby customers are not external actors in the business communication process but an integral part of an organization's plan for survival through effectiveness and efficiency.

Thirdly, in 1993, Normann and Ramirez published their seminal work on how new information and communication technologies (ICTs) and changing consumer lifestyles transform the notion of business value from Porter's (1985) traditional model of the sequential value chain into their new model of *value constellation*. There, consumers and other partners, suppliers, etc., actively co-produce relationships along with the enterprise. In their model, the business model is meant to be actively co-created between the various actors involved. To support this, interactive network technologies would potentially open organizations towards customers' involvement for value generation. Prahalad and Ramaswamy (2000, 2002, 2003, 2004), another two comprehensive business thinkers, have further elaborated on changes in the traditional logic of governance in electronic commerce as analytically depicted by the concept of the linear and horizontal value chain. Briefly, they claim the need for producers to establish interaction platforms for "co-creating unique value with customers". Only this would achieve sustainable competitive advantage for the business firm. Likewise, German and Scandinavian researchers in business and management have focused on *customer integration* (Kleinaltenkamp et al. 1996;

Lampel and Mintzberg 1995; Wikstroem 1996a, b), *value webs* (Reichwald et al. 2004) and *interactive value creation* (Reichwald and Piller 2009), a general research perspective which this present study is based on conceptually.

Adoption of the concept of interactivity within the research domain of electronic commerce can be found in studies investigating business-to-customer relationships in e-commerce research traditions (Romano and Fjermestad 2003; Kuk and Yeung 2002; Essler and Whitaker 2001; Sukpanich and Chen 2000; Yadav and Varadarajan 2005a) and the marketing and advertising activities of firms (Blattberg and Deighton 1991; Coviello et al. 2001; Day 1998; Ha and James 1998; Novak et al. 2000; Iacobucci 1998; Liu and Shrum 2002; Ko et al. 2005; Webster 1996, 1998). Naturally, the possible thematic scope of interactivity within an e-commerce context is broad and rather scattered, discussing structural, processual, and perceptual dimensions across various issues. To start with, Choi, Stahl, and Winston (1997) saw interactivity as a defining criterion for digital products: "Products that are downloaded at once or in a piecemeal fashion, such as through daily updates, can be called delivered products. Interactive products, on the other hand, are products or services, such as remote-diagnosis, interactive games, and tele-education" (p. 76). Bezjian-Avery et al. (1998) defined interactivity as part of "the immediately iterative process by which customer needs and desires are uncovered, met, modified, and satisfied by the providing firm" (p. 23). Interactivity can push users to actively engage in the communication process and thus build sustainable relationships between consumer and advertiser/message provider. Romano and Fjermestad (2003) identified a number of current and emergent technologies for internet-based electronic customer relationship management (e-CRM). They developed an e-CRM IT classification scheme from the consumer's perspective based on how consumers communicate to develop and maintain relationships via three specific levels of participation along a continuum ranging from passive to interactive. For them, interactive emergent technologies such as e-mail, forums, online focus groups, interactive interviews, survey panels, auctions, trade shows, and shopping agents are participatory. Essler and Whitaker (2001) pointed to the need of rethinking e-commerce business models impacted by interactivity in the era of cyberspace. They argued that, in the future, interactivity would drive changes from enterprise infrastructure to the so-called '*interactional agitecture*' described as a process of reciprocal interactivity and influence between firm and customer. Alba et al. (1997) conceptualized interactivity from an e-commerce point of view as "a continuous construct capturing the quality of two-way communication between two parties [...]. In the case of interactive home shopping (IHS), the parties are the buyer and seller. The two dimensions of interactivity are response time and response contingency. Because IHS involves electronic communication, the response can be immediate – similar to response time in face-to-face communications. Response contingency is the degree to which the response by one party is a function of the response made by the other party" (p. 38).

2.3 The Concept of Customer Integration

The concept of *customer integration* dates back to the mid-1990s, when several researchers in management theory began to work on the belief that new technologies, increased competition, and more assertive customers are leading firms towards customization of their products and services. By integrating customers into design, research and product development, manufacturing, assembling, or sales activities, companies, it is believed, will get efficient support to improve products for more customer satisfaction, and identify and unlock new sources of revenue (Kleinaltenkamp et al. 1996). Customer integration can be defined as a value creation process where "consumers take part in activities and processes which used to be seen as the domain of the companies" (Wikstroem 1996a, p. 360). Value webs enable both customers and suppliers to be co-operatively active in team-based product and process innovation activities, as well as in product design, re-design, development, and, finally, electronically mediated transactions between organizations and customers (Chesbrough et al. 2006; von Hippel 2005). Social network effects and transaction cost efficiencies resulting from these value webs are said to emerge if customers are actively involved in and integrated into the respective e-business processes (Economides 1996; Klemperer 2008; Yadav and Varadarajan 2005a).

3 The Role of Transaction Costs

Transaction cost theory (TCT) provides a useful theoretical framework for analyzing whether particular business firm activities should be organized internally (e.g. within news journalists of an online web news portal) or externally (e.g. through collaborative creation of user generated content).

Conceptually introduced in Ronald Coase's 1937 paper *The Nature of the Firm* (1937), transaction costs are generally defined as costs incurred when using the market mechanism in buying or selling a good or service. Coase noted that there were costs using the price system, costs we know as transaction costs. Coase reasoned that firms emerge when the transaction costs associated with coordinating particular exchanges using markets exceeded those of coordinating the same exchanges using managers. In the absence of transaction costs, Coase (1937/1988) wrote, "the firm has no purpose" (p. 34). Oliver Williamson (1975, 1985, 2005) later developed transaction cost theory (TCT) more fully. The primary concern of TCT is with the relative efficiency of internal versus external organization of activities and with the conditions affecting the efficiency of the two organizational governance forms: 'Market' (i.e. external market mechanism) or 'Hierarchy' (i.e. internal organizational structure).

Presenting a minimalist version of the theory, Williamson based TCT on two assumptions of human behavior: 'bounded rationality' and 'opportunism' (also see Table 1). Bounded rationality refers to the difficulty of making fully informed decisions. Opportunism is the tendency for one party of an exchange to change the terms in their favor once the other party has committed itself. Transactions are

Table 1 TC constructs and description

TC constructs	Description
Governance structure	The term was coined by Williamson in his 1979 paper "Transaction cost economics: The governance structures are examples of institutions, defines as sets of laws, rules, customs, and norms that guide human behaviour". 'Market' and 'hierarchy' are the two main governance mechanisms
Transaction	Economic exchange requires transaction, that is, transfers of goods and services across "technologically separable interface(s)" (Williamson 1981, p. 552). Transactions are thus all explicit and implicit negotiations on property rights transfers between at least two economic actors
Transaction costs	The effort, time, and costs incurred in searching, creating, negotiating, monitoring, and enforcing a product or service contract between buyers and sellers (Williamson 1991; Allen 1991; Rindfleisch and Heide 1997)
Asset specificity	The degree to which an asset can be redeployed to alternative uses and by alternative users without sacrifice of productive value (Williamson 1976, 1991). In other words, transactions require specific investments in support of the transaction for which the investment has been made. Different types of asset specificity exist: site specificity, physical asset specificity, human asset specificity, temporal specificity and brand name capital (Williamson 1991)
Frequency	The number of times a client organization initiates a transaction, typically categorized as either occasional or frequent (Williamson 1991)
Uncertainty	The degree of unpredictability or volatility of future states as it relates to the behavioural or environmental factors of a transaction (Williamson 1991)
Bounded rationality	Human decision making is limited by the ability to process information. "While their actions are 'intendedly rational', cognitive limitations render them only limitedly so" (Simon 1957, p. xxiv)
Decision	Essentially, a 'make-or-buy' decision in which a client organization decides to keep a transaction in-house or decides to contract with an outsourcing supplier for all or part of the transaction (Williamson 1991)
Information asymmetry	Information of relevance to transaction is not always shared equally by all parties (Arrow 1963)
Opportunism	Economic agents seek "self-interest ... with guile" (Williamson 1975, p. 26). "This includes but is scarcely limited to more blatant forms, such as lying, stealing, and cheating. Opportunism more often involves subtle forms of deceit" (Williamson 1985, p. 47)

Source: The author

further characterised by three critical dimensions on the basis of which evaluations can be undertaken as to whether the transaction can be better executed within a firm or on the market (Williamson 1973). The dimensions are (1) uncertainty, (2) the frequency with which transactions recur, and (3) the degree to which durable, transaction-specific investments are required to realise least-cost supply (asset specificity). Uncertainty (1) mainly resides in the missing of adequate information about a subject. For example, uncertainty can emerge in case the future behaviour of a cooperating actor is not predictable. Hence, uncertainty generally drives the formation of hierarchies, where actors are bound to certain behaviour by contract (Williamson 1973). Similarly, high levels of transaction frequency (2) foster the emergence of hierarchies (Rindfleisch and Heide 1997), as forming identical co-operations again and again is not efficient. As a high level of asset specificity (3) raises the danger of opportunistic behaviour and fosters the emergence of hierarchies.

In what follows, selected constructs of TCT relevant for the present study shall be briefly summarized:

The following sample propositions offer suggested research directions in analyzing potential impacts of web interactivity on customer integration with a view to be further hypothesized against the role of transactions costs involved in such an integration process.

Proposition 1: Web interactivity enhances consumer value

Reviewing the interactivity concept has shown that it potentially offers greater product choices for consumers by offering a wider range of options for consumption to customers. Proposition 1 is supported by the following arguments as drawn from a review of the literature:

First, that interactivity enhances consumer value is plausible if one considers the importance of the technology dimension of interactivity when predicting a positive impact relationship between interactivity and consumer value. Following the interactivity as technology school of thought, which focuses on functions of technology features, interactivity is based on how many and what types of features are available for online users to fulfil interactive communication (Steuer 1992; Sundar 2004). Simply speaking, once interactive technology infrastructures are in place, the more interactive features offered, the bigger the choice and thus value for the consumer.

A range of theories from neighbouring disciplines such as marketing science, journalism, and advertising support this proposition (Deuze 2003; Ghose and Dou 1998; Liu 2003; Woodruff 1997; Wu 2006). There, greater choice would improve the general attractiveness of a website by improving the consumer's choice of options and active control over the type of product sought after and selected. On closer inspection, however, interactivity sub-dimensions may each impact differently on consumer value. *Bi-directionality*, *bandwidth*, and *synchronicity* may serve as necessary *but not sufficient* conditions for interactivity. As exemplified by Song and Bucy (2008), "it might be possible that one perceives communication through asynchronous e-mail as more interactive than synchronous communication through Instant Messenger (IM) even though objectively (technologically) the opposite appears true" (p. 7). Further, *timeliness* as interaction speed is perceived as a positive predictor of interactivity-induced business value. However, when defined as communication speed, the construct becomes particularly valuable for the consumer (Kiousis 2002). In fact, consumers may wish to determine their own message timing and thus increase their control over technology and communication process (Downes and McMillan 2000; Kiousis 2002). Consumer value may thus eventually depend on the perceptual aspects of interactivity that may mediate the effects of technology on certain outcomes (Bucy and Tao 2007).

Past research has also indicated that greater *complexity of choice available* may have an effect on consumer choice difficulty and choice overload (Ariely 1998, 2000; Heeter 1989; Kim and LaRose 2004). Interactivity thus also implies that consumers may have to afford higher amounts of effort to seek, self-select, process, use, and respond to information (Heeter 1989; Stewart and Pavlou 2002). In this case, consumers may have to undertake (significant) cognitive activities when trying to satisfy some need or goal (e.g., navigating the website and pulling information from it) (Heeter 1989; McMillan and Hwang 2002; Zaichkowsky 1985). This may act as a further impediment on consumer value.

Proposition 2: Web interactivity drives customer integration
As indicated, the role of the customer is changing from a pure consumer of products or services to that of equal partner in a process of adding value: consumers are becoming co-producers and co-designers (Berger et al. 2005; Picot et al. 1998; Reichwald et al. 2004; Tseng and Piller 2003). Both e-business partners are thus tied together in these value webs.

The firm's relationship with the customer, thus the business value of any customer integration, is crucially dependent on interaction with him or her. Here, interactivity is an essential building block for enhancing an electronic commerce relationship with the customer. More strongly, interactivity may even be considered as the engine of this the new fabric of interaction. Theoretically, customer integration is the ultimate form of this kind of customer orientation. Its goal is to provide customized products or services that exactly meet the desires and wishes of each individual customer (Milgrom and Roberts 1990).

Among other issues, the economic view of customer integration identifies interactive value creation as an emergent paradigm at the interface of research into strategic management, innovation management, and marketing management (Kotha 1995; Reichwald and Piller 2009). Hence, customer integration may become a strategic necessity of business companies as electronic transactions may impact the characteristics of these markets in ways that overall efficiency gains (e.g., lower information search costs for consumers) and/or improvements in effectiveness (e.g., greater ability of consumers to purchase products better suited to their specific needs) may result from transactions in electronic marketplaces in various industries (Bakos 1991; Lampel and Mintzberg 1996; Yadav and Varadarajan 2005b; Zeithaml 1988). Business companies may benefit from so-called *economies of integration* (Noori 1990; Piller et al. 2004; Wind and Rangaswamy 2001; Vandermerve 2000). These are defined as "cost savings potentials as a result from the direct interaction between each customer and the firm" (Piller and Moeslein 2002, p. 6). These economies of integration arise from a process called *mass customization* which essentially means differentiation through customization, i.e. the production of goods in so many variants that the wishes of each relevant customer are fulfilled. A customized product can lead to lower costs when a combination of economies of scale and economies of scope is attained. The differentiation option leads to greater product attractiveness. In addition, the individual contact between supplier and customer offers possibilities of building up a lasting relationship with the customer.

One can reasonably expect web interactivity-induced online transactions to push customer integration. This integration would then have potential effects on transaction costs involved, contingent upon type and intensity of web interactivity and thus the type and level of customer integration. As for customer integration to economize on this underlying trend of low transaction costs in electronic market exchanges, three areas of common concern are, however, worth specifying:

First, while web interactivity may reduce transaction costs, customer integration is, however, characterized by a high intensity and volume of information exchange between publisher and consumer. As web interactivity allows consumers to feel higher perceived sensory, cognitive, and affective affiliation with online site content, their perceived value of the site may be improved (Kalyanaraman and Sundar 2006). A corollary is that this generally improves the site's stickiness, i.e. the site's ability to retain online customers and prolong their duration of each stay. It is obvious, however, that the more intense and the larger the volume of transactions between producer and consumer become the higher will the investments necessary to deliver a satisfying and frustration-free experience for the consumer. A longer duration of stay, a higher engagement of the consumer, a bigger volume of transactions, simply, the more the customer is integrated and the more likely web interactivity is pushing this integration, the more complex will be the governance of relations between them two and the underlying transaction cost situations thereof.

In contrast to the popular thesis that internet-enabled business exchange would *automatically* lead to transaction costs efficiencies (Bakos 1991; Brynjolfsson and Smith 2000; Cordella and Simon 1997) (also see proposition 3 below), it may thus be argued that although web interactivity may potentially reduce transaction costs, exchanges differ in their affinity to generate particular types of transaction costs (see, above) and governance structures necessary to organize these transactions cost-efficiently. This is to say that full-fledged electronic market transactions require adequate interactive communication technology architecture. But while interactive broadband infrastructures provide a more efficient flow of information and facilitate transaction under complex and uncertain circumstances, and thereby reduce transaction costs (Benjamin and Wigand 1995), transactional risks remain prevalent in relation-specific investments. Opportunism and loss of resource control (Clemons and Row 1992; Clemons et al. 1993) over content quality and brand reputation come as impediments for online transaction to be organized exclusively via markets.

Proposition 3: Web interactivity reduces transaction costs
Reviewing the relevant literature on interactivity alludes to the possibility that it has various effects on transaction costs in online news publishing. Web interactivity-driven interactions between news provider and user involve various types of transaction costs, ranging from initiation to monitoring costs. When information is costly, various activities related to the exchange of property rights between the exchange partners give rise to transaction costs. In order for the transaction to be initiated, consumers face search costs for the product/content they demand (Stigler 1961). The publisher, on his side, needs to communicate the product value to the consumer by signaling price and quality components of the information good demanded. The consumer faces search and first assessment costs of product samples. Second, agreement costs are bargaining costs which arise when contracts are designed and duration of usage of the information goods to be exchanged are to be established.

Table 2 Transaction costs types and occurrence in online publishing—a selection

Transaction cost type	Occurrence in online publishing
Initiation	Consumer search costs for content of information goods
	Assessment of content samples
Agreement	Negotiation of contract design and duration of usage
Execution	One-time or recurring delivery of content
	Transfer of property rights
Monitoring	Monitoring of content quality, IPR, copyright infringement, social costs (Coase 1960)
Adjustment	Re-definition and re-negotiation of contract (Picot et al. 1998)
Motivation	Informational asymmetry and imperfect commitment (Milgrom and Roberts 1992)
Thinking	Cognitive costs (Shugan 1980)
Perception	Mental accounting costs (Thaler 1985)

Source: The author (following Anding and Hess 2002)

Execution costs relate to temporal types of content delivery and the actual transfer of property rights. Further, monitoring of content quality on the supply side as well as monitoring consumers to see whether they abide by the forms of contract (e.g. copyright infringement, costs of cheating and opportunistic behavior) come as another transaction cost component (Williamson 1975). Monitoring social costs (i.e. costs or benefits on others which are not reflected in the prices charged for the goods and services being provided and consumed; Coase 1960), and illicit copying and intellectual property theft further are perennial problems. Following TCT, contracts need to be adjusted again and again (Picot et al. 2001). Motivation costs are costs related to information asymmetries and incomplete commitment (Milgrom and Roberts 1992), mental accounting costs are some sort of psychological transaction costs that arise when humans make decisions under the impression of perceptual fallacies (Thaler 1985). Cognitive costs are costs related to mental effort and choice processing (Shugan 1980).

The following Table 2 presents potential transaction cost types in an online publishing context.

Conclusion

This article reviewed and synthesized selected literature on web interactivity and the management of customer integration with a view to evaluating both concepts against the role of transaction costs involved in social and economic transactions in the electronic marketplace. I hope to have made the following three contributions to discussions surrounding theory development in social media management research:

First, reviewing the concept of interactivity has identified a variety of themes from various scholarly perspectives. Although there are disciplinary differences in observing, defining, and interpreting interactivity, which obviously makes comparisons of different studies difficult, interactivity must be analyzed from these multiple sources in order to link the concept of interactivity with the concept of customer integration in exchanges in the electronic marketplace.

I adopted the dominant three-dimensional view of interactivity and conceptualized it as an intrinsic attribute of the communication technology, as a constituent part of a social interaction and communication process between users or between users and technology interfaces and designs, and as a process of subjective user perception (McMillan 2002, 2005, 2006; Quiring and Schweiger 2008). This three dimensional approach has become the canonical standard in researching the phenomenon of interactivity (Bucy and Tao 2007; Gleason and Lane 2009; McMillan 2005).

I conclude from the review of current literature that interactivity is highly heterogeneous in nature and thus covers a broad variety of challenging issues in building value webs through customer integration. However, the literature bodies of both concepts are wide and yet have to be researched more systematically. The problems are manifold but the most pressing seems to be the nature of the concept of web interactivity itself, which remains multi-faceted and difficult to operationalize. Theoretically, web interactivity may widen a publisher's strategic options focusing on customer integration, cooperation, and, eventually, sourcing of business value. Customer integration may also help achieving product differentiation thereby reducing the pressure of competition from identical products or close substitutes (Bakos 1991, 1997). Transaction cost theory may deliver a solid theoretical base for integrating both concepts more soundly. It was shown that web interactivity potentially drives up the interaction frequency of online transactions (e.g. because of open standards, anyone can interact with anyone else), reduces transaction uncertainty (by providing a wealth of transaction-specific information or establishing new contacts on a targeted basis; Richter et al. 2010), and is dependent on the type of economic and social transaction contracted. A corollary is that publishers need to carefully decide on type and organization of customer integration in order to successfully build a consumer marketplace for information goods and services. This would be strongly built on the media firm's ability in identifying the actual consumer need and ensuring a stable and sustainable relationship with him/her. It should have become clear that offering web interactivity may involve transaction costs that exceed efficiency thresholds on both sides of the transaction which will negatively affect the welfare of both news publisher and online consumers. Planned extensions and future research of this study shall include improving the validity of analysis by generating more insightful and testable theoretical propositions to be examined against empirical evidence. This would imply to establish a structural model which postulates effects between the technological, communicative and perceptual determinants of web interactivity, customer integration strategies, and the perceived impacts on transaction costs measured on both sides of the equation.

To conclude, a more nuanced investigation needs to be made into the transaction cost effectiveness of interactive media and communications in online publishing, since these costs can become critical for overall business success in digital media markets.

References

Alba, J. W., Lynch, J., Weitz, B., Janiszewski, C., Lutz, R., & Sawyer, A. (1997). Interactive home shopping: Consumer, retailer, and manufacturer incentives to participate in electronic marketplaces. *Journal of Marketing, 61*, 48–53.
Allen, D. W. (1991). What are transaction costs? *Research in Law and Economics, 14*, 1–18.
Amit, R., & Zott, C. (2001). Value creation in e-business. *Strategic Management Journal, 22*(6–7), 493–520.
Anding, M., & Hess, T. (2002). Online content syndication - eine transaktionskostentheoretische Analyse. In R. Gabriel & U. Hoppe (Eds.), *Electronic business. Theoretische Aspekte und Anwendungen in der betrieblichen Praxis* (pp. 163–189). Heidelberg: Physica.
Ariely, D. (1998). Combining experiences over time: The effects of duration, intensity changes, and on-line measurements on retrospective pain evaluations. *Journal of Behavioral Decision Making, 11*, 19–45.
Ariely, D. (2000). Controlling the information flow: Effects on consumers' decision making and preferences. *Journal of Consumer Research, 27*, 233–248.
Arrow, K. J. (1963). Uncertainty and the welfare economics of medical care. *American Economic Review, 53*(5), 941–973.
Baecker, R. M. (1980). Towards an effective characterization of geographical interaction. In R. A. Guedj, P. W. T. ten Hagen, F. R. Hopgood, H. Tucker, & D. A. Duce (Eds.), *Methodology of interaction* (pp. 127–147). Amsterdam, The Netherlands: North-Holland.
Baecker, R. M., & Buxton, W. A. S. (1987). *Readings in human-computer interaction: A multidisciplinary approach*. San Mateo, CA: Kaufmann.
Bakos, J. Y. (1991). A strategic analysis of electronic marketplaces. *MIS Quarterly, 15*(3), 295–310.
Bakos, J. Y. (1997). Reducing buyer search costs: Implications for electronic marketplaces. *Management Science, 43*(12), 1676–1692.
Bandulet, M., & Morasch, K. (2005). Would you like to be a Prosumer? Information revelation, personalization and price discrimination in electronic markets. *International Journal of the Economics of Business, 12*, 251–271.
Barnard, C. (1948). *Organization and management*. Cambridge, MA: Harvard University Press.
Benjamin, R., & Wigand, R. (1995). Electronic markets and virtual value chains on the information highway. *Sloan Management Review, 36*, 62–72.
Berger, C., Moeslein, K., Piller, F. T., & Reichwald, R. (2005). Co-designing modes of cooperation at the customer interface: Learning from exploratory research. *European Management Review, 2*, 70–87.
Bezjian-Avery, A., Calder, B., & Iacobucci, D. (1998). New media interactive advertising vs. traditional advertising. *Journal of Advertising Research, 38*(4), 23–32.
Blattberg, R. C., & Deighton, J. (1991). Interactive marketing: Exploiting the age of addressability. *Sloan Management Review, 32*(1), 5–14.
Brynjolfsson, E., & Smith, M. D. (2000). Frictionless commerce? A comparison of Internet and conventional retailers. *Management Science, 46*(4), 563–585.
Bucy, E. P. (2004a). Interactivity in society: Locating an elusive concept. *The Information Society, 20*(5), 375–387.
Bucy, E. P. (2004b). The interactivity paradox: Closer to the news but confused. In E. P. Bucy & J. E. Newhagen (Eds.), *Media access: Social and psychological dimensions of new technology use* (pp. 47–72). Mahwah, NJ: Erlbaum.
Bucy, E. P., & Tao, C. C. (2007). The mediated moderation model of interactivity. *Media Psychology, 9*, 647–672.
Burgoon, J. K., Bonito, J. A., Bengtsson, B., Cederberg, C., Lundeberg, M., & Allspach, L. (2000a). Interactivity in human-computer interaction: A study of credibility, understanding, and influence. *Computers in Human Behaviour, 16*, 553–574.

Burgoon, J. K., Bonito, J. A., Bengtsson, B., Ramirez, A., Dunbar, N. E., & Miczo, N. (2000b). Testing the Interactivity model, communication processes, partner assessments and the quality of collaborative work. *Journal of Management Information Systems, 16*(3), 33–56.

Burke, K., & Chidambaram, L. (1999). How much bandwidth is enough? A longitudinal examination of media characteristics and group outcomes. *MIS Quarterly, 23*(4), 557–580.

Carey, J. (1989). Interactive media. In E. Barnouw (Ed.), *International encyclopaedia of communications* (pp. 328–330). New York: Oxford University Press.

Chen, K., & Yen, D. C. (2004). Improving the quality of online presence through interactivity. *Information Management, 42*(1), 217–226.

Chesbrough, H., Vanhaverbeke, W., & West, J. (2006). *Open innovation: Researching a new paradigm*. Oxford, UK: Oxford University Press.

Choi, S.-Y., Stahl, D. O., & Winston, A. B. (1997). *The economics of electronic commerce*. London: Macmillan Technical Publishing.

Clemons, E. K., Reddi, S. P., & Row, M. C. (1993). The impact of information technology on the organization of economic activity: The "move to the middle" hypothesis. *Journal of Management Information Systems, 10*(2), 9–35.

Clemons, E. K., & Row, M. C. (1992). Information technology and industrial cooperation: The role of changing transaction costs. *Journal of Management Information Systems, 9*(2), 9–28.

Coase, R. H. (1937). The nature of the firm. *Economica, 4*, 386–405. Reprinted in Coase, R. H. (1988). The nature of the firm: Influence. *Journal of Law, Economics, and Organization, 4*, 33–47.

Coase, R. H. (1960). The problem of social cost. *Journal of Law and Economics, 3*, 1–44.

Cordella, A., & Simon, K. A. (1997, August). *The impact of information technology on transaction and coordination cost*. Paper presented at the Conference on Information Systems Research in Scandinavia (IRIS 20), Oslo, Norway.

Coviello, N., Milley, R., & Marcolin, B. (2001). Understanding IT-enabled interactivity in contemporary marketing. *Journal of Interactive Marketing, 15*(4), 18–33.

Coyle, J. R., & Thorson, E. (2001). The effects of progressive levels of interactivity and vividness in web marketing sites. *Journal of Advertising, 30*, 65–77.

Day, G. (1998). Organizing for interactivity. *Journal of Interactive Marketing, 12*(1), 47–53.

Dennis, A. R., Fuller, R. M., & Valacich, J. S. (2008). Media, tasks, and communication processes: A theory of media synchronicity. *MIS Quarterly, 32*(3), 575–600.

Dennis, A. R., & Kinney, S. (1998). Testing media richness theory in the new media: The effects of cues, feedback, and task equivocality. *Information Systems Research, 9*(3), 256–274.

Dennis, A., & Valacich, J. S. (1999). Rethinking media richness: Towards a theory of media synchronicity. *Proceedings of the 32nd Hawaii International Conference on System Science*, IEEE Computer Society, Los Alamitos, CA.

Deuze, M. (2003). The web and its journalisms: Considering the consequences of different types of newsmedia online. *New Media Society, 5*(2), 203–230.

Downes, E. J., & McMillan, S. J. (2000). Defining interactivity: A qualitative identification of key dimension. *New Media and Society, 2*(2), 157–179.

Durlak, J. T. (1987). A typology for interactive media. In M. L. McLaughlin (Ed.), *Communication yearbook* (Vol. 10, pp. 743–757). Mahwah, NJ: Erlbaum.

Economides, N. (1996). The economics of networks. *International Journal of Industrial Organization, 14*(6), 673–699.

Essler, U., & Whitaker, R. (2001). Re-thinking e-commerce business modelling in terms of interactivity. *Electronic Markets, 11*(1), 10–16.

Fortin, D. R., & Dholakia, R. R. (2005). Interactivity and vividness effects on social presence and involvement with a web-based advertisement. *Journal of Business Research, 58*(3), 387–396.

Franz, C. R., & Robey, D. (1986). Organizational context, user involvement, and the usefulness of information systems. *Decision Sciences, 17*(4), 329–356.

Fulk, J., Schmitz, J., & Steinfield, C. W. (1990). A social influence model of technology use. In J. Fulk & C. Steinfield (Eds.), *Organizations and communication technology* (pp. 117–140). Newbury Park, CA: Sage.

Ghose, S., & Dou, W. (1998). Interactive functions and their impacts on the appeal of internet presence sites. *Journal of Advertising Research, 38*(2), 29–43.
Gleason, J. P., & Lane, D. (2009, November). *Interactivity redefined: A first look at outcome interactivity theory.* Paper presented at the annual meeting of the NCA 95th Annual Convention, Chicago, IL. Retrieved February 24, 2010, from http://people.eku.edu/gleasonj/Outcome_Interactivity_Theory.pdf
Goffman, E. (1967). *Interaction ritual.* Chicago: Aldine.
Gouldner, A. W. (1960). The norm of reciprocity: A preliminary statement. *American Sociological Review, 25*(2), 161–178.
Grunig, J. E., & Grunig, L. A. (1989). Toward a theory of public relations behavior of organizations: Review of a program of research. In J. E. Grunig & L. A. Grunig (Eds.), *Public relations research annual* (pp. 27–63). Hillsdale, NJ: Erlbaum.
Guedj, R. A., tenHagen, P. J. W., Hopgood, F. R., Tucker, H. A., & Duce, D. A. (1980). *Methodology of interaction.* Amsterdam, The Netherlands: North Holland.
Ha, L., & James, E. L. (1998). Interactivity reexamined: A baseline analysis of early business web sites. *Journal of Broadcasting and Electronic Media, 42*(4), 457–474.
Hanssen, L., Jankowski, N. W., & Etienne, R. (1996). Interactivity from the perspective of communication studies. In N. W. Jankowski & L. Hanssen (Eds.), *Contours of multimedia: Recent technological, theoretical, and empirical developments* (pp. 61–73). London: University of Luton Press.
Hartson, H. R. (1998). Human-computer interaction: Interdisciplinary roots and trends. *Journal of Systems and Software, 43*(2), 103–118.
Hartwick, J., & Barki, H. (1994). Explaining the role of user participation in information system use. *Management Science, 40*(4), 440–465.
Heeter, C. (1989). Implications of interactivity for communication research. In J. L. Salvaggio & B. Jennings (Eds.), *Media use in the information age: Emerging patterns of adoption and consumer use* (pp. 53–75). Mahwah, NJ: Erlbaum.
Heeter, C. (2000). Interactivity in the context of designed experiences. *Journal of Interactive Advertising, 1*(1). Retrieved March 25, 2005, from http://jiad.org/vol1/no1/heeter/
Iacobucci, D. (1998). Interactive marketing and the meganet: Networks of networks. *Journal of Interactive Marketing, 12*(1), 5–16.
Jaeckel, M. (1995). Interaktion. Soziologische Anmerkungen zu einem Begriff [Interaction. Sociological comments on a concept]. *Rundfunk und Fernsehen, 43*(4), 463–476.
Jee, J., & Lee, W.-N. (2002). Antecedents and consequences of perceived interactivity: An exploratory study. *Journal of Interactive Advertising, 3*, 1–18.
Jensen, J. F. (1998). Interactivity – tracking a new concept in media and communication studies. *Nordicom Review, 19*(1), 185–204.
Johnson, G. J., Bruner, G. C., II, & Kumar, A. (2006). Interactivity and its facets revisited: Theory and empirical test. *Journal of Advertising, 35*(4), 35–52.
Kalyanaraman, S., & Sundar, S. S. (2006). The psychological appeal of personalized content in web portals: Does customization affect attitudes and behavior? *Journal of Communication, 56*, 110–122.
Kim, J., & LaRose, R. (2004). Interactive e-commerce: Promoting consumer efficiency or impulsivity? *Journal of Computer-Mediated Communication, 10*(1). Retrieved July 9, 2006, from http://jcmc.indiana.edu/vol10/issue1/kim_larose.html
Kiousis, S. (2002). Interactivity: A concept explication. *New Media and Society, 4*(3), 355–383.
Kleinaltenkamp, M., Fließ, S., & Jacob, F. (1996). *Customer Integration – Von der Kundenorientierung zur Kundenintegration.* Wiesbaden, Germany: Gabler.
Klemperer, P. D. (2008). Network effects. In S. N. Durlauf & L. E. Blume (Eds.), *The New Palgrave: A dictionary of economics* (pp. 915–917). Basingstoke, UK: Palgrave-Macmillan.
Ko, H., Cho, C.-H., & Roberts, M. S. (2005). Internet uses and gratifications: A structural equation model of interactive advertising. *Journal of Advertising, 34*(2), 57–70.
Kotha, S. (1995). Mass customization: Implementing the emerging paradigm for competitive advantage. *Strategic Management Journal, 16*, 21–42.

Kuk, G., & Yeung, F. T. (2002). Interactivity in e-commerce. *Quarterly Journal of Electronic Commerce, 3*(3), 223–235.

Lampel, J., & Mintzberg, H. (1996). Customizing customization. *Sloan Management Review, 38*(1), 21–30.

Laurel, B. (1991). *Computers as theatre*. Reading, MA: Addison-Wesley.

Lee, T. (2004). The impact of perceptions of interactivity on customer trust and transaction intentions in mobile commerce. *Journal of Electronic Commerce Research, 6*(3), 165–180.

Lee, C.-H., Barua, A., & Whinston, A. B. (2000). The complementarity of mass customization and electronic commerce. *Economics of Innovation and New Technology, 9*(2), 81–110.

Liu, Y. (2003). Generating value through online interaction. Individual and situational differences. *Competitive Paper Submitted to the 2003 AMS Annual Conference.* Retrieved July 9, 2006, from http://jcmc.indiana.edu/vol3/issue2/ lombard.html

Liu, Y., & Shrum, J. L. (2002). What is interactivity and is it always such a good thing? Implications of definition, person, and situation for the influence of interactivity on advertising effectiveness. *Journal of Advertising, 31*(4), 53–64.

Lombard, M., & Ditton, T. (1997). At the heart of it all: the concept of presence. *Journal of Computer-Mediated Communication, 3*(2). Retrieved July 9, 2006, from http://jcmc.indiana.edu/vol3/issue2/lombard.html

Lowry, P. B., Romano, N. C., Jr., Jenkins, J. L., & Guthrie, R. W. (2009). The CMC interactivity model: How interactivity enhances communication quality and process satisfaction in lean-media groups. *Journal of Management Information Systems, 26*(1), 155–195.

McMillan, S. J. (1998). Who pays for content? funding in interactive media. *Journal of Computer Mediated Communication, 4*(1). Accessed December 20, 2012. http://www.ascusc.org/jcmc/vol4/issue1/mcmillan.html

McMillan, S. J. (1998). Who pays for content? Funding in interactive media. *Journal of Computer Mediated Communication, 4*(1). Retrieved July 24, 2009, from http://www.ascusc.org/jcmc/vol4/issue1/mcmillan.html

McMillan, S. J. (2000). Interactivity is in the Eye of the Beholder: Function, Perception, Involvement, and Attitude toward the Web Site, http://web.utk.edu/~sjmcmill/Research/research.htm.

McMillan, S. J. (2000a). Interactivity is in the eye of the beholder: Function, perception, involvement, and attitude toward the Website. In M. A. Shaver (Ed.), *Proceedings of the 2000 Conference of the American Academy of Advertising* (pp. 71–78). Michigan State University: East Lansing. http://web.utk.edu/~sjmcmill/Research/mcmillsj.doc.

McMillan, S. J. (2000b). The microscope and the moving target: the challenge of applying content analysis to the World Wide Web. *Journalism and Mass Communication Quarterly, 77*(1), 80–98.

McMillan, S. J. (2002). A four-part model of cyber-interactivity: Some cyber-spaces are more interactive than others. *New Media and Society, 4*(2), 271–291.

McMillan, S. J. (2005). The researchers and the concept. Moving beyond a blind examination of interactivity. *Journal of Interactive Advertising, 5*(2), 1–4.

McMillan, S. J. (2006). Exploring models of interactivity from multiple research traditions: Users, documents, and systems. In L. L. Lievrouw & S. Livingstone (Eds.), *Handbook of new media* (pp. 205–230). London: Sage.

McMillan, S. J., & Hwang, J.-S. (2002). Measures of perceived interactivity: An exploration of the role of direction of communication, user control, and time in shaping perceptions of interactivity. *Journal of Advertising, 31*(3), 41–54.

Milgrom, P. R., & Roberts, J. (1990). The economics of modern manufacturing: Technology, strategy and organization. *American Economic Review, 80*(3), 511–528.

Milgrom, P. R., & Roberts, J. (1992). *Economics, organization, and management*. Englewood Cliffs, NJ: Prentice-Hall.

Nickerson, R. S. (1977). On conversational interaction with computers. In *User-oriented design of interactive graphic systems* (pp. 101–113)). New York, NY: ACM. Reprinted in Baecker, R. M., & Buxton, W. A. S. (Eds.). Readings in human-computer interaction: A multidisciplinary approach. Los Altos, CA: Morgan-Kaufmann.

Neumann, W. R. (2008). Interactivity, concept of. In W. Donsbach (Ed.), *The international encyclopedia of communication*. Blackwell Publishing, Blackwell. Reference Online

Retrieved October 10, 2010, from http://www.blackwellreference.com/public/tocnode?id=g9781405131995_yr2010_chunk_g978140513199514_ss44-1
Nielsen, J. (2000). *Designing web usability: The practice of simplicity.* Indianapolis, IN: New Riders.
Noll, A. M. (2003). Television over the Internet: Technological challenges. In E. Noam (Ed.), *Internet television* (pp. 19–30). Mahwah, NJ: Erlbaum.
Noori, H. (1990). Economies of integration: A new manufacturing focus. *International Journal of Technology Management, 5*(5), 577–587.
Normann, R., & Ramirez, R. (1993). From value chain to value constellation: Designing interactive strategy. *Harvard Business Review, 71*, 65–77.
Novak, T. P., Hoffman, D. L., & Yung, Y.-F. (2000). Measuring the customer experience in online environments: A structural modeling approach. *Marketing Science, 19*(1), 22–42.
Picot, A., Reichwald, R., & Wigand, R. (1998). *Information, organization, and management: Expanding markets and corporate boundaries.* New York: Wiley.
Picot, A., Reichwald, R., & Wigand, R. T. (2001). *Die grenzenlose Unternehmung.* Gabler: Wiesbaden.
Picot, A., Reichwald, R., & Wigand, R. T. (2008). *Information, organization and management.* Berlin: Springer.
Piller, F. T. (2002). Customer interaction and digitizability – a structural approach. In C. Rautenstrauch, R. Seelmann-Eggebert, & K. Turowski (Eds.), *Moving towards mass customization: Information systems and management principles* (pp. 119–138). Berlin/New York: Springer.
Piller, F. T., & Moeslein, K. (2002). *From economies of scale towards economies of customer integration. Value creation in mass customization based electronic commerce.* Unpublished working reports of the Chair of Industrial and Business Economics at the Technical University of Munich.
Piller, F. T., Moeslein, K., & Stotko, C. (2004). Does mass customization pay? An economic approach to evaluate customer integration. *Production Planning and Control, 15*(4), 435–444.
Porter, M. E. (1985). *Competitive advantage: Creating and sustaining superior performance.* New York: The Free Press.
Porter, M. E. (2001). Strategy and the internet. *Harvard Business Review, 79*(3), 62–78.
Prahalad, C. K., & Ramaswamy, V. (2000). Co-opting customer competence. *Harvard Business Review, 79*(1), 79–87.
Prahalad, C. K., & Ramaswamy, V. (2002). The co-creation connection. *Strategy and Business, 27*, 50–61.
Prahalad, C. K., & Ramaswamy, V. (2003). The new frontier of experience innovation. *MIT Sloan Management Review, 44*(4), 12–18.
Prahalad, C. K., & Ramaswamy, V. (2004). *The future of competition: Cocreating unique value with customers.* Boston, MA: Harvard Business School Press.
Quiring, O. (2009). What do users associate with 'interactivity'? A qualitative study on user schemata. *New Media and Society, 11*(6), 899–920.
Quiring, O., & Schweiger, W. (2008). Interactivity: A review of the concept and a framework for analysis. *Communications, 33*(2), 147–167.
Rafaeli, S. (1988). Interactivity: From media to communication. In R. P. Hawkins, J. M. Wieman, & S. Pingree (Eds.), *Advancing communication science: Merging mass and interpersonal communication* (pp. 110–134). Newbury Park: Sage.
Rafaeli, S., & Sudweeks, F. (1997). Networked interactivity. *Journal of Computer-Mediated Communication, 2*(4). Retrieved March 3, 2007, from http://jcmc.huji.ac.il/vol2/issue4/rafaeli.sudweeks.html
Rangaswamy, A., & Pal, N. (2003). Gaining business value from personalization technologies. In N. Pal & A. Rangaswamy (Eds.), *The power of one: Gaining business value from personalization technologies* (pp. 1–9). Victoria, Australia: Trafford.
Reichwald, R., & Piller, F. T. (2000). Mass customization-Konzepte im electronic business. In R. Weiber (Ed.), *Handbuch electronic business. Informationstechnologien – electronic commerce – Geschäftsprozesse* (pp. 359–383). Wiesbaden, Germany: Gabler.
Reichwald, R., & Piller, F. T. (2009). *Interaktive Wertschoepfung: Open Innovation, Individualisierung und neue Formen der Arbeitsteilung.* Wiesbaden: Gabler.

Reichwald, R., Seifert, S., & Walcher, D. (2004, January). *Customers as part of value webs. Towards a framework for webbed customer innovation tools*. Paper presented at the Hawaii International Conference on Computer Sciences (HICSS), Maui.

Rice, R. E., & Williams, F. (1984). Theories old and new: The study of new media. In R. E. Rice (Ed.), *The new media* (pp. 55–80). Beverly Hills, CA: Sage.

Richter, D., Riemer, K., & vom Brocke, J. (2010). *Social transactions on social network sites: Can transaction cost theory contribute to a better understanding of internet social networking?* Paper presented at the 23rd Bled eConference, Bled, Slovenia.

Rindfleisch, A., & Heide, J. B. (1997). Transaction cost analysis: Past, present, and future applications. *Marketing, 61*(4), 30–54.

Robey, D. (1979). User attitudes and management information system use. *Academy of Management Journal, 22*(3), 527–538.

Romano, N. C., & Fjermestad, J. (2003). Electronic commerce customer relationship management: A research agenda. *Information Technology and Management, 4*, 233–258.

Shaw, T., Aranson, K., & Belardo, S. (1993). The effects of computer mediated interactivity on idea generation: An experimental investigation. *IEEE Transactions on Systems, Man, and Cybernetics, 23*(3), 737–745.

Short, J. A. (1974). Effect of medium of communication on experimental negotiation. *Human Relations, 27*, 225–234.

Short, J., Williams, E., & Christie, B. (1976). *The social psychology of telecommunications*. New York: Wiley.

Shugan, S. M. (1980). The cost of thinking. *Journal of Consumer Research, 75*, 99–111.

Simon, H. A. (1957). A behavioural model of rational choice. *Quarterly Journal of Economics, 69*(1), 99–118.

Song, I., & Bucy, E. P. (2008). Interactivity and political attitude formation. A mediation model of online information processing. *Journal of Information Technology and Politics, 4*(2), 29–61.

Stanoevska-Slabeva, K. (2011). *Enabled innovation: Instruments and methods of internet-based collaborative innovation*. Draft paper prepared for the first Berlin Symposium in Internet and Society, Berlin, October 25–27, 2011.

Steuer, J. (1992). Defining virtual reality: Dimensions determining telepresence. *Journal of Communication, 42*(4), 73–93.

Stewart, D. W., & Pavlou, P. A. (2002). From consumer response to active consumer: Measuring the effectiveness of interactive media. *Academy of Marketing Science, 30*(4), 376–396.

Stigler, G. J. (1961). The economics of information. *Journal of Political Economy, 69*(3), 213–225.

Sukpanich, N., & Chen, L.-D. (2000). Interactivity as the driving force behind e-commerce. *AMCIS 2000 Proceedings* (Paper 163). Accessed December 20, 2012. http://ais.bepress.com/amcis2000/163

Sundar, S. S. (2004). Theorizing interactivity's effects. *The Information Society, 20*(5), 355–383.

Taylor, F. W. (1911). *The principles of scientific management*. New York: Harper & Row.

Thaler, R. H. (1985). Mental accounting and consumer choice. *Marketing Science, 4*, 199–214.

Toffler, A. (1980). *The third wave*. New York: Bantham Books.

Tseng, M., & Jiao, J. (2001). Mass customisation. In G. Salvendy (Ed.), *Handbook of industrial engineering* (pp. 684–709). New York: Wiley.

Tseng, M. M., & Piller, F. T. (2003). *The customer centric enterprise. Advances in mass customization and personalisation*. Berlin: Springer.

Vandermerve, S. (2000). How increasing value to customers improves business results. *Sloan Management Review, 42*, 27–37.

Varadarajan, P. R., & Yadav, M. S. (2002). Marketing strategy and the internet: An organizing framework. *Journal of the Academy of Marketing Science, 30*(4), 296–313.

von Hippel, E. (1998). Economics of product development by users. *Management Science, 44*(5), 629–644.

von Hippel, E. (2005). *Democratizing innovation*. Cambridge, MA: MIT.

Walther, J. B. (1992). Interpersonal effects in computer-mediated interaction: A relational perspective. *Communication Research, 19*(1), 52–89.

Webster, F. E., Jr. (1996). Perspectives - the future of interactive marketing. *Harvard Business Review* (November–December), 156–157.
Webster, F. E., Jr. (1998). Commentary: Interactivity and marketing paradigm shifts. *Journal of Interactive Marketing, 12*(1), 54–55.
Wigand, R. T. (1997). Electronic commerce: Definition, theory, and context. *The Information Society, 13*, 1–16.
Wigand, R. T., Benjamin, R. I., & Birkland, J. L. H. (2008). Web 2.0 and beyond: Implications for electronic commerce. *Electronic Commerce ACM*, New York, NY, USA, Innsbruck, Austria.
Wikstroem, S. (1996a). Value creation by company-consumer interaction. *Journal of Marketing Management, 12*, 359–374.
Wikstroem, S. (1996b). The customer as co-producer. *European Journal of Marketing, 30*(4), 6–19.
Williams, F., Rice, R. E., & Rogers, E. M. (1988). *Research methods and the new media*. New York, NY: Free Press.
Williamson, O. E. (1973). Markets and hierarchies: Some elementary considerations. *The American Economic Review, 63*(2), 316–325.
Williamson, O. E. (1975). *Markets and hierarchies, analysis and antitrust implications*. New York: The Free Press.
Williamson, O. E. (1976). Franchise bidding for natural monopolies in general and with respect to CATV. *Bell Journal of Economics, XXVI*(3), 497–540.
Williamson, O. E. (1979). Transaction cost economics. The governance of contractual relations. *Journal of law and Economics, 22*, 233–261.
Williamson, O. E. (1981). The economics of organisation: The transaction cost approach. *The American Journal of Sociology, 87*, 548–577.
Williamson, O. E. (1985). *The economic institutions of capitalism: Firms, markets, relational contracting*. New York: The Free Press.
Williamson, O. E. (1991). Comparative economic organization: The analysis of discrete structural alternatives. *Administrative Science Quarterly, 36*(2), 269–296.
Williamson, O. E. (1996). *The mechanism of governance*. New York, NY: Oxford University Press.
Williamson, O. E. (2005). Transaction cost economics. In C. Menard & M. M. Shirley (Eds.), *Handbook of new institutional economics* (pp. 41–65). Dordrecht, Netherlands: Springer Press.
Wind, J., & Rangaswamy, A. (2001). Customerization: The next revolution in mass customization. *Journal of Interactive Marketing, 15*(1), 13–32.
Woodruff, R. B. (1997). Customer value: The next source for competitive advantage. *Journal of the Academy of Marketing Science, 25*(2), 139–153.
Wu, G. (2006). Conceptualizing and measuring the perceived interactivity of websites. *Journal of Current Issues and Research in Advertising, 28*(1), 87–104.
Yadav, M. S., & Varadarajan, P. R. (2002). Understanding product migration to the electronic marketplace: A conceptual framework. *Journal of Retailing, 81*(2), 125–140.
Yadav, M. S., & Varadarajan, P. R. (2005a). Interactivity in the electronic marketplace: An exposition of the concept and implications for research. *Journal of the Academy of Marketing Science, 33*(4), 585–603.
Yadav, M. S., & Varadarajan, P. R. (2005b). Understanding product migration to the electronic marketplace: A conceptual framework. *Journal of Retailing, 81*(2), 125–140.
Zaichkowsky, J. L. (1985). Measuring the involvement construct. *The Journal of Consumer Research, 12*(3), 341–352.
Zaichkowsky, J. L. (1986). Conceptualizing involvement. *Journal of Advertising, 15*(2), 4–34.
Zeithaml, V. A. (1988). Consumer perceptions of price, quality, and value: A means-end model and synthesis of evidence. *Journal of Marketing, 52*(3), 2–22.

All Businesses are Media Business: The Impact of Social Media on the Healthcare Market

Alexander Schachinger

A healthcare market related article in a book of social media in media markets may not fit into context at first hand. Contrariwise especially in the healthcare market one can observe the changing and partly disrupting impact of social media and social network phenomenons on this market and its stakeholders, distribution and communication structures quite exemplary. We can see that for example the information monopoly feature of experts medical information and research and the physician as the partriarchal disposer and controller of medical knowledge, diagnose and therapy in opposite to the passive and therapy regimes receiving patient is slowly breaking open through online connected patients and their free access to health information, yet unobservable on how this change will impact on the healthcare system or even does at all. As Bernhard Heitzer, President of the Federal Antitrust Agency of Germany described it: in a free market customer information evolves automatically but in the healthcare industry the information asymmetry between care provider and patients did not improve even after 50 years of planning.[1] Furthermore new forms of patientcentric internetbased services and products in the healthcare segment evolve that go beyond communicational aspects of social media, building new product and service innovation trajectories and value chains that improve medicare with digital means. However, these innovations are mainly developed and offered by nontraditional player that are yet not linked to the traditional medicare provider of a healthcare system. Parallel to relevant social media aspects mentioned in the introduction of this book focusing on the evolution of middle media, community forming, ROI issues and disruptive moments, all these aspects also occur for the impact of social media on the healthcare market. They can exemplary be observed and first e-strategical learnings deduced.

---

[1] http://www.berliner-zeitung.de/archiv/der-praesident-des-bundeskartellamts--bernhard-heitzer--fordert-die-abschaffung-des-gesundheitsfonds-und-mehr-marktwirtschaft--das-monopol-der-aerzte-muss-gebrochen-werden-,10810590,10649004.html

A. Schachinger (✉)
Humboldt University, Berlin, Germany
e-mail: alexander.schachinger@gmail.com

The audience paradigm shift described by Jay Rosen as "the people formerly known as the audience" can be adapted to healthcare via the people formerly known as patients.[2] We observe for example that those mobile applications for chronically ill who offer best relevance for a daily coping with a dedicated disease thus new forms of therapy and care is offered by patients who do have access or knowledge of producing software and apps and not from the traditional caregiver like hospitals, doctors or pharma companies. Leveraging these examples onto a higher and systemic market level, aspects of disruption, loss of formerly unrestrained control and the entrance of nontraditional player into the traditional sphere of a nations healthcare and medicare system occur. Exactly this scenario is described by Clayton Christensen, known as an innovation theorist for disruptive technologies, in his book "The Innovators Prescription—A Disruptive Solution for Healthcare".[3]

In the following text an observational and on the theory side a microsociological approach will be used to separately analyse the internetbased behaviour of healthcare surfers as the demand side aside the evolving digital products and services they find online, defined as the supply side, followed by hypothetical consequences of these two sides onto the traditional healthcare system.

A step back: what means healthcare system? (example: Germany)

Coming from the partly known belief that all consumer centered businesses are media business, the traditional healthcare industry and especially the care provider (e.g. hospitals, medical technology and medication producers) are mainly not. The impact of the internet to different market segments and industries, for example the cultural industry started around the very late nineties of the last century and had quite a disruptive impact to its distribution channels and sales models. But the healthcare market or the healthcare system in general, besides the evolution of online pharmacies, was yet quite untouched of the internet.

Furthermore if one assumes that the currency of gained customer centered market or brand awareness and thus market success besides the product quality is a condition of revenue and thus return on media spendings, in healthcare it is not. Because the majority of European and many other healthcare systems of the developed countries are by regulation run by governmental solidary systems where the funding is strictly regulated by tax and mandatory insurance fees for the employer and employees and the spending side by mandatory licensing and approval regulatory authorities defining who can be a care provider and what he can prescribe and what he gets in return for that (also known as a fee-for-service economy).[4] Thus this market is regulated and is also called as the first healthcare market. This is mainly the market for medications or other medical diagnoses or therapies prescribed by a physician. He is thus the main advertising target audience for the products and its manufacturer that by licencing can only be distributed via a physicians prescription and paid by the

---

[2] http://www.economist.com/node/18904124

[3] Christensen (2009).

[4] See exemplary Busse and Riesberg (2005).

health insurance. The second healthcare market is the classical healthcare consumer market which is free of mandatory subscription and where the demand side can liberaly buy healthcare related products and services (e.g. fitness clubs, health food, wellness products and holidays and similar).

Both markets in size gain about 16 % of Germanys GDP in 2010 with a value of roughly 280 billion euros and having grown since 1970 with a price adjusted growth rate of a factor about 11.7. Yes, by the western demographical shift, ongoing medical innovations and a lifestyle and social value shift towards health, the healthcare market is growing.

1 The Demand Side and its Impact

For the impact analysis of social media in healthcare the first market is the more interesting one especially because of its regulation.

Curiously not before late 2009 a German market research company analyzed, that 79 % of the German internet users (about 77 % of the German population over age 14) uses the internet for healthcare topics, which is overall about 60 % of the population over 14 years of age.[5] The 2011 ITU report gives a comparable percentage of online health care surfers among countries with a digitally relatively high developed infrastructure, which are for example the majority of the EU27 countries.[6] A sociodemographic explanation of an assumed growth in using the internet for healthcare is based on the fact that the growth of internet users in general happens mainly in the age segments of 40–50 years and above, where health topics increasingly play a relevant role of interest and especially those age segments have a relatively high share of the total population of Germany compared to younger age segments. Furthermore it generally can be observed that the longer a person is online the higher the chance that this person uses the internet also for health topics.[7]

The contemporary institutionalized academic disciplines have yet not implemented the research field of digital healthcare, also known as health 2.0 or the medical or health related usage of digital channels and platforms from patients and healthcare professionals. A lot of influencing publications like from the social scientist Manuel Castells on the network society[8] or from Yochai Benkler on the wealth of networks[9] analyzed the societal and economical influence of the internet. It seems as if the scientific analytical break down into sub topics or sub systems of a society and its relation to the digital age is the next step of academic research.

---

[5] Press Release of Psychonomics AG, Cologne on September 27, 2009.
[6] International Telecommunication Union (2011).
[7] xx pew als Quelle rein.
[8] Castells (2004).
[9] Benkler (2006).

Starting in the last years of the twentieth century the research papers covering these areas are coming either from the social, medical or computer sciences. The globally leading publication organisation covering this research area is the journal of medical internet research at the University of Toronto, which was founded by Gunther Eysenbach in 1999.[10] In the United States the Society for Participatory Medicine with its Journal of Participatory Medicine (founded 2008) covers aspects of how digital media can shift the existing healthcare system towards a more patient- and health outcome-centric medicare approach.[11]

Thomas William Ferguson was one of the first who described the phenomenon called "e-patient" in his comprehensive and meta-analytica white paper on this issue in 2006.[12] Thus e-patients are people who surf on the net for healthcare reasons. They either have an acute or chronic condition or surf on behalf their relatives as a form of caregiver. E-patients inform, exchange and learn from each other online in all aspects of a diseases diagnose, symptoms, therapies, doctors, hospitals and of course alternatives to those aspects their doctor told them. Because the concernment of having a chronic disease, the personal data aspects gets a different priority if one chats or posts messages on behalf ones condition in the internet. Furthermore, the majority of patients forums and social networks work on an anonymous profile base which makes the sharing of personal disease data easier. Due the fact that e-patients speak the same social language in a comparable context, seek similar disease coping information, mainly among other likeminded patients having the same disease, the information exchange is perceived as highly relevant, comprehensive and helpful. Especially patients who have experience since many years within a dedicated chronic indication become a new form of patient opinion leader. On the other side, aspects of orientation on where to find what and aspects of transparence and quality are still an inhibitor of getting fast and comprehensive gratification while surfing on the net for health topics.

Thus in many aspects e-patients who learn online among each other can be described as a social "community of practice", based on the microsociological and collaborative learning theory of Etienne Wenger.[13] Wenger sees the "like-me" phenomenon, the same aspects of a groups situation, problems, shared symbols, meanings and resources as those preconditions that form a community of practice, where learning can happen, independent of the place or the used medium. This collaborative aspect of learning stands in opposition to the institutionalized learning paradigm where collaboration is mere a reason for penalty. According to Wenger, a community of practice defines by self regulation which agenda, goals, means to learn and even which learning architecture is relevant and in which forms, artefacts and language it is communicated.

---

[10] See online: http://www.jmir.org

[11] See online: http://www.jopm.org

[12] Ferguson and White Paper der e-Patient Scholar Working Group (2006).

[13] Wenger (2008).

A yet unpublished online-survey as the empirical part of my Ph.D. thesis, focusing on the impact of online exchange with likeminded e-patients among 1946 self-selected users of the major German healthcare online portals reveiled that
- About every second participant exchanges health related issues in forums and uses the mutual help from other patients online
- 72 % of the participants can better deal with their disease due health related online surfing
- 80 % can better decide for or against a special treatment or health product due health related online surfing
- 81 % change the way they talk to and with their doctors due health related online surfing

Furthermore it seems that those internet users who use the internet for health issues are parallel also consumers of health related content in the traditional mass media and are thus recruiting themselves from a generally socioeconomic higher positioned milieu.[14] The upcoming question is, how is an assumed digital divide, separating the offliners from the onliner within a dedicated country, influencing or amplifying a digital healthcare divide? Unfortunately the phenomenon of the e-patient is not covered within the academic research field of public health.

Switching to the side of the doctors, in discussions with them at medical congresses in Germany, Austria and Switzerland they all seem to be unprepared and lack time and regulatory resources in coping the new phenomenon of the educated and connected e-patient which can be seen as a small disruptive moment toward an institutionalized health authority.[15] As discussed with several healthcare practitioner at the Charité Hospital in Berlin, this should be a topic and a call-for-action for the national medical associations delivering orientation to their members.

Summing it up, the evolving e-patient phenomenon and its aftermath at the contact points of the medicare providers is a very new situation which mid future impacts are yet hard to forecast.

2 The Supply Side and its Development

Broadcast media companies and publishing houses with its audience centric and content rich approach are generally those stakeholders in the online healthcare market who generate the highest traffic and thus audience market share. Examples are content rich healthcare portals linked by their name and branding to health related broadcast or magazine brands that have since years or decades a strong share of voice in the mass media on a national level. Additionally and before the spread of social

---

[14] Fox (2008).

[15] See for example the ehealth panel in the programme of the 42nd Annual Conference of The Austrian Society for Internal Medicine, Oct 5th in Innsbruck, online:http://www.oegim.at

media and its web-based features technically defined by web 2.0,[16] usually text-based forums like the yahoo groups for example next to the content based health portals mentioned above were the standard internetbased supplies that health surfers could find. An example for a health-related text forum in Germany is med1.de which was founded in 1999 and gathers around 3.5 million visits on a monthly base in 2010 and is one of the leading healthcare portals in reach. The portal was found and is run by a retired physician. An example of the publishing industry is the health website of the leading health and pharmacy magazine in Germany the Apotheken Umschau, with about 2.6 million visits a month.[17] Complementary the traditional stakeholder of the healthcare system (hospitals, health insurances, med.tech and pharma industries to name the most relevant one) in their majority simply offer till today a corporate representation as a website, mainly because of the communicative regulations mentioned above. Compared to health-related websites like the ones mentioned, the traffic of these stakeholder website have generally visits in a range of 10–50 thousand on an monthly base,[18] except the leading national relevant health insurances who also have visits reaching the millions. A content analysis of every healthcare system relevant stakeholder and health related websites independent of the legal form of the stakeholder with a traffic above around 30–40 thousand visits a month revealed that about 70 % of the whole health related traffic happens on websites outside the healthcare system and thus in the sector of the private media market.[19] The majority of the leading health portals from the private stakeholders do have a forum or a social network to exchange on health related questions. The conclusion of these observations are twofold: the awareness goes to the health websites of the private media market and not to the traditional stakeholder of the healthcare system and the exchange and participation on questions from e-patients within forums happens also outside the websites of the traditional healthcare stakeholders also because of their regulatory limited scope of communication possibilities.

The advent of social media and thus collaboratively evolved new forms of data and information enabled new user-centered services of information and evaluation for example user generated votings of hospital performance, physicians and even medications and medical side effects. These consumer-centric information are very new qualities that laymen have access to. An example of this mainly user-generated new information quality is the German website sanego.de where registered and unregistered patients evaluate medication they took based on their sociodemographics, personally perceived efficiency and reported side effects. The result is a website where everybody can search for a medication, its brand name, which by the

---

[16] O'Reilly (2005).
[17] Visits Data from http://www.ivw.de for December 2011.
[18] See note no. 8, additional source: Google Analytics for Germany.
[19] Source: google ad planner and http://www.ivw.de

way is usually only communicated to the doctor from regulatory authorities or the medical industry, and the reported efficiency and side effects based on user feedbacks often based in the upper three digit area. This new form of medication transparency combined with an evaluation describable as a form of comparative effectiveness, accessible for patients who usually and by law have no access to prescription drug names and professional background data is just one example of a new form of health-related data on the internet that may have a disruptive potential towards the existing structures of the healthcare system. The consequence is thus an informed patient who comes to the doctor and persists on having a medication regime change based on his online experience. On the other hand this example illustrates the potential of collaboratively working online masses and e-patients to improve and give feedback on medications, therapies and related medicare services, which is one approach of the paradigm of participatory healthcare.[20] The Danish healthcare company Coloplast was within the EU obviously the first company who used proactively the experience of patients as the users and experts of their main product, a temporary, invasive stoma care supplement. In a closed patients-only online community, patients gave feedback and collaboratively worked on improving ideas on the stoma product and the medicare service linked to it. This approach can also be described as an open innovation or user innovation approach which Eric von Hippel describes.[21] The two examples of e-patients gathering new forms of medication data in an independent online community and a medical product company uses the experience of their product´s users to improve its product within a medicare environment both show the disruptive but also the chances to use digital paradigms to improve medicare.

A content focused and patient-centric approach using the simple benefits of the web to window and tailor digital content by time, person and digital device is rolled out mainly in the United States by hospitals who implement an internet based "information therapy" approach, based on the concept of Kemper and Mettler.[22] The basic idea is a software which allows the doctor to send out digitally the right information to the right patient at the right time and the optimal consumable format. This approach takes into account that a patient has a different knowledge level at the beginning of the therapy and a different media usage behaviour which is also challenged especially if new therapy regimes are prescribed. Information therapy leads to a more educated, involved and adherent patient thus also reducing non-adherence costs which occur due false patient therapy behavior and increase the healthcare costs in Germany for about ten billion euros per year.[23]

---

[20] See for example: http://participatorymedicine.org/; see the press release of Coloplast at http://www.coloplast.com/about/news/stomainnovationwebsiteasuccess

[21] von Hippel (1986).

[22] Kemper and Mettler (2002).

[23] Bundesverband Deutscher Apothekerverbände (2012, March), online: http://www.abda.de/303.html

3 Hypothetical Disruptions and Chances of Health 2.0

A structured analysis of the status quo and especially the development of internetbased healthcare products and services, simply by the online accessible health related assets reveals that the majority of innovations happen outside the healthcare system and its traditional stakeholders; in other words the media industry, startups, the information- and telecommunication industry are those market segment from where the evolution of health 2.0 services come from. This development is an indicator of the scenario that Clayton Christensen described for disruptive technology innovation and its impact on the healthcare systems.[24] Christensen sees the highly regulated and with relatively strong industry lobby activities affected healthcare systems as incapable to find a intrinsic solution for the exponential rising medicare costs and the increasing number of chronic people in an aging society. He arguments that technological innovations, mainly described as digital facilitated networks help to manage patients medicare, communication and coordination from diagnose to therapy and rehabilitation, and those patient-centered technological innovations probably come from a stakeholder network outside the healthcare system thus from a so called nontraditional player. A digital personal and patient-centered health record, for example may be the information and coordination hub for this network, says Christensen. With "sundhed" Denmark already implemented such a nationwide personal health record where any patient and any medicare related doctor can have access to the whole history of medical documentation of a patient's case. In comparison the debate of similar patient-centered projects in Germany runs since decades. Furthermore one has to take into account the mindset of the healthcare industry which is since decades grown in and comparable to a closed-system view onto the healthcare system. The institutional independence and openness of internet based healthcare resources and its usage by collaboratively working patients and also doctors is a quite open network paradigm. Clayton Christensen mentioned the problem of new and disruptive technologies to a culture or a network which was in control of it before the new technologies arrived.

> We cannot ask people running traditional systems to evaluate a new technology for its radical benefits; people committed to keeping the current sytem will tend, as a group, to have trouble seeing value in anything disruptive.

Summing it up on a global scale, digital innovation trajectories and new value chains in healthcare of different kinds enter the stage from heterogeneous players and in different phases of innovation, varying from already existing nationwide personal health records, to pilots of user innovation approaches to improve medicare products to websites gathering medication reports to improve clinical medication research up to software products delivering tailored and prescribable information as a reimbursable service over different digital channels preferring the patients device, format and state of education.[25]

---

[24] Christensen (2009).

[25] Kemper and Mettler (2002).

4 Outlook

Even a midterm perspective in the area of digital healthcare innovations cannot evaluate the impact or disruptive change that it may have on the structures of a healthcare system like the one for example in Germany. The existing regulations are in place, strongly integrated and thus control the focus of the traditional stakeholders entrepreneurical orientation based on the fee-for-service economy in place. On the other hand the spread and usage intensity of the internet users and thus patients using internetbased healthcare tools and services will probably increase and with this, increasing also the effect of connected patients, their mutual learning and their behaviour on the healthcare market.

Probably the physician will be the traditional stakeholder being confronted with an increasingly informed and connected patient using enhanced digital healthcare tools and realizing that a new generation of patients demand a healthcare system that progressively integrate these tools into its medicare structures. It is yet hard to evalute at which place or moment this integration will start and if at all.

References

Baumann D (2009, June 27–28) Berliner Zeitung, No 147. p. 12: Das Monopol der Ärzte muss gebrochen werden. http://www.berliner-zeitung.de/archiv/der-praesident-des-bundeskartellamts–bernhard-heitzer–fordert-die-abschaffung-des-gesundheitsfonds-und-mehr-marktwirtschaft–das-monopol-der-aerzte-muss-gebrochen-werden-,10810590,10649004.html

Benkler, Y. (2006). *The wealth of networks. How social production transforms markets and freedom*. New Haven: Yale University Press.

Bundesverband Deutscher Apothekerverbände. (2012, March). http://www.abda.de/303.html

Busse, R., & Riesberg, A. (2005). *Gesundheitssysteme im Wandel: Deutschland*. Kopenhagen: WHO Regionalbüro für Europa im Auftrag des Europäischen Observatoriums für Gesundheitssysteme und Gesundheitspolitik.

Castells, M. (2004). *The network society*. England: EE Publishing Limited.

Christensen, C. M. (2009). *The innovator's prescription. A disruptive solution for health care*. New York: McGraw-Hill.

Ferguson, T. & White Paper der e-Patient Scholar Working Group. (2006). e-Patients. How they can help us heal healthcare. New York: Association of Cancer Online Resources. Retrieved November 16, 2009 from http://e-patients.net/

Fox, S. (2008, August). The engaged E-patient population. Washington: PEW Research Center. http://www.pewinternet.org/Reports/2008/The-Engaged-Epatient-Population.aspx

International Telecommunication Union. (2011). Measuring the Information Society. http://www.itu.int

Journal of Medical Internet Research: JMIR Publications Inc. Toronto, Canada. http://www.jmir.org

Kemper, D. W., & Mettler, M. (2002). *Information therapy. Prescribed information as a reimbursable medical service*. Healthwise: Idaho.

O'Reilly, T. (2005). *What is Web 2.0?* Sebastopol, CA: O'Reilly Media.

Psychonomics AG. (2009, 4 November) Köln, Berlin: Pressemitteilung vom 27 October 2009: "Zum Thema Gesundheit fragen Sie Ihren Arzt oder das Internet"; unter http://www.presseportal.de/pm/25608

von Hippel, E. (1986). Lead users: A source of novel product concepts. *Management Science, 32*(7), 791–805.

von Hippel, E. (1995). *The sources of innovation* (p. 1088). England: Oxford University Press.

Wenger, E. (2008). *Community of practice learning, meaning and identity* (17th ed.). Cambridge: Cambridge University Press.

The Impact of Facebook on News Consumption

Agnes Urban and Tamas Bodoky

1 Introduction

The rise of Facebook is undoubtedly a success story of recent years. The social media website is not just a successful application used by millions of people all over the world, but it has also emerged as a major actor in the public sphere. Politicians often publish announcements on it, while it also serves as a news source for many users as well as a major distribution channel of media content.

This study does not concern itself with many notable aspects of the Facebook phenomenon. We do not analyze Facebook's marketing communication aspects, even though social networking is widely used by companies to build brands and reach target markets. We don't deal either with the political impacts of Facebook, for example its well-known application during the Obama-campaign prior to the 2008 U.S. presidential election or the role it played during the recent Arab revolutions.

Our scope instead is how social networking, and in particular Facebook, has reshaped media consumption habits and what happens if a social networking site (SNS) becomes so significant as Facebook has in terms of internet usage. SNSs are both a threat and an opportunity for media companies at the same time. On the one hand, they are an effective tool for sharing news, enabling media content to reach many more users than before. On the other hand, media companies lose control over the distribution channels: it is the users themselves who decide what to share and in which way. Research studies and academic papers are already available about trends in SNS usage. They show how these sites have grown in importance, especially among young people. In parallel, media companies are attracting more and more visitors from these sites.

A. Urban (✉)
Corvinus University Budapest, Budapest, Hungary

T. Bodoky
Karoli Gaspar University Budapest, Budapest, Hungary

Opinions about the role of citizen journalism are divided. While its significance in recent years is not in question, some worry about its impact on the professionalism of news making, while others look on it more positively as it increases the supply of content. The role of users in distribution, however, appears to be more significant than their role in content creation. Social filtering has a greater impact on the news market than citizen journalism. It appears that users trust more in their personal friends than in unknown editors.

Media companies are struggling to find the right answers to the challenges posed by social media sites. Many companies poorly use SNS, they merely create a Facebook page because they feel it is a 'must' and leave it at that, while others actively aim to build a community. The long term effects of the different strategies are not yet known. It is also as yet uncertain how Facebook can stablize its dominant role on the SNS market, and how it changes media consumption habits in long run.

This chapter includes a short case study illustrating the role of social media in the news market.

We will look at how Facebook contributed to the market entry of a Hungarian watchdog portal (http://www.atlatszo.hu/) which was launched in early July 2011.

2 Social Networking Sites

The rise of social networking sites is clearly related to Web 2.0; an era characterized by the active participation of users. There were forerunners in the nineties when a number of SNSs were launched, such as classmates.com in 1995). Start-up social networking sites were launched in the last decade in smaller communities. Facebook was set up in 2004 on Harvard University and became open in 2006 for all users above 18.[1] Thematic SNSs for niche audiences still exist, for example LinkedIn for professional networks.

The geographical origin of SNSs has influenced their diffusion; in some countries or in some cultures certain sites are more popular than others. In recent years this factor has weakened due to the global dominance achieved by Facebook. Hargittai (2007) analyzed users of four different social networking sites (Facebook, MySpace, Xanga and Friendster). She found that the demographic characteristics and social circumstances of users can be related to the particular social network sites they use.

The diffusion of social networking sites was first explained by Rogers's innovations theory. It describes the diffusion of innovation among different types of users: first innovators and early adopters start using the new technology, and, partly based on the influence of these, others (early majority, late majority) also adopt the innovation. All of these groups have their own particular characteristics; innovators and early adopters, for example, are more open and willing to take on risk than the majority. (Rogers 2003)

---

[1] Age limit today is 13.

In the case of SNSs, a network effect has a definite impact on diffusion, both in direct and indirect forms. A direct network effect operates in the value to a product generated by the growing number of users (in the case of an SNS this means an increasing number of friends). An indirect network effect can be explained by market success: in Facebook's case, application providers develop complementary products and services, improving the functionality of Facebook, and increasing its attractiveness further in a virtuous circle. (Cachia 2008, 9)

As a result of these network effects, the success of an innovation is based on reaching a critical mass. There is no benchmark figure for critical mass, e.g. in the case of broadband services, Goff (2002) defined a 15 % threshold for critical mass. It is practically impossible to define an exact proportion for an online service that has no clear geographical borders. A social networking site is not related to infrastructure or special equipment; it has a global market and is widely used in countries with different levels of development. By January 2012, Facebook had more than 800 million active users[2] and a market leading position on the SNS market. It is not in question whether Facebook has reached a critical mass.

While network effects in large part explain the current success of Facebook, it is more interesting how it was able to beat its competitors in the early stages of development. One of the main competitive advantages of Facebook was that its clear focus was on communication: it did not merely link users together to create a network of different relationships, but it became a space for personal, group and mass communication. An area or space able to cope with different levels of communications has proved to be highly attractive for users, hence Facebook has managed to gain a high level of internet-usage minutes.[3] The second attractive feature was its development of applications: who would have imagined that virtual gardening and other games would be so popular among users. The third competitive advantage of Facebook was the early recognition of the potential of mobile technologies. Facebook has been available on mobile devices from the very beginning. This has proved to be an important factor for users who increasingly use smartphones and tablets for social networking.

Without any doubt Facebook is the most successful SNS today, but we cannot be sure, however, that this position is sustainable in the long run. As Rose (2011) points out, internet companies are often overvalued: while financial data can be temporarily impressive, this does not guarantee economic sustainability, especially in the field of social networking sites. AOL bought Bebo in 2008 for 850 million dollars, but within two years it had lost its value (AOL sold it for 10 million dollars[4]). News Corp. acquired MySpace for 580 million dollars in 2005, but by

---

[2] http://www.facebook.com/press/info.php?statistics
[3] http://techland.time.com/2011/12/05/the-beginning-of-the-end-for-facebook/
[4] http://techcrunch.com/2010/06/16/aol-to-sell-bebo-for-around-10-million/

July 2011 it was worth only 35 million dollars. Based on these experiences, a bright future for Facebook isn't guaranteed: the real questions are what will be the next success story and what kind of services will attract users in the coming years.

3   Characteristics of Facebook Users

As social networking sites build mass audiences, the socio-demographic characteristics of users converge on those of average internet-users. Research conducted in the US found that between 2008 and 2010, the average age of an SNS user increased from 33 years to 38 years (Hampton et al. 2011). Users are still young, but it can no longer be said that SNSs are merely a teenage fad. An infographic of Community 102[5] shows the high proportion of young users on Facebook: 40 % of the user base is comprised of 13–17 years olds (11 %) and 18–25 years olds (29 %). Above these age groups, the proportion of active users falls, 25–34 years old (23 %), and 35–44 years old (18 %) have smaller representations. The 45+ age group represents just 19 % of all Facebook users.

Hampton et al. (2011) found that 52 % of Facebook users engage with the platform on a daily basis (Twitter 33 %, MySpace 7 %, LinkedIn 6 %). In addition, Facebook users are also regularly active on the site each day:
- 15 % of Facebook users update their own status;
- 22 % comment on another's post or status;
- 20 % comment on another user's photos;
- 26 % "Like" another user's content;
- 10 % send another user a private message.

Widespread usage of social networking sites is a relatively new phenomenon, but academic papers are already available and numerous. Ryan and Xenos (2011) conducted a survey of Australian internet users. They found that registered Facebook users are more extroverted and narcissistic, but less conscientious and socially lonely, than non-users. Extroversion was significantly positively correlated with communicative features of Facebook (chat, massage, comment, and wall functions). Interestingly, socially lonely people tend to spend more time on Facebook but prefer the passive features of the site.

Underwood et al. (2011) analyzed communicative and broadcasting interaction patterns among undergraduate students in the UK. In terms of Facebook usage, both interactions were typical and the creation of user types was possible; communicators are group-focused while broadcasters seek to present a more positive image of themselves to their network. Surprisingly, cluster analysis identified a third group which was characterized by a high level of interaction. Members of this group are cautious, and, while they are keen to self-project, are uncomfortable with the risks attached to such behavior.

---

[5] http://news.community102.com/how-different-age-groups-interact-online

4 News Consumption on Facebook

As the technological environment and media content supply have evolved, consumption habits have also changed. Users have turned from the once-dominant print media to electronic media and new electronic media. Content supply is continuously increasing and media has become a global market: availability of content is not a technological question any more, although economic barriers have remained (Gálik 2003).

Social networking sites do not only change the communication habits and network of users, but also have a growing importance in content distribution. It is especially true for Facebook: its high number of registered users and the Facebook user walls make it extremely effective for sharing and distributing news as well as other types of content. Brian Stelter, reporter of The New York Times described in 2008 the experience of the Obama campaign, and found that the role of SNS filtering had become significant. Younger users in particular are not only consumers of news and current events but are also sending news content links via e-mail or simply sharing them on SNSs. They tend to prefer clicking on links coming from friends instead of visiting different websites and searching for content. Hence it appears that social filtering via personal networks can partly take the place of professional filtering. Stelter used the expression 'social media generation' and illustrated changing news consumption habits with a quotation from a focus group research: 'If the news is that important, it will find me.' (Stelter 2008).

A Financial Times writer wrote about a similar phenomenon. According to Gelles (2009), traditional internet portals (e.g. Yahoo and AOL) are losing their position as front doors to the online world as social sites take over this role. It can be explained by the simple fact, that users prefer new ways of filtering and are interested in news shared by friends. On the one hand this can work in the favor of media companies, since users share their content and generate visitors for their online portals. On the other hand it has limited benefits from a business perspective: there are as yet no precise statistics about sharing through social networks due to the fact that links are being shared on multiple platforms, and that new services such as link-shorteners are complicating efforts to monitor the flow of traffic.

Another problem, one that has not been proved empirically but has been experienced by the authors of this paper is that users often check their Facebook wall throughout the day to keep informed about the latest news, but do not click on the original sources to read entire articles. In this case the SNS and the monitoring of headlines and lead paragraphs (as well as comments of friends) can take the place of visiting the original source and content-providers, which is clearly disadvantageous for media companies and content providers.

This substitution effect has been analyzed in academic papers in the context of substitution and complementary usage between print newspapers and online portals; but no general answer for this dilemma has been found, since users' habits determine consumption. This is the case with social networking sites too: reading headlines and lead paragraphs can be enough for many users to feel informed, although others still prefer to read whole articles and search for background information. The analysis of this substitution effect of social networking sites clearly merits further research.

Research from recent years proves the significant role of SNSs in the distribution of news. Purcell et al. (2010) analyzed news consumption in the US, and found that 92 % use multiple platforms to get news while 59 % combine online and offline sources. The internet is ranked third as a news source, after local TV stations and national networks/cable TVs. The data shows that 37 % of internet users are participatory news consumers; in other words, they contribute to the creation of news, comment on it or disseminate it. 17 % of internet users (30 % of SNS users) post links and thoughts about news on social networking sites. 51 % of SNS users who are also online news consumers say that on a typical day they get news from people they follow. Another 23 % of this group follow news organizations or individual journalists on social networking sites. Using social networks as a source of news is more typical among younger people, suggesting in the long run, the importance of SNS in news consumption will grow.

Olmstead et al. (2011) analyzed the traffic of 25 websites in the US, including print media sites, TV channels, news portals and online portals. The proportion of direct traffic is 60–65 % (including cross-links from other articles in the same portal) while 35–40 % of the traffic comes from external links. With regard to external sources, the dominance of Google is clear (accounting for 30 % of all traffic of websites). In some cases Facebook is relevant source: Huffingtonpost.com generates 8 % of its traffic from Facebook (8 %), while CNN, New York Times and ABC News all generate above 6 % of their traffic from the site. Facebook is less relevant however (ca. 1 %) for news aggregators (YahooNews.com, AOLNews.com, MSNBC.com and local aggregator Topix).

In the case of Hungary, the evidence indicates that entertainment media companies are more dynamic users of Facebook than news media. On the list of top Hungarian Facebook pages we can find TV shows, radio stations, and music television channels. This can be explained by the popularity of Facebook among young users who clearly focus more on entertainment content than news content.

With regard to serious content, the news portal of the political/business weekly magazine HVG (hvg.hu) has the most 'likes' (55.000 in January 2012), far more than any other political site. It should be noted here that, surprisingly, the two market-leading Hungarian news portals (index.hu and origo.hu) are not active on Facebook, and appear to have given up this area to their smaller competitors.

5 Community Building Strategy of a Non-Profit News Portal

In July 2011, the authors of this chapter co-founded a Hungarian NGO and online news portal site called atlatszo.hu (atlatszo means transparent in Hungarian), which deals with freedom of information requests and investigative journalism. Among many other aims, the project is testing the effect of Facebook on internet news consumption. We summarize the empirical observations and experiences of the first half year of the site's existence as follows (Fig. 1). (The manuscript of this study closed in January 2012.)

Fig. 1 Facebook page of atlatszo.hu (17 January 2012)

The site produces investigative reports, accepts information from whistleblowers, files requests for data on the basis of freedom of information laws, and starts freedom of information lawsuits in the case of refusal. Atlatszo.hu publishes all its relevant findings on the internet, and organizes transparency campaigns with the involvement of the public.

The mission statement of atlatszo.hu is very critical towards the mainstream Hungarian press: "Mainstream media in Hungary has become a toy of political and economic interest groups, and it is often not the journalists, but the owners of the media and the circles behind them who decide what can be published, and what can become an issue in a publication. Our governments handle mass media as a propaganda tool, public service media is controlled by the appointees of political parties, and the new media law gives almost unlimited power to the politically controlled Media Authority to silence dissent voices. The result is a very limited freedom of the press in Hungary: there are many taboos and forbidden themes, political circles leak minor corruption cases to the media close to them, while in fact, behind the scenes they cooperate—regardless of their political affiliation—in corrupt dealings that involve billions of forints, joining forces in muzzling the media that begins to investigate their big time operations. Meanwhile many important stories remain untold, numerous corruption cases go undisclosed, even if there are whistleblowers and they have evidence."[6]

This critical view led atlatszo.hu to choose partnership with similar new grassroots media projects rather than mainstream news portals with a high number of

---

[6] http://atlatszo.hu/2011/07/01/about-us/

visitors. This stance however has limited the visibility of the website. While the media partners of high ranking Hungarian news portal sites are able to reach thousands, or even tens of thousands of visitors by appearing on the front page of these popular services, without a powerful media partner or costly online marketing campaign a startup website is barely visible and struggles to attract even a few hundred visitors per day. At the same time, atlatszo.hu defines itself as a community project, not only by opening up every article or blogpost for user comments, but also by trying to build an online community from internet users who support the cause of the website and are willing to take part by volunteering in atlatszo.hu's efforts.

An obvious strategy was to turn to Facebook, where similar Hungarian new media initiatives have been able to build fanclubs of 5–10,000 users in recent years. Integrating Facebook into the website served several purposes: to let Facebook users know when atlatszo.hu published new content, to interact with our visitors by engaging them in conversations about topics covered by the website, to invite them into the information gathering process (crowdsourcing), to launch donation campaigns, and to recruit volunteers to the project.

On the technical side, integrating Facebook into a website is no longer a difficult task: installing a number of "social plugins" into the WordPress powered content management system makes every piece of content and the site as a whole "likeable on Facebook, and vice versa, it also makes the content feed on Facebook visible on the website. We created two Facebook pages for the project: an official Facebook page as a Non-Profit Organization (facebook.com/atlatszo.hu), and a community Facebook page (facebook.com/atlatszo.volunteer) for those volunteers who are not only interested in reading our articles, but are willing to work with us to realize atlatszo.hu's mission.

From the outset, we have distributed new content from the website on the official Facebook page of the project, and hence have been able to analyze the usage statistics of the Facebook page. However, it is worth noting that the number of members of the project's volunteer Facebook page has grown together with the official page, and that this number represents approximately 10 % of the membership of the official page. This means that one out of ten Facebook fans of the project is willing to volunteer to the project, a fact we exploited by asking volunteers to take part in solving various problems to do with the project.

According to traffic and usage statistics collected by Google Analytics, the website of atlatszo.hu generated ca. 597.000 page views, 269.000 visits and 150.000 unique visitors in the first half year of its existence. Visitors to atlatszo.hu downloaded 2,22 webpages, and spent approximately 3 min on the website on average. The extraordinarily high visitor numbers that were achieved in the first week following the launch of the website on 4th July 2011 can be attributed to a buzzword, "MagyarLeaks", a service of the website intended to provide advice on secure digital whistleblowing. This feature attracted a lot of hype and media attention to the project, due to its resemblance to the well-known whistleblowing website WikiLeaks. MagyarLeaks soon generated police inquiries. After news was leaked about a hacker attack, the Organised Crime Unit of the Hungarian Police

Fig. 2 Website traffic diagram of atlatszo.hu between 4th July 2011 and 17th January 2012 (*Source*: Google Analytics)

wanted to know the identity of the informant. We claimed reporter's privilege and regularly updated our readers about what was happening, which generated more attention and an even higher number of visitors than our core business, namely requesting and publishing government data under the freedom of information legislation. The site achieved its highest number of visitors in October 2011, when we leaked a secret application for the directorship of a publicly owned theatre, by an actor well known for his extreme right political views. The volume of traffic to the site was so large that the webserver froze and was brought down. Another popular piece of content was our photograph of our external hard drive being seized by the police—the device would be ruined in the course of the investigation, which again generated media attention. Our most read investigative article concerned the state-owned gambling monopoly Szerencsejatek Ltd. paying billions of Hungarian forints to the private company which produces it's television commercials. We were able to discover that this private company is controlled by political appointees of the largest political parties of Hungary (Fig. 2).

The content of atlatszo.hu is bilingual and includes English abstracts of Hungarian news pieces. This has helped to attract visitors to the site from 122 different countries around the world. Most of our visitors unsurprisingly come from Hungary (91 %), but there was also significant traffic, approximately 1 % each, from Germany, the United Kingdom and the United States. The main traffic source is referral traffic (47 % of visits), meaning that people arrive on atlatszo.hu from other websites referring to the site. A further 37 % of visits is direct traffic, meaning people enter the internet address of the site (atlatszo.hu) into their browsers. The remaining 16 % is search engine traffic, in other words people make a search in search engines and end up on our website.

We found out that the main referral traffic source is Facebook, which accounts for 14 % of all traffic, and 30 % of referral traffic according to data gathered by Google Analytics. Facebook is followed by the mainstream news portal sites index.hu and hvg.hu which represent 12 % and 5 % of referral traffic respectively, which are then followed by a number of prominent Hungarian blogs representing less than 5 % of referral traffic each, but more than 20 % of referral traffic together. The statistics prove that Facebook delivered more traffic to the website than any mention or reference in the mainstream or citizen online media.

The Facebook page of atlatszo.hu was launched together with the website in July 2011. The number of fans has grown steadily ever since. The exceptional peaks and lows of visitor numbers of the website don't seem to have affected the number of

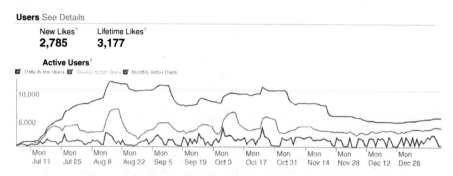

Fig. 3 Number of daily, weekly and monthly active users of atlatszo.hu Facebook page between 4th July 2011 and 15th January 2012 (*Source*: Facebook Insights)

Facebook fans. It is worth noting that the number of fans grew markedly when a prominent Hungarian Facebook group, "One million people for press freedom in Hungary" discussed atlatszo.hu, and also after we released a campaign video in which we asked the community to like our Facebook page and donate (Fig. 3).

As well as being the main content distribution channel of atlatszo.hu, the official Facebook page serves as the primary forum of discussions: our Facebook posts generated more comments than the referred articles on the website. While our website generated 597,000 page views, data gathered by Facebook Insights shows that our Facebook posts were published 1,637,941 times on a user's wall. For commercial websites, this can be a problem, as they cannot generate advertisement revenues on Facebook and therefore website traffic is more valuable. However, in the case of a non-profit organization which isn't reliant on the advertising market, reach and traffic on Facebook are equally valuable. Facebook statistics show that the growing number of fans of atlatzso.hu's Facebook page generate more and more likes and comments on the site's Facebook posts as well (Fig. 4).

The Facebook page also enables us to receive feedback from the community in different ways. We are experimenting with crowdsourcing to get additional information on data gathered from public institutions by means of freedom of information requests. Maintaining communication channels with the community enables us to develop a more personal relationship with the audience: the editors of atlatszo.hu appear as public persons and engage in conversations, which engage the audience and generate more connection with the brand. However, this strategy can be controversial: if you don't respect limits and post too much or irrelevant content, users may revoke their 'likes' and disappear from the community. In the first half year, the Facebook page of atlatszo.hu had less than twenty revoked likes, which suggests that we haven't alienated our audience with the frequency of our posts.

Integrating Facebook also means we obtain more accurate demographic data about our fans and audience. With Facebook Insights we found out that 33 % of our Facebook fans are women, while 65 % are men—this can be explained by the nature of our topic, investigative journalism, which tends to attract more men than women. The majority of the fans of atlatszo.hu are between 24 and 45 years of age,

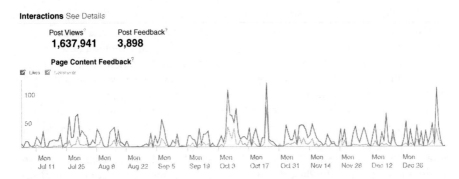

Fig. 4 Feedback from the atlatszo.hu Facebook page between 4th July 2011 and 17th January 2012 (Facebook Insights)

Demographics

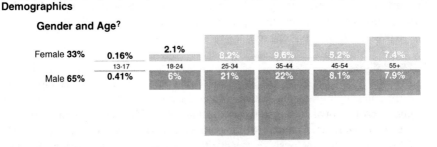

Fig. 5 Demographics of atlatszo.hu fans on Facebook, 15th January 2012 (*Source*: Facebook Insights)

as are the contributors in the project—however, we have a sizeable number of fans older than 45. A significant majority, 2,843 out of 3,187 of atlatszo.hu fans live in Hungary, 1,669 of them in the capital Budapest. Countries with the most people who 'like' us are Germany, United Kingdom, United States and Austria (Fig. 5).

Summarizing our experiences of the first half year, it is clear that the decision to choose Facebook was a good one for atlatszo.hu in terms of building an audience and a community. Our target group, the educated Hungarian middle class, has a significant presence on Facebook and appears to have welcomed our initiative. After the encouraging initial results with Facebook we expanded our community-building efforts to Twitter and Tumblr microblogs in October 2011. Since then, we have attracted 127 followers on Twitter, and 136 followers on Tumblr. We have not, however, automized our presence on these sites by publishing everything from the website—instead a human editor decides on what content is cross-posted. We believe that it makes no sense to be present on a social networking site by automatically posting everything, but rather one has to engage with the community on a personal basis. As with Facebook, on Twitter and Tumblr we try to attract visitors to the website with excerpts from our articles, but neither has emerged yet as a significant traffic source in our website usage statistics. However, some elements of our content have had their 15 min of fame on these social networks as well. The picture of our hard drive damaged by the police investigation, for example, went viral and ended up on mainstream news portals, resulting in our webserver being brought down. Social networks also proved to be excellent emergency communication channels in such circumstances—when the webserver of atlatszo.hu went down, we were still able to communicate with the audience via Facebook and the microblogs.

Turning to the financial side of the experiment, our fundraising campaign raised approximately USD 12,000 from more than a hundred individual donors, who donated small amounts via PayPal, Flattr or bank transfer to our NGO. It remains, however, an open question if it is possible to build a sustainable, community based business model on individual donors reached by online networks and social networking sites. Investigative journalism is a time-consuming and costly business, while the internet is full of free content supported by advertisement. These factors make it exceptionally difficult to ask money for quality journalism and freedom of information advocacy. Examples do exist on the international level of NGOs like ours succeeding with donation based business models, but we still don't know if this is possible or not in Hungary.

Conclusion

In recent years, the impact of user-generated content on media consumption has been a hot topic in media studies. More pessimistic authors have predicted the end of professional editing in the media and the devaluation of journalism, since the citizen-generated content will inevitably come to dominate the online world. Others emphasize the positive aspects: there is more available content than ever before, no one can control distribution channels anymore, and popularity depends on creativity and talent. We cannot read the future, but it seems that coexistence of citizen-generated and professional content can be sustainable in long run, since both content types have their benefits for the users.

Up until recently, the debate has been mainly about the role of users in content creation. Now it appears that the issue of content dissemination is becoming even more interesting: with regard to the social networking sites, users have a much larger role in distribution. In short, users take the place of editors rather than journalists. As Arianna Huffington, a co-founder of Huffington Post news site said: "They don't just consume news, they share it, develop it, add to it—it's a very dynamic relationship with news" (The Economist 2011). It seems there is a new ecosystem on the news market, where users have different roles.

It is hard to predict how social media will influence the dissemination of the news in the long run. Media consumption habits are continuously evolving but the future of the social media market is also uncertain. Facebook is certainly a dominant player today, but the online service market is dynamic: new companies and new services can appear at any time.

It will remain a considerable challenge for media companies how to use and get the best out of social media. Many websites today remain passive in the field of social communities, others meanwhile actively use it to build competitive advantage in the news market. Examples like Huffington Post or atlatszo.hu in Hungary prove that Facebook can be a useful tool to introduce a service. There is a paradigm shift in this field: not only well-known content providers can build a community based on their audiences. Newcomers as well are building communities via social media, which can then be transformed to audiences in the long run. What is clear, is that there are many open questions, for example the viability of the business models of these newcomers. We are convinced, however, that usage of social media in the news market has an impact on news consumption at least in the short to medium term.

References

Cachia, R. (2008). *Social computing: study on the use and impact of online social networking.* IPTS Exploratory Research on the Socio-economic Impact of Social Computing. EUR 23565 EN–2008. 64. o.

Community 102: *How Different Age Groups Interact Online.* Infografika. 2011. június 28, http://news.community102.com/how-different-age-groups-interact-online, Újra letöltve 2011. augusztus 29.

Gálik, M. (2003). *Médiagazdaságtan.* Budapest: Aula Kiadó.

Gelles, D. (2009). Friends, not editors, shape internet habits. *Financial Times.* September 02

Goff, D. H. (2002). An assessment of the Broadband Media Strategies of Western European Telecoms. In R. G. Picard (Ed.), *Media firms structures, operations, and performance.* Mahwah, NJ: Lawrence Erlbaum Associates.

Hampton, K. N., Sessions Goulet, L., Rainie, L., Purcell K. (2011) *Social networking sites and our lives.* How people's trust, personal relationships, and civic and political involvement are connected to their use of social networking sites and other technologies. Pew Research Center 85. o.

Hargittai, E. (2007). Whose Space? Differences among users and non-users of social network sites. *Journal of Computer-Mediated Communication, 13,* 276–297.

Olmstead, K., Mitchell, A., Rosenstiel, T. (2011) *Navigating news online: where people go, how they get there and what lures them away.* Pew Research Center, Project for Excellence in Journalism.

Purcell, K., Rainie, L., Mitchell, A., Rosenstiel, T., Olmstead, K. (2010). *Understanding the participatory news consumer.* How internet and cell phone users have turned news into a social experience Pew Research Center, Project for Excellence in Journalism.

Rogers, E. M. (2003). *Diffusion of innovations* (5th ed.). New York: Free Press. 552.

Rose, C. (2011). Internet valuations and economic sustainability. *Journal of Business and Economics Research, 9,* 49–53.

Ryan, T., & Xenos, S. (2011). Who uses Facebook? An investigation into the relationship between the Big Five, shyness, narcissism, loneliness, and Facebook usage. *Computers in Human Behavior, 27,* 1658–1664.

Stelter, B. (2008). Finding political news online, the Young Pass It On. *The New York Times.* March 27, http://www.nytimes.com/2008/03/27/us/politics/27voters.html

The Economist 2011. Bulletins from the future. *The Economist,* July 9

Underwood, J. D. M., Kerlin, L., & Farrington-Flint, L. (2011). The lies we tell and what they say about us: Using behavioural characteristics to explain Facebook activity. *Computers in Human Behavior, 27,* 1621–1626.

The Usage and Advertising Effects of Social Media in China

Li-Chuan Evelyn Mai

1   Introduction

In China, the number of the netizens was 477 million in 2011, reaching 34.5 % of Chinese population, with representing 23.3 % of the worldwide users (Xinhua Net 2011a). Simultaneously, the number of the mobile users was 303 million in 2010 (Gongchang.com 2010). China became the country with the largest number of the netizens. On the other hand, the revenue of the e-business was over 200 billion in 2010, and over 775 billion in 2011, indicating both internet users and e-business grew rapidly in China.

Since 2004, the new media—Social Network System (SNS), such as facebook or Twitter developed sharply in the worldwide, because of China's policy, these foreign social media are blocked, and Chinese users could not access these SNS easily. The domestic social media, Sina Weibo and Tengxun Weibo were launched in 2008 and 2010 that attracted a large number of users becoming members and using those of Weibo (microblog) to generate contents and connect friends. The increasing members of these social media also attract commercial businesses advertised their products on the media, leading to those of domestic social media become one of marketing channels in China.

Therefore, the aims of this research are to understand the usage of the social media in China, and to investigate the advertising effect of the social media.

L.-C.E. Mai
Beijing Normal University-Hong Kong Baptist University United International College (UIC), Zhuhai, Guangdong, China
e-mail: evelyn_mai2000@yahoo.com

2 Social Media in China

In last few years, the web has sifted towards user-driven technology, such as blogs, social networks and video sharing platform (Smith 2009a, b) that enabled the netizens generating contents and have been being the most important functions of the social media. In China, the domestic social media are encompassed in different functions and characteristics. In terms of the microblogs, Sina Weibo and Tengxun Weibo are two of the main sites. Similar to Facebook or Twitter, members could type 140-character messages in the microblgs and share the contents with their friends. Some social media aim to specific users, for instance, the members of the Kaixin Net or Renren Net are mainly aimed to university students, the websites are not only provided information and the function of the microblogs, but also provided internet games. QQ or Feixin are generally used as the instant messengers in China. Like YouTube, Youku and Tudou provided video contents which are generated by their members. As Internet Search Engines, such as Baidu and Sina also provide forums for their members. Similar to e-Bay and Amazon, some e-shops such as TaoBao and JingDong are also applied the technology and functions of Web 2.0 to establish their websites, members are able to post comments, share experiences, contact sellers and evaluate products, etc. These social media are generally used by young netizens in China.

Moreover, the members of these Chinese social media were increasing rapidly, this phenomenon also indicates the restrictions on some foreign websites and social media have resulted in flourishing home-grown, government-approved systems in which Chinese-owned properties succeed (Crampton 2011). For instance, Sina Weibo was launched 1 year later in August 2009, its members grew up to one million, following 3 months later, the members was 50 million; until Feb 2011, the members were 100 million. The phenomenon is similar to other global social media over the world. According to Neilsen Report (2010), 74 % of the respondents from 11 countries visited social media and spent about 6 h per month on these sites, and the netizens of the social media were increasing. Furthermore, the largest of the global online brands, three out of seven were social media, i.e. Facebook, Wikipedia and YouTube. Facebook had 500 million users and the revenue was 175 billion in 2010 that meant the social media have great business values and benefits.

On the other hand, the e-commerce is growing and the internet shoppers are continuously increasing in China. In the late 2010, the economic scale of e-business was 45.67 billion that was raising 53.7 % compared to the same period of 2009 (Gongchang.com 2010). Following the growth of the social media, the advertising and marketing of the e-business started transforming to those of social media in China (Jiang 2011); this trend will be extended onto the near future. According to iReserach Report (2011a), VANCL spent 11.97 million RMB advertised on the internet last November, its 1 month amount of advertising expenses stood at the first place among fashion e-shops. VANCL mostly advertised its brand on the search engines such as Sohu and Sina; and social media, such as Sina Weibo, Skype, RenRen Net, etc. In 2010, VANCL spent 400 million RMB ($58.82 million) on advertising and in 2011 about 1,000 million RMB ($147.06 million), utilizing online advertising to establish its brand image and promote its products online (Zhang 2011). More and more e-shops are applied VANCL model to advertise product information online. However, there is a need to further examine the effectiveness of the online advertising.

3   Social Media Advertising

Social media became a new hybrid component of integrated marketing communications, providing a cyber space for organisations to advertise products or establish strong relationships with their customers (Chu and Kim 2011). Many studies are concerned with the commercial effectiveness of the social media, focusing on advertising effects (Bergh et al. 2011; Campbell et al. 2011b; Ha 2011; Taylor et al. 2011) or branding issues of the word-of-mouth (WOM) and marketing communications (Smith 2009b; Kozinets et al. 2010; Moran and Gossieaux 2010; Chi 2011; Colliander and Dahlen 2011; Li and Zhan 2011; Phan 2011; LaPointe 2011). Some studies are interested in the topic of the social media as a new tool of the market research (Casteleyn et al. 2009; Hardey 2009).

In terms of advertising effectiveness of social media, Taylor et al. (2011) found that social networking advertising can be effective when users accept it, but the perception of excessive commercialisation may lead to user abandonment. For the further research in consumer generated advertising of social media, Campbell et al. (2011a) developed two approaches, correspondence and learning-bases to analyse the contents of the consumer-generated advertising. Moreover, Campbell et al. (2011b) focused on consumer-generated advertising to analyse and interpret these comments on the social media by using a new text analysis tool, Leximancer. They concluded the consumer generated ads can be conceived into two dimensions, one is conceptual which is concerned with effective or cognitive components, and the other is emotional which can be either collaborative or oppositionary.

Chu (2011) examined the potential link of Facebook group participation with viral advertising responses, she found Facebook members involved in higher level of self-discourse and had more favourable attitudes toward social media and advertising in general. In other words, advertising on social media is more effective to those of users than non users. Similarly, Chi (2011) found users' motivation for online social networking had varying effects on their social media marketing responses. However, those of online advertising whether can attract to social media users that will be examined in this research.

With respect to the issue of the branding or online WOM, Chu and Kim (2011) found that SNSs provide a channel for establishing a brand-consumer relationship. They suggested advertisers should take social relationship factors into account and develop marketing strategic communication to fulfil SNS users' needs. Li and Zhan (2011) analysed the contents of the online product reviews by using several variables, such as language style, organisational structure and other content features in order to understand whether those of generated-contents affect online users. He found generated-contents have significant effectiveness on consumer behaviours.

Lapointe (2011) suggested online social media and offline WOM should work together that would be even more powerful. Kozinets et al. (2010) found network communication offers four social media communication strategies-evaluation, embracing, endorsement, explanation. They indicated that communal WOM does not simply increase or amplify marketing message, marketing message and meanings are systematically altered in the process of embedding them. Jones et al. (2009) investigated how companies manage their corporate reputation and branding in the new online environment of the social web. Simth (2009a, b) even argued to build up social media platform for growing brands, as well as Kuo (2009) suggested to succeed business in China, investors must understand China's social media environment.

The results and implications of the most previous studies indicate the positive effectiveness or online word-of mouth of the social media generally affects the online users. But Phan (2011) researched the social media users and found no impact of social media investments on consumer's perceptions and purchase intentions of luxury fashion brands. The contradictory results are valuable to be examined in this research. Therefore, the research questions of this research are concerned two main issues of social media. One is the usages of the social media in China, and the other is related to the effectiveness of social media advertising, and further to discuss the influences of the generated-contents.

4 Research Methodology

Online questionnaires were undertaken to collect primary data. Phan (2011) stated that social media is extremely popular especially among the Young adults who have actually grown up with new communication technologies. Hence, this research targeted young people mainly from age 18 to 32. Moreover, VANCL spent a large number of advertising expenses to promote its products and build up its brand among the clothing industry in the past 2 years. It was selected as the case study of this research, in order to examine the advertising effects.

A snow balling was employed to select samples who were required to answer the questions online. The questionnaire was comprised of four parts, demographics, social media usages, social media advertising and generated-contents effects, and effectiveness of VANCL advertising.

The survey was conducted from 28th of May to 27th of June 2011, receiving 594 respondents from different geographical areas of China. The valid questionnaires were 586, and the validity rate was 98.65 %.

5 Data Analysis

The software package SPSS was used to analyze the data. Frequencies were employed to draw a descriptive analysis of demographics of respondents, social media usages, the effects of the advertising and generated-contents, and effectiveness of VANCL advertising. Correlations were employed to analyse the relationships between usages and effectiveness, and T-test was employed to compare the differences between usages and effects.

5.1 The Usages of Social Media in China

355 out of 586 respondents were females (60.6 %), majority of respondents were between age 22 and 24, presenting 49.70 % of respondents. Among the respondents, 57.50 % were students, 17.60 % were organisational staff. These respondents were from overall of China, but 59.90 % of them were from Southern China.

In terms of the usages of the social media, 518 out of 586 respondents regularly used social media, representing 88.40 % of respondents. 39.60 % of respondents spent on social media between 1 and 2 h per day, and 26.5 % of respondents were spending 3–4 h. The results indicate the social media is popular among Young people, and the netizen spend quite a lot time on social media. Based on the results and following the trends of social media, China E-Business Centre (2011) even predicted that e-business marketing will move to social media.

236 (45.56 %) out of 518 respondents were using social media because social media provided abundant useful information; 36.68 % of them indicated the reason because there were many friends online (See Table 1). The main purposes of they using social media were 'contacting with friends' (65.19 %) and 'killing rest of time' (50.51 %, see Table 2). These results show the characteristics of the social media and the reasons of social media developing rapidly in China. Users use social media to contact with friends and obtain generated-contents from their friends, using social media they also can get friend information or some other information which is not able to show on the traditional media. These reasons of the usage are mainly concerned with the social medium's social functions and characteristics, not much concerned with business or consuming products.

6.1 % of respondents have used social media before but for some reasons, they stopped to use them. The reasons were mainly 'not interested in the activities' (17 out of 35). 5.5 % (32) out of 586 interviewees have never used social media because they were lack of knowledge about social media or did not know how to use social media.

43.70 % of them used both computer and mobile devices logging social media. Regarding to the contents, most of the social media users paid attentions on their friends and classmates, presenting 73.20 % of respondents. 10.10 % of them paid attentions on professionals. Only 1.90 % of them paid attentions to brand official webpage on social media. The results indicate those of brand official pages did not attract majority of social media users, and the impacts of soft-advertising on the official webpage might be limited.

But from most of respondents' perspectives, 57.7 % out of 586 respondents thought the first priority of social media was 'Weibo', 18.10 % of them thought that it was 'Instance Massager'. The two forms of social media also were used the most by the respondents. 77.80 % of respondents used 'Sina Weibo', 47.80 % of them

Table 1 The reasons of using social media

Reasons	Frequencies	Percentage
Many friends on social media	190	36.68
Interested in activities on social media	37	7.14
Abundant information	236	45.56
Many games	9	1.74
Have same issues for discussing	27	5.21
Other reasons	19	3.67
Total	518	100

N = 518, Person, %

Table 2 The purposes of using social media (multiple answers)

Purposes	Frequencies	Percentage
Killing rest of time	296	50.51
Contacting with friends	382	65.19
Understanding friends' life	197	33.62
To Know more friends	82	14.00
Finding self emotional space	57	9.73
Presenting self comments	176	30.03
Discussing hot issues with others	108	18.43
Everybody using, if I am not using it I am out	36	6.14
Get information	211	36.01

N = 586, Person, %

Table 3 Respondents with different ages and their usages

Relationship	Visit official webpage	Pay attention to product information	Forward to social media	Share product information to social media	Recommend to friends	More attractive
Ages	$r = -.098^*$ $P < .05$	$r = -.127^{**}$ $P < .01$	$r = .080$ $P > .05$	$r = .085^*$ $P < .05$	$r = .057$ $P > 0.5$	$r = .152^{***}$ $P < .001$

N = 586, $P < .05^*$, $P < .01^{**}$, $P < .001^{****}$

used 'Renren', and 43.00 % of them used 'QQ space'. These three could be seen as the most popular social media in China. Among the three social media, 'Sina Weibo' is similar to 'Facebook', and 'QQ space' is similar to 'My Space'.

The results indicate that respondents with different ages have different usages of social media (see Table 3). The result shows the elder users tend not to visit preferred product's or brands' webpage ($r = -.098$, $P < .05$); on the other words, younger users more tend to visit preferred product's or brand's official webpage on social media. These younger users more tend to pay attention on updated information of preferred brand or product ($r = -.127$, $P < .01$). Furthermore, the elder users more tend to share preferred brand or product information on social media ($r = .085$, $P < .05$), and they more tend to agree that the products or brands shown on social media are more attractive (r = .152, P < .001), this result also demonstrates the effectiveness of the social media, i.e. products or brands shown on social media are more attractive.

In terms of relationships between the respondents spending time online and their social media usages (Table 4), the statistical results show that the respondent spent more time online, the more use social media (r = .505, P < .001), the more visited preferred brand and product official webpage (r = .103, P < .05), and the more paid attention on these brand or product updated information (r = .106, P < .05). But those of respondents tended to less recommend their preferred brand and product to friends (r = −0.94, P < .05).

On the other hand, the respondents more tended to be social media heavy users that they tended to spend more expenses on social media (r = 136, P < .001). But the same, they tended to less share preferred brand or product information with friends (r = −.088, P < .05); and less recommended their preferred brand or product to their friends (r = −.093, P < .05). Moreover, the respondents were the more spending money on social media, they were less forwarding (r = −.127, P < .01), sharing (r = −.123, P < .01), or recommending (r = −.135, P < .001) their preferred brand or product to their friends.

According to above results, the respondents spend more time online or on social media, or spend more expense on social media, who tend to be less sharing their preferred brand or product information with friends, less recommending these brand or product to their friends. The results indicate that the respondents spend more time online or on social media might be not only for buying or sharing consuming information. They might tend to share other information in their life. Therefore, these results difficult to demonstrate that heavy social media users tend to generate more preferred brand or product information to share or recommend their friends. They might use social media in social orientated function rather than business or consuming orientated function. Therefore, the effects of the advertising on social media might be limited.

In short, there were near 90 % of respondents using social media, and about 40 % of them spent 1–2 h every day. Over 65 % of respondents indicated that the main purpose of using social media was for contacting friends. Near 50 % of respondents used social media because social media provided abundant information. Most of respondents paid attentions on their friends, only very few of them pay attentions on brand or product official webpage. The majority of respondents frequently used Sina Weibo, Renren and QQ Space. The results show the respondents with different ages have different usages of the social media. Those of elder users tend to share preferred products or brands information on social media and recommend products or brands to their friends. All respondents agree that products or brands shown on social media is more attractive, demonstrating the advertising effects of the social media is existed. On the other hand, the respondents spent more time online or on social media, they were less forwarding or recommending preferred brands or products to their friends. These respondents used more social media in the social orientated functions rather than the business or consuming purposes.

Table 4 Respondents with different time spending and their usages

Relationship	Online time	S M time	Expense on SM	Visit webpage	Pay attention	Forward information	Share information	Recommend to friends	More attractive
Online time	1	r = .505*** P < ..001	r = .073 P > .05	r = .103* P < .05	r = .106** P < .01	r = -.013 P > .05	r = -.053 P > .05	r = -.094* P < .05	r = -.018 P > .05
Using SM time	r = .505*** P < .001	1	r = .136*** P < .001	r = .044 P > .05	r = .044 P > .05	r = -.056 P > .05	r = -.088* P < .05	r = -.093* P < .05	r = -.051 P > .05
Expense on SM	r = .073 P > .05	r = .136*** P < .001	1	r = .032 P > .05	r = .022 P > .05	r = -.127** P < .01	r = -.123** P < .01	r = -.135*** P > .001	r = .044 P > .05

N = 586, P < .05*, P < .01**, P < .001****
SM Social media

5.2 Effects of Social Media Advertising

432 (73.7 %) out of 586 respondents have paid attentions on advertisement of social media, only 154 (26.3 %) of respondents never paid attentions on them. Within these 432 respondents, 173 (39.77 %) out of them have never clicked advertisement in the past 1 month, 192 (44.44 %) out of them have clicked 1–3 times, 38 (6.83 %) out of them clicked 4–6 times, 9 (2.08 %) out of them clicked 7–9 times, and 20 (4.63 %) out of them clicked more than ten times. The results show most of social media users pay attentions on advertising, but most of them seldom click those of digital advertisement to see details, indicating the effective way of advertisement is showing the contents on the webpage directly, if the advertising is required users to click it that might not have effectiveness. In other word, viral marketing might be the better way to deliver brand or product information to social media users rather than the clicking advertisement.

Moreover, 74.60 % of respondents have never spent money on social media, and 10.10 % of respondents spent less than 5 RMB monthly. The result indicates that most of respondents did not spend money on social media, but few of them spent little money on communication fares, such as QQ or Skype.

331 (56.4 %) out of the 586 respondents were the fans of some brands or products on social media, but 255 (43.5 %) out of 586 respondents were not. In other words, over half of the users are the fans of some brands or products. They have higher intentions to get more related information. Among these 331 respondents who had preferred brands or products, 132 (39.88 %) out of them were 'interested' in the brands or products; 98 (29.60 %) out of them wanted to 'have different views and obtain more information' about the brands or products. Regarding to the official webpage of these brands or products, 134 (40.48 %) out of these 331 respondents visited some of them, 47 (14.20 %) visited all of them, and 43 (13 %) visited most of them. According to these results, more than 60 % of brand or product fans of social media visited the official webpage of their preferred brands or products, indicating there are some relations linked with social media and brand's or product's official webpage.

42.70 % of 586 respondents 'sometimes' forwarded information of preferred brands on social media and 13.30 % of them 'always' or 'often' did it. Moreover, 45.20 % of respondents 'sometimes' shared product information or generated-contents of preferred brands on social media and 15 % of them 'always' or 'often' did it. 51.4 % of them 'sometimes' recommended product information or generated-contents of preferred brands to others, 13.70 % of them 'always' or 'often' did it.

With respect to those of sharing or recommended information or generated-contents from friends on social media, the respondents have different views. 28.70 % of respondents indicated that the recommended information or generated-contents increased their interests in the brands or products. The result means that online word-of-mouth from friends strengthens the brands or products images in some respondents' minds. 25.10 % of them took the brands or products as one of the purchasing choices. 19.60 % of them considered those of recommended products or brands as their first priority when they were shopping. The result indicates that online word-of-mouth from friends increases some users' purchasing intentions, and it might change their shopping choices if their first priority is not the recommended products or brands. The results demonstrate online 'word-of-mouth' from friends is strongly affecting some of the respondents in terms of brand or product consuming. But as well as the same percentage, 19.60 % of respondents said the information did not affect their consuming behaviours. The results demonstrated that generated-contents from friends are more attractive and effective to social media users rather than advertising.

Regarding to those of product promotional or on sale information were shown on social media, 39.6 % of respondents believed it and sometimes purchased it, but 49.8 % of them believed it but never tried it and 10.6 % of them did not believe such kind of advertising. The results demonstrate that promotional advertising on social media can attract some users to purchase products, but more than half number of them has never been encouraged by those of promotional advertising, indicating the effectiveness of social media advertising is existed, but not strong enough to encourage or attract to the majority of the respondents to buy the products.

On the other hand, 41.30 % of respondents agreed that productions or brands showing on social media are more attractive, as well as the same proportion of respondents was slightly disagreed, strongly agreed was 3.20 % and disagreed was 6.8 %.

In terms of generated-contents, the results demonstrate that those of users the more frequently visiting official webpage of products or brands tended not to share their preferred product's or brand's information on social media ($r = -.085$, $P < .05$; see Table 5). These respondents also tended not to recommend their preferred products or brands to their friends ($r = .-108, P < .01$), but they agreed that products or brands shown on social media were more attractive ($r = .160$, $P < .001$). Adversely, those of users who frequently sharing preferred product's or brand's information to social media tended to recommend the products or brands to their friends ($r = .646, P < .001$). They also agreed that products or brands shown on social media are more attractive ($r = .306, P < .001$).

In summary, more than 70 % out of 586 respondents have paid attentions on social media advertising, and most of social media users pay attentions on advertising, but seldom click those of digital advertisement to see details. Over half number of the users is the fans of some brands or products. Among these respondents, more than 60 % of brand or product fans of social media visited the official webpage of their preferred brands or products, demonstrating there are some relations linked with social media and brand's or product's official webpage. With respect to those of sharing or recommended information or generated-contents from friends on social media, the respondents have different views. The results demonstrate that online word-of-mouth from friends strengthens the brands or products images in some respondents' minds; increases some users' purchasing intentions, and it might change their shopping choices if their first priority is not the recommended products or brands. The results demonstrate online 'word-of-mouth' from friends is strongly affecting some of the respondents in terms of brand or product consuming.

Table 5 Relationships among different usages of social media

Relationship	Visit official webpage	Pay attention to product information	Forward to social media	Share product information to social media	Recommend to friends	More attractive
Visit official webpage	1	r = .872*** P < .001	r = −.085* P < .05	r = −.110 P > .05	r = −.108** P < .01	r = −.160*** P < .001
Pay attention to product information	r = .872*** P < .001	1	r = −.053 P > .05	r = −.079 P > .05	r = −.080 P > .05	r = −.166*** P < .001
Forward to social media	r = −.085* P < .05	r = −.053 P > .05	1	r = .825*** P < .001	r = .646*** P < .001	r = .328*** P < .001
Share product information	r = −.110 P > .05	r = −.079 P > .05	r = .825*** P < .001	1	r = .735*** P < .001	r = .310*** P < .001
Recommend to friends	r = −.108** P < .01	r = .080 P > .05	r = .646*** P < .001	r = .375*** P < .001	1	r = .306*** P < .001
More attractive	r = −.160*** P > .001	r = −.166*** P < .001	r = .328*** P > .001	r = .310*** P < .001	r = .306*** P < .001	1

N = 586, P > .01*, P > .05**, P > .001***

5.3 The Effects of Social Media Advertising in China: The Case Study of VANCL

For further demonstrating the effectiveness of social media advertising, the e-shop brand- VANCL was used to examine the brand image and advertising effects. The results show 80.5 % of the respondents knew the brand of VANCL, and 388 (66.1 %) out of 586 respondents paid attentions on VANCL advertising. These respondents received the VANCL advertising from search engines (24.48 %), video websites (21.90 %), or social media (22.64), presenting 69.02 % of those of respondents. The results show that VANCL utilized the online adverting to promote their products attracting more than half of respondents' attentions. The adverting effects are shown.

Moreover, 256 (65.98 %) out of 388 respondents have clicked the VANCL advertisement, 57 (14.70 %) out of them have shared the advertisement with their friends on social media, 152 (39.18 %) out of 388 through social media understood product information of VANCL. The results show that among these respondents paid attention on VANCL, more than half of them clicked VANCL's advertisement and some of them intended to get VANCL product information, and some of them also shared the advertisement with their fans online.

173 (29.52 %) out of 586 have bought VANCL products online. They bought VANCL products because of reasonable price (53.56 %), good quality (11.56 %) and easily to pay (10.98 %). 123 (71.10 %) out of 173 agreed to continue buying VANCL products. Among these respondents who paid attentions on VANCL brand (471 out 586), they thought the brand image of the VANCL is reasonable price (63.06 %), design individualism (11.25 %), and good quality (9.13 %). These images are coincided with these respondent perceived with VANCL's official website, 51.59 % of the respondents thought VANCL's website is 'simple but practical'. 52.26 % of them believe the publicity of VANCL is higher than other online fashion brand. 34.18 % of them will choose VANCL fashion shop as the first priority. The results show the effectiveness of the VANCL online advertising and their brand image building.

Based on the research of VANCL case, the above results provide some implications about online advertising:
1. Online advertising shown on social media could attract more than 60 % of users' attentions, and brand publicity will be extended.
2. Among these respondents who paid attention on online advertising, 60 % of them may click the advertising to get information, and about 15 % of them might share the information with their fans on social media. In this stage, the advertising becomes online word-of-mouth through some sharing contents.
3. The products of e-shop should be price reasonable, good quality, and easily to pay. The products of the fashion shop might be required design individualism, simultaneously. These reasons could keep a number of consumers stably and they put the shop in the first priority.

Conclusions

According to the results and discussions, social media is generally used by young adults in China. Because it develops rapidly, most of advertisers or marketers see it as a new medium able to advertise product information. Although most of social media users have seen the advertising on the social media, they were not interested in advertising because near half proportion of respondents never clicked those of advertising. Therefore, these advertising only can bring the names of the brands or products to users that will extend brand publicities and enhance the surface of brand image in users mind. But users will not spend time to see more detailed information; hence, the effects of the clicking advertising on the social media are limited, suggesting to use the viral marketing providing brand or product information on the social media directly is more effective.

Users pay more attentions on shared information from their fans or idols, therefore, generated-contents are more effective for those of users. Social media users sometimes share or recommend their preferred brands or productions to their followers and fans, the information will increase these receivers purchasing intentions which is supported by the results of this research, suggesting advertisers or marketers can use these generated-contents or create contents to attract users by using the concepts of the online word-of-mouth that would be more effective than digital advertising.

Based on the VANCL case, VANCL advertised large number of the advertisement on search engines and social media to build up their brand and extend brand publicity. Moreover, about 15 % of the respondents often shared VANCL product information to their friends that became online word-of-mouth in affecting and circulating to the individual social communities, the effectiveness could be strong. VANCL is the case both involved in the large number of digital advertising and online word-of-mouth, and the brand is successful in China. The case might be providing one of the online branding models by using both digital advertising and online word-of-mouth to succeed e-businesses.

References

Bergh, B. G. V., Lee, M., Quilliam, E. T., & Hove, T. (2011) 'The Multidimensional Nature and Brand Impact of User-Generated Ad Parodies in Social Media', International Journal of Advertising , 30(1), 103–131.

Campbell, C., Pitt, F. L., Parent, M., & Berthon, P. (2011a). Tracking back-talk in consumer-generated advertising: An analysis two interpretative approaches. Journal of Advertising Research, 51(1), 224–238.

Campbell, C., Pitt, F. L., Parent, M., & Berthon, P. (2011b). Understanding consumer conversations around ADS in A Web 2.0 World. Journal of Advertising, 40(1), 87–102.

Casteleyn, J., Mottart, A., & Rutten, K. (2009) 'How to Use Facebook in Your Market Research", International Journal of Market Research, 51(4), 439–447.

Chu, S. C., & Kim, Y. (2011). Determinants of consumer engagement in electronic word-of-mouth (EWOM) in social networking sites. *International Journal of Advertising, 30*(1), 47–75.

Chu, S. C. (2011). Virtual advertising in social media: Participation in Facebook groups and responses among college-aged users. *Journal of Interactive Advertising, 12*(1), 30–43.

Chi, H. H. (2011). Interactive digital advertising vs. virtual brand community: exploratory study of user motivation and social media marketing responses in Taiwan. *Journal of Interactive Advertising, 12*(1), 44–61.

Colliander, J., & Dahlen, M. (2011). Following the fashionable friends: The power of social media. *Journal of Advertising Research, 2011*, 313–320.

Crampton, T. (2011). Social media in China: The same, but different. *The China Business Review*, Jan. 2011

Gongchang.com (2010) A research report on Chinese Netizens. *Behaviour in E-commerce*. World Gongchang, No. 4

Ha, A. (2011). Trends: social media advertising. *Adweek, 52*(36), 29.

Hardey, M. (2009). The social context of online market research: Introduction to the sociability of social media. *International Journal of Market Research, 51*(4), 562–564.

http://www.thomascrampton.com/china/social-media-china-business-review/

Jiang, R. (2011). E-commerce marketing will move to social media. *China Buisness Journal*, 14 December.

Jones, B., Temperley, J., & Lima, A. (2009). Corporate reputation in the era of Web 2.0: The case of Primark. *Journal of Marketing Management, 25*(9–10), 927–939.

Kozinets, R., de Valck, K., Wojnicki, C. A., & Wilner, J. S. S. (2010). Networked narrative: Understanding word-of-mouth marketing online communication. *Journal of Marketing, 74*, 71–89.

Kuo, K. (2009) Blogs, bulletin boards and business, *China Business Review*. Com, Jan–Feb, 28

LaPointe, P. (2011). The rock in the pont: How online buzz and offline WOM can make a strong message even more powerful. *Journal of Advertising Research, 51*, 456–457.

Li, J., & Zhan, L. (2011). Online persuasion: How the written words drives WOM: Evidence from consumers-generated product reviews. *Journal of Advertising Research, 51*, 239–257.

Moran, E., & Gossieaux, F. (2010). Marketing in hyper social world. *Journal of Advertising Research, 2010*, 232–239.

Neilsen Report (2010) Research on the trends of the social media in Asia. June.

Phan, M. (2011). Do social media enhance consumer's perception and purchase intention of luxury fashion brands? *VIKALPA, 36*(1), 81–84.

Smith, H. (2009a). Building social media platforms for growing brands. *Marketing, 177*, 26–28.

Smith, T. (2009b). The social media revolution. *International Journal of Market Research, 51*(4), 559–561.

Taylor, G. D., Lewin, E. J., & Strutton, D. (2011). Do ads work on social network? How gender and age shape receptivity? *Journal of Advertising Research, 51*, 258–275.

Xinhua Net (2011a) 'China Netizen Reached 477 Million', 16 May 2011. http://news.xinhuanet.com/tech/2011-05/16/c_121421711.htm

Web

China E-Business Centre (2011) E-Business Marketing Will Move to Social Media. *China Business Operation*, 25th Dec. http://b2b.toocle.com/detail-6016361.html

http://news.itxinwen.com/internet/inland/2011/0315/252950.html

Iresearch Report (2011a) *Internet Brand Advertising* in November 2011.

Zhang, Y. (2011). VANCL spent 1000 million RMB on advertising and involved in high investment on advertising industry. *IT Business Magazine Online* (IT Xinwen.com), 15 March.

Part VI
Conclusion

What Social Media Are Doing and Where They Are Taking Us

Robert G. Picard

Social media are inextricably altering how we as individuals, organizations and enterprises communicate. We use them to convey information and thoughts about the trivial and the momentous occurrences in our lives, our communities, and society, to share our thoughts, hopes, and wishes, and to access and share information about products, services, companies and organizations.

These communications themselves are not new. We have always engaged in personal communications and talked with family members at home, chatted with neighbours, conversed with friends in cafes and taverns, chattered with co-workers in our workplaces, and written letters and made phone calls to family, friends, and colleagues at distant locations. What is new in the era of social media is that the forms in which these communications take place are different, that they are much more socially inclusive than before, they are not limited to speech and text and can involve distant persons.

Social media are part of the parallel world of digital media. We work in it; we buy and sell in it; we seek and exchange information in it; we play and entertain ourselves in it; we engage with friends and colleagues in it; we meet and develop relationships in it; we fall in love in it; we discuss and debate in it; we act politically in it; we behave badly and commit crimes in it; we practice religion in it; and we sin in it.

The digital world frees us from the material world of physical objects and activity and the restraints of distance and time. We are able to move in and out of the immaterial world at will and to operate simultaneously in both the material and immaterial world. This can sometimes be disconcerting and disorienting because the norms of the two worlds vary. The norms of the material world are based on concepts of structure, privacy and concealment, property, hierarchy, control and formality, whereas the norms of the immaterial world are based on amorphous

R.G. Picard (✉)
Reuters Institute, University of Oxford, Oxford, UK
e-mail: robert.picard@politics.ox.ac.uk

arrangements, revelation and transparency, sharing, empowerment, collaboration, and informality.

The different cultures of the parallel worlds are leading to increasing disputes and struggles over the norms of immaterial world. Businesses are trying to infuse the property norms of the material world into the immaterial; governments are trying to assert norms of control over content and the scope of transparency that are similar to those of the material world. These efforts are met by resistance from those who perceive the norms of the immaterial world as natural and desirable.

As a consequence, social media exist in an uneasy situation today. They are pulled between the desires of users upon whose existence the social media are dependent and the desires of other interests such as companies—including many media firms—who wish to commercially exploit the social networks and governments that wish to structure interactions and controls along the lines of the material world.

Media firms recognize that their audiences are increasingly using social media, that they provides new ways for information and opinion to be conveyed among the public and to share content produced by media firms in the material world. Concurrently they recognize that digital media of all types are stripping economic value from legacy media firms. For legacy media, social media are thus a two-side sword offering new marketing and sales opportunities, but creating a competing activity for the audiences that legacy media traditionally dominated.

Social media also provide mechanisms for firms that provide all kinds products and services and to engage in a range of activities from marketing to customer relations and from product development to brand development. All of these functions existed in the material world, but social media offer distinct advantages in carry them out.

To use them effectively, one must comprehend how social networks fundamentally differ from other digital platforms. Although constructed by commercial firms, they differ from websites and apps because social media communications are primarily influenced by individual users rather than organizers of the networks or companies that employ them. The fundamental purpose and structure of social networks is increase users' abilities to communicate and establish and maintain relationships with persons of their choosing.

The primary purposes of social communications are to extend interpersonal communications that had previously been done in person, letters, telephone calls or messaging to individuals or limited number of persons to a wider group, thus facilitating interpersonal communication among a broader social network. Uses of social networks for commercial gain are thus secondary purposes of such networks rather than being primary functions as in mass media and communications.

The chapters in this handbook have shown how social media differ from mass media, but that they do not replace it. Instead, they supplement mass media by creating capabilities for social interaction. The chapters have shown the issues and challenges that social media present for commercial users and their implications.

The operation of social networks is today dominated by major global players, but—as authors of this handbook have shown—effective regional and national networks are coexisting and flourishing. They do so by serving users with different linguistic bases, but also by receiving the support of national policies that seek domestic economic benefits and national influence over the social networks.

From the commercial standpoint social networks are another avenue for mass media content to be brought to the attention of people and be accessed by them. More importantly, however, they provide means for engaging with customers and potential customers outside the settings of markets and exchange.

The fundamental basis of all human relationships—whether personal, social or market based—are interactions and transactions. These require shared values and interest, acceptance, reciprocity and trust. The extent to which these develop is based on frequency of interaction and scale of interaction. The functionalities of mass media constrained their abilities to facilitate interactions and transactions, but digital media—and especially social media—are founded on technologies designed to connect people and facilitate both. This gives them great flexibility and increases their social influence.

1 Implications of Individual Use of Social Media

Because users of social media are active rather than passive, facilitating users' interactions and satisfaction must the central objective of network organizers and those who intend to use it commercial purposes. Absent this user-centric approach participation in social networks loses authenticity and cannot provide the communication legitimacy that users seek. Unless those participating in networks provide voice and opportunities for other users to influence and control the interactions, relationships will prove unsatisfying.

Users primarily view social media as a facilitator of their own personal and social communication. It enables exchange of views and recommendations from other network members with whom relationships pre-exist or are developed in the digital network. These relationships allow users to bring ideas and content to the attention of others in their networks, to identify satisfying diversionary and leisure content and activities; to contribute to information and knowledge flow on topics of mutual interest; and to holding companies and authorities to account.

These social communication processes also allow participants to bypass constraints in traditional media channels that have limited access to content that does not fit established formats or commercial imperatives. Numerous chapters in the handbook have shown that social media prove particularly adept at diffusing non-conformist youth and underground culture in the form of music, video, humour and other discourses, in allowing users to bypass social and political constraints on information and discussion in formal media systems, and in permitting commercial interests to communicate in less formal and aloof manners.

The myriad of opportunities provided by social media are not universally employed by users, however. As research in this handbook and cited literature shows, social media users are not a homogeneous group: they differ in terms of characteristics, the uses they make of social media, the levels of engagement they pursue, and the satisfactions they seek. These differences are particularly significant in social media because they permit users to exercise levels of individuality unavailable to users of mass media. Although network users can be grouped by certain broad characteristics and patterns, they are ultimately individuals with individual aspirations, desires, tastes, and preferences.

2 Implications of Company and Organizational Use of Social Media

Social media clearly provide new types of communication activity that lie somewhere between interpersonal communication and mass communication. Social media cannot merely be seen as another communication tool by companies, however, because doing so disregards the ways it is altering communication processes and patterns and the hierarchies of communications resident in legacy media and how it empowers individual and aggregate users.

Users of social media are not homogenous. Some use them more often than others and some are more willing to engage with firms than others. Organizational strategies for using social media need to account for those use differences; variations in ways user interact with producers of various types of products and services, and more precisely target consumer contact than in mass media.

Inaccurate targeting and use of non-relational content by companies and organizations is increasing conflicts with users over privacy and commercial exploitation. If the contacts are seen more in the interests of organizational and firm interests than of mutual benefit, resistance arises.

Nevertheless, social media are important marketing channel for products and services. Research presented in this handbook shows they have particular value for single production products such as books and recordings. These marketing capabilities differ from those afforded in the material world, where producers have greater control over the messages. The digital world is much more influenced by users themselves who may judge products or services negatively or provide significant word-of-mouth marketing for those they appreciate.

Many media companies are also using social media as a way of gathering information and content that can be used in the creation of their own content and then distributed via their various distribution platforms. This has proved particularly important for news organizations and for other media firms that can aggregate and redistribute video clips. However, the techniques, processes, and tools for effectively using social media for these purposes for remain immature and need significant development.

Because social media magnify the voices of consumers they increase the importance of customer relations and producing customer satisfaction. But social media also provide means for companies pursue those goals as well. It becomes a complimentary tool to pursue customer relations objectives. Creating truly interactive and engaging social media contacts becomes critical because of the importance of inducing users to voluntarily become followers and participants in a relationship with the company or organization. Effectively using social media for marketing and customer relations is, in many ways, more complex than pursuing those functions through mass media.

Companies are also feeling the impact of social media within themselves. Although company structures and organizations exist to facilitate internal communication and interaction, they can concurrently restrict it with social norms that limit employee ability to express themselves freely. When social media are employed, some of the communication restraints can be removed and some organizational impediments to communicating more informally across operating units and among hierarchies and thus bypassing restraints. Social media thus can make internal communications less formal and structure and multidirectional. However, when social media are employed, leadership may become more diffused in the organization and will not always reside in actors with parallel official leadership position in the organization—thus challenging hierarchy and authority, which is seen sometimes seen as threatening.

Social media are increasingly deployed by 'official' leaders in organizations with varying effect and tend to produce expectations that they will communicate more often and directly with employees. The communication, however, must be authentic, respecting employees as individuals, and providing them licence to engage in conversation with leaders—exchanges that are sometimes uncomfortable for the leaders.

These new communication patterns created by digital and social media shake many who are rooted in practices of orchestrating communication. This has led some companies to attempt to direct or restrict the use of social media to avoid conflicts and destabilization of hierarchy and authority—thus effectively denying themselves its benefits as well. This pattern is often not only seen for internal communications, but external communications as well.

Social media thus offer companies and organizations opportunities to enhance their information gathering, marketing, customer relations and internal communications activities. But such uses must be strategic and provide something beneficial for all users. Otherwise it risks just increasing the noise level in an already bustling communication environment.

3 The Importance of Value Creation and Value Configuration Through Social Media

If social media are to produce effective results for enterprises and organizations they must ensure that uses create value for users and themselves and be willing to engage with others in collaborative value creation.

As contributors to this volume have shown, social media can strengthen pre-existing relations between companies and consumers and establish new ones. However, the choice of relationship in social media resides in the consumer; although companies may want a relationship with a consumer, the consumer may not have reciprocal desires. Thus, establishing a social media relationship requires clearly offering value that induces them to engage.

To do so, commercial users must do more than send self-interested, one-way, impersonal messages that primarily benefit themselves. Social media also cannot be effective if they are employed as a mere feedback mechanism rather than a tool designed for engagement and conversation. These challenges require meeting the expectation of social media users for more personalization and specialization of messages and for exercising less control over message construction, distribution and reception.

Social media companies themselves are struggling to find how to create value in the networks they have made possible. They are increasingly trying to benefit from the user aggregation created for social purposes by turning them into aggregate audiences. This is occurring because advertising has become the main revenue source for social media companies. Although they recognize the usefulness of analysing and targeting users, the advertising still tends to be rather broadly targeted.

Social media firms, and other enterprises engaging through social media, must not allow desires for income production to interfere with the benefits of regular connections and solidifying relationships with users.

Because users' expectations of social media are primarily influenced by interpersonal communication norms, overtly commercial contacts or communication control that chiefly benefits firms lose effectiveness in the environment. This should be a particular concern of all those employing social media based apps as a means of exploiting and monetizing users of social media.

Many firms are attempting to overcome resistance to contact in social media by linking them to other platforms and communication experiences. These are beginning to produce networked business models—often micro business models—in which attention captured in social media are moved to other platforms and interactions were commercial purposes produce less resistance.

There is rising use of social media for non-exchange activities such as product development and customer service. Through these relationships, firms engage with customers to co-create value by allowing and encouraging consumers and others to improve existing products, develop add-ins and new products, and obtain information to enhance their uses of products.

Although social media provide mechanisms to create economic opportunities for entrepreneurs and economies, and to create additional value for users, the value creation must result from the relationships with users rather than managing users—a factor that requires careful planning and operationalization of contacts in social networks.

4 Navigating the Social Media Environment

Social media are now clearly established as an important means of communication for individuals, enterprises, and organizations. Companies that provide all types of digital services are integrating social media utilities to increase their functionality for users and induce more non-users to engage. Although they users of all kinds clearly perceive the value of social media use, we have much to learn about the incentives, practices, and effectiveness of employing them.

Individual and commercial users of social media are clearly using them to obtain new opportunities to speak and be heard, to increase access to free and paid content as well as other products and services, to gather information about what customers think and their values and concerns, and to learn what is happening in networked community.

For existing media firms, social media enables unbundling content and this is hastening the breakdown of long-established business strategies and cost recovery models. It is also facilitating richer and more niched contacts and relationships, and increasing links to their mass market—and often offline—products and services.

Network economics offer significant advantages to dominant organizers of social media platforms—which is producing struggles among operators to ensure they are global and national market leaders. Because these companies are increasingly reliant on capital from share markets and impatient investors pressures are growing on them to find ways to exploit their users commercially—and creating risks that their users may resist.

Commercial and organizational users of social media are also feeling pressured to produce results. Many are struggling to establish strategies and performance measures that produce and reveal impact. But because of the importance of social media to company brands and reputations, addressing consumer issues and comment, and generating recommendations and word-of-mouth marketing, they dare not discount social media.

Clearly, new and costly tools and techniques needed for analysing and evaluating communications in social media is critical for those who wish to understand and respond to the aggregate of what is being discussed and how it is being framed. Social media are much more difficult to monitor than traditional media because of the number of users and volume of communications, but it has great value because it represents the individual and collective concerns of the public. Nevertheless, the emphasis on uses of social media must remain their benefits to individual users and the ability to establish meaningful relationships with and for them lest social media migrate from their original purposes and norms of personal social communication to those that remain primary in mass media.

About the Authors

Alan B. Albarran (Prof. Dr.) is Professor and Chair of the Department of Radio, Television and Film at the University of North Texas in Denton, Texas, USA. He is the author/editor of 15 books and numerous articles and book chapters related to topics in media management and economics. He served a total of 12 years as Editor of the Journal of Media Economics (1997–2005) and The International Journal on Media Management (2005–2008). His research interests center on the managerial and economic aspects of the media industries with an emphasis on electronic and new media. Albarran has been recognized with several awards including the Award of Honor from the Journal of Media Economics representing lifetime contributions to the field (2008), the Broadcast Education Association's Distinguished Scholar Award (2009), and the Distinguished International Education Award from the University of North Texas (2010).

Piet Bakker studied Political Science at the University of Amsterdam. He worked as a journalist for several newspapers, magazines and radio stations and was a teach-er at the School for Journalism in Utrecht. He also organized workshops for newspapers publishers, gave lectures and works as a consultant on newspaper innovation. From 1985 to 2007 he worked at the Department of Communications at the University of Amsterdam/Amsterdam School of Communications Research (ASCoR) as an associate professor. He is now (from September 2007 on) professor Cross Media Content at the School of Journalism and Communication at the Hogeschool Utrecht. He is still member of ASCoR in Amsterdam as well. He edited and published books and articles on reading habits, media history, local journalism, internet, Dutch media, international news, investigative journalism, the music industry and free newspapers. He teaches mass communication and journalism at undergraduate and MA-level.

Cristóbal Benavides Almarza is Assistant Professor of media management at the School of Communication at Universidad de los Andes, Santiago de Chile. He studied Journalism and worked in several newspapers and Canal 13 (national tv station) as a business journalist and as a manager of new platforms and new businesses. He has a PhD in Communication Studies from the University of Navarra. He got his master degree in media management in the same university. He has published papers and book chapters about research on the field of media management and new technology in the media industry. He also is a well know consultant for newspaper publishers and for the National Association of Newspapers (Chile).

About the Authors

Marianna Blinova (Ph.D., Dr.) is an Associate Professor of Advertising and Media Economics at the Faculty of Media Communications National Research University Higher School of Economics. In 1996 she graduated with honour the Faculty of Journalism Moscow State University. In 1999 she defended her doctoral dissertation "The Advertising in Japanese Press: from the National Features to the Globalization". Her main research interests include Advertising Markets, Media Economics, Japanese Media Market, New Media Technologies, Business Journalism and Social Media. She got twice the Moscow University grant as one of the most successful young researcher and professor. Also was awarded by The Japanese Fond Association as one of the most successful researcher and educator. She is author of numerous monographs, articles and analytic materials on history of foreign journalism, communication, advertising (specially Japanese and Russian), business journalism, information society, Japanese culture. Contact: mblinova@hse.ru

Andreas H. Bock is Senior Strategist Social Media at Telekom Deutschland GmbH. He is responsible for the Social Media Roadmap of the division Sales & Service and the program management of "Telekom hilft". Andreas has been in the online business since 1995. He started as a "Project Manager Electronic Publishing" at Axel Springer Verlag AG, where he setup pioneering internet projects. This followed editorial and project management roles across different companies (e.g. for T—Online, Telefonica, Entertainment Media Verlag and Ganske Verlagsgruppe)—covering content, community, and commerce projects. Andreas is also a visiting lecturer and a speaker at conferences. In 2012 he published a book with O'Reilly Germany on "customer service in the social web". Prior to his work in the online industry Andreas had worked as a journalist for diverse German newspapers and magazines specialized on media topics. He holds a Magister Artium degree in Communication Science from Freie Universität Berlin. Contact: @AndreasHBock

Tamás Bodoky (Ph.D.) is freelance investigative journalist based in Budapest, Hungary. He covers science and technology, environmental and human rights issues, corruption and organized crime cases, misuse of power and police brutality, and green politics. Bodoky has been a journalist since 1996. Before joining Index.hu, where he worked for 9 years in different journalistic and editorial positions, he was a science and technology journalist at the Magyar Narancs weekly. Bodoky won the Gőbölyös Soma Prize for investigative journalism in 2008, the Szabadság Prize in 2009 for his articles on Hungary's 2006 unrest and police brutality, the Iustitia Regnorum Fundamentum and the Hungarian Pulitzer Memorial Prize for his investigative articles on corruption cases. Bodoky holds an MSc degree in Agricultural Sciences and a Ph.D. degree in Language Sciences. He is an editor of the Hungarian media studies quarterly, Médiakutató, and teaches journalism at Károli Gáspár University, Budapest. Bodoky is a Marshall Memorial Fellowship alumnus, and a member of the international investigative journalism network "Organized Crime and Corruption Reporting Project". As member of the OCCRP, he won the Daniel Pearl Global Investigative Journalism Award in 2011. He is the co-founder and editor in chief of the non-profit Hungarian investigative journalism portal, atlatszo.hu.

Charles Brown is the creator and leader of the University of Westminster's MA Media Management, a programme designed to provide media professionals with the managerial, commercial and strategic skills and knowledge they require in order to deal with the challenges facing their organisations. Charles Brown has been a media consultant and journalist for over 20 years and has worked with a wide range of media organisations in North America and Europe, advising them on the development of strategy and commercial solutions. Charles has worked with a wide range of media and entertainment clients, helping organisations develop digital products and identify and secure commercial opportunities. He has worked with companies in publishing, online services, music and broadcasting. Between 1998 and 2001 Charles Brown was a director of the iGroup, the eBusiness services and software development arm of Computacenter (UK) Ltd. where he played a led the development of applications for digital content distribution, digital rights management, knowledge management and content management. He has published widely and his work includes Co-production International (a guide to international production finance), The New Economics of Audiovisual Production and The Future of International Television Funding.

About the Authors

Sylvia M. Chan-Olmsted (Prof. Dr.) received her Ph.D. degree from Michigan State University with an emphasis in media economics and marketing. She is the author of the book, Competitive Strategy for Media Firms and co-editor of two books, Media Management and Economics Handbook and Global Media Economics. She has published over 50 refereed articles in the Journal of Broadcasting and Electronic Media, Journalism & Mass Communication Quarterly, Telecommunications Policy, New Media and Society, Journal of Media Economics, International Journal on Media Management, and others. Her research focuses on new media adoption and marketing strategy, brand management, mobile media industry and audience, and strategic management in emerging media industries. Her current research projects involve the development and marketing of mobile media, cross-platform media strategy and audience behavior, and brand management via social/mobile media. Recipient of over 15 national research awards, Dr. Chan-Olmsted also held the University of Florida Research Foundation Professorship and the Al and Effie Flanagan Professorship at the University of Florida.

Moonhee Cho (Prof. Dr.) is an assistant professor in the School of Mass Communications, University of South Florida. She received her Ph.D. degree from University of Florida. As a former fundraiser and nonprofit public relations manager, her research interests are public relations management of both for-profit and nonprofit organizations, emerging media as a tool for branding and public engagement, and public empowerment. During her doctoral studies, she was named the Emerging Scholar by the Association for Research on Nonprofit Organization and Voluntary Action in 2010, and won best paper awards at the AEJMC for three consecutive years. Also, her master's thesis won the Northwestern Mutual 2009 Best Master's Thesis Award, sponsored by the Institute for Public Relations. She has published research in scholarly journals and she has presented at numerous conferences.

Eleftheria (Roila) Christakou is a Ph.D. Candidate at the Panteion University of Social and Political Sciences, in Athens, Greece. Her research interest focuses on the impact of Social Media and Blogs on Organizational Reputation. She holds an M.A. in Cultural Management, from City University of London and a B.A. in French Language and Literature, from the National and Kapodistrian University of Athens. She is currently working as a Communication Officer at the European Stability Mechanism (ESM) in Luxembourg. She has held Communications positions in Eurobank, the Foundation of the Hellenic World, Pharmaserve—Lilly, the Ministry of Finance of the Hellenic Republic, as well as in the Greek Embassy in London. For 6 years, she has been a part-time lecturer at the CMA College for Management, covering Marketing and Public Relations topics. Contact: roila1@yahoo.gr

Cinzia Dal Zotto is Professor of Media Management at the Faculty of Economics and Business at the University of Neuchâtel, Switzerland. She was director of the Academy between 2010 and 2012. Before that, from January 2004 to December 2008 she was Research Director at the Media Management and Transformation Centre and Assistant Professor at the Jönköping International Business School, Sweden. In 2000 Dal Zotto received her Ph.D. in Organizational and Human Resource Development at the University of Regensburg in Germany. Between 2001 and 2003 her research on new ventures' growth in the media sector was funded by the German Ministry of Education. Within that program she was a consultant for start-up firms. During 2002 Cinzia Dal Zotto was a visiting scholar at UC Berkeley, USA. She has published four books, various book chapters, and papers in the fields of organizational behavior, human resource management, entrepreneurship and strategy. She has taught at various universities in Sweden, Germany, UK, Italy, and France.

Patricia Diego is Professor of TV Drama Production and TV Programming at the School of Communication, University of Navarra (Spain), as well as Vice-director of the Departament of Film, TV & New Media. She got a Ph.D. in 2004 with a thesis entitled Production of TV fiction in Spain (1990–2002). History, industry and market, which received the Outstanding Doctoral Thesis Award. She has been Visiting Researcher at University of Westminster and has published several articles and books about TV production and history of TV Fiction in Spain.

Sergio Roncallo Dow, Ph.D (Philosophy) and M.A (Communications) from the Pontificia Universidad Javeriana, Bogotá Colombia. He has been professor and researcher at several universities in Colombia and is now assistant professor at the School of Communication at Universidad de La Sabana. He is a board member of Palabra Clave journal. His research interests are the philosophy of technology and communication as well as contemporary aesthetics and, in particular, the relationship between art and technology. In recent years he has dedicated his research to the thought of Marshall McLuhan.

Paul Dwyer is Course Leader for the MA International Media Business and Senior Lecturer in Media Management at the University of Westminster. He is a member of CAMRI, the highest ranked media research institute in the UK. Paul is currently on the steering group of Radio Connected, an industry R&D consortium developing Connected Radio platforms and applications, and a consultant to television production companies and broadcasters. Previously he was Head of Development in the BBC's Documentaries and Specialist Factual Department, developing new TV and multiplatform content for all genres of factual programming. He spent 11 years at the BBC as an award winning TV producer and director where he produced flagship investigative programmes like Panorama and Rough Justice, drama documentaries like The Plot Against Harold Wilson and Windscale: Britain's Biggest Nuclear Disaster. He also worked in radio news as editor of the Financial World Tonight and producer of In Business. Paul gained his Ph.D. from Imperial College, University of London, where is research was a management study of pirate radio.

Tom Evens studied Communication Sciences and Business Administration. He lecturers in New Media Markets and Economics at Ghent University, Belgium. Tom works as a senior researcher at the Research Group for Media and ICT (MICT), which is affilliated to the Interdisciplinary Institute for Broadband Technology (IBBT). His research focuses on the political economy of new media and ICT, business model analysis and public policy aspects of new media. He has published widely on media management issues in diverse international journals (including New Media & Society, Telematics and Informatics, Media Culture & Society, Journal of Media Business Studies, International Journal of Digital Television, Javnost—The Public, and other) and contributed to numerous edited volumes. Together with Petros Iosifidis and Paul Smith, he co-authored 'Playing to Win: The Political Economy of Television Sports Rights' (published by Palgrave Macmillan, 2013). (contact: Tom.Evens@UGent.be).

About the Authors

Paulo Faustino teaches marketing in Porto University and media management, economics and marketing in School of Mass Communication of Lisbon and Polytechnic Institute of Leiria. He is visting professor in several international universities, namely in Brasil and Macau/China. He was professor on management, economics and marketing in Portuguese Catholic University (here he also coordinated one masters in media& entertainment). He has Ph.D. in Media Management, from Complutense University of Madrid. Paulo Faustino holds a MSc in Economic and Organizations Sociology, from Technique University of Lisbon. He was President of Media XXI/Formalpress (Consulting, Research & Publishing Company), board member of the International Journal on Media Management and board member of the European Association of Media Management Education. Previously, he was advisor of State Secretary and Presidency Minister of the XV and XVI Constitutional Governments. Paulo Faustino has conducted consultancy work for several private and public institutions like, for example, World Bank and to Portuguese Media Regulatory Entity. He was also a board adviser of Lusomundo Media's Administration (Portugal Telecom's Group). He is the author of several scientific articles published in national and international magazines, as well as books in the media area studies.

Mike Friedrichsen (Prof. Dr.) is a professor of media economics and media business at the Stuttgart Media University and President at the Humboldt Media Business School in Berlin. He studied Business Administration, Political Economics, Journalism and Political Sciences in Kiel, Mainz and Berlin. He earned his doctorate at the Free University of Berlin in 1996 at the Institute of empirical Market and Communication Research. His main research interests are Media Management and Media Economics, Digital Radio and Television, Opinion Research, New Media Technologies und Business Communication. Mike Friedrichsen emphasizes transfer between the University and Economy and in leads several Networking Organisations. He is author and editor of several books and has also published in different journals. Contact: Friedrichsen@mbtc.eu

German Antonio Arango Forero, Doctoral candidate in communication studies at Austral University, Buenos Aires Argentina. He also attended the Media and Entertainment Management program at the Insitute for Media and Entertainment, New York, USA. Associate professor at the School of Communication at Universidad de La Sabana, Colombia. He is a board member of the Journal of Media Management and the Journal of Spanish Language Media. He has published several papers and book chapters about research on the field of media industries and audiences' analysis. Currently he manages the multimedia production center at Universidad de La Sabana, Colombia.

Christoph Fritsch is a case officer for media and media networks at the German antitrust authority (Bundeskartellamt). He teaches Media Economics at the University of Cologne and at the Fresenius University of Applied Sciences and holds lectures in Public Finance at the Sofia University St. Kliment Ohridski. He received his Ph.D. (Dr. rer. pol.) from the University of Cologne in 2010 for his research in "Economic Analysis of Broadband TV-Markets". During his doctoral studies, he worked at the department for Competition Theory and Media Economics at the University of Cologne and went to India and China for research and working purposes.

Marco Gambaro is associate professor of Media Economics and Economics of Communication at the Department of Economics and Business at the Università degli Studi di Milano (Italy) where he is in the board of the School of Journalism. He was visiting professor at George Mason University, University of Trento, IULM University and University of Parma. He is part of the Advisory Board at Florence School of Regulation for Media and Telecommunication Section and in the scientific committee of Patti Chiari the self regulation board of Italian Bank Association. He is member in the editorial board of The International Journal of Media Management, Communication and Strategies, Consumatori Diritti e Mercato. Previously he worked as a journalist, economic analyst, management consultants in media companies. His research interest include: television industry, Italian and international film industry, competition in the communication markets, economics of information and advertising.

Richard Ganahl (Professor, Ph.D.) is a professor in mass communications at Bloomsburg University, PA. Ganahl is a former publisher, entrepreneur, media manager, and marketing consultant. He is co-editor with Dr. Louisa Ha of the award-winning Webcasting Worldwide (2007), and the founding faculty advisor of BUNow, a pure-play, multi-media, student-managed news site. In its first 3-years, more than 187,808 visitors from over 168 countries have viewed over 434,243 pages. BUNow is nearly unique among student news sites because it stands-alone from, and is independent of other campus media. His column GANAHL ON MEDIA is an occasional column about media issues that first appears on BUNow. He is a graduate of the School of Journalism at the University of Missouri, and a former Visiting Scholar at Yonsei University, South Korea.

Stavros Georgiades is a Lecturer of Management at the Department of Economics Accounting and Finance, Frederick University, Cyprus. He holds a Ph.D. in Management and a BA in Accounting and Economics from Henley Business School, University of Reading, UK, having conducted his research in media organizations in the US and Brazil. Prior to his current appointment he was a Manager in a Business Consultancy firm in London, UK, for several years, his clients including media organizations. Stavros Georgiades has worked in several research programs with US and European media organizations, including the operationalization of online business models and the development of an online platform through the interaction of users and collaborators. His research interests are in the area of organizational change. He is particularly concerned with the way management in the media industry can achieve employee involvement and contributions towards organizational decisions and operations via changes in the provision of information and influence to employees. He has presented in several international conferences including the Academy of Management.

Richard A. Gershon, Ph.D., (Ohio University) is Professor and Co-Director of the Telecommunications & Information Management program at Western Michigan University where he teaches courses in Telecommunications Management and Communication Technology & Innovation. Dr. Gershon is the author of Telecommunications & Business Strategy (2009) and The Transnational Media Corporation: Global Messages and Free Market Competition, winner of the 1998 book of the year sponsored by the National Cable Television Center. Dr. Gershon has twice been selected for national teaching honors, including the Steven H. Coltrin Professor of the Year Award (2000) by the International Radio& Television Society (IRTS) and the Barry Sherman Award for Teaching Excellence (2001) by the Management and Economics division of the Association for Education in Journalism and Mass Communication (AEJMC). In 2007, he was the recipient of the Distinguished Teaching Award at Western Michigan University. Dr. Gershon is a founding member of the International Telecommunications Education & Research Association (ITERA) and currently serves as the Chairman of the Board of Directors.

About the Authors

Birgit Gray (M.A.) has over 17 years experience in the media sector, with over 13 years of experience in strategic media research and consulting to broadcasters and media companies in Europe. Her area of expertise spans across traditional television/radio to digital media services. Her recent work focused on digital strategies for broadcasters, television related interactive services and new forms of multiplatform programming. As innovation manager Birgit works with Deutsche Welle as innovation manager (New Media Division—Innovation Projects) and as an independent Media Consultant. She held positions as Senior Consultant and Consulting Director in the UK, following employment at broadcasters in both the UK and Germany (covering TV, Radio and New Media). Birgit is the author of several consultancy reports on broadcast related digital media strategies and developments. She has a Masters degree in media studies and business administration from the Free University of Berlin.

Johanna Grüblbauer, Postgraduate in Media- and Communication Studies, University of Vienna, has worked as Research Manager for Market and Media Research. Project Manager and Lecturer at the Institute of Media Economics, University of Applied Sciences St. Poelten. Research focus: media use & media effects as a gateway of Stakeholder Value Management.

Enrique Guerrero received his Ph.D. degree in Audiovisual Communication (2009) from the University of Navarra and got a certificate in Entertainment Media Management (2007) from the University of California Los Angeles (UCLA). His doctoral research consisted on a study about production standards of entertainment TV shows. Currently, he is professor in Entertainment Production and in Multimedia Content Management. His research is focused on the audiovisual industry, specially on the development of multiplatform entertainment formats from different perspectives: creativity, production and business models. In addition, he has worked for some of the main television broadcasters in Spain, in the production of TV programmes such as quiz shows, magazines and documentaries. Besides he is a member of the Spanish Academy of Television Arts & Sciences. He has recently published two books, "El entretenimiento en la televisión española. Historia, industria y mercado" (Barcelona: Deusto, 2010) and "Guion y producción de programas de entretenimiento" (Pamplona: Eunsa, 2013), and several articles about digital television and entertainment contents.

Louisa Ha is a professor and chair of the Department of Telecommunications at Bowling Green State University, Ohio, U.S.A. and associate editor of Journalism and Mass Communication Quarterly. Her edited book, Webcasting Worldwide: Business Models of an Emerging Global Medium, received the AEJMC 2007 Robert Picard Award for Books and Monographs in Media Management and Economics. She is also the recipient of the 2006 Barry Sherman Teaching Award in Media Management and Economics. She received her Ph.D. in Mass Media from Michigan State University. Her bachelor's and M. Phil degrees in Communication were from the Chinese University of Hong Kong. Her research interests are emerging media business models, social media and media management, international and online advertising and audience research.

About the Authors

Min Hang is an Associate Professor in the School of Journalism and Communication in Tsinghua University, China. She also works as director of the East Asia Institute of the Media Management and Transformation Center of Jönköping University (MMTC-EA), Sweden. Hang holds doctoral degree in Business Administration from Jönköping University, Sweden, master degree of European Business Administration and Business Law from Lund University, Sweden. Hang had also been working in the Ministry of Communications and Hohai University in China. Her research interests include cross-national management, strategy in the media companies and market differences in the media industries. Hang is the author of several books and book chapters, journal articles and conference papers on New Media Venturing, International Media Product Portfolios Management, Media Economics Research, Media and Entrepreneurship, and Media Human Resources Management.

Dr. Peter Haric, educated editor, Consultant for Marketing and Brand Management with focus international and middle sized companies in the financial and creative industries. Research on marketing/trend management and metrics as well as brand centric management and Management 2.0. Ph.D. on strategic thinking.

About the Authors

Mónica Herrero is an Associate Professor of Media Management and Media Markets at the School of Communication (University of Navarra, Spain). She holds a MSc in Media Management from the University of Stirling (Scotland). She won the annual Award for her doctoral dissertation in the University of Navarra and she also holds the honorific title of European Ph.D. She has been a Visiting Researcher at the University of Westminster (London, 2004); the University of Glasgow (2005, 2007) and the University of Lugano (Lugano, 2010). She has been a Visiting Professor at the University of Missouri and at the International Institute of Social Sciences (Sao Paolo). She is the Dean of the School of Communication at the University of Navarra since June 2008. Her research focuses on television economics, new television products and on the new relationships in the digital era. She has participated in three public funded research projects regarding quality and competition in the audiovisual market.

Sanne Hille studied Art & Culture Studies (BA) and Media and Journalism (MA) at Erasmus University Rotterdam. After graduating in 2005 she became lecturer New Media and Journalism and researcher (2008) at the Research Centre for Communication and Journalism at the HU University of Applied Sciences. This research group aims specifically at the consequences of digitalization and the impact of cross-media for the journalistic sector. In 2011, she received a Ph.D. grant from the HU for a project "Sixteen Million Reporters? Determinants of Success and Failure of Audience Participation in Journalism". This study focuses on (traditional) news media (e.g. daily newspapers, weeklies, television/radio broadcasters and news programs) and how they deal with audience participation on their online platforms, blogs, Facebook and Twitter.

About the Authors

Xiao Hu is a doctoral student in the School of Media and Communication, Bowling Green State University Ohio, U.S.A. She received her MA in Communication from Communication University of China and BA in Broadcasting and TV journalism, Zhengzhou University, China. Her research interests include media economics and media technologies, advertising and business model of new media. She teaches video production courses.

Datis Khajeheian (Ph.D.), is an assistant Professor from University of Tehran and a Media Management Scholar. In regard with the Background of M.A in Entrepreneurship; New Venture Creation and B.A in Business Administration; He focused on Media Entrepreneurship and Media Businesses in developing countries, especially in the Middle East, and working theoretical and Practical on development of Digital Media as a platform for filling the gaps in the region. He published many articles in Persian and English and is author of some International Journal Articles and Book Chapters and also and member of the board in some Iranian research institutes in the field of Media, Communications and Entrepreneurship. The major interests includes: Media Entrepreneurship and Businesses, Media Policy, Business Models and Strategies for digital media and Globalization of Media. He also publish serial articles on Media Enterprise issues in his personal site at http://www.datiki.com

About the Authors

George Michael Klimis B.Sc (Hons), PGDip. Sc, MBA, Ph.D., is currently lecturer at Panteion University, Athens Greece, where he teaches Strategic Management, Marketing and Change management. He studied mathematics in Aristotle University, Thessaloniki, Greece. He moved to the UK to study for a Postgraduate Diploma in Music Information Technology (City University, London) and also earned an MBA from Cass Business School (former City University Business School, London). He was then offered a scholarship to study for a Ph.D. at Cass Business School, while researching for the Economic and Social Research Council (ESRC) funded programme "Globalisation, Technology and Creativity: Current Trends in the Music Industry". He has been visiting lecturer at Cass Business School and also taught at the University of Athens, Open University in Greece, the Technological Educational Institute (TEI) of Peiraus and the national School of Public Administration among others. He has also worked as a freelance management consultant to various companies in Greece, the UK and Sweden. George M. Klimis has published extensively in academic journals such as the European Management Journal, British Journal Management, European Journal of Communication, New Media and Society and others.

Arne H. Krumsvik (Ph.D.) is Associate Professor in Journalism at Oslo and Akershus University College of Applied Sciences and Adjunct Associate Professor in Media Management and Innovation at Gjøvik University College. He is Vice Chairman of the Appeals Board at the Norwegian Media Authority and member of the board of Centre for Research on Media Innovatons (Univeristy of Oslo). He has published several articles on media management, media policy, and online journalism. His latest book 'Media Innovations' was co-edited with professor Tanja Storsul.

About the Authors

Reinhard Kunz (Prof. Dr.) is a junior professor in Media Management at the University of Bayreuth (Germany). He wrote his doctoral thesis on the influencing factors of mobile TV with a special focus on sport content. Both his teaching and research on media management have an emphasis in sport media. Reinhard Kunz lectures on the management of the audiovisual digital media and the marketing-management of sport media for master and Ph.D. students in media culture and media economy, business administration and sport economics programs. Research is focused on media marketing, media management, and interdisciplinary questions and phenomena in the media sector. His research interest especially concerns the behavior of consumers and recipients as well as new business models in the areas of digital TV, the Internet and mobile telecommunication. Theoretical and empirical analyses on media usage and management of media networks are one part of his research. Contact: Kunz@uni-bayreuth.de.

Moonhaeng Lee (Ph.D., Dr.) is an Associate Professor at the Faculty of Journalism and Communication, University of Suwon (Korea). In 1999 she received her Ph.D. degree from Paris 2 University (France) with an emphasis in media economics. With 10 years' field experience in Broadcasting company, her main research interests include Broadcasting Industry, Media Economics, Media Market, TV Content Business and Entertainment industry. She got the Suwon University award as one of the most outstanding researcher and professor in 2009. Contact: moonhlee@suwon.ac.kr...

Prof. Dr. Artur Lugmayr describes himself as a creative thinker and his scientific work is situated between art and science. Starting from July 2009 he is full-professor for entertainment and media production management at the Department of Business Information Management and Logistics at the Tampere University of Technology (TUT): EMMi—Entertainment and Media Production Management (http://webhotel2.tut.fi/emmi/web/). He is the head and founder of the New AMbient MUltimedia (NAMU) research group at the Tampere University of Technology (Finland) which is part of the Finnish Academy Centre of Excellence of Signal Processing from 2006 to 2011 (http://namu.cs.tut.fi). He is holding a Dr.-Techn. degree from the Tampere University of Technology (TUT, Finland), and is currently engaged in Dr.-Arts studies at the School of Motion Pictures, TV and Production Design (UIAH, Helsinki). He chaired the ISO/IEC ad-hoc group "MPEG-21 in broadcasting"; won the NOKIA Award of 2003 with the text book "Digital interactive TV and Metadata" published by Springer-Verlag in 2004; board member of MindTrek (http://www.mindtrek.org), EU project proposal reviewer. He is founder of the production company LugYmedia Inc. (http://www.lugy-media.tv). More about him on http://www.tut.fi/emmi

Li-Chuan Evelyn Mai is a Professor and Associate Dean of Division of Humanities and Social Sciences at Beijing Normal University-Hong Kong Baptist University United International College (UIC). She is also in charge of Centre of Cultural Creative Industry and Cinema and Television Programme at UIC. Prof. Mai obtained her Ph.D. degree from School of Media, Art and Design, University of Westminster, UK. Her specialization is in media management focusing on the fields of the media operation, corporate culture, strategy, global media and new media. She was the Executive Chairman of 7th World Media Economics Conference (Beijing), a member of the Editorial Board of International Journal of Media Management, a visiting professor of University of Bedfordshire. She serves as the Ph.D. supervisor of Hong Kong Baptist University-UIC Ph.D. Joint Programme, and the External Examiner of the MBA programme of University of Wales. She has started teaching in Taiwan from 1987 and in mainland China from 2003. She was the Vice Dean of Communication School, Arts and Communication School, and International Faculty; Director of Cultural Creative Industry Research Centre of Beijing Normal University, Zhuhai, respectively.

About the Authors

Mikhail Makeenko, Ph.D., associate professor at the Chair of Media Theory and Media Economics, Faculty of Journalism, Lomonosov Moscow State University. Author of more than 30 articles and chapters in Russian and English and two monographs. Research interests include media economics, media industries, economic history of media, American and European media systems, television programming, online entrepreneurship.

Stéphane Matteo is a Research and Teaching Assistant at the Academy of Journalism and Media, University of Neuchâtel, Switzerland. His research focuses on brand content or how new brand management strategies make companies become media. His interests extend towards nonlinear and transmedia storytelling. Previously he has been conducting research on cultural journalism on a mandate for the Swiss Federal Office of Culture (BAK) and now collaborates with an independent audiovisual production house. He holds a M.A in Journalism from University of Neuchâtel and received a M.Sc in Marketing and Corporate Communication from USI, University of Lugano, Switzerland.

Mercedes Medina (Ph.D. University of Navarra; MSc University of Westminster) is an Associate Professor and Director of Media Management Master at the School of Communication (University of Navarra, Spain). She is the author of Valoración publicitaria de los programas de televisión (1998), European Television Production. Concentration and Pluralism (2004), Estructura y gestión de empresas audiovisuales (2011 2ª), Calidad y contenidos audiovisuales (2006) and the editor of Creating, Producing and selling TV shows. The case of the most popular dramedies in Spain (2009); The Changing Media Business Environment (2008) and Series de televisión. Médico de Familia, Cúentame y Los Serrano (2008). Her last publications include "The Effects of Competition in the profitability of European Television Channels" (2010), "The Transformation of Public TV Companies into Digital Services at the BBC and RTVE" (2011). Her research has focused on media management and economics, globalization, and audiovisual business. She has been member of the editorial board of The International Journal on Media Management and currently she is an external reviewer of Palabra Clave, Innovative Marketing and Comunicación y Sociedad.

Terry Moellinger received his Ph.D. from the University of Oklahoma. His dissertation was entitled To Think Different: The Unexpected Consequences of the Personal Computer and Internet use. His primary area of research grew out of his dissertation work and focuses on how Internet-based communication has affected the perception of time and space for its users, as well as the changing patterns of both communication and interpersonal relations that these communication modalities have influenced, and the affects of the use of digital technology on cognitive processing. A second line of research deals with media content and examines media presentations for their semiotic meaning. A third line of research deals with the historical entrance of new technology into society and focuses on its acceptance, how it becomes adapted by users, and its potential as a major component of popular culture. He is currently teaching Communication Studies and Speech at North Central Texas College.

About the Authors

Wolfgang Mühl-Benninghaus (Prof. Dr.) is a professor of Film Theory and History at the Humboldt-University of Berlin and President at the Humboldt Media Business School in Berlin. He studied Economics, Business Administration and History in Berlin. He earned his doctorate at the Humboldt-University of Berlin in 1981 at the Institute for Cultural Studies. His main research interest are History of Media, Media Economics, New Media and Business Communication. Wolfgang Mühl-Benninghaus emphasizes transfer between the University and Economy. He is author and editor of several books and has also published in different journals.

Paul C. Murschetz, born in Salzburg/Austria, is consultant for the University of Westminster's China Media Centre and adjunct associate professor of business administration at University of New York, Tirana. He earned his Ph.D. from the Vienna School of Economics and Business Administration (commerce). He also holds a master's degree in media and communication (London School of Economics and Political Science). Besides research and consulting on higher education management, his current research in media management focuses on issues of strategic e-commerce management, media interactivity, WebTV, public financial subsidies on media firms, and game theory. Research results have appeared in journals such as: The International Journal on Media Management, the European Journal of Communication, the Communication Yearbook and in conference proceedings of the German Association of Communication (DGPuK). Paul is member of the European Media Management Education Association (EMMA).

François Nel is the founding director of the Journalism Leaders Programme at the School of Journalism, Media and Communication, University of Central Lancashire, UK, co-founder of the Digital Editors Network, UK, and a winner of the International Press Institute's News Innovation Contest sponsored by Google. He is an author of the annual World Newsmedia Innovation Study, initiated in 2009 in collaboration with the World Association of Newspapers and News Publishers (WAN-IFRA), and two Oxford University Press texts. His research into innovation in newsrooms, boardrooms and classrooms has also been published in journals such as *Journalism Practice*, *Journalism Studies*, *Journalism and Mass Communication Educator* and the *Rhodes Journalism Review*.

Astrid Nelke (Dr.) is a visiting lecturer at the MHMK University for Media and Communication in Berlin. She studied communication science and psychology at Free University of Berlin and sociology at Humboldt University of Berlin. She earned her doctorate at Free University of Berlin in 2008 at the institute of communication science. Her main research interests are internal communication, online communication of organisations and gender and diversity management with a special focus to its communicative aspects. Astrid Nelke is managing director of [know:bodies] ltd., a Berlin based consultancy for communication and education, which she founded in 2010.

Nicholas Nicoli is an Assistant Professor at the University of Nicosia's Department of Communications. He currently teaches undergraduate, and post-graduate students of communications, public relations, marketing and advertising. His research areas are on social media, creativity and creative processes, media management, the future of public service broadcasting and corporate communications. Before entering academia Nicholas spent a large part of his career working in corporate communications in the USA, in the UK and in Cyprus. He is also a qualified Charter Institute of Public Relations Instructor where he teaches public relations practitioners in Cyprus, Greece and Romania. He completed his B.A. with honours in Communications from the University of South Florida, Tampa, his M.A. in communication policy and his Ph.D. in Sociology, both at City University, London.

José Luis Orihuela is Ph.D. in Communication and MA in Journalism. Professor of Multimedia Communication and New Media at the School of Communication, University of Navarra (Pamplona, Spain). Visiting professor and speaker in Latin America. Writer and blogger focused on the impact of internet on media, enterprise and education. Author of "Mundo Twitter" (2011), "80 claves sobre el futuro del periodismo" (2011) and "La revolución de los blogs" (2006). Editor of the blogs "eCuaderno" (since 2002) and "Digital Media Weblog" (since 2009), and active Twitter user: @jlori (since 2007).

Alejandro Pardo is Professor of Production for Film & TV (undergraduate students) and Audiovisual Project Management (graduate students) at the School of Communication, University of Navarra (Spain). Former Head of the Department of Film, TV & Digital Media. He holds Certificate Programs in Production for Film and Television (UCLA Extension) and in Entertainment & Media Management (UCLA Anderson School of Management). In addition, he is graduated from the European Master in Audiovisual Management (Media Business School, Madrid). He has been Visiting Researcher at the UCLA School of Theater, Film & TV, as well as Guest Scholar at the DeSantis. Among his publications, it accounts *The Europe-Hollywood Coopetition: Cooperation and Competition in the Global Film Industries* (2007), and *The Audiovisual Management Handbook* (2002, editor). He has also written a number of contributions to collective books and journal articles, like *The International Journal on Media Management*, *Film International* and *Wide Screen*. He is member of the Society of Cinema and Media Studies (SCMS), the European Network for Cinema and Media Studies (NECS), and the European Media Management Association (EMMA). His research is focused on the entertainment industry, and more particularly on the impact of digitization and globalization on the film and TV industries.

Francisco J. Pérez-Latre, Ph.D., is Director of International Relations and Professor of advertising at the School of Communication of the University of Navarra, Spain. He is also Master of Arts en Marketing Communications/Advertising, Emerson College, Boston (1993), and has served as academic director at the Institute of Media and Entertainment, New York. He sits on the Board of the European Foundation for Commercial Communications Education (EFCCE). He is the author of "Advertising fragmentation: the beginning of a new paradigm?" in Handbook of Advertising, Routledge, London 2009, and Issues on Media and Entertaiment, Media Market Monographs, Pamplona 2006. He has written seven books in Spanish and his works include 20 book chapters and 53 articles on media management, advertising and communication strategy. Some of his articles have been published in international journals like the Journal of Media Business Studies, Journal of Spanish Language Media or The International Journal on Media Management. His research is now focused on social responsibility and social media technologies.

About the Authors

Robert G. Picard, Prof. Dr., is one of the world's leading academic experts on media economics and management and government communications policies. He is Director of Research at the Reuters Institute, Department of Politics and International Relations, University of Oxford, and a research fellow at Green Templeton College, Oxford. He is also on the faculties of the Media Management and Transformation Centre, Jönköping International Business School, Sweden, the Institute of Media and Entertainment, IESE Business School, in New York, and the Center for Media Management and Economics at Tsinghua University in China, and University of Tampere, Finland.

Harald Rau, Prof. Dr. phil. habil., is heading the program for media management at Ostfalia University of applied sciences. He published four books and a high number of articles and reports on management, media economics and journalism. His in 2007 published framework on media quality presents an economically driven approach to content production. Besides his academic career (Universities of Hagen, Dortmund and Leipzig), Rau worked for German broadcasters as presenter and reporter, he developed several television formats and was member of the management team heading a business radio station with newsrooms in Berlin, Frankfurt and Munich. In corporate communications of internationally renowned companies like ABB, BASF or SAP he responsibly headed more than 500 communication projects—(most of them television or movie based). His current research projects are focusing on media quality, the efficiency of social networks and a newly founded concept for creating news value in converging media environments. http://www.ostfalia.de/imm/Team/Rau

Alfonso Sanchéz-Tabenero (astabernero @unav.es) is President of the University of Navarra and Professor of Media Management at the School of Communication in the same university. He is also Doctor in Public Communications (University of Navarra, 1988). He got the Diploma in Business Administration (IESE Business School, 1996). He has been professor of Strategy at the Institute for Media and Entertainment (New York), Visiting Fellow at the European Institute for the Media (Düsseldorf) and President of the European Media Management Education Association. He has been Dean of the School of Communications (1996–2005) and Director of a Master in Media Management (2001–2006) at the University of Navarra. He has published more than forty articles about media management and media economics in scientific journals. His latest books are Media Concentration in Europe. Commercial Enterprise and the Public Interest, European Institute for the Media,1993; Dirección estratégica de empresas de comunicación, Cátedra, 2000; Media Concentration in the European Market: new trends and challenges (with M. Carvajal), Media Markets Monographs, 2003; The Content of Media: Quality, Profits and Competition, Formalpress, 2009).

Alexander Schachinger, an Austrian in Berlin, is a digital healthcare resesarcher within the German speaking countries. After studying communication science in Berlin and Toronto, Alexander worked in international pharma and digital advertising companies. Since 2009 he is a Ph.D. candidate on the e-patient phenomenon in Germany and is working on digital healthcare research and pilot projects together with health related institutions and companies from the media and healthcare industry.

About the Authors

Holger Sievert (Dr.) is Professor for Media Management, especially PR and Communication Management, at the Cologne Campus of the MHMK University. Furthermore, he works as a communication consultant on strategic issues to some larger German companies and as a certified senior management coach. His main areas of expertise are international, integrated, internal and interactice PR. Previously to his current academic position, he was Director at the agency group komm.passion, Düsseldorf, held a leadership role at the Bertelsmann Foundation, Gütersloh, and worked as a management consultant for Roland Berger Strategy Consultants in Düsseldorf, Paris and Rio de Janeiro. He had studied communication science in Münster and Aix-en-Provence.

Jochen Spangenberg (M.A.) has been working in the media industry since the early 1990s both on the journalistic and strategic side. From 1994 to 1998 he was a frequent contributor to BBC Radio & TV programmes. Then, he set up and ran the streaming media and media consulting business of Altus Analytics AG, Berlin, being also responsible for all R&D projects of the company. In 2003, Jochen joined Germany's international broadcaster Deutsche Welle (http://www.dw.de), working first in the Online department and, since January 2006, in the Distribution Directorate. His main tasks at Deutsche Welle to date included strategy development and subsequent implementation of digital media services, and co-ordination of the broadcaster's innovation projects. Jochen is also a Visiting Lecturer at various Universities, a frequent speaker at conferences, and moderator of events and workshops that cover issues in the digital media, telecommunications and information technology sector (more on http://www.me-mod.de). He is the author of the book *The BBC in Transition*.

Giulia Spolaor is a doctoral student and teaching assistant at the Academy of Journalism and Media at the University of Neuchâtel, Switzerland. She studied Business Administration at the Università Bocconi, Italy, and holds a Master degree in Economics and Business Administration with a specialization in Strategic Market Creation of the Copenhagen Business School, Denmark. Her main research interests include pan-regional television networks, media branding, social networks and sport broadcasting.

George Tsourvakas holds a licentiate degree in business administration from University of Piraeus, a degree in Sociology and a master of Law and Economics from Hamburg and Stockholm Universities. He earned his doctoral degree from the Panteion University of Athens on media. He is Assistant Professor of media economics at the Aristotle University of Thessaloniki, department of Journalism and Mass Communications and his current research interests focus on the media management and marketing communications. He has published articles in journals such as the International Journal on Media Management, Journal of Media Economics, Journal of Media Business Studies, Communications, the European Journal of Law and Economic, Journal of Radio and Audio Media.

About the Authors

Agnes Urban (Ph.D.) is Assistant Professor at the Corvinus University of Budapest (CUB). She has a master degree in Business Administration, and she got her Ph.D. degree (summa cum laude) on the Corvinus University in 2006. The title of the Ph.D. thesis was 'The market of new media services'. She is a lecturer at the CUB (Media Economics, Media and Audience Research). Her primary research interest are diffusion of new media, reshape the business models and change of media consumption habits. In the last years she conducted researches about the restructuring of Hungarian television market, change of media consumption of teenagers and impact of new technologies on media markets. She participated in a pan-European COST project (COST298: Participation in the Broadband Society). She is the author of ca. 30 Hungarian and English publications including academic papers, book chapters, and conference proceedings.

Elena Vartanova (Prof. Dr.) is Full Professor, Dean and Chair in Media Theory and Media Economics at the Faculty of Journalism, Moscow State University. Her Ph.D. was on Finnish Newspaper System (1982), her Doctoral dissertation on Information Society Concepts and Their Impact on Media Practice in EU and Nordic Countries (1999).Her research interests include media systems in Nordic countries, information society, post-Soviet transformation of Russian media, media economics. Vartanova is an author of three books and an editor of six books (in Russian) on Nordic media systems, Information society, media economics. Published more than 150 research articles in Russian academic magazines. Editor of five monographs in English. Editor-in-chief of the Faculty research journal Mediaalmanac, online research magazine Mediascope and bulletin for experts MediaTrends.

Marco van Kerkhoven is a Ph.D. candidate at the University of Amsterdam/ASCoR. He studies online business models and market strategies of regionale news media. He worked as a science and innovation editor for different newspapers, magazines and (online) business publications in the Netherlands, Belgium and the US. In 2003 he set up a new training center for journalists in Iraq. He wrote and co-authored several books on science communication and other science related topics. He teaches journalism at the Utrecht School of Journalism (HU University of Applied Sciences) and is a researcher at the Research Centre for Communication and Journalism in Utrecht.

Hans van Kranenburg is full professor of Corporate Strategy and chair of Business Administration at Radboud University Nijmegen, Nijmegen School of Management, the Netherlands. He has been a visiting scholar at Media Management and Transformation Center at Jönköping International Business School (Sweden) and the University of Chicago (USA). He published on strategic behaviour of companies, industry dynamics, alliances and networks, foreign direct investments, non-market strategies, and intellectual property rights. He also is an expert in media management and economics. He has published in books and international journals like Journal of Law and Economics, Journal of International Business Studies, International Business Review, British Journal of Management, Industry and Corporate Change, Journal of Media Economics, Managerial and Decision Economics, International Journal of Industrial Organization, Journal of Economic Behaviour and Organization, Telecommunications Policy. He also is co-author of the book Management and Innovation in the Media Industry (2009).

Aldo van Weezel is a media business consultant based in Santiago, Chile. He is currently advising the Chilean National Press Association and representing German software company ppi Media GmbH in Latin America. He got his Ph.D. in Business Administration from Jönköping University (Sweden). He also holds the degrees of Industrial Engineer and MSc in Engineering from Pontificia Universidad Católica de Chile, and a Master in Media Management from University of Navarre (Spain). His research interests include strategy and entrepreneurship in media firms. His work has been published in the International Journal on Media Management and the Journal of Media Business Studies.

Julián Villanueva is the Director of the Department of Marketing at IESE Business School. He has a Ph.D. in Management (Marketing) from UCLA and an MBA from IESE Business School; he took an undergraduate degree in Economics at the Complutense University in Madrid. His main teaching and research interests include client management, new media, sales force management and, more generally, how investments in marketing may generate results in the long term. His research papers have been published in Journal of Marketing Research, Journal of Marketing and Quantitative Marketing and Economics, among other publications. Prof. Villanueva has also authored a number of books and more than 20 case-studies and technical manuals. His consultancy work has addressed market research, control panels, positioning recommendations, as well as international expansion and general marketing strategy. He is a member of the European Marketing Association, and acts as a reviewer for Journal of Marketing, Journal of Marketing Research, Marketing Science and Management Science. He is a member of the Editorial Review Board for the International Journal of Research in Marketing and a member of the Editorial Committee for IESE Insight Review. In 2006, he received the award for outstanding research project from the European Marketing Academy.

About the Authors

Zvezdan Vukanovic (Prof. Dr) is an Associate Professor and the Director of Master's Program in Media Economy at the University of Donja Gorica (UDG), Podgorica, Montenegro where he teaches courses in New Media Management and Economy and Network Economy in Media Industry and Business at the faculty of International Economics, Finance and Business and Faculty of Information Systems and Technology. He obtained a post-doctoral fellowship at the McLuhan Program in Culture and Technology, Coach House Institute, Faculty of Information, University of Toronto in 2008. Vukanovic received a Ph.D. in economics at the Faculty of Business—The Megatrend University of Applied Sciences, Belgrade in 2006; M.A. in Arts and Media, The University of Arts, Belgrade 2004 and B.A. in Arts and Media, University of Victoria, British Columbia, Canada in 1999. During 2008–2009 he was a visiting lecturer at the School of Business and Economics, Thompson Rivers University, Canada. Vukanovic is the author/editor of 7 books and numerous articles and book chapters related to topics in media management.

Andrei Vyrkovsky is a Senior Lecturer at the Faculty of Journalism, Moscow State University. Graduated MSU Faculty of Journalism in 2004, Ph.D. since 2007 (his Ph.D. dissertation was on Comparative Analysis of Russian and American business magazines). His research interests include business journalism, media systems, economic issues of media business. Published about 20 articles and monographs on business journalism in Russia and abroad, media business issues.

About the Authors

Stefan Werning (Dr.) is an assistant professor for applied media studies at the University of Bayreuth. He received his Ph.D. degree from Bonn University in 2004 with a thesis about the exchange of technologies and concepts between the digital games industry and the military entertainment complex. He is a fellow of the Futures of Entertainment program at MIT and a member of the working group 'digital games' of the German association for media studies. His main areas of interest include structural aspects of digital games, the interplay of media theory and practice as well as the effects of economic contexts on media use.

Oscar Westlund holds a joint affiliation as associate professor at the University of Gothenburg (Sweden) and the IT University of Copenhagen (Denmark). He is an interdisciplinary researcher focusing on the transformations and relationships between old and new media. He has specialized in qualitative and quantitative longitudinal studies of media organizations, media content and services, and usage patterns. He researches the evolving dynamics and interplay of journalism, internet and ICTs, in general, and the intersection of journalism and mobile media, in particular. Westlund has published widely in Swedish and English, including original articles in more than a dozen international peer-reviewed journals. Moreover, he has authored "Cross-media news work—Sensemaking of the Mobile Media (R)evolution" (2011) and guest edited a special issue in *Information, Communication & Society* (2012) titled "Transforming tensions: legacy media towards participation and collaboration".

Steven S. Wildman is the James H. Quello Professor of Telecommunication Studies and Director of the James H. and Mary B. Quello Center for Telecommunication Management & Law at Michigan State University. At the time this book went to press, he was on leave from Michigan State to serve as Chief Economist for the U.S. Federal Communications Commission. Prior to joining Michigan State in Fall 1999, Dr. Wildman was Associate Professor of Communication Studies and Director of the Program in Telecommunications Science, Management & Policy at Northwestern University. Earlier positions include Senior Economist with Economists Incorporated and Assistant Professor of Economics at UCLA. Dr. Wildman holds a Ph.D. in economics from Stanford University and a BA in economics from Wabash College. He is well-known for his research and publications on economics and policy for communication industries, including the broadcasting, cable television, and recording industries. In addition to numerous articles and book chapters, Dr. Wildman is an author or editor for the following books: Making Universal Service Policy: Enhancing the Process Through Multidisciplinary Evaluation (Lawrence Erlbaum Associates, 1999); and Rethinking Rights and Regulations: Institutional Responses to New Communications Technologies (MIT Press, 2003).

About the Authors

Sonya Yan Song is an experienced researcher in online news media and emerging technologies. She joined the Media and Information Studies program at Michigan State University in the fall of 2009. In 2013, Song was selected as one of the eight Knight-Mozilla Fellows across the globe. In the previous year, she was awarded a Google Fellowship to study Internet censorship in Hong Kong, as the only winner of a worldwide competition. In 2008, Song conducted her research in comparative business models of online media companies in China at The University of Hong Kong. Song possesses a Bachelor's and Master's degree in Computer Science from Tsinghua University in Beijing, the country's leading university, and Master of Philosophy in Journalism from The University of Hong Kong. She began her career in Internet start-ups in 1999, at the peak of the dotcom bubble. Later, Song worked as a journalist and columnist focusing on the Internet, online media and technology sectors. Her writings have touched on a full range of China's new media sector, including coverage of companies as diverse as CCTV, Google China, Baidu.com, Sohu.com, QQ.com, Sina.com, Taihe Rye Music, and numerous start-ups. Moreover, her work experience obtained at various news outlets has endowed her with a wide view of the journalistic practice in China. Song is also an avid photographer, graphic designer and devotee of literature and films.

Mark Yi-Cheon Yim (Ph.D., University of Texas at Austin) is an assistant professor of Marketing in Richard J. Wehle School of Business at Canisius College. His research interests focus on diverse current issues in the domain of digital marketing and marketing communications. He recently worked on projects exploring how in-store digital signage and stereoscopic 3-D advertising can be effectively adopted as a marketing tool with prominent companies, such as CJ Powercast and Pavonine Korea. His work has been published in Journal of Advertising, Journal of Advertising Research, and Social Science Review, among others.

Biser Zlatanov (Asst. Prof. Dr.) teaches Media Management, Business Communication and prepares workshops in E-mail Marketing at Sofia University. He studied Journalism, Financial Management, Business and Finance in Sofia. He earned his doctorate in 2009. His main research interests are in the fields of Media Economics, Media Innovation, Institutional Economics, Investment Valuation and Relationship Marketing. Biser Zlatanov explores the effect of prioritization between market power and efficiency on innovation adoption and value creation in media. He regularly publishes articles in different journals and is a co-author of books and scientific research projects.

Gerrit Willem Ziggers (Dr.) is an assistant professor of Strategy at the Institute for Management Research, Nijmegen School of Management at the Radboud University Nijmegen, The Netherlands. He earned his doctoral degree from Wageningen University on entrepreneurship. His work predominantly deals with strategic aspects of business networks with particular interest in the dynamics, governance and performance of those networks.

Lightning Source UK Ltd.
Milton Keynes UK
UKOW050649210613

212590UK00001B/70/P